T0387237

EARLY
NEW TESTAMENT
APOCRYPHA

Ancient Literature *for* New Testament Studies

═══ VOLUME **9** ═══

EARLY
NEW TESTAMENT
APOCRYPHA

J. CHRISTOPHER EDWARDS, EDITOR

CRAIG A. EVANS AND CECILIA WASSÉN, SERIES EDITORS

ADELA YARBRO COLLINS, JOHN J. COLLINS,

AND GRANT MACASKILL, CONSULTING EDITORS

NATHAN C. JOHNSON, MANAGING EDITOR

ZONDERVAN ACADEMIC

Early New Testament Apocrypha
Copyright © 2022 by J. Christopher Edwards, Craig A. Evans, and Cecilia Wassén

Requests for information should be addressed to:
Zondervan, *3900 Sparks Dr. SE, Grand Rapids, Michigan 49546*

Zondervan titles may be purchased in bulk for educational, business, fundraising, or sales promotional use. For information, please email SpecialMarkets@Zondervan.com.

Library of Congress Cataloging-in-Publication Data

Names: Edwards, J. Christopher, 1982- editor.
Title: Early New Testament apocrypha / J. Christopher Edwards, editor ; Craig A. Evans, Cecilia Wassén,
  series editors.
Description: Grand Rapids : Zondervan, 2022. | Series: Ancient literature for New Testament studies, volume 9
  | Includes bibliographical references and index.
Identifiers: LCCN 2022014478 (print) | LCCN 2022014479 (ebook) | ISBN 9780310099710 (hardcover) |
  ISBN 9780310099727 (ebook)
Subjects: LCSH: Apocryphal books (New Testament)--Criticism, interpretation, etc. | BISAC: RELIGION /
  Biblical Reference / Handbooks | RELIGION / Biblical Studies / New Testament / General
Classification: LCC BS2840 .E27 2022 (print) | LCC BS2840 (ebook) | DDC 229/.92--dc23/eng/20220524
LC record available at https://lccn.loc.gov/2022014478
LC ebook record available at https://lccn.loc.gov/2022014479

Cover design: Brian Bobel
Cover image: © Universität Heidelberg
Interior design: Kait Lamphere

Printed in the United States of America

22 23 24 25 26 27 28 29 30 31 32 /TRM/ 15 14 13 12 11 10 9 8 7 6 5 4 3 2 1

CONTENTS

CONCLUSION

SERIES PREFACE

The several volumes that make up the Ancient Literature for New Testament Studies series provide introductions to the diverse bodies of literatures that are in various ways cognate to biblical literature, especially to the New Testament. These volumes have been written to serve the needs of advanced students who aspire to become New Testament interpreters, as well as the needs of veteran scholars who lack expertise in some of the fields these volumes treat.

The last two generations have witnessed the discovery and publication of a remarkable amount of ancient literature that in various ways is relevant to New Testament interpretation. Scholarly research has made it abundantly clear that much of this material proves to be contextually and exegetically helpful in the interpretation of the writings that make up the New Testament. But the sheer magnitude and diversity of this material have also proven to be intimidating to many students. Indeed, there are many scholars and teachers of biblical literature who are not sure exactly what makes up this literature, how it is relevant, and how it is to be accessed. It is the purpose of Ancient Literature for New Testament Studies to address this challenge.

The editors and contributors believe that if one is to interpret New Testament literature in full context, one must know something of these diverse writings and their relevance for the New Testament. Some of these writings are vital for understanding the literature of the New Testament, some much less so. But all are referred to in scholarly discourse. Thus, intelligent reading of New Testament scholarship more broadly requires familiarity with these writings.

The general editors are grateful to the many contributors and volume editors who have made this important work possible. We are also grateful to our colleagues at Zondervan Academic, and we thank our consulting editors Adela Yarbro Collins, John J. Collins, and Grant Macaskill.

Craig A. Evans
Cecilia Wassén

EDITOR'S PREFACE

The ALNTS series was created to introduce key ancient texts that form the cultural, historical, and literary context for the study of the New Testament. Scholars differ in their opinions regarding how long the temporal context for understanding the New Testament extends past its composition. Needless to say, the closer in time a text is to the New Testament the better its chances of maintaining the earliest meanings assigned to the New Testament. For this reason, I initially conceived of this volume as devoted to Christian apocryphal literature written within the first three to four centuries CE, hence the title, *Early New Testament Apocrypha*. However, as I began looking at the available literature, I found myself irresistibly tempted also to include a few slightly later texts, and some much later. How could I possibly omit essays on the Apocalypse of Thomas, Gospel of Barnabas, and Toledot Yeshu? While most of the texts introduced below still fall within the timeframe of the first four centuries CE and therefore may be useful for uncovering the earliest meanings assigned to the New Testament, the later texts serve as reminders of how the meanings of the New Testament continue to evolve in subsequent centuries. Indeed, the contemporary quest for the earliest meanings of the New Testament is itself simply another bend in the river of reception history.

I believe the organization of the texts in this volume is fairly standard. Some texts, such as *Epistula Apostolorum* or *Protevangelium of James*, will raise an eyebrow no matter where I place them. As to the categories of genre, while the list could be expanded, I thought it best to squeeze all the texts into the genres included in the canonical New Testament—Gospels, Acts, Letters, and Apocalypses—and then to organize them alphabetically. While not all the texts introduced in this volume are orthodox, or even Christian, there has been no attempt to include the texts from Nag Hammadi or other literature typically identified as gnostic. This literature is introduced in a separate volume of ALNTS. The texts in the Apostolic Fathers are also included in a separate volume. Finally, concerning this volume's title, Dale Martin's essay ably demonstrates the problems with using "New Testament Apocrypha" as a defined category. While I find myself in full agreement with Martin's criticisms, I have chosen to maintain "New Testament Apocrypha" in the title of this volume simply because its usage has become standard in contemporary scholarship.

I am very pleased with the high quality of the essays in this volume, which simply reflects the all-star cast of contributors. I would personally like to thank Craig Evans for his generous invitation to edit the volume. I would also like to thank Katya Covrett for her skillful editing and prompt correspondence. I am dedicating this volume to my close friends and colleagues at St. Francis College. The personal isolation required by the COVID-19 pandemic has reminded me how much I value working alongside the folks I love.

J. Christopher Edwards
New York, 19 March 2021

CONTRIBUTORS

Reidar Aasgaard is professor of history of ideas/intellectual history at IFIKK, faculty of humanities, University of Oslo. He has written and edited several books, among them *Beloved Brothers and Sisters! Christian Siblingship in the Apostle Paul* (2004); *The Childhood of Jesus: Decoding the Apocryphal Infancy Gospel of Thomas* (2009); and *Childhood in History: Perceptions of Children in the Ancient and Medieval Worlds* (with C. B. Horn and O. M. Cojocaru; 2018). He was director of the international project "Tiny Voices from the Past: New Perspectives on Childhood in Early Europe" (2013–2017) and has published Norwegian translations of early Christian works, among them the New Testament, Augustine, and apocryphal writings.

William Adler received his PhD from the University of Pennsylvania in 1982. He is currently distinguished university professor of religious studies in the department of philosophy and religious studies at North Carolina State University. He has published seven books and editions, including *The Cambridge History of Religions in the Ancient World*, vol. 2 (2013), *The Chronography of George Synkellos* (2002), *The Jewish Apocalyptic Heritage in Early Christianity* (1996), and *Time Immemorial: Primordial History in Christian Chronography from Julius Africanus to George Syncellus* (1989).

Harold W. Attridge is Sterling Professor of Divinity emeritus and served as dean of Yale Divinity School from 2002 to 2012. He has made scholarly contributions to the study of the New Testament, Hellenistic Judaism, and early Christianity. Educated at Boston College, Cambridge University, and Harvard University, he has been active in the Society of Biblical Literature, the Catholic Biblical Association, the Society of New Testament Studies, and on the editorial boards of the *Catholic Biblical Quarterly*, *Harvard Theological Review*, *Journal of Biblical Literature*, *Novum Testamentum*, and Hermeneia commentaries. In 2017 he was elected to the American Academy of Arts and Sciences.

Dan Batovici is a research associate at KU Leuven and UC Louvain, having received his PhD from the former in 2015. He has published broadly on early Christian manuscripts and patristic exegesis. He is the author of *The Shepherd of Hermas in Late Antiquity* (2022) and *Parabiblical Papyri: Secondary Spaces and the Reception of Early Christian Literature* (2022).

Jan N. Bremmer is emeritus professor of religious studies at the University of Groningen, Netherlands. His areas of specialization are in Greek, Roman, and early Christian religion. His most recent monographs are *Maidens, Magic and Martyrs in Early Christianity* (2017), *The World of Greek Religion and Mythology* (2019), and *Becoming a Man in Ancient Greece and Rome* (2021).

J. Christopher Edwards is professor of religious studies at St. Francis College, Brooklyn. He is the author of *The Ransom Logion in Mark and Matthew* (2012) and *The Gospel according to the Epistle of Barnabas* (2019).

Keith Elliott received his DPhil from the University of Oxford, under the supervision of George Kilpatrick, then its Dean Ireland Professor. Since then, until his retirement, he taught at the University of Leeds, UK. Currently, he is the emeritus professor of textual criticism. He edited *The Apocryphal New Testament* (1993) and also a selection of his own work in *Textual Criticism of the New Testament* (2010). He is the author of many articles and reviews.

Eric M. Vanden Eykel is associate professor of religious studies at Ferrum College in Virginia. His area of research is early Christian apocryphal literature, with a special focus on texts and traditions about the infancies and childhoods of Jesus and Mary, his mother.

Paul Foster is professor of New Testament and early Christianity in the school of divinity at the University of Edinburgh. His work centers on the emergence of the Jesus-movement in the first two centuries of the common era. His publications include *The Apocryphal Gospels: A Very Short Introduction* (2009); *The Gospel of Peter: Introduction, Critical Edition and Commentary* (2010); and *Colossians* in the Black's New Testament Commentaries series (2016).

Florence Gantenbein received her MA in biblical studies from Durham University and her Master of Theology from the University of Zurich. She is presently a doctoral candidate at the University of Bern, Switzerland.

Andrew Gregory is chaplain at University College, Oxford. He is author of *The Gospel according to the Hebrews and the Gospel of the Ebionites* (2017), *The Reception of Luke and Acts in the Period before Irenaeus* (2003), and chapters and articles on the New Testament and other early Christian literature. His edited books include *The Oxford Handbook of Early Christian Apocrypha* (2015), and he is a series editor of the Oxford Early Christian Gospel Texts and Oxford Apostolic Fathers.

Sarit Kattan Gribetz is associate professor in the theology department at Fordham University. Her first book, *Time and Difference in Rabbinic Judaism*, received the National Jewish Book Award in Scholarship.

Katharina Heyden has been full professor for ancient history of Christianity and inter-religious encounters at the University of Bern since 2014. Her publication list includes the volumes *Die Erzählung des Aphroditian: Thema und Variationen einer Legende im Spannungsfeld von Christentum und Heidentum* (2009); *Orientierung: Die westliche Christenheit und das Heilige Land in der Antike* (2014); *Eine Religionskonferenz in Perisen—De gestis in Perside* (2019); and, as coeditor, *Jerusalem in Roman-Byzantine Times* (2021) and *Claiming History in Religious Conflicts* (2021).

Philip Jenkins received his doctorate from Cambridge University. He is presently distinguished professor of history at Baylor University, where his main appointment is in the Institute for Studies of Religion (ISR). He has published thirty books, including *The Next*

Christendom: The Coming of Global Christianity (2002); *The Lost History of Christianity* (2008); *The Many Faces of Christ: The Thousand-Year Story of the Survival and Influence of the Lost Gospels* (2015); and *Crucible of Faith: The Ancient Revolution That Made Our Modern Religious World* (2017).

Mary Julia Jett is an Episcopal priest and scholar in New York City. She works with under-resourced congregations in the Bronx, while teaching at St. Francis College, Brooklyn. Her research and publications focus on Old Testament biblical exegesis in late antique and Anglican contexts. She is currently working on a project to increase accessibility to late antique North African religious history with an open-access website for English speakers.

Nathan C. Johnson holds a PhD from Princeton Theological Seminary and is assistant professor of religion at the University of Indianapolis, having previously served as a teaching fellow at Princeton Theological Seminary and a research specialist at Princeton University. His articles have appeared in venues such as the *Journal of Biblical Literature, Catholic Biblical Quarterly, New Testament Studies,* and the *Journal of Theological Studies.* His publications include *"To Recover What Has Been Lost": Essays on Eschatology, Intertextuality, and Reception History in Honor of Dale C. Allison Jr.* (coeditor; Brill, 2020) and *The Suffering Son of David in Matthew's Passion Narrative* (Cambridge University Press, forthcoming).

F. Stanley Jones is emeritus professor of religious studies at California State University, Long Beach. He was educated at Yale, Oxford, and Göttingen. His specialization is New Testament and ancient Christianity, and he serves on the scientific committee of the journal *Apocrypha.*

Jon C. Laansma holds a PhD from the University of Aberdeen and is the Gerald F. Hawthorne Professor of New Testament Greek and Exegesis at Wheaton College. His publications include *I Will Give You Rest: The Rest Motif in the New Testament with Special Reference to Mt 11 and Heb 3–4* (1997), *The Letter to the Hebrews: A Commentary for Preaching, Teaching, and Bible Study* (2017), *Christology, Hermeneutics, and Hebrews: Profiles from the History of Interpretation* (coeditor; 2014), and *So Great a Salvation: A Dialogue on the Atonement in Hebrews* (coeditor; 2019).

Petri Luomanen is professor of New Testament and early Christian culture and literature at the Faculty of Theology, University of Helsinki. He has published widely on the Gospel of Matthew, early Jewish Christianity, and socio-cognitive study of early Christianity, including *Recovering Jewish-Christian Sects and Gospels* (2012) and *Christianity and the Roots of Morality: Philosophical, Early Christian, and Empirical Perspectives* (coedited with A. B. Pessi and I. Pyysiäinen; 2017).

Dale B. Martin is Woolsey Professor Emeritus, Yale University. He has published numerous books, articles, essays, and reviews, including *Sex and the Single Savior: Gender and Sexuality in Biblical Interpretation* (2006); *New Testament History and Literature* (2012); and most recently *Biblical Truths: The Meaning of Scripture in the Twenty-First Century* (2017). He currently resides in Galveston, Texas.

Christopher R. Matthews is editor of *New Testament Abstracts* and research professor of early Christianity at the Boston College School of Theology and Ministry. He received his doctoral degree from Harvard in 1993. He is the author of *Philip: Apostle and Evangelist: Configurations of a Tradition* (2002), and with François Bovon, *The Acts of Philip: A New Translation* (2012). He also serves as editor-in-chief of Oxford Bibliographies: Biblical Studies.

Tobias Nicklas is professor of New Testament and director of the Centre for Advanced Studies "Beyond Canon" at the University of Regensburg, Germany. He has published several books (most recently *Studien zum Petrusevangelium* [2021]) and *Sola Scriptura Ökumenisch* (with Stefan Alkier and Christos Karakolis [2021]), is coeditor of more than thirty volumes and author of around 150 scholarly articles. He is research associate at the University of the Free State, Bloemfontein, South Africa.

Catherine Playoust lectures in biblical studies at Catholic Theological College (Melbourne, Australia) within the University of Divinity. Her doctorate is from Harvard University. Among her publications are works on John's Gospel, gospel infancy traditions, the Acts of Thomas, the letters of Paul, and Hebrews.

Robert F. Stoops Jr. is professor emeritus in the department of global cultures and religions at Western Washington University. He received his BA in religion from UNC-Chapel Hill, his MDiv from Harvard Divinity School, and his PhD in the study of religion from Harvard University. His research has focused on early Christianity in the context of Greco-Roman religions and society.

Philip L. Tite teaches religious studies at Eastside Catholic School in Sammamish, WA, and is an online instructor for Youngstown State University, as well as an instructor for occasional graduate and undergraduate courses at the University of Washington and Seattle University. He holds a PhD degree from McGill University and has authored several books and articles, notably *The Apocryphal Epistle to the Laodiceans: An Epistolary and Rhetorical Analysis* (2012) and *Valentinian Ethics and Paraenetic Discourse: Determining the Social Function of Moral Exhortation in Valentinian Christianity* (2009). As a specialist in the study of early Christianity, Tite has a strong interest in apocryphal texts, ancient Gnosticism, martyr accounts, New Testament epistles, and the social history of the early Christians.

Robyn Whitaker is senior lecturer in New Testament at Pilgrim Theological College, the University of Divinity, Australia. She received her PhD from the University of Chicago Divinity School and has published several books and articles, including her monograph *Ekphrasis, Vision, and Persuasion in the Book of Revelation* (2015).

ABBREVIATIONS

ABD	*Anchor Bible Dictionary*. Edited by David Noel Freedman. 6 vols. New York: Doubleday, 1992
ABRL	Anchor Bible Reference Library
ANRW	*Aufstieg und Niedergang der römischen Welt: Geschichte und Kultur Roms im Spiegel der neueren Forschung*. Part 2, *Principat*. Edited by Hildegard Temporini and Wolfgang Haase. Berlin: de Gruyter, 1972–
ANTF	Arbeiten zur neutestamentlichen Textforschung
BBR	*Bulletin for Biblical Research*
BEHER	Bibliothèque de l'École des Hautes études: Sciences religieuses
BHS	*Biblia Hebraica Stuttgartensia*. Edited by Karl Elliger and Wilhelm Rudolph. Stuttgart. Deutsche Bibelgesellschaft, 1983
BibInt	Biblical Interpretation Series
BJS	Brown Judaic Studies
BR	*Biblical Research*
BZNW	Beihefte zur Zeitschrift für die alttestamentliche Wissenschaft
CBQ	*Catholic Biblical Quarterly*
CCSA	Corpus Christianorum Series Apocryphorum
CCSL	Corpus Christianorum: Series Latina. Turnhout: Brepols, 1953–
CIL	*Corpus Inscriptionum Latinarum*. Berlin, 1862–
CSCO	Corpus Scriptorum Christianorum Orientalium. Edited by Jean Baptiste Chabot et al. Paris, 1903
CSEL	Corpus Scriptorum Ecclesiasticorum Latinorum
DACL	*Dictionnaire d'archéologie chrétienne et de liturgie*. Edited by Fernand Cabrol. 15 vols. Paris: Letouzey et Ané, 1907–1953
ECA	Early Christian Apocrypha
ECCA	Early Christianity in the Context of Antiquity
EL	*Ephemerides liturgicae*
FRLANT	Forschungen zur Religion und Literatur des Alten und Neuen Testaments
GCS	Die griechischen christlichen Schriftsteller der ersten [drei] Jahrhunderte
GECS	Gorgias Eastern Christian Studies
HBS	History of Biblical Studies
HR	*History of Religions*
HTR	*Harvard Theological Review*
Hug	Hugoye: Journal of Syriac Studies
ITQ	Irish Theological Quarterly
JAC	Jahrbuch für Antike und Christentum
JBL	*Journal of Biblical Literature*
JCT	Jewish and Christian Texts
JCTCRS	Jewish and Christian Texts in Context and Related Studies

JECS	*Journal of Early Christian Studies*
JQR	Jewish Quarterly Review
JSHRZ-NF	*Jüdische Schriften aus hellenistisch-römischer Zeit, Neue Folge*
JSJ	Journal for the Study of Judaism in the Persian, Hellenistic, and Roman Periods
JSJSup	Journal for the Study of Judaism Supplement Series
JSNT	*Journal for the Study of the New Testament*
JSNTSup	Journal for the Study of the New Testament Supplement Series
JSP	*Journal for the Study of the Pseudepigrapha*
JTS	*Journal of Theological Studies*
LNTS	The Library of New Testament Studies
LSTS	The Library of Second Temple Studies
MTSR	*Method and Theory in the Study of Religion*
NHMS	Nag Hammadi and Manichaean Studies
NHS	Nag Hammadi Studies
NovT	*Novum Testamentum*
NovTSup	Supplements to Novum Testamentum
NTApoc	*New Testament Apocrypha.* 2 vols. Revised ed. Edited by Wilhelm Schneemelcher. English trans. ed. Robert McL. Wilson. Cambridge: Clarke; Louisville: Westminster John Knox, 1991
NTS	*New Testament Studies*
OCP	*Orientalia christiana periodica*
OLA	Orientalia Lovaniensia Analecta
OrChr	*Oriens Christianus*
PG	Patrologia Graeca [= *Patrologiae Cursus Completus: Series Graeca*]. Edited by Jacques-Paul Migne. 162 vols. Paris, 1857–1886
PGM	*Papyri Graecae Magicae: Die griechischen Zauberpapyri.* Edited by Karl Preisendanz. 2nd ed. Stuttgart: Teubner, 1973–1974
PL	Patrologia Latina [= *Patrologiae Cursus Completus*: Series Latina]. Edited by Jacques-Paul Migne. 217 vols. Paris, 1844–1864
PTS	Patristische Texte und Studien
PW	*Paulys Real-Encyclopädie der classischen Altertumswissenschaft.* New edition by Georg Wissowa and Wilhelm Kroll. 50 vols. in 84 parts. Stuttgart: Metzler and Druckenmüller, 1894–1980
PWSup	PW Supplement. See PW above.
RB	*Revue biblique*
RBPH	*Revue belge de philologie et d'histoire*
RGG	*Die Religion in Geschichte und Gegenwart.* Edited by Hans Dieter Betz. 4th ed. 8 vols. Tübingen: Mohr Siebeck, 1998–2007
RHE	*Revue d'histoire ecclésiastique*
RHPR	*Revue d'histoire et de philosophie religieuses*
RJFTC	The Reception of Jesus in the First Three Centuries
RSR	*Recherches de science religieuse*
RTP	*Revue de Théologie et de Philosophie*
SAC	Studies in Antiquity and Christianity
SBLDS	Society of Biblical Literature Dissertation Series
SBLSBS	Society of Biblical Literature Sources for Biblical Study
SBLSP	Society of Biblical Literature Seminar Papers

SBLTT	Society of Biblical Literature Texts and Translations
SBLSymS	Society of Biblical Literature Symposium Series
SJLA	Studies in Judaism in Late Antiquity
SMSR	*Studi e materiali di storia delle religioni*
SNTSMS	Society for New Testament Studies Monograph Series
StT	Studi e Testi, Biblioteca apostolica vaticana
TENTS	Texts and Editions for New Testament Study
ThH	Théologie historique
TLG	*Thesaurus Linguae Graecae: Canon of Greek Authors and Works.* Edited by Luci Berkowitz and Karl A. Squitier. 3rd ed. New York: Oxford University Press, 1990
TS	Texts and Studies
TSAJ	Texts and Studies in Ancient Judaism
TUGAL	Texte und Untersuchungen zur Geschichte der altchristlichen Literatur
TU	Texte und Untersuchungen
TU NF	Texte und Untersuchungen, Neue Folge
UALG	Untersuchungen zur antiken Literatur und Geschichte
VC	*Vigiliae Christianae*
VCSup	Vigiliae Christianae Supplements
WGRW	Writings from the Greco-Roman World
WGRWSup	Writings from the Greco-Roman World Supplement Series
WUNT	Wissenschaftliche Untersuchungen zum Neuen Testament
ZAC	*Zeitschrift für Antikes Christentum*
ZNW	*Zeitschrift für die neutestametliche Wissenchaft unde die Kunde der älteren Kirche*
ZPE	*Zeitschrift für Papyrologie und Epigraphik*
ZWT	*Zeitschrift für wissenschaftliche Theologie*

PART 1

APOCRYPHAL GOSPELS

CHAPTER 1
AGRAPHA

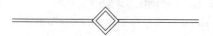

ANDREW GREGORY

1. INTRODUCTION

The term *agrapha* is widely used to refer to sayings that are attributed to Jesus but are not found in the canonical Gospels, and that is how I use the term here.[1] Such sayings have been identified in a wide range of written sources, including manuscripts of the canonical Gospels that contain variant readings, other books included in the New Testament, noncanonical Gospels, a variety of other Christian texts, and also Jewish and Muslim writings.[2]

Since these agrapha are preserved as quotations in written texts,[3] the critical study of these sayings begins necessarily with the study of the texts in which they are found and not with any postulated source from which they may or may not have been excerpted. Agrapha are almost always presented as isolated or stand-alone quotations, so the starting point for interpreting these sayings is the context in which, and the purpose for which, they were quoted. That context may or may not fairly reflect and may or may not offer any evidence for or access to any earlier context that the quotation may have had, for example in a narrative about Jesus or in a collection of sayings attributed to him.

---

1. It is also sometimes used in a wider sense, to refer to sayings attributed to Jesus that are not found in the New Testament. I reject that approach, for reasons that I explain below.

2. Recent collections of these sayings include Klaus Berger and Christiane Nord, *Das Neue Testament und frühchristliche Schriften* (Frankfurt: Insel, 2005), 1114–202, which presents 413 agrapha in German; Mauro Pesce, *Le Parole Dimenticate di Gesù*, Scrittori Greci e Latini (Milan: Fondazione Lorenzo Valla and Arnoldo Mondadori, 2004), which presents 542 agrapha in Latin and Greek, with facing Italian translation, plus commentary (also in Italian); William D. Stroker, *Extracanonical Sayings of Jesus*, SBL Resources for Biblical Study 18 (Atlanta: Scholars Press, 1989), which presents 266 agrapha, many listed with parallels, in Greek, Latin, and Coptic, with English translations, preceded by a short but useful introduction. Older collections that remain of value include Alfred Resch, *Agrapha: Aussercanonische Schriftfragmente*, 2nd ed., TU NF 15.3–4 (Leipzig: Hinrichs, 1906; repr., Darmstadt: Wissenschaftliche Buchgesellschaft, 1976), and James Hardy Ropes, *Die Sprüche Jesu: die in den kanonischen Evangelien nicht überliefert sind: eine kritische Bearbeitung des von Alfred Resch gesammelten Materials*, TUGAL 14.2 (Leipzig: Hinrichs, 1896). An extensive collection of sayings attributed to Jesus in Muslim sources may be found in Miguel Asín Palacios, *Logia et agrapha Domini Jesu apud moslemicos scriptores asceticos praesertim usitata*, ed. R. Graffin and F. Nau, Patrologia Orientalis (Paris: Firmin-Didot, 1916–1929), 13.3 (1919), pp. 335–441, and 19.4 (1926), pp. 531–624.

3. We may note that the term *agrapha*, meaning "unwritten [sayings]," is certainly therefore unfortunate. But it is widely used and performs the useful function of labeling a body of material that falls within a broadly understood set of parameters. I do not think that the term needs to be abandoned, but critical analysis of this material does require the sort of careful definition and qualification that I seek to provide in what follows, in which I take account of the measured assessment of Tobias Nicklas, "Zur Problematik der so genannten 'Agrapha': Eine Thesenreihe," *RB* 113.1 (2006): 78–93, and try to avoid the methodological pitfalls noted by Giovanni Bazzana, "Replaying Jesus's Sayings in the 'Agrapha': Reflections on the *Neu-Inszenierung* of Jesus's Traditions in the Second Century between *2 Clement* and Clement of Alexandria," in *Gospels and Gospel Traditions in the Second Century: Experiments in Reception*, ed. Jens Schröter, Tobias Nicklas, and Joseph Verheyden, BZNW 235 (Berlin: de Gruyter, 2019), 27–43.

These questions that arise in the interpretation of agrapha are similar to those that sometimes arise in the study of the canonical Gospels. This means that reflection on how such questions help us to understand better the texts that we identify as agrapha is not only an end in itself but may also help to shed light on how to understand certain aspects of the development of the canonical Gospel tradition.

2. SUMMARY OF CONTENT: DEFINITION AND SCOPE

For the purposes of this discussion, I shall define *agrapha* as follows:

> Discrete sayings that are attributed to the earthly Jesus but are not included in what is normally received as the standard critical text of any of the four canonical Gospels. They are usually presented as quotations, which means that they are transmitted independently of their context in any earlier source from which they may have been taken.

Four points may be noted. First, this definition excludes sayings that have been transmitted in noncanonical Gospels or other texts that present the life or teaching of the earthly Jesus and that survive in a manuscript tradition of their own, since those sayings can be interpreted in the literary context of the texts in which they are transmitted. Thus the definition has genuine heuristic value, since it serves to exclude a large number of sayings that are sometimes included among agrapha but are better studied separately because of the different (but sometimes related) methodological questions that their sources raise.

Second, the definition excludes sayings attributed to the risen Jesus and spoken only after his death. It thus excludes sayings found in texts sometimes known as resurrection dialogues, as well as the sayings of the risen Jesus recorded in Revelation. Such sayings might in any event be excluded because they are embedded in a literary context, but the definition seeks to make a clear distinction between teaching from before and after Jesus's resurrection, even if it is not always easy to maintain that distinction in practice—as we shall see below.

Third, it is important to note that the definition includes the slightly cumbersome reference to agrapha as texts that "are not included in what is normally received as the standard critical text of any of the four canonical Gospels." This qualification arises because the texts inscribed in our very many manuscript witnesses to the canonical Gospels differ at a large number of points, usually in minor ways. Among the more lengthy or substantial variant readings in the manuscript tradition are some that have been considered agrapha, and I discuss several of these variants below. They may be noted in the apparatus at the bottom of critical editions of the Greek New Testament, but they are not normally included in the reconstructed critical text or in most modern vernacular translations based on that critical text.[4]

Fourth, the definition also includes sayings of Jesus that were not inscribed in the canonical Gospels but may be found elsewhere in the New Testament. Among them are possible sayings of Jesus that may be transmitted or reflected in the letters of Paul, which were written at an earlier date than the canonical Gospels and therefore have the potential to shed light on the development of the gospel tradition before it was inscribed in the Synoptic Gospels or in John. Also included are sayings found elsewhere in the New Testament, for example in Acts, where Luke attributes to Jesus two sayings that he did not record Jesus saying in his Gospel. This means that this chapter will discuss canonical

---

4. A partial exception is the *Pericope Adulterae*, on which see below on p. 12.

as well as noncanonical texts with a view to how they cast light on the interpretation of the canonical Gospels, but I hope that the advantages of doing this will be apparent and that the discussion of some New Testament agrapha will not seem out of place in a volume devoted to noncanonical writings. My working definition of agrapha presumes the existence of the canonical boundary around the books of the New Testament, and I accept it as a well-documented historical given, but the definition requires that the canonical status of the source of an agraphon should play no role in the process of evaluating the literary or historical significance of any particular saying of Jesus that was transmitted "outside the standard critical text of any of the four canonical Gospels."

3. INTERPRETIVE ISSUES

At least three reasons for scholarly interest in agrapha may be noted, and each raises interpretive issues of its own. First, they are evidence for the ongoing collective memory of Jesus, or the reception of Jesus tradition and its impact on the development of early Christian history and literature (and sometimes on Jewish and Muslim sources too). Second, they may be considered sources to be mined in search of evidence for what the historical Jesus may have said. Third, the way in which they appear to have been used and to have developed may be analyzed to see whether by analogy they may shed light on how canonical traditions developed. We shall consider each of these approaches in turn.

3.1 Evidence for Collective Memory about Jesus and for Different Communities Who Preserved It

The first approach begins with the texts in which agrapha are transmitted and concerns itself with the wider issues that those writings raise. It draws on these texts as sources that are useful for investigating the reception of traditions about Jesus and how different communities formed and passed on their collective memories of him. Thus it seeks not to isolate the agrapha from the texts in which they are transmitted but to interpret them as sayings that are embedded in and are therefore integral elements of larger texts. Those texts are treated as sources that are significant in themselves and that may be considered in their own historical and literary contexts as potential witnesses to the contemporary lives and beliefs of those who quoted the agrapha that they contain, not merely as sources from which agrapha may be extracted and studied in isolation.

This is arguably the most productive way in which to approach the study of the agrapha, as it addresses them as parts of the texts in which they were transmitted and does not seek to remove them from the context in which they are accessible to readers today. It has the potential to make an important contribution to our understanding of the development of Christian (and sometimes Jewish and Muslim) literature, and it fits neatly with current interest in the reception of Jesus traditions, and with current interest in collective memory broadly understood. Yet this approach, with its interest in a wide range of literature, takes us away from the immediate concerns of this volume and its focus on the interpretation of the New Testament. This puts it beyond the scope of this chapter, so although it is important to be aware of this way of approaching the agrapha, it will not feature very much in the discussion that follows.

3.2 Potential Evidence for the Historical Jesus

A second reason for studying agrapha is their potential as evidence for the historical Jesus. Scholars who draw on agrapha in search of sayings that might be attributed to the historical Jesus need to have some sort of criteria with which to assess the likelihood that any saying might go back to Jesus and for that reason be considered "authentic." One criterion may be a relatively early date, although it is widely recognized that a late text may transmit early tradition. Another criterion may be whether a particular saying can make sense in a first-century Galilean or Judean context, since that is where Jesus lived and taught. A third may be the extent to which a saying is consistent or congruent with Jesus's teaching as presented in the Synoptic Gospels, or elsewhere, depending on which texts a scholar sees as the most important starting place for any attempt to reconstruct the teaching of the historical Jesus. A fourth is whether the saying is proverbial or otherwise known in other contexts, in which case it may have been attributed erroneously to Jesus. Through the application of these criteria, scholars are able to eliminate a large number of sayings included in different collections of agrapha and other sources and to produce a much smaller sample on which to focus their attention. This may be seen in the work of scholars such as Joachim Jeremias, who brought his collection of agrapha down to eighteen,[5] and Otfried Hofius, who has reduced this number to seven, of which he considers only three to be eligible for consideration as authentic sayings of Jesus.[6]

3.3 Evidence for the Development of Gospel Traditions

A third reason for studying these texts is their potential to shed light on the development of the canonical Gospels and the Jesus tradition that they contain. Scholars who are interested in the development of the canonical Gospels may be interested in the agrapha in order to increase the data set that they may investigate, in order to try to understand the development of gospel (and particularly Synoptic Gospel) tradition. Their primary interest in the development of the canonical gospel tradition tends to mean that they focus on agrapha that are closest to canonical sayings in content or in form, and they may not be unduly concerned about whether noncanonical sayings analogous to their canonical counterparts are preserved in late or in early sources. Many of the agrapha that I discuss below are susceptible to be used in this way.

4. KEY PASSAGES FOR NEW TESTAMENT STUDIES AND THEIR SIGNIFICANCE

Any selection of agrapha needs to be ordered in some way. William Stroker orders his list according to their content and form, drawing on form-critical categories developed by Rudolf Bultmann. Another approach would be to present them in the chronological order of the authors who quoted the sayings (which may not be the same as the chronological order of the manuscripts in which their writings have been preserved), beginning with the letters of Paul, and moving forward through early Christian authors such as Clement of Rome, Justin Martyr, Irenaeus, and Tertullian, as well as later Christian authors and also Jewish and Muslim sources, attempting to slot in the evidence from Gospel variants at appropriate points.

No one approach is self-evidently better than any other, although it is important to note how any particular order may affect how readers interpret the selection of texts that it presents. In what follows, I take a schematic approach that is informed but not dictated by the relative dating of the sources. Thus I begin with New Testament texts other than the Gospels, before moving to the evidence of variant readings within the manuscript tradition

---

5. Joachim Jeremias, *Unknown Sayings of Jesus*, 2nd ed., trans. Reginald H. Fuller (London: SPCK, 1964).

6. Otfried Hofius, "Isolated Sayings of the Lord," in *NTApoc* 1:88–91. For a fuller statement of his position, see his essay, "Unknown Sayings of Jesus," in *The Gospel and the Gospels*, ed. Peter Stuhlmacher (Grand Rapids: Eerdmans, 1991), 336–60, in which he discusses nine sayings, four of which he considers eligible for consideration as authentic sayings of the historical Jesus.

of some of the canonical Gospels. I then take a broadly chronological approach to a selection of sayings found in texts and authors as follows: the Didache, 1 and 2 Clement, the Letter of Barnabas, Justin Martyr, Clement of Alexandria, and Origen.[7]

4.1 Agrapha in the New Testament

In what follows I begin with two texts from Acts, which was almost certainly written by the same author as the Gospel of Luke. This raises the intriguing possibility that he chose to use in his second volume sayings that he could have used in his Gospel. I then consider examples from the letters of Paul. These are our earliest surviving Christian texts, written before the canonical Gospels (and before Acts). It is therefore possible either that Paul drew on early forms of tradition that the Gospel writers later used independently of his writings, or that the Gospels were influenced by traditions that they knew in the form that Paul recorded them. Finally, I discuss some agrapha that are found in certain manuscripts of the canonical Gospels but are not usually thought to belong to the earliest attainable version of their texts. The selection of texts reflects both the intrinsic interest of each saying that I include as well as the methodological issues that they raise. Other New Testament texts that may contain agrapha include James, 1 Peter, and 2 Peter, but I do not discuss them here because of lack of space.

4.1.1 The Acts of the Apostles
Acts 11:16

"John baptized with water, but you will be baptized with the Holy Spirit."[8]

Toward the end of his speech to the church at Jerusalem, in which he explains why he went to the house of Cornelius in Caesarea and ate there, Peter appeals to a "word of the Lord" that he had remembered when he witnessed the gift of the Spirit to Cornelius and his household: "John baptized with water, but you will be baptized with the Holy Spirit."

The saying has no parallel with any saying of Jesus found in the canonical Gospels, although a similar saying is found at Acts 1:5, where the risen Jesus tells the apostles, "John baptized with water, but you will be baptized with the Holy Spirit not many days from now." Since it is the risen Jesus who speaks, this instance would not be considered an agraphon on the definition set out above, which requires agrapha to be attributed to Jesus during his earthly life (i.e., prior to his resurrection). However, Luke's introduction of a forty-day period between the resurrection and the ascension, and his presentation of the risen Jesus using this time to teach his disciples much as he had done before (Acts 1:3), problematizes the strict application of this definition and the distinction on which it rests, and may justify discussing this saying alongside other texts that clearly fit the definition of agrapha that I employ.

The passage in Acts is of particular interest because a very similar saying is found in all three Synoptic Gospels, in passages which appear to reflect an overlap between Mark (Mark 1:8) and double tradition (Matt 3:11 and Luke 3:16). This suggests that the saying, which all three Synoptic Gospels attribute not to Jesus but to John the Baptist, goes back

---

7. The sources of my English translations of these texts are as follows: New Testament texts (including John 8:7)—NRSV; textual variants—Bruce M. Metzger, *A Textual Commentary on the Greek New Testament*, 2nd ed. (London: United Bible Societies, 1994); Apostolic Fathers—Michael W. Holmes, *The Apostolic Fathers: Greek Texts and English Translations*, 3rd ed. (Grand Rapids: Baker Academic, 2007); Justin Martyr, Clement of Alexandria, and Origen—Stroker, *Extracanonical Sayings*.

8. Cf. Mark 1:8//Matt 3:11//Luke 3:16; Acts 1:5.

to the earliest stages of the tradition. Luke clearly knew this, since in his Gospel he attributes these words to John, which raises the question why in Acts he twice attributes them to Jesus—once directly to the risen Jesus at Acts 1:5, and once indirectly to Jesus at Acts 11:16, where Peter refers to something that he remembers Jesus to have said either before or after his resurrection.

At least two explanations may be considered as to why, in Acts, Luke presents these words as a saying of Jesus. First, Luke may have encountered the saying in a form in which it was already attributed to Jesus, whether during his earthly ministry or after his resurrection. Jesus may have repeated words that John had spoken about him, and Luke may have chosen to present them when they refer to something that is imminent (Acts 1:5) or that has happened already (Acts 11:16). If so, Luke has chosen to hold over until his second volume a tradition that he received as a saying of Jesus because he considered it better suited for the second rather than the first volume of his work. Or, second, Luke may have known the tradition only as a saying attributed to John, but he chose to repurpose it as a saying of Jesus. This would be consistent with his widely recognized editorial interest in associating Jesus with John, but subordinating John to Jesus. Just as Luke removed John schematically from the scene (Luke 3:20) before he introduced the ministry of Jesus (Luke 3:21–23a), so now he is clear that it is the baptism promised by Jesus, and not by John, that is foundational for the mission and expansion of those who followed Jesus (Acts 1:5; 11:16, cf. 19:1–7).

Two further points may be noted about how Luke frames this saying that Peter attributes to Jesus. The first is his appeal to memory, which may be compared with similar appeals in 1 Clement and in Polycarp's *Letter to the Philippians* (on each of which, see below). The second is that Peter appeals to a saying of Jesus toward the very end of his speech as a way of strengthening the argument that he has made. Paul does something very similar in Acts 20:35 (on which, see below), so these two apostolic appeals to words of Jesus that Peter and Paul remember and commend to their hearers may be part of a wider pattern of parallels in Luke's presentation of these two apostles in the Acts of the Apostles. This underscores just how carefully Luke crafted his narrative account as well as his belief in the importance of the teaching of Jesus for those who followed him.

Acts 20:35

"It is more blessed to give than to receive."

At the end of his speech to the Ephesian elders, Luke has Paul appeal to his own example as one who through his own toil helped the weak, as he implores his addressees to do. Then, to seal his argument, Luke has Paul appeal to them to remember the words of the Lord Jesus: "It is more blessed to give than to receive." The saying has no parallel in any of the canonical Gospels, although its command to give is consistent with Jesus's teaching about how his followers should share their wealth and possessions, which is a particularly prominent theme in the Gospel of Luke. Paul speaks of how through his own labor he earned an income that he was able to share with others, rather than relying on their financial support (Acts 20:33–34), and he appeals to the teaching of Jesus as the reason why he did so and why the Ephesian elders should follow his example as he followed the example of his Lord (v. 35).

The fact that this saying fits so neatly with much of the teaching of Jesus in Luke, particularly in single tradition, makes it plausible to believe that Luke took the saying from oral traditions or written sources that he may have used when composing his Gospel, but chose to hold it back in order to use it when writing Acts. According to James Ropes, it "possesses the same right to be accepted as any saying in the Gospel of Luke."[9]

Yet Ropes's claim does not preclude the possibility that it may have been Luke who attributed the saying to Jesus rather than any prior tradition or source on which he drew. This possibility gains credence from the fact that the same sentiment is expressed in a number of ancient texts and that there is a close verbal parallel in Thucydides, from which it appears to have been taken up by other authors.[10] Thus it is possible that Luke has taken a proverbial saying and attributed it to Jesus, as commentators on Acts such as Haenchen and Pervo suggest,[11] and as Hofius concludes: "We are dealing with a maxim that circulated in the Graeco-Roman world, as a wealth of evidence shows, which is erroneously attributed to Jesus."[12] If so, Luke may not have been doing anything unusual, whether his transference of the saying from another source should be considered "erroneous" or "deliberate."[13]

4.1.2 The Letters of Paul
1 Thessalonians 4:15–17

> For this we declare to you by the word of the Lord, that we who are alive, who are left until the coming of the Lord, will by no means precede those who have died. For the Lord himself, with a cry of command, with the archangel's call and with the sound of God's trumpet, will descend from heaven, and the dead in Christ will rise first. Then we who are alive, who are left, will be caught up in the clouds together with them to meet the Lord in the air; and so we will be with the Lord forever.

First Thessalonians is arguably the earliest letter of Paul. It includes this teaching about the fate of the Christian dead that Paul introduces with what may be an appeal to the explicit teaching of Jesus. Two difficulties in interpreting this passage may be noted. The first is that Paul writes in the third person, so he paraphrases the content of the "word of the Lord" to which he refers. This means that if we are to try to recover any words that Paul may have received as a saying of Jesus, then we would need at the very least to rephrase them in the first person. The second is that it is difficult to determine how much of it corresponds to "the word of the Lord" to which Paul refers, and how much of it corresponds to Paul's own commentary on it. The words that Paul paraphrases might be found only in verse 15, only in verses 16–17, or in all three verses, but his use of the third person makes it very difficult to know where the teaching of the Lord may end and that of Paul may begin (cf. 1 Cor 7:10–12, 25 where the distinction is explicit and clear).

None of this material has any clear parallel in the canonical Gospels or in other sources that attribute similar teaching to Jesus, so it is the sole surviving early witness to this tradition. It is impossible to determine whether Paul means to refer to teaching of the earthly Jesus (as he clearly does in some places where he refers to the Lord, on which see further below) or to that of the risen and exalted Christ (cf. Gal 1:11–12), so this uncertainty raises the question of whether the tradition meets the definition of agrapha set out above. Paul could be appealing to a saying of the earthly Jesus that is otherwise unrecorded,

---

9. James Hardy Ropes, "Agrapha," in *Dictionary of the Bible*, ed. James Hastings, 5 vols. (Edinburgh: T&T Clark, 1904), 5:344.

10. See Ernst Haenchen, *The Acts of the Apostles* (Oxford: Basil Blackwell, 1971), 594n5, and Richard I. Pervo, *Acts*, Hermeneia (Minneapolis: Fortress, 2009), 528–29.

11. See previous note.

12. Hofius, "Unknown Sayings," 344.

13. See, with further examples, Jeremias, *Unknown Sayings*, 32–35; Hofius, "Unknown Sayings," 343–46.

to something that he received directly from the risen Lord, or to words spoken by an early Christian prophet that either the prophet or Paul designated a "word of the Lord." For Jeremias, this passage contains the earliest known agraphon;[14] for Hofius, however, no agraphon is to be found in this text.[15]

1 Corinthians 9:14

In the same way, the Lord commanded that those who proclaim the gospel should get their living by the gospel.

This is one of four points in 1 Corinthians in which Paul appeals to teaching of Jesus that has clear parallels in the Synoptic Gospels.[16] His statement that "the Lord commanded that those who proclaim the gospel should get their living by the gospel" appears to reflect the saying of Jesus at Matthew 10:10//Luke 10:7 that the worker is worthy of his hire. The use of the noun "gospel" for the proclaimed message of good news is found very frequently in Paul, but never in the double tradition found in Matthew and Luke (and only four times in Matthean single tradition, and never in Luke, although it is found twice in Acts).

The fact that the distinctively Pauline form of this tradition differs from that found in Matthew and Luke may be interpreted in different ways. It could mean that Paul was paraphrasing an early form of the tradition that was actually much closer to the form in which it was received by Matthew and by Luke than the form in which they handed it down. If so, the form of the saying found in the Synoptic tradition could be directly dependent on the saying in 1 Corinthians 9:14. However, that seems unlikely, not least because it would require us to believe that someone had taken a distinctively Pauline expression and purged it of its characteristically Pauline vocabulary before recasting it in a form closer to other sayings of Jesus as presented in the Synoptic tradition. Therefore, it seems better to see the Pauline saying and the Synoptic saying as independent of each other but making a similar point.

The saying, in a form close to that of the Synoptic tradition, is also found at 1 Timothy 5:18. There it follows a quotation of Deuteronomy 25:4 and is presented with it as a quotation from Scripture. This suggests that the author of the letter valued the saying as authoritative and thought that it came from the Jewish Scriptures; it is unlikely that he was referring to the Gospels in this way. Here we see how a saying can be easily misattributed, possibly because it circulated with other sayings or excerpts arranged not by source but by subject matter.

4.1.3 Textual Variants

Agrapha transmitted as textual variants are found in a number of manuscripts, prominent among which is Codex Bezae. This is a bilingual codex of the New Testament with

---

14. Jeremias, *Unknown Sayings*, 80–83.

15. Hofius, "Unknown Sayings," 338–41.

16. Commentaries on 1 Corinthians and Paul's other letters discuss his possible knowledge of sayings of Jesus where the question arises. Longer discussions of these issues, together with further bibliography, may be found in a wide range of other secondary literature, including David Wenham, "Jesus Tradition in the Letters of the New Testament," in *Handbook for the Study of the Historical Jesus*, ed. T. Holmén and Stanley E. Porter, 4 vols. (Leiden: Brill, 2010), 3:2041–57; idem, *Paul: Follower of Jesus or Founder of Christianity?* (Grand Rapids: Eerdmans, 1995); Dale C. Allison, "The Pauline Epistles and the Synoptic Gospels: The Pattern of the Parallels," *NTS* 28 (1982): 1–32; David L. Dungan, *The Sayings of Jesus in the Churches of Paul* (Oxford: Basil Blackwell, 1971).

Greek and Latin facing text.[17] It was likely written about 400 CE, and it includes a Latin text that may go back to the third century. The character of this text varies between different books of the New Testament, but it seems to have been a fresh translation of the Greek, not based on an earlier Latin text. It may have offered an opportunity for its translators and scribes to introduce some additional sayings of Jesus, some of which would eventually make their way from its Latin text into Greek manuscripts of the Gospels.[18] Four examples may be noted.

Matthew 20:28

"But seek to increase from that which is small, and from the greater to become less."

This saying is found in Codex Bezae and, with minor variations, some other witnesses. According to Metzger, this interpolation is "a piece of floating tradition," so potentially an agraphon by another name. It is to be explained, he continues, as "an expanded but inferior version of Luke 14:8–10."[19] But even if the bulk of the passage may depend on Luke (and not on any source on which he may have drawn) and is therefore not an independent witness to material found also in the Synoptic tradition, this does not apply to the opening part of this passage, which has no parallel in any canonical Gospel. Thus, the words quoted above are an agraphon, and we may note how a scribe or translator was prepared to conflate a noncanonical tradition with a paraphrase of part of one Synoptic Gospel in order to produce a new passage in a second Synoptic Gospel. The material based on Luke shows how Jesus's saying might be applied, but it is difficult to decide which, if either, had any form of priority before they were brought together. Does the saying depend on the teaching that follows and possibly derive from it, thus allowing a scribe to introduce it in this context? Or did a scribe know the saying and decide that Jesus's teaching about the etiquette of seating at banquets was a suitable text with which to illustrate the meaning of an otherwise isolated saying?

Mark 9:49

"Every sacrifice will be salted with salt."

This addition to Mark 9:49, found in Codex Bezae and some other manuscripts, may be compared to Leviticus 2:13, which instructs worshipers to offer salt with all their offerings to God. Metzger suggests that a scribe may have thought that the text in Leviticus helped to explain the meaning of Jesus's statement in Mark that "everyone will be salted with fire" and therefore wrote it in the margin of his copy of Mark at 9:49. Later scribes may then have moved the marginal reading into the main part of the text, which explains both this textual form found in Bezae and also another textual variant found in other witnesses at this point, "For everyone will be salted with fire, and every sacrifice will be salted with salt."[20] If so, this is an example of how a text from the Hebrew Bible came to be identified accidentally as a saying of Jesus, through a scribal error.

---

17. On the manuscript and its text, see David C. Parker, *Codex Bezae: An Early Christian Manuscript and Its Text* (Cambridge: Cambridge University Press, 1992).

18. Parker, *Codex Bezae*, 257, 279–80.

19. Metzger, *Textual Commentary*, 43.

20. Metzger, *Textual Commentary*, 87.

Luke 6:5

"Man, if you know what you are doing, you are blessed; but if you do not know you are accursed and a transgressor of the Law."

These words of Jesus are addressed to a man working on the Sabbath, who is introduced in Codex Bezae instead of the usual text at Luke 6:5, which Bezae places elsewhere. This situates the incident immediately after Luke's account of Jesus and his disciples in the grainfields, in a passage in which Bezae makes a number of changes to the text. The fact that in Codex Bezae the saying circulates with its own narrative context, albeit very short ("On the same day, he saw a man performing a work on the Sabbath. Then he said to him . . ."), could tell against its inclusion as an agraphon. But I present it here because it provides a useful point of comparison to other sayings preserved as textual variants. It also serves as an example of a saying that Jeremias considered to be an early tradition that goes back to the historical Jesus.[21]

John 8:7

"Let anyone among you who is without sin be the first to throw a stone at her."

This saying, found in Codex Bezae and other witnesses[22] and part of the story often known as the *Pericope Adulterae*, should be considered alongside the words that Jesus addresses to the woman condemned for adultery: "Woman, where are they? Has no one condemned you?" (John 8.10) and "Neither do I condemn you. Go your way, and from now on do not sin again" (John 8:11b). Its inclusion here may be questioned. Since the sayings have a literary context of their own—in the narrative in which they are embedded—they may be excluded as agrapha by the definition of that term. The whole passage might be considered more like the sort of brief narrative found in P.Oxy840, or compared to some of the material attributed to the Gospel according to the Hebrews, rather than to free-floating sayings of Jesus. However, this strict application of our definition may be set against the fact that this passage is not only comparable to the additions to Matthew and Luke noted above but is by far the best known of such passages. This may be seen in its inclusion in most vernacular translations of the New Testament as well as in critical editions of the Greek text, even though no one claims that this passage is anything other than an interpolation in the text of John, and there is widespread agreement that it did not originate there.

The fact that sayings embedded in a narrative could be added to the text of a canonical Gospel demonstrates that at least in this one instance the texts of those Gospels could be expanded or supplemented, even after they had been in circulation for some time. It therefore raises the question of whether (and, if so, when and how) other sayings or traditions may have been incorporated into earlier forms of the Gospel tradition.

---

21. Jeremias, *Unknown Sayings*, 61–65. Hofius judges the historicity of the scene presupposed at Luke 6:5d to be quite improbable and considers the saying to be one of the few examples of where the early church minted a new dominical saying ("Unknown Sayings," 357, 359–60).

22. This passage has generated an enormous amount of discussion, both in commentaries on John and elsewhere. For a recent and comprehensive treatment, with further bibliography, see Jennifer Knust and Tommy Wasserman, *To Cast the First Stone: The Transmission of a Gospel Story* (Princeton: Princeton University Press, 2019).

4.2 Agrapha in Other Early Christian Literature
4.2.1 The Didache

The Didache is an early Christian text that contains a number of sayings that have parallels in the Synoptic Gospels, especially in the Sermon on the Mount and the Sermon on the Plain.[23] It may be among the earliest noncanonical writings that contain sayings of Jesus, but the questions of its date relative to the Synoptic Gospels and whether its author drew on Matthew and/or Luke are contested. It does not explicitly identify all this material as sayings of Jesus, which raises the question of whether that is how the author (or editor or compiler) of this text understood its content. The title of the book in one manuscript is "The Teaching of the Lord to the Gentiles by the Twelve Apostles," but we do not know at what point this title was ascribed to the text.

There are two points where the text appeals to material as the Lord's command or word, and we may consider each in turn.

Didache 8.2

> Our Father in heaven,
> hallowed be your name,
> your kingdom come,
> your will be done
>   on earth as it is in heaven.
> Give us today our daily bread,
> and forgive us our debts,
>   as we also forgive our debtors;
> and do not lead us into temptation,
> but deliver us from the evil one;
> for yours is the power and the glory forever.'

In this first instance, the author exhorts his readers to "pray like this, just as the Lord commanded in his Gospel," then quotes the prayer above. It is very similar to the Lord's Prayer as found in Matthew, and readers of the Didache are enjoined to say it three times daily. It is possible that the very significant similarities between the Didache and Matthew are because the former quotes the latter, which would mean that this quotation should not be considered an agraphon. However, if the author of the Didache is quoting a version of the Lord's Prayer that was known to him through communal worship and is earlier than or otherwise independent of the form found in Matthew's Gospel, or if Matthew is drawing on the Didache, this could be an example of an agraphon that overlaps with material found in the Synoptic Gospels and that might shed light on the development of that tradition.

Didache 9.5

"Do not give what is holy to dogs."

The second quotation that the Didache attributes explicitly to the Lord raises similar issues. The same saying is found verbatim in single tradition at Matthew 7:6, but it is very

---

23. For fuller discussions of these parallels, with bibliography, see Christopher M. Tuckett, "The *Didache* and the Writings that Later Formed the New Testament," in *The Reception of the New Testament in the Apostolic Fathers*, ed. Andrew F. Gregory and Christopher M. Tuckett (Oxford: Oxford University Press, 2005), 104–6, and Stephen E. Young, *Jesus Tradition in the Apostolic Fathers*, WUNT 2.311 (Tübingen: Mohr Siebeck, 2011), 201–25, 227–29.

difficult to prove literary dependence, or which text may be dependent on the other. It is therefore unclear whether either text should be considered an agraphon; the merit of discussing it here, together with the prayer above, is that they illustrate some of the difficulties that arise when a saying of Jesus is found both in the canonical Gospels and elsewhere, but we are unable to determine if one form of the tradition has influenced the other, or if they might each independently reflect a common source.

4.2.2 First Clement

First Clement is conventionally dated in the 90s CE, but it could have been written at almost any point in the last quarter of the first century CE or in the first quarter of the second. If dated in the first century, it could be the earliest or among the earliest noncanonical writings that may contain sayings of Jesus.[24]

1 Clement 13.2

[a] "Show mercy, so that you may receive mercy; [b] forgive, so that you may be forgiven. [c] As you do, so shall it be done to you. [d] As you give, so shall it be given to you. [e] As you judge, so shall you be judged. [f] As you show kindness, so shall kindness be shown to you. [g] With the measure you use, it will be measured to you."

Its author explicitly attributes this string of teaching to Jesus and appeals to his audience to remember these words of the Lord Jesus, which suggests that it may have been widely known as oral tradition. The saying itself is deceptively straightforward in the form in which the author presents it, in the sense that one instruction follows another, and they may be read together as one whole. However, when the composite saying is broken down into its constituent parts and each is compared with parallels elsewhere, the potential complexity of the tradition history of this carefully crafted saying becomes apparent. Three sayings have close verbal parallels in Synoptic tradition ([g], cf. Mark 4:24; Luke 6.38; [e], cf. Matt 7:1–2; Luke 6:37; [d], cf. Luke 6:38), two sayings have less close verbal parallels ([b], cf. Matt 6:14; Mark 11:25; Luke 6:37; [a], cf. Matt 5:7; Luke 6:36), and there are two with no close verbal parallels, one of which conveys a similar idea to a saying found in Synoptic tradition ([c], cf. Matt 7:12; Luke 6:31) and one which has no parallel at all (f). Where there are parallels with Synoptic tradition, it is not possible to demonstrate literary dependence, and the combined weight of the differences between the parallel sayings, the presence of material without parallel, and the appeal for readers to remember these sayings have led most scholars who have studied this material to conclude that they originate in a sayings collection that was probably earlier than, and independent of, the Synoptic Gospels.[25] Thus it is an agraphon that may give access to an earlier form of the Synoptic tradition than found in the canonical Gospels, and to at least one saying attributed to Jesus at an early date that was not transmitted in any canonical text. It is significant both because of its early date and because it combines tradition found also in canonical texts with tradition that is not.

A very similar tradition is found in Polycarp's *Letter to the Philippians* 2.3, which may be dated to about 110 to 140 CE. Polycarp may have taken the material from a source shared

---

24. Fuller discussions of these sayings in 1 Clement, with further bibliography, include Donald M. Hagner, *The Use of the Old and New Testaments in Clement of Rome*, NovTSup 32 (Leiden: Brill, 1973), and Andrew Gregory, "*1 Clement* and the Writings that Later Formed the New Testament," in Gregory and Tuckett, *Reception*, 129–57.

25. For further discussion, with bibliography, see Gregory, "*1 Clement* and the Writings," 131–34.

with the author of 1 Clement, or may have taken it from 1 Clement, and may perhaps have modified it under the influence of the wording found in Matthew and possibly in Luke.[26]

1 Clement 46.8

(a) "Woe to that person! (b) Rather than cause one of my elect to sin (c) it would have been good for that one not to have been born. (d) It would have been better for that person to have been tied to a millstone and cast into the sea (e) rather than pervert one of my elect."

The author also appeals to his readers to remember these words of the Lord Jesus (1 Clem. 46.7). The phrases identified as (a) and (c) may be compared to Synoptic tradition found at Matthew 26:24//Mark 14:21//Luke 22:22, and the phrases identified as (b) and (d) may be compared to Synoptic tradition found at Matthew 18:6//Mark 9:42//Luke 17:2. The phrase identified as (e) contains the verb "pervert," which is not found in any of the Synoptic parallels but conveys an idea similar to Matthew 18:6, Mark 9:42, and Luke 17:2 where they use the verb "cause to sin [NRSV: 'stumble']" (as 1 Clement does here in phrase [b]). It is possible that the author of 1 Clement (or the tradition or source that he shares with his readers) may conflate and abbreviate two very different sayings that he takes from one or more of the canonical Gospels, but it is also possible (and many scholars judge more likely) that he appeals to a noncanonical and possibly oral tradition.[27] If so, this is not a loose quotation but an agraphon that may give us access to a saying of Jesus not recorded elsewhere, or to an earlier stage in the development of the Synoptic tradition than that found in the passages in the triple tradition noted above.

4.2.3 Second Clement

Second Clement, which is usually dated somewhere around the middle of the second century CE, includes a number of quotations that it attributes to Jesus,[28] at least two of which (3.2; 4.2) likely presuppose the form in which the tradition was presented in the Gospel according to Matthew.[29] It also contains a number of sayings that may be considered agrapha, but for reasons of space I discuss only the following example.

2 Clement 4.5

"If you are gathered with me close to my breast, yet you do not keep my commandments, I will throw you out and say to you: 'Get away from me; I do not know where you are from, you evildoers.'"

As this quotation appears in 2 Clement, it is clearly one saying of Jesus. The second half has a parallel in the canonical Gospels (Matt 7:23//Luke 13:27; cf. Ps 6:9 LXX), but the first half does not; its use of the word "breast" may be compared with John 13:25 and 21:20 but hardly proves dependence. Further, the first half has a well-known parallel elsewhere, in a marginal gloss found at Matthew 7:5 in manuscript 1424, which says that it may be found

---

26. Further discussions include Michael Holmes, "Polycarp's *Letter to the Philippians* and the Writings That Later Formed the New Testament," in Gregory and Tuckett, *Reception*, 190–93; and Paul Hartog, *Polycarp's Epistle to the Philippians and the Martyrdom of Polycarp: Introduction, Text and Commentary*, Oxford Apostolic Fathers (Oxford: Oxford University Press, 2013), 107–12.

27. For further discussion, with bibliography, see Gregory, "*1 Clement* and the Writings," 134–37.

28. For further discussion, with bibliography, see Christopher M. Tuckett, ed., *2 Clement: Introduction, Text and Commentary*, Oxford Apostolic Fathers (Oxford: Oxford University Press, 2012), and idem, "*2 Clement* and the Writings That Later Formed the New Testament," in Gregory and Tuckett, *Reception*, 252–78.

29. Tuckett, "*2 Clement* and the Writings," 257–60.

in the "Jewish Gospel." Since the author of 2 Clement presents this quotation as one saying of Jesus, the question to be asked is whether the whole saying should be considered an agraphon. The answer to this is yes, since the first part of the quotation has no canonical parallel, and the marginal gloss found at Matthew 7:5 in manuscript 1424 notes that this saying is found in a source that it appears to distinguish from the Gospel according to Matthew.

Yet the canonical parallels to the second part of the quotation raise further questions about the history of the tradition that the author of 2 Clement quotes as a saying of Jesus. If he knew either of these Gospels (and evidence elsewhere suggests that other quotations presuppose Matthew, and possibly Luke) he, or his source, may have taken a tradition from one of them and combined it with a tradition from elsewhere to produce the one agraphon that he quotes. Alternatively, regardless of whether he drew elsewhere on Matthew or on Luke, he may here quote a saying that is independent of and possibly earlier than the version found in Matthew and in Luke. If so, we may ask whether Matthew and Luke (or the person responsible for their source, if they are drawing on a written Q) knew a version of the saying that included the first half of the quotation found in 2 Clement 4.5, but chose not to use it.[30] On either hypothesis, the breakdown and analysis of this agraphon, and careful comparison with parallels elsewhere, points to the very complex nature of the development of the gospel tradition, either before or after much of it was given a particular written form (or forms) in the Synoptic Gospels.

4.2.4 The Letter of Barnabas

The Letter of Barnabas is usually dated sometime between 70 CE and 135 CE, so it too could be the earliest or among the earliest noncanonical writings that may contain sayings of Jesus. It may once quote from the Gospel according to Matthew (Barn. 4.14), and it also includes some other material with parallels in the Synoptic tradition, but the source on which it draws most frequently is the Jewish Bible.[31] Many passages from Jewish Scripture are identified as words of the Lord, who is almost always Yahweh, the God of Israel. A good example is at 6.13, where the author quotes "the Lord" as saying, "See I am making the final things like the first." This may be compared with the saying of the earthly Jesus found at Matthew 20:16 (cf. Matt 19:30//Mark 10:31) and the saying of the risen Jesus at Revelation 21:4–5, but its context in Barnabas suggests that the author attributes the words to Yahweh, not to Jesus.

Two potential agrapha may be noted, each in Barnabas 7, which expounds the meaning of the suffering and death of Jesus, understood as a past event that was foretold beforehand in Scripture (Barn. 7.1–2). We will consider them together.

Barnabas 7.5 and 7.11

"Since you are going to give me, when I am about to offer my flesh for the sins of my new people, gall with vinegar to drink, you alone must eat, while the people fast and lament in sackcloth and ashes." (v. 5)

---

30. Similar issues arise at 2 Clem. 8.5. Here the author quotes a saying that includes material with no canonical parallel ("If you do not keep what is small, who will give to you what is great?") and material that has a partial parallel at Luke 16:10 ("For I say to you that the one who is faithful in very little is faithful also in much"). In this instance he introduces it with the phrase "the Lord says in the Gospel," which suggests a written source and raises the question whether this might be a citation from a written text that no longer survives rather than an agraphon, as defined above.

31. On Barnabas and its sources, see James Carleton Paget, *The Epistle of Barnabas: Outlook and Background*, WUNT 2.64 (Tübingen: Mohr Siebeck, 1994), 71–185.

"Those who desire to see me and to gain my kingdom must receive me through affliction and suffering." (v. 11)

The first quotation, at Barnabas 7.5, is introduced in the context of the author's account of what the priests of the temple revealed in advance of the one who was given vinegar and gall to drink when he was crucified (vv. 3–4) and of what "the Lord," who intended to offer himself, said about the self-offering that he would make for the sins of his new people. Thus the speaker looks forward to the cross, but is more likely to be understood as the preexistent Christ, not as the earthly Jesus. Therefore, by definition, the status of the saying as an agraphon is at best uncertain, and probably doubtful, unless its attribution to the preexistent Christ is considered the author's imposition upon a saying that he may have received as the words of the earthly Jesus.

The status of the speaker to whom should be attributed the saying found at Barnabas 7.11 is also unclear, but it is more likely the preexistent Christ who speaks through the prophets than the earthly Jesus. This means that it, too, should probably not be considered an agraphon, at least as the author of the epistle presents it.

Of considerable interest, however, is the way in which the author of the letter draws on identifiable passages from the Jewish Scriptures, on traditions about the crucifixion of Jesus that may be compared to the accounts in the canonical Gospels, and on the two sayings discussed above for which no source may be identified, and brings them all together in support of the argument that he wishes to make. No other text provides an identifiable source for either of the two sayings, and we cannot altogether exclude the possibility that the author of Barnabas received these forms of words as sayings of Jesus that were handed down to him as part of oral tradition or in a written source. Yet the extent to which they fit their literary context and advance the argument of the author (especially at 7.11, which provides a fitting conclusion to the discussion in the chapter) may suggest that they originated with him. If so, both sayings may show how an early Christian theologian was prepared to attribute words of his own devising to the preexistent Christ, which raises the question of whether other theologians would also attribute words of their own devising to the earthly Jesus by including them alongside or as part of gospel traditions known to them.[32]

4.2.5 Justin Martyr

Justin Martyr's *Dialogue with Trypho* may be dated to the middle of the second century. Both in it and in his *Apology*, Justin quotes a great deal of material that may reflect knowledge of the Synoptic Gospels. He also quotes traditions that may be identified as agrapha, three of which may be considered here.

Dialogue with Trypho 35.3

"There will be divisions and factions."

In this passage Justin attributes four sayings to Jesus. The first, third, and fourth, which are all warnings about false prophets, have parallels in Synoptic tradition (Matt 7:15; 24:5, 11, 24; Mark 13:22). The second, which is quoted above, does not. A similar quotation also appears as a saying of Jesus in the Syriac *Didascalia Apostolorum* and as an unattributed

---

32. For further discussion of these sayings, and the full range of Jesus traditions in Barnabas, see J. Christopher Edwards, *The Gospel according to the Epistle of Barnabas: Jesus Traditions in an Early Christian Polemic*, WUNT 2.503 (Tübingen: Mohr Siebeck, 2019), esp. 34–42, 96–98.

quotation in Didymus, and there are references to "divisions and factions" in other texts, including the Pseudo-Clementine *Homilies* (16.21, in a saying of Jesus) and Lactantius (*Inst.* 4.30). Paul also refers to divisions and factions at Corinth (1 Cor 11:18–19), and some scholars have argued that later Christians identified Paul's words as some sort of prophecy of Jesus that they then portrayed as a saying of the Lord. If so, this agraphon shows how material in the letters of Paul could influence the development of the gospel tradition without being mediated through the form of the tradition that was found in the canonical Gospels.[33]

Dialogue with Trypho 47.5

"In whatever circumstances I come upon you, in them I will also judge you."

Justin quotes this saying, which he attributes explicitly to Jesus, while answering a question about whether followers of Jesus who follow the Mosaic law may be saved. Others who quote similar words as a saying of Jesus (but with "find" instead of "come upon you") include Pseudo-Athanasius (*Quaestiones ad Antiochum* 36). Clement of Alexandria (*Quis div.* 40) also quotes the saying (with "find," like Pseudo-Athanasius), but he attributes it to God the Father, not to Jesus. Other authors quote similar words, but they identify them as coming from the prophet Ezekiel (7:8; cf. 18:30; 33:20). If they are correct, the saying in Justin appears to be an agraphon that arose when a prophetic text which was part of Jewish Scripture was attributed to Jesus. Both Clement and Justin quote the saying in a context in which they drew on material taken from Ezekiel 33, so it is easy to see how either Justin or the source on which he drew came to attribute this saying to Jesus—either inadvertently, or perhaps because of a belief that the preexistent Logos was speaking through the prophet Ezekiel.

Dialogue with Trypho 51.2

And Christ ... also himself preached, saying that the kingdom of heaven was near and that he must suffer many things from the scribes and Pharisees and be crucified and rise on the third day and appear again in Jerusalem and then eat and drink again with his disciples, and foretold in the time between his (first and second) advent, as I have said before, that priests and false prophets would appear in his name.

Here Justin tells Trypho how Christ came to the Jordan, while John the Baptist was still there. Justin says that Christ spoke of his crucifixion, resurrection, and second coming, and of the rise of heresies and false prophets before his second coming (*parousia*). The reference to priests (which several modern editors have suggested should read "heresies"; the two Greek words sound very alike, which could explain how a scribe wrote "priests" rather than "heresies") and false prophets may be compared to the agraphon in *Dialogue with Trypho* 35.3 and its parallels elsewhere, where Jesus speaks of divisions and heresies, and most of what Jesus says here has parallels in Synoptic tradition. Justin's explicit reference to Jesus eating and drinking may be compared not only to canonical passages such as Luke 24:42–43, John 21:13–15, and Acts 10:41, but also to Ignatius's *To the Smyrnaeans* 3.3 and other noncanonical texts that might offer independent testimony to similar traditions.

---

33. For a much fuller discussion, with further bibliography, see Enrico Norelli 'Déchirements, "Un *agraphon* derrière 1 Corinthiens 11,18–19," in *Nuove Testamento: Teologie in Dialogo Culturale*, ed. N. Ciola and G. Pulcinelli, FS for Romano Penna, Supplementi all Rivista Biblica (Bologna: Edizioni Dehoniane Bologna, 2008), 265–85.

This text might be rejected as an agraphon since it contains reported speech, not a direct quotation, but its form reflects its literary context in Justin's *Dialogue*. It shows how Justin was prepared to appeal to teachings that look very much like material found in the Synoptic tradition, but to insert them in a context where they are not found in the Synoptic Gospels (Jesus's encounter with John at the Jordan) and so to provide an expanded version of the Synoptic account, in which Jesus prophesies his death, resurrection, and parousia at the very beginning of his ministry as well as the struggles that his followers would face before he returned. Justin's willingness to expand the Synoptic tradition in this way raises the questions of whether other authors did the same, and if any of their expansions may have been incorporated in any textual witnesses to the Synoptic Gospels.

4.2.6 Clement of Alexandria
Excerpta ex Theodoto 2.2

"Save yourself, you and your soul."

Clement of Alexandria quotes this saying in his *Excerpta ex Theodoto*, or *Excerpts from Theodotus*, a text in which he engages with the work of the Valentinian theologian Theodotus. It has no later parallels in sayings attributed elsewhere to Jesus, but the saying may be compared to the words of warning given to Lot in Genesis 19:17a LXX, where the angel tells Lot, "Save your own soul." In the canonical Gospels, Jesus draws on the story of the destruction of Sodom and the flight of Lot and his wife in Luke's account of Jesus's apocalyptic discourse (Luke 17:28–32). Elsewhere he refers explicitly (Matt 10:15//Luke 10:12; Matt 11:23–24) and perhaps implicitly to the judgment of Sodom (e.g., Mark 9:49; Luke 12:49) and to the flight of Lot to the hills (Matt 24:16//Mark 13:14//Luke 21:21; cf. Gen 19:17b). According to Jeremias, this makes this agraphon an early tradition that may go back to Jesus, since it "fits in perfectly with a definite cycle of ideas in the tradition of Jesus's eschatological sayings."[34]

If this is correct, it could suggest that Theodotus drew on a source used also by Luke (and possibly Mark or Matthew) and quotes a saying that none of them included in their Gospels. However, it is also possible that Theodotus knew Luke's Gospel, saw the allusion to Genesis 19:17a, and attributed to Jesus a saying very similar in meaning to the warning to Lot in Genesis 19:17b. If so, this agraphon would be an example of how a Christian author could draw on the Jewish Scriptures and find in them sayings or other texts that they attributed to Jesus. On either interpretation, it points to the difference between identifying a plausible literary explanation of the origin of a saying and determining whether that saying may be traced back to the historical Jesus.

Stromata 3.15.97.4

"Let him who is married not send (his wife) away, and let him who is not married not marry."

This saying, which Clement attributes explicitly to Jesus ("Again the Lord said"), is quoted in the context of a discussion of various biblical texts on marriage and celibacy. It has no parallel in any canonical Gospel, but it does look very much like the words of Paul

---

34. Jeremias, *Unknown Sayings*, 78. Cf. Hofius, "Unknown Sayings," 337n6, who rejects the saying as an agraphon and construes it instead as a free quotation from Genesis 19:17 LXX that Theodotus understood as a saying of the preexistent Savior (not the earthly Jesus). Stroker, *Extracanonical Sayings*, 207, includes it as an agraphon that may be considered an example of a community rule.

in 1 Corinthians 7:27, in which he addresses issues facing unmarried people, having stated explicitly that he has no instructions from the Lord (1 Cor 7:25). It also follows immediately from a quotation of 1 Corinthians 7:33 that Clement attributes explicitly to Paul, so its attribution to Jesus may simply reflect an error on Clement's part, where he should have written, "Again the apostle said." As Roukema observes, Resch and Ropes each suggest that this saying may have come from the *Gospel of the Egyptians*,[35] but it seems much easier to interpret it as an instruction from Paul that has been misattributed to Jesus.[36] If so, it serves to illustrate how maxims from different sources may have found their way into sayings attributed to Jesus.

4.2.7 Origen
Commentary on John 19.7.2
> "Be skillful moneychangers."

The earliest quotation of the saying "Be skillful moneychangers" is found in Clement of Alexandria (*Strom.* 1.28.177.2), but there it is attributed to Scripture rather than to a named speaker. The earliest, securely datable instance of the saying attributed to Jesus is in the writings of Origen, who quotes it as a saying of Jesus in his *Commentary on John* (19.7.2, quoted above), but attributes it to Scripture in his *Commentary on Matthew* 17.31.

These words may also be identified as a saying of Jesus in some other texts that transmit material that may go back to the second or third century. The fourth-century Pseudo-Clementine *Homilies*, which likely draws on a second- or third-century source, refers to it twice as a saying of their teacher, who may be identified with Jesus (2.51.1; 18.20.4), and once in a passage where the context identifies the speaker as Jesus (3.50.2). The fourth-century heresiologist Epiphanius says that the second-century Apelles quoted the saying as something said "in the Gospel" (*Panarion* 44.2.6). Some sources associate the saying of Jesus with the words of Paul at 1 Thessalonians 5:21–22 about the need to test all things (e.g., Origen, *Commentary on John* 19.7.2; Socrates Scholasticus, *Hist. eccl.* 3.16; Jerome, *Epist.* 119) and others attribute the saying about skillful moneychangers not to Jesus but to Paul (e.g., Cyril of Alexandria, *Comm. Isa.* 1.2; Dionysius of Rome, in Eusebius, *Hist. eccl.* 7.7.3). The use of the metaphor of a moneychanger to illustrate the need for careful discernment is also found in non-Christian texts that predate its attribution to Jesus (e.g., Aristotle, *Rhetoric* 1.15.7 [1375b]; Philo, *Spec.* 4.77), so it was a proverbial saying that Christians repurposed as a saying of Jesus or sometimes of Paul.

As may be seen by its frequent use and the variety of purposes in support of which it was deployed, the metaphorical saying about moneychangers and its call for discernment lends itself to be used in different ways, according to the interests and concerns of each author who quoted it. As Bazzana notes, it could be used to establish doctrinal points, to exhort Christians to distinguish between acceptable and unacceptable moral behavior, and also as a reminder of the need to establish which texts have the authority of Scripture and which do not.[37]

---

35. Riemer Roukema, "Jesus Tradition in Early Patristic Writings," in Holmén and Porter, *Handbook*, 3:2142, citing Resch, *Agrapha*[2], 182–83, and Ropes, *Sprüche Jesu*, 107–8.

36. For further discussion, see J. Ruwet, "Les 'Agrapha' dans les Oeuvres de Clément d'Alexandrie," *Biblica* 30 (1949): 136–38.

37. Giovanni Bazzana, "'Be Good Moneychangers': The Role of an Agraphon in a Discursive Fight for the Canon of Scripture," in *Invention, Rewriting, Usurpation: Discursive Fights over Religious Traditions in Antiquity*, ed. Jörg Ulrich, Anders-Christian Jacobsen, and David Brakke, ECCA 11 (Frankfurt am Main: Peter Lang, 2012), 297–98. For further discussion of this agraphon, see also Johan S. Vos, "Das Agraphon 'Seid kundige Geldwechsler!' bei Origenes," in *Sayings of Jesus: Canonical and Non-Canonical*, ed. William L. Petersen, Johan S. Vos, and Henk J. de Jonge, FS T. Baarda, NovTSup 89 (Leiden: Brill, 1997), 277–302.

4.3 Conclusion

As we have seen, very many sayings are attributed to Jesus in a wide range of early Christian (and other) texts. The working definition followed here allows us to distinguish between those sayings that are preserved in texts where they are inscribed in a narrative or other literary context, and those that appear as isolated quotations where their only setting is the immediate context in which they are cited. These latter sayings are those that we have referred to as agrapha, provided that they have no parallel or source in the standard critical text of any of the four canonical Gospels.

As sayings that are not part of the critical text of the canonical Gospels, these agrapha may be evaluated as potential independent evidence for the teaching of the historical Jesus, although there are in fact very few that have been considered useful for this purpose. More fruitfully, they may be used as comparative data to shed light on sayings that are found in the fourfold canonical Gospel tradition; if other authors may be shown to have used sayings that they attributed to Jesus in a certain way, might that cast light on or raise questions about how any or all of the Gospel writers may have used sayings of Jesus?

Yet their real value for the historian, and for anyone interested in how Christians and others remembered Jesus and drew on his authority in situations that they and their communities faced, lies elsewhere. The number and variety of agrapha point to the conviction that Jesus was someone whose teaching was of continuing relevance for those who followed or valued him as a teacher or prophet and that his authority as a teacher could be brought to bear in new situations beyond those addressed by the Gospel writers. Thus, these sayings may cast light not only on the development of gospel tradition but also on the collective memory of the communities that shaped and adapted traditions through which they could appeal to Jesus to address issues and situations that they faced. In this way, the study of the agrapha helps us to understand the impact of the New Testament, for it helps us to grasp its ongoing importance and effect and the enduring significance of its witness to Jesus and to what Christians believe that God did and does through him.

5. BIBLIOGRAPHY

5.1 Primary Sources: Edited Collections of Agrapha

Hofius, Otfried, "Isolated Sayings of the Lord." Pages 88–91 in *New Testament Apocrypha, Volume One: Gospels and Related Writings*. Rev. ed. Edited by W. Schneemelcher and R. McL. Wilson. Cambridge: Clarke; Louisville: Westminster John Knox, 1991.
———. "Unknown Sayings of Jesus." Pages 336–60 in *The Gospel and the Gospels*. Edited by Peter Stuhlmacher. Grand Rapid: Eerdmans, 1991.
Jeremias, Joachim. *Unknown Sayings of Jesus*. 2nd ed. Translated by Reginald H. Fuller. London: SPCK, 1964.
Pesce, Mauro. *Le Parole Dimenticate di Gesù*. Scrittori Greci e Latini. Milan: Fondazione Lorenzo Valla and Arnoldo Mondadore, 2004.
Stroker, William D. *Extracanonical Sayings of Jesus*. SBL Resources for Biblical Study 18. Atlanta: Scholars Press, 1989.

5.2 Secondary Sources

Klauck, Hans-Josef. Pages 6–21 in *Apocryphal Gospels: An Introduction*. London: T&T Clark, 2003.
Norelli, Enrico. "Étude Critique: Une Collection de Paroles de Jésus non comprises dans les Évangiles Canoniques." *Apocrypha* 17 (2006): 223–44.
Roukema, Riemer. "Jesus Tradition in Early Patristic Writings." Pages 2119–47 in volume 3 of *Handbook for the Study of the Historical Jesus*. Edited by T. Holmén and Stanley E. Porter. Leiden: Brill, 2010.
Stroker, William D. "Agrapha." Pages 92–95 of volume 1 in *Anchor Bible Dictionary*. Edited by David Noel Freedman. 6 vols. New York: Doubleday, 1992.
Walt, Luigi. "Agrapha of Jesus." e-Clavis: Christian Apocrypha. www.nasscal.com/e-clavis-christian-apocrypha/agrapha-of-jesus/.
Young, Stephen E. *Jesus Tradition in the Apostolic Fathers*. WUNT 2.311. Tübingen: Mohr Siebeck, 2011.

CHAPTER 2

GOSPEL FRAGMENTS ON PAPYRUS

TOBIAS NICKLAS

1. INTRODUCTION

Among the most fascinating evidence we have for the partly lost varieties of what we call "early Christianity" is a series of fragments of Jesus stories, most of which were discovered at the end of the nineteenth century. It is not clear in every case whether these fragments comprise otherwise lost Gospels related to certain communities. Some of them may simply be fragments of excerpts, homilies, or re-narrations of Jesus stories by unknown, ancient Christian authors. In any case, these fragments offer us important insights into the development of early Jesus traditions. They transmit Jesus material outside the canonical Gospels and help us to understand how different groups of second-century (and later) Christians understood the figure of Jesus and his impact. Some of these fragments may even be relevant for the reconstruction of the historical Jesus. We will, however, see that this is only a minor dimension of their impact.

As the number of possible candidates is too big to allow me to be exhaustive, this essay will concentrate on a few of the most important fragments. These include P.Egerton 2 (plus P.Köln 255); P.Oxy. II 210; P.Oxy. V 840; P.Oxy. X 1224; the newly edited P.Oxy. LXXVI 5072; P.Vindob. G 2325, the so-called *Fayûm Gospel*; P.Berol. 11710; P.Mert. II 51; and the somewhat later P.Cair.Cat. 10735. This is certainly not everything that exists, and we can be quite certain that new fragments will be discovered in the future.

Excluded from this essay are fragments attributed to an otherwise known Gospel, such as P.Oxy. L 3525 and P.Ryl. III 463 (Gospel of Mary); P.Oxy. XLI 2949 (Gospel of Peter); P.Oxy. VIII 1081 (Wisdom of Jesus Christ); P.Dura 10 (Tatian's Gospel, usually labeled *Diatessaron*); and P.Oxy. I 1; IV 654; and IV 655 (Gospel of Thomas). The Coptic P.Stras. I 5–7 was identified as connected to the Berlin-Strasbourg Apocryphon (= the former "Unknown Berlin Gospel"), a so-called "apostolic memoir" from the post-Chalcedonian Miaphysite Church of Egypt.[1] In addition, P.Oxy. LX 4009 has been discussed controversially as a part of the Gospel of Peter. A few other fragments should be mentioned, but will not be extensively discussed for different reasons: PSI XI 1200bis and P.Ryl. III 464 simply contain too little text to offer real insights. P.Oxy. XI 1384 (= *PGM* II 7) inserts two apocryphal stories in a medical recipe, but it is highly improbable that any of these go back to an extracanonical Gospel. P.Gen. III 125 offers a free reenactment of Matthew 10:11–13//Luke 10:5–6, but no narrative frame.

---

1. Alin Suciu, *The Berlin-Strasbourg Apocryphon: A Coptic Apostolic Memoir*, WUNT 370 (Tübingen: Mohr Siebeck, 2017).

2. SUMMARY OF CONTENT, INTERPRETIVE ISSUES, AND CONNECTIONS TO NEW TESTAMENT STUDY

2.1 The "Unknown Gospel" on P.Egerton 2 (plus P.Köln 255)

P.Egerton 2 consists of four fragments of papyrus with writings on both sides; it thus belonged to a codex. While the *editio princeps* by H. I. Bell and T. C. Skeat regarded P.Egerton 2 as the earliest Christian papyrus (and dated it in the middle of the second century),[2] later editors were somewhat more cautious. This caution resulted from the discovery and edition of another part of the same papyrus—that is, P.Köln VI 255 by M. Gronewald, which shows features suggesting a somewhat later date.[3] The latest paleographical analysis points to a date between 150 and 250 CE as most plausible.[4] However, even with this later dating, P.Egerton 2 remains one of the earliest extant Christian papyri. It is certainly the most impressive of all the extracanonical Gospel fragments known today. The tiny fragment 4 offers only remains of one letter, while only a few words can be found on fragment 3 (size: 2.5 x 6 cm), which could have a parallel in John 10:30. It is for this reason that we may concentrate on fragments 1 (8.5 x 11.5 cm) and 2 (10 x 12.5 cm). As the original order of the fragments is still a matter of debate, I will present the fragments in the artificial order: 1 *verso* (plus P.Köln VI 255 *verso*), 1 *recto* (plus P.Köln VI 255 *recto*), 2 *verso*, and 2 *recto*.

Fragment 1 *verso* narrates a dispute between Jesus and a group of νομικοί, that is, "experts in the (Jewish) law." While they seem to attack him as a transgressor of the law, he addresses them, now called the "leaders of the people," with the words, "Search the Scriptures, in which you think you have life! These are the ones which bear witness about me. Do not think that I have come to accuse you before my Father. There is already someone who accuses you: Moses, in whom you have hope,"[5] a very clear parallel to a combination of John 5:39 and 5:45. Following the leaders' response, which is a close parallel to John 9:29, Jesus answers with a saying closely resembling John 5:46: "But when they said: 'We know that God has spoken to Moses, but of you we do not know where you come from,' Jesus responded to them and said: 'Now accusation will be made against your unbelief in relation to what he gave testimony. For if you believed Moses, you would also have believed me. Because he has written about me to your/our forefathers [. . .]." After these words the extant fragment breaks off.

Fragment 1 *recto* starts with the remaining lines of a story according to which "the leaders" try to arrest Jesus, while (probably) the crowd wants to stone him. Jesus, however, "got out from their hands and withdrew himself from them." Again, the text offers its own story, but shows parallels to John 7:30 and 44 (plus John 8:20; 10:39a; and see Luke 20:17–20). After this, the narrative turns quite abruptly to another scene, the healing of a leper: "And behold, a leper came to him and said: 'Teacher Jesus, I made my way together with lepers and ate with them in the inn; then I myself became leprous. If you then will, I will be clean.' And the Lord said to him, 'I will, be clean!' And immediately his leprosy left him. Jesus said to him: 'Go and show yourself to the priests and offer for your purification,

---

2. H. I. Bell and T. C. Skeat, eds., *Fragments of an Unknown Gospel and Other Early Christian Papyri* (London: Trustees of the British Museum, 1935), 1–42, esp. 1.

3. M. Gronewald, "P.Köln VI 255: Unbekanntes Evangelium oder Evangelienharmonie (Fragment aus dem 'Evangelium Egerton')," in *Kölner Papyri (P.Köln), Volume VI* (Opladen: Westdeutscher, 1987), 136–45, esp. 138.

4. L. Zelyck, *The Egerton Gospel (Egerton Papyrus 2 + Papyrus Köln VI 255): Introduction, Critical Edition, and Commentary*, Texts and Editions for New Testament Study 13 (Leiden: Brill, 2019), 46.

5. Translations in this essay are from T. Nicklas, "The 'Unknown Gospel' on *Papyrus Egerton* 2 (+ *Papyrus Cologne* 55)," in *Gospel Fragments*, ed. T. J. Kraus, M. J. Kruger, and T. Nicklas, Oxford Early Christian Gospel Texts (Oxford: Oxford University Press, 2009), 11–120.

as Moses commanded. And do not sin again.'"[6] While fragment 1 *verso* matches Johannine texts almost verbatim, this story parallels Mark 1:40–45 (//Matt 8:1–4//Luke 5:12–16), but offers additional elements, such as a sentence wherein the leper says that he became leprous because of contact with other lepers, and the command from Jesus not to sin again (see John 5:14; 8:11). Jesus, who is called a "teacher" by the leper, neither touches him nor shows any emotions. This apocryphal story, though shorter than its canonical parallels, thus contains certain elements that cannot be found in those Gospels.

Fragment 2 *verso* offers the biggest riddle surrounding P.Egerton 2. The extant text does not have any clear parallels in the canonical Gospels and is full of lacunae. It therefore has not been possible to reconstruct it properly. This only changed with the new edition by Lorne Zelyck, who relates the second half of the fragment to Josephus's version of 2 Kings 2:19–22 (*Jewish War* 4.460–64).[7] In his recent commentary, he observes that several late antique pilgrimage accounts (Theodosius, *Topography* 1 and 8; *Piacenza Pilgrim* 13–14) identify the spring of Elisha, mentioned in the miracle told in 2 Kings 2:19–22, with a place called "the Lord's field" close to Jericho. The *Piacenza Pilgrim* even speaks of a miracle related to the Lord's field: "In front of the basilica [close to Jericho] is a plain, the Lord's field, in which the Lord sowed with his own hand. Its yield is three pecks, and it is reaped twice in the year, but it grows naturally, and is never sown."[8] This combination of a miracle related to grain at the Lord's field plus Elisha's spring forms the background of Zelyck's fascinating reconstruction.

The reconstructed text starts with a Jesus logion: "When the farmer has enclosed a single seed of grain in the field, so that it is invisibly buried, how can its abundance become an immeasurable bushel?"[9] When the audience becomes "perplexed about this strange question," Jesus provides an illustration by a miracle: "Then Jesus, as he walked, stood on the bank of the Jordan River. He reached out his right hand, took salt, and scattered it upon the river. Then he poured out much water on the ground. He prayed and it was filled before them. Then it brought forth a crop of great abundance, produced by an everlasting gift for all these people."

Fragment 2 *recto*, finally, presents another conflict scene according to which an unspecified group approaches Jesus to test him with a question: "Teacher Jesus, we know that you have come from God. For what you do bears witness beyond all the prophets. So tell us: Is it allowed to hand over to the kings what belongs to their government? Shall we pay them or not?" While the first sentence closely parallels the opening of Nicodemus's speech (John 3:2b), the following questions evoke scenes like Mark 12:13–17 (//Matt 22:15–22//Luke 20:26) and Matthew 17:25b. The verbal parallels to the Synoptics, however, do not go very far, and Jesus's response does even less. Instead of pointing to the image of the emperor on a coin, he becomes angry and rebukes his enemies with a quote of Isaiah 29:13: "Why do you call me teacher with your mouth, but not hear what I say? Well did Isaiah prophesy about you: 'This people honors me with their lips but their heart is far away from me—in vain do they worship me.'"

All the above creates the image of a Gospel that is influenced by the Gospel of John (perhaps even literarily dependent), knows stories that are paralleled in the Synoptic Gospels, and transmits independent Jesus traditions. As far as we can discern from the

---

6. Translation adapted from Nicklas, "The 'Unknown Gospel,'" 43.

7. L. Zelyck, "Elisha Typology in Jesus's Miracle on the Jordan River (Papyrus Egerton 2, 2v.6–14)," *NTS* 62 (2016): 149–56.

8. *Piacenza Pilgrim* 13. Translation is mine.

9. All translations of fragment 2 *verso* adapted from Zelyck, *Egerton Gospel*.

form of the extant text, the Egerton Gospel was a Synoptic-like text consisting of clearly defined pericopes. The author seems to have used Synoptic-like material in a very free manner. I call this way of free rewriting of (probably) already existing texts a "re-enactment" (*Neuinszenierung*). By speaking about a "re-enactment," and not just a re-narration, I am emphasizing interactive and performative aspects of the processes that lead to the emergence of the new story.[10] I use this term when an author probably knew about written Gospels or Jesus stories, but the new story does not reveal a clear redactional attitude toward the older ones. The new story follows main lines and includes decisive motifs from the older versions, but it deals so freely with them that we cannot determine the extent of the new author's access to already-existing written texts. In other words, s/he may have heard or even read these stories at a certain time, or perhaps s/he only knew about their existence in written form, but they were not available to him/her as written *Vorlage* when s/he wrote down the new story. This becomes possible as soon as a story becomes part of the collective or even cultural memories of a group.

We can find comparable developments in the Gospel of Peter, the *Epistula Apostolorum*, other extracanonical Gospel fragments (see below), and also sayings material.[11] While the stories of the healing of the leper and (probably) the dispute over taxes can be understood with the help of the above paradigm, the (reconstructed) miracle story at the Jordan River tells us about the life and emergence of local Jesus traditions *besides* the canonical Gospel. The (much later) evidence in the sixth-century *Piacenza Pilgrim* quoted above, in turn, shows that some of this material could survive at least in the form of local traditions.

What else can we learn from the "Unknown Gospel" on P.Egerton 2? And why is it important for New Testament studies? Even if we can never be certain regarding the overall theology of a partly lost writing, several topics seem to be especially interesting for the remaining text.

First, although we do not know whether the original plot of the Egerton Gospel concluded with a story about Jesus's passion and resurrection, the remaining text shows us a Jesus in a life-and-death conflict. Comparable to the Gospel of John, the Egerton Gospel creates the image of Jesus as a Jewish teacher who provokes opposition. This can probably be linked to his way of teaching the Torah (even if the extant text only seems to presuppose a conflict with the "experts of the law"), as well as to his self-understanding as someone about whom "Moses has written." Different from, for example, texts like the Gospel of Judas or the Gospel of Marcion, Jesus and his opponents share the same Scriptures and refer to the same God, but they disagree about the correct interpretation of Israel's traditions.[12] Perhaps we can say even more. If Francis Watson is right, and the last lines of fragment 1 *verso* read "our forefathers" instead of "your forefathers," then the Egerton Gospel describes Jesus as even closer to his opponents than the parallels in the Gospel of John do, since they can still speak about a shared ancestry.[13]

---

10. T. Nicklas, "Second Century Gospels as 'Re-Enactments' of Earlier Writings: Examples from the Gospel of Peter," in *Modern and Ancient Literary Criticism of the Gospels: Continuing the Debate on Gospel Genre(s)*, ed. R. Calhoun, D. Moessner, and T. Nicklas, WUNT 451 (Tübingen: Mohr Siebeck, 2020), 471–86.

11. G. Bazzana, "Replaying Jesus's Sayings in the 'Agrapha': Reflections on the *Neu-Inszenierung* of Jesus's Traditions in the Second Century between *2 Clement* and Clement of Alexandria," in *Gospels and Gospel Traditions in the Second Century: Experiments in Reception*, ed. J. Schröter, T. Nicklas, J. Verheyden, BZNW 235 (Berlin: de Gruyter, 2019), 311–30.

12. See also T. Nicklas, "Jesus and Judaism: Inside or Outside? The *Gospel of John*, the *Egerton Gospel*, and the Spectrum of Ancient Christian Voices," in *Connecting Gospels: Beyond the Canonical/Non-Canonical Divide*, ed. F. Watson and S. Parkhouse (Oxford: Oxford University Press, 2018), 125–41.

13. F. Watson, *Gospel Writing: A Canonical Perspective* (Grand Rapids: Eerdmans, 2013), 295.

Second, much of the conflict has to do with scriptural interpretation. Fragment 1 *verso*, for example, seems to witness to an interpretive methodology wherein the Scriptures of Israel (or at least parts of them) must be understood in the light of the "Christ event." The idea that Moses—that is, the Torah—is all about Jesus and thus requires a reading different from traditional, non-Christian Jewish interpretations comes close not only to comparable developments in the Gospel of John but also to those in Ignatius of Antioch, the Epistle of Barnabas, or Justin Martyr.[14] Other passages are less explicit, but go in the same direction; if we trust Zelyck's reconstruction, fragment 2 *verso* describes Jesus as a kind of "new Elisha,"[15] while fragment 2 *recto* understands Isaiah 29:13 as a prophecy about Jesus's time.

Third, the Egerton Gospel's Jesus is still understandable as a kind of Jewish teacher who can work miracles. While the extant fragments do not say anything about his teaching on the kingdom of God, both the leper (fragment 1 *recto*) and his opponents (fragment 2 *recto*) address him as a teacher. Interestingly, in both cases the text does not use the term "rabbi," but the Greek expression διδάσκαλος. Even if it is not clear whether the text regards this as an appropriate title for Jesus, it is noticeable that he can at least be understood in such a manner. Perhaps one can go a bit further and link this both with the fact that Jesus discusses with "experts of the law" and with the way he deals with the leper. He does not even touch him and seems to understand his sickness as a sign of a former sin, perhaps his former contact with other lepers, which made him impure. Does the Egerton Gospel understand Jesus as a teacher of the Torah? This cannot be excluded, but it also cannot be fully proven. The extant fragments neither call Jesus the Messiah (or Christ), nor the Son of Man, nor use the title Son of God explicitly (but see frag. 1 *verso* calling God Jesus's father). The title κύριος, Lord, does occur twice (both times frag. 1 *recto*) and could also underlie the story of fragment 2 *recto*. It is thus possible that "the UG [Unknown Gospel] shows remnants of a christological 'leitmotif': Jesus reveals himself as the 'Lord,' but is not recognized."[16]

If we put all this together and presuppose that the extant manuscript is not the original copy of the Egerton Gospel, we may conclude that the text goes back perhaps to the middle of the second century. While I previously wanted to exclude a Palestinian provenance because of the Gospel's alleged lack of interest in the country's topography,[17] Zelyck's recent reconstruction of fragment 2 *verso* makes such a provenance possible. In the end, we cannot really know where the text came from. Was it produced and used by a group of Christ-believing Jews? This is possible, but even here we cannot be sure.

2.2 Papyrus Oxyrhynchus 210 (P.Oxy. II 210)

Papyrus Oxyrhynchus 210 was edited in the year 1899 by B. P. Grenfell and A. S. Hunt in the second volume of the *Oxyrhynchus Papyri*.[18] The manuscript (17.2 x 9.4 cm), which probably dates to the third century, offers writing on both of its sides. Grenfell-Hunt's proposal that it could be part of the Gospel of the Egyptians—several quotations of which survive in the oeuvre of Clement of Alexandria—was rejected and the manuscript forgotten.

---

14. T. Nicklas, *Jews and Christians? Second Century 'Christian' Perspectives on the 'Parting of the Ways'*, Annual Deichmann Lectures 2013 (Tübingen: Mohr Siebeck, 2014), 124–41.

15. Zelyck, "Elisha Typology."

16. Nicklas, "The 'Unknown Gospel,'" 108.

17. Nicklas, "The 'Unknown Gospel,'" 113.

18. B. P. Grenfell and A. S. Hunt, *The Oxyrhynchus Papyri II* (London: Egypt Exploration Society, 1899), 9–10.

Only a new edition by C. H. Roberts[19] and an article by S. E. Porter[20] reopened a modest discussion of this text. As the text is very fragmentary, it is not easy to reconstruct its narration. Its *recto* side speaks about an angel and a sign given for the people—a possible parallel to Matthew 1:24 and Luke 2:10, 12. The *verso* contains the remains of a dialogue between (probably) Jesus and an unknown partner. It is obviously interested in the question of what is good (see Matt 19:16–17//Mark 10:17–18//Luke 18:18–19). Following the dialogue are remnants of a parable reminiscent of Matthew 7:17–19//Luke 6:43–44. It reads: "The good fruits which God produces [. . .] But good fruit of a good tree produces [. . .] under the good."[21] After this follow two "I am" sayings similar to the Gospel of John: "I am [. . .] I am the image [. . .] in the form of God [. . .]." The remaining words seem to play with the motifs of "image," "God," and "visibility," but no other sentence can be reconstructed with certainty.[22]

Of course, all this does not allow more than speculation about the text's profile and provenance. Porter, who sees possible parallels in Proverbs 7:26, Romans 1:20, 1 Corinthians 1:26–27, 2:6–8, and Philippians 2:6, concludes that the text presupposes an extensive collection of Christian Scripture. The text seems to witness to a high Christology, understanding Jesus as God's image on earth.[23] Many questions regarding the original extent of P.Oxy. II 210—Is it remnants of a formerly full Gospel (perhaps originating in Egypt), or fragments of a homily quoting Scripture?—must remain open.

2.3 Papyrus Oxyrhynchus 840 (P.Oxy. V 840)

Papyrus Oxyrhynchus 840 was discovered in the year 1905 by B. P. Grenfell and A. S. Hunt, who edited it in the fifth volume of the *Oxyrhynchus Papyri* (1908).[24] Although this little piece of parchment (8.5 x 7 cm; fourth or fifth century CE) was sometimes described as an amulet, it can be safely understood as a fragment of a miniature codex.[25] It presents the text of an otherwise unknown story about Jesus, perhaps a part of a longer Gospel text. It starts with remnants of Jesus-sayings, probably directed to the disciples about evildoers and their future fate. After this, Jesus and his disciples enter a place of purification in the temple (obviously of Jerusalem), where they meet a Pharisaic high priest (or chief priest), whose name can probably be reconstructed as Levi. This priest accuses Jesus, "Who allowed you to enter this place of purification and view these holy vessels when you did not bathe yourself, nor did your disciples immerse their feet? But being defiled you entered this holy place, which is pure, where no one else except one who bathed himself and changed

---

19. C. H. Roberts, "An Early Christian Papyrus," in *Miscel·lània papirològica Ramon Roca-Puig en el seu vuitantè aniversari*, ed. S. Janeras (Barcelona: Fundació Salvador Vives Casajuana, 1987), 293–96.

20. S. E. Porter, "POxy II 210 as an Apocryphal Gospel and the Development of Egyptian Christianity," in *Atti del XXII Congresso Internazionale di Papirologia: Firenze, 23–29 agosto 1998*, ed. I. Andorlini et al. (Florence: Istituto Papirologico G. Vitelli, 2001), 1095–1108; see also idem, "Der Papyrus Oxyrhynchus II 210 (P.Oxy. 210)," in *Antike christliche Apokryphen in deutscher Übersetzung I: Evangelien und Verwandtes*, ed. C. Markschies and J. Schröter (Tübingen: Mohr Siebeck: 2009), 387–89. Porter argues that the manuscript could offer the remnants of an apocryphal Gospel that originated in Egypt.

21. My translation.

22. But see the far-going proposal by B. Landau and S. E. Porter, "Papyrus Oxyrhynchus 210," in T. Burke and B. Landau, eds., *New Testament Apocrypha: More Noncanonical Scriptures*, vol. 1 (Grand Rapids: Eerdmans, 2016), 109–24.

23. Porter, "Papyrus Oxyrhynchus II 210," 388.

24. B. P. Grenfell and A. S. Hunt, eds., "840. Fragment of an Uncanonical Gospel," in *The Oxyrhynchus Papyri V* (London: Egypt Exploration Society, 1908), 1–10.

25. T. J. Kraus, "*P.Oxy. V 840*—Amulett oder Miniaturkodex? Grundsätzliche und ergänzende Anmerkungen zu zwei Termini," *Zeitschrift für Antikes Christentum* 8 (2005): 485–97.

clothes enters or dares to see these holy vessels."[26] This begins a debate about purity. Jesus, who is called the Savior (σωτήρ), asks the priest whether he is clean. The priest responds: "I am pure, as I bathed in the Pool of David and went down by one stairway and went up by another. I put on white and pure clothes. Then I came and looked upon these holy vessels." The Savior's response is harsh:

> Woe to you blind ones who do not see! You bathed in these outpoured waters wherein dogs and pigs lie night and day. And when you washed yourself, you wiped your outer skin, which even prostitutes and flute girls anoint, wash, wipe, and beautify for the lust of men. Inside, however, they are full of scorpions and all wickedness. But I and my disciples, who you have said did not bathe, have been bathed in living waters from heaven, which are from the Father above.

Jesus's argument, of course, should not be misunderstood. He does not point to dogs and pigs in the water of David's Pool; this would certainly be inconceivable. Instead, he argues that the quality of water in the Pool of David does not differ from that of any other natural water wherein dogs and pigs bathe yet remain impure. In other words, according to Jesus, impurity is an inner characteristic, which cannot be removed by ways of outward cleansing. This is illustrated by his second example, the saying about prostitutes and flute girls who wash and beautify themselves more extensively than most other people, but, according to the saying, are "full of scorpions and all wickedness" inside. Real purification is only possible with the help of the "living waters," given from the heavenly Father. Does this refer to the gift of the Spirit? We cannot be certain.

While this story does not have a clear parallel in the canonical Gospels, its main subject—the question of cultic purity—is discussed in texts like Mark 7:1–23 (//Matt 15:1–20). While Jesus's woe against the Pharisee parallels Matthew 23:27–28, his concluding words about "living waters" are reminiscent of John 4:14; 7:37–38 and perhaps even Revelation 22:17 (but see also Jer 2:13; Zech 14:8).[27] Very soon after its publication, a debate about the text's date and its relevance for the reconstruction of the historical Jesus broke out. Perhaps the most influential voice came from Joachim Jeremias, who argued that both the setting (including reference to the Pool of David) and Jesus's response point to the scene's authenticity.[28] After a long time of silence, the most important countervoice came from François Bovon, who argued that the whole passage has nothing to do with matters of Jewish purity. Instead, he related the text's description of the alleged Jerusalem Temple to the structure of ancient Christian baptisteries and pointed to the text's relation to liturgical terminology.[29] He argued that the text could have been produced by an ancient Christian group that criticized water baptism—he explicitly mentions the Ophites, Perates, and Naassenes.[30] In two extensive studies, Michael J. Kruger rejected this view.[31] According to Kruger, the text shows clear knowledge of the purity practices of Pharisaic

---

26. Translations of P.Oxy. V 840 are my own.

27. For more details see M. J. Kruger, *The Gospel of the Savior: An Analysis of P.Oxy. 840 and Its Place in the Gospel Traditions of Early Christianity*, TENTS 1 (Leiden: Brill, 2005), 161–88.

28. J. Jeremias, *Unbekannte Jesusworte* (Gütersloh: Gerd Mohn, 1948), 50–60.

29. F. Bovon, "Fragment Oxyrhynchus 840: Fragment of a Lost Gospel Witness of an Early Christian Controversy over Purity," *JBL* 119 (2000): 705–28, esp. 717–20.

30. Bovon, "Fragment Oxyrhynchus," 723–27.

31. Kruger, *Gospel of the Savior*, and idem, *"Papyrus Oxyrhynchus 840,"* in *Gospel Fragments*, ed. T. J. Kraus, M. J. Kruger, and T. Nicklas, Oxford Early Christian Gospel Texts (Oxford: Oxford University Press, 2009), 123–215.

(and rabbinic) Judaism, which he also understands as the main opponent behind the text.[32] That's why he places it within an early second century "orthodox" Jewish-Christianity, probably the Nazarenes.[33]

I am quite reluctant to accept Kruger's view. First, the description of a Pharisaic chief, or even high priest, with the name Levi does not sound as if it refers to a real person but to a kind of artificial figure that combines prejudices of a "Jewish" enemy of Jesus. Second, even if we know of *mikvaot*—that is, Jewish ritual baths—both close to the Jerusalem Temple and on the Temple Mount itself, and even though these ritual baths had divided steps as presupposed in the manuscript, we do not have evidence for a "Pool of David." Third, the term used for the "place of purification" (ἁγνευτήριον) is very rare. In two of its three occurrences, it refers to a church building. Fourth, it is not clear under which circumstances the "holy vessels" of the Temple could be viewed. I thus tend to follow a recent publication by Harald Buchinger and Elisabeth Hernitscheck, who argue that the special language used in the manuscript presupposes fourth-century developments in the church's rituals of baptism. According to Buchinger and Hernitscheck, P.Oxy. 840 can be seen as a cult-critical voice in the debates emerging around these developments.[34] The authors argue that the motif of a baptismal *pedilavium*, that is, a "washing of the feet" (as presupposed by the high priest), is documented from the fourth century. At this time we also have the earliest evidence for Christian baptismal architecture, with double stairways to descend and ascend.[35] They add evidence for the use of white garments for the neophytes—that is, the newly baptized Christians. Even the motif of "seeing the holy vessels" can be explained:

> One may speculate about the importance of contemplating sacred vessels in the initiation to mystery cults. Another context may be sought in the practice of 4th-century mystagogy, which used things that lay before the eyes of the newly initiated as a starting-point for their sacramental theology. In turn, it was not until the later 4th century that the Christian liturgical mysteries were protected from common sight by curtains and other fittings, and it was in the same period that liturgical dishes . . . were first called "holy vessels."[36]

Should these results disappoint us? Is P.Oxy. 840 thus of only minor interest for the study of ancient Christianity? I think this is not the case. Although we would certainly like to have more material about the earliest periods and want to know more about the historical Jesus, the history of later periods is by no means less important. The text is interesting on many levels. It gives evidence for the use of extracanonical literature even after the (more or less clear and official) closure of the New Testament canon in the middle of the fourth century. If we trust Buchinger and Hernitscheck, the text shows how even after the second century new Jesus-material emerged and was used as authoritative argument in the debates of the time. Perhaps even more interesting is the fact that an inner-Christian debate could be mirrored in the narration of a conflict between Jesus and one of his Jewish opponents. In this case, the "mainstream" Christian view that (natural) water is important for the sacrament of baptism is mirrored in the argument of the Jewish high priest. In other words,

---

32. Kruger, *Gospel of the Savior*, 212.

33. Kruger, *Gospel of the Savior*, 245, 257–58.

34. H. Buchinger and E. Hernitscheck, "P.Oxy. 840 and the Rites of Christian Initiation: Dating a Piece of Alleged Anti-Sacramentalistic Polemics," *Early Christianity* 5 (2014): 117–24.

35. Buchinger and Hernitscheck, "P.Oxy. 840," 121.

36. Buchinger and Hernitscheck, "P.Oxy. 840," 123.

from the perspective of the fragment, "orthodox" ideas about baptism are simply too Jewish to be accepted.[37]

2.4 Papyrus Oxyrhynchus 1224 (P.Oxy. X 1224)

Papyrus Oxyrhynchus 1224 was edited by Grenfell and Hunt in volume 10 of the *Oxyrhynchus Papyri* (1914).[38] The manuscript was dated to the fourth century CE. It consists of two fragments with writing on both sides (frg. 1: 4.6 x 4.1 cm; frg. 2: 13.1 x 6.3 cm), including remnants of pagination. The preserved page numbers 139 and 174 show that these fragments must have been part of a larger codex. While the remains of fragment 1 do not allow the reconstruction of a proper text, fragment 2 offers several lines of an otherwise unknown Jesus story, which is divided in two columns. Unfortunately, the question of the original order of fragment 2 *recto* and *verso* must remain open. The below sequence follows the reconstruction by Kraus and Foster.[39]

On fragment 2, column 2 *recto*, we find five lines representing a few sentences that can only partially be reconstructed. After the sentence "[he? it?] weighed me down," Jesus appears in a vision and speaks to the storyteller: "Why are you depressed? Because not [. . .] but he [. . .] who gives [. . .]." Foster's edition goes a bit further than Kraus and suggests the sentence "which the other visions" instead of "but he."[40] We should, however, be aware that after the word ἀλλά ("but" or "other") only an o—that is, the first letter of ὁράματα ("visions")—is visible. Kraus points to Acts 9:10 as a possible parallel.[41] It seems that the text relates a (post-resurrection?) vision of Jesus to a single person who is depressed (about Jesus's death?). The question whether Jesus's response refers to any other visionary experiences must remain open.

Fragment 2, column 1 *verso* appears to transmit a series of accusations against Jesus. The fragmentary state of the text does not permit identification of the subjects of these accusations. It is possible, however, that they are the same groups mentioned in fragment 2, column 2 *verso* (below). The exact meaning of the text depends on reconstructions of missing passages: "You [sa]id without answ[ering. What then] have you renounced? What is, [as they say,] the new tea[ching you teach and what is the] new b[aptism you proclaim? Ans]wer and [. . .]." The motif of Jesus's "new teaching" parallels Mark 1:27 (but see also the more friendly Acts 17:19), and there is a proclamation of a baptism in Mark 1:4 (//Luke 3:3). The whole passage creates the impression of a conflict or even a trial scene.

Fragment 2, column 2 *verso* parallels Mark 2:15–17 (//Matt 9:10–12; Luke 5:29–31). However, we should note that the key words ὑγιαίνοντες ("healthy ones"), ἰατροῦ ("physician"), and χρείαν ("need") are almost completely reconstructed. As Jesus hears that scribes, Pharisees, and priests are upset about his relation to sinners (probably during meals), he says: "The h[ealthy ones] do not have [need of] [the physician]." Foster writes: "The meaning of this proverbial maxim remains unaltered from the intended sense in the canonical narratives."[42]

---

37. Nicklas, *Jews and Christians*, 35–40.
38. B. P. Grenfell and A. S. Hunt, "1224. Uncanonical Gospel," in *The Oxyrhynchus Papyri X* (London: Egypt Exploration Society, 1914), 1–10.
39. T. J. Kraus, "Other Gospel Fragments," in Kraus, Kruger, and Nicklas, *Gospel Fragments*, 219–80; and P. Foster, "Papyrus Oxyrhynchus X 1224," in *Early Christian Manuscripts: Examples of Applied Method and Approach*, ed. T. J. Kraus and T. Nicklas, Texts and Editions for New Testament Study 5 (Leiden: Brill, 2010), 59–96.
40. Foster, "Papyrus Oxyrhynchus X 1224," 75.
41. Kraus, "Other Gospel Fragments," 269.
42. Foster, "Papyrus Oxyrhynchus X 1224," 86.

Fragment 2, column 1 *recto*, finally, offers remnants of three sayings, the first of which can be related to Matthew 5:44 and Luke 6:27–28 (see also Did. 1.3). The second saying comes close to the ones preserved in Mark 9:40//Luke 9:50, Matthew 12:30//Luke 11:23, and Justin, *First Apology* 15.9. The third saying offers an otherwise unknown tradition, perhaps parallel to Jeremiah 2:5 LXX or Gospel of Thomas 82:

> [A]nd pray for your ene[mies]. For he who is not [against yo]u is for you. He who is far off [toda]y, tomorrow will be [close to yo]u and in . . . the adversary.

Of course, it is very difficult to give an exact date for the origin of such a fragmentary writing. While some favor an extremely early date (already in the middle of the first century CE), Foster tries to show that the "for and against" saying in fragment 2, column 1 *recto* comes closest to the form of the saying in Luke 9:50. Moreover, if we accept the reading ὑγιαίνοντες in the saying about those who need the doctor (frg. 2, col. 2 *verso*), this passage seems dependent on Luke 5:31.[43] If this is correct, the original text of P.Oxy. X 1224 must be younger than Luke, which is usually dated to the end of the first century. Questions about the text's provenance or its primary social setting or function cannot be answered.

2.5 Papyrus Oxyrhynchus 5072 (P.Oxy. LXXVI 5072)

While most of the fragments discussed in this essay were discovered at the turn of the nineteenth to the twentieth century (or only a bit later), Papyrus Oxyrhynchus 5072 is a new finding. The fragment (7 x 7 cm; 24 fragmentary lines), which preserves text on both sides and was thus probably part of a codex, was edited by Juan Chapa in 2011.[44] Paleographical investigations make a date between the second half of the second century and the middle of the third century probable. In other words, P.Oxy. LXXVI 5072 is one of the earliest fragments of an extracanonical Jesus-text. Its provenance is unclear.

The *recto* side offers remnants of an exorcism, which can be reconstructed as follows:[45]

> . . . before [the crowd?]. But he fell down [. . .]. He cried out saying: "Son [of God, what do you have to do with me?] Did you come before the time [to destroy] us?" He [Jesus] rebuked him say[ing: "Be silent!] Leave the man [. . .]." Going out he sat down. [two lines missing] someone to him [. . .].

As we can see, this text shows many motifs of an exorcism story like we find in the Synoptic Gospels. The demoniac seems to be brought before Jesus, falls down (perhaps due to the demon's powers), recognizes Jesus as "Son" (of God?), and tries to repudiate him but is forced to go out of the man only by Jesus's word. After this the healed man sits down.

If we take a closer look into the text, almost every line shows parallels to Synoptic stories about Jesus's exorcisms. At the same time, it is impossible to say which of the exorcisms in the canonical Gospels comes closest to what we find in the remaining text. While some parallels point to Mark 5:1–20 (and parr.), it is clear that this story did not contain the miracle of the pigs jumping into the Sea of Galilee. At the same time, the demon's saying comes closest to Mark 1:21–28 (and parr.). That's why I have suggested elsewhere that we

---

43. Foster, "Papyrus Oxyrhynchus X 1224," 90–92.

44. J. Chapa, "Uncanonical Gospel?," in *The Oxyrhynchus Papyri 76*, ed. J. Chapa and D. Colomo, Graeco-Roman Memoirs (London: Egyptian Exploration Society, 2011), 1–20.

45. For an even more detailed reconstruction, see R. Ponder, "Papyrus Oxyrhynchus 5072," in Burke and Landau, *New Testament Apocrypha*, 125–39, esp. 137–38.

should not understand the author of this text as a "redactor" of written miracle stories like those we find in the canonical Gospels, but as a person who may have known one or more of the Synoptic Gospels and who was able to tell his own story about Jesus as a great exorcist. Perhaps we can understand this story as a "re-enactment" (*Neuinszenierung*) of stories that made it into the canon but at the same time became part of the collective (or perhaps already cultural) memories of many Christians.[46]

The *verso*, in turn, offers remnants of a speech of Jesus about discipleship that, even though the speaker does not change, seems to be addressed to different audiences. Ross Ponder presents a very far-reaching reconstruction:

> After the […], you will confess that I am your teacher, but I myself will deny that you are my disciple. And you will be ashamed eternally, Yes, I say to you, the one who loves his soul more than me is not worthy to be my disciple. If then, you are a scribe, go to Jerusalem; although, if you are a wise man, go forth into the courts (of heaven). But in fact, the kingdom of God is before you. My father conceals these things from the wise and intelligent ones. He spoke to his disciples … .[47]

Even if this sounds very convincing and offers a smooth text full of parallels to the Gospels,[48] we must be aware that no line of P.Oxy. LXXVI 5072 is without lacunae. The manuscript thus certainly shows how Jesus-sayings that we know from the canonical Gospels could be rewritten and recombined to form new clusters of speeches. Again, however, even though some of the parallels are quite evident, I do not think that we should speak about a redaction of canonical Gospel material but rather about a free recombination of remembered Jesus-sayings under a common topic—perhaps "proper discipleship."

2.6 The *Fayûm Gospel* (P.Vindob. G 2325)

This small third-century fragment (3.5 x 4.3 cm) from the Vienna papyrus collection was edited by G. Bickell in the year 1885.[49] Interestingly, it has writing only on its *recto* side and thus could stem from a scroll (instead of the usual codex). Since the name "Peter" is shortened to πετ and distinguished from the remaining text by red ink, it was suggested that this short text could have been part of the apocryphal Gospel of Peter. While we cannot exclude this possibility (which also influenced some reconstructions of the text), it is also not possible to prove.

The extant text presents a dialogue between Jesus and Peter, which closely resembles Mark 14:26–27, 29–30 and the parallel of Matthew 26:30–31, 33–34 (both quoting Zech 13:7 LXX)—that is, Jesus's prophecy of Peter's denial. The following translation and reconstruction was completed by Thomas J. Kraus:[50]

> While going out as he said: "In this night all of you will take offense at me according to what is written: 'I will strike the shepherd and the sheep will be scattered,'" Peter said, "And if all not I." Says Jesus: "Before the cock will have crowed twice you will deny me three times today."

---

46. T. Nicklas, "Eine neue alte Erzählung im Rahmen antiker Jesustraditionen: Reste eines Exorzismus auf P.Oxy. lxxvi 5072," *Annali di storia dell'Esegesi* 29 (2012): 13–27; see above on P.Egerton 2.

47. Ponder, "Papyrus Oxyrhynchus 5072," 139.

48. Matt 10:32–33//Luke 12:8–9; Mark 8:38//Luke 9:26; Luke 14:26–27//Matt 10:37–38; Luke 17:21 et al.

49. G. Bickell, "Ein Papyrusfragment eines nichtkanonischen Evangeliums," *ZKT* 9 (1885): 498–504.

50. T. J. Kraus, "*P.Vindob.G* 2325: The So-Called Fayûm-Gospel—Re-edition and Some Critical Conclusions," in: *Ad fontes: Original Manuscripts and Their Significance for Studying Early Christianity*, Texts and Editions for New Testament Study 3 (Leiden: Brill, 2007), 89, and Kraus, "Other Gospel Fragments," 222.

While earlier authors speculated whether the text could be a harmony, a paraphrase, or even a source of New Testament Gospel material, Kraus points to several differences between the *Fayûm Gospel* and the Synoptic parallels. First, the text does not contain Jesus's reference to his future resurrection (Mark 14:28; Matt 26:32). Second, its language shows two interesting features. Instead of the word ἀλεκτώρ ("cock"), as used in the Synoptic Gospels, it has ἀλεκτρυών. Even more striking is its use of the verb κοκκύζω (instead of φωνέω), which never occurs in the Greek Bible to describe a cock's cry.[51] If we take all this into account, it is improbable that the *Fayûm Gospel* used Mark or Matthew as its written *Vorlage*. Why, for example, should in this case the prophecy about Jesus's resurrection have been omitted? Instead, the *Fayûm Gospel* shows a clearer focus on Peter's denial and uses more uncommon language than the canonical Gospels. While we cannot know whether this short passage was originally part of a full extracanonical Gospel, it at least seems to be a free retelling (or again, a "re-enactment") of a story which had made it into the collective (or even cultural) memories of many early Christians and was thus not only read but retold in different contexts. Again, it is not possible to say anything reliable regarding the original text's date and provenance.

2.7 Papyrus Berolinensis 11710 (P.Berol. 11710)

This papyrus, which is currently kept in the Egyptian Museum and Papyrus collection of Berlin, consists of two leaves of miniature size (ca. 6.5 x 7.5 cm) and was probably used as an amulet.[52] The manuscript, which was first edited by Hans Lietzmann in the year 1923,[53] is likely quite late, perhaps sixth century CE, or even later.[54] This is supported by the fact that the text of leaf B *recto* is in Coptic ("Jesus Christ, great God . . .").

The text offers remnants of a dialogue between Jesus and Nathanael with close parallels to the Gospel of John. If we connect the leaves in the order A *verso*, A *recto*, and B *verso*—B *recto* is the Coptic line mentioned above—we get the following short text; the first saying is probably by Nathanael:[55]

[A *verso*] [. . .] and said: "Rabbi, Lord, you are the Son of God." The Rabbi answered to him and said: "Nathanael, [A *recto*] walk in the sun." Nathanael answered to him and said: "Rabbi, Lord, you are the Lamb [B *verso*] of God which carries the sins of the world." The Rabbi answered to him and said [. . .]

Nathanael's first sentence comes close to his saying in John 1:49 (though it adds the title "Lord" [*kyrios*] and omits the reference to the "king of Israel"). Jesus, who is again called "Rabbi," offers a strange response. His command to "walk in the sun" can refer to very different things. While some interpreters have suggested a Manichaean background (and pointed to Augustine, *Haer.* 46.6 as a possible parallel), the easiest solution is to connect this sentence to Johannine passages. One could, for example, consider John 1:48, where Jesus perhaps commands Nathanael to leave the shadow of the fig tree and "walk in the sun." One could also see a more symbolic meaning of "walking in the sun" as a way of "walking in the light" or "coming to the light," as in John 3:21.[56] Nathanael's answer,

---

51. Kraus, "Other Gospel Fragments," 224–25.
52. Kraus, "Other Gospel Fragments," 238.
53. H. Lietzmann, "Ein apokryphes Evangelienfragment," *ZNW* 22 (1923): 153–54.
54. Kraus, "Other Gospel Fragments," 229.
55. See also Kraus, "Other Gospel Fragments," 232–33.
56. Kraus, "Other Gospel Fragments," 234.

finally, takes over John the Baptist's well-known address to Jesus (John 1:29). Instead of the Johannine singular "sin of the world," P.Berol. 11710 uses the plural "sins of the world."

The extant text seems to be highly influenced by passages from the first chapter of the Gospel of John. The text does not want to tell an interesting Jesus-story or transmit logia but is interested in putting together as many christological titles as possible (including the Coptic text on B *recto*!). Perhaps the owner of the amulet understood them as "names of power," which could protect from evil. All in all, it is quite probable that this text is not an excerpt of a longer, otherwise lost Gospel. Instead, it was likely composed for its present purpose, the use as an apotropaic amulet. Interestingly, the maker of this papyrus (or the client) seems to have been interested in motifs from the Fourth Gospel without quoting them slavishly. This is an example of a broader trend, which can be seen in several papyri from late antique Egypt. With the increasing success of Christianity, old beliefs in magic were not simply abandoned. Instead, Christian texts and motifs were combined with old names of power or replaced them. In many cases, texts like Psalm 90 LXX[57] or the Lord's Prayer were used. At least in some cases, the fact that a New Testament passage was used as an amulet led to changes in its text form. Papyrus Oxyrhynchus VIII 1077, for example, offers a text of Matthew 4:23–24. It both shortens its Matthean *Vorlage* as well as stresses Jesus's healing activities: "And he healed every disease and every disease [sic!] and every sickness among the people."[58] At least in some cases this freedom toward Jesus-material went so far as to create new Jesus-stories. This was, for example, probably the case with P.Oxy. XI 1384 (fifth or sixth century CE), which combines several medical recipes, a short Jesus-story (probably invented just for this purpose), and a story about angels asking for a medicine against eye-disease.[59] Like P.Oxy. XI 1384, the text of P.Berol. 11710 is probably not part of an early apocryphal Gospel but was composed for the amulet. As such, it does not tell us anything about the historical Jesus, but it does tell us quite a lot about late antique Christians' lived religion.

2.8 Papyrus Merton 51 (P.Mert. II 51)

Papyrus Merton 51 was edited in the year 1959 by B. R. Rees, who dated this tiny fragment (3.9 x 5.3 cm) to the third century CE.[60] If we follow the reconstruction by Kraus (who comes close to Rees), the following text emerges. On the *recto* side, Kraus reconstructs the text as follows:

> And the whole people and even the tax collectors when they heard (him?) they acknowledged that God is just and confessed their sins. But the Pharisees were not baptized by John. They rejected the counsel of God and the command of God. But a Pharisee (?) asked him to eat with him [...][61]

---

57. T. J. Kraus, "Hebrew Psalm 91 / Greek Psalm 90: Collections and Contexts, and a Text of Authority," in *Authoritative Writings in Early Judaism and Early Christianity*, ed. T. Nicklas and J. Schröter, WUNT 441 (Tübingen: Mohr Siebeck, 2020), 289–312.

58. T. Nicklas, "Zur historischen und theologischen Bedeutung der Erforschung neutestamentlicher Textgeschichte," *NTS* 48 (2002): 145–58, esp. 150–51.

59. R. Mazza, "P.Oxy. XI, 1384: Medicina, rituali di guarigione e cristianesimi nell'Egitto tardoantico," *Annali di Storia dell' Esegesi* 24 (2007): 437–62, and T. Nicklas, "Fragmente christlicher Apokryphen und die Geschichte des frühen Christentums," in *Shadowy Characters and Fragmentary Evidence*, ed. J. Verheyden, T. Nicklas, and E. Hernitscheck, WUNT 388 (Tübingen: Mohr Siebeck, 2017), 69–88, esp. 81–87.

60. H. Rees, "51. Christian Fragment," in *Descriptive Catalogue of the Greek Papyri in the Collection of Wilfred Merton II*, ed. H. I. Bell and J. W. B. Barns (Dublin: Hodges Figgis, 1959), 1–4.

61. Kraus, "Other Gospel Fragments," 256, 258. The translation is my own.

On the *verso* we have:

> [...] the bad man, who generates from evil, generates evil fruit like an evil tree from evil. And when you send out from the good treasure of the heart its good fruit does perish. Do not call [pl.] me "Lord, Lord" while you do not do what I say nor listen to what the prophet says.

Of course, we should be aware that these rather smooth texts are the result of a far-reaching reconstruction of this fragment's lacunae. That said, several parallels to New Testament passages can be observed, the clearest of which is Luke 7:29–30 (see again P.Mert. II 51 *recto* above). Other passages, such as Mark 7:9, Luke 7:36; 1 Corinthians 10:2, and 1 John 1:9 can be added.[62] The *verso* comes closest to Luke 6:45–46 (plus parallels in Matt 12:35; Gospel of Thomas 45; and even P.Oxy. II 210).

At least in the reconstruction, the text of P.Mert. II 51 differs only slightly from Luke. Even if we consider the *recto* as following the *verso* side, it must be clear that the original text of P.Mert. II 51 did not offer a version of Luke (or an extracanonical Gospel rewriting Luke).[63] While it is not impossible that it was part of an otherwise unknown extracanonical Gospel (which at least in this part was related to the Gospel of Luke), it is more likely that we have parts of a homily or a free excerpt (perhaps for exegetical purposes?) related to the Gospel of Luke.

2.9 Papyrus Cairensis 10735 (P.Cair.Cat. 10735)

Papyrus Cairensis 10735 was edited in the year 1903 by B. P. Grenfell and A. S. Hunt, who dated it to the sixth or seventh century CE.[64] The little fragment (5.3 x 6.3 cm) transmits remains of text on both sides. While Grenfell and Hunt identified it as the remnants of an otherwise unknown apocryphal Gospel, it could also be part of a homily or another Christian text. Its few remaining lines show parallels to the New Testament infancy stories. Interestingly, the *recto* offers a passage that seems to record a story about the Holy Family's flight to Egypt:

> The Angel of the Lord said: "Joseph, take Mary, your wife and flee to Egypt" [two lines lacking] every present and when [...] his friends [...] of the king.[65]

The text on the *verso* appears to recall the annunciation of Mary:

> The [Archistrategos] said to the virgin: "Behold, Elizabeth, your relative, has conceived as well and she is in the sixth month, she, who had been called barren." In the sixth, that is [in the month of Thoth the mother has] conceived John. But the Archistrategos [had to preannounce] John as the servant who goes ahead [...]

While it is impossible to decide if these fragments belonged to an originally full Gospel, an otherwise lost infancy story, or just a homily or something comparable, some of the text's

---

62. See Kraus, "Other Gospel Fragments," 257.

63. Kraus writes, "But what happened to Luke 6.47–7.28? The passage cannot have been between the text preserved on the recto and the verso according to the probable page dimensions of the codex leaf. Consequently, the papyrus did not contain a continuous coverage of Luke" ("Other Gospel Fragments," 262).

64. B. P. Grenfell and A. S. Hunt, eds., *Catalogue général des antiquités égyptiennes du Musée du Caire: Nos. 10001–10869*, vol. 10 (Oxford: Oxford University Press, 1903), 90.

65. Greek texts according to Kraus, "Other Gospel Fragments," 244, 246; translations are adapted.

features point to an origin in Egypt, which during late antiquity developed a kind of "landscape of memories"[66] full of sites that wanted to remember the story of the Holy Family's flight to Egypt. In this context a whole series of "new" apocryphal stories were written and related to places in Egypt.[67] It makes sense to understand the text of P.Cair.Cat. 10735 as part of this thought world, which remains attractive for Coptic Christians still today.

The *verso*, in turn, presupposes the idea of a hierarchy of angels, among which the archangel Gabriel takes over the role of a highest-ranking officer—that is, an *archistrategos*. The dating of Elizabeth's conception to the sixth month is usually a sign for a later development when apocryphal writings related to aspects of an emerging Holy Year. Papyrus Cairensis 10735 is a witness for how ancient Jesus-stories known from the canonical Gospels could be retold and reshaped by later Christians without looking exactly like the wording of "what is written."

3. CONCLUSION

Why should we read these texts, which are often very fragmentary and sometimes strange? Perhaps we may be disappointed when we see how little additional information about the historical Jesus they offer us. Of course, one could consider whether P.Egerton 2 preserves additional, and perhaps independent, evidence for material we also know from the Synoptic Gospels. But we should not concentrate on this question alone. Much more is to be discovered. The Gospel fragments mentioned above give us fascinating material for our understanding of the history of the New Testament canon.[68] They show, in different ways, that the development of Jesus-material did not stop with the emergence of the four Gospels. Texts like P.Cair.Cat. 10735, and probably P.Oxy. V 840, show that this production did not come to an end even after the more or less universally acknowledged closure of the New Testament canon in the second half of the fourth century.

Even though some of the fragments discussed above were probably not part of otherwise lost full Gospels, they also witness to how long it was possible to retell and rewrite Jesus-stories, which already must have existed in written form. I think that in many cases we should neither speak too quickly of traditions independent of the canonical Gospels nor refer to these writings as the results of redactions of one or more literary *Vorlagen*. In many cases, I think it is best to describe them with the term *re-enactment*, which comes close to what is sometimes expressed with the term *second orality*.

Other cases, like P.Oxy. V 840 and P.Egerton 2, fragment 2 *verso*, offer evidence of the production and transmission of otherwise unknown Jesus-stories. In the case of P.Egerton 2, we can even see how Old Testament and early Jewish stories about Elisha and local traditions in the Jericho region formed the background of a fascinating miracle story.

Not only the texts, but also the manuscripts themselves, tell stories about the people who produced and used them. If P.Oxy. V 840 was part of a miniature codex, it was certainly not read openly in a liturgical context. If P.Berol. 11710 was an amulet, the text could be understood in the context of ancient (even Christian) magical practices.[69]

---

66. T. Nicklas, "New Testament Canon and Ancient Christian 'Landscapes of Memory,'" *Early Christianity* 7 (2016): 5–23, esp. 9–18.

67. For example, there is a story about a sycamore tree in Mataria (Al Matariyyah) close to today's Cairo, which was allegedly a place of rest for the Holy Family or a place where Joseph had to sell the presents given to him by the magi to get the "tickets" for a Nile boat.

68. See also T. Nicklas, "Christian Apocrypha and the Development of the Christian Canon," *Early Christianity* 5 (2014): 220–40.

69. One could give even more information, but this would have made very precise and detailed paleographical descriptions necessary. For this, see, e.g., Kraus, Kruger, and Nicklas, *Gospel Fragments*.

To conclude, the fragments of extracanonical Gospels (or at least Jesus-stories) may not provide us with much of otherwise unknown material for the reconstruction of the historical Jesus, but they do offer us intriguing insights into the varieties of early Christianity.

4. BIBLIOGRAPHY

Chapa, J. "Uncanonical Gospel?" Pages 1–20 in *The Oxyrhynchus Papyri 76*. Edited by J. Chapa and D. Colomo. Graeco-Roman Memoirs. London: Egyptian Exploration Society, 2011.

Foster, P. "Papyrus Oxyrhynchus X 1224." Pages 59–96 in *Early Christian Manuscripts: Examples of Applied Method and Approach*. Edited by T. J. Kraus and T. Nicklas. Texts and Editions for New Testament Study 5. Leiden: Brill, 2010.

Gronewald, M. "P.Köln VI 255: Unbekanntes Evangelium oder Evangelienharmonie (Fragment aus dem 'Evangelium Egerton')." Pages 136–45 in *Kölner Papyri (P.Köln), Volume VI*. Opladen: Westdeutscher, 1987.

Kraus, T. J. "Other Gospel Fragments." Pages 219–80 in *Gospel Fragments*. Edited by T. J. Kraus, M. J. Kruger, and T. Nicklas. Oxford Early Christian Gospel Texts. Oxford: Oxford University Press, 2009.

———. "P.Oxy. V 840—Amulett oder Miniaturkodex? Grundsätzliche und ergänzende Anmerkungen zu zwei Termini." *Zeitschrift für Antikes Christentum* 8 (2005): 485–97. Republished as "*P.Oxy*. V 840—Amulet or Miniature Codex? Principal and Additional Remarks on Two Terms." Pages 47–68 in *Ad fontes: Original Manuscripts and Their Significance for Studying Early Christianity*. By T. J. Kraus. Texts and Editions for New Testament Study 3. Leiden: Brill, 2007.

———. "*P.Vindob.G* 2325: The So-Called Fayûm-Gospel—Re-edition and Some Critical Conclusions." Pages 69–94 in *Ad fontes: Original Manuscripts and Their Significance for Studying Early Christianity*. By T. J. Kraus. Texts and Editions for New Testament Study 3. Leiden: Brill, 2007.

Kraus, T. J., M. J. Kruger, and T. Nicklas, eds. *Gospel Fragments*. Oxford Early Christian Gospel Texts. Oxford: Oxford University Press, 2009.

Kruger, M. J. *The Gospel of the Savior. An Analysis of P.Oxy. 840 and Its Place in the Gospel Traditions of Early Christianity*. Texts and Editions for New Testament Study 1. Leiden: Brill, 2005.

———. "*Papyrus Oxyrhynchus 840*." Pages 123–215 in *Gospel Fragments*. Edited by T. J. Kraus, M. J. Kruger, and T. Nicklas. Oxford Early Christian Gospel Texts. Oxford: Oxford University Press, 2009.

Nicklas, T. "The 'Unknown Gospel' on *Papyrus Egerton 2* (+ *Papyrus Cologne 55*)." Pages 11–120 in *Gospel Fragments*. Edited by T. J. Kraus, M. J. Kruger, and T. Nicklas. Oxford Early Christian Gospel Texts. Oxford: Oxford University Press, 2009.

Zelyck, L. *The Egerton Gospel (Egerton Papyrus 2 + Papyrus Köln VI 255): Introduction, Critical Edition, and Commentary*. Texts and Editions for New Testament Study 13. Leiden: Brill, 2019.

CHAPTER 3

GOSPEL OF BARNABAS

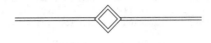

PHILIP JENKINS

1. INTRODUCTION

Even by the standards of noncanonical Scriptures and pseudepigrapha, the Gospel of Barnabas is a controversial and paradoxical work. We remain uncertain about many critical matters concerning its origin and its stages of composition, or of its purpose, so that remarkably few statements about it can be made without qualifications. Yet Barnabas is surprisingly influential in shaping popular views of Christian origins, especially in the Islamic world.

1.1 Provenance

The first known reference to Barnabas was written in 1634 by Ibrahim al-Taybili, in what is now Tunisia.[1] The Gospel became known in Europe in the early eighteenth century, where it was cited in Italian and Spanish versions. We cannot certainly say which language represents the original text. Although the Spanish text was lost, large portions survive in transcription. Early references to an Arabic version are unsubstantiated and generally viewed with suspicion.[2]

The Italian manuscript came to light in Amsterdam around 1709, when it was reported by the Irish deist and religious radical John Toland. Its earlier history is unknown, although it probably circulated within Europe's covert but widespread elite networks of skeptical anti-Trinitarian thinkers. Toland claimed that it had come from the library of "a person of great name and authority in that said city," whose identity has resisted scholarly inquiry. Toland used Barnabas as part of his controversial work *Nazarenus* (1718), which promised a survey of "Jewish, Gentile, and Mahometan Christianity" that contained "the history of the antient Gospel of Barnabas, and the Modern Gospel of the Mahometans."[3] *Nazarenus* was a landmark in the modern critical study of Christian origins. Besides introducing the groundbreaking concept of "Jewish Christianity," Toland challenged the whole concept of the New Testament canon by advocating Barnabas as equal or superior to the familiar Gospels.[4]

---

1. Gerald A. Wiegers, "Muhammad as Messiah: A Comparison of the Polemical Works of Juan Alonso with the Gospel of Barnabas," *Bibliotheca Orientalis* 52 (1995): 245–91; idem, "Gospel of Barnabas," in *Encyclopedia of Islam*, 3rd. ed., ed. Kate Fleet et al. (Leiden: Brill, 2013). For Taybili, see Teresa Soto, "Poetics and Polemics," in *Polemical Encounters*, ed. M. García-Arenal and G. Wiegers (University Park: Pennsylvania State University Press, 2019).

2. Luis F. Bernabé Pons, *El texto morisco del Evangelio de San Bernabé* (Granada: Universidad de Granada, 1998).

3. John Toland, *Nazarenus, or Jewish, Gentile and Mahometan Christianity* (London: J. Brown, 1718), title page.

4. See David Sox, *The Gospel of Barnabas* (London: Allen & Unwin, 1984); J. A. I. Champion, *The Pillars of Priestcraft Shaken* (Cambridge University Press, 1992).

1.2 Text and Translations

The standard English edition and translation of Barnabas was published in 1907 by Lonsdale Ragg and Laura Ragg.[5] A scholarly edition by Luigi Cirillo and Michel Frémaux appeared in 1977, which included a facsimile of the original text, together with a French translation. Other editions and translations have followed subsequently.[6]

Although it takes the form of a Gospel narrative, the central purpose of the Gospel of Barnabas as we have it is to make Jesus proclaim the future coming of Muhammad and the truth of Islam. The Gospel condemns St. Paul as the effective inventor of historical Christianity and its theology, which betrayed the pristine truth. So powerful a weapon did the text appear against Christian orthodoxy that in 1908, Islamic reformer Rashid Rida used the Ragg version as the basis of an Arabic translation. Muslims around the world have since widely adopted the work as the *Injil*, the primitive lost *evangelium* that Christians supposedly distorted in their own canonical texts. Among other enthusiasts, the work attracted the advocacy of Maulana Mawdudi, one of the key funders of modern political Islamism. Muslims deploy Barnabas in polemic and proselytizing, a trend that has been vastly boosted by the coming of the Internet. Mass media in Islamic countries regularly report the discovery of new texts purporting to reveal the true origins of Christianity, finds that generally turn out to be versions of Barnabas. So extensively is it read and cited for these ends that Barnabas exercises a global popular influence at least equal to any alternative Gospel.[7]

1.3 Origins and Authorship

The work's origins are so puzzling that we almost seem to be dealing with a fictional (or metafictional) writing by Umberto Eco. Key areas of debate include the date at which the text emerged in something like its extended narrative form. Beyond argument, the work was not originally written as a unity. Scholars have identified multiple stages of composition, which in their earliest layers include various narratives and discourses and which were integrated at different stages between the fourteenth and late sixteenth centuries. Both the nature and number of these building blocks is open to debate. Also uncertain is the stage at which a Christian original or originals acquired the present "Islamic" shape and content, with its strong polemics against orthodox Christian theology.[8]

---

5. Lonsdale Ragg and Laura Ragg, eds., *Gospel of Barnabas* (Oxford: Clarendon, 1907). All quotations from Barnabas in this present introduction are drawn from the Raggs' translation. I have engaged in very minor, silent editing throughout those quotations, e.g., changing "Mohammed" to "Muhammad." I have also Americanized spelling, e.g., with "splendor" for "splendour."

6. Luigi Cirillo and Michel Frémaux, eds., *Évangile de Barnabé* (Paris: Beauchesne, 1977). Frémaux also edited a second revised and updated edition of this work (Paris: Beauchesne, 1999), which took full account of recent textual discoveries and which is much more readily available than the first. However, the second edition omits the very extensive introductory materials of the first. Ideally, both editions need to be consulted together. See also Eugenio Giustolisi and Giuseppe Rizzardi, *Il Vangelo di Barnaba: Un vangelo per i musulmani?* (Milano: Istituto Propaganda Libraria, 1991).

7. Jan Slomp, "The Gospel in Dispute," *Islamochristiana* 4.1 (1978): 67–111; Oddbjørn Leirvik, *Images of Jesus Christ in Islam*, 2nd ed. (London: Continuum, 2010); idem, "History as a Literary Weapon: The *Gospel of Barnabas* in Muslim-Christian Polemics," *Studia Theologica* 56.1 (2010): 4–26. Rida's work is described in Umar Ryad, *Islamic Reformism and Christianity* (Leiden: Brill, 2009), 213–42. Mawdudi's work is described in Jan Slomp, "The 'Gospel of Barnabas' in Recent Research," under the section "Barnabas, More Authentic? Maulana Mawdudi," Christlich-Islamische Gesellschaft e.V., www.chrislages.de/barnarom.htm#KKK. For modern rediscoveries of Barnabas, see Annette Yoshiko Reed, "'Muslim Gospel' Revealing the 'Christian Truth' Excites the *Da Vinci Code* Set," *Religion Dispatches*, May 22, 2014, https://religiondispatches.org/muslim-gospel-revealing-the-christian-truth-excites-the-da-vinci-code-set/.

8. For ongoing debates, see Jan Slomp, "The Gospel of Barnabas in Recent Research," *Islamochristiana* 23 (1997): 81–109.

Another debate involves the Christian originals that were thus adapted and whether these included early alternative or apocryphal Gospels, singular or plural. Speculation has focused on possible Jewish-Christian or Ebionite sources underlying the present Barnabas. In addition, the presence of early materials is particularly likely in the very distinctive account presented of the crucifixion. Finally, many parts of the text incorporate biblical readings that differ from the conventional Latin Vulgate, and which point rather to the tradition of the *Diatessaron*. It is unknown whether any hypothetical predecessor texts had any relationship to the lost Gospels cited under the name of Barnabas by various early church writers, up to the seventh century. (There is no relationship to the Epistle of Barnabas, or to the Acts attributed to the same figure.)[9]

Barnabas is not in whole, or even a large part, an "ancient" Gospel, but many aspects of the work point to earlier origins, and perhaps to primitive Gospels.

1.4 Circumstances of Writing: (1) Medieval

In seeking to establish the development of Barnabas, scholars have focused on the affairs of Latin Christendom during the fourteenth century. Many portions of the text seem to allude to the ecclesiastical politics of that era and in particular to the affairs of the Carmelite Order. The Order was founded as part of the medieval Crusading venture, and, as such, members were forced to flee the Near East after the Crusader collapse in 1291. When they returned to Europe, survivors were shocked to find that local houses of the Order had largely abandoned their eremitical tradition, which they struggled to restore. Matters such as the severity of fasting were singularly contentious. Over the next century, Carmelite reformers and scholars created an influential mythology concerning the roots of the Order, which they traced to the followers of the ancient prophet Elijah and linked firmly to the Hebrew prophetic tradition. Polemical writings accumulated as the movement faced outright suppression.[10]

That history may be reflected in the Gospel of Barnabas, in which Jesus so often quotes Elijah and other prophets beloved of the Carmelites. In his prolix sermons and teachings, Jesus shows deep concern about questions of religious discipline and self-control, especially fasting (from a great many examples, see ch. 107, 110–11). As we will see, Barnabas also draws a stark distinction between faithful and faithless followers of religion, the true and false Pharisees, who may be coded representations of the competing sides in medieval factional struggles. Those true Pharisees would thus correspond with the Carmelite rigorists. The Gospel specifically cites "Mount Carmel, where the prophets and Pharisees abode." Reading those materials, we are immersed in a conventional world of late medieval mendicant piety, with its homilies and sermons.

Also indicating parallels to Barnabas, the Carmelite literature of this era drew heavily on invented pseudohistorical ancient texts in order to promote their views. The most significant reformer was the Catalan Felip Ribot, author around 1380 of the influential treatise *Liber de Institutione Primorum Monachorum* or *Book of the Institution of the First Monks*, which he credited falsely to an ancient Christian patriarch. But other Carmelite writers freely plundered Christian antiquity in support of their Order, inventing authorities and

---

9. For the *Diatessaronic* elements, see Jan Joosten, "The Gospel of Barnabas and the Diatessaron," *HTR* 95 (2002): 73–96; but see also the critique in August den Hollander and Ulrich Schmid, "The Gospel of Barnabas, the Diatessaron, and Method," *VC* 61 (2007): 1–20. For earlier gospels of Barnabas, see R. Blackhirst, "*Barnabas* and the Gospels," *Journal of Higher Criticism* 7 (2000): 1–22.

10. Theodore Pulcini, "In the Shadow of Mount Carmel," *Islam and Christian-Muslim Relations* 12.2 (2001): 191–209.

authors. Some early tract of this nature—even a "Carmelite Gospel"—might be preserved in Barnabas, where it occupies a substantial part of the text.[11]

A fourteenth-century context would explain many features of the Gospel of Barnabas, which draws so heavily not just on the Christian Bible but the Bible as it would have been known and interpreted in the later Middle Ages. Jesus quotes the Old Testament in the Vulgate translation, proving that we cannot be dealing with a very primitive text. But if these quotes are not very early historically, neither do they belong to a later stage of composition or revision by a Muslim editor. As quoted, the great majority speak to Christian concerns and traditions and to conventional moral lessons and preaching, and as such they have no relevance to the Islamizing arguments we find elsewhere. We also find many allusions in passing to New Testament texts, including most of Paul's letters.

The Gospel of Barnabas closely resembles other medieval Christian writings in its ignorance of the authentic history of Jesus's era. The Gospel makes many factual and geographical errors that were characteristic of this later age and that commonly arose from retrojected Catholic practice and belief. Barnabas thinks that Second Temple-era Jews practiced a forty-day fast like the Christian Lent (ch. 91), and other examples record medieval Latin Christian practice and belief. Nor does this Gospel seem to understand that the term *Christ* is synonymous with *Messiah*. Among other features, a fourteenth-century date would explain the Gospel's odd cosmic structure, which seems to stem from Dante.

The exact limits of this "Carmelite" portion of Barnabas are difficult to determine with any confidence, and they may or may not have included the substantial portions of apocalyptic, together with Jesus's descriptions of paradise and hell. Such accounts were common enough in European Christian literature of that era and usually accompanied exhortations to piety and proper living. If they did, the original descriptions would have differed from the present content in omitting some of the explicitly Islamic material. Nor is it clear whether the authors of this layer of the work would have used a contemporary Gospel harmony to frame the material, but that is likely. Sections of Barnabas resemble Italian writings of that era, including Gospel harmonies of a *Diatessaronic* character.[12]

1.5 Circumstances of Writing: (2) Early Modern

From this perspective, much of Barnabas is conventional, orthodox, and Catholic, and the only difference from many other writings of the era is the attribution to Jesus and his contemporaries. But if such a "Carmelite" layer of the text did exist, it presumably did not include other material that is so conspicuously present in the version that we have. That would include the Islamic declarations of faith and the predictions of Muhammad, the diatribes about the superiority of Ishmael to Isaac, and the preaching of distinctively non-Christian customs, such as circumcision.

Probably by the end of the fourteenth century, a manuscript existed that included large portions of the present text of Barnabas but was lacking those elements that have subsequently made the work so daring, and even scandalous. At some point before the late sixteenth century, there was at least one thorough and sweeping process of editing and augmentation, taking it in a definitively Islamic direction. Just when and where that occurred is much debated, but the contents of Barnabas suggest a region marked by religious exchange, a world in which Jewish, Christian, and Muslim traditions were in contact and contention. The knowledge of multiple faiths implied by our present Barnabas points

---

11. Andrew Jotischky, *The Carmelites and Antiquity* (Oxford: Oxford University Press, 2002).
12. Jan Joosten, "The Date and Provenance of the Gospel of Barnabas," *JTS* 61 (2010): 200–215.

to an author or authors with personal knowledge of various strands, presumably a convert or a crypto-believer. The text is thus richly illustrative of religious debates and interchange, most likely—but not necessarily—in the Mediterranean world.

As to determining a date for the Islamization of the Gospel of Barnabas, we could be dealing with the work of a medieval Christian convert to Islam, perhaps during the fourteenth century. This would require an educated person, so presumably a cleric, and perhaps a defector from the Carmelites. Although a credible case can be made for such an early chronology, most scholars focus on later dates, particularly in the later sixteenth century.[13]

The two possible languages of composition are suggestive in determining origins, but they are not definitive. There is convincing evidence that parts of Barnabas were translated from an original Italian into Spanish, but this does not mean this applied to the whole text. We might even imagine a two-stage process. If we assume that the Catholic and late medieval sections were in Italian, then they could have been translated into Spanish and combined with other materials in order to create the Islamized whole that we know subsequently. This new Gospel would then have been turned into Italian. The fact that we do not possess the whole Spanish text means that we can never entirely resolve this question.[14]

Ultimately, any attempt to locate the origins of Barnabas with any precision founders on the extreme mobility of Europe in the century or so after 1530, a time of frequent religious purges, persecutions, and expulsions, when scholars and clergy, besides ordinary believers, were very likely to end their days in countries other than the ones in which they had been born. If indeed Italian was the language of the final Gospel as we have it, this final editing could have occurred in Italy itself, or in many other regions. Italian was widely spoken by educated elites across Europe.

One credible theory grounds Barnabas in anti-Trinitarian circles in Transylvania, where radical theological views were tolerated and even enjoyed mainstream status. Supporting that view are passages in Barnabas that seem to refer to theological debates within contemporary European Protestantism. Jesus condemns ideas of predestination and expresses firmly anti-Calvinist opinions that fitted well with the Socinian and anti-Trinitarian thought of the time (ch. 164). As we have seen, Barnabas continued to circulate in such circles over the following century, until achieving public visibility in Toland's work. Yet it is not clear how an anti-Trinitarian or Unitarian approach should have traveled so totally to the explicitly and comprehensively Islamic declarations that we find in Barnabas (although as I will note, the work's Islamic qualities are more nuanced than they might appear at first blush)..

If we assume a Spanish-language origin, another and perhaps more plausible setting would be among Spain's Moriscos. These were Muslims who accepted conversion to Christianity after 1492 and who lived in an increasingly tense relationship with the regime until their decisive expulsion in 1614. Meshing well with that chronology, the same era produced other examples of literary and archaeological forgery presenting religious apologetics, notably the so-called Lead Books of Sacromonte, which were purportedly discovered near Granada around 1600. As interpreted by their Morisco translators, these sensational texts recorded statements and visions of the Virgin Mary, which offered an alternative version of early Spanish Christian history. In that distinctive account, moreover, the Lead Books offered no role for Saint Paul, whom Barnabas would likewise portray as a deceiver and falsifier. One obvious purpose of the Lead Books was to enhance the role of the Arab-derived

---

13. Theodore Pulcini, "In the Shadow of Mount Carmel," *Islam and Christian-Muslim Relations* 12.2 (2001): 191–209.

14. Joosten, "Date and Provenance of the Gospel of Barnabas."

Morisco people themselves. Barnabas in turn writes at length of the virtues and importance not just of Muhammad but of the descendants of Ishmael in general—that is, of the Arabs.[15]

So familiar was the stereotypical association of Morisco scholars with invented or imaginary texts that it famously appears around the very time of the Sacromonte affair in *Don Quixote*, when the actual author Miguel de Cervantes claims he is using a work by the fictitious Cide Hamete Benengeli. Cervantes was satirizing both the contemporary taste for forging polemical documents as well as the credulity of Christian authorities in accepting them.[16] As I will suggest, issues of forgery, authenticity, and scribal integrity surface repeatedly in Barnabas, as we might expect in a culture where such controversies were ongoing. Barnabas is ideally suited for a society in which conversion is a very live issue, but in which the relative value and authenticity of Scriptures and texts were fiercely debated. Texts, as well as individuals, readily crossed religious frontiers. Barnabas assumes a world in which multiple competing Scriptures bid for people's attention and loyalty. Even if it is not the only candidate for such an environment, sixteenth-century Spain fits that model very well.[17]

That Moriscos knew and valued Barnabas is beyond doubt. Ibrahim al-Taybili, mentioned earlier in the essay as the one who offered the first evidence of knowledge of Barnabas, was a Spanish Morisco. An English reference to Barnabas in 1734 notes that "of this Gospel, the Moriscos in Africa have a translation in Spanish." (We can challenge the word "translation.")[18]

Complicating the matter is a preface to the Spanish Barnabas that claims it was translated from an Italian original purloined from the papal library by a disaffected Catholic cleric, "Fra Marino," who had developed troubling doubts about the canonical Gospels. The value of that story is highly dubious, particularly as it so closely resembles origin legends that are frequently added to forged texts in order to enhance their authenticity. No less frequent in such a context are claims that highly sensitive documents had been translated from other languages, in order to confuse potential persecutors. Significantly, even in the text of Barnabas itself, a pious scribe reports having discovered an authentic version of sacred Scripture that priestly authorities circulated in bogus form, and he found it in the library of the high priest. It is curious, to say the least, that "Fra Marino" is so exactly duplicating the experience portrayed in the very text that he supposedly steals.

Confirming a Spanish interpretation, our Barnabas includes anti-Judaic as well as anti-Christian materials and arguments. This must have been written in an environment in which Jews were a sufficiently potent presence to be worth combating. Although the new Spanish kingdom formally expelled its Jews in 1492, substantial populations remained as converts to Christianity as *conversos*, or as crypto-Jews, Marranos.[19]

---

15. Mercedes García-Arenal and Fernando Rodríguez Mediano, *The Orient in Spain* (Leiden: Brill, 2013); Elizabeth Drayson, *The Lead Books of Granada* (New York: Palgrave, 2013); A. Katie Harris, "Material and Textual Forgery in the Lead Books of Granada," in *Literary Forgery in Early Modern Europe, 1450–1800*, ed. Walter Stephens and Earle A. Havens (Baltimore: Johns Hopkins University Press, 2018); L. P. Harvey, *Muslims in Spain, 1500 to 1614* (Chicago: University of Chicago Press, 2005); Mikel de Epalza, "Garcia Gómez und die Autorschaft des Barnabas-Evangeliums," *Religionen im Gespräch* 6 (2000): 10–13.

16. Carroll B. Johnson, "Phantom Pre-texts and Fictional Authors," *Cervantes* 27.1 (2007): 179–99.

17. For other forgery scandals in this era, see Ingrid D. Rowland, *The Scarith of Scornello* (Chicago: University of Chicago Press, 2004). For the spread of Iberian texts and controversies to Northern Europe, see Gerard A. Wiegers, "Polemical Transfers: Iberian Muslim Polemics and Their Impact in Northern Europe in the Seventeenth Century," in *After Conversion: Iberia and the Emergence of Modernity*, ed. M. García-Arenal (Leiden: Brill, 2016), 229–49. Cf. Miriam Eliav-Feldon, *Renaissance Impostors and Proofs of Identity* (New York: Palgrave Macmillan, 2012).

18. George Sale, *The Koran: Commonly Called the Alcoran of Mohammed* (London: C. Ackers, 1734).

19. Mercedes García-Arenal and Gerard Wiegers, eds., *Polemical Encounters* (University Park: Pennsylvania State University Press, 2019).

1.6 Genre and Purpose

As with so much about Barnabas, even simple statements require caution. Although the work so enthusiastically praises Muhammad, this does not necessarily imply a simplistic Muslim propagandist. Key differences separate Barnabas from authentic Islam, notably the stern denial that Jesus was the Messiah and that Muhammad instead fulfilled this role. In fact, the Qur'an has no difficulty in ascribing the messianic title to Jesus, *al-Masih* (sura Al Imran 3:45). Barnabas's Gospel actually differs from the Qur'an in many points of detail. The Virgin, for instance, suffers no pain when she delivers Jesus, an idea derived from mainstream Catholic doctrine but alien to the Qur'an. Taken together, such deviations might imply that the author or editor was ill-informed or followed a sectarian variant of Islam, or even that he was a non-Muslim making his best effort to imagine how a Muslim might write. Conceivably, the editor has treated the original text in a hurried or superficial way without even noticing the contradictions of Islamic doctrine that he was failing to purge or revise. Alternatively, it has been argued that the work stemmed from a circle of skeptical critics of mainstream orthodox Christianity, who used Muhammad as the ultimate subversive symbol.

That we are not dealing with a straightforward Islamic appropriation is further indicated by the Arabic writings found throughout the Italian manuscript, which are often ungrammatical to the point of bizarre.[20] For the sake of convenience, I will refer throughout to the "Islamic" editor or compiler, but these qualifications should be borne in mind.

That a Christian text has to some degree—in some form—been Islamized is beyond debate, but the nature of the adapted original (or originals) is not clear, nor is the degree of editing or rewriting. We are dealing with multiple layers of subterfuge and of misrepresentation.

2. SUMMARY OF CONTENT

2.1 Structure

The Gospel of Barnabas is a very sizable work. The Italian manuscript contains five hundred pages, and in the Ragg English translation the text includes some 87,000 words, divided into 222 chapters. Of itself, that extensive quality makes any kind of summary difficult, but there are special factors that make it all but impossible to offer the straightforward summary of contents that we might expect for such a document, divided for instance according to events, visions, or discourses.

Barnabas incorporates most of the material in the canonical Gospels, except in the areas of the crucifixion and resurrection. The author or editor might have used the Gospels individually, but there are clear signs of the presence of a Gospel harmony. But besides presenting the individual stories and teachings, Barnabas has lost the essential structure that we know from the Gospels, and an alternative structure has not been imposed with any degree of consistency. In consequence, the reader finds it extremely difficult to navigate the text.

The presence of a harmony is indicated by the first few chapters that integrate the birth stories of Matthew and Luke. We read about the annunciation to Mary, the birth of Jesus, and the visitations by both the magi and the shepherds (chs. 1–9). Throughout the text, we can find all the classic events of the Christian story, the familiar miracles and parables, culminating in the entry to Jerusalem and the story of Holy Week. Particularly in the early sections of the work, Barnabas includes such stories as the temptation in the wilderness (ch. 14), the marriage at Cana and the Beatitudes (chs. 15–16), and the usual collection of

---

20. Cirillo and Frémaux, *Évangile de Barnabé* (2nd ed.), 11–13.

miracle stories (chs. 19–21, 30–34). Barnabas includes the Last Supper, the prophecy of the betrayal, and temptations by Satan (chs. 72–80). Many of these stories are reproduced with few structural revisions, such as the miracle of the man born blind, who is healed at the Pool of Siloam (chs. 156–58).[21]

But the author/editor shows no sense of chronology or development in the narrative. Completely lacking is the narrative structure that we find in the canonical Gospels that divides events before and after Jesus's entry into Jerusalem, and the ensuing story of Holy Week. In Barnabas, the arrival in Jerusalem seemingly makes no difference in locating events that the canonical Gospels portray much earlier in the narrative. In fact, there are multiple arrivals in the city, as Jesus and his followers casually travel back and forth to Galilee.

To cite an egregious example, the story of Jesus's meeting with the Samaritan woman at the well occurs *after* the discourse with the disciples that John situates at the Last Supper (chs. 81–82). In turn, something like that Supper occurs at an early point in Barnabas as we have it. The feeding of the five thousand occurs not in an early phase of Jesus's mission, as in the canonical Gospels, but after he has entered Jerusalem and confronted the priestly authorities. In the days leading up to the crucifixion, Jesus mysteriously returns to Galilee in order to tell the parable of the Sower (ch. 132). There are many other such incongruities. This random distribution of events means that most of Barnabas follows no real logical progression.

In the great majority of cases, the final editor of Barnabas has incorporated earlier Christian materials without paying any great attention to adapting or integrating those materials to his purpose. The exception to this statement involves one theme that the Islamic editor has introduced into the text, in which Jesus must respond to claims of his divine status, which he rejects utterly and strives to suppress. This story shapes the narrative in encouraging Jesus to visit Jerusalem to confront the falsifiers and even helps determine the mission of the apostles. But it is poorly integrated with the other material.

2.2 Jesus's Discourses and Teachings

Much of the text involves sermons or dialogues by Jesus himself, commonly scenes in which he teaches the disciples and responds to their questions (see, e.g., chs. 49–70, 84–90, 99–134). Major themes include the proper means of prayer and fasting, but Jesus also discourses on such matters as lust, impurity, avarice, and vain talk (chs. 115–34) and controlling the flesh (chs. 24–29). As I have suggested earlier, most of these discourses would fit well with the suggested medieval monastic context and with the debates in the Carmelite order. However, some passages use similar styles and formats to present very distinctive messages, notably the lessons on the absolute necessity of circumcision (chs. 22–23) and the question of predestination (chs. 164–65). Jesus also offers glorious visions of paradise (chs. 171–79) and dreadful pictures of hell (chs. 59–61). In some cases, the author/editor adapts well-known Gospel passages for his own purposes, such as the rich man and Lazarus (chs. 24–29), but in many instances the theological purpose or tendency is far from clear.

Reading the text, we commonly find themes or motifs pursued intensely for some length—perhaps ten or twenty chapters—which then vanish, never to be revisited. Far from being a unified work, much of Barnabas as it stands looks like a collection or

---

21. But see Jan Joosten, "Jésus et l'aveugle-né (Jn 9, 1–34) dans l'Évangile de Barnabas et dans le Diatessaron," *RHPR* 80.3 (2000): 359–69.

anthology of Jesus's stories and sermons, without any worldly setting or context. These have been drawn from very diverse sources, which the final editor has not incorporated with much skill or success. The fact that so much of the text involves teachings offered by Jesus to the apostles recalls the familiar pattern of the post-resurrection discourses so often found in early alternative Gospels, although the substance of material discussed in Barnabas is radically different.

Also marking a stark difference from those ancient accounts is the lack of major female characters in Barnabas, beyond the specific instances recorded in the canonical Gospels. Apart from some additional materials concerning the Virgin Mary and her relationship with her Son, Barnabas has no interest in such stock female characters of the apocryphal tradition as Mary Magdalen or Salome. Again, this is in keeping with what we might expect if so many of the discourses were drawn from late medieval monastic sources.

3. INTERPRETIVE ISSUES

Fundamental to our interpretation of Barnabas as we have the text is the Islamic approach that is apparently so dominant. Unraveling these Islamic themes is critical to understanding the nature and purpose of the original work and the later stages of revision and editing. That task also allows us to assess claims that have been made about other nonorthodox Christian elements in the text, including purportedly Jewish or Jewish-Christian materials.

3.1 Islamizing

As we read the Gospel, the process of Islamizing begins slowly but soon becomes near total. Initially, a Christian reader would find little surprising or unorthodox in the text, as the Islamic elements are introduced very gradually and quite subtly; for instance, with a reference to Abraham planning to sacrifice his son Ishmael rather than Isaac (ch. 13). The first significant change from the standard narrative occurs in chapter 10, in which Jesus receives his prophetic call in a scene that replaces the canonical story of the baptism by John. At the age of thirty, Jesus visits the Mount of Olives with Mary, when he is surrounded by angels praising God, and he receives a visitation from the angel Gabriel. Gabriel "presented to him as it were a shining mirror, a book, which descended into the heart of Jesus, in which he had knowledge of what God hath done and what he hath said and what God willeth insomuch that everything was laid bare and open to him." As he tells Barnabas, everything Jesus says comes from that book. Jesus accepts his prophetic commission, although he knows the suffering it will entail, and he receives Mary's approval. The critical role of the revealed heavenly book presumably foreshadows the eternal truth of the Qur'an.

Only in a discourse in chapters 17–18 do we first encounter an explicit reference to a future prophet who is clearly Muhammad. In response to questions by Philip, Jesus condemns false prophecies and the distortion of the true faith. He declares that "after me shall come the Splendor of all the prophets and holy ones, and shall shed light upon the darkness of all that the prophets have said, because he is the messenger of God."

Muhammad's specific name first appears somewhat later, and after that Jesus speaks at length about his qualities and glories. Jesus tells the story of the fall and rebellion of the angels after Satan refused to venerate the raw material out of which God would make his prophets on earth (ch. 35–41). That naturally leads to the story of the creation of Adam and Eve and their temptation and fall. Adam sees writings proclaiming that "there is only one God, and Muhammad is the Messenger of God," which is the first appearance of Muhammad's name in the text (ch. 39). It is also, of course, the standard form of the

Muslim proclamation of faith, the *shahadah*. Again, after Adam leaves paradise, "turning around, [he] saw written above the gate, 'There is only one God, and Muhammad is Messenger of God.'"

Thereafter, Muhammad makes frequent appearances in the text. The word "messenger" occurs ninety-two times in the text, virtually always in the context of Muhammad, and Muhammad's actual name features on fifteen occasions. Muhammad features prominently in the accounts of the end times and last judgment that appear so strongly in Jesus's preaching (chs. 49–60). Muhammad thus stands at the beginning of human history as well as at its end. Jesus prophesies that in those days, the Messenger will draw together the prophets. God will speak with him "even as a friend to a friend when for a long while they have not met" (ch. 55). The Messenger holds the book that God will open.

The process of gradual unveiling culminates after Jesus has entered Jerusalem and is in dialogue with the Jewish priests:

> Then said the priest: "How shall the Messiah be called, and what sign shall reveal his coming?" Jesus answered: "The name of the Messiah is admirable, for God himself gave him the name when he had created his soul, and placed it in a celestial splendor. God said: 'Wait Muhammad; for your sake I will to create paradise, the world, and a great multitude of creatures, whereof I make you a present, insomuch that whoever shall bless you shall be blessed, and whoever shall curse you shall be accursed. When I shall send you into the world I shall send you as my Messenger of salvation, and your word shall be true, insomuch that heaven and earth shall fail, but your faith shall never fail.' Muhammad is his blessed name." Then the crowd lifted up their voices, saying: "O God, send us your Messenger: O Muhammad, come quickly for the salvation of the world!" (ch. 97)

When the disciples inquire on another occasion,

> Jesus answered with joy of heart: "He is Muhammad, Messenger of God, and when he comes into the world, even as the rain makes the earth to bear fruit when for a long time it has not rained, even so shall he be occasion of good works among men, through the abundant mercy which he shall bring. For he is a white cloud full of the mercy of God, which mercy God shall sprinkle upon the faithful like rain." (ch. 163)

Muhammad will liberate the virtuous dead from hell and in the process defeat the devil, in what appears to be an appropriation of the Christian apocryphal story of the harrowing of hell (chs. 136–37).

3.2 The Qur'an

The yet unborn Muhammad would be the vehicle of the Qur'an, the book that contains all truth, and which supersedes all rivals and predecessors. Suggestive is the treatment of the so-called Book of Moses, which is referred to often in Barnabas in passages that are intended to be anti-Judaic rather than anti-Christian. Despite the singular form, the phrase "Book of Moses" refers collectively to the books of the Torah. Jesus is circumcised "according to the law of the Lord, as it is written in the book of Moses" (ch. 5), and he and his disciples behave according to that Book (e.g., ch. 61; 92). The phrase occurs no fewer than ten times in the puzzling story of Hosea and Haggai (chs. 185–89; discussed below).

But as Jesus emphasizes, that original Book of Moses had been corrupted, as had its successor, the Book of David, so that anyone relying on it would be misled (chs. 189–91).

In particular, the deceivers had veiled or distorted its core Islamic message as well as the pivotal role of Ishmael in the story of salvation. The culprits were the "false Pharisees and doctors." "Every prophecy have they corrupted, in so much that today a thing is not sought because God has commanded it, but men look whether the doctors say it, and the Pharisees observe it, as though God were in error, and men could not err." The faithful scribe Nicodemus admits that he has seen what must have been a copy of an original and true Book of Moses, "written by the hand of Moses and Joshua" and located in the library of the high priest (ch. 191). In this version, Moses tells how "God showed him his Messenger in the arms of Ishmael, and Ishmael in the arms of Abraham. Near to Ishmael stood Isaac, in whose arms was a child, who with his finger pointed to the Messenger of God, saying: 'This is he for whom God has created all things.'" I will return to the character of Nicodemus the scribe, whom I will suggest is critical in understanding the nature and intent of Barnabas, but who is curiously underemphasized in the scholarly literature.

That history of textual contamination had required God to send new prophets and messengers, such as Jesus, to restate the original truth. That process would end with a new revelation, and a new book. As Jesus declares, "The Lord our God is unchangeable, and hath spoken but one message to all men. Wherefore, when the Messenger of God shall come, he shall come to cleanse away all wherewith the ungodly have contaminated my book" (ch. 124).

Alongside Muhammad and the Qur'an, we find other echoes of Islamic belief. Barnabas offers abundant and quite diverse references to Abraham, not just in his familiar biblical role as the forefather of Israel but as an exemplar often cited by Jesus in stories and legends. In these different contexts, Abraham's name is mentioned 109 times throughout the Gospel, significantly more than Moses (for Abraham, see, e.g., chs. 24–29). This reflects Abraham's significance in the Qur'an, as the father of Ishmael and the Arab peoples: Ishmael's own name occurs on twenty-four occasions. In the eyes of temple authorities, the final sin of Jesus—and the cause of his condemnation to death—is his avowal to the high priest that "the son of Abraham was Ishmael, from whom must be descended the Messiah promised to Abraham, that in him should all the tribes of the earth be blessed" (ch. 208).

3.3 Denying Divinity

The corollary of that stress on Muhammad is Jesus's rejection of any special role for himself. That denial is central to the whole Gospel of Barnabas, and it is proclaimed by Barnabas in the Gospel's opening promise to recount the story of the great prophet Jesus, about whom so much falsehood has circulated: "Many, being deceived of Satan, under pretense of piety, are preaching most impious doctrine, calling Jesus Son of God, repudiating the circumcision ordained of God for ever, and permitting every unclean meat: among whom also Paul hath been deceived" (opening prologue).

Jesus repeatedly denies being the Son of God, the prospect of which reduces him to tears of grief (ch. 47). He even rejects claims of messiahship. He is rather a voice crying in the wilderness for the true Messenger of God who would come in the future and who would be born of Ishmael, not Isaac. Jesus clarifies the prophecies made about the future Messenger, which have been distorted by the Jewish teachers (chs. 42–44). When Peter acknowledges him as Christ, Son of God, Jesus furiously denounces him and struggles to suppress the absurd doctrines that were emerging among the people (ch. 70). These denials of divine claims echo Qur'anic texts concerning Jesus, especially those in sura 5, Al-Ma'idah.

This issue becomes critical after Jesus travels toward Jerusalem, where his miracles cause great excitement and spawn myth-making about his divine qualities. When he enters the city, Roman and Jewish authorities confront him. Although they expect Jesus to make superhuman claims, his preaching to repentance proves that he holds correct and orthodox views about God, and he is allowed to preach to the people (chs. 91–98). In his confrontations with priestly authorities, Jesus repeatedly denies ever having claimed that he is other than human or more than a mere man. "For I am a man, born of a woman, subject to the judgment of God; that lives here like as other men, subject to the common miseries" (ch. 94). "As God lives, in whose presence my soul stands, I am not the Messiah whom all the tribes of the earth expect." The priests agree to tell the Romans that Jesus makes no claim to be God, or Son of God, and they post notices sternly forbidding making any such assertion.

Similar confrontations and denials recur on several occasions, and as noted, Barnabas does not confine itself to a single epochal entry into Jerusalem. Jesus realizes with growing horror just how widespread is the growing belief in his divinity, despite all the efforts he can make to combat it. He particularly blames the distortion of gentile foreigners and warns his followers, "I say, brethren, that Satan, by means of the Roman soldiery, deceived you when you said that I was God" (ch. 128).

The whole Gospel concludes with the dispersion of the disciples and their persecution by enemies of the truth (ch. 222). Particularly grievous was the spread of false doctrine concerning Jesus:

> For certain evil men, pretending to be disciples, preached that Jesus died and rose not again. Others preached that he really died, but rose again. Others preached, and yet preach, that Jesus is the Son of God, among whom is Paul deceived. But we—as much as I have written—we preach to those that fear God, that they may be saved in the last day of God's Judgment.

3.4 Jewish or Ebionite?

The Islamic nature of Barnabas is obvious and pervasive, but other emphases and influences have been proposed. Some scholarship on Barnabas links it to Jewish-Christian influence, perhaps through the Ebionite sect that existed in the early Christian centuries. There are even theories that posit very long-term continuities from early Jewish sects through later hermit communities, and to the Carmelites who so proudly vaunted their prophetic origins. This Jewish-Christian emphasis goes back to Toland in 1718, and indeed we can find resemblances between those ancient sectarian views and Barnabas. Some such Judaizing view might underlie the basic decision to attribute the Gospel to Barnabas, who in the book of Acts engaged in such ferocious contention with Paul that the two separated in sharp disagreement (Acts 15:36–41). In Galatians, Barnabas adheres to Paul's Judaizing opponents (Gal 2:11–14). Barnabas thus becomes a corrector of Pauline falsehoods, an anti-Paul.

The Ebionite theory suffers from several problems, not least that modern scholars differ greatly on how they reconstruct the Ebionite movement, and about which ancient writings might actually express its opinions. Even given what we can say with any confidence, Barnabas differs from the Ebionite stance on such fundamental issues as the nature of Jesus. Ebionites denied that Jesus was God, but they had no doubt that he was the Messiah, the Christ, a view sternly and repeatedly denied by Barnabas.

No less troubling, most of the elements of Barnabas that might seem Jewish-Christian are very difficult indeed to disentangle from Islam. Hypothetical Ebionite readers would have appreciated Barnabas's powerful stress on circumcision, a law that according to Jesus was originally laid down by Adam and revived by Abraham (chs. 22–23). Just as appropriate is the radical and repeated denial that any human being could share God's divinity. But such views are also quintessentially Islamic.

It is all but impossible to assign much material in Barnabas to either Jewish or Islamic tradition with any confidence, as so many of the stories recounted in this Gospel originated in a Jewish apocryphal context, often in the Second Temple era, but were subsequently incorporated into the Qur'an, or into Islamic tradition. This includes the detailed stories about the childhood and youth of Abraham and his struggles with his father about making and worshiping idols. These derive from the (Jewish) Genesis Rabbah, but they also appear in the Qur'an's sura 21, Al-Anbiya'.

Similar remarks apply to the Gospel's pervasive emphasis on the role of Satan and the legends concerning his fall and that of Adam. Satan is referred to over 150 times throughout the whole work, compared to just fourteen times in the four canonical Gospels combined. Satan in Barnabas often serves as a generalized driving force for evil, but the Jesus of this Gospel also repeatedly places the narrative in the larger fall mythology (chs. 35–41, 49–60). The lore concerning Satan and the fall of the angels originally derived from the writings now known as the Life of Adam and Eve. Although Life of Adam and Eve stemmed from a Jewish environment, it became an indispensable component of both Christian and Islamic thinking, and the twin falls—of Satan and of Adam—are described at length in the Qur'an, in sura 7, Al-A'raf. That presence justified and encouraged Islamic scholars to expound those stories in the qur'anic commentaries, the *tafsir*, and in so doing they drew widely on available lore and literature, much of which was also Jewish.

Equally difficult to distinguish between Jewish and Islamic origins are God's faithful angels, such as Gabriel and Michael, who are referred to so frequently throughout Barnabas. Although the archangel Gabriel was of course a key figure in Jewish religious thought, he was central to Islamic belief as the revealer of heavenly truth to Muhammad, and he features frequently in Barnabas in providing Jesus advice and direction (see, e.g., ch. 13). Little or nothing here need have come from Jewish sources directly rather than being mediated through Islam.

If an Ebionite or Jewish-Christian context for Barnabas cannot be disproved or eliminated, it is hard to substantiate.

3.5 Reading the Old Testament

Some elements in Barnabas assuredly point to non-Islamic connections, and one is the heavy use of Old Testament passages, particularly in Jesus's teaching and preaching. But this material is far more likely to be Christian rather than Jewish in origin, and almost certainly derives from the "Carmelite" layer of the Gospel. Tellingly, all follow the readings of the Latin Vulgate rather than the Hebrew text or the Septuagint.

The Jesus of Barnabas quotes Old Testament passages far more than his canonical counterpart, offering more detailed quotations and more extensive allusions. Besides Abraham and Moses, the Jesus of the Gospel of Barnabas is saturated in the Hebrew Prophets, above all Elijah (forty-nine references), the special focus of Carmelite tradition and devotion. Jesus also makes frequent allusions to Isaiah, Jeremiah, Micah, Amos, Joel, Ezekiel, Job, Daniel, and Elisha; Isaiah alone receives twenty mentions, Job fifteen.

Jesus has a special taste for the historical books of Samuel and Kings, which in Protestant Bibles appear as 1 and 2 Samuel and 1 and 2 Kings, and which for Jews formed part of the Former Prophets. Jesus refers often to David, not just as the author of psalms that he quotes and as a prophet, but with detailed allusions to the king's career in the books of Samuel. He refers to David's relationships with Saul, Shimei, Mephibosheth, and Uriah, and the story of Absalom is mentioned on several occasions. Jesus cites the story of Micaiah the prophet and his dealings with Ahab and Jehoshaphat, as reported in 1 Kings—although he credits the book's authorship to "Daniel the prophet" (ch. 160). As these books supply the original biblical sources for the accounts of Elijah and Elisha, they would naturally have appealed to a Carmelite readership.

One odd portion of Barnabas recounts at some length the relationship between Obadiah, Hosea, and Haggai, presumably the Hebrew prophets of those names, who in reality lived in very different eras (chs. 185–89). The teenaged Haggai serves the aged Obadiah as a pupil and offers an excellent moral example to other students. Hosea in turn serves Haggai, and we are told edifying tales of their piety and generosity, all of which are attributed to the influence of "the Book of Moses"—the Torah. Jesus orders the scribe Nicodemus to recount the story, which he does reluctantly on the grounds that "many believe it not, although it is written by Daniel the prophet." That indicates that the author/editor regards the tale as at best apocryphal or a folk tale, and he does not wish to place it in the mouth of Jesus himself—who nevertheless confirms its truth by means of a miracle.

The source of this material is unknown, and a Jewish rabbinic origin is conceivable. Hosea and Haggai were both very significant figures in Jewish tradition, and rabbinic scholars regarded Hosea in particular as one of the greatest of the prophets. We might also imagine an otherwise unknown Carmelite legend in a community that likewise venerated Hosea. But whether Carmelite or rabbinic, the story does not derive from Islam. Neither Hosea nor Haggai have any prominence in Islamic tradition, either in the Qur'an itself or the commentaries. It is not obvious why a writer seeking to Islamize the tale of Jesus would incorporate such a story, unless he found it already present in an earlier version of Barnabas.

As they appear in Barnabas, these Old Testament-derived materials are overwhelmingly likely to be Christian rather than Islamic in origin and are preserved from an earlier medieval layer of composition. The Qur'an, of course, makes heavy use of Old Testament figures such as Moses and Abraham, and many others, although many are recalled only generically as prophets. Despite his enormous significance in the Hebrew Bible and in Jewish tradition, Elijah receives only a brief mention in the Qur'an, in the context of his struggle with the worshipers of Baal (Qur'an, sura 37, As-Saaffat 123–30). David is cited sixteen times in the Qur'an, but usually as a prophet and a just ruler, with no real awareness of the turbulent political career so often mentioned in Barnabas, nor of the individual characters with whom he is associated. The Micaiah reference is particularly striking. Because of the heavenly vision associated with his story as well as its depiction of a heavenly throne room, Micaiah attracted considerable interest among rabbinic scholars as well as in popular Jewish tradition. In contrast, he does not feature in Islamic lore.

These copious references are very unlikely to have been the work of a Muslim editor or reviser, not least because they serve no obvious purpose in promoting his theological goals. Rather, they point to the work of a late medieval Christian writer, which underlies subsequent Islamic adaptations or appropriations.

3.6 True and False Pharisees

The references to "Pharisees," a term that mattered greatly to the author's theological and controversial approaches, likely also stems from the same period.

The canonical Gospels record many interactions between Jesus and other Jewish schools of thought of the time, especially the Pharisees. Barnabas takes over some of these and adds a great many more. After telling the canonical story of Zacchaeus, the Gospel reports Jesus's polemic against not just the Pharisees but the "false Pharisees," who are the deadly enemies of faith. In contrast, Haggai and Hosea—whom we encountered earlier—represent the true Pharisee (chs. 185–88). The sectarian label of Pharisee thus expands to encompass those who hold and practice true or false religion (chs. 143–51). Pharisees, broadly defined, feature often in the Gospel, especially in its second half.

These references are neither Muslim nor Jewish in origin. However familiar they might be to readers of the New Testament, Pharisees do not feature in Islamic scripture or tradition, and they are little known in Jewish discourse after the fall of the temple, chiefly because the sect's views gained such an absolute hegemony within Judaism. In medieval and early modern times, the only people who would write about Pharisees in any light, favorable or not, would be Christians, who derived their idea of the sect entirely from the canonical Gospels. The rhetoric would be unintelligible to non-Christians.

But if these references are indeed Christian, several possible explanations might account for their presence in Barnabas. The most probable is that the Pharisaic distinction originated in the controversial rhetoric of the late medieval Carmelite writings. Alternatively, at least some instances originated in the inter-Christian polemic of a still later era. When Jesus condemns predestination, and with it the Calvinist system, he denounces the people who hold such views as Pharisees "who contradict God altogether" (ch. 165).

4. KEY PASSAGES FOR NEW TESTAMENT STUDIES AND THEIR SIGNIFICANCE

That distinction between true and false Pharisees is intimately related to the larger questions of truth and falsehood that run through Barnabas. These questions are manifested in issues of authenticity and deception, of forgery and falsification, of truths hidden and made manifest. Although those contrasts originate in the medieval Christian layers of the work, the later Islamic editor builds substantially upon it for his own ends. Such themes of deception and subterfuge would be very fitting if, as suggested earlier, the author was himself living in a society in which outward religious conformity was demanded upon pain of death or exile. Throughout the text, these issues are presented in the context of characters and stories from the four canonical Gospels. The Pharisees offer one example, but still more significant is the scribe Nicodemus, who derives from the Jewish leader described in the canonical Gospel of John (John 3) but who as he appears in Barnabas is arguably a key to understanding the whole work. The deception theme returns finally with the depiction of the crucifixion itself.

4.1 Nicodemus and the Final Truth

Fundamental to the final editor's vision is the untrustworthiness of texts and particularly of the Scriptures, not because they have been inaccurately delivered to humanity—an intolerable thought—but because they have been subsequently falsified. Among their other sins, the false Pharisees are the ones who have contaminated the sacred Jewish Scriptures, the Books of Moses and David. Only such deception could have prevented people of wisdom and intelligence from understanding such key truths as the nature of the future Messiah and his descent from Ishmael. The fact that Nicodemus was able to read an authentic version of the text shows that the true Books really had been concealed from the people, for sinister purposes—ultimately, the work of Satan. So flawed are the books of the time that they must be supplemented by prophetic revelation until the final arrival of the ultimate Book of Truth, which is the Qur'an. Nicodemus thus becomes a herald of final truth, and its vehicle.

A reader of Barnabas might easily miss the pivotal role of Nicodemus because of the oblique way in which the text introduces him. Through many chapters, Jesus is in dialogue with a nameless scribe, who is eventually identified parenthetically as Nicodemus (chs. 180–93, 211–17). As Cirillo and Frémaux aptly note, this is a *révélation bien tardive*.[22] Only when we retroactively compile the deeds and sayings of "the scribe" who is Nicodemus does his full role become apparent. He is a key recurring character in Barnabas, in a way that his namesake is not in the canonical Gospel of John. John's Nicodemus only reappears to assist in Jesus's burial (John 19:39).

In the Gospel of John, Nicodemus is a secret follower of Jesus who meets him by night, and that theme of clandestine faith made him a byword for early modern Christian thinkers.[23] In 1544 John Calvin famously denounced *Messieurs les Nicodémites*, those cowards who refused to make bold public assertion of their faith. Other observers were far more sympathetic to discreet or crypto-believers, especially those who, like the Moriscos, had no option but to conceal their real religious sentiments upon pain of persecution and death. In various ways, Nicodemites and Nicodemism have been major themes in recent scholarship on the religious history of early modern Europe. As on so many other issues, the approach to this topic in Barnabas is explicitly anti-Calvinist.[24]

The Nicodemus of the Gospel of Barnabas is a wholly sympathetic character. He understands concealed truth. He appreciates when a document is likely to be forged or misleading, as we have seen in the legend of Hosea and Haggai. He can discern truthful and bogus writings. But his honesty can only take him so far, and he needs the miraculous aid of Jesus to allow him to make the final leap to accepting the truth of the texts. As the story progresses, he becomes Jesus's follower, and his host. In his openness to divine truth and his willingness to penetrate the veil of literary deception, he is a model true Pharisee. The truth he accepts and asserts is also Islamic, making him in fact a crypto-Muslim *avant la lettre* and arguably thereby reinforcing the argument for the Spanish Morisco origin of Barnabas.

Reading this account, we must always recall that these words are all present in a book that is itself bogus or deceptive. Even if the author was presenting the words that he felt most sincerely that Jesus would have said, he knew that he was not presenting an authentic history or reproducing the actual words of Barnabas as he claimed. A forger is thus assuring his readers that even the most ostensibly authoritative texts have been contaminated, a warning that extended to the Scriptures. Perhaps he saw himself in Nicodemus, reading out a story that he knew or suspected to be false, but acting under a divine command. That context might explain the otherwise strange inclusion of the obscure story of the prophet Micaiah, with its stress on true and false visions and prophecies. That passage includes the theologically troubling statement that an angel or spirit might inspire the speaking of false words or bogus prophecy.[25]

---

22. Cirillo and Frémaux, *Évangile de Barnabé* (2nd ed.), 281.

23. For early modern approaches to the biblical Nicodemus, see Paul Cefalu, *The Johannine Renaissance in Early Modern English Literature and Theology* (New York: Oxford University Press, 2017).

24. The modern literature on Nicodemism in this era dates from the rediscovery of the phenomenon in Carlo Ginzburg, *Il Nicodemismo* (Turin: Giulio Einaudi, 1970). See Federico Zuliani, "The Other Nicodemus," in *Discovering the Riches of the Word*, ed. S Corbellini, M. Hoogvliet, and B. Ramakers (Leiden: Brill 2015), 311–34; M. Anne Overell, *Nicodemites* (Leiden: Brill, 2018); Kenneth J. Woo, *Nicodemism and the English Calvin, 1544–1584* (Leiden: Brill, 2019); Michael W. Bruening, "Calvin, Farel, Roussel, and the French Nicodemites," in *Calvin and the Early Reformation*, ed. B. C. Brewer (Leiden: Brill, 2020), 113–24. Diarmaid MacCulloch discusses Nicodemism in his biography of *Thomas Cromwell* (New York: Viking, 2018). For various manifestations of "dissimulation, persecution and conformity" in this era, see Perez Zagorin, *Ways of Lying* (Cambridge: Harvard University Press, 1990).

25. For debates over forgery and pseudonymous writings, see Anthony Grafton, *Forgers and Critics* (Princeton: Princeton University Press, 1990); Bart D. Ehrman, *Forgery and Counterforgery* (New York: Oxford

4.2 Judas and the Crucifixion

That theme of divinely inspired deception culminates in the crucifixion narrative, where not even the noblest and holiest characters can penetrate the illusion that leads people to see Judas as if he is Jesus, and to kill him accordingly (chs. 215–20). That blindness extends to the narrator Barnabas himself, who in this instance at least admits to being thoroughly unreliable. That deception continues after Judas's death, when Nicodemus and Joseph of Arimathea bury that body in the exact manner described for Jesus in the canonical Gospels. In every sense, Christianity is founded upon a deception, a lie.

That crucifixion story in Barnabas poses critical questions about the original sources deployed in the work (chs. 215–20). Here particularly we encounter motifs that closely resemble ideas from early Christian times and from a range of movements that were stigmatized as heretical. If anywhere, it is here that we find the most likely example of the compiler of Barnabas including a genuinely old or independent text.

As we would expect from a work intended to promote Islam, the account follows the qur'anic story of the passing of Jesus, who does not actually die, and the crucifixion as such is an illusion:

> They did not slay him, and neither did they crucify him, but it only seemed to them [as if it had been] so; and, verily, those who hold conflicting views thereon are indeed confused, having no [real] knowledge thereof, and following mere conjecture. For, of a certainty, they did not slay him: nay, God exalted him unto Himself—and God is indeed almighty, wise. (Qur'an, sura 4, An-Nisa 4:157–58, Muhammad Asad translation)[26]

This follows the ancient docetic doctrine of the illusory quality of Christ's life and death, a view that is repeatedly denounced in the New Testament (e.g., at 1 John 4:1–3; 2 John 7). In itself, this continuity is not surprising, as Islamic tradition drew heavily on the diverse forms of Christianity that flourished in the Near East in the sixth and seventh centuries. But Barnabas goes far beyond the meager qur'anic account of that event and includes many other details not found in the Qur'an itself—critically, the central role accorded to Judas Iscariot. In this text, Judas is disillusioned when it becomes clear that Jesus does not intend to seek worldly power or kingship, and he agrees to betray him for thirty pieces of gold.

But in Barnabas it is Judas, not Jesus, who is tortured and crucified, because a divinely caused illusion has caused all observers to view him as Jesus (chs. 215–18). The deception even extends to Jesus's closest intimates, to the Virgin and the apostles, including Barnabas himself. Not even Judas's most desperate pleas can persuade observers to realize who he is. Jesus, meanwhile, has escaped from Gethsemane, and angels have taken him to heaven. The same angels restore him to be seen by his followers, in this Gospel's divergent version of resurrection appearances.

The idea that another man suffered in the place of Jesus is commonplace in early Christian writings, from between the second and fourth centuries. In the gnostic Apocalypse of Peter, found at Nag Hammadi, the true Jesus mocks the deluded persecutors who are crucifying his illusory self. The Judas of the Gospel of Barnabas likewise perishes amid laughter, from those amused at his seemingly ridiculous attempts to deny that he is Jesus.

University Press, 2013); Walter Stephens and Earle A. Havens, eds., *Literary Forgery in Early Modern Europe, 1450–1800* (Baltimore: Johns Hopkins University Press, 2018).

26. "Comparative Study 4:157," Islamicity, www.islamicity.org/quransearch/index.php?q=chapter:4#id_COMPARE-157.

Many Christian sects had cultivated such ideas about Jesus's end, although they differed as to who might have substituted for Jesus on the cross. Some early readers of the Synoptic Gospels note the account of Simon of Cyrene, who is forced to carry Jesus's cross on the way to Calvary, and they suggest that subsequent references to what "he" suffered refer to Simon rather than Jesus. Already in the 170s CE, the anti-heretical writer Irenaeus knew of such an interpretation, which he credited to the Egyptian gnostic Basilides. Jesus, in this account, stands by the cross and laughs at the error. Among the Nag Hammadi Gospels, in the Second Discourse of Great Seth, Jesus says:

> Yes, they saw me; they punished me. It was another, their father, who drank the gall and the vinegar; it was not I. They struck me with the reed; it was another, Simon, who bore the cross on his shoulder. It was another upon whom they placed the crown of thorns. But I was rejoicing in the height over all.[27]

The Gospel of Barnabas differs from these accounts in choosing Judas as the victim, on the moral principle that he suffers the evil he intended for another.

> Probably in the ninth century, a narrative of Christ's Life and Passion was falsely credited to the early church father Cyril of Jerusalem. Among the fragment's surprising features, we read that Pilate and Jesus were on excellent terms, to the extent that the two dined together the night before Jesus's arrest. Pilate even offered to give his only son to be crucified in Jesus's place. Apart from reinforcing the substitution theme, that recalls Barnabas's statement that Pilate "secretly loved Jesus." (ch. 217)[28]

The echoes of early Christian writings permeate the crucifixion account in Barnabas, and they go far beyond what an early modern writer could have constructed drawing only on the New Testament and the Qur'an. Two explanations suggest how those ancient ideas might have been transmitted and preserved. One is through Islamic tradition, and particularly the role of the Qur'anic commentators, *muffassirin*, who over the centuries wrote works of interpretation or explanation (*tafsir*) on every portion of the sacred text, and they expounded the passage about the crucifixion. These writers explored a variety of ideas about the illusory nature of the crucifixion, and the identity of a victim who perished in the place of Jesus—either one who looked like him naturally or who was made to resemble him. Among the many names offered for the substitute was Judas Iscariot.[29]

4.3 An Alternative Gospel Tradition?

The other possibility is that the authors/editors who created the Gospel of Barnabas were actually drawing on an alternative Gospel with its roots in early sectarian or heretical Christianity. If that is correct, then we can readily suggest means by which such an early work could have found its way to Italy and the western Mediterranean in the Middle

---

27. Joseph A. Gibbons and Roger A. Bullard, "The Second Treatise of the Great Seth," in *The Nag Hammadi Library in English*, ed. James M. Robinson, 4th rev. ed. (Leiden: Brill, 1996), 332.

28. Roelof van den Broek, ed., *Pseudo-Cyril of Jerusalem on the Life and the Passion of Christ* (Leiden: Brill, 2013).

29. Aman Daima Md. Zain, Muhammad Lukman Ibrahim, Hasan Al-Banna Mohamed, and Jaffary Awang, "Yahuza al-Iskhriyuti (Judas Iscariot) according to the Views of Quranic *Muffassirin* Scholars," *Journal of Research in Islamic Studies* 2.2 (2015): 18–25. See also A. H. Mathias Zahniser, *The Mission and Death of Jesus in Islam and Christianity* (Eugene, OR: Wipf & Stock, 2017), 79–94.

Ages, not long before the time of our hypothetical "Carmelite" Gospel. Obviously, the fact that any such writing would have been so severely proscribed means that the process of transmission would have been clandestine, so that any reconstruction must of its nature be speculative. But we know that other alternative scriptures circulated underground in this era, including in the western Mediterranean regions in which the Gospel of Barnabas was created.

Between the twelfth and the fourteenth centuries, a variety of heretical and sectarian movements flourished in the western Mediterranean, most celebrated among whom were the Albigensians or Cathars. In documented instances, such western Mediterranean groups obtained texts or scriptures from Balkan movements like the Bogomils, and some of these materials were genuinely primitive. The well-known story of the modern discovery of the Slavonic pseudepigrapha suggests just how diverse was the range of early Jewish and Christian writings circulating in the Balkans in that era, many of which are not attested elsewhere. Dualist and even possibly Manichaean texts found their way from this region to Italy and southern France. The *Secret Supper* (or *Questions of John*) was a dualist Bogomil Gospel composed around 1100, which was seized by the Inquisition in Languedoc.[30]

Whatever the source of their beliefs, these various sects shared views with many parallels to the early Christian movements, and the western Albigensians held docetic views about Christ and the crucifixion. Like their Bogomil allies, they held that "Christ our God was born . . . as an illusion, and as an illusion he was crucified." They would have welcomed a Gospel that reported the triumphant escape from death of the true spiritual Christ.[31]

Although condemned by church authorities, local groups actually had cordial relations with particular Catholic orders whom they admired for their stern asceticism, and in Italy that meant the Carmelites. Despite the fundamental nature of their differences, the different movements and orders remained in dialogue.[32] If any Catholic group had access to such an alternative Gospel, it would have been the Carmelites.

Of course, all this is in the realm of conjecture. An early alternative Gospel *could* feasibly have been imported to Italy to provide the basis for the Gospel of Barnabas that we know—which does not mean that it actually did so or that such a hypothetical text even existed. The multiply subversive and illicit nature of the Gospel of Barnabas makes it difficult to state anything about it with certainty, about its origins or subsequent development. Whichever interpretation we favor—whether or not a Muslim writer appropriated an early heretical Gospel—the Gospel of Barnabas that we presently have offers startling evidence of the survival of alternative versions of Christianity into the early modern world, and beyond.

5. BIBLIOGRAPHY

Bernabé Pons, Luis F. *El texto morisco del Evangelio de San Bernabé*. Granada: Universidad de Granada, 1998.
Blackhirst, R. "*Barnabas* and the Gospels." *Journal of Higher Criticism* 7 (2000): 1–22.
Cirillo, Luigi, and Michel Frémaux, eds. *Évangile de Barnabé*. 2nd rev. ed. Paris: Éditions Beauchesne, 1999.
Epalza, Mikel de. "Garcia Gómez und die Autorschaft des Barnabas-Evangeliums." *Religionen im Gespräch* 6 (2000): 10–13.
Giustolisi, Eugenio, and Giuseppe Rizzardi. *Il Vangelo di Barnaba: Un vangelo per i musulmani?* Milano: Istituto Propaganda Libraria, 1991.

---

30. Philip Jenkins, *The Many Faces of Christ* (New York: Basic, 2015); Janet Hamilton and Bernard Hamilton, eds., with Yuri Stoyanov, *Christian Dualist Heresies in the Byzantine World, c. 650–c. 1450* (Manchester, UK: Manchester University Press, 1998).

31. Jenkins, *Many Faces of Christ*, 211.

32. Susan Taylor Snyder, "Cathars, Confraternities and Civic Religion," in Michael Frassetto, ed., *Heresy and the Persecuting Society in the Middle Ages* (Leiden: Brill, 2006), 241–51.

Hollander, August den, and Ulrich Schmid. "The Gospel of Barnabas, the Diatessaron, and Method." *VC* 61 (2007): 1–20.

Joosten, Jan. "The Date and Provenance of the Gospel of Barnabas." *JTS* 61 (2010): 200–215.

———. "The Gospel of Barnabas and the Diatessaron." *HTR* 95 (2002): 73–96.

———. "Jésus et l'aveugle-né (Jn 9, 1–34) dans l'Évangile de Barnabas et dans le Diatessaron." *RHPR* 80.3 (2000): 359–69.

Leirvik, Oddbjørn. "History as a Literary Weapon: The *Gospel of Barnabas* in Muslim-Christian Polemics." *Studia Theologica* 56.1 (2010): 4–26.

———. *Images of Jesus Christ in Islam*. 2nd ed. London: Continuum, 2010.

Pulcini, Theodore. "In the Shadow of Mount Carmel." *Islam and Christian-Muslim Relations* 12.2 (2001): 191–209.

Ragg, Lonsdale, and Laura Ragg, eds. *Gospel of Barnabas*. Oxford: Clarendon, 1907.

Reed, Annette Yoshiko. "Muslim Gospel Revealing the 'Christian Truth' Excites the *Da Vinci Code* Set." *Religion Dispatches*. May 22, 2014.

Slomp, Jan. "The Gospel in Dispute." *Islamochristiana* 4.1 (1978): 67–111.

———. "The Gospel of Barnabas in Recent Research." *Islamochristiana* 23 (1997): 81–109.

Sox, David. *The Gospel of Barnabas*. London: Allen & Unwin, 1984.

Toland, John. *Nazarenus, or Jewish, Gentile and Mahometan Christianity*. London: J. Brown, 1718.

Wiegers, Gerald A. "Gospel of Barnabas." In *Encyclopedia of Islam*. Edited by Kate Fleet et al. 3rd ed. Leiden: Brill, 2013.

———. "Muhammad as the Messiah." *Biblitheca Orientalis* 52.3–4 (1995): 245–91.

CHAPTER 4

GOSPEL OF PETER

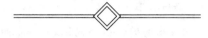

PAUL FOSTER

1. INTRODUCTION

The Gospel of Peter is a relatively extensive fragment of a noncanonical Gospel that relates the events of Jesus's death and resurrection. It occupies nine pages of the small codex in which it is written (P.Cair. 10759). The fragment breaks at a point when it appears to be about to narrate a post-resurrection appearance of Jesus. Surviving noncanonical Gospels have come down to modern readers either through repeated copying in antiquity and the medieval period, or through archaeological discoveries in the modern period. The Gospel of Peter is in the latter category. It was one of the first noncanonical Gospel texts to be discovered as part of an archaeological excavation in 1886–1887. Its discovery was a sensation not just in academic circles but more widely. There was a flurry of interest in this text in the immediate years following its discovery. This soon abated. Then, with some notable exceptions, there was a paucity of scholarly interest in this text until recent decades, when there has been renewed interest in the noncanonical Gospels as literary texts in their own right. Due to the extensive nature of this fragmentary text, the Gospel of Peter has gained significant attention in recent research.

Under the auspices of La Mission archéologique française au Caire, an archaeological excavation was undertaken at Akhmîm along the upper Nile. In the early Christian era, the area developed into a center for monasticism. The city is located approximately 310 miles (500 km) almost due south of Cairo. The French team, led by Eugene Grébaut during the winter-season dig of 1886–1887, excavated several graves in the Christian cemetery at Akhmîm. In the course of these excavations, two ancient manuscripts were discovered. One was a mathematical text, containing geometric and arithmetic problems. The second manuscript was a codex containing a number of early Christian writings. The editing of this codex was entrusted to Urbain Bouriant.

This codex comprised thirty-three unnumbered leaves of parchment, as well as two parchment pages glued to the inner sides of both the front and rear leather covers. The result was a codex containing sixty-eight pages available for writing. The dimensions of the pages are approximately 15.5–16.5 cm in height and 12.0–12.5 cm in width. The codex contains fragments of four texts, including two overlapping fragments of the third text.

While there is a connection between the first two texts in the codex in terms of the putative apostolic author of the two documents, there is no clear connection with the remaining two writings. This is a miscellaneous codex. It appears to have been assembled from writings or fragments of writings that were written separately. The first two texts may have been written by the same hand, but the remaining writings appear to have been written by different scribes in comparison with the first two documents. The contents are as follows:

Page	Contents
Inside front cover	Blank
1	Decoration, including Coptic crosses
2–10	The Gospel of Peter
11–12	Blank
13–19 (20–14)	The Apocalypse of Peter
20 (13)	Blank
21–66	Two fragments of 1 Enoch
Inside back cover	Martyrdom of St Julian of Anazarbus

FIG. 1: Contents of the Akhmîm Codex—P.Cair. 10759

2. SUMMARY OF CONTENT

The portion of the Gospel of Peter that is extant commences mid-sentence and likewise ends with an incomplete sentence. There is space for further writing after the final sentence, but this has been filled with decorative swirls. This suggests that the copy of this text was made from what might have been an incomplete exemplar rather than representing the partial preservation of a manuscript that was itself more extensive. The reason for a scribe copying a defective manuscript remains unclear. However, the broken text suggests that the form of the Gospel of Peter at some stage prior to the surviving text in the Akhmîm codex must have been more extensive, although one cannot ascertain the extent of the larger narrative with any certainty. While some have suggested that the original form of the Gospel of Peter would have encapsulated an account of the ministry and perhaps the birth of Jesus, this is at best a speculative inference based on a fleeting comment in the writings of Origen. In his commentary on the Gospel of Matthew, Origen makes the following comment:

> But some say the brothers of Jesus are, from a tradition based upon the Gospel according to Peter, as it is entitled, or the Book of James, sons of Joseph from a former wife, who was married to him before Mary. (Origen, *Comm. Matt.* 10.17)

Since the surviving portion of the text of the Gospel of Peter contains no reference to the sons of Joseph from a former marriage, if Origen is correct in his comment then the Gospel of Peter may have contained this detail perhaps prior to the section of the passion narrative that is preserved. However, certainty is far from possible.

Therefore, as it stands in the surviving manuscript evidence, the Gospel of Peter preserves an account of the passion of Jesus presumably at a point just after Pilate washed his hands in the Matthean sequence (Matt 27:24). It then narrates the events of Jesus being handed over to Jewish leadership figures, tells of the mockery of Jesus, his crucifixion, and the burial of his body with heightened security measures. It offers an expanded version of the Matthean guard-at-the-tomb story, narrates the moment of the resurrection and the visit of the women to the tomb, and it appears to be about to describe a post-resurrection appearance of Jesus beside the sea when the text breaks off mid-sentence. This surviving portion presents a creative retelling of the crucifixion and resurrection of Jesus.

There are several excellent editions of the Greek text of the Akhmîm fragment of the

Gospel of Peter.[1] In what follows, the comments are provided under each of the standard fourteen chapter divisions of the text.

Chapter 1

The text begins mid-sentence, with the statement that the trio of "Jews," Herod Antipas, and his judges refused to wash their hands. There is no parallel to this detail in the canonical Gospels, but it makes sense as a contrast to a detail unique to the Gospel of Matthew, which presents the scene of Pilate washing his hands (Matt 27:24). Here it appears that the author of the Gospel of Peter has read the Matthean description of Pilate washing his hands as a genuine declaration of innocence and a demonstration that the Roman governor did not wish to be involved in the condemnation of Jesus. By contrast, in this scene unique to the Gospel of Peter depicting the combined and stylized characters of Jews, Herod, and the judges refusing to wash their hands, the text portrays these people as responsible for the death of Jesus and as the key actors in organizing the execution of Jesus. While this is unlikely to reflect the historical reality of the circumstances surrounding the execution of Jesus, such a shift reflects wider tendencies in second-century Christianity. Thus, the text to a certain extent exonerates Pilate, thereby distancing Romans from responsibility for the death of Jesus. At the same time, it transfers the blame for the death of Jesus onto the Jewish leaders. Such a strategy may have had a double benefit for early Christian apologetic concerns. First, lack of involvement of Pilate in the death of Jesus may be intended to show that Jesus was not executed as one considered subversive to the Roman authorities. Second, in the aftermath of the Jewish rebellion of 70 CE and the later Jewish rebellions in the time of Trajan, the text implies that Jesus was killed at the hands of a duplicitous Jewish leadership that was itself subsequently viewed by many as the true enemy of the Roman state. As such, the Gospel of Peter engages in an exercise of blame-shifting by portraying Jewish leaders as responsible for the death of Jesus. At the same time, it not only exonerates Roman leaders but also has them declare Jesus innocent (cf. Luke 23:4).

The text portrays Herod Antipas as taking control of the ensuing events. Among the canonical Gospels, the figure of Antipas is present during the events of Jesus's trial only in the Gospel of Luke (Luke 23:7–12).

Chapter 2

The next scene is a chronological reordering of an event reported in the canonical Gospels. After the death of Jesus, according to all four canonical Gospels (Matt 27:57–60; Mark 15:43–46; Luke 23:50–53; John 19:38–40), Joseph of Arimathea comes to Pilate to ask for the body of Jesus for burial. By contrast, in the Gospel of Peter the narrative of the involvement of Joseph's role in the burial of Jesus is split into two parts that are separated by the account of Jesus's scourging and crucifixion. In the first of those scenes, before Jesus is scourged, Joseph asks Pilate for the body of the soon-to-be crucified Jesus (Gos. Pet. 2.3). In the second scene, after the death of Jesus and the removal of his corpse from the cross, "the Jews" who have carried out the crucifixion hand the body of Jesus over

---

1. For early editions of the Greek text, see J. A. Robinson and M. R. James, *The Gospel according to Peter, and the Revelation of Peter: Two Lectures on the Newly Recovered Fragments Together with the Greek Texts* (London: C. J. Clay and Sons, 1892), 83–88; H. B. Swete, *The Akhmîm Fragment of the Apocryphal Gospel of St Peter* (London: Macmillan, 1893), 1–24; A. Harnack, *Bruchstücke des Evangeliums und der Apokalypse des Petrus*, TU 9.2 (J. C. Hinrichs: Leipzig, 1893), 8–12. For more recent editions, see Thomas J. Kraus and Tobias Nicklas, *Das Petrusevangelium und die Petrusapokalypse: Die griechischen Fragmente mit deutscher und englischer Übersetzung* (Berlin: de Gruyter, 2004), 32–48.

to Joseph for burial (6.23). This rearrangement allows the author of the Gospel of Peter to connect Joseph more closely with Pilate, whose actions are also positive in seeking an honorable burial for Jesus. Furthermore, by bringing the timing of the request forward, the preparations for the burial of Jesus are not entirely reactive. In this manner, such a degree of proactive planning demonstrates that Jesus was buried in a planned and known location, "Joseph's garden" (6.24). It may be the case that this change of chronology responded to the charge that his followers mistakenly found an empty tomb and that this was the origin of the story that Jesus was risen. If that were part of the reason for the chronological trans-position, it would mean that one of the motivations for the temporal reordering was to create a version of the story that was more apologetically robust.

This section continues to narrate the preparations that are made in advance of his death for the burial of Jesus. Acting upon the request, Pilate, who is now removed from the events of the abuse and death of Jesus, sends to Antipas to ask for the body of Jesus. Although reported as direct speech, the narrative requires the response from Herod to have been sent back to Pilate. Initially there appears to be a humane concern for the corpse expressed in the reply, "Even if somebody had not asked for him, we would have buried him" (Gos. Pet. 2.5).[2] However, as the reply unfolds it is revealed that the response is not motivated out of respect for Jesus but by self-concern not to transgress "the law" (2.5). Here the legal ruling invoked appears to be reflective of a halakic principle in Deuteronomy: "And if a man has committed a sin worthy of death, and he is put to death, and you hang him on a tree, his corpse shall not hang all night on the tree, but you shall surely bury him on the same day (for he who is hanged is accursed of God), so you do not defile your land which the Lord your God gives you as an inheritance" (Deut 21:22–23 NASB [1977]).

This section concludes with a description of Herod handing Jesus over to the people. At this point Herod disappears from the narrative.

Chapter 3

Next, the Gospel of Peter describes the scene of the mockery of Jesus paralleled in the canonical Gospels, replete with elements of verbal and physical abuse. Here various actions pertaining to the mocking garb and regalia remain consistent with descriptions in the canonical accounts. However, the three instances of reported direct speech attributed to groups within the mob are unparalleled in the four New Testament Gospels.

The first verbal utterance of the crowd, "Let us drag the son of God having authority over him," contains a number of significant elements. The narrator typically refers to Jesus as "Lord." By contrast, opponents use various other christological titles, but in a manner that does not come from acceptance of Jesus's status. The title "son of God" is employed in the passion narrative of the Gospel of Matthew as a challenge from passers-by to Jesus to prove that he is indeed the son of God (Matt 27:40, 43). Here, the status is not explicitly questioned or mocked. Rather, the title is used descriptively. However, the actions of the angry mob demonstrate that they do not accept the claim of the title that Jesus is God's son.

The Gospel of Peter, following the descriptions in Mark and John, names the color of the robe as "purple" (Mark 15:17; John 19:2; cf. Matt 27:28, "scarlet"; Luke 23:11, "white" or "shining"). The Markan description of a purple robe is probably intended to convey royal associations. Whether the author of the Gospel of Peter has intentionally reverted to the color purple to retain the royal designation or has done so because purple was the more

---

2. All translations of the Gospel of Peter are from Paul Foster, *The Gospel of Peter: Introduction, Critical Edition and Commentary* (Leiden: Brill, 2010).

familiar element in the version of the story he recalled is difficult to determine. This is followed by a reference to a seat of judgment. Although using different Greek terminology, in the Fourth Gospel during the trial before Pilate there is also a reference to a "judgment seat" (John 19:13). While it is perhaps more natural to understand John's account as describing Pilate sitting on the judgment seat to pass a verdict on Jesus, the syntax is ambiguous, and it could refer to Jesus sitting on the judgment seat. The Gospel of Peter appears to exploit the ambiguity of the Johannine scene by having the mob place Jesus on the judgment seat. This is a moment of bitter irony. When they invoke Jesus to "judge justly, King of Israel," they are unaware that he is the absolute judge and that their request is a judgment on themselves. There is a striking parallel in the writings of Justin Martyr: "Dragging him along they sat him on the judgment seat and said, 'Judge for us'" (*1 Apol.* 35.6).

At this point, the description of the mockery returns to material that most closely parallels the Matthean account with the crown of thorns being placed on Jesus's head (Matt 27:29a), coupled with spitting on and striking Jesus (29:30), and the reference to a reed (27:29b). However, whereas in Matthew's account the reed functions as a mock scepter, the Gospel of Peter transforms it into a weapon of torment. The regalia of robe, crown, and reed are again presented as instruments that are used to mock Jesus's status as son of God, in much the same manner as the Roman soldiers mocked Jesus as "king of the Jews" (Matt 27:29) with the same items.

Chapter 4

A striking detail that is unique to the Gospel of Peter is the description of the manner in which Jesus underwent crucifixion: "And he was silent as though feeling no pain" (Gos. Pet. 4.10). This description portrays Jesus as a noble figure quietly enduring suffering.

Another significant feature is the change in wording on the titulus of the cross. Instead of "king of the Jews" as in the canonical accounts, the Gospel of Peter changes this to "king of Israel." Once again the author seeks to distance Jesus and his followers from contemporary Judaism, while having no concern about identifying Jesus with historic Israel. The division and the casting of lots for Jesus's clothes is reminiscent of the canonical accounts (cf. Matt 27:35). However, the Gospel of Peter adds the additional detail that the clothes were laid out before Jesus while he was being crucified. This makes the action more vivid and perhaps reflects a further degree of callousness on the part of those executing Jesus.

The text then focuses on the two people crucified alongside Jesus. These figures are present in the canonical accounts, but the Gospel of Peter re-narrates the story in a different form. Both Matthew and Mark have the two thieves mocking Jesus (Matt 27:44; Mark 15:32). Luke changes and extends the Markan account by having only one of the thieves cast insults at Jesus, while the other declares Jesus's innocence (Luke 23:39–43). The Gospel of Peter goes even further in the rewriting of the tradition with three highly significant changes. First, the author removes any element of abuse or insult coming from either of the co-crucified thieves. Second, the one criminal who speaks does not speak to Jesus but to those who are executing Jesus. Third, he describes Jesus using the theologically perspicacious christological title "savior of men." He also asks a challenging question to those performing the execution concerning Jesus: "What wrong has he done you?" The implications are clear. Jesus is innocent, he has not wronged his executioners in any way, and on the cross he is recognized by the criminal as being the savior of humanity.

Chapter 5

This section largely parallels material contained in Matthew 27:45–51a, albeit with transpositions, additions, and the creative rewriting of source material. The Gospel of Peter employs the tradition of the darkness that came over the land but names the geographical location as Judaea. An addition is made to the canonical material at this juncture. First, to make the story more vivid, the narrative recounts the emotional state of those carrying out the crucifixion, stating that they were "troubled and distressed." Second, it explains the cause of this emotional state by harking back to the same scriptural rationale that Herod gave for why Jesus would be given a proper burial (Deut 21:22–23).

The drink offered to Jesus appears to conflate two scenes contained in the Matthean account. Immediately prior to the crucifixion, Matthew states that Jesus was given "wine to drink, mingled with gall" (Matt 27:34 NASB [1977]). Then again, just prior to Jesus's death, the First Gospel reports that Jesus was given sour wine to drink on a sponge (27:48). The latter action is apparently in response to a misunderstanding of the cry of Jesus, which the crowd takes to be a calling for Elijah. In the Gospel of Peter, the cry of Jesus is delayed till after the drink, and all reference to Elijah is omitted. There is no explanation in the Gospel of Peter for the provision of a drink, and in some ways this would only make sense to those who already knew the canonical accounts. Here, the drink of gall and vinegar is mixed on site for Jesus. This same combination of gall and vinegar brings the wording of the Gospel of Peter into even closer alignment with the text of LXX Psalm 68:22 than the Gospel of Matthew. This same combination is also cited in the Epistle of Barnabas (Barn. 7.5).

The last part of this section presents Jesus's only spoken words recorded in the entire surviving portion of the Gospel of Peter, along with the immediate event following the death of Jesus. In this part of the narrative, up to this point, although Jesus was present on the cross, he had fallen into the background. Instead, the author focused on the actions of those executing Jesus. Now attention returns to Jesus, with a report of his final words. As is well-known in the accounts of Matthew and Mark, with the former using the Hebrew *Eli, Eli* as his opening two words (Matt 27:46), and the latter using the Aramaic *Eloi, Eloi* (Mark 15:34), both cite LXX Psalm 21:2. The cry, "My God, my God, why have you forsaken me?" is not without theological challenges. This probably explains why Luke replaces this psalm text with an alternative "into your hands I place my spirit" (Luke 23:46; see LXX Ps 30:6). It appears that for a similar reason the Gospel of Peter replaces the version of a cry where Jesus speaks of his sense of being forsaken by God, and in its stead the author rewrites this tradition with a statement from Jesus wherein he recognizes the departure of his life force: "My power, the power, you have left me" (Gos. Pet. 5.19). Jesus simply observes that this is the moment when his life is ending.

This section concludes with a description of the temple curtain being ripped in two. This detail occurs in all three of the Synoptic Gospels (Matt 27:51a; Mark 15:38; Luke 23:45). The Gospel of Peter specifies that this was the Jerusalem Temple. Perhaps this clarification was made for gentile readers, for whom there were many temples. However, unlike Matthew and Mark, the Gospel of Peter does not state that the curtain was ripped in two "from top to bottom." Perhaps the author has missed the theological significance of this detail, which reveals the action comes from above and reflects both judgment on the temple and an opening up of access to the divine presence.

Chapter 6

This section of the Gospel of Peter describes in greater detail than its canonical parallels the process of removing the body from the cross and its initial preparation and burial. In the Gospel of Peter, there is reference to nails, which were used to affix Jesus to the cross. This is unparalleled in the canonical accounts, although in a post-resurrection scene in the

Gospel of John, Thomas refuses to believe unless he sees "in his hands the imprint of the nails" (John 20:25). Furthermore, an extra supernatural phenomenon is described that is not mentioned in the New Testament Gospels. When the body of Jesus is removed from the cross and placed on the ground, the earth shakes in response. This may be an embellishment of one of the additional phenomena that Matthew narrates as accompanying the Markan account of the rending of the temple veil. The first of these additional events is only briefly described by Matthew, namely, "the earth shook" (Matt 27:51b). If this is the basis of the tradition in the Gospel of Peter, it has been moved from the moment of death to the time when the body was placed on the earth. According to the narrative description, the ground itself quakes in response to the placement of the body of Jesus on its surface. The Gospel of Peter provides a number of scenes where apparently inanimate objects move in response to the events surrounding Jesus. This represents a clear tendency of the author to heighten or to add miraculous elements to the tradition, presumably as a means of commending belief and verifying the status of Jesus.

The reappearance of the sun not only ends the premature darkness but further establishes that its cause was the crucifixion of Jesus. The darkness is therefore to be understood as a sign of divine displeasure in response to the execution of Jesus and as judgment on those carrying it out. The rejoicing of those carrying out the crucifixion is in reaction to the return of daylight. Their legalistic concern over the inadvertent transgression of a halakic ruling is shown not to have occurred. Here the author no doubt wishes readers to recognize the irony of the misplaced sense of piety over any real concern for true justice. At this point, the body of Jesus is handed over to Joseph as agreed upon earlier in the narrative. Having washed and wrapped the body, the corpse is placed in a known location. In this way the narrative begins to establish an apologetic that defends against the charge that the place of burial was unknown or that the body was removed by the followers of Jesus.

Chapter 7

The author depicts the leaders as self-interested. It appears that the miraculous phenomena of the earth tremor and the return of daylight have caused them to realize that their actions had caused divine displeasure. However, the cry they collectively utter, "Woe to our sins, the judgment and the end of Jerusalem is at hand," is not repentance over the injustice committed but desperation upon realizing that their action will bring about an end to Jerusalem and their religious system. Here the text appears to promote early Christian polemic that the destruction of Jerusalem was judgment upon the city because of the death of Jesus.

The self-concern of the leaders, rather than their true repentance, is further illustrated by what follows. The disciples are forced to hide because they, according to the narrative, were being sought as evildoers. Again, the Gospel of Peter is interested to describe the emotional state of the characters. Thus the disciples are said to be grieving and wounded in mind. These graphic descriptions may do more than simply portray the emotional state of Jesus's followers. Being in such a state, it is unlikely that they could have stolen the body of Jesus while they were concealing themselves from the authorities. Here, for the first time in the extant portion of text, the narrative breaks into the first-person voice. The unnamed narrator speaks of "I with my companions" to describe the state of grief and the action of hiding themselves. It is not until the end of the surviving portion of the narrative that this first-person narrator is clearly identified as Peter (Gos. Pet. 14.60). The accusation that the followers of Jesus wished to burn the temple may have a double resonance. First, unlike the canonical Gospels where no mention of fire occurs with Jesus's declarations on the destruction of the temple, such flammable destruction is prominent in the writings of Josephus, who was writing after the events of 70 CE (*J.W.* 6.406). Second, the accusation that followers of Jesus were stigmatized as would-be arsonists is also known in the writings of Tacitus. According to Tacitus, in relation to the fire in Rome during the reign of Nero, blame was falsely shifted onto the Christians (Tacitus, *Ann.* 15.44).

Chapter 8

Here the Gospel of Peter commences an extended narrative depicting the security measures put in place at the burial place of Jesus (Gos. Pet. 8.28–11.49). The story in the Gospel of Peter is based on three separate scenes in the Gospel of Matthew (Matt 27:62–66; 28:2–4, 11–15). Whereas Matthew has the guard-at-the-tomb narrative interwoven with the story of the visit of the women followers (Matt 28:1, 5–10), these stories are kept separate in the Gospel of Peter.

Once again, the Gospel of Peter displays its concern to describe the emotional state and mood swings in various characters. Another trio of leadership groups, here "the scribes and the Pharisees and the elders" assemble in response to the general populace becoming unsettled due to the events involving Jesus that have transpired. The people are disquieted, they express their dissatisfaction with their leaders by grumbling, and their action of beating their chests appears to be genuine within the context of the narrative. Moreover, they recognize the signs that accompanied Jesus's death as demonstrating the innocence of Jesus. In response the elders call upon Pilate, who has been absent from the narrative for some time. The reintroduction of Roman authority at this point allows the author to involve characters with whom the readers might have identified more readily. Furthermore, Pilate is portrayed by the author as a more objective figure, and hence his involvement underscores the veracity of the account that follows. The elders come to Pilate and request that a guard be placed at the tomb. In contrast with the Matthean account, where the theft of the body from the tomb is said to be invented after the resurrection (Matt 28:13), in the Gospel of Peter the elders envisage this possibility prior to the resurrection and take precautionary measures to prevent it from happening. Self-protection is also presented as a motivating factor in the request, along with the desire to prevent an act of deception.

The rest of the section details the measures taken to secure the tomb. These are much more involved than those described in the Gospel of Matthew. Here a centurion is provided, and several soldiers. Making the narrative more vivid, the centurion is named as Petronius. The Roman troops attend the tomb along with the elders and the scribes. Furthermore, the burial place is made secure with elaborate precautions. The apologetic aim of this version of the story is transparent.

Chapter 9

The canonical accounts do not narrate the events of the intervening Sabbath day to any great extent, although Matthew alone commences his account of the request for guards on "the next day" (Matt 27:62). Thus, the new narrative account fills the temporal gap by describing the visit of a crowd from Jerusalem and surrounding areas. This has the effect of increasing the number of witnesses who saw the tomb sealed and guarded, and who also knew the location of the burial place of Jesus.

The next set of events occur during the night prior to dawn on the following day. That next day is described as "the Lord's day," a term used only once in the New Testament writings, when in Revelation John describes himself as "in the Spirit on the Lord's day" (ἐν τῇ κυριακῇ ἡμέρᾳ) when he received his vision (Rev 1:10). The usage is slightly different in the Gospel of Peter since the adjective κυριακή functions as a substantivized noun. This terminology is shared with other early Christian texts (Did. 14.1; Ign. *Magn.* 9.1; Acts Pet. 29; Acts Paul 7). Along with the presence of the guards, the celestial phenomenon of a great voice is noted, although there is no record of what the voice might have said. The occurrence of this voice is an innovation in the Gospel of Peter. By contrast, the presence of heavenly or unknown figures is a feature of the Synoptic accounts. In Mark the women, upon entering the tomb, find an unnamed young man sitting down, wearing white and proclaiming Jesus to be risen (Mark 16:5–6). In Matthew, after the occurrence of an earthquake, "an angel of the Lord" descends from heaven and physically moves the stone from the entrance of the tomb (Matt 28:2). That figure is described in the following manner: "His appearance was like lightning, and his garment as white as snow" (v. 3 NASB [1977]). However, in many respects the description in the Gospel of Peter is closest in details to the Lukan account. Unlike the Matthean and Markan accounts, the Gospel of Peter and the Gospel of Luke both describe the appearance of two figures rather than one, and both call these figures men rather than angels, as in Matthew (Luke 24:4). Unlike Matthew, the stone is not moved by either of these figures. The Gospel of Peter also heightens miraculous elements in the narrative by having inanimate objects move of their own volition.

Chapter 10

This section is perhaps the most startling, innovative, and memorable scene in the Gospel of Peter. In none of the canonical Gospels is the actual moment of resurrection narrated. Although readers are not taken inside the tomb with the two figures who have descended from heaven, they are taken as close as possible to the actual resurrection events without being inside the tomb itself.

First, the group of witnesses to these events is enlarged, since the two soldiers on duty rouse their compatriots who are also present. These witnesses are presented as being impartial Roman guards. They are present and awake to witness the emergence from the tomb of not only the two men who entered but the reappearance of those two men supporting a third man. This is coupled with a further embellishment to the tradition for which the Gospel of Peter is rightly famous. The text narrates the group of three men being followed by a self-animating cross. Whether the implication is that the cross was buried in the tomb with Jesus or that it has miraculously appeared is not resolved in the details of the account. In many ways such a clarification would detract from the impact of the depiction of the moving cross following the group out of the tomb (Gos. Pet. 9.39).

Some space is devoted to describing the transformed appearance of the three figures who have emerged from the tomb. Whereas upon entry the two men were marked out by their extreme brightness, now on departure their bodily proportions have been metamorphized so that their heads "reached as far as heaven" (Gos. Pet. 9.40). These gargantuan proportions are dwarfed, however, by the third man in the middle whose head "surpassed the heavens" (Gos. Pet. 9.40). These highly visual depictions of transformation are intentional. Not only does depiction of the risen Jesus communicate the qualitative difference of the central figure in comparison to the two supporting heavenly figures, but it also presents him as a figure whose resurrected being spans the earthly and heavenly realms. It is striking that whereas the canonical accounts are relatively measured and circumspect in their depictions of the risen Jesus (although the Fourth Gospel has Jesus materialize miraculously and pass through locked doors, see John 20:19, 26), there is by comparison in the Gospel of Peter something of the "comic book" in the way Jesus is now depicted.

The following two verses continue the heightened miraculous elements, with emphasis on the interplay between the earthly and heavenly domains. Moreover, the material here is generative for certain Christian traditions. For a second time in this resurrection account (cf. Gos. Pet. 9.35) a heavenly voice is heard. Here the words of utterance are recorded, and the celestial voice asks, "Have you preached to those who sleep?" (Gos. Pet. 9.41). At this stage it is unclear to whom the question is directed, though one might assume it is asked of the risen Jesus. However, it is the cross that answers with the one-word affirmation "yes" (Gos. Pet. 9.42). The visual and auditory embellishments to the canonical version of events are memorable and sensational. To modern minds such a heightening of miraculous elements might be considered to make the resurrection scene less believable than the relatively unadorned Synoptic accounts. However, the impact on ancient readers may have been different. A more miraculous account might have been considered as a more believable story. The direct and visual intervention of the heavenly realm would perhaps be seen as a demonstration and a vindication of Jesus. Thus readers were assured that because of decisive divine action the claim of Jesus's resurrection and the affirmation of his status were assured.

The heavenly question about preaching to those who sleep perhaps has a single partial parallel in the New Testament. In 1 Peter 3:18–19 the text describes Christ as being put to death in the flesh but transformed into a mode of existence in the spirit "in which also he went and made proclamation to the spirits in prison." This statement, along with the question in the Gospel of Peter, appears to reflect the beginning of the so-called "harrowing of hell" tradition that became prominent in certain Christian writings and works of art. The flowering of this tradition can be found in texts such as the Gospel of Nicodemus 17–29. Here Christ, during the intervening period between his burial and resurrection, descends into hell and releases the righteous (typically figures depicted in the Hebrew Bible) from the power of death and Hades. In the Gospel of Nicodemus, they are led forth by Adam, who is given the sign of the cross on his forehead (presumably a baptismal symbol) and leads forth the righteous from hell as the outcome of Christ's defeat of death.

Chapter 11

This scene opens with the soldiers deciding to make a report to Pilate. There then follows what might be a piece of clumsy editing of source materials. The narrative has just described the descent of two heavenly figures along with their re-ascent to heaven. Hereafter, in Gospel of Peter 12–13, the author returns to following the canonical accounts more closely. The source material depicts the women encountering a young man sitting in the tomb (cf. Mark 16:5). However, having removed all heavenly figures from the scene, this is problematic. Therefore, the author narrates a second opening of the heavens and a second descent of a heavenly figure who simply enters the tomb and waits there without explanation (Gos. Pet. 11.44). Having repaired the narrative gap created by the innovative account of Gospel of Peter 10, the author then returns to narrate the actions of the Roman soldiers.

Within the story line, the second heavenly appearance serves to motivate the soldiers to leave their post and report to Pilate the events they had witnessed. The report is devoid of details and reduced to one summary statement that communicates the implication of the events by underscoring the status of Jesus: "Truly this was God's son" (Gos. Pet. 11.45). In Matthew and Mark, a similarly worded confession is made by a Roman centurion, but in a different context. It occurs at the moment of Jesus's death and is placed on the lips of an unnamed centurion (Matt 27:54//Mark 15:39). In the Gospel of Peter, the recognition of Jesus's divine sonship comes not at the moment of his death but rather after the events of his resurrection. Therefore, for the Gospel of Peter it appears that the vindication of Jesus through his resurrection elicits this elevated christological confession. Mark's theology is different. From the Markan perspective, in his obedient suffering and death on the cross Jesus is to be recognized as son of God.

Pilate's reaction to the report is voiced in a statement that occurs in another context in the Gospel of Matthew. Prior to the crucifixion in the Gospel of Matthew, Pilate offers to release Jesus, but in the end he acquiesces to the crowd calling for Jesus to be crucified. He then washes his hands (cf. Gos. Pet. 1.1) and declares, "I am innocent of this man's blood" (Matt 27:24). The declaration in the Gospel of Peter is similar, but instead of referring to Jesus as "this man," he affirms the declaration of the soldiers by also referring to Jesus as "the son of God" (Gos. Pet. 11.45). The aim here appears to present impartial Romans, both common soldiers and a member of the officer class, as recognizing the divine status of Jesus.

At this point, following the report from the soldiers, the local leaders who oversaw the execution of Jesus arrive to speak with Pilate. They are portrayed in the narrative as being cowardly and conniving. These unnamed figures implore Pilate to cover up the details of the resurrection of Jesus. Without explanation, the text simply states that Pilate complied with this request and ordered the soldiers to keep silent.

Chapter 12

The material in Gospel of Peter 12.53 contains significant verbal parallels to Mark 16:3. While the material in Gospel of Peter 12.50–13.57 weaves together elements from each of the Synoptic parallels, the story is based most closely on Mark 16:1–8, albeit in a rewritten form reflecting the authors own redactional interests.

The narrative continues its tendency to shift blame onto the Jews. Whereas the canonical accounts state that the women had delayed attending to the body because of observance of the Sabbath, in the Gospel of Peter the delay is attributed to fear of the Jews. It describes that group as being "inflamed with rage" (Gos. Pet. 12.50). The Gospel of Peter is more fulsome in its description of the purpose of the visit of the women to the tomb. In the Gospel of Mark, the purpose is simply to anoint the body (Mark 16:1). By contrast, the Gospel of Peter portrays the women as visiting the burial site since they "had not done at the tomb of the Lord those things which women are accustomed to do over those who have died and for those who are loved by them" (Gos. Pet. 12.50). Here the text appears to expand the Markan description by assigning a stereotypical depiction of the role of women in the burial process in accordance with what was typical in ancient Mediterranean culture. Where the Synoptic accounts provide the names of several women, the Gospel of Peter mentions only Mary Magdalene.

The Gospel of Peter makes use of Markan language with the rhetorical question, "But who will roll away the stone for us?" (cf. Mark 16:3). However, this detail is expanded to include a reason for the desire to open the tomb. The women yet again declare their desire to "do the things that are necessary" (Gos. Pet. 12.53). The author is concerned to emphasize the piety of the women in carrying out the correct burial rites for the corpse. For Hellenistic readers such a determined action to carry out burial rites may have resonated with Antigone's disregard for her safety when she performed the required rites for her deceased brother Polyneices (Sophocles, *Ant.* 21–39).

Unlike the Synoptic accounts, the women note that the stone at the entrance is large and that they may require help to move it aside. They make a contingency plan in the likely case that they cannot enter the tomb. Here the purpose appears apologetic. The narrative presents the women at this stage of being unaware of the open tomb and the resurrection, and as being incapable of removing the stone by themselves. Both these factors are designed to show readers that it was not the women who opened the tomb or removed the body.

Chapter 13

The story of the women at the tomb continues with the description of their arrival at the burial place (Gos. Pet. 13.55). Upon arriving, the Gospel of Peter relates that the women found the tomb open, so they approached, stooped down, and discovered the young man whose entry into the tomb had been described in 11.44. This material is a rewritten version of the events contained in Mark 16:4–5, yet it differs in important respects from the account in Matthew 28:1–3. There are also elements of the Johannine story of the women at the tomb that can be seen to have influenced the Gospel of Peter.

The following verse (Gos. Pet. 13.56) in the manuscript presents several difficulties. The manuscript contains erasures, overwriting, insertions, and repetitions. It appears that the scribe has fatigued in his task of copying the exemplar. The verse opens with a series of three questions spoken by the young man to the women: "Why did you come? Whom do you seek? Not that one who was crucified?" However, these questions remain unanswered. Only the second question finds a close parallel in the canonical accounts. In the Markan account, the male figure makes a statement telling the women that "you seek Jesus the Nazarene" (Mark 16:6; for different expressions, cf. Matt 28:5; Luke 24:5). By contrast, in the Fourth Gospel, like the Gospel of Peter, this is framed as the question, "Whom do you seek?" (John 20:15). The final question in the sequence in the Gospel of Peter, "Not that one who was crucified?" appears to transform the reference to Jesus in Mark 16:6 as the one "who was crucified" into this third question.

The remainder of Gospel of Peter 13.56 is confusing because of its poor state of transcription. It may well be an expansion and rewriting of the statement in Mark 16:6b: "He is risen; he is not here; behold the place where they laid him." If that is the case, then in the Gospel of Peter the young man first invites the women to inspect the empty tomb to satisfy their doubts, before declaring Jesus to be risen. This section concludes by describing the response of the women in Markan terms (cf. Mark 16:8): "Then the women, fearing, fled" (Gos. Pet. 13.57). This terse conclusion reflects the women's surprise at the events that had transpired. In Mark's account the emphasis might fall more heavily on the fear of the women. In the Gospel of Peter, it appears to focus on the outcome of that fear, namely, the women fleeing from the tomb. At this point, both the young man and the women disappear from the narrative, and one is left uninformed of the actions of the women after departing from the tomb.

Chapter 14

The opening verse of the final surviving portion of the Gospel of Peter is transitional. It describes the pilgrims to Jerusalem quitting the city to return home at the end of the Festival of Unleavened Bread. If the author of the Gospel of Peter has a correct understanding of the duration of the Festival of Unleavened Bread, then eight days would have elapsed from the beginning of Passover to the end of the weeklong Festival of Unleavened Bread that commenced the day after Passover. This would mean that this scene takes place five days after what the narrative calls "the Lord's day," when the women encountered the young man in the previous scene. This is not impossible, but this would create the largest temporal gap in the narrative and leave the intervening days unexplained. Alternatively, it might be the case that the author of the Gospel of Peter may not have been properly informed concerning the duration of the festival. If that were correct, then he may present it as ending on the same day as the events just narrated. Certainty is not possible at this point. The chief purpose is to signal the end of the events that took place in Jerusalem around Passover season when Jesus was crucified.

In Gospel of Peter 14.59–60, for the second time the story is presented using a first-person narrator (cf. Gos. Pet. 7.26). Whereas on the previous occasion the identity of that narrator was not explicitly stated, here the narrator is named as being Simon Peter. It is this detail that led to the text being identified as the Gospel of Peter, the title of which was otherwise known from antiquity, but until the discovery of the Akhmîm codex none of the text was preserved. The group of Jesus's associates who gather are described as "the twelve disciples of the Lord" (Gos. Pet. 14.59). The title "the Twelve" was a standard way of designating a group of Jesus's earlier followers, with slightly differing lists being presented in the Synoptic accounts (Matt 10:2–5//Mark 3:16–19//Luke 6:14–16). It has been suggested that the use of the term "the Twelve" at this point in the Gospel of Peter means that the author either deleted or was yet to narrate the story of the death of Judas. However, while in certain places the canonical Gospels and Acts carefully designate eleven disciples after the death of Judas (Matt 28:16; [Mark 16:14]; Luke 24:9, 33; Acts 1:26; 2:14), at other times the designation "the Twelve" is frequently retained (cf. Acts 6:2; 1 Cor 15:5). The author of the Gospel of Peter is at times imprecise in designations. Therefore, it is not possible to determine whether the author is ignorant of or does not narrate the death of Judas, or whether he simply used "the Twelve" as a familiar title for the group that was closely associated with Jesus during his earthly ministry.

Much like the description in Gospel of Peter 7.26–27, the followers of Jesus are depicted as being in a state of continuing grief. As a result, the text states that each returned to his own house. The locations of these homes are not disclosed. Here the imprecision in geographical details means that the audience must yet again supply background information. If information from the canonical accounts is meant to be used to understand this description, then presumably the destination was Galilee in general, and in the case of at least Peter and Andrew perhaps readers are meant to understand them as now being back home in Capernaum (Mark 1:21). The following verse probably requires this understanding, since when Peter decides to return to fishing, he takes his nets, which were presumably not with him in Jerusalem, and he sets out for the sea. At least three of the disciples are named as taking part in this fishing trip: Peter, Andrew, and Levi. The text breaks off abruptly at this point, so it is unclear whether any other members of the Twelve were described as present.

Although ultimately unanswerable, it is interesting to reflect on the question of what elements may have come next and concluded the narrative. The device of moving the disciples from Jerusalem to the sea and Peter taking his nets is highly suggestive of the Johannine narrative, where Peter likewise declares, "I am going fishing," and does so in the company of six other disciples (John 21:2–3). Therefore, it is likely that the Gospel of Peter may have continued with a version of the story of Jesus's appearance on the beach while the disciples are fishing (John 21:1–14). If this is the case, this is significant because it shows that the author of the Gospel of Peter was familiar with material contained in the final chapter of the Gospel of John, and therefore he was probably familiar with the complete text of the Fourth Gospel. Beyond this, the contents of the text are difficult to determine. Now that the disciples are in Galilee, and having seen that the Gospel of Peter is so heavily dependent on the Gospel of Matthew, it is possible that the Gospel of Peter might have drawn on Matthew for the scene of Jesus's last words to the disciples on a mountain in Galilee (Matt 28:16–20). However, that remains a mere possibility, and without further manuscript discoveries it is probably better to concede ignorance concerning the ending of the text.

3. INTERPRETIVE ISSUES
3.1 Initial Reaction and Publication

When Bouriant published the first edition of the codex in 1892,[3] he focused more attention on the fragments of 1 Enoch since he considered this to be a more significant discovery. This was due to the fact that, prior to the discovery, only Ethiopic versions of 1 Enoch were known. However, once the *editio princeps* was published, scholars in Germany, France, and England devoted more attention to the first two texts in the codex—the Gospel of Peter and the Apocalypse of Peter.

In Britain the flurry of early interest, primarily in the form of academic lectures and short publications, was generated by a circle of Cambridge scholars. Studies and editions of the text were produced by J. Armitage Robinson (mentioned earlier),[4] H. B. Swete (mentioned earlier),[5] and J. Rendel Harris.[6] The first two volumes printed the Greek text with an accompanying English translation of the Gospel of Peter, whereas the "popular account" of Harris presents only an English translation of the text. Thus, the works of Robinson and Swete have maintained a greater impact on scholarly discussions of the text. A similar flurry of activity occurred in Germany during 1892–1893. Chief among the publications arising in German scholarship was Harnack's edition,[7] with printed versions of the Greek text of both the Gospel of Peter and the Apocalypse of Peter. Both German and English scholarship contributed to the standard referencing system for the text. Robinson divided the text of the Gospel of Peter into fourteen paragraphs of chapter divisions; by contrast Harnack divided the text into sixty shorter units or verses. The convention for referencing sections of the text has been to use both Robinson's fourteen-chapter system and Harnack's sixty-verse system together, without the verse numbering recommencing at the beginning of each larger chapter.

Following this initial interest in the text, for the first three decades of the twentieth century relatively little scholarly work was undertaken on the text. The major contribution was the magisterial commentary of Léon Vaganay, published in French with the title *L'Évangile de Pierre*.[8] There then ensued a period of approximately forty years in which the text was almost totally neglected. Various publications appeared in the 1970s, but the text came to prominence again in the 1980s. In a highly innovative monograph, J. D. Crossan suggested that the Gospel of Peter contained an earlier source that he termed the Cross Gospel.[9] According to Crossan, this source formed the bulk of the Gospel of Peter, which itself was a light expansion of this source. The creative suggestion proposed by Crossan was that the Cross Gospel source predated the canonical accounts and in various ways was

---

3. U. Bouriant, "Fragments du texte grec du livre d'Énoch et de quelques écrits attribués à saint Pierre," in *Mémoires publiés par les membres de la Mission archéologique française au Caire*, vol. 9 (Paris: Ernest Leroux, 1892), 93–147.

4. J. A. Robinson and M. R. James, *Gospel according to Peter, and the Revelation of Peter*.

5. Swete, *Akhmîm Fragment of the Apocryphal Gospel of St Peter*.

6. J. R. Harris, *A Popular Account of the Newly Recovered Gospel of St Peter* (London: Hodder and Stoughton, 1893).

7. Harnack, *Bruchstücke des Evangeliums und der Apokalypse des Petrus*.

8. L. Vaganay, *L'Évangile de Pierre*, Etudes Biblique (Paris: Gabalda, 1929).

9. J. D. Crossan, *The Cross that Spoke: The Origins of the Passion Narrative* (San Francisco: Harper & Row, 1988).

used as a source for the passion narratives in the canonical Gospels as well as by the Gospel of Peter. Crossan's work was of great importance for refocusing scholarly attention on the Gospel of Peter as an early Christian Gospel writing, even if his source theories are not widely accepted.

Since this resurgence of interest in the noncanonical Gospels in general and the Gospel of Peter specifically, numerous editions,[10] studies,[11] and commentaries have appeared. This intellectual turn toward studying Gospel literature more widely as part of the larger field of Christian origins continues. Amid this interest in the noncanonical Gospels, a steady stream of further studies on the Gospel of Peter appears regularly.[12]

3.2 Date, Place of Composition, and Other Possible Manuscripts

Two dates are important in terms of describing the textual history of the Gospel of Peter. The first is the date of the manuscript P.Cair. 10759. That is the date when the scribe copied the exemplar text and produced the physical manuscript in which the text is now preserved. The second date of importance is when the text of the Gospel of Peter was composed and first put in written form. It appears to be the case that several centuries had elapsed between these two dates. During that intervening period, it is quite possible that the form of the text had changed. However, without additional manuscript evidence the degree of change is impossible to determine.

In relation to when the manuscript P.Cair. 10759 was written, a number of factors can assist in determining the approximate date. Since the manuscript is undated, one must rely primarily upon paleographical analysis. Such analysis involves comparing the style of handwriting with similar scribal hands preserved in manuscripts where a date is given or where there is a clear reference to some contemporary event that allows the time of composition to be determined. Other factors have also been considered, such as the period of Christian presence at the Akhmîm site and the location of the specific grave in which the manuscript was discovered. This is relevant because the burial sites moved up the hill over the centuries, since in general the burials started at the closer sites before moving up the hill. However, such archaeological indicators lack precision. The result of this data has been to suggest a broad spectrum of dates from as early as the fifth century to as late as the twelfth century for the possible composition of the manuscript. On the basis of handwriting styles, the later centuries have largely been abandoned as serious possibilities for dating the time of copying. The Leuven database of ancient books, apparently drawing on the analysis of Cavallo and Maehler,[13] also rejects the fifth century as a possible date, but it still places the composition in the early range of sixth or seventh century. This, however, is in all likelihood an overly narrow and too confident range of dates. Therefore, while the date of the manuscript remains an open question, it does appear that a date of the late sixth to the early ninth century provides a highly probable period for the composition of the text.

Perhaps the more interesting question, especially for understanding the Gospel of Peter in relation to other early Christian Gospel literature, is the date of the initial composition

---

10. E.g., see T. J. Kraus and T. Nicklas, *Das Petrusevangelium and die Petrusapokalypse: Die griechischen Fragmente mit deutscher und englischer Übersetzung* (Berlin: de Gruyter, 2004).

11. T. P. Henderson, *The Gospel of Peter and Early Christian Apologetics*, WUNT 2.301 (Tübingen: Mohr Siebeck, 2011); P. Augustin, *Die Juden im Petrusevangelium: Narratogische Analyse und theologiegeschichtliche Kontextualisierung*, BZNW 214 (Berlin: de Gruyter, 2015); J. J. Johnston, *The Resurrection of Jesus in the Gospel of Peter: A Tradition-Historical Study of the Akhmîm Gospel Fragment*, JCT 21 (London: T&T Clark, 2016).

12. E.g., see R. G. T. Edwards, "The Theological Gospel of Peter?," *NTS* 63 (2019): 477–95.

13. G. Cavallo and H. Maehler, *Greek Bookhands of the Early Byzantine Period A.D. 300–800* (London: Institute of Classical Studies, 1987), 75.

of the text. Here a different type of evidence must be analyzed. This relates to possible references to the Gospel of Peter in other Christian writings as well as indications of literary relationships between the Gospel of Peter and other early Christian texts. Here Eusebius's *Historia ecclesiastica*, written in the early fourth century, is significant. In one place it refers to various writings attributed to the apostle Peter, including "the Gospel named according to him [i.e. Peter]" (Eusebius, *Hist. eccl.* 3.3.1–2). Eusebius's second reference to the Gospel of Peter is far more extensive, and it is valuable to cite this piece of evidence in full. Here Eusebius refers to one of the literary works of Serapion, bishop of Antioch, around the last decade of the second century or perhaps into the opening decade of the third century. The work of Serapion to which Eusebius refers is known by the title *Concerning the So-called Gospel of Peter*. Eusebius makes his own introductory comment and then claims to cite a paragraph from Serapion's work as follows:

> And another book has been composed by him: *Concerning the so-called Gospel of Peter*, which he has written refuting the false statements in it, because of certain in the community of Rhossus, who on the ground of the said writing turned aside into heterodox teachings. It will not be unreasonable to quote a short passage from this work, in which he puts forward the view he held about the book, writing as follows:
>
> "For our part, brothers, we receive both Peter and the other apostles as Christ, but the writings which falsely bear their names we reject, as men of experience, knowing that such were not handed down to us. For I myself, when I came among you, imagined that all of you clung to the true faith; and without going through the Gospel put forward by them in the name of Peter, I said, 'If this is the only thing that seemingly causes captious feelings among you, let it be read.' But since I have now learnt, from what has been told me, that their mind was lurking in some hole of heresy, I shall give diligence to come quickly to you; wherefore brothers expect me to come quickly. But we, brothers, gathering to what kind of heresy Marcianus belonged (who used to contradict himself, not knowing what he was saying, as you will learn from what has been written to you), were enabled by others who studied this very Gospel, that is, by the successors of those who began it, whom we call Docetae (for most of the ideas belong to their teaching)—using [the material supplied] by them, were enabled to go through it and discover that the most part indeed was in accordance with the true teaching of the Saviour, but that some things were added, which also we place below for your benefit."
>
> Such are the writings of Serapion. (Eusebius, *Hist. eccl.* 6.12.2–6)

If Eusebius provides accurate information about a text titled the Gospel of Peter being known to Serapion, and if that document is broadly identical although perhaps more extensive than the Akhmîm text, then one may infer that the Gospel of Peter was in existence by the time of Serapion in the late second century. How much earlier it may have existed is more difficult to tell. Others have found links with the writings of Justin Martyr,[14] and thus inferred the existence of the Gospel of Peter by the mid-second century. More radically, as has been mentioned, Crossan proposed that much of the Gospel of Peter in the form of the "Cross Gospel" was in fact a source for the canonical Gospels. This would necessitate a date at least as early as the middle of the first century. Such theories have

---

14. In his *Dialogue with Trypho*, Justin refers to "the memoirs of Peter" (*Dial.* 106). While some have argued this could be a reference to the Gospel of Peter, it could equally refer to the Gospel of Mark, given Papias's statement that "Mark, having become Peter's interpreter, wrote down accurately everything he remembered, though not in order, of the things either said or done by Christ" (Eusebius, *Hist. eccl.* 3.39.15).

different levels of plausibility, but all fall far short of certainty. Returning to the statement from Eusebius, this may imply that the Gospel of Peter had been in existence for sufficient time to gain a following and to warrant a response. Thus, the most secure suggestion for the date of composition of the Gospel of Peter is sometime in the second half of the second century, prior to Serapion's written refutation. That would be approximately between 150 and 190 CE.

Determining the location of composition is even more difficult. The manuscript discovered in Akhmîm in Egypt may have been composed between the late sixth to the early ninth century. A text known as the Gospel of Peter appears to be in circulation in the late second century in Rhossos in Syria, in the region of Antioch. However, both Akhmîm and Rhossos are locations of reception, not places of composition. The details of the text betray no indication of the place of composition. In fact, the lack of precision regarding Judean or Galilean topography may count against these areas being possible places of composition. The text is written in Greek, which is suggestive of composition in the broad area of the eastern Mediterranean. Perhaps the links with Rhossos suggest a Syrian composition, and its appearance in Egypt may reflect the connections between Syrian and Egyptian monasticism. In the end, however, there is no evidence that permits a specific location of composition to be proposed.

Several other texts or artifacts have been suggested as possible witnesses to the text of the Gospel of Peter. The two manuscripts that have been most frequently proposed as fragments of the Gospel of Peter are both from Oxyrhynchus, also in Egypt. These are the papyrus fragments P.Oxy. 2949 and P.Oxy. 4009. Taking the latter first, P.Oxy. 4009 is a small slither of a papyrus manuscript written on both sides. The reconstruction of the *verso* is problematic, and what can be reconstructed on the *recto* is a little more certain, but the identification of the text it carries is not secure. The text of P.Oxy. 4009 does not overlap in any respect with the text preserved in the Akhmîm manuscript. Therefore the identification of P.Oxy. 4009 as part of the Gospel of Peter can only be correct if it preserves a part of the Gospel of Peter otherwise unknown. However, since the contents of the Gospel of Peter are unknown apart from what is contained in the Akhmîm manuscript, this results in a circular argument. Hence, it appears best not to identify P.Oxy. 4009 as a fragment of an otherwise nonextant portion of the Gospel of Peter.[15]

The second Oxyrhynchus fragment, P.Oxy. 2949, is certainly worthy of fuller consideration. It consists of two fragments, the smaller of which perhaps preserves ten letters over four lines. These fragments are typically dated to the second or early third centuries. The larger fragment preserves the partial remains of nine lines of text. The first lines preserve lexical items that are certainly shared with the text of Gospel of Peter 2.3–5a. Common elements include a figure called "the friend of Pilate," this figure "coming to Pilate," and reference to some burial rite, "the body to a tomb." It is also possible that the ending of an incomplete word might also refer to "Herod." Given these similarities, there is certainly some connection with the story in the Gospel of Peter 2.3–5a. However, there are also numerous differences in wording between the text of P.Oxy. 2949 and the apparent parallel material in the Gospel of Peter. There are several ways to interpret this data. P.Oxy. 2949 could be a portion of an early form of the text of the Gospel of Peter. It might be a source tradition incorporated into the Gospel of Peter when it was composed. Or, perhaps P.Oxy. 2949 more accurately reflects the text of the Gospel of Peter, and it is the Akhmîm

---

15. For a fuller discussion of this problem, see P. Foster, "Are There Any Early Fragments of the So-called Gospel of Peter?," *NTS* 52 (2006): 1–28.

text that modified and developed the earlier Gospel of Peter. It is particularly noteworthy that lines ten to thirteen of P.Oxy. 2949 provide virtually no similarities with the proposed parallel from Gospel of Peter 2.3–5a. Hence, one is certainly not dealing with two copies of an identical text. What this illustrates is the fluidity in the form of various traditions that were in circulation during the second century. Again, it is possible to glimpse the activity of early Christian writers in that period, as they rewrote and combined versions of the Jesus story into creative, entertaining, and theologically reassuring resources.

In the end, the principal witness to the Gospel of Peter remains P.Cair. 10759, the Akhmîm text. Other proposals that various manuscripts preserve portions of the Gospel of Peter are typically unpersuasive. Only the case of P.Oxy. 2949 deserves fuller attention, since there are certainly overlaps with a small portion of the Akhmîm text.

3.3 A Docetic Christology?

Under the influence of the comment from Eusebius attributed to Serapion that those called *Docetae* used the Gospel of Peter in support of their theological view, scholars attempted to identify docetic elements in the text. While acknowledging that the label *docetic* probably covers a range of ideas, its central claim was that while Christ was fully divine his humanity was adopted only in appearance. Probably part of the motivation for this belief was a desire not to contaminate the higher heavenly nature of Christ with what presumably was viewed as a corrupt material from the physical world. Moreover, there was a desire to protect the divine Logos from the experience of human suffering. Taking Serapion's comment as indicating that the Gospel of Peter was docetic in outlook, early scholarship on the text sought to identify elements that aligned with such a theology. Three main features were proposed. First, it was observed that during the mockery the Lord was said to suffer "as though feeling no pain" (Gos. Pet. 4.10). Second, it was noted that during the crucifixion, unlike the canonical Gospels, there was no declaration of "I thirst" (John 19:28). Thus, a very human reaction to suffering is removed from the account in the Gospel of Peter. Third, the cry, "My God, my God, why have you forsaken me?" (Matt 27:46//Mark 15:34) is replaced with, "My power, the power, you have left me" (Gos. Pet. 5.19). These changes or omissions were seen as creating a portrait of a Jesus who was spared pain and suffering. Hence they were interpreted as being docetic in orientation.

Such an interpretation is questionable on several levels and has been abandoned by virtually all scholars. First, Serapion's comment does not say that the Gospel of Peter was docetic. Rather, it states that the *Docetae* were able to read the material in this text in a manner that aligned with their views. Second, the three examples cited are all dubious. The omission of the statement "I thirst" perhaps has more to do with the relative neglect of the Fourth Gospel as a source for the passion narrative in the Gospel of Peter. The comment that Jesus faces his torments "as though feeling no pain" (Gos. Pet. 4.10) aligns with the common trope of the noble sufferer. In fact, a highly significant parallel to this statement occurs in the Martyrdom of Polycarp, where Polycarp injures his leg when pushed out of the wagon in which he is being transported on the way to martyrdom. The narrator reports that he walked on "as suffering no pain" (Mart. Pol. 8.3). Therefore, such comments concerning suffering as though having no pain are not a reflection of docetic theology but align with the widely known portrayal of noble death. Finally, what was seen as the key passage, understood as the divine power of the Logos leaving the human shell of Jesus to die, is a strange way to read the text. It hardly preserves the divine element from suffering, given that it has experienced the full range of torment and the actual crucifixion itself.

By contrast, in the Coptic Nag Hammadi text the Apocalypse of Peter, during the crucifixion Peter encounters three Jesus-like figures. With one Peter conducts a conversation, one is glad and laughing on or above the tree, and the third Jesus-figure is being crucified. Regarding the third figure, the text states, "But the one into whose hands and feet they are driving the nails is his fleshly part, which is the substitute, being put to shame, the one who came into being in his likeness" (Apoc. Pet. NHC VII.3.81).[16] Whereas this text removes the divine Christ from the entire experience of suffering, thereby articulating a docetic Christology, the Gospel of Peter presents the Lord as subject to the full torment and pain of mockery and crucifixion. For these reasons it is inaccurate to describe the contents of the surviving portion of the Gospel of Peter as docetic.

4. KEY PASSAGES FOR NEW TESTAMENT STUDIES AND THEIR SIGNIFICANCE

The text overlaps extensively with the canonical passion narratives, especially the Matthean form of the story. However, the Gospel of Peter tells its own story in its own way. Notwithstanding the redactional creativity employed by the author, the text appears to be dependent on each of the canonical accounts to a greater or lesser extent, and it preserves elements that are unique in the three Synoptic Gospels. For this reason, it seems that the Gospel of Peter knows and uses the canonical Gospels as the basis and framework for its expansionist and more fantastic version of the passion narrative. As such, the Gospel of Peter provides important insights into the ways in which early Christians handled traditions concerning Jesus. It reflects a desire to fill gaps in existing stories, to increase miraculous elements, and to make the story of the passion and resurrection more robust for apologetic purposes and more appealing to gentile readers by shifting the blame for the death of Jesus far more squarely onto the Jewish leaders in Jerusalem.[17]

Various authorial aims have been detected that account for the reason why the author of the Gospel of Peter undertook the task of rewriting and supplementing the traditions preserved in the canonical passion and resurrection accounts. At times, more than one of the author's aims can be achieved by the same modification to the tradition received from the source material. The following seven factors can be seen as prominent and repeated concerns in the surviving portion of the text.

1. Shifting blame for the crucifixion from Roman authorities to Jewish figures
2. Producing a Christology that aligns with the author's elevated understanding of Jesus
3. Heightening miraculous elements as a means of commending belief
4. Resolving problematic theological features in the canonical form of the passion narratives
5. Creating a form of the tradition that is more robust for apologetic purposes
6. Filling gaps in the narrative to satisfy the curiosity of the pious
7. Producing a stylistically more developed text with greater points of narrative tension

---

16. For a fuller discussion of this text, see P. Foster, "Polymorphic Christology: Its Origins and Development in Early Christianity," *JTS* 58 (2007): 66–99, here 97.

17. For a discussion of these motivations, see P. Foster, "Passion Traditions in the *Gospel of Peter*," in *Gelitten, Gestorben, Auferstanden: Passions- und Ostertraditionen im antiken Christentum*, ed. T. Nicklas, A. Merkt, and J. Verheyden, WUNT 2.273 (Tübingen: Mohr Siebeck, 2011), 47–68. The summary of motivations for rewriting this account of the passion is provided toward the conclusion of this discussion.

The prominence of blame-shifting from Roman figures to Jewish leaders is apparent throughout the entire surviving portion of the narrative. In many ways, this tendency aligns with wider perspectives in second-century and later Christianity, where there is a desire to attribute the death of Jesus to Jewish figures while also exonerating gentiles or Romans of guilt.

The elevated Christology is a feature than can already be detected in later canonical Gospels such as the Gospel of Matthew or the Gospel of John, where these authors explore new ways of expressing their belief in the divine status of Jesus. In the Gospel of Peter, the narrator reserves the title "Lord" for his own comments about Jesus, and it never occurs on the lips of characters in the text. This title may have been the primary way in which the author and his community referred to Jesus.

The heightening of miraculous elements is striking, and this tendency is perhaps one of the most memorable aspects of this text. Inanimate objects move of their own volition, in particular the cross is not only self-animating but is also able to speak, and the body proportions of heavenly figures can metamorphize into gigantic proportions. These startling innovations need to be understood in the context of an ancient worldview. From that perspective, the more miraculous a story the more it demonstrated divine action and vindication.

The Gospel of Peter is a historical text. However, the historical window it provides is not primarily onto the events surrounding the crucifixion and resurrection of Jesus in the first century. Rather, its main historical insights are in relation to depicting the piety of believers in Jesus in the second century and as a reflection of the ways in which they handled the gospel traditions from earlier accounts. The Gospel of Peter has it own themes or theological perspective. Some are developments of ideas already present in the canonical Gospels, while others resonate with concerns arising in the period in which it was written. As such, the Gospel of Peter has much to teach those interested in the history of early Christianity and in the transmission and reception of traditions concerning Jesus.

5. BIBLIOGRAPHY

Augustin, P. *Die Juden im Petrusevangelium: Narratogische Analyse und theologiegeschichtliche Kontextualisierung.* BZNW 214. Berlin: de Gruyter, 2015.

Bouriant, U. "Fragments du texte grec du livre d'Énoch et de quelques écrits attribués à saint Pierre." Pages 93–147 in *Mémoires publiés par les membres de la Mission archéologique française au Caire.* Vol. 9. Paris: Ernest Leroux, 1892.

Brown, R. E. *The Death of the Messiah: From Gethsemane to the Grave.* 2 vols. ABRL. New York: Doubleday, 1994. See esp. vol. 2, appendix 1, pp. 1317–49.

Crossan, J. D. *The Cross That Spoke: The Origins of the Passion Narrative.* San Francisco: Harper & Row, 1988.

Foster, P. *The Gospel of Peter: Introduction, Critical Edition and Commentary.* Leiden: Brill, 2010.

Harnack, A. *Bruchstücke des Evangeliums und der Apokalypse des Petrus.* TU 9.2. J. C. Hinrichs: Leipzig, 1893.

Henderson, T. P. *The Gospel of Peter and Early Christian Apologetics.* WUNT 2.301. Tübingen: Mohr Siebeck, 2011.

Johnston, J. J. *The Resurrection of Jesus in the Gospel of Peter: A Tradition-Historical Study of the Akhmîm Gospel Fragment.* JCT 21. London: T&T Clark, 2016.

Kraus, T. J., and T. Nicklas, eds. *Das Petrusevangelium and die Petrusapokalypse: Die griechischen Fragmente mit deutscher und englischer Übersetzung.* Berlin: de Gruyter, 2004.

Mara, M. G. *Évangile de Pierre: Introduction, Texte Critique, Traduction, Commentaire et Index.* Sources Chrétiennes 201. Paris: Cerf, 1973.

Robinson, J. A., and M. R. James. *The Gospel according to Peter, and the Revelation of Peter: Two Lectures on the Newly Recovered Fragments Together with the Greek Texts.* London: C. J. Clay and Sons, 1892.

Swete, H. B. *The Akhmîm Fragment of the Apocryphal Gospel of St Peter.* London: Macmillan, 1893.

Vaganay, L. *L'Évangile de Pierre.* Études Biblique. Paris: Gabalda, 1929.

CHAPTER 5

INFANCY GOSPEL OF THOMAS

REIDAR AASGAARD

1. INTRODUCTION

The Infancy Gospel of Thomas, one of the so-called "infancy gospels," deals with the childhood of Jesus. The other main infancy gospel is the Protevangelium of James, which describes the family, childhood, and youth of Mary until she has given birth to Jesus.[1] The Infancy Gospel of Thomas, which covers about six to seven modern book pages, consists of a number of miracle stories and some discourses. It begins with the five-year-old Jesus playing by a brook and ends with the well-known episode from the Gospel of Luke about Jesus at the age of twelve discussing Scripture with the learned in the temple (Luke 2:41–52). In the story, Jesus mainly interacts with his parents, teachers, and other children, partly performing healing miracles and blessings, partly cursing his opponents so that they wither and even die—the latter repeatedly bringing him into grave conflict with others. Eventually, however, when people realize who Jesus is, the one sent by God, all things end well.[2]

The Infancy Gospel of Thomas, which is of no value for the study of the Jesus of history, is the only story to relate his childhood years at some length. In the Early Middle Ages, it was incorporated together with the Protevangelium of James into larger narratives about the childhoods of Mary and Jesus, in particular the Gospel of Pseudo-Matthew.[3]

1.1 Authorship

Traditionally, the story is attributed to Thomas. The apostle Thomas is probably intended, possibly Thomas as Jesus's legendary twin brother, or Thomas, a disciple of Mani.[4] In one main variant or recension of the story (Gd), Jesus's brother James is named as its author. The prologue, which is the only place where the author is mentioned, is only loosely integrated into the story and clearly secondary and is lacking in many of the earliest versions.[5] The author thus remains unknown. It may even be the kind of story that has

---

1. See ch. 9 on the Protevangelium of James in the present volume.

2. For a general introduction to various topics in the work, see Reidar Aasgaard, *The Childhood of Jesus: Decoding the Apocryphal Infancy Gospel of Thomas* (Eugene, OR: Cascade, 2009). For a specialized presentation, see the standard text-critical edition: Tony Burke, *De Infantia Iesu Evangelium Thomae, Graece*, CCSA 17 (Turnhout: Brepols, 2010). See also Tony Burke, "Infancy Gospel of Thomas," North American Society for the Study of Christian Apocryphal Literature, www.nasscal.com/e-clavis-christian-apocrypha/infancy-gospel-of-thomas/; Burke's web page is an extremely useful gateway to resources for research on the Infancy Gospel of Thomas.

3. See Bart D. Ehrman and Zlatko Pleše, *The Apocryphal Gospels: Texts and Translations* (Oxford: Oxford University Press, 2011), 73–113, for a brief introduction with Latin text (without the second part, the *pars altera*, which contains the Infancy Gospel of Thomas) and an English translation.

4. See Burke, *De Infantia Iesu*, 205–7 on authorship.

5. The ascription to Thomas is, for example, absent in the Georgian manuscript and some Syriac and Latin manuscripts.

been developed and embellished over time by scribes, narrators, or others, so that it is more adequate to speak of an "originator" or "originators" rather than an author.[6]

1.2 Language

The original language of the infancy gospel was very likely Greek, although Syriac has also been proposed.[7] The story, and variants of it, survives in several other languages, particularly in Latin, Syriac, Armenian, Georgian, Ethiopic, Irish, Arabic, and Slavonic, among which the Latin and Syriac manuscripts are the oldest surviving witnesses (both third century, with a retranslation to Latin by the seventh century); the other preserved translations were probably made during the sixth to tenth centuries.[8]

1.3 Provenance

The place of origin for the story is uncertain. Considering the very general and limited information given about geography, regional cultures, and other things, not much can be said about its geographical origin. Traditionally, Syria (and Antioch in particular) has been suggested, based on the assumed association of the apostle Thomas with this area. In addition, Egypt, Palestine, Asia Minor, and Jewish diaspora centers (the last because of the story's use of material from the Gospel of Luke) have been argued, with Asia Minor or Syrian Antioch being perhaps the best guesses.[9]

More rewarding than this, however, has probably been the quest for the social and topographical location of the story. Based on studies of its language, descriptions of social relations and structures, theology, and cultural concepts and values, the infancy gospel seems to mirror a setting among common people rather than the social elite. The milieu of the story also reflects a rural, village-like world, which was the main whereabouts for a large majority of the population in late antiquity, rather than an urban setting.[10]

1.4 Date

Because the origin and transmission of the infancy gospel is hard to trace, it is very difficult to date. At least in core, it goes back to the middle of the second century. Justin Martyr in *Dialogue with Trypho* 88 refers to Jesus "doing carpentry, making plows and yokes" (ca. 150 CE).[11] The *Epistula Apostolorum* 4, or the *Epistle of the Apostles* (mid-second century CE),[12] mentions a scene in which Jesus's parents follow him to a place where he gets to learn letters. Irenaeus in *Against Heresies* 1.20.1 describes a similar episode, and in more detail (before 180 CE). It seems also to be hinted at in the Gospel of Truth I 19.17–32 (140–180 CE) and in Acts of Thomas 79 (early third century). Most of these texts refer to the episode(s) about Jesus learning the letters. A number of sources from the fourth century also refer to other episodes in the infancy gospel, thus attesting awareness of a story containing a broader range of material. The most important of these are Epiphanius, *Refutation of All Heresies* 51.20.2–3; John Chrysostom, *Homilies on John* 17; and *History*

---

6. Aasgaard, *Childhood of Jesus*, 27–34.
7. Burke, *De Infantia Iesu*, 174–88.
8. Aasgaard, *Childhood of Jesus*, 180–85; Burke, *De Infantia Iesu*, 144–71. Apart from the Greek edition, the other language to have a text-critical edition is Syriac; see Tony Burke, *The Syriac Tradition of the Infancy Gospel of Thomas: A Critical Edition and English Translation*, GECS 48 (Piscataway, NJ: Gorgias, 2017).
9. Burke, *De Infantia Iesu*, 206–12.
10. Aasgaard, *Childhood of Jesus*, 166–91 (also 53–85).
11. Aasgaard, *Childhood of Jesus*, 174.
12. See ch. 23 of the present volume.

of Joseph the Carpenter 17.[13] It is not possible to say for sure whether the infancy gospel existed as a combination of various episodes already in the second century or developed over time from a core that consisted primarily of the episodes with Jesus being instructed in the letters; the former seems to be somewhat more probable.

1.5 Text

The earliest witnesses to the Infancy Gospel of Thomas are in fifth- to sixth-century Latin (Vindob. 563) and Syriac (SyrG; SyrW) manuscripts; they contain parts of the story and probably reproduce material translated from Greek in the third century. Late manuscripts in Latin and Syriac, as well as Armenian, Georgian, and Ethiopic, may also reproduce considerably earlier material, probably from the sixth century.[14]

The oldest known manuscript in Greek containing the infancy gospel is Codex Sabaiticus 259 (dated 1089 or 1090), which also preserves the full story; very probably, it reflects a text from between the fourth to the seventh century. Most scholars believe it preserves the oldest attainable form of the story. All other Greek manuscripts are considerably later (thirteenth to sixteenth century), with texts that reflect later stages of transmission (ninth through fifteenth century).[15]

The fourteen Greek manuscripts preserving the infancy gospel (complete and in part) can be divided into four main variants or recensions: Gs (1), Ga (8), Gb (2), and Gd (3), with "G" signifying "Greek."[16] Codex Sabaiticus 259 is the sole witness of Gs, but with a manuscript fragment within Ga having some affinity to it. In a fairly similar way, the Latin and Syriac manuscripts can be divided into variants or recensions: Lv, Lm, and Lt, and SyrW, SyrP, SyrG, and SyrB, respectively.[17]

1.6 Genre

Form critically, the infancy gospel—according to Gs—consists of three main types: prologue, miracles, and discourses. The short and secondary prologue shares many features with related early Christian works, such as apocryphal Gospels and Acts. The miracles are of two kinds: nature and health miracles, five in the former category and seven in the latter, of which four are instances of cursing and three of healing. Although miracles are the more frequent in number, the discourses add up to more than 60 percent of the total story and consist both of dialogues and of short sayings and speeches, mostly by Jesus.

As for the genre of the infancy gospel as a whole, no simple categorization is possible. It clearly shares some features with ancient biographies on holy men and political leaders, such as Philo's *On the Life of Moses* (ca. 10–40 CE), Suetonius's emperor biographies (ca. 120 CE), and Hellenistic novels (first through third century CE), but none of these deal at any length with the childhood of their main characters. The story has some elements in common with fable literature such as *Life of Aesop*, but unlike them it has no animals in its main cast. It shares some, but not very significant, traits with ancient fairytales, myths, and legends, yet it also has a simple and matter-of-fact form that makes it differ considerably from most of them.[18]

---

13. Aasgaard, *Childhood of Jesus*, 174–80, also 252–53 (appendix 6); Burke, *De Infantia Iesu*, 3–44; 201–5.

14. Burke, *De Infantia Iesu*, 144–71.

15. Burke, *De Infantia Iesu*, 127–44; Aasgaard, *Childhood of Jesus*, 14–16, 248–51.

16. The term *recension* is somewhat problematic, and potentially misleading, in the case of this material, since it implies that the material has undergone conscious revisions, which is clearly not the case. Even though the term *recension* can be understood in a relatively open sense, I find it more appropriate to speak of *variants* (see Aasgaard, *Childhood of Jesus*, 15, 32–33).

17. Burke, *De Infantia Iesu*, 144–67; also Burke, *Syriac Tradition*, 1–122.

18. For discussions of genre, see Aasgaard, *Childhood of Jesus*, 49–52; J. R. C. Cousland, *Holy Terror: Jesus*

The Infancy Gospel of Thomas has some elements in common also with other Jewish and early Christian literature, such as Tobit (third to second century BCE), Joseph and Aseneth (first century BCE), Acts of Paul and Thecla (mid-second century CE), and Acts of Peter (late second century CE), and with hagiographical writings such as *Life of Antony* (356–362 CE), but the similarities are not very close. The same is the case with its relation to the Protevangelium of James. Despite their shared focus on childhood, the two works are quite different in form and style. The early Christian material to come the closest to the story as concerns genre is in fact the canonical Gospels, with their biographical and chronological approach, their similar mixture of miracles, discourses, and Jesus-sayings, and the explicit link to the Jesus-in-the-temple episode in Luke 2.

In sum, the Infancy Gospel of Thomas appears to be a mixture of Gospel and belief legend, with some elements in common with ancient biography. This is probably the closest one can (and needs to) get to a genre classification. Being the single story from antiquity to focus exclusively on a character's childhood, it appears to be unique.[19] This is also indicated in that the oldest designation of the story is not as a Gospel (*euangelion*), but as *paidika megaleia*, a story about Jesus's "great childhood deeds."[20] Even though it is not fully adequate, I here—for sake of simplicity—nonetheless refer to the story as the Infancy Gospel of Thomas or as an "infancy gospel."

2. SUMMARY OF CONTENT

The transmission history of this infancy gospel in Greek and in its versions is very complicated: it is marked by fluidity both structurally and in content.[21] Here, I take my point of departure in the text that very probably reflects the earliest attainable stage of the story, at least in Greek—namely, Gs. Structurally Gs differs from the other main variants or recensions at two points: it lacks two miracle episodes, and it has a different sequence of some chapters.[22]

Gs has a simple and clearly set out structure. It can be outlined like this:

---

in the Infancy Gospel of Thomas (London: Bloomsbury T&T Clark, 2018), 14–18; Burke, *De Infantia Iesu*, 268–84; Sharon Betsworth, *Children in Early Christian Narratives* (London: Bloomsbury T&T Clark, 2015), 148–50. See Graham Anderson, *Fairytale in the Ancient World* (London: Routledge, 2000), for a survey of fairytale traditions.

19. In comparison, the Protevangelium of James allots much more space to descriptions of the ancestry and the youth and early adulthood of Mary than of her childhood.

20. Gs and Gb, see Burke, *De Infantia Iesu*, 303, 455.

21. Certain main forms are nonetheless visible. The manuscripts reflect four such forms (see Burke, "Infancy Gospel of Thomas"; Aasgaard, *Childhood of Jesus*, 14–16):

1. A short form, containing fifteen units (Gs 2–15, 17). This is found in most of the versions.
2. An intermediate form, with two units added (Gs 1 and 16). This is found in one Greek manuscript (H, Codex Sabaiticus 259).
3. A long form with two additional units placed before the final episode, nineteen units in all. This form is found in most Greek manuscripts.
4. A combined form, namely, together with other infancy stories.

Very likely the short form is the oldest, with various kinds of material being added over time, though some occasionally also being taken away, and all of this taking place in a long and complex process. For a survey of the structure and composition of the infancy gospel in recent translations and editions, see the synopsis in Geert van Oyen, "Rereading the Rewriting of the Biblical Traditions in the *Infancy Gospel of Thomas (Paidika)*," in *Infancy Gospels: Stories and Identities*, ed. C. Clivaz et al., WUNT 281 (Tübingen: Mohr Siebeck, 2011), 504–5.

22. The naming of the full and short titles are mine, as is the translation of the Gs text; see Aasgaard, *Childhood of Jesus*, 245–47 and 219–42 (appendices 1 and 2). Gs has the same structure as most of the versions (with Gs 1 and 16 added). Ga and Gd differ from Gs in that they have Gs 16 placed after Gs 9 as well as two additional episodes after Gs 15 and Gs 17: "Raising of a Dead Baby" (01) and "Raising of a Dead Laborer" (02); see Aasgaard, *Childhood of Jesus*, 241–42 and 243–44 (appendix 3). Gb is shorter than the others (Gs 11 and 13–17 are missing).

The Structure of Gs Infancy Gospel of Thomas

Gs	Full title	Short Title
1 Heading/Prologue		
2–3 Three Miracles		
2.1	Cleaning of Pools	Pools
2.2–5	Vivification of Sparrows	Sparrows
3.1–3	Curse on Annas's Son	Annas's Son
4–5 A Miracle and the Responses to It		
4.1–2	Curse on Careless Boy	Careless Boy
5.1–3	Joseph Rebukes Jesus	Joseph's Rebuke
6–8 First Teacher Discourse		
6.1–7	Dialogue	1 Teacher (dial.)
6.8–10	Alpha Lesson	1 Teacher (alpha)
7.1–4	Lament	1 Teacher (lam.)
8.1–2	Exclamation	1 Teacher (exclam.)
9 A Miracle and the Responses to It		
9.1	Raising of Zeno	Zeno
9.2–4	Parents' Dialogue with Jesus	Zeno
10–12 Three Miracles		
10.1–2	Carrying Water in Cloak	Water in Cloak
11.1–2	Miraculously Great Harvest	Harvest
12.1–2	Miraculous Repair of Bed	Bed
13–14 Second and Third Teacher Discourses		
13.1–3	Second Teacher	2 Teacher
14.1–4	Third Teacher	3 Teacher
15–16 Two Miracles		
15.1–2	Healing of James's Snakebite	Snakebite
16.1–3	Healing of Injured Foot	Injured Foot
17 Final Discourse (Epilogue)		
17.1–5	Jesus in the Temple	Jesus in Temple

In what follows as a summary of the content of the Infancy Gospel of Thomas, the titles mentioned in the table above will be employed.

The prologue (1) attributes the infancy gospel to "the Israelite" Thomas and functions as a solemn opening, giving it an air of authenticity and authority by linking it up with a well-known figure. It situates the story in the geographical context of Nazareth; the prologue, however, is only loosely integrated into the narrative. Throughout the story there are no explicit references to Thomas.

In the story itself, the narrator emerges as omniscient (he knows what Jesus and others feel and think) and omnipresent (as having direct access to all the events). The narrator does not take part in the story but tells it from outside of the events taking place. Nevertheless, what is told is presented as reliable and as reflecting Jesus's own point of view.

After the introduction, the main body follows, with its alternation of miracles and discourses. The first triplet of miracles, "Pools," "Sparrows," and "Annas's Son" (2–3), is performed by Jesus at the age of five. On a Sabbath, Jesus is playing at the ford of a stream, making pools. He miraculously purifies the polluted water in the pools and then forms twelve sparrows out of clay, which he—to the marvel of a Pharisee—makes come alive. The son of the high priest Annas observes the events, destroys the pools with a twig, and accuses Jesus of breaking the Sabbath. The result is that Jesus curses him so that he withers away, and most probably dies.

The three miracles are closely knit together, in an A–B–A structure: Annas's son acts in relation to Jesus's first miracle, "Pools," and without explicit reference to the second, "Sparrows." The insertion of this miracle enhances the total effect of the account, both by heightening the impression of Jesus's miraculous power and by juxtaposing two different responses—namely, that of the marveling Pharisee and that of the averse son of Annas. Climax and conclusion to the events finally occur in the third miracle: the death of Annas's son.

After this follow "Careless Boy" (4) and "Joseph's Rebuke" (5), which have central features in common with "Annas's Son." When Jesus is on his way from the ford, another boy runs by and bumps into him, and he too is cursed and dies. Whereas this episode also involves a boy who dies, it differs from the preceding by developing the reaction of those witnessing it. As for motif, it is linked up with "Annas's Son," but it takes the issue of audience response much further. There is a threefold response: first from "the people," then from the boy's parents who accuse Jesus, and finally from Joseph. The last response is the longest by far, thus indicating a narrative *tricolon crescens*.

Now "First Teacher Discourse" (or "1 Teacher," 6–8) commences, with Zacchaeus being introduced. He stands listening to Jesus's words and is inspired to impart even more wisdom to the boy. The result is near fatal—not for Jesus, but for the teacher imagining that he was able to teach the pupil something he did not already know. Zacchaeus ends up by professing his uttermost despair and shame: he must "die, or have to flee from this village" (7.3). He also proclaims that the boy must be something great, "whether a god, an angel, or whatever else" (7.4).

After this confession, there is a turning point in the story. Jesus first assures that now the "unfruitful [will] bear fruit, the blind see, and the foolish in heart become wise" (8.1). Interestingly, this saying appears to correspond, even in sequence, to the earlier instances of cursing: the withered Annas's son, the blinded accusers (5.5, probably the parents of the careless boy), and stupid Zacchaeus (7.3–4)—all will be restored, as they, respectively, bear fruit, see, and become wise. Read this way, the saying serves as an implicit analepsis that ties the first half of the story together. Jesus then breaks out in praise: "I have come from above in order to rescue those below and call them to what is above, just as the one who sent me to you ordered me" (8.1).

As a result, the cursed are saved, and Jesus wins the respect of all: "No-one dared to make him angry after that" (8.2). Thus, the untimely deaths are made good again, and they seem to have had their effect as warnings toward unbelieving spectators. With this climax, tensions created earlier in the plot are solved and balance reestablished. Jesus's first day at school is also over, without any hints of further visits. The matter seems to be held in suspension, however: the unsuccessful event can indicate that new attempts will be necessary.

The next episode, "Zeno" (9), is more loosely tied to the preceding: it happens "many days later." The tension level is now considerably lower. Again, a miracle takes place, and again a dead boy is involved, in a way similar to "Careless Boy" (4). This time it is not Jesus who causes the death: Zeno himself falls from a roof while at play. Nevertheless, the boy's parents accuse Jesus: "You pushed our child down." No flashback to Jesus's previous "murders" is given, but clearly they are implied as the reason for their accusation. Jesus, however, acquits himself by waking Zeno from the dead and having him confirm his innocence. After this Jesus commands Zeno to "sleep," so that he dies again. Nonetheless, his parents praise God and worship Jesus (9.3).

After this, the next stage of Jesus's childhood is introduced. He has become seven years old and performs a string of three miracles (10–12: "Water in Cloak," "Harvest," "Bed"). The first two miracles are briefly narrated, whereas the third is more elaborate and functions as a climax within the unit. The miracles are thematically related; they all deal with domestic activities (water fetching, sowing/harvesting, handiwork), places (house/hometown, field, workshop), and figures (mother and father). They are also linked together by the similar reactions of Mary (10.2) and Joseph (12.2): both kiss Jesus and pray that God bless the child. Thus, although these miracles are not as integrated as the first group of three (2–3), they are nevertheless strongly interconnected.

By the time of this last miracle, Jesus has become eight years old, and, seeing the boy's wisdom, Joseph thinks it time to take him to school again, three years after the first attempt, so that he shall not "be unacquainted with letters" (13.1). The return to this issue serves to create narrative cohesion in the infancy gospel as a whole and contributes to the push in its plot. A brief reference back to the first teacher discourse—the boy is handed over to "another" master—also establishes a link to the first episode and raises expectation as to what will now happen. At the same time, the introduction to "2 Teacher" (13) gives the narrative a fresh start, as no indication is given of Joseph having realized from Jesus's first visit to school that he already knew the letters and would have no need of education. Although the audience of the story knows better, the characters in the story—Joseph in particular—do not appear to have learned anything from the previous incident.

The second teacher discourse ("2 Teacher") is briefly narrated and clearly functions as a passageway to the climax of the third teacher discourse ("3 Teacher"). But it also serves to heighten the tension in this part of the story in two ways. First, by its fatal result: the second teacher is not only shamed like the first teacher, but he is even cursed to death after having hit Jesus (13.2). Second, it heightens the tension by its dramatic break with what was stated at the end of 1 Teacher, that "no-one dared to make him angry after that" (8.2). What the narrator has "promised" in fact turns out not to hold good: Jesus is nevertheless made angry and is now confined to the house in order to avert the death of others who might instigate him.

After some days of confinement—a modest punishment for the deed!—the third teacher offers to take Jesus to school. He is a wise man who immediately acknowledges Jesus's superiority, and instead of doing the teaching lets Jesus teach him and the bystanders. As a result of his truthful witness, the previous teacher too is "saved," which probably means that he is brought back to life (14.4). With "3 Teacher," a new climax is reached, and tensions are resolved again. The last teacher has proven his competence, the former has been revived, and—most importantly—a main point in 1–3 Teacher is stated, namely, Jesus's superior "grace and wisdom" (14.3).

Then, two somewhat less related miracles follow (15–16; "Snakebite," "Injured Foot"). Still, there is a certain narrative coherence and development even here: both episodes deal with work activities (wood fetching and wood splitting) and with young men being healed, namely, Jesus's brother James and "a young man." There is also a rise in drama; whereas James is at the verge of dying when rescued, the young man is already dead after having cut his foot. And whereas no audience reaction is reported in the first episode, this is central in the second and even presages the adult Jesus of the canonical Gospels—the crowd exclaims that he will go on saving "all the days of his life" (16.3).

Thus, the final miracle also leads up to the last episode (17; "Jesus in Temple"), which is the story's most explicit and elaborate narrative link to the canonical tradition. Clearly, it is meant to lend authority to the infancy gospel as a whole; it does not compete with the more established Gospels but shows them due respect by making the story from Luke 2 its ending. However, "Jesus in Temple" is not only an appendix but is also slightly reworked to serve as a rounding off, highlighting some of the features characteristic of the boy Jesus according to the infancy gospel.

In earlier research, this infancy gospel has generally been viewed as primarily a collection of loosely related episodes about Jesus as a child. A closer analysis, however, shows that the story—at least in its main variants—has an ordered structure and a coherent story line, with narrative climaxes and instances of analepses and anticipations.[23] There is also a fairly regular alternation of form-critical types of episodes (miracles and discourses) and subtypes (different miracle categories), which lends variation to the story, but also secures unity. In addition, some episodes are intertwined ("Pools," "Sparrows," and "Annas's Son") in ways that provide keys for interpretation, serving to emphasize Jesus's miraculous power and the differing reactions to him. Yet related episodes are also split and postponed so as to maintain narrative tension (e.g., "1–3 Teacher"). Finally, the main characters add to the cohesion: they are limited in number and appear repeatedly throughout the story. At the same time, the cast is broad enough to keep up interest in the story. Thus, the Infancy Gospel of Thomas in structure, story line, and plot turns out to have far more narrative quality than has previously been assumed.

3. INTERPRETIVE ISSUES
3.1 General

The Infancy Gospel of Thomas does not contain anything about Jesus that can add to what may already be ascertained or assumed from the Gospels of the New Testament. Its merits lie elsewhere, and within several fields of research the story—given its special topic and character—is of considerable value. First, it is important for the post-New Testament views it reflects of Jesus, theologically (later Christology) and socially (as a person, child, boy, and family member). The story is also interesting for its depiction of social and cultural milieus, such as the glimpses it seems to give of ancient everyday life, whether work or play. Furthermore, it is important for the ideas that it reflects about social relations and roles in the contexts it was transmitted, particularly about children, but also about family mentalities and social values. In addition, the Gospel's focus on Jesus's childhood evokes questions about its audience: Who would be interested in a story like this? The story is also of great interest tradition-historically in what can be learned from its development through the centuries; this has transfer value for similar ancient sources. Unlike much other material from late antiquity, the story has enjoyed a varied and unbroken history of reception from the second century until the present. And finally, this infancy gospel is of much value for how it makes use of biblical texts. Below, I present some main discussion

---

23. See Aasgaard, *Childhood of Jesus*, 35–52 (esp. 35–38 and 52).

topics within recent scholarship as well as some that have received less attention but that will benefit from closer scrutiny.

3.2 Theology and Views of Jesus

Theology has been a main focus in research on the Infancy Gospel of Thomas. The story has traditionally been considered to be weak on theology and even been slighted for lacking it.[24] A comparison with the fairly contemporary Protevangelium of James can illustrate this. Whereas the virginity of Mary is of crucial importance there, it is in the Infancy Gospel of Thomas of no importance, and not even noted. More recent research has, however, demonstrated that this infancy gospel has more theological substance than previously conceded. Despite its relatively unassuming narrative form, it contains distinct ideas about creation theology, ethics, epistemology, and hermeneutics.[25] Its main theological focus, however, is clearly on Christology. In earlier research, the depiction of Jesus in the Gospel has been variously assessed; it has particularly been associated with gnostic, docetic, and Ebionite thinking, and for such reasons also occasionally labeled heretical.[26] These views have mainly been based on the seemingly deviant elements in the story's portrait of Jesus: his "negative" cursing miracles and his anger and vindictiveness toward others.

Recent research has taken a markedly different direction in this. Most scholars have rejected previous views and rather see in the story a more "mainstream" Christology, maintaining that its portrait has much more in common with perceptions of Jesus in the canonical Gospels, in which he also occasionally pronounces curses and woes. Based on research on some of the Greek manuscripts, the present scholarly consensus seems to be that there is little deviance in the story's depiction of Jesus. More research is still needed, however. It may be that other manuscripts, for example in languages other than Greek, display types of Christology that differ more expressly from this.

To many modern readers, scholars as well as non-scholars, the strangeness, or even the offensiveness, of Jesus in the infancy gospel has been difficult to come to terms with. In early twentieth-century history-of-religions research on the infancy gospel, this was explained through exchange with Eastern religion, in particular similarities with Buddha as a child.[27] The offensive Jesus has also been accounted for by interpreting the infancy gospel as an anti-Christian work, similar to the Jewish *Toledot Yeshu* ("The Life Story of Jesus").[28] Some recent research has followed up this history-of-religions approach by pointing to similarities between the infancy gospel and popular perceptions of the Greco-Roman gods, with the gods often avenging human hubris far beyond the gravity of the actual transgression.[29] In this interpretation, some of the burlesque features in the infancy

---

24. For a brief survey of negative assessments, see Ursula Ulrike Kaiser, "Die sogenannte 'Kindheitserzählung des Thomas': Überlegungen zur Darstellung Jesu als Kind, deren Intention und Rezeption," in Clivaz, *Infancy Gospels*, 461–63.

25. Aasgaard, *Childhood of Jesus*, 149–65.

26. See Cousland, *Holy Terror*, 75–103, for a survey and references; also Andries Van Aarde, "The Ebionite Perspective in the *Infancy Gospel of Thomas*," in *The Apocryphal Gospels within the Context of Early Christian Theology*, ed. Jens Schröter (Leuven: Peeters, 2013), 611–26.

27. See Aasgaard, *Childhood of Jesus*, 87–88.

28. Peter Schäfer, Michael Meerson, and Yaacov Deutsch, eds., *Toledot Yeshu ("The Life Story of Jesus") Revisited*, TSAJ 143 (Tübingen: Mohr Siebeck, 2011); Philip Alexander, "Jesus and His Mother in the Jewish Anti-Gospel (the *Toledot Yeshu*)," in Clivaz, *Infancy Gospels*, 588–616; Frédéric Amsler, "Les *Paidika Iesou*, un nouveau témoin de la rencontre entre judaïsme et christianisme à Antioche au IVᵉ siècle?," in Clivaz, *Infancy Gospels*, 433–58; Kristi Upson-Saia, "Holy Child or Holy Terror? Understanding Jesus's Anger in the *Infancy Gospel of Thomas*," *Church History* 82.1 (2013): 1–39. See ch. 10 on the Toledot Yeshu in the present volume.

29. Cousland, *Holy Terror*, 33–47.

gospel are regarded to mirror a humor similar to that found in various Greco-Roman descriptions of the gods.[30]

3.3 Social and Cultural Setting

What may have been the social and cultural context of the Infancy Gospel of Thomas? In what kind of milieus can it have originated and been transmitted? Despite the importance of such questions, the matter has until recently received limited attention. This is the more striking, considering the central place that discussions about the social and cultural settings of the canonical Gospels have had among scholars over the last decades. One reason for this neglect is obviously that other concerns have been more pressing, especially the need for text-critical editions that could serve as a sound basis for research on the material. Another reason may be the relative brevity of the infancy gospel and that it has seemed to contain few elements that could link it up with specific social and cultural milieus. Nevertheless, some early scholars did touch on such matters, noting its popular nature and realistic portrayal of everyday life.[31] And during the last decade, a number of scholars have followed up on this, and have—sometimes from the perspectives of social history and cultural anthropology—developed and argued similar points in much more detail.[32]

In one version of this view, the Infancy Gospel of Thomas (in the Gs variant) is seen to be socially and culturally reflecting an early Christian "middle class" setting, probably situated in an eastern Mediterranean rural village milieu.[33] Interpreted in this way, this Gospel can serve as more of a source to other layers and segments of society than many, or maybe most, other writings from the ancient world. It may even be representative of most people in the ancient world, who lived in rural areas, and not of the very small group of urban elites. Recent scholarly interest in popular and non-elite early Christianity, sometimes termed "the second church," has also given support to this kind of approach.[34] So far, few scholars have developed and discussed this in the case of the Infancy Gospel of Thomas.

3.4 Audience and Aim

Who would be interested in a story such as the Infancy Gospel of Thomas? And for what reasons? These are issues that have been much more debated in recent research than its social and cultural settings. Two main, and partly opposing, views can be found, each of them related to, but not necessarily dependent on, different interpretations of the Jesus-figure in this Gospel. Common for both views is that they focus on the function of Jesus's "human" side, how he is depicted as a human being.

---

30. Cousland, *Holy Terror*, 43–45; also Aasgaard, *Childhood of Jesus*, 140–48.

31. See, e.g., van Oyen, "Rereading the Rewriting," 495–97, for references to this.

32. In particular, Aasgaard, *Childhood of Jesus*; Betsworth, *Children in Early Christian Narratives*; Cousland, *Holy Terror*, 105–16 (on popular Christianity); also Stevan Davies, *The Infancy Gospels of Jesus: Apocryphal Tales from the Childhoods of Mary and Jesus—Annotated and Explained* (Woodstock: Skylight Paths, 2009), xxvi–xxviii.

33. This view is argued in detail in Aasgaard, *Childhood of Jesus*, chs. 4, 5, and 11. I am fully aware of the risks of mirror reading, but I maintain that such an approach is tenable; it has also been a continual prerequisite within modern New Testament research.

34. See, e.g., Ramsay MacMullen, *The Second Church: Popular Christianity A.D. 200–400* (Atlanta: SBL, 2009), and many of the chapters in Virginia Burrus, ed., *Late Ancient Christianity*, A People's History of Christianity 2 (Minneapolis: Fortress, 2005), 95–116; Stevan Davies, *The Revolt of the Widows: The Social World of the Apocryphal Acts* (Carbondale: Southern Illinois University Press, 1980; repr., Dublin: Bardic, 2012); also Reidar Aasgaard, "The *Protevangelium of James* and the *Infancy Gospel of Thomas*: Orthodoxy from Above or Heterodoxy from Below?," in *The Other Side: Apocryphal Perspectives on Ancient Christian "Orthodoxies,"* ed. T. Nicklas et al. (Göttingen: Vandenhoeck & Ruprecht, 2017), 75–97.

In one view, the depiction of Jesus as a child is seen as representing a common *topos* in ancient biography, that of a *puer senex*, a child as a miniature adult without the characteristics associated with a child. Within this model, famous political and religious figures (e.g., emperors and so-called "holy men") are portrayed as being endowed with the wisdom of an adult already from their earliest childhood, thus foreshadowing their future greatness. According to supporters of this view, the depiction of Jesus in the infancy gospel is fundamentally defined and shaped by this *topos*.[35]

In the other view, which is less traditional, Jesus is not considered a *puer senex* but reflects children as they were commonly experienced by adults in everyday life, and he is to a considerable extent portrayed as a real child.[36] This is argued from close readings of the text; in it, Jesus is depicted as playing with other children, helping his parents, going to school, being chastised, responding emotionally to others, and maturing as he grows older.[37] The description also very much agrees with depictions of children in other ancient sources.[38] The only feature that makes Jesus differ from other children is his speeches (and his miracles, but here he also differs from ordinary adults). In one formulation of this view, Jesus is—pointedly stated but in agreement with New Testament tradition—described as both divine and childish, both true God and a true child.[39]

In the *puer senex* view, the audience of the infancy gospel—usually assumed to be adult readers—would consciously or unconsciously recognize the *topos* and be edified in their understanding of Jesus as an ideal in maturity and wisdom already in his childhood. In the other view, the depiction of Jesus as a child is more closely related to the question about audience. Some supporters of this approach argue in favor of a different target group for the story, a group that could easily and meaningfully relate to it: children in early Christianity.[40] In this interpretation, the story is parallel to other material that formed part of children's "culture" in antiquity, such as fables, riddles, and fairytales.[41] Whereas adherents of a *puer*

35. See Burke, *De Infantia Iesu*, 247–89; Stephen J. Davis, *Christ Child: Cultural Memories of a Young Jesus* (New Haven: Yale University Press, 2014), 7–14; also Christopher A. Frilingos, *Jesus, Mary, and Joseph: Family Trouble in the Infancy Gospels* (Philadelphia: University of Pennsylvania Press, 2017).

36. See Aasgaard, *Childhood of Jesus*, 88–102; Cousland, *Holy Terror*, 49–74; Betsworth, *Children in Early Christian Narratives*, 153–55; Kaiser, "Die sogenannte 'Kindheitserzählung des Thomas,'" 468–81; Davies, *Infancy Gospels of Jesus*.

37. E.g., Cousland, *Holy Terror*; Reidar Aasgaard, "From Boy to Man in Antiquity: Jesus in the Apocryphal *Infancy Gospel of Thomas*," *THYMOS: Journal of Boyhood Studies* 3 (2009): 3–20; Ursula Ulrike Kaiser, "Jesus als Kind: Neuere Forschungen zur Jesusüberlieferung in den apokryphen 'Kindheitsevangelien,'" in *Jesus in apokryphen Evangelienüberlieferungen: Beiträge zu außerkanonischen Jesusüberlieferungen aus verschiedenen Sprach- und Kulturtraditionen*, ed. Jörg Frey and Jens Schröter, WUNT 254 (Tübingen: Mohr Siebeck, 2010), 264–69.

38. For introductions to research on children and childhood in antiquity, see Sharon Betsworth and Julie Faith Parker, eds., *T&T Handbook of Children in the Bible and the Biblical World* (London: T&T Clark, 2019), with chapters on research history (Reidar Aasgaard), apocryphal Acts (Anna Rebecca Solevåg), and infancy gospels (Tony Burke). See also Cornelia B. Horn and John W. Martens, *"Let the Little Children Come to Me": Childhood and Children in Early Christianity* (Washington, DC: Catholic University of America Press, 2009); Christian Laes, *Children in the Roman Empire: Outsiders Within* (Cambridge: Cambridge University Press, 2011); Ville Vuolanto, Reidar Aasgaard, and Oana Maria Cojocaru, "Children in the Ancient World and the Early Middle Ages: A Bibliography (eighth century BC–eighth century AD)," 9th edition, www.hf.uio.no/ifikk/forskning/prosjekter/barndom/dokumenter/bibliography.pdf.

39. Aasgaard, *Childhood of Jesus*, 152–57; Betsworth, *Children in Early Christian Narratives*, 155–56; Davies, *Infancy Gospels of Jesus*, 116–21.

40. Aasgaard, *Childhood of Jesus*, 192–213; Isolde Kurzmann-Penz, *Zur literarischen Fiktion von Kindheit: Überlegungen zu den apokryphen Kindheitsevangelien Jesu im Rahmen der antiken Biographie* (Stuttgart: Franz Steiner, 2018), 78–81; see also Kaiser, "Jesus als Kind," 264–69, for some reflections on this.

41. Reidar Aasgaard, "Uncovering Children's Culture in Late Antiquity: The Testimony of the *Infancy Gospel of Thomas*," in *Children in Late Ancient Christianity*, ed. C. B. Horn and R. R. Phenix (Tübingen: Mohr

senex view argue that little can be retrieved of children's world beyond the (supposedly) generally negative adult perceptions of them, scholars of the other view take their point of departure in recent childhood studies, which make use of a broad variety of historical material and also ascribe to adults in the ancient world considerable ability of insight into children's lives and needs.[42] In this interpretation, the Infancy Gospel of Thomas can be viewed as an entertaining, and even edifying, story for children—but also for many adults.[43] Speaking of the story as some kind of a "children's book," however, would of course be anachronistic.[44] From its inception and in the following centuries the Infancy Gospel of Thomas is—parallel to its written forms—likely to have had its own life as a widely transmitted oral tale.

3.5 History of Transmission

The transmission history of the infancy gospel is both very complex and extremely fascinating, and calls for much more research. Two areas of study, which are fairly distinct but still interrelated, seem to stand out: the relation between oral and written transmission of the story, and the development of the material into larger narrative cycles. Within both areas, questions about how the material has been received, transformed, and adapted to new contexts are of great interest. Like many other early Christian apocryphal works, the infancy gospel material was fluid in both its content and organization, far more fluid than was the case with the canonical Gospels.[45]

As indicated above, it is a matter of discussion whether there was an original core to the story, and if so what it was, and whether the material has its origin in oral storytelling or was a literary work from the outset. In the preserved texts, at least the Greek variants, features from both forms of transmission are present, and it is very likely that this has been an ongoing and parallel interchange between the two, in varying combinations of oral retelling, scribal copying, and editorial reworking.[46] Some episodes about Jesus's childhood are also less established in the written transmission, and seem—in various disguises—to float in and out of it. In addition, the story was, in written and probably also oral form,

---

Siebeck, 2009), 1–27; Cornelia B. Horn, "Children's Play as Social Ritual," in Burrus, *Late Ancient Christianity*, 95–116; Anderson, *Fairytale in the Ancient World*.

42. See Laurel W. Koepf Taylor, "Accessing Childhoods: Interdisciplinary Tools at the Intersection of Biblical Studies and Childhood Studies," in Betsworth and Parker, *Children in the Bible and the Biblical World*, 39–63; John W. Martens, "Methodology: Who Is a Child and Where Do We Find Children in the Greco-Roman World," in Betsworth and Parker, *Children in the Bible and the Biblical World*, 223–43; Reidar Aasgaard, "How Close Can We Get to Ancient Childhood? Methodological Achievements and New Advances," in *Children and Everyday Life in the Roman and Late Antique World*, ed. Christian Laes and Ville Vuolanto (London: Routledge, 2017), 321–34.

43. Aasgaard, *Childhood of Jesus*, 192–213 (ch. 12). Without adult (oral and written) transmission, it would clearly not have survived. As a story, the infancy gospel can be compared to modern "all-ages literature" (in Norwegian *allalder-litteratur*), which is intended to appeal not only to children but also to adults.

44. Aasgaard, *Childhood of Jesus*, 212–13. Some scholars have erroneously criticized and even rejected the "children's story" view as if the infancy gospel was a kind of book written for children.

45. On this kind of fluidity in apocryphal material, see Christine M. Thomas, *The Acts of Peter, Gospel Literature, and the Ancient Novel: Rewriting the Past* (Oxford: Oxford University Press, 2003), and in biographical works, see Tomas Hägg, *The Art of Biography in Antiquity* (Cambridge: Cambridge University Press, 2012), 99–147 (ch. 3, *Life of Aesop*) and 175–76 (Infancy Gospel of Thomas); also Betsworth, *Children in Early Christian Narratives*, 145 (esp. note 9). Kaiser, "Die sogenannte 'Kindheitserzählung des Thomas,'" 463–68, presents many interesting examples from the infancy Gospel.

46. Aasgaard, *Childhood of Jesus*, 14–34 (ch. 2). See also Kurzmann-Penz, *Zur literarischen Fiktion von Kindheit*, 77–78; Pamela Scheingorn, "Reshapings of the Childhood Miracles of Jesus," in *The Christ Child in Medieval Culture*, ed. M. Dzon and T. M. Kenney (Toronto: University of Toronto Press, 2012), 254–92, with examples from art, such as manuscript illuminations.

translated into various languages from early on and even retranslated at later points of time, for example in Latin. It has even left traces in the Qur'an (sura 3:49 and 5:110). Some research has been done, but the oral-written relationship clearly merits further study.

In the course of its written transmission, the infancy gospel has also gone through a number of transformations, and it has proven very difficult to come up with a stemma for the relationship between the various manuscripts, both in the early versions and in the Greek variants, or recensions, of the story.[47] In addition, the story has undergone special developments during its transmission in non-Greek languages. It has at times been loosely combined with other writings, such as in Latin with the Protevangelium of James in the Gospel of Pseudo-Matthew, as well as in the Arabic Gospel of the Infancy, but it also has been more radically transformed and incorporated into larger narrative cycles, such as the Syriac Life of Mary and the Ethiopic *Ta'amra 'Iyasus* (Miracles of Jesus). Tracing these forms of transmission is important, but even more interesting and probably more promising may be to study how the infancy gospel material is received in later historical periods and other language areas, as regards Christology, ideas about children and childhood, and adaptation to cultural context. Some interesting studies of the reception history of the material have been done on late antiquity,[48] Syriac and Arabic material,[49] Byzantium,[50] and the Latin Middle Ages.[51]

3.6 Other Topics of Discussion

Other important topics have also entered the discussion, such as the story's depiction of family dynamics,[52] social values,[53] gender,[54] and ideas about the formation of children.[55] More specialized issues have also been taken up and debated, such as the miracle episodes,[56] the passage in "1 Teacher" in which Jesus gives an explanation of the meaning of the alpha (6.8–10),[57] and the "Jesus in Temple" episode (17).[58]

In addition, terminological matters are in need of discussion, particularly the title of the story. In recent research, scholars partly use Infancy Gospel of Thomas and partly

---

47. For a stemma, see Burke, *De Infantia Iesu*, 220–22.

48. See Davis, *Christ Child*, 129–92 (Christian/Jewish/Muslim relations).

49. See Cornelia B. Horn and Robert R. Phenix, "Apocryphal Gospels in Syriac and Related Texts Offering Traditions about Jesus," in Frey and Schröter, *Jesus in apokryphen Evangelienüberlieferungen*, 527–55 (esp. 537–44); Cornelia B. Horn, "Apocryphal Gospels in Arabic, or Some Complications on the Road to Traditions about Jesus," in Frey and Schröter, *Jesus in apokryphen Evangelienüberlieferungen*, 583–609 (esp. 589–602).

50. See Marijana Vuković, *Survival and Success of an Apocryphal Childhood of Jesus: Reception of the Infancy Gospel of Thomas in the Middle Ages* (Berlin: de Gruyter, 2022).

51. See Mary Dzon, *The Quest for the Christ Child in the Later Middle Ages* (Philadelphia: University of Pennsylvania Press, 2017); Dzon and Kenney, *Christ Child in Medieval Culture*. For other language areas, see chapters in Frey and Schröter, *Jesus in apokryphen Evangelienüberlieferungen* (Peter Nagel, Coptic; Igor Dorfmann-Lazarev, Armenian; Tedros Abraha and Daniel Assefa, Ethiopic; Christfried Böttrich, Slavonic; Martin McNamara, Irish).

52. See Frilingos, *Jesus, Mary, and Joseph*.

53. See Aasgaard, *Childhood of Jesus*, 73–85.

54. See Betsworth, *Children in Early Christian Narratives*, 156–63; Aasgaard, "From Boy to Man in Antiquity"; Eric Stewart, "Sending a Boy to do a Man's Job: Hegemonic Masculinity and the 'Boy' Jesus in the Infancy Gospel of Thomas," *HTS Teologiese Studies/Theological Studies* 71.1 (2015), Art. #2817, http://dx.doi.org/10.4102/hts.v71i1.2817.

55. See Davis, *Christ Child*, esp. 92–108.

56. See Ruben Zimmermann et al., eds., *Kompendium der frühchristlichen Wundererzählungen, Band 1: Die Wunder Jesu* (Gütersloh: Gütersloher, 2013), 781–92, 827–68.

57. See Davis, *Christ Child*, 108–21; Aasgaard, *Childhood of Jesus*, 143–46; also Frilingos, *Jesus, Mary, and Joseph*, 69–74.

58. See J. R. C. Cousland, "Soundings in the Christology of the *Infancy Gospel of Thomas*: The Rewriting of Luke 2:41–52 in *Paidika* 17," *CBQ* 81.4 (2019): 657–78; van Oyen, "Rereading the Rewriting," 485–91.

Paidika. In early scholarship, the story was usually designated the Gospel of Thomas. With the Nag Hammadi discovery in 1945 of the Coptic Gospel of Thomas, it was called the Infancy Gospel of Thomas so as to distinguish it from this sayings Gospel.[59] Since this title is based on a late, non-original attribution to Thomas, several scholars instead prefer a title borrowed from some of the early Greek manuscripts, *Paidika tou Iēsou* ("Jesus's childhood deeds"), but in the short form *Paidika*.[60] Whereas Infancy Gospel of Thomas is historically misleading, *Paidika* is indefinite and cryptic in meaning, particularly to nonspecialists. In some cases, the Childhood of Jesus has also been used.[61] Even though the standard Greek and Syriac text-critical editions use the title Infancy Gospel of Thomas (abbreviated IGT), the issue of how to designate the story is still not settled.[62] The matter clearly deserves more discussion. Both research in the field and public interest in the story would profit from a general agreement on nomenclature.[63]

4. KEY PASSAGES FOR NEW TESTAMENT STUDIES AND THEIR SIGNIFICANCE

In earlier research, the Infancy Gospel of Thomas has usually been viewed as theologically slender and as offering few connections with the New Testament. On a closer look, however, the story has considerably more substance than previously assumed; this is clearly the case with its reception of the Bible, and the New Testament in particular.[64] Above, I have already touched on matters of genre and form-critical types: the infancy gospel's narrative is obviously akin to the canonical Gospels, and it shares with them main forms such as miracles, discourses, and Jesus-sayings, and with an equal variety. The influence from the New Testament, however, goes much further than this, and I shall deal with the most evident instances in the following.[65]

The most explicit, and very extensive, reference in the story is to the Gospel of Luke 2:41–52. The passage is reproduced in its entirety in "Jesus in Temple" (17), but with some reformulations, omissions, and expansions so as to highlight its own special concerns.[66] In this episode, the infancy gospel also borrows phrases and terms from other parts of Luke (1:42; 2:19; 11:27; "wisdom"; "glory"). The other explicit reference is to 1 Corinthians 13:1 and its "a noisy gong or a clanging cymbal," which occurs in Jesus's response to his teacher hitting him in the head (1 Teacher 6.8); with this, Jesus seems to be criticizing the teacher's hypocrisy and lack of insight.[67]

In addition to these explicit references, there are also several allusions to specific biblical texts, particularly expressions, phrases, and patterns of thought typical of the Gospel of John, such as "from where was this child born" (4.1; John 7:27–28); "to seek and find" (5.3;

---

59. This is, e.g., used by Burke, *De Infantia Iesu* (usually abbreviated IGT); Frilingos, *Jesus, Mary, and Joseph*; Aasgaard, *Childhood of Jesus*.

60. This is used by Davis, *Christ Child*, and Cousland, *Holy Terror* (except in the main title of his book); Kaiser, "Die sogenannte 'Kindheitserzählung des Thomas,'" 459–81.

61. Burke, www.nasscal.com/e-clavis-christian-apocrypha/infancy-gospel-of-thomas/; Aasgaard, *Childhood of Jesus* (book title).

62. Burke, *De infantia Jesu*; idem, *Syriac Tradition of the Infancy Gospel of Thomas*.

63. For reflections on this, see Kaiser, "Jesus als Kind," 253–57.

64. The infancy gospel also appears to build on a number of Hebrew Bible/Old Testament passages, in 2:1–3:3 on Gen 1–3, and in its miracle episodes on 1–2 Kgs (on Elijah and Elisha); see Aasgaard, *Childhood of Jesus*, 128–29.

65. See Aasgaard, *Childhood of Jesus*, 113–36 (ch. 8); van Oyen, "Rereading the Rewriting," 491–97, and 499–503 (which is a very helpful table on similarities between the Infancy Gospel of Thomas and biblical—and a few non-biblical—texts).

66. See Aasgaard, *Childhood of Jesus*, 115–18.

67. Aasgaard, *Childhood of Jesus*, 118–20.

John 7:34–36); "when you were born, I existed" (6.4b and 6.6; John 8:58; 17:5, 24); "I came into this world for judgment so that those who do not see may see, and those who do see may become blind" (8.1a; John 9:39); and "I have come from above to rescue those below" (8.1b; John 3:3). Allusions to the Synoptics are more limited, but Jesus's proclamation in 6.4 that "I am from outside of you, but I am also within you" may mirror Luke 17:21 (cf. also Gos. Thom. 3). Apart from 1 Corinthians 13:1, the infancy gospel also occasionally alludes to the letters of Paul—for example, "to bless and not to curse" (4.2; Rom 12:14; cf. Deut 11:26); "do not be worried" (6.3; 1 Cor 7:21); and "noble birth in the flesh" (6.4; Rom 15:27; 1 Cor 3:3).[68]

On the basis of explicit references and allusions to specific New Testament texts, it appears that the creator of the infancy gospel was particularly familiar with the Gospels of Luke and John, and to an extent also with Paul's letters. There may, however, also be a few references to other parts of the New Testament (e.g., at 7.3; see Rev 21:6), but these are more remote. The repeated use of Luke and John seems to mirror familiarity with various parts of them, or maybe even the whole, whereas the use of the letters of Paul is sparser and more haphazard. Whether the New Testament references in the infancy gospel reflect knowledge of these writings from reading or from hearing (orally) is unclear; it may be either, the only exception possibly being "Jesus in Temple" (17).[69]

There are also, however, other elements that mirror knowledge of the New Testament, and which seem to aim at evoking true-to-life scenes from the world of Jesus and his family. Among the most important are obviously the names of main figures such as Jesus, Mary, and Joseph. Interestingly, Mary has a more inferior role in the story than Joseph and a far more inferior role than in the Gospel of Luke. James, Jesus's brother, is also part of the story (15, "Snakebite"). It is not stated that James is his brother; knowledge of this is tacitly assumed. James also seems to be older than Jesus; in the episode, he appears to be in the lead.[70]

Two other biblical figures are also mentioned by name in the infancy gospel: Zacchaeus (6.1) and Annas (3.1). Zacchaeus is probably borrowed from Luke 19:1–10, but he has on the way undergone vocational rehabilitation from tax collector to teacher ("1 Teacher"). And the outcome of his encounter with Jesus is far less favorable than in Luke: he is shamed in front of all who are present. Annas, who may be the high priest mentioned in Luke-Acts and John (Luke 3:2; Acts 4:6; John 18:13, 24), is presented in a way much closer to biblical usage and to historical reality: he held this position in 6–15 CE, at the actual time of Jesus's childhood and youth. The historical fit is probably incidental, given the infancy gospel's general vagueness. It is more likely to represent another example of its use of Luke. In Luke, Annas appears immediately after the passage with Jesus in the temple. Equally interesting, however, is John's mention of Annas; there, Annas is the high priest interrogating Jesus in the passion narrative. If the name is primarily borrowed from John, it may be because Annas there functions as one of Jesus's main opponents. In any case, these names again appear to attest to the infancy gospel's familiarity with material from Luke and John.[71]

The infancy gospel also makes use of the ethnic term "Jew"/"Jews" and of words that signify occupations and social roles: "Pharisees," "scribes," and "high priest." Of special interest are "lawyer" (6.4, *nomikos*) and "teacher of the law" (6.5, *nomodidaskalos*). In the

---

68. Aasgaard, *Childhood of Jesus*, 120–22.
69. Aasgaard, *Childhood of Jesus*, 118, 122.
70. Aasgaard, *Childhood of Jesus*, 125–27.
71. Aasgaard, *Childhood of Jesus*, 125–27.

canonical Gospels these terms occur (almost) only in Luke, and they are very rare elsewhere, whether in the New Testament, the Septuagint, or early Christian and other ancient literature. Again, this indicates that the Infancy Gospel of Thomas is particularly familiar with this Gospel. Apart from the secondary prologue, which speaks of Bethlehem and Nazareth, the only location mentioned is Jerusalem. The scarcity of geographical names suggests that the creator of the story may have had very limited knowledge of the landscape of Palestine.[72]

In addition to this, the infancy gospel also makes use of various terms and concepts that are common in the New Testament: soteriological terms such as "rescue" (*rhyomai*), "save" (*sōzō*), "salvation" (*sōtēria*), "bless" (*eulogein*), "glory" (*doxa*), and "grace" (*charis*); and anthropological terms such as "soul" (*psychē*) and "flesh" (*sarx*). Epistemological terms and concepts are quite frequent: "know" (*ginōskō*), "ignorance" (*agnoia*), "light" (*phōs*), "understanding" (*epistēmē*), "wisdom" (*sophia*), "teaching" (*paideia*), and others. The Sabbath and Sabbath observance are also touched on (2.2–4). Christological terms, however, are very few: "lord" (*kyrios*; 1.1; 9.3) and "the name" (*to onoma*; 6.4). Again, some of the words above are more common in Luke than in the other canonical Gospels.[73]

There are also many instances in which the infancy gospel seems to imitate biblical style and phraseology: in cursings (3.2), various exclamations (5.3; 6.5, 6), and formulations such as "take him with salvation to your house" (7.4; 14.3; cf. Luke 19:9 et al., and Matt 9:6; Mark 2:11), and "Jesus . . . cried out in a loud voice (9.3; cf. Rev 19:17). Some passages appear to echo biblical accounts: the parable of the sower (11.1–2; cf. Mark 4:3–8 par.), Jesus's rejection in Nazareth (14.1–3; cf. Luke 4:16–30), and the cursing of the fig tree (3.3; cf. Matt 21:18–19 par.). Finally, the infancy gospel seems to reflect some biblical narrative patterns in a more general way, such as the number twelve (2.2), accusations against Jesus (2.3; 5.1; 9.2), the trial against him (6.4, 8; 13.2), Jesus being deserted (9.1), and the turning-of-tables motif ("1–3 Teacher").[74]

In its creative use of material from the New Testament, and from Luke and John in particular, the infancy gospel emerges as an interesting case among early Christian works. It also appears to contain little material that can be traced back to other early Christian or other ancient sources.[75] The reception of the New Testament in the Infancy Gospel of Thomas clearly deserves more study, particularly the usage in other Greek variants than Gs and in the various versions.

5. BIBLIOGRAPHY

Aasgaard, Reidar. *The Childhood of Jesus: Decoding the Apocryphal Infancy Gospel of Thomas*. Eugene, OR: Cascade, 2009.

———. "The *Protevangelium of James* and the *Infancy Gospel of Thomas*: Orthodoxy from Above or Heterodoxy from Below?" Pages 75–97 in *The Other Side: Apocryphal Perspectives on Ancient Christian "Orthodoxies."* Edited by T. Nicklas et al. Göttingen: Vandenhoeck & Ruprecht, 2017.

Burke, Tony. *De Infantia Iesu Evangelium Thomae, Graece*. CCSA 17. Turnhout: Brepols, 2010.

———. *The Syriac Tradition of the Infancy Gospel of Thomas: A Critical Edition and English Translation*. Piscataway, NJ: Gorgias, 2017.

Clivaz, Claire et al., eds. *Infancy Gospels: Stories and Identities*. WUNT 281. Tübingen: Mohr Siebeck, 2011.

Cousland, J. R. C. *Holy Terror: Jesus in the Infancy Gospel of Thomas*. London: Bloomsbury T&T Clark, 2018.

Davis, Stephen J. *Christ Child: Cultural Memories of a Young Jesus*. New Haven: Yale University Press, 2014.

---

72. Aasgaard, *Childhood of Jesus*, 125–27.
73. Aasgaard, *Childhood of Jesus*, 123–24.
74. Aasgaard, *Childhood of Jesus*, 124–25, 127–32.
75. But see van Oyen, "Rereading the Rewriting," 499–503, for some examples; also Aasgaard, *Childhood of Jesus*, 137–48 (ch. 9).

Dzon, Mary, and Theresa M. Kenney, eds. *The Christ Child in Medieval Culture.* Toronto: University of Toronto Press, 2012.

Frey, Jörg, and Jens Schröter, eds. *Jesus in apokryphen Evangelienüberlieferungen: Beiträge zu außerkanonischen Jesusüberlieferungen aus verschiedenen Sprach- und Kulturtraditionen.* WUNT 254. Tübingen: Mohr Siebeck, 2010.

Frilingos, Christopher A. *Jesus, Mary, and Joseph: Family Trouble in the Infancy Gospels.* Philadelphia: University of Pennsylvania Press, 2017.

Kurzmann-Penz, Isolde. *Zur literarischen Fiktion von Kindheit: Überlegungen zu den apokryphen Kindheitsevangelien Jesu im Rahmen der antiken Biographie.* Stuttgart: Franz Steiner, 2018.

Vukovíc, Marijana. *Survival and Success of an Apocryphal Childhood of Jesus: Reception of the Infancy Gospel of Thomas in the Middle Ages.* Berlin: de Gruyter, 2022.

CHAPTER 6

JEWISH-CHRISTIAN GOSPELS

PETRI LUOMANEN

1. INTRODUCTION
1.1 The Structure of the Essay

There are two difficult interpretive issues related to early Jewish-Christian Gospels: the reconstruction of the Gospels themselves, and the question of defining Jewish Christianity. Because none of the Jewish-Christian Gospels have survived, their contents have to be reconstructed from the fragments preserved in the writings of the church fathers. In this essay, I provide a concise historical overview of the reconstructions and present the New Two Gospel Hypothesis (N2GH; see sec. 1.2 below), which provides the framework for the Gospels treated in this essay. A description of *indicators of early Jewish Christianity* follows as a solution to the problem of definition (sec. 1.3). Further introductory questions, description of the contents, and passages relevant for New Testament studies are treated in the subsequent sections devoted to the Gospel of the Ebionites (sec. 2) and the Gospel of the Hebrews (sec. 3), the latter also including a reconstruction of the Nazarenes' anti-rabbinic collection. The final section (sec. 4) contains a description of the Jewish-Christian profiles of the Gospel of the Ebionites and the Gospel of the Hebrews. Unless otherwise indicated, translations of the fragments are mine.

1.2 Two or Three Early Jewish-Christian Gospels?

Throughout the twentieth century, the most common reconstruction in English and German scholarly literature assumed three Jewish-Christian Gospels: the Gospel of the Ebionites (Gos. Eb.), the Gospel of the Hebrews (Gos. Heb.), and the Gospel of the Nazarenes (Gos. Naz.).[1] In reality, only one of these titles, the Gospel of the Hebrews (or the Gospel according to the Hebrews),[2] appears in ancient sources; the others are simply names given to gospel traditions that were supposedly used by the Nazarenes and the Ebionites, two Jewish-Christian groups that patristic writers assumed to have existed and that they regarded as more or less "heretical." Scholars largely agree that the surviving remnants of the Gospel of the Ebionites appear in Epiphanius's *Panarion* (*Pan.* 30), but the problem is whether the other fragments are from one or two Gospels.

From the beginning of the twenty-first century, critical remarks have been advanced against the Three Gospel Hypothesis (= 3GH) because it was constructed on the basis of questionable presuppositions. Originally, the hypothesis, which was first presented by

---

1. See, Philipp Vielhauer and Georg Strecker, "Jewish-Christian Gospels," in NTApoc 1:134–78.
2. In the sources, the name is often the Gospel according to the Hebrews. For the sake of convenience, the present essay uses the shorter title.

Hans Waitz in the 1920s,[3] argued that passages with "gnostic" orientation (a term used by Waitz) cannot come from the same Gospel as traditions that resemble passages in the Synoptic Gospels, especially in the Gospel of Matthew. When the Gospel of Thomas was found at Nag Hammadi in 1945, the assumption was actually proven wrong, because the Gospel of Thomas includes both "gnostic" and Synoptic types of sayings, but this escaped the notice of the proponents of the hypothesis.[4]

The present survey is based on the hypothesis that there were only two distinctively Jewish-Christian Gospels, the Gospel of the Hebrews and the Gospel of the Ebionites. In addition, the New Two Gospel Hypothesis (= N2GH) assumes that Jerome received a collection of anti-rabbinic sayings from contemporary Nazarene Christians who had found them in a slightly modified Semitic (Western Aramaic or Syriac) translation of Matthew's Gospel.[5] In this regard, the N2GH differs from an earlier version of the Two Gospel Hypothesis (2GH) that simply assigned all the surviving fragments to two Gospels: the Gospel of the Ebionites and the Gospel of the Nazarenes/Hebrews.[6]

Andrew Gregory's critical edition in the Oxford Early Christian Gospel Texts series agrees with the N2GH by attributing the fragments to only two Gospels, the Gospel according to the Hebrews and the Gospel of the Ebionites.[7] Jörg Frey continues to support the 3GH in the German successor to the influential Hennecke-Schneemelcher collection (cf. note 1 above).[8] However, Frey is to be credited for abandoning the most vulnerable earlier arguments and for excluding the "Jewish" readings, the so-called *to Ioudaikon* variants, which were collected from the margins of some Gospel manuscripts and counted among the fragments in the earlier versions of the 3GH and the 2GH. The N2GH and Gregory's edition also exclude these. Because the reconstruction of the Gospel of the Hebrews is still debated, section 3 below also casts light on the arguments that support the reconstruction.

1.3 Jewish Christianity in Early Christian Sources

In ancient sources, Jews who had become Christ-followers without abandoning their ancestral beliefs and practices were regularly called "those of the Jews/Judeans who believed (in Jesus)" (see John 8:31; Origen, *Cels.* 2.1). The terms "Jewish Christianity" and "Jewish Christian" became standard formulations in English (scholarly) literature only from the late sixteenth century onward.[9]

---

3. Hans Waitz, "Die judenchristlichen Evangelien in der altkirchlichen Literatur," in *Neutestamentliche Apokryphen*, ed. Edgar Hennecke (Tübingen: J. C. B. Mohr, 1924).

4. For the history of reconstructions, see Petri Luomanen, *Recovering Jewish-Christian Sects and Gospels*, VCSup 110 (Leiden: Brill, 2012), 83–89. In the new situation, some introductions have preferred to provide only expositions of individual fragments in their literary and historical contexts. See, e.g., Craig A. Evans, "The Jewish Christian Gospel Tradition," in *Jewish Believers in Jesus: The Early Centuries*, ed. Oskar Skarsaune and Reidar Hvalvik (Peabody, MA: Hendrickson, 2007), 245–58. Thus, the "consensus view" of the 3GH has been effectively challenged from the beginning of the twenty-first century, contra Edwin Broadhead, *Jewish Ways of Following Jesus*, WUNT 266 (Tübingen: Mohr Siebeck, 2010), 257.

5. Luomanen, *Recovering*, summarizes the argumentation for the N2GH that was developed in a series of earlier articles.

6. E.g., Simon C. Mimouni, *Le judéo-christianisme ancien: Essais historiques* (Paris: Cerf, 1998), 209–11, 215–16.

7. Andrew Gregory, ed., *The Gospel according to the Hebrews and the Gospel of the Ebionites*, Oxford Early Christian Gospel Texts (Oxford: Oxford University Press, 2017).

8. Jörg Frey, "Die Fragmente judenchristlicher Evangelien," in *Antike christliche Apokryphen in deutscher Übersetzung I: Evangelien und Verwandtes*, ed. C. Markschies and J. Schröter (Tübingen: Mohr Siebeck, 2012).

9. For the history of the terminology, see Matti Myllykoski, "'Christian Jews' and 'Jewish Christians': The Jewish Origins of Christianity in English Literature from Elizabeth I to Toland's *Nazarenus*," in *The Rediscovery of Jewish Christianity: From Toland to Baur*, ed. F. S. Jones, HBS 5 (Atlanta: Society of Biblical Literature, 2012).

The concept of Jewish Christianity is often criticized as anachronistic.[10] Andrew Gregory has also raised the question of whether the surviving fragments themselves actually include features that would justify the attribute "Jewish Christian."[11] In the following, these problems are addressed by focusing on *indicators of Jewish Christianity*. The indicators approach is qualitative and practical; in each case under examination, the type of Jewish Christianity is to be determined only after a critical evaluation that brings together several indicators in order to summarize a Jewish-Christian profile of a text or a group. The outcome is that there is not just one type of ancient Jewish Christianity but several different ones, each of them resembling ancient and present forms of Judaism and Christianity to some degree. Despite its anachronistic character, the concept of Jewish Christianity provides a useful starting point for historical analysis because it directs attention to a phenomenon that falls in between Judaism and Christianity as they are known today.[12]

The study of the indicators of Jewish Christianity implies the following questions:

1. Are characteristically Jewish practices such as (Jewish) circumcision, the Sabbath, and purity laws observed?
2. Are characteristically Jewish ideas such as Yahweh as the only God, the temple as Yahweh's abode, or the Torah maintained?
3. What is the pedigree of the group/person? Jewish or not?
4. What is the role of Jesus in the worship and ideology of the community? Is Jesus considered as a Jewish prophet or is he more a divine being, worshiped as *kyrios* ("Lord"), an equal to God?
5. Is baptism in the name of Jesus (or the triune God) an entrance rite to the community?
6. To what extent are these or other issues important for inter- or intra-group relations? What roles do they play in defining the borders and identity of the group in question?

Undoubtedly, several additional indicators could also be listed, but the above examples form a core of questions that help form a picture of the Jewish-Christian profile of a group or a text. The approach is provided here primarily to inspire readers to make their own observations and judgments based on the fragments presented in this essay, in addition to the draft of the profiles sketched at the end of the essay.

2. THE GOSPEL OF THE EBIONITES
2.1 Date and Language of the Gospel of the Ebionites

Because the fragments that can reasonably be attributed to the Gospel of the Ebionites are available only in Epiphanius's *Panarion*, it is clear that the dating of *Panarion*,

---

10. For critical overviews, see Matt Jackson-McCabe, "What's in a Name? The Problem of 'Jewish Christianity,'" in *Jewish Christianity Reconsidered*, ed. Matt Jackson-McCabe (Minneapolis: Fortress, 2007), 1–38; Oskar Skarsaune, "Jewish Believers in Jesus in Antiquity: Problems of Definition, Method, and Sources," in Skarsaune and Hvalvik, *Jewish Believers*, 3–21; James Carleton Paget, "The Definition of the Terms Jewish Christian and Jewish Christianity in the History of Research," in Skarsaune and Hvalvik, *Jewish Believers*, 22–52.

11. Andrew Gregory, "Hindrance or Help: Does the Modern Category of 'Jewish-Christian Gospel' Distort Our Understanding of the Texts to which It Refers?," *JSNT* 28 (2006): 387–413. See also Gregory, *Gospel*, 21–23, 168, 260–61.

12. The approach is presented in detail in Luomanen, *Recovering*, 8–15. Annette Yoshiko Reed also sees heuristic value in the analytical use of the term "Jewish Christianity": Annette Yoshiko Reed, *Jewish Christianity and the History of Judaism*, TSAJ 171 (Tübingen: Mohr Siebeck, 2018), xxi–xxvii, 110–15.

ca. 376–378 CE,[13] also sets the final date before which the Gospel of the Ebionites must have been composed. However, at least two second-century authors seem to have been aware of the Gospel of the Ebionites even before Epiphanius: Irenaeus, who wrote his *Against Heresies* around 180 CE, and the author of an early source that was included in the Pseudo-Clementine *Recognitions* (in Ps.-Clem. *Rec.* 1.27–71; composed ca. 200 CE).[14] Irenaeus obviously thought that the Ebionites used only the canonical Gospel of Matthew (Irenaeus, *Haer.* 1.26.2), but he did not have any firsthand knowledge about them and therefore mixed up the Ebionites' Gospel of Matthew with the canonical one.[15] The Ebionites themselves seem to have called their Gospel something like the "Hebrew Gospel according to Matthew" (cf. Epiphanius, *Pan.* 30.13.2–3).

Because the Gospel of the Ebionites uses canonical Gospels, combining and harmonizing their readings, it must have been written after them. The most likely earliest date is the beginning of the second century, when harmonizing readings start to appear in gospel traditions.[16] Thus we may safely conclude that the Gospel of the Ebionites was written in the first half of the second century.

Although Epiphanius's Ebionites probably characterized their Gospel as a Hebrew Gospel of Matthew, scholars agree that it was not written in Hebrew or in any other Semitic language, but in Greek.[17] This is clear because the Gospel combines wordings from the Greek Gospels of Matthew and Luke, possibly also from Mark, and one of the fragments includes a verbal play that presumes the Greek translation of the Old Testament (LXX) and is understandable only in Greek: locusts (sg. *akris*) in John the Baptist's diet are replaced by wild honey (*enkris*).

Because the Gospel of the Ebionites uses material and phrases from all the Synoptic Gospels, it has sometimes been characterized as a Gospel harmony. This, however, is not a suitable label, because the main goal of the writing is not to combine the different canonical Gospels in order to form a more harmonious narrative. Rather, the Gospel of the Ebionites is best understood as a new composition that makes a clear Jewish-Christian statement, as a response to the canonical Gospels, by creatively combining their secondary oral and written traditions.[18]

2.2 Fragments from the Gospel of the Ebionites

In the following translations, Epiphanius's own introductory words and other comments appear in italics.

---

13. Aline Pourkier, *L'Hérésiologie chez Épiphane de Salamine*, Christianisme Antique 4 (Paris: Beauchesne, 1992), 47–51.

14. For the Pseudo-Clementine source, see F. Stanley Jones, *An Ancient Jewish-Christian Source on the History of Christianity: Pseudo-Clementine Recognitions 1.27–71*, SBLTT 37; Christian Apocrypha Series 2 (Atlanta: Scholars Press, 1995), 148–49.

15. I agree with Richard Bauckham that Irenaeus's information concerned the Ebionites' Gospel of Matthew, not the canonical Matthew. See Richard Bauckham, "The Origin of the Ebionites," in *The Image of the Judaeo-Christians in Ancient Jewish and Christian Literature*, ed. Peter J. Tomson and Doris Lambers-Petry, WUNT 158 (Tübingen: Mohr Siebeck, 2003), 164.

16. Tatian's *Diatessaron*, which combined all the canonical Gospels, was composed ca. 172–175 CE. It was most likely based on Justin Martyr's Greek harmony that did not include the Gospel of John. See William L. Petersen, *Tatian's Diatessaron: Its Creation, Dissemination, Significance and History in Scholarship*, VCSup 25 (Leiden: Brill, 1994), 426–28.

17. A. F. J. Klijn, *Jewish-Christian Gospel Tradition*, VCSup 17 (Leiden: Brill, 1992), 68; Jörg Frey, "Die Fragmente des Ebionäerevangeliums," in Markschies and Schröter, *Antike christliche Apokryphen*, 612. Gregory, *Gospel*, 183, 222.

18. For discussion, see Gregory, *Gospel*, 184–89.

1. The Beginning of the Gospel of the Ebionites

But the beginning of the Gospel that they have says:

In the time of Herod the king of Judea, John came baptizing with a baptism of repentance in the Jordan River. John was said to be from the family of Aaron the priest, a son of Zechariah and Elizabeth, and all went out to him. (Epiphanius, *Pan.* 30.13.6)[19]

2. John's Diet

And:

When John was baptizing, Pharisees went out to him and were baptized, and all of Jerusalem. John had a garment made of camel's hair and a leather belt around his waist. His food was, *it says,* wild honey, which tastes like manna, like a cake in olive oil, *so that they really would turn the word of truth into a lie by replacing locusts with a honey cake.* (Epiphanius, *Pan.* 30.13.4–5)

3. The Baptism of Jesus

After having said many things, it adds:

When the people had been baptized, Jesus also came and was baptized by John. When he came up from the water, the heavens opened, and he saw the Holy Spirit in the figure of a dove descending and entering into him. A voice from the heavens said: "You are my beloved son, in you I am well pleased." And again: "I have begotten you today." A great light immediately shone around the place. Having seen this, *it says,* John said to him: "Who are you, Lord?" And again a voice from the heavens said to him: "This is my beloved son, in whom I am well pleased." Then, *it says,* John said, falling down before him: "I beg you, Lord: Baptize me!" But he prevented him saying: "Let it be, because it is appropriate to fulfill everything this way." (Epiphanius, *Pan.* 30.13.7–8)

4. The Savior's True Brothers and Mother

They also deny that he is a man, supposedly because of the word that the Savior said when it was reported:

"See, your mother and your brothers are standing outside." He said: "Who are my mother and brothers?" He stretched his hand toward his disciples and said: "These are my brothers and my mother, and my sisters, these who do the will of my Father." (Epiphanius, *Pan.* 30.14.5)

5. Jesus Abolishes Sacrifices

As the writing called Gospel among them says,

"I came to put down the sacrifices. If you do not leave off sacrificing, the wrath will not leave off from you." (Epiphanius, *Pan.* 30.16.5)

6. Did Jesus Eat Passover?

They have themselves hidden the true sequence by altering what is said, as is evident to all from the words that are tied together. They have made the disciples to say:

"Where do you want us to prepare the eating of Passover for you?" *and made him to say:*

"I truly did not desire to eat meat with you this Passover."

---

19. Epiphanius also quotes the opening in *Pan.* 30.14.3 in a slightly different form. For a composite text of these two citations, see Gregory, *Gospel*, 208–9.

How their wickedness could remain undetected when the sequence cries out that the mu *and the* eta *are additions!*[20] *For instead of "I truly desired" they have imposed an additional* "not." *But he really said, "I truly desire to eat this Passover with you." But writing, in addition,* "meat," *they have led themselves astray, saying recklessly,* "I truly did not desire to eat meat with you this Passover." (Epiphanius, *Pan.* 30.22.4–5)

7. The Call of Disciples (Epilogue of the Gospel or an Introduction to the Ebionite Acts of the Apostles?)

In the Gospel that is called among them according to Matthew—although it is not whole or complete but corrupted and mutilated—and they call it Hebrew Gospel, it is said:

There was a man whose name was Jesus, about thirty-years old, and he chose us. He came to Capernaum, went into the house of Simon, also called Peter, opened his mouth and said: "When I walked by the Lake of Tiberias, I chose John and James, the sons of Zebedee, and Simon and Andrew and Thaddeus and Simon the Zealot, and Judas the Iscariot. And I called you, Matthew, when you were sitting at the customs house, and you started following me. I want you to be twelve apostles for testimony to Israel." (Epiphanius, *Pan.* 30.13.2–3)

2.3 Main Themes of the Gospel of the Ebionites

Because Epiphanius wanted to show how the Ebionites had "distorted" the canonical Gospel, even the limited selection he offers highlights themes that make the Gospel of the Ebionites distinctive.

First, Epiphanius complains that because the Ebionites did not accept the virgin birth they had deleted the infancy narrative in the beginning of the Gospel of Matthew, starting it with the baptism of John (*Pan.* 30.1.5; 30.14.3). According to Epiphanius, the Ebionites taught that Christ came into Jesus in the form of a dove at his baptism (see frag. 3 above)

Second, Epiphanius finds examples of the Ebionites' vegetarianism in their Gospel. They have changed John the Baptist's diet from locusts to honey cakes (*Pan.* 30.13.4–5; see frag. 2 above), and they have made Jesus say that he "truly did not desire to eat meat" with the disciples at Passover (*Pan.* 30.22.4–5; see frag. 6 above).

Third, fragment seven indicates that Jesus chose the twelve apostles for the testimony of Israel (*Pan.* 30.13.2–3). This accords with the mission instructions in chapter 10 of the Gospel of Matthew, which, however, closes its narrative with the universal mission command (Matt 28:19–20). Although we cannot be sure if the mission was also described in more universal terms in the Gospel of the Ebionites, the mission to Israel was clearly emphasized in it, which suits well the Gospel's Jewish-Christian profile.

Fourth, Jesus's critical statement on sacrificing (frag. 5) does not have any parallels in the canonical tradition, but similar criticism appears in Pseudo-Clementine *Recognitions* 1.27–71. As noted above, this is hardly coincidental; there seems to be a tradition-historical connection between the Gospel of the Ebionites and the source behind *Recognitions* 1.27–71.[21]

2.4 Key Passages for New Testament Studies in the Gospel of the Ebionites
2.4.1 Fragments 2, 5, and 6: On Diets and Sacrificing

Apart from being examples of asceticism, which is a widely attested phenomenon in early Christianity, the fragments relating to the Ebionites' vegetarianism and criticism of

---

20. The letters *mu* and *ēta* refer to the Greek word *mē*, which denotes negation.
21. See note 14 above; Bauckham, "Origin," 168.

sacrifices may cast light on some variant readings in the New Testament textual tradition concerning the institution of the Eucharist.

First, we know that there was a description of preparations for the Last Supper where Jesus says that he does not want to eat meat (frag. 6). Consequently, because the Gospel of the Ebionites seems to have been a narrative akin to the Synoptic Gospels, we can also surmise that there was an institution of the Eucharist in the immediately following verses. Because fragment five reveals that the Ebionites opposed sacrifices, it is unlikely that they would have granted sacrificial value to Jesus's blood. This assumption coheres with Epiphanius's remark a bit earlier in *Panarion* about the Ebionites' practice of celebrating Passover with unleavened bread and water (*Pan.* 30.16.1). All this leads to the hypothesis: if there was an institution of the Eucharist in the Gospel of the Ebionites, its wording could not have referred to Jesus's eucharistic cup of blood.

The other side of the story is that, in the Synoptic traditions about the institution of the Eucharist, there are variants in the manuscripts of the Gospel of Luke that have puzzled scholars. In Codex Bezae as well as in Old Latin and Old Syriac translations, the words of institution are shortened as follows:

> He said to them, "I have eagerly desired to eat this Passover with you before I suffer; for I tell you, I will not eat it until it is fulfilled in the kingdom of God." Then he took a cup, and after giving thanks he said, "Take this and divide it among yourselves; for I tell you that from now on I will not drink of the fruit of the vine until the kingdom of God comes." Then he took a loaf of bread, and when he had given thanks, he broke it and gave it to them, saying, "This is my body, which is given for you. [Do this in remembrance of me." And he did the same with the cup after supper, saying, "This cup that is poured out for you is the new covenant in my blood."] (Luke 22:15–20 NRSV, square brackets added)

The words in square brackets are missing in Codex Bezae (fifth century) and Old Latin and Old Syriac manuscripts. Thus, the text conveniently ends at the point that would have become problematic from an Ebionite point of view (for v. 15, see also frag. 6). Textual critics have disputed whether the shorter reading of Codex Bezae might represent an older tradition.[22] These observations do not help solve the problem, but they suggest that Ebionite theology may have influenced the canonical textual tradition. Notably, textual critics who have argued that the longer version is original have found it difficult to explain the genesis of the shorter version. Ebionite influence provides one possible reason. If the longer version is original, a later copyist or editor sympathetic to Ebionite ideas may have shortened the text. Interestingly, in the fragments of the Gospel of the Ebionites there is also another link to the same group of manuscripts that support the shorter reading in Luke's institution of the Eucharist, as becomes clear in the following.

2.4.2 Fragment 3: The Baptism of Jesus

In the description of Jesus's baptism (*Pan.* 30.13.7–8), the Gospel of the Ebionites describes how the Spirit descends *into* Jesus in the form of a dove. This accords with the wording of the Gospel of Mark as well as the wording of Codex Bezae in the Gospel of Luke. Mark's version is the oldest, but it is clear that the wording in the Gospel of the Ebionites is not coincidental—the result of a random pickup from Mark—because it

---

22. For discussion, see Luomanen, *Recovering*, 147–50.

accords with the beliefs of the Ebionites as they are reported by Irenaeus (*Haer.* 1.26.2) and Epiphanius (*Pan.* 30.3.4–6; 30.16.3–4).[23]

If Mark's description of Jesus's baptism expresses possessionist Christology—that is, Christ/ Spirit enters the man Jesus—as has been suggested,[24] then it is possible to see possessionist Christology as a rival to the tradition about Jesus's divine conception through the Virgin Mary. Matthew and Luke suppressed the Markan formulations that suggested possessionist Christology. The Ebionites took over the Synoptic narrative, making creative use of all three Synoptic Gospels and reedited their Gospel to accord again with their christological views.

The same tendency is again, as in the case of the Eucharist, also detectable in Codex Bezae (and Old Latin), which says that the Spirit descended *into* Jesus. Furthermore, the wording of the Gospel of the Ebionites also agrees with Codex Bezae and Old Latin manuscripts of the Gospel of Luke 3:22 by including Psalm 2:7 at the end of the words sounding from the heaven: "Today I have begotten you."[25] This highlights the idea that the divine element, the Spirit, started working in Jesus on the day of his baptism.

If the writers of the Gospel of the Ebionites worked consistently in their remodeling of the Synoptic narratives, we can also ask if there was, at the end of the Gospel, a similar description of the departure of the Spirit as in the Gospel of Peter. In the Gospel of Peter 19, the Lord cries: "My power, my power, you have forsaken me," and after that he was taken up. A story like this is surely possible, but it remains unprovable because we do not know how the narrative in the Gospel of the Ebionites ended.

3. THE GOSPEL OF THE HEBREWS
3.1 Date and Language of the Gospel of the Hebrews

Eusebius transmits information about two second-century authors who help set the date before which the Gospel of the Hebrews must have been written: Papias of Hierapolis (ca. 60–130 CE) and Hegesippus (ca. 110–180 CE).[26] According to Eusebius, Papias "presented a story about a woman who was accused of many sins in front of the Lord, which is in the Gospel according to the Hebrews" (*Hist. eccl.* 3.39.17, translation mine). Hegesippus, for his part, "presents some things from the Gospel according to the Hebrews, and also from the Syriac, and especially from the Hebrew language" (*Hist. eccl.* 4.22.8, translation mine). The latter passage indicates that Hegesippus quoted from a Greek Gospel of the Hebrews. Greek is not mentioned explicitly, but because Syriac and Hebrew are listed as supplements, the Gospel of the Hebrews must have been in Greek.[27]

---

23. In the Gos. Eb., the idea of the Spirit going *into* Jesus is expressed not only with the Greek preposition *eis* ("into"), as in Mark (see Mark 1:10), but also by adding the same prefix to the verb (*eiselthousēs eis auton*), which makes the idea of entering very clear. See Luomanen, *Recovering*, 21–22.

24. Michael D. Goulder, *A Tale of Two Missions* (London: SCM, 1994), 128–42; Sakari Häkkinen, "Ebionites," in *A Companion to Second-Century Christian "Heretics,"* ed. A. Marjanen and P. Luomanen, VCSup 76 (Leiden: Brill, 2005), 266–69.

25. Justin Martyr's *Dialogue with Trypho* (See *Dial.* 88.3; 88.8) supports the same wording in the description of Jesus's baptism, which proves that this kind of description was known already by the middle of the second century, close to the time when the Gos. Eb. is likely to have been composed (see above).

26. In addition, Eusebius claims that the Ebionites used the Gospel according to the Hebrews (*Hist. eccl.* 3.27), but this information is not historically reliable. Irenaeus, who was Eusebius's source here, claimed that the Ebionites used only the Gospel of Matthew (Irenaeus, *Haer.* 3.11.8–9). Eusebius probably replaced the Gospel of Matthew with the Gospel according to the Hebrews, because for him it was unthinkable that heretics could have based their teaching on a canonical Gospel. See Luomanen, *Recovering*, 122–23; Gregory, *Gospel*, 76–77.

27. This is the most natural conclusion, although some scholars have argued that Hippolytus already knew the "Syriac Gospel according to the Hebrews." For discussion, see Luomanen, *Recovering*, 126–27; Gregory, *Gospel*, 82–85.

Together these passages suggest that the Gospel of the Hebrews was composed in Greek, in the first quarter of the second century, probably in the Syro-Palestinian area. Later on it also found its way to Egypt, where Clement of Alexandria and Origen quoted it.[28]

Both Clement and Origen cite the Gospel of the Hebrews in Greek (Clement of Alexandria, *Strom.* 2.9.45.5; 5.14.96.3; Origen, *Comm. Jo.* 2.12; *Hom. Jer.* 15.4). Because Origen wrote his *Commentary on John*, in which he quoted this Gospel, at the time he was still in Alexandria (cf. Eusebius, *Hist. eccl.* 6.24.1), the quotations indicate that the Gospel of the Hebrews was known there toward the end of the second and at the beginning of the third century.

Although Hegesippus, Clement of Alexandria, Origen, and most likely Papias knew the Gospel of the Hebrews in Greek, there is also evidence suggesting that at some point it must have been translated into a Semitic language, Syriac and/or West Aramaic. A Latin translator has added at Origen's *Commentary on Matthew* 15.14 a story about "another rich man" from the Gospel of the Hebrews. Although the story is now in Latin, it was most likely preceded by a Semitic version. (For more on this, see sec. 3.6.2, below.)

3.2 How to Reconstruct the Contents of the Gospel of the Hebrews?

As pointed out earlier, the titles that the church fathers gave to Jewish-Christian Gospel fragments cannot always be trusted. Jerome is particularly challenging in this respect, as becomes clear in the following case.

> In the Gospel according to the Hebrews, which is written in the Chaldaic[29] and the Syriac language but with Hebrew letters, and which the Nazarenes use even today, [the Gospel] according to the apostles, or, as many say, according to Matthew, which is also in the library of Caesarea, the story runs... (Jerome, *Pelag.* 3.2)

The collection of titles Jerome presents here indicates that, in his opinion, there was only one Jewish-Christian Gospel, which had several names. Although scholars generally agree that Jerome himself assumed only one Jewish-Christian Gospel, many think that the fragments transmitted by him came from at least two Gospels.[30] The crucial question is whether it is possible to trace Jerome's sources, and if so, to develop reliable criteria for attributing the surviving fragments to different Gospels.

Where did Jerome find all his fragments? If his own information is taken at face value, he learned the contents when he copied the Gospel of the Hebrews and translated it from the original Hebrew into Latin and Greek. In *On Illustrious Men* (*De viris illustribus*), Jerome shares his knowledge about the original Hebrew copy of the Gospel of Matthew:

> The actual Hebrew has been stored until today in the library of Caesarea, which Pamphilus the martyr carefully collected. The Nazarenes who use this book in Beroia, a city of Syria, gave me an opportunity to copy it. (Jerome, *Vir. ill.* 3)

---

28. For possible routes, see Luomanen, *Recovering*, 138–39.

29. Jerome's "Chaldaic" refers to biblical Aramaic. See Edmon L. Gallagher, *Hebrew Scripture in Patristic Biblical Theory: Canon, Language, Text* (Leiden: Brill, 2012), 125–26.

30. Vielhauer and Strecker, "Jewish-Christian Gospels," 146; Klijn, *Jewish-Christian*, 16–19; Hans-Josef Klauck, *Apocryphal Gospels: An Introduction* (London: T&T Clark International, 2003), 36–37; Frey, "Die Fragmente judenchristlicher Evangelien," 582.

In a previous passage that celebrates the work of James the brother of Jesus, Jerome has already informed us that some knowledge about James is also preserved in

> the Gospel which is called according to the Hebrews and which was recently translated by me into Greek and Latin, and which Origen also often uses... (Jerome, *Vir. ill.* 2)

Unfortunately, these self-testimonies of Jerome are not reliable. First, if he really had translated the entire Hebrew Gospel of Matthew into Latin and Greek, there would surely be more references to this work in his writings. Second, it can be proved that he received some of the fragments directly from his predecessors, especially Eusebius and Origen.[31]

However, if Jerome only passed on information that he assumed to be from the Gospel of the Hebrews, why would he want to claim to have recently translated that Gospel? Given Jerome's eagerness to excel, it is not entirely impossible that he invented the whole story, but it is more likely that he was only planning to translate the Gospel that he believed to be available in the library of Caesarea. This would accord with the optimism expressed in his own list of publications in *On Illustrious Men* (*Vir. ill.* 135). There he boasts of having translated the entire Old Testament and the New Testament into Latin, although he never completed the translation of the New Testament, and the Old Testament translation was finished a decade after the writing of *On Illustrious Men*.[32]

Jerome must have met Nazarene Christians,[33] whose Gospel he claims to use, during his first trip to the East (ca. 374–377 CE) when he tried the life of a monk in the neighborhood of Chalcis.[34] There he picked up some elementary Syriac from local people and received instruction in Hebrew from a Jew who had converted to Christianity. Later in Bethlehem he also had Hebrew mentors, whose knowledge of rabbinic exegesis he was able to use in his Old Testament commentaries.[35] Thus, it is conceivable that Jerome received his passages from the "Hebrew Matthew" "that the Nazarenes also use" from his instructors, either in Chalcis or in Bethlehem.

If Jerome not only passed on information he had picked up from the writings of his predecessors but had also really received some "Hebrew" gospel traditions from the Nazarenes, is there any way to distinguish these genuine Nazarene fragments from other traditions?

The classic version of the 3GH assumed that signs of Semitic language or content similar to the Gospel of Matthew indicated that a fragment was most likely from the Gospel of the Nazarenes, whereas Greek language and "gnostic" ideas signaled that the fragment was from the Gospel of the Hebrews.[36] As shown above, it is not justifiable to distribute the fragments to two different Gospels simply on the basis of whether they resemble Synoptic Gospels or "gnostic" ideas. Furthermore, fragments that the 3GH assumed to

---

31. See note 39 below; Luomanen, *Recovering*, 89–103; Frey, "Die Fragmente judenchristlicher Evangelien," 581–87. Overall, Jerome used Origen widely in his literary production. See J. N. D. Kelly, *Jerome: His Life, Writings, and Controversies* (New York: Harper & Row, 1975), 164.

32. Kelly, *Jerome*, 161–62.

33. In the Syriac language, a Christian is *natsraya*. Therefore, the "Nazarenes" to whom Jerome is referring in the context of the Gos. Heb. may simply have been (Jewish) Christians whose native language was Syriac. For the artificial character of Epiphanius's Nazarenes, see Luomanen, *Recovering*, 71–79.

34. Luomanen, *Recovering*, 90–92. For the chronology of Jerome's visit to the East, see Kelly, *Jerome*, 46–80.

35. Jerome, *Epist.* 7.2; 125.12; see Kelly, *Jerome*, 49–50. For mentors in Bethlehem, see, e.g., Jerome, *Epist.* 84.3; *Comm. Eccl.* 4.13/16; 9.5/6; see Kelly, *Jerome*, 50–51; 134.

36. Vielhauer and Strecker, "Jewish-Christian Gospels," 148. Frey, who continues to support the 3GH, has modified the argumentation. For him, the decisive criterion seems to be the linguistic background (Frey, "Die Fragmente judenchristlicher Evangelien," 590).

resemble especially the Gospel of Matthew include expressions that are also paralleled in other Synoptic Gospels.[37] Thus, an alternate set of criteria needs to be applied in order to distinguish what Jerome received from the Nazarenes.

The N2GH builds on the observation that in many cases Jerome's introductions to the fragments include references to Latin *and Greek* as the target languages as well as signal that other translators were at work in addition to Jerome by having the *subject in the first-person plural* (see *Comm. Mich.* 7.6; *Vir. ill.* 2; *Comm. Matt.* 12.13, and their parallels). Because Jerome was reluctant to credit his sources, Greek as a target language (unnecessary for Jerome who was writing in Latin) and the recognition of other active subjects (by an author who was eager to reap all the possible glory for himself) may betray that the passage was picked up from a predecessor who was writing in Greek.[38] In addition to these, a passage that is clearly from Eusebius (*Vir. ill.* 16),[39] as well as the fragments that Jerome presented before he started to refer to the Gospel that the Nazarenes used (*Epist.* 20.5; *Comm. Eph.* 5.4; dated before 391–392 CE), can also be removed from the group of possible Nazarene fragments. Furthermore, the extraordinarily long list of possible titles in *Pelagius* 3.2 (see above) suggests that the passage was not from the Nazarenes but from another source.[40]

After the above eliminations, the list of possible fragments includes mainly short notices about variant readings to Matthew's Gospel. At first sight, the collection appears quite random, but when the alternative readings are set in their Matthean contexts, it becomes clear that the readings were derived from passages that propagate the hostility of the Jewish people and the judgment upon them (read the fragments below in their Matthean contexts). The corollary of this collection is Jesus's judgment by Pilate in front of all the people. In the canonical version, the people vote for Barabbas, which means "the Son of the Father," but the Nazarenes had made it so that the people required the release of "the son of our Rabbi" (*barrabban*). This justifies the hypothesis that Jerome received a collection of anti-rabbinic passages from his Nazarene contacts. The collection was from a Semitic translation of the Gospel of Matthew where some wordings were touched up and interpreted in order to better serve the Nazarenes' fierce criticism of contemporary rabbis. The hypothesis is also supported by the fact that in his *Commentary on Isaiah*, Jerome is able to present several quotations from the Nazarenes' explanation of Isaiah that provide examples of similar play with Hebrew words and letters, serving the Nazarenes' anti-rabbinic polemics.[41]

3.3 Fragments from the Nazarenes' Anti-Rabbinic Collection

In the following translations, Jerome's own introductions and other comments appear in italics.

---

37. For the problems of the criteria used in the 3GH, see Luomanen, *Recovering*, 84–89.

38. Since Jerome was using secretaries who were both reading and writing for him, he probably found it necessary to explain why the passage that he claimed to have translated from Hebrew was also (or only) available in Greek in one of his predecessors' writings; see Luomanen, *Recovering*, 104. For Jerome's assistants, see Kelly, *Jerome*, 48–49, 306–8.

39. This is a classic example of Jerome's use of Eusebius. Jerome copied the information from Eusebius (*Hist. eccl.* 3.36.11), but reveals his source accidentally, by presenting exactly the same sentences as Eusebius, without realizing where the borderline between Eusebius's paraphrasing of Ignatius and the actual quotation lies. See, e.g., Gregory, *Gospel*, 274–77.

40. Jerome probably collected all the names into the introduction because he needed extra support for his case against Pelagius.

41. For the details of the reconstruction process, see Luomanen, *Recovering*, 103–19.

1. In Bethlehem of Judea

And they said to him: "In Bethlehem of Judea." This is a copyist's error because we think that the evangelist wrote in his first edition as we read in the original Hebrew: Judah *and not* Judea. (Jerome, *Comm. Matt.* 2.5)

2. Bread for Tomorrow

In the Gospel called according to the Hebrews, I found, instead of "bread necessary to support life," maar, *which means "for tomorrow," so that the meaning is "our bread for tomorrow," that is, "bread for the future, give us today."* (Jerome, *Comm. Matt.* 6.11; *Tract. Ps.* 135)

3. Zacharia Son of Jojada

In the Gospel which the Nazarenes use, we find written son of Jojada, *instead of son of* Barachia. (Jerome, *Comm. Matt.* 23.35)

4. Son of Their Master

In the Gospel that is written according to the Hebrews the name of the man who was condemned because of insurrection and homicide is interpreted as "son of their master." (Jerome, *Comm. Matt.* 27.16)

5. The Lintel of the Temple

In the Gospel, which we have often mentioned, we read that a lintel of an enormous size was broken and split. (Jerome, *Comm. Matt.* 27.51; *Epist.* 120.8)

3.4 Fragments from the Gospel of the Hebrews

The following reconstruction of the Gospel of the Hebrews is based on the view that after the genuine Nazarene anti-rabbinic fragments have been located among the fragments that Jerome transmitted, it is reasonable to attribute the remaining collection to the Gospel of the Hebrews. Because it is impossible to provide definite proof, in many cases it is surely possible to speculate with other possible sources.[42] However, when these fragments are viewed together, they reveal distinctive theological notions with a reasonable amount of coherence. As such, they serve as the best available approximation of how Jesus-traditions were developed and interpreted in a Gospel used by "the Hebrews who have accepted Christ" (cf. Eusebius, *Hist. eccl.* 3.25.5). In the following translations, comments by the transmitters of the traditions from the Gospel of the Hebrews appear in italics.

1. The Baptism of Jesus

1a. *But the Nazarenes read, according to the Gospel written in the Hebrew language:* The whole fountain of the Holy Spirit came upon him ...

Further, in the Gospel which we mentioned above, we find written this:

It happened, when the Lord ascended from the water, that the whole fountain of the Holy Spirit descended and rested upon him and said to him: "My son, in all the prophets I expected you, that you would come and that I would rest in you. You are my rest; you are my firstborn son who will reign for all eternity." (Jerome, *Comm. Isa.* 11.1–3)

Below is a second text that touches on Jesus's baptism:

---

42. Cf. Gregory, *Gospel,* 140–46.

1b. *In the Gospel according to the Hebrews, which is written in the Chaldaic and the Syriac language but with Hebrew letters and which the Nazarenes use even today, [the Gospel] according to the apostles, or, as many say, according to Matthew, which is also in the library of Caesarea, the story runs:*

See, the mother of the Lord and his brothers said to him: "John the Baptist baptizes for the remission of sins, let us go and let us be baptized by him." He said to them: "What is the sin I have committed, so that I should go and be baptized by him? Unless, perhaps what I have said is in itself ignorance." (Jerome, *Pelag.* 3.2)

2. The Holy Spirit Takes Jesus to Tabor

If somebody accepts the Gospel according to the Hebrews, where the Savior himself says,

"My Mother, the Holy Spirit, just took me by one of my hairs and carried me over to the great hill, the Tabor,"

he will ask how the Holy Spirit, which was born through the Word, can be the mother of Christ. (Origen, *Comm. Jo.* 2.12; paralleled in Origen, *Hom. Jer.* 15.4; Jerome, *Comm. Mich.* 7.5–7; *Comm. Isa.* 40.9–11; *Comm. Ezech.* 16.13)

3. Matthias and Levi are the Same

Matthew seems to be called Levi in the Gospel according to Luke. However, they are not the same, but Matthias who replaced Judas and Levi are the same with a double name. This becomes clear in the Gospel according to the Hebrews. (Didymus, *Comm. Ps.*)[43]

4. Jesus Chooses the Good Ones

He himself taught about the necessity of the divisions of the souls which takes place in the houses, as we have found somewhere in the Gospel which exists among the Jews in the Hebrew language, in which it is said:

"I choose for myself the good ones, the good ones whom my Father in heaven has given to me." (Eusebius, *Theophania syriaca* 4.12)

5. Attaining Rest

As it is also written in the Gospel according to the Hebrews:

He who has become astonished will rule and he who has ruled will rest. (Clement of Alexandria, *Strom.* 2.9.45.5; paralleled in 5.14.96.3 and Gos. Thom. 2)

6. Mason's Prayer

In the Gospel which the Nazarenes and the Ebionites use, which we recently translated from Hebrew to Greek and which very many call the authentic Matthew, it is written that the man who has a withered hand is a mason, praying for help with words like this:

"I was a mason earning my living with my hands. I pray for you, Jesus, to restore my health so that I will not shamefully beg for food." (Jerome, *Comm. Matt.* 12.13)

7. Distressing One's Brother

In the Gospel which is according to the Hebrews and which the Nazarenes are accustomed to read, among the worst crimes is regarded he who saddens the spirit of his brother. (Jerome, *Comm. Ezech.* 18.5–9)

---

43. M. Groenewald, ed., *Didymos der Blinde: Psalmenkommentar [Tura-Papyrus]. Teil III. Kommentar zu Psalm 29–34*, Papyrologische Texte und Abhandlungen (Bonn: Habelt, 1969), 184.

8. How to Look at One's Brother

As we read in the Hebrew Gospel, the Lord said to the disciples:

"And never be happy," he said, "unless you have looked at your brother with love." (Jerome, *Comm. Eph.* 5.4)

9. Woman Accused of Many Sins

Papias also used evidence from 1 John and from 1 Peter and provides another story of a woman falsely accused before the Lord of many sins, which is in the Gospel of the Hebrews. (Eusebius, *Hist. eccl.* 3.39)[44]

10. Even Anointed Prophets Sinned

And in the same volume [cf. frag. 1b above]:

He said: "If your brother has sinned with a word and has made amends to you, accept him seven times a day." Simon, his disciple, said to him: "Seven times a day?" The Lord answered and said to him: "I say to you, even as much as seventy times seven. For even among the prophets, after they were anointed with the Holy Spirit, there was found sinful speech." (Jerome, *Pelag.* 3.2; paralleled in codices 566 and 899, Matt 18:22)

11. The Rich Man

It is written in a certain Gospel which is called according to the Hebrews—if someone sees good to accept it, not as an authority but in order to clarify the question that has been put:

The second rich man said to him: "Master, what good must I do, that I may live?" He said to him: "Man, do the Law and the Prophets." He answered him: "That I have done." He said: "Go, sell all that you have and distribute it to the poor, and come and follow me." But the rich man started to scratch his head, and he was not satisfied with it. The Lord said to him: "How can you say: 'I have done the Law and the Prophets?' For it is written in the Law 'Love your neighbor as yourself,' and see, many of your brothers, sons of Abraham, are clothed with dung, dying from hunger. Your house is full of many good things, but nothing at all comes out of it for them." He turned and said to Simon, his disciple, who was sitting by him: "Simon, son of Jonah, it is easier for a camel to go through the eye of a needle than for a rich man to enter the kingdom of heaven." (Origen, *Comm. Matt.* 15.14)

12. The Parable of the Talents

However, the Gospel which has come to us in Hebrew letters, does not direct its threat against the one who had hidden [the talent] *but against the one who led a profligate life.*

For he had three slaves, one who spent the fortune of the master with harlots and flute girls, one who multiplied his trade, and one who hid his talent. One was then accepted, one only rebuked, and one sent to prison.

I wonder whether the threat in Matthew, which according to the letter was spoken against the one who did nothing, applies not to him but, by way of resumption, to the first one who was eating and drinking with those who were drunk. (Eusebius, *Theoph.* 4.22; Migne, PG 24:685–88)

---

44. The story quoted by Papias is often linked with the story about an adulteress that was later added to the Gospel of John (John 7:53–8:11; in some manuscripts after 7:26 or 21:25, or after Luke 21:25). However, the connection is far from sure, because the fragment from Papias refers to "many sins" and expresses the accusation with a Greek word that could also refer to presenting false accusations (*diaballō*). If so, the setting in Papias's version would be different, possibly closer to what we can find in Luke 7:36–50, where Jesus defends the actions of an unnamed woman who anoints him against the "false" accusation of a Pharisee, forgiving the "many sins" (Luke 7:47) of the woman.

13. Jesus Breaks Bread for James the Just

The Gospel which is called according to the Hebrews and which was recently translated by me into Greek and Latin, and which Origen also often uses, says after the resurrection of the Lord:

But when the Lord had given the linen cloth to the priest's servant, he went to James and appeared to him. For James had sworn that he would not eat bread after the hour when he drank the cup of the Lord until he would see him rising from those who sleep.

And again, a little later, it says: "Bring the table and bread," said the Lord. *And immediately it is added:* He took the bread, blessed it, broke it, and gave it to James the Just saying: "My brother, eat thy bread for the Son of Man is risen from those who sleep." (Jerome, *Vir. ill.* 2)

3.5 The Main Themes of the Gospel of the Hebrews

One of the most distinctive features of the Gospel of the Hebrews is its affinity with Wisdom traditions. In the classic version of the 3GH, this was the key criterion that indicated the "gnostic" character of the Gospel.[45] By the present standards of gnostic studies, however, the content of the Gospel of the Hebrews hardly fulfills the criteria for classification as gnostic literature because there is no indication of the idea of the demiurge, a lower creator god responsible for the material world from which men may become saved if they realize their divine origins.[46] Yet the presence of Jewish Wisdom theology is present in fragments one, two, four, and five (see above). The fundamental myth pictures Wisdom as God's envoy, even an independent divine being, who seeks a person worthy of its descent and presence among humans (Sir 24). On the other hand, from the human perspective, the search for Wisdom may be seen as hard labor and toil that will finally lead to rest.

In fragments one and two, Jesus is pictured as the son of his mother, the Holy Spirit, who has been waiting for him and who endows him with her full presence in his baptism. Fragment five, which promises rest for those who become astonished, has a parallel in the Gospel of Thomas (logion 2), but it is still clearly within the confines of traditional Wisdom thinking. Fragment four, concerning the chosen ones, can also be interpreted in the same light. Eusebius seems to quote fragment four to support a distinction between the morally good and bad, but in the Gospel of the Hebrews the passage was more likely referring to those who are worthy of Wisdom's revelation.[47]

Another notable topic is love toward one's brother. Distressing one's brother is one of the worst crimes (frag. 7), and rejoicing is not allowed if one cannot look at one's brother with love (frag. 8). Fragment ten reveals a wider theological horizon behind these admonitions. The passage first presents a combination of the Lukan and Matthean versions of Jesus's words on reconciliation (Matt 18:15, 21–22; Luke 17:3–4), but elaborates it by giving an example from the history of prophets that supports the admonition to forgive one's brother his sinful words; even the prophets, after they were anointed with the Holy Spirit, uttered sinful words. This passage also reveals how the understanding of the Spirit in the Gospel of the Hebrews differed from the Gospel of Thomas. In the Gospel of Thomas, the term

---

45. Vielhauer and Strecker, "Jewish-Christian Gospels," 173–74.

46. For discussions on the definition and the character of Gnosticism, see Antti Marjanen, ed., *Was There a Gnostic Religion?*, Publications of the Finnish Exegetical Society 87 (Helsinki: Finnish Exegetical Society, 2005), and Antti Marjanen, "Gnosticism," in *The Oxford Handbook of Early Christian Studies*, ed. Susan Ashbrook Harvey and David G. Hunter (Oxford: Oxford University Press, 2008), 203–11.

47. For the relationship between the Gos. Heb. and the Gos. Thom., see Luomanen, *Recovering*, 133–35, 223–31.

"spirit" is used to describe the divine light in men (Gos. Thom. 50), while in the Gospel of the Hebrews the Spirit is received through anointing or baptism (frags. 1 and 10).[48]

3.6 Key Passages for New Testament Studies in the Gospel of the Hebrews
3.6.1 The Gospel of the Hebrews and Q

Because the classic 3GH detached the Wisdom sayings of the Gospel of the Hebrews from the Synoptic tradition, scholars have not paid much attention to the possible relation of the Gospel of the Hebrews to Q traditions. However, the reconstruction of the Gospel of the Hebrews in the N2GH shares several features with Q. The understanding of the prophets in the Gospel of the Hebrews (frag. 10) seems to presuppose the Deuteronomistic scheme—typical of Q—of a series of God's envoys from the Old Testament, through John and Jesus, to the disciples. Admonitions to forgive one's brother and not to judge, central themes in the Gospel of the Hebrews, appear in Q 6:41–42 and Q 17:3–4.[49] Furthermore, the criticism targeted at the rich and the exhortation to give up one's property, thus becoming a poor follower of Jesus (frags. 10 and 12), conform to the central ethos of Q as it appears in Q's sermon (Q 6), Q's mission instructions (Q 10), and Q 12:22–34. The perspective from which the Gospel of the Hebrews views poverty-related issues also has its own distinctive edge that differs from what is observable in the canonical Gospels, as becomes clear in the following section.[50]

The points of contact listed above suggest that the framers of the Gospel of the Hebrews were preoccupied with the same topics as those behind Q and were therefore possibly their post-Synoptic successors.[51] However, the topics also have clear connections to Matthew's Gospel. The Deuteronomistic scheme is further emphasized in Matthew's redaction (parables in Matt 21:28–22:14) and the exhortations to forgive one's brother (Matt 18:23–35). Furthermore, the passage where Jesus promises rest to his followers (Matt 11:28–30) can be located in Matthew's special tradition. Thus, from the viewpoint of the N2GH it is easy to agree with James M. Robinson, who saw a close relationship between Q, Matthew, and later Jewish-Christian groups.[52]

3.6.2 Fragment 11: The Rich Man

The story about "another rich man" is derived from the Latin translation of Origen's commentary on Matthew (Origen, *Comm. Matt.* 15.14). The unknown translator probably added it, sometime between the fifth and ninth centuries, because it does not appear in the Greek original. Because the passage is longer than many other surviving fragments, a careful comparison with its parallels reveals more details about its background.

The opening of the passage, "another rich man," indicates that the Gospel of the Hebrews must have included at least two stories about rich men in the same context. Its Synoptic counterparts have only one story, but there were more stories about rich men in

48. Also, the gender of the Spirit is different in the Gos. Thom., where the Spirit is usually the Father's Spirit. The Spirit as a mother may appear in Gos. Thom. 101. In any case, within Thomasine traditions, it is more prominent in the Acts of Thomas. See Luomanen, *Recovering*, 227–31.

49. Q's verse numbers are from the Gospel of Luke.

50. For a more detailed description of the relationship between Gos. Heb. and Q, see Luomanen, *Recovering*, 139–44.

51. As noted above, the Gos. Heb. was most likely composed in the Syro-Palestinian area. The observed affinities with the Q-tradition accord with this hypothesis, because Q seems to presume Galilee as its social setting. See John Kloppenborg Verbin, *Excavating Q: The History and Setting of the Sayings Gospel* (Minneapolis: Fortress, 2000), 214–61.

52. James M. Robinson, *Jesus according to the Earliest Witness* (Minneapolis: Fortress, 2007), 158, 200.

the same context in Tatian's *Diatessaron*. Furthermore, a comparison with Syriac translations and other *Diatessaronic* witnesses show that the passage also shares many wordings with this branch of Gospel tradition, so much so that it was most probably translated from Syriac into Latin.[53]

Some scholars have suggested that the passage may include pre-Synoptic Jesus-traditions,[54] but a comparison with Matthew's and Luke's Gospels shows that the passage includes formulations that derive from the final editors of these Gospels. This clearly shows that the passage was composed after the Synoptic Gospels.[55]

The fact that the passage was also available in Syriac and that it uses the Semitic version of Peter's name ("Simon, son of Jonah") already suggests its use by Jewish Christians. The Jewish background of its modifiers becomes clear when it is analyzed in the light of other indicators of Jewish Christianity.

There is no doubt about the Jewish starting point of the discussion, since the love commandment, around which the discussion revolves, is in Leviticus 19:18. However, by the time the passage was added to Origen's commentary it was also a crucial part of Christian tradition. Is there anything to suggest whether the love commandment was interpreted from a Jewish or a Christian point of view? The formulation "do the law and the prophets" slightly favors the Jewish option, because the verb "do" (*poieō*) is used, for instance, in the Greek (LXX) translation of Deuteronomy 27:26 where anyone who does not "do" the law is cursed. "Fulfill" (*plēroō*), for its part, is preferred by Christian writers who refer to the principle of fulfilling the law or its core intention.[56] The use of the verb "do" suggests that the passage in the Gospel of the Hebrews takes the love commandment more as one of the Old Testament commandments than as a "Christian" summary of the law.

In contrast to the Synoptic versions, the fragment does not list any of the Ten Commandments. In Gospels directed mainly to gentile audiences, it is natural to list the individual commandments, and in the Synoptic Gospels this is the only place where Jesus lists them—whereas for a Jewish audience this is not so crucial, especially if the focus is elsewhere, as it seems to be in this passage.

Another omission in the Gospel of the Hebrews also suits a Jewish context very well. In the Synoptic version of Mark and Luke, Jesus takes up the address "Good teacher" in the rich man's question, to remind his audience that only God is good (Mark 10:17; Luke 18:18). The monotheistic note ("only one is good") is still present in Matthew's Gospel (Matt 19:17), but the Gospel of the Hebrews totally skips this opportunity to give a short lesson on monotheism, which, naturally, was less important in a Jewish context.

In the Synoptic versions of the story, Jesus urges the rich man to sell his property and to follow him. Jesus requires this in addition to traditional Jewish piety—Matthew makes this very clear by referring to perfectness (Matt 19:21). This exhortation gives the story its Christian edge and turns it into a conflict story that points out where the border between Jesus's followers and traditional Jewish Torah obedience lies. However, although Jesus first advises the man to sell everything in the Gospel of the Hebrews too, the rest of the story is more occupied with the question of showing mercy. In the final analysis, the crucial

---

53. Luomanen, *Recovering*, 175–99.

54. Klijn, *Jewish-Christian*, 59–60.

55. E.g., the address "Teacher, what good . . . ," "came and said," and "teacher" are clearly typical of the editor of Matthew's Gospel. Furthermore, the passage shares phrases with Luke's version of the lawyer's question in Luke 10:25–28, which clearly derives from the editor of Luke's gospels. See Luomanen, *Recovering*, 179–83.

56. See, e.g., Matt 5:17. For the discussion of Paul's possible distinction between "doing" and "fulfilling," see Heikki Räisänen, *Paul and the Law* (Philadelphia: Fortress, 1986), 63–64n104.

question is not the following of Jesus but alleviating the desperate situation of his brothers. Notably, the rich man should show mercy to his fellow Jews, "sons of Abraham."

3.6.3 Fragment 12: The Parable of the Talents

Eusebius only summarizes the main points of the parable as it stood in the Gospel of the Hebrews. However, the sequence in which he describes the actions of the servants and their judgments is surprising and has troubled interpreters. Eusebius describes the actions of the servants in the order (1) spent, (2) multiplied, (3) hid, and he describes the punishment of the first servant last, giving the impression that the judgment was described in the reversed order.

The Gospel of the Hebrews		The Gospel of Matthew 25:14–30	
Servant	*Judgment (Eusebius's order reversed)*	*Servant*	*Judgment*
1. spent the fortune with flute girls	thrown into prison	1. doubles five talents	was praised
2. multiplied the trade	rebuked	2. doubles two talents	was praised
3. hid the talent	accepted	3. hid the talent	was thrown into darkness

Some scholars have found this problematic because it seems then that the servant who hid the talent would have been the one who was accepted, not the one who was able to multiply the entrusted fortune as in the canonical versions and which also better meets modern expectations.[57] However, as Bruce Malina and Richard Rohrbaugh have argued, the order implied in Eusebius's summary is understandable in the ancient Mediterranean culture where the idea of limited good was one of the shared cultural convictions.[58] Because the amount of goods was limited, all those who were trying to get more for themselves were necessarily stealing from others. Notably, Deuteronomy prohibits charging interest (Deut 23:19–20), and in later rabbinic tradition burying was considered a perfectly responsible way of taking care of someone else's money (b. B. Meṣ 40a).[59] The version in the Gospel of the Hebrews accords with these values. From the viewpoint of limited good, both the man who spent his money on the flute girls and the servant who made a profit with the entrusted money are morally despicable persons.

If the version in the Gospel of the Hebrews suits the ancient Mediterranean culture better, should we regard it as the more original one? In the light of the idea of limited good, the Matthean and Lukan versions of the parable do not present morally exemplary persons but set dubious characters as examples in order to give a lesson on what God requires of men. As such, they resemble the parable of the dishonest manager (Luke 16:1–13) and the parable of the unjust judge (18:1–8).[60] Because of these morally dubious features, it is easier

---

57. Klijn, e.g., has suggested that Eusebius's first listing does not follow the order in the Gos. Heb. He thinks that Eusebius focused on the servant who was punished and therefore mentioned him first. Klijn, *Jewish-Christian*, 61.

58. Bruce J. Malina and Richard L. Rohrbaugh, *Social Science Commentary on the Synoptic Gospels* (Minneapolis: Fortress, 1992), 148–50.

59. Thus, e.g., Ulrich Luz, *Das Evangelium nach Matthäus, Mt 18–25* (Zürich: Benziger; Neukirchen-Vluyn: Neukirchener, 1997), 500–1.

60. Thus Luz, *Das Evangelium nach Matthäus*, 497–98, who thinks that these parables may well be derived from the historical Jesus.

to understand a tradition-historical development from the Matthean/Lukan "immoral" version to the parable in the Gospel of the Hebrews where the judgment conforms better to ancient Mediterranean cultural values. When the parable of the talents in the Gospel of the Hebrews is interpreted in the light of limited good, it also becomes clear that it is, just like the story about the rich man in Gospel of the Hebrews, against becoming rich at the expense of others.

4. JEWISH-CHRISTIAN PROFILES OF THE GOSPEL OF THE EBIONITES AND THE GOSPEL OF THE HEBREWS

4.1 The Gospel of the Ebionites

The Gospel of the Ebionites includes features that would well suit communities following its principles in a marginal position regarding both formative Christianity and formative Judaism. The surviving passages do not reveal how circumcision, Sabbath, or everyday Jewish practice were interpreted in the Gospel of the Ebionites, but its interpretation of the Passover/Easter traditions is distinctive. If Jesus's words on eating Passover (frag. 6) were followed by the institution of the Eucharist as suggested above, it shows that the Jewish Passover tradition is transforming into the Christian Eucharist. Although vegetarianism could be interpreted as a sign of protecting the purity of meals in a pagan environment,[61] Jesus's outward rejection of the supposedly correctly slaughtered Passover lamb places him on the margins of common Judaism. The same holds true regarding his rejection of the sacrifices. On the other hand, the possessionist Christology and (possibly) exclusive mission to Israel signal the Gospel's close ties to Jewish traditions, but these have made it suspicious in the eyes of the heresiologists of the formative Christianity.

The lack of evidence relating to the observance of Jewish purity and practice, beyond sacrifice, makes it impossible to judge the degree of Jewishness of the Gospel of the Ebionites. However, the evidence we have about its relation to Passover suggests that the Gospel was not Jewish enough for many of its Jewish contemporaries. If the institution of the Eucharist did not include words referring to the sacrificial blood of Jesus, this was not necessarily interpreted as a "heresy" among early followers of Christ, since communal meals without a sacrificial aspect are also known in the Didache (Did. 9–10).

In the surviving fragments, there is nothing that would tie the Gospel with Jewish ethnicity or Hebrew/Aramaic tradition. As such, this does not speak against its Jewishness, since its profile would suit well a Hellenistic (Jewish) setting.

On the basis of the limited evidence, it is not possible to say for sure if the Gospel was likely to be too Jewish for Christians or too Christian for Jews in the formative traditions of these religions. However, it is likely that for many doctrinally oriented leaders within these traditions it was either not Jewish enough or not Christian enough.

4.2 The Gospel of the Hebrews

The fragments from the Gospel of the Hebrews give slightly more material for sketching its Jewish-Christian profile. The Wisdom thinking that characterizes many of its fragments places the Gospel squarely within Jewish tradition. The Gospel is also more closely tied to a Semitic context: it pictures the Spirit as feminine, addresses Peter as Simon (frag. 11), and it is occasionally referred to as a Gospel in Hebrew/Hebrew letters—which is also confirmed by the tradition history of some of its fragments (frags. 1, 4, 10, 11, and 12). The passage that describes Jesus's conversation with "another rich man" is rich in detail relating

---

61. Thus Gregory, *Gospel*, 260–61.

to a Jewish social-historical and theological setting. The discussion seems to take mono-theism and the knowledge of the Ten Commandments more for granted than its canonical counterparts. Its main point is not so much to urge its readers or hearers to follow Jesus as to exhort them to take action to help their "brothers," the "sons of Abraham," in their economic despair and social shame. The themes of honor and shame are also accentuated in the story of the mason, who must beg for his living (frag. 6), as well as in the parable of the talents (frag. 12). Clearly the fragments of the Gospel of the Hebrews are more Jewish than their canonical counterparts, and the overall profile of the collection has distinctively Jewish characteristics. Was the Gospel of the Hebrews perhaps too Jewish to be classified as a Christian Gospel? In light of the reception history of the Gospel, this is not the case.

In the third book of his *Ecclesiastical History* (*Hist. eccl.* 3.25), Eusebius classifies the New Testament and related writings into three categories: (1) generally accepted books (*homologoumena*), (2) disputed books (*antilegomena*), and (3) writings used by the heretics but not quoted by the writers of the church. The Gospel of the Hebrews is placed in the second category together with such writings as Revelation, which eventually ended up in the New Testament canon, as well as books that were valued and largely used later on, like the Shepherd of Hermas, Barnabas, and Didache. In the light of this classification, the profile of the Gospel of the Hebrews is somewhere between the clearly "heretical" Gospel of Thomas and the Synoptic Gospels of Matthew, Mark, and Luke.

5. BIBLIOGRAPHY

Frey, Jörg. "Die Fragmente des Ebionäerevangeliums." Pages 607–22 in *Antike christliche Apokryphen in deutscher Übersetzung I: Evangelien und Verwandtes*. Edited by C. Markschies and J. Schröter. Tübingen: Mohr Siebeck, 2012.

———. "Die Fragmente judenchristlicher Evangelien." Pages 560–92 in *Antike christliche Apokryphen in deutscher Übersetzung I: Evangelien und Verwandtes*. Edited by C. Markschies and J. Schröter. Tübingen: Mohr Siebeck, 2012.

Gregory, Andrew, ed. *The Gospel according to the Hebrews and the Gospel of the Ebionites*. Oxford Early Christian Gospel Texts. Oxford: Oxford University Press, 2017.

Jackson-McCabe, Matt, ed. *Jewish Christianity Reconsidered*. Minneapolis: Fortress, 2007.

Jones, F. Stanley, ed. *The Rediscovery of Jewish Christianity: From Toland to Baur*. HBS 5. Atlanta: Society of Biblical Literature, 2012.

Klijn, A. F. J. *Jewish-Christian Gospel Tradition*. VCSup 17. Leiden: Brill, 1992.

Luomanen, Petri. *Recovering Jewish-Christian Sects and Gospels*. VCSup 110. Leiden: Brill, 2012.

Marjanen, Antti, and Petri Luomanen, eds. *A Companion to Second-Century Christian "Heretics."* VCSup 76. Leiden: Brill, 2005.

Mimouni, Simon C. *Le judéo-christianisme ancien: Essais historiques*. Paris: Cerf, 1998.

Reed, Annette Yoshiko. *Jewish Christianity and the History of Judaism*. TSAJ 171. Tübingen: Mohr Siebeck, 2018.

Skarsaune, Oskar, and Reidar Hvalvik, eds. *Jewish Believers in Jesus: The Early Centuries*. Peabody, MA: Hendrickson, 2007.

Vielhauer, Philipp, and Georg Strecker. "Jewish-Christian Gospels." Pages 134–77 in *New Testament Apocrypha, Volume One: Gospels and Related Writings*. Rev. ed. Edited by W. Schneemelcher and R. McL. Wilson. Cambridge: Clarke; Louisville: Westminster John Knox, 1991.

CHAPTER 7

THE LEGEND OF APHRODITIAN

KATHARINA HEYDEN

1. INTRODUCTION

The Legend of Aphroditian is an imaginative narration about the magi who came to adore the newborn Christ and his mother Mary in Bethlehem (cf. Matt 2:1–12). In its first part, it describes the appearance of a star and a revelation in a temple of Hera in Persia. In the second part, it illustrates the magi's journey to Judah and their encounter with Mary along with her child in Bethlehem. Thus, the Legend belongs to the group of apocryphal childhood narratives. A rich manuscript tradition indicates the popularity of the Legend in the medieval Byzantine as well as Slavic worlds.

1.1 An Unknown Author in Western Syria

The author of the text remains unknown. In Greek and Slavic traditions, the Legend is attributed to a certain Aphroditian. This attribution goes back to the sixth-century work *De gestis in Perside*.[1] A few manuscripts mention an *Afrikanos* as the author of the narrative. However, this presumably traces back to a misunderstanding of the Greek abbreviation Αφρ in some manuscripts and does not point to the second-century Christian historiographer Julius Africanus. Philip of Side, the compiler of a Christian universal history in Constantinople in the fifth century,[2] is mentioned as the author in some manuscripts, although he is most likely not the inventor but the transmitter of the Legend of Aphroditian.

The story presents itself as a faithful copy of a report, which is "inscribed upon the golden tablets and laid up in the royal temples" (Leg. Aphr. 1.1; ὡς γὰρ ἐν ταῖς χρυσαῖς ἀρκλαρίαις κεκόλαπται καὶ κεῖνται ἐν τοῖς ἱεροῖς βασιλείοις). But there can be no doubt about its fictional, not to say fantastic, character, which is to be recognized by the fact that a temple of Hera in Persia is historically impossible.

The place of origin is probably western, Greek-speaking Syria. The early reception of the text as a table reading at the patriarch's court on Christmas in Antioch, as well as a close

---

1. This disputation romance presents a competition between Hellenes, Christians, Jews, and a Zoroastrian magician at the court of the Sassanids. In this, Aphroditian, an educated Greek philosopher, is arbitrator and king's court chef (see Eduard Bratke, *Das sogenannte Religionsgespräch am Hof der Sassaniden*, TU NF 4/3 [Leipzig: Hinrichs, 1899]; Katharina Heyden, *Die "Erzählung des Aphroditian": Thema und Variationen einer Legende im Spannungsfeld von Christentum und Heidentum*. Studien und Texte zu Antike und Christentum 53 [Tübingen: Mohr Siebeck, 2009]).

2. See Katharina Heyden, "Die christliche Geschichte des Philippos von Side. Mit einem kommentierten Katalog der Fragmente," in *Julius Africanus und die christliche Weltchronistik*, ed. M. Wallraff, TU 157 (Berlin: de Gruyter, 2006), 209–43.

connection to the cult of the goddess Dea Syria in Hierapolis/Mabbug, points to this.[3] Another reference to Syria as the place of origin can be found in the second part of the Legend. There it is told that a gifted slave made a portrait of Mary with the child, which was set up in the temple of Hera after the magicians returned to Persia. This has its parallel in the Doctrine of Addai, which was probably composed in fifth-century Syria. It adds the motif of the portrait of Jesus made by Hannan, which was brought by the sick King Abgar to Edessa, where it was set up in the royal palace according to the so-called Legend of Abgar.[4]

1.2 Apologetic-Missionary Intention

The unknown author of the Legend of Aphroditian appears to draw his inspiration from his knowledge of the cult in Hierapolis. But with what intention did he do this? Are we dealing with a satirical parody of a pagan author or rather with a Christian apologetic-missionary text linked to the cult of Dea Syria? This question cannot be answered with ultimate certainty. However, it is more likely that the Legend originated and was received in Christian circles. This is indicated most strongly by the concluding statement of the magi, in which they make a clear confession to Christ, claiming: "We know that Christ has become our Savior" (Leg. Aphr. 9.2; οἴδαμεν Χριστὸν σωτῆρα ἡμῶν γενόμενον). But already on the basis of the programmatic first sentence, "To Persia Christ was known from the beginning" (Leg. Aphr. 1.1; Ἐκ Περσίδος ἐγνώσθη Χριστὸς ἀπ' ἀρχῆς), it stands to reason that the Legend wants to illustrate when and how Christianity came to Persia. At the same time, the Legend testifies to respect for Persian wisdom in proclaiming Christian truth. However, the text shows no knowledge of real Persia. Furthermore, it was originally written in Greek and therefore cannot have been addressed to a Persian readership. Rather, it seems to be directed to an audience that has a great affinity to pagan culture and cult. Its purpose is to show by means of popular literature that Christianity can fit into paganism and at the same time surpass it. This story and such intentions are quite plausible in the border area between the Roman and Persian Empires, which was a melting pot of cultures and cults.[5]

1.3 Pre-Constantinian Origin?

While uncertainties abound, the parallels to the cult of Hierapolis are possibly indications of the Legend's date. The *terminus ante quem* is the formation of *De gestis in Perside*, which probably falls into the period between the sixth and seventh century. But this text indicates that the Legend was already read in the *Historia Christiana* of Philip of Side written in the 420s, and it is unlikely that Philip, who processed a lot of source material, invented the story himself. The parallels to the cult of Dea Syria could be traced to an origin in the second or third century, the heyday of the sanctuary of Dea Syria in Hierapolis. This early date is supported by the close similarities with the epitaphs of Abercius from the early third century, in which the motifs of spring, fish, and food occur in a similar way as in the Legend (see below). In addition, the interest in Jesus's childhood and the discussions about his divinity were intense at this time, as apocryphal writings like the Protevangelium of James, as well as other sources, show.[6] But it remains questionable whether the intensity of Marian devotion, as expressed in the Legend of Aphroditian, is already conceivable in

---

3. See below in more detail.
4. See ch. 20 in this volume.
5. Cf. Touraj Daryaee, *Sasanian Persia: The Rise and Fall of an Empire* (London: I. B. Tauris, 2009).
6. For the Protevangelium of James, see ch. 9 of this present volume.

the second or third century. Overall, it cannot be excluded that the Legend of Aphroditian, similar to the Doctrine of Addai, was composed in the fourth or fifth century, using older, pre-Constantinian material, especially in the first part of the text.

It is impossible to assign the Legend of Aphroditian to a specific theological school. It is most plausible that the Legend combines elements of various theological ideas and doctrines in an epoch, which might be called a "laboratory of Christian theology."[7]

1.4 Creative Reception

The Legend refers to a rich and fascinating history of transmission and reception. The *De gestis in Perside*, mentioned above, passes down the oldest written version of the Legend. Therein, the Legend is told by the Hellenic arbiter Aphroditian and is crucial for the confirmation of Christianity by "Hellenic oracles." A scholion on *De gestis in Perside* ascribes the Legend to the *Historia Christiana* of Philip of Side, in which it was perhaps part of a book titled "Hellenic Oracles" (Χρησμῳδίαι ἑλληνικαί) and was thus available to the author of *De gestis in Perside* as a source.[8]

The medieval manuscript tradition of *De gestis in Perside* already indicates a particular interest in the Legend. Eight of the forty-four known Greek manuscripts of *De gestis in Perside* only pass on this part of the text. The narrative seems to have gradually emerged from the context of *De gestis in Perside* in the manuscript tradition. In the eighth century, John of Damascus included the Legend in a sermon, *De nativitate domini*, as a pagan prophecy for the birth of Christ.[9] Two magnificently illuminated manuscripts from the Macedonian Renaissance in Constantinople exist due to the Legend: Codex Esphigmenou 14 and Codex Taphou 14.[10] These also contain miniatures of the Legend.[11] In the twelfth century at the latest, the Legend was transmitted separately in Byzantium.

In the Slavic tradition, the Legend was widely used in various versions, which is reflected in ninety-two manuscripts known to date.[12] Different closing sentences show editorial redactions with image-friendly, liturgical, or dogmatic emphases. The so-called Pre-Mongolian translation was possibly produced in Bulgaria as early as the tenth century and is now available in fifty-eight manuscripts. The so-called South Slavic translation, which is extant in thirty-four manuscripts, is based on a Serbian translation of an original Greek translation made in Constantinople, or on Mount Athos, in the fourteenth century at the latest. Until the sixteenth century, the Legend was in regular liturgical use in the Slavic world on Christmas. In the collective codices, it is indicated as a reading at the end of the service or as a table reading in monasteries and private houses for December 25th.

Later, the Legend was again received in other Slavic writings, for example, in a christological adaptation by the Ladder of Jacob, in which various elements of the Legend are

---

7. Christoph Markschies, "Alte Kirche," *RGG* 1:353.

8. Heyden, *Die "Erzählung des Aphroditian"*, 171–225.

9. Bonfatius Kotter, ed., *Die Schriften des Johannes von Damaskos, Volume 5: Opera Homiletica et Hagiographica*, PTS 29 (Berlin: de Gruyter, 1988).

10. Both date from the second half of the eleventh century.

11. See Heyden, *Die "Erzählung des Aphroditian"*, 67–93, and fig. 5–49; cf. Jacqueline Lafontaine-Dosogne, "L'illustration du cycle des Mages suivant l'homélie sur la Nativité attribuée à Jean Damascène," *Muséon* 100 (1987): 208–18.

12. Alexander G. Bobrov, *Апокрифическое Сказание Афродитиана в литературе и книжности Древней Руси. Исследование и тексты* (St. Petersburg: Nauka, 1994); Pauline Bringel, "Interprétation et réécritures dans la tradition manuscrite du Récit d'Aphroditien," in *Entré Actes. Regards croisés en sciences humaines. Réalités et représentations: les pistes de la recherche. Actes du Ier Colloque international des jeunes chercheurs en sciences humaines et sociales de Strasbourg, 10 et 11 mai 2004*, ed. Laurent Angard (Strasbourg: Université Marc Bloch, 2005), 285–96.

taken up in the mode of prophecy and presented to a fictitious Jew as proof of the biblical announcement of the incarnation. It states, for example: "But when he comes, the idols, who are angry, stone and any sculpture, will make their voices sound for three days. There they will tell those wise men to also recognize the future on earth, and they will find their way to him through a star."[13] In an anonymously transmitted "Speech on the Star of Hera,"[14] elements of the story are linked to biblical motifs, such as Balaam's prophecies (Num 22–24), as well as to Neo-Platonic philosophical ideas. These traces of reception bear witness to the great popularity of the Legend in medieval Russia. The Persian Aphroditian was also highly regarded in the rising Russia of the fifteenth and sixteenth centuries. He appears in a series with other pagan and biblical authorities as a prophet of Jesus's birth on the bronze doors of Blagoveshchensky Sobor and Uspensky Sobor, the two most important cathedrals on the Kremlin.

In the sixteenth century, the monk Michael Trivolis, alias Maksim Grek (1470–1556), who immigrated from Athos, triggered a debate in opposition to the popular Legend. Maksim's polemic, "On the Accusation and Conviction of the False Thinking Persian Aphroditian,"[15] with which he tried to curb liturgical use, was part of a comprehensive literary and political campaign for the "Greekization" of the Russian Church. His attack against the Legend had different consequences. From some codices the corresponding pages were removed with reference to the "lying character" of the writing. In others, Maksim's objections were recorded as marginals. Nevertheless, and at the same time, the story was included in the *Great Reading Menologia* compiled by the Moscow metropolitan Makarij in 1554, in which Russia's literary heritage was to be fixed and thus legitimized as the heir to the lost Byzantium.

Little is known about the reception of the Legend in the Latin West. The similarity in name between Ἀφροδιτιανός and *Affrodisius*, prefect of the Egyptian city of Sotinen, in which, according to the Gospel of Pseudo-Matthew 22–24 (written not earlier than in the seventh century), the statues of the gods fell down in the temple when Mary and Joseph entered the city with the newborn child, is probably one trace of reception.

Finally, academic research on the Legend of Aphroditian began at the end of the nineteenth century, mainly driven by Russian[16] and German[17] scholars of the Religionsgeschichtliche Schule ("history-of-religions school") who were particularly interested in relations to pagan cults in the first part of the Legend. The Legend's significance for New Testament studies and the history of early Christianity is still largely undiscovered.

2. SUMMARY OF CONTENT

The Legend is not an extensive writing. Its language and content allow it to be divided into two parts of approximately equal length. The following structure and headings correspond to those of Katharina Heyden's translation in *New Testament Apocrypha* edited by Tony Burke and Brent Landau.[18]

---

13. Ladder of Jacob 4.37–75 (translation mine). On this work, see Christfried Böttrich and Sabine Fahl, eds., *Leiter Jakobs*, Jüdische Schriften aus hellenistisch-römischer Zeit, Neue Folge 1/6 (Gütersloh: Gütersloher, 2015).

14. Слово о звезде Ираны. Edition and introduction by Jurij K. Begunov, Новонайденное апокрифическое "Слово о звезде Ираны," *Zeitschrift für Slawistik* 28 (1983): 238–57.

15. Bobrov, *Апокрифическое*, 138–49.

16. Pavel E. Schegoljev, "Очерки истории отреченной литературы. Сказание Афродитиана," *Извѣстія отдѣленія русскаго языка и словесности Императорской Академіи наукъ* 4 (1899): 148–99; 1304–344.

17. See the works by Schwartz, Bratke, and Usener in the bibliography at the end of this essay; cf. Adolf von Harnack, *Zur Abercius-Inschrift*, TU 12/4b (Leipzig: Hinrichs, 1895).

18. Katharina Heyden, "The Legend of Aphroditianus: A New Translation and Introduction," in *New

First Part: The Miracle in the Persian Temple of Hera

1. Introduction. The first part tells of a miracle in the temple of Hera at the time of the birth of Christ. The Persian king, who remains unnamed, arrives at the temple built by King Cyrus to have his dreams interpreted.

2. The miracle of the dancing statues. The priest, Proupippos, welcomes the king with the words: "Rejoice, because Hera is pregnant." He then tells the king about the events in the temple during the night: the images of the gods had danced and sung "because Hera was loved by Zeus." Therefore, her name was no longer Hera, but Urania (Οὐρανία, i.e., "Queen of Heaven"). However, a dispute arises between the female and the male images of the gods about Hera-Urania. The female statues make fun of her, saying that a carpenter did not impregnate Hera but Pege (Πηγή, i.e., "Fountain," or "Source"). But the male gods instruct the (apparently jealous) female gods that Hera-Urania can also be called Pege, because "as a water source she is also a source of spirit, which contains a fish that feeds the whole world with its flesh."

3. The appearance of the star above the statue of Pege. While the images of the gods still quarrel, the Persian king attends another miracle in his temple: a shining star appears above the statue of Hera-Pege, a heavenly voice announces the birth of a savior, and a crown of precious stones is found on the head of Pege. As a result, the other images of the gods fall down before her.

4. Interpretation of the miracle by the wise men of Persia. The king then orders the wise men of his kingdom, who interpret the events in the following way. Pege is the daughter of Karia of Bethlehem, who will bear a king in Judah. The prostration of the gods before Pege is a sign that the end of the worship of the images of the gods has come with this birth.

5. The apparition of Dionysus. In the evening, the god Dionysus appears in the same temple, confirms the interpretation of the Persian scholars, and sings a hymn of submission to Hera-Pege together with the other images of the gods.

6. The Persian king sends the magi to Judah. Impressed by these miraculous events, the king sends magi with gifts to Judah, while a star leads the way.

Second Part: The Narration of the Magi

The second part is designed as a self-report of the magi about their journey and encounter with Mary and the child.

7. The conversation between the magi and the Jews. Arriving in Jerusalem, they announce to the "leaders of the Jews" the birth of the Messiah and the annihilation of the synagogues. An attempt at bribery with gifts to prevent the magicians from spreading this message fails. A meeting with the "King of the Jews," unnamed until then, is also briefly mentioned.

8. The magi in Bethlehem. In Bethlehem, the magi find Mary with the help of the star. They question and then worship her. The report also contains a description of Mary's appearance—perhaps the most ancient description we have of Mary—and a note that a slave had painted a portrait of Mary and the child, which had been placed in the Persian temple of Hera-Pege after the magi returned home. The child, who is "almost two years old," sits on the floor and laughs and jumps when the magicians give him gold, take him in their arms, caress him, and boast. In some versions, among others by John of Damascus,

Testament Apocrypha: More Noncanonical Scriptures, vol. 1, ed. T. Burke and B. Landau (Grand Rapids: Eerdmans, 2016), 3–18.

a conversation among the magi about the Christ's "polymorphism" follows. The magi discover that he had appeared to one as a newborn, to the other as a young adult, to the third as an old man.

9. The departure of the Magi. In the evening, an angel appears in the residence of the magi and warns that Herod is pursuing them. Therefore, they flee home on their strong horses. The Legend ends with a confession and an accusation formulated in the second-person plural: "We know that Christ is our Savior. But you resist him by your way of life, you slander his preaching at every hour."

An Image as a Link

The two parts of the Legend can be clearly distinguished from each other by the change of location and persons, but they are also connected by certain motifs, so that their original common bond is beyond question. The most important link is the portrait of Mary and the child, painted by a slave in Bethlehem, that the magi, upon their return, affix to the temple where the star appeared and the fall of the idols took place (καὶ ἀνετέθη ἐν τῷ ἱερῷ, ἐν ᾧ ἐχρηματίσθη). The apologetic point of this short remark is that the fallen Persian-Hellenistic statues of the gods are replaced by the image of the mother of God with the newborn Christ.

3. INTERPRETIVE ISSUES

Apart from the uncertainty concerning time, place, and authorship, the content and interpretation of the Legend of Aphroditian also provide puzzles. The most scholarly attention has been paid to the description of the star miracle in the Persian Temple of Hera and to the identification of Hera with Urania and Pege in the first part of the Legend. Eduard Bratke, using the parallels to Lucian of Samosata's treatise *De Dea Syria*, convincingly demonstrated that the depiction of the cult and the description of the images of the gods are probably inspired by the cult of Dea Syria in Hierapolis/Mabbug. He interpreted the story of Aphroditian as an ironic Christian replica of Lucian's writing and as an apologetic transformation of the very popular cult of the Astarte-Kybele of Hierapolis.[19] However, Lucian's writing itself is already a parody of the religious excesses of his time, and an ironic refraction would only harm the apologetic intention of a Christian author. If one considers other literary and archaeological sources for the cult of Hierapolis,[20] it can be concluded that the parallels to Hierapolis are not of literary but of factual character.

At the center of the sanctuary of Hierapolis stood the statues of Zeus and Hera, the latter uniting the characteristics of many female goddesses and being named accordingly with different names (Atargatis, Aphrodite, Athena, Artemis, Rhea, Selene). According to Lucian, a belt also identified her as "Queen of Heaven" or Urania (Οὐρανία). On her head, surrounded by rays of light, was a tower-shaped crown, and at night a fire-colored gemstone above her filled the temple with light. As food, the priests offered the goddess a fish from a nearby spring every day, because a special relationship to this animal was attributed to her. The other images of the gods in the temple, including those of Apollo and Dionysus, moved and gave oracles of their own accord. There was also a throne of Helios. All these

19. Bratke, *Das sogenannte Religionsgespräch am Hof der Sassaniden*, 177–78.

20. See Paul-Louis Van Berg, *Répertoire des sources greques et latines: Corpus Cultus Deae Syriae*, Études préliminaires aux religions orientales dans l'empire romain 28 (Leiden: Brill 1972); Sabine Fick, "Hierapolis/Bambyce (Membidj)," in *Religionsgeschichte Syriens: Von der Frühzeit bis zur Gegenwart*, ed. P. Haider, M. Hutter, and S. Kreuzer (Stuttgart: Kohlhammer, 1996), 210–16; J. L. Lightfoot, *Lucian, On the Syrian Goddess: Edited with Introduction, Translation, and Commentary* (Oxford: Oxford University Press, 2003).

elements and motifs also appear in the Legend of Aphroditian. The author of the Legend may have known the cult of Hierapolis firsthand.

3.1 Christian Persianism

There can be no doubt that the existence of a Hera temple in the Sassanid palaces is an impossibility. But why, then, did the author transfer the events to Persia and not leave them in Syrian Hierapolis? The reason probably lies in the fact that he was keen to locate the origin of the wise magi in Persia. For Romans of this time, Persia was, on the one hand, the military archenemy, and on the other hand, the epitome of the origin of old wisdom. King Kyros, to whom the construction of the Hera Temple is ascribed in the Legend of Aphroditian, was regarded as the ideal ruler with a tolerant religious policy. In the first centuries, religious movements came from the Orient to the West, such as the Mithras cult and Manichaeism. The programmatic first sentence of the Legend—"To Persia Christ was known from the beginning, for nothing escapes the learned lawyers of that country, who investigate all things with eagerness"—testifies to an esteem for Persian wisdom and scholarship, which is quite typical of this period for Romans interested in religion. Thus, the Legend of Aphroditian fits into late antique "Persianism."[21]

3.2 Mariology: Hera-Urania-Pege

What kind of Marian conception and veneration is associated with the connection to the goddess Dea Syria and the description of the magi's encounter with Mary? The report of the priest Proupippos on the events in the temple (2–3) are decisive in this respect. He tells the Persian king that over the whole night the images in the temple continued dancing, both the males and the females, saying to each other, "Come, let us rejoice with Hera," and to the priest, "Prophet, come and rejoice with Hera, for she has been loved. She has come to life again and is no longer called Hera, but Urania ('Queen of Heaven'). For the Mighty Helios ('Great Sun') has loved her." This leads to a dispute between the female images and the male ones about the right understanding of that holy wedding of Hera and Helios. The males claim, "That she was rightly called Hera, we admit. But her name is Myria ('Thousandfold'), for she bears in her womb, as in the sea, a vessel burdened with a myriad. And if she is also called Pege, let it be understood thus: a fountain of water continuously sends forth a fountain of spirit, containing a single fish, which is taken with the hook of divinity and which sustains with its own flesh the whole world, dwelling there as though in the sea."

This discussion between the female and the male images of gods may reflect christological-Mariological disputes of the Legend's own time.

The Greek goddess Hera, who mythically regained her virginity through a bath after each meeting with Zeus, was identified in Hellenistic times with different mother deities, and in Hierapolis she was identified with Atargatis, Artemis, and Rhea, among others. The fact that she is given the epithet Urania ("Queen of Heaven") is perhaps already a consequence of the identification with the Syrian Atargatis, who, for her part, has a close relationship to springs and to fish.[22] The female deities seem to want to protect Hera, the mother of the gods par excellence, from being devalued by the claimed pregnancy by referring to the apparently lower goddess Pege. But in their response, the male deities offer an interpretation for the epithet Pege, which helps her even more to fame (see below).

---

21. See Rolf Strootman and Miguel John Versluys, eds., *Persianism in Antiquity* (Stuttgart: Franz Steiner 2017).

22. Heyden, *Die "Erzählung des Aphroditian"*, 264–65.

3.3 Christology I: The Eucharistic Fish

The connection of the Pege with the fish "which sustains with its own flesh the whole world" contains a complex of motifs, which is also testified by the epitaphic poem of Abercius of Hierapolis. It was composed in 215 or 216 CE and is transmitted both epigraphically and literarily.[23] The epigram reports on the deceased's long journeys, including to Syria, and then continues:

> [12] I had Paul [...] Faith everywhere led me forward,
> [13] and everywhere provided as my food a fish
> [14] of exceeding great size, and perfect, which a holy virgin drew with her hands from
>   a fountain
> [15] and this it ever gives to its friends to eat,
> [16] it having wine of great virtue, and giving it mingled with bread.[24]

The close parallels to the etiology for the Urania-Myria-Pege in the Legend of Aphroditian are obvious. They were first noticed by Adolf von Harnack but interpreted in a misleading way as pagan testimonies to the cult of Hierapolis.[25] Their significance lies rather in the Christian eucharistic use of the fish symbol. In both texts, the fish (ἰχθύς) is offered by a fountain (πηγή) that is also declared a virgin. But while in the Abercius inscription the virgin and fountain are identified with the faith, πίστις, in the Legend she stands for Mary, the mother of Jesus. The fish established itself very early in ancient Christianity as a symbol of Christ, not least because of the popular acrostic: Ἰησοῦς Χριστὸς Θεοῦ Υἱὸς Σωτήρ—Jesus Christ Son of God, Savior.[26] In the epigram of Abercius, as well as in the Legend, it is used as a eucharistic symbol, emphasizing the large size of the fish and its universal power. The way of fishing, however, is different: In the Abercius inscription, the virgin takes the fish alone with her hands. In the Legend, however, the fish is taken with the hook of divinity. According to Gregory of Nyssa, the "fishhook of deity" (τὸ ἄγκιστρον τῆς θεότητος) symbolizes the divine nature of Jesus, which is veiled by his humanity so that he can redeem the world as God-Man (Gregory of Nyssa, *Oratio catechetica* 24). This is a concise symbolic declaration concerning Mary, by which the divinity of her child is wrapped in human flesh and thus becomes the redeemer of humanity.

3.4 Christology II: The Carpenter

The second key christological passage in the Legend of Aphroditian is related to the carpenter. In their explanation of the events, the male gods say, "You have well said: 'She has a carpenter' [τέκτονα ἔχει ἐκείνη]—but the carpenter whom she bears does not come from a marriage-bed. For this carpenter who is born, the child of the chief carpenter, has built the triple-constructed celestial roof with most wise skills [ὁ τοῦ τεκτονάρχου παῖς, τὸν

---

23. See Vera Hirschmann, "Untersuchungen zur Grabinschrift des Aberkios," *Zeitschrift für Papyrologie und Epigraphik* 129 (2000): 109–16; Reinhold Merkelbach, "Grabepigramm und Vita des Bischofs Aberkios von Hierapolis," *Epigraphia Anatolica* 28 (1995): 125–39.

24. Παῦλον ἔχων ἔποχον. Πίστις πάντη δὲ προῆγε / καὶ παρέθηκε τροφὴν πάντη ἰχθὺν ἀπὸ πηγῆς / πανμεγέθη καθαρὸν, ὃν ἐδράξατο παρθένος ἁγνή / καὶ τοῦτον ἐπέδωκε φίλοις ἔσθειν διὰ παντός / οἶνον χρηστὸν ἔχουσα κέρασμα διδοῦσα μετ' ἄρτου.

25. Harnack, *Zur Abercius-Inschrift*; see the critics in Heyden, *Die "Erzählung des Aphroditian"*, 243–46.

26. See Franz-Josef Dölger, *Ichthys: Der heilige Fisch in den antiken Religion und im Christentum*, vol. 2 (Münster: Aschendorff, 1922); Gedalyahu Stroumsa, "The Early Christian Fish Symbol Reconsidered," in *Messiah and Christos: Studies in the Jewish Origins of Christianity*, ed. I. Gruenwald, S. Shaked, G. Stroumsa, Texte und Studien zum antiken Judentum 32 (Tübingen: Mohr Siebeck, 1992), 199–205.

τρισύστατον οὐράνιον ὄροφον ἐτεκτόνησε πανσόφοις τέχναις], establishing this three-fold inhabited dwelling by the Logos [τὴν τρικάτοικον ταύτην στεγότητα λόγῳ πήξας]" (Leg. Aphr. 2.3).[27]

The reference to the profession of Joseph put forward by the female gods has been raised by both Jewish-Christian groups and pagan apologists against the emerging worship of Jesus as God (see Eusebius, *Hist. eccl.* 3.27; Origen, *Cels.* 6.34). Here the carpenter is applied to God as the heavenly Father of the newborn king: The child is descended from the divine carpenter, the master builder of the world. Trinitarian terms and allusions, such as "built the triple-constructed celestial roof" (τὸν τρισύστατον οὐράνιον ὄροφον ἐτεκτόνησε) and "establishing this threefold inhabited dwelling by the Logos" (τὴν τρικάτοικον ταύτην στεγότητα λόγῳ πήξας), reinforce the statement, and a proximity to Sabellian modalism can be detected.[28]

Elsewhere, there are other, more clearly orthodox expressions of Christology. Thus, the designation of Jesus as "Son of the All-Ruler, who is born in the flesh of the female arms" emphasizes the child's human side (Leg. Aphr. 2.3; see Col 2:9). The Persian interpreters emphasize this humanity particularly strongly when they announce to the king that in Bethlehem he will find "the son of the Omnipotent, carried in bodily form in the bodily arms of a woman" (Leg. Aphr. 4.2; εὑρήσεις γὰρ τὸν υἱὸν τοῦ παντοκράτορος σωματικῶς σωματικαῖς ἀγκάλαις γυναικείαις βασταζόμενον). In addition, Judeo-Christian idioms appear in phrases like "Christ the Son of the Most High" (Leg. Aphr. 7.3; ὁ γὰρ Χριστὸς ὁ τοῦ ὑψίστου παῖς; see Luke 1:32), as well as in Mary's praise as "Mother of the First of all orders" (Leg. Aphr. 3.1; μήτηρ τοῦ πρώτου πάντων τῶν ταγμάτων; see Col 1:15), and as "divine and royal root that shapes the image of the heavenly and earthly king" (Leg. Aphr. 4.2; ῥίζα ἔνθεος καὶ βασιλικὴ ἀνέκυψεν, οὐρανίου καὶ ἐπιγείου βασιλέως χαρακτῆρα φέρουσα; see Isa 11:1–10; cf. Sib. Or. 8.264–69; 439–79).

Overall, no mature Christology or Trinitarian doctrine can be discerned in the Legend of Aphroditian. The Legend associates motifs that emphasize the divinity of Jesus and his mother (through identification with gods in the first part) with those that accentu-ate human appearance and behavior (in the encounter with Mary and the child). These conflicting aspects in christological and Mariological terms are perhaps an argument for the early origin of the Legend.

3.5 Soteriology

The theological punch line of the Legend is of soteriological character. This becomes obvious in a number of places, first by the voice that accompanies the wonder of the star (3) that claims:

> Mistress Pege [Δέσποινα Πηγή], the Mighty Helios has sent me to announce to you and at the same time to serve you in your giving birth, for he produces a blameless childbirth for you, who is becoming mother of the first of all ranks, bride of the triple-named single

---

27. τέκτονα ἔχει ἐκείνη, ἀλλ' οὐκ ἐκ λέχους, ὃν τίκτει τέκτονα· οὗτος γὰρ ὁ γεννώμενος τέκτων, ὁ τοῦ τεκτονάρχου παῖς, τὸν τρισύστατον οὐράνιον ὄροφον ἐτεκτόνησε πανσόφοις τέχναις, τὴν τρικάτοικον ταύτην στεγότητα λόγῳ πήξας.

28. See Manlio Simonetti, "Sabellio e il Sabellianismo," *Studi storico-religiosi* 4.1 (1980): 7–28. The confes-sion made by Dionysos, "We are going to be exposed as false by an acting person" (μέλλομεν ὑπὲρ ἐμπράκτου προσώπου ἐλέγχεσθαι ὡς ψευδεῖς), reminds one of the Sabellian distinction of the three πρόσωπα of God. Also, the designation of the Pege as "bride of the triple-named single divinity" (νύμφη τριωνύμου μονοθείας) points in this direction.

divinity [νύμφη τριωνύμου μονοθείας]. And the unbegotten new-born is called Beginning and End—the beginning of salvation, the end of destruction.

Here the christological formula "Beginning and End" (cf. Rev 22:13, "the Alpha and the Omega") is recorded and interpreted in a soteriological way.

In the interpretation of the miracle by Dionysus, it becomes clear how salvation happens: "He re-creates the ancient image, and puts together image with image, and the unlike he brings to likeness" (ὁ τὴν παλαιὰν εἰκόνα ἀνακτίζων καὶ τὴν εἰκόνα τῇ εἰκόνι συντιθεὶς καὶ τὸ ἀνόμοιον ἐφ᾽ ὁμοίωσιν διδούς; cf. Gen 1:26–27). In the background stands the doctrine of the restoration of man's original image of God through incarnation as a condition for the salvation of mankind. This doctrine was developed especially by Athanasius of Alexandria (in *De incarnatione verbi*) and appears here in a more narrative mode.

3.6 With the Pagans against the Jews

A fundamental question of interpretation is how pro-pagan and anti-Jewish aspects of the Legend are to be related to each other. One gets the impression that the positive reference to the pagan cult is directly linked to anti-Jewish polemics. This becomes clear in both the characterization of persons and the wording of proclamations. As already shown, the first sentence emphasizes immediately the wisdom of the Persians: "To Persia Christ was known from the beginning. For nothing escapes the learned lawyers of that country, who investigate all things with eagerness." By contrast, in their encounter with Jewish authorities, the magi announce that the newborn Christ is "annulling your law and your synagogues" (Leg. Aphr. 7.3; ὁ γὰρ Χριστὸς ὁ τοῦ ὑψίστου παῖς ἐγεννήθη, καταλύων τὸν νόμον ὑμῶν καὶ τὰς συναγωγάς). In reply, the Jews appear unreasonable in their attempt at bribery.

However, in the interpretation of the star miracle by the Persian scholars, the end of both pagan and Jewish tradition is announced: "Out of Judah a kingdom has arisen which will abolish all the memorials of the Jews. The prostration of the gods upon the floor prefigured the end of their honor. For he who comes is of more ancient dignity and will shake those who are new in it" (Leg. Aphr. 4.2). Nevertheless, there seems to be a difference in how the respective authorities relate to this revelation. While the pagan god Dionysus proclaims his own end and that of all overthrown deities, and all of them sing of their fall as perfection, the Jewish authorities seem to resist recognizing their own end.

From a linguistic point of view, however, it is not clear whether the Legend's closing words from the magi—"Behold then, such great things we have told you regarding Christ and we know that Christ has become our Savior. But you, by your ways, are opposed to him, all the time slandering his pain" (9.2)—refer to the Jews, Persians, or the audience of the Legend. This depends on how one interprets the prior sentence "and we reported all that we had seen in Jerusalem" (καὶ πάντα ἀπηγγείλαμεν, ἃ εἴδομεν ἐν Ἰερουσαλήμ). If the place "in Jerusalem" is linked to ἃ εἴδομεν ("what we had seen"), the following sentence may mean either the Persians or the audience. However, if the location is linked to πάντα ἀπηγγείλαμεν, one has to imagine the accusatory speech not after the return of the magi in their homeland but always in Jerusalem—that is, to the Jews. It seems to me that the latter is the more plausible reading, because the magi did not actually see something worth telling in Jerusalem but in Bethlehem. If that is true, then the positive connection to the pagan cult is in fact combined with a clear anti-Jewish tendency. The promise of Dionysus that "salvation has come for the gentiles and foreign peoples, there is plenty of refreshment for the afflicted" seems to apply exclusively to pagans.

4. KEY PASSAGES FOR NEW TESTAMENT STUDIES AND THEIR SIGNIFICANCE
4.1 An Anti-Jewish Alternative to Matthew 2:1–12

Like many other apocryphal writings, the Legend of Aphroditian fills a narrative gap left by the Gospels. In its second part (7–9), the Legend provides an alternative narration to Matthew's magi pericope (Matt 2:1–12) and thus contributes to contextualizing Matthew in the early Christian discourse on the magi. Interest in the tradition of the magi from the east flourished in the second and third centuries among Christians, because it offered possibilities for dealing with the non-Jewish environment more than almost any other Gospel text. At the same time, Matthew left open many questions that could be answered differently depending on the historical context and theological goal: Who were the magi? Where did they come from? Where had they identified the star, and on what knowledge could they interpret it correctly?

Few Christian authors followed the positive image that Matthew had drawn of the magi. Most of them followed an interpretation inspired by Isaiah 8:4, according to which the magi, who were identified as the "power from Damascus," had actually come to Judah with malicious intent and were converted only through the encounter with the Son of God (see Justin, *Dial.* 78.2; Tertullian, *Marc.* 3.13.8; Didymos, *Comm. Ps.* 64.1–7). Other authors refer to the biblical tradition, mostly to the prophet Balaam (Num 22–24), whose descendants were considered magicians (see Origen, *Cels.* 1.60; *Hom. Num.* 13.7.4; Justin, *Dial.* 106.4; *1 Apol.* 32.12–13; Eusebius, *Dem. ev.* 9.417–21). Only Theodot and Clement of Alexandria identify the magi as Persians independently of Balaam; Clement even ranks them among the ancestors of Greek philosophy (see Clement, *Exc.* 75.1–12; *Strom.* 1.15.71.3–4).

It cannot be clearly stated whether the author of the Legend knew the Gospel of Matthew. Since the second century, different traditions about magicians have been documented, and not all can be traced back to the Gospel of Matthew.[29] But if the author of the Legend knew the Gospel of Matthew, he not only supplemented but corrected it, and he did so with an anti-Jewish intention. One could say that the Legend is a pagan counternarrative to the Gospel of Matthew. The birth of Jesus Christ is revealed not by Jewish prophecy but by pagan cult, and more precisely, by Persian wisdom.

Matthew 2:1–9 simply states that "magicians from the Orient" came to Jerusalem to worship the newborn king of the Jews because of the appearance of a star. Thereupon Herod makes inquiries among the Jewish scribes and is referred by them to the prophecy of Micah 5:1, which is why he sends the magi to Bethlehem. In contrast, in the Legend of Aphroditian the magi are identified as Persians and are not dependent on the help of the Jewish scribes. They already know from the revelation in their homeland, and thanks to the star that shows them the way, where to look for the newborn king.

Upon their arrival in Jerusalem, they proclaim the birth of the Messiah even before they have seen him, and they announce the end of the Jewish religion: "You are suffering from unbelief [ἀπιστίαν νοσεῖτε], and neither without an oath nor with an oath do you believe, but you follow your own thoughtless goal. For the Christ, the son of the Most High is born, annulling your law and your synagogues [ὁ γὰρ Χριστὸς ὁ τοῦ ὑψίστου παῖς ἐγεννήθη, καταλύων τὸν νόμον ὑμῶν καὶ τὰς συναγωγάς]. And for this reason, struck by a most excellent oracle, you do not hear with pleasure this name which has come upon you unexpectedly" (Leg. Aphr. 7.3).

---

29. Thomas Holtmann, *Die Magier vom Osten und der Stern: Mt 2,1–12 im Kontext frühchristlicher Traditionen*, Marburger Theologische Studien 87 (Marburg: Elwert, 2005).

The Jewish authorities are portrayed negatively from the outset as they try to silence the magi with gifts of money so that there won't be a riot among the people.[30] King Herod, who has the role of the enemy of Christ in the Gospel of Matthew, plays a subordinate role in the Legend of Aphroditian in comparison with the scribes. The magi meet him only for a short conversation but do not care about him and "pay him no more attention than to an insignificant person" (Leg. Aphr. 7.5; καὶ ἀπέστημεν ἀπ' αὐτοῦ, μὴ προσέχοντες αὐτῷ εἰ μὴ ὡς ἑνὶ εὐτελεῖ). The role of the wicked enemy of the newborn Christ is thus shifted from Herod to the religious authorities of the Jews.

The second part of the story narrates the meeting of the magi with Mary and the child, which is only outlined in a few words in the Gospel of Matthew (2:11). When the magi question Mary, she refers to the annunciation of the birth by an angel, which is reported in Luke 1:26–38.[31]

A special focus is on Mary's appearance: she is described as dainty, with grain-colored skin, and a beautiful and simple hairstyle. Her portrait, made for the magicians by a "servant quite skilled in painting" (Leg. Aphr. 8.5; εὐφυῆ παῖδα ζωγράφον) and placed in the Persian temple after their return, serves as proof of the encounter. The description of the child Jesus emphasizes his childlike behavior: he sits on the floor, plays, and laughs, while the magi caress and praise him. Whereas Matthew mentions gold, incense, and myrrh as gifts of the magi, the original version of the Legend of Aphroditian probably spoke only of gold. Later manuscripts, however, adapted the text to match the Gospel of Matthew and added incense and myrrh.

The closing words of the Legend, discussed above, provide an alternative or a correction to the Gospel of Matthew. Matthew emphasizes that the magicians, for fear of Herod, do not return to their homeland via Jerusalem, but that they went on a different path. The Legend, in contrast, ends with a report by the magi in Jerusalem and an accusatory statement against the Jews in Jerusalem for their unbelief.

In the context of early Christian discourse on the magi, the Legend of Aphroditian is one of the few texts that grant the magi their own wisdom, independent of biblical revelation.

In the combination of the revelation to the magicians and the travelogue, as well as in some narrative and theological details, the Legend resembles a writing that only recently came into the focus of research: the so-called Revelation of the Magi, which is handed down within the framework of the Syrian Chronicle of Zuqnin. In the Revelation of the Magi, it is not Persia but the land of Shir (presumably China) that is the home of the magi, but many other motives are similar: the detailed description of the "prehistory" of the star appearance, the appreciation of pagan oracles, the emphasis on the appearance of Jesus and Mary, the motif of Jesus's polymorphism (which, however, does not appear in the earlier versions of the Legend), the reproduction of the conversation between the magi and Mary, and the missionary closing sermon of the magi on their return home.

Brent Landau suspects that the original version of the Revelation of the Magi was written in Syriac in Edessa in the second or third century and is intended to demonstrate the connection of Christianity with pre-Christian religious traditions of the Orient.[32] The Legend of Aphroditian pursues a very similar intention, whereby the missionary intention

---

30. The mention of rioting may show a trace of knowledge of Matt 26:5.
31. But even here it cannot be clearly decided whether there is a specific reference to the Gospel of Luke in the background or only a general knowledge of the tradition of the annunciation.
32. Brent Landau, "The Revelation of the Magi," in Burke and Landau, *New Testament Apocrypha*, 19–38.

of a synthesis of pagan religion and Christianity is accompanied by anti-Jewish polemics. If the assumption is correct that the Legend was originally written in Greek, then one could regard the Revelation of the Magi and the Legend as two complementary apocryphal narratives, which in late antique Syria, a linguistically, culturally, and religiously plural world, took the biblical magi pericope as an opportunity to connect Christianity to existing religious traditions. In the Legend, however, this positive link is accompanied by an anti-Jewish tendency that is alien to the Synoptic Gospels.

5. BIBLIOGRAPHY

Bobrov, Alexander G. *Апокрифическое Сказание Афродитиана в литературе и книжности Дрвней Руси. Исследование и тексты.* St. Petersburg: Nauka, 1994.

Bratke, Eduard. *Das sogenannte Religionsgespräch am Hof der Sassaniden.* TU NF 4/3. Leipzig: Hinrichs, 1899.

Bringel, Pauline. "Interprétation et réécritures dans la tradition manuscrite du Récit d'Aphroditien." Pages 285–96 in *Entré Actes. Regards croisès en sciences humaines. Réalités et représentations: les pistes de la recherche. Actes du Ier Colloque international des jeunes chercheurs en sciences humaines et sociales de Strasbourg, 10 et 11 mai 2004.* Edited by Laurent Angard. Strasbourg: Université Marc Bloch, 2005.

Gaster, M. "Die rumänische Version der Legende des Aphroditian." *Byzantinisch-Neugriechische Jahrbücher* 14 (1938): 119–28.

Heyden, Katharina. "Die Christliche Geschichte des Philippos von Side. Mit einem kommentierten Katalog der Fragmente." Pages 209–43 in *Julius Africanus und die christliche Weltchronistik.* Edited by M. Wallraff. TU 157. Berlin: de Gruyter 2006.

———. *Die "Erzählung des Aphroditian": Thema und Variationen einer Legende im Spannungsfeld von Christentum und Heidentum.* Studien und Texte zu Antike und Christentum 53. Tübingen: Mohr Siebeck, 2009.

———. "The Legend of Aphroditianus: A New Translation and Introduction." Pages 3–18 in *New Testament Apocrypha: More Noncanonical Scriptures.* Vol. 1 Edited by T. Burke and B. Landau. Grand Rapids: Eerdmans, 2016.

Monneret de Villard, Ugo. *Le leggende orientali sui magi evangelici.* Studi e Testi 163. Vatican: Biblioteca apostolica vaticana, 1952.

Schwartz, Eduard. "Aphroditianos." PW 1: 2788–93.

Usener, Hermann. *Religionsgeschichtliche Untersuchungen: Das Weihnachtsfest.* 2nd ed. Bonn: Friedrich Cohen, 1911.

Veder, William R. "The Slavonic Tale of Aphroditian: Limitations of Manuscript-Centred Textology." *Търновска книжовна школа* 9 (2011): 344–58.

CHAPTER 8

PILATE CYCLE

J. K. ELLIOTT

1. INTRODUCTION

Pilate is a New Testament character whose role in the trial of Jesus and whose subsequent career figure extensively in the apocryphal literature. Reasons for this interest in Pilate's place in the Jesus story are not hard to find. As will be shown below, the same motives lie behind the earlier New Testament interest in him.

The earliest surviving apocryphal texts to include Pilate are also the two longest yarns: the Acts of Pilate (*Acta Pilati*) and the originally unrelated Descent [of Christ] into the Underworld (*Descensus ad Inferos*). As separate documents, the *Descensus* was written about the fifth or sixth century, and the (earlier Greek "A") Acts of Pilate was written about the fourth century. Tischendorf's volume includes both these texts, as well as some of the later texts in the Pilate Cycle, such as letters to and from Emperor Claudius, to and from Emperor Tiberius, to Herod and his reply, the Report (*Anaphora*), the Handing Over (*Paradosis*), and the Vengeance of the Savior (*Vindicta Salvatoris*).[1]

The Acts of Pilate was combined with the *Descensus* in the Middle Ages and survives as the first half of the Gospel of Nicodemus, a book that was popular in an Anglo-Saxon version. As such, it was (and still is) hugely popular in the English-speaking world—and rightly so.

The Gospel of Nicodemus that also goes on in its second half to tell of Jesus's descent to the underworld (the *Descensus ad Inferos*) was translated by the fifteenth century into Latin from an original Greek text. But it was the Latin from which modern vernacular translations (like that into Anglo-Saxon) were normally translated. Like many of the texts in the Pilate Cycle, the original provenance of the Gospel of Nicodemus is disputed by academics, as too is its date of composition.

While the Acts of Pilate and the *Descensus* are the longest and, to many readers, the most important literature that contains Pilate's name, "The Pilate Cycle" includes many more texts mentioning Pilate. My work titled *The Apocryphal New Testament*, following M. R. James's edition and example, includes such texts. Under the heading "The Pilate Cycle," I include the twelve apocrypha that deal with the end of Jesus's life and beyond; each extract and full Gospel (bar one, the *Descensus ad Inferos*, or The Descent [of Christ] into the Underworld, which is also known as The Harrowing of Hell[2]) feature the Roman governor, the prefect Pontius Pilate.[3]

---

1. C. de Tischendorf, *Evangelia Apocrypha*, 2nd ed. (Leipzig: Avanarius and Mendelssohn, 1876; repr., Hildesheim: Olms, 1966; 1987), 210–486.

2. Not that "hell" is the most appropriate translation here, as I shall explain below.

3. J. K. Elliott, *The Apocryphal New Testament* (Oxford: Clarendon, 1993), 164–225.

The two relatively full apocryphal Gospels in the Cycle, the Acts of Pilate and the *Descensus ad Inferos*, usually stand together, and as already indicated, they are collectively known in combination, especially in medieval manuscripts, as the Gospel of Nicodemus. Modern paragraph numbering has given the Acts of Pilate the chapters 1–16 and the *Descensus* chapters 17–27 (or, according to the tradition and translation known by modern scholars as Latin A, chs. 17–29). The titles of both books, the Acts of Pilate and the *Descensus*, are found in the medieval Gospel attributed to Nicodemus and are the names normally used in modern scholarship. These titles arose first in the introductions to certain medieval Latin manuscripts.

In antiquity, Justin Martyr and Eusebius both seem to refer to a work called the Acts of Pilate (respectively, in *1 Apol.* 35.9; 48.3; and in *Hist. eccl.* 9.5.1), but this is unlikely to be an early version of our currently available Acts of Pilate. Both halves of the Gospel of Nicodemus seem to be much later, at least from the fifth or sixth century. (The second half, the *Descensus*, is a quasi-appendix to the first part.) That there is no real connection between the two halves is clear from our reading of both.

Part of the reason for these two apocryphal "confections" (to adopt M. R. James's definition of several of such bizarre writings, and indeed for all such works) was because Pilate's role in the Christian drama intrigued believers. Was Pilate a good man, a mere cog in a divine drama that required Jesus's death, and prior to that Jesus's arrest, trials, and sentence of execution? Or was he an agent of Satan, essentially a malevolent ruler, who performed that most heinous of crimes, deicide? The fact, moreover, that Jesus of Nazareth, Christianity's proclaimed Savior and Lord, had been convicted of a serious crime and had been put to death by order of the Roman governor called for explanation. The Pilate legends invited a number of explanations.

2. SUMMARY OF CONTENT
2.1 The Acts of Pilate

In the first part of the Gospel of Nicodemus known as the Acts of Pilate, we are in a different, albeit familiar, biblical world. This apocryphon is part of the library of rewritten biblical books, a genre familiar to those who know the Qumran literature.[4] In these rewritings of Jesus's trials, which drew extensively on the canonical Gospels, it is Pilate who becomes the main center of attention, as one would expect to find in this cycle of texts.

The Acts begins with accusations about Jesus's alleged sorcery (because of his having healed numerous people on the Sabbath) and his having apparently been born "of fornication." Pilate is reluctant to judge Jesus but eventually does so. On entering the praetorium, where Pilate sits in judgment, the heralds find that their standards automatically bow down (on two separate occasions) to honor Jesus. This frightens Pilate, who then receives word from his wife—who piously observes the Jewish faith, we are told!—warning him to have nothing to do with Jesus. Pilate now debates the question of Jesus's guilt with the Jewish leaders and whether Jesus had been born out of wedlock. Pilate consults Jesus. Then a woman named Bernice comes forward, stating that Jesus had healed her of her hemorrhage. Pilate again bickers with the Jewish leaders. Pilate declares that he finds no fault in Jesus. Nicodemus and Veronica separately also plead for him. Pilate again rebukes the

---

4. E.g., see James Charlesworth's series, *The Dead Sea Scrolls: Hebrew, Aramaic and Greek Texts*, The Princeton Theological Seminary Dead Sea Scrolls Project (Tübingen: Mohr Siebeck; Louisville: Westminster John Knox, 1994–). Such expansions of Old Testament narratives and traditions created a precedent for similar literary activities on the part of Christian scribes and teachers.

Jewish leadership, and on it goes until, frustrated and weary, the governor gives in and allows Jesus to be crucified. Two men are crucified with Jesus, and the one who rebukes the other for reviling Jesus is given the name Dysmas.

The crucifixion of Jesus results in strange omens. Pilate is agitated and asks if the Jewish leaders witnessed what had happened. Pilate and his wife are grieved and fast. The Jewish leaders persecute Joseph of Arimathea for daring to request the body of Jesus for burial. The description of the resurrection—and the deliverance of Joseph of Arimathea, who had been locked in a room—is quite dramatic. Everyone is talking about the appearances of Jesus.

As is typical of many apocryphal texts, the Acts of Pilate expands the canonical Gospels' accounts of the trials and death of Jesus. Here Pilate's role is central, of course, but it is the persuasiveness of the Jewish leaders that makes Pilate allow Jesus to be crucified. What is hinted at in the canonical Gospels becomes explicit and exaggerated in the Acts of Pilate. The effect is to shift the blame for Jesus's condemnation squarely onto the Jewish leaders. Pilate may have been weak, but his culpability in the death of Jesus is to some extent mitigated.

2.2 The *Descensus ad Inferos*

The Christian affirmation of belief in Jesus's descent to Hades is in the Apostles' Creed and in the so-called Athanasian Creed, as well as being article 3 in the Anglican Thirty-Nine Articles of 1563. The biblical origin for this belief, which is a major and normal part of Christian tradition, seems to be based on a particular interpretation of 1 Peter 3:19 ("In the spirit he [Christ] went and preached to the imprisoned spirits"). Not surprisingly, that statement encouraged later generations of Christians to elaborate what was meant by Jesus's appearance before "imprisoned spirits." The apocryphal stories of Jesus's descent to the underworld reflect those elaborations.

The main text describing these events is the fifth- or sixth-century *Descensus ad Inferos*. In this tradition Jesus's arrival in Hades after his death by crucifixion spells the end of death as a permanent state. Hades by transference is the domain of the character Hades (known elsewhere in mythology as Pluto). He rules over the world of departed spirits. This realm seems close to the idea of the Hebrew Sheol. (In the creeds the word "hell" is erroneous and confusing.) Hades is not hell or Tartarus—those are names for the place of eternal punishment and are the opposite of "heaven," the place of the eternally blessed.

The two characters, Satan (that supreme embodiment of evil, the devil, the adversary of God) and Hades, aware of Jesus's imminent arrival in their midst, are powerless to stop his descent. Following Jesus's arrival and his triumph over Satan, the faithful are then released. The whole narrative is presented as a written account commissioned by the chief priests of the Jerusalem Temple from the newly resurrected sons of Simeon: the men tell their story as eyewitnesses of the events in Hades.

Now we refer, albeit only briefly, to another apocryphon that parallels in part the *Descensus*—namely, the Questions of Bartholomew, dated perhaps from as early as the second century. In that apocryphon Bartholomew confronts Jesus in the period before his ascension; his questioning concerns Jesus's whereabouts after his crucifixion (when he is said to have "vanished" from the cross). Jesus's reply is remarkably consistent with the story in the *Descensus*, and one wonders if the Questions could later have influenced the *Descensus*. Other queries posed by the eponymous hero of the Questions of Bartholomew include his request to meet the adversary of man—called there Beliar. Beliar is usually known as Belial in the Bible, in the Dead Sea Scrolls, and also in Milton's *Paradise Lost*, where he is the fallen angel who represents impurity.

Let us now return to the *Descensus*, attributed to Leucius and Carinus (Karinus), the sons of Simeon, the elderly worthy in Luke 2:25–35.[5] We are now dealing with an apocryphal text proper, in the sense that the writing seems to have originated to complete a perceived hiatus in the story of Jesus's death. The New Testament's own passion narratives fail to tell us what Jesus was doing between his dying on the cross on the afternoon of Friday and the finding of his empty tomb on the Sunday following. In other words, the *Descensus* fills in a gap. The apocryphon has Jesus gainfully occupied between Good Friday and his resurrection announced on the first Easter Day. No doubt readers may well have been puzzled, as indeed are modern commentators, what precisely was in his mind when the author of 1 Peter wrote 3:19 with its oblique reference to Jesus in the underworld, but detail is lacking. And it is this alleged gap that this apocryphon tries to fill. We find the same impulse in the Gospel of Peter, which tells us that when Jesus emerged from the tomb a heavenly voice asked if he had preached to the dead.[6]

In this apocryphon, Jesus meets Adam and Eve and leads them out of Hades, holding their hands. He conducts them into their long-awaited paradise. Others follow: patriarchs and other Old Testament worthies and characters, including martyrs and prophets. Adam and Eve are duly shocked at and are understandably surprised by the endless (and potentially doomed) fallen progeny that they have created. The righteous among them are led to paradise to rejoin Adam and Eve. The sinful go into hell, and punishments are duly meted out. Apocryphal apocalypses go to great lengths to describe the punishments of hell handed out to sinners (and, to a lesser extent, the joys of heaven that await the pious).

Other characters from the New Testament include the penitent "good thief" from the canonical Gospels, who is a figure beloved of the apocryphal accounts in the Pilate Cycle. He is described here as "humble" and is still alive when Jesus leads the dead into paradise—just as Elijah and Enoch are. (These characters make small reappearances in the Acts of Pilate. All such worthies were understood not to have died—hence their special category.)

2.3 Shorter Texts

Among the shorter texts are the following ten writings. These ought to be read alongside the introductory remarks in this essay, especially for those books that consider Pilate's part in the death of Jesus. All should normally be understood together with the Gospel of Nicodemus part 1, the Acts of Pilate. First comes the Letter of Pilate to Claudius as well as that from Pilate to Tiberius, and its reply; the letters from Pilate to Herod and his reply to Pilate, which precede the narratives; and a few more texts that fill out details relating to the passion, the resurrection, and especially the aftermath of these events. The shorter texts are as follows:

1. The Letter of Pilate to [Emperor] Claudius (*Epistula Pilati ad Claudium*)
2. The Letter of Pilate to [Emperor] Tiberius (*Epistula Pilati ad Tiberium*)
3. The Letter of [Emperor] Tiberius to Pilate (*Epistula Tiberii ad Pilatem*)
4. The Letter of Pilate to Herod (*Epistula Pilati ad Herodem*)
5. The Letter of Herod to Pilate (*Epistula Herodi ad Pilatem*)
6. The Handing Over of Pilate (*Paradosis Pilati*)

---

5. The two names, Leucius and Carinus (Karinus), were associated in the early church with the authorship of all five early apocryphal Acts (of Andrew, John, Paul, Peter, and Thomas).

6. The interest in what Jesus did in the underworld is paralleled in a number of apocryphal texts, where the eponymous heroes and heroines of their own, named, Gospels, books of apocryphal acts, and apocryphal apocalypses experience visions of heaven and hell and encounter angels, the righteous, and/or the damned.

7. The Report of Pilate (*Anaphora Pilati*)
8. The Vengeance of the Savior (*Vindicta Salvatoris*)
9. The Death of Pilate (*Mors Pilati*)
10. The Narrative of Joseph of Arimathea (*Hyphēgēsis Iōsēph*)

2.3.1 The Letter of Pilate to Claudius

This "letter" may have been composed in the fourth or fifth century, possibly in Latin. Later copies survive in that language. In this letter Pilate attempts to excuse himself in the execution of Jesus, saying that the Jewish leaders misled him. This was clearly a popular letter and is reproduced in numerous places, including the Acts of Peter and Paul 40–42, and Ps.-Marcellus's Passion of Peter and Paul 19. The letter appears today in differing guises (including in Latin) and in Greek. Versions also occur in Armenian and in Syriac.

It, like so many apocrypha, is vehemently anti-Jewish, especially against the chief priests who are here accused of lying; the Jews *en bloc* are described as wicked, and it is they who are said to have crucified Jesus. In this last, bizarre point the composer is clearly copying Luke 23:25. Our author obviously did not understand that crucifixion was a distinctively Roman form of capital punishment. If Jews were indeed allowed to carry out judicial state killings, death by stoning was the preferred and normal method of corporal punishment. In any case, in Acts 7:59 the death of Stephen by stoning, whether his death was carried out as a mob-lynching or not, is, nevertheless, described as the normal or expected way in which Jews eliminated malefactors or opponents. However, the beneficence of the Romans marks this text as being from an Eastern church provenance.

2.3.2 The Letter of Pilate to Tiberius

We note the emperor here has a different name to that in the letter immediately above. This writing may have originated in the seventh century. The letter survives in both Greek and Latin manuscripts. The Greek is, arguably, the earlier. In his letter Pilate tells the emperor that Jesus was pious and that when he was crucified, supernatural signs appeared. He acknowledges the injustice of executing Jesus, but he feared the multitude. Pilate regrets that he did not strive to the utmost of his power to prevent the loss and suffering of righteous blood. He fears destruction will come, as the Scriptures testify.

2.3.3 The Letter of Tiberius to Pilate

This writing is Western in provenance. The text is not translated in my *Apocryphal New Testament*.[7] In the letter, Pilate is cast as a criminal. He has "no pity" and is "deceitful"; he is accidentally killed when out hunting. The emperor's alleged response is also included. In the Greek version, Tiberius tells Pilate without qualification that his condemnation of Jesus "was completely unjust."

2.3.4 The Letter of Pilate to Herod

The text is known in Greek and in Syriac. The Syriac may be as old as the sixth or seventh century, although our Greek manuscripts are late medieval. (One manuscript combines this letter with the Handing Over of Pilate [*Paradosis Pilati*] and the Report of Pilate [*Anaphora Pilati*].) The text was possibly written in the fourth or fifth century in Latin and in Syriac. As is common in modern discussions, it is difficult to be precise about dates or the original language. In this letter Pilate admits that he committed a grave error

---

7. See Elliott, *Apocryphal New Testament*, 225, where a summary of contents is provided.

in sending Jesus to the cross. Pilate says his wife, Procla, and Longinus went to hear Jesus teach and were deeply moved.

2.3.5 The Letter of Herod to Pilate

This writing survives from the fifteenth century and was written in Greek. Several Syriac manuscripts are also extant, which have been dated by paleographers to the seventh and eighth centuries. Again, anti-Jewish rhetoric is normal in this letter, although Herod is described as sympathetically disposed to Pilate. In the letter we learn that vengeance will come on the Jewish priests and that gentiles will inherit the kingdom. This is the hopeful message received by its Christian believers. In his response, Herod (i.e., Antipas, tetrarch of Galilee until deposed in 39 CE) acknowledges the grievous nature of what was done. The tetrarch notes that one calamity after another has occurred since the crucifixion of Jesus: the accidental decapitation of his step-daughter who had asked for the head of John the Baptist, the horrible death of the Roman Longinus, who thrust his spear into the side of Jesus, and the appearance of worms within Herod himself portending his soon death.[8]

2.3.6 The Handing Over of Pilate

This writing, too, may be of Eastern provenance; it is extant in Greek. According to Tischendorf, both versions, designated A and B, were probably written originally in Greek in the seventh century, though the oldest extant manuscripts date to the twelfth century.[9] In my *Apocryphal New Testament*, I followed the Latin text published by Tischendorf.[10] At the end of some manuscripts is also to be found the Letter of Pilate to Claudius. This interesting text deserves a somewhat longer treatment.

The Handing Over of Pilate tells the story of Pilate's recall to Rome, as a prisoner, for the part he played in condemning Jesus to the cross. The enraged emperor demands to know why Pilate ordered the crucifixion of Jesus. Pilate did what he had to do, he explains, only because he feared an uprising of the Jewish people. Jesus is presented as pious and upright, whereas the Jewish scribes, chiefs, and elders are motivated by animosity against Jesus. The later followers of Christ—that is, the gentiles, including Romans—are a beneficent presence and are temperate. Jesus himself is of righteous blood and entirely guiltless.

Again, this is another text that has a high regard for Pilate. It will be seen that Caesar pronounces that Pilate should not have crucified Jesus. Nonetheless, the text is probably also of Eastern provenance. It is an early text, although surviving manuscripts are medieval. We see here that Pilate is imprisoned because he is lawless. "The impious one" is a common description of Pilate, and the adjective "insatiable" is also repeatedly used to describe him; these adjectives are, therefore, used almost like Homeric epithets. But despite such descriptions, he is "innocent," whereas it is "the Jews" (including Herod, Archelaus, Philip, Annas, Caiaphas, the chief priests, and "the multitudes") who collectively are the ones who are rebellious, reckless, and guilty of Jesus's death. One may indeed pause to ask: Where would Christianity be had Jesus been acquitted? In fact, his preordained death, allegedly through divine planning, was essential for Christianity's theology—as, of course, was his resurrection.

On the second day of Pilate's "trial" before Caesar, we are informed that he acted only because of "lawless and godless" Jews. This was the party line, especially in the

---

8. Recall that Herod's nephew Agrippa I, King of Judea, Samaria, and Galilee, and killer of the Apostle James, was "eaten by worms and died" (Acts 12:23).

9. Tischendorf, *Evangelia Apocrypha*, lxxix–lxxx.

10. Elliott, *Apocryphal New Testament*, 208–11.

Eastern churches. Pilate was "forced" into his action against Jesus. Although justice requires Pilate's death (by decapitation), his ultimate fate is favorable: an angel receives his severed head. Pilate's wife, Procla, sees this event and dies immediately to join her husband in heaven. The Jews are the ones described as the real sinners. In one paragraph toward the end of this letter, a divine proclamation from heaven states, "All generations and families of the gentiles will call you blessed."

2.3.7 The Report of Pilate

This text was often added to the Handing Over of Pilate. It is another writing that is close to the Letter of Pilate to Claudius and the Letter from Tiberius to Pilate. It was probably written in Greek somewhere in the fifth to the seventh centuries, although Syriac and early Latin manuscripts have also been found. The writing purports to be Pilate's official report to Emperor Tiberius, in which he tries to explain that despite his many miracles Jesus was nevertheless condemned to the cross.

2.3.8 The Vengeance of the Savior

The Vengeance of the Savior is one of several medieval texts that refers to Veronica, with her wonder-working kerchief onto which is implanted the face of Jesus *en route* to Calvary. Written in Latin and anti-Jewish, the Vengeance of the Savior tells of the conversion of one Tyrus and his household, Vespasian's capture of Jerusalem, and, anachronistically, the agitation of Herod the Great and his son Archelaus. One Volosianus, the emperor's kinsman, is sent to Judea to enquire into events, including (once again anachronistically) interrogation of Pilate. It is in the execution of his mission that Volosianus comes into possession of Veronica's cloth with the image of the face of Jesus. Acquisition of this cloth, or kerchief, results in the healing of the emperor.

As in several apocrypha, Veronica, or Ber(e)nice in the Latin tradition, is another minor character in the New Testament proper who is elevated in status in later texts. She is identified as the woman whom Jesus heals of an "issue of blood" in Matthew 9:20 and Mark 5:25 (cf. Luke 11:27).

From the eighth century onward, a "veil of Veronica" was preserved in Rome, and specifically from the end of the thirteenth century it was housed in St. Peter's Basilica. In the fourteenth and fifteenth centuries it was the object of much veneration and was believed to effect cures. Veronica has been given a place of continuing devotion in Christian practice because of the stations of the cross. Once the fourteen stations became a standard and popular pictorial means of encouraging meditation on the passion of Christ, station six, depicting the wiping of Jesus's face by Veronica, helped to perpetuate the fame of this woman.

Popular etymology explains that Veronica means "true image" (*vera icon*)—as opposed to spurious images of Christ, apparently to be found elsewhere. The name is applied to the cloth and to the woman whose headcloth it was. (A sudarium with the image of Christ printed on it is known in English as a *vernicle*, and one of the torero's movements with his cape used to flourish in a bullfight is called a *veronica*.)

To return to the Vengeance of the Savior, we have a tale of yet another (re-)telling of Pilate's alleged death. It is a story apparently originating in Aquitaine by the fourteenth century, in which again we find another version of a yarn in which Jesus's real enemies are Jews. Tiberius himself is (eventually) healed by Veronica with her kerchief. Her story is recalled when she captures the image of Christ on a sudarium as he was on his way to Calvary and his death. Again here we note the popularity of the theme that shows the power of Christianity over paganism.

2.3.9 The Death of Pilate

The Death of Pilate is a medieval concoction, presumably written originally in Latin (or even in Ethiopic). Like the Vengeance of the Savior, the story in the Death of Pilate tells of Tiberius, who is ill and who sends his emissary Volusianus (probably the same person mentioned in the previous writing), to seek out the healer Jesus. Having learned of Jesus's death, Volusianus instead meets Veronica, whose vernicle holds the image of Jesus's face; he then takes her with him to Rome, where Tiberius is subsequently healed. The emperor is enraged at Pilate and has him bound and brought to Rome. Imprisoned, Pilate takes his own life. The dead man is first buried in the Tiber in Rome but must be removed because of the ensuing earthquakes associated with the burial there of this despised deicide. Even hauntings are reported. The corpse then goes to Vienne in France, and inevitably there are earthquakes there too. Finally, it is dispatched to Losania (Mount Pilatus on Lake Lucerne in Switzerland), where further disturbances are also reported. The story is virulently anti-Pilate in tone and is therefore deemed to be Western Christian in origin.

Visitors to Lucerne in Switzerland may well wonder why a mountain nearby is called Mont Pilatus (Mount Pilate). The reason is the belief found in this apocryphon that Pilate lies, safely, beneath its huge bulk.

2.3.10 The Narrative of Joseph of Arimathea

This yarn, originally written in Greek, is likely to have originated in the twelfth century. As a rewriting of the New Testament stories about the death of Jesus, it is clearly important and significant, especially for scholars currently enamored of "reader response" theories. Once again, the main theme running throughout it is that it is virulently anti-Jewish (cf. Luke 23:25, when Jesus is handed over "to their [i.e., the Jewish leaders'] will"). Much is made of the two criminals crucified alongside Jesus. We are told that the names of the two robbers crucified with Jesus are Gestas and Demas (presumably the man called Dysmas in the Acts of Pilate). The good thief, like Jesus himself, will be translated immediately to paradise.

3. INTERPRETIVE ISSUES

A brief summary of these apocrypha *in toto* reveals the following themes:

a. They have anti-Jewish sentiments. The chief priests and the scribes are singled out for special condemnation, but the whole Jewish "mob" follows their lead. "The whole multitude's" words and actions occur in unison. The most malevolent of them inevitably include Judas (of course).

b. By contrast, Pilate is usually described sympathetically, as in the New Testament itself. He sees Jesus as a king and treats him as such.

c. Coupled with Pilate's sympathetic hearing of Jesus in the trial and the general antagonism to the Jews are the figures of (Jesus) Barabbas and the role of Herod (on these two figures, see sec. 4 below).

d. Charges against Jesus include (i) Sabbath healing[11] and (ii) fornication. Twelve Jews (obviously a significant number) are "allies" of Jesus. They defend him against the charge of his being illegitimate.

---

11. Nina L. Collins, *Jesus, the Sabbath and the Jewish Debate in the First and Second Centuries C.E.*, LNTS 474 (London: Bloomsbury, 2014).

THE ACTS OF PILATE AND THE PASSION
ACCOUNTS OF THE CANONICAL GOSPELS

The Acts of Pilate elaborates the passion accounts familiar to us from the canonical Gospels, and these are seen principally in manuscripts from the medieval period. The accounts contain textual citations that regularly follow the wording and story line in the New Testament Gospels. In one sense these citations, like patristic commentaries on the canonical works,[12] may well be of use to textual critics of the canonical Gospels. In the early apocryphal citations, we could also well learn much about the way(s) in which the quotations from Matthew, Luke, and John were remembered, used, and copied.

Literary criticism may use all these recurring themes to plot how stories were repeated with differing nuances and therefore altered, or even sometimes very carefully reproduced. Historians, too, should be allowed their contributions. At the very least, one could deduce that the earliest stories—that is, the accounts that were sufficiently familiar, early, and popular—were the versions selected for the canonical corpus. They were thus the very words copied or expanded by later writers. As is common in ancient literature, especially with apocryphal rather than canonical Scripture, embellishments and elaborations, as well as abridgments, can be readily spotted in later copying.

Another theological conundrum that is "solved" by the *Descensus* is the issue concerning the fate of those who had died prior to Jesus's incarnation. As the statement in either the Apostles' Creed or in the Athanasian Creed makes clear,[13] Christians believe that Jesus "descended into Hell." The apocryphon is set in Hades itself, a limbo for *all* dead people, righteous and unrighteous. It is a waiting room and not purgatory in the sense that Hades, as a place, is *not* for punishing sinners.

Hades here is not only a place but is, as already indicated above, also personified. As a character, Hades is engaged in conversation with Satan throughout the apocryphon. Both await the arrival of Jesus after his crucifixion, Satan with foreboding and Hades with joy. Jesus duly arrives and breaks down the gates of Hades *en route*. This is what medievalists call the Harrowing of Hell. The English "mystery" plays were popular dramatic representations of the biblical accounts and were usually performed by trade guilds from carts pulled through medieval cities; they included the apocryphal scene when Jesus enters Hades. In the English city of York, the Saddlers' Company traditionally performed this scene.

There are also many iconic representations of the *Descensus ad Inferos*, such as in Chora (in modern-day Turkey), and frescoes in the famous Scrovegni Chapel in Padua (the "Arena Chapel") may depict this scene. Utrecht University Library has a manuscript containing the Psalter; this includes an illumination of the ninth century as an illustration to Psalm 10:12. It has Jesus carried from his tomb by two figures and is sometimes said to illustrate the scene found in the apocrypha. Today's visitors to the famous wooden churches of Romania are similarly confronted by paintings of the choices awaiting people and affecting

---

12. The terms "apocryphal" and "canonical" are understood here as anachronisms. Any alternatives seem to be clumsy in English. (German usage may encourage our saying something like "texts deemed, or destined to become, apocryphal/canonical.")

13. This belief is not enunciated in the Nicene Creed.

them in their afterlives, just as those leaving the Scrovegni Chapel in Padua see Giotto's famous fresco of the end-time on the inside west wall of the "Arena Chapel" on their departure into the world outside.

Modern-day America is familiar with the event. For example, the church of Hagios Giorgios in Knoxville, Tennessee, has in a transept a twentieth-century window showing the Anastasis (i.e., the Harrowing of Hell).[14] There are many comparable examples throughout the world. Modern Westerners who read novels in English may know *The Lion Country* by Frederick Buechner, which draws heavily on M. R. James's *Apocryphal New Testament*.[15]

The age-old cycle of death and decay inaugurated by Adam's sin is now said to have been reversed by Christ's inability to be bound by death. This orthodox belief, so strongly present in the New Testament Gospels and in Paul's writings, is in effect dramatized in the *Descensus*. Another orthodox belief dramatized in this apocryphon is that the faithful will be raised from death because Christ is the firstfruits of those raised. This belief is graphically illustrated.

The apocryphal writings are, for the most part, orthodox in their theological teachings, strange though some details be. One must admit that even though these stories have occasionally been contaminated by Gnosticism or docetism, most of these apocryphal writings and their contents are "normal, middle of the road" expressions of Christian beliefs and practices. For texts that originated for the most part in the second and third centuries when many syncretistic beliefs were emerging and when much in Christianity was still being hammered out by church fathers and theologians, a person in the pew took canonical stories into their own hands, modeling them to fit into their own beliefs, experiences, and practices. What modern readers need to recognize is that much of what we may describe as "history" in these accounts is the history of Christian ideas held not by intellectuals but by ordinary believers. This history of Christian ideas is reflected in their beliefs, hymns, and liturgical practices (such as baptism, marriage, death, exorcisms, sealing, etc.), as well as the stories they tell of the founders of the faith and its churches.[16]

4. KEY PASSAGES FOR NEW TESTAMENT STUDIES AND THEIR SIGNIFICANCE

Crucifixion was known as a distinctively Roman form of capital punishment. In any telling of Jesus's story, his manner of death could not be avoided, and as it was a death by crucifixion, Roman involvement at some stage in the judicial process had to be explained. Hence all the New Testament accounts (as given below) tell how Pontius Pilate was the Roman official who passed the death sentence on Jesus. If one reads those accounts in the likeliest chronological sequence of composition, first Mark, then Matthew, Luke, and finally John, one can discern a developing tradition regarding Pilate. The evangelists' differing emphases reflect the early church's sensitivity in handling Pilate's involvement in the trial of Jesus at a time when a growing number of converts to Christianity were coming from a non-Jewish background, when the church was spreading throughout the empire,

14. David R. Cartlidge and J. Keith Elliott, *Art and the Christian Apocrypha* (London: Routledge, 2001). Other comparable scenes exist elsewhere in which the broken-down doors of Hades are clearly visible.

15. *The Lion Country* is the first part of a trilogy called *The Book of Bebb*, written in 1971. In one of his chapters, Buechner, using James's *Apocryphal New Testament*, imagines the speeches of Satan and of the personified Hades in terms of an opera. It is thus a scene that the author expects to be relatively familiar to at least a modern and educated readership.

16. Jacobus de Voragine, *The Golden Legend: Readings on the Saints*, 2 vols. (Princeton: Princeton University Press, 1993), e.g., chs. 53 and 54.

and when Christianity was becoming increasingly dependent on the goodwill of the Roman authorities.

Basically, the evangelists were embarrassed or reluctant to blame Pilate entirely for the death of Jesus, as we observe in each of the canonical Gospels. We thus read that Pilate's wife dreams of Jesus's blamelessness, that Pilate himself declares that Jesus is innocent three times, and that he washes the guilt for his judgment from his hands. By the time the Fourth Gospel was written toward the end of the first century, Pilate is described as reluctantly accepting his constitutional role as the only legally established figure able and qualified to pronounce a judicial death sentence.

Already we have drawn attention above to the part that the New Testament has played in the apocrypha. But the popular theme of the whitewashing or exonerating of Pilate especially has as its counterpoint the blaming of the Jewish race for the fate of Jesus in the canonical Gospels. Collectively the Jews are said to accept guilt for the death. Throughout the Gospels it is "the Jews" who become increasingly hostile to Jesus and his message. At the trial before the Sanhedrin, it is the Jewish leadership that pronounces Jesus worthy of death even before the Roman trial has begun; at the Roman trial itself, when Pilate offers an amnesty limited to the freeing of one prisoner, the Jews elect to have the murderer Barabbas released rather than Jesus. The Jews force Pilate to have Jesus crucified. By these means, Pilate is portrayed as a mere cog in the divine drama that requires Jesus to die on a cross and be raised.

As far as the New Testament itself is concerned, the Acts of Pilate not only expands the New Testament accounts of Jesus's trials and death but also adds the story of Veronica. There this apocryphon, the *Descensus*, explains what Jesus was doing between Good Friday and Easter morning. In that sense it is a "proper" apocryphon. Many other apocryphal yarns try to fill in perceived gaps in the story of Jesus's life. Thus citations from the New Testament may be seen as amplifying the Jesus narrative in the Acts of Pilate but not so in the case of the *Descensus*.

The Acts of Pilate expands the biblical narrative about Jesus's trials and death. Unlike the *Descensus*, we may read there the biblical accounts alongside the apocryphal elaborations. They do not control one another. The trial before Pilate precedes the one before Herod in Luke's Gospel alone, but when he is returned to Pilate we are then given in all the canonical accounts and in the Acts of Pilate the episode in which Jesus and Barabbas are the only choices offered by Pilate to the (Jewish) mob. Jesus is later described in the Ecce Homo episode and then is mocked by the Roman soldiers, prior to Pilate's condemning him to death by crucifixion. The Acts of Pilate is partly an expansion of that narrative, but it is also a retelling of the whole story.

Barabbas is mentioned in the New Testament's accounts of Jesus's death. The way he is introduced is peculiar even by the standards of the New Testament, although one can readily see how and why later apocryphal accounts lapped up such a text in their attempts to exonerate Pilate. Pilate oddly must "remind" the Jews that they have a custom of asking the Romans to pardon one person every Passover, as in Matthew 27:15–17 (cf. Mark 15:6; John 18:39). It is indeed strange (to me at least) that Pilate in the New Testament must tell Jews of their (otherwise) unknown convention and, even more peculiarly, that his alleged amnesty is limited to only one man, even though we read *in all four canonical Gospels* (i.e., Matt 27:38; Mark 15:27; Luke 23:33; John 19:18) that at least two other men were in custody at the same time, awaiting their deaths. The Jews choose the murderer Barabbas rather than the two thieves, subsequently said to have been crucified alongside Jesus (the "good thief" and the other, unrepentant, robber); "the Jews" then demand that Pilate crucify Jesus of Nazareth.

If there is historical value in this story, it *could* perhaps be that Pilate was here confronted by two men called Jesus—a relatively popular Jewish name at that time. He must ask the Jews calling for "Jesus's" death: "Which Jesus are you talking about, Jesus of Nazareth (or "the Nazarene") or Jesus Barabbas?" Here textual criticism may play a vital role. Some manuscripts at Matthew 27:16 and 17 read Jesus before the name Barabbas. It is likely that the longer text giving Barabbas his proper double name, "Jesus son of Barabbas," is original, but that soon after Christian scribes deleted "Jesus" before "Barabbas" in the belief that it would be inappropriate to use what had by then become a distinctive Christian name (par excellence) of another, especially of Barabbas, a murderer. Hence the shorter text, reading only Barabbas, was left *simpliciter*.

Another story added to the Pilate story in the New Testament is the episode with Herod. Pilate discovers that Jesus comes from Galilee and so readily tries to relieve himself of the responsibility of sentencing Jesus by sending him off to the puppet ruler, Herod (Luke 23:6–12). This is yet another contrivance to show that Pilate is doing all that he is able to do constitutionally, in order to avoid having to pass sentence on Jesus. It was entirely suitable to have the Jewish vassal-king Herod try Jesus and pronounce him worthy of death in place of Pilate. This tale is expanded in the apocrypha. This exonerating of the Romans and concurrent vilifying of Jews are, as we keep reading in these apocrypha, elaborations of the New Testament accounts. Here in the Acts of Pilate, the Roman prefect tried to free himself of all responsibility for the death of Jesus by blaming the verdict that Jesus must die on Herod and on the Jews, as in the New Testament itself.

What begins in the biblical tradition as an ambivalent attitude toward Pilate has become fixed, and Pilate is now a mere puppet in the hands of the Jewish mob. Better and more tactful to portray the Roman governor as a weak and vacillating man than as a murderous deicide! This way of resolving the "Pilate problem" by the New Testament authors did not, however, finally settle the issue. The later apocryphal tradition reflects a continuing dilemma in judging his character. Possibly the changed attitude, especially in Western European sources, was because the earlier goodwill of the Roman authorities had by then turned to an official persecution. The ambiguous ways of treating Pilate are at their most apparent when the apocryphal legends come to the death of Pilate. When a document, like the Acts of Pilate, is treating of the events of Jesus's passion, we can still see the influence of the canonical traditions: the picture of Pilate in these Acts is close to the New Testament's portrayal. The version in the Acts of Pilate is an elaboration of the canonical Gospels' trial narrative. We again see that the apologetic tendency in the account in the Acts of Pilate is to show how Pilate tried to free himself from all responsibility for the death of Jesus by blaming the events that led to his death on Herod and the Jews.

One may assume that Luke 13:1 (the only occurrence in the canonical Gospels where Pilate's name is *not* in the passion narrative) had remembered Pilate as a ruthless tyrant. If so, then, of course, Christians could claim that God subsequently reversed the result of Jesus's punishment for any alleged crimes against the Roman state by raising him from the dead. Jesus's resurrection from death meant that for Christians he lives on forever, affecting the lives and futures of all believers. Accounts of Jesus's post-Easter appearances by the faithful occur in all the canonical Gospels. Those accounts obviously satisfied readers, and we have no apocryphal additions to those stories, and we may indeed ask why that should be so. One may wonder if early believers needed further accounts. However, legitimate questions remain(ed): Where was Jesus when he was not being seen after Easter by the faithful? Was he hiding, or merely unrecognized? And why did Luke have the resurrected Jesus appear only within the restricted period of forty days, however symbolic and significant such a duration would have been to those familiar with that number from the Old Testament? The stories in the canonical Scriptures were, nevertheless, clearly adequate, and no *addenda* to them were even partly concocted to form New Testament apocryphal accounts.

The role of Pilate obviously remained highly important and was dealt with in differing ways. Although the churches in the West tried to be sympathetic to Pilate, it was the Eastern church traditions, particularly those early churches such as the Coptic and Ethiopic, that felt that he was essentially a "good" man, to the extent that the Ethiopic Church ultimately canonized him. Saint Pilate in that church was ultimately the most blessed of all men. His wife, Procla, was similarly canonized by that church too.

In both accounts, Eastern and Western, one can trace aspects of these two lines of judgment on Pilate, reflected in stories that go back to the New Testament itself where Pilate tries to reason with implacably hostile Jews; we also read of Pilate's wife's dream about Jesus's innocence. The episode in which Pilate washes his hands publicly of the issue occurs in the New Testament (Matt 24:27).

These incidents recur in the apocrypha. It is, however, in the New Testament where Pilate's words are followed by the Jews' own response with the words, "His blood be upon us and on our children" (Matt 27:25; words that have had tragic consequences for Jews ever since). Also, it is in the New Testament where Pilate declares Jesus innocent in Luke 23:22, giving this, the *third* and final such declaration.[17] There was therefore an issue which these apocryphal texts tried to explain. Most of the writings, canonical or apocryphal, are indeed theological and not histories (as commonly defined today). We should therefore not expect the New Testament to include precise court transcripts of the trial(s) of Jesus.

Yet, as far as Pilate's later story is concerned, where a judgment on his career is expected, he is treated variously as a saint or as an outcast. In the Eastern church, particularly in the Coptic and Ethiopic tradition, he was portrayed favorably (as already stated above). The Handing Over of Pilate shows how one Eastern legend treated Pilate and his wife, named here as Procla. Although Caesar has Pilate beheaded, Pilate's destiny there is a triumph. The Western church judged Pilate harshly. That tradition is represented above. It is also shown in the Death of Pilate, which is the text that explains how Mount Pilatus on Lake Lucerne (Losania in the text) was so named. (In that same context another place-name is explained: Vienne is also said to be a name that is derived from the words *via Gehenna* ["Hell Road"]. That folk etymology also made this location an appropriate, albeit temporary, resting place for the man who condemned Jesus to death.)

In addition to these contradictory accounts of Pilate's end are those letters allegedly written by Pilate. The letters sympathetic to Pilate suggest an Eastern origin. The letter addressed to the Emperor Claudius appears in various contexts, thereby revealing its popularity. Like many apocryphal writings this one is also anti-Jewish. In it an attempt is made to see the condemnation of Jesus from Pilate's point of view.

We ought also to read the canonical accounts of Jesus's passion in their entirety to see possible parallels to and developments in the later apocryphal stories examined here. The canonical Gospels' passion stories proper may be read in Matthew 26–28; Mark 14–16; Luke 22–24; and John 12–21 (omitting chs. 14–17).

---

17. See also J. K. Elliott, "The Case of the 'Rule of Three' in the Gospels," in *The New Testament in Antiquity and Byzantium: Traditional and Digital Approaches to Its Texts and Editing. Festschrift for Klaus Wachtel*, ed. H. A. G. Houghton, D. C. Parker and H. Strutwolf, ANTF 52 (Berlin: de Gruyter, 2019), 123–34.

5. BIBLIOGRAPHY

Bovon, François, and Pierre Geoltrain, eds. *Écrits apocryphes chrétiens*. Vol. 1. Bibliothèque de la Pléiade 442. Paris: Gallimard, 1993.

Cartlidge, David R., and J. Keith Elliott. *Art and the Christian Apocrypha*. London: Routledge, 2001.

Charlesworth, James H., ed. *The Dead Sea Scrolls: Hebrew, Aramaic and Greek Texts*. The Princeton Theological Seminary Dead Sea Scrolls Project. Tübingen: Mohr Siebeck; Louisville: Westminster John Knox, 1994–.

Collins, Nina L. *Jesus, the Sabbath and the Jewish Debate in the First and Second Centuries CE*. LNTS 474. London: Bloomsbury, 2014.

Elliott, J. K. *The Apocryphal Jesus: Legends of the Early Church*. Oxford: Oxford University Press, 1996.

———. *The Apocryphal New Testament*. Oxford: Clarendon, 1993.

Erbetta, Mario. *Gli apocrifi del Nuovo Testamento*. Casale Monferrato: Marietti, 1975.

Geoltrain, Pierre, and Jean-Daniel Kaestli, eds. *Écrits apocryphes chrétiens*. Vol. 2. Bibliothèque de la Pléiade 516. Paris: Gallimard, 2005.

Klauck, Hans-Josef. *Apocryphal Gospels: An Introduction*. London: Continuum T&T Clark, 2003.

Moraldi, Luigi. *Apocrifi del Nuovo Testamento*. Casale Monferrato: Piemme, 1994.

Santos Otero, Aurelio de. *Los evangelios apócrifos*. 6th ed. Madrid: Biblioteca Autori Cristianos, 1963.

Voragine, Jacobus de. *The Golden Legend: Readings on the Saints*. 2 vols. Princeton: Princeton University Press, 1993.

CHAPTER 9

PROTEVANGELIUM OF JAMES

ERIC M. VANDEN EYKEL

1. INTRODUCTION

The Protevangelium of James (sometimes known as the "Infancy Gospel of James") is an early Christian apocryphon about the birth of Jesus as well as the birth and childhood of Mary his mother. Although it is sometimes grouped with the Infancy Gospel of Thomas, the only thing that these two narratives share is that they both have children as their protagonists. The focus of the Infancy Gospel of Thomas is the sometimes impish Jesus, who abuses his power even to the point of killing his teachers and playmates. The Protevangelium of James instead focuses on a deeply pious portrait of Mary and the circumstances surrounding her birth and childhood. While Jesus does appear in this text, he is a relatively peripheral character. Yet it would be a mistake to claim that the author of this text is interested in Mary for Mary's own sake; the details of Mary's childhood are brought into focus because of the identity of her son. The portrait that this author paints of Mary (and Jesus) is so "orthodox" that it has achieved a quasi-canonical status both in some of the traditions it espouses as well as in its influence on Christian iconography through the centuries.[1]

1.1 Author

As is the case with many early Christian texts, the circumstances of the Protevangelium's authorship are largely mysterious to us. In the epilogue (Prot. Jas. 25.1–3), the author claims to be Jesus's brother James, and they claim to be writing from Jerusalem, just after the death of Herod the Great. Scholars are in general agreement that these claims are as fallacious as they are fantastic. The claim that the author is Jesus's brother serves to give the account a measure of authority that it wouldn't otherwise enjoy. James in this story is clearly to be understood by readers as a half-brother to Jesus, the son of Joseph from

---

1. See, e.g., the frescos in the Scrovegni Chapel in Padua, Italy, which contain a number of scenes from the Protevangelium. David R. Cartlidge and J. K. Elliot catalog this and other examples of apocrypha influencing art in *Art and the Christian Apocrypha* (London: Routledge, 2001). Michael Peppard has argued that the Protevangelium inspired some of the imagery on the walls of the *domus ecclesia* at Dura Europos (see Peppard, *The World's Oldest Church: Bible, Art, and Ritual at Dura-Europos, Syria* [New Haven: Yale University Press, 2016], esp. 155–201; idem, "Illuminating the Dura-Europos Baptistry: Comparanda for the Female Figures," *JECS* 20 [2012]: 543–74). Preceding Peppard in this argument is Dominic E. Serra, "The Baptistery at Dura-Europos: The Wall Paintings in the Context of Syrian Baptismal Theology," *EL* 120 (2006): 67–78. Certain Mariological dogmas (e.g., Immaculate Conception, Perpetual Virginity) may also originate with this narrative. When the French humanist Guillaume Postel "rediscovered" this text in the mid-sixteenth century, he is rumored to have heard it being read as part of a liturgy at a church in Constantinople (so W. J. Bouwsma, *Concordia Mundi: The Career and Thought of Guillaume Postel, 1510–1581*, Harvard Historical Monographs 33 [Cambridge: Harvard University Press, 1957], 36–37).

an earlier marriage, and he is likely present at a number of points in the story (e.g., Prot. Jas. 18.1). Thus, this specific claim of authorship not only heightens the *gravitas* of the narrative but frames much of it as a firsthand, eyewitness account.

1.2 Date

The claim that this account dates from not long after Jesus's birth is likewise optimistic and part of the author's attempt to locate the narrative in closer proximity to the events it purports to narrate. Yet because the author shows an awareness of certain canonical materials—among them the Gospels of Matthew, Luke, and John—we can comfortably assign it a second-century *terminus post quem*. And because our earliest extant copy of the text is in the Bodmer V codex—which dates from the third or fourth century—a third-century *terminus ante quem* seems reasonable. Many are comfortable narrowing that range based on possible citations of it in other early Christian literature. Clement of Alexandria, for example, references the story of the midwife who examines Mary's body after the birth of Jesus in order to validate that she retains her virginity postpartum (*Strom.* 7.16; see Prot. Jas. 20). Similarly, Origen refers to a "Book of James" as a possible root of the tradition that Joseph already had several children from a previous marriage when he and Mary were wed (*Comm. Matt.* 10.17). If Clement and Origen do indeed reference the Protevangelium, that would indicate a date of composition in the latter half of the second century.[2]

1.3 Provenance

In terms of the epilogue's final claim that the text was written in Jerusalem, most scholars continue to doubt that there is any truth to be found here. Often cited in support of a provenance other than Jerusalem is the author's lack of familiarity with Palestinian geography in general and the topography of Jerusalem in particular.[3] Against the claim that the author is ignorant of such things, Malcom Lowe has argued (as a resident of Jerusalem) that the author of the Protevangelium is actually quite accurate in terms of how they describe the geography of Jerusalem. Those who claim otherwise, he argues, are themselves ignorant of the geography of Jerusalem.[4] Lowe's arguments have failed to gain any serious traction among scholars of this text. In terms of provenance, the most likely candidates are Egypt or Syria. Émile de Strycker suggests Egypt as the more likely option because of the alleged connection between this text and the works of Clement and Origen, as well as what he considers to be the modesty of the author's Greek and the presence of certain "Coptic elements."[5] Lily Vuong, by contrast, has made a compelling case for Syria as the

---

2. Issues related to date are outlined more fully in P. A. van Stempvoort, "The Protevangelium Jacobi, the Sources of Its Theme and Style and Their Bearing on Its Date," in *Studia Evangelica III*, ed. F. L. Cross, TU 88 (Berlin: Akademie, 1964), 410–26; Eric M. Vanden Eykel, *"But Their Faces Were All Looking Up": Author and Reader in the Protevangelium of James*, RJFTC 1 (London: Bloomsbury T&T Clark, 2016), 23–24; Lily Vuong, *Gender and Purity in the Protevangelium of James*, WUNT 2.358 (Tübingen: Mohr Siebeck, 2013), 32–39.

3. Examples of such statements in Gerhard Rauschen, *Monumenta minora saeculi secundi* (Bonn: Sumptibus Petri Hanstein, 1914), 14; Johannes Quasten, *Patrology: The Beginnings of Patristic Literature* (Utrecht: Spectrum, 1950), 121; Wilhelm Michaelis, *Die Apokryphen Schriften zum Neuen Testament*, 2nd ed. (Bremen: Carl Schunemann, 1958), 71.

4. See Malcom Lowe, "Ἰουδαῖοι of the Apocrypha: A Fresh Approach to the Gospels of James, Pseudo-Thomas, Peter and Nicodemus," *NovT* 23 (1981): 56–90.

5. Full argument in de Strycker, *La Forme la plus ancienne du Protévangile de Jacques*, Subsidia hagiographica 33 (Brussels: Société des Bollandistes, 1961), 419–21. Proponents of an Egyptian provenance include Edouard Cothenet ("Le Protévangile de Jacques: origine, genre et signification d'un premier midrash chrétien sur la Nativité de Marie," *ANRW* 2.25.6 [1988]: 4267) and Philipp Vielhauer (*Geschichte der urchristlichen Literatur* [Berlin: de Gruyter, 1975], 668).

more likely place of composition. Citing the author's interest in varying types of purity and ritual practice, as well as the need to portray Mary as both a perpetual virgin and a mother, Vuong argues persuasively that this text fits well into what we know of second-century Christianity in Syria.[6]

2. SUMMARY OF CONTENT

The story begins with Mary's parents, Anna and Joachim, who are depicted as a wealthy, pious, and infertile Israelite couple. At the start of the narrative, the reader's focus is on Joachim, whom the author describes as both wealthy and generous. And these features are linked with temple practice, for Joachim is said to offer twice what is expected. "One portion from my abundance," he says, "will be for all the people; the other portion for forgiveness will be for the Lord God as my sin-offering" (Prot. Jas. 1.1).[7] But conflict soon comes when Joachim is told that because he is childless, he must wait to offer his gifts until others have first offered theirs. Dismayed by this, he consults "the Book of the Twelve Tribes of the People" in order to confirm whether all the righteous in Israel's history had borne children. To his further dismay, he finds that this is, in fact, the case. He leaves the city and takes to the wilderness in order to pray, fast, and lament (1.10).

At this point the reader's focus is redirected to Anna, who in addition to mourning her lack of a child mourns her current lack of a husband. No stranger to hyperbole, Anna conceives of her condition as one of widowhood (2.1). Following a strange interaction with her slave Juthine, Anna dons her wedding clothes and heads to her garden. She sits down underneath a tree there and offers a lengthy lament, comparing her barrenness to what she perceives as the universal fecundity of every created thing: the birds, the wild animals, the waters, and even the ground itself. All these things, in her view, are fruitful and therefore blessed by God. As Anna concludes her lament, an angel appears to her and announces that she too will conceive and bear a child (3.1–8). And this child will be unique, "spoken of throughout the world" (4.1). Anna vows to offer her child, whether male or female, as a gift to God. Joachim reenters the story when two additional angels announce to Anna that he is on his way home, having received the same message.[8] When he returns home, he prepares a huge sacrifice in celebration (5.1–4).

Mary is born to Anna after a short, seven-month pregnancy (Prot. Jas. 5.5).[9] The author is careful to frame the account of her birth in a way that emphasizes her purity. After she is born, for example, Anna refrains from breastfeeding her until she can cleanse herself

---

6. See Vuong, *Gender and Purity*, 193–239. Others who have argued for a Syrian provenance include Hans von Campenhausen (*Die Jungfrauengeburt in der Theologie der alten Kirche* [Heidelberg: Winter, 1962], 14–15) and Richard Bauckham (*Jude and the Relatives of Jesus in the Early Church* [Edinburgh: T&T Clark, 1990], 27–28).

7. All English translations of the Protevangelium of James are taken from Lily Vuong, *The Protevangelium of James*, ECA 7 (Eugene, OR: Cascade, 2019). The chapter and verse references likewise follow Vuong's translation.

8. There is an important textual variant in the angel's message. Some MSS have the angel telling Joachim that "Anna *will* conceive," while in others the angel says that "Anna *has* conceived." The former (future tense) indicates that the action of conception has yet to occur, while the latter (perfect) indicates that the action has already been completed, presumably by miraculous means, in Joachim's absence. To be sure, when the author notes later (in 4.10) that Joachim "rested . . . in his home," this certainly could suggest a "natural" conception and would tip the scales in favor of the future tense. Yet it is also notable that our earliest MS (Bodmer V) has the perfect tense. The variant serves as a reminder not only of the fluidity of the MS tradition but also of the remarkably high view of Mary espoused by the author and the scribes who transmitted it.

9. The length of Anna's pregnancy is a matter of disagreement among the manuscript tradition, but as Vuong notes, "Seven months is widely attested and is aligned with narrative tropes that depict divine or miraculous births. Thus it is likely to be the more original reading" (Vuong, *Protevangelium*, 59).

"when the required days were completed" (5.9). And not long after her birth, Mary reveals to the world that she is no ordinary child. For when she is but six months old, and to the astonishment of her mother, she begins to walk. From this day on, Mary's childhood is remarkable by any standard. Once Mary has taken her first steps, Anna sweeps her off her feet and exclaims: "As the Lord my God lives, you will not walk on this ground at all until I take you into the temple of the Lord" (6.3). She then builds a sanctuary in her bedroom and keeps Mary there, separated from anything that might risk threatening the purity she has enjoyed since her birth (6.4). While she lives in the sanctuary, Mary is entertained by a mysterious group of women the author calls "the undefiled daughters of the Hebrews" (6.4).

When Mary turns three, Joachim and Anna bring her to the temple in Jerusalem in fulfillment of Anna's vow to the angel who delivered news of her impending pregnancy (see Prot. Jas. 4.2). When they arrive, Mary is blessed by the priest and placed upon the steps of the altar, where she dances in front of the people of Israel (7.9). Nine years then pass in the span of one verse: "Mary was in the temple of the Lord, nurtured like a dove, receiving her food from the hand of an angel" (8.2). When she turns twelve, the reader finds the temple priests in crisis, trying to figure out what to do with the girl who is on the eve of becoming a woman. Their concern seems to be with the onset of her menstrual cycle, which they fear will "defile" the temple (8.3–4). The high priest enters the holy of holies and is instructed by an angel to summon all of the widowers from the land so that a suitable husband might be chosen through a process of divination (8.6–8).

An elderly Joseph is among those widowers summoned to the temple, and he is selected to take Mary into his care when a dove sprouts from his walking stick and lands on his head (Prot. Jas 9.5–6). He protests by noting that he has children older than Mary and by expressing concern that taking on such a young bride will make him a spectacle (9.8). The high priest counters his resistance by calling to mind the story of Dathan, Korah, and Abiram, who rebel against Moses and Aaron and are swallowed up by the earth because of their actions (Num 16:1–35). "Be afraid, Joseph," the high priest warns, "lest these things also happen in your house" (Prot. Jas. 9.10). Hearing this, Joseph concedes and brings the young virgin home with him. But no sooner than they arrive, Joseph leaves Mary so that he can continue building houses (9.12). His actions here could be interpreted in two ways: first, that Joseph is an irresponsible steward and that by leaving Mary alone he is being reckless; and/or second, that Joseph has no interest in pursuing any sort of sexual relationship with Mary and that he sees his responsibility as that of a reluctant guardian, not a "husband."

Following this scene, the reader's attention shifts back to the temple, where a council of priests discusses the need for a new veil or curtain in the temple. The high priest commands that a group of undefiled virgins from the "tribe of David" be brought to the temple in order to spin thread that will be used in the construction of this veil (Prot. Jas. 10.1–4).[10] Mary is among those who are called, and when all are gathered they cast lots in order to determine who will spin what thread. The purple and scarlet fall to Mary, and she returns home to begin spinning (10.6–10). It is at this point in the narrative that the author begins attempting to bring the story in line with the Gospel of Luke. In a brief aside, the narrator comments, "It was at this time that Zechariah became mute and Samuel took his place, until Zechariah could speak again" (Prot. Jas. 10.9). This is a clear reference to the Lukan

---

10. An overview of issues related to the designation "tribe of David" can be found in Vanden Eykel, *"But Their Faces"*, 105–7.

dialogue between Zechariah and the angel in the temple, wherein Zechariah is told that his wife Elizabeth will become pregnant. When Zechariah is astonished by this news, he becomes mute until his son John (the Baptist) is born (so Luke 1:8–20, 57–64).

During a break from her spinning, Mary goes outside to draw water, and she hears a voice that says, "Greetings, favored one! The Lord is with you! You are blessed among women" (Prot. Jas. 11.1–2). Terrified, she runs back into her house and resumes spinning. At this point an angel appears to her and announces that she has found favor with God and that she will "conceive from his Word" (11.5). Mary seems puzzled by this and asks, "If I conceive by the Lord, the living God, will I give birth like all other women give birth?" (11.6).[11] The angel assures her that this birth will not be "normal" and that her son will be called "Son of the Most High" and "will save his people from their sins" (11.7). Mary replies to this news in Lukan fashion: "Let it happen to me according to your word" (11.8).

When she is finished spinning the scarlet and purple threads for the veil, she brings them to the temple, where they are received enthusiastically by the high priest, who blesses her: "Mary, the Lord God has magnified your name, and you will be blessed among all the generations of the earth" (Prot. Jas. 12.2). As this episode follows closely on the tail of the annunciation dialogue, the author likely intends for the reader to see the priest's blessing as unintentionally appropriate given the identity of the child in her womb. Mary goes straight from the temple to visit her relative Elizabeth, who likewise blesses her and refers to her as "the mother of my Lord," claiming that "the child in [her] sprang up" (12.5). In what is certainly one of the narrative's stranger moments, Mary is bewildered by this because she "forgot the mysteries that the angel Gabriel had spoken" (12.6). The inexplicably forgetful virgin becomes frightened once her belly begins to grow, and she returns home to hide herself from public view (12.8).

Joseph returns home when Mary is in her sixth month, and he is horrified when he finds her pregnant. He berates himself, because he presumes that her "condition" is the result of his negligence; he left her alone and failed to fulfill his duty to protect her. He goes so far as to invoke the story of Eve and the serpent in Genesis 3: "Just as Adam was in the hour of his praising when the serpent came and found Eve alone and deceived her and defiled her, so too has the same happened to me" (Prot. Jas. 13.5). But his self-deprecation is short lived, for he quickly turns his attention to Mary and lambastes her for betraying her privileged upbringing in the temple: "You who have been cared for by God—why have you done this?" (13.6). Mary denies that she is responsible and insists that she is still a virgin. Joseph asks what most would agree is a reasonable question, namely: "How then are you pregnant?" And keeping with the forgetfulness so strangely introduced earlier Mary responds: "I do not know from where it came to me" (13.10).

At this point the author attempts to bring the narrative into alignment with the Gospel of Matthew by portraying a fearful Joseph in crisis. On the one hand, he wants to expose Mary because he is afraid of being held accountable for any sin that *she* may have committed. But on the other hand, he is worried that her child is "angelic" and that by exposing her he may risk betraying an innocent person. His solution: divorce her secretly (Prot. Jas. 14.4). His plan is quickly troubled when an angel appears to him in a dream and warns him against such action by revealing the divine origin of the child inside her (14.5–6). Joseph awakes with a new resolve, determined to guard the young Mary (14.8).

A previously unknown character called Annas the scribe arrives on the scene following this and asks Joseph, "Why have you not attended our council?" As Joseph is explaining

---

11. Notably, Mary's question here concerns not the conception itself but the manner of parturition.

that he is weary from recent travel, the tension rises as Annas turns his head and beholds a visibly pregnant Mary (Prot. Jas. 15.1–3). He goes to the high priest and reveals that Joseph appears to be in violation of his commitment to guard the young virgin he received from the temple. Here it becomes clear what Joseph was agreeing to when he agreed to take Mary as his "wife." In contrast to the accounts in Matthew and Luke, for example, where it is assumed that Mary and Joseph have a "normal" married relationship (and all that implies) after Jesus is born, the author of the Protevangelium sees their relationship quite differently. In this text, Mary is understood as Joseph's ward, not his spouse.

Mary and Joseph are brought to the temple to give an account, and the high priest begins his questioning with Mary: "Why have you done this? Why have you humiliated your soul and forgotten the Lord your God?" (Prot. Jas. 15.10–11). Mary weeps and maintains that she remains pure and innocent of what she is accused of (15.13). The high priest's attention then turns to Joseph, who responds that he as well is innocent and has not forsaken his vow to protect the young virgin. The high priest accuses him of lying, and Joseph is silent (15.18).

The high priest determines that the best way to determine guilt in this instance is to administer a drink test that he terms "the Lord's water of conviction" (Prot. Jas. 16:1). The reference seems loosely based on a drink test described in Numbers 5:11–31, which was administered in order to determine whether a woman had been unfaithful to her husband. If she had, and had become pregnant, then the test would cause an abortion (Num 5:27). The test that Mary and Joseph are given is different insofar as the drink is given to Mary *and* Joseph, and it is administered without any specification of outcomes. Both drink the water, are sent into the wilderness, and come back "whole" (Prot. Jas. 16.4–5). The witnesses are in awe when neither is affected, and Joseph and Mary return home, vindicated and rejoicing (16.8).

The author points the reader back toward the Gospel of Luke with the announcement, "An order came out from King Augustus that everyone in Bethlehem of Judea be registered for a census" (Prot. Jas. 17.1). In contrast to the census in Luke, which applies to the entirety of the Roman world (so Luke 2:1), in the Protevangelium the census would seem to apply only to those in Bethlehem. Joseph's anxiety returns, as he puzzles over how he will register Mary; her age makes him embarrassed to claim her as his wife, and he can't claim her as his daughter because everyone knows she's not actually his daughter (Prot. Jas. 17.2–3). Nevertheless, he puts Mary on a donkey, and he and his sons begin the journey to register. Halfway into their journey, Mary indicates that she is going into labor (17.10).

Joseph helps Mary off the donkey and brings her to a cave so that she is not exposed in the process of giving birth. He leaves her there with his sons (who are traveling with them), and he sets out to the hill country to find a Hebrew midwife (Prot. Jas. 18.1–2). As he leaves the cave, Joseph has a peculiar vision of the created world stopped in its tracks, like a diorama. He sees birds hanging still in the air, workers in the field in the act of enjoying a meal, goats with their mouths in the river but not drinking, among other things. Aside from the unusual contents of Joseph's vision, it is also curious that the entirety of the vision is narrated in first person, from Joseph's point of view (18.3–10).[12]

The action in the narrative resumes suddenly, and Joseph encounters a woman coming

---

12. Prompting some to suggest this as a secondary addition to the text. The scene is absent from a number of important MSS. François Bovon's analysis of this scene (in "The Suspension of Time in Chapter 18 of *Protevangelium Jacobi*," in *The Future of Early Christianity: Essays in Honor of Helmut Koester*, ed. B. A. Pearson [Minneapolis: Fortress, 1991], 393–405) provides a helpful overview of the MS tradition as well as references to similar scenes in cognate literature.

down from the hill country. After some initial questioning, the woman—later called a midwife—asks about who is giving birth in the cave, and Joseph invites her to follow him back to that place (Prot. Jas. 19.1–11). As soon as they arrive, a cloud fills the cave, and the midwife exclaims, "My soul has been magnified today because my eyes have seen an incredible sign; for salvation has been born to Israel" (19.14). The cloud departs and is replaced with a blinding light, and when the light recedes Joseph and the midwife behold the infant Jesus feeding at the breast of his no-longer-pregnant mother (19.16). The midwife rejoices, "How great is this day for me, for I have seen this wondrous sight" (19.17).

The midwife rushes from the cave and encounters a character—a woman called Salome—who at this point in the narrative has yet to be named or make an appearance. The midwife announces to her, "A virgin has given birth, something that is contrary to her physical nature" (Prot. Jas. 19.18). What precisely the midwife is trying to impart to Salome is not clear, but it would seem as if her claim concerns the fact that Mary's physical "intactness" as a virgin has been affected neither by conceiving nor by giving birth to a child. Faced with this incredible claim, Salome says that she will not believe "unless I insert my finger and examine her physical condition" (19.19). Salome enters the cave, and the midwife instructs Mary to prepare for an examination. Salome wastes no time and thrusts her finger into Mary (20.2). It quickly becomes evident to Salome as well as to the reader that this plan was ill-conceived, for Salome's hand bursts into flames and begins to wither away in the blaze (20.4). Salome cries out to God in her anguish and prays for deliverance, at which point an angel appears to her and instructs her to pick up the infant Jesus and be healed (20.5–9). She does this, is healed, and leaves the cave "justified" (20.11).

After the birth of Jesus and the Salome episode, the author's attention shifts to other "supporting characters." The material in chapters 21–22 follows Matthew's account closely, though with some embellishments. As Joseph is getting ready to return home, the magi arrive, asking about the whereabouts of the king of the Jews (Prot. Jas. 21.2). Herod is troubled by this question, and he calls together the high priests to seek council. The magi describe to Herod the star that they saw, a star so bright that it eclipsed all other stars in the sky (20.8). Herod sends them to Bethlehem with instructions that they are to report back to him with the new king's whereabouts, and the star leads them to the cave and stops directly over Jesus's head (20.10). They present their gifts and then return home by another route (20.11–12).

When Herod realizes that the magi have defied him, he gives the order that all infants two years old or younger be killed (Prot. Jas. 22.1–2). In an effort to harmonize Matthew's account with Luke's, the author has Mary place Jesus in a manger in order to hide him and so spare him from the slaughter (22.3). Elizabeth and a newborn John (the Baptist) appear on the scene as well, also fleeing from the wrath of Herod. Finding no hiding place for her son, Elizabeth approaches a mountain and prays, "Mountain of God, take me in, a mother with her child" (22.7). The mountain splits open without hesitation and allows her to enter, and they are protected there by an angel (22.8).

In his search for John, Herod sends his servants to the temple to question Zechariah on his whereabouts. Zechariah responds, "I am a minister of God, serving in his temple. How would I know where my son is?" (Prot. Jas. 23.3). The servants report back to Herod, who becomes enraged. He sends his servants back to remind Zechariah that he has the power to determine whether he lives or not (23.5–6). Zechariah persists in his refusal to cooperate: "I am a witness of God. Take my blood, for the Master will receive my spirit because you are shedding innocent blood at the entrance of the Lord's temple" (23.7–8). As a result, Herod's servants murder Zechariah in the temple (23.9).

The narrative closes in the temple, with the priests arriving in anticipation of being blessed by Zechariah. They begin to worry when he does not appear, and one priest enters the sanctuary and finds blood there. A voice exclaims, "Zechariah has been murdered and his blood will not be wiped away until his avenger comes" (Prot. Jas. 24.3–6). All the priests enter the sanctuary at this point, and they and the temple itself begin to lament in unison, "The ceiling panels of the temple cried out and they ripped their clothes from top to bottom" (24.7–8). The priests then discover that Zechariah's blood has become stone, and the people lament his death for three days and three nights (24.9–11). After three days, Simeon is chosen by lot to replace Zechariah as high priest, and the narrative draws to a close here (24.14).

The author concludes with a brief epilogue in which he claims to be James the brother of Jesus, writing in or around Jerusalem around the time of Herod's death. This is followed by a short blessing: "Grace will be with all those who fear the Lord. Amen" (Prot. Jas. 25.4).[13]

3. INTERPRETIVE ISSUES

There are a number of interpretive issues that appear frequently in scholarship on the Protevangelium of James. Here I should like to address two of the most significant: text-critical issues, and audience/intended function.

3.1 Text-Critical Issues

It has become commonplace for studies on the Protevangelium to lament the lack of a critical edition of this text. In the 1924 edition of his *Apocryphal New Testament*, for example, M. R. James comments that "there is as yet no really critical edition of the text, in which all manuscripts and versions are made use of."[14] Roughly thirty years later, in the preface to his important text-critical dissertation on the Protevangelium of James, Boyd Lee Daniels notes that when he read these words from M. R. James, "this dissertation was conceived."[15] And thirty years after that, George T. Zervos framed his own dissertation (also at Duke University) as completing the work that Daniels was unable to.[16] Now thirty years after his dissertation was completed at Duke, and nearly one hundred years after M. R. James noted the lack of a definitive critical edition, Zervos has published a new volume on the Protevangelium of James, and in the preface to this volume he writes, "It is my hope that this work will facilitate the eventual production by future scholars of the elusive definitive critical edition of this most important New Testament Apocryphon."[17] Part of what may stand behind the "elusiveness" of a definitive critical edition is the impressive number of manuscripts in which this text is preserved as well as the number of languages in which it was transmitted. We have around 140 MSS in Greek alone, and others in Arabic, Armenian, Coptic, Ethiopic, Georgian, Latin, and Syriac. The ambitious task of assembling all MSS into a definitive critical edition of the Protevangelium will be a welcomed addition to Christian Apocrypha scholarship.

---

13. Our oldest extant copy of the text, in the Bodmer V codex, includes a title following the epilogue: "Birth of Mary. Apocalypse of James."

14. M. R. James, *Apocryphal New Testament* (Oxford: Oxford University Press, 1924), 38–39. There do exist a number of good, usable versions of this text, but all of these are self-consciously partial and tentative.

15. Boyd Lee Daniels, "The Greek Manuscript Tradition of the Protevangelium Jacobi" (PhD diss., Duke University, 1956), i.

16. George T. Zervos, "Prolegomena to a Critical Edition of the Genesis Marias (Protevangelium Jacobi)" (PhD diss., Duke University, 1986), vii–xii.

17. George T. Zervos, *The Protevangelium of James: Greek Text, English Translation, Critical Introduction*, vol. 1, Jewish and Christian Texts in Context and Related Studies 17 (London: T&T Clark, 2019), viii.

Even in the absence of a definitive critical edition, there exist a number of questions regarding the textual integrity of the Protevangelium, as literary "seams" appear visible at a number of points. One of the most well-known examples is the so-called Vision of Joseph in chapter 18. The abrupt shift in narration from third- to first-person suggests that this episode may have originated elsewhere or at a later date, and its absence from a number of important textual witnesses may support this conclusion as well. Similarly, some have suggested that the final portion of the narrative (chs. 21–25) is a secondary addition because of the sudden change in subject matter. This final portion of the narrative has been underanalyzed by scholars, at least in comparison to the material that precedes it.

3.2 Intended Audience/Function

An important question in the study of any text (ancient or otherwise) concerns the intended audience and function. Put another way: To whom is this addressed, and for what purpose was it created? These questions are in many ways two sides of the same coin, and there are a number of possible answers to them. In terms of function, a strong case can be made that the author of the Protevangelium writes in order to "fill out" the scant portraits of Mary in the canonical materials. The need to do so arises not necessarily from an interest in Mary *per se* but as an almost natural consequence of christological reflection. If the canonical Gospels portray Jesus as somehow God in human form yet also as the son of a human mother, then this raises crucial questions about this woman. What sort of woman is capable of giving birth to a god? Surely a woman who gives birth to a god must have had an extraordinary childhood, right? Since the canonical Gospels are silent on these issues, it is possible that the author of the Protevangelium seeks to provide details for the curious reader.

Another possibility is that the author of the Protevangelium writes in order to praise Mary and so defend her from slander. This has been most influentially argued by P. A. van Stempvoort, who suggests that the Protevangelium is essentially a point-by-point refutation of the accusations of Celsus, a second-century philosopher who refuted various tenets of Christianity in his major work *The True Word*.[18] Where Celsus claims that Mary comes from a poor family, the author of the Protevangelium suggests that the opposite is true: Joachim is so wealthy that he can offer in the temple twice what is required of him. Where Celsus claims that Mary had to spin thread in order to make ends meet, the Protevangelium shows her spinning only the finest thread, that which will be used for the construction of the temple veil. And finally, where Celsus posits that Mary became pregnant after she was raped by a Roman soldier, the author of the Protevangelium goes to great lengths to show that her purity and physical integrity are guarded for the entirety of her young life.

To be sure, all these possible functions have significant overlap, and we need not settle on one to the exclusion of the others. A point they share is that the intended reader of this text is one with a keen interest in Mary as a person, both as an individual and by virtue of her role as the mother of Jesus.

---

18. So van Stempvoort, "Protevangelium Jacobi," 410; see also Cothenet, "Protévangile de Jacques," 4256–57. Ronald Hock has suggested that while the Protevangelium contains some apologetic elements, these are only secondary in importance; the author's primary purpose is not to *defend* Mary but to *praise* her. Hock argues that the narrative overall shares much in common with ancient encomiastic literature (*The Infancy Gospels of James and Thomas*, Scholars Bible 2 [Santa Rosa: Polebridge, 1995], 15–20). Both these theories have gained fairly standard acceptance in the field.

4. KEY PASSAGES FOR NEW TESTAMENT STUDIES AND THEIR SIGNIFICANCE

The author of the Protevangelium betrays familiarity with a number of New Testament texts.[19] The most obvious and prominent among those are the Gospels of Matthew, Luke, and John.[20] In terms of this text's significance for the study of the New Testament, I address three broad avenues of exploration below: first, the appropriation of Old and New Testament stories and characters; second, the harmonization of canonical infancy narratives; and third, the author's desire to revise portions of those canonical accounts.

4.1 Appropriation

One of the Protevangelium's primary sources for material is the Old Testament, and much like the New Testament evangelists, its author uses Old Testament narratives as a basis for their own stories. One example of this is found in the story of Mary's parents, Joachim and Anna, which is based on the story of Elkanah and Hannah from 1 Samuel 1–2. Elkanah and Joachim are both introduced as men who sacrifice more than is expected of them (1 Sam 1:4–5; Prot. Jas. 1.1–3). And Hannah and Anna—aside from sharing a remarkably similar name—both lament their inability to have children (1 Sam 1:9–11; Prot. Jas. 3). And just as Elkanah and Hannah are able to conceive a child (Samuel) once God intervenes, so too are Joachim and Anna able to conceive their child (Mary) under similar circumstances. The consequence of this is that the reader of the Protevangelium is prompted to see Mary as a sort of Samuel figure.

The author does not limit themselves to the Old Testament as a source for narratives to reuse, as there are a number of points at which the author borrows from the New Testament as well. Some of these instances are straightforward and reproduce narratives in more or less their "standard" form. Mary's visit to Elizabeth in Protevangelium 12.2–6 is one such instance; while the author employs this scene to different ends and makes some minor adjustments, the story is more or less what we find in Luke's Gospel (Luke 1:39–56). There are other points at which the author is more brazen in their repurposing. The episode involving Salome and her postpartum examination, for example, is patterned off the Johannine pericope of "Doubting Thomas" (Prot. Jas 20; John 20:24–29). Just as Thomas refuses to believe the message that the disciples deliver to him (i.e., "We have seen Jesus alive"), so Salome refuses to believe the message that the midwife delivers to her (i.e., "A virgin just gave birth, and her body shows no evidence of it"). And like Thomas, Salome suggests that she would be open to believing if she had the opportunity to investigate matters for herself. For Thomas this involves seeing the wounds of Jesus and putting his finger inside those wounds; for Salome this involves putting her finger inside of Mary (Prot. Jas. 19.18–19; John 20:25). Both pericopes end with a validation of the original message as well as a statement of belief from their protagonists. When Thomas sees the resurrected Jesus, he exclaims, "My Lord and my God!" (John 20:28). And when Salome goes to touch Jesus

---

19. It is, of course, anachronistic to speak of the author's familiarity with "The New Testament" or with "canonical materials" as such, as this collection did not exist when the author was writing. Yet it is clear that certain texts that would be included later in the New Testament do occupy a place of prominence in the author's source material. As such, when I use the designation "New Testament" in what follows, this should be interpreted as indicating those texts that would later constitute the New Testament canon.

20. The argument has been made that Mark is perhaps the only canonical Gospel with which the author is not explicitly familiar (so Édouard Massaux, *The Influence of the Gospel of Saint Matthew on Christian Literature before Saint Irenaeus*, trans. N. J. Belvel and S. Hecht, 3 vols., New Gospel Studies 5 [Macon: Mercer University Press], 1:236). The case has also been made that the author is quite familiar with the Epistle to the Hebrews (so Vanden Eykel, *"But Their Faces"*, 131–34).

in order to be healed from her affliction, she says, "I will worship him, for he has been born a great king to Israel" (Prot. Jas. 20.10).

4.2 Harmonization

In addition to appropriating various narrative bits for their own purposes, the author of the Protevangelium also seeks to harmonize the sometimes disparate canonical accounts of Jesus's birth. This "harmonizing impulse" is visible at a number of points. As noted above, the first attempt to bring Mary's story in line with the canonical accounts occurs in the tenth chapter, when Zechariah becomes mute before the birth of John the Baptist (Prot. Jas. 10.9; see Luke 1:21–23). After this comes the annunciation (Prot. Jas. 11) and Mary's visit to Elizabeth (Prot. Jas. 12), neither of which have narrative counterparts in Matthew. It is only in Protevangelium 13–14, when Joseph returns home to find Mary pregnant and then puzzles over what to do with her, that the author must determine how to combine Matthew's account with Luke's. In Luke's Gospel, Mary knows the nature of her pregnancy because she herself receives these details from the angel (Luke 1:26–38). But in Matthew there is no annunciation narrative and no reason to presume that *either* Mary or Joseph has been told of the nature of Mary's pregnancy. In Matthew, this is only revealed to Joseph once he decides to "dismiss [Mary] quietly" (Matt 1:19).

The challenge in combining these two narratives, of course, is that doing so requires explaining how Mary, on the one hand, could receive news of her impending pregnancy, but Joseph, on the other hand, remains ignorant. The author of the Protevangelium accomplishes this in a rather unusual and possibly clumsy way by simply stating that Mary forgot what the angel had told her between the time of the annunciation and her visit to Elizabeth (Prot. Jas. 12.6). So the news is still delivered to Mary, but Joseph cannot determine the nature of her pregnancy because when he asks about it, Mary doesn't know either. Other instances of harmonization are less forced and far more subtle. The author is able to combine the Lukan census/journey to Bethlehem with the Matthean magi without much difficulty, for example (Prot. Jas. 17; 21). Similarly, the manger (from Luke) integrates easily into Herod's slaughter of children (from Matthew); in the Protevangelium it merely becomes a place in which to hide the infant Jesus from Herod's assassins. In this instance the manger also allows the author of the Protevangelium to simplify the story of Jesus's birth, as it eliminates the need for the family's flight to Egypt (Matt 2:13–18).

4.3 Revision

In the author's attempt to incorporate as much as possible from the canonical accounts of Jesus's birth, it is also striking to note the degree to which they attempt to revise another part of the canonical tradition—namely, the notion that Joseph and Mary's relationship was relatively "normal" after the birth of Jesus, and that additional children, brothers and sisters of Jesus, were a result. While Matthew goes to great lengths to emphasize that Mary is a virgin when Jesus is conceived and born, he also states quite clearly that there is no expectation for her to remain a virgin after the birth of Jesus. In the retelling of Joseph's dream, the narrator of Matthew comments: "[Joseph] took [Mary] as his wife, but had no marital relations with her *until* she had borne a son" (Matt 1:24–25 NRSV). The "until" suggests that he "had no marital relations with her" is a condition that ceases to exist once Jesus is born.

The idea that Jesus had brothers and sisters—presumably, fruits of this normal sexual relationship—is one that is expressed in both Matthew and Mark. In Mark, those gathered in the Nazareth synagogue to hear him speak remark to one another: "Is not this the carpenter, the son of Mary and brother of James and Joses and Judas and Simon? And are not his sisters here with us?" (Mark 6:3 NRSV). The same story appears with minor variations in Matthew 13:54–58. Paul likewise speaks of James as "the Lord's brother" (Gal 1:19 NRSV), and he references multiple brothers of the Lord in 1 Corinthians 9:5. In the fifth century CE, Jerome argued quite vehemently that references such as these are to be understood as references to "cousins," not "siblings" (*Helv.* [PL 23.181–206]). Before Jerome, in the late-fourth century CE, Epiphanius argued that such references are indeed to siblings, but that these siblings should be understood as "half siblings," or children of Joseph from a previous marriage (*Pan.* 29.3.9; 29.4.1). The solution posed by the author of the Protevangelium likely stands behind Epiphanius's own thoughts on the matter.

In their desire to harmonize and revise the accounts of Matthew and Luke, the author of the Protevangelium shows not only that these accounts were available as literary sources but that they enjoyed a place of prominence in the author's own "canon" in the late-second century. So while the "official" New Testament canon does not take shape until later, it is possible at least to speak of a sort of "proto-canon" from a much earlier period. Yet the author's desire to push back on portions of these narratives (most conspicuously in the depiction of Mary's virginity as a permanent state, and not one that goes away after Jesus is born) illustrates that much of what would become the canonical tradition is still very much in flux when the Protevangelium first took shape.

5. BIBLIOGRAPHY

Daniels, Boyd Lee. "The Greek Manuscript Tradition of the Protevangelium Jacobi." PhD diss., Duke University, 1956.

Foskett, Mary F. *A Virgin Conceived: Mary and Classical Representations of Virginity.* Bloomington: Indiana University Press, 2002.

Hock, Ronald F. *The Infancy Gospels of James and Thomas.* Scholars Bible 2. Santa Rosa: Polebridge, 1995.

Smid, H. R. *Protevangelium Jacobi: A Commentary.* Translated by G. E. Van Baaren-Pape. Assen: Van Gorcum, 1965.

Strycker, Émile de. *La Forme la plus ancienne du Protévangile de Jacques.* Subsidia hagiographica 33. Bruxelles: Société des Bollandistes, 1961.

Testuz, Michel. *Papyrus Bodmer V: Nativité de Marie.* Geneva: Bibliotheca Bodmeriana, 1958.

Vanden Eykel, Eric M. *"But Their Faces Were All Looking Up": Author and Reader in the Protevangelium of James.* The Reception of Jesus in the First–Three Centuries 1. London: Bloomsbury T&T Clark, 2016.

Vuong, Lily. *Gender and Purity in the Protevangelium of James.* WUNT 2.358. Tubingen: Mohr Siebeck, 2013.

———. *The Protevangelium of James.* Early Christian Apocrypha 7. Eugene, OR: Cascade, 2019.

Zervos, George T. *The Protevangelium of James: Greek Text, English Translation, Critical Introduction.* JCTCRS 17. London: T&T Clark, 2019.

CHAPTER 10

TOLEDOT YESHU

SARIT KATTAN GRIBETZ

1. INTRODUCTION

The term "Toledot Yeshu" refers to a set of texts written from a Jewish anti-Christian perspective that share a basic narrative about Jesus's life.[1] Each version narrates and elaborates on this story in somewhat different ways. Manuscripts employ a variety of titles for these works, including the *Book of Nazoreans, as decreed concerning Yeshua, the son of Pandera*; *Book of the Governor and Yeshu ha-Notsri*; *Story of Yeshua ha-Notsri*; *Ma'aseh Yeshu*; and so on. Only one subgroup of manuscripts consistently uses the title *Toledot Yeshu* as this collection of texts has now come to be known.[2]

While one manuscript recension only narrates Jesus's ministry and crucifixion, most manuscripts begin with an account of Mary's conception of Jesus, and then describe Jesus's childhood as a precocious troublemaker who stirs tension in the rabbinic study house. Jesus presents himself as the son of God, performing miracles to prove his status and gain a following. He is eventually defeated by Judas in a flying contest and condemned to death, after which his followers erroneously believe that he has been resurrected, when in fact his tomb has been robbed by a gardener. Some versions append a section about Peter and Paul's roles in the development of the Jesus-movement after Jesus's death; this section narrates the decisive schism that both these men enact between Jewish Jesus-followers, who become Christians, and those who do not follow Jesus and remain Jews.

---

1. Thanks to J. Christopher Edwards for the invitation to contribute to this volume, and to Naomi Koltun-Fromm and Jonathan Gribetz for helpful feedback.

The first scholarly works about Toledot Yeshu include Samuel Krauss, *Das Leben Jesu nach jüdischen Quellen* (Berlin: S. Calvary, 1902; repr., Hildesheim: Olms, 1977, 2006); William Horbury, "A Critical Examination of the Toledoth Yeshu" (PhD diss., University of Cambridge, 1970), and related articles; Riccardo Di Segni, "La tradizione testuale delle 'Toledòth Jeshu': Manoscritti, edizioni a stampa, classificazione," *Rassegna Mensile di Israel* 50 (1984): 83–100; idem, *Il vangelo del ghetto* (Rome: Newton Compton, 1985). The past decade has seen renewed interest in Toledot Yeshu, including a critical edition, translation, and introduction to the Hebrew and Aramaic manuscripts in Peter Schäfer and Michael Meerson, eds., *Toledot Yeshu: The Life Story of Jesus*, 2 vol. (Tübingen: Mohr Siebeck, 2014) as well as two edited collections of essays: Peter Schäfer, Michael Meerson, and Yaacov Deutsch, eds., *Toledot Yeshu ("The Life Story of Jesus") Revisited: A Princeton Conference* (Tübingen: Mohr Siebeck, 2011), and Daniel Barbu and Yaacov Deutsch, eds., *Toledot Yeshu in Context: Jewish-Christian Polemics in Ancient, Medieval, and Modern History*, TSAJ 182 (Tübingen: Mohr Siebeck, 2020), with an appendix that contains a complete index of all Toledot Yeshu manuscripts. Extensive bibliographies of previous scholarship on Toledot Yeshu can be found in these volumes.

2. Schäfer and Meerson, *Toledot Yeshu*, 1:40–42; William Horbury, "Titles and Origins of *Toledot Yeshu*," in Barbu and Deutsch, *Toledot Yeshu in Context*.

1.1 Languages

Manuscripts of Toledot Yeshu, which number well over a hundred, exist in numerous languages. The earliest extant manuscripts, found among the remains of the Cairo Geniza, were composed in Aramaic and probably represent the earliest versions of this tradition, though manuscripts in other languages do occasionally preserve older traditions than those found in Aramaic manuscripts. Other early versions of Toledot Yeshu appear in Hebrew, Judeo-Arabic, and Latin.[3] Versions of Toledot Yeshu also appear in Yiddish, Judeo-Persian, Ladino, French, and German.[4]

1.2 Authorship

Almost nothing about Toledot Yeshu's authorship, provenance, and date is known for certain, and scholars provide a variety of perspectives about each of these aspects of Toledot Yeshu's origins. The Toledot Yeshu traditions do not have a single author, nor are the authors of these traditions known by name. While we do not know the names of any of the authors of these traditions, what seems clear is that the texts were written and transmitted by Jews, primarily for Jews, in order to disparage Christian narratives about Jesus, refute Christian theological claims about Jesus's status, or discourage Jews from embracing Christianity. In some regions, particularly the Islamic Middle East, versions of Toledot Yeshu functioned as Jewish folk-narratives that, while still parodical and polemical, were likely told for entertainment rather than exclusively or even primarily as religious argumentation.[5] Some of the earliest textual attestations of Toledot Yeshu, however, appear as quotations in Christian writings that seek to highlight Jewish blasphemy. In fact, one fascinating dimension of studying Toledot Yeshu is identifying unique aspects of a manuscript or group of manuscripts and imagining who might have authored, transmitted, read, or heard it—and what that might teach us both about the text and the people who interacted with it.

---

3. On Hebrew, Aramaic, and Arabic manuscripts, see Schäfer and Meerson, *Toledot Yeshu*, 1:28–39; 2:45–46; on the relationship between some Hebrew and Aramaic versions, see Yaacov Deutsch, "New Evidence of Early Versions of *Toldot Yeshu*," *Tarbiz* 69 (2000): 177–97 (in Hebrew); on Arabic manuscripts and their relationship to other manuscripts, see Miriam Goldstein, "Judeo-Arabic Versions of *Toledot Yeshu*," *Ginzei Qedem* 6 (2010): 9–42; idem, "A Polemical Tale and Its Function in the Jewish Communities of the Mediterranean and the Near East: Toledot Yeshu in Judeo-Arabic," *Intellectual History of the Islamicate World* 7 (2019): 192–227; idem, *A Judeo-Arabic Parody of the Life of Jesus: The* Toledot Yeshu *Helene Narrative* (Tübingen: Mohr Siebeck, forthcoming); Gideon Bohak, "Jesus the Magician in the 'Pilate' Recension of *Toledot Yeshu*" and Daniel Stökl Ben Ezra, "On Some Early Traditions in *Toledot Yeshu* and the Antiquity of the 'Helena' Recension," in Barbu and Deutsch, *Toledot Yeshu in Context*; on the earliest Latin versions, see Peter Schäfer, "Agobard's and Amulo's *Toledot Yeshu*," in Schäfer, Meerson, and Deutsch, *Toledot Yeshu Reconsidered*, 27–48.

4. A list of Yiddish, Judeo-Persian, and Ladino manuscripts can be found in Schäfer and Meerson, *Toledot Yeshu*, 2:42–44, 47–48; on Yiddish versions, see Michael Stanislawski, "A Preliminary Study of a Yiddish 'Life of Jesus' (*Toledot Yeshu*): JTS Ms. 2211," in Schäfer, Meerson, and Deutsch, *Toledot Yeshu Reconsidered*, 79–87; Evi Michels, "Yiddish *Toledot Yeshu* Manuscripts from the Netherlands" and Claudia Rosenzweig, "The 'History of the Life of Jesus' in a Yiddish Manuscript from the Eighteenth Century (Ms. Jerusalem, NLI, Heb. 8°5622)," in Barbu and Deutsch, *Toledot Yeshu in Context*; on a French translation of *Toledot Yeshu*, see Daniel Barbu and Yann Dahhaoui, "Un manuscrit français des *Toledot Yeshu*: Le ms. lat. 12722 et l'enquête de 1429 sur les juifs de Trévoux," *Henoch: Historical and Textual Studies in Ancient and Medieval Judaism and Christianity* 40 (2018): 223–88; idem, "The Secret Booklet from Germany: Circulation and Transmission of *Toledot Yeshu* at the Borders of the Empire," in Barbu and Deutsch, *Toledot Yeshu in Context*; a German version appears in Franz F. Engelsberger, *Dieses Buch offenbaret die Geheimnussen Gottes den verstokten blinden Juden* (Vienna: Rickhesin, 1640).

5. Miriam Goldstein, "A Polemical Tale and Its Function in the Jewish Communities of the Mediterranean and the Near East: *Toledot Yeshu* in Judeo-Arabic," *Intellectual History of the Islamicate World* 7 (2019): 192–227.

1.3 Provenance

Toledot Yeshu probably originated in Jewish Babylonia. In his linguistic analysis of the Aramaic fragments of Toledot Yeshu, Michael Sokoloff concluded that the morphology and vocabulary of these manuscripts are "permeated by JBA [Jewish Babylonian Aramaic] and TA [Targumic Aramaic] to such an extent that it is extremely improbable to contend that it was originally written anywhere else except in Jewish Babylonia."[6] Locating the origins of Toledot Yeshu in Jewish Babylonia corresponds well with anti-Jesus sentiments and stories found in the Babylonian Talmud (which are largely though not entirely absent in Jewish Palestinian texts). This location also helps explain the fact that several Judeo-Arabic translations of Toledot Yeshu seem to preserve versions of Toledot Yeshu that are most similar to the earliest Aramaic and Hebrew manuscripts and that sometimes even contain language that appears older than any extant manuscripts in other languages.[7] In a different linguistic analysis of the same Aramaic fragments, Willem Smelik has suggested that the tradition originated in Palestine, moved to Babylonia, and then returned to Palestine—that is, that certain aspects of the text suggest some Palestinian linguistic presence.[8] These differing conclusions might point to the complicated transmission history of this text, of which we have so many versions, and even perhaps suggest that there were several transmission paths very early in its history.[9] Regardless of the original place of Toledot Yeshu's composition, however, the texts soon spread widely and became popular among Jews in Christian Europe, the Muslim Middle East, and North Africa through the medieval and early modern periods.

1.4 Date

Toledot Yeshu traditions are notoriously difficult to date. This is true both for proposing a date for the earliest version(s) of Toledot Yeshu as well as for dating the various versions of the narrative that circulated in later periods, the manuscripts of which are often undated and, in any case, might preserve older texts (though more recent manuscripts are easier to date than those from the earlier medieval period). Scholars have relied on a number of strategies for dating Toledot Yeshu: linguistic and paleographic analysis of the earliest manuscripts; literary and narrative style; and references to or excerpts from the text in other relatively early works.

Extant evidence largely points to a date of composition in the early medieval period, after the mid-sixth century and before the early ninth century CE. From a linguistic perspective, Sokoloff contends that in the early Aramaic manuscripts of Toledot Yeshu, "the absence of known morphological elements from Geonic JBA [Jewish Babylonian Aramaic] and the presence of morphological elements from TA [Targumic Aramaic] point to its having been composed sometime before the Geonic period"—that is, sometime in the middle of the first millennium CE.

From a literary perspective, Eli Yassif has pointed out that Toledot Yeshu's narrative form is most compellingly contextualized among Hebrew narrative texts of the early medieval period, when independent halakic and midrashic traditions were placed into whole,

---

6. Michael Sokoloff, "The Date and Provenance of the Aramaic *Toledot Yeshu* on the Basis of Aramaic Dialectology," in Schäfer, Meerson, and Deutsch, *Toledot Yeshu Reconsidered*, 13–26, at 16. Sokoloff notes that one Aramaic manuscript contains occasional JPA (Jewish Palestinian Aramaic) morphological forms.

7. On portrayals of Jesus in the Babylonian Talmud, see Peter Schäfer, *Jesus in the Talmud* (Princeton: Princeton University Press, 2007).

8. Willem Smelik, "The Aramaic Dialect(s) of the Toldot Yeshu Fragments," *Aramaic Studies* 7.1 (2009): 39–73.

9. As suggested in Bohak, "Jesus the Magician."

independent stories. This trend, Yassif points out, "is associated with a major cultural development in the medieval Islamic east—the emergence of distinct disciplines. Thus, starting in the eighth century, we find works devoted to specific disciplines, including prayer and liturgy, history, linguistics, philosophy, and commentary. The first autonomous narratives, such as *Midrash Aseret ha-Dibrot* and *The Alphabet of Ben-Sira*, belong to this category, and the same can be said for *Toledot Yeshu*."[10] There are also interesting correspondences between Toledot Yeshu and *Sefer Yosippon*, as Saskia Donitz has observed, as well as resonances with *Sefer Zerubavel*, texts both composed during this period (and that, similar to Toledot Yeshu, build on traditions from the late Second Temple and rabbinic periods).[11]

In addition to contemporaneous Jewish literature, Toledot Yeshu's emergence as a narrative about Jesus's life corresponds as well to renewed interest in narrating Jesus's childhood in the early medieval period in Christian contexts, as exemplified by the Arabic Infancy Gospel and the Gospel of Pseudo-Matthew (both from the eighth or early ninth century), which adapted earlier infancy gospel traditions from late antiquity.[12] Alexandra Cuffel has argued that Toledot Yeshu can also be contextualized in light of Sīra literature, which narrated the prophet Muhammad's biography as well as the lives of other prophets, from the Fatimid and Mamluk Middle East.[13] The noteworthy generic similarities between Toledot Yeshu and these Christian and Islamic literary traditions also highlight that Toledot Yeshu likely functioned both as anti-Christian and anti-Islamic polemic, given that Jesus is venerated in both traditions (though differently so, as the Qur'an is clear that Jesus was not the son of God) and that Toledot Yeshu circulated in areas populated by both Christians and Muslims.

Finally, Peter Schäfer has noted that while the earliest Aramaic fragment is a tenth-century text preserved in the Cairo Geniza, the earliest quotations of and references to Toledot Yeshu appear in the Latin writings of Agobard, bishop of Lyon, and his successor, Amulo, in the early ninth century.[14] Schäfer notes that these bishops' writings serve as a terminus ad quem, given that they preserve translations of a text that appears to be an early version of Toledot Yeshu (quite similar, in fact, to the earliest Aramaic fragments). Yassif further argues that had Toledot Yeshu circulated long before the eighth or early ninth century, when these first references appear, we would expect it to have been mentioned, even in passing, by someone, given how controversial the text would have been.

Other scholars prefer earlier or later dates. Samuel Krauss, in his early twentieth-century study of Toledot Yeshu, proposed a composition date in the fifth century, while William Horbury has suggested that the text likely dates to late antiquity, perhaps as early as the third century.[15] Earlier readers of Toledot Yeshu, among them German Protestant Hebraist

---

10. Eli Yassif, "*Toledot Yeshu*: Folk-Narrative as Polemics and Self-Criticism," in Schäfer, Meerson, and Deutsch, *Toledot Yeshu Reconsidered*, 104.

11. Saskia Dönitz, *Überlieferung und Rezeption des Sefer Yosippon* (Tübingen: Mohr Siebeck, 2013), 53–58.

12. Sarit Kattan Gribetz, "Jesus and the Clay Birds: Reading *Toledot Yeshu* in Light of the Infancy Gospels," in *Envisioning Judaism: Studies in Honor of Peter Schäfer on the Occasion of His Seventieth Birthday*, ed. R. Boustan et al. (Tübingen: Mohr Siebeck, 2013), 1021–48.

13. Alexandra Cuffel, "*Toledot Yeshu* in the Context of Polemic and Sīra Literature in the Middle East from the Fatimid to the Mamluk Era," in Barbu and Deutsch, *Toledot Yeshu in Context*. On Toledot Yeshu in Muslim contexts more generally, see also Philip Alexander, "The *Toledot Yeshu* in the Context of Jewish-Muslim Debate," in Schäfer, Meerson, and Deutsch, *Toledot Yeshu Reconsidered*, 137–58.

14. Schäfer, "Agobard's and Amulo's *Toledot Yeshu*," 27–48; idem, "Introduction," in Schäfer, Meerson, and Deutsch, *Toledot Yeshu Reconsidered*, 3.

15. Krauss, *Das Leben Jesu*, iii–iv, 2–5; Horbury, "Titles and Origins of *Toledot Yeshu*," 13–42; idem, "Critical Examination," 16.

Johann Christoph Wagenseil (who published Toledot Yeshu for the first time in 1681) and the Jewish philosopher Moses Mendelssohn, dated the composition of Toledot Yeshu firmly in the medieval period, denying it both the coveted status of an ancient text and the insight of a modern enlightened work.[16]

One unresolved question is whether the diversity of Toledot Yeshu versions suggests that there was an early core text that was variably adapted by later transmitters, or whether from an early date Toledot Yeshu circulated in a variety of forms (without an "original text" but rather an organic process of the accumulation of traditions in different recensions). The question of Toledot Yeshu's date is further complicated by the fact that discrete traditions within the narrative are almost certainly older than the full narrative. Daniel Stökl Ben Ezra has identified, for example, a list of festivals in some recensions of Toledot Yeshu that includes names of certain festivals, including the Feast of Ascension in late spring and the Invention of the Cross and the Circumcision in the fall, which accord with Christian festival practices and dates specific to the late fourth and early fifth century rather than earlier or later centuries—the implication being that this textual unit is more ancient than the full text into which it was later embedded.[17] When scholars discuss the date of Toledot Yeshu, however, they generally refer to the date when a full narrative of Jesus's life was composed (probably between the mid-sixth and early ninth century) rather than the date of individual portions of the text, many of which seem to be older or to draw on earlier sources.

1.5 Genre

Scholars have characterized Toledot Yeshu's genre in various ways. Toledot Yeshu's unmistakably polemical tone, found across manuscripts, easily casts it as a polemic and a parody.[18] Because Toledot Yeshu tells a version of Jesus's life story that refutes those presented in the canonical Gospels, scholars sometimes refer to it as an "anti-gospel" or a "counter-history."[19] Toledot Yeshu's narrative style, which suggests that it could have been recited or shared in communal and familial settings, and its malleability in different historical and cultural contexts—variably told and retold, adapted and adopted, details changed and dimensions added, even as the core narrative arc remained fairly stable— remind scholars of folktales.[20] Yet other versions of Toledot Yeshu read more like scholarly

16. Horbury, "Titles and Origins of *Toledot Yeshu*," details early views about Toledot Yeshu's composition. Another version of Toledot Yeshu was published by Johann Jacob Huldreich in Leiden in 1705.

17. Daniel Stökl Ben Ezra, "An Ancient List of Christian Festivals in *Toledot Yeshu*: Polemics as Indication for Interaction," *HTR* 102.4 (2009): 481–96. Further discussion of this text and Stökl Ben Ezra's assessment of it appears in Schäfer and Meerson, *Toledot Yeshu*, 1:105–8.

18. Sarit Kattan Gribetz, "Hanged and Crucified: The Book of Esther and *Toledot Yeshu*," in Schäfer, Meerson, and Deutsch, *Toledot Yeshu Reconsidered*, 159–80.

19. Amos Funkenstein, "Anti-Jewish Propaganda: Pagan, Medieval and Modern," *Jerusalem Quarterly* 19 (1981): 56–72; idem, *Perceptions of Jewish History* (Berkeley: University of California Press, 1993); David Biale, "Counter-History and Jewish Polemics against Christianity: The *Sefer Toledot Yeshu* and the *Sefer Zerubavel*," *Jewish Social Studies* 6.1 (1999): 130–45; Alexandra Cuffel, "Between Epic Entertainment and Polemical Exegesis: Jesus as Antihero in *Toledot Yeshu*," in *Medieval Exegesis and Religious Difference: Commentary, Conflict, and Community in the Premodern Mediterranean*, ed. R. Szpiech (New York: Fordham University Press, 2015), 155–70; Daniel Barbu, "The Case about Jesus: (Counter-)History and Casuistry in *Toledot Yeshu*," in *A Historical Approach to Casuistry: Norms and Exceptions in a Comparative Perspective*, ed. C. Ginzburg and L. Biasori (London: Bloomsbury, 2018), 65–98.

20. Eli Yassif, "*Toledot Yeshu*: Folk-Narrative as Polemics and Self Criticism," Galit Hasan-Rokem, "Polymorphic Helena—*Toledot Yeshu* as a Palimpsest of Religious Narratives and Identities," and Paola Tartakoff, "The *Toledot Yeshu* and Jewish-Christian Conflict in the Medieval Crown of Aragon," all in Schäfer, Meerson, and Deutsch, *Toledot Yeshu Reconsidered*, 101–35, 247–82, and 297–309; Gribetz, "Hanged and

treatises, as they frequently quote biblical and rabbinic prooftexts. Such generic variability accords well with the wide array of literary styles and languages in which Toledot Yeshu appears.

Toledot Yeshu's focus on Jesus's birth, family, and childhood escapades is reminiscent as well of apocryphal gospel traditions, in particular the infancy gospels, even though the Toledot Yeshu tradition seeks, through these tales of his early life, to defame and discredit Jesus rather than valorize him.[21] Categorizing Toledot Yeshu among other apocryphal Gospels highlights a number of important features of this textual tradition beyond its focus on aspects of Jesus's life that are not addressed in the canonical Gospels. First, certain stories about Jesus's life are shared between Toledot Yeshu and other apocryphal Gospels. For example, most recensions of Toledot Yeshu recount an episode in which Jesus performs a series of miracles, including forming birds out of clay and causing them to fly.[22] This same miracle appears as early as the second or third century in the Infancy Gospel of Thomas, and then in the Qur'an, the Arabic Infancy Gospel, the Latin Gospel of Pseudo-Matthew, as well as in later works based on these infancy gospels, such as *Liber de infantia salvatoris*, the *Evangelica historia*, *Evangile de l'Enfance*, and *Les Enfaunces de Jesu Crist*. That Toledot Yeshu contains this story, not found in canonical Gospels but so popular in apocryphal Gospels, suggests that there was a shared reservoir of traditions about Jesus's life that these texts, including Toledot Yeshu, tapped into. Second, placing Toledot Yeshu alongside other apocryphal Gospels highlights the types of texts and traditions that the various recensions of Toledot Yeshu sought to refute—it was not exclusively the canonical works in the New Testament or the writings of the church fathers that the stories in Toledot Yeshu aimed to challenge. Toledot Yeshu also engaged with and refuted the widespread narratives preserved in apocryphal texts, which became important features of popular piety and liturgy in Christian communities. This categorization also brings to light certain traditions and viewpoints about Jesus (such as those found in Toledot Yeshu) against which apocryphal Gospels might have been composed or used for refutation.[23] Finally, the categorization of Toledot Yeshu as an apocryphal Gospel also illuminates aspects of the fluidity of Toledot Yeshu's composition and transmission. Unlike canonical texts (which, by definition, cannot easily be amended or expanded), and similar to other apocryphal Gospels (which were indeed revised and elaborated upon with greater ease), Toledot Yeshu did not have a single author or a straightforward transmission trajectory; it was a tradition that transformed as it traveled to new places and contended with different challenges. The study of apocryphal literature, and of the infancy gospels in particular, is enriched when we add apocryphal narratives of Jesus's life not only from within Christian communities but also from those who contended with them.

Crucified"; Natalie E. Latteri, "Infancy Stories of Jesus: Apocrypha and Toledot Yeshu in Medieval Europe," in *Essays on the History of Jewish-Christian Relations*, ed. J. P. Brown (San Francisco: University of San Francisco Press, 2020), 15–51; Goldstein, "Polemical Tale," 192–227.

21. On which, see William Horbury, "The Depiction of Judaeo-Christians in the Toledot Yeshu," in *The Image of the Judaeo-Christians in Ancient Jewish and Christian Literature*, ed. P. J. Tomson and D. Lambers-Petry (Tübingen: Mohr Siebeck, 2003), 280. Toledot Yeshu is sometimes included in studies about the infancy gospels, e.g., Philip Alexander, "Jesus and His Mother in the Jewish Anti-Gospel (the *Toledot Yeshu*)" and Daniel Barbu, "Voltaire and the *Toledoth Yeshu*," both in *Infancy Gospels: Stories and Identities*, ed. C. Clivaz, A. Dettwiler, L. Devillers, and E. Norelli (Tübingen: Mohr Siebeck, 2011), 588–627; Stephen Davis, *Christ Child: Cultural Memories of a Young Jesus* (New Haven: Yale University Press, 2014), 143–51.

22. Gribetz, "Jesus and the Clay Birds."

23. This point is developed in Pierluigi Piovanelli, "The *Toledot Yeshu* and Christian Apocryphal Literature: The Formative Years," in Schäfer, Meerson, and Deutsch, *Toledot Yeshu Reconsidered*, 89–100.

These characterizations of Toledot Yeshu's genre—as polemic, anti-gospel, counter-history, folktale, or apocryphal gospel—are by no means mutually exclusive. Indeed, articulating these diverse generic possibilities helps capture Toledot Yeshu's complexity as a tradition that developed over the course of hundreds of years and as it was employed by diverse audiences in different times and places.

1.6 Textual Recensions, Editions, and Translations

The texts and translations of many representative Hebrew and Aramaic manuscripts of Toledot Yeshu have been published by Peter Schäfer and Michael Meerson in *Toledot Yeshu: The Life Story of Jesus* (Tübingen: Mohr Siebeck, 2014); Miriam Goldstein has published Judeo-Arabic manuscripts; Claudia Rosenzweig has published an edition and translation of a Yiddish manuscript; Daniel Barbu and Yann Dahhaoui have published a Middle French version.[24] Each manuscript has its own history. Those interested in researching Toledot Yeshu should consult multiple manuscripts to understand the range of ways that Toledot Yeshu has been constructed, the variety of contexts in which the manuscript appears (e.g., in what types of codices and among which other texts Toledot Yeshu is bound), and the different purposes for which it has been used.

Because of the great variability among manuscripts, scholars have divided Toledot Yeshu manuscripts into a number of recensions.[25] Riccardo Di Segni identified two major recensions, which he titled "Pilate" and "Helena" (with a minor third recension titled "Herod"), referring to the names of the rulers of Jerusalem featured in the manuscripts. Schäfer and Meerson, in their recent edition, largely follow Di Segni but propose three manuscript groups: "Group I" (which corresponds to Di Segni's "Pilate" manuscripts) includes fragmentary Aramaic, Hebrew, and Judeo-Arabic manuscripts from the Cairo Geniza, along with a few complete early modern manuscripts. This group of manuscripts narrates Jesus's trial and execution. "Group II" and "Group III" manuscripts (which correspond to Di Segni's "Helena" recension) represent two different recensions, each of which tells a fuller and generally longer version of Jesus's life, starting from Mary's conception of Jesus and Jesus's birth through his death or thereafter.[26] According to Schäfer and Meerson, the two groups frame the core story of Jesus's life in different ways: Group II downplays the role of the sages and amplifies the role of Queen Helena, the reigning figure in the text, while according to Group III "Israel is displayed as a far more independent and aggressive protagonist ... able to defeat Christianity and to confront the government on its own," without a strong monarch.[27] Each of these three main recensions can be further subdivided, and readers interested in a detailed analysis of each subgroup are encouraged to consult Schäfer and Meerson's edition.

---

24. Goldstein, "Judeo-Arabic Versions"; idem, *A Judeo-Arabic Parody of the Life of Jesus*; Rosenzweig, "'History of the Life of Jesus'"; Barbu and Dahhaoui, "Un manuscrit français." I have published a partial translation of a more recent Judaeo-Arabic manuscript in Sarit Kattan Gribetz, "'When Miriam Heard Rabbi Shimon ben Shetah's Words She Became Very Scared': Emotions in the Conception Narrative of a Judaeo-Arabic Version of *Toledot Yeshu*," Fordham Research Commons (Fordham University), *History of Emotions/Emotions in History*, Early Modern Workshop: Jewish History Resources, https://research.library.fordham. edu/cgi/viewcontent.cgi?article=1148&context=emw.

25. On which, see Schäfer and Meerson, *Toledot Yeshu*, 1:28–39, upon which the summary here is largely based; a history of scholarship about the manuscripts is found on pp. 19–27. Schäfer and Meerson's classification is based on and expands that found in Di Segni, *Il vangelo del ghetto*.

26. Schäfer and Meerson, *Toledot Yeshu*, 1:28–39, and Bohak, "Jesus the Magician," suggest that Group I probably dates earlier than Groups II and II, though other scholars, such as Stöckl Ben Ezra, "On Some Early Traditions," prefer to regard them as more or less contemporaneous traditions.

27. Schäfer and Meerson, *Toledot Yeshu*, 1:36.

2. SUMMARY OF CONTENT

The following summary of the Toledot Yeshu narrative is based on the Strasbourg manuscript (BnU 3974 [héb. 48], folios 170a to 175b). I chose this manuscript because it is among the best-known and widely circulated versions of Toledot Yeshu, and because it contains a comprehensive narrative of Jesus's life from birth to death as well as an extensive account of the Jesus-movement following Jesus's death (belonging as it does to the "Helena" recension).[28] The following section ("Interpretive Issues") incorporates notable episodes not included in this manuscript but featured in other manuscripts, including the "Pilate" recension, to provide a more comprehensive overview of Toledot Yeshu's contents. In the summary, I use the English versions of character names, such as Mary and Jesus, rather than transliterations of the names found in the manuscripts, such as Miriam/Maryam and Yeshu, in order more organically to place Toledot Yeshu's narrative alongside the other narratives of Jesus's life in this volume.

The story of Jesus's life begins with a story about his mother, Mary (Miriam). Mary, a young Jewish woman, is engaged to a learned God-fearing man named John (Yohanan), who hails from the royal house of David. Next door to Mary lives a good-looking but villainous neighbor named Joseph (Yosef) ben Pandera. One Sabbath eve, Joseph drunkenly enters Mary's house, where he hugs and kisses her. Mary assumes that the man who has entered her home is her fiancé John, and she asks him not to touch her because she is menstruating. According to Jewish laws of purity a woman cannot come into physical contact with others during her period of menstruation, and Mary is portrayed in this text as a pious Jewish woman who tries diligently to observe these laws. Joseph, however, ignores her pleas to stop, disregarding her impure status. Joseph rapes Mary, and Mary conceives a child from this sexual assault.

In the middle of the night, Mary's fiancé John returns home and, like Joseph had done a few hours earlier, initiates a sexual encounter with her, not knowing that she is menstrually impure. Confused, because she believes that she has already endured an unwanted and prohibited sexual encounter with John earlier that evening, Mary confronts John, telling him that since their betrothal he has not come to her twice in a single night. John explains that this is his first attempt this evening; soon they realize that Joseph had broken in and violated Mary. Immediately John seeks the assistance of Rabban Shimon ben Shetah, a prominent rabbinic figure. The rabbi advises John to keep this event quiet. Eventually, despite their best efforts to keep the sexual assault a secret, news of Mary's pregnancy spreads. John disavows the pregnancy and, fearing his own disgrace, flees to Babylonia.

Mary eventually gives birth to a son, whom she names Joshua (Yehoshua). "When his defect was discovered," however, this child came to be called Jesus (Yeshu). Jesus is a bright student, and his mother hires a teacher to instruct him in Scripture and Talmud. Jesus's academic giftedness and disregard for rabbinic authority, however, end up causing him trouble. The text recounts an event in which Jesus passes before his rabbis sitting at the gate with his head uncovered, in defiance of the prevalent custom that students reverently cover their head in front of their teachers. As he does so, one of the sages calls him out as a "bastard" (*mamzer*, someone born from an adulterous union and thus not considered a full member of the Jewish community; the term functions not only as a slur but also

---

28. Dates proposed for this version of Toledot Yeshu range from antiquity through the thirteenth century, on which see Stöckl Ben Ezra, "On Some Early Traditions." For text and translation, I rely on Schäfer and Meerson, *Toledot Yeshu*, 1:167–84; 2:82–95. On this manuscript, see also William Horbury, "The Strasbourg Text of the *Toledot*," in Schäfer, Meerson, and Deutsch, *Toledot Yeshu Reconsidered*, 49–59.

to designate a legal status, as a *mamzer* is not permitted to marry Jews of non-*mamzer* status). Another sage joins these taunts by adding that Jesus is not only a "bastard" but also "the son of a menstruating woman" (*ben niddah*), a disparaging epithet disclosing that his mother conceived him during her period of menstrual impurity. The following day, Jesus challenges his teachers' authority while they are studying the talmudic tractate *Neziqin*. The discussion in the study house centers on the relationship between Moses and Jethro and, by extension, between students and teachers; Jesus subversively suggests that sometimes students are those who instruct their supposed teachers, upsetting the pedagogical and cultural hierarchy that the rabbis represent. This second event angers the sages so much that they decide to conduct a formal inquiry into Jesus's birth status.

The sages summon Mary to testify about Jesus's birth father. At first, Mary claims that John fathered Jesus and that he had fled to Babylonia before Jesus's birth. But the sages pressure her to confess, noting that they have witnesses to the fact that Jesus is a "bastard" and "the son of a menstruating woman." Finally, Shimon ben Shetah steps forward and recounts his conversation with John years earlier. He admits that Joseph is Jesus's biological father, but also that Mary is not culpable for punishment because she committed the transgression unintentionally—and that it is Joseph who is, in fact, liable for punishment. Once Mary understands that she will not be held accountable for the sin of Jesus's birth, she corroborates the rabbi's story and confesses Jesus's identity as the son of Joseph ben Pandera. With this information now public, Jesus is officially called "the bastard son of a menstruating woman" and sentenced to death for his disrespectful behavior. Jesus therefore flees from his hometown to Jerusalem, in an attempt to distance himself from this event and its consequences.

The next part of the narrative shifts to Jerusalem, where the text reveals that a powerful woman, Helena, ruled over the Jews at the time (the text likely refers to Queen Helena of Adiabene, who never served as a monarch of Jerusalem but who lived in Jerusalem during Jesus's lifetime and who is remembered in Josephus and rabbinic sources both as an enthusiastic convert to Judaism and as a generous benefactor of the city and the region more generally, especially during times of famine and hardship; but the text also might evoke Helena mother of Constantine, who, according to Eusebius, Rufinus, and other late antique Christian sources, played an important role in the Christianization of Jerusalem in the fourth century).[29] Jerusalem was the site of the Jewish temple, in which lay the foundation stone containing the letters of God's ineffable name. Those who memorized these letters gained infinite power, and so the sages, fearing that some would seek to abuse the power of God's name and destroy the world, closely guarded the foundation stone with the help of copper dogs stationed at two iron columns at the gate of the temple. These supernatural dogs would bark at anyone who succeeded in entering the temple and learning the letters; indeed, the very sight of the dogs would make the intruder instantaneously forget the memorized letters. Jesus, however, outsmarts the sages and their copper dogs. When he enters the temple and accesses the ineffable name, he not only memorizes the letters but also inscribes them on a piece of parchment, which he then painlessly inserts into his thigh with the help of the very letters he has memorized. When Jesus leaves the temple, the sight of the barking dogs causes him to forget the letters, but that poses no problem, for he is able to relearn them with the help of parchment that he removes from his thigh once he is safely outside the temple precinct.

---

29. On Queen Helena, see, e.g., Josephus, *Ant.* 20.49–52, m. Yoma 3:10; m. Nazir 3:6; t. Sukkah 1:1; b. Sukkah 2b–3a; b. Yoma 37b–38a; Eusebius, *Vit. Constantini* 3.25–47; Rufinus, *Hist.* 10.7–8.

Armed with the magical letters of God's ineffable name, Jesus seeks out crowds of young men and claims to be the Messiah. His audiences express skepticism at his claims, and they challenge him to show them signs proving that he is in fact the Messiah they have been expecting (this exchange is reminiscent of the Israelites in Egypt demanding that Moses perform signs to prove that he is God's prophet and their redeemer from slavery). Jesus is more than eager to display his magical abilities, made possible by the letters of God's ineffable name that he has memorized. He asks his audience what miracles they would like to witness. They bring him a man who has never been able to stand on his feet; immediately, Jesus recites the letters, and this man is able to stand up. Those in attendance swiftly prostrate themselves and proclaim Jesus the Messiah. Jesus continues performing miracles, such as curing a leper, and consequently he gains a large following of disciples.

The sages take notice and are not pleased by the popular following that Jesus has cultivated. They arrest him and bring him to Queen Helena, accusing him of sorcery and leading the people astray. Jesus defends himself before the queen by claiming that he is the fulfillment of earlier biblical prophecies and that he can perform miracles as great as raising people from the dead. The queen asks him to perform such a feat, and Jesus succeeds, amazing the queen, who praises Jesus and rebukes the sages. This event mortifies the sages and increases the number and fervor of Jesus's followers. While Jesus finally returns with his following to the Galilee, the sages request a meeting with the queen.

Again, the sages lobby the queen for support against Jesus, and Queen Helena recalls Jesus back to Jerusalem. His followers are eager to physically defend Jesus, but Jesus encourages them to remain nonviolent, assuring them that he can prove his status as Messiah through divine rather than human power. Jesus forms birds of clay and animates them with the letters of the ineffable name; the birds fly. Jesus takes a millstone, causes it to float on the sea, and then uses it as a boat; the wind raises him and miraculously returns him to shore. The queen's horsemen witness these miracles in amazement and recount the events to the queen, who begins to doubt the sages' testimonies of Jesus as a deceitful sorcerer. The sages thus challenge Queen Helena to summon Jesus so that they can prove to her that he is a fraud. Meanwhile, the sages send Judas Iscariot (Yehudah Iskariota) to the temple to acquire the ineffable name, implanting it into his thigh, using the same method that Jesus had done not long before. Once the queen has gathered the competing parties, Jesus demonstrates his divinity by flying into the air "between the heaven and the earth." The sages encourage Judas to follow Jesus into the air, and the two men engage in a dramatic flying contest. Judas soon realizes that neither man will win until one of them loses his magical powers; he thus decides to urinate on Jesus and defile him (either soiling him with urine or ritually polluting him with semen), bargaining that defilement will neutralize the power of the ineffable name.[30] His reasoning proves correct. Jesus promptly falls to the ground, demonstrating, according to the narrative, his charlatanry. The authorities arrest him, call for his death, and cover his head with a cloth—a clever return to the earlier incident in which Jesus refused to cover his head in reverence of his rabbinic teachers.

Queen Helena leaves Jesus's fate in the hands of the sages. They bring him to a synagogue in Tiberias and tie him to the ark. His followers try to rescue their leader, but to no avail. Jesus requests water and is served vinegar; a crown of thorns is placed upon his head.

---

30. On this tradition, which appears for the first time in Thomas Ebendorfer's fifteenth-century Latin translation of Toledot Yeshu, see Ruth Mazo Karras, "The Aerial Battle in the *Toledot Yeshu* and Sodomy in the Late Middle Ages," *Medieval Encounters* 19 (2013): 493–533; Ora Limor and Israel J. Yuval, "Judas Iscariot: Revealer of the Hidden Truth," in Schäfer, Meerson, and Deutsch, *Toledot Yeshu Reconsidered*, 197–220; on earlier traditions upon which this story draws, see Schäfer and Meerson, *Toledot Yeshu*, 1:84–87.

Jesus continues to proclaim himself as Messiah, and his followers throw stones at the sages. Unrest unfolds, and Jesus's followers sneak Jesus to Antioch until Passover.

On Passover eve, Jesus returns to Jerusalem with his disciples. He enters Jerusalem on an ass, all those with him weeping and prostrating themselves. Jesus and his followers make their way to the study house, where Jesus is betrayed by a man named Geisa. Jesus is arrested and killed. When the authorities decide to hang his body from a tree, however, they encounter a problem: each tree they try to use breaks under the weight of his body. This happens, the text explains, because Jesus knew that he would eventually be hanged, and so before his death he used the ineffable name to ensure that no tree would agree to host his body. Not considering the cabbage stalk as a tree, however, Jesus had not made such an arrangement with it. Therefore, he is finally hanged on a cabbage stalk. Jesus is then buried.

Jesus's followers mourn at his grave and soon discover that it is empty. They rush to share the news of Jesus's resurrection with Queen Helena. The sages begin to panic when Queen Helena asks them for an explanation, for they do not know where Jesus's body is. As it happens, a gardener had stolen Jesus's body to use as a barrier in his garden to stop a water leak, and then buried the body to conceal the theft. The queen demands that the sages produce Jesus's body or face devastating consequences; she gives them three days to complete this task. The people of Israel fast and pray for God's mercy. A certain Rabbi Tanhuma bumps into the gardener, who confesses his theft. They share the news with those in Jerusalem, dragging Jesus's body through the streets of the city all the way to Queen Helena. This final disgrace to Jesus's body proves definitively that Jesus was not the Messiah and had not ascended to heaven.

At this point, the narrative shifts from retelling the life of Jesus to recounting the events that transpired in the years after Jesus's death. Jesus's disciples travel far and wide, to the mountains of Ararat, to Armenia, to Rome, and to other places, but none of them survive. Those followers who stay in town accuse the people of Israel of killing God's Messiah, while the people of Israel accuse them of believing in a false prophet. The text is quick to note, however, that even though three decades have passed since Jesus's crucifixion, the two groups of people—those who follow Jesus and those who reject him—still form a single community, and that those who belong to one or the other group are not easily distinguishable. And therein lie two interrelated problems: the Jesus-followers cause continual strife within the community, and they cannot be readily weeded out of the community. The two groups regularly quarrel.

The sages attempt to solve this conundrum creatively. They resolve to remove the Christians, who desecrate the Sabbath and festivals, from their community. They collaborate with a sage named Elijah (Eliyahu), tasking him with convincing the Christians to part ways with the people of Israel. They assure him that he can serve as a double agent, pretending publicly to be Jesus's apostle while privately remaining a pious sage. Elijah travels far and wide, from Tiberias to Antioch, proving through a series of miracles that he is Jesus's messenger and declaring that everyone who believes in Jesus should follow him. With a robust following, Elijah begins his program of separating Jesus-followers from the people of Israel. He commands them, in Jesus's name, to abandon the congregation of Israel, replace the Jewish Sabbath and annual festivals with the Christian Sunday and annual festivals, avoid circumcision, eat all animals (thus violating the laws of *kashruth*), and ignore the criticisms of Jews who find these choices offensive. Elijah succeeds in his mission; the Christians longingly call him Paul (yes, it turns out that he is the Paul of the New Testament, apostle to the gentiles!).

Just when the story seems to come to an end, with Jesus dead and the Jesus-followers safely separated from the Jewish community, another wrench is thrown into the narrative. Elijah/Paul's mission faces a challenger named Nestor, who claims that Jesus never advocated rejection of Jewish law and in fact believed that his followers ought to practice circumcision, just as Jesus himself was circumcised. A schism forms between Nestor's followers and Elijah/Paul's followers over this and other issues.

Finally, the narrative introduces another character, Shimon Kepha, the head of the Sanhedrin (who is also the apostle Peter). Christians become jealous that the Jews have such a charismatic spiritual leader. When Shimon Kepha makes a pilgrimage to Jerusalem during the festival of Sukkoth, all the governors and Christian elders assemble at the Mount of Olives on Hoshana Rabbah, determined to convert him to Christianity, threatening his life if he does not convert. The narrative suggests that Christian proselytizing and oppression of the Jews was a persistent problem. The Jews convince Shimon Kepha to become yet another double agent, similar to Elijah/Paul, with the goal of teaching Christians to treat Jews with more respect and to leave them alone. The Jews assure Shimon Kepha that if he pretends to convert to Christianity, they will nonetheless consider him a pious Jew. Shimon Kepha therefore makes a deal with the Christians: he will join their community if they agree never to beat or kill another Jew and to let Jews freely enter and exit the temple (perhaps an allusion to restrictions or the alleviation of restrictions on Jewish movement in Jerusalem in the period when this tradition developed). That is, Shimon Kepha is willing to sacrifice his own life as a Jew for the well-being and safety of his fellow Jews. He also convinces the Christians to build him a tall tower in which he can dwell for the remainder of his life, sustaining himself exclusively on bread and water. He devises this plan so that he can continue observing all the Jewish laws of purity without associating with Christians (he tells the Christians, however, that he leads such a secluded, ascetic lifestyle in mourning of Jesus). In this tower, Shimon Kepha composes Jewish liturgical poetry (including the famous Nishmat prayer and liturgy for Yom Kippur), disseminating his writings to the elders of Israel, who incorporate them into Jewish prayer both in Palestine and Babylonia. While Elijah/Paul caused the separation of Christians from Jews, Shimon Kepha/Peter assured that Christians stopped persecuting Jews. And so the story of Toledot Yeshu, according to the Strasbourg manuscript, ends—not only with the death of Jesus but also with the decisive schism between Judaism and Christianity and with some form of protection for the remaining Jewish community.

3. INTERPRETIVE ISSUES
3.1 Relationship of Toledot Yeshu to Other Texts and Traditions

Discussion of Toledot Yeshu's engagement with specific passages from the New Testament is addressed in section four below. But Toledot Yeshu's engagement with earlier sources expands far beyond the New Testament. The manuscripts frequently allude to narratives from the Hebrew Bible; incorporate rabbinic concepts, idioms, and vignettes; and draw on early (and not necessarily Jewish) anti-Christian polemics.

One of the biblical narratives on which Toledot Yeshu draws most heavily is the book of Esther.[31] The most striking similarity, and the correspondence on which the broader comparison between the two stories rests, is the similar manner of Haman and Jesus's deaths by hanging and crucifixion. Drawing on an account of Haman's hanging in an Aramaic

---

31. The correspondences between Toledot Yeshu and the book of Esther are documented in detail in Gribetz, "Hanged and Crucified."

targum of the book of Esther and rabbinic midrashim, in which many different trees refuse to be used for Haman's hanging until the puniest tree or bush is finally found, Toledot Yeshu constructs a similar scenario in which all of the trees upon which the authorities try to hang Jesus break until they finally find the cabbage stalk, the least distinguished among all of the plants and not even a tree.[32] Haman's hanging and Jesus's crucifixion thus end up similarly humiliating. Other references to the book of Esther include the ways in which the narrative refers to or describes characters. For example, Jesus is often referred to as *yeshu harasha'* ("the evil Jesus"), *ha'arur yeshu* or *yeshu ha'arur* ("the accursed Jesus"), allusions to epithets used for Haman (*haman harasha'*) in classical and postclassical rabbinic literature and liturgical poetry; Mary is described as belonging to the tribe of Benjamin, like Esther, and being *yefah to'ar vetovat mar'eh* ("beautiful"), almost the same words that the book of Esther uses in its description of Esther's beauty in Esther 2:7.[33] In Toledot Yeshu, the Jews send letters, fast, and pray for three days before meeting with a royal figure, just as Esther, Mordecai, and the Jews of the Persian Empire do in the biblical narrative. These and other allusions set up a parallel between the narratives in the book of Esther and Toledot Yeshu: in both texts, Jews face an existential threat to their community, their religious convictions, and their standing within the empire, and just as the Jews of Shushan prevailed over Haman, so too the Jews of Palestine prevail over Jesus. By alluding to the book of Esther, the authors of Toledot Yeshu suggest that the threat of Christianity is just as dangerous to the Jewish community as were Haman's genocidal plans to exterminate the Jews—and thus require just as vigilant and focused a response.

Toledot Yeshu also alludes to the story of Joseph and Potiphar in Genesis 39 when it describes Joseph's rape of Mary. In both Genesis 39 and some versions of Toledot Yeshu, the two Josephs are each described as good-looking, and a specific allusion to Genesis 39:18 appears in at least one manuscript of Toledot Yeshu.[34] When Jesus begins defying the authority of the sages, he does so through a subversive interpretation of Exodus 18's depiction of the relationship between Moses and Jethro—even though Moses was the most important prophet, he learned about effective governance from his father-in-law Jethro. Certain manuscripts extensively cite biblical prooftexts from across the Hebrew Bible, especially from the book of Psalms and Isaiah (texts central in New Testament and early Christian sources), especially in scenes in which Jesus continually insists that he is the Son of God and the Messiah who has come to fulfill biblical prophecies.[35]

Toledot Yeshu likewise incorporates late antique and medieval rabbinic ideas, passages, and narratives. For example, Jesus's status as the son of a menstruating woman (*ben niddah*, attested in Kallah Rabbati 2:2) is grounded in rabbinic law, which deems children conceived when a woman is menstrually impure to be "blemished" (e.g., Shulchan Arukh, Even HaEzer 4:13).[36] His status as a *mamzer* is based on the biblical category (Deut 23:3) and rabbinic discussions (e.g., m. Yevamot 4:13) of the lower status of such a person.

---

32. In the Second Targum of Esther, the cedar tree suggests that Haman and his ten sons be hung on the cedar gallows that Haman prepared for Mordecai, while in Midrash Esther Rabbah, Haman is hung on a thorn bush. This portion of the narrative and additional intertexts are discussed in Ernst Bammel, "Der Tod Jesu in einer 'Toledot Jeschu'-Überlieferung," *Annual of the Swedish Theological Institute* 6 (1968): 124–31; Hillel I. Newman, "The Death of Jesus in the 'Toledot Yeshu' Literature," *JTS* 50 (1999): 59–79.

33. The Toledot Yeshu manuscripts have *yefah* instead of the biblical *yefat*.

34. MS New York JTS 2221, 24, discussed in Schäfer and Meerson, *Toledot Yeshu*, 1:186n6.

35. Lists of biblical passages are provided in Schäfer and Meerson, *Toledot Yeshu*, 1:71–72, 81–84, 93–94.

36. On which, see Schäfer and Meerson, *Toledot Yeshu*, 1:48; Mika Ahuvia and John G. Gager, "Some Notes on Jesus and His Parents: From the New Testament to the *Toledot Yeshu*," in Boustan et al., *Envisioning Judaism*, 997–1119.

The figure Shimon ben Shetah, who appears frequently in rabbinic sources, plays a prominent role in the narrative as the character to whom John confides his wife's pregnancy and who ultimately testifies about Jesus's true parentage. This ultimately marks Jesus as an inferior member of the Jewish community, only able to marry a fellow *mamzer*, and whose children will forever bear the label and status of *mamzer*.

Sifra Shemini 1, Leviticus Rabbah 20:6, and b. Eruvin 63a explain that a student who teaches before his rabbis is liable for death, which is precisely Jesus's first transgression in Toledot Yeshu; the implication is that even just this single sin is enough to justify Jesus's execution.[37] A medieval interpretation of b. Berakhot 27b suggests that young men ought to prostrate themselves or bow in the presence of rabbis (though the rabbinic text itself does not advocate this behavior), a norm that Jesus is accused of transgressing in Toledot Yeshu.[38] The trial of Jesus's five disciples (Mattai, Naqi, Buni, Netser, and Todaah), each of whom advocate for a different aspect of Jesus's messianic identity, appears in some manuscripts of Toledot Yeshu and is based on a narrative from b. Sanhedrin 43a–b.[39] The copper dogs that guard the temple might allude to a tradition in Exodus Rabbah 17:20, in which Joseph's tomb in Egypt is guarded by two golden dogs who bark at passersby to protect the tomb, and only Moses is able to pass them.[40] God's ineffable name, which Jesus steals from the temple, is a prominent feature in ancient and medieval Jewish magical and mystical traditions, and Jesus's magical feats draw a close connection between him and Moses, who performed miracles in Egypt.[41] In t. Shabbat 11:15, a certain Ben Stada (identified in other texts as Jesus), learns by scratching his flesh, and in y. Shabbat 12:4 and b. Shabbat 104b he uses this method of learning to bring knowledge of sorcery back from Egypt.[42]

In some manuscripts, when Jesus enters the temple, he goes straight to the Foundation Stone (*even shetiya*), which is said to contain God's ineffable name. Rabbinic texts develop traditions about a "foundation stone" located in the holy of holies, believed to be the spot from which the world was created and where the ark of the covenant stood in Solomon's temple (e.g., m. Yoma 5:2; t. Yoma 2:14; y. Yoma 5:3, 42c; b. Yoma 54b; in y. Sanhedrin 10:2, 29a, King David discovers a clay pot, which seals the waters of *tehom*, when he digs the foundations of the temple; in b. Sukkah 53a–b, David engraves God's name on a shard of pottery in order to seal the unruly waters of *tehom*), and postclassical rabbinic texts present this foundation stone as the place subduing the chaotic waters that threaten the world's continued existence (e.g., Pirqe de Rabbi Eliezer 10.9; 35.8; Targum Pseudo-Jonathan to Exodus 28:30; Tanhuma Kedoshim 10).[43] It is this piece of bedrock to which Toledot Yeshu refers in its narrative about Jesus stealing God's ineffable name. As Naomi Koltun-Fromm has demonstrated, Jerusalem's rocks (both the rock under the holy of holies and the

---

37. These rabbinic texts are discussed in Schäfer and Meerson, *Toledot Yeshu*, 1:58.

38. On which, see Schäfer and Meerson, *Toledot Yeshu*, 1:58; on sage veneration, see Rachel Neis, *The Sense of Sight in Rabbinic Culture: Jewish Ways of Seeing in Late Antiquity* (Cambridge: Cambridge University Press, 2013), 231–39.

39. Schäfer and Meerson, *Toledot Yeshu*, 1:89–91.

40. Schäfer and Meerson, *Toledot Yeshu*, 1:65.

41. See the extensive discussion and citations in Schäfer and Meerson, *Toledot Yeshu*, 1:66–69, and the discussion of magic in Bohak, "Jesus the Magician."

42. Schäfer and Meerson, *Toledot Yeshu*, 1:67.

43. The tradition that the foundation stone contains the ineffable name appears in Targum Pseudo-Jonathan on Exodus 28:30 and Targum Ecclesiastes 3:11, discussed in Schäfer and Meerson, *Toledot Yeshu*, 1:66. Toledot Yeshu mentions that the foundation stone is the very place at which Jacob "poured oil," a tradition found as well in Pirqe de Rabbi Eliezer 35. On rabbinic traditions of the foundation stone, see Naomi Koltun-Fromm, "Imagining the Temple in Rabbinic Stone: The Evolution of the 'Even Shetiya," *AJS Review* 43:2 (2019): 355–77.

Dome of the Rock as well as that under the Anastasis in the Church of the Holy Sepulchre) were sites of interreligious (Jewish-Christian, and ultimately Jewish-Christian-Muslim) traditions and tensions in late antiquity and the medieval period.[44] The foundation stone's centrality in Toledot Yeshu's narrative corresponds well with this broader interreligious discourse about Jerusalem's sacred rocks.

In addition to biblical and rabbinic traditions, certain passages in Toledot Yeshu also suggest knowledge of earlier anti-Christian polemics. For example, Celsus and Tertullian both refer to theories that Jesus's birth was not a miracle but rather the product of an illicit relationship between a carpenter and a prostitute (Tertullian, De spectaculis 30) or a poor countrywoman and a Roman soldier (Celsus, quoted in Origen, Cels. 1.28–32), theories that reappear in polemical texts thereafter, including the Vita Silestri, the writings of Jerome, the Babylonian Talmud, and medieval disputations.[45] In "Group II" manuscripts, the ruling authority in Jerusalem is Queen Helena, who seems to be a blend of Queen Helena of Adiabene, known from the writings of both Josephus and the rabbis, and Helena the mother of Emperor Constantine, famous from texts such as Eusebius's Vita Constantini and the legends of her finding the true cross, such as that told by Rufinus, which over time were depicted on reliquaries, incorporated in popular Christian piety, and celebrated on the liturgical calendar.[46] One version of Toledot Yeshu parodies more explicitly the legend of the finding of the true cross,[47] while several engage with the Nestorius legend.[48]

3.2 Notable Feature of the "Pilate"/"Group I" Recension

One of the most fascinating episodes in Toledot Yeshu appears only in the "Pilate"/"Group I" recension. The early manuscripts in this recension generally begin with Jesus's adult ministry and miracles and do not contain a narrative of Jesus's birth. A different birth narrative, however, is nevertheless embedded into this text.[49] When Pilate and the Jewish authorities challenge John (the Baptist) and Jesus, the two men are summoned to the emperor Tiberius Caesar, who questions them. John and Jesus claim to be sons of God, able to perform miracles such as miraculously impregnating a woman who has never borne a child. The emperor thus challenges Jesus to impregnate the emperor's virgin daughter, which Jesus agrees to do. The emperor arrests Jesus and John for the nine months of his daughter's pregnancy, while those who brought Jesus to the emperor grow increasingly worried that Jesus will succeed in his promised miracle. The emperor's daughter conceives a child, who slowly grows in her womb. As the Jews mourn and pray to God for salvation, however, that fetus slowly transforms into a stone. When the woman does not give birth at the end of the expected nine-month period of gestation (because, by then, her fetus has fully calcified), Jesus assures the emperor that his daughter will eventually give birth, perhaps after twelve months rather than nine. At the end of a full year, Jesus decides to perform a

---

44. Naomi Koltun-Fromm, "Rock over Water: Pre-Historic Rocks and Primordial Waters from Creation to Salvation in Jerusalem," in Jewish and Christian Cosmogony in Late Antiquity, ed. Lance Jenott and Sarit Kattan Gribetz, TSAJ 155 (Tübingen: Mohr Siebeck, 2013); idem, "Jerusalem Sacred Stones from Creation to Eschaton," Journal of Late Antiquity 10.2 (2017): 405–31.

45. Schäfer and Meerson, Toledot Yeshu, 1:45–46.

46. On which, see Hasan-Rokem, "Polymorphic Helena."

47. On which, see Schäfer and Meerson, Toledot Yeshu, 1:120–24.

48. On which, see Stephen Gero, "The Nestorius Legend in the Toledoth Yeshu," Oriens Christianus 59 (1975): 108–20.

49. A comprehensive analysis of this episode is the subject of Sarit Kattan Gribetz, "The Mothers in the Manuscripts: Gender, Motherhood and Power in the Toledot Yeshu Narratives," in Barbu and Deutsch, Toledot Yeshu in Context.

caesarean section and, much to the surprise of everyone present, he pulls out a large stone rather than a baby from the woman's womb (the woman herself dies from this experiment, her life seemingly disposable to the whims of both Jesus and her emperor father).

This story has been contextualized within the history of medieval medicine (because calcified fetuses and caesarean sections play such central narrative roles in the tale) as well as intertextually among other references to stones in New Testament and Toledot Yeshu narratives (e.g., Jesus's stoning and the fact that Peter's name, *Petros*, means "stone").[50] As I have argued elsewhere, the story not only pokes fun at Jesus's magical shortcomings but also functions as an articulation of Toledot Yeshu's attitude toward Jesus's ministry writ large and the Christianity that emerged from it:

> According to the gospels, Jesus's birth narrative is an important piece of evidence that the child is the son of God, the Jewish Messiah who ushers in a new era. According to *Toledot Yeshu*, this birth narrative suggests that that child is not a son of God, nor an heir to the emperor, nor an inheritor of the kingdom, but a stone. In the absence of his own birth narrative, Jesus is put in parallel with the stone fetus: the hoped-for redeemer who fails to return, who transforms from a being filled with life and movement into a calcified lifeless mass, a malignancy that causes discomfort and suffering and ultimately death.[51]

This story does not appear in other recensions of Toledot Yeshu, all of which contain Jesus's birth narrative.

3.3 History, Legend, and Reception

The introduction to Daniel Barbu and Yaacov Deutsch's volume about Toledot Yeshu poses generative questions for the study of Toledot Yeshu:

> The question we must ask . . . is not if there is any truth in a story like *Toledot Yeshu* . . . It is: Who felt the need to express this particular truth? What does it tell us about those who wrote and told such a story, as well as those who read it, copied it, transformed it, and perhaps even enjoyed it? And conversely, who felt the need to revile it, attack it, or fear it?[52]

This intervention is especially important because it redirects conversations about Toledot Yeshu away from discussion about its date of origin (when was it first composed?) and its historicity (are certain aspects of the text historically accurate and do they shed light on the historical Jesus?), to more productive engagement with the texts' content and the reasons for Toledot Yeshu's continued relevance in so many historical contexts.

To that end, it is worth noting some of the purposes for which Toledot Yeshu was likely composed, preserved, transmitted, translated, and told. It is difficult to determine the purposes of the earliest versions of Toledot Yeshu, because we do not have extant manuscripts that provide textual and paratextual clues for contextualization. Later manuscripts and references to Toledot Yeshu provide helpful indications for how the text functioned in later periods. For example, some versions of Toledot Yeshu are preserved in codices with midrashim, suggesting that the text was placed among rabbinic compositions that expand

---

50. Michael Meerson, "Yeshu the Physician and the Child of Stone: A Glimpse of Progressive Medicine in Jewish-Christian Polemics," *Jewish Studies Quarterly* 20 (2013): 297–314; Schäfer, "Agobard's and Amulo's *Toledot Yeshu*," 35.

51. Gribetz, "Mothers in the Manuscripts."

52. Barbu and Deutsch, *Toledot Yeshu in Context*, 3.

and comment on biblical and rabbinic passages, and in collections of folk narratives, told alongside other Jewish lore. Other versions appear in codices of liturgical material, raising the possibility that Toledot Yeshu might have been studied or recited as part of worship or recitation. Toledot Yeshu traditions also found their way into the Zohar and other kabbalistic writings.[53] Some sources mention that Toledot Yeshu was studied on particular days of the year, most often Christmas Eve.[54] Translations of and references to Toledot Yeshu appear in Christian anti-Jewish polemical works, such as in the writings of Abogard, Amulo, Raymond Martí, Thomas Ebendorfer, Martin Luther, Wagenseil, and Voltaire, indicating that there was robust engagement with Toledot Yeshu among Christian bishops, apologists, and Hebraists who sought to use Toledot Yeshu to expose the blasphemous traditions of Jews.[55] Some inquisitorial records accuse Jews of teaching Toledot Yeshu within their communities or using its biting tales to convince Jews to reject Christianity or to reconvert recent apostates back to Judaism.[56] In each of these contexts, Toledot Yeshu was likely regarded by its audiences as (variably) accurate history, persuasive counternarrative, polemics or parody, sophisticated midrash, fanciful tales, good stories, decisive proof of blasphemy, and more.

4. KEY PASSAGES FOR NEW TESTAMENT STUDIES AND THEIR SIGNIFICANCE

Because Toledot Yeshu offers a counternarrative to the canonical Gospels, especially the Synoptic Gospels, and in a more limited fashion the book of Acts, the entire text is relevant for the study of the reception of the New Testament. Certain parts of the gospel narratives, however, figure most prominently in Toledot Yeshu's retelling of Jesus's life story, and therefore these episodes are reviewed here.

4.1 Birth Narrative

None of Paul's epistles mention Jesus's parents. The Gospel of Mark (6:3) refers to Jesus's siblings and reveals that Mary is Jesus's mother (no mention is made of his father), while the Gospel of John (1:45 and 6:42) mentions that Jesus is the son of Joseph even as, at various points in the text, Jesus also insists that his Father is in heaven. Yet neither of these Gospels contains Jesus's birth story. The Gospels of Matthew and Luke, in contrast, each provide their own genealogies of Jesus's ancestry (Matthew 1:1–17; Luke 3:23–34), and they each tell a different birth narrative. In Matthew 1:18–25 Mary miraculously conceives Jesus by the Holy Spirit, and Joseph decides not to expose her pregnancy publicly for fear

---

53. Jonatan M. Benarroch, "'A Real Spark of Sama'el': Kabbalistic Reading(s) of Toledot Yeshu," in Barbu and Deutsch, *Toledot Yeshu in Context*; idem, "'Son of an Israelite Woman and an Egyptian Man'—Jesus as the Blasphemer (Lev. 24:10–23): An Anti-Gospel Polemic in the Zohar," *HTR* 109 (2016): 100–124; idem, "'Piercing What Has Been Closed Up'—The Story of the One Who Blasphemes by Invoking the Name (Lev. 24:10–16) and *Toledot Yešu*: From the Homilies of the Zohar to *And I came this Day unto the Fountain*," ed. P. Maciejko (Los Angeles: Cherub, 2014), 243–77 (in Hebrew).

54. Sid Z. Leiman, "The Scroll of Fasts: The Ninth of Tebeth," *JQR* 74.1 (1983): 174–95; Marc Shapiro, "Torah Study on Christmas Eve," *Journal of Jewish Thought and Philosophy* 8.2 (1999): 319–53.

55. Schäfer, "Agobard's and Amulo's *Toledot Yeshu*"; Brigitta Callsen et al., *Das jüdische Leben Jesu—'Toldot Jeschu': Die älteste lateinische Übersetzung in den 'Falsitates Judeorum' von Thomas Ebendorfer* (Wein: Oldenburg, 2003); Stephen Burnett, "Martin Luther, *Toledot Yeshu* and 'the Rabbis,'" in Barbu and Deutsch, *Toledot Yeshu in Context*; Daniel Barbu, "Voltaire and the *Toledoth Yeshu*: A Response to Philip Alexander," in Clivaz, *Infancy Gospels: Stories and Identities*, 588–627; idem, "Some Remarks on Toledot Yeshu (The Jewish Life of Jesus) in Early Modern Europe," *Journal of Religion, Film, and Media* 5.1 (2019): 29–45; Martin Lockshin, "Translation as Polemic: The Case of *Toledot Yeshu*," in *Minhah le-Nahum: Biblical and Other Studies Presented to Nahum M. Sarna in Honour of His 70th Birthday*, ed. M. Brettler and M. Fishbane (Sheffield: JSOT Press, 1993), 226–41.

56. Tartakoff, "*Toledot Yeshu*"; Barbu and Dahhaoui, "Un manuscrit français"; idem, "Secret Booklet from Germany."

of disgracing her, while in Luke 1:26–38 the angel Gabriel informs Mary of her pregnancy, also by the Holy Spirit.

John G. Gager and Mika Ahuvia note that the question of Jesus's paternity must have been raised by early readers of Mark, who wondered why Joseph is an absent figure in the Gospels (John 8:19 even articulates this question explicitly when it states, "Where is your father?")—and that the narratives of a virgin birth offered in Matthew and Luke sought to provide answers that were acceptable to Jesus-followers.[57] Ancient texts, including the writings of Tertullian (*De spectaculis* 30), Celsus (Origen, *Cels.* 1.28–32), and other writers, explicitly cite doubts about Jesus's parentage that circulated among critics of the early Jesus-movement; such critics answered questions about the identity of Jesus's father not by positing that the Holy Spirit impregnated Mary, as Matthew and Luke do (perhaps even in response to such circulating questions or rumors), but rather alleging illicit sexual relations of various sorts (e.g., that Jesus was a prostitute's son, according to an opinion cited by Tertullian, or the son of a poor woman guilty of adultery with a soldier named Panthera, as per Celsus). The infancy gospels, too, grapple with the story of Jesus's birth and his complicated relationships to his relatives.

Many Toledot Yeshu manuscripts, most consistently in the "Group II" and "Group III" manuscripts, participate in telling a story of Jesus's birth that aligns with its composers' own communal and theological commitments. Thus they feature versions of Jesus's birth narrative that either correspond closely with (and were likely drawn from) early traditions in which Jesus is conceived from an adulterous union or that expand on them into far more elaborate narratives.[58] It is clear that the composers of these birth narratives were familiar with the gospel narratives and that they sought to undermine them by drawing on competing traditions about Jesus's birth, such as those preserved by Tertullian and Celsus, rabbinic sources (e.g., m. Shabbat 12:4; t. Shabbat 11:15; y. Shabbat 12:4/3, fol. 13d; b. Shabbat 104b; b. Sanhedrin 76a), and other contemporary literature.[59]

4. 2 Jesus's Miracles

In most Toledot Yeshu versions, as in the Gospels, Jesus develops his following in the Galilee. Toledot Yeshu describes Jesus as leading crowds of followers, perhaps with Matthew 14:13–21 in mind.[60] In both Toledot Yeshu and the Gospels, one of the primary ways that Jesus convinces people of his status as Messiah is through miracles; in Toledot Yeshu, Jesus performs many of the same miracles that are described in the Gospels: healing a leper (Matt 8:2–4; Mark 1:40–45; Luke 5:12–15; 12:11–19), healing a crippled man (Matt 9:2–8; Mark 2:1–12; Luke 5:17–26), healing a blind man (Matt 9:27–31; 20:29–34; John 9:1–12), and resurrecting the dead (Matt 9:18–26; Mark 5:22–24; Luke 7:11–17; 8:40–56; John 11:38–44).[61] Certain recensions also describe Jesus feeding multitudes

---

57. Ahuvia and Gager, "Some Notes on Jesus and his Parents," 997–1119.

58. On the range of birth narratives told in different Toledot Yeshu manuscripts and their engagement with the Gospels and other ancient and medieval sources, see Ahuvia and Gager, "Some Notes on Jesus and his Parents"; Gribetz, "Mothers in the Manuscripts"; Schäfer and Meerson, *Toledot Yeshu*, 1:7, 45–56; Peter Schäfer, "Jesus's Origin, Birth, and Childhood according to the *Toledot Yeshu* and the Talmud," in *Judaea-Palaestina, Babylon and Rome: Jews in Antiquity*, ed. B. Isaac and Y. Shahar, TSAJ 147 (Tübingen: Mohr Siebeck, 2012), 139–64; Adina M. Yoffie, "Observations on the Huldreich Manuscripts of the *Toledot Yeshu*," in Schäfer, Meerson, and Deutsch, *Toledot Yeshu Reconsidered*, 61–77.

59. Ahuvia and Gager, "Some Notes on Jesus and His Parents," 997–1119. On rabbinic sources about Jesus's parents, see Schäfer, *Jesus in the Talmud*, 15–24.

60. Schäfer and Meerson, *Toledot Yeshu*, 1:70–71.

61. This list of citations appears in Schäfer and Meerson, *Toledot Yeshu*, 1:74–75.

(Matt 14:13–21; 15:32–39; Mark 6:31–44; 8:1–9; Luke 9:12–17; John 6:5–14) and turning water into wine (John 2:1–11).[62] Gideon Bohak has noted that "one of the central features of *Toledot Yeshu*'s anti-Christian polemics is that it does not deny the claim that Jesus performed many miracles, but insists that he did so by using magic"—in other words, accusing Jesus of magic (rather than acknowledging his actions as miracles) served both to explain how Jesus was able to accomplish these deeds and to polemicize against him because his abilities stemmed from sorcery rather than divinity.[63] Bohak also notes that in particular cases, such as Jesus's attempt to impregnate the emperor's daughter or the aerial battle against Judas (which both fail), the pious practices of the Jews or their careful planning end up preventing Jesus's magical acts from succeeding. But regarding miracles reported in the New Testament, Toledot Yeshu always describes Jesus as succeeding in these acts but doing so through magical, rather than miraculous, means.

4.3 Death, Burial, and Resurrection

In Toledot Yeshu, as in the Gospels, Jesus endures a trial, is sentenced to death, executed, hanged, buried, and eventually his followers discover an empty tomb—the general narrative is the same in both sets of texts, though as usual Toledot Yeshu inverts the significance of the events. The manner of Jesus's execution differs in Toledot Yeshu from the narrative told in the Gospels (Mark 15:21–41; Matt 27:32–56; Luke 23:26–43; John 19:16–42). The "Pilate"/"Group I" recension notes that Jesus is hanged and then stoned, rather than crucified, which Schäfer and Meerson suggest may "be the result of the confluence of the New Testament tradition, according to which Jesus was crucified, and the Talmudic tradition, according to which Yeshu was stoned."[64] In the "Group II" recension, Jesus suffers flagellation, as he does in Mark 15:15, Matthew 27:26, and John 19:1. Jesus's crucifixion is recast so that Jesus is hanged on a cabbage stalk.[65]

Jesus's burial, too, alludes to the gospel narratives (Matt 27:57–61; Mark 15:42–47; Luke 23:50–24:12; John 19:38–42), though in Toledot Yeshu Jesus's body is buried in a water channel or aqueduct ("Pilate"/"Group I") or is buried first in a grave, then stolen, and then secretly reburied in a garden, possibly as part of an irrigation or sewer system ("Group II" and "Group III"). As in the Gospels, Jesus's empty tomb is discovered by his followers, but in Toledot Yeshu the quest to determine whether Jesus has been resurrected or his body stolen occupies a suspenseful part of the narrative that ends in proving that Jesus was not the risen Messiah but an ordinary charlatan.[66]

4.4 Paul's Legacy and the Fate of Simon Peter

"Group II and III" recensions continue the story of Jesus's life by focusing on his afterlife—that is, on the development of his movement following his death. This section is often called the "Acts of the Apostles" section, for it focuses on Peter and Paul. In Toledot Yeshu, Peter is called Shimon Kepha, a reference to the names (Simeon, Simon, Simon Peter, and Kephas/Cephas) used for him in the New Testament (e.g., Matt 4:18; 8:14; 16:18; Mark 1:16; John 1:24; 21:15; Acts 15:14; Gal 2:11; 2 Pet 1:1, and in dozens of other passages across the corpus), and as the Peshitta of the Gospels and some other Syriac texts

---

62. Schäfer and Meerson, *Toledot Yeshu*, 1:75.
63. Bohak, "Jesus the Magician."
64. Schäfer and Meerson, *Toledot Yeshu*, 1:92, referring specifically to b. Sanhedrin 43a.
65. See the extensive discussion in Newman, "Death of Jesus."
66. For a comparison of Toledot Yeshu and the gospel accounts, see John G. Gager, *Who Made Early Christianity? The Jewish Lives of the Apostle Paul* (New York: Columbia University Press, 2017), 131–32.

call him. Paul's name is Elijah, but Christians call him Paul. Both these characters are modeled after their counterparts in the New Testament, but Toledot Yeshu employs these characters to new ends. Gager explains, for example, the role that Peter plays in the Toledot Yeshu texts:

> In the official Christian version of history, Peter is the immediate successor to Jesus, the first Christian pope, and the first Christian martyr in Rome. In the Jewish versions of history, Peter undergoes a complete transformation. He becomes a subversive double agent, a pretend Christian, commissioned by the Jews to undermine Christianity by delivering false instructions in Rome. Far from being a pious Christian, he lives his entire life as an observant Jew, isolated in his special tower. One day a year, he emerges to deliver false teachings of his own making, the most important of which is that Christians should leave Jews in peace and stop persecuting them.[67]

Gager argues further that ambivalence in the Gospel of Mark about the figure of Peter and suspicion that he might be a false believer lay the groundwork on which Toledot Yeshu could develop its own myths about Shimon Kepha's role.[68] Shimon Kepha's ascetic lifestyle and his residence in a tower also evoke the figure of Simeon Stylites, who lived in strikingly similar conditions.[69] In Toledot Yeshu, Paul's character, too, becomes a figure who presents himself as an apostle. In truth, though, he seeks to drive Jesus-followers out of the Jewish community by convincing them to stop observing Jewish festivals, dietary laws, and circumcision—in this case alluding to Paul's epistles, including the letters to the Galatians (e.g., 4:10–11; 5:2–6) and Romans (2:25–27) in particular.

5. CONCLUDING REFLECTIONS

Toledot Yeshu narrates a devastatingly nasty version of Jesus's life story, which begins with Jesus's conception through an adulterous rape and ends with his body dumped in a sewer, or variations on this theme. The text was and remains controversial—in Jewish communal contexts, in Christian confessional settings, and in the field of Jewish studies—for it exposes a Jewish literary tradition that not only disrespects but mocks Jesus and Christian origins and that, moreover, was popular, if kept mostly secret, for hundreds of years.

Why, then, study Toledot Yeshu? Scholars study this text not because it contains truth about the historical Jesus or necessarily reflects ancient Jewish attitudes about Jesus, given that the full narrative postdates antiquity. Rather, Toledot Yeshu provides a lens into the stories that some Jews told about Jesus in the medieval and early modern periods, both in contexts in which relations between Jews and Christians were relatively civil and at times when tensions between Jews and Christians ran high or when Jews felt particularly threatened or persecuted. In all of the contexts in which Toledot Yeshu circulated, Jews lived as minorities in majority Christian or Muslim societies, and their interest in this text reminds us of the sorts of "hidden transcripts" that sustained Jews in those situations and that allowed them to narrate Christian history, especially its earliest moments, in ways that empowered them.[70] Placing Toledot Yeshu within these contexts helps us better understand

---

67. Gager, *Who Made Early Christianity?*, 133. See also John G. Gager, "Simon Peter, Founder of Christianity or Saviour of Israel?," in Schäfer, Meerson, and Deutsch, *Toledot Yeshu Reconsidered*, 221–45.

68. Gager, "Simon Peter," 233.

69. Schäfer and Meerson, *Toledot Yeshu*, 1:114–15.

70. James C. Scott, *Domination and the Arts of Resistance: Hidden Transcripts* (New Haven: Yale University Press, 1990).

those who composed and transmitted this story. Thus, scholars who study Toledot Yeshu acknowledge that in order to appreciate Jewish-Christian relations in nuanced ways, we ought not shy away from or ignore challenging texts and histories, such as Toledot Yeshu, even when they reveal unsavory stories that Jews told each other about Jesus and the beliefs of those among whom they lived.

6. BIBLIOGRAPHY

Ahuvia, Mika, and John G. Gager. "Some Notes on Jesus and His Parents: From the New Testament to the *Toledot Yeshu*." Pages 997–1119 in *Envisioning Judaism: Studies in Honor of Peter Schäfer on the Occasion of his Seventieth Birthday*. Edited by Ra'anan Boustan et al. (Tübingen: Mohr Siebeck, 2013).

Barbu, Daniel, and Yaacov Deutsch, eds. *Toledot Yeshu in Context: Jewish-Christian Polemics in Ancient, Medieval, and Modern History*. TSAJ 182. Tübingen: Mohr Siebeck, 2020.

Deutsch, Yaacov. "New Evidence of Early Versions of *Toldot Yeshu*." *Tarbiz* 69 (2000): 177–97 (in Hebrew).

Di Segni, Riccardo. "La tradizione testuale delle 'Toledòth Jeshu': Manoscritti, edizioni a stampa, classificazione." *Rassegna Mensile di Israel* 50 (1984): 83–100.

Goldstein, Miriam. "Judeo-Arabic Versions of *Toledot Yeshu*." *Ginzei Qedem* 6 (2010): 9–42.

Gribetz, Sarit Kattan, "Jesus and the Clay Birds: Reading *Toledot Yeshu* in Light of the Infancy Gospels." Pages 1021–48 in *Envisioning Judaism: Studies in Honor of Peter Schäfer on the Occasion of his Seventieth Birthday*. Edited by Ra'anan Boustan et al. Tübingen: Mohr Siebeck, 2013.

Horbury, William. "A Critical Examination of the Toledoth Yeshu." PhD diss., University of Cambridge, 1970.

Krauss, Samuel. *Das Leben Jesu nach jüdischen Quellen*. Berlin: S. Calvary, 1902. Repr., Hildesheim: Olms, 1977, 2006.

Rosenzweig, Claudia. "The 'History of the Life of Jesus' in a Yiddish Manuscript from the Eighteenth Century (Ms. Jerusalem, NLI, Heb. 8°5622)." in Daniel Barbu and Yaacov Deutsch, eds., *Toledot Yeshu in Context: Jewish-Christian Polemics in Ancient, Medieval, and Modern History*. TSAJ 182. Tübingen: Mohr Siebeck, 2020.

Schäfer, Peter, and Michael Meerson, eds. *Toledot Yeshu: The Life Story of Jesus*. 2 vol. Tübingen: Mohr Siebeck, 2014.

Schäfer, Peter, Michael Meerson, and Yaacov Deutsch, eds. *Toledot Yeshu ("The Life Story of Jesus") Revisited: A Princeton Conference*. Tübingen: Mohr Siebeck, 2011.

Tartakoff, Paola. "The *Toledot Yeshu* and Jewish-Christian Conflict in the Medieval Crown of Aragon." Pages 297–309 in *Toledot Yeshu Reconsidered*. Edited by Peter Schäfer, Michael Meerson, and Yaacov Deutsch. Tübingen: Mohr Siebeck, 2011.

CHAPTER 11

REVELATION OF THE MAGI

CATHERINE PLAYOUST

1. INTRODUCTION

The Revelation of the Magi (Rev. Magi) is a narrative account written from the perspective of the magi who appear in Matthew 2. As well as recounting the magi's visit to Herod in Jerusalem and then to the Christ-child and his family in Bethlehem, it presents their life in the remote eastern land of Shir before and after their great journey. The earliest conceivable dating for the text is the late second century CE, and so it is unlikely to contain historical information about the magi or the events around Jesus's birth. However, the text is theologically notable for its christological interpretation of the star of Bethlehem and for its ideas about a kind of proto-Christian faith among a certain gentile community in the era prior to the birth of Jesus.

1.1 Source, Manuscript, Editions, Translations, and Title

While there are good reasons for thinking that the Revelation of the Magi existed as a separate text at some stage, it survives only as a portion of a larger work, the Chronicle of Zuqnin, also known as the Chronicle of Pseudo-Dionysius of Tel-Maḥrē.[1] The Chronicle is a substantial account of world history from creation to the late eighth century CE and seems to have been written in the Zuqnin Monastery in eastern Turkey. The document incorporates what appear to be several preexisting texts, including the one of concern here. Immediately before and after the Revelation of the Magi material are short notes about what happened in particular years, quite different in style from the account about the magi, so it is evident that the magi account in the Chronicle comes from a source, although this is not said explicitly. According to Witold Witakowski's analysis, the customary practice of the author of the Chronicle was to incorporate sources fully and without change, so it is likely that this holds in the present case.[2]

In turn, this Chronicle survives only in one manuscript, a vellum codex written in Syriac as a palimpsest over Septuagint fragments.[3] This manuscript, Vat. sir. 162, was added to the Vatican Library's collection by Assemani in the eighteenth century.[4] The *editio princeps* of

---

1. Witold Witakowski, *The Syriac Chronicle of Pseudo-Dionysius of Tel-Maḥrē: A Study in the History of Historiography*, Acta Universitatis Upsaliensis 9; Studia Semitica Upsaliensia 9 (Uppsala: Uppsala University, 1987).
2. Witold Witakowski, "The Magi in Syriac Tradition," in *Malphono w-Rabo d-Malphone: Studies in Honor of Sebastian P. Brock*, ed. G. Kiraz, Gorgias Eastern Christianity Studies 3 (Piscataway, NJ: Gorgias, 2008), 810.
3. Witakowski, *Syriac Chronicle*, 30; Brent Christopher Landau, "The Sages and the Star-Child: An Introduction to the *Revelation of the Magi*, An Ancient Christian Apocryphon" (ThD diss., Harvard Divinity School, 2008), 4–5.
4. A scan of Vat. sir. 162 is available in the Vatican Library's digital collection (https://digi.vatlib.it/view/MSS_Vat.sir.162).

the Chronicle was made by Tullberg and his students in the nineteenth century.[5] Another critical edition of the Chronicle was made by Chabot in the early twentieth century, together with a Latin translation.[6]

The magi portion of the manuscript of the Chronicle (folios 17^r–25^r) is generally well preserved, though it seems to have been in better condition at the time of the *editio princeps* than when Chabot did his edition.[7] It is this portion that is often called the Revelation of the Magi. The most recent critical edition of this portion is by Landau, who also made the first translation into English and assigned chapter-and-verse divisions.[8] Earlier translations of the magi section into modern languages were done by Giorgio Levi Della Vida (Italian)[9] and Witakowski (Polish).[10]

The title of the Revelation of the Magi is a modern title of convenience, and not all recent scholars use this designation. The magi section of the Chronicle does not bear a title but begins with this description: "About the revelation of the Magi, and about their coming to Jerusalem, and about the gifts that they brought to Christ" (1.1). It is from this incipit that Reinink adopted the title *Die Offenbarung der Magier* and Landau followed with the Revelation of the Magi.[11]

1.2 Genre and Structure

The Revelation of the Magi is a narrative text. Over its thirty-two short chapters, the narration is by the magi in the first-person plural for most of chapters 3–27. The rest of the text is told in the third person. In addition to the narrative material, the text includes dialogues, substantial speeches, a quotation from the magi's ancestral teaching, a quotation from a book attributed to Seth, and a prayer of epiclesis (invocation of the Holy Spirit) over oil for baptismal sealing.

To the extent that the Revelation of the Magi reimagines Matthew 2 (and, to a lesser extent, the early chapters of Genesis) for its own theological and creative purposes, it belongs to the category of compositional activity often called "rewritten Bible." The narrative starts with an explanation of who the magi are, how they pray, and why they await the star; this includes a flashback to the time of Adam and Seth. The storyline of Matthew 2:1–12 follows, but from the magi's perspective: the coming of the star and the associated visions the magi have; their journey to Jerusalem and meeting with Herod; their journey

---

5. O. F. Tullberg et al., *Dionysii Telmahharensis Chronici liber primus: e codice Ms. syriaco Bibliothecae Vaticanae transcriptus notisque illustratus* (Uppsala: Royal Academy, 1848–1851).

6. I.-B. (J.-B.) Chabot, ed., *Chronicon anonymum pseudo-Dionysianum vulgo dictum I*, CSCO 91, Scriptores Syri 43 (Leuven: Peeters, 1927). This is a Syriac critical edition of the Chronicle of Zuqnin. The following volume is the Latin translation of this Syriac critical edition: I.-B. (J.-B.) Chabot, ed., *Incerti auctoris Chronicon Pseudo-Dionysianum vulgo dictum I*, CSCO 121, Scriptores Syri 66 (Leuven: Peeters, 1949). These two volumes will be referred to together in the following notes as *Chronicon*.

7. Landau ("Sages and the Star-Child," 19) observes that Chabot leans on Tullberg's edition particularly for folios 24^r, 24^v, and 25^r, near the end of Rev. Magi.

8. Landau, "Sages and the Star-Child," 23–74 (critical edition) and 75–136 (English translation). His published version of the English translation is available in Brent Landau, *Revelation of the Magi: The Lost Tale of the Wise Men's Journey to Bethlehem* (New York: HarperOne, 2010), 35–98, and it is this work that is cited for translations given here. Landau is developing a new critical edition of Rev. Magi for the Corpus Christianorum Series Apocryphorum, published by Brepols.

9. Found in Ugo Monneret de Villard, *Le leggende orientali sui Magi evangelici*, StT 163 (Vatican City: Vatican Library, 1952), 27–49.

10. Witold Witakowski, "Syryjska Opowiesc o Magach," in *Apokryfy Nowego Testamentu: Ewangelie apokryficzne, 1: Fragmenty, narodzenie i dziecinstwo Maryi i Jezusa*, ed. Marek Starowieyski (Kraków: WAM, 2003), 352–83.

11. G. J. Reinink, "Das Land 'Seiris' (Šir) und das Volk der Serer in jüdischen und christlichen Traditionen," *JSJ* 6.1 (1975): 72–85 (75n8); Landau, "Sages and the Star-Child," 2n3.

to Bethlehem to encounter the child as well as to converse with Mary and Joseph; and their return home. Lastly, Judas Thomas comes to the magi's land (chs. 29–32). The key innovation is that the star is itself a manifestation of the Son of God and therefore a central character in all phases of this narrative.

1.3 Authorship, Language, Place, and Date

The authorship of the Revelation of the Magi is unknown, and so the author's characteristics can be sketched only obliquely from the concerns of the text and from theories about the language, date, and place of composition.

The home of the magi according to this text is Shir (perhaps China, as discussed in sec. 4 below), but nobody suggests that the text actually came from there. The Revelation of the Magi as we have it is written in Syriac, and this seems to be its original language, for it contains some Syriac wordplay and there are no indications that it has been translated. The text probably comes from Edessa in eastern Syria, which was an active center for the production of Christian literature in the early centuries CE and had a particular connection to the apostle Judas Thomas.[12]

The Revelation of the Magi is much older than the Chronicle of Zuqnin, but it is difficult to pin down the date. The text refers to the Holy Spirit, using feminine constructions (Rev. Magi 21.10; 30.6; 31.1), which is characteristic of Christian texts in Syriac prior to 500 CE only.[13] The story has a notable similarity to a brief Latin account of the magi and the star-child, called *Liber apocryphum nomine Seth* and preserved in a fifth-century Matthean commentary known as the *Opus imperfectum in Matthaeum*.[14] The epiclesis and the interest in Judas Thomas as apostle suggest a similar date for the Acts of (Judas) Thomas, which is from around the third century, but not a detailed knowledge of it, since the latter text says that his mission was to India. If the final section (chs. 29–32) was added later, as discussed in section 3 below, then the shared milieu with the Acts of Thomas pertains specifically to that level of the redaction. Putting these details together and considering some additional factors, Witakowski has dated the Revelation of the Magi to the mid-fourth century,[15] while Landau has dated it to the late second or early third century.[16]

2. SUMMARY OF CONTENT

The account of the magi in the Revelation of the Magi is clearly modeled on the narrative of the magi in Matthew 2, but it comes with many distinctive features and considerable detail. In this work, the magi are sages and rulers who live in the remote eastern land of Shir. While the central part of the story is about the magi who go to Bethlehem, they are members of a familial religious group known as "magi" (in the Syriac text, *magūšē*) that has existed for many generations. They describe themselves as having the distinctive practice of praying in silence, which they connect to the meaning of *magūšē* in the language of Shir.[17] These magi provide most of their account themselves. There are twelve of them,

12. Monneret de Villard, *Le leggende orientali sui Magi evangelici*, 67. Brent Landau, "*The Revelation of the Magi*: A Summary and Introduction," in vol. 1 of *New Testament Apocrypha: More Noncanonical Scriptures*, ed. T. Burke and B. Landau (Grand Rapids: Eerdmans, 2016), 21, 23.

13. Witakowski, "Magi in Syriac Tradition," 814.

14. Migne, PG 56:637–38.

15. Witakowski, "Magi in Syriac Tradition," 833; cf. 813–14.

16. Landau, "*Revelation of the Magi*: A Summary and Introduction," 21–23.

17. Rev. Magi 1.2; 2.1. Modern scholars have not been able to find an explanation for this etymology in any likely language. See the discussion of Matt 2 in sec. 4 for μάγοι in that text. The word *magūšē* is simply the Syriac translation of μάγοι in Matt 2:1 as found in, for example, the Peshitta.

and their names are listed early in the text (2.3), but these names do not reappear.[18] Indeed, the magi are barely individuated; an exception to their collective speech and action may be found at 14.3–8, where we hear eight brief testimonies to the diverse visions that they had experienced.[19]

The magi belong to a long line of sages and rulers, tracing their ancestry and their calling back to Adam's son Seth. They explain that Adam passed on commandments to Seth, counseling him to live righteously, after describing to him how he and Eve had sinned and giving warnings about the end times. Seth wrote the whole account of this in a book, which is given verbatim (chs. 6–10). This book, in conjunction with other commandments and revelations by ancestors such as Seth and Noah (ch. 3), constitutes the collection of books of mysteries that their "fathers" have passed on through the generations. These books are stored in Shir on the Mountain of Victories, in the Cave of Treasures of Hidden Mysteries.[20]

For generations, the magi have carried out a special religious practice each month (ch. 5). They ascend the mountain, and after purifying themselves and praying silently, they enter the cave, going to the treasures and reading from the revelations. They then descend the mountain and take care to instruct their families as well as teaching the people of the land. When one of the magi dies, the group renews itself by installing that member's "son" or one of their "sons" as a replacement (5.10).

In addition to engaging in these practices of prayer, tradition, and renewal, these generations of magi have been awaiting a specific event (ch. 4). They expect that one day a light in the form of a star will shine forth and come to rest in the cave. This light will be "the great mystery of the Son of the exalted majesty, who is the voice of the Father; the offspring of his hidden thought; the light of the ray of his glory" (4.4). Hence this star (which will later be the star of Bethlehem) is not merely a pointer to the Son of God but is itself a manifestation of him. Adam had seen this star descending over the tree of life while he was in paradise, before he sinned (ch. 6). When this light comes, the magi should take the Son's "own pure gifts" (4.7), which their fathers have put in the cave, and should go where the light leads them. It will take them to a frail and lowly child, who is God in the form of a human being. They should worship in his presence and offer him the gifts they have brought from the cave. In return, the child will give them joy and salvation.

In due course, the star appears at the cave and speaks to the generation of magi who are telling this story (chs. 11–15). While they are on the mountain, they see a brightly shining star that descends onto a pillar of light and then enters the cave. They follow inside and see the star "in the bodily form of a small and humble human" (13.1). The star explains who he is and tells them to journey where he will be born; he will be there, is already with them here, will be their guide along the way, and is also with the Father (13.8–9). In their conversations soon after, the magi realize that each of them saw the star differently, having visions of various phases of the Son's life: infancy; adulthood as a humble, unsightly, and poor man; hanging upon the cross as a person of light; descending to Sheol; opening the graves; and ascending to heaven in glory (ch. 14). They also hear the voice of the Father,

---

18. All twelve are male, with names in the form "N. son of N." (e.g., "Zaharwandad son of Artaban"). The language about their family traditions (e.g., "fathers" and "sons") is masculine plural, which in Syriac is used for male groups and mixed-gender groups, so it is not certain to what extent the female members of the family also take part in the traditional observances described by the text. The language at 5.10 about replacing a deceased member (see below) indicates that male replacements are preferred and possibly required.

19. The people of the magi's homeland who eat the marvelous provisions of the magi have an analogous experience of diverse visions at 28.1–4, but they also are not otherwise distinguished from each other.

20. The precise name of this cave in Shir has slight variations throughout the text, but clearly the same cave is meant in each instance.

who confirms that the star-child is his "beloved Son ... the revealer of the secrets of the Father for his beloved ones" (15.4).

As planned, the magi take the gifts from the cave and follow the star on a swift and safe journey, without weariness but supported with ample provisions (ch. 16). It leads them first to Jerusalem, where they tell their story to its nobles and rulers (ch. 17). Herod asks the elders what the scriptural expectation is about where the Messiah is to be born, and he is told it will be in Bethlehem. The magi see the star once again and go to Bethlehem in joy, but they are made aware that Herod and the scribes are "blind," neither believing what the Scriptures say nor seeing this light. Despite Herod's request, the star tells them not to return to him afterward, since "he was not worthy for the worship of the light that was born, because he was a dwelling of error" (17.9).

They come now to Bethlehem, where the house of Mary and Joseph is, to a cave that resembles their cave back in Shir (ch. 18).[21] They follow the star-child into the cave and worship him there, putting their crowns under his feet and bringing their treasures "before him, who is the treasure of salvation" (18.8). Then "the glorious infant and the ancient light" (19.1) greets them, saying they have been found worthy to see him and he will remain with them until the end. After they hear voices praising the child, as if the cave is in another world (ch. 20), the star says they have completed the task commanded by their fathers and tells them that later he will send them some of his chosen ones and have them baptized to be missionaries in the East (ch. 21).

Mary and Joseph are concerned that the magi have come to take the child away in exchange for their gifts (ch. 22; 24.4), but the magi reassure her that the child is not only traveling away with them but is also inside her (still!), as well as awaiting her and Joseph in the house (chs. 22–23). Mary enters the house and is greeted by the child, who says that in bearing him she was "deemed worthy to be blessed among women" (25.1) and has brought hope and salvation to Eve and her offspring (25.2).[22]

The magi return home, guided and assisted by the star once more (ch. 26). They spread the message of what has happened to the people of Shir, and they share with them the special provisions from the star (ch. 27). Those who eat these provisions have visionary experiences of Christ's deeds, and day by day the people in this land of the East grow in faith, love, and mighty works (ch. 28).

Considerably later, after Christ's ministry and saving work are accomplished, the apostle Judas Thomas is sent by the Lord on mission. He arrives in Shir, doing mighty works, and faith increases even more. The magi greet him and tell him of their experiences. He recognizes that "the gift of our Lord had overflowed upon them" (29.4) and shares his own account of the Savior's deeds and the various forms he took in his appearances. At the magi's request, he gives them the "seal" (29.5–6), saying a prayer of epiclesis over oil (ch. 30) and baptizing them "in the name of the Father and the Son and the Holy Spirit" (31.1). An apparition of Christ (as a child, then as a young man) gives them bread in a Eucharist-like ritual, saying, "Behold the consummation and sealing of your birth of salvation. From now and forever, be confirmed in my promise" (31.2). He then departs to heaven, after which Judas Thomas and the new disciples praise him. At the apostle's invitation, the newly sealed magi go forth to every place, preaching and doing mighty works through the gift of

---

21. The wording of the text is awkward regarding locations in Bethlehem, but probably no distinction is being made between the house and the cave in that town.

22. The conversation of Mary and the child in chs. 24–25 belongs theoretically to the account given by the magi, but it is unclear whether the magi actually witness their interaction.

the Holy Spirit, encouraging their hearers to "flee from the darkness and come to the light that does not pass away" (32.2).

3. INTERPRETIVE ISSUES
3.1 Redactional History of the Text

The structural divisions of the Revelation of the Magi, certain shifts in vocabulary and theology, and some related early Christian texts have prompted questions about whether the work incorporates any preexisting sources.[23]

In the narrative world of the text, it is stated that two sources are incorporated, and thus it is worth considering whether any of this material existed prior to the Revelation of the Magi. In chapter 4, the magi quote a detailed command, passed on from generation to generation, to await the fulfillment of a prophecy that a light in the form of a star will appear. This is directly on topic for the Revelation of the Magi, and its style resembles its surroundings, so this passage is likely to have been written by the main author of the text. The other quoted material (6.1–10.7) is represented as a book by Seth, one of the ancestral books that they keep in the Cave of Treasures of Hidden Mysteries. This section of the text begins as an account of how Adam was deprived of the light of the star after he was expelled from paradise (ch. 6) and then becomes a speech from Adam to Seth, counseling him not to sin (chs. 7–10). From a historical-critical viewpoint, nobody would wish to argue that the passage came from Adam or Seth, but it could be investigated to see if it predates the Revelation of the Magi. In particular, Adam's speech is quite long for the role it serves, and while a cautionary tale not to sin is suitable on the lips of Adam, the wider text does not share that concern strongly.

At 30.2–9, during a baptismal sealing, Judas Thomas makes an epiclesis over oil. This prayer stands out from its surroundings in its style and its choice of metaphors. However, it is reminiscent of two epicleses over baptismal oil in the Acts of Thomas.[24] It may perhaps have originated in a Syriac liturgical context and been included as a preexisting source in the Judas Thomas section.

The shift in narration between first-person plural and third person may also be a sign of redactional activity. Most of chapters 3–27 is in the first-person plural, so perhaps what comes before and after has been added to it. The third-person material in chapters 1–2 is introductory in character. (Furthermore, the names of the magi, given in 2.3 but never used again, could have been added during the development of the text.[25]) Late in chapter 28, some changes take place that endure until the end of the whole text: the narration shifts to third person; the magi are called "nobles" instead of "magi"; explicit reference to "Jesus" begins; and more frequent use of the terms "Christ" and "our Lord" commences.

The most likely contender for redactional development in the text is the Judas Thomas section at the end of the narrative (chs. 29–32). Landau has argued that this section was added after the rest of the text was written and that the oddities just noted about the latter part of chapter 28 are caused by editing done in connection with this.[26] On their return

---

23. Reinink, "Das Land 'Seiris' (Šir)," 75n13; Landau, "Sages and the Star-Child," 175–202.

24. S. P. Brock, "An Archaic Syriac Prayer over Baptismal Oil," in *StPatr 41: Papers Presented at the Fourteenth International Conference on Patristic Studies held in Oxford 2003*, ed. F. Young, M. Edwards, and P. Parvis (Leuven: Peeters, 2006), 3–12.

25. Despite the setting in Shir, the names are based on those of Iranian and Babylonian kings and deities. Some other texts in Syriac have similar lists of names for the magi; see Witakowski, "Magi in Syriac Tradition," 811, 839–43.

26. Landau, "Sages and the Star-Child," 175–202.

home, the magi give their testimony, do mighty works, and bring many people to faith, and the impression given at the end of chapter 28 is that nothing further is required. However, the Judas Thomas section abruptly takes up the story one generation later. In addition to favoring the new terminology and presenting a distinct narrative perspective, the section gives the impression that more is needed theologically. Now it seems important that the "nobles" (the magi) should receive standard Christian initiation. Judas Thomas comes to them as an apostle sent by Jesus, presumably after Jesus's resurrection. The apostle and the nobles tell one another of their experiences, and the nobles ask to receive "the seal of our Lord" (i.e., a rite of Christian initiation in the Syriac style, involving anointing with oil, baptism, and the Eucharist). After they are sealed, Judas Thomas sends them out to preach and do mighty works in the Lord's name. Since this mission is not so different from what they had already been doing, this final section has perhaps been added to bring the magi's missionary role within the customary apostle-led timeframe of the early church, the effect being to "domesticate" the theology of revelation in the rest of the text.[27]

3.2 The Relationship of This Text to Other Early Christian Texts

The Revelation of the Magi has points of contact with many extracanonical early Christian writings. In some cases, these are indicative of shared traditions; in others, one text may be a source for another. The *Liber apocryphum nomine Seth* (within the *Opus imperfectum in Matthaeum*) has already been mentioned as a particularly important text for considering the development and transmission of the star-child story. It was via the *Opus imperfectum*, which used to be attributed to St. John Chrysostom, that the star-child legend of the magi made some headway into medieval European art and literature.[28]

Many infancy gospels exist, across several languages, from late antiquity and beyond. The most famous of these, the second-century Protevangelium of James, shares a few traditions with the Revelation of the Magi: a cave as Jesus's birthplace (Prot. Jas. 17–19 [see also Justin Martyr, *Dial.* 78]; cf. Rev. Magi 18); and Mary's hearing of God's word being the way that her conception took place (Prot. Jas. 11.5; cf. Rev. Magi 22.2). Unlike the Revelation of the Magi, however, the Protevangelium of James sets out to harmonize the Matthean and Lukan infancy narratives. Another infancy gospel, now known as the *Liber de nativitate Salvatoris*, has attracted attention for its multiple connections to the Revelation of the Magi; both texts speak of the magi's history and experience, and they describe the star in similar ways.[29]

The tendency of Jesus to take on multiple appearances, even at the same time, is found in several other early Christian texts, including some of the apocryphal acts of the apostles. The Acts of Thomas, already mentioned, is one such text, and another is the Acts of John.[30] In these examples, as with the Revelation of the Magi, the polymorphy of Jesus operates as a way to depict the many facets of his saving works as well as to show his power.

---

27. Brent Landau, "'One Drop of Salvation from the House of Majesty': Universal Revelation, Human Mission and Mythical Geography in the Syriac *Revelation of the Magi*," in *The Levant: Crossroads of Late Antiquity: History, Religion and Archaeology*, ed. E. B. Aitken and J. M. Fossey (Leiden: Brill, 2014), 87.

28. Landau, *Revelation of the Magi: The Lost Tale of the Wise Men's Journey to Bethlehem*, 91–96.

29. Jean-Daniel Kaestli, "Mapping an Unexplored Second Century Apocryphal Gospel: The *Liber de Nativitate Salvatoris* (CANT 53)," in *Infancy Gospels: Stories and Identities*, ed. C. Clivaz et al. (Tübingen: Mohr Siebeck, 2011), 506–33. The name is from Kaestli, or rather, he has matched this infancy gospel to a record of a text by this name. The text was initially investigated by M. R. James in connection with medieval Latin and Irish infancy gospels; see Landau, "Sages and the Star-Child," 201–14.

30. Paul Foster, "Polymorphic Christology: Its Origins and Development in Early Christianity," *JTS* 58 (2007): 66–99.

The magi's Cave of Treasures in Shir is not unique to the Revelation of the Magi. Several texts, most obviously a late antique Syriac text called the Book of the Cave of Treasures, speak about a cave of that name from the early stages of creation in which treasures were stored.[31] Typically these treasures included the bodies of antediluvian ancestors, but also gold, myrrh, and frankincense. The flood complicates what happens to these treasures, but there are at least indications in the Cave of Treasures traditions that the ancient gold, myrrh, and frankincense are in continuity with those that the magi bring to Jesus. Some sections of the Chronicle of Zuqnin before the Revelation of the Magi should be regarded as belonging to this complex of traditions, since they have close verbal links to it. Early in the Chronicle, it says that Adam and Seth sealed up gold, myrrh, and incense with their rings and placed them in the Cave of Treasures, which was located on a mountain called Shir—a mountain, not a country, but its location is described similarly to that of Shir in the Revelation of the Magi.[32] (In Rev. Magi 4.1, this cave is on the Mountain of Victories, located within the land of Shir.) These gifts are said to be the ones that Jesus will later be given by the magi.[33] This poses an interesting interpretative puzzle. The Revelation of the Magi has generally been studied as a text excerpted from and independent of the rest of the Chronicle of Zuqnin, but it is only known to us via that larger text, so perhaps the independence can be pushed too far. The Revelation of the Magi refers to the sealed gifts that the magi bring to Bethlehem without ever naming them, which has caused discussion about whether they are the canonical three gifts or quite different items (as occurs in some infancy gospels).[34] But if the Revelation of the Magi is read in its extant context, then it is clear that they are indeed gold, myrrh, and frankincense.

The Revelation of the Magi cannot be described as gnostic, even if that much-vexed word is still capable of a definition, but it inclines toward absolute and deterministic language in describing the nature and destiny of various categories of people. For instance, Herod is not just ignorant or sinful but "a dwelling of error" (Rev. Magi 17.9; cf. Gos. Truth 16.31–17.36), and it is for this reason that he is "not worthy" to see or worship the light. Conversely, the magi are "from the race of light" (Rev. Magi 21.9), and the privileging of their Sethian descent is reminiscent of several texts from Nag Hammadi, such as the Secret Book of John or the Three Steles of Seth. However, the absolutist language needs to be interpreted alongside the idea that the Son comes to illuminate and to save, which is also strong in the text's theology.[35]

---

31. Alexander Toepel, "*The Cave of Treasures*: A New Translation and Introduction," in *Old Testament Pseudepigrapha: More Noncanonical Scriptures*, vol. 1, ed. R. Bauckham, J. R. Davila, and A. Panayotov (Grand Rapids: Eerdmans, 2013), 531–84.

32. Chronicle of Zuqnin, folio 3ʳ, according to Chabot, *Chronicon* (Syriac, p. 6; Latin, p. 4). Chabot transliterates the location as *Seïr* here but as *Šīr* in Rev. Magi 2.4 and 4.1. However, the same Syriac word underlies these.

33. Admittedly, as tends to happen with the Cave of Treasures texts, there is some roughness in the continuity after the flood. Adam's body and the gifts are taken onto Noah's ark: Chronicle of Zuqnin, folio 4ʳ–4ᵛ, according to Chabot, *Chronicon* (Syriac, p. 9; Latin, p. 6). However, it is unclear what happens to the gifts afterward. Readers of the Chronicle are left to trust that the earlier statement is correct that the gifts will later be given to the infant Jesus.

34. Landau, "Sages and the Star-Child," 85 note a.

35. Albrile has considered the extent to which Rev. Magi can be regarded as exhibiting gnostic syncretism; see Ezio Albrile, "Il mistero di Seth: sincretismo gnostico in una perduta apocalisse," *Laurentianum* 39.1–3 (1998): 413–53; idem, "I Magi e la 'madre celeste': Appunti per una teologia del sincretismo Iranico-Mesopotamico," *Antonianum* 75 (2000): 311–32.

3.3 Selected Themes

The Revelation of the Magi is a theologically rich text. It takes up and transforms a small episode from Matthew's Gospel in order to make profound claims about God, God's Son in relation to the Father and the world, revelation, salvation, universality, and mission. These are discussed in section 4 below. In the present section, it has also been argued that the Judas Thomas portion of the narrative provides a way to bring these far-distant people, privileged with an extraordinary revelation from early days, into the framework of the church as conventionally understood.

It is also worth considering the ethical impact of the Revelation of the Magi on early Christian readers, and here the starting point must be to ask what the purpose of the magi's journey is in this narrative. Why do the magi need to go to Bethlehem to worship the child when they have already encountered the child back in their own land and are being guided on their journey by the child in the form of a star?

The narrative technique may provide an answer: the bulk of the text is told by the magi themselves. For the intended Christian readers of this text, particularly those living far from Bethlehem, this invites a partial identification with the magi, so that their way of responding to the star-child can be in some ways a model for Christian life. The magi gather regularly as a community in a holy place to read the books of hidden mysteries handed down by their ancestors. When they are told to go on a long journey to worship the child, a command that corresponds to their expectations in the hidden mysteries, they respond in joy, setting out at once (14.2). The journey could have been presented as an arduous pilgrimage with only intermittent divine guidance, but this is not the choice made by the narrator; instead, the journey is swift and pleasant, and their guide stays close (16.5–6).

The text implies, then, that for believers who practice the virtues of community life, constancy, trust, prayer, and scholarship, God will provide an easy road. When the magi arrive in Bethlehem and worship the child there, they are praised for accomplishing what they were commanded and are rewarded by seeing the child and hearing the heavenly praises he receives. The magi's story is not yet finished, whether on earth or in heaven, but this major phase of their life has been accomplished successfully and triumphantly, so encouraging and fostering the faith of the readers of this text.

4. KEY PASSAGES FOR NEW TESTAMENT STUDIES AND THEIR SIGNIFICANCE

The Revelation of the Magi shows wide familiarity with many biblical materials, and, given the text's date, we can be confident that the influence is from the biblical books to this text. (The relationship to extracanonical early Christian traditions is more complex and is discussed in the previous section.) Old Testament connections can be noted only briefly here. The text traces the ancestry and mission of the magi to the characters and events of the early chapters of Genesis, and there are brief allusions to verses from Exodus, the prophets, and the Psalms.[36] As to the New Testament, all its major sections have exercised at least a passing influence, and some have been strongly influential, as will be seen below. Perhaps surprisingly, no attempt has been made to incorporate the story line of the Lukan infancy narrative, but a few expressions have made their mark (e.g., descriptions of Mary from Luke 1:28, 42 in Rev. Magi 25.1–2).

This section will focus on two kinds of connections with the New Testament: the magi story in Matthew's Gospel, which underpins the narrative, and the use of other New Testament materials to support the text's Christology and soteriology.

---

36. For details, see Landau, "Sages and the Star-Child," 239–43.

4.1 Use of the Magi Story in the Gospel of Matthew

The text's most fundamental New Testament connection is with the magi story in Matthew 2, which provides the backbone of the magi's journey in chapters 11–26. The broad shape of their journey is the same as in the Matthean account. Led by the star from their home in the east, the magi go first to Jerusalem, where they have an audience with King Herod. They next go to Bethlehem, where they see the child and bring him gifts in homage. Lastly, they return home, but by a different route, so as to avoid Herod. The Revelation of the Magi does not mention the material later in Matthew 2 about the massacre of the innocents at Herod's instigation[37] or the consequent flight into Egypt of the Holy Family. As a text that is largely from the magi's perspective, however, it provides considerable detail about the backstory of the magi and the star (chs. 1–10), and it follows the journey with a narrative of the events once they arrive home, both in the short term and a generation afterward (chs. 27–32).

Matthew calls these visitors "magi" (in Greek, μάγοι, plural of μάγος). The word μάγος is usually considered by modern scholars to be a Persian loanword ("magician, sage, astrologer"), and modern translations of Matthew 2 therefore often read "sages" or "wise men," though it has been debated whether this fits their portrayal in the Matthew passage.[38] The magi in the Revelation of the Magi describe themselves as "sages" (2.1), which is in keeping with their careful custody of special books and knowledge over the generations. A relic of the astrologer idea may be found in 17.2, in which the nobles and rulers of Jerusalem think the visitors must be "magi" (in Syriac, *məgūšē*) because of how they are looking at and praying to the star, but this supposition is presented as if it is a mistake; the magi of the Revelation of the Magi do not claim to study the stars in general but to be waiting for the one special light in the form of a star. However, *məgūšē* in the early chapters of the Revelation of the Magi is a self-descriptive name for the journeying magi and their ancestors who awaited the coming of the star, and they explain the name in terms of their habit of praying in silence (1.3; 2.1). Furthermore, in 1.2 they describe themselves as "rulers" (or "kings"), although this features in the story only at 18.5 (when they lay their crowns before the child) and seems not to affect how they interact with the people in their own land. While the Matthean account does not refer to the magi as kings, the idea that they were kings developed early in the reception history of Matthew 2, probably under the influence of Psalm 72:10 and Isaiah 60:1–18.[39]

Matthew never indicates how many magi there are (except that the word is plural), nor does he report any of their names. However, many retellings and artistic interpretations of Matthew's account depict three magi, probably because three gifts are mentioned in Matthew 2:11.[40] In the Revelation of the Magi, there are twelve magi, all named, though they are barely distinguished beyond the initial listing of their names.[41] They travel with an "encampment" (16.2)—that is, a large group of travelers,[42] presumably their attendants.

---

37. However, just after the Rev. Magi portion concludes, this event is briefly noted in the Chronicle of Zuqnin, folio 25ʳ, according to Chabot, *Chronicon* (Syriac, p. 91; Latin, p. 70).

38. Ulrich Luz, *Matthew 1–7: A Commentary*, trans. J. Crouch, Hermeneia (Minneapolis: Fortress, 2007), 112–13.

39. The existence of this interpretation was known already to Tertullian (*Marc.* 3.13).

40. See, e.g., the famous mosaic of the three magi from the Basilica of Sant'Apollinare Nuovo in Ravenna, Italy.

41. If the number twelve bears any significance here, it could be to imply that the magi will act as apostles when they return to the east, as has been suggested by Monneret de Villard, *Le leggende orientali sui Magi evangelici*, 54.

42. Landau, "Sages and the Star-Child," 107 note h.

The Matthean magi are "from the east," without further specification. This would mean east relative to the Levant, and the use of the word "magi" suggests that they may be from Parthia (the Persian region of that time), but Isaiah 60 and Psalm 72 push in other directions, suggesting in the end that what is crucial is that they are gentiles from afar. In the Revelation of the Magi, the magi's homeland is Shir (*Šir*), which is described as "the outer part of the entire East of the world inhabited by human beings, at the Ocean, the great sea beyond the world, east of the land of Nod" (Rev. Magi 2.4). The physical description (with its suggestion of a great ocean beyond the Asian continent) implies China, which in several ancient languages of the Mediterranean and Near East was called something like "Sir" or "Shir."[43] Yet the text presents an imagined country far to the east of both Judea and Syria and is not engaging with any specific culture. In both Matthew and the Revelation of the Magi, the point here is that people from far away have had greater insight into the Christ-child than many of the Jews have had.

Given its focus on the magi, the Revelation of the Magi says more about their journey to Judea than that they "came" (Matt 2:1). Their journey can be told briefly, however, since it is miraculously easy and swift (Rev. Magi 16), without challenges of fatigue, hunger, or threatening animals. The star guides them and illuminates their path all the way, and they can still see it when they arrive in Jerusalem and before they leave that city, which means they do not really need to ask for advice when they reach Jerusalem. By contrast, the Matthean magi see his star ἐν τῇ ἀνατολῇ, *en tē anatolē* (Matt 2:2), and whether this means that they see the star when it rises in the eastern sky or when they are in the east, the implication in that case is that their long westward journey is not explicitly led by the star. The prophecy-based advice to go to Bethlehem is genuinely helpful, and then confirmed by the star, which now acts as a more precise guide for them by going ahead and then stopping over the place; this is presumably the kind of guiding behavior that has influenced what the Revelation of the Magi describes. Lastly, the magi of the Revelation of the Magi are guided home again by the star, whereas the Matthew account is silent about the return, beyond the dream warning to take a different route.

Matthew's account places considerable emphasis on the encounter of the magi with King Herod, as they ask about the child born "king of the Jews." The episode provides the evangelist with a way to quote Micah 5:2 as a prophecy that a ruler of Israel will be born in Bethlehem (Matt 2:6). By contrast, in the Revelation of the Magi 17 the magi arrive with considerable knowledge and confidence already, explaining their mission, though without mentioning the star, let alone that the star is the same as the Son to whom they are journeying. The implication is that the star is invisible to everyone else in Jerusalem (Rev. Magi 17.2, 8; cf. 11.7). Herod asks his city elders, "Where is it written that the king messiah, and savior, and life giver of the worlds is to be born?" (17.6), and the elders tell him that the birth will be in Bethlehem, but they credit the prophet inaccurately as being David. Hence the scope of Jesus's reign is universalized, although the memory of Israel in terms of David and the messiah title is preserved. In Matthew, the motive behind Herod's desire to find the child is left open for some verses, until the magi are warned in a dream not to return to him, and Herod goes on to attempt to kill Jesus by killing the male infants in the region. For the Revelation of the Magi, the encounter with Herod is rounded off with an immediate criticism of his deceitfulness and spiritual blindness (along with the failure of his scribes to believe their own books—the text here indulges in an anti-Jewish stereotype)

---

43. Reinink, "Das Land 'Seiris' (Šir)," 78.

and his unworthiness to see and worship the child. This is why these magi do not return to Herod, and nothing more is said of him.

In Matthew, the star halts over the house in Bethlehem where Jesus is, and the magi rejoice, go inside to see him and his mother, worship him, and offer him gifts. All this is true for the magi in the Revelation of the Magi as well, but their experience is more complicated. Having followed the star to the cave-house in Bethlehem, they see the star go into the cave ahead of them, and they follow to worship it—or rather, to bow down before the infant who is also the star. They give him "hidden treasures" from the cave in Shir as gifts, but they clearly recognize that within this cave in Bethlehem they are receiving a greater gift in him, the "treasure of salvation" (18.7–8). The nature of their gifts is unspecified in the Revelation of the Magi alone, but if the text is read in the context of the rest of the Chronicle of Zuqnin (see sec. 3 above), then the gifts are gold, myrrh, and frankincense, as in Matthew's account.

The Matthean star has served its purpose as guide and is no longer mentioned after this point in the narrative, but for the Revelation of the Magi the star remains active, since it is identical to "the glorious infant and the ancient light" (19.1). The infant assures the magi that he is the one who has been with them both before and during the journey. After angelic praises and further speeches, the magi leave his presence, and with them go Mary and Joseph, who are mentioned here for the first time but who, in retrospect, must have been with the infant in the cave (cf. "with Mary his mother," Matt 2:11 NRSV). The magi acclaim Mary for bringing forth this child, but the strangeness of the Son's omnipresence in this scenario is accentuated by their explanation that he is simultaneously in the house, within her, and with them. Mary rejoices that the child is not leaving her, even though she also saw his holy form traveling with the magi.

The magi return home, guided by the star, and this brings to an end the close connections with Matthew 2. Since there is no massacre of the innocents narrated in the Revelation of the Magi, there is also no need for Joseph to be warned in a dream to take the family and flee to Egypt. His role in this narrative is to accompany and support Mary, though she is the one who receives the principal attention from the magi and makes the speeches in response.

4.2 Use of Other Parts of the New Testament for the Text's Christology and Soteriology

Even beyond the Matthean magi episode, the Revelation of the Magi is thoroughly steeped in the New Testament. The following passage, which comes from a speech about the Son that the Father makes to the magi, may serve as an example:

> This is the one in whose name signs and portents take place through his believers. This is the perfect Son, doing the will of he who sent him. This one is the way and the gate of light for those who enter by it. This is the one who is in everything and is named and spoken of above all. This is the bread of life that comes down from me for believers; he is the sower of the word of life, and he is the shepherd of truth who gives himself as ransom for his flock. He is the great priest who by his blood absolves the worlds; he is a drink of the vine of life. This is the one that you saw who is in many forms that appeared to you, but is not deprived of either my love or the person of his glory. And no one exists over him or over his majesty to speak of how he is, except me, and I and he, we are one in unspeakable glory. (Rev. Magi 15.8–10)

In this passage can be heard versions of several "I am" statements" from John's Gospel (John 6:51; 8:12; 10:7, 11; 14:6; 15:1), as well as some other Johannine material (John

1:3–9; 5:30; 10:30; 17:5) and hints of Matthew 26:27–29, Mark 4:14, Acts 4:30, and Hebrews 10:19–22. The density of biblical texture in this passage is higher than average for the text but by no means uncharacteristic.

The biblical allusions in the Revelation of the Magi play a major role in undergirding the text's Christology and soteriology. The use of the New Testament to support the identification of the star with the Son of God is an important example of this. Consequently, this identification concretizes the Johannine "I am" metaphors of "way" and "light" (noted above), for the star provides the illumination and the path for the magi to follow. Just as in Johannine theology it is only believers who can follow Jesus (John 10:26–27), likewise the star that the magi follow is not visible to all but can be seen by the magi because they know and believe in the "mysteries" that their ancestors have handed down (Rev. Magi 11.7).

The radiance of this star is beyond the normal range for stellar bodies. Indeed, it is brighter than the sun (Rev. Magi 11.7), which may perhaps be a connection to the verse in the Benedictus about God's visitation in Jesus being like the dawn from on high, visiting those in darkness and guiding their feet (Luke 1:78–79). The brightness is so extreme because of the source of the light. In a key phrase, the star describes himself as "a ray of light" from the Father:

> I am both there and with the majesty of my Father. And I am everywhere, because I am a ray of light whose light has shone in this world from the majesty of my Father, who has sent me to fulfill everything that was spoken about me in the entire world. (Rev. Magi 13.9–10)

This quotation comes from a speech by the star when he is sending the magi on their journey to worship him in human form, and it has multiple implications.

The first implication is the intimate connection of the Son with the Father. As a ray of light that comes from the Father, the Son is, to quote Hebrews 1:3, "the radiance of God's glory" (NIV). This idea belongs to a group of descriptions whereby the Son is, in some fashion or other, an emanation from the Father. The Son explains: "For the Father of majesty does not have an image and form in this world, except I who am an epiphany from him, since I am his will, and his power, and his wisdom, since I am in my Father and my Father is in me" (Rev. Magi 21.8). The reciprocal indwelling at the end of this quotation is directly from John 14:10 and expresses the close bond between them. The emanation concept, however, is closely related to the Son being the divine Word (John 1:1–18) and "the image of the invisible God" (Col 1:15 NRSV), and both of these expressions probably developed in the context of Second Temple Jewish tradition about the personified Wisdom of God, active in the world (Prov 8:22–31; Sir 24:1–22). In all cases, these texts speak of the divine emanation being active along with God even at the time of creation, and the same holds for the Revelation of the Magi, in which the divine infant in Bethlehem is hailed by the angels as the one "through whom everything came into being . . . and all the worlds seen and unseen were brought to completion" (Rev. Magi 20.3).

The next implication is that the Son is present everywhere. The "ray of light" idea supports this in that the light is present at its source and in each place in every direction where the light has traveled. Specifically for the course of the narrative, the Son is with the magi in Shir, soon to be in Bethlehem, and throughout all this still with the Father too. The text's identification of the star with the Son puts a certain strain on the Matthean story, since we might wonder why the magi would need to make this great journey in order to encounter someone they have already met. Rather than covering over this problem, the text makes a theological feature of the Son's omnipresence.

For the most part in the New Testament, by contrast, Jesus Christ is present in only one place at a time. Even after his death and resurrection, when he is seated at the right hand of the Father in heaven, the transition involves a departure from earth and a heavenly ascent, according to multiple New Testament passages (e.g., John 16:5–7; 20:17; Acts 1:9–11; Eph 4:8–10). At the end of Matthew, however, Jesus sends out his apostles in various directions to "make disciples of all nations" and then adds, "I am with you always" (Matt 28:19–20 NRSV). The omnipresence of the Son in the Revelation of the Magi resolves the tension that exists across the New Testament and in early Christian experience as to how Jesus can be in many places at once in some mode or other, and also in heaven, by declaring that the Son is not separated from any believer.[44]

The idea that the Son is present in all times and places also explains the knowledge that the magi have. They come from the east to Bethlehem, not as foreigners who have been granted an isolated message through an unexpected star, but as people who have long treasured a revelation given to their ancestors by the Son. The magi explain, "He commanded us in a great vision to come to this land to worship him in reverence, because he has worshipers in every country" (17.5). Using this quotation among others, Landau has argued that the text is promoting the idea of "universal divine revelation" and that "Christ is the reality behind all divine revelations throughout human history."[45] The behavior of the magi on their return home matches this idea well; they confidently and successfully spread the good news in keeping with the notion that they are recipients of the necessary revelation. When Judas Thomas arrives much later in the final section, the timetable of post-Easter apostolic preaching (cf. Matt 28:19) is imposed more strictly on the narrative, which is one reason why Landau argues that this portion of the text was added later. An earlier statement by the Son to the magi holds these two views together: "You will be witnesses for me in the land of the East together with my disciples, those who are chosen by me to preach my gospel" (19.6).

The third implication of the "ray of light" image derives from the directionality of the ray: the Son is sent by the Father with a purpose. His goal can be described variously. At 21.6 he revisits the previous image, stating, "I am a ray of [the Father's] light and I was sent to you to enlighten you." The use of enlightenment language to speak of knowledge revealed to Christians by Jesus can be found in passages such as 2 Corinthians 4:4–6 and Ephesians 5:8–14, as well as the Johannine "light of the world" texts noted above. The Revelation of the Magi also says the Son has been sent to save and redeem all people in the world (19.9; 23.4). This too is very familiar language from the New Testament (e.g., Mark 10:45; John 3:16; Acts 4:12; Rom 3:21–25). Furthermore, his coming is according to God's ultimate purpose, as shown by the fulfillment of prophecy: he has been sent "to fulfill everything that was spoken about [him] in the entire world" (13.10). The Revelation of the Magi contains some possible allusions to Old Testament texts that are interpreted as prophecies of Jesus in the New Testament, but during the dialogue with Herod about Bethlehem as the expected birthplace, it does not imitate Matthew 2:6 in providing a biblical prophecy. Perhaps the magi's own traditions are dominant in the prophecies being fulfilled.

---

44. Rev. Magi may also be developing an idea in the longer textual form of John 3:13, which was known to the Syriac New Testament tradition. In this verse Jesus says, while speaking on earth to Nicodemus and discussing heavenly ascent and descent, that he (the Son of Man) is in heaven. This is remarkably similar to a Rev. Magi statement by the Son: "And when I have completed the will of my Father regarding everything that he commanded me, (I will go up) in the glory in which I was with him. Yet even now, while I am speaking with you, I am with him and have not become separated from the majesty of the Father" (Rev. Magi 19.7).

45. Landau, "'One Drop of Salvation,'" 83–103, esp. 87–88 and 94.

The understanding of salvation in this text deserves further attention, but first it is necessary to explore the implications and consequences of the Son's powers. The identification of the Son with the star is the clearest example of a concept that is essential to the text's Christology: not only can this Christ be present in multiple places but he can take on any form. What is more, the way he appears depends on the viewer, so witnesses can report seeing different forms during the same interval of time.[46] This happens in Shir, when each of the magi sees the Son at a different stage of his saving work (Rev. Magi 14; cf. 28). The forms chosen by the Savior thus constitute part of how he enlightens them, revealing various aspects of himself and of the salvation story to them. A polymorphic Christ along these lines can be found in several early Christian apocryphal texts, as noted earlier, and within the New Testament the idea exists in the accounts of the transfiguration (Mark 9:2–8 and parr.; 2 Pet 1:16–18). These various forms also provide a type of protection, reminiscent of the tradition in a certain stream of the biblical tradition that nobody can see God and live, at least not if they see God's face (Exod 33:20). Just as John's Gospel finds a way for believers to see the Father by seeing the Son (cf. John 1:18 and 14:9), so too in the Revelation of the Magi the Son reveals God in forms that protect the viewers, whether they are humans or angels:

> I am never separated from you, nor from the presence of the Father, because I am a ray of his light, and I was sent to you to enlighten you. And behold, you are amazed as frail human beings—how much more when I have come to you in the majesty of my Father. As for you not being able to stand before me, neither (could) the angels and powers that are above you when I descended upon them, and they saw a vision of wonders and stood in fear and trembling. Even as it was fitting for them I appeared to them, and for you I appeared as you were able to see. (Rev. Magi 21.6–7)

Since the Son in this text is polymorphic and omnipresent, the question arises as to how to consider his life on earth theologically. Clearly the Son is divine, but can he be described as having taken on human flesh or having emptied himself (cf. John 1:14; Phil 2:7), or does he merely appear to be human? The traditional phrasing of such a question is to ask whether the Christology is docetic, but this category has recently been critiqued,[47] and its reevaluation could well be extended to the present text. For the Revelation of the Magi, the evidence points at first glance in the direction of a Christ who takes on mere semblance of flesh, as shown in the quotation above about the Son's free choices of "appearance." Similarly, when the magi come to Bethlehem, the ostensible infant not only utters substantial speeches but also says about the angels they have just heard, "For you they are mighty because you are clothed in weak flesh, yet for me they are very small things" (Rev. Magi 21.2).

Notwithstanding this, the text also holds that salvation is effected by the Son's death (and the following events). Consequently, the Son must indeed be capable of dying. How this works remains unexplored by the narrative, but perhaps the connection is the willingness to appear in a humble and unsightly form, a christological commonplace that probably

---

46. Herod and the scribes are not considered worthy to see the star at all. They are said to be "blind" and "dwelling in darkness" (Rev. Magi 17.8–9), according to the metaphor of spiritual blindness that is often found in the NT (e.g., Mark 4:11–12 [cf. Isa 6:9–10]; John 9:40–41; 2 Cor 4:3–6). The star is visible to the magi in Jerusalem (Rev. Magi 17.2), but apparently not to these others.

47. Joseph Verheyden, Reimund Bieringer, Jens Schröter, and Ines Jäger, eds., *Docetism in the Early Church: The Quest for an Elusive Phenomenon*, WUNT 402 (Tübingen: Mohr Siebeck, 2018).

goes back to Isaiah 52:13–53:12. When the people of Shir are speaking, after they hear from the magi and eat the wondrous provisions they have given them, one of them sees the Son as "a human being whose appearance is more unsightly than a man, and he is saving and purifying the world by his blood and by his humble appearance" (Rev. Magi 28.2). But even the crucifixion can be regarded as a moment for light to shine forth (and this idea probably comes from the glorious "lifting up" of Jesus spoken of in John 12:27–33); one of the magi sees "a cross and a person of light who hung upon it, taking away the sins of the entire world" (Rev. Magi 14.6).

As the previous quotation indicates, what the Son does has the effect of forgiving sins and prevailing over error and death. Regarding forgiveness and death, this is quite reminiscent of Pauline theology (e.g., Rom 5:18–21; 8:1–4; 1 Cor 15:24–26), even down to the phrasing at times:

> This is the one who was humbled and became a human being for the salvation of human beings so that they would not perish. He put on, by his will, a body, a humble form, that with it he might slay death and take away the dominion of death, to give eternal life to those who love him and believe in him. (Rev. Magi 15.7)

The reason that death has been prevailing is expressed early in the text, in the speech of Adam to Seth. Adam explains that his sin of eating the forbidden fruit caused death but that he expects to be granted life again through God's mercy (Rev. Magi 10.1–4); this is reminiscent of the Romans 5 interpretation of Genesis 3 as well.

These predictions, visions, and interpretations of the Son's crucifixion and resurrection are of special importance for the narrative of the Revelation of the Magi, since the magi as viewpoint characters have returned home long before the events occur. This does not mean that the magi have no further role in salvation; indeed, they become both missionaries and recipients of the good news. The Son sends them back from Bethlehem with their own mission that the text has modeled on Matthew 28:18–20, but also with a promise of apostolic messengers to come after he has ascended:

> And again, you have been deemed worthy to be witnesses for me in the East with my disciples, who were chosen by me before the world came to be. And when I have completed the will of my Father regarding everything that he commanded me and have ascended to him in glory, I shall send to you some of my chosen ones who have been chosen by me for your land. And they shall speak and witness the truth with you that it may be your seal with one accord. (Rev. Magi 21.5)

The magi carry out this mission faithfully and with considerable success back in their own land of Shir. A generation later, Judas Thomas arrives there on mission. What the apostle does, in the wake of the crucifixion and beyond, is to bring them into the fold of formally initiated Christians, in the mode of the Acts of the Apostles and with the particular flavor of Syriac sacramental rites, thus gathering the magi and the local people into the church.

5. BIBLIOGRAPHY

Brock, S. P. "An Archaic Syriac Prayer over Baptismal Oil." Pages 3–12 in *StPatr 41: Papers Presented at the Fourteenth International Conference on Patristic Studies Held in Oxford 2003*. Edited by F. Young, M. Edwards, and P. Parvis. Leuven: Peeters, 2006.

Chabot, I.-B. (J.-B.), ed. *Chronicon anonymum pseudo-Dionysianum vulgo dictum I*. CSCO 91, Scriptores Syri 43. Leuven: Peeters, 1927. This is a Syriac critical edition of the Chronicle of Zuqnin.

———, ed. *Incerti auctoris Chronicon Pseudo-Dionysianum vulgo dictum I*. CSCO 121, Scriptores Syri 66. Leuven: Peeters, 1949. This is the Latin translation of the Syriac critical edition listed above.

Chronicle of Zuqnin, Vaticanus Syriacus 162. Scan of the manuscript at https://digi.vatlib.it/view/MSS_Vat. sir.162.

Foster, Paul. "Polymorphic Christology: Its Origins and Development in Early Christianity." *JTS* 58 (2007): 66–99.

Kaestli, Jean-Daniel. "Mapping an Unexplored Second Century Apocryphal Gospel: The *Liber de Nativitate Salvatoris* (CANT 53)." Pages 506–33 in *Infancy Gospels: Stories and Identities*. Edited by Claire Clivaz et al. Tübingen: Mohr Siebeck, 2011.

Landau, Brent. "'One Drop of Salvation from the House of Majesty': Universal Revelation, Human Mission and Mythical Geography in the Syriac *Revelation of the Magi*." Pages 83–103 in *The Levant: Crossroads of Late Antiquity: History, Religion and Archaeology*. Edited by Ellen Bradshaw Aitken and John M. Fossey. Leiden: Brill, 2014.

———. "*The Revelation of the Magi*: A Summary and Introduction." Pages 19–29 in volume 1 of *New Testament Apocrypha: More Noncanonical Scriptures*. Edited by Tony Burke and Brent Landau. Grand Rapids: Eerdmans, 2016.

———. *Revelation of the Magi: The Lost Tale of the Wise Men's Journey to Bethlehem*. New York: HarperOne, 2010. Includes English translation, substantially the same as in Landau (2008) below.

———. "The Sages and the Star-Child: An Introduction to the *Revelation of the Magi*, An Ancient Christian Apocryphon." ThD diss., Harvard Divinity School, 2008. Includes Syriac critical edition and English translation. Available from https://utexas.academia.edu/BrentLandau

Monneret de Villard, Ugo. *Le leggende orientali sui Magi evangelici*. StT 163. Vatican City: Vatican Library, 1952. Includes an Italian translation of the text by Giorgio Levi Della Vida (pp. 27–49).

Reinink, G. J. "Das Land 'Seiris' (Šir) und das Volk der Serer in jüdischen und christlichen Traditionen." *JSJ* 6.1 (1975): 72–85.

Witakowski, Witold. "The Magi in Syriac Tradition." Pages 809–43 in *Malphono w-Rabo d-Malphone: Studies in Honor of Sebastian P. Brock*. Edited by George Kiraz. Gorgias Eastern Christian Studies. Piscataway, NJ: Gorgias, 2008.

PART 2

APOCRYPHAL ACTS

CHAPTER 12

ACTS OF ANDREW

NATHAN C. JOHNSON

1. INTRODUCTION

Among the five major apocryphal Acts—those attached to Andrew, John, Paul, Peter, and Thomas—the Acts of Andrew is the longest, and textually the most complicated.[1] The collections of stories related to the apostolic figure of Andrew tell of his various travels, miracles, and teachings. And like the other apocryphal Acts of the apostles, Andrew's ends in martyrdom—in this case, with the martyr being tied to a cross from which he teaches for several days. In the following, I begin by answering a simple question—What is the Acts of Andrew?—that has a complex answer, before describing the contents of the Acts of Andrew, laying out its key interpretive issues, and then discussing its relationship to the New Testament.

1.1 What Is the Acts of Andrew?

Ancient and modern people alike have wondered what happened to the apostle Andrew after the few things reported about him in the canonical Gospels and Acts.[2] The various texts, tales, and traditions housed under the title "The Acts of Andrew" would have gone some way in addressing that curiosity. Yet one of the simplest questions to ask concerning the Acts of Andrew is also one of the most difficult to answer: What is the Acts of Andrew? Or, asked differently, what comprises the Acts of Andrew, and what is not included in that title?

The answer is complicated by the number of fluid traditions concerning the apostolic figure of Andrew and their relation to what ancient and modern readers refer to with the title "The Acts of Andrew." Therefore, before exploring the content of the Acts of Andrew, it will be useful to survey the textual traditions associated with the apostle Andrew and what ancient and modern readers mean by this title. Finally, I will define what I signify with this title throughout this chapter.

1.2 Texts

The number of traditions, tales, and texts associated with Andrew are legion. Thus, in this section I briefly enumerate the most important texts concerning Andrew. This will then be of use in describing what the Acts of Andrew does and does not comprise.

---

1. So already M. R. James: "I suspect it was the most prolix of all the five" (M. R. James, ed., *The Apocryphal New Testament: Being the Apocryphal Gospels, Acts, Epistles and Apocalypses, with Other Narratives and Fragments* [Oxford: Clarendon, 1924], 337). Even Gregory of Tours speaks of the original Acts's "excessive verbosity" (James, *Apocryphal New Testament*, 337).

2. On which, see "Andrew in the New Testament" below.

The textual traditions break down according to three broad categories: martyrdom texts, collections of wondrous deeds, and biographical texts. Here I focus only on the former two categories, which tend to be earlier (perhaps deriving from the second to sixth centuries).[3]

1.2.1 Martyrdom Texts

The Martyrdom of Andrew, also called the Passion of Andrew, is not represented in a single manuscript, recension, or version but is rather a complex of traditions with numerous textual witnesses, the most important of which include:

- *Manuscripts J and S*: The longest of the Passion versions is represented in portions of two manuscripts: Codex Sinai Gr. 526 (tenth century) and Codex Jerusalem St. Sabas 103 (twelfth century), often together referred to as "JS" (Jerusalem/Sinai).
- *Vatican Gr. 808* (tenth or eleventh century): Seen by some as the most important witness to the primitive Acts of Andrew, this mutilated manuscript ends just before Andrew is martyred.[4]
- *MS Ann Arbor 36*: This fragment incidentally begins approximately where Vatican Gr. 808 leaves off and describes Andrew's crucifixion.
- *Martyrium prius* ("The Earlier Martyrdom"): This late eighth-century Greek text reports how Andrew converts the city of Patras and its proconsul (Lesbius) and includes Andrew's speech to the cross upon which he will be crucified.
- *Martyrium alterum* ("The Alternate Martyrdom"): A Greek version represented by manuscripts from the eleventh to the fourteenth century, of which two recensions exist (*A* and *B*).
- *Armenian Passion*: Though derivative, the Armenian account (sixth century) of the passion includes some sections not found in any of the Greek witnesses and may attest to a textual tradition before the extant Greek witnesses in several sections.[5]

1.2.2 Collections of Wondrous Deeds

- Gregory of Tours's (ca. 540–594) epitome, *Liber de miraculis beati Andreae apostoli* ("Book of the Miracles of the Blessed Apostle Andrew," hereafter *Epitome*), describes Andrew's miracles and travels from Achaia to the city of cannibals, then to Byzantium, and finally back again to Achaia.
- *Papyrus Coptic Utrecht 1* (fourth century) tells of a single "act of Andrew," the exorcism and conversion of a young soldier (cf. *Epitome* 18).
- The "Acts of Andrew and Matthias in the City of the Cannibals"[6] tells of Andrew rescuing Matthias from his imprisonment among cannibals. The rollicking tale is well attested in antiquity. Two text-types are present: an Eastern text-type based on

---

3. The latter category stems primarily from the eighth to ninth century and is represented by the ninth-century *Vita Andreae* of Epiphanius the Monk (not to be confused with the fourth-century heresiologist Epiphanius of Salamis); and the *Narratio* and *Laudatio* texts. See further Lautaro Roig Lanzillotta, "The Acts of Andrew," in *The Oxford Encyclopedia of the Books of the Bible*, 2 vols., ed. M. Coogan (Oxford: Oxford University Press, 2011), 1:34–35.

4. See Lautaro Roig Lanzillotta, "The Acts of Andrew: A New Perspective on the Primitive Text," *Cuadernos de Filología Clásica* 20 (2010): 247–59.

5. Jean-Marc Prieur, "Acts of Andrew," *ABD* 1:245.

6. Greek: Πράξεις Ἀνδρέου καὶ Ματθεία εἰς τὴν πόλιν τῶν ἀνθρωποφάγων (*Praxeis Andreou kai Mattheia eis tēn polin tōn anthrōpophagōn*, "Acts of Andrew and Matthias in the city of the cannibals"); Latin: *Acta Andreae et Matthiae apud anthropophagos* ("Acts of Andrew and Matthias among the cannibals").

the Greek witnesses (e.g., Ottoban 415, P.Oxy. 851)[7] and a Western text-type based on Latin witnesses (e.g., Bologna 1576 [eleventh century], Recensio Casanatensis 1104 [twelfth century], and Recensio Vaticana 1274 [twelfth century]).[8]

As can be seen, the figure of Andrew attracted a considerable range of texts and traditions. So what does "the Acts of Andrew" signify? The answer depends on who is asked. For example, some scholars attach this name to Gregory's *Epitome*, while others attach it only to texts and traditions concerning Andrew's martyrdom.[9] Still others argue that the primitive Acts of Andrew was originally a larger unity that was later split up; thus, the "Acts of Andrew" refers to what is now the Acts of Andrew and Matthias, *Epitome*, and Martyrdom of Andrew.[10]

If the matter is confused in modern scholarship, another angle on the question is provided by investigating what the Acts of Andrew constituted for *ancient* authors. The issue, unfortunately, is that ancient authors mentioning the Acts of Andrew by title do not typically quote from the text. Eusebius, for example, simply names "the Acts of Andrew" before condemning it as "the fiction of heretics" that is "so completely out of accord with true orthodoxy" it must "be cast aside as absurd and impious" (*Hist. eccl.* 3.25.6–7). Yet even here we find a clue: whatever "the Acts of Andrew" signified for Eusebius offended his theological sensibilities. This likely points to the Acts of Andrew including unorthodox elements later stripped from or neutralized within the text by later tradents. Put differently, Eusebius's evidence may indicate that the text grew more "orthodox," not less, as time passed and that, conversely, more primitive forms of the tradition were also more heterodox.

We find something along these lines in the works of the later heresiologist Epiphanius (ca. 310–403 CE), who refers to the Acts of Andrew along with the Acts of Thomas and the Acts of John (on which, see the respective chapters in this volume). The Acts of Andrew stands among the principal Scriptures of the ascetic Encratites, who, among other things, eschew marriage as "plainly the work of the devil."[11] The Acts of Andrew has statements against sex in Gregory's *Epitome* (e.g., Andrew speaks "at length against fornication," Acts Andr. 28.12; cf. Acts Thom. 57, where marriage is "the work of the serpent"), but the strongest anti-marriage statements come in the Martyrdom of Andrew.[12] Thus, when Epiphanius speaks of the apocryphal Acts of Andrew being against marriage, the question is what text he is referring to. Is he referring to a primitive form of Gregory's *Epitome* that spoke more stridently against marriage, or a harsher form of the Martyrdom of Andrew?

The case is difficult to decide with Epiphanius, but clearer with another patristic source, that of Evodius of Uzala. In a treatise against the Manichaeans, he clearly refers to an episode from the Martyrdom of Andrew:

---

7. Reconstructed in Maximilian Bonnet, *Acta apostolorum apocrypha II/1: Passio Andreae, Ex actis Andreae, Martyria Andreae, Acta Andreae et Matthiae, Acta Petri et Andreae, Passio Bartholomaei. Acta Ioannis, Martyrium Matthiaei* (Leipzig: Hinrichs, 1898), 65–116.

8. Reconstructed in Franz Blatt, ed., *Die lateinischen Bearbeitungen der Acta Andreae et Mattiae apud anthropophagos*, BZNW 12 (Giessen: A. Töpelmann, 1930). Dating of the Latin manuscripts accords with Aurelio de Santos Otero, "Acta Andreae et Matthiae apud anthropophagos," in *NTApoc* 2:446; cf. Dennis R. MacDonald, *The Acts of Andrew and the Acts of Andrew and Matthias in the City of the Cannibals*, SBLTT 33.1 (Atlanta: Scholars Press, 1990), 63–65.

9. E.g., Roig Lanzillotta, "Acts of Andrew: A New Perspective."

10. So MacDonald, *City of the Cannibals*. Acts Andr. Mth. 11–15 are excluded from the original in his view.

11. Epiphanius, *Pan.* 2.47.1 (trans. Frank Williams, *The Panarion of Epiphanius of Salamis: Books II and III, De Fide*, 2nd ed., NHMS 79 [Leiden: Brill, 2013], 3).

12. On the Acts Andr. and Encratism, see sec. 3.2 below, "Heretical Tendencies: Encratism and Asceticism."

Observe, in the Acts of Leucius which he wrote under the name of the apostles, what manner of things you accept about Maximilla the wife of Egetes: who, refusing to pay her due to her husband (though the apostle had said "Let the husband pay the due to the wife and likewise the wife to the husband" 1 Cor 7:3), imposed her maid Euclia upon her husband, decking her out, as is there written, with wicked enticements and paintings, and substituted her as deputy for herself at night, so that he in ignorance used her as his wife.[13]

The ruse of Euclia taking Maximilla's place in bed is from the Martyrdom of Andrew (ch. 17). Significantly, Evodius's reference is textual ("as is there written"), hinting that what he refers to as an "act" was indeed a written text.[14] Evodius condemns the encratistic tendencies of the text by citing Paul against the Acts of Andrew, intimating to us once again that the primitive form of the text known to ancient readers was readily adaptable to encratistic groups.

Below we shall explore the Encratite tendencies of the various forms of the Acts of Andrew more thoroughly. And as shall be seen, this propensity is detectable even in Gregory's more orthodox *Epitome*, but it is more obvious in the Martyrdom of Andrew, especially as represented by Vatican Gr. 808. Thus, when ancient authors such as Eusebius refer to the Acts of Andrew, this reference perhaps includes encratistic-friendly forms of the Martyrdom of Andrew as well as a primitive Acts of Andrew (i.e., a pre-Gregorian version of Andrew's travels and miracles). What we do not possess, however, is an ancient reference to the "Acts of Andrew" that includes something like the Acts of Andrew and Matthias. Thus, on the current evidence the "Acts of Andrew" to these ancient authors signified a text that included elements of a pre-Gregorian *Epitome* and the Martyrdom of Andrew, but not the Acts of Andrew and Matthias, and which had ascetic tendencies useful to the Encratites.

Considering the diversity of views on what the "Acts of Andrew" signifies in modern and ancient usage, how do we proceed? Rather than attempt either to find the "earliest" recension or text of the Acts of Andrew[15] or to reconstruct the original text as much as possible,[16] given the diversity of the extant evidence a productive approach would be to view the Acts of Andrew as a fluid and open textual field. The Acts of Andrew is textually elusive, and the terms "earliest" and "original" ill suit the complicated and plastic textual evidence. Instead, we would do well to approach the Acts of Andrew as ancient audiences did: the term houses several traditions and tales, but all of them relate to the apostolic figure of Andrew. Thus, what Julia Snyder says of the Acts of Andrew and Matthias nicely applies to the entire complex of Acts of Andrew traditions: "Moving forward, we need to take fluidity in the manuscript tradition more seriously."[17]

In the following, the Acts of Andrew is taken broadly to refer to the early traditions related to the apostolic figure—that is, the Acts of Andrew and Matthias, the account of Andrew's peregrinations and miracles contained in Gregory of Tour's *Epitome*, and the Martyrdom of Andrew. This is done, however, without making a claim (à la Dennis

---

13. J. K. Elliott, "The Acts of Andrew," in *The Apocryphal New Testament: A Collection of Apocryphal Christian Literature in an English Translation* (Oxford: Clarendon, 1993), 232.

14. Evodius's reference to the "Acts of Leucius" rather than Andrew accords with the ancient tradition that Leucius wrote the text on Andrew's behalf.

15. This is the approach of Roig Lanzillotta, which is based primarily on Vatican Gr. 808 (Roig Lanzillotta, "Acts of Andrew: A New Perspective").

16. This is the approach of MacDonald, *City of the Cannibals*.

17. Julia A. Snyder, "Christ of the Acts of Andrew and Matthias," in *Christ of the Sacred Stories*, ed. P. Dragutinović et al., WUNT 2.453 (Tübingen: Mohr Siebeck, 2017), 249n10.

MacDonald) that these three textual compilations originally made up *the* Acts of Andrew. Instead, the Acts of Andrew is regarded as a fluid textual field loosely united by association with Andrew, but bounded by time (texts deriving from the third to the eighth centuries)[18] and language (primarily Greek and Latin, with some consideration of the early offshoots in Coptic and Armenian).

1.3 Authorship

M. R. James's argument that the Acts of Andrew, of Peter, and of John all had the same author, "who may be called, for the sake of convenience, Leucius," has not gained acceptance in scholarship.[19] Dennis MacDonald has a cleverer solution to the problem.[20] In condemning the Acts of Andrew, Pope Innocent I (early fifth century) believed it to be the work of "the philosophers Xenocharides and Leonides." MacDonald finds further corroboration for the plural authors in Philaster of Brescia's attribution of the work to "disciples who followed the apostles." Given the text's "sophisticated Christian Platonis[m]," MacDonald supposes that it could indeed have been written by those known as philosophers (i.e., Xenocharides and Leonides). MacDonald then deals with the text's singular scribal postscript ("Hereabouts *I* should make an end of the blessed tales," Martyrdom of Andrew 65.1) by conjecturing that the text was *authored* by one of the philosophers, while the other served as a putative eyewitness.

However, MacDonald himself concedes that his reconstruction is "hypothetical" and that "the evidence precludes firm conclusions," and his solution strikes the current author as more ingenious than convincing.[21] Given the current data, I join most other scholars in leaving the question of authorship open and undecided.[22]

1.4 Language

Because the "Acts of Andrew" can refer to so many different texts in antiquity, the linguistic situation is similarly diverse: witnesses survive in Greek, Latin, Syriac, Ethiopic, Coptic, Armenian, Arabic, Georgian, various Slavonic dialects, and Anglo-Saxon. Our best witnesses tend to be in Greek and Latin, though exceptions may be the Coptic of Andrew's run-in with the proconsul Varianus (P.Copt. Utrecht 1; cf. *Epitome* 18) and the Armenian Passion, especially its parable of the eagle (cf. Martyrdom of Andrew 53). Arguably the best critical edition of the Greek text of the Martyrdom of Andrew and the Latin of Gregory's *Epitome* is Jean-Marc Prieur's *Acta Andreae* (with French translation).[23] For the Acts of Andrew and Matthias, look to MacDonald's eclectic text, which has the added benefit of including texts and translations of the other tales associated with Andrew (i.e., *Epitome* and Martyrdom of Andrew).[24] References to and quotations of the Acts of Andrew throughout this chapter derive from MacDonald's updated 2005 translation.[25]

---

18. This is not to say that the manuscripts must derive from this period—few do.

19. M. R. James, *Apoc. Anec.* 2:xxxi, cited in Elliott, "Acts of Andrew," 235.

20. Here and throughout this paragraph, I refer to MacDonald, *City of the Cannibals*, 47–51.

21. MacDonald, *City of the Cannibals*, 51.

22. So Elliott, "Acts of Andrew," 235.

23. Jean-Marc Prieur, *Acta Andreae*, 2 vols., CCSA 5–6 (Turnhout: Brepols, 1989). Texts and translations appear in vol. 2 (CCSA 6).

24. MacDonald, *City of the Cannibals*.

25. Dennis R. MacDonald, *The Acts of Andrew*, Early Christian Apocrypha 1 (Santa Rosa, CA: Polebridge, 2005).

1.5 Provenance

The provenance is, in a word, unknown.[26] Further, based on the present information and according to current estimates, it is perhaps unknowable. This too fits with the character of a composite text: even if one were to identify the provenance of one textual tradition, that would not account for the others. So even if one traced the primitive Acts of Andrew back to, for example, Alexandria, that would likely not account for the provenance of the Acts of Andrew and Matthias, nor of the Martyrdom of Andrew. And since the primitive Acts of Andrew is itself the result of scholarly conjecture, this would be building speculation atop speculation. It is better to follow those who are content to leave the matter unresolved, as we have done here.[27]

1.6 Date

As seen above, the earliest mention of the "Acts of Andrew"—and thus the text's *terminus ante quem*—is by Eusebius of Caesarea (ca. 250–340 CE).[28] A near quotation of Achilles Tatius in Vatican Gr. 808 provides a *terminus post quem*, about 170 CE.[29] Thus most scholars date the origins of the Acts of Andrew to the late second or early third century, though the textual complex branched out and grew from that starting point.

1.7 Genre

What Harry Attridge writes of the Acts of another apostle in this volume applies, *mutatis mutandis*, to the Acts of Andrew:

> Like other apocryphal Acts, the Acts of Thomas combines tales of the exotic, the miraculous, the sublimated erotic,[30] along with an account of the noble death of the martyred apostle. They thus resemble ancient romances and other forms of popular fiction, although they have distinctive features, including constant echoes of early Christian gospel literature.[31]

Links to romantic literature are especially striking in the Martyrdom of Andrew; typically, the fires kindled in a romance end in the consummation of a marriage, a unit of social stability in the Roman Empire. However, in the Martyrdom of Andrew, Maximilla's relationship with Andrew both plays on these tropes (Andrew as the object of affection) and subverts them: the "romance" is actually with God, and the outcome is an ascetic

---

26. Prieur wisely notes: "So far as place of origin is concerned, there is nothing to compel us to decide for one particular region rather than another. The text may have been composed just as well in Greece as in Asia Minor, Syria or Egypt," before adding that "Alexandria especially could have afforded the spiritual and intellectual surroundings in which a text like the [Acts of Andrew] could have come into being" (Jean-Marc Prieur and Wilhelm Schneemelcher, "The Acts of Andrew," in *NTApoc* 2:115).

27. So Elliott, "Acts of Andrew," 235.

28. Origen (d. 254 CE), as quoted by Eusebius, mentions Andrew's mission to Scythia, but not to any of the places the apostle travels in the Acts Andr. As with Origen's failure to mention India for Thomas (see Harry Attridge, "The Acts of Thomas," in this volume), Origen's omission of these places would seem to indicate that the Acts Andr.'s version of Andrew's activity was not widely known in the third century. The Manichaean Psalter, approximately contemporary with Eusebius's account, recounts a narrative thought to resemble those in the Acts of Andr., and, as seen above, the heresiologist Epiphanius was aware that some (to him, heretical) groups used the Acts Andr. in the fourth century (Epiphanius, *Pan.* 2.47.1; 2.61.1; 2.53.2).

29. So Roig Lanzillotta, "Acts of Andrew," 1:38.

30. On which, see T. Adamik, "Eroticism in the *Liber de miraculis beati Andrea apostoli* of Gregory of Tours," *The Apocryphal Acts of Andrew*, ed. Jan N. Bremmer (Leuven: Peeters, 2000), 35–46.

31. Attridge, "Acts of Thomas," 292.

"marriage" between believer and deity that undermines the elite marriage and thereby the social stability that marriage provides.[32]

Gregory's *Epitome* is more closely related to peregrination accounts of ancient figures—it is, in its current form, a travelogue punctuated by miracles and exorcisms. Finally, the Acts of Andrew and Matthias reads as a single "act" of the apostle (so *Epitome* 1), a rescue tale that bears striking similarities to the Septuagint version of Jonah.[33]

2. SUMMARY OF CONTENT

Given the textual complications described above, the Acts of Andrew is difficult to summarize as one continuous story. Instead, I here present the content of three important subsets of the Acts of Andrew tradition: (2.1) the Acts of Andrew and Matthias (33 chs.); (2.2) the *Epitome* of Gregory of Tours (33 chs.); and (2.3) the Martyrdom of Andrew (approx. 65 chs.). The text for each is based on the reconstructed text and translation of Dennis MacDonald, with reference to the aforementioned critical editions as needed.[34]

2.1 Acts of Andrew and Matthias

This tale begins with the twelve apostles casting lots to determine what region each would evangelize, with the lot falling to Matthias to go to "Myrmidonia" (so the Latin witnesses) or "the city of the cannibals" (so the Greek witnesses; 1.2). The residents of the city live up to their reputation, and upon his arrival Matthias is captured, blinded, drugged, and imprisoned for thirty days in order to fatten him up for his grisly fate. Miserable, Matthias prays that the Lord would rescue him, if it be God's will. Matthias's prayer is partially answered in his eyesight returning, and a light/voice in the prison assures him that he has not been abandoned but will be rescued by Andrew.

Twenty-seven days later, the Lord appears to Andrew in Achaea, calling him to rescue Matthias before he is devoured three days hence. To facilitate the journey, Jesus and two angels charter a vessel and invite Andrew and his disciples aboard, though they do not recognize Jesus and his angelic crew "because Jesus was hiding his divinity and appeared to Andrew as a human captain" (5.5). Like the Road to Emmaus story (Luke 24:13–35), the narrative device of disguise delights by making the reader privy to something to which the characters are not, and the narrator draws out the trope with a number of back-and-forth exchanges between Andrew and captain Jesus that also recount Andrew's time with the pre-Easter Jesus (chs. 7–15). On arriving in Myrmidonia, Jesus enlists the angels to place Andrew and his disciples, now asleep, on land (ch. 17). Only then does Andrew realize who his captain was ("the Lord was with us in the boat and we did not know him, for he transformed himself [μετεμόρφωσεν ἑαυτόν, *metemorphōsen heauton*] into a captain in the boat"; 17.4). Nevertheless, Jesus reappears to Andrew as a small child, showing him that "I can do anything and appear to each person in any form I wish" and warning him that he will suffer but that "I endured and forgave in order to provide a model also for you" (18.10, 15).

As Andrew enters the city, the action increases: he approaches the prison and slays the guards with prayer, then marks the prison door with the sign of the cross, making it open

---

32. So Caroline T. Schroeder, "Embracing the Erotic in the Passion of Andrew: The Apocryphal Acts of Andrew, the Greek Novel, and Platonic Philosophy," in *The Apocryphal Acts of Andrew*, ed. J. Bremmer (Leuven: Peeters, 2000), 110–26.

33. On the parallels with Jonah, see further MacDonald, *City of the Cannibals*, 4–6.

34. MacDonald, *City of the Cannibals*.

automatically. He frees Matthias, but not content to leave others behind, the two apostles free nearly three hundred other inmates, also restoring their sight (cf. Luke 4:18).

Meanwhile, the residents of the city, finding their guards dead and their prison empty, begin preparing the guards' bodies for consumption; however, Andrew foils their preparations with prayer (ch. 22). Hungry, they round up the elderly in the city, one of whom begs that his young son take his place, but Andrew again prayerfully intervenes (ch. 23). Finally, the devil—disguised as an old man—incites the residents to end the problem at its source by finding and destroying Andrew. Andrew makes the former task easy by showing himself to the residents, but the latter proves impossible, even after the cannibals drag Andrew through the streets for three days (chs. 25–28). After the second day, the devil, accompanied by seven demons (cf. Matt 12:45 par.), takes it on himself to kill Andrew, but he cannot because of the godly seal on the apostle's forehead. The demonic foes thus content themselves to tempt Andrew to use his power to save himself (27.12; cf. Matt 4:3 par.). Andrew finally is left for dead in prison, but the Lord visits him in prison and restores his health (29.1). Andrew then avenges himself on the Myrmidonians by commanding a statue to spew forth a flood of water that, with poetic justice, consumes human flesh (29.10). After many deaths and as the flesh-devouring waters rise to their necks, the city's citizens repent (ch. 30). The flood finally abates upon Andrew's command that the earth open and "devour" it (along with the filicidal old man and the executioners). Andrew then revives all those killed in the flood—both humans and animals—and, after baptizing the citizens, establishes a church and "hand[s] onto them the commands of our Lord Jesus Christ" (ch. 32). Despite pleas for him to stay, Andrew leaves town, only to be met and rebuked by Jesus, who appears as a "beautiful small child" (33.1).[35] Duly chastened, Andrew returns to the Myrmidonians, teaching them for seven days and presumably raising the men from the abyss as Jesus commanded (cf. 33.4).[36]

2.2 Gregory's Epitome of the Acts of Andrew

The first act in Gregory's abbreviated version is a much-shortened version of the Acts of Andrew and Matthias (ch. 1). Thereafter, Gregory presents the myriad acts of Andrew. Since in what follows I give an epitome of an epitome, descriptions of the episodes are necessarily quite short, giving only the essential details.

Andrew's Acts from Myrmidonia to his Allotted Region, Achaia (chs. 2–21)

- A blind man, who does not deign to ask Andrew to heal his blindness, is nevertheless healed by the apostle and given new clothes (ch. 2).
- In Amasia, Andrew raises the dead boy of the community leader, causing all unbelievers to believe and be baptized (ch. 3)
- Secretly, a young Christian (Sostratus) tells Andrew of his mother's incestuous advances. But like Potiphar's wife, she turns the accusation around, taking Sostratus to court. Though Andrew defends him from her "blazing lust" (4.11), the proconsul sides with the mother, condemning both Andrew and Sostratus to death. Andrew's response is swift: by prayer he summons an earthquake, which convinces the proconsul to convert and be baptized, and lighting, which strikes the boy's mother dead (ch. 4).

---

35. As MacDonald points out, the text here echoes LXX Jonah's cycle of preaching, repentance, conversion, and prophetic discontent (*City of the Cannibals*, 4–6).

36. On the abrupt ending in our current versions, see MacDonald, *City of the Cannibals*, 171–77.

- In Sinope, Andrew sets the household of Gratinus in order, exorcizing the son, healing the parents, and confronting the latter two about their extramarital affairs. As a result, all in the household are converted, causing Gratinus to lavish gifts on the apostle, which he redirects to the poor (ch. 5).

- Traveling now to Nicaea, Andrew expels seven demons who are in the form of dogs, who prowl the roadside tombs. In response, all the locals are baptized and given a bishop—an ecclesial element that likely comes from Gregory himself (ch. 6).[37]

- The seven demonic hounds, however, continue their reign of terror elsewhere by mangling a youth in Nicomedia. On entering the city, the apostle encounters his bier and revives him, to the astonishment of onlookers (ch. 7).

- Next, sailing to Byzantium, Andrew calms a storm on the way and saves all aboard (ch. 8).

- Going from Byzantium to Thrace, the apostle is then confronted by a band of brigands. After Andrew makes the sign of the cross, an angel disarms them, and he passes by, now adored by his would-be attackers (ch. 9).

- Arriving at Perinthus in Thrace, Andrew immediately embarks for Macedonia, converting the crew on the way (ch. 10). The action of chapters 11–21 then centers on Macedonia.

- In Philippi, Andrew breaks up the incestuous wedding of several cousins and enjoins them to hold fast to his teaching to gain everlasting life (ch. 11).

- A young Thessalonian, Exochus, follows Andrew, but his parents attempt to kill both of them by setting the house they are in ablaze. After Andrew easily extinguishes the fire, the parents attack with the sword, but are blinded. Though these wonders cause the crowd to convert, the parents persist in their rejection, dying soon thereafter. Newly rich, Exochus redistributes his inheritance to the poor (ch. 12).

- Andrew then journeys with Exochus to the latter's hometown, Thessalonica. There, Exochus preaches—the first time someone other than Andrew does so—and Andrew heals an invalid, to the delight of the crowd (ch. 13).

- Delight turns to wholesale conversion after the apostle next raises a young man killed by a demon (ch. 14). The crowd is then taught "the essential things about God" for three days (14.11). As is typical of Gregory's *Epitome*, the contents of this teaching are not given.

- An old man named Medias then begs Andrew to come to Philippi to heal his crippled son. Obliging, Andrew enters Medias's home only to find people imprisoned in squalor. Andrew convinces Medias to repent and release the captives and then heals his son, who himself heals many in the city (ch. 15).

- Next, a Philippian named Nicolaus offers Andrew his dearest possessions (a gilded carriage with white mules and horses) in exchange for healing his diseased daughter. Andrew refuses the visible gifts, instead requesting the invisible gift of Nicolaus's soul. His speech leads to the conversion of all listening even before he goes on to heal Nicolaus's daughter, and reports of his wonder-working spread through Macedonia (ch. 16).

- Andrew's reputation is such that a demon voluntarily leaves a possessed boy in Andrew's presence. Matching his spiritual powers, his teachings are reported as being so sophisticated that "even philosophers would come and debate with him; no one could oppose his teaching" (ch. 17), though again the contents are not given.

---

37. So Prieur and Schneemelcher, "Acts of Andrew," 122.

- The lack of adequate opponents quickly changes with the introduction of the proconsul Varianus. The best witness to this next "act of Andrew" appears in Papyrus Coptic Utrecht 1, though Gregory's account is broadly similar. Learning of Andrew's reputation as a troublemaker and destroyer of the gods' temples, Varianus sends infantry and cavalry to capture him. However, much to Varianus's vexation, the soldiers fall at Andrew's feet terrified when they see his face aglow. Unable to arrest Andrew, they instead arrest some of his followers. While Andrew confronts them about this, the demon in one of the soldiers comes forward and confesses his prior misbehavior, then kills the soldier when leaving his body. Andrew raises the soldier, but not even this placates Varianus, who arrests Andrew and throws him to the beasts in the stadium. But the beasts do not harm the apostle. In fact, the final beast, a leopard, instead kills Varianus's own son, whom Andrew naturally raises. While the people glorify God, Varianus storms off, defeated but unchanged (ch. 18).
- Andrew next comes to a region where a 150-foot, man-eating snake is on the loose and has killed a boy. He exterminates the snake and has a previously unmentioned convert (the "proconsul's" wife, perhaps referring to Varianus) raise the boy to life, to the delight of his parents (ch. 19).
- In a break from the action, Andrew then recounts a dream-vision: Peter and John appear on a mountain and cryptically inform Andrew of his martyrdom ("you will drink Peter's cup," 20.4). After praying with and teaching his followers, he returns to Thessalonica for two days (ch. 20), then to Patras in Achaia. En route, he calms a storm and rescues a man fallen overboard (ch. 21).

Andrew's Acts in and around Achaia (chs. 22–33)

- As with the previous proconsul Varianus, Patras's proconsul Lesbius is disturbed by Andrew's arrival. However, this time an angel appears to the proconsul, who is struck dumb, healed by Andrew, and converted along with the rest of the town. True to reputation, Andrew's presence leads to the town destroying their temples and idols (ch. 22).[38]
- Among the converted is Lesbius's former mistress, Trophime, who leaves her (unnamed) husband to follow Andrew. Her husband ironically responds to her newfound chastity by condemning her to prostitution at the urging of the proconsul's wife Callisto. But Trophime manages to resist the advances of the male clientele by holding a written Gospel to her breast, even leading to the death of one man (whom she later raises). Meanwhile, Callisto (tellingly with Trophime's pimp) is found beaten to death by a demon in a public bath. Andrew raises her, and she repents of the wrong done to Trophime and is apparently converted.
- While on the seashore with Lesbius, Andrew discovers a corpse, which he revives. The newly resuscitated man, Philopater, reports that he and his crew were sailing in search of the teacher of the true God when a storm arose and drowned them all. Andrew prays, and a wave casts ashore the bodies of Philopater's thirty-nine companions, which Philopater himself and a close friend revive, to the astonishment of onlookers (ch. 24).

---

38. This is the account in the *Martyrium prius* and *Laudatio*. Gregory's account differs in that it tells of Lesbius's failed attempted to capture Andrew in Macedonia and of his conversion.

- We are then introduced to Calliope in Corinth, who conceives a child outside of marriage with a murderer. Having difficulty in labor, she calls upon the goddess Diana for help, but instead the devil appears. Surprisingly, he refers Calliope to Andrew instead (!). Andrew arrives and scolds Calliope for the way in which she conceived and for consulting "demons." Her baby is stillborn—a tragic point that does not seem to bother Gregory—but she is "relieved of her suffering" and lives (25.11).
- Next Philopater's father, Sostratus, prompted by a vision, seeks Andrew out and is converted (ch. 26).
- Andrew, while bathing, then exorcizes an old and young man, warning the bystanders to be constantly vigilant against "the enemy of humankind" (27.7).
- An old man named Nicolaus confesses to Andrew his lengthy struggle with various forms of sexual immorality. Compared to the instant transformation in other episodes, the conversion is agonizingly slow: God takes five days to reply to Andrew's prayer for mercy, resulting in Nicolaus "tortur[ing] himself" with a penitential bread-and-water diet for six months and finally passing from this world in haggard peace (ch. 28).
- A citizen of Megara named Antiphanes next asks Andrew to heal his wife, who was severely beaten by Antiphanes's possessed servants. Andrew goes a step further, arriving in Megara and healing not only Antiphanes's wife but also exorcizing all in the house (ch. 29).
- Recalling the martyrdom vision of chapter 20, Andrew receives a vision of Christ calling him to give the Spirit to his protégé Lesbius and to prepare for martyrdom in Patras the next day (ch. 29).
- Andrew dutifully returns to Patras, healing a paralyzed person upon reentry. Reports of the healing spread, reaching the proconsul's wife, Maximilla, who soon after falls ill with a fever and summons Andrew. Andrew heals her and characteristically refuses payment from the proconsul Aegeates (ch. 30).
- Andrew then heals another paralyzed man, though he finally begins to feel his own bodily limitations and must be propped up by his disciples (ch. 31).
- In rapid succession, Andrew next restores sight to an entire family struck with demonic blindness, to the delight of the crowd (ch. 32).
- A final challenge awaits Andrew: the rehabilitation of a leprous old man of noble descent dwelling on a dung heap. Oozing with pus, the man washes in the sea and is restored body and soul. He runs through the streets naked proclaiming God's mercy until Andrew catches up and orders him to dress. He becomes a follower of Andrew, and all are astonished (ch. 33).

There ends Gregory's *Epitome*—notably missing an account of the martyrdom in Patras forecasted by the vision of chapter 29. For that, we turn now to what we have called the "Martyrdom of Andrew," itself confusingly labeled by some as the "Acts of Andrew."

2.3 The Martyrdom of Andrew

Andrew's martyrdom account begins by gesturing to events and characters already described: "At the same time that his wife was healed, the proconsul Aegeates took leave for Rome, to the emperor Nero" (1.1). Concurrently, Aegeates's brother Stratocles arrives from Italy to Patras, having been given leave from the army by Nero to study philosophy (1.2). On arriving, Stratocles's servant is overcome by a demon, but Andrew arrives to expel the demon before a crowd. Witnessing the exorcism and hearing Andrew's teachings set in motion Stratocles's conversion, a "birth" of which Andrew is the midwife (chs. 7–8). Thereafter, Stratocles becomes inseparable from the apostle and his teachings, even giving up all his possessions (12.8). Unlike in Gregory's *Epitome*, throughout the martyrdom Andrew's teachings are described in rich philosophical detail. Here, a block of teaching (chs. 9–12) includes injunctions about the Lord's seal on the soul, which is to be loosed from the body (11.2) on the way back to God (12.1), foreshadowing Andrew's own fate (see 63.6 and below).

The golden times of learning together night and day are interrupted when Aegeates returns home from Rome, and Maximilla panics that their group will be exposed and broken up. But Andrew miraculously intervenes, cloaking the believers in invisibility and enabling all but Maximilla to exit the house undetected (13.8). Alone with her husband, Maximilla must now face one of the central challenges in the Martyrdom of Andrew: avoiding "filthy intercourse" with Aegeates (14.7).[39] She temporarily evades him on the pretext that lips should not kiss after prayer (14.8). But Aegeates—called "that savage lion" (13.6), "that insolent and hostile snake" (16.2), and "our savage and perpetually boorish enemy" (16.4)—and his appetites are animalistic (cf. 46.5), and he is not easily rebuffed. Thus, Andrew returns to pray over Maximilla so she can "sleep apart from her visible husband and be wed to her inner husband" (16.4). But how? Maximilla takes matters into her own hands, enlisting "a shapely, notoriously wanton servant-girl named Euclia" to "sleep with Aegeates in her stead" (17.1, 4). The ruse works for eight months until it backfires: Euclia finally realizes that she can blackmail Maximilla (ch. 18). However, it is not Euclia who discloses the scheme, but Maximilla's own servants. They first extort her for their silence and then tell Aegeates (chs. 20–21). Aegeates's effort to contain the news is draconian: he tortures and mutilates Euclia and crucifies the informant servants. He then begs Maximilla to tell him if there is "another man" (23.4). Maximilla uncovers her romantic relationship in strikingly erotic language: "I am in love, but the object of my love is not of this world.... Night and day it kindles and enflames me with love for it.... So then, let me have intercourse and take my rest with it alone" (23.6–8).

This revelation makes Aegeates even more enraged, but he has nowhere to direct his anger since his wife outstrips him in rank (and deicide proves impossible). Finally, an attendant informs him of Maximilla's relationship with Andrew (25.5). Incidentally, Andrew walks by just then, and immediately the servant seizes him and Aegeates locks him up, to the dismay of the adoring crowd (ch. 26). Aegeates then gloats to Maximilla that he has imprisoned her teacher, destined to die "a horrible death" (27.2). Nonplussed, Maximilla informs him, essentially, that her *real* teacher is not of this world: "He can't be 'caught,' just as he can't be seen" (27.3).

Nevertheless, she sends her believing servant Iphidama to reconnoiter the prison so that they can visit Andrew. Iphidama is miraculously able to enter the prison undetected, where she finds Andrew encouraging his fellow inmates (ch. 28). He prays protection over her and sends her to retrieve Maximilla, which Iphidama does with haste (ch. 29). Aegeates, however, guesses their plans and arranges to have her bedroom door and the gates of the prison carefully guarded (ch. 31). An apparent answer to the women's prayer for safe passage, they leave the bedroom and are led by a beautiful young boy (an angel as in Mark 16:5? Or Jesus himself as in Acts Andr. Mth. 18.4?) into the prison, evidently unbeknownst to Aegeates's lackeys. The boy enjoins them to be edified by Andrew's "speech"

---

39. See sec. 3.2, "Heretical Tendencies: Encratism and Asceticism," below.

(32.4), the lengthy contents of which appear in Vatican Gr. 808 as a sort of "testament of Andrew" before his execution the next day (chs. 33–50). In it, he first addresses the "brethren" (chs. 33–36), then Maximilla (chs. 37–41), Stratocles (chs. 42–45), and finally the brethren again (chs. 47–50). A narrative interlude tells of Maximilla's return to the praetorium and final rejection of Aegeates's ultimatum for sex in exchange for Andrew's freedom, causing him to hate Andrew all the more and settle upon a supremely painful punishment—crucifixion (ch. 46). The next morning, Aegeates has Andrew flogged and sent to be crucified, though not "with nails" but "with ropes" and uncut knees, thus prolonging the punishment (ch. 51). However, Stratocles intercepts Andrew on the way to the cross and fights off his captors. Ultimately, though, he understands that enduring afflictions is godlier than resisting them, and he leads his teacher to the place of execution (ch. 52). On the way, Andrew instructs Stratocles on how to overcome the world through detachment rather than anger (ch. 53), and here the Armenian Passion includes a lengthy conceit comparing the soul to an eagle that ascends to luminous heights only by leaving behind all that is earthbound. Arriving at the cross and fully in control of his fate, Andrew then greets it and welcomes death, inviting the believers to have the executioners carry out their orders (ch. 54). On the cross, Andrew appears to experience no pain, but rather smiles and laughs (ch. 55). Indeed, despite the intent to prolong Andrew's torture, the ropes and uncut knees succeed only in prolonging his final oration, which lasts for three days and three nights (chs. 56–58; cf. 59.3). Now instructed in Andrew's ways, on the fourth day the crowd rails against Aegeates's injustice, such that he fears a revolt and promises to release Andrew (ch. 60). But Andrew refuses an escape from death, committing instead to "escape what's earthly" (61.2). After upbraiding Aegeates, Andrew, ever the master of his fate, hands his spirit over to God (chs. 62–63).

A brief denouement follows: after burying Andrew, Maximilla separates from Aegeates, choosing instead a quiet and holy life with the other believers. Dejected, Aegeates leaves his house (ironically undetected by those in his household; cf. ch. 31) and throws himself to his death. Since Aegeates was childless, Stratocles inherits his wealth but rejects it as evil (ch. 64). A narrator's coda concludes the work with a prayer about the account's veracity ("I pray ... that I heard what was actually said") and that those convinced by its contents may enjoy fellowship and the gifts of God (ch. 65).

3. INTERPRETIVE ISSUES
3.1 History and Use

Insofar as one is seeking to gain reliable information about the post-Easter life of the apostle Andrew, the historical value of the Acts of Andrew is essentially nil. But that is not to say the texts lack historical value for other endeavors. As Roig Lanzillotta tells it:

> The production of new texts based on the primitive *Acts of Andrew* gained a new impulse during the eighth and ninth centuries, a period in which Andrew's figure acquired an almost political character. In its rivalry with the West, Byzantium claimed the authority of the apostle as founder of the Oriental Church with a view to counteracting the authority of Simon Peter, the legendary founder of the Christian community of Rome.[40]

Since, according to the Gospel of John, Andrew was the first to be called by Jesus rather than Peter, Andrew's association with Byzantium could be leveraged in debates about

---

40. Roig Lanzillotta, "Acts of Andrew," 1:35.

apostolic priority. As such, the historical import of the Acts of Andrew is significant in later ecclesial politics.

3.2 Heretical Tendencies: Encratism and Asceticism

As noted above, a fascinating feature of the Acts of Andrew is the text's asceticism and occasional anti-marriage views. This ascetic, anti-marriage perspective is particularly associated with the Encratites, a second-century Christian group. Later heresiologists condemned the group and included Tatian, author of the Gospel harmony the *Diatessaron*, among their ranks. As seen above, Epiphanius of Salamis (ca. 310–403 CE) reports that the group held as scriptural the Acts of Andrew, John, and Thomas, each of which has anti-marriage content felicitous to the group's perspective.[41]

This encratistic tendency is represented most stridently in the Martyrdom of Andrew, even in the secondary forms that we possess. Maximilla's prayer is that God "rescue me at last from Aegeates's filthy intercourse and keep me pure and chaste" (Mart. Andr. 14.7). Likewise, Andrew himself prays that the Lord "protect her especially, Master, from this disgusting pollution" (Mart. Andr. 16.3)—that is, intercourse with her (unbelieving) husband.[42] Since the plot is based on Maximilla's conversion and attempt to avoid being sexually reunited with Aegeates, the ascetic tendencies are woven so deeply into the fabric of the martyrdom tale as to prove inextricable—pull out the anti-marriage thread, and the plot of the tale unravels.

The encratistic tendencies of the Martyrdom of Andrew are also especially prevalent in Vatican Gr. 808, which Roig Lanzillotta and others reckon resembles a more primitive form of the Acts of Andrew before its heretical tendencies were more effectively purged.[43] For example, Andrew solemnly enjoins Maximilla to "resist *any* proposition of sexual intercourse and wish to be disassociated from so foul and filthy a way of life," to "not commit this act"—again, the act being *intramarital* sex (Mart. Andr. 37.3, 5 [Vatican Gr. 808 5.3, 5]).[44]

If the earliest stratum of the Acts of Andrew textual stream contains encratistic tendencies, this aspect of the text is notably "expurgated and catholicized over the centuries" in later textual forms.[45] Thus, Gregory appears to address and correct the anti-marriage perspective of the primitive Acts of Andrew. For example, when Andrew crashes the wedding of four cousins in *Epitome* 11, there are tantalizing clues that Gregory has corrected a text that originally forbade marriage tout court. Gregory's suspiciously orthodox version, with his probable interpolations italicized, reads: "Repent, for you have sinned against the Lord by wanting to unite *blood relatives* in marriage. *It is not that we forbid or shun weddings*—from the beginning God commanded the male and the female to be joined together—but *we do condemn incest*" (*Epitome* 11.12–13). However, the Epistle of Titus (not to be confused with the canonical "Epistle *to* Titus") witnesses to a similar wedding-crashing episode. There, Andrew is focused on breaking up the marriage, full stop: "At last, when Andrew arrived at a wedding, he, too, to demonstrate God's glory, disjoined men and women whose marriages had been arranged and taught them to continue being holy

---

41. See Epiphanius, *Pan.* 2.47.

42. Maximilla's solution to the problem is itself quite problematic: she enlists "a shapely, notoriously wanton servant-girl named Euclia" to "sleep with Aegeates in her stead" (Mart. Andr. 17.1, 4).

43. Roig Lanzillotta, "Acts of Andrew: A New Perspective."

44. Similarly, "If you become won over by the seductions of Aegeates and the flatteries of the serpent, his father, so that you return to your former sexual acts, know this . . ." (Mart. Andr. 40.5 [Vatican Gr. 808 8.5]).

45. Elliott, "Acts of Andrew," 234.

as singles."[46] Unlike the Acts of Andrew version, it is clear here that the affianced depart in singleness. A second text, possibly inspired by the primitive Acts of Andrew account, describes Thomas breaking up a wedding between two noble youths so that they avoid "filthy intercourse" (Acts Thom. 4–16, here 12). Both episodes likely reflect an earlier, anti-marriage version of the episode, which was later sanitized by Gregory. Ultimately, however, Gregory's efforts could not save the Acts of Andrew; indeed, it had already been condemned as heretical by Pope Innocent I over a century earlier.[47]

3.3 Theology and Philosophy of the Acts of Andrew

Since the theology and soteriology of the Acts of Andrew and Matthias and Gregory's *Epitome* are much more occasional and less developed, here we will focus primarily on the theological system of the Martyrdom of Andrew. In Andrew's numerous, lengthy speeches, the Martyrdom presents a coherent symbolic world around the interrelated topics of God, anthropology, revelation, and salvation. Previous generations of scholars likened it to a gnostic redeemer myth, wherein an enlightened individual (Andrew) reveals to trapped souls their true origin and destination in God. However, a "gnostic" cosmogony in which the material world was created by an evil entity (i.e., demiurge) is entirely absent in the Martyrdom of Andrew, and "Gnosticism" is in any case a fraught category in contemporary scholarship.[48] A better setting for the text is within the world of Christian Middle Platonism.[49] The theological outlook is that the soul is destined for the higher plane of ideals rather than the current, corrupted forms of the material plane (the realm of "external forms," Mart. Andr. 58.1). Escape from the material plane comes through "knowledge [γνῶσις, *gnosis*] of our God," which is revealed by God's apostle Andrew (58.6). The anthropology is therefore based on body-soul dualism. While not going as far as saying material was created by an evil being, nevertheless the body is a worthless "prison" (40.2). As Andrew says to Maximilla, "You are immaterial, holy, light, akin to the unbegotten, intellectual, heavenly, transparent, pure, beyond the flesh, beyond the world" (38.7). This understanding of "the mysteries of [one's] proper nature" (47.7) allows the soul to return to God and "rest" upon separation from the body in death, "as we fly off to those things which are properly ours" (50.11).[50]

However, the devil schemes to keep people trapped in what is fleeting and ephemeral rather than to attain what is permanent and enduring. His key ploy is to use "immediate pleasure" to distract and entice humans, even and especially in the bonds of marriage, which involves not only sex but also, through it, the birth of children—a painful obstacle to the simple life and a distraction from the soul's focus on God (56.10). Thus, Andrew's disciples need to be "at war with pleasures" (50.3), thereby weakening the devil's schemes.

If the way to overcome pleasures is through worldly detachment, this is especially true

---

46. MacDonald, *Acts of Andrew*, 49. The epistle lacks chapter and verse markers.

47. The Acts Andr. is also associated with the Manicheans by Philaster of Brescia and Augustine.

48. The watershed study in the debate is Michael Allen Williams, *Rethinking "Gnosticism": An Argument for Dismantling a Dubious Category* (Princeton: Princeton University Press, 1999).

49. As Roig Lanzillotta observes, the "AA's cosmology, theology, anthropology, ethics, and epistemology show a marked influence from Middle Platonism, notably from those Middle Platonists who incorporated Aristotelian thought into the common Platonic heritage" (Roig Lanzillotta, "Acts of Andrew: A New Perspective," 255).

50. Cf. the Armenian fragment of Andrew's parable of the eagle: "Like the eagle, we fly toward our natural heavenly light and adorn ourselves with luminous commandments. . . . They will put off the earthly body and the next time rise clothed in heavenly glory, and then into coveted paradise they will enter" (Mart. Andr. 53.17, 25).

when the soul gains freedom in death. Andrew serves as the exemplar here: "Learn from me!" he calls from the cross, "I exhort you all instead to rid yourselves of this life . . . and hurry to overtake my soul which speeds toward things beyond time" (57.5, 7). In so doing, Andrew (echoing Jesus in John 14:2, 6) leaves "to prepare [his followers'] routes to God" (58.5; see also 63.5). Andrew is so intent to escape this life that he prays to prevent Aegeates from untying him from the cross before he expires, and he ultimately hands his own spirit over to God (Mart. Andr. 63).

Since a central concern of the Martyrdom of Andrew is to present the beliefs of the author(s) as a coherent philosophical theology, the text must also oppose and prove itself preferable to pagan philosophy. The initial conduit for this is Stratocles, who is on leave from the army to study "philosophy" but discovers in Andrew a new, superior philosopher. This finding makes his former pagan pursuits seem "hollow," "destitute and worthless" (7.8). Yet even in opposing pagan philosophy, the Martyrdom nevertheless traffics in its terminology and conceptual field.

Whereas the Martyrdom narrates Andrew's lengthy speeches and presents him as a "Christianized Socrates"—principled to the point of dying for his philosophy[51]—neither the Acts of Andrew and Matthias nor Gregory's *Epitome* participate in the high-minded conceptual world of Middle Platonism. In their present form, these are naive in philosophical matters: "To say it pointedly: the [Martyrdom of Andrew] is a treatise in philosophical religion whereas the [Acts of Andrew and Matthias]"—as well as Gregory's *Epitome*—"is just a juicy story."[52]

3.4 Masculinity and Gender Roles

Recent scholarship on the Acts of Andrew has drawn attention to the subversion of certain gender roles in the narrative, especially in the Martyrdom of Andrew.[53] If masculinity in the Greco-Roman world is defined in part by a man's mastery over his household (οἶκος, *oikos*) and its affairs, the Martyrdom of Andrew represents Aegeates as stripped of this mastery: over his wife, his brother, his slaves, and even his emotions and appetites.[54] Because Aegeates lacks self-mastery, he is no longer deserving of this role: the master of the household is shown to be master of none. By contrast, Maximilla exhibits extreme moderation and self-control, as represented most pointedly in her celibacy. Though this contrast might seem to "render the woman masculine and the man feminized," in fact the text focuses more on Aegeates's emasculated character than Maximilla's masculinity. As Jennifer Eyl argues, the author retrains the reader to think of ethical matters "such that the Christian message alone supplies a supreme ethos and overrides any person's presumed

---

51. Dennis R. MacDonald, *Christianizing Homer: The Odyssey, Plato, and the Acts of Andrew* (Oxford: Oxford University Press, 1994), 301.

52. A. Hilhorst and P. Lalleman, "The Acts of Andrew and Matthias: Is It Part of the Original Acts of Andrew?," in *The Apocryphal Acts of Andrew*, ed. J. Bremmer, Studies on the Apocryphal Acts of the Apostles 5 (Leuven: Peeters, 2000), 9.

53. See Virginia Burrus, *Chastity as Autonomy: Women in the Stories of the Apocryphal Acts*, Studies in Women and Religion 23 (Lewiston, NY: Mellen, 1987); Jennifer Eyl, "Apocryphal Acts of the Apostles," in *The Oxford Handbook of New Testament, Gender, and Sexuality*, ed. B. Dunning (Oxford: Oxford University Press, 2019), 387–404; Schroeder, "Embracing the Erotic in the Passion of Andrew"; Saundra Schwartz, "From Bedroom to Courtroom: The Adultery Type-Scene and the *Acts of Andrew*," in *Mapping Gender in Ancient Religious Discourses*, ed. T. Penner and C. Vander Stichele (Leiden: Brill, 2006). On the relationship between Andrew and Stratocles, see Christy Cobb, "Madly in Love: The Motif of Lovesickness in the Acts of Andrew," in *Reading and Teaching Ancient Fiction: Jewish, Christian, and Greco-Roman Narratives*, ed. S. Johnson, R. Dupertuis, and C. Shea, WGRWSup 11 (Atlanta: SBL Press, 2018), 29–42.

54. Eyl, "Apocryphal Acts of the Apostles," 400.

'nature.' As a practitioner of ascetic Christianity, even a woman can excel like a man"; on the other hand, "if that ascetic Christian message is rejected, even the most powerful and ideal man suffers the moral weaknesses of women."[55]

4. KEY PASSAGES FOR NEW TESTAMENT STUDIES AND THEIR SIGNIFICANCE
4.1 Andrew in the New Testament

The apostle Andrew is mentioned twelve times in the New Testament. Often it is merely in passing as the brother of Peter (Matt 4:18//Mark 1:16, 29) and/or listed among the other apostles (Matt 10:2//Mark 3:18//Luke 6:14; Acts 1:13). However, Mark and John, by their unique references to Andrew, appear to have more interest in this apostle than Luke and Matthew (Mark 1:29; 13:3; John 6:8; 12:22). John's Gospel recounts perhaps the most important canonical Andrean story (which is absent from the Synoptic Gospels), the "finding" of the Messiah by Andrew, who then introduces his brother Simon Peter to Jesus. Thus, in John, Andrew is the first of the Twelve to follow Jesus (John 1:40).

Despite these references to Andrew in the New Testament, the diverse texts comprising the Acts of Andrew arguably do not depend on any of them.[56] This is not to say that the Acts of Andrew has no knowledge of Andrew in the New Testament texts—that would be an argument from silence. Rather, whatever its knowledge of Andrew traditions, the Acts of Andrew builds upon and goes beyond the New Testament in a variety of creative directions.

4.2 The Acts of Andrew and the New Testament

Many of the parallels to the New Testament are of a general sort that could either reflect a casual link to the New Testament or merely the common idiom of the Mediterranean religious world of late antiquity. For instance, Andrew's exhortation for Maximilla and Iphidama to "rejoice in the Lord" echoes Philippians 4:4, but the parallel has little significance. Other connections, however, appear to be more substantial. These we will explore in each of the three Andrean corpora we have been considering: the Acts of Andrew and Matthias, Gregory's *Epitome*, and the Martyrdom of Andrew.

4.3 The Acts of Andrew and Matthias and the New Testament

On the one hand, the Acts of Andrew and Matthias "contains no introductory formulae that refer to written texts and no extended citation that exactly replicate canonical wording."[57] On the other hand, the work constantly echoes the New Testament.[58] For instance, Jesus's past actions are recounted—some of which recall events from the canonical Gospels, while others are not found there. As an example of the former, Andrew recalls how Jesus performed various healings and miracles, including the feeding of the five thousand with loaves and fish, echoing the account found in the fourfold canonical Gospels (10.5–9). As an instance of the latter, Andrew recounts how he went to "the temple of the gentiles"

---

55. Eyl, "Apocryphal Acts of the Apostles," 400.

56. According to MacDonald, Acts Andr. Mth. 10.7–8 is the only possible reference to any of the NT passages that directly mention Andrew. Yet even here Acts Andr. Mth.'s account more closely parallels the Synoptic feedings of the five thousand (which do not mention Andrew) than John's account where Andrew plays an active role (John 6:8–9).

57. Snyder, "Christ of the Acts of Andrew and Matthias," 250. The issue is complicated by ancient media, what Snyder calls "the dynamic, multi-media nature of the ongoing Christian conversation about Jesus. Producers of [Acts Andr. Mth.] may well have read Gospel texts, but they had also heard stories about Jesus recounted in oral form" (250).

58. Snyder, "Christ of the Acts of Andrew and Matthias," 250.

with Jesus and was confronted by the high priests. The religious elite challenged Jesus, who enlivened a sphinx in the gentile temple to prove to them that he is "God and not a human" (13.5). The sphinx even goes so far as to raise the patriarchs to prove that Jesus called them. Predictably, the priests still do not believe. The episode, calculated to prove Jesus's divinity, echoes New Testament texts about Jesus's origin (Mark 6:3 parr.; John 6:42), the primacy of Jesus over Abraham (John 8:56–58), and the ineffectiveness even of one returning from the dead to produce belief (Luke 16:31). Yet it does not precisely match any of these texts. Thus, the Acts of Andrew and Matthias appears to access the language and symbolic world of the New Testament at times to bolster points about Jesus's status, or to communicate in the increasingly well-known language of the Gospels, but it rarely develops these references in a sustained way.[59]

In addition to alluding to the Gospels, the Acts of Andrew and Matthias echoes the canonical Acts of the Apostles in ways that help the text make a case for its legitimacy. Thus, the Acts of Andrew and Matthias begins by clearly evoking Acts: "At that time, all the apostles were gathered together in one place" (1.1; see Acts 2:1). Similarly, the lot assigning the city of the cannibals "falls to Matthias," just as the lot falls to him in Acts (1.2; see Acts 1:26). Like the Paul of Acts, Andrew is shown what he must suffer (18.10; see Acts 9:16), and Jesus speaks to Matthias out of a light before he regains his sight (3.1; see Acts 22:6, 13). Matthias, like Paul and Barnabas, sings in prison (3.6; see Acts 16:25). Andrew even challenges God's faithfulness with words from Luke-Acts, lamenting while tortured, "Lord, where are your words which you spoke to us to strengthen us, telling us, 'If you walk with me, *you will not lose one hair from your head*'?" (28.6; see Luke 21:18; Acts 27:34). Thus, alluding to the canonical Acts of the Apostles proved to be a useful, if ultimately ineffective, strategy for establishing the Acts of Andrew and Matthias's legitimacy in the mind of readers.

4.4 Jesus in the Acts of Andrew and Matthias

Before turning to the relationship of Gregory's *Epitome* with the New Testament, a special note is required on a feature peculiar to the Acts of Andrew and Matthias (as compared to Gregory's *Epitome* and the Martyrdom of Andrew)—namely, its characterization of Jesus. Unlike the other Andrean texts, in the Acts of Andrew and Matthias Jesus appears as a flesh-and-blood, present character "who plays an active participatory role in almost every scene [of the Acts Andr. Mth.], and who is characterized as directing and determining the course of events."[60] Perhaps the most memorable example is Jesus's sending of Andrew to rescue Matthias from the city of the cannibals. Jesus brings about Andrew's arrival by preparing a boat, and "he himself was in the boat like a human captain, and he had brought on board two angels whom he had transformed to look like humans" (Acts Andr. Mth. 5.2). The literary device of an unrecognizable Jesus, familiar from the Road to Emmaus account (Luke 24:13–35), heightens narrative suspense—*When will the characters realize it is Jesus?*—and thus the reader's enjoyment. What the readers are privy to takes Andrew thirteen more chapters to discover, and only after Jesus has the angels put Andrew ashore while the apostle sleeps and Jesus returns to heaven (16.6). As with Emmaus, Jesus is unrecognizable when present and recognizable only after departing.

---

59. On parallels between the Acts Andr. Mth. and the NT, see further Hilhorst and Lalleman, "Acts of Andrew and Matthias," 7.

60. Snyder, "Christ of the Acts of Andrew and Matthias," 256. She also notes that the Acts Andr. Mth. "highlights Jesus's divinity and his ongoing presence with his people."

Unlike Emmaus, however, here the apostle asks the Lord to forgive his ignorance, and Jesus immediately reappears "like a most beautiful small child" (18.4), proving to Andrew that "I can ... appear to each person in any form I wish" (18.8).[61]

The resulting Christology of the Acts of Andrew and Matthias is mixed. On the one hand, the text makes clear that Jesus is divine and "can do anything" (18.8). On the other hand, Jesus's full humanity is, as Snyder observes, "strikingly absent."[62] As Prieur and others have noted, in stepping into the world of the Acts of Andrew, we are not in the world of precise theological definitions, nor of late-antique christological and Trinitarian debates. Whether those behind the text would have denied the validity of these debates is unknowable; all that can be said is that the text does not weigh in on them and instead presents a playful, simple Christology convenient to the needs of the story.[63]

4.5 Gregory's *Epitome* and the New Testament

The deeds of wonder narrated in Gregory's *Epitome* inevitably echo the miracles and exorcisms of Jesus in the canonical Gospels. Oftentimes the connections are idiomatic and simple, as when Andrew tells Gratinus to "*get up* in the name of the Lord Jesus Christ, *stand up* whole, and *sin no more, lest you incur a worse ailment*" (*Epitome* 5.7; see John 5:8, 14). Similarly, Lysimachus's confession that "truly Christ, whom his servant Andrew preaches, is the Son of God" invariably calls to mind the centurion's confession at the cross (*Epitome* 12.22; see Mark 15:39 par.), though recognizing the parallel adds little depth to one's interpretation of the text.[64]

A more sustained intertextual relationship occurs in *Epitome* 27: a possessed young boy falls at Andrew's feet, and the demoniac's address to the apostle echoes Legion's plea in the canonical parallels: "What do we have to do with you, Andrew? Have you come here to tear us from our dwellings?" (27.2; see Mark 5:7 parr.). Andrew tells onlookers, "Don't be afraid, but believe in Jesus our Savior," calling to mind Jesus's words from the same chapter in Mark (27.3; see Mark 5:36). Having rebuked the demons, Andrew then permits the youth to go home, again recalling the conclusion of the Legion pericope (27.6; see Mark 5:19 par.). Thus, these intertextual parallels are sustained and consistent, showing that Andrew does what Jesus did and is therefore trustworthy. Ultimately, however, it is difficult to know if the parallels with the New Testament in the *Epitome* reflect the primitive Acts of Andrew or merely Gregory's orthodox handling of the text.[65]

In addition to these textual parallels, Gregory's *Epitome* also notably includes copies of "the Gospel" as a device for warding off evil. In addition to the aforementioned woman sold into prostitution who repels men with "the Gospel" (*Epitome* 23), the lecherous old man Nicolaus unwittingly carries "the Gospel" into a brothel, causing a prostitute to see him as an angel and flee (*Epitome* 28). Thus, the Gospels are not only textual fields of

---

61. As Snyder rightly points out, even "Jesus's adopting human form in [Acts Andr. Mth.] is thus part of its depiction of him as divine" ("Christ of the Acts of Andrew and Matthias," 258). What Lalleman calls Jesus's "polymorphy" in the Acts of John applies equally well to the Acts Andr. Mth. (Pieter J. Lalleman, "Polymorphy of Christ," in *The Apocryphal Acts of John*, ed. J. N. Bremmer, Studies on the Apocryphal Acts of the Apostles 1 [Kampen: Kok Pharos, 1995], 97–118).

62. Snyder, "Christ of the Acts of Andrew and Matthias," 259.

63. Prieur and Schneemelcher, "Acts of Andrew," 115.

64. The text also evokes the canonical Acts in a similarly shallow way: *Epitome* 11.15 (Acts 6:15); *Epitome* 12.18 (Acts 7:54); *Epitome* 17.7 (Acts 13:26); *Epitome* 24.13 (Acts 4:8); *Epitome* 29.10 (Acts 10:34); *Epitome* 30.12 (Acts 16:28).

65. Of interest on this point is the Coptic account of the exorcism of Varianus, which contains a parallel to the parable of the ten virgins independent of Gregory (*Epitome* 18b.36 [Matt 25:6]). Likewise, *Epitome* 18b.14 is in Armenian and echoes Acts 10:9.

reference in Gregory's *Epitome* but also material objects brandished in the ongoing war with the devil.

4.6 The Martyrdom of Andrew and the New Testament

Of the Andrean textual traditions, the parallels between the Martyrdom of Andrew and the New Testament are the least numerous and developed. Nevertheless, a few striking references echo from the text:

- Andrew says that Aegeates's father is the devil (Mart. Andr. 40.2); similarly, a group of wicked servants has the same parentage (21.4; see also 49.3), recalling the invective of John 8:44: "You are from your father the devil, and you choose to do your father's desires" (NRSV).
- Andrew's question as to whether the inner man in Maximilla has "anywhere to lay his head" (Mart. Andr. 42.6) brings to mind the logion in Matthew 8:20 par.[66]
- "After all, what benefit is there for you who gain for yourselves external goods but don't gain your very selves?" (Mart. Andr. 57.1) echoes Jesus's warning about gaining the whole world at the cost of one's soul (Mark 8:36 parr.).
- Though Andrew essentially eclipses Jesus in the Martyrdom of Andrew, he is also likened to Christ: before dying on a cross, the crowd is in uproar over Andrew's sentence, taking Pilate's sentiment as their own: "What crime did the man commit? What evil has he done?" (59.8; see Mark 15:14 parr.).
- Finally, Andrew, like Jesus, commits his spirit to God (63.6; see Matt 27:50 par.).

Beyond these Gospel allusions, the Martyrdom of Andrew develops a conceit in which Maximilla is likened to Eve and Andrew to Adam. Unlike the original pair, their relationship is passionless and does not produce progeny. As such, they avoid the things that "tripped up" the original couple since "it is ordained that each person correct his or her own fall" (36.12). The analogy calls to mind the new-Adam typology of Romans 5:12–17. Indeed, comparison with Paul reveals how different the Martyrdom of Andrew's soteriology is and the limited role Christ plays therein, since it is Andrew, not Jesus, who plays the role of the second Adam. Overall, however, the Martyrdom of Andrew evinces the fewest connections to the canonical New Testament of the Andrean texts, causing some to regard it as the earliest stratum of the Acts of Andrew traditions—from a time purportedly before the New Testament had canonical status and influence.[67]

5. BIBLIOGRAPHY

Bremner, Jan N., ed. *The Apocryphal Acts of Andrew.* Studies on the Apocryphal Acts of the Apostles 5. Leuven: Peeters, 2000.

Elliott, J. K. "The Acts of Andrew." Pages 231–302 in *The Apocryphal New Testament: A Collection of Apocryphal Christian Literature in an English Translation.* Oxford: Clarendon, 1993.

MacDonald, Dennis R. *The Acts of Andrew.* Early Christian Apocrypha 1. Santa Rosa, CA: Polebridge, 2005.

———. "*The Acts of Andrew and Matthias* and *The Acts of Andrew.*" *Semeia* 38 (1986): 9–26.

---

66. Hilhorst and Lalleman, "Acts of Andrew and Matthias," 7.

67. Thus Roig Lanzillotta writes: "The most primitive text [i.e., Vatican Gr. 808] does not seem to include any relevant NT references.... At the time of the [Acts Andr.]'s composition, the New Testament as such did not exist" (Lautaro Roig Lanzillotta, "The Acts of Andrew and the New Testament: The Absence of Relevant References to the Canon in the Primitive Text," in *Christian Apocrypha: Receptions of the New Testament in Ancient Christian Apocrypha*, ed. T. Nicklas and J.-M. Roessli, Novum Testamentum Patristicum 26 [Göttingen: Vandenhoeck & Ruprecht, 2014], 187–88).

———. *The Acts of Andrew and the Acts of Andrew and Matthias in the City of the Cannibals.* SBLTT 33.1. Atlanta: Scholars Press, 1990.

Prieur, Jean-Marc. *Acta Andreae.* 2 vols. CCSA 5–6. Turnhout: Brepols, 1989.

———. "Les Actes apocryphes de l'apôtre André: Présentation des diverses traditions apocryphes et état de la question." *ANRW* 25.6:4383–414. Part 2, *Principat*, 25.6. Edited by H. Temporini and W. Haase. Berlin: de Gruyter, 1988.

———. "Acts of Andrew." *ABD* 1:244–47.

Prieur, Jean-Marc, and Wilhelm Schneemelcher. "The Acts of Andrew." Pages 101–51 in volume 2 of *NTApoc*.

Roig Lanzillotta, Lautaro. "The Acts of Andrew: A New Perspective on the Primitive Text." *Cuadernos de Filología Clásica* 20 (2010): 247–59.

Santos Otero, Aurelio de. "Acta Andreae et Matthiae apud anthropophagos." Pages 443–47 in volume 2 of *NTApoc*.

Snyder, Julia A. "Christ of the Acts of Andrew and Matthias." Pages 247–62 in *Christ of the Sacred Stories*. Edited by Predrag Dragutinović, Tobias Nicklas, Kelsie G. Rodenbiker, and Vladan Tatalović. WUNT 2.453. Tübingen: Mohr Siebeck, 2017.

CHAPTER 13

ACTS OF JOHN

HAROLD W. ATTRIDGE

1. INTRODUCTION

The Acts of John tells a story of the apostolic activity of John, the son of Zebedee, understood to be the Beloved Disciple prominent in the Fourth Gospel. The work survives in segments with different histories of transmission that have been reassembled by modern editors. The Acts of John shows affinities with other popular accounts of the lives of the apostles, although at least one section seems to have affinities with ancient gnostic literature. While showing how traditions about the apostle developed in Christian circles that valued celibacy and had distinctive views about Christ's divinity, it also suggests ways in which the Fourth Gospel influenced some second-century Christians.

1.1 Authorship

By the time of the Byzantine scholar Photius (d. 893), all the major apocryphal Acts were attributed to Leucius Charinus, an unlikely attribution given their diversity. The original author of the Acts of John remains unknown, and the very assumption of a single author for that work is problematic, since the extant evidence of the Acts of John suggests that it developed over time.

1.2 Language

The original language of the Acts of John was certainly Greek. Portions of the work, especially the concluding *Metastasis*, or "departure" of John to heaven, were translated into other Christian languages, and portions survive in Latin, Syriac, Armenian, Coptic, Georgian, and Arabic.[1]

1.3 Provenance

The setting of John's story is eastern Asia Minor, particularly Ephesus, where tradition held that the apostle was buried.[2] That setting may indicate the place of composition, but there is little, if any, local detail in the story that would support such a provenance. Other locations are possible, including the interior of Asia Minor, Syria, and Egypt, but definite evidence is lacking.

---

1. For a detailed account of the versions, see Kurt Schäferdiek, "Acts of John," in *NTApoc* 2:159–62.
2. Eusebius, *Hist. eccl.* 3.39.1–7, citing the testimony of Papias. The tombs of the apostle and the presbyter John are also mentioned in a letter of Dionysius, bishop of Alexandria (248–264 CE), in Eusebius, *Hist. eccl.* 7.25.15.

1.4 Date

The Acts of John is first explicitly attested by Eusebius (*Hist. eccl.* 3.25.1–6) in a discussion of recognized, non-genuine, and absolutely impious books. The last category included the Acts of John. There is also evidence of its use in the Manichaean Psalter from the late third century. That the Acts of John took original shape in the second century is likely, but a more precise date is debated. The work has affinities with second-century gnostic texts that share views of Christ's polymorphous nature. Pieter Lalleman finds the form of Gnosticism in the Acts of John to be pre-Valentinian and therefore dates the work to the early second century.[3] There are certainly connections with second-century speculative theology, but their imprecise character may reflect not the development of a theological system but the genre of the Acts of John, which is content to allude to a conceptual system and not to present it in detail. Some scholars suggest a mid-second century date.[4] The major modern editors, Eric Junod and Jean-Daniel Kaestli, plausibly date the Acts of John to the late second century, finding traces of it in works of the late second and third centuries— namely, the Acts of Peter, the Acts of Thomas, and the Acts of Paul.

1.5 Text

The first critical edition of the Acts of John by Maximilian Bonnet appeared in the late nineteenth century.[5] The most thorough modern edition is by Eric Junod and Jean-Daniel Kaestli.[6] Several English translations are available,[7] using the chapter numbers originally assigned by Bonnet, even when subsequent editors have decided on a different order of the surviving materials.

The text produced in modern critical editions is based on a complex array of manuscript evidence.[8] Four segments, chapters 18–36, 37–55, 58–86, and 106–115, were transmitted through the Acts of John of Ps.-Prochorus, a work of the fifth or sixth century focusing on the miracles of John on Patmos. The final segment, chapters 106–115, containing the story of the death and departure (*Metastasis*) of John, was transmitted with the Acts of John in Rome, which provides the introductory chapters in Bonnet's edition. The *Metastasis* also appeared as an independent piece used in liturgical celebrations of the saint.[9] A small section, chapters 56–57, appears with the beginning of the Acts of John of Ps.-Prochorus and in an Armenian translation of that work. The segment of the text with the most interesting and potentially controversial theology, chapters 87–105, was transmitted separately in a hagiographical collection dating to 1319. This segment has been variously located in modern critical editions. In addition to these manuscript witnesses, there is one papyrus

---

3. Pieter J. Lalleman, *The Acts of John: A Two-Stage Initiation into Johannine Gnosticism* (Leuven: Peeters, 1998), 208–12, 268–70.

4. Charles Hill, *The Johannine Corpus in the Early Church* (Oxford: Oxford University Press, 2004), 259.

5. Maximillian Bonnet, in Albert Lipsius and Maximillian Bonnet, *Acta Apostolorum Apocrypha II.1* (Leipzig: Mendelssohn, 1889; repr., Hildesheim: Olms, 1972), 151–216.

6. Eric Junod and Jean-Daniel Kaestli, *Acta Iohannis*, 2 vols., CCSA 1–2 (Turnhout: Brepols, 1983), 2:694–700.

7. Schäferdiek, "Acts of John," 2.215–58; M. R. James, *The Apocryphal New Testament: Being the Apocryphal Gospels, Acts, Epistles and Apocalypses, with other Narratives and Fragments* (Oxford: Clarendon, 1926), 228–70, revised and updated by J. K. Elliott, *The Apocryphal New Testament* (Oxford: Oxford University Press, 1993), 303–49; and, most recently, Richard I. Pervo with Julian Hills, *The Acts of John*, Early Christian Apocrypha 6 (Salem, OR: Polebridge, 2016).

8. See Junod and Kaestli, *Acta Iohannis*; Schäferdiek, "Acts of John," 2.156–57.

9. For the complex manuscript tradition of this portion of the Acts of John, see Junod and Kaestli, *Acta Iohannis*, 317–43.

fragment, P.Oxy. 850, which reports another episode in John's life that may belong in a lacuna in the narrative.

2. SUMMARY OF CONTENT

2.1 Preliminary: Acts of John in Rome

Chapters 1–14 of Bonnet's edition are based on the Acts of John in Rome, probably dating from the fifth century or later and surviving in two recensions.[10] Although not part of the original Acts of John, it helped to preserve the older work and is summarized here.

This story reports that Emperor Domitian, informed by Jews living in Rome about the new Christian sect and its apocalyptic prophet, ordered John arrested and brought from Ephesus to the capital (chs. 1–4). John travels to Rome, fasting all the way, to the amazement of the accompanying soldiers (chs. 5–6). Presented to Domitian and asked about his prophecy, John responds with a proclamation of Christ's future kingship (chs. 7–8). Domitian reacts by giving him a cup of poison, which John drinks with no ill effects (ch. 9). The scene dramatizes Jesus's prediction in the longer ending of Mark that if his disciples "drink any deadly thing, it will not hurt them" (Mark 15:18 NRSV). This account inspired the popular icon of John with poisonous cup in hand. To assure a suspicious Domitian that the poison was real, John gives it to a condemned criminal, who dies but is immediately raised by the apostle, showing that God's power overcomes any evil (chs. 10–11). This account parallels the miraculous resurrections featured in the Acts of John proper.

Impressed by what he sees, Domitian does not condemn John to execution but only exiles him to a distant island. Before departing, John raises from the dead a servant of the emperor stricken suddenly by an unclean demon (chs. 12–13). John travels to Patmos, where he resides until Trajan's reign, when he returns to Ephesus. There he dies in old age, leaving the leadership of the community to Polycarp (ch. 14).

One recension of this version of John's story has three more chapters that serve to transition to the account of the original Acts of John.[11] These chapters report that after coming ashore in Asia, John evangelizes a small village while seated on a rock (ch. 15). He then goes to Miletus, performs miracles, and again drinks a poisonous cup unharmed (ch. 16). The villagers erect a memorial to the apostle, incorporating the rock on which he once sat. That rock regularly emits fragrant myrrh as a sign of the belief of the faithful (ch. 17). The final verse introduces the narrator's first-person voice, which tells the story of the travel from Miletus to Ephesus.

2.2 The Surviving Acts of John

What remains of the original Acts of John falls into five large blocks (A: 18–35; B: 87–105; D: 37–55; F: 58–86, G: 106–115) and two small segments (C: P.Oxy. 850; E: 56–57) of narrative. The location of B (87–105) is based on the narrative logic of the conversion of Drusiana and Andronikos.[12]

Block A, Chapters 18–35: John Arrives in Ephesus and Raises the Dead

The surviving text of the Acts of John begins with John coming to Ephesus. Prior to this section there may have been a story, such as that found in other apocryphal Acts, of the apostles casting lots to determine who will evangelize what part of the world.

---

10. See Bonnet, *Acta Iohannis*, 151–60; Junod and Kaestli, *Acta Johannis*, 862–86.
11. Bonnet, *Acta Johannis*, 160.
12. Schäferdiek, "Acts of John," 178–79.

Or there may have been an account of resurrection appearances of Jesus to his apostles. The surviving text begins (ch. 18) with the voice of a narrator who tells of the apostle's progress. John, impelled by a vision, was departing from Miletus to travel to Ephesus. Several characters, Damonikos, a relative named Aristodemos, Kleobios, and the wife of Marcellus, convince John to rest with them for a day. These characters may have been part of the lost material that preceded this account, which probably told of John's travel to and activity in Miletus. Rising at dawn, John hears a voice promising a glorious time for him and those Ephesians who come to belief through him. The apostle moves ahead, filled with joy.

When John arrives in Ephesus, Lykomedes, a local nobleman, greets him outside the city and prostrates himself in supplication. His wife, Kleopatra, had just tragically died, and Lykomedes had experienced a vision in which a mysterious messenger predicted John's coming and promised that the apostle could assist him. John follows Lykomedes, while a companion from Miletus, Kleobios, deals with local arrangements (ch. 19).

At home Lykomedes delivers a melodramatic speech lamenting Kleopatra's death. He threatens to take his own life and then complains before the throne of divine justice that Kleopatra had treated him unjustly by her untimely death (ch. 20). Melodrama continues as Lykomedes, after one last rhetorical outburst, falls dead beside his wife. John then offers his own self-pitying lament, claiming that he would be blamed for the nobleman's death. He finally converts his sorrow to a prayer that his Lord would restore the deceased husband and wife (ch. 21).

Upon the news of Lykomedes's demise, a large crowd assembles. Seeing the opportunity to make an impression, John beseeches Christ in his usual rhetorical style. Citing Jesus's teaching, "Ask and it will be given you," the apostle approaches Kleopatra, and in the name of Jesus Christ tells her to arise (ch. 22). A simple command, however, is not enough. So John touches Kleopatra's face and offers a more elaborate summons. Dead for seven days, Kleopatra responds, amazing the Ephesian crowds. When she asks about her husband, John reassures her that she will see him soon (ch. 23).

John and Kleopatra approach the corpse of Lykomedes, provoking Kleopatra's profound grief. John tells her to command her husband to rise. Obedient to his wife, Lykomedes does so and falls at the feet of the apostle, who tells him to worship God instead (ch. 24). The resuscitated husband and wife invite the apostle to stay with them, an invitation that John, along with his Milesian companions, accepts (ch. 25).

A Portrait of John

The next four chapters constitute a discrete vignette with a particular point. In response to the apostle's miracle, Lykomedes commissions the apostle's portrait (ch. 26). The artist executes a sketch and on the next day adds colors and presents it to Lykomedes, who decks it with flowers and installs it in his private chamber. Wondering what Lykomedes is about, John visits the room, where he sees an old man's portrait decorated with flowers surrounded by burning lamps. He asks Lykomedes if he still worships a pagan deity. The noble responds that he only worships the one who raised him from the dead, an earthly benefactor whom he acknowledges as a "god" (ch. 27). Amazed to see his portrait, John challenges Lykomedes to prove that the picture accurately portrays him. When the noble responds with a mirror, John proclaims that while the image may resemble him, it does not capture his essence, the virtues by which he lives (ch. 28). He challenges Lykomedes to paint a portrait using such colors, an image of a living being in his own soul. By comparison, physical art is ridiculous (ch. 29).

John Assembles Elderly Women in the Theatre

The next seven chapters also constitute a discrete story. John begins by commissioning a believing servant, Verus, who remains with John to the end, to gather the elderly women of Ephesus. Verus does so, with the assistance of Kleopatra and Lykomedes. Only four sexagenarians are in good health; the rest suffer from various illnesses and disabilities. John asks that they be brought to the famous theater of Ephesus (ch. 30). Having told the crowds at Lykomedes's home to join him, John arrives to find the Roman governor present along with Andronikos, a leading citizen. Apparently suspecting that John is a magician, Andronikos challenges him to come to the theater naked and refrain from using his favorite magical name (ch. 31). John responds by ordering the women to be brought in (ch. 32) and then delivers an address explaining his purpose, which is not to make a magical display but to turn unbelief to belief (ch. 33). He continues, warning the crowds not to assemble treasures on earth, which only cause grief (ch. 34). He sternly admonishes them to repent of their sins of adultery, greed, anger, and drunkenness, to abandon their commitment to luxury and whatever evil deeds they enjoy. They should know that even emperors and princes will depart this world naked (chs. 35–36).

The account breaks off before describing the impact of John's rhetoric. The magistrate, Andronikos, along with his wife, Drusiana, will appear in chapter 37, but as believers. The story of their conversion, perhaps resulting from whatever wonder John worked in the theater, has probably been lost. Drusiana's prayer in chapter 82 alludes to a number of events in her life perhaps contained in the missing section, including her conversion to celibacy, the resistance by her husband Andronikos, his attempt to rape her, and his conversion.

Block B, Chapters 87–105: John's Gospel
A Remembrance of Jesus's Last Song and Dance

This section contains the most distinctive theological elements of the Acts of John, presented as an explanation by John of a vision experienced by Drusiana. The story's placement in Bonnet's edition was probably based on the reference to the Drusiana-Callimachus interaction appearing in chapters 63–86, but Drusiana's claim to have seen Jesus does not match anything in that account.[13] The segment consists of two major parts. The first is based on Jesus's last interactions with his disciples in the Farewell Discourse in the Fourth Gospel (John 13–17). The second segment parallels the Fourth Gospel's account of the passion, with its own special perspective. As in the canonical Gospel, the two segments reinforce one another.

Drusiana's report that Jesus both resembled John and a youth causes consternation (ch. 87). John offers an explanation that will enable his disciples to perceive the "glory" that ever envelops Jesus, a category at the heart of the Fourth Gospel. John's testimony consists of a series of reports of the multiple forms in which Jesus appeared to him, beginning with his own call to discipleship. Jesus had invited John and his brother, James, to approach him. James thought he saw a little child; John, a handsome man (ch. 88). Jesus later appeared to John as an old man, bald and bearded, but to James as a youth with a new beard. John then notices that Jesus's eyes never blinked and that he sometimes appeared as a small, unattractive person gazing at the sky, perhaps a recollection of the famous depiction of Socrates sketched by Plato (*Symposium* 220 C–D). Echoing the Fourth Gospel's account of the Last Supper (John 13:23), the apostle reports that he used to lie on Jesus's chest, which sometimes felt smooth, sometimes hard, perhaps suggesting that Jesus transcended

---

13. As argued by Schäferdiek, "Acts of John," 179.

traditional gender markers. The chapter ends on an unfinished note that John wondered about this polymorphism (ch. 89).

John then reports a series of appearances of Jesus on mountain tops. In one such appearance, Jesus was enshrouded in light; in another he seemed to be naked, but with snow-white feet and head extended to the heavens. John reacted in terror, and Jesus responded by pulling John's beard, which ached for months. At the same time, Jesus admonished John to be "not faithless but believing" (ch. 90). Peter and James did not enjoy the same vision, since they asked John who was the old man with whom he had been speaking. John replied that they should ask him (ch. 91).

Not all John's recollections have obvious connections to familiar gospel accounts. He reports hearing a nocturnal conversation between Jesus and someone else who complained that the disciples did not believe in him, to which Jesus responded that they were only human (ch. 92).

John reports that Jesus was sometimes tangible, sometime incorporeal. He then reports a special example at a meal in the house of a Pharisee. While all received a loaf of bread from the hosts, Jesus distributed his loaf in small pieces to the disciples, totally satisfying them, while their own loaves remained untouched. The allusion to Christian eucharistic practice is clear, and the play on tangible and intangible serves as a comment on that ritual.

John also tried to see Jesus's footprints, but never found one, anticipating a famous description of the Christ of the Fourth Gospel by Ernst Käsemann as a "god walking above the earth" (ch. 93). John's observation, like Käsemann's quip, poses the question of how seriously this text takes the incarnation and the human reality of Jesus.

John then recalls what Jesus said before he was arrested by the "lawless Jews," intensifying the Gospel's anti-Jewish polemic. Jesus does not simply speak with his disciples, as in the Johannine Farewell Discourse, but leads them in song and dance. As they circle round holding hands, they offer communal praise, addressing the divine with multiple epithets: Father, Word, Grace, Spirit, Holy One, Light (ch. 94). The referents of these designations are unclear, since the divine world is complex. The hymn will also refer to the "one Ogdoad" and to a "Duodecad," presumably of heavenly beings. After the doxology, Jesus expresses his hope through balanced, sometimes paradoxical couplets, asking to be saved and to save, to be freed and to free, to be wounded and to wound, to be born and to beget, to eat and to be eaten, combinations all suggesting his mediatorial role in the salvific process. After a celebration of participation in heavenly realities, Jesus makes a series of paradoxical affirmations. He has no house, place, or temple, but possesses many. Evoking Johannine imagery, he declares himself to be lamp, mirror, door, and path (ch. 95). He then invites the dancers to see themselves in him, to understand what he does, embracing the suffering of humankind, to which he gives meaning; though shaken, they have rest in him. Jesus declares that once he departs his disciples will discover who he is, something not now obvious. Knowledge about him is also knowledge about suffering, from which he offers an escape. He declares himself their God, not the "god of the betrayer," and renews an invitation to share his celestial song and learn his wisdom. The hymn closes with another doxology, glorifying Father, Word, and Spirit, and then the Father alone, a somewhat more "orthodox" pattern than evident earlier (ch. 96).

John's Experience of the Cross

John's recollection then continues to follow the arc of the Fourth Gospel, moving to the crucifixion. The narration moves quickly, apparently assuming a knowledge of stories of Jesus's passion and offering its own perspective on the testimony of the Beloved Disciple.

After the song and dance, the disciples flee. John sees Jesus suffering, but, unlike the Gospel, he does so from a distance, having taken refuge on the Mount of Olives. There Jesus appears to him in a cave and tells him that he has been hung on a cross, pierced and given vinegar and gall to drink. John thus has a report about the crucifixion, from divine teacher to human pupil, not an immediate perception. The insistence on the roles of teacher and pupil and the goal of transcending, immediate experience to discover deeper meaning will pervade the following discourse (ch. 97).

John then sees a vision of a luminous cross surrounded by a mass of people. Jesus's voice tells him to distinguish the ultimate reality from the images used to depict it. The divine teacher, condescending to the limited capabilities of his pupils, has used images to point to the reality: word, mind, Christ, door, way, bread, seed, resurrection, son, father, spirit, life, truth, faith, and grace. Jesus tells John that the results of the educative enterprise are to create a distinction between the "left," its principalities, powers, demons, and passions, and the "right," who are in line with Wisdom (ch. 98).

Jesus summarizes his message about the true cross, which is not the wooden artifice used for execution but, by implication, a principle to distinguish cosmic truth and falsehood. If the true cross is something other than the wooden structure, so too the true Jesus is not the body hanging on the cross but the revealer who speaks to John, an ineffable reality (ch. 99). The teaching about the cross and the nature of Christ has implications for human salvation, which Jesus proceeds to explain. The people around the cross are the "lower nature." Authentic humanity is of a higher, nonmaterial nature that unites with Jesus and is taken up to the spiritual realm with him. The notion of mutual indwelling, so prominent in the Johannine Farewell Discourse, here comes into play. Jesus proclaims that all those who belong to him will be like him. He is with the Father and the Father with him. So, by implication, those who believe in him are united with the Father (ch. 100).

Jesus then explains his suffering on the cross, which did not happen as commonly reported. He was not really pierced, injured, or crucified. He says that he is speaking enigmatically, unlike the Jesus of the Farewell Discourse. He then challenges John to understand all the aspects of the passion—arrest, piercing, blood, wounding, hanging, suffering, nailing, and death—as attributes of the Word or Logos, the key term of the Johannine Prologue. Understand that Word, Jesus says, and one will understand both the Lord and his "humanity" (ch. 101).

John then reports that Jesus invisibly ascended to heaven. The apostle descended from the mountain, laughing at all who had spoken about Jesus in their uncomprehending way. He understood that Jesus had done things as symbols for the salvation of humankind (ch. 102). The apostle closes his instruction with an exhortation to worship Jesus not with bodily parts but with souls correctly disposed. Believers should be vigilant in all the trials and tribulations that they suffer, since the Lord is with them in their pain (ch. 103). The heart of his message is that John is not proclaiming a human being for them to worship but the invincible God himself. Knowing that, they will have an imperishable soul (ch. 104). The episode ends with John walking away with Andronikos. Drusiana and the other faithful follow at a distance.

Segment C, P.Oxy. 850

The fragment of a narrative about John found among the papyri unearthed in the nineteenth century in Oxyrhynchus, Egypt, was probably a part of the Acts of John. Locating its contents is a matter of conjecture, but it may be placed after the account of Jesus's teaching and before the rest of the story of John's activity in Ephesus.

One side (the *verso*) of the fragmentary papyrus involves an encounter between John and a man named Zeuxis, to whom the apostle had just given the Eucharist, and a Roman proconsul. Exactly what the interaction involved is uncertain. The other side (*recto*) of the papyrus reports an encounter between John and a threatening soldier. John tells the man that the Lord will quench his anger, and the man disappears. John then goes to his assembled disciples and bids them celebrate God's victory over the enemy.

Block D, Chapters 37–55: More Activity in Ephesus
The Destruction of the Temple of Artemis

The apostle's companions from Miletus suggest that they have spent enough time in Ephesus and should go to Smyrna. Andronikos, by now a disciple, responds that they should defer to their teacher. John suggests that they should instead visit the Temple of Artemis (ch. 37).

Two days later, John and his disciples arrive at the temple, where a festival of dedication is underway. John, wearing black among worshipers clad in white, causes offense and is arrested. The Ephesians want to kill him. Telling them that they are mad, John climbs a platform and preaches (ch. 38). He tells the Ephesians that they are behaving like rivers and springs made bitter by the ocean. Their ancient pieties have prevented them from seeing the miracles that John has done in their midst. He challenges them to ask Artemis to slay him. If that does not work, he will ask his God to punish their unbelief with death (ch. 39). The Ephesians, familiar with John's power and obviously not confident in their deity, ask for mercy. John responds that he will beg God's mercy, but they should abandon their deception (ch. 40). John offers a prayer to that end, asking God to destroy the demon that has deceived the multitude (ch. 41). The prayer is successful. The altar shatters, and statues fall to the ground in pieces; part of the building collapses, killing a priest. The people respond, confessing belief in John's God and begging for mercy (ch. 42). John glorifies Jesus, "the only true God," and bids the crowd acknowledge his power while he mocks Artemis (ch. 43). The newly converted crowd completes the destruction of the temple, acknowledges what they have come to understand, and begs for the apostle's acceptance (ch. 44). John responds that he will not leave for Smyrna until he has weaned his converts from nurse's milk and given them something solid, not food but a rock on which to stand (ch. 45).

John and a Priest of Artemis

In the aftermath of the temple's destruction, a relative of the dead priest brings his corpse to the home of Andronikos, where the apostle is presiding over a Eucharist. The man leaves the corpse outside and enters the home during the ceremony. After the ceremony, John congratulates the man on his concern for true salvation rather than for taking care of his dead relative (ch. 46). John rewards him in a now familiar way. Taking his hand, the apostle leads him to the corpse and, as he told Drusianna, bids the man to command the priest to rise. John then tells the risen priest that he is not fully alive and invites him to believe in the Lord Jesus. The priest does so and becomes a disciple of the apostle (ch. 47).

Deadly Lust

Prompted by a dream, John goes for a walk outside the city, where he meets a young man involved in an adulterous relationship. The man's father had tried to convince him to end that affair. Rejecting the advice, the man angrily kicked his father to the ground and left him lifeless (ch. 48). The man fled, sickle in hand. John met him and asked about the tool.

The man acknowledged his evil deed and indicated that he intended to kill his lover, her husband, and himself (ch. 49). John tells the young man to show him his dead father. The man promises that if his father is restored to life, he will leave his lover (ch. 50). When they find the corpse, John reproves the man for his crime. Torn by grief, the man begs for his father's life and asks for mercy (ch. 51). Risen from the dead, the old man complains that he is being restored to misery. John reassures him that he is rising to a better situation. When they return to the city, the old man becomes a believer (ch. 52). The youth, meanwhile, uses his sickle to castrate himself and delivers the severed genitals to his former lover, denouncing her in the process (ch. 53). He reports his actions to John, who condemns the act of self-castration as another work of the evil power that had prompted the youth to commit adultery and murder. John admonishes the man to cut off instead the shameful impulses that led him to sin in the first place. The young man repents and becomes another of John's devoted disciples (ch. 54). At this point John receives an invitation from the Smyrnaeans to come to their city and instruct them about his God (ch. 55).

Segment E, Chapters 56–57: Activity in Smyrna

This segment of the Acts of John, transmitted independently, describes the apostle's arrival in Smyrna and one episode there. Upon his arrival, John is greeted by a prominent citizen, Antipatros, who has twin sons, thirty-four years of age, demon-possessed since birth, whom he will poison if they cannot be healed. He offers John a hundred thousand pieces of gold to cure them. John notes that his "physician" does not accept money (ch. 56). With a brief prayer, John exorcizes the demons and baptizes the sons in the name of Father, Son, and Holy Spirit. They depart, praising God (ch. 57).

Block F, Chapters 58–86: Back to Ephesus

The brief account of an exorcism at Smyrna was hardly the only miracle that John performed there, but his other activity at that site has been lost. In what follows there are references to individuals who will travel to Ephesus with John. The stories of their conversions and other adventures have been lost.

Departure from Smyrna

John announces his departure from Smyrna, telling the locals that he had promised the Ephesians that he would return to them. The Smyrnaeans grieve, but John consoles them, promising that their love for Jesus will ensure continuing fellowship with him (ch. 58). The list of John's traveling companions includes Andronikos and Drusiana, familiar from earlier segments. Others, Aristoboula, whose husband had died, Aristippos, Xenophon, and a "chaste prostitute" no doubt became disciples during John's time in Smyrna (ch. 59).

John and the Bedbugs

The narrator's "we" recounts an incident on the way from Smyrna to Ephesus. In a lonely inn, John's companions let him sleep on the single bed in their room. During the night he is bothered by a horde of bedbugs. His companions are amused to hear John rebuke the insects (ch. 60). In the morning, they see a large group of bugs gathered by the door. When John awakes and rises from the bed, he courteously tells the insects that they may return to their home in the bed, which they immediately do. He draws a moral from the story that humans should be as obedient to the word of God as the insects were to a human's request (ch. 61).

In Ephesus, with Drusiana and Kallimachos

John receives a warm reception at the home of Andronikos (ch. 62). Among the guests is a young man, Kallimachos, who is obsessed with love for Drusiana, the now celibate wife of Andronikos. Conversations between Kallimachos and other guests, who are trying to dissuade him from his fixation, reveal details of the story of the conversion of Drusiana and her husband. Andronikos had resisted Drusiana's attraction to celibacy, confining her to a tomb and threatening her with death if she did not continue as his wife. Drusiana obviously won that test of wills. Recollection of that experience does not restrain Kallimachos (ch. 63). Drusiana staunchly resists the pleas of Kallimachos, sending him into a listless despair. She grieves that she has become a source of temptation, falls ill, and dies. The apostle is unaware of all these developments (ch. 64). Andronikos laments, and John provides conventional solace that Drusiana has passed to a better state. Andronikos is consoled, knowing his beloved sister in Christ died in a state of purity (ch. 65).

Finally learning of the circumstances of Drusiana's demise, John is perturbed (ch. 66). He offers a reflection, invoking different professions, a ship's captain, a sower, a racer, a boxer. All are acknowledged as successes only when they have reached their goal (ch. 67). John argues that people of faith are similar and have many obstacles to face before attaining their goal. These obstacles include vices, vanity, anger, laziness, lust, and human conditions, wealth and pretensions that distract them from their goal (ch. 68). Believers must keep their eyes on the prize. John assembles an array of other illustrations of the point, a general at war, a physician working to heal. He offers a catalogue of the ways in which souls can fail to meet their goal, misled by longing for what is transient, temporal, or valueless. He concludes with a summons to extol the soul that perseveres and is not misled by money, lust, or anger (ch. 69).

While John preaches, Kallimachos plots. He bribes a servant to open Drusiana's tomb and allow him to sexually assault her corpse, mocking her as he attempts to do so (ch. 70). A serpent stymies his assault. Emerging from the tomb, it strikes and kills the bribed servant. It does not, however, strike Kallimachos, but winds round his feet, hissing. When Kallimachos collapses, the serpent settles on his chest (ch. 71). John, Andronikos, and some other faithful companions visit Drusiana's tomb. Unable to find the keys to the tomb, John suspects, incorrectly at least at a physical level, that Drusiana may not be in it and predicts that the doors will be open (ch. 72). The doors of the tomb do open at John's command, and a smiling youth seated by Drusiana's grave greets them. He reports that he has brought Drusiana to his realm for a short time and then ascends to heaven. John sees the corpse of the servant, now named Fortunatus, and the serpent coiled on the chest of Kallimachos. He wonders why his Lord has kept him in the dark about what has happened (ch. 73). Andronikos, remembering the threats of Kallimachos and knowing his desire for Drusiana, explains the situation to John. He says that Fortunatus does not merit salvation but asks that John raise up Kallimachos to confess what he has done (ch. 74). John dismisses the serpent and bids Kallimachos to rise. He does so but remains silent (ch. 75). John enquires about why he had come to the tomb. Kallimachos confirms what Andronikos had surmised. John then asks whether Kallimachos had been successful. The youth then explains what happened after the encounter with the serpent. After tearing off Drusiana's burial garments, he had attempted to rape her but was prevented by a luminous young man who protected her with his cloak. He told Kallimachos, "Die that you may live!" which is the command that put him into the condition in which John found him. Now raised by John, Kallimachos, in a lengthy speech, dramatically begs for forgiveness, proclaims that his sinful self has died, and promises that he will live as one faithful to God (ch. 76). John then offers an emotional prayer of thanks and praise to Jesus Christ, who preserved Drusiana and brought about the repentance of Kallimachos (ch. 77). John welcomes Kallimachos, confirming his call to a new life (ch. 78). Andronikos and the other faithful then ask that John do to Drusiana what he had done to Kallimachos and raise her from the dead (ch. 79). John goes to the grave, takes Drusiana's hand, offers a prayer celebrating God's supreme power over all creation, and asks for Drusiana's restoration. He then commands her to rise. She does so, somewhat puzzled about why she is so scantily clad. Andronikos explains what has taken place, and Drusiana joins the joyous assembly (ch. 80).

The Dire Fate of Fortunatus

Drusiana is not the only one to benefit from divine mercy. She sees Fortunatus and, displaying exemplary compassion, asks John to raise him as well, even if he did betray her. Kallimachos protests, arguing that the heavenly voice that spoke to him mentioned only Drusiana, not the servant. John rebukes him and offers a little sermon on the pity and compassion that God shows and expects of the faithful. He tells Kallimachos that if he will not allow John to raise Fortunatus, Drusiana will have to do the deed (ch. 81). Drusiana prays to Jesus, recalling the major events in her story, the appearance of Jesus in many forms, his protection from and the conversion of Andronikos, and her resurrection. She asks Jesus to raise Fortunatus as well (ch. 82). She then takes the servant's hand and bids him rise. Fortunatus reacts differently from the other beneficiaries of divine power. He views the faithful people surrounding him as dreadful, says he had no desire to be raised, and flees from the tomb (ch. 83). John delivers a condemnatory tirade, declaring Fortunatus a hopelessly lost soul, naturally unsuited for salvation, a Satan to be forever excluded from the fellowship of the faithful and all their rituals (ch. 84). The mention of rituals introduces a eucharistic celebration, where John brings bread (but not wine) into the grave. He offers a eucharistic prayer, praising the name of the Lord and giving thanks to Jesus for giving his people the unshakable conviction that he alone is God (ch. 85). John distributes the Eucharist to the faithful and returns to the home of Andronikos. He tells the faithful that Fortunatus will die from the serpent's bite and sends people to check on him. Someone does go and finds Fortunatus three-hours dead, his body, including his heart, decaying. John dismisses him as an offspring of the devil (ch. 86).

Block G, Chapters 106–115: John's Departure

John's farewell sermon begins by recalling all the signs and wonders God has done for the faithful in Ephesus through him. He asks them to remember God in all they do, knowing that Jesus understands sin and treachery (ch. 106). John admonishes his faithful to a life of virtue by invoking God, Jesus Christ, who will rejoice with them when they live nobly. The virtues John enjoins include purity, celibacy, sharing goods, self-denial, and love of God. John also reassures the faithful by enumerating what they have, God's pledges, his generous gifts, his presence, his mercy. He finally warns them that return to their old ways will result in punishment (ch. 107).

John then offers a prayer, invoking with a series of images the God and Lord, Jesus Christ, who wears a woven crown and an imperishable bouquet, who has sown seeds, protected his servants, and heals without charge. John beseeches him to assist his servants (ch. 108). He then offers a prayer over the eucharistic bread, praising Jesus in names spoken by him, Father and Son, and describing him with multiple images and titles familiar from the Gospels. He explains how that multiplicity of terms works, enabling the faithful to comprehend the invisible majesty of Jesus, which can only be apprehended by those formed by him (ch. 109). John distributes the Eucharist, offers a greeting of peace to the congregation, and then departs with his faithful companion, Verus, and two servants, equipped with baskets and shovels (ch. 110).

John instructs the servants to dig a deep trench, while he continues preaching and praying. The narrator's voice emerges and notes that none of "us" understood what the trench was for. When the trench is complete, John removes his outer garments and lays them at the bottom (ch. 111). John then prays to his God, the Lord Jesus, listing the ways Jesus has made himself known to the world, and asks him to receive his soul (ch. 112). He continues praying, rehearsing his own history of interaction with Jesus, providing details not recorded elsewhere, that Jesus prevented John from marrying, that he blinded John for two years, that he taught John, sight restored, not even to look at a woman. John celebrates Jesus who guided him to look to what is eternal and spiritual and worked in many other salvific ways. The apostle, his work declared complete, then again asks Jesus to grant him salvation (ch. 113). He adds a poetic prayer that inimical powers be overcome, the fires of Gehenna quenched, the devil muzzled, and his offspring banned. John's journey then may end without harm (ch. 114). With his prayers concluded, John asks Jesus to be with him, wishes peace to his brethren, lies in the grave, and like his master gives up his spirit, rejoicing (ch. 115).

Possible Citations

Three passages in a fifth-century Latin apocryphon, the Epistle of Pseudo-Titus, report episodes about John, perhaps connected to the Acts of John. In the first, John before his death gives thanks that he has been kept pure from the touch of a woman. The second reports that demons declared to the deacon Dyrus (presumably Verus) that they could possess those who boast of their continence. The third reports an address by John to a bride and groom at a wedding, persuading them to embrace celibacy.[14]

3. INTERPRETIVE ISSUES
3.1 History and Johannine Legend

John the son of Zebedee was one of the earliest disciples of Jesus, recruited with his brother James as a disciple from the shores of the Sea of Galilee early in Jesus's career (Matt 4:21; Mark 1·19; Luke 5:10). The brothers, nicknamed Boanerges, or "Sons of Thunder" (Mark 3:17), were listed among the Twelve (Matt 10:2; Mark 3:17; Luke 6:14; Acts 1:13) and in their naivete were not afraid to ask for a special place in Jesus's kingdom (Mark 10:35). The brothers were companions of Jesus at critical moments of his ministry, his transfiguration (Matt 17:1–9; Mark 9:2–10; Luke 9:28–36) and his agony in the garden (Matt 26:37; Mark 14:33). The sons of Zebedee were explicitly named as among the disciples to whom the resurrected Jesus appeared (John 21:2).

The Fourth Gospel tells of a disciple whom Jesus loved, who reclined close to him at his last supper (John 13:33), who stood at the foot of the cross (19:26), who outran Peter to the tomb on Easter morning (20:2–4), and who, unlike Peter, "believed" when he saw the burial cloths (v. 8). This disciple also told Peter who it was that appeared to them while fishing (21:7). Tradition identified this beloved disciple with John, the son of Zebedee, although the Gospel itself does not do so, a situation that has stimulated considerable speculation.[15]

---

14. For these citations, see Elliott, *Apocryphal New Testament*, 346–47.
15. Speculation about the identity of the Beloved Disciple is carefully catalogued by James H. Charlesworth, *The Beloved Disciple: Whose Witness Validates the Gospel of John?* (Valley Forge, PA: Trinity Press International,

In the second century, Papias, cited in Eusebius's *Ecclesiastical History*,[16] reported on his efforts to identify the authors of early Christian texts. He mentioned both John the son of Zebedee and another John, the elder or presbyter, a disciple of the apostle, who like the apostle was also buried in Ephesus. Little survives from any legends about the apostle that Papias may have discovered.

Legends about the apostle did, however, circulate among second-century Christians.[17] At least one of these stories resembles the content of the Acts of John. Eusebius records that an opponent of the late second-century prophetic movement known as Montanism reported on a resurrection performed by John at Ephesus.[18] Other stories bear little relationship to what remains of the Acts of John. Clement of Alexandria tells of John's relationship with a young man whom he leaves in the care of a bishop. The young man goes astray and leads a lawless life until the apostle seeks him out and secures his repentance.[19] Tertullian reports that, in an effort to kill him, John was cast into a tub of boiling water, which did him no harm.[20]

The heresiologist Irenaeus, writing around 180 CE, reports of an encounter in the baths of Ephesus between John and a gnostic teacher, Cerinthus, from whom John flees in disgust.[21] That story may reflect debates about the authentic theological interpretation of the Fourth Gospel echoed in the theology of the Acts of John and the Johannine Epistles.

Apart from the discrete legends found in patristic sources, some "gnostic" sources such as the Apocryphon of John frame their distinctive theology with a report of an appearance of the resurrected Jesus to the apostle John in which he conveys cosmic secrets to the apostle.[22]

Later apocrypha continue the development of the Johannine legend, sometimes preserving elements of the Acts of John.[23] These include the sixth-century Pseudo-Abdias, *Virtutes Iohannis*;[24] Pseudo-Melito, *Passio Iohannis*;[25] the fifth- or sixth-century Syriac Acts of John;[26] and the *Liber Flavus Fergusiorum*, a fifteenth-century Irish work dependent on Pseudo-Melito but with independent traditions.[27]

1995). On the literary function of the anonymous disciples, see Harold W. Attridge, "The Restless Quest for the Beloved Disciple," in *Early Christian Voices: In Texts, Traditions, and Symbols: Essays in Honor of François Bovon*, ed. D. H. Warren, A. G. Brock, and D. W. Pao, BibInt 66 (Leiden: Brill, 2003), 71–80, reprinted in Harold W. Attridge, *Essays on John and Hebrews*, WUNT 264 (Tübingen: Mohr Siebeck, 2010), 20–29.

16. Eusebius, *Hist. eccl.* 3.39.1–7.

17. On traditions about John the apostle in general, see R. Alan Culpepper, *John the Son of Zebedee: The Life of a Legend*, Studies on Personalities of the New Testament (Columbia: University of South Carolina Press, 1994; repr., Minneapolis: Fortress, 2000).

18. Eusebius, *Hist. eccl.* 5.18.14.

19. Clement of Alexandria, *Quis div.* 42.

20. Tertullian, *Praescr.* 36.3.

21. Irenaeus, *Haer.* 3.3.4. On the Fourth Gospel in Irenaeus, see Bernhard Mutschler, *Irenäus als johanneischer Theologe: Studien zur Schriftauslegung bei Irenäus von Lyon*, Studien und Texte zu Antike und Christentum 21 (Tübingen: Mohr Siebeck, 2004), and idem, *Der Corpus Johanneum bei Irenäus von Lyon: Studien und Kommentar zum dritten Buch von Adversus Haereses*, WUNT 189 (Tübingen: Mohr Siebeck, 2006).

22. See Ap. John NHC II 1 1.1–2.23, translated in Bentley Layton, with David Brakke, *The Gnostic Scriptures* (New Haven: Yale University Press, 2021), 30–31. On the appropriation of the Fourth Gospel in that text, see David Creech, *The Use of Scripture in the Apocryphon of John*, WUNT 2.441 (Tübingen: Mohr Siebeck, 2017).

23. For a survey, see Elliott, *Acts of John*, 347–49.

24. Junod and Kaestli, *Acta Johannis*, 799–834, containing Acts of John chs. 62–86 and 106–115.

25. Junod and Kaestli, *Acta Johannis*, 764–71.

26. Junod and Kaestli, *Acta Johannis*, 109–12.

27. James, *Apocryphal New Testament*, 469–70.

Whatever their relationship with the Acts of John, the various surviving legends indicate that the apostle continued to provide fertile territory for the Christian imagination. That fact reflects the larger phenomenon of the widespread popularity of the Fourth Gospel, and therefore of its reputed author, in the second century and beyond.[28]

3.2 The Acts and Other Second-Century Christians

Much of the narrative of the Acts of John resembles legends found in other apocryphal Acts. These include the adaptation of popular tropes of ancient novels to foster extreme asceticism, and the interaction between humans and animals, or in this work, insects.[29] There are, however, some distinctive conceptual elements rooted in second-century strands of Christian theology.

3.2.1 Theology

One of the most complex theological elements of the Acts of John is its understanding of God. Some passages display an apparent Trinitarian prayer, naming Father, Son, and Holy Spirit (57). A more complex picture appears when John expounds his gospel (block B: 87–105). A triad, similar to that of the baptismal formula, stands at the beginning (93) and end (96) of the hymn that John sings as he dances with his disciples, but within that hymn, he refers to an Ogdoad of heavenly powers and to "the twelfth number" that "dances on high." These seem to be elements of the heavenly world like the array of aeons or emanations from the ultimate source of all being found in descriptions of the celestial world attributed to Valentinians, "gnostic" teachers active in Rome and Egypt in the mid-second century.[30] Other elements of the theology of the Acts of John also point to some connection with Valentinians.

3.2.2 Christology: Polymorphism and Docetism

Perhaps the most distinctive theological element of the Acts of John is its Christology, which echoes second-century teachings criticized by heresiologists such as Irenaeus and Tertullian. The Acts of John makes two significant and related affirmations about Christ: (1) that he is so divine as to be indistinguishable from the Father, and (2) that his physical manifestation, transient and unstable, and what happens to it, is insignificant. The first position is often labeled Sabellianism or Patripassianism (the claim the Father suffers on the cross); the second, docetism.

The intimate relationship of Jesus and the Father is grounded in the Johannine affirmation that Jesus and the Father are one (John 10:30). The Acts of John affirms that intimate unity in John's recollection of Jesus's address to his disciples, telling them that they will know that he is their God when he departs (ch. 96). To the crowds in the theater of Ephesus, John proclaims Jesus, "the only true God" (ch. 43). John prays to Jesus as God alone (ch. 85) and repeats that address in his final prayer (chs. 107, 108, 111).

Several third-century teachers, known primarily through their opponents, expressed a

---

28. On the early history of the Fourth Gospel, see Hill, *Johannine Corpus*, who rejects the claim that the Fourth Gospel was primarily popular among "gnostics," and Tuomas Rasimus, *The Legacy of John: Second-Century Reception of the Fourth Gospel*, NovTSup 132 (Leiden: Brill, 2010).

29. On the role of animals, see Janet Spittler, *Animals in the Apocryphal Acts of the Apostles: The Wild Kingdom of Early Christian Literature*, WUNT 2.247 (Tübingen: Mohr Siebeck, 2007).

30. See Irenaeus, *Haer.* 1.1.1–2. On Valentinians in general, see Einar Thomassen, *Spiritual Seed: The Church of the "Valentinians"* (Leiden: Brill, 2006). On connections with the school, see Lalleman, *Acts of John*, and Gerard Luttikhuizen, "A Gnostic Reading of the Acts of John," in Bremmer, *Apocryphal Acts of John*, 119–52.

similar position and explained the distinction between Father and Son as one of different "modes" of being. A teacher named Noetus, originally from Smyrna and thus perhaps an heir to the tradition represented in the Acts of John, was active in Rome in the early third century and was criticized by the heresiologist Hippolytus.[31] Tertullian, writing in North Africa around the same time, criticized a Roman teacher named Sabellius, whose position resembled that of Noetus.[32] The Alexandrian bishop Dionysius (248–264 CE), cited by Eusebius, also criticized Sabellius.[33] Interpretation of Johannine traditions is clearly involved in these debates. Thus, Hippolytus notes of John 10:30, "the Father and I are one," that the verb is plural, indicating that there are two persons and one power. He also interprets Jesus's comment to Philip that whoever has seen him has seen the Father (John 14:9), arguing that the verse implies knowledge of the Father, not directly but *through* the Son.[34]

Even more clearly articulated in the Acts of John is the position that the physical manifestation of Jesus is unimportant. This judgment is supported by the polymorphism of Jesus. The segment of the Acts of John highlighting John's teaching begins with a description of the apostle's experiences of Jesus in various shapes and forms (chs. 88–89). In the beginning of the segment on Drusiana and Kallimachos, the heroine summarizes her experience of Jesus in similar terms, perhaps alluding to a lost part of the Acts of John (ch. 82).

The theme of multiplicity reappears when John reviews his teaching, first in the dance hymn (ch. 94) and then in his recollection of the passion (ch. 98). In both passages the variety of images for Jesus, largely derived from the Fourth Gospel, makes the point. The implications of that multiplicity are clear in the teaching about the spiritual character of the cross and the Savior's body (chs. 99–100).

Other second-century Christian literature presented a similar understanding of the spiritual character of Christ. At least one other apocryphon offers a close parallel. Eusebius cites a work by Serapion, bishop of Antioch at the end of the second century (191–211 CE), condemning the docetism of the Gospel of Peter.[35] That Gospel, rediscovered in the nineteenth century, contains an account of the passion resembling that of the Acts of John.[36]

It is possible that on the point of its Christology, the Acts of John conforms to at least part of the Valentinian tradition, since "eastern" Valentinians taught that Christ was "spiritual," although their position may have had more to do with the character of Jesus's true self than with the physical character of his body.[37] Some Valentinian texts apparently affirm the reality of the incarnation.[38]

3.2.3 Anthropology

In one other doctrine, the Acts of John apparently represents the Valentinian theory that humankind was divided into three types: "spiritual" people, saved by nature; "hylic" or "material" people, condemned by nature; and "psychics," who had to choose whether or not to be saved. The theory combines elements of predestination and free will. How

---

31. See Hippolytus, *Contra haeresin Noeti.*
32. Tertullian, *Adversus Praxean.*
33. Eusebius, *Hist. eccl.* 7.6.1; 7.26.1.
34. Hippolytus, *Contra haeresin Noeti* 7.
35. Eusebius, *Hist. eccl.* 6.12.1–6.
36. For the text, see Elliott, *Apocryphal New Testament,* 150–58. For a recent assessment, see Jeremiah Johnston, *Resurrection of Jesus in the Gospel of Peter: A Tradition-Historical Study of the Akhmîm Gospel Fragment* (London: Bloomsbury T&T Clark, 2016).
37. See Thomassen, *Spiritual Seed.*
38. See the third-century Tripartite Tractate NHC I 5 115.3–11.

the two blended differed among different Valentinian teachers.[39] Such a theory seems to lie behind the description of Fortunatus as "hopelessly lost" and "naturally unsuited" for salvation. The same anthropological background seems to be involved in John's vision of the physical cross, surrounded by people of a "lower nature," while authentic humanity ascends on high with Christ to its spiritual home (ch. 100).

3.2.4 Christian Life

While distinctive doctrinal positions appear in the Acts of John, it shares with other apocrypha a concern with a virtuous life and a radical sexual ethic focused on chastity. The allusion preserved in Acts of John 62 suggests that the lost story of the conversion of Drusiana and Andronikos involved the summons to renounce marital relations, like that of other apocrypha.[40] A similar concern appears in the third citation of the Acts of John in the Epistle of Pseudo-Titus. The Acts of John also paints a lurid portrait of sexual desire in the story of Kallimachos's attempt to rape Drusiana's corpse. Yet the Acts of John shows disapproval of the self-castration (ch. 54); triumph over lust should take place through heroic self-control.

4. KEY PASSAGES FOR NEW TESTAMENT STUDIES AND THEIR SIGNIFICANCE
4.1 Relationship to the New Testament

The Acts of John alludes to various New Testament passages, but its major source for imagery and language is the Fourth Gospel. Its teachings also may reflect the position of members of the Johannine community who separated from those to whom the first epistle of John was addressed.

Several items recall the Synoptics and especially Matthew. The series of appearances of Jesus on mountain tops evokes the transfiguration (Matt 17:1–5; Mark 9:1–8; Luke 9:28–29). Before raising Kleopatra (Acts John 22), John recalls the saying of Jesus, "Ask and it will be given you" (Matt 7:7; Luke 11:9). The action of the self-castrating youth (Acts John 53) dramatizes the saying about eunuchs (Matt 19:12), although the Acts of John disapproves. Jesus's promise of "rest" to his followers (Acts John 96) echoes Matthew 11:28–29. The trinitarian baptismal formula (Acts John 57) recalls the Great Commission (Matt 28:19).

Lukan allusions are less prominent. The setting of a dinner conversation with a Pharisee (Acts John 93) recalls several Lukan stories (Luke 7:36; 11:37; 14:1). There are faint echoes of the canonical book of Acts. John's command to Kleopatra to arise (Acts John 22) recalls the command to a lame man in the Jerusalem Temple spoken by Peter, in John's company (Acts 3:6). The reminiscence may reflect the rivalry between Peter and the Beloved Disciple in the Fourth Gospel; the resurrection of Kleopatra is a more impressive miracle than healing a cripple. The name of the wicked servant who facilitated Kallimachos's attempted rape of Drusiana was Fortunatus (Acts John 70–86). The name is the Latin equivalent of Greek Eutychus, in English "Lucky," the name of Paul's disciple. Lulled to sleep by the apostle's preaching, he fell to his death (Acts 20:7–12) but enjoyed a more lasting resurrection than that of Fortunatus.

---

39. See Jean-Daniel Dubois, "Once Again, the Valentinian Expression 'Saved by Nature,'" in *Valentinianism: New Studies*, ed. C. Markschies and E. Thomassen, NHMS 96 (Leiden: Brill, 2020), 193–204. On the debate between Origen and Heracleon, the Valentinian commentator on the Fourth Gospel, see Harold W. Attridge, "Heracleon and John: Reassessment of an Early Christian Hermeneutical Debate," in *Biblical Interpretation, History, Context, and Reality*, ed. C. Helmer (Leiden: Brill, 2005), 57–72. Free will, at least in the spiritual realm, is emphasized in the Tripartite Tractate (NHC I 5); see NHC I 5 75.35.

40. See the treatment of Encratism in the introduction to the Acts of Thomas in this volume (ch. 17).

The Acts of John uses some expressions familiar from the Pauline corpus. The trope contrasting milk and solid food as stages of learning (1 Cor 3:1–2; Heb 5:12) appears with a twist, contrasting nurse's milk with a solid rock on which to stand (Acts John 45). The saying thus also evokes the Matthean simile of the house built on rock (Matt 7:24–27) and the designation of Peter as the church's foundation stone (Matt 16:18). In the Acts of John, however, it is John on whom correct tradition rests. The command given to Kallimachos to die that he might live (Acts John 77) echoes Paul's metaphor of baptismal death (Rom 7:4–8).

Imagery from Revelation appears in one account of the polymorphism of Jesus, who is seen with "snow white feet and head" (Acts John 90), evoking Revelation 1:14.

4.2 The Fourth Gospel[41]

The literary framework of the Acts of John, with a narrator speaking in the first person (Acts John 19), recalls the "we" passages of canonical Acts (16:10–13; 20:6, 13–15; 21:1–8), but also the "we" of the Fourth Gospel's prologue and final epilogue (John 1:14, 16; 21:24).

While there are such allusions to New Testament texts, connections to the Fourth Gospel are abundant. Some seem to be incidental. The notion that Fortunatus was considered an "offspring of the Devil" (Acts John 86), although probably reflecting a complex anthropology, evokes the polemical language used against Jesus's adversaries in John 8:44. Following the Johannine pattern, "the Jews" also appear as enemies responsible for the arrest of Jesus (Acts John 94). That Jesus claims to be speaking enigmatically (Acts John 101) recalls, by contrast, his declaration that he is then speaking *plainly* to his disciples (John 16:25). Jesus indicated that he did not always do so, and in fact the Fourth Gospel abounds in riddles.

More important connections are prominent. John's major miracle, done repeatedly, is to raise people from the dead (Acts John 22–23; 25; 47; 75; 80; 83). While the Gospels contain other resurrection stories, the raising of Lazarus is the most dramatic display of divine power in the Fourth Gospel (John 11:1–44) and serves as the model for the apostle's actions.

The structure and content of the major theological section of the Acts of John (87–105) abounds in Johannine elements. The overall pattern, moving from dialogue with disciples to the crucifixion, recalls the Fourth Gospel's structure and its Farewell Discourse anticipating the passion. Elements within the discourse clearly evoke the Gospel. The passage begins with John telling his disciples that he will enable them to see and understand Christ's "glory" (Acts John 88), a major theme in the Gospel (John 1:14; 2:11), intimately connected with the proper understanding of the cross (John 12:28–33; 17:1). Jesus's declaration that his disciples will discover who he is once he departs recalls a theme in the Gospel (John 2:22) emphasized in the Farewell Discourse (John 14:3–7, 20). Quite striking is the list of metaphors for Jesus: word, mind, Christ, door, way, bread, seed, resurrection, son, father, spirit, life, truth, faith, and grace (Acts John 98). Most of these terms, familiar from the Fourth Gospel,[42] reflect its characteristic pattern of complex imagery.[43] Some

---

41. On the Fourth Gospel in the Acts of John, see Lallemann, *Acts of John*, 110–23, and Harold W. Attridge, "The Acts of John and the Fourth Gospel," in *From Judaism to Christianity: Tradition and Transition*, ed. P. Walters, NovTSup (Leiden: Brill, 2010), 255–65.

42. Word: John 1:1; Christ: 1:17, 41; 4:25; 20:31; door: 10:7, 9; way: 14:6; bread: 6:35, 41, 48; resurrection: 11:25; Son: 3:16 and frequently; Spirit: 1:32; life and truth: 14:6; grace and truth: 1:14, 16–17.

43. On which, see Harold W. Attridge, "The Cubist Principle in Johannine Imagery: John and the Reading of Images in Contemporary Platonism," in *Imagery in the Gospel of John*, ed. J. Frey, J. G. Van der Watt, and

exceptions convey the distinctive theology of the Acts of John: "mind" (*nous*), connected to its anthropology, and "Father," expressing its high Christology. Some derive from other New Testament sources, including "seed" (Mark 4:26; Luke 8:5) and "faith" (perhaps Rom 1:5 and frequently), but the overall tenor is Johannine, and the Johannine stamp is clear in the several references to Jesus as Word (Acts of John 93; 95; 98; 101) or Wisdom (95; 98). All these images are framed with "educational" language, capturing the Gospel's rhetorical thrust.[44] Jesus, the spiritual instructor, aims to unite believers with the Father (Acts John 100), applying the Gospel's ideals of mutual indwelling (John 14:11; 17:21). The note that John's work has been completed marks the apostle's end (Acts John 113). When John lays himself in the tomb (115), he gives up his spirit. John's final remarks echo the Johannine crucifixion scene (John 19:30). Other elements of the passion account of the Acts (Acts John 97–105) recall canonical stories—namely, that Jesus was given vinegar (Mark 15:36; Luke 23:36; John 19:29) or wine mixed with gall (Matt 27:34) to drink (Acts John 97). The note that Jesus was "pierced" (Acts John 97; 101) is highlighted in the Johannine account (John 19:34–37), as is the report that John was a witness. Here, however, John does not stand by the cross (John 19:26) but observes from afar, distant from physical suffering (Acts John 97). Jesus's command to Thomas, "Do not doubt, but believe" (John 20:27) finds an echo in Jesus's initial encounter with John (Acts John 90).

Johannine connections are obvious, but the theology and Christology of the Acts of John stands at odds with the Gospel's insistence that the Word became flesh (John 1:14).[45] It is likely that the Johannine Christianity represented in the Acts of John bears some relationship to the schismatics mentioned in 1 John 2:19. They are probably the false prophets who do not confess that Jesus Christ has come in the flesh (1 John 4:1–2). Their tradition lives on in this text.

5. BIBLIOGRAPHY

Attridge, Harold W. "The Acts of John and the Fourth Gospel." Pages 255–65 in *From Judaism to Christianity: Tradition and Transition*. Edited by Patricia Walters. NovTSup. Leiden: Brill, 2010).

Bremmer, Jan N., ed. *The Apocryphal Acts of John*. Studies on the Apocryphal Acts of the Apostles 1. Kampen: Kok Pharos, 1995.

Cartlidge, David R. "Transfiguration of Metamorphosis Traditions in the Acts of John, Thomas and Peter." *Semeia* 38 (1986): 53–66.

Culpepper, R. Alan. *John, The Son of Zebedee: The Life of a Legend*. Studies on Personalities of the New Testament. Columbia, SC: University of South Carolina Press, 1994. Repr., Minneapolis: Fortress, 2000.

Lalleman, Pieter J. *The Acts of John: A Two-Stage Initiation into Johannine Gnosticism*. Leuven: Peeters, 1998.

Luttikhuizen, Gerard. "A Gnostic Reading of the Acts of John." Pages 119–52 in *The Apocryphal Acts of John*. Edited by Jan N. Bremmer. Studies on the Apocryphal Acts of the Apostles 1. Kampen: Kok Pharos, 1995.

MacDonald, Dennis R. "Jesus and Dionysian Polymorphism in the Acts of John." Pages 97–104 in *Early Christian and Jewish Narrative: The Role of Religion in Shaping Narrative Forms*. Edited by Ilaria Ramelli and Judith Perkins. WUNT 348. Tübingen: Mohr Siebeck, 2015.

MacNamara, Martin. *The Apocrypha in the Irish Church*. Dublin: Institute for Advanced Studies, 1975.

Pervo, Richard I. "Johannine Trajectories in the Acts of John." *Apocrypha* 3 (1992): 47–68.

Pervo, Richard I., with Julian Hills, *The Acts of John*. Early Christian Apocrypha 6. Salem, OR: Polebridge, 2016.

Schäferdiek, Kurt. "Acts of John." Pages 152–258 of volume 2 of *NTApoc*.

Schneider, P. G. *The Mystery of the Acts of John: An Interpretation of the Hymn and the Dance in the Light of the Acts' Theology*. San Francisco: Mellen Research University Press, 1991.

R. Zimmermann, WUNT 2.200 (Tübingen: Mohr Siebeck, 2006), 47–60, reprinted in idem, *Essays on John and Hebrews*, 79–91.

44. On this topic in the Gospel and its interpreters, see Jason S. Sturdevant, *The Adaptable Jesus of the Fourth Gospel: The Pedagogy of the Logos*, NovTSup 162 (Leiden: Brill, 2015).

45. Udo Schnelle, *Antidocetic Christology in the Gospel of John*, trans. L. Maloney (Minneapolis: Fortress, 1992).

CHAPTER 14

ACTS OF PAUL

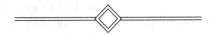

HAROLD W. ATTRIDGE

1. INTRODUCTION

The Acts of Paul tells of Paul's missionary activities, many involving prominent women, the foremost of whom is a determined ascetic and missionary, Thecla. It also enshrines a letter ascribed to Paul propounding a decidedly orthodox theology, and it recounts the circumstances of his martyrdom. The three major segments of the Acts of Paul—namely, the Acts of Paul and Thecla, 3 Corinthians, and the Martyrdom of Paul—were transmitted independently until modern times. They appear together in a Coptic papyrus now in Heidelberg, dating to the fifth or sixth century, discovered and published in the twentieth century.[1] This papyrus contains other stories of Paul's missionary activity in addition to the three major segments. Another papyrus, now preserved in Hamburg, contains the Martyrdom of Paul, two episodes immediately preceding it in the Heidelberg papyrus, and another episode not otherwise attested. This text, written in Greek in the fourth century, was also published in the twentieth century.[2] As with similar literature about other apostles, various accounts of Paul's activity and death circulated in antiquity. Whether all three segments were part of an original composition is unclear. It is likely that segments such as the Corinthian correspondence were additions to the stories about Paul's ministry and martyrdom. The whole collection first represented in the Heidelberg papyrus may have developed in stages.[3]

1.1 Authorship and Date

By the time of the Byzantine scholar Photius (d. 893), all the major apocryphal Acts—Andrew, Peter, Paul, John, and Thomas—probably collected together by Manichaeans in the fourth or fifth century, were attributed to one Leucius Charinus, an unlikely attribution given their diversity.[4] The textual history of the Acts of Paul complicates the question

---

1. Carl Schmidt, *Acta Pauli: Aus der Heidelberger koptischen Papyrushandschrift Nr. 1*, 2 vols. (Leipzig: Hinrichs, 1904). The second edition of volume one was published in 1905 and was reprinted by the publisher Olms in 1965.

2. Carl Schmidt and Wilhelm Schubart, *PRAXEIS PAULOU: Acta Pauli nach dem Papyrus der Hamburger Staats-und Universitäts-Bibliothek* (Glückstadt-Hamburg: Augustin, 1936); Erik Peterson, "Einige Bemerkungen zum Hamburger Papyrus-Fragment der Acta Pauli," *VC* 3 (1949): 33–35; reprinted in idem, *Frühkirche, Judentum, Gnosis* (Rome: Herder, 1959), 183–208.

3. Such is the general assessment of the work by Glenn E. Snyder, *The Acts of Paul*, WUNT 2.352 (Tübingen: Mohr Siebeck, 2013).

4. On the attribution, see Knut Schäferdiek, "The Manichean Collection of Apocryphal Acts Ascribed to Leucius Charinus," in *NTApoc* 2:87–100.

of authorship. At least one version of the Acts of Paul, however, is attested in the late second century by Tertullian:[5]

> Now should certain *Acts of Paul*, which are a fabrication, appeal to the example of Thecla as authorizing women to teach and to baptize, note that the Asian presbyter who concocted that document, aspiring to enhance Paul's standing, was exposed and, despite his plea that he acted out of love for Paul, renounced his office.[6]

Tertullian thus confirms that by about 190 CE a version of the Acts of Paul featuring Thecla circulated in western Asia Minor and that a local presbyter had claimed responsibility for the work. The Acts of Paul were known to Origen[7] in the third century and Eusebius in the fourth.[8]

1.2 Language

The original language of the Acts of Paul and its various components was certainly Greek,[9] but the work was translated into various languages, including Coptic,[10] Latin,[11] Armenian,[12] Syriac,[13] and Ethiopic.[14]

1.3 Provenance

The author of the version of the Acts of Paul mentioned by Tertullian resided in the Roman province of Asia (Western Turkey), the focus of much of Paul's missionary activity. According to the canonical Acts (19:10), he spent more than two years teaching in Ephesus, and it is highly likely that a Pauline "school" formed there, collecting his letters and producing others in his name. Ephesus, or any of the other centers of Christian activity in the province, would be a likely location for the composition of the Acts of Paul.

1.4 Text

The first critical edition of the Acts of Paul in the nineteenth century was based on the three independently transmitted segments:[15] the Acts of Paul and Thecla, which survives in some fifty manuscripts and numerous versions; 3 Corinthians, which survives in Greek,[16] Coptic, Armenian, and Latin versions; and the Martyrdom of Paul, which

---

5. Willy Rordorf, "Tertullien et les Actes de Paul (à propos de bapt. 17, 5)," in *Autour de Tertullien: Hommage à René Braun*, 2 vols., Publications de la Faculté des Lettres et Sciences Humaines de Nice 56 (Paris: Les Belles Lettres, 1990), 2:151–60.

6. Tertullian, *Bapt.* 17 (translation by Pervo, *Acts of Paul*, 43).

7. *Comm. John* 20.12; *Princ.* 1.2.3.

8. *Hist. eccl.* 3.3.5, "not among the uncontested works," and 3.25.4, "among the illegitimate writings."

9. For details of the versions, see J. K. Elliott, *The Apocryphal New Testament* (Oxford: Oxford University Press, 1993), 357–62.

10. Rudolph Kasser, "Acta Pauli 1959," *RHPR* 40 (1960): 45–57.

11. Otto von Gebhardt, *Passio S. Theclae virginis: Die lateinischen Übersetzungen der Acta Pauli et Theclae nebst Fragmenten, Auszügen und Beilagen* (Leipzig: Hinrichs, 1902).

12. See Samuel Berger and A. Carrière, "La correspondance apocryphe de saint Paul et des Corinthiens: Ancienne version latine et traduction du texte arménien," *RTP* 24 (1891): 333–51.

13. William Wright, *Apocryphal Acts of the Apostles: Edited from Syriac Manuscripts in the British Museum and Other Libraries*, 2 vols. (London: Williams and Norgate, 1871), 1:128–69; 2:116–45 (English translation).

14. E. J. Goodspeed, *The Book of Thekla* (Chicago: University of Chicago Press, 1901).

15. Richard Adelbert Lipsius and Maximillian Bonnet, *Acta Apostolorum Apocrypha*, 2 vols. (Leipzig: Mendelssohn, 1889; repr., Hildesheim: Olms, 1972), 1:235–72.

16. The most important witness is P.Bodmer 10, edited by M. Testuz, *Papyrus Bodmer X–XII* (Geneva: Bibliotheca Bodmeriana, 1959), also edited in Robert Matthew Calhoun, "The Resurrection of the Flesh in

survives in three Greek manuscripts, the earliest dating to the ninth century, and Latin, Coptic (P.Heidelberg), Syriac, Arabic, Ethiopic, Armenian, and Georgian versions. The manuscript discoveries of the twentieth century, the Hamburg, Heidelberg, and Bodmer papyri, as well as smaller finds,[17] have occasioned several reconstructions of the Acts of Paul and various English translations.[18] A new critical edition is in preparation in the series Corpus Christianorum Series Apocryphorum.[19]

2. SUMMARY OF CONTENT

The remains of the Acts of Paul may be conveniently arranged in fourteen chapters or episodes, each of which has a different setting.[20] The numbers of the subsections found in modern editions of the three blocks of material that survive in manuscripts are retained. For materials that survive primarily on papyri, the page numbers are indicated. Chapter 9, which is based on two papyri, also has subsection numbers, as in the translation of Richard Pervo.

1. From Damascus to Jerusalem[21]

In this fragmentary chapter, Paul enters Damascus, where he finds the community fasting. He then travels to Jerusalem via Jericho. He later (Acts Paul 9) tells of an encounter with a lion that occurred on this journey, perhaps originally reported here.

2. In Antioch on the Orontes[22]

This fragmentary chapter recounts the resurrection of a dead boy apparently related to Paul's converts, Anchares and his wife. After the miracle Paul is expelled from the city.

3. Paul and Thecla in Iconium (Acts Paul Thecla 1–25)[23]

1. After fleeing Antioch, Paul arrives at Iconium in the company of Demas and Hermogenes, who are false disciples. 2–3. Onesiphoros, his wife Lektra, and their two

---

Third Corinthians," in *Christian Body, Christian Self: Concepts of Early Christian Personhood*, ed. C. Rothschild and T. Thompson, WUNT 2.284 (Tübingen: Mohr Siebeck, 2006), 235–57.

17. See H. A. Sanders, "A Fragment of the Acta Pauli in the Michigan Collection," *HTR* 31 (1938): 70–90 [= P.Mich. 1317]; idem, "Three Theological Fragments," *HTR* 36 (1941): 165–67 [= P.Mich. 3788]; G. D. Kilpatrick and C. H. Roberts, "The Acts Pauli: A New Fragment," *JTS* 47 (1946): 196–99 [= P.Mich. 3788]; C. H. Roberts, "The Acts of Paul and Thecla," in C. H. Roberts, ed., *The Antinoopolis Papyri: Part 1* (London: Egypt Exploration Society, 1950), 26–28; M. Gronewald, "Einige Fackelmann-Papyri," *ZPE* 28 (1978): 274–75; Willy Rordorf, "Les Actes de Paul sur papyrus: problemes liés aux P. Mich. 1317 et 2788," *Proceedings of the XVIII International Congress of Papyrology 1986* (Athens: Greek Papyrological Society, 1988), 453–56.

18. Wilhelm Schneemelcher, "The Acts of Paul," in *NTApoc* 2:213–70; Elliott, *Apocryphal New Testament*, 364–89. The most complete recent translation is Richard I. Pervo, *The Acts of Paul: A New Translation with Introduction and Commentary* (Cambridge, UK: James Clarke, 2014).

19. The organization of the CCSA edition is illustrated in Snyder, *Acts of Paul*, 4–5, and reflected in Pervo's translation.

20. Willy Rordorf, "Tradition and Composition in the Acts of Thecla: The State of the Question," in *The Apocryphal Acts of Apostles*, Semeia 38 (Atlanta: Scholars Press, 1986), 43–52; idem, "Was wissen wir über Plan und Ansicht der Paulusakten?" in *Oecumenica et Patristica: Festschrift für Wilhelm Schneemelcher zum 75. Geburtstag*, ed. D. Papandreou, W. Bienert, and K. Schäferdiek (Stuttgart: Kohlhammer, 1989), 71–82.

21. From P.Ryl.; P.Heid. 59–62.

22. From P.Heid. 1–6. The pages in the Heidelberg papyrus have two numbers, one based on the extant papyrus leaves, used here, and one that reflects a hypothetically reconstructed codex, used in Willy Rordorf, "Actes de Paul," in *Écrits apocryphes chrétiens*, ed. F. Bovon and P. Geoltrain, vol. 1 (Paris: Gallimard, 1997), 1115–77, and noted in Pervo's translation.

23. From P.Heid. 6–20. See Jeremy W. Barrier, *The Acts of Paul and Thecla: A Critical Introduction and Commentary*, WUNT 2.270 (Tübingen: Mohr Siebeck, 2009).

children, Simias and Zeno, come to greet Paul, having been informed about his arrival by his disciple Titus. The account includes a famous description of Paul's appearance, inspiring a tradition of visual representations: "Short, bald, bow-legged, healthy-looking, single browed, a bit long-nosed, and bursting with beneficence. Sometimes he looked like a mortal; at other times he had the glowing countenance of an angel."[24] 4. Onesiphoros warmly greets Paul; Demas and Hermogenes take offense that Onesiphoros does not welcome them. 5–6. At home with Onesiphoros, Paul breaks bread and preaches about sexual continence and resurrection. The teaching takes the form of beatitudes, expanding the traditional formulas. "Blessed are the pure in heart" becomes a series focusing on renunciation of the world and the embrace of chastity.

7. Thecla, a virgin seated near a window of her home, listens to Paul's preaching for three days and nights. 8–9. She had been promised by her mother, Theiocleia, to a man named Thamyris. Summoning him, Theiocleia informs him that Thecla is spellbound and "sticks to the window like a spider," while Paul upsets the Iconians. 10. Thecla's mother and fiancé, fearing Thecla is mentally disturbed, appeal to her in vain. The household is cast into mourning.

11–15. Leaping into action, Thamyris finds Demas and Hermogenes. He invites them home for food and wine and inquires about Paul's teaching. They advise Thamyris to bring Paul to the governor, Castellius. They also report about Paul's belief in a future resurrection, deeming it an error; resurrection takes place through one's children.

16. An angry Thamyris leads a crowd to the home of Onesiphorus, seizes Paul, brings him to the proconsul, and accuses him of preventing women from marrying. Demas and Hermogenes urge him to add that Paul is a Christian, but the governor intervenes and, echoing Pilate, remarks on the severity of the accusation. 17. Paul defends his teaching as a divine message for the salvation of humankind. The governor imprisons him, pending another hearing. 18–19. Thecla bribes her own family's servants and the prison guards in order to visit the apostle. Thamyris and Thecla's family search for her and find her "bound with affection" to Paul.

20. The governor orders Paul brought to him. Thecla remains behind, languishing in Paul's seat until the governor also summons her. The crowds denounce Paul as a sorcerer, but the governor is favorably impressed. He asks Thecla why she refused to marry Thamyris, prompting her mother to call for Thecla's execution.

21. The governor has Paul scourged and expelled from the city but condemns Thecla to be burned alive in the theater. Like a sheep longing for her shepherd, she looks for Paul in the crowd. Instead, she sees Jesus looking like Paul, but he quickly disappears. 22. A pyre is prepared; Thecla, naked, mounts it, making the sign of the cross. The fire is lit, but an earthquake intervenes. A storm with heavy rain and hail quenches the fire, saving Thecla while endangering the crowd.[25]

23. Meanwhile, Paul, Onesiphorus, and his family have been fasting in an open tomb on the road from Iconium to Daphne. When the children complain of hunger, Paul gives them his cloak to sell and buy bread. On the errand the boy meets Thecla and informs her of Paul's whereabouts. 24. Reaching the tomb, Thecla finds Paul praying for her.

---

24. Translation is from Pervo, *Acts of Paul*, 89. See Robert M. Grant, "The Description of Paul in the Acts of Paul and Thecla," *VC* 36 (1982): 1–4, and Abraham J. Malherbe, "A Physical Description of Paul," *HTR* 79 (1986): 170–75; János Bolyki, "The Description of Paul in the Acta Pauli," in *The Apocryphal Acts of Paul and Thecla*, ed. J. Bremmer (Kampen: Kok Pharos, 1996), 1–15.

25. Margaret P. Aymer, "Hailstorms and Fireballs: Redaction, World Creation, and Resistance in the Acts of Paul and Thecla," *Semeia* 79 (1997): 45–61.

She in turn thanks God for letting her live to see him. 25. Paul, Thecla, and the family of Onesiphorus share a vegetarian meal with water. Thecla undertakes to shave her head and follow Paul, who counsels against the action, worried that Thecla might succumb to temptation. When she asks to be baptized, Paul advises patience.

4. Paul and Thecla in Antioch (Acts Paul Thecla 26–43)[26]

26. Paul and Thecla arrive together in Antioch where a powerful noble, Alexander, is smitten by Thecla and tries to buy her from Paul, who denies knowing her. Alexander tries to seize Thecla, but she rips his cloak and snatches away his crown. 27. Alexander brings Thecla to the governor, who promptly condemns her to the beasts. Thecla requests that she be kept pure till her execution. A noblewoman, Queen Tryphaena, an imperial relative whose daughter had recently died, gives her refuge. 28. Thecla is brought to the arena, bound on the back of a lioness, who licks her feet. The women of the city denounce the charge of sacrilege, while Tryphaena, encouraged by her dead daughter in a dream, again takes Thecla under her wing. 29. Tryphaena asks Thecla to pray for her deceased daughter, now named Falconilla. Thecla prays that Falconilla might live forever, while Tryphaena mourns the imminent execution of the beautiful Thecla.

30. Alexander fetches Thecla for her battle with the beasts, but Tryphaena drives him away. She then prays for the safety of Thecla, now "her child." 31. Soldiers are sent to bring Thecla to the arena. In a melodramatic exchange, Tryphaena laments her new daughter's fate while Thecla earnestly prays for her patroness. 32–33. A divided crowd and roaring beasts greet Thecla, who is stripped of her clothing, given a girdle, and thrown to the animals. A lioness lies down before her, then defends her against a marauding bear and a lion trained by Alexander. Both lion and lioness perish in a fight. 34. While other beasts are sent in, Thecla sees a pit full of water. Extending her hands in prayer, she casts herself into it, baptizing herself in the name of Jesus Christ on what she takes to be her last day. The crowd and the governor are aghast, since the pit is full of carnivorous seals, but a flash of lightning kills the seals and saves Thecla.

35. More beasts enter but are overpowered by the perfume from flowers cast into the arena by supportive women. Alexander volunteers to supply his own bulls to tear Thecla apart; the governor agrees. Thecla is tied to the bulls, who are prodded with hot irons. As they lunge forward, a flame surrounding Thecla burns through the ropes, freeing her. 36. Queen Tryphaena faints and is deemed dead. The people, including Alexander, panic and beg the governor to release Thecla, fearing the emperor's revenge. 37–38. Brought before the governor, Thecla praises the God who has saved her. Supplying clothes, the governor bids Thecla dress. When he decrees her release, the people thunderously praise the one God who delivered her. 39. Tryphaena, revived, takes Thecla home, confesses her belief in resurrection, and promises Thecla all her wealth. For eight days Thecla instructs Tryphaena and her household in God's word, amid abundant joy.

40–41. Missing Paul, Thecla, in men's clothing,[27] searches for him in Myra. She finds him and tells him of her baptism and of her plans to visit Iconium, her hometown. Paul then bids Thecla go and preach the gospel, which she does, supported by Tryphaena's resources. 42. In Iconium Thecla visits Onesiphorus and prays. 43. Thamyris has died,

---

26. From P.Heid. 20–28.

27. On the symbolism of the clothing, see Sebastian P. Brock, "Clothing Metaphors as a Means of Theological Expression in Syriac Tradition," in *Typus, Symbol, Allegorie bei den östlichen Vätern und ihren Parallelen im Mittelalter*, ed. M. Schmidt and C. Geyer (Regensburg: Pustet, 1981), 11–40.

but Thecla's mother still lives, and Thecla asks her to believe in God. She then departs for Seleucia, where she preaches the word of God before she finally sleeps a noble sleep.

5. Paul in Myra[28]

(p. 28) Teaching in Myra, Paul encounters a certain Hermocrates, suffering from edema, which the apostle heals. The man's son, Hermippos, having hoped to inherit his father's wealth, is angry at Paul and plots against him. Another son, Dion, dies, plunging his mother, Nympha, into mourning. (p. 31) [As is clear from the later narrative, Paul revives Dion, an event reported on a lost leaf of papyrus.] Paul then has a vision of coming persecution, soon followed by the approach of Hermippos leading an armed crowd. Paul responds with a challenge and a prayer. (p. 32) Charging at Paul, Hermippos suddenly goes blind and then repents. (p. 33) Hermippos is taken to his parents' home, where Hermocrates and Nympha are celebrating Dion's revival by feeding the poor. (p. 34) Paul finally restores the sight of the repentant Hermippos, (p. 35) then departs for Sidon.

6. Paul Travels to Sidon[29]

(p. 35) Paul's departure from Myra saddens the local brethren. Traveling with two couples from Perga, Paul stops for a meal. [At this point the papyrus becomes fragmentary. Other people apparently join the meal, and Paul preaches.] (p. 36) An elderly man stands and challenges Paul, citing examples of others punished for their disregard of the gods. [The vignette apparently foreshadows conflict to come in Sidon.]

[After several missing pages the narrative continues.] An unknown speaker, Paul or one of his companions, (pp. 37–38) cites the example of God's punishment of Sodom and Gomorrah for their mistreatment of strangers. The Sidonians, unimpressed, imprison Paul and his companions in the Temple of Apollo, awaiting trial the next day. As Paul and his companions pray, the temple collapses. Proclaiming that Apollo has fallen, the crowd demands that Paul and his party be brought to the theater. [What happens there has been lost.]

[When the papyrus resumes] (p. 39) Paul, apparently vindicated, is concluding a speech, mentioning "Christ's polity." A character named Theudas requests the "seal" of baptism. Paul then departs for Tyre.

7. Paul in Tyre[30]

This fragmentary section mentions that Paul encountered a crowd of Jews, including two individuals, Amphion and Chrysippus. Paul apparently exorcises demons and encounters a man with a son born dumb.

8. Paul in Jerusalem and Smyrna[31]

These fragmentary pages tell of Paul's travels to and activity in Jerusalem and Smyrna.[32] The state of the papyrus makes it impossible to trace a coherent narrative. There is mention

---

28. From P.Heid. 28–35.
29. From P.Heid. 35–39.
30. From P.Heid. 40.
31. From P.Heid. 67–83.
32. The section appears in Willy Rordorf, "Actes de Paul," in *Écrits apocryphes chrétiens*, ed. F. Bovon and P. Geoltrain, vol. 1 (Paris: Gallimard, 1997), 1115–77, with a translation of the Coptic by Pierre Cherix; and Pervo, *Acts of Paul*, but not in earlier translations.

of Cilicia (pp. 67–68), Jerusalem (p. 73), and Cyrenaica, as well as a reference to the persecution of apostles outside of Jerusalem (p. 81).

9. Paul in Ephesus[33]

1. (P.Bodmer) Having traveled from Smyrna to Ephesus, Paul comes to the house of
Aquila and Priscilla for a night of prayer. An angel appears to all but speaks in tongues
only to Paul. Paul interprets and tells of fiery distress to come but encourages the believers
to trust in the "God Jesus Christ." Paul preaches a Pentecost sermon, recalling his time in
Damascus as a persecutor of believers, his conversion to life in Christ by a message from the
Father, his welcome by Jude, the Lord's brother, and his initial success as a preacher.

Paul then tells how he traveled to "Jericho in Phoenicia,"[34] in the company of two
women, a widow, Lemma, and her daughter, Ammia. A lion confronts them[35] but does
not disturb their prayers. When they finish, the lion asks to be baptized. Overcoming
his concerns, Paul prays earnestly, grabs the beast's mane, and throws him into a nearby
stream. The lion emerges and says, "Grace be with you," to which Paul replies, "And also
with you." The lion departs for the forest, while it is revealed to Paul that the lion avoided
contact with any lioness. Paul concludes his account with encouraging words for Aquila
and Priscilla.

Paul baptizes another woman, Procla, along with her household. As believers increase
in number, the locals grow angry that Paul is destroying their gods. Paul is arrested and
brought to the proconsul, charged with destroying the gods of Rome.

2. (P.Hamburg, p. 1) During interrogation, Paul responds that the proconsul,
Hieronymus, has authority only over his body, none over his soul. Paul condemns idolatry
and proclaims Jesus the one Lord. Hieronymus reacts favorably, but the crowds want Paul
burned or sent to the beasts. Hieronymus has Paul flogged and condemns him *ad bestias*,
but the believers rejoice. Arriving in a cage, a fierce lion terrifies the crowds with his roar
and even makes Paul pause.

3. (p. 2) Two women are intrigued by Paul, Eubula, the wife of a Christian freedman
in the service of Hieronymus, and Artemilla, the proconsul's wife. Artemilla wants to
hear Paul's prayers, so the two, dressed in dark clothing, pay him a visit. Paul preaches to
Artemilla, denouncing her feigned modesty and calling on her to abandon her wealth and
her idols and serve the true God. Artemilla begs for immediate baptism.

(p. 3) While the women attend to Paul, Hieronymus learns of their visit and aims to
hasten the sentence. The women volunteer to engage a smith to free Paul from his chains
so that he might baptize them. Declining the offer, Paul prays for deliverance. God answers
his prayer when a mysterious boy releases Paul from his bonds. Guided by this luminous
youth, Paul and the women exit while the guards sleep. They approach the sea, where Paul
baptizes Artemilla, but turbulent waters make her faint. (p. 4) Paul's prayer that he not be

---

33. From P.Bodm. 41 [Coptic] and P.Hamb. [Greek] 1–5. Concerning the Coptic, see Rodolphe Kasser
and Philippe Luisier, "Le Papyrus Bodmer XLI en Édition Princeps l'Épisode d'Èphèse des Acta Pauli en Copte
et en Traduction," *Le Muséon* 117 (2004): 281–384. In *NTApoc* 2:263–65, a translation of the unpublished
Bodmer papyrus appears in an appendix. Pervo, *Acts of Paul*, 21–28, combines them, with part 1 coming from
the Bodmer papyrus.

34. The text may be corrupt.

35. On this episode, see Willy Rordorf, "Der getaufte Löwe und die Theologie der Acta Pauli," in *Carl-
Schmidt-Kolloquium an der Martin-Luther-Universität 1988*, ed. P. Nagel (Halle: Wissenschaftliche Beiträge
der Martin-Luther-Universität Halle, 1990), 181–89, and Tamás Adamik, "The Baptized Lion in the Acts of
Paul," in Bremmer, *Apocryphal Acts of Paul and Thecla*, 60–74.

blamed for her death, along with the smiling youth, revives Artemilla. Paul returns to the prison, breaks bread with her, and restores her to her husband.

4. The next day Hieronymus orders Diophantes to deliver Paul to the stadium. Artemilla and Eubula are distressed by these developments, while Hieronymus is concerned about his reputation. The crowds apparently clamor for Paul's death as the papyrus here becomes fragmentary.

The narrative resumes with Paul conversing with the lion sent to kill him, who happens to be the beast whom he had baptized before coming to Ephesus and whom he now greets with a kiss. Hieronymus sends other animals to dispatch Paul. A fierce hailstorm intervenes, sparing Paul and the baptized lion, but killing all the other beasts in the arena and striking off an ear of Hieronymus. Paul escapes and boards a boat bound for Macedonia; the lion retires to the hills.

5. (p. 5) The episode closes with Hieronymus, Eubula, and Artemilla together, the women fasting and wondering about Paul, the proconsul nursing his severed ear. An apparition, presumably the child who had played a role earlier, tells the women of Paul's departure and restores the ear, bidding Hieronymus to treat himself to some honey.

10. Paul at Philippi (3 Cor)[36]

1. (p. 44) The fragmentary beginning of the episode sets the scene in Philippi. (p. 45) After a prayer, Paul receives a communication from the Corinthians. They were disturbed by two teachers, Simon and Cleobios, who had been propounding a number of problematic views: that there is no resurrection of the body but only of the spirit, that neither the world nor the body were created by God, that Jesus was not really crucified, nor was he born of Mary or of the seed of David. (p. 46) Two deacons, Threptus and Eutychus, deliver the letter.

2. (Letter of the Corinthians). The letter, written by Stephen and several other elders, requests Paul's aid either in person or in writing to deal with the teaching. It then lays out the problematic positions, adding a few points to the narrator's introduction. These include a rejection of the prophets and a claim that the cosmos is the work of angels.

3. Paul is in prison because of Stratonike, wife of Apollophanes. The precise offense is not specified but probably followed the usual pattern of a husband annoyed at his wife's attraction to Paul's message of sexual discipline. Paul receives the letter, laments that it would be better for him to be with the Lord than to hear such things, then responds with his own missive.

4. (3 Corinthians). Paul begins by denouncing the teachings of the Evil One, who will soon be subject to Christ's judgment. He then reviews what he taught the Corinthians from the beginning, doctrines that he had received from the apostles: that Christ, of the seed of David, was born of Mary when the Holy Spirit came upon her. He came to free all flesh by his own fleshly death and resurrection. His mission was to save human beings, who had been made by his Father. He erected a righteous temple in his own body through which people are redeemed. Those who deny that God created the world are children of wrath; those who deny the physical resurrection have no resurrection. Bodies are like seeds, but Paul says that if such a comparison is not convincing the Corinthians should remember Jonah, who rose from the belly of a whale after three days, or the dead man raised by contact with Elisha's bones. Paul concludes by pointing to his own bonds and the bodily

---

36. From P.Heid. 44–50; P.Bodm. 10.

marks that foretell the resurrection. He promises that those who accept his gospel will be rewarded; the vipers who do not will be punished.

11. Paul Revives Frontina[37]

The precise setting of this fragmentary episode is unclear, but it involves a mine where Paul has been imprisoned. A young woman, Frontina, daughter of Longinus and Firmilla, had died after being cast down into the mine. After reviving her with prayer, Paul leads her back to the home of Longinus, while the people acclaim the one God who created heaven and earth.

12. Paul Travels from Philippi to Corinth[38]

(P.Hamb. p. 6) Paul arrives in Corinth and stays at the home of Epiphanius, delighting the brethren. After teaching for forty days, Paul prepares to depart for Rome, consoling his congregation that his departure is necessary. They pray that he remain with them. (p. 7) A woman named Myrta assures the believers that Paul will save many in Rome. The congregation feasts on bread and sings Davidic psalms. The next day Paul bids them farewell.

13. Paul Travels to Italy[39]

1. (P.Hamb. p. 7) Paul sails to Italy in a boat captained by Artemon. During the night Jesus appears to him, walking on the water, lamenting that he is to be crucified again, but he tells Paul to encourage believers in Rome to be faithful.

2. (p. 8) Upon arriving in Italy, Paul is greeted by Claudius, who takes him home. There Paul preaches to the congregation about God's salvific action in Israel's history, echoing Deuteronomy but with a note that Israel had lost its eternal inheritance. Believers can be confident in Christ, who was truly incarnate of Mary, the Galilean, and who came to proclaim God's coming kingdom. Paul encourages the congregation to accept the light, inspired by the wonders that Christ performed.

3. (P.Heid. pp. 79–80 and P.Mich. 3788) The next scene, whose beginning is lost, shows Paul recounting a story in which Jesus tells of his miraculous deeds and admonishes his hearers to have the faith that will move mountains. (p. 80) Jesus then dialogues with Simon, who here receives the name Peter, and Philip, in which a comparison is made between the miracles done by Jesus and something "greater than these." The papyrus ends before that greater deed is explained.

14. Paul's Martyrdom[40]

1. In Rome Luke, from Gaul, and Titus, from Dalmatia, greet Paul, who rents a barn outside the city in which to teach. His pupils include many of Caesar's household. Among them is a youthful cupbearer, Patroclus, who finds a seat on a high window to listen to Paul. When Patroclus falls and dies, the mishap is immediately reported to Nero. Warning of demonic opposition, Paul orders the youth brought to him. He then revives Patroclus and sends him to Caesar.

2. The scene shifts to Nero's palace. Emerging from his bath, Nero looks for someone else to serve him wine. Learning that Patroclus is alive and present, Nero summons the

---

37. From P.Heid. 41–42.
38. From P.Hamb. 6–7; also P.Heid. 44/43; 51/52.
39. From P.Hamb. 7–8; P.Heid. 79–80; P.Oxy. 1602; P.Berl. 13893; P.Mich. 1317 + 3788.
40. From P.Hamb. 9–11 and P.Heid. 53–58. Sections are numbered according to the modern editions of the Mart. Paul.

youth and questions him. Patroclus proclaims that Jesus Christ, the "king of the ages," restored him to life. Nero asks if this king will destroy other kingdoms, and Patroclus responds that he will. Asked by the emperor if he is in this king's army, Patroclus declares that he is, along with three other prominent imperial servants, Barsabbas Justus, Orion from Cappadocia, and Festus from Gaul. Nero reacts by imprisoning and torturing his servants and decreeing that all Christians be persecuted.

3. The military imagery continues as Paul is arrested and interrogated by Nero. The emperor queries him about his recruiting practices. Paul declares that he recruits soldiers for his king from the world over. He bids Nero submit to Christ, otherwise he will perish when Christ wages war on the world with fire. Nero responds by ordering Christians in general to be burned, but Paul, as a Roman citizen, is to be beheaded. Paul does not keep silent but shares his message with a prefect, Longus, and a centurion, Cestus. Mob violence ensues, killing many Christians. Rallying in support, the people plead with Nero to stop the killing. He does so, pending further investigation.

4. After Nero confirms Paul's sentence, the apostle predicts his resurrection. Longus and Cestus ask about his king. Paul responds with a proclamation of apocalyptic judgment, when that king will cleanse the world of sin by fire. Longus and Cestus offer to free Paul if he spares them. Paul replies that he is not a deserter. The Romans wonder how they will survive.

5. Nero sends two more servants, Parthenion and Feritas, to report on Paul's execution. Paul invites them to believe in the living God. They mock the apostle, saying they will believe when he is resurrected. Longus and Cestus seem more interested in learning from Paul, who tells them to return the next morning to hear from Luke and Titus. Paul then prays in Hebrew and stretches out his throat for the executioner. After his decapitation, milk spurts onto the soldiers, amazing all, who then glorify God.

6. The execution is reported to a marveling Nero. At the ninth hour, Paul appears to the emperor, surrounded by philosophers and centurions. Paul declares that he is alive to God and predicts dire punishments for the emperor. Nero in distress frees other prisoners, including Patroclus and those around Barsabbas.

7. The next day Longus and Cestus visit Paul's tomb and, as predicted, find Luke and Titus, but Paul as well. The Christians run in fear, but Longus and Cestus assure them that they only want what Paul promised. Luke and Titus grant them the seal of baptism, giving glory to God and to Jesus Christ. A doxology concludes the text.[41]

3. INTERPRETIVE ISSUES
3.1 History and Pauline Legends

Paul's apostolic activity spanned roughly three decades from his encounter with the resurrected Christ around 33 CE to his martyrdom in Rome, which probably occurred around 64 CE during the Neronian persecution. Paul's memory lived on, through disciples who edited his correspondence,[42] compiled it into a collection, and supplemented it.

---

41. On the episode, see János Bolyki, "Events after the Martyrdom: Missionary Transformation of an Apocalyptic Metaphor in *Martyrium Pauli*," in Bremmer, *Apocryphal Acts of Paul and Thecla*, 92–106.

42. Interpolations have been suspected throughout the Pauline corpus. For a general review, see William O. Walker, *Interpolations in the Pauline Letters* (London: Sheffield Academic, 2001). Several letters show evidence of a complex composition history. On 2 Corinthians, see Hans Dieter Betz, *2 Corinthians 8–9*, Hermeneia (Minneapolis: Fortress, 1985), 3–36, for a more complex theory; see Victor Paul Furnish, *II Corinthians*, AB 32A (Garden City: Doubleday, 1984), for a simpler theory. On a possible similar history in Philippians, see Paul Halloway, *Philippians*, Hermeneia (Minneapolis: Fortress, 2017), 10–19.

Exactly what was added remains debated, but it is most likely that the deutero-Pauline texts are 2 Thessalonians, Colossians, 1 and 2 Timothy, Titus, and Ephesians. This body of correspondence preserved Paul's memory, at times modified his teaching, as is certainly the case regarding women's roles, and systematized his theology, particularly in Ephesians. The process of producing letters in Paul's name did not end with the epistles that became canonical. In addition to 3 Corinthians, included in the Acts of Paul, there remain the Epistle to the Laodiceans, written in Greek sometime before the fourth century but surviving in Latin, Slavonic, and Arabic,[43] and the correspondence of Paul and Seneca.[44] Other pseudepigraphic epistles are known only by name.[45]

Paul's memory also generated narratives.[46] For later believers, the canonical Acts of the Apostles, a companion volume to the Gospel of Luke, became the most important source. The Lukan Acts, however, was not alone in preserving Pauline tradition. Paul's death, absent from Acts, had already become the stuff of legend by the end of the first century. It is first mentioned in 1 Clement (ca. 90–110), an anonymous letter written from the church at Rome to settle a disagreement among Corinthian Christians. First Clement 5.1–7 links Paul with Peter as founders of the Roman church. Ignatius of Antioch, on his way to martyrdom in Rome about 110–115 CE, recalls Paul's experience,[47] as does Polycarp of Smyrna in the mid-second century.[48] Paul's foundational role continued to be celebrated by proto-orthodox Christians of the second century, such as the heresiologist Irenaeus of Lyon, writing around 180 CE (*Haer.* 3.3.1–3).

Paul's death was recalled both in writing and in material culture, with memorials at two Roman sites that later accommodated church structures, and in a Roman catacomb.[49] Oral traditions about Paul, evident in reports of his death,[50] contributed to the accounts enshrined in the canonical and apocryphal Acts. The Acts of Paul participates in this complex tradition.

3.2 Paul and Women

Paul's relationship to Thecla, at the heart of the surviving Acts of Paul, reflects significant tensions within Paul's relationships with women as well as the development of women's roles in the early church. Paul believed that God had intervened in human history through Jesus to create a new reality that anticipated the final establishment of divine rule over creation (1 Cor 15:28). In this realm, the body of Christ (1 Cor 12:12), conventional

---

43. Elliot, *Apocryphal New Testament*, 544–45. On this letter, see Philip Tite, *The Apocryphal Epistle to the Laodiceans: An Epistolary and Rhetorical Analysis* (Leiden: Brill, 2012).

44. Elliot, *Apocryphal New Testament*, 547–53.

45. An Epistle to the Macedonians, mentioned in Clement of Alexandria (*Protr.* 9.87.4); an Epistle to the Alexandrians, and another, Marcionite, Epistle to the Laodiceans, mentioned in the Muratorian Canon 39–40, on which see Geoffrey Smith, *Guilt by Association: Heresy Catalogues in Early Christianity* (Oxford: Oxford University Press, 2015), 21–26.

46. Dennis R. MacDonald, *The Legend and the Apostle: The Battle for Paul in Story and Canon* (Philadelphia: Westminster Press, 1983); idem, "Apocryphal and Canonical Narratives about Paul," in *Paul and the Legacies of Paul*, ed. W. Babcock (Dallas: Southern Methodist University Press, 1990), 55–70; Richard I. Pervo, *The Making of Paul: Constructions of the Apostle in Early Christianity* (Minneapolis: Fortress, 2010); Andrew Gregory, "The Acts of Paul and the Legacy of Paul," in *Paul and the Second Century*, ed. M. Bird and J. Dodson (London: T&T Clark, 2011).

47. Ign. *Eph.* 12.1–2; Ign. *Rom.* 4.1–3.

48. Pol. *Phil.* 9.1–2. For later references to Paul's martyrdom, see Tertullian, *Praescr.* 36; *Scorp.* 13–15.

49. See Snyder, *Acts of Paul*, 35–36, and David L. Eastman, *Paul the Martyr: The Cult of the Apostle in the Latin West*, WGRWSup 4 (Atlanta: SBL Press, 2011).

50. Jean Zumstein, "L'apôtre comme martyr," *RTP* 112 (1980): 371–90; Judith Perkins, "The Apocryphal Acts and Early Christian Martyrdom," *Arethusa* 18 (1985): 211–30.

distinctions were erased. At Galatians 3:28 Paul cites what is probably a baptismal formula proclaiming that in Christ there is neither Jew nor Greek, male nor female, slave nor free, but all are one. Equality of some sort prevailed in the ecclesia. Working out the implications of that proclamation was not a simple matter.

Several practical issues appear in Paul's Corinthian correspondence. Some there apparently understood Paul's proclamation that they were "called to freedom" (Gal 5:13 NRSV) to imply that old norms of sexual behavior no longer obtained. Paul insists that they do. Hence, a man involved with his stepmother should be severely disciplined (1 Cor 5:1–5).

At the other end of the spectrum stood people who rejected any sexual activity, appealing to the principle cited at 1 Corinthians 7:1: "It is well for a man not to touch a woman" (NRSV). The Corinthians had questioned Paul about this declaration and its consequences. Where they learned the principle is not totally clear, though it is probably from Paul himself, who here clarifies his position. Husbands and wives can remain sexually active (1 Cor 7:3–4), although they may abstain temporarily (v. 5). Paul prefers that people be like himself, presumably celibate, but he recognizes that people have different gifts (vv. 6–7). Paul's position on sexual activity thus resembles Stoic moral categories. The practice is neither prohibited nor required, but is a matter of ethical indifference, although celibacy is preferred.

Similar reflections continue through 1 Corinthians 7. Following a "word of the Lord," Paul prohibits divorce, except in the case of an unbelieving partner, though he hopes that such marriages might last (vv. 8–16). He sketches his fundamental conviction that the shape of the world is passing away and that believers should therefore remain as they were called (vv. 17–24). The time is short; people should be free from this life's cares, ready to serve the Lord (vv. 29–35). Ever pragmatic, Paul does not make his preference absolute but allows virgins (vv. 25–28) and widows (vv. 39–40) to marry. In the Acts of Paul, Paul's preference for celibacy has become more pronounced.

Paul's attempt to balance the ideal of equality between male and female (Gal 3:28) with life in a world that groans for redemption (Rom 8:22) characterizes his treatment of the Corinthians' worship. The presenting issue was how women, who pray and prophesy (1 Cor 11:4) and thus play active roles in the assembly, should appear. Paul's bottom line is clear; they should behave decorously, as do worshipers elsewhere (v. 16). He particularly wants them to wear something on their heads, perhaps concerned that they would otherwise appear like bacchants, ecstatic worshipers of Dionysus. That headgear Paul labels an *exousia*, which generally means "authority." The term suggests that he wants women to have a mark of authorization for their public roles. Paul's concern about unbridled behavior in worship and his overall aims are clear enough, even if details remain obscure.

Paul's arguments reveal tensions. He begins by sketching the cosmic hierarchy of God, Christ, man, and woman, where each is the "head" or authority over what follows (1 Cor 11:3). He then plays on the word "head," arguing that an uncovered female head is repugnant, but the head of a man, made in God's image, reflects divine glory (vv. 5–7). The argument then focuses on the process of creation. Women, or at least the first, was "from man" (vv. 8–9). The grounds for *exousia* on a female head established (v. 10), Paul issues a corrective that "in the Lord" a woman is not "independent of man," nor a man from a woman (v. 11 NRSV). The creation story in Genesis receives another interpretive twist. The woman was "from" the man, but the man was "through" the woman, and both are "from" God (v. 12 NRSV). Mutuality prevails, both "in the Lord"—that is, in the believing community—and in the created order itself. Paul then appeals to custom, cloaked in the garb of what "nature" teaches: long-haired men are dishonored, but women should keep their hair long as a covering. So a woman praying or prophesying should "naturally" have something on her head.

The issue of women's behavior in the assembly surfaces again when Paul reflects on the practice of tongues, or glossolalia, one of many Corinthian charisms (1 Cor 12:28, 30). His overall position displays characteristic political sensitivity. Speaking in a mysterious, perhaps angelic (13:1), language at worship is certainly acceptable, and Paul has done it himself (14:18). Yet to prophesy, or speak in intelligible language, is preferable, since it edifies both insiders and outsiders (14:4). Paul then advises people with the charism of tongues to use it only with an interpreter present (vv. 27–28).

Paul's advice about glossolalia hardly seems relevant to women's roles. A few verses—1 Corinthians 14:33b–36—make it so. This brief passage denies women the right to say anything in the worship assembly. If they have a question, they should ask their husbands at home. Contradicting the assumption of 1 Corinthians 11:4 that women prayed and prophesied, these verses place women in a distinctly subordinate role, subject to their husbands' authority. The verses are almost certainly not by Paul himself but by a later hand, not unlike that of 1 Timothy 2:11–12, probably placed here because of the immediately following verse (1 Cor 14:37). There Paul affirms that what he advises is not his own word but a command of the Lord. As the text stands, it is not Paul but Jesus himself who prohibits women's speech in worship.[51]

While some of Paul's arguments, particularly in 1 Corinthians 11, could support the subordination of women and suppression of their voices, his letters attest the significant role that women actually played in his orbit. "Chloe's people" (1 Cor 1:11), who brought him news from Corinth, were probably household slaves and freedmen of a woman of means, perhaps with business interests in Ephesus and Corinth. Phoebe at Cenchreae, the port of Corinth, receives Paul's commendation in Romans 16, a list of greetings that accompanied a version of Romans probably sent to Ephesus. Paul labels Phoebe a "deacon" (16:1 NRSV), a position that may not have had its later connotations of formal ordination. Yet the term certainly indicates Phoebe's prominence in her community, and Paul labels her a "benefactor" of many, himself included (v. 2 NRSV). The following greetings mention several women: "Prisca [the short form of Priscilla]" (v. 3); "Mary who has worked very hard among you" (v. 6 NRSV); Junia, with her husband Andronicus, both "relatives" of Paul, "prominent among the apostles" and believers prior to him (v. 7 NRSV).[52] Paul's use of "apostle" is not limited to the Twelve, as in Luke; for Paul an apostle is anyone commissioned by the risen Christ. Other women are Tryphaena (v. 12), a name that appears in Acts of Paul; Tryphosa (v. 12); the mother of Rufus, who was "a mother to me also" (v. 13 NRSV), and the sister of Nereus (v. 15).

Women also play significant roles in other Pauline communities. In his letter to the Philippians, Paul urges Euodia and Syntyche, who "have struggled beside me in the work of the gospel" (Phil 4:3 NRSV), to be of the same mind (v. 2). Their disagreement may have occasioned the letter. Acts also tells of a couple who appear in the Acts of Paul, Aquila and Priscilla, occasionally thought to be the author of the Epistle to the Hebrews.[53] The couple sailed with Paul from Cenchreae to Ephesus, where they remained while Paul continued

---

51. Tertullian, *Bapt.* 17, cites 1 Cor 14:34–35 after his comment on the author of the Acts of Paul.

52. On Junia, see Eldon Jay Epp, *Junia, The First Woman Apostle* (Minneapolis: Fortress, 2005).

53. Adolf von Harnack, "Probabilia über die Adresse und den Verfasser des Hebräerbriefes," *ZNW* 1 (1900): 16–41; Ruth Hoppin, *Priscilla: Author of the Epistle to the Hebrews and Other Essays* (New York: Exposition, 1969).

to Jerusalem (Acts 18:18–19). In Ephesus they met Apollos, an eloquent Alexandrian preacher, whose inadequate understanding of baptism they corrected (vv. 24–28).

3.3 Thecla Remembered

The heirs of Paul, involved in the continuing discussion of gender,[54] were less welcoming of women in leadership roles. Yet in the late antique environment where ideals of virginity held sway,[55] ascetical women remained influential.[56] Such women pervade the apocryphal Acts,[57] but Thecla stands out.[58] As a dedicated virgin and an itinerant preacher, she was celebrated by numerous church fathers, including, in the east, Athanasius,[59] Gregory of Nazianzus,[60] Gregory of Nyssa,[61] and John Chrysostom,[62] and, in the west, Augustine[63] and Jerome.[64] She plays a prominent role in the *Symposium* or *Treatise on Chastity* of Methodius of Olympus, an early fourth-century bishop.[65] This Christian adaptation of the symposiast genre records the speeches and dialogues of eleven women ascetics. In Logos 8 Thecla is praised by Arete (Virtue) as "second to none in your grasp of philosophy and universal culture . . . instructed in divine and evangelical doctrine by Paul himself."[66] Thecla then praises virginity, offers an account of the ascent of the soul, an exegesis of Revelation 12, and a refutation of astrology and astral determinism. Hagiographers would continue to celebrate the life and miracles of this special virgin, particularly in *Life and Miracles of Thecla*.[67]

---

54. Rosemary Radford Reuther, "Misogynism and Virginal Feminism in the Fathers of the Church," in *Religion and Sexism: Images of Woman in the Jewish and Christian Traditions*, ed. R. R. Reuther (New York: Simon and Schuster, 1974), 150–83, and Caroline Vander Stichele and Todd Penner, *Contextualizing Gender in Early Christian Discourse* (London: Bloomsbury, 2009).

55. Peter Brown, "The Notion of Virginity in the Early Church," in *Christian Spirituality: Origins to the Twelfth Century*, ed. B. McGinn, J. Meyendorff, and J. Leclercq, World Spirituality 16 (New York: Crossroad, 1986), 427–43; Susanna Elm, *"Virgins of God": The Making of Asceticism in Late Antiquity* (Oxford: Clarendon, 1994).

56. Rosemary Radford Reuther, "Mothers of the Church: Ascetic Women in the Late Patristic Age," in *Women of Spirit: Female Leadership in the Jewish and Christian Traditions*, ed. R. R. Reuther and E. McLaughlin (New York: Simon and Schuster, 1979), 71–98; Elizabeth Castelli, "Virginity and Its Meaning for Women's Sexuality in the Ancient Church," *Journal of Feminist Studies in Religion* 2 (1986): 61–88.

57. See Stevan L. Davies, *The Revolt of the Widows: The Social World of the Apocryphal Acts* (Carbondale, IL: Southern Illinois University Press, 1980), and Virginia Burrus, *Chastity as Autonomy: Women in the Stories of the Apocryphal Acts*, Studies in Women and Religion 23 (Lewiston, NY: Edwin Mellen, 1987).

58. Susan E. Hylen, *Modest Apostle: Thecla and the History of Women in the Early Church* (New York: Oxford University Press, 2015). Hylen rightly notes that chaste modesty did not necessarily remove women from leadership roles.

59. Athanasius, *On Virginity*, on which see Stephen J. Davis, *The Cult of Saint Thecla: A Tradition of Women's Piety in Late Antiquity* (Oxford: Oxford University Press, 2001), 87–94.

60. *Praesc. ad virg.* 190; *Exh. ad virg.* 87; *Or.* 4.69; 24.10. The patristic sources are noted in Snyder, *Acts of Paul*, 102. In general, see Monika Pesthy, "Thecla in the Fathers of the Church," in Bremmer, *Apocryphal Acts*, 164–78.

61. *Hom. in Cant.* 14.

62. *Hom. Acts* 25, and on an encomium attributed to Chrysostom, see Dennis R. MacDonald and Andrew D. Scrimgeour, "Pseudo-Chrysostom's *Panegyric to Thecla*: The Heroine of the Acts of Paul in Homily and Art," *Semeia* 38 (1986): 151–59.

63. *Faust.* 30.4; *Virginit.* 1.44.

64. *Epist.* 22.41.

65. See Herbert Musurillo, *St. Methodius, The Symposium, a Treatise on Chastity*, Ancient Christian Writers (New York: Newman, 1958).

66. Musurillo, *St. Methodius*, 105.

67. Gilbert Dagron, *Vie et miracles de sainte Thècle: Texte grec, traduction, et commentaire*, Subsidia Hagiographica 62 (Brussels: Société des Bollandistes, 1978), and Scott Fitzgerald Johnson, *The Life and Miracles of Thekla: A Literary Study*, Hellenic Studies Series (Washington, DC: Center for Hellenic Studies; Cambridge: Harvard University Press, 2006), 113–71.

In addition to the literary references, Thecla's memory was preserved in the popular imagination and in monasteries and cultic sites around the Christian world. She was especially prominent in Egypt, in the vicinity of Alexandria, up the Nile River, and beyond.[68] Tokens of her importance as a model of virginity for late antique Christians are pieces of material culture, paintings, combs, lamps, and pilgrim flasks, which often show her as described in the Acts of Paul, surrounded by respectful lions.[69] Her close encounters with death gained her martyr's honors. The major site of her veneration was a shrine, the Hagia Thecla, in Seleucia in the southeast of Turkey, visited by the famous fourth-century pilgrim Egeria and numerous others. There was also a pilgrimage site in her memory in Egypt, where her memory generated another, indigenous, Thecla.[70]

3.4 Theology of the Acts of Paul

Although the Acts of Paul focuses on the deeds and dramatic encounters of Paul and the characters with whom he interacts, the work also clearly defends several theological positions. Different parts of the Acts of Paul emphasize different points. The stories of Paul and Thecla focus on the role of ascetical women. Third Corinthians in Acts of Paul 10 is particularly interested in presenting Paul as a defender of orthodoxy,[71] a role that his character plays in his farewell to the Ephesian elders visiting him in Miletus in Acts 20:18–35 and in the denunciation of false teachers in 1 Timothy 4:1–5.

The fundamental belief in one true God as opposed to old idols grounds Paul's Ephesian preaching (Acts Paul 9.2). Third Corinthians (Acts Paul 10.4) emphasizes that God created the cosmos and especially the human body, a position that repudiates the denigration of creation and of the flesh characteristic of many other sources. Similarly, 3 Corinthians and Paul's subsequent preaching strongly emphasizes the true humanity of Jesus. Jesus, who is of the seed of David, was born of Mary and the Holy Spirit (10.4; 13.2). The kind of docetism that appears in works such as the Acts of John is here rejected, although the resurrected Christ can appear to his followers in various forms (3.21, and perhaps 9.3). Yet Jesus also shares in the status of the creator and can be called God (9.1). He came into the world for the salvation of humankind (3.17), or as 3 Corinthians puts it, to free all flesh by his fleshly death and resurrection. Salvation involves a real corporal resurrection, which Paul's false pupils deny (3.15; 10.1–2) and true converts like Tryphaena affirm (3.39). The Acts of Paul echoes the historical Paul's eschatology not only through the emphasis on physical resurrection but also in the expectation of a future fiery judgment (9.1; 10.4), when unbelievers will be punished (12) and hostile forces eliminated (14.4).

Life in expectation of Christ's kingdom (Acts Paul 13.2) has distinctive characteristics. Dedication to sexual purity, prominent in the Thecla stories (3.5–6), is assumed in Paul's encounters with other women. Service of the one true God also involves the independence from parents (3.10, 20) and abandonment of wealth (9.3), exemplified by Thecla.

---

68. Davis, *Cult of Saint Thecla*, 83–148, and Jeremy W. Barrier, Jan N. Bremmer, Tobias Nicklas, Armand Puig, *Thecla, Paul's Disciple and Saint in the East and West* (Leuven: Peeters, 2017).

69. On the artistic evidence, see Claudia Naureth and Rudiger Warns, *Thekla: Ihre Bilder in der frühchristlichen Kunst* (Wiesbaden: Harrassowitz, 1981); Annewies van den Hoek and John Hermann Jr., "Thecla the Beast Fighter: A Female Emblem of Deliverance in Early Christian Popular Art," *Studia Philonica Annual* 13 (2001): 212–49; and Davis, *Cult of Saint Thecla*, 195–200.

70. See Davis, *Cult of Saint Thecla*, 36–80 on Seleucia, and 149–94 on other Egyptian traditions.

71. Gerard Luttikhuizen, "The Apocryphal Correspondence with the Corinthians and the Acts of Paul," in Bremmer, *The Apocryphal Acts of Paul and Thecla*, 75–91; Vahan Hovhanessian, *Third Corinthians: Reclaiming Paul for Christian Orthodoxy*, Studies in Biblical Literature 18 (New York: Lang, 2000).

The account of Paul's martyrdom emphasizes Christ's kingship, participation in his "polity" (6) that challenges Roman imperial authority with a new king, leading a new army (14.2).

4. KEY PASSAGES FOR NEW TESTAMENT STUDIES AND THEIR SIGNIFICANCE
4.1 Relationship to the Canonical Acts
Significant parallels to the Lukan Acts appear in Acts of Paul episodes 9 and 14. The Ephesus segment (9) reports the story of Paul's call and gives an account of his activity in Ephesus, where he meets Priscilla and Aquila and occasions a riot. A story of an unfortunate disciple, Patroclus, which leads to Paul's martyrdom (14), resembles the account of a similarly unlucky disciple in Acts. Each merits attention.

4.2 Paul's Apostolic Commission
Three passages in the canonical Acts recount, with slight variations, Paul's encounter with the resurrected Christ on the road to Damascus. In Acts 9:1–9, written in the narrator's voice, a heavenly light surrounds Paul, who falls to the ground and hears the question, "Saul, Saul, why do you persecute me?" (v. 9 NRSV). The speaker, Jesus, commands Paul to rise and go to the city, where he will learn what to do. Paul's companions hear the voice but see nothing. Blinded, Paul goes to Damascus, where Ananias, sent by Jesus, teaches and baptizes him (vv. 10–19). In Acts 22:3–21, Paul, addressing a hostile crowd in Jerusalem, reports that his companions saw the light but did not hear the voice. He then tells of being instructed and baptized by Ananias (vv. 10–16) and of another vision of Christ (vv. 17–21). At his trial before Herod Agrippa II (26:12–20), Paul tells of a light, brighter than the sun, which grounded everyone. Paul hears Jesus's question, which now adds, "Why do you kick against the goad?" probably echoing Euripides.[72] Jesus immediately commissions Paul.

In the Acts of Paul, the apostle refers to his call in the Bodmer papyrus that begins the extant text of chapter 9. The event does not happen on the road to Damascus but in the city where Paul was persecuting Christians. No light or words of Jesus are involved, but only "mercy from the Father who proclaimed the message of his son to me."[73] There is no mention of Ananias. Instead, Paul finds support in Jude, the Lord's brother, who brings Paul to the Christian assembly. The Acts of Paul here at least seems likely to rely on a tradition that differs from canonical Acts.

4.3 Paul's Ephesian Mission
Other details of the Ephesus account evoke Acts and Pauline letters. The story is set in the house of Aquila and Priscilla, who appear prominently in Acts 18 as believers expelled from Rome under Emperor Claudius (Acts 18:2). They share Paul's tent-making or leatherworking trade, which explains Paul's stay with them. They later play a role educating Apollos (vv. 24–28). Nothing of their background or activity in Ephesus is part of the Acts of Paul, where they are simply described as believers (9.1, 14).

The temporal setting is Pentecost,[74] originally a Jewish festival seven weeks (hence Hebrew *Shavuoth* or "Weeks") after Passover, the time that the Holy Spirit first descended on believers (Acts 2:1). The approach of Pentecost also marked the time of Paul's last trip

---

72. On the evocation of *Bacchae* 794, see Harold W. Attridge, "Paul and Pentheus: What's in a Possible Allusion," in *Delightful Acts: New Essays on Canonical and Non-Canonical Acts: In Memory of Richard I. Pervo*, ed. H. Attridge, D. MacDonald, and C. Rothschild, WUNT 2.391 (Tübingen: Mohr Siebeck, 2017), 7–18.

73. Pervo, *Acts of Paul*, 215.

74. Pervo, *Acts of Paul*, 215, translates as "Eastertide," capturing the Christian significance of the reference (9.4) but not the possible allusion to Acts.

in the vicinity of Ephesus (Acts 20:16). Intending to be in Jerusalem for the festival, he did not then stay in Ephesus. Instead, he summoned the elders of the community to Miletus for a final admonition (vv. 16–17). The Acts of Paul identifies an earlier visit at the same time of year.

On Paul's first night in Ephesus, an angel appears to him, speaking in tongues, which Paul interprets as eschatological prophecy (9.3). The episode dramatizes Paul's suggestion that ecstatic speech involves the language of angels (1 Cor 13:1), of which he had personal experience (1 Cor 14:18). He also insists that such speech requires interpretation (1 Cor 14:5).

Paul's critique of pagan gods (Acts Paul 9.1) leads to his arrest and trial before the Roman governor, Hieronymus. In the trial, the goldsmiths cry out for Paul to be thrown to the beasts (9.2). Exactly why they do so is unclear. The combination evokes the episode in Acts in which Demetrius, a silversmith who made shrines of Artemis, led a demonstration by those whose livelihood Paul's preaching threatened (Acts 19:23–41). In that account, the town clerk quiets the demonstrators, and Paul departs for Macedonia. The account in the canonical Acts clarifies the hostility of the craftsmen in the Acts of Paul.

In prison the night before being thrown to the beasts, Paul is visited by Eubula and Artemilla (Acts Paul 9.3). Rejecting their offer of assistance to escape, Paul is freed by a heavenly youth, while the guards sleep. Paul returns to prison after baptizing Artemilla. The story resembles the prison break in Acts 12:1–11, where Peter escapes confinement in Jerusalem when an angel wakens him and guides him past sleeping guards. In the Acts of Paul, Paul returns to prison, as in Acts 16:25–40, when an earthquake in Philippi presents Paul the opportunity to escape prison, which he rejects, much to the guards' amazement. The Acts of Paul apparently combines elements of the two prison stories of Acts.

Highlighting the Ephesian episode is the encounter with the beasts (Acts Paul 9.4) and Paul's surprising deliverance by the previously baptized lion. The story's imaginative details rest on a tradition of Paul's Ephesian challenges reported in 1 Corinthians 15:32, "If with merely human hopes I fought with wild animals at Ephesus, what would I have gained by it?" (NRSV). Paul's expression may have been metaphorical, but the Acts of Paul took it literally, then explained how Paul survived.

While there are certainly echoes of Acts and Pauline letters in the Ephesian episode, there is also at least one other obvious echo of another tradition of the New Testament. The hailstorm that finally frees Paul and his friendly lion also injures the ear of the governor Hieronymus, recalling what happened to the high priest's servant, Malchos or "king," in Gethsemane (John 18:10; cf. Matt 26:51; Mark 14:47). As in Luke 22:50–51, the ear is healed.

4.4 Patroclus and Eutychus

As the Martyrdom of Paul begins, Paul rents a barn outside Rome in which to preach. During a service, a servant of Nero, Patroclus, seated in a high window, falls and dies. Paul revives him and sends him back to the emperor, who learns from him about the politically subversive preacher. The story's role in setting up the encounter between Paul and Nero is unique to the Acts of Paul, but its details resemble the canonical Acts's account of Eutychus (whose name means "Lucky"), a youth who was also seated in a window, dozed off while Paul preached, and fell to an apparent death. Eutychus, unlucky in his choice of seating, was aptly named because Paul, recognizing that "his life is in him," restored him (Acts 20:7–12). One of the deacons who delivered 3 Corinthians to Paul is named Eutychus.

In addition to larger thematic parallels, there are numerous particular expressions and plot elements echoing the canonical Acts.[75] There are also elements of Acts that are absent in the Acts of Paul, such as the resistance of Jews to Paul's mission. The relationship continues to intrigue scholars.[76] Some suggest that the parallels are best explained by common oral traditions.[77] At least one has argued that some stories, such as that of Patroclus, circulated independently and was a source used by the author of canonical Acts.[78] Most argue that the Acts of Paul knows the canonical Acts but adapts elements from it freely.[79]

4.5 Other New Testament Echoes

In addition to the parallels to the Lukan Acts, the Acts of Paul, and particularly the Acts of Paul and Thecla, echo other parts of the New Testament. Some echoes are superficial. The character of Onesiphorus (Acts Paul 3.2) bears a name attested in 2 Timothy 1:16; 4:19. Others are more substantive. Paul's opening sermon (3.5) in the Paul and Thecla story consists of a series of beatitudes, beginning with "blessed are those with unadulterated hearts, for they shall see God," from Matthew 5:8. Another echo appears later in the declaration that the merciful will obtain mercy (Matt 5:7).[80] Much of the sermon argues for chastity, evoking other biblical texts. Thus, those who "keep the flesh pure" will be God's temple, a familiar Pauline image (1 Cor 3:16–18; 2 Cor 6:16). That those who have wives should not engage in sex with them recalls 1 Corinthians 7:29. The promise near the homily's end (Acts Paul 3.6) that virgins will not lose their reward echoes Matthew 10:42.

The claim that "the resurrection has already taken place" (Acts Paul 3.14) recalls the teaching attributed to Hymenaeus and Philetus in 2 Timothy 2:18. The denial of a future bodily resurrection reappears in Acts of Paul 10, attributed to another pair, Simon and Cleobios.

The Corinthians' concern (Acts Paul 10) that Paul wants to commit suicide reflects Philippians 1:23, where Paul expresses his desire to "depart and be with Christ." The language of 3 Corinthians, that Paul "delivered to you first of all what I received from the apostles," repeats his solemn formula in 1 Corinthians 15:3. Third Corinthians also echoes the use of the image of "seeds" for dead bodies that will be raised, which appeared in Paul's explanation of bodily resurrection in 1 Corinthians 15:42–44. The author of 3 Corinthians worries that it might not be persuasive and adds the allusion to the story of Jonah emerging from a sea monster's belly (Matt 12:40–41). Echoes of Paul's original correspondence thus pervade the Acts of Paul.

75. So Acts Paul 3.1: "great acts of Christ" (Acts 2:11); Acts Paul 3.17: Paul's second hearing (Acts 24:25); Acts Paul 3.17: Paul scourged and expelled (Acts 13:50; 14:19). Descriptions of God are familiar from Acts: Acts Paul 3.17: "living" (Acts 14:15 etc.); Acts Paul 24: "who made heaven and earth" (Acts 4:24; 14:15); "knower of hearts" (Acts 1:24; 15:8).

76. For possible parallels, see Snyder, *Acts of Paul*, 262. Cf. Willy Rordorf, "In welchem Verhältnis stehen die apokryphen Paulusakten zur kanonischen Apostelgeschichte und zu den Pastoralbriefen?," in *Text and Testimony: Essays on New Testament and Apocryphal Literature in Honour of A. F. J. Klijn*, ed. T. Baarda et al. (Kampen: Kok, 1988), 225–41.

77. MacDonald, *Legend and the Apostle*, 25–26.

78. Snyder, *Acts of Paul*, 54–64.

79. Richard Bauckham, "The Acts of Paul as a Sequel to Acts," in *The Book of Acts in Its Ancient Literary Setting*, ed. Bruce W. Winter and Andrew D. Clarke, vol. 1 of *The Book of Acts in Its First Century Setting*, ed. B. Winter (Grand Rapids: Eerdmans, 1993), 105–52; idem, "The Acts of Paul: Replacement of Acts or Sequel to Acts?," *Semeia* 80 (1997): 159–68; Julian Hills, "The Acts of Paul and the Legacy of the Lukan Acts," *Semeia* 80 (1997): 145–58; Daniel Marguerat, "The Acts of Paul and the Canonical Acts: A Phenomenon of Rereading," *Semeia* 80 (1997): 169–89; Richard I. Pervo, "A Hard Act to Follow: The Acts of Paul and the Canonical Acts," *Journal of Higher Criticism* 2 (1995): 3–32; idem, *Acts of Paul*, 67–70.

80. P.Heid. lacks this parallel, perhaps indicating a later addition.

5. BIBLIOGRAPHY

Barrier, Jeremy W. *The Acts of Paul and Thecla: A Critical Introduction and Commentary*. WUNT 2.270. Tübingen: Mohr Siebeck, 2009.

Bremmer, Jan N., ed. *The Apocryphal Acts of Paul and Thecla*. Kampen: Kok Pharos, 1996.

Davis, Stephen J. *The Cult of Saint Thecla: A Tradition of Women's Piety in Late Antiquity*. Oxford: Oxford University Press, 2001.

Hylen, Susan E. *Modest Apostle: Thecla and the History of Women in the Early Church*. New York: Oxford University Press, 2015.

Klauck, Hans-Josef. *The Apocryphal Acts of the Apostles: An Introduction*. Translated by Brian McNeil. Waco, TX: Baylor University Press, 2008. See pages 47–79.

MacDonald, Dennis R., ed. *The Apocryphal Acts of Apostles*. Semeia 38. Atlanta: Scholars Press, 1986.

McLarty, J. D. *Thecla's Devotion: Narrative, Emotion and Identity in the Acts of Paul and Thecla*. Cambridge, UK: James Clark, 2018.

Pervo, Richard I. *The Acts of Paul: A New Translation with Introduction and Commentary*. Cambridge, UK: James Clarke, 2014.

Rordorf, Willy. "Actes de Paul." Pages 1115–77 of volume 1 of *Écrits apocryphes chrétiens*. Edited by François Bovon and Pierre Geoltrain. Paris: Gallimard, 1997.

Sellew, Philip. "Paul, Acts of," and "Paul, Martyrdom of," in *ABD* 5:202–3; 204–5.

Snyder, Glenn E. *Acts of Paul*. WUNT 2.352. Tübingen: Mohr Siebeck, 2013.

CHAPTER 15

ACTS OF PETER

ROBERT F. STOOPS JR.

1. INTRODUCTION

The Acts of Peter narrates a series of engaging stories built around the conflict between the apostle Peter and Simon Magus.[1] The action takes place in Jerusalem and Rome. Peter is not so much a missionary as a defender of the faith, who demonstrates through words and deeds that Christ is the one true God.[2] Simon, identified as a Jew, offers commonplace criticisms of Christian beliefs: How can a mere carpenter be the Christ (Acts Pet. 14; 23)? Can God be crucified (Acts Pet. 23)? At the same time, Simon declares himself to be the "Great Power of God" and wins many followers, including Christians, through his wonder working (Acts Pet. 4). Peter exposes Simon's trickery and produces greater wonders through prayer. In between his confrontations with Simon, Peter preaches and works additional miracles to restore and strengthen the faith of believers. The possibility of repentance, even after apostasy, is an important theme throughout the Acts of Peter, second only to the repeated assertion that Christ can and will care for his own.

1.1 Author

All five of the early apocryphal Acts came to be attributed to a single author, Leucius, probably by the fourth century.[3] However, the differences among these Acts show that they cannot be from the same author. Several sources identify Clement of Rome as the author of the Acts of Peter because of its association with the Pseudo-Clementine texts. The unknown author shows some familiarity with popular literary forms and techniques but was not necessarily highly educated.

1.2 Audience and Purpose

The Acts of Peter is a Christian apology in the form of an entertaining narrative. Like other apologies, it is aimed first and foremost at an audience of believers. It is meant to bolster their faith and present Peter as a model for Christian living. Neither Peter nor Simon offers a detailed theology, so the author does not seem to be engaged in polemic against any specific opponents. The use of Old Testament prooftexts and multiple allusions to writings

---

1. All translations of the Acts of Peter are my own.
2. The Christology of the Acts of Peter is modalist. The Father and Son are understood to be manifestations of one God, not separate persons. See, e.g., Peter's prayer: "We confess that you <Jesus> alone are God and no other" (Acts Pet. 39). In Christ, God takes on human form and genuinely suffers while remaining transcendent and beyond suffering. This mystery is expressed in the antitheses in Acts Pet. 20.
3. Knut Schäferdiek, "The Manichaean Collection of Apocryphal Acts Ascribed to Leucius Charinus," in *NTApoc* 2:87–100.

of the New Testament suggest that the author is closer to the emerging "orthodoxy" than are the other early apocryphal Acts.

The treatment of Jews as outsiders indicates that the author was writing for a largely gentile church. Paul is said to have overcome the Jewish teachers in Rome and overturned their Sabbath and traditions before Simon's arrival in Rome (Acts Pet. 1). The public contests between Peter and Simon take place on the Sabbath, before a mixed crowd of Jews and gentiles, showing disregard for Jewish practices (Acts Pet. 16; 18; 22; 25).[4]

1.3 Date

The earliest explicit reference to the Acts of Peter appears in Eusebius's *Ecclesiastical History* 3.3.2. Eusebius rejects the Acts of Peter (*Praxeis Petrou*), along with other Petrine apocrypha, on the grounds that they were not cited by ancient Christian writers. Less direct evidence suggests that the Acts of Peter was known earlier. Origen's *Commentarii in Genesim* 3 refers to Peter's inverted crucifixion in Rome.[5] The Acts of Peter is probably the source of this tradition. The Muratorian canon list may provide even earlier evidence if it belongs to the end of the second century rather than the fourth. The list argues that Luke reported only things that he had himself witnessed. It offers as evidence the absence of Peter's martyrdom and Paul's departure from Rome for Spain. These two items may have been known from the Acts of Peter. If so, the disputed first three chapters were part of the text known to this author. The canon list also observes that Luke wrote the Acts of *all* of the apostles in *one* book, implying that the author knew Acts devoted to individual apostles. L. H. Westra has offered another line of evidence that the Acts of Peter should be dated to the second century. He notes that the nascent creedal formulae in the Acts of Peter, which ignore the Holy Spirit, have their closest parallels in the second century, particularly in North Africa.[6]

The most secure date in the development of the apocryphal Acts is provided by the Acts of Paul, specifically the portions involving Thecla. Tertullian claimed that the text was a recent invention by a presbyter in Asia Minor (*Bapt.* 17). This suggests that some version of the Acts of Paul and Thecla was written between 180 and 200 CE. Because Origen connected the *Quo vadis* to Paul (*Comm. John* 20.91), earlier scholars assumed that the Acts of Peter borrowed the scene from the Acts of Paul and should, therefore, be dated to the first decades of the third century.[7] In 1930 Carl Schmidt argued that the relationship was the reverse on the basis of the Hamburg papyrus, which contains the full *Quo vadis* from the Acts of Paul.[8] The encounter between Paul and Christ seems to borrow from two unrelated episodes in the Acts of Peter: the *Quo vadis* scene (Acts Pet. 35) and Christ's appearance to Peter and Theon after the captain's baptism (Acts Pet. 5).[9] Most scholars now accept the date of 180 to 190 CE for the Acts of Peter on the assumption that it was

---

4. Christian gatherings for worship take place on the first day of the week, i.e., on Sunday, the Lord's day (P.Berol. 8502.4; Acts Pet. 7; 29; 30).

5. Eusebius, *Hist. eccl.* 3.1.2.

6. L. H. Westra, "*Regulae fidei* and Other Creedal Formulations in the Acts of Peter," in *Apocryphal Acts of Peter: Magic, Miracles and Gnosticism*, ed. J. Bremmer, Studies on the Apocryphal Acts of the Apostles 3 (Louvain: Peeters, 1998), 134–47.

7. Carl Ludwig Schmidt, *Die alten Petrusakten im Zusammenhang der apokryphen Apostelliteratur, nebst einem neuentdeckten Fragment, untersucht*, TU 24.1 (Leipzig: Hinrichs, 1903), 82–86. Léon Vouaux, *Les actes de Pierre: Introduction, textes, traduction et commentaire*, Documents pour servir a l'étude des origines chrétiens: Les apocryphes du Nouveau Testament (Paris: Letouzey et Ané, 1922), 52–53, 203–6.

8. Carl Ludwig Schmidt, "Zur Datierung der alten Petrusakten," *ZNW* 29 (1930): 150–55.

9. Robert F. Stoops Jr., "The Acts of Peter in Intertextual Context," *Semeia* 80 (1997): 73–79.

used by the author of the Acts of Paul. However, some scholars still argue that the Acts of Paul is the earlier text.[10] The picture is further complicated by the fact that the relevant sections, Paul's journey to Rome and martyrdom, may not have been part of the work that Tertullian knew. And it is always possible that similar motifs in the apocryphal Acts are based on shared oral traditions rather than literary dependence.[11]

Similar questions complicate the understanding of the relationship between the Acts of Peter and the Acts of John. Both texts include a denunciation of Satan, a linkage between the story of Christ's transfiguration and polymorphism, and extended lists of christological titles.[12] These elements are similar but not identical, and they are used quite differently in the two Acts.[13] So, again, it is hard to either define the direction of influence or identify common traditions behind these sections. Eric Junod and Jean-Daniel Kaestli believe that the heterodox views expressed in Acts of John show that it should be dated early in the second century.[14] However, there is no reason to believe that the development of the apocryphal Acts of the Apostles always moved in the direction of orthodoxy. The fourth-century Acts of Philip, which makes use of the Acts of Peter, provides a clear counterexample.[15] There is general agreement that the Acts of Andrew and the Acts of Thomas were written after the Acts of Peter. Portions of the Acts of Andrew appear to be inspired by the Acts of Peter, including Andrew's address to the cross.[16] The influence of the Acts of Peter on the Acts of Thomas is more difficult to determine, but there are a number of potential examples.[17]

Attempts at dating the Acts of Peter must also take into account the possibility that the text may not all have been written at the same time. Vouaux,[18] following Adolf von Harnack,[19] argued that the first three chapters describing Paul's activity in Rome, the other mentions of Paul, and the final chapter, which associates Peter's martyrdom with Nero, are later additions intended to bring Paul into closer association with Peter.[20] Some version of this theory could explain the relationship between the Acts of Peter and the Acts of Paul. The Acts of Paul could have borrowed details of Peter's voyage and the *Quo vadis* encounter from an earlier version of the Acts of Peter. A later redactor of the Acts of Peter could have added the final chapter on the basis of the Acts of Paul. Variations of this hypothesis have been defended by Gérard Poupon and Christine Thomas. Poupon argues that the strong interest in the forgiveness of serious sins committed after baptism belongs to a late level of editorial activity, dating from the first decades of the third century. He finds additional signs of this redaction

---

10. Dennis R. MacDonald, "Which Came First? Intertextual Relationships among the Apocryphal Acts of the Apostles," *Semeia* 80 (1997): 13–24.

11. Christine M. Thomas, "Word and Deed: The *Acts of Peter* and Orality," *Apocrypha* 3 (1992): 125–64. Willy Rordorf believes that a common stock of oral tradition can explain any perceived parallels between these two Acts apart from Acts Pet. 41, which he believes is modeled on Mart. Paul ("The Relation between the *Acts of Peter* and the *Acts of Paul*: The State of the Question," in Bremmer, *Apocryphal Acts of Peter*, 191).

12. MacDonald, "Which Came First?," 28–33; Robert F. Stoops Jr., *The Acts of Peter* (Salem, OR: Polebridge, 2012), 33–35.

13. Judith Perkins, "The *Acts of Peter* as Intertext: Response to Dennis MacDonald," in *Society of Biblical Literature 1993 Seminar Papers*, ed. E. Lovering, SBLSP 32 (Atlanta: Scholars Press, 1993), 627–33.

14. Eric Junod and Jean-Daniel Kaestli, *Acta Iohannis*, CCSA 2 (Turnhout: Brepols, 1983), 695.

15. François Bovon and Christopher R. Matthews, *The Acts of Philip: A New Translation* (Waco, TX: Baylor University Press, 2012).

16. MacDonald, "Which Came First?," 33–35.

17. Stoops, *Acts of Peter*, 35–36.

18. Vouaux, *Actes de Pierre*, 26–35.

19. Adolf von Harnack, *Mizellen zu den Acta Pauli*, TUGAL 20.3 (Leipzig: Hinrichs, 1900), 100–106.

20. Acts Pet. 41 is represented in all of the translations of the Martyrdom of Peter. There is no evidence that the Martyrdom of Peter continued beyond this point; some Syriac manuscripts append a section from the Martyrdom of Paul after Acts Pet. 41.

in Acts of Peter 30, the Chryse episode, and the characterization of Marcellus as a lapsed believer in Acts of Peter 8 and 10.[21] Thomas agrees with Poupon that the emphasis on the repentance of apostates belongs to a late level of redaction, but she dates that redaction to the end of the second century,[22] and dates the core composition to the 170s.[23]

On the other hand, Marietheres Döhler argues in detail that the Acts of Peter is a well-integrated text with no clear redactional seams. She points to the coherence of the narrative and the consistent treatment of characters throughout and notes that the theme of forgiveness is present at every supposed redactional level.[24] The issues of apostasy and repentance have a natural connection to the figure of Peter. They are important throughout the Acts of Peter; it is unlikely that they belong to a separate layer of redaction.

The Acts of Peter can reasonably be dated to the second half of the second century. The letters of Dionysius of Corinth, written around the year 170 CE, address many of the issues that are important in the Acts of Peter: persecution, the return of apostates, moderation on the question of celibacy, and resisting the appeal of Marcion.[25] Apostasy in the Acts of Peter is presented as a response to seduction rather than persecution, which suggests a date of 160–175 CE, before the more systematic persecutions under Marcus Aurelius began.[26] According to Richard Bauckham, the date could be as early as 150 CE.[27] Alternatively, the Acts of Peter could reflect the last two decades of the second century when the threat of persecution had subsided.[28]

1.4 Provenance

Although a great deal of the action takes place in Rome, a Roman provenance seems difficult to defend. The author's knowledge of Roman geography is imprecise at best.[29] The Acts of Peter does share with Justin Martyr Simon's use of the title "Standing One" and the notion of a statue dedicated "Simon, the New God" in Rome.[30] However, the Acts of Peter situates the statue in the courtyard of a private house rather than a public shrine, so it does not represent local knowledge.[31] Alternatives to Rome include Syria[32] and North Africa.[33]

---

21. Gérard Poupon, "Les 'Actes de Pierre' et leur remaniement," *ANRW* 25.6:4374–78.

22. Christine M. Thomas, *The Acts of Peter, Gospel Literature, and the Ancient Novel: Rewriting the Past* (Oxford: Oxford University Press, 2003), 37–54; idem, "The Prehistory of the Acts of Peter," in *The Apocryphal Acts of the Apostles: Harvard Divinity School Studies*, ed. François Bovon, Ann Graham Brock, and Christopher R. Matthews, Religions of the World (Cambridge: Harvard University Center for the Study of World Religions, 1999), 39–62.

23. Thomas, *Acts of Peter*, 28.

24. Marietheres Döhler, *Acta Petri: Text, Übersetzung und Kommentar zu den Actus Vercellenses* (Berlin: de Gruyter, 2018), 27–34.

25. Eusebius, *Hist. eccl.* 4.23.1–12.

26. Stoops, *Acts of Peter*, 31.

27. Richard Bauckham, "The Martyrdom of Peter in Early Christian Literature," *ANRW* 26.1:578.

28. Jan N. Bremmer, "Aspects of the *Acts of Peter*: Women, Magic, Place and Date," in Bremmer, *Apocryphal Acts of Peter*, 18; Stoops, *Acts of Peter*, 31.

29. Gerhard Ficker, *Die Petrusakten: Beiträge zu ihrem Verständnis* (Leipzig: Barth, 1903), 35–36.

30. Justin Martyr, *1 Apol.* 26.2. The statue tradition is probably based on a misinterpretation of the inscription on the base of a statue dedicated to *Semo Sancti*. The misconstrual was repeated often in second-century Christian writings. See Otto Zwierlein, *Petrus in Rom: Die literarischen Zeugnisse. Mit einer kritischen Edition der Martyrien des Petrus und Paulus auf neuer handschriftliche Grundlage*, 2nd ed., UALG 109 (Berlin: de Gruyter, 2010), 129–33.

31. There is no evidence of the tradition linking Peter's martyrdom to the Vatican Hill before the very end of the second century (Zwierlein, *Petrus in Rome*, 4–6). Its absence from the Acts of Peter is only relevant on a late dating of the text.

32. Poupon, "Actes de Pierre," in *Écrits apocryphes chrétiens*, ed. F. Bovon et al., 2 vols., Bibliothèque de la Pléiade 442, 516 (Paris: Gallimard, 1997, 2005), 1:1043.

33. Westra, "*Regulae fidei*," 147.

The best case can be made for Asia Minor, placing the Acts of Peter in the vicinity of the Acts of Paul. Gerhard Ficker first argued that several details point more specifically to Bithynia.[34] Ficker suggested that the hospice of the Bithynians mentioned in Acts of Peter 4 might reflect local interests. The most intriguing argument is the possible connection between the senator Marcellus of the Acts of Peter 8–15 and M. Granius Marcellus, praetor and then governor of Bithynia. In 15 CE, this Marcellus was charged with treason (*maiestas*) for speaking disrespectfully of Tiberius and replacing the head on a statue of Augustus with that of the new emperor. He was also charged with extortion (*repetundia*) in connection with his service as governor in Bithynia (Tacitus, *Ann.* 1.74). The combination of the name and charges is striking. Bremmer has endorsed these lines of argument. He also notes that a child senator (Acts Pet. 28) would be plausible only in the eastern part of the empire.[35] Bremmer suggests that interest in Christianity among the senatorial class may have arisen earlier in Asia Minor than in Rome, especially after the ranks of senators were greatly expanded in the later second century.[36]

Pliny the Younger shows that already in the first decades of the second century religious competition was an issue in Bithynia, that Christians were to be found in every social class (*ordo*), and that many Christians were willing to abandon their faith when pressure was applied (*Ep.* 10.96). During the second century, northern and central Asia Minor spawned a range of new religious groups. Marcion came out of Pontus, Alexander of Abonoteichus established the dramatically successful cult of Glykon in Paphlagonia, and Montanism arose in Phrygia. Christians in this region encountered both sporadic persecution and lively competition of the type represented by Simon. Canonical Acts has the Holy Spirit direct Paul away from Bithynia (Acts 16:7). Bithynia, with its substantial Jewish population, may have been fertile ground for Petrine Christianity (cf. 1 Pet 1:1).

1.5 Religious and Social Context

The Acts of Peter attempts to show that Christ offers benefits in both the material and spiritual realms that are superior to those available from either competing cults or Roman society. Stories in which opponents are overcome and new converts won are primarily meant to strengthen the faith of believers. If such stories persuade outsiders, so much the better. Simon Magus, who is greeted as "Savior of the Romans" (Acts Pet. 4), represents the challenges posed by the new religious movements of the time.[37] The second century was also a time of active competition within the Christian movement. Simon could easily stand for Valentinus, Marcion, or Montanus, but it impossible to tell which, if any, is intended.

The competition for adherents takes place within the framework of Roman society. Believers face no demands to demonstrate loyalty by worshiping the gods of Rome. There is only one direct attack on Greco-Roman gods (Acts Pet. 28). While idols are shown to be material objects whose gold can be melted (Acts Pet. 17), no temples are destroyed. Rather the statue of Caesar is restored in a way that confirms Marcellus's standing as a Christian (Acts Pet. 11). Roman officials are either friendly (Paul's guard, Acts Pet. 1) or neutral (the prefect Agrippa initially, Acts Pet. 25). Converts are made among the highest classes, and their resources benefit the Christian community. In the Acts of Peter, only Paul (before his conversion) and Simon Magus are identified as persecutors. Even in the case of Nero, it is made clear that he is killing Christians out of irrational anger rather than state policy.

---

34. Ficker, *Petrusakten*, 38–39, 43–44.
35. Bremmer, "Aspects," 15.
36. Bremmer, "Aspects," 17–18.
37. Döhler also notes the religious pluralism of the period (*Acta Petri*, 321–22).

1.6 Language, Text, and Genre

The Acts of Peter was composed in Greek. However, the only witness for the majority of the text is a Latin translation preserved in a single manuscript, the *Actus Vercellenses*. Because the Martyrdom of Peter (Acts Pet. 33–41) remained important for liturgical use, it survives as an independent text in three Greek manuscripts and numerous translations.[38] The Mount Athos manuscript begins with the story of Chryse (Acts Pet. 30) and shows knowledge of Simon's first flight above the city of Rome (Acts Pet. 4). So it must have been extracted from a more complete version of the Acts of Peter. The other witnesses to the Martyrdom of Peter begin with Acts of Peter 33.

Portions of the Greek text of chapters 25 and 26 are preserved on a single vellum leaf from Egypt dated to the late third or early fourth century (P.Oxy. 849).[39] The fourth-century *Vita Abercii* somewhat loosely incorporates speech material from several parts of the Acts of Peter.[40] The portions of the Acts of Peter that survive in Greek show that the *Actus Vercellenses* is a relatively faithful translation. Overall, it is somewhat abbreviated, but the translator or a later scribe had a penchant for adding the title Lord (*dominus*) in references to God and Christ. The Vercelli manuscript dates from the seventh century. In it the Acts of Peter follows Rufinas's translation of the Pseudo-Clementine *Recognitions*, but it is treated as a separate text. Poupon notes some characteristic mistakes in the rendering of *nomina sacra* that suggest that the Latin translation was made in the late third or early fourth century, possibly for use by Manichaeans.[41] Marginalia in West Gothic show that the manuscript was in Spain before coming to Italy.[42]

In 1891 Richard Lipsius published this Vercelli manuscript together with the previously known Greek Martyrdom of Peter.[43] Lipsius's edition quickly displaced earlier efforts to reconstruct the Acts of Peter from traditions found in the ante-Nicaean fathers, especially the hypothetical common source (*Grundschrift*) behind the Pseudo-Clementine *Homilies* and *Recognitions*. Because the stichometry of Nicephorus indicates that the text it knows as the Journeys (*Periodoi*) of Peter was approximately the same length as the canonical Acts of the Apostles, it appears that as much as a third of the original Greek text is not reflected in the Latin version. In 1903, Carl Ludwig Schmidt published the Coptic "Act of Peter" (P.Berol. 8502.4), an account of Peter's daughter's paralysis, which seems to match Augustine's apparent reference to the Acts of Peter (*Adim.* 17).[44] Schmidt argued that this story had belonged to a section of the Acts of Peter that narrated Peter's activity in Jerusalem before his travel to Rome. The story of the gardener's daughter, which Augustine mentions alongside the story of Peter's daughter, probably belonged to the Jerusalem section as well. This story survives only in a very brief summary found in the Pseudo-Titus

38. Details in J. K. Elliott, *The Apocryphal New Testament: A Collection of Apocryphal Christian Literature in an English Translation Based on M. R. James* (Oxford: Clarendon, 1993), 390–430.

39. B. P. Grenfell and A. S. Hunt, *Oxyrhynchus Papyri 6* (London: Egypt Exploration Fund, 1908), 6–12.

40. See Mathew Baldwin, *Whose Acts of Peter? Text and Historical Context of the Actus Vercellenses*, WUNT 2.196 (Tübingen: Mohr Siebeck, 2005), 197–241, for text, translation, and discussion of the relevant passages.

41. Gérard Poupon, "L'Origine africaine des Actus Vercellenses," in Bremmer, *Apocryphal Acts of Peter*, 192–99.

42. Döhler, *Acta Petri*, 5–6.

43. Richard A. Lipsius, "Actus Petri cum Simone" and "Μαρτύριον τοῦ ἀγίου ἀποστόλου Πέτρου," in *Acta apostolorum apocrypha: post Constantinum Tischendorf denuo ediderunt*, ed. R. Lipsius and M. Bonnet, 2 vols. in 3 parts (Leipzig: Herrmann Mendelssohn, 1891–1903; repr.; Hildesheim: Olms, 1959, 1972), 1:44–103.

44. Schmidt, *Alten Petrusakten*, 14–16, 21–25. See James Brashler and Douglas M. Parrott, "The Act of Peter," in *Nag Hammadi Codices V, 2–5 and VI with Papyrus Berolinensis 8502, 1 and 4*, ed. D. Parrott, NHS 11, The Coptic Gnostic Library (Leiden: Brill, 1979), 473–93; Michel Tardieu, *Écrits gnostiques: Codex de Berlin*, Sources gnostiques et manichéens 1 (Paris: Cerf, 1984), text 217–22; commentary 403–10.

epistle, a seventh-century tract on virginity that incorporates material from several of the apocryphal Acts, including the Acts of Peter.[45]

Léon Vouaux's edition of the Acts of Peter together with a French translation and commentary was published posthumously in 1922.[46] It included the Latin text through chapter 29 but followed the Greek Martyrdom of Peter with reference to other ancient translations. Vouaux suggested that Peter's speech in Acts of Peter 17 concerning Eubula had originally belonged to the Jerusalem section. This hybrid text, together with the Coptic "Act of Peter" and the episode of the gardener's daughter, remained the accepted definition of the Acts of Peter until recently.

Against this consensus, Andrea Molinari has argued that the Coptic "Act of Peter" is a wholly separate text, with no connection to the Acts of Peter represented in the Vercelli manuscript.[47] Matthew Baldwin has argued that there is no evidence for an early text that can be identified as the Acts of Peter.[48] He assigns the *Actus Vercellenses* to a Priscillianist author writing in Spain in the fifth century. While it is certainly worthwhile to interpret this manuscript as one "performance" of the text, it is going too far to deny that it has any relationship to the Acts of Peter rejected by Eusebius. In 2010, Otto Zwierlein published a critical edition of a third Greek manuscript of the Martyrdom of Peter.[49] In 2018, Marietheres Döhler published a critical edition of the whole of the *Actus Vercellenses* with extensive notes.[50] She includes the Greek parallels from P.Oxy 849, the *Vita Abercii*, and the Greek Martyrdom of Peter separately. In this way she preserves the integrity of the Latin text while providing the resources for detailed comparison with the Greek. Poupon is currently preparing a critical edition of the Acts of Peter for the *Corpus christianorum* series. His understanding of the text is reflected in the French translation he published in 1997,[51] and in the critical apparatus in Döhler's edition.

1.7 Genre

Although it is difficult to assign the Acts of Peter to a specific genre, it was not out of place in the larger literary environment of its time. Literary genres, including romance and biography, to which the apocryphal Acts are often compared, were both eclectic and fluid in the second and third centuries CE.[52] The Acts of Peter has fewer elements characteristic of the Hellenistic novels than do the other early Acts. Travel is not important to the structure of the Acts of Peter. Peter only makes one journey and is never in danger during it. The Acts of Peter also places less emphasis on asceticism and chastity, which have been seen as substitutes for the erotic motifs in the novels.

The Acts of Peter presents a well-integrated narrative. Transitions, cross-references, and consistent characterization are used to stitch together a variety of sources. The narrative is punctuated by speeches, prayers, and visions that interpret the events. In terms of genre, the

---

45. Domitien de Bruyne, "Nouveaux fragments de Actes de Pierre, de Paul, de Jean, d'André, et de l'Apocalypse d'Élie," *Revue bénédictine de critique, d'histoire et de littérature religieuses* 25 (1908): 149–60; esp. 151–53. Aurelio de Santos Otero, "The Pseudo-Titus Epistle," in *NTApoc* 2:57.

46. Vouaux, *Actes de Pierre*.

47. Andrea Lorenzo Molinari, *"I Never Knew the Man": The Coptic Act of Peter (Papyrus Berolinensis 802,4), Its Independence from the Apocryphal Acts of Peter, Genre and Origins*, Bibliothèque copte de Nag Hammadi, Section Études 5 (Quebec: Université Laval, 2000).

48. Baldwin, *Whose Acts of Peter?*

49. Zwierlein, *Petrus in Rome*, 403–25.

50. Döhler, *Acta Petri*.

51. Poupon, "Actes de Pierre," 1:1041–114.

52. See Judith Perkins, "This World or Another? The Intertextuality of the Greek Romances, the Apocryphal Acts and Apuleius' *Metamorphoses*," *Semeia* 80 (1997): 247–60.

Acts of Peter was probably most influenced by canonical Acts, which in turn was modeled on the Gospels. The closest parallel outside of the New Testament might be Philostratus's *Apollonius of Tyana*. Lucian's *Alexander the False Prophet* and *The Passing of Peregrinus* also offer interesting parallels if allowance is made for the level of satire.

2. SUMMARY OF CONTENT
2.1 Summary

The Acts of Peter depicts a series of confrontations between the apostle Peter and Simon Magus, first in Jerusalem, then in Rome. Only a few episodes from the Jerusalem section survive. The story of Peter's daughter found in the Coptic "Act of Peter" (BG8502,4)[53] probably belonged to this section. It shares many motifs with the *Actus Vercellenses*. Peter's young daughter had been abducted by Ptolemy, who was attracted by her beauty. When Peter prayed, his daughter was paralyzed on one side, so Ptolemy returned her to her parents. In order to convince an audience that God has the power to heal, Peter first cures his daughter, then returns her to paralysis. Peter explains that his daughter's paralysis is "beneficial" both for him and for her. It saves her from the sexual advances of men and will save men from temptation, a classic example of blaming the victim. Ptolemy, who had abducted the girl, is blinded by the tears he sheds over losing the girl. Both his physical blindness and his spiritual blindness are later healed, and he is converted. His story demonstrates the possibility of forgiveness, even after serious offenses. The story also illustrates the proper use of material riches. Ptolemy left a plot of land to Peter's daughter in his will, which Peter sold for the benefit of the poor. Peter explains that God cares for his own even when they are not aware of it, an idea that is important throughout the Acts of Peter. Augustine refers to a story of a gardener's daughter alongside the story of Peter's daughter (Augustine, *Adim.* 17), which probably belonged to the Jerusalem section too.[54] When a gardener asks Peter to pray for his daughter, she dies. At the father's insistence, Peter restores her to life. A few days later she runs off with a stranger. The implication is that death would have been beneficial because it would have protected her purity.

The culmination of the Jerusalem section, in which Simon flees Judea, is reflected in Peter's report of how he stopped Simon's efforts to defraud the rich widow Eubula (Acts Pet. 17). Eubula's experiences expose Simon as a greedy charlatan. Her story also shows how prominent people can recognize Peter's God and turn their wealth to the service of poor believers, especially the widows. It appears that the major interests of the Acts of Peter were well-established before the action moved to Rome.

The *Actus Vercellenses* begins with Paul rather than Peter ministering to the Christians in Rome. Although the believers beg him to stay, Paul leaves Rome in order to minister to the people of Spain (Acts Pet. 1–3). Shortly after Paul's departure, Simon Magus appears in Rome and seduces the masses, including most of the Christians, by means of his wonders and his claim to be the "Great Power of God" (Acts Pet. 4). In response, Christ directs Peter to go to Rome to counter Simon once again. Peter's voyage is smooth, giving him a chance to convert and baptize the ship's captain (Acts Pet. 5–6). Once in Rome, Peter encourages the lapsed believers, citing himself as an example of one whose loss of faith had been forgiven (Acts Pet. 7).

A subplot around the senator Marcellus (Acts Pet. 8–15) amplifies the theme of reliance on Christ by demonstrating the spiritual weakness of Marcellus, who had been a patron of

---

53. Brashler and Parrott, "Act of Peter."
54. Wilhelm Schneemelcher, "The Acts of Peter," *NTApoc* 2:279.

the Christians before he was won over by Simon. The story of Marcellus's return to faith is interwoven with Peter's rebukes of Simon by means of a speaking dog and an infant who curses Simon and drives him from the city. With Simon out of the way for the moment, Peter encourages the community through additional preaching and miracle working (Acts Pet. 16–22). This section contains Peter's sermon on the transfiguration and the healing of a group of blind widows. When Christ appears in a different form to each woman, both their physical and spiritual eyes are opened.

In their first public competition, Simon denounces Jesus on the grounds of his obscurity and the ignominy of his death. Peter responds with arguments that include the fulfillment of prophecy, the miracles worked by Jesus during his earthly career, and the mighty works that God/Christ is now accomplishing through his apostle (Acts Pet. 23–24). When the prefect proposes a contest of miracles, Simon kills a young slave by whispering into his ear. Peter demonstrates the superiority of his God by raising not only that man from the dead but two others as well. Both are sons of widows, one rich, the other poor. Again, Christ's benefits, both material and spiritual, are shown to be available to all. While the wealthy son and his mother make substantial monetary donations, it is the son of the poor widow who will become a deacon (Acts Pet. 27, 29).

Later, Peter preaches on the Lord's Day to a crowd that includes many wealthy and high-ranking men and women. When Chryse brings ten thousand gold pieces in response to a vision, Peter accepts the money despite her reputation for lascivious behavior (Acts Pet. 30). A transitional section summarizes Peter's continued success at both healing and exposing Simon's deceptions. The second public confrontation takes place when Simon attempts to demonstrate his divine nature by flying up to heaven. He is lifted into the air but is then brought down by Peter's prayer. Simon dies of his injuries a few days later (Acts Pet. 32).

The text reaches its climax with Peter's martyrdom at the hands of the prefect Agrippa and his friend Albinus (Acts Pet. 33–40). Peter's message of purity includes abstinence from sex, or more accurately, abstinence from inappropriate sexual relations. Among those who accept Peter's preaching on purity are four concubines of the prefect Agrippa. Agrippa's friend Albinus, who is described as mad with lust, complains that his wife, too, has withdrawn from his bed as a result of Peter's preaching. The two men conspire against the apostle. The whole section is meant to demonstrate the base motives of those responsible for Peter's martyrdom.

When the plot against the apostle is discovered, the believers convince Peter to leave Rome for the sake of his safety (cf. Mart. Pol. 5.1). As he leaves the city, Peter encounters Christ and asks the famous question: "Lord, where are you going?" Christ answers that he is coming "to be crucified again," which Peter recognizes as a reference to his own impeding martyrdom. Christ returns to heaven, and the apostle cheerfully returns to the city (Acts Pet. 35–36). Many of the elements most commonly found in early Christian martyrdom accounts are missing from the Martyrdom of Peter. There is no trial, nor any confession of "the name" (of Christ).

Before his execution, Peter explains the mystical meaning of the cross and then asks to be crucified head downward. From the cross he gives a second, longer speech, interpreting his inverted position as a sign of the human condition and the need for conversion and repentance (Acts Pet. 37–39). These speeches emphasize the distinction between the physical and spiritual realms in language borrowed from Middle Platonism. Salvation is understood in terms of reversing the consequences of ignorance.

Marcellus shows his continued lack of understanding when he carefully tends to Peter's corpse and places it in his own tomb. Peter appears to Marcellus at night to let him know that what he has spent on the dead is wasted (Acts Pet. 40). In the final chapter (Acts Pet. 41), Nero persecutes the believers in Rome because he is angry that Peter had not suffered sufficiently, but he is stopped by a vision of a figure scourging him.[55] As a result, the believers enjoy peace.

2.2 Themes

The Acts of Peter differs from the other early apocryphal Acts in that it is not focused on carrying the gospel to new territory. Peter is active only in Jerusalem and Rome. The work is apologetic in the sense of supporting existing believers. Convincing outsiders is only a secondary interest. Simon Magus challenges the Christians with both ridicule and demonstrations of power. Peter shows how such challenges are to be met. He defends the faith with arguments from the prophets, denunciations of Satan, and praise of Christ. But Peter concedes that deeds are more powerful than words, so miracle-working takes precedence.

Simon is depicted as a Jew who fails to understand the prophets or recognize the power of the true God at work in the miracles worked by Jesus or through Peter (Acts Pet. 23–24). Simon undermines the confidence of believers by denouncing Jesus as a mere carpenter who died in obscurity and ignominy (Acts Pet. 24). At the same time, Simon offers an alternative means of accessing divine power with his demonstrations of magical power. Simon's use of the titles "Great Power of God" and "Standing One" suggest that he might even be the true Christ (Acts Pet. 4). Simon's success at winning converts among the believers whom Paul left behind sets up the issues of apostasy and forgiveness. Peter can use his own doubts while walking on water (Matt 14:28–31) and his denial of Jesus at the trial (Luke 22:55–62) as evidence of the Lord's compassion and the possibility of repentance (Acts Pet. 7).

One reason that sins as serious as adultery and apostasy can be forgiven is the understanding that all sin originates in ignorance. Paul asserts that sins done in ignorance can be forgiven (Acts Pet. 2). As the motif gets repeated throughout the Acts of Peter, it becomes clear that ignorance is a metaphysical principle. After the first man mistook evil for good and good for evil (Acts Pet. 38), Satan "ensnared the first human with desire" and "bound him in bodily chains" (Acts Pet. 8).[56]

The material world, or realm of becoming, is not fundamentally evil or hostile to the spirit, though it is inferior to the spirit. The relationship between the two realms is expressed in the modalist Christology of the Acts of Peter. In an act of compassion, God sent his Son into the world (Acts Pet. 7), or alternatively God "shone forth in the world," in order to eliminate "all ignorance and every activity of the devil" (Acts Pet. 7). The Father and Son are not separate persons. The one God takes on another form, the image of a man (Acts Pet. 20). God genuinely appears as a human—without losing his divine nature. The virgin birth and passion are both real, although their reality is qualified. This mystery is expressed in the series of antitheses in Acts of Peter 20. Because God as Christ has an ongoing engagement with the world, the Holy Spirit does not play a significant role in the Acts of Peter. Christ, rather than the Spirit, is the source of guiding visions.

Both the transcendence and the accessibility of the one God are demonstrated in Christ's polymorphism. When Peter prays that the inner eyes of the blind widows be

---

55. *Actus Vercellenses* identifies the mysterious figure as *angelus dei*. The same terminology is applied to Peter in Acts Pet. 12, but there it must mean a messenger of God.

56. The language of ignorance and illumination reflects an appropriation of Middle Platonism.

opened, Christ appears in radiant splendor, displaying a form suitable to each recipient simultaneously (Acts Pet. 21). Polymorphism illustrates the compassion and accessibility of God rather than underscoring differences in spiritual capacity, as is the case in Acts of John 91.[57] According to the Acts of Peter, even though no human is capable of comprehending God or Christ, both material aid and spiritual illumination are available to all who are faithful.

The rejection of radical dualism is further illustrated in the miracle stories. Miracles performed on the physical level confer practical benefits that are real, but most of them are also signs of the greater spiritual benefits available from the same source. The healings, resurrections, and other miracles are also a mechanism by which Christ cares for the financial needs of the community. Wealthy individuals who receive miraculous aid through Peter frequently devote a significant portion of their wealth to the support of the community, especially the widows and the poor.

The mystery of salvation can be apprehended only by the spirit, so it is appropriate that Peter communicates this knowledge, as far as is possible, to the crowd at the cross. It is a very public lesson, which is accepted with a collective "amen" (Acts Pet. 38). The Acts of Peter does not distinguish between ordinary believers and a spiritual elite.

3. INTERPRETIVE ISSUES

Lipsius believed the *Actus Vercellenses* to be an orthodox revision of an earlier gnostic version of the Acts of Peter.[58] Debate over the gnostic or, more generally, heretical character of the Acts of Peter continued for several decades.[59] Although Gnosticism is now recognized as a problematic category, disagreement continues concerning the extent to which the Acts of Peter demonstrates an attitude of world rejection or an ethic of asceticism. These questions center around Peter's speech from the cross, the polymorphic appearances of Christ, the absence of wine from the Eucharist, and the view of sexuality.

The Acts of Peter does not treat the cosmos as inherently evil or opposed to God. The distinction between the material and spiritual realms is important; it explains why God cannot be fully comprehended by the eyes and ears of the flesh. But the distinction is not as radical as that found in Plato, "Gnosticism," or the other early Acts. As Flamion suggested, the Acts of Peter lives with the tension between early Christian creedal formulations and Middle Platonism.[60] For the Acts of Peter, evil is the product of ignorance, which leads to erroneous judgments (Acts Pet. 7; 8; 38). Peter advocates a Platonic turning away from the realm of "appearances" and toward the spiritual in order to begin to understand what "truly exists." Believers must ultimately abandon the bodily organs of perception and communication so that the spiritual faculties of their souls can perceive the nature of salvation (Acts Pet. 37).

The distinction between body and spirit takes on heightened importance as Peter approaches death. After insisting that his impending death is the Lord's will (Acts Pet. 36), Peter announces that he will reveal the previously hidden mystery of the meaning of the cross (Acts Pet. 37). Peter is then crucified upside down at his own request.[61] From the

---

57. David Cartlidge, "Transfigurations of Metamorphosis Traditions in the Acts of John, Thomas and Peter," *Semeia* 38 (1986): 62–66.

58. Lipsius, "Actus Petri cum Simone," 109–42.

59. For a summary of the early debate, see Döhler, *Acta Petri*, 42–43.

60. Flamion, "Les actes apocryphes de Pierre," *RHE* 10 (1909): 251.

61. The tradition that Peter requested to be crucified upside down out of humility arises centuries later in the Pseudo-Linus Martyrdom of Peter.

cross he delivers another lengthy speech on the need for repentance. Peter's speech from the cross is more esoteric than what has come before, but it is delivered in a very public way, and much of the content has been alluded to earlier (Acts Pet. 7; 8; 21). Peter explains his inverted position by saying he presents an image of the first man (*anthropos*) as he fell into the world of becoming. Peter is showing the onlookers their present condition and need for repentance; he is not an image of Christ or a redeemed redeemer.[62] This first man entered the world with the wrong orientation, mistaking left for right and evil for good. Because of these errors, the first human became imprisoned through desire inspired by the devil (Acts Pet. 8). Under the influence of Satan, people continue to mistake evil for good, valuing the material rather than the eternal. This is the fundamental linkage between ignorance and sin.

A substantial portion of the speech is constructed on the basis of the apocryphal saying of Jesus: "Unless you make the things on the right as the things on the left, and the things on the left as the things on the right, and the things above as the things below, and the things behind as the things in front, you will not recognize the kingdom."[63] Partial parallels to this saying are found in the Gospel of Thomas 22 and 2 Clement 12.2. The closest parallel occurs in the Acts of Philip 140, which is probably dependent on the Acts of Peter at this point.[64] It appears as a saying of Jesus embedded in the speech given by Philip while he hangs upside down. Philip explains that he is an image of the first man and represents the way that souls forget heavenly things when they occupy bodies, which is a direct, if overly simplistic, way of summarizing the first part of Peter's speech.

Peter goes on to explain that the cross—that is, the one apprehended by the spirit—is both the image and means of salvation. The cross is the point of connection between the two worlds rather than a boundary marking their separation. The nail at the center of the cross connects the crossbeam, human nature, to the upright Word. This is the sense in which human nature "cannot be separated from God" (Acts Pet. 37). The single nail makes the necessary reorientation possible. The crossbeam of human nature can be turned around this axis through repentance and conversion (Acts Pet. 38). This rotation reorients human nature toward the divine and restores right and left to their proper places.

Peter's death does not involve suffering, but the Acts of Peter is not docetic. Whereas docetism stresses Christ's freedom from the constraints of the material world, the modalist Christology of the Acts of Peter emphasizes the paradoxical nature of God. God, in the form of Christ, shows concern for the material well-being of believers as well as their ultimate salvation.

Compared to the other early apocryphal Acts, the Acts of Peter contains very little that points to an ascetic ethic or spiritual practice. Fasting is practiced in preparation for challenging tasks, but no dietary restrictions appear. Wine is not mentioned alongside the

---

62. So also Döhler, *Acta Petri*, 309–10.

63. The Patmos manuscript and Pseudo-Linus read "*recognize* or *know* [Gk. *epiginōskō*; Latin *cognosco*] the kingdom of God." *Actus Vercellenses* reads "enter [*intro*] the kingdom of heaven." The Ochrid manuscript, as well as the Coptic and Slavic versions, reads "enter [*eiserchomai*] the kingdom of God." The saying is not present in the Athos manuscript. See Zwierlein, *Petrus in Rome*, 416 notes. Kingdom language is not typical of the Acts of Peter. It appears only here, in Acts Pet. 7, and in Acts Pet. 24, where the kingdom of God is said to come to completion through a mystery along with the promise that "these things will be revealed to you later," a probable reference to Peter's speech from the cross.

64. The saying has a slightly different form in each of the three recensions of the Mart. Phil. See Christopher R. Matthews, "Peter and Philip Upside Down: Perspectives on the Relation of the *Acts of Philip* to the *Acts of Peter*," in *Society of Biblical Literature 1996 Seminar Papers*, SBLSP 35 (Atlanta: Scholars Press, 1996), 31–34.

eucharistic bread, but there is no polemic against wine. Celebrating the Eucharist with just bread or with bread and water was not limited to strongly ascetic Christians.

The situation is more complicated when it comes to sexual norms. Yves Tissot has argued that the Acts of Peter cannot be described as Encratite because the theme of disrupting marriages appears abruptly in the Martyrdom of Peter.[65] He considers it to be a literary motif and therefore not representative of the author's viewpoint. However, concern for sexual purity is more than a literary motif. The stories of Peter's daughter and the gardener's daughter both place a very high value on maintaining the sexual purity of the two young girls. Rufina's adultery disqualifies her from participation in the Eucharist (Acts Pet. 2). Lust and adultery are both condemned, which is typical of most philosophies at the time, but celibacy is never said to be a requirement for salvation in the Acts of Peter.

Peter's martyrdom does not need to be seen as a condemnation of marriage or even of sexual relations within marriage, as long as they are not driven by lust.[66] Concubinage would be deemed impure by most Christians, and Albinus is explicitly described as driven mad by lust. Justin Martyr tells a similar story concerning the martyrdom of the Christian teacher Ptolemy in 2 Apology 2. A Christian wife refuses to engage in the sexual excesses in which the couple had previously indulged. When she seeks a divorce, her husband denounces her as a Christian.[67] She is able to avoid execution, so the enraged husband denounces her teacher, who is executed. It is important to note that Justin is arguing for the reasonableness of Christianity, not an Encratite ethic.

Rather than rejecting the larger Roman social order, the Christians in the Acts of Peter seem to operate largely within it. Ann Graham Brock makes this clear in laying out important differences between the Acts of Peter and the Acts of Paul. She addresses the lack of hostility toward political authorities,[68] as shown by the presence of several Christian senators,[69] especially Marcellus, the restoration of an imperial statue, and the apolitical tone of Peter's martyrdom. Brock then turns to issues of cultural accommodation.[70] She notes the absence of autonomous action by female characters apart from making donations to the community, conformity to the expected familial and social relations within Roman society, and the more frequent mentions of ecclesiastical officeholders.[71] All of these contrasts, apart from the question of female leadership, would apply equally well in a comparison with the Acts of John, Andrew, or Thomas.

3.1 Reception History

The Acts of Peter influenced a broad range of later literature, both directly and through derivative texts such as the Pseudo-Linus and Pseudo-Marcellus martyrdoms.[72]

---

65. Yves Tissot, "Encratisme et actes apocryphes," in Bovon et al., Les actes apocryphes, 109–19.

66. Husbands refusing to sleep with their wives is an unusual motif and may reflect the influence of 1 Cor 7:5.

67. The name of Christ or Christian plays a role in Justin's story that it does not have in the Acts of Peter.

68. Ann Graham Brock, "Political Authority and Cultural Accommodation: Social Diversity in the Acts of Paul and the Acts of Peter," in Bovon et al., Apocryphal Acts of the Apostles, 145–52.

69. The senators do not give up their civic rank, but two of them are held back from full participation in Christian life by the obligations of their political offices (Acts Pet. 3; 22).

70. Brock, "Political Authority," 155–68.

71. Church officials play a very limited role in Acts Pet. In contrast to the Pastoral Epistles, there is no discussion of their qualifications, duties, or authority.

72. For the manuscript witnesses for these later texts, see J. K. Elliott, "The Acts of Peter," in Elliott, Apocryphal New Testament, 427–30; Maurice Geerard, "Acta Petri," in Clavis Apocryphorum Novi Testamenti, Corpus Christianorum (Turnhout: Brepols, 1992), 109–12; Aurelio de Santos Otero, "Later Acts of Apostles," in NTApoc 2:436–43.

Peter and Simon meet again in the Pseudo-Clementine *Homilies* and *Recognitions*. Both texts are usually dated to the mid-third century.[73] It is possible that the Pseudo-Clementines drew on the lost first section of the Acts of Peter, but this is unlikely. The geography is different. Peter ends his travel in Antioch rather than Rome. The arguments are more elaborate and address different issues. Peter's martyrdom is not reported. Similarly, the itinerary and depiction of Satan make it unlikely that the fragment published by Bovon and Bouvier belonged to the Acts of Peter.[74]

It is clear that the five apocryphal Acts were valued by Manichaeans and that the canonical Acts was not. While the existence of a fixed Manichean collection of the early apostolic Acts has been questioned,[75] it appears that Herakleides used such a collection near the beginning of the fourth century. The Manichean psalm book dating from the mid-fourth century seems to know all five of the "Leucian" Acts, but none of this means that these Acts formed part of a Manichaean canon. No outside texts had the status of Mani's revelations. The Manichaeans were interested in the apostles and other characters appearing in the apocryphal Acts as forerunners of Mani—that is, as examples of the ascetic lifestyle and endurance in the face of suffering or persecution. The Acts of Peter had less to offer than some of the other Acts. Only two allusions to the Acts of Peter found their way into the Manichean psalm book,[76] and one, the reference to Eubula, may be to the character of the same name in the Acts of Paul.[77]

The *Vita Abercii*, composed in Asia Minor in the mid-fourth century, incorporated passages from Paul's speech in Acts of Peter 2 and Peter's speeches in Acts of Peter 7, 20, and 21 for use against Manicheans.[78] The Acts of Philip was written in the fourth or fifth century, probably in Phrygian Hierapolis. A brief report of the story of Peter's daughter and materials adapted from Acts of Peter 28 and 38 are reused in this Encratite setting.[79] The Pseudo-Titus epistle drew on several of the early apocryphal Acts in advocating virginity. It alludes to the story of Rufina (Acts Pet. 2) and provides the only surviving version of the story of the gardener's daughter. It is probably from a Priscillianist writing in Spain during the fifth century.[80] The Syriac Teaching of Simon Cephas in the City of Rome, also written in the fourth or fifth century, made use of elements of Peter's contest in the forum.[81]

In the Roman church, the early Acts of Peter was supplanted by versions that linked the deaths of Peter and Paul. The Pseudo-Hegesippus *De excidio Hierosolymitano*,[82] composed

---

73. F. Stanley Jones, *The Syriac Pseudo-Clementines: An Early Version of the First Christian Novel*, Apocryphes 14 (Turnhout: Brepols, 2014).

74. François Bovon, and Bertrand Bouvier, "Une fragment grec inédit des actes de Pierre?," *Apocrypha* 17 (2006): 9–54.

75. Jean-Daniel Kaestli, "L'utilisation des actes apocryphes des apôtres dans le manichéisme," in *Gnosis and Gnosticism: Papers Read at the Seventh International Conference on Patristic Studies (Oxford, September 8th–13th, 1975)*, ed. M. Krause, NHS 8 (Leiden: Brill, 1977), 107–16; Baldwin, *Whose Acts of Peter?*, 98.

76. Peter Nagel, "Die apokryphen Apostelakten des 2. und 3. Jahrhunderts in der manischäischen Literatur: Ein Beitrag zur Frage nach den christlichen Elementen im Manichäismus," in *Gnosis und Neues Testament: Studien aus Religionswissenschaft und Theologie*, ed. K.-W. Troeger (Gütersloh: Gütersloher, 1975), 149–82. See also Schäferdiek, "Manichaean Collection," 88–90.

77. Kaestli, "L'utilisation," 111.

78. See Baldwin, *Whose Acts of Peter?*, 197–241, for text and translation of the parallel passages.

79. See Frédéric Amsler, François Bovon, and Bertrand Bouvier, trans., *Actes de l'apôtre Philippe: Introduction, traduction et notes*, Apocryphes: Collection de Poche de L'AELAC 8 (Turnhout: Brepols, 1996); see also Bovon and Matthews, *Acts of Philip*.

80. Aurelio de Santos Otero, "The Pseudo-Titus Epistle," *NTApoc* 2:54.

81. David L. Eastman, *The Ancient Martyrdom Accounts of Peter and Paul*, WGRW 39 (Atlanta: SBL Press, 2015), 367–75.

82. Vincentius Ussani, *Hegesippi qui dicitur historiae libri V*, CSEL 66 (Vienna: Hoelder-Pichler-Tempsky, 1932).

around 370 CE in Rome, employs material from the contest in the forum and Peter's martyrdom, including a version of the *Quo vadis* scene. Simon is presented as a friend of Nero, and Paul is brought into the story, though with few details. The two apostles suffer martyrdom on the same day. The Pseudo-Linus Martyrdom of Peter from late fourth-century Rome elaborates on the Greek Martyrdom of Peter and includes some material from Pseudo-Hegesippus.[83] It circulated together with the Martyrdom of Paul, created on the basis of the martyrdom from the Acts of Paul. The Acts of Nereus and Achilleus uses a good deal of material from the Acts of Peter, including a greatly expanded version of the story of Peter's daughter.[84] The author, writing in Rome in the fifth or sixth century, may have also known the Pseudo-Linus Martyrdom.[85] The sixth-century Pseudo-Marcellus texts, the Martyrdom of Peter and Paul, and the Acts of Peter and Paul are based largely on the Pseudo-Linus Martyrdom.[86] In Pseudo-Marcellus, conflicts with the Jews motivate the martyrdoms of both apostles, but no specific confrontations that might reflect missing portions of the Acts of Peter are narrated. Book 1 of the Pseudo-Abdias Apostolic History, possibly written in Gaul in the sixth century, also employs material from the Acts of Peter.[87] The Acts of Xanthippe and Polyxena, another sixth-century text of uncertain provenance, makes extensive use of Acts of Peter 1–5.[88]

4. KEY PASSAGES FOR NEW TESTAMENT STUDIES AND THEIR SIGNIFICANCE

The Acts of Peter shows some of the ways that New Testament and related traditions were employed in the second half of the second century, a period when the New Testament canon was still under formation. The Acts of Peter draws material from the Pauline letters, the canonical Gospels, and the book of Acts, but does not treat any of these texts as author-itative. The Pauline epistles contribute names and phrases but no extensive quotations. There are possible allusions to all the canonical letters in the name of Paul, apart from 2 Thessalonians and Philemon. These Pauline elements occur throughout the Acts of Peter, but naturally are more numerous in the first three chapters, which deal with Paul in Rome. Despite the frequency of these echoes, none of Paul's characteristic ideas are evident. Both canonical and noncanonical sayings of Jesus are explicitly cited as sayings of the Lord. They are treated as authoritative but appear without settings in the life of Jesus. Isolated motifs from Acts and the Gospels appear throughout the Acts of Peter. It is rather free in its appropriation of narrative elements from the canonical Gospels and Acts. A few details are characteristic of the Gospel of Luke, but there is more evidence of the influence of the Gospel of Matthew. Stories such as Peter's walking on water can be referenced briefly as though they are familiar to the audience (Acts Pet. 7; 10). Other stories found in the New Testament appear in significantly different forms, as is the case with the transfiguration (Acts Pet. 20) and the encounter between Peter and Simon in Acts 8 (Acts Pet. 23).

Christine Thomas has argued that the differences in the ways biblical materials are treated correspond to the redactional layers she identifies. The earliest layer makes use of the Hebrew prophets. The second employs sayings of Jesus. The third shows freer

---

83. Eastman, *Ancient Martyrdom Accounts*, 27–65.

84. Text in Hans Achelis, *Acta SS. Nerei et Achillei: Texte und Untersuchung*, TUGAL 11.2 (Leipzig: Hinrichs, 1893). Discussion with translation of the parallel passages can be found in Baldwin, *Whose Acts of Peter?*, 61–80. See also Thomas, *Acts of Peter*, 45–46.

85. J. Flamion, "Les actes apocryphes de Pierre," *RHE* 11 (1910): 450–53.

86. Eastman, *Ancient Martyrdom Accounts*, 221–341.

87. Eastman, *Ancient Martyrdom Accounts*, 67–101.

88. Montague Rhodes James, *Apocrypha anecdota*, TS 2.3 (Cambridge: Cambridge University Press, 1893; repr., 1956), 43–85.

adaptation of New Testament narratives.[89] However, these differences may have more to do with the nature of the materials than with layers of editorial activity.

Clearly the Hebrew prophets, possibly known through testimony collections, are treated as authoritative. In his public refutation of Simon's slanders against Jesus (Acts Pet. 24), Peter offers quotations from the Psalms, Isaiah, and Daniel, most of which are familiar from the New Testament. In addition, a quotation attributed to Ezekiel by Tertullian (*Carn. Chr.* 22) and another from the Ascension of Isaiah 11.4 are cited to support a paradoxical understanding of the virgin birth. The Acts of Peter is explicit about the need to properly interpret these prophecies. The Roman crowd in the forum are not expected to understand their significance.

Dominical sayings have a similar oracular quality. They are treated as independent units, used without attention to their context in the Gospels. This may reflect the continued oral circulation of the sayings or the use of sayings collections similar to Q or the Gospel of Thomas. Like the words of the Hebrew prophets, the sayings of Jesus need interpretation, which is often provided by the new narrative context. In Acts of Peter 10, Marcellus attempts to justify his own lapse of faith by reminding Peter that Jesus had said, "If you have faith like a grain of mustard, if you say to this mountain, 'Move!', it will move immediately" (cf. Matt 17:20). Marcellus points out that despite this assurance, Peter doubted while walking on water. Marcellus then adds a noncanonical saying attributed to Jesus: "Those who are with me do not understand me" (cf. Acts John 92).

In the contest in the forum, Peter stops the crowd from attacking Simon by saying, "We have not learned to return evil for evil; rather we have been taught to love our enemies and to pray for our persecutors" (Acts Pet. 28). The first clause appears as ethical advice in New Testament letters (Rom 12:17; 1 Thess 5:15; 1 Pet 3:9). This aphorism also plays an important role in the Acts of Philip. More broadly, it was a philosophical commonplace, one important in the Socratic tradition. Here it is combined with a recognizable saying from the Sermon on the Mount (Matt 5:44). Although neither saying is explicitly attributed to Jesus, that seems to be implied.

Peter's speech from the cross employs two noncanonical sayings of Jesus. The saying about making "the things on the right as the things on the left" (Acts Pet. 38) has been discussed above under "3. Interpretive Issues." It fits the image of Peter's inverted crucifixion so well that one must wonder whether it lies behind that tradition. It is a powerful image of both the wrong-headed thinking that characterizes life dominated by the senses and the need for a complete reorientation in order to align oneself with the divine.[90] Peter goes on to say that those who take refuge in Jesus will receive "things which neither the eye has seen nor the ear heard nor has it entered the human heart" (Acts Pet. 39). Here, as in Gospel of Thomas 17 and 1 Clement 34.8, the saying is attributed to Jesus. The same phrase is cited as Scripture in 1 Corinthians 2:9. Origen says that Paul read it in the lost Apocalypse of Elijah (Origen, *Comm. Matt.* 5.29). The attribution of isolated sayings could be fluid.

After his death, Peter appears to Marcellus, who has given lavish attention to Peter's corpse. Peter asks Marcellus if he remembers the word of the Lord: "Let the dead be buried by their own dead" (cf. Matt 8:22; Luke 9:60).[91] The saying is no longer related to following Jesus. It is used here to support the belief that the body is worthless once the spirit has

---

89. Christine Thomas, "Canon and Antitype: The Relationship Between the *Acts of Peter* and the New Testament," *Semeia* 80 (1997): 185–205.

90. In Gos. Thom. 22, a longer version of the saying is linked to a related motif, becoming childlike.

91. The scene is reminiscent of Socrates's chastising Crito for asking how the philosopher wished to be buried (Plato, *Phaed.* 115c–116a).

left it. The saying has lost any sense of apocalyptic urgency, as is true of all the sayings of Jesus in the Acts of Peter. The sayings of Jesus have unchallenged authority in the Acts of Peter, but their meaning depends almost entirely on the context in which they are quoted.

The comments made by Peter in Acts of Peter 20 concerning the written testimony of the apostles show that narratives were seen as necessarily limited expressions of higher truths. So they have less authority for the writer than Old Testament prophecies or sayings of Jesus. The Acts of Peter, as represented by the *Actus Vercellenses*, shows significant influence from the canonical Acts. The clearest examples are the Lukan motif of the regular addition of large numbers of believers as a result of Peter's preaching and thaumaturgy, the image of Peter and Paul working in parallel, and the figure of Simon Magus. The opening three chapters relating Paul's activity in Rome (cf. Acts 28:30–31) and departure for Spain (cf. Rom 16:23) could easily follow the end of Acts. Vouaux speculated that the text was truncated for just that purpose.[92] Peter's encounter with Simon in Judea (Acts Pet. 17) loosely parallels Philip's encounter with Simon in Samaria reported in Acts 8:5–24. In the Acts of Peter 23, Simon never converts, but he offers money for the gift of healing. Healing is accomplished through the laying on of hands, which strongly suggests that the canonical story is in the background.[93] The freedom with which the author of the Acts of Peter treats the Lukan Acts indicates that Acts was recognized but not authoritative. Bovon has even suggested that the Acts of Peter, along with the other apocryphal Acts, is rooted in resistance to the movement toward the canonization of the Lukan Acts of the Apostles.[94]

The miracle stories in the Acts of Peter generally follow the patterns identified by New Testament form criticism. The miracles are signs of the power of Peter's God. However, in the Acts of Peter, miracles only rarely depend on the faith of the recipient. Rather, miracles engender faith by winning over pagan onlookers, restoring the faith of apostates, or bolstering the faith of believers. A few miracles are treated primarily as signs. A dried fish is brought to life in response to a crowd's demand for another sign before they will believe (Acts Pet. 13). Peter's compliance stands in stark contrast to the reply Jesus gives the Pharisees when they demand a sign in the Synoptic Gospels (Mark 8:11–13 and parr.). Peter's daughter is temporarily relieved of her paralysis in order to convince a questioning crowd that God has the power to do it (P.Berol. 8502.4). In most cases, however, the miracles produce important physical benefits. The blind receive sight. Widows have their deceased sons restored to them. At the same time, the miracles confer spiritual benefits, not only conversion but also deeper understanding. In the case of the blind widows in Marcellus's house, the healing of their physical sight is almost incidental to the spiritual insight that is gained through their vision of the polymorphous Christ (Acts Pet. 21).

The resurrection of the poor widow's son (Acts Pet. 27) is reminiscent of the raising of the widow's son in Luke 7:12–16. The story follows a traditional pattern, with some additions that integrate it into the context. It is not necessarily directly dependent on Luke, because the features they have in common are stock elements, including the son of a widow. Stories of miraculous resurrections in the ancient world typically involve young men, especially widow's sons, or slaves. The reason for the choice of these subjects is made plain by Artemidorus Daldianus in his book on dream interpretation. To dream that those

---

92. Vouaux, *Actes de Pierre*, 27–33.

93. Christopher R. Matthews, "The *Acts of Peter* and Luke's Intertextual Heritage," *Semeia* 80 (1997): 207–22.

94. François Bovon, "Vie des apôtres," in François Bovon et al., eds., *Les actes apocryphes des apôtres: Christianisme et monde païen*, Publications de la Faculté de Théologie de l'Université de Genève 4 (Geneva: Labor et Fides, 1981), 150.

who were dead live again signifies tumult (ταραχή; *tarachē*) and harm (βλάβη; *blabē*), because those who return to life would demand their possessions back (*Onir.* 3.62.). The resurrection of property owners is associated with disruptions of the social order because the norms around the transfer of property are not prepared to deal with it.[95] One episode in the Acts of Paul plays this theme out (P.Heid. 28). When Hermocrates is saved from imminent death, his son, who hoped to inherit the property, is angry and looks for a way to kill Paul. In the later apocryphal Acts, the rich and powerful are more frequently raised from the dead. In these texts, resurrection is associated with a new way of life, which often includes the renunciation of property. Here, the disruption of a society that is antithetical to Christianity is viewed positively.

The story of the poor widow's son is one of three resurrection stories worked into Peter's public contest with Simon in the forum (Acts Pet. 24–28). The framing story involving the prefect's slave is created for the context. The raising of the young senator, however, is constructed to parallel the story of the poor widow's son in many of its details. The two resurrections taken together show Christ's ability to care for his own and how that care affects groups differently. The son of the ordinary widow is destined to become a leader in the church after supporting his mother. The senator and his mother become donors, while the slaves who were freed for his funeral retain their freedom.

Not surprisingly, some of the traditions most closely associated with Peter in the New Testament appear in the Acts of Peter. Peter points to his experience of walking on water as an example of the power of faith (Acts Pet. 7). The story is referred to again in Acts of Peter 10. This time Peter's doubts on the water, found only in Matthew in the New Testament (Matt 14:28–31), are cited as evidence of the availability of forgiveness. This second reference is closely linked to Peter's triple denial of Jesus at his trial. Although it is a very compressed retelling, it includes the detail of Jesus turning toward Peter after the cock crows for the third time, which is found only in Luke (Luke 22:61). This is the kind of detail that could have been added by a copyist or translator at a later date, but it probably shows the author's familiarity with the Gospel of Luke.

The use of Christian texts and traditions in worship is portrayed in the complex of stories in Acts of Peter 20–21. As he enters a gathering of believers at the house of Marcellus, Peter encounters a blind widow being led by her daughter. Peter prays that Jesus, "through whom we have unapproachable light," will give his right hand to the woman (Acts Pet. 20). She immediately regains her sight. Vision, light, and helping hands are recurring motifs that unify this section. Inside the house, a reading from a Gospel is underway. With a gesture that resembles the synagogue scene in Luke 4:16–21, Peter rolls up the scroll. He refers to it as "holy Scripture," if that phrase is not a later addition. Peter comments that the things written about Jesus, even by those who knew him, are conditioned by the capacities of their authors.[96] This seems to imply the recognition of multiple Gospels and their inconsistencies. There are Christian Scriptures, but no canon is in place. Peter proceeds to explain the text by giving an account of the transfiguration that is significantly different from the canonical versions (Mark 9:2–8; Matt 17:1–8; Luke 9:28–36; 2 Pet 1:16–18). It includes the Matthean motif of Jesus giving his hand to Peter (Matt 17:1–8), so it is likely that at least this version is in the background. As in 2 Peter, neither Moses nor Elijah is

---

95. Lazarus is the only head of a household raised in the New Testament. While his return to life is presumably good for his sisters, the association with social unrest may help to explain the negative reaction of the Jewish authorities (John 11:38–48).

96. Acts of John 88 has a similar motif, but there the incapacity of the audience is blamed rather than that of the apostle.

mentioned. However, the two Old Testament figures are not relevant or necessary to the point in either version.

Peter's retelling of the story emphasizes the transcendence of God/Christ over against the weakness of human beings by focusing on the overpowering light and the indescribable voice of God/Jesus.[97] Peter is unable to comprehend—he can barely endure—the splendor, and he fears that he will lose his physical sight. Christ, however, is accommodating. He lifts Peter by the hand and returns to a form that the apostle can apprehend.[98]

Peter's account of the transfiguration is followed immediately by a series of antithetical statements underscoring the paradox of the divine presence in the world. Then Peter praises Christ with a list of titles. Many have parallels in the Gospel of John. Others are key terms from the Synoptic parables that are used here as christological titles, which may imply a tradition of applying these parables to Jesus rather than to the kingdom.

The section is finished by the healing of a group of blind widows. In response to Peter's prayer, the room is filled with an overwhelming, "ineffable, invisible light which no one can describe" (Acts Pet. 21). The women experience Christ appearing as a male figure of different ages who touches their eyes to restore their sight. The widows' experience of the polymorphic Christ reinforces what Peter said in his account of the transfiguration and in his mini sermon. The true nature of God and Christ remains beyond human comprehension, while the care given to believers demonstrates God's compassion.

5. BIBLIOGRAPHY

Baldwin, Matthew C. *Whose Acts of Peter? Text and Historical Context of the Actus Vercellenses.* WUNT 2.196. Tübingen: Mohr Siebeck, 2005.

Bauckham, Richard J. "The Martyrdom of Peter in Early Christian Literature." *ANRW* 26.1:539–95. Part 2, *Principat*, 26.1. Edited by H. Temporini and W. Haase. New York: de Gruyter, 1992.

Bovon, François, et al., eds. *Les actes apocryphes des apôtres: Christianisme et monde païen.* Publications de la Faculté de Théologie de l'Université de Genève 4. Geneva: Labor et Fides, 1981.

Bovon, François, Ann Graham Brock, and Christopher R. Matthews, eds. *The Apocryphal Acts of the Apostles: Harvard Divinity School Studies.* Religions of the World. Cambridge: Harvard University Center for the Study of World Religions, 1999.

Brashler, James, and Douglas M. Parrott. "The Act of Peter." Pages 473–93 in *Nag Hammadi Codices V, 2–5 and VI with Papyrus Berolinensis 8502,1 and 4.* Edited by Douglas M. Parrott. NHS 11, Coptic Gnostic Library. Leiden: Brill, 1979.

Bremmer, Jan N., ed. *The Apocryphal Acts of Peter: Magic, Miracles and Gnosticism.* Studies on the Apocryphal Acts of the Apostles 3. Louvain: Peeters, 1998.

Döhler, Marietheres. *Acta Petri: Text, Übersetzung und Kommentar zu den Actus Vercellenses.* Berlin: de Gruyter, 2018.

Eastman, David L. *The Ancient Martyrdom Accounts of Peter and Paul.* WGRW 39. Atlanta: SBL Press, 2015.

Poupon, Gérard. "Les 'Actes de Pierre' et leur remaniement." *ANRW* 25.6:4363–82. Part 2, *Principat*, 25.6. Edited by H. Temporini and W. Haase. Berlin: de Gruyter, 1988.

Stoops, Robert F., Jr. *The Acts of Peter.* Salem, OR: Polebridge, 2012.

Thomas, Christine M. *The Acts of Peter, Gospel Literature, and the Ancient Novel: Rewriting the Past.* Oxford: Oxford University Press, 2003.

Zwierlein, Otto. *Petrus in Rom: Die literarischen Zeugnisse. Mit einer kritischen Edition der Martyrien des Petrus und Paulus auf neuer handschriftliche Grundlage.* 2nd ed. UALG 109. Berlin: de Gruyter, 2010.

---

97. What is spoken by the voice is not reported, so the Father/Son dichotomy is avoided.

98. Acts of John 90 gives a similar and possibly related account of the transfiguration, but there John's special relationship with Christ and consequent superiority to Peter and James is emphasized.

CHAPTER 16

ACTS OF PHILIP

CHRISTOPHER R. MATTHEWS

1. INTRODUCTION

Raising the dead, healing the sick, pronouncing beatitudes, promoting virtue and chastity, touring the underworld, traveling with talking animals, battling dragons—the protagonist of the Acts of Philip both emulates the deeds and sayings of his Lord as found in the New Testament and breaks new ground, sometimes in wildly imaginative ways. Both the traditional and innovative aspects of his portrayal contribute to the crafting of an image of this disciple of Jesus that creatively depicts him as engaging and confronting the world in which some Christian believers of the earliest centuries found themselves.

1.1 Attestation

The text of the Acts of Philip presents many challenges to interpreters used to dealing with the relatively abundant supply of manuscript evidence for the texts of the New Testament. As is the case with apocryphal New Testament texts in general,[1] what manuscript evidence is available for the Acts of Philip shows that it, like many other texts that did not possess the cloak of canonicity, exhibits various degrees of fluidity as well as censorship in its textual presentation. A number of the acts in the second main part of the text have only recently become known to scholarship and are extant only in one manuscript, the recently edited Xenophontos 32 from Mt. Athos.[2] This manuscript appears to offer the most unexpurgated text for the Acts of Philip, with the exception of the martyrdom account at the end, and it will be used as the principal representative of the Acts of Philip in this overview. Apart from three discernable Greek recensions of the martyrdom account,[3] and variations between the Greek witnesses in other sections of the text where multiple witnesses exist, there are also numerous early "versions" of the Acts of Philip (e.g., Latin, Coptic, Syriac, Arabic, and Ethiopic).[4] But just as there is an evident fluidity in the

---

1. See François Bovon, "Editing the Apocryphal Acts of the Apostles," in Bovon, Brock, and Matthews, *Apocryphal Acts of the Apostles: Harvard Divinity School Studies*, ed. F. Bovon, A. Brock, and C. Matthews, Religions of the World (Cambridge: Harvard University Center for the Study of World Religions, 1999), 1–35.

2. François Bovon, Bertrand Bouvier, and Frederic Amsler, *Acta Philippi: Textus*, CCSA 11 (Turnhout: Brepols, 1999).

3. Joseph Flamion, "Les trois recensions grecques du Martyre de l'apôtre Philippe," in *Mélanges d'histoire offerts à Charles Moeller à l'occasion de son jubilé de 50 années de professorat à l'Université de Louvain 1863–1913*, vol. 1, *Antiquité et moyan âge*, Recueil de travaux publiés par les membres des conférences d'histoire et de philologie 40 (Louvain: Bureaux de Recueil, 1914), 215–25.

4. For a good overview of the manuscripts and versions, see the introduction in François Bovon and Christopher R. Matthews, *The Acts of Philip: A New Translation* (Waco, TX: Baylor University Press, 2012), 1–16.

transmission of the episodes in Greek, so too one encounters different levels of fluidity in the versions, which in some cases offer rather pronounced rewritings that significantly alter the thrust of the "original" text.

1.2 Provenance, Acts of Philip 1–7

As is already intimated by the state of the Greek manuscript evidence and that of the early versions, attempts to answer the standard array of introductory questions regarding the authorship of the Acts of Philip, its date, its provenance, and so forth, are frustrated by a variety of complications that apply to the Acts of Philip as it has come down to us. In broad terms, the full document is manifestly a composite construction that, in both its individual components and larger redactional presentation, has undergone a number of levels of elaboration. The first seven "acts" cannot be said to form anything other than a very loose unity, which is achieved simply by providing the designations "act one," "act two," and so forth, to the sequential presentation of the discrete scenes. In these vignettes Philip, ordinarily identified as the apostle, appears in various circumstances where he takes on roles and speaks words that are reminiscent of familiar New Testament episodes. In combination with this obvious intertextual engagement with the New Testament, one also finds positions and emphases that are much less familiar or even discordant with the main thrust of New Testament teaching. It is not at all obvious that these "tales" of Philip can be traced back to the same source in terms of their authorship, date, audience, and so forth. A partial exception is offered by Acts of Philip 5–7, however, which do exhibit narrative unity, sharing characters and a continuous story line across their borders. The concerns brought forward in these acts seem to offer some possibilities for discerning the basic contours of a sociohistorical or socioreligious context in which the scenario that plays out in their shared story line might have emerged.[5] Points of contact exist between Acts of Philip 5–7 and the "episodes" in Acts of Philip 1–4, but the divergences (especially in the case of act 2) raise questions about the feasibility of positing a common origin for everything that has been knit together to form the sequence of Acts of Philip 1–7. While one might speculate on a number of possible prehistories for the separate story lines of Acts of Philip 1–7, about all that seems certain is that at some point subsequent to their individual elaborations (granting that 5–7 likely forms a unit from the start), some person or group joined these seven acts together, and presumably intended them to form a composite portrait of Philip that was deemed useful to the redactors and their audience(s).

1.3 Provenance, Acts of Philip 8–15 and the Martyrdom

It is clear that with Acts of Philip 8 one makes a new beginning in the larger text, insofar as Acts of Philip 8–15 as well as the concluding Martyrdom present a unified novelistic account of Philip's journey to the mythical city of Ophioryme (or, Ophiorymous),[6] though the majority of manuscripts identify this name as a stand-in for Hierapolis, where Philip fulfills his destiny.[7] This section features a cast of constant companions for Philip, unlike

---

5. See Christopher R. Matthews, *Philip: Apostle and Evangelist: Configurations of a Tradition*, NovTSup 105 (Leiden: Brill, 2002), 186–89; and Debra J. Bucher, "Converts, Resisters, and Evangelists: Jews in the Acts of Philip V–VII," in *A Most Reliable Witness: Essays in Honor of Ross Shephard Kramer*, ed. Susan Ashbrook Harvey et al., BJS 358 (Providence, RI: Brown Judaic Studies, 2015), 9–16.

6. On the variation of the name of the city in which the martyrdom takes place, see Bovon, Bouvier, and Amsler, *Acta Philippi: Textus*, 244n12, and the references there.

7. On the possible engagement of these acts with the socioreligious situation in Hierapolis, see Frédéric Amsler, "Les Actes de Philippe: Aperçu d'une compétition religieuse en Phrygie" in *Le mystère apocryphe: Introduction à une littérature méconnue*, ed. J.-D. Kaestli and D. Marguerat, Essais Bibliques 26 (Geneva: Labor

the diverse situations presented in the first seven acts in which Philip essentially appears as an independent operator. Beginning in Acts of Philip 8, Philip receives a mission to carry out, in which he will be accompanied by Bartholomew, a disciple who tends to be closely associated with Philip in the various canonical lists of the Twelve, and Mariamne, a figure bearing traits of Mary Magdalene but who in this text plays the role of Philip's sister.[8] Soon after the story is underway, Philip and his associates are joined by two further traveling companions, a leopard and a kid goat, who represent the reconciliation of wild and domesticated animals under the sway of the universal Christian message, in this case fulfilling an expectation traced back to scriptural texts in Isaiah 11:6–9 and 65:25. These two animals acquire speech, assisted in their diction by Philip's prayerful intervention, and also insist on joining the apostolic mission, tearfully beseeching their human counterparts to baptize them and (it seems) allow them to partake in the small band's eucharistic celebration.[9]

1.4 Ancient Sectarian Context

There has been a fairly consistent assessment among researchers, even before the "rediscovery" of portions of the text in MS Xenophontos 32 unknown to most twentieth-century scholars, that the Acts of Philip was cultivated by certain fourth-century sectarian groups.[10] Eric Peterson had earlier made the case for connecting the particular contour of asceticism found in the text with the promotion of this ideal in Messalian texts and Ps.-Makarios.[11] Research on the apotactic and apostolic sectarian movements in fourth-century Asia Minor adds further context for the currents visible in our text.[12] Thus encratistic accents throughout much of the text, the incorporation of liturgical language in support of unorthodox theological and social positions, and critiques of majority ecclesial practices are among the clues found in the text that suggest it was prized by those who called on the authority of the apostle Philip to sanction their forms of worship and belief.[13] Indeed, opposition to what was viewed as extreme asceticism in the writings of Basil of Caesarea and others provides

---

et Fides, 1995), 125–40; idem, "The Apostle Philip, the Viper, the Leopard, and the Kid: The Masked Actors of a Religious Conflict in Hierapolis of Phrygia (*Acts of Philip* VIII–XV and *Martyrdom*)," in *Society of Biblical Literature 1996 Seminar Papers*, SBLSP 35 (Atlanta: Scholars Press, 1996), 432–37; and idem, "Remarques sur la réception liturgique et folklorique des *Actes de Philippe* (*APh* VIII–XV et *Martyre*)," *Apocrypha* 8 (1997): 251–64.

8. François Bovon, "Mary Magdalene's Paschal Privilege," in *New Testament Traditions and Apocryphal Narratives*, ed. F. Bovon, trans. J. Haapiseva-Hunter (Allison Park, PA: Pickwick, 1995), 228–35; and idem, "Mary Magdalene in the *Acts of Philip*," in *Which Mary? The Marys of Early Christian Tradition*, ed. F. S. Jones, SBLSymS 19 (Atlanta: Society of Biblical Literature, 2002), 75–89. See also idem, "Women Priestesses in the Apocryphal *Acts of Philip*," in *Walk in the Ways of Wisdom: Essays in Honor of Elisabeth Schüssler Fiorenza*, ed. S. Matthews, C. Kittredge, and M. Johnson-Debaufre (Harrisburg, PA: Trinity Press International, 2003), 109–21.

9. See Christopher R. Matthews, "Articulate Animals: A Multivalent Motif in the Apocryphal Acts of the Apostles," in Bovon, Brock, and Matthews, *Apocryphal Acts of the Apostles*, 225–31.

10. See François Bovon, "Les Actes de Philippe," *ANRW* 25.6:4521–23; and Bovon and Matthews, *Acts of Philip: A New Translation*, 8–9.

11. Erik Peterson, "Zum Messalianismus der Philippus-Akten," *OrChr* 7 (1932): 172–79; and idem, "Die Haretiker der Philippus-Akten," *ZNW* 31 (1932): 97–111.

12. See A. Lambert, "Apotactites et Apotaxamenes," *DACL* 1.2:2604–26; and Georges Blond, "L'heresie encratite vers la fin du quatrieme siecle," *RSR* 32 (1944): 157–210.

13. In addition to the studies cited in the previous notes, see Frédéric Amsler, "Amphiloque d'Iconium, Contre les hérétiques encratites et apotactites: Traduction française," in *Poussières de christianisme et de judaïsme antiques: Études réunies en l'honneur de Jean-Daniel Kaestli et Éric Junod*, ed. A. Frey and R. Gounelle, Publications de l'Institut romand des sciences bibliques 5 (Prahins, Switzerland: Zebre, 2007), 7–40; Constantine Bonis, "What Are the Heresies Combatted in the Work of Amphilochios Metropolitan of Iconium (ca 341/5–ca 395/400) 'Regarding False Asceticism'?," *Greek Orthodox Theological Review* 6 (1963): 79–96; and Richard N. Slater, "An Inquiry into the Relationship between Community and Text: The Apocryphal *Acts*

some confirmation for this supposition. It seems that it was some fourth-century ecclesial situation such as this that provided the environment in which such strange stories could be cultivated and also amalgamated with additional "adventures" of Philip to form the larger document that we today know as the Acts of Philip.

2. SUMMARY OF CONTENT[14]

Acts of Philip 1 opens abruptly with Philip encountering a widow carrying out her only son for burial. Moved by her dreadful appearance, the apostle asks what religion her son had practiced. The woman recounts her religious observances on behalf of numerous gods, their failure to respond to her cries, and her consultation of a seer who only foretold lies. She admits that she has despised the Christians; but now she has lost her only son (§1). Philip replies that this is how the devil leads people astray and promises to raise her son by the power of his God, Jesus Christ. Taking heart, the old woman reflects that perhaps it is profitable not to marry, and to eat bread and water instead of wine and meat (§2). Philip suggests that her words show that the Savior is already speaking through her about purity, observing that God associates with purity itself, and speaks a beatitude. The woman responds with a profession: "I believe in Jesus and in holy virginity" (§3). Philip commands the young man to arise, and the latter gets up as if from sleep and asks how, through Philip's intervention, an angel was able to extract him from the prison of judgment (§4). In a succession of scenes, the young man describes in great detail the horrendous punishments and torments he has witnessed in the underworld; the rescuing angel or the victims themselves provide commentary on the suitability of the diverse agonies for particular sins (§5–14). Philip urges the young man to protect himself from such a fate through baptism (§15). The young man recounts one more particularly gruesome torture—two men burning in a frying pan and forced to drink molten lead "because they were intoxicated with all evils" (§16). The young man notes that the way of the righteous leads into the place of refreshment (§17). As the scene ends, the boy and his mother believe, many are converted, abundant provisions are given to the apostle for the road, and the young man follows Philip, exulting in his daily miracles and glorifying God.

Acts of Philip 2 presents an entirely new scene. Philip arrives in the city of the Athenians, and three hundred philosophers ask whether he can present something new (§§1–2). Philip recounts how Jesus chose twelve to preach the good news, which accounts for his arrival (§§3–4). The philosophers confer for three days about the name Jesus and send for the high priest of the Jews to debate Philip (§§5–6). Ananias, the great high priest of the Jews in Jerusalem, is enraged when he receives their letter about Philip's miracles and spreading fame; Mansemat, or Satan, secretly enters him. Ananias consults with teachers of the law and Pharisees, who advise him to go to Athens with five hundred strong men and eliminate Philip (§§7–8). Ananias arrives in Hellas with great pomp and labels Philip a sorcerer and magician (§9). He speaks of the heresy taught by Jesus, who was crucified for destroying the law. He claims that his disciples stole his body to proclaim his resurrection and spread "the magic of Jesus" throughout the world. He announces that he has come to take Philip back to Jerusalem where Archelaus the king seeks to execute him (§10). Philip

---

of Philip I and the Encratites of Asia Minor," in Bovon, Brock, and Matthews, *Apocryphal Acts of the Apostles*, 281–306.

14. The following paragraphs provide an indication of the content of the various acts of the Acts Phil., according to the structure outlined above. The summary follows the text of Xenophontos 32 (A) wherever possible, filling in lacunae with the evidence of various other witnesses. Numbers in parentheses refer to the paragraphs in the critical edition of Bovon, Bouvier, and Amsler, *Acta Philippi: Textus.*

tells the Athenians that he has come not with words but wonders (§11). When Ananias attempts to whip Philip, his hand withers and his eyes are blinded; his five hundred men are likewise blinded (§12). Philip calls on Jesus to expose the current madness (§13). Ananias asks whether Philip really expects them to turn from "our fathers" to follow the Nazarene Jesus. Philip replies that he will pray for God's manifestation, and if Ananias persists in unbelief, he will descend alive into Hades (§14). Suddenly Jesus descends in fantastic glory, and all the idols of Athens are broken and the demons in them flee. But Ananias refuses to believe (§15). Jesus reascends, and an earthquake splits the ground. The crowd and the five hundred men beg for mercy, the latter noting that it is impossible for sinful people to fight with God (§16). A voice from heaven announces that the Father will do whatever Philip asks. Philip restores Ananias's sight in the name of Jesus and asks whether he now believes. Ananias replies that he cannot be persuaded through such magical arts (§17). The apostle prays to Jesus: "Zabarthan, sabathabat, bramanouch, come quickly!" and immediately the ground swallows Ananias up to his knees. He protests loudly but maintains his resolve not to believe (§18). Philip angrily commands the earth to swallow Ananias up to his navel (§19). Philip gestures over the five hundred men in the name of Jesus, and they regain their sight. Ananias laughs scornfully (§20). Philip commands the earth to swallow him up to his neck (§21). A leading citizen tells the "blessed apostle" that a demon has killed his son in retaliation for Philip's destruction of demonic worship in the city (§22). Philip promises to restore the man's son through Christ. When Ananias claims he will not believe even if the boy is raised, Philip commands his immediate departure into the abyss. The high priestly garment detaches itself from Ananias and flies off, never to be seen again. Then Philip restores the young man living to his father (§23). The crowds acclaim the God of Philip as the only God. Philip stays in Athens for two years, builds a church, and leaves to evangelize Parthia (§24).[15]

Acts of Philip 3 opens in a city of Parthia. Philip encounters Peter, other disciples, and women who imitate the male faith, and he requests that they strengthen him to evangelize and live in continence. They rejoice at Philip's resolve to complete his apostleship and deaconship (§1). John tells Philip, "his brother and fellow apostle," that Andrew has gone to Achaia and Thrace, Thomas to India and the murderous flesh eaters, and Matthew to the Troglodytes. He urges Philip not to be dejected (§2). Philip asks John and Peter to pray for him so that he may fulfill his apostleship. He prepares for a long journey, and Jesus travels with him in secret (§3). Philip offers a lengthy prayer, asking that Jesus manifest himself in his glory: "Physician of our inner self, strengthen me in your wisdom" (§4). A large eagle is perched in a great tree with its wings extended in a type of the true cross (§5).[16] Perceiving that the Lord Jesus Christ is revealing himself in this great image, Philip offers a series of reflections on how the eternal Lord could have known birth and suffered on the cross (§6). Philip falls to his knees and worships (§7). Jesus speaks as though from the mouth of the eagle and confirms that he has blessed him and displayed his glory to him. He promises to guide Philip as he guides his apostolic brethren (§8). Jesus tells Philip to rise and proceed: "Behold, I am with you." (§9). Philip travels by sea to the borders of the Candacians and boards a boat there to sail to Azotus (§10). A storm endangers the ship, and locusts afflict

---

15. The note about Parthia appears to be an editorial insertion to smooth the transition to act three when these acts were joined together; see Matthews, *Philip: Apostle and Evangelist*, 168–70.

16. For a multifaceted analysis of the miraculous aspects of Acts Phil. 3.5–19, see Christopher R. Matthews, "Kreuzformiger Adler und leuchtendes Siegel (Sturmstillung und sprechender Adler): ActPhil 3,5–19," in *Die Wunder der Apostel*, vol. 2 of *Kompendium der frühchristlichen Wundererzählungen*, ed. R. Zimmermann (Gütersloh: Gütersloher, 2017), 927–34.

the sailors (§11). Philip calls out to Christ. A shining signet in the form of a cross appears and illuminates the sea. The creatures in the sea form a circle and make obeisance to the light, howling out hymns in their language. The air becomes still, and the locusts perish (§12). Philip offers a lengthy prayer, punctuated by a series of contemplations on the hidden glory of the incarnated Jesus (§13). All these events astonish those on the ship, who fix their eyes on heaven (§14). When the boat arrives at Azotus, the sailors comment that the city will be blessed by Philip's presence. Philip, in simple dress, addresses those at the city gate. He speaks of the beneficial effects of continence and abasement of the flesh on the soul. With reference to the image of eagles teaching their young, he urges his listeners to focus on the essence above. Many are restored to health and baptized (§§15–19).

As Acts of Philip 4 begins, Philip's fame as a miracle worker spreads in Azotus. Some suppose him to be a magician, while others criticize him for dividing spouses with his teaching about chastity leading to a vision of God (§1). When Philip prays to Jesus about his lodging, a beautiful child appears and indicates some storehouses owned by a certain Nikokleides, a friend of the king (§2). Philip speaks at length to his soul about the benefits of the food of the Spirit (§3). Nikokleides's daughter Charitine, who suffers from a deformity in her right eye, listens to Philip through the night and weeps. In the morning she insists to her father that the strange doctor residing in his storehouses can heal her. Nikokleides brings Philip to her, and she has her house purified for the entrance of Philip's doctor, Jesus (§4). Philip tells Charitine that Jesus will make known to her the tents in the highest places where there is eternal rest. He asks her to pass her right hand before her face and say, "In the name of Jesus Christ, let the deformity of my eye be cured." She is immediately cured and glorifies God (§5). Father and daughter believe and are baptized. Charitine adopts a male appearance and clothing and follows Philip (§6).

In Acts of Philip 5, the arrival of Philip with a band of disciples in Nicatera creates a disturbance in the city (§§1–2). When "the brothers" ask where they will stay, Philip offers a short exhortation on Christ's assistance (§3). When they are distressed by the turmoil in the city, Philip assures them that Jesus, the "just athlete," is with them (§4). An angry crowd, worried about Philip's teaching about the separation of husbands and wives on the principle that purity consorts with God, decide to oppose his stay in the city (§5). Jews also voice harsh words against Philip and his undoing of their traditions, but one of them, Ireos, counsels restraint (§6). When Ireos asks Philip what will happen if he follows him, Philip replies that he and his house will be saved (§7). Ireos announces that he has prepared his soul for salvation, and Philip tells him to bid farewell to his wife, Nerkella (§8). Ireos expresses to Nerkella his wish that their house become a dwelling place for Philip's God, but she worries that Philip separates husbands and wives (§9). Ireos responds that Philip offers them better things than their vain wealth (§10). When Nerkella asks whether Philip's God is made of gold and is secure in a temple, Ireos replies that Philip's God is the God who lives in the heavens (§11). Ireos invites Philip to stay in his house, and Philip describes everything that had just transpired between him and his wife (§12). Philip announces that Jesus has directed him to go to Ireos's house (§13). The city rulers and the multitude are troubled when they see Philip and his companions conducted to Ireos's house with honor. Ireos advises his wife to shed her seven layers of clothing interwoven with gold and put on others proper for immortality (§14). Philip rejects the gold chairs brought for him and his companions, explaining that gold and silver are unnecessary things that will be consumed by fire (§15). When Ireos expresses anxiety about his former sins, Philip assures him that Jesus can remove sins committed in ignorance (§16). The doorkeeper believes in Christ when she realizes that Philip knows the things spoken by his mistress in private. When the maidservant Marklaina thinks to herself about repentance and salvation, Philip informs her that she will be saved (§17). Ireos goes to his wife and urges her to see the man of God, who knows what happens in private (§18). Philip, aware of Ireos's concern over his wife, prays to Jesus for guidance. The Savior appears to him and announces that both will be saved (§19). Nerkella's unbelief falls away, and she says to Ireos, "Blessed is the one who is not undecided" (§20). Her beautiful daughter Artemilla declares that she, too, wishes to participate in this alternative life. Nerkella and her daughter put on humble clothing (§21). Only their eyes are uncovered when Ireos leads them out, and they all see Philip as a great light, encircled by his disciples (§22). When Philip returns to his usual appearance, Nerkella invites him into the house and voices regret for her previous unbelief (§23). Philip declares that all will be saved by Jesus. Nerkella and Artemilla renounce their possessions and beauty (§24). At this, Philip pronounces three beatitudes, and all are filled with joy (§25). Ireos brings bread and vegetables, but Philip declines to eat in preparation for an upcoming contest (§26). A great crowd assembles at Ireos's house, listens to Philip's word, and believes (§27).

In Acts of Philip 6, all the Jews and idolaters in Nikatera are agitated because Ireos and his household have believed in Christ. They identify Philip as a magician who has deceived many (§1). Seven men of the highest status are sent to fetch Ireos, who follows them, smiling and unconcerned (§2). The rulers are amazed by Ireos's humble dress and modest contingent of twelve servants. One, named Onesimus, acknowledging his unworthiness to address Ireos, asks how he has been deceived by the stranger, who separates married couples, preaches chastity, and maintains the resurrection of the dead (§3). Ireos asks why he is being interrogated on account of a just man (§4). He informs Philip that the whole city is against them and offers to write to the governor for help. Philip tells him that Jesus is able to contend on his behalf (§5). The rulers and all the city seize Philip at Ireos's house and lead him, followed by three hundred of Ireos's slaves, to the council chamber to be flogged (§6). Ireos warns them not to strike Philip without cause, for Caesar will hear of it. The crowd refers to Philip's strange instruction about remaining chaste to live as stars in heaven, and about the crucified God (§7). The crowd is aware that Philip is highborn and gave up a fortune to follow Jesus. They are afraid he will strike them blind (§8). The Jews grumble at Philip's words, and the most prominent among them, Aristarchus, proposes a public debate about Jesus (§9). He grabs Philip's beard to drag him, and while Philip feels no pain, Aristarchus's hand withers, he becomes deaf, and his right eye is blinded. He pleads with his Jewish companions to intercede with Philip, "For truly, human beings cannot fight with God" (§§10–11). Philip directs Ireos to make the sign of the cross on Aristarchus's head, and the latter tells of seeing a child from heaven go to Philip and speak to him to sanction the healing. Aristarchus renews his debate proposal (§12). Aristarchus, the president of the synagogue, goes first, reciting various scriptural texts and inquiring about the virgin birth, Jesus's divine identity, and Philip's contending on behalf of Christ (§13). Philip quotes his own series of scriptural texts, arguing that all the prophets and patriarchs proclaimed Christ's coming (§14). The rulers announce that Philip has guided them to the truth and that there is no basis for action against him. Both he and Aristarchus have revealed Christ with certainty (§15). When the funeral procession of the only son of a wealthy couple appears, carried by twelve slaves who are to be burned with him, a contest is proposed to see whether God is in Philip (§16).[17] Philip asks what the weeping parents

---

17. For a multifaceted analysis of the miraculous aspects of Acts Phil. 6.16–22, see Julia A. Snyder, "Sieg durch Wunder (Totenerweckung in Nikatera): ActPhil 6,16–22," in Zimmermann, *Die Wunder der Apostel*, 935–52.

will do if he raises their son. They are not only willing to grant his request for the lives of the twelve slaves but also promise to divest themselves of their wealth, smash their idols, and believe in the God of Philip (§17). Philip asks Aristarchus to attempt to raise the dead boy, Theophilus. He touches his face, spits on him a great deal, and drags him by the hand, but the corpse is unaffected (§18). Nereus, the boy's father, offers to fight against the Jews if his son is raised. Philip demands, rather, that he promise not to do wrong to the Jews (§19). Philip places his hands on the boy and prays. Theophilus rises and cries out, "There is only one God, that of Philip, Jesus Christ, who gave me life." The crowd affirms this (§20). Three thousand souls believe in Christ, the prefect confers freedom on the slaves, and Philip's disciples prepare bread and vegetables so he can break his fast (§§21–22).

As Acts of Philip 7 opens, Ireos's wife Nercella and her daughter Artemilla rejoice over Philip (§1). Ireos asks Philip where he wishes to build a synagogue in the name of Christ. Ireos and Nereus agree on construction plans and spend much gold. The Jews are jealous but decide to keep their distance. All the believers come into the meeting place and are amazed and rejoice at Philip's teaching about the magnificent things of Christ (§§2–4). Philip directs the brothers to associate with one another in purity, warning them not to forget his words but to keep them in their hearts. They weep because Philip has told them he is departing. Philip tells them not to let their hearts be distressed, for he must also go to other cities to fulfill the will of Christ (§§5–6). Twenty stadia into his journey, the multitudes still follow Philip. Then, taking only five loaves and invoking Jesus, he orders them to return to the city with the camels and their abundant provisions. A voice comes out of heaven, "Press on, Philip! I, Jesus, am waiting for you on the ship in the upper harbor, because I will not abandon you" (§§7–8).

As Acts of Philip 8 opens, the apostles are dispersing to their respective missionary territories: Peter to Rome, John to Asia, Thomas to Parthia and India, and so forth, ending with Philip to the land of the Greeks (§1).[18] Philip grumbles and weeps over his harsh lot. John and Mariamne, Philip's sister, are present. She speaks with the Savior about Philip's displeasure (§2). The Savior comments on her manly soul and blessedness among women, and he commissions her to accompany Philip in all his travels. Bartholomew will also go with him. John will later embolden them in martyrdom (§3). The Savior instructs Mariamne to change her appearance and dress as a man and proceed with her brother to the city of Opheorymos ("Promenade of the Serpents"), where people worship the Viper. The serpents there must not see her in the form of Eve, given the hostility that arose at the time of Eve and Adam (§4). The Savior continues an extended commissioning discourse, treating a variety of topics, supporting his promise to be with them in every place. A short natural-history disquisition on the sun, moon, stars, lower air, and four winds illustrates God's providence (§5). The Savior will aid them when harassed, and if their blood is shed, he will collect it in his shining robe and offer it to the Father. Their tombs will be called the dwelling places of the saints (§6). They are not to fear the bite of the serpents or their poison, for their mouths will be shut and their boasts will be in vain (§7). Philip is still crying in view of the persecution that awaits him, fearing that he will repay evil with evil (§8). The Savior extols the grace received by the one who repays good to the one who has done him evil (§9). The Savior offers a lesson on the nature of the world to show that that which does good increases, not that which does evil (§10). He indicates how this applied

---

18. Xenophontos 32 breaks off here, amid this list, where pages have been torn from the codex. The order of the names and particular places are somewhat different in Athens 346 (G), which ends with the reference to Philip.

in the condemnation of the Watchers, when Noah gathered seven pairs of clean animals, but only two pairs of unclean (§11). It was Noah's model that Peter recalled when he asked about forgiving up to seven times (§12). After additional "natural-history" illustrations, the Savior calls Philip to imitate all good things (§§13–14). Rejoicing over these lessons, Philip goes forth with Bartholomew and Mariamne, to the land of the Ophianeans (§15).[19] In the wilderness of the she-dragons, a great leopard comes out of the mountain forest, throws itself at the apostles' feet, and speaks with a human voice (§16).[20] It recounts how it seized a kid from a herd of goats and dragged it off to eat it, but the wounded kid, taking on a human voice, urged it to put on mildness, because the apostles of the divine greatness were nearby. And the leopard's fierceness turned to gentleness. The leopard asks to be permitted to accompany Philip everywhere and to lay aside his beast-like nature (§17). When the leopard leads the apostles to where the kid is lying under a tree, Philip and Bartholomew acknowledge the unsurpassed compassion of the philanthropic Jesus. They pray that the animals might receive human hearts and follow the apostles everywhere. The leopard and the kid stand and raise up their forefeet and glorify God with human voices. The apostles glorify God and resolve that the animals will travel with them (§§18–21).[21]

At the start of Acts of Philip 9, Philip, Bartholomew, Mariamne, the leopard, and the kid proceed on their way for five days. After midnight prayers, a strong wind brings on a murky gloom, out of which a great and dark dragon emerges, accompanied by multitudes of snakes (§1). Philip tells his companions to recall Christ's words to fear nothing (§2). They take their cup and offer a prayer. Philip instructs them to lift their hands with the cup and sprinkle the air with the sign of the cross. A flash like lightning dries up the dragon and the beasts with it, and the apostles continue on their way, praising the Lord (§§3–5).

Acts of Philip 10 currently remains lost, and the beginning of Acts of Philip 11 is missing. The extant text of Acts of Philip 11 starts with the end of a prayer by Philip. Bartholomew and Mariamne, about to receive the Eucharist, have fasted for five days to become worthy (§1). Suddenly an earthquake occurs, and voices emerge from a group of broken stones. They reveal that they are fifty demons sharing one nature and that the slaves of Christ now travel everywhere with Jesus, destroying their race (§2). When the apostle asks that they show their ancient nature, the dragon among them replies that it was cursed in paradise, lurked in Cain, and with feminine beauty brought down angels from heaven; it notes that their current nature was engendered when the rod of Moses refuted the wise men and magicians of Egypt (§3). The apostle prays to Jesus and then adjures the demons to show their number and form. The demons exit the pile of broken stones in the form of serpents; then, after a tremendous earthquake, a great dragon appears in their midst (§§4–5). It addresses Philip as "son of thunder" and requests not to be destroyed but that its demonic power, which once served Solomon in Jerusalem in the construction of the temple, be transformed to serve Philip by building a church (§6). Philip inquires how serpents can build, and the dragon replies about their nature and a series of demonic attributes. They work unseen for three hours and produce fifty high columns (§7). The church is finished in six days, and streams like rivers flow from it. After a few more days, about three thousand

---

19. Athens 346 (G) breaks off here; Vaticanus graecus 824 picks up at paragraph sixteen.

20. For the following episodes dealing with the talking animals, see Matthews, "Articulate Animals," in Bovon, Brock, and Matthews, *Apocryphal Acts of the Apostles*, 205–32; see also François Bovon, "The Child and the Beast: Fighting Violence in Ancient Christianity," *HTR* 92 (1999): 372–76.

21. For a multifaceted analysis of the miraculous aspects of Acts Phil. 8.16–21, see Christopher R. Matthews, "Ein veganes Evangelium fur Tiere (Bekehrung des Leoparden und der jungen Ziege): ActPhil 8,16–21," in Zimmermann, *Die Wunder der Apostel*, 953–58.

men and many women and infants gather and worship Christ. The dragon informs Philip that it is departing (§8). Philip prays in his soul, enumerating various attributes of the Lord. Then he distributes the Eucharist to Bartholomew and Mariamne (§§9–10).

Acts of Philip 12 opens with Philip, Bartholomew, and Mariamne rejoicing over the Eucharist, while the leopard and the kid look on, weeping excessively (§1). The leopard begins a defense of the animals' grief, relating how his savage nature has changed to goodness (§2). He and the kid are weeping because they have not been deemed worthy of the Eucharist. Yet they have used human speech and prayed to God, and when the Only-Begotten killed the dragon and the serpents by the beauty of his form, they were not excluded from his mystery or the wonder of his face (§3). The leopard continues with his impassioned plea: "Show us mercy . . . since he is in everyone." He is confident that this will happen through the apostles (§§4–5). As the leopard and kid continue to weep, the apostle observes that God has visited everything through his Christ, not only human beings but also animals of every sort (§6). Philip raises his hands and prays to Jesus that he might make the animals appear to themselves as human. He takes the cup and sprinkles the animals with water, and little by little the forms of their faces and bodies become human. They stand, stretch out their forefeet in place of hands, and glorify God for their birth into immortality in the receipt of a human body in place of that of a beast (§§7–8).

The apostles and animals are journeying toward the city as Acts of Philip 13 begins, the leopard leading the way. As they approach, seven men advance to meet them, each with a serpent on his shoulder that will bite any who do not share their worship of the Viper (§1). When the men let down their serpents to assess the apostles, the serpents bow their heads to the ground and bite their own tongues, leading the men to conclude that the apostles also worship the Viper. Philip and company proceed; the men are amazed by the speaking animals (§2). Philip looks at the two large dragons guarding the city gate, and they see the ray of the light of the Monad shining in his eyes; turning their heads aside, they expire (§3). The apostles find a vacant clinic near the gate, and Philip suggests that they establish themselves there and practice healing. He then offers an extended prayer to the "living voice of the highest" (§§4–5).

At the start of Acts of Philip 14, a rich man named Stachys, blind for forty years, hears Philip's prayer through his window. He asks his children to take him to those at the clinic since they can restore his sight (§1).[22] Led by his sons and their slaves to the apostles, Stachys prostrates himself before them. He relates that before he became blind he persecuted strangers and Christians and surpassed all who worshiped the Viper (§2). He tells the tale of his blindness. His eyes were first inflamed for ten years after applying supposedly therapeutic liquid from serpents' eggs. His wife used to collect dew from the mountain to assuage his affliction, but she was killed by a large beast. Since then, Stachys has been blind (§3). He next relates a dream in which a voice told him to find the physician at the city gate who would give him light. In his dream, he does as instructed and regains his sight; he sees the likeness of a handsome young man with three faces: a beardless youth, a woman in glorious apparel, and an old man. Everyone in the city is baptized by the young man, and their bodies become bright (§4). Philip responds with another prayer, then he explains that Stachys's vision was from the Holy Spirit and prior to it he had been bound by Satan, who had kept him blind (§§5–6). Philip draws Stachys near and extends his hand and dips his

---

22. For a multifaceted analysis of the miraculous aspects of Acts Phil. 14.1–7, see Christopher R. Matthews, "Heilkraftige Schmiere (Wunder in Opheorymos. Die Heilung des blinden Stachys mit Mariamnes Speichel): ActPhil 14,1–7," in Zimmermann, *Die Wunder der Apostel*, 959–65.

finger in Mariamne's mouth and smears . . .[23] . . . and Stachys prepared a great reception for them (§7). A great crowd gathers at Stachys's house, witnessing the healing of those sick and demon possessed. Philip was baptizing the men, Mariamne the women, and the leopard and the kid were pronouncing the amen (§§8–9).

Acts of Philip 15 sets up the situation that leads to the martyrdom. Nicanora, the Syrian wife of Turannognophos, the governor of the city, had been bitten by the city serpents as a stranger and suffered from their venom. Hearing about Stachys's cure, she goes secretly to his house where the apostles are present (§1). Philip points out to Stachys that he must adjust his diet, avoid indulging in wine, not boast in silver or gold, and cultivate continence and asceticism (§2). He informs Stachys that the peace of God has taken root in his house; his sons are to be useful, his daughters virgins, and his servants taught continence (§§2–3). Philip places his staff in Stachys's courtyard, prays, and it buds and becomes a laurel plant. Three jars are filled with grain, wine, and olive oil to care for the poor (§§4–5). Nicanora hears the apostle's words, sees the signs being done, and forgets her ailment. Her servants warn her about Turannognophos's brutality, and she returns home, grieving. At night she prays to God that Turannognophos might believe or die. Turannognophos tells her that if he discovers that she has gone to the apostles, he will take vengeance on them and shut her in a dark place (§§6–7). Philip, Bartholomew, Mariamne, the leopard, and the kid remain in the house of Stachys (§8).

The martyrdom opens with a chronological note placing Philip in Trajan's eighth year and locating him in the cities and regions of Lydia (§1). He reaches the city of Ophioryme, which is identified as Hierapolis, and is welcomed by Stachys. Bartholomew, Mariamne, and his disciples are with him. Many assemble at the house of Stachys for instruction about Jesus by Philip and Bartholomew (§2). Mariamne, sitting at the entrance to the house, invites those approaching to listen to the apostles. An extended account of their message is provided (§3). "Trample down the snares of the enemy and the coiling serpent" (§4). "Become faithful, doers of good, free from deceit" (§5). "God has become present through us to you, to show you mercy and deliver you from the evil snare of the enemy" (§6). Philip's words, aimed at those who from time immemorial revered the serpents and the Viper, are effective, and a great multitude is added to Philip and those around him (§7). Nicanora, the proconsul's wife, who suffers from various ailments, hears about Philip and believes in Jesus. She is delivered from her afflictions when she calls on Jesus's name. Leaving her house by the side door, her slaves carry her in a silver litter to Stachys's house (§8). At the entrance to the house, Mariamne delivers a short speech in Hebrew to her "twin sister" about the latter's redemption (§9). Nicanora cries out: "I am a Hebrew and a daughter of Hebrews"; she reveals that her disease has been cured (§10). Philip prays for her to God together with Bartholomew and Mariamne and those with them (§11). Suddenly Tyrannos, Nicanora's husband, arrives enraged and threateningly inquires about her presence with "these magicians," the healing of her eyes, and the identity of her doctor (§12). She responds with an extended appeal for his reform from the ways of the "cruel dragon and his desires" (§13). But Tyrannos drags her by the hair and kicks her, declaring, "It is better for you to die by the sword than for you to be seen by me fornicating with these magicians." By his orders Philip, Bartholomew, and Mariamne are brought to the proconsul's place (§14). After they are flogged with rough leather straps, they are bound by the feet and dragged through the city

---

23. It seems that folios from the manuscript have been intentionally removed at this point, presumably to eliminate the account of the healing of Stachys by Mariamne's saliva. See Bovon, Bouvier, and Amsler, *Acta Philippi: Textus*, 328n33.

streets before large crowds (§15). After the proconsul has the saints around Philip tortured, he orders them to be secured in the temple of the Viper (§16). The priests of the Viper and a crowd of some seven hundred men demand that the proconsul avenge them against the seducers who have led the people astray. They complain about lack of wine to offer to the Viper, the slain dragons at the city gate, and the teaching about living in purity and holiness (§17). Further angered, the proconsul complains about his wife's enchantment, her night-time prayer, and a bright ray of light that momentarily blinded him (§18). He orders Philip and the others brought out from the temple, stripped, and searched for the instruments of their magic. Philip is hung by his ankles on a tree before the temple; Bartholomew faces him, pinned by his hands on the wall of the temple gate (§19). Philip and Bartholomew smile at one another, for their punishments are prizes and crowns. When Mariamne is stripped, her body is immediately changed, and a cloud of fire surrounds her (§20). Philip asks Bartholomew in Hebrew about John's whereabouts. Observing Stachys's house ablaze, he asks whether they should call down fire upon their tormentors (§21). Just then, John enters the city, as though a resident, and learns what is happening (§22). Led to the scene of the apostles' torture, he says, "The mystery of the one who was hung in the middle between heaven and earth, will be with you" (§23). He then delivers a short speech on how the people of "Ophioryme Hierapolis" have been led astray by error (§24). Those who attempt to seize John find their hands paralyzed. John urges Philip not to return evil for evil, but Philip declares he cannot hold back (§25). John, Bartholomew, and Mariamne try to calm him by recalling several examples from the life of Jesus. But Philip begins to curse the locals in Hebrew and utters a long prayer to open Hades so that the great abyss can swallow up the city's godless residents (§26). Suddenly the abyss opens and the whole place where the proconsul sat is swallowed up, along with the temple, the Viper, the priests, and about seven thousand men, let alone women and children. Only the apostles remain unmoved. Pleas for mercy rise from the abyss with acknowledgments of the unjust crucifixion of the apostles. A voice declares, "I will be merciful to you by my luminous cross" (§27). Stachys and his household, Nicanora and fifty other believing women, and various others remain above, as they had been marked with the seal of Christ (§28). The Lord then appears to Philip and asks why he has disobeyed and returned evil for evil. He delivers a series of sayings to exploit this teachable moment (§29). Philip suggests that he has only done what was warranted (§30). The Savior explains that as punishment for his disobedience, at his passing, Philip will be barred from paradise for forty days. Bartholomew will depart for Lycaonia, where he will be crucified, and Mariamne's body will be placed in the Jordan River (§31). The Savior sketches out a cross in the air, from the heights to the abyss. It appears like a ladder, and all those in the abyss come back up; but the proconsul and the Viper remain. When the returning crowds see Philip hanging head downward, they mourn their lawless act (§32). Philip speaks to them about his rash act and urges them to reject evil (§33). When some of the faithful move to take Philip down, he explains that this is to be the fulfillment of his life. He refers to himself as bearing the type of the first human, brought head downward upon the earth and once more made alive through the cross of wood. This fulfills the Lord's saying to him: "Unless you make your things below as the things above, and the things on the left as the things on the right, you will not enter into my kingdom" (§34). Philip continues to address the returnees with references to the gospel message (§35). He then commands that Bartholomew be released and gives extensive instructions regarding what will happen when he departs from the body, including the eventual burial of the leopard and the kid close to the porch of the church. He also issues various warnings regarding the temptations of Satan, including reference to the story of Peter's prayer that his own daughter be paralyzed to prevent deception (§36). Bartholomew is to appoint Stachys as bishop and undertake various preparations for Philip's burial and its aftermath (§37). Philip offers one more extended prayer (§38), and then gives up his spirit (§39). Bartholomew and Mariamne take down his body and do as Philip had commanded (§40). After three days, a grapevine sprouts where the blood of the apostle Philip had dripped (§41). After forty days the Savior appears in the form of Philip to Bartholomew and Mariamne. When they depart to their destinies, Stachys and those with him hold fast to the church in Christ Jesus (§42).

3. INTERPRETIVE ISSUES

It becomes clear when reading through a text such as the Acts of Philip that what one might seek to establish in the case of a New Testament narrative or epistolary text cannot serve as a reliable guide for the analysis of a composite text with multiple levels of editorial involvement. An eclectic approach must be employed, in which various segments of the text may be approached with attention to the rhetorical signals that have been woven into the text. The latter may allow the interpreter, perhaps, to say something meaningful about the ostensible time and circumstance when such a text would have been formulated in the way that it is frozen in the manuscripts that we have.

3.1 Primitive Remnants

Even if one grants that the broad contours of the Acts of Philip seem quite amenable to the fourth-century Christian ascetical context noted above, there remain features of the text that appear to signal the greater antiquity of some materials that have been sutured into the various scenes depicted. While the running narration and dialogues that form the bulk of the text are written in a somewhat unsophisticated Koine Greek, numerous examples of more finely crafted compositions are embedded within the flow of the text. The segments of text that stand out as of a higher linguistic quality are various liturgical-looking formulations that appear on the characters' lips, notably the remarkable prayers that are recorded at key points in the plot to mark the onset or conclusion of a significant event in which divine intervention has enabled the apostolic group to continue its mission without obstruction. Unfortunately, it is not possible to say with any precision at what place or date such material was first formulated, but it is possible that what we have in these "citations" are survivals from the third or even second century.[24] Thus the Acts of Philip informs us to some degree about certain liturgical emphases that were part of the practice of some Christian groups in these earlier periods and serves as a witness to the reception of such materials into the practice of various nonconforming Christian groups into the fourth century.[25] For that matter, the fact that we have numerous manuscripts of various sorts dedicated to Philip (e.g., the various *Menologia* and *Synaxaria*) is a testimony to the ongoing interest in this figure (along with all the other apostolic and ecclesial figures) among monastic groups up through the medieval period. As François Bovon notes, even if the more theologically suspect portions of a text like the Acts of Philip were not a regular part of ongoing church services, nevertheless such materials were heard during meal times in the refectory and thus were considered edifying in their own ways.[26]

---

24. See, e.g., François Bovon, "The Synoptic Gospels and the Noncanonical Acts of the Apostles," *HTR* 81 (1988): 19–36.

25. See Bovon, "Actes de Philippe," 4501; and idem, in Bovon and Matthews, *Acts of Philip: A New Translation*, 21.

26. François Bovon, "Beyond the Canonical and the Apocryphal Books, the Presence of a Third Category: The Books Useful for the Soul," *HTR* 105 (2012): 125–37.

3.2 Intertextual Engagements

Apart from obvious instances of intertextual engagement with texts we know from the New Testament, some of which will be examined in more detail below, it is clear that those responsible for formulating the stories about Philip found in the Acts of Philip were also aware of accounts and traditions about other apostolic figures.[27] Notable instances among dozens of such appropriations are the appearance of a redacted version of the Hymn of Christ from Acts of John 94–96 in Acts of Philip 11,[28] and Philip's upside-down crucifixion and speech from that position that takes up the circumstances and words of Peter from the martyrdom scene in Acts of Peter 38. Rather than judging such parallels between one of the other apocryphal Acts and the Acts of Philip as merely uncreative borrowings, such instances offer an opportunity to engage in some reception-historical analysis of the utilization of such texts in new narrative and rhetorical situations. Regarding Philip's "performance" in Acts of Philip Martyrdom 34 of Peter's saying about making the things below like the things above and what is on the left as what is on the right,[29] what is particularly noteworthy is that the original import of this saying seems to have survived only with its reception in the Acts of Philip. As Jonathan Z. Smith's analysis of the upside-down motif found, "Philip gives a dogmatic formulation which is a major key to this upside-down tradition: 'Imitate me in this, for all the world is turned the wrong way and every soul that is in it.' . . . In such a world, *to be upside down is in fact to be right side up*. . . . The call of Philip . . . is thus a gospel of rebellion and liberation."[30] Other instances of the reception of the Acts of Peter by the Acts of Philip offer similar examples of "rereadings" of the antecedent text that resituate its meaning and thus must be judged as more complex hermeneutical operations than simple borrowing or imitation.[31]

3.3 Redactional Developments

Additional interpretative issues arise at many points within the text of the Acts of Philip. Space permits reference to only a couple of illustrative examples. It is not difficult to detect several seemingly abrupt shifts in the narrative presentation of Acts of Philip 1 that potentially mark various stages at which dialogue material was elaborated to introduce a further theme of interest to a redactor. It could be that the lengthy tour of hell found in 1.4–17 marks a major interpolation into what originally was a more straightforward account of Philip's raising of a dead man.[32] That a miracle such as the latter was quite early associated with Philip is clear because of the information provided about Philip by Papias (see Eusebius, *Hist. eccl.* 3.39.9). The supplementation of the resurrection account echoing

---

27. See François Bovon, "Facing the Scriptures: Mimesis and Intertextuality in the *Acts of Philip*," in *Mimesis and Intertextuality in Antiquity and Christianity*, ed. D. MacDonald, SAC (Harrisburg, PA: Trinity Press International, 2001), 138–53.

28. See Frédéric Amsler, *Acta Philippi: Commentarius*, CCSA 12 (Turnhout: Brepols, 1999), 348–54.

29. "And now I am fulfilling what was assigned to me, for the Lord said to me: 'Unless you make your things below as the things above, and the things on the left as the things on the right, you will not enter into my kingdom'" (Bovon and Matthews, *Acts of Philip: A New Translation*, 104).

30. Jonathan Z. Smith, "Birth Upside Down or Right Side Up?," *HR* 9.4 (1970): 290, 297, 301; also in idem, *Map Is Not Territory: Studies in the History of Religions*, SJLA 23 (Leiden: Brill, 1978), 156, 164, 169 (emphasis original). Smith goes on to explain that the upside-down motif points not to "an exercise in humility" but is rather "an *act of cosmic audacity* consistent with and expressive of a Christian-gnostic understanding and appreciation of the structures of the cosmos and of the human condition" ("Birth Upside Down," 286 = *Map*, 152–53, emphasis original). For more details on the relation between Acts Pet. 38 and Acts Phil. 34, see Matthews, *Philip: Apostle and Evangelist*, 189–96.

31. Matthews, *Philip: Apostle and Evangelist*, 195–96.

32. Matthews, *Philip: Apostle and Evangelist*, 176.

Luke 7:11–17 with the extended vision of the punishments in the underworld may have appealed to the heterodox audience of the fourth century, taking into account how many of the victims of torture are associated with mainstream clergy. It might be suggested that the relationship between Acts of Philip 6 and Acts of Philip 2 could be profitably explored as an instance of literary development (a rewriting or rereading) that moves from an earlier scenario in Acts of Philip 6, which depicts the achievement of a certain accommodation between Jews and Christians (quite prejudiced, to be sure, in favor of the latter), to a later scenario in Acts of Philip 2, which removes various elements of "restraint" in the literary depiction of the Christian position in Acts of Philip 6 in favor of a rather crude supersessionism. The matter is even more complicated, insofar as features shared by Acts of Philip 2 and 6 also appear in the Martyrdom.

3.4 Visual Reception

A further example of reception moves outside of the text to Byzantine art. In the small town of Arsos on the island of Cyprus, an icon of the apostle Philip survives (from the thirteenth century), surrounded by eighteen narrative scenes that depict his various deeds and his martyrdom. As Bovon observes, these images amount to "a witness to the long text of the *Acts of Philip*."[33] His analysis suggests that "the iconographer and his commissioners had in their hands a copy of the *Acts of Philip*."[34] He further notes that the Arsos icon offers a graphic witness to many of the episodes from the Acts of Philip: "From the resurrection of the widow's son in Galilee and the dangerous sailing episode to the healing of Charitine and the restoration of sight to Stachys; from the presence of the two animals to Ireos's hospitality and the opposition of the town meeting; from the apostle's instructions to wrap his body with strips of paper from Syria to his agony of being hung upside-down."[35]

3.5 Philip as Authorizing Figure

It is reasonable to suppose that those who thought it meaningful to accumulate a range of stories and traditions under the name of Philip perceived this figure as in some sense a patron for their particular theological preferences, as has been suggested above. Though some earlier scholarship seemed to locate the value of apocryphal texts for researchers mainly in what primitive details such texts might retain from the earliest period, texts such as the Acts of Philip are rather most beneficial for the access they afford to a longer span of socioreligious development in early Christianity. It seems not unlikely that the Acts of Philip participates in a larger tendency among early Christians to gather and "substantiate" certain traditions and perspectives under the name of an apostolic guarantor. Texts such as the Gospel of Philip, the Letter of Peter to Philip, and Pistis Sophia, though not formally part of an intentional trajectory, nevertheless illustrate the desirability of employing this name in particular to serve as a validation for the materials contained in the respective texts.[36] It is not unfeasible to suppose that the appearance and utilization of Philip's name in various controversial contexts in the earlier part of the second century added impetus in later periods to the generation of additional narratives involving his words and deeds to authorize further developments in tradition.[37]

---

33. François Bovon, "From Vermont to Cyprus: A New Witness of the *Acts of Philip*," *Apocrypha* 20 (2009): 13.
34. Bovon, "From Vermont to Cyprus," 24.
35. Bovon, "From Vermont to Cyprus," 25.
36. Matthews, *Philip: Apostle and Evangelist*, 129–55.
37. Matthews, *Philip: Apostle and Evangelist*, 15–34.

4. KEY PASSAGES FOR NEW TESTAMENT STUDIES AND THEIR SIGNIFICANCE

A survey of the entire content of the Acts of Philip as represented by the critical edition of the Greek text shows frequent contact with the Bible, both Old Testament and New Testament, in many parts of the text. But, on the whole, the connections are more superficial than substantive. In several places a familiar New Testament scene furnishes a starting point for the Philip story in question. While such allusions are surely intended, in most instances the Philip narrative pursues its own particular emphases. The opening of Acts of Philip 1, for example, is immediately reminiscent of Jesus's encounter with the widow of Nain in Luke 7:11–17. But that familiar scenario mostly serves as a convenient frame within which to present an argument for an ascetic form of Christian belief and practice, with some beatitudes echoing Matthew 5 (see Acts Phil. 1.3 and Matt 5:11) to show that Philip's teaching is patterned after that of Jesus. While it is true that Philip also imitates Jesus in deed with the raising of the widow's son, it is the latter's recounting of his angelic tour of the underworld on his way back to life that dominates the version of the story that survives in MS Xenophontos 32. Acts of Philip 2 can almost be characterized as a burlesque retelling of Paul's visit to Athens in Acts 17:16–34. This superficial similarity is efficiently achieved by weaving a few familiar elements from Luke's narrative into the Philip story, but the latter is a rather crude reception that seems designed to endorse a supersessionistic relationship between Christians and Jews in the post-Constantinian era. Acts of Philip 3 and 4 include some details deriving from or inspired by canonical Acts 8 to describe and situate Philip (e.g., an encounter with Peter and the disciples with him in 3.1; travel to the borders of the Candaceans and to Azotus in 3.10; arrival and entry into Azotus in 3.15 and 4.1), as well as features of the shipwreck scene in Acts 27 (3.11–12; but also including echoes of the stories of Jonah and Jesus's stilling of the storm), but the bulk of the material appearing in the accompanying stories betrays no particular relation to the canonical narratives.

The editors of the critical Greek text have provided a rather extensive listing of possible allusions (and in a couple of cases, citations) of New Testament texts in the Acts of Philip. Of the nearly six hundred instances, only about a dozen appear to be something more than just a staccato reference to some familiar New Testament topic or theme; such allusions provide a "biblical" flavor to the narrative but do not serve to relay some traditional information or exegetical point. It is interesting to observe, using the possible allusions assembled by the critical-text editors, that recourse to potential New Testament allusions is more prominent in Acts of Philip 1–7 than in Acts of Philip 8–15. The Martyrdom seems more closely aligned with Acts of Philip 8–15, betraying fewer New Testament allusions, in relative terms of the length of the respective texts, than one finds in Acts of Philip 1–7. One can also observe in the Martyrdom, for which we have textual evidence of three different recensions, that those recensions that are considered to be more recent include a number of biblical allusions that do not appear in what is judged to be the most ancient version (Vaticanus). This very broad-based observation about the presence or absence of New Testament allusions in the various parts of the Acts of Philip may offer some independent confirmation of the idea that Acts of Philip 1–7 and Acts of Philip 8–15 went through initially different redactional channels before being joined to create the larger text we know as the Acts of Philip.

Some examples of the hundreds of allusions that appear in the text that might be considered "one offs" are as follows: Galilee in 1.1 (Matt 28:16; [Mark 16:7]; John 1:45; 12:21);[38]

---

38. The references are those indicated in the apparatus of the critical edition (Bovon, Bouvier, and Amsler, *Acta Philippi: Textus*).

"it avails nothing" in 1.8 (1 Cor 13:3); "run in vain" in 1.9 (Gal 2:2; Phil 2:16); "refreshment" in 1.17 (Acts 3:20); Athens in 2.1 (Acts 17:16); "listen to something novel" in 2.2 (Acts 17:21); "the old human being" in 2.3 (Rom 6:6; Eph 4:22; Col 3:9); "demonstration of wondrous deeds" in 2.4 (1 Cor 2:4; 2 Cor 10:11; 1 John 3:18); "with great pomp" in 2.9 (Acts 25:23); son of thunder in 2.9 and 11.6 (Mark 3:17); two years in 2.24 (Acts 28:30); "the new human being" in 3.3 (2 Cor 4:16; Eph 2:15; 4:24; Col 3:10); "unskilled in speech" in 3.3 (Acts 4:13; 1 Cor 2:4); "where can I lay my head" in 4.2 (Matt 8:20; Luke 9:58); Philip appears as a great light in 5.22 (Matt 17:1–9 parr.); Onesimus in 6.3 (Col 4:9; Phlm 10); "three thousand souls believed" in 6.21 (Acts 2:41); "the brothers and sisters . . . wept" in 7.6 (Acts 20:36–38; 21:12–14); Mariamne in 8.2 (Matt 28:1, 9–10; [Mark 16:9–11]); Martha in 8.2 (Luke 10:38–42; John 11:1–44; 12:2); "blessed among women" in 8.3 (Luke 1:42); "flogged in their synagogues" in 8.6 (Matt 10:17); "you are the bread" in 11.9 (John 6:35); "the image of truth" in 11.9 (2 Cor 3:18; 4:4; Col 1:15); "the abyss" in 12.7 (Rev 1:18); "the Most High has visited us" in 13.5 (Luke 1:68, 78); "he is . . . the way" in 13.5 (John 14:6); "the Lamb" in 13.5 (Rev 5:6); "images of the invisible" in 14.5 (Col 1:15); "snares of Satan" in 15.2 (1 Tim 3:7; 2 Tim 2:26); "the city above" in Martyrdom 3 (Gal 4:26; Rev 3:12; 21:1–22:5); "call down fire" in Martyrdom 21 (Luke 9:54–55); "living water" in Martyrdom 23 (John 4:10–11); "hand to the plow" in Martyrdom 29 (Luke 9:62); "great is the harvest" in Martyrdom 29 (Matt 9:37–38 [Luke 10:2]); "they spit upon him and gave him gall to drink" in Martyrdom 35 (Matt 26:67; 27:34); "a sign for those who believe" in Martyrdom 36 (1 Cor 14:22); "meet you in the air" in Martyrdom 38 (1 Thess 4:17); and "gave up his spirit" in Martyrdom 39 (John 19:30).

Various of the allusions verge over into the territory of, or in fact are, citations: "Blessed are you when people speak every lie against you. Rejoice and be glad, because your reward is great in the heavens" in 1.3 (Matt 5:11–12);[39] "As my Lord said: 'It is not possible to put new wine into old wineskins'" in 2.3 (Matt 9:17 parr.); "As human beings we cannot fight with God" in 2.12 and 6.11 (Acts 5:39); "Blessed are those who are straightforward in the word of Jesus" in 5.25 [with two additional beatitudes] (Matt 5:3–12); "This is also why your brother Peter . . . said to me: 'Do you wish me to forgive my brother up to seven times?'" in 8.12 (Matt 18:21–22 [Luke 17:4]); "For our Lord while teaching us said: 'Whoever gazes at a woman and desires her in his heart has committed adultery'" in Martyrdom 36 (Matt 5:28). This last citation is followed by a concise recap of the story of Peter's daughter attested in Coptic P.Berol. 8502, judged by C. Schmidt as part of the lost Acts of Peter,[40] which seems to implicate Peter in untoward behavior regarding his own daughter.[41] Especially noticeable are several sections in the Acts of Philip that feature a dense employment of allusions: in Ananias's version of the story of Jesus and the activity of Philip in 2.10 (where up to fifty allusions may be involved), and in the Scripture debate that takes place in 6.13–14, which includes both New Testament allusions and multiple citations of Old Testament texts (about fifty OT/Apocrypha texts are cited or alluded to in Acts Phil. 6 as a whole). Across the full range of the Acts of Philip, references to the Old Testament or Old Testament Apocrypha (and a few other related texts) appear in a pattern somewhat similar to the situation observed with New Testament texts. Out of a total of about two hundred allusions or citations (as identified by the editors of the critical text of

---

39. Translations of the Acts of Philip are taken from Bovon and Matthews, *Acts of Philip: A New Translation*.

40. See Wilhelm Schneemelcher, "The Acts of Peter," in *NTApoc* 2:278–79.

41. Christopher R. Matthews, "Peter's Daughter: Daddy Dearest?," in *"The One Who Sows Bountifully": Essays in Honor of Stanley K. Stowers*, ed. C. Hodge et al., BJS 356 (Providence, RI: Brown Judaic Studies, 2013), 319–28.

Acts Phil.), the majority (ca. 129) occur in Acts of Philip 1–7, with a bit less than half of that number (ca. 57) appearing in Acts of Philip 8–15, and an additional fourteen or so in the Martyrdom. A number of the suggested allusions in the apparatus of the critical text are, at best, possible (e.g., Luke 15:17 in 3.6; Matt 15:13 at 7.5; Luke 4:43–44 at 7.5; Eph 2:14 at Mart. Phil. 13; Matt 26:73 at Mart. Phil. 25), though some appear very unlikely or far-fetched (e.g., Luke 14:28 at 11.8; 1 Cor 12:17 and Rev 5:6 at 13.5; Rev 12:5 and 19:15 at 15.4).

5. BIBLIOGRAPHY

Amsler, Frédéric. *Acta Philippi: Commentarius*. CCSA 12. Turnhout: Brepols, 1999.

Amsler, Frédéric, François Bovon, and Bertrand Bouvier. *Actes de l'apôtre Philippe*. Apocryphes 8. Turnhout: Brepols, 1996.

——. "Les Actes de Philippe." Pages 1179–320 in vol. 1 of *Écrits apocryphes chrétiens*. Edited by François Bovon and Pierre Geoltrain. Bibliothèque de la Pléiade 442. Paris: Gallimard, 1997.

Bovon, François. "Les Actes de Philippe." *ANRW* 25.6:4431–527. Part 2, *Principat*, 25.6. Edited by H. Temporini and W. Haase. Berlin: de Gruyter, 1988.

——. *New Testament and Christian Apocrypha*. WUNT 237. Tübingen: Mohr Siebeck, 2009.

——. *Studies in Early Christianity*. WUNT 161. Tübingen: Mohr Siebeck, 2003.

Bovon, François, Bertrand Bouvier, and Frédéric Amsler. *Acta Philippi: Textus*. CCSA 11. Turnhout: Brepols, 1999.

Bovon, François, Ann Graham Brock, and Christopher R. Matthews, eds. *The Apocryphal Acts of the Apostles: Harvard Divinity School Studies*. Religions of the World. Cambridge: Harvard University Center for the Study of World Religions, 1999.

Bovon, François, and Christopher R. Matthews. *The Acts of Philip: A New Translation*. Waco, TX: Baylor University Press, 2012.

Lipsius, Richard Adelbert, and Maximilien Bonnet. *Acta Apostolorum Apocrypha*. Vol. 2.2. Leipzig: Mendelssohn, 1903. Repr., Darmstadt: Wissenschaftliche Buchgesellschaft, 1959.

Matthews, Christopher R. *Philip: Apostle and Evangelist. Configurations of a Tradition*. NovTSup 105. Leiden: Brill, 2002.

Zimmermann, Ruben, ed. *Die Wunder der Apostel*. Vol. 2 of *Kompendium der frühchristlichen Wundererzählungen*. Gütersloh: Gütersloher, 2017.

CHAPTER 17

ACTS OF THOMAS

HAROLD W. ATTRIDGE

1. INTRODUCTION

The Acts of Thomas, one of the five major apocryphal Acts, describes the missionary activity of Didymus Judas Thomas[1] in India, where he preaches a gospel advocating sexual celibacy. He takes his message primarily to the elites of at least two kingdoms, focusing on upper-class women. The conversion of noble women, Mygdonia, wife of a general, and Tertia, wife of King Mizdai, is particularly troublesome and leads eventually to the apostle's martyrdom. The story is replete with dramatic encounters not only with human beings in an exotic land but also with various talking animals and demonic forces. Embedded in the text are significant blocks of poetic material, including symbolic hymns and liturgical invocations.

1.1 Authorship

The medieval encyclopedist, Photius, attributed all the major apocryphal Acts to Leucius Charinus.[2] Given the variety of literary styles among the Acts, such an attribution is impossible, and the identity of the author or authors remains unknown. It has been suggested that the author may have been influenced by Bardaisan, a well-known sage in early Edessa,[3] active at the time of King Abgar VIII (177–212 CE), but that connection is also speculative.

1.2 Language

The Acts of Thomas survive primarily in Greek and Syriac. Which version came first remains a matter of debate. The presence of Syriac idioms in the Greek suggests that the current Greek version was translated from a Syriac source and that the text was originally composed in Syriac.[4] That sequence is not certain, however, and some scholars argue for the

---

1. The name varies in the manuscript tradition. The oldest Syriac witnesses favor "Judas," corrected to Thomas in later witnesses. The Greek martyrdom uses the name of Thomas with only three exceptions, while the Syriac version uses Judas exclusively. See J. J. Gunther, "The Meaning and Origin of the Name 'Judas Thomas,'" *Le Museon* 93 (1980): 113–48.

2. Photius, *Bibliotheca* 114.

3. See Jan N. Bremmer, "The Acts of Thomas: Place, Date, Women," in Jan N. Bremmer, ed., *The Apocryphal Acts of Thomas* (Leuven: Peeters, 2001), 74–90, esp. 78.

4. Harold W. Attridge, "The Original Language of the Acts of Thomas," in Harold W. Attridge, John J. Collins, and Thomas H. Tobin, eds., *Of Scribes and Scrolls: Studies on the Hebrew Bible, Intertestamental Judaism and Christian Origins*, College Theology Society Resources in Religion 5 (Lanham, MD: University Press of America, 1990), 241–50. The treatment of money, with the Greek using "bullion" instead of coinage, also reflects late third-century conditions. See Nathanael J. Andrade, *Journey of Christianity to India in Late Antiquity: Networks and the Movement of Culture* (Cambridge: Cambridge University Press, 2018), 32–42.

priority of a Greek version.[5] It is possible that a Greek original was translated into Syriac and then retranslated into Greek or that the current Acts of Thomas is based on earlier accounts. Evidence of an original Greek version may be found in the account of Thomas's martyrdom (chs. 159–70), which circulated independently. Whatever the original, the Acts of Thomas was soon translated into the other major language of late antique upper Mesopotamia, and both versions continued to develop.[6] In general, the current Greek version preserves a less pious version of the work, with fewer explicit scriptural references than the current Syriac.

1.3 Provenance

The association of the text with the cosmopolitan city of Edessa (modern Urfa, Turkey) in what had been the independent kingdom of Osrhoene (132–246 CE), is based on the connection of the apostle Thomas with that city attested in several fourth-century sources.[7] The *Carminia Nisibena* 42 of Ephrem (306–373 CE) celebrates the transfer of Thomas's bones from India to Edessa.[8] The *Pilgrimage of Egeria* (ca. 381–384 CE) reports interesting details. After visiting the holy sites in Jerusalem and the Holy Land, Egeria made a special trip to Edessa to visit the martyrium or burial place of Judas Thomas.[9] During her time in Edessa, she read literature "of Thomas," possibly the Acts of Thomas, unless the phrase suggests another first-person account.[10] She also records the Abgar legend, which tells how Jesus received a request for assistance from the ailing king of Edessa. Jesus responded by promising to send Thomas after his resurrection. Eusebius, who cites the exchange (*Hist. eccl.* 1.13.6–9), reports that the correspondence was preserved in Edessa in his day—that is, the first decades of the fourth century. In the Eusebian version, Judas Thomas, one of the Twelve, dispatched Thaddeus, known in Syriac tradition as Addai, to Abgar (*Hist. eccl.* 1.13.4, 11). The fact that Eusebius is silent on Thomas's presence in Edessa suggests that the connection with the city was made later in the fourth century. Whether the Acts of Thomas was composed there is uncertain, and other venues, such as Nisibis, are also possible. In favor of the latter are details such as the name of the noblewoman Mygdonia, derived from the River Migdon that runs through Nisibis.[11]

1.4 Date

The fact that Origen (d. 254 CE), followed by Eusebius in the early fourth century, mentions only Thomas's mission to Parthia, not India, indicates that the version of his

---

5. Lautaro Roig Lanzillotta, "A Syriac Original for the Acts of Thomas? The Hypothesis of Syriac Priority Revisited," in *Early Christian and Jewish Narrative: The Role of Religion in Shaping Narrative Forms*, ed. I. Ramelli and J. Perkins, WUNT 348 (Tübingen: Mohr Siebeck, 2015), 105–34.

6. Note the extensive poetic passages found only in the Syriac, translated in Harold W. Attridge, *The Acts of Thomas*, Early Christian Apocrypha 3 (Salem, OR: Polebridge, 2010), 124–32.

7. For the connection with Edessa, see Bremmer, "Acts of Thomas," 77.

8. Ephrem thus specifies the "western regions" of Acts Thom. 170. Cf. also Ephrem, *Madrasha* 2.1, and see Johnson Thomaskutty, *Saint Thomas the Apostle, New Testament, Apocrypha and Historical Traditions* (London: Bloomsbury T&T Clark, 2018), 162–63.

9. *The Pilgrimage of Egeria* 17–19, on which see Anne McGowan and Paul F. Bradshaw, *The Pilgrimage of Egeria: A New Translation of the Itinerarium Egeriae, with Introduction and Commentary* (Collegeville, MN: Liturgical Press Academic, 2018), 133–36. On the dating of the *Itinerarium*, see pp. 22–27.

10. On the phenomenon of pilgrimage and Egeria's readings, see Scott Fitzgerald Johnson, *Literary Territories: Cartographical Thinking in Late Antiquity* (Oxford: Oxford University Press, 2016), 82–88.

11. On provenance, see Susan Myers, "Revisiting Preliminary Issues in the Acts of Thomas," *Apocrypha* 17 (2006): 95–112; and Pierluigi Piovanelli, "Thomas in Edessa? Another Look at the Original Setting of the Gospel of Thomas," in *Myths, Martyrs, and Modernity: Studies in the History of Religions in Honor of Jan Bremmer*, ed. J. Dijkstra, J. Kroesen, and Y. Kuiper (Leiden: Brill, 2010), 443–62.

activity found in the Acts of Thomas was not assumed in the third century in Alexandria or Palestine. Fourth-century sources know of the apostle's activity in India, probably reflecting the Acts of Thomas.[12] The varying awareness of Thomas's association with India suggests that the Acts of Thomas in its final form was created in upper Mesopotamia late in the century,[13] while earlier accounts told only of Thomas in Parthia.[14]

1.5 Text

The earliest witnesses to the text are a fifth-century Syriac palimpsest and testimonies by Epiphanius (*Pan.* 47.1; 60.1.5), Augustine (*Serm. Dom.* 1.20.65; *Adim.* 17; *Faust.* 14), and the Manichaean Psalter. A tenth-century Syriac (BM add. 14,645, dated to 936 CE) and a twelfth-century Greek (Romanus Vallicellanus B 35) manuscript preserve the complete text, including the well-known "Hymn of the Pearl," possibly added later. Shorter versions survive in Greek, Syriac, Latin, Armenian, Coptic, and Arabic. Basic critical editions[15] have been followed by an annotated edition,[16] and a new critical edition is in preparation.

1.6 Genre

Like other apocryphal Acts, the Acts of Thomas combines tales of the exotic, the miraculous, the sublimated erotic, along with an account of the noble death of the martyred apostle. They thus resemble ancient romances and other forms of popular fiction, although they have distinctive features,[17] including constant echoes of early Christian gospel literature.[18]

2. SUMMARY OF CONTENT

The first six episodes of the Acts of Thomas (chs. 1–61) consist of discrete tales with editorial touches that connect them to what follows. The last six acts (chs. 62–149) comprise an integrated novella about Thomas at the court of King Mizdai (also Mazdai, Misdaeus). The first episode (chs. 1–16) begins with the apostles casting lots to determine their assignments to various parts of the globe. Judas, "the twin," Didymus in Greek and Thomas in

---

12. For patristic sources, see George Nedungatt, *The Quest for the Historical Thomas: A Re-Reading of the Evidence* (Bangalore: Theological Publications in India, 2008), 181–212. Nedungatt (187) notes one third-century source placing Thomas in India, the *Doctrine of the Apostles*, citing William Cureton, *Ancient Syriac Documents Relative to the Earliest Establishment of Christianity in Edessa and Neighboring Countries* (London: Williams and Norgate, 1864), 33. A third-century date is hardly secure for that church order. Thomaskutty, *Saint Thomas*, 165–66, mistakenly cites the same passage as part of the third-century *Didascalia apostolorum*, which contains no reference to Thomas. See R. Hugh Connolly, *Didascalia apostolorum: The Syriac Version Translated and Accompanied by the Latin Verona Fragments* (Oxford: Clarendon, 1929; repr., 1969).

13. Myers, "Revisiting Preliminary Issues," argues for a late third-century date; Bremmer, "Acts of Thomas," 77, defends the early third century.

14. See Andrade, *Journey of Christianity*, 50–54, who accepts the late third-century date, suggesting that Edessenes wanted to associate their local hero, Addai, not Thomas, with Parthia.

15. The Greek: Maximillian Bonnet, *Acta Philippi et Acta Thomae Accedunt Acta Barnabae*, ed. R. Lipsius and M. Bonnet, Acta Apostolorum Apocrypha 2.2 (Leipzig: Mendelssohn, 1903; repr., Darmstadt: Wissenschaftliche Buchgesellschaft, 1959). The Syriac: W. Wright, "The Acts of Judas /Thomas (or the Twin) the Apostle," in W. Wright, *Apocryphal Acts of the Apostles Edited from Syriac Manuscripts in the British Museum and Other Libraries*, 2 vols. (London: Williams and Norgate, 1871; repr., Amsterdam: Philo, 1968).

16. A. J. F. Klijn, *The Acts of Thomas: Introduction, Text and Commentary*, 2nd ed. (Leiden: Brill, 2003).

17. Jason König, "Novelistic and Anti-Novelistic Narrative in the *Acts of Thomas* and *Acts of Andrew and Matthias*," in *Fiction on the Fringe: Novelistic Writing in the Post-Classical Age*, ed. K. Grammatiki (Leiden: Brill, 2009), 121–50.

18. Craig Morrison, "The Text of the New Testament in the Acts of Judas Thomas," in *The Peshitta: Its Use in Literature and Liturgy. Papers Read at the Third Peshitta Symposium*, Monographs of the Peshitta Institute 15 (Leiden: Brill, 2006), 187–205.

Aramaic, draws the lot for India, but resists traveling to such a distant, alien land. Having no patience with such resistance, Jesus sells the reluctant apostle into slavery to Chaban, a merchant from a kingdom ruled by King Gundafar (also Gudnafar, Goundaphoros).[19] As the Syriac version explains, Jesus had the right to do so because he had purchased Judas by his blood (Acts 20:28). Chaban happily buys Thomas, since his king has told him to acquire a well-trained carpenter, a trade that Thomas would have learned at home.

Although the reader might know the identity of Thomas's twin, the story will soon make the relationship abundantly clear. Sailing east from Jerusalem,[20] Thomas accompanies his master to the city of Andrapolis (Syriac: Sandaruk),[21] where a royal wedding is taking place. Chaban and his slave attend. After the banquet a Hebrew flute girl greets the apostle, occasioning a major poem (6–7). This "Hymn of the Bride," or the "Wedding Hymn,"[22] celebrates a young woman, "the daughter of light." Surrounded by an array of luminous bridegrooms and bridesmaids, she symbolizes an unspecified heavenly reality, wisdom perhaps. Deeper meaning is hidden from the audience at the banquet, since Thomas sings the hymn in Hebrew (8). Only the flute girl understands, and she becomes enamored of the apostle, like many other women in the Acts of Thomas. Another servant who slapped Thomas before his hymn meets a more gruesome fate, devoured by a lion.

Meanwhile, the bride and groom, having retired to their wedding chamber, experience a vision of a figure looking exactly like the apostle. Thomas's twin convinces the bride and groom to forsake sexual pleasure and embrace a life of celibacy, which they do after fervent prayer (chs. 11–16). Their decision enrages the bride's father, who seeks to arrest Thomas, but the apostle has moved on to India, joined by bride, groom, and flute girl. The conversion of the couple in their "bridal chamber" is the first of many similar decisions to embrace celibacy. For the Acts of Thomas, true marriage is not a matter of fleshly union but a connection of the self to its heavenly spouse.

The second episode (chs. 17–29) records Thomas's experience at Gundafar's court. Having examined Thomas's carpentry credentials, the king, promising abundant resources, commissions him to build a magnificent palace. Thomas promises to begin the project in October and finish by April, a schedule that astounds the king (18), who nonetheless provides funding. Thomas then distributes the king's money to the poor. When Gundafar enquires about the progress of his commission, Thomas gives a positive report, and the king sends more funds. Eventually the king arrives for an inspection. Discovering that Thomas had done nothing but give away his money, the enraged king imprisons him and contemplates an extremely painful execution. The king's brother, Gad, equally offended by Thomas's deed, urges the king to take action. In his distress Gad falls ill and dies. Upon entering heaven, he finds a glorious palace where he asks to dwell. Angels tell him that he cannot do so, since it has been constructed for his brother (22). Gad asks to return to earth to purchase the palace from Gundafar, who has no idea what a magnificent home awaits him. The angels agree, Gad returns, and light dawns on the king about what Thomas has done. The two brothers free Thomas and ask to become "worthy residents" of the heavenly abode. Thomas then initiates them, first with a ritual of anointing that involves an elaborate epiclesis of the Spirit (27). Some forms of address are familiar: the "holy name

---

19. See Jennifer Glancy, "Slavery in the *Acts of Thomas*," *Journal of Early Christian History* 2 (2012): 3–21.

20. The oddity may be a narrative abbreviation or a reflection of an earlier tale with a different port of embarkation (so Andrade, *Journeys of Christianity*, 49).

21. Andrade, *Journeys of Christianity*, 47, suggests the site was the island of Kharg in the Persian Gulf.

22. Miroslav Marcovich, "The Wedding Hymn of the Acta Thomae," *Illinois Classical Studies* 6 (1981): 367–85.

of Christ," the "power of the Most High." Others are less familiar: the "Merciful Mother," "fellowship of the male,"[23] and the "Mother of the Seven Houses," probably reflecting the fact that in Syriac "Holy Spirit" is feminine.[24] The initiation, which had taken place by night, is followed by the Eucharist at dawn. Thomas continues to preach, admonishing repentance from sin and a life of virtue, and on the following day celebrates the Eucharist for all (28–29).[25]

The next four segments feature encounters between Thomas and exotic and sometimes dangerous beings. In the third act, having set out for an unnamed venue, the apostle encounters a deadly serpent, who has killed a handsome young man who had engaged in sexual intercourse with a beautiful young woman (chs. 30–38). Thomas confronts the serpent, who describes himself with an "aretalogy," celebrating his amazing accomplishments from the seduction of Eve to Judas's betrayal of Christ (32). Thomas forces the serpent to suck the poison from the dead youth, leading to the youth's revival and the serpent's demise. The grateful young man reports a vision he had experienced of Thomas and another person, no doubt his twin, who told Thomas to revive the young man. The youth then celebrates his release from the grasp of death and sin. He then accompanies Thomas as the apostle enters the new venue, preaching repentance from sin and deliverance to a new life (36–37). The serpent is the first of several animals endowed with speech in the Acts of Thomas.[26]

In the fourth episode (chs. 39–41), Thomas encounters a talking ass, who hails him as Christ's twin and invites him to mount and ride to his next destination. Thomas offers a lengthy prayer thanking Jesus for his benefactions. He then questions the beast, learning that he is a descendant of Balaam's famous talking ass (Num 22). Thomas does not wish to ride, but the ass insists and Thomas agrees. Upon reaching the city, the ass dies. Thomas's companions urge him to revive the animal, but the apostle refuses, saying that what has happened is beneficial for the ass, who is then formally buried.

In the fifth episode (chs. 42–50), Thomas enters the unnamed city and encounters a woman possessed by a demon who had sexually abused her. Thomas summons the inimical power, who turns out to be a pack of demons that had already experienced the exorcistic power of Thomas's twin (45), probably an allusion to the Gerasene demoniac (Matt 8:28–34; Mark 5:1–13; Luke 8:26–39). After the exorcised demon disappears in a puff of fire and smoke, Thomas offers a two-part prayer to Jesus (47–48). He then initiates the woman and many bystanders with the seal in the name of the Trinity and then celebrates the Eucharist (49). The ceremony begins with a solemn epiclesis (50), calling on a heavenly power to "come" to the table. While using many of the same terms for the Holy Spirit as in chapter 27, this prayer adds others, including "Highest Charism" and "Mother of the Seven Houses."

The sixth episode (chs. 51–61) occurs at a Eucharist, when a youth's hands shrivel after he receives communion unworthily (51). Bidden by Thomas to confess his sins, the young man tells how he was attracted to the apostle's call to celibacy. Unsuccessful in persuading

---

23. On this expression, see Harold W. Attridge, "Masculine Fellowship in the Acts of Thomas," in *The Future of Early Christianity*, ed. B. Pearson (Minneapolis: Augsburg Fortress, 1991), 406–13.

24. On the epithets, see Susan Myers, *Spirit Epicleses in the Acts of Thomas*, WUNT 2.281 (Tübingen: Mohr Siebeck, 2010), esp. 181–220.

25. On the eucharistic passages, see Gerard Rouwhorst, "La celebration de l'eucharistie selon les Actes de Thomas," in *Omnes circumdastantes: Contributions towards a History of the Role of the People in the Liturgy*, ed. C. Caspers and M. Schneiders (Kampen: Kok, 1990), 51–77.

26. On the phenomenon, see Janet Spittler, *Animals in the Apocryphal Acts of the Apostles: The Wild Kingdom of Early Christian Literature*, WUNT 2.247 (Tübingen: Mohr Siebeck, 2007).

his lover to embrace that call, he murdered her. Thomas bids the youth wash his hands; they then go together to the inn where the murder took place (52). The woman's corpse is brought to them, Thomas prays to Jesus (53), and the woman miraculously revives. Like the youth bitten by a serpent in the third episode, the woman had a postmortem experience of Thomas's twin, who brought her to the apostle (54). Thomas then inquires about her experience of death. She responds that she went on a tour of hell (55–57), where she saw the grisly punishments of various sinners.[27] The apostle uses the occasion to preach repentance to the woman and the bystanders, cataloguing the kinds of sins whose punishments the woman had witnessed (58). The crowd responds appropriately, and Thomas continues to teach, offering a brief creedal summary of the faith (59). He concludes with a hymn glorifying the "only begotten of the Father," beseeching him to look on his people with favor (60–61).

The next six episodes (chs. 62–149) comprise a more integrated novella, focusing on the activity of Thomas at King Mizdai's court. In episode 7 (62–67), a general of the king, Sifor, approaches Thomas while the apostle is preaching. The general asks for Thomas's help, explaining that his wife and daughter, possessed by demons, are now confined to their house (63–64). Thomas challenges Sifor to profess faith in Jesus (65) and then bids farewell to his congregation, bidding them to live in virtuous poverty, hoping in Christ (66). Thomas departs with the general, leaving his flock to a deacon named Xanthippos.

Episode 8 (chs. 68–81) begins with Sifor and Thomas traveling in the general's chariot. Sifor shows great respect to the apostle, volunteering to serve as his driver until Thomas asks him to take his proper seat. Working in the heat of the day, the animals drawing the chariot tire and refuse to move (69). Thomas solves the problem by sending Sifor to a herd of wild asses. When told that the apostle Judas Thomas needs them, they rush to help (70) and remain prominent throughout this episode. Thomas instructs Sifor to harness the strongest four and return the rest to their pastures. The team of asses draws the chariot to Sifor's residence, amazing the local population (71). Thomas dismounts and prays to Jesus, invoking his incarnation and redemptive action (72). Sifor's demon-possessed wife and daughter are present, limp and dazed. Thomas bids one of the asses to exorcise the demons (73), which the beast does with an elaborate speech (74). Thomas adds his word of exorcism to that of the ass. The demon emerges, berating Thomas for harassing him again. This response leads Thomas to suspect that he had previously encountered the same demon (act 5). In his reply to the ass's exorcism, the demon argues for an equivalence between competing spiritual factions, Thomas and Christ versus the demon and his "father" (76). The speech, which recalls the opposed spirits of the Dead Sea Scrolls and the cosmic divisions of Zoroastrianism and Manichaeism, is fruitless. Thomas gives a firm command in Jesus's name for the demon to leave the women, and he does so, not without a bitter complaint (77). The oratorically sophisticated ass is not finished. He delivers one more speech, urging Thomas to do the deed of healing (78) and the assembled crowd to believe in Christ, the teacher of truth (79). His summons evokes episodes from the canonical Gospels, especially Luke, and from the Infancy Gospel of Thomas, which contains a famous episode of the child Jesus teaching his teacher. The ass concludes with a warning about false teachers, echoing similar admonitions in the canonical Gospels. Thomas responds with a prayer glorifying Christ (80). Resembling the famous Christ hymn of Philippians 2:6–11, the prayer celebrates Christ, who humbled himself to save humankind by his death, resurrection,

---

27. On this motif in general, see Martha Himmelfarb, *Tours of Hell: An Apocalyptic Form in Jewish and Christian Literature* (Philadelphia: University of Pennsylvania Press, 1983).

and exaltation. The act concludes with Thomas restoring Sifor's wife and daughter and returning the asses to their pastures, taking care that no one harm them on the way.

Act 9, the longest section of the work (chs. 82–118), begins with a noble couple of King Mizdai's realm, Carish, a relative of the king, and his wife, Mygdonia. The scene begins with Thomas preaching to the crowds to avoid adultery and arrogance and to embrace meekness and "holy chastity" (84–86). Captivated by the exotic apostle, Mygdonia throws herself at his feet and begs for his aid. Thomas exhorts her to abandon "filthy intercourse" and embrace chastity (87–88). Back at home, Mygdonia, claiming to feel out of sorts, excuses herself from her husband's bed (89–90). Carish reluctantly spends the night alone, dreaming of an eagle that snatches delicate birds from himself and the king. In the dream the king responds by shooting the eagle with an arrow, which does the raptor no harm (91). In the morning, before leaving home, Carish ties the left sandal on his right foot. He asks Mygdonia what such a dream and such an ominous mistake might portend. She responds that a change for the better is coming (92).

The next day Mygdonia goes forth and meets the apostle, now informed of her identity and her husband's harshness (ch. 93). Mygdonia indicates that she has accepted his message, and Thomas responds with a hymn celebrating the bodies and souls of chaste saints (94). Evening in the home of Carish and his wife is difficult. She refuses to join her husband for dinner (95). He then confronts her and bitterly denounces Thomas as a poor magician, a wretch who does not even have bread for the day (96). He merely does tricks in the name of Father, Son, and Holy Spirit. Mygdonia remains resolute. Before retiring, she prays to her "Master" and "merciful Father," Christ, for the strength to remain committed to holy chastity (97). Carish tries unsuccessfully to force himself on Mygdonia (97), but she flees naked, wrapping herself in a veil (98). Carish spends the night in melodramatic self-pity, plotting revenge on the "sorcerer" (99–100).

The next day of confrontation brings the various characters together. In an audience with the king, Carish tells him of the Hebrew wizard and requests that he summon Sifor and Thomas (ch. 101). King Mizdai sends messengers, who find the apostle teaching in Sifor's house, with the general and Mygdonia among those at his feet. Thomas tells Sifor to fear not and go (102). The apostle then questions Mygdonia about her husband's anger and encourages her for the trial ahead (103). The scene shifts to the king's interrogation of Sifor, who tells how Thomas healed his possessed wife and daughter. He then gives a concise summary of Thomas's message: the apostle teaches that people must fear the one God and his Son Jesus Christ and thus, living in faith and holy chastity, gain eternal life (104).

The king sends soldiers to arrest Thomas, but, deterred by large crowds, they return empty-handed. Carish then leads a mob to seize the apostle (ch. 105). He apprehends Thomas, ties him with his turban, and drags him to the king. Mizdai questions Thomas, who, like his twin before Pilate (Matt 27:12; Mark 15:5; Luke 23:9), says nothing. The king, like Pilate, orders that Thomas receive 128 lashes and then casts him into prison, while discussing with Carish how to kill him (Acts Thom. 106). While in prison, Thomas sings the Hymn of the Pearl (108–113), which deserves separate attention.

While Thomas languishes in prison, Carish returns home to find Mygdonia with hair shorn and clothing torn (114). His questions and complaints produce yet more lamentation from his grieving wife. Meanwhile, Carish wallows in pathetic self-pity and tries to regain Mygdonia's affection (115–16). She in turn disdains his worldly wealth and status and professes her love for Jesus alone (117). When Carish falls asleep, Mygdonia takes ten denarii as a bribe for the guards and goes to visit Thomas in prison, but instead encounters him along the way (118).

The tenth act tells of Mygdonia's baptism and its consequences.[28] When a stunned Mygdonia wonders how she can be meeting Thomas, who is supposed to be in prison, the apostle assures her that Jesus Christ is more powerful than any earthly authority (ch. 119). Mygdonia asks for the "seal" of baptism. Prompted by Thomas, she goes to rouse her nurse, Narkia (Greek: Markia or Marcia). Initially reluctant, Narkia agrees to give her what she needs, including abundant bread and wine. Mygdonia requests a small piece of bread, some water, and some oil (120). Thomas then uses all the elements in a ritual of initiation, first anointing Mygdonia with oil, then baptizing her in water in the name of Father, Son, and Spirit, and finally sharing Eucharist with her (121). Thomas then returns to prison. In a scene reminiscent of Acts 16:25–28, the guards find the doors open and, to their amazement, Thomas still within (122).

The next morning, Carish finds Mygdonia at prayer. Ever the persistent husband, he begs her once more to return to him as his wife (123). She offers a poetic response contrasting carnal marriage with a bridal chamber that remains forever (124). The language recalls the initial scene of the marriage that Thomas and his twin disrupted. Carish goes to the king and asks him to give Thomas one last try to persuade Mygdonia to return to him (125).

Mizdai proceeds to interview Thomas, asking about his challenge to live a pure life. Thomas's defense compares his message to the king's requirements that his servants keep themselves clean (126). Mizdai then bids Thomas go and persuade Mygdonia to return to Carish or face death (127). The apostle responds by telling the king that if Mygdonia has really accepted his teaching, nothing earthly will change her mind. To the king's threat, Thomas responds that "this life is given on loan," while the life about which he teaches is imperishable. On the way to Mygdonia, Carish again pleads with the apostle, threatening that if Thomas does not agree, he will kill him, then commit suicide (128). Finding Mygdonia and her nurse, Thomas surprisingly tells her to "obey what your brother Carish tells you" (130). Given what he told King Mizdai about the firmness of a true believer, his command must simply be a test to prove Mygdonia's commitment. Mygdonia responds, quoting the apostle's teaching back to him and asking whether he has now become fearful. Thomas repairs to the house of the general, Sifor, who with his wife and daughter commits to living the chaste life advocated by Thomas (131). The apostle proceeds to initiate them, using the same combination of oil and water used for Mygdonia (132). He concludes with a eucharistic prayer, invoking both the name of Jesus and the name of "the Mother," presumably the Holy Spirit (133).

The struggle for the souls of the royal family continues in act 11 (chs. 134–38). Upon returning home, King Mizdai tells his wife, Tertia, about recent events and sends her to advise Mygdonia to return to her husband (134). Tertia finds Mygdonia sprawled on the floor, in sackcloth and ashes. In response to the queen's plea, Mygdonia tells her that she does not understand about eternal life, salvation, and an imperishable communion (135). Intrigued, Tertia asks to be introduced to the apostle. Mygdonia sends her to Sifor's home. There she meets the apostle who tells her of Jesus, the "Son of the living God," who gave his life for humankind. Thomas invites her to believe and become "worthy of his mysteries" (136). Tertia returns to the king and invites him to join her in a commitment to chastity. Mizdai is not persuaded (137). Instead, the king finds Carish, and together they go to Sifor's house, beat Thomas, and take him into custody (138).

---

28. On baptismal rituals in the Acts of Thomas, see A. J. F. Klijn, "Baptism in the Acts of Thomas," in *Studies on Syrian Baptismal Rites*, ed. J. Vellian, Syrian Churches Series 6 (Kottayam: CMS, 1973), 57–62.

Encounter with another royal follows in act 12 (chs. 139–49) when Vizan, the son of Mizdai, seeks out Thomas. The prince asks Thomas to share his magical power and offers to secure the apostle's release. Thomas responds with an exhortation to "take refuge in the Living God," not in worldly wealth (139). While the prince ponders how to release Thomas, his father arrives and puts Thomas on trial. Like the son, he asks Thomas by whose power he performs his marvelous deeds. Thomas responds that he relies on Jesus. To Mizdai's threat of execution, Thomas responds that the king has no authority over him, paraphrasing his twin's remark to Pilate (John 19:11). Mizdai orders Thomas to be stood on heated stone slabs, but as soon as the stones arrive, the earth miraculously pours forth water, scaring away the king's servants (140). Also frightened by the flood, Mizdai asks Thomas to pray for divine rescue. Thomas responds with a poetic appeal to God, which of course works, but Mizdai simply sends him back to prison (141).

The remainder of the act focuses on the apostle's last hours. In prison, surrounded by Sifor, his wife and daughter, and Prince Vizan, Thomas offers a series of farewell prayers. The first (ch. 142), like the Farewell Discourse of John 14–17, sounds as if he is actually at the point of death, "being released from care and grief, to live in repose." He repeatedly celebrates the "now" of his entry into the heavenly kingdom, anticipating what is soon to come. Having caught the attention of his audience, he preaches to them to entrust themselves to Christ, whose salvific life, death, and victory over death are celebrated in festive prose (143). Thomas then offers the Lord's prayer, embellished with an affirmation of his commitment to chastity (144), and a review of his life's work. That review begins with a simple catalogue of his toils and suffering (145), followed by a set of evocations of gospel stories (146), and a rich bouquet of images (147). He concludes with a final prayer and farewell to his companions (148–49).

Act 13 (chs. 150–158) tells of the baptism of Prince Vizan, who visits Thomas in prison and reveals his own history. He was wedded at the age of fourteen to a woman, Mnesara, with whom he never had sex in the seven years of their marriage (150). They are joined by the rest of Thomas's followers, Queen Tertia, Mygdonia, and her nurse, who bribed the jailers to gain entrance (151). Sifor and his wife and daughter are already with Thomas. Tertia tells of the king's reaction to her attraction to Thomas (152). The guards order the prisoners to extinguish their lights. Thomas prays to Jesus, and while the unbelievers sleep in darkness, the believers are bathed in bright, heavenly light (153). Thomas sends Vizan to prepare what is necessary for his baptism. Trusting in Jesus, he is able to exit the prison and encounters his wife Mnesara, who has been led to him by the vision of a mysterious youth (155). Thomas offers another prayer to Jesus, invoking his guidance for Vizan, Tertia, and Mnesara (156). Assisted by Mygdonia, who, like a deaconess, strips and vests the women, Thomas then baptizes them, following the now familiar pattern. He first offers an invocation over the sacred chrism, "seals" the initiates with the holy oil, and then baptizes them in water with the name of the Trinity (157). Thomas then celebrates the Eucharist for the newly sealed, offering them first the cup, then the bread (158).

The Acts of Thomas concludes with the martyrdom of Thomas, here regularly named Judas. After his last Eucharist, the apostle returns to prison, accompanied by Mygdonia, Tertia, and Narkia. He gives them a little homily, telling them that he is ready to go and receive his reward from the just paymaster (159). He then encourages them to abide in the faith of Christ and resist the inimical force that wants to worm its way into them and destroy their minds (160). With Judas Thomas back in prison, the guards, afraid that he might use his magical power to free all prisoners, resolve to go tell King Mizdai that the apostle has converted his wife and son (161–62). Mizdai comes and engages in one more round of questioning. The interrogation focuses on Thomas's status as slave or free, and the apostle is happy to claim his status as a slave of the Lord of heaven and earth. Finally, Mizdai decides to eliminate the sorcerer and cleanse his land, an effort that the apostle assures him will be futile (163). Fearing the response of people who have accepted the new message, Mizdai takes the apostle away along with four soldiers, an officer, and Vizan, his son (164). As he is led away, Judas Thomas finds symbolic significance in the number of the execution team. The four men correspond to the four elements of which he is made, and the one who leads them reminds the apostle that he is from a single source (165). His situation, with four men who will strike him, contrasts with that of his Lord who, since he was from a single source, was only struck by one man (165). At the spot of execution, the apostle first preaches to his executioners, bidding them to open their eyes and ears (166). With Vizan's assistance he then secures a moment of private prayer away from his executioners, asking his Lord to receive him and not let his soul be delayed by "toll-keepers" (167). The soldiers then come and slay him. His brethren retrieve his body, adorn it, and bury it in an old royal tomb (168). While Sifor and Vizan conduct a vigil at the tomb, the apostle appears to them and separately to Mygdonia and Tertia, promising them aid from Jesus. The believers proceed to ordain Sifor a presbyter and Vizan a deacon, guaranteeing the orderly life of the community (169). A brief epilogue reports an event that took place "after much time had passed." When a demon possesses the son of King Mizdai, the king decides that he will use a bone of the apostle as a remedy. A touch of the sacred relic will, he hopes, exorcise the evil power. Unfortunately for the king, the apostle's bones have been removed "to the western regions," a note that aligns with the connection of Thomas to Edessa, although that site is not explicitly named.

Embedded in act 9 is the "Hymn of the Pearl" (chs. 108–113), probably an adaptation of a traditional Parthian or Mesopotamian tale.[29] Preserved in only two manuscripts,[30] the poem is probably a redactional addition to the story.[31] As already noted, Thomas recites it after he has been flogged and imprisoned by King Mizdai. The poem tells of a Parthian prince brought up in luxury at the royal court. His parents send him on a mission to Egypt, lavishly equipped for the journey, but stripped of a splendid robe made especially for him. The mission's goal is to retrieve a pearl guarded by a dangerous serpent. If successful, the prince will be restored to his position, recover his robe, and rule along with his brother. The prince tells of his travel to Egypt, where he encamps by the serpent's lair. While waiting to see if he might snatch the pearl, he befriends a local prince, adopts the native costume, and eats the local food. All of this induces forgetfulness of the prince's origins and mission, and he falls into a deep sleep. Back in Parthia his father, mother, and brother learn of his fate, gather together, and compose a letter. They tell the prince to awaken and remember who he is and what he is supposed to do. They urge him to recall his special cloak and the book of heroes in which his name is written. The letter flies to him like an eagle and awakens him. He casts a spell on the serpent, seizes the pearl, and returns home, guided by the letter. The climax of his return is the encounter with his special robe, in which he sees himself as in a

29. Simo Parpola, "Mesopotamian Precursors of the Hymn of the Pearl," in *Mythology and Mythologies: Methodological Approaches to Intercultural Influences*, ed. R. Whiting (Helsinki: Neo-Assyrian Text Corpus Project, 2001), 181–94.

30. Greek U and Syriac L. For the texts, see P.-H. Poirier, *L'Hymne de la Perle des Actes de Thomas: Introduction, Text, Traduction, Commentaire* (Louvain: Pierier, 1981); Johan Ferreira, *The Hymn of the Pearl: The Syriac and Greek Texts with Introduction, Translation, and Notes* (Sydney: St. Paul's, 2002).

31. G. P. Luttikhuizen, "The Hymn of Judas Thomas, the Apostle, in the Country of the Indians," in *The Apocryphal Acts of Thomas*, ed. J. Bremmer (Leuven: Peeters, 2001), 101–14.

mirror. He dons the robe and enters his father's glorious kingdom, prepared to present the pearl before the king. Presumably, he lives happily ever after.

3. INTERPRETIVE ISSUES
3.1 Tracing the Development of the Text

The composite character of the text has often been noted.[32] The marked difference between the discrete episodes of the first six acts and the integrated novella of the last seven suggests that the current work has been compiled from earlier traditions. The potpourri of narratives, rhetorical pieces, poems, and various types of prayer is characteristic of the popular literary genre, but also suggests a complex compositional history. One clear indication of development is the insertion of the Hymn of the Pearl, appearing in only two of the major witnesses to the Acts of Thomas with superficial connections with its narrative context.

The epicleses resemble liturgical forms associated with initiation and eucharistic rituals, especially as attested in eastern or Syriac Christianity. It is likely that some of the epicleses are derived from actual liturgical practices but were adapted for use in this story.[33] The accounts of initiation all highlight the role of oil in the process, a prominent feature of Syrian initiation rituals. The initiation of Mygdonia (ch. 121) is the most complex. The heroine had asked for the "seal," and the ceremony begins with the apostle anointing her and offering an epiclesis over the oil, addressing it as what "reveals hidden treasures." He then proceeds to baptize her with water in the name of Father, Son, and Spirit, after which he shares the Eucharist with her. The account involves two ritual actions, which reflect different stages in a single initiation process. The primary focus is on the anointing, the "seal" to which Mygdonia had referred. The same sequence of anointing, followed by water baptism and Eucharist appears in the initiations of Sifor and his wife (132) and Prince Vizan (157).

The prayer in the scene of the initiation of Sifor and Mygdonia succinctly summarizes what the rite was understood to achieve. Thomas says, "This baptism is the remission of sins. It gives birth to the light poured out; it gives birth to the new person and mixes a new spirit into the person's soul; it thus triply generates the new person and involves a share in the remission of sins." The baptismal theology of this formula combines discrete traditional elements, including the belief that baptism cleanses from sin (cf. Mark 1:4; Luke 3:3; Rom 6:3, 18) and that it involves a "rebirth" with "spirit" (cf. John 3:3–5). If such prayers were not simply imported from rituals common in Syrian Christianity, they were surely inspired by them.

3.2 History and Legend

A major issue regarding the Acts of Thomas is the relationship of literary imagination and history. The Acts of Thomas is set in four major contexts, an unnamed port on the way to the kingdom of Gundafar (act 1), King Gundafar's court (act 2), on the road to and in an

---

32. Yves Tissot, "Les Acts de Thomas: exemple de recueil composite," in *Les Actes apocryphes des Apôtres: Christianisme et monde païen*, ed. F. Bovon et al. (Geneva: Labor et Fides, 1981), 223–32.

33. See Myers, *Spirit Epicleses*, 87–107. See also Gerard Rowhorst, "Hymns and Prayers in the Apocryphal Acts of Thomas," in *Literature or Liturgy? Early Christian Hymns and Prayers in Their Literary and Liturgical Context in Antiquity*, ed. C. Leonhard and H. Löhr, WUNT 2.363 (Tübingen: Mohr Siebeck, 2014), 195–212, and Caroline Johnson, "Ritual Epiclesis in the Greek Acts of Thomas," in *The Apocryphal Acts of the Apostles*, ed. F. Bovon, A. G. Brock, and C. Matthews, Harvard Divinity School Studies (Cambridge: Harvard University Press, 1999), 171–200.

unnamed city in the realm of King Mizdai (acts 3–6), and finally in King Mizdai's court (acts 7–10), also in an unnamed locale. The narrative is framed by reference to two other sites, Jerusalem after the death and resurrection of Jesus (ch. 1), and the "western regions," probably Edessa, where the bones of Thomas are finally buried (ch. 170).[34]

Indian Christians have long revered the apostle Thomas as the founder of Christianity in India and hold that the Acts of Thomas has at its core a remembrance of Thomas's missionary activity in the first century, a position defended by many modern scholars.[35] Others, however, are skeptical, finding in the Acts of Thomas legends that reflect later traditions.[36]

The Acts of Thomas does contain details reflecting first-century historical conditions. Coins attest the presence of a King Gundafar (or Greek Gundaphoros), and his brother Gad (Gudana on the coins[37]), in the Indus valley in the early first-century, reigning about 21–46 CE.[38] Equally important is the fact that there were well-known first-century trade routes from the Mediterranean to India, some by land and one important sea route to the Malabar coast on the southwest of India.[39] Pliny's *Natural History* 6.26 offers a detailed description, also recorded in the *Periplus of the Erythrean Sea*, a handbook for seafarers from around 60 CE. Traders would have sailed with their goods down the Nile from Alexandria to Coptos, moved their cargo overland to a port such as Berenice, sailed down the Red Sea, and then turned to the east, taking advantage of a monsoon wind, the Hippalus, that blew from the west during midsummer. This trade wind was discovered in Ptolemaic times[40] and used by the Romans in the first century CE. The merchants' voyage ended forty days later at a port, Muziris, probably at the site of modern Kodungallur (or Cranganore) at the mouth of the Periyar River, north of what has been the major port in the region since the fourteenth century, Kochi (Cochin). Traders returned in January, driven by winds from the east. While there may have been earlier connections between India and the Mediterranean,[41] there were certainly known trade routes and trading relations in the early Roman imperial period. Such relations also included official embassies, including one sent from the Island of Taprobane, modern Sri Lanka, to the emperor Claudius (Pliny, *Nat.* 6.24).

The fact that known trade routes existed in the first century creates the possibility that Christian missionaries traveled to India at that time.[42] Scholars who find history behind

---

34. For a general review of the early history of Christianity in India, see Robert Frykenberg, *Christianity in India: From Beginnings to the Present* (Oxford: Oxford University Press, 2008), 91–115.

35. See most recently Thomaskutty, *Saint Thomas*, with earlier literature.

36. Most recently, Andrade, *Journey of Christianity*, with earlier literature.

37. On the interpretation of the name as a title, see James McGrath, "History and Fiction in the Acts of Thomas: The State of the Question," *JSP* 17 (2008): 297–311, esp. 300.

38. A. D. H. Bivar, "Gondophares and the Indo-Parthians," in *The Age of the Parthians*, ed. V. Curtis and S. Steward (London: Tauris, 2007), 26–36. Bivar notes an image of Gundafar in the cathedral of Troyes, France (30). He also discusses the possibility that there was more than one king with this name (32).

39. For a detailed assessment of the trading situation, see Andrade, *Journey of Christianity*, 101–12.

40. Strabo, *Geogr.* 2.3.4, attributes the discovery to Eudoxus of Cyzicus under Ptolemy VII in the second century BCE.

41. Thomaskutty, *Saint Thomas*, 130, suggests connections already in the time of Solomon. See also George Nedungatt, "India Confused with Other Countries in Antiquity," *Orientalia Christiana Periodica* 76 (2010): 315–37, here 323–25.

42. For exotic settings in other texts, see Gary Roger, "On the Road to India with Apollonios of Tyana and Thomas the Apostle," in *Greek and Roman Networks in the Mediterranean*, ed. I. Malkin et al., 2nd ed. (London: Routledge, 2009), 249–63, and Janet Spittler, "Christianity at the Edges: Representations of the Ends of the Earth in the Apocryphal Acts of the Apostles," in *Rise and Expansion of Christianity in the First Three Centuries of the Common Era*, ed. C. Rothschild and J. Schröter, WUNT 301 (Tübingen: Mohr Siebeck, 2013), 353–75.

the Acts of Thomas have mapped its account onto the geopolitical scene of first-century India. One recent reconstruction argues that Thomas traveled first (chs. 1–16) to a location in south India, where his port of arrival, Andrapolis in Greek and Sandaruk in Syriac, was situated on the Malabar Coast in old Kerala, possibly Maliankara, near Kodungallur, the probable site of ancient Muziris.[43] From there, Thomas traveled to north India and the court of Gundafar (chs. 17–61). He then returned to south India (chs. 62–170) and the realm of King Mizdai, perhaps on the Coromandel Coast in the southeast of India.[44] The latter suggestion reflects the Christian tradition of the subdistrict of Mylapore, located in the city of Chennai of the state of Tamil Nadu, on the southeast coast of India, where there is a shrine at the site of Thomas's martyrdom and the Cathedral of St. Thomas, which houses his tomb.[45]

While the existence of trade routes suggests that a first-century Christian mission to the Malabar Coast in particular was possible, some details of the story are ill-suited for southern India. When Thomas arrives in the kingdom of Mizdai (ch. 87), Thomas is told, "You have come to a barren country, for we dwell in a desert," hardly the topography of either southern coast. Some readers find in the Acts of Thomas evidence of specifically Indian customs, such as bathing before dinner, but these are all attested in the west as well.[46] Names may also be significant. "Mizdai" is more at home in a Zoroastrian context where Ahura Mazda was the chief deity than a Hindu environment. Similarly, Carish, King Mizdai's kinsman, a leading character in the last part of the Acts of Thomas, is probably related to the name Cyrus, also more at home in Parthia than India. The geographical details and the names might be appropriate for the kingdom of Gundaphoros, in the Indus River area, but not for a more southerly region, on the Malabar or Coromandel Coasts. As already noted, Origen (*Hom. Gen.* 3) and Eusebius (*Hist. eccl.* 3.1) knew of a Parthian, not Indian, mission, and the details of the account are more compatible with such a venue.

Other data suggest a different origin for Christianity in India. A report, cited as a "tradition" by Eusebius (*Hist. eccl.* 5.10.3), records a trip to India by Pantaenus, a respected Alexandrian Christian teacher in the late second century.[47] He is said upon his arrival to have found Christians who revered Bartholomew rather than Thomas as their founding apostle. Complicating the testimony is the fact that "India" for some ancients referred not to the subcontinent but to east Africa and southern Arabia, since Ethiopia and India were closely associated in their climate, flora, fauna, and human inhabitants.[48] If so, Pantaenus may have encountered Christians with a memory of Bartholomew in the Arabian Peninsula or on the east coast of Africa. The report of his voyage would then be irrelevant to the historicity of Thomas traditions. Others argue that most ancients understood

---

43. For discussion, see James Kurikilamkatt, "The First Port of Disembarkation of the Apostle Thomas in India according to the Acts of Thomas," *Ephrem's Theological Journal* 8 (2004): 3–20.

44. Thomaskutty, *Saint Thomas*, 130–31. On local traditions, see Nedungatt, *Quest*, 258–367; A. C. Perumalil, *The Apostles in India: Fact or Fiction*, 2nd ed. (Patna: Catholic Book Crusade, 1971); Joseph Kolangadan, "The Historicity of Apostle Thomas' Evangelization in Kerala," *The Harp* 8–9 (1995–1996): 8–9; 305–27.

45. On ancient traditions and modern archeology of the site, see Carlo Cereti, Luca Olivieri, and Joseph Vazhuthanapally, "The Problem of the St. Thomas Crosses and Related Questions: Epigraphical Survey and Preliminary Research," *East and West* 52.1 (2002): 285–310, esp. 303–9. The identification of the location of Thomas's death and burial as Calamina or Kalamene, perhaps a version of Cholomandalam, the source of "Coromandel," is a late antique development that then became widely accepted. Andrade, *Journey of Christians*, 222–30, notes other purported burial sites of Thomas.

46. See McGrath, "History and Fiction," 305–9.

47. The visit is also noted by Jerome, *Vir. ill.* 36, and *Epist.* 70.4.

48. Andrade, *Journey of Christianity*, 73–84.

the geographical distinction between India and Ethiopia, despite their similarities.[49] If Pantaenus in the second century did travel to India via the trade route described by Pliny and found Christians on the Malabar Coast, they did not revere Thomas as their apostle.

The Acts of Thomas, therefore, is hardly a reliable source for a mission of Judas Thomas to southern India in the first century. It is possible that the apostle was active in the Indo-Parthian kingdom once ruled by Gundafar. It is also possible that, after the demise of the kingdom around 50 CE, Thomas did travel south, as oral traditions in southern India testify.[50] It is far more probable that his arrival was later and symbolic. By late antiquity Christians from Syria, where Thomas's tomb was revered, or from northern India, where Thomas may have evangelized, arrived on the Malabar and Coromandel Coasts. They brought with them an apostle's memory, preserved in Syria, about his mission to a part of India. The memory of Thomas in India took root and was adopted by local Christians, like the memory of James in medieval Spain, giving them an intimate connection to the origins of the faith. By late antiquity, with the Acts of Thomas in circulation, Thomas was widely understood to be responsible for Christianity throughout India.[51]

3.3 The Relationship of the Acts of Thomas to Other Early Christian Works

Whatever its relationship to the history of Indian Christianity, the Acts of Thomas displays themes attested in other representatives of early Christianity. Attention to the apostle Thomas is shared with other literature that includes one long familiar text and two discoveries of the twentieth century. The Infancy Gospel of Thomas, which recount Jesus's childhood, describes Thomas as one like Jesus, in whom the Lord's Spirit dwells (10.2; 15.2). The Coptic literature discovered at Nag Hammadi in 1945 includes the Gospel of Thomas (NHC II 2) and the Book of Thomas (NHC II 7).[52] The Gospel of Thomas contains 114 sayings attributed to Jesus, some known from other early Christian literature, some otherwise unattested. The collection was reportedly recorded (saying 1, Coptic[53]) by "Didymus Judas Thomas," the name familiar from the Acts of Thomas. In saying 13, Thomas describes Jesus as an ineffable reality. Jesus in turn acknowledges Thomas as one who has "drunk and become intoxicated from the bubbling wellspring that I have personally measured out."[54] The Book of Thomas purports to contain teaching delivered to

---

49. Nedungatt, "India Confused"; Ilaria Ramelli, "Early Christian Missions from Alexandria to 'India': Institutional Transformations and Geographical Identifications," *Augustinianum* 51 (2011): 221–31; and Pierre Schneider, "The So-Called Confusion between India and Ethiopia: The Eastern and Southern Edges of the Inhabited World from the Greco-Roman Perspective," in *Brill's Companion to Ancient Geography: The Inhabited World in the Greek and Roman Tradition*, ed. S. Bianchetti et al. (Leiden: Brill, 2016), 184–202.

50. On oral traditions about Thomas, see Nedungatt, *Quest*, 258–396. More critical is Andrade, *Journey of Christianity*, 207–13, noting how such traditions often depend on Acts Thom. Thus, the opening scenes of the *Thomas Parvam*, first transcribed in 1601, mirror the first chapter of Acts Thom. but change the setting to southern India.

51. See Thomaskutty, *Saint Thomas*, 161–70, finding the traditions reliable; and Andrade, *Journeys of Christianity*, 60–64, 223–25, arguing that the movement of Christians to the region was a fifth-century phenomenon.

52. For connections among these texts, see Bentley Layton, with David Brakke, *The Gnostic Scriptures* (New Haven: Yale University Press, 2021), 555–600; P. H. Poirier, "*Évangile de Thomas, Actes de Thomas, Livre de Thomas*, une tradition et ses transformations," *Apocrypha* 7 (1996): 9–26; Birger Pearson, *Ancient Gnosticism: Traditions and Literature* (Minneapolis: Fortress, 2007), 256–72; Thomaskutty, *Saint Thomas*, 89–150, who reviews all the Thomasine literature, including the Infancy Gospel of Thomas.

53. The Greek has simply "Judas Thomas." For the critical edition, see Harold W. Attridge, "Gospel of Thomas: Appendix: The Greek Fragments," in *Nag Hammadi Codex II,2–7*, ed. B. Layton, NHS 20 (Leiden: Brill, 1989), 95–128.

54. Translation from Layton, *Gnostic Scriptures*, 563.

Judas Thomas, the "brother" and "twin" of Jesus (138.2–11), but is written by Matthias. The work consists of dialogue between Jesus and Thomas, in which Jesus preaches against attachment to fleshly desires and pronounces woes on those who refuse his gospel. The Book of Thomas favors an ascetic form of Christianity, with a sharp dualism of flesh and spirit, although it does not explicitly maintain the Encratite position of "holy chastity" found in the Acts of Thomas.

The rigorous sexual ethics of the Acts of Thomas is not limited to literature associated with Thomas. Many Christian apologists and writers of more popular Christian literature defended a countercultural teaching of sexual restraint,[55] and some went to the extreme represented by the Acts of Thomas. The prohibition of marriage surfaced early. In 1 Corinthians 7, Paul had to clarify his teaching for his Corinthian converts. He did not forbid marriage but recommended that they "remain in the condition in which you were called" (v. 20 NRSV), preferring, on pragmatic grounds, that they remain unmarried. He did, however, allow marriage, which was better "than to burn with passion" (v. 9 NIV). Other teachers in the Pauline tradition prohibited marriage, as the polemic against them in 1 Timothy 4:3 indicates.[56]

In the second century, Encratites emerge as a distinctive group. Around 180 CE, Irenaeus, later cited by Eusebius, claimed that Tatian, an apologist from Syria, disciple of Justin Martyr, and author of the gospel harmony the *Diatessaron*, taught that marriage was "a corruption and fornication."[57] Irenaeus added that other "heretical" second-century teachers, Saturninus and Marcion, maintained this position. In the fourth century, Eusebius (*Hist. eccl.* 4.28–29) quotes Irenaeus and then claims that the Encratite position was developed by a certain Severus. The heresiologist Epiphanius of Salamis (ca. 310–403 CE) echoes Eusebius in criticism of Tatian. He suggests that Encratites were increasing in number in Pisidia and Phrygia and in other parts of the Christian east, and he notes that they used as scriptures the Acts of Andrew, John, and Thomas.[58] He also reports that they celebrate mysteries with water, not wine, which is absent from all but one of the Eucharists in the Acts of Thomas (ch. 158). Thus, while the rigorous position of the Acts of Thomas prohibiting sex and even marriage seems extreme to modern ears, it was not unique in the early Christian scene. As Epiphanius noted, other apocryphal Acts shared the rigorously ascetical stance of the Acts of Thomas, as well as the reinterpretation of sexual attraction characteristic of the Greek romances.[59]

3.4 The Meaning of the Hymn of the Pearl

The Hymn of the Pearl is a classic folktale about a mission, its challenges, and its ultimate success. Interpreters have explored various possibilities for reading it allegorically.[60] One option, popular in the early twentieth century, was to see in it a classic form of "gnostic mythology," telling of a "redeemed redeemer," a notion then thought to be a central

---

55. See Helen C. Rhee, *Christ and Culture in the Second and Third Centuries* (London: Routledge, 2005), esp. 128–36.

56. For more on issues of sexuality in the Pauline tradition, see the Acts of Paul in ch. 14 of this volume.

57. Irenaeus, *Haer.* 1.28. Cf. also Clement of Alexandria, *Paed.* 2.2.33; *Strom.* 1.91.5; 3.76.25; 7.108.2; Hippolytus, *Haer.* 8.7; Origen, *Cels.* 5.65.

58. *Pan.* 2.47. See Frank Williams, *The Panarion of Epiphanius of Salamis: Books II and III (Sects 47–80, De Fide)*, NHMS 36 (Leiden: Brill, 1994), 3–6.

59. On this literature, see Brian P. Reardon, *The Collected Ancient Greek Novels* (Berkeley: University of California Press, 2008), and Tim Whitmarsh, *The Cambridge Companion to the Greek and Roman Novel* (Cambridge: Cambridge University Press, 2008).

60. For the range of opinion, see Ferreira, *Hymn of the Pearl*, 4–9.

"gnostic" myth.[61] The prince would be the revealer, sent to earth (Egypt), to redeem spiritual beings (the pearl), from material bondage (the dragon). But before completing his mission, the redeemer himself needed to be redeemed, by "gnosis" about his origin and destiny. An alternative, more likely reading finds in the poem not the hypothetical gnostic myth but a more general statement about the human condition and its remedy. All human beings, like the prince, are souls embedded in the beguiling material world that erases the memory of their true, heavenly home. A sacred message of divine revelation reminds them of their origin and destiny and guides them along the way to reunification with their heavenly selves. Versions of this philosophically grounded myth of spiritual alienation and restoration also appear in the other Thomasine texts, the Gospel of Thomas and the Book of Thomas.[62]

Either reading involves doctrinal elements absent from the Acts of Thomas. The motif of a "twin" is probably the point of contact with the story of Thomas, although the way in which the image is developed in the Hymn of the Pearl, however its symbolism is construed, differs from the account of the relationship between Judas Thomas and Jesus. Jesus is not Thomas's heavenly *alter ego*, a notion also found in Manichaeism. Other elements of the hymn could be correlated with the story of Thomas, such as the prince's forgetfulness and Thomas's reluctance to evangelize India, or the prince's future rule with his brother and Thomas's postmortem relationship to his twin. But unlike the prince in the hymn, Thomas does not immerse himself in the pleasures of "Egypt," nor does he hear an illuminating message from on high within the story.

4. KEY PASSAGES FOR NEW TESTAMENT STUDIES AND THEIR SIGNIFICANCE

Several individuals in the New Testament relate to the figure of Didymus Judas Thomas in the Acts of Thomas. The lists of the Twelve (Matt 10:2–4; Mark 3:16–19; Luke 6:14–16) include a Thomas, though he is not also named Didymus in these texts. Thomas plays a more substantial part in the Fourth Gospel. Didymus Thomas appears at the resurrection of Lazarus (John 11:16) and at Jesus's final appearance (21:2). After the Last Supper, Thomas asks Jesus about the "way" (14:5). Most famously, Didymus Thomas appears as "doubting Thomas" who, absent from Jesus's first appearance to his disciples, sought empirical evidence of the resurrection (20:24–25). Perhaps Thomas's hesitation to travel to India echoes that doubt, although some question whether the Johannine passage was intended to present a negative portrait of Thomas.[63]

Alongside Thomas or Didymus Thomas, several individuals in the New Testament bear the name Judas (or Jude). Judas Iscariot, who betrayed Jesus,[64] is not part of this Thomas tradition, but there are others. The lists of Jesus's brothers include Judas (Matt 13:55; Luke 6:16) alongside James, Joses, and Simon. The Fourth Gospel mentions a Judas, "not Iscariot," who queries Jesus after the Last Supper (John 14:22), shortly after Thomas asks his question. A Jude, the "brother of James," is the purported author of a brief letter included among the Catholic Epistles (Jude 1). If, as is likely, the James mentioned in that title is the "Lord's brother" (Gal 1:19), who was a leader of the early Jerusalem community

---

61. For the gnostic interpretation see, e.g., Hans Jonas, *The Gnostic Religion: The Message of the Alien God and the Beginnings of Christianity* (Boston: Beacon, 1963; repr., 2001), 112–29, and Werner Foerster, *Gnosis: A Selection of Gnostic Texts* , trans. R. McL. Wilson, 2 vols. (Oxford: Clarendon, 1972), 1:337–64, esp. 341.

62. Layton, *Gnostic Scriptures*, 535–54, esp. 536–37.

63. See Thomaskutty, *Saint Thomas*, 54–74.

64. Cf. Matt 10:4; 26:25; 27:3; Mark 3:19; 14:10, 43; Luke 22:3, 47–48; John 6:71; 12:4; 13:2, 26, 29; 18:2–5.

(Gal 2:9, 12; cf. Acts 15:13), then the epistle's Jude or Judas is probably also the Jude mentioned among Jesus's brothers in Matthew and Mark. Yet this Jude is not identified as anyone's "twin." These data suggest that the Didymus Judas Thomas of the Acts of Thomas conflates two first-century figures, the Didymus Thomas of the Gospel of John and Judas from the Synoptics.

If the Acts of Thomas focuses on Thomas, his twin is never far from the scene. Jesus plays an active role at the start of the story and then appears to many characters as they experience visions (chs. 11–16, and possibly 155) or brushes with death (36–37; 54). These scenes assume that Jesus is the twin of Judas Thomas, ignoring the tradition of the virgin birth. Otherwise, the Acts of Thomas displays an orthodox third-century Christology, which affirms that Jesus is the Son of God (104), although without the post-Nicene insistence on his "consubstantiality" with the Father. The Acts of Thomas celebrates Jesus's humble incarnation (72; 79; 80; 143), his teaching (79; 143), his redeeming, liberating death (72; 80; 143), his resurrection (59; 80), and his ascension (80). The work uses traditional apocalyptic language (80), but its eschatological hope focuses on union with Jesus and participation in heavenly life (104; 136). The desired salvation is mediated through a ritual system that includes both baptism, with its focus on anointing, and Eucharist (27–29; 120–21; 132–33; 157–58).

The rhetorically elaborate sermons, replete with such figures as anaphora, balanced clauses, and parallelism, often allude to the New Testament.[65] This is particularly true of Thomas's speeches in the final portion of the Acts of Thomas. These include the sermon that Thomas preaches after healing Sifor's wife and daughter (ch. 80), evoking the Christ hymn of Philippians 2:6–11, and the lengthy sermon that the apostle delivers when Mygdonia appears. Thomas tells the assembled crowds (Acts Thom. 82.6) that they have eyes and see not, ears and hear not (cf. Matt 13:13). He then (Acts Thom. 82.7) admonishes those who have ears to listen (cf. Matt 11:15) and invites those who are burdened to come and find rest (cf. Matt 11:28), which grounds an extended exhortation to embrace meekness and, above all, "holy chastity" (Acts Thom. 85–86). The sermon ends as it began, with clear allusions to the Gospels. Thomas evokes both Jesus's forty-day fast (Matt 4:2; Mark 1:13; Luke 4:2) and his command to Peter to sheathe his sword since, had Jesus wished, the Father would have sent twelve legions of angels to his aid (Acts Thom. 86.10; cf. Matt 26:52; John 18:11).

Some allusions are more subtle. Thomas at one point describes his gospel of chaste celibacy as "seed" sown in Mygdonia (Acts Thom. 93). She responds that the seed has indeed been planted and will soon bear fruit (94), evoking the parable of the Sower (Matt 13:3–9; Mark 4:1–9; Luke 8:4–8). The resemblances to the passion of Jesus in Thomas's trial (Acts Thom. 106) include the apostle's silence and flogging. Thomas's prayer in prison (107.4) recalls the beatitude about those who suffer for Christ's sake (Matt 5:11). Even the apostle's adversaries ironically allude to the New Testament, as does Carish when calling Thomas a pauper who lacks even "bread for the day" (Acts Thom. 86.7). Carish unknowingly invokes the Lord's prayer, which grounds Thomas's own prayer in Acts of Thomas 144. The Acts of Thomas thus constantly echoes the New Testament, though it does so with its own emphasis on the dichotomy of flesh and spirit and its emphatic summons to chastity.

---

65. See Harold W. Attridge, "Intertextuality in the Acts of Thomas," *Semeia* (1999): 87–124.

5. BIBLIOGRAPHY

Andrade, Nathanael J. *Journey of Christianity to India in Late Antiquity: Networks and the Movement of Culture.* Cambridge: Cambridge University Press, 2018.

Attridge, Harold W. *The Acts of Thomas.* Early Christian Apocrypha 3. Salem, OR: Polebridge, 2010.

Klijn, A. J. F. *The Acts of Thomas: Introduction, Text and Commentary.* 2nd ed. Leiden: Brill, 2003.

McGrath, James F. "History and Fiction in the Acts of Thomas: The State of the Question." *JSP* 17 (2008): 297–311.

Myers, Susan. "Revisiting Preliminary Issues in the Acts of Thomas," *Apocrypha* 17 (2006): 95–112.

———. *Spirit Epicleses in the Acts of Thomas.* WUNT 2.281. Tübingen: Mohr Siebeck, 2010.

Nedungatt, George. "The Apocryphal Acts of Thomas and Christian Origins in India," *Gregorianum* 92 (2011): 533–57.

———. *The Quest for the Historical Thomas: A Re-Reading of the Evidence.* Bangalore: Theological Publications in India, 2008.

Roig Lanzillotta, Lautaro. "A Syriac Original for the Acts of Thomas? The Hypothesis of Syriac Priority Revisited." Pages 105–34 in *Early Christian and Jewish Narrative: The Role of Religion in Shaping Narrative Forms.* Edited by Ilaria Ramelli and Judith Perkins. WUNT 348. Tübingen: Mohr Siebeck, 2015.

Spittler, Janet. *Animals in the Apocryphal Acts of the Apostles: The Wild Kingdom of Early Christian Literature.* WUNT 2.247. Tübingen: Mohr Siebeck, 2007.

Thomaskutty, Johnson. *Saint Thomas the Apostle, New Testament, Apocrypha and Historical Traditions.* London: Bloomsbury T&T Clark, 2018.

CHAPTER 18

THE DEPARTURE OF MY LADY MARY FROM THIS WORLD
(The Six Books Dormition Apocryphon)

J. CHRISTOPHER EDWARDS

1. INTRODUCTION

According to Stephen Shoemaker, the Six Books Dormition Apocryphon[1] is "a narrative packed with nearly every sort of Marian devotion," and is "every bit as important as the *Protevangelium of James* for understanding the rise of Marian piety in early Christianity."[2] Despite its importance, and its availability—it was translated into English in the mid-nineteenth century—Shoemaker observes that it has been largely ignored in the study of early Christianity and Christian late antiquity. In 2016 he was able to state that "prior to the last decade or so, this text was virtually unknown outside of studies on the early Dormition traditions. Even works on Mary in early Christian tradition would generally afford it no more than a brief mention or footnote."[3] Shoemaker credits this lengthy disregard to anti-Catholic tendencies within earlier scholarship on Christian history.[4]

The Six Books is the oldest exemplar of a literary family of Dormition traditions called the Bethlehem traditions, due to the amount of narrative occurring in Bethlehem.[5] The text of the Six Books is originally composed in Greek,[6] although no Greek manuscripts of the text survive.[7] The earliest extant manuscripts are preserved in Syriac and date from the

---

1. The standard title for this work is the Six Books Dormition Apocryphon. Above, I also include the title used by William Wright in his English translation because it better describes the content for those who are not familiar with the text. However, in the body of the essay, I maintain the standard title.

2. Stephen Shoemaker, *Mary in Early Christian Faith and Devotion* (New Haven: Yale University Press, 2016), 130. It behooves me to say that my essay would not be possible if it were not for Shoemaker's extensive work on this text and other Marian traditions. Most of this essay is simply a distillation of his work.

3. Shoemaker, *Mary in Early Christian Faith*, 131.

4. Shoemaker, *Mary in Early Christian Faith*, 131; idem, "Death and the Maiden: The Early History of the Dormition and Assumption Apocrypha," *St Vladimir's Theological Quarterly* 50 (2006): 95–97.

5. For a discussion of other independent families of Dormition traditions, see Shoemaker, "Death and the Maiden," 90–91.

6. The text itself claims to have been translated from Greek into Syriac (see below, "2. Summary of Content"). Also, the Tübingen Theosophy, an apologetic text written around 500 CE, mentions a text called "the birth and assumption of our lady the immaculate Theotokos," which likely refers to an earlier Greek version of the Six Books narrative (Stephen Shoemaker, *Ancient Traditions of the Virgin Mary's Dormition and Assumption*, Oxford Early Christian Studies [Oxford: Oxford University Press, 2002], 28–29, 54—drawing on the work of Pier Franco Beatrice).

7. A later Greek text was made to abbreviate the much longer Six Books narrative. This text is known as *Ps.-John Transitus Mariae* or Ps.-John Dormition of Mary. According to Shoemaker, this later abridgment "survives

fifth and sixth centuries. Shoemaker notes at least five Syriac manuscripts, two of which are complete, and three sets of palimpsest fragments.[8] There are two major English translations of these earliest Syriac texts, each undertaken in the nineteenth century. William Wright translated one of the complete Syriac manuscripts, and A. Smith Lewis translated a fragmentary palimpsest codex.[9] Shoemaker is now producing a much-needed critical edition and translation of the Six Books narrative.[10]

The Six Books must have been written sometime before the middle of the fifth century, since the extant Syriac manuscripts are from the late fifth century, and they were translated from an earlier Greek text.[11] The Six Books must have been written sometime after Constantine, since the traditions about the relic of the True Cross and Mary's practice of praying at Jesus's tomb are only conceivable after Constantine's mother, Helena, journeyed to the Holy Land.[12] Shoemaker argues that the Greek original and its traditions can be more specifically dated "almost certainly to the middle of the fourth century, if not perhaps even earlier."[13] The reasons for this more specific dating are somewhat complicated, but can be summarized in the following two points.

First, the Six Books is dependent on the *Doctrina Addai*. After 400 CE, this text begins to include a story of the discovery of the True Cross, known as the Protonike legend, which is derivative of the Helena legend. Because the Six Books includes a story of the True Cross that is different than the Protonike legend, it must be dependent on a version of *Doctrina Addai* that lacked this legend—that is, a version existing before the year 400 CE.[14]

Second, among the heresies addressed by the fourth-century writer Epiphanius of Salamis in his *Panarion* are the so-called "Kollyridians." This group offered Mary a degree of veneration that Epiphanius finds unacceptable. Shoemaker demonstrates the high likelihood that Epiphanius obtained his understanding of the Kollyridians from his acquaintance with the Six Books.[15] Shoemaker conjectures that "Epiphanius encountered the Six Books traditions in Palestine, where he lived prior to becoming metropolitan of Cyprus in 367."[16]

Finally, although this is not a rationale for dating the Six Books in the mid-fourth century provided by Shoemaker, Richard Bauckham argues for a date "from the fourth century at the latest, but perhaps considerably earlier," based on the position of the dead

---

in as many as one hundred Greek manuscripts and over one hundred known Church Slavonic manuscripts, as well as in Georgian, Latin, and Arabic versions," and therefore rivals the Protevangelium of James's popularity (*Mary in Early Christian Faith*, 131).

8. Shoemaker, *Mary in Early Christian Faith*, 133.

9. William Wright, "The Departure of My Lady Mary from This World," *The Journal of Sacred Literature and Biblical Record* 6–7 (1865): 417–48 and 129–60; Agnes Smith Lewis, *Apocrypha Syriaca*, Studia Sinaitica 11 (London: C. J. Clay, 1902). For a discussion of these and other editions of fragments and versions, see Shoemaker, *Ancient Traditions*, 46–51; *Mary in Early Christian Faith*, 267.

10. *The "Six Books" Dormition Narrative in Syriac: Critical Edition, Translation, and Commentary*, CCSA (Turnhout: Brepols), in preparation.

11. Shoemaker, *Ancient Traditions*, 57.

12. Shoemaker, *Mary in Early Christian Faith*, 134. For a discussion of the Six Books' version of the True Cross story, see Shoemaker, "A Peculiar Version of the *Inventio Crucis* in the Early Syriac Dormition Traditions," *Studia Patristica* 41 (2006): 75–81.

13. *Mary in Early Christian Faith*, 25. It should be noted that in his earlier work, Shoemaker opposed a fourth-century date (*Ancient Traditions*, 56, 286–87).

14. Shoemaker, "Peculiar Version," 80.

15. Stephen Shoemaker, "Epiphanius of Salamis, the Kollyridians, and the Early Dormition Narratives: The Cult of the Virgin in the Fourth Century," *JECS* 16 (2008): 371–401; cf. idem, *Mary in Early Christian Faith*, 145–65.

16. Shoemaker, "Epiphanius of Salamis," 398.

in the Six Books as "waiting for the last judgment and resurrection," which he says can be found in "no other apocalypse [...] later than the mid second century."[17]

2. SUMMARY OF CONTENT[18]

The Syriac manuscript translated by William Wright opens with a short sermon extolling God, who sent his Son, "who migrated from heaven and dwelt in Mary." The author describes the Virgin Mary as "holy and elect of God from (the time) when she was in her mother's womb; and she was born of her mother gloriously and holily; and she purified herself from all evil thoughts, that she might receive the Messiah her Lord." In the middle of the sermon, the author asks his readers to call to mind "the exit of my Lady Mary from this world."[19]

Following the sermon, the author mentions a "book of my Lady Mary," and then proceeds to narrate how it was discovered. According to the author, three holy men, David, John, and Philip, who officiate at the shire on Mount Sinai, write a letter to Cyrus, bishop of Jerusalem, concerning the book of Mary's departure from this world. After searching for the book, those in Jerusalem are unable to find it, but they do find a text written by James, the earlier bishop of Jerusalem. This text describes how in the year that Mary departed from this world "there were written concerning her six books, each book by two of the apostles," and "John the young used to carry them." In response, Cyrus assembles the people of Jerusalem to beseech Jesus so that John, the beloved disciple, might appear to them. After the people fall asleep, John appears and says, "Rise, take the book of the mother of my Lord [...] and go to Mount Sinai [...] and say to them: 'John has sent you this book in order that there may be a commemoration of my Lady Mary three times in the year, because, if mankind celebrate her memory, they shall be delivered from wrath.'" When the people awake, they find the promised volume, which was "written in Hebrew and Greek and Latin." The narrative concerning the discovery of the book concludes by noting that the book was "translated from Greek into Syriac at Ephesus; and was written out and sent to Mount Sinai." The content of the book follows the narrative of its discovery.[20]

According to the book of Mary's departure from this world, in the year 345 (i.e., 33–34 CE), Mary goes, as is her daily custom, to the tomb of the Messiah to weep and pray. In opposition to Mary are the Jews, who barricade the tomb door and install guards with orders to kill anyone who attends the tomb to pray. Inevitably, Mary is spotted praying and is reported to the authorities.[21]

---

17. Richard Bauckham, *The Fate of the Dead: Studies on Jewish and Christian Apocalypses*, NovTSup 93 (Leiden: Brill, 1998), 58–60. In his early work on the Dormition traditions, when Shoemaker himself opposed a fourth-century date, he found Bauckham's reasoning wanting (*Ancient Traditions*, 55–56). However, in his later work, once he changed his own mind about the date, he refers to Bauckham approvingly (e.g., "Peculiar Version," 80n25; *Mary in Early Christian Faith*, 134).

18. My summary follows William Wright's text and translation. There are many ways in which the text and translation of Smith Lewis differs from Wright's. Most obviously, Smith Lewis's manuscript consistently contains much longer versions of the same stories. There are several places in the below summary where I add (in italics) narrative material from Smith Lewis, which is not paralleled in Wright (see the above introduction for a discussion of the textual history of the Six Books). I should emphasize that my additions from Smith Lewis are very minimal. It is for this reason that anyone wishing to utilize the Six Books in their research must closely examine for themselves the earlier work of both Wright and Smith Lewis—that is, until Shoemaker's critical edition is published.

19. Wright, "Departure," 129–30; cf. Smith Lewis, *Apocrypha Syriaca*, 12–15.

20. Wright, "Departure," 130–33; cf. Smith Lewis, *Apocrypha Syriaca*, 15–19. According to Shoemaker, the story of the narrative's discovery "seems designed to introduce an unfamiliar text and to apologize for its apparent newness" (*Mary in Early Christian Faith*, 135).

21. Wright, "Departure," 133–34; cf. Smith Lewis, *Apocrypha Syriaca*, 19–21.

While the authorities deliberate Mary's fate, letters come from Abgar, king of Edessa, addressed to the Roman official, Sabinus. Abgar, who had been healed by one of the seventy-two apostles, and who loves Jesus, is grieved to hear that the Jews killed him. In response, he rises to lay Jerusalem waste. However, in order that there not be conflict between him and the emperor, before crossing the Euphrates Abgar sends letters, informing Sabinus and Emperor Tiberius of Jerusalem's crimes against the Messiah and asking them to "do me justice on the crucifiers." Upon reading the letters, Tiberius resolves to "destroy and kill all the Jews."[22]

When the people of Jerusalem learn of Tiberius's plans, they become insistent that Mary not pray at the tomb, since presumably her custom reveals the crime of the Jews—earlier in the narrative the author reports that the Jews had hidden the cross, spear, nails, and the robe, in order to hide their actions. Fortunately for the people of Jerusalem, Mary becomes sick and is forced to depart for her house in Bethlehem, accompanied by virgins from Jerusalem, who were "the daughters of rich men and rulers."[23]

These virgins spend their time serving Mary. They wash her feet, fold her clothes, and make her bed. They themselves sleep on carpets spread around her bed. Every day they ask her "how our Lord Jesus Christ was born from thee without intercourse with man." And the Lady Mary tells them everything.[24]

Once in Bethlehem, Mary becomes distressed. Taking a censer of incense, she prays to the Messiah: "Hear the voice of Thy parent, and send to me John the young [. . .] and send to me the apostles his fellows." Once Mary prays thus, John, who is living in Ephesus, is told by the Holy Spirit that he is to go to Mary, since the time of her departure is near. After praying, John is snatched by a cloud of light and brought to Mary in Bethlehem. Arriving, John offers Mary a blessing, after kissing her "on her breast and on her knees"—a common greeting to Mary throughout the text.[25]

The Holy Spirit next summons the other apostles "wherever they were, that they should sit upon decorated steeds and on clouds of light, and go to Bethlehem to the blessed one"—Peter in Rome, Paul in Tiberius, Thomas in India, Matthew in Yābūs, James in Jerusalem, Bartholomew in Thebais, and Mark in an unspoken location. Several of the apostles are already dead—Andrew, Philip, Luke, and Simon the Canaanite. To these, the Holy Spirit says: "Rise from Sheōl [. . .] Do not suppose that the resurrection is come; but your rising today from your graves is wholly that you may go to greet the mother of your Lord, for the time draws nigh for her to leave the world."[26]

The miraculous nature of the apostles' journey to Bethlehem draws a crowd to Mary's house. Women come from as far as Athens and Rome. Daughters of kings and rulers bring her gifts. The sick and demon-possessed approach her, and she heals them. The afflicted cry out, "My Lady Mary, mother of God, have mercy on us." Eventually, Mary's activities come to the attention of the authorities. The priests persuade the local judge to bring Mary and the apostles to them for judgment. However, the Holy Spirit reveals the plot to the apostles and enables them and Mary to fly over the heads of those en route to arrest them.[27]

After five days, Mary is once again in Jerusalem, and the people of the city observe angels

22. Wright, "Departure," 134; cf. Smith Lewis, *Apocrypha Syriaca*, 21–22.

23. Wright, "Departure," 134–35; cf. Smith Lewis, *Apocrypha Syriaca*, 22–24. On Mary's additional home in Bethlehem, see Shoemaker, "Death and the Maiden," 69–75.

24. Smith Lewis, *Apocrypha Syriaca*, 24.

25. Wright, "Departure," 136; cf. Smith Lewis, *Apocrypha Syriaca*, 25–27.

26. Wright, "Departure," 137–41; cf. Smith Lewis, *Apocrypha Syriaca*, 27–33.

27. Wright, "Departure," 141–43; cf. Smith Lewis, *Apocrypha Syriaca*, 33–37.

coming to visit her. They begin to implore her to ask her Son for healing. In response, the priests warn a Roman judge that "there will be a great uproar concerning this woman." They obtain his permission to "take fire, and go and burn the house in which she dwells." However, when they approach her house, an angel "dashed his wings in their faces, and fire blazed forth [...] and the faces and hair of the persons who came up to the door of the house were burned, and many people died there." Upon observing this event, the Roman judge acknowledges "the Son of the living God, who was born of the Virgin Mary." He then upbraids the people of Jerusalem as "the wicked nation that crucified God," and he forbids them to go near Mary's dwelling.[28]

Following the judge's rebuke, a man named Caleb, "the chief of the Sadducees, who believed in the Messiah and in my Lady Mary," approaches the judge and advises him to have the people swear by God and the holy books, and to declare what they call the child of Mary, whether a prophet, a righteous man, or the Messiah, the son of God. The judge follows Caleb's advice, and the people are divided into two parties, those who believe the child is the Messiah and the "unbelievers." After an extended back and forth between the "lovers of the Messiah" and the unbelievers, in which the two sides debate the status of the Messiah versus Abraham, Isaac, Jacob, Elijah, and Moses, the judge determines that the unbelievers have lost the argument, and four of their number are "severely scourged."[29]

After the scourging, the lovers of the Messiah question the unbelievers as to the whereabouts of the crucifixion relics: the wood, nails, sponge, spear, crown of thorns, and robe. The judge himself presses the unbelievers to disclose the location of these items. The unbelievers reply that they had cast lots for the items and then buried them. Over the spot where the cross is buried, they left a hole so that a person could reach their hand down the hole and touch the cross. By this means, many thousands had been cured of their afflictions. In response, the judge commands that huge stones be laid upon the place where the items are buried, "ten times the height of a man, [...] so that help shall not go forth from the cross of the Christ to the children of Israel."[30]

The next day, the judge goes to Mary's house, along with his son, who has an abdominal disease. The judge offers Mary extended praise. After Mary blesses the judge, the apostles enter the scene and speak approvingly of his punishment of the crucifiers.[31]

Like the earlier virgins from Jerusalem, the judge questions Mary "about thine election and thy virginity, and how God dwelt in thee." Mary replies that she does "not know whence He entered the palace of my members." She then recounts the events of the Annunciation, when she was at home making the curtain of the temple door, and the angel of the Lord came to her and called her "blessed among women." The scene ends with Mary healing the judge's son.[32]

Upon leaving Mary's home, the judge travels to Rome and speaks of Mary's miracles to "the emperors and the great." The disciples of Peter and Paul hear the judge's words and write to the apostles in Jerusalem, testifying that Mary often "appears to the human beings who believe in her prayers." They relate many stories in which people who are in trouble cry out, "My Lady Mary, have mercy on me/us," and she appears in order to deliver them from their distress.[33]

Back in Jerusalem, the apostles are instructed by the Holy Spirit to take Mary out of

28. Wright, "Departure," 143; cf. Smith Lewis, *Apocrypha Syriaca*, 37–39.

29. Wright, "Departure," 143–46; cf. Smith Lewis, *Apocrypha Syriaca*, 39–43.

30. Smith Lewis, *Apocrypha Syriaca*, 43–46. For a discussion of the manuscripts of the Six Books containing this version of the True Cross story, and those lacking it, see Shoemaker, "Peculiar Version," 78–79.

31. Wright, "Departure," 146–47; cf. Smith Lewis, *Apocrypha Syriaca*, 46–47.

32. Smith Lewis, *Apocrypha Syriaca*, 47–48.

33. Wright, "Departure," 147–48; cf. Smith Lewis, *Apocrypha Syriaca*, 48–50.

the city to a location where there are "three caves and a raised seat of clay." They are to place Mary on that seat and serve her. The villain in this story, at least initially, is a "powerful Jew" named Yūphanyā, whom the scribes of Israel recruit to oppose Mary. As the apostles carry Mary on her bed, Yūphanyā seizes the bed "so that the Jews might carry it off and burn it with fire." However, an angel of the Lord appears with a sword and cuts off Yūphanyā's arms at the shoulders, "and they hung like ropes on the bed." Yūphanyā weeps and cries out, "My Lady Mary, mother of God, have mercy on me!" Mary instructs Peter to reattach Yūphanyā's arms. Peter then gives Yūphanyā a stick and tells him to go and "show the power of the Son of God to all the Jews, and tell of my Lady Mary." The story concludes with an exhortation: "Let no one who loves God and my Lady Mary, who bore Him, be a companion and friend of the Jews; for if he is so, the love of the messiah is severed from him."[34]

Taking the stick, Yūphanyā travels to Jerusalem to witness to the Jews. Arriving, he strikes the stick on the city gate and immediately it puts forth buds and leaves. He informs the Jews of his new convictions about Mary. In order to validate his preaching, he permits those afflicted with various maladies to touch the stick, and they are instantly healed.[35]

Once the apostles install Mary upon her seat in the cave, a group of Jews approach the entrance and see the apostles and angels serving Mary. When three of them enter the cave, fire bursts forth and consumes them, and the earth swallows their bodies. The remaining Jews flee, and the priests bribe them not to reveal what had happened. "They had a custom that every time that one of the Jews went near the mother of God, and was healed, they gave him a bribe and said to him: 'Do not tell that Mary has healed thee! But say that the priests have laid the Torah on me, and I am healed.'"[36]

While in the cave, the Holy Spirit reminds the apostles of the great events that have occurred on Sundays: the Annunciation, Jesus's birth, his arrival in Jerusalem, and his resurrection. Now, once again on a Sunday, Jesus will come from heaven and glorify his mother. And so, on the following Sunday, there appears around Mary's bed Eve, Mary's mother, and Elizabeth. Next arrives Adam, Seth, Shem, and Noah. Then comes Abraham, Isaac, Jacob, and David, followed by the prophets and "created beings without number." Finally, the Great King Jesus arrives, calls to his mother, and blesses her. He also grants her request that he "show mercy to everyone who calls upon thy [i.e., her] name." For Mary's last moment, Jesus asks all present to "sing with the voice of Halleluiah," and immediately Mary's soul leaves her and ascends "to the mansions of the Father's house." Jesus then commands that Mary's body be placed in a chariot of light and taken to the paradise of Eden.[37]

Following Mary's assumption, the apostles give extensive commandments about the dates and the liturgical details for her commemoration. They also command that a book should be written concerning her, "six books, each by two of the apostles." Lastly, they call on Jesus to return them to the countries from which they had come.[38]

The final section of the text concerns the afterlife of Mary. In the paradise of Eden, Jesus comes to Mary's body and says, "'Mary, rise.' And straightway she was restored to life and worshipped Him." Mary is then given a tour of the place prepared for the just, from the "lowest heaven" to the "heaven of heavens." She also sees Gehenna, a place of darkness and fire, which is kindled for the wicked who have disregarded Jesus's commands. When she

---

34. Wright, "Departure," 148–49; cf. Smith Lewis, *Apocrypha Syriaca*, 50–51.
35. Smith Lewis, *Apocrypha Syriaca*, 50–52.
36. Smith Lewis, *Apocrypha Syriaca*, 52.
37. Wright, "Departure," 150–52; cf. Smith Lewis, *Apocrypha Syriaca*, 53–59.
38. Wright, "Departure," 152–56; cf. Smith Lewis, *Apocrypha Syriaca*, 59–64.

hears the voice of those whose destiny it is to be cast into Gehenna crying out for mercy, she says to Jesus, "Have mercy upon the wicked when you judge them at the day of judgment; for I have heard their voice and am grieved."[39]

The text concludes with Mary revealing all that Jesus had shown her to John the young, the beloved disciple.[40]

3. INTERPRETIVE ISSUES
3.1 The Assumption of Mary

Both the sixth-century manuscript used by Wright, and the much later nineteenth-century manuscript used by Smith Lewis to fill in the gaps of her fragmented fifth-century palimpsest codex, narrate Mary's death as follows: Mary's soul departs from her, and Jesus sends it to the mansions of the Father's house. Mary bids Jesus farewell and states, "I am looking to Thy coming which is at hand." Jesus commands the apostles to place Mary's body in a chariot of light. Her body is taken to the paradise of Eden, where later in the narrative Jesus approaches the body, commands Mary to rise, and she worships him.[41] The reader is never told that Mary is reunited with her soul, although this may be assumed when Jesus resurrects her in the paradise of Eden.[42]

Some scholarship has attempted to demonstrate a doctrinal development within the ancient Dormition traditions from those with a supposedly assumptionless Mary to those that confirm a bodily assumption.[43] The key claim on the part of this developmental view is that early Dormition traditions, like the Six Books, portray Mary's resurrection in the paradise of Eden as temporary, in order to provide her a tour of the heavens and Gehenna. It is true that earlier in Smith Lewis's palimpsest codex Jesus says to Mary, "I will make thy body go into the Paradise of Eden, and there it will be until the resurrection."[44] This statement could be understood as referring to the participation of Mary's uncorrupted body in a future general resurrection. However, there is nothing in either Wright's manuscript, nor in the much later manuscript used by Smith Lewis to complete her palimpsest codex, stating that after Jesus resurrects Mary's body in the paradise of Eden, she resumes her bodily separation in anticipation of a future general resurrection.[45] Therefore, Jesus's statement may be best understood as simply referring to Jesus's upcoming resurrection of Mary in the paradise of Eden.

Shoemaker surveys the perspectives on Mary's assumption in the various Dormition traditions, from those which clearly support Mary's bodily assumption to those, like the Six Books, that some scholars have understood as supporting an assumptionless Mary. According to Shoemaker, not only is the assumptionless understanding of the Six Books mistaken, because Mary is not separated from her body after her tour, but so is the argument that there is a demonstrable development in the assumption theologies of the ancient Dormition traditions. Shoemaker argues that the variety in the Dormition traditions regarding Mary's assumption is not due to theological development. Rather, there was an initial diversity in theological differences concerning the exact nature of Mary's final state,

---

39. Wright, "Departure," 156–60; cf. Smith Lewis, *Apocrypha Syriaca*, 64–68.
40. Wright, "Departure," 160; cf. Smith Lewis, *Apocrypha Syriaca*, 68–69.
41. Wright, "Departure," 152, 156; cf. Smith Lewis, *Apocrypha Syriaca*, 58, 64.
42. It is not the purpose of this essay to determine how the Six Books narrative aligns with twentieth-century Catholic dogma.
43. Shoemaker, *Ancient Traditions*, 147–51.
44. *Apocrypha Syriaca*, 55.
45. See Shoemaker, *Ancient Traditions*, 197–200.

so that one tradition cannot claim to be the original from which the others evolved. He states that "the various narrative types are best understood as coexistent, rival traditions [. . .] with none having a substantial claim to priority over the others, and with no evidence of any tradition having developed or decayed from the others."[46]

3.2 Anti-Judaism

Throughout the Six Books, the Jews are portrayed as fierce opponents of Mary. They crucified her Son and desire her death, preferably by burning. According to Shoemaker, we have over sixty different accounts of Mary's Dormition before the tenth century, spread across nine languages, and one of the unifying motifs across these accounts is extreme Jewish opposition to the Virgin and their subsequent punishment, either from God or from the state.[47]

Jewish communities were spread throughout the Byzantine Empire, and regular social contact with Christian communities can be assumed. While the stories in the Six Books are fictions, they almost certainly reflect real tensions between Jews and Christians.[48] For example, Shoemaker argues that the desire of the Jews to burn Mary's body reflects the Christian awareness of Jewish opposition to relics, such as the bodies of holy people.[49]

The greatest source of tension between Jewish and Christian views of Mary concerned her virginity. Both Jewish and Christian sources admit that Mary's sexual status was a subject of ongoing debate. Jews had long insisted that Mary's child was illegitimate. The accusation of Mary's sexual promiscuity can be perceived as early as the Gospel of Mark (6:3). It is also well known that Celsus reports learning from a Jewish source that Mary had been caught in adultery with a Roman soldier named Panthera. Early rabbinic texts refer to Jesus as either "ben Pantera" or "ben Stada."[50] Of course, Jewish populations made their arguments about Mary's sexual status in response to what they perceived was the absurd claim that she had given birth to the messiah of Israel and that they were obliged to recognize him as such.

As is clear from the above "Summary of Content," one Christian response to Jewish denials of Mary's status as the Virgin Mother of God was to create narratives in which Jews are depicted as archenemies of Christian piety toward the Virgin.[51] Such narratives had political consequences for Jewish populations. As veneration of the Virgin was cemented into the imperial establishment, Jews become enemies of the Christian state.[52] It is clear that the Dormition narratives support state action against the Jews from their projection of current tensions between Jews and Christians back into the first century, with pagan proto-Christian rulers defending Christian teaching. In the Six Books, rulers such as Abgar and the Roman emperor Tiberius desire to kill all the Jews, and a Roman judge finds Christian theology far superior to Judaism, and scourges the unbelieving Jewish

---

46. Shoemaker, *Ancient Traditions*, 146–47. For the entire discussion, see 148–51; 179–204. Although not discussed above, Shoemaker also addresses the question of how ancient Christians understand the temporal nature of paradise.

47. Stephen Shoemaker, "'Let Us Go and Burn Her Body': The Image of the Jews in the Early Dormition Traditions," *Church History* 68 (1999): 777. Shoemaker argues that anti-Judaism of the Dormition traditions lays the foundation for the frequent anti-Judaism in medieval Marian piety (776).

48. Shoemaker, "'Let Us Go and Burn Her Body,'" 777.

49. Shoemaker, "'Let Us Go and Burn Her Body,'" 798–800, 808–10.

50. Shoemaker, "'Let Us Go and Burn Her Body,'" 792.

51. For other responses, see Shoemaker, "'Let Us Go and Burn Her Body,'" 794–98.

52. According to Shoemaker, "Mary emerged as a primary focus of imperial Christian identity—a powerful, celestial patroness whose favors fell especially on the empire, its capital, and its rulers" ("'Let Us Go and Burn Her Body,'" 817).

opponents. Shoemaker notes that as the Roman Empire increasingly Christianized, the laws giving Jews the right to abstain from imperial religion waned.[53] The result is that the very same religious persecution that the empire had placed upon Christians in the second half of the third century is later directed by Christians at their religious opponents, increasingly Jews.[54]

3.3 Liturgy

Immediately after the assumption of Mary's body into the paradise of Eden, the apostles command that there should be a "commemoration of the blessed one three times in the year."[55] Then follows what amounts to an instructional guide for the observance of these holy days on which no work should be done.[56] The instruction for each holy day revolves around the blessing of bread in commemoration of Mary, and is as follows:

> And the apostles also ordered that any offering offered in the name of my Lady Mary should not remain over the night, but that at midnight of the night immediately preceding her commemoration, it should be kneaded and baked; and in the morning let it go up on the altar, whilst the people stand before the altar with psalms of David, and let the New and Old Testaments be read, and the volume of the decease of the blessed one [the *Six Books*]; and let everyone be before the altar in the church, and let the priests celebrate (the holy Eucharist) and set forth the censer of incense and kindle the lights, and let the whole service be concerning these offerings; and when the whole service is finished, let everyone take his offerings to his house. And let the priest speak thus: "In the name of the Father, and of the Son, and of the Holy Spirit, we celebrate the commemoration of my Lady Mary." Thus let the priest speak three times; and (simultaneously) with the work of the priest who speaks, the Holy Spirit shall come and bless these offerings; and when everyone takes away his offering, and goes to his house, great help and the benison of the blessed one shall enter his dwelling and establish it forever.[57]

Of note in this passage is the instruction that the Six Books be read as part of the ceremony. This makes sense of the fact that the Six Books opens with what might be called a sermon or a prayer before narrating the events of Mary's departure. The apostles' command for a commemoration also shows that regular liturgies for the Virgin were established by the fourth century, if not earlier.[58] It may be that the Six Books itself was created for liturgical purposes. This is certainly true of *Ps.-John Transitus Mariae*, the Greek abbreviation of the Six Books, which according to Shoemaker, survives in hundreds of Greek and Church Slavonic manuscripts, the overwhelming majority of which are liturgical collections."[59]

---

53. Shoemaker, "'Let Us Go and Burn Her Body,'" 779.

54. Shoemaker, "'Let Us Go and Burn Her Body,'" 778.

55. According to Shoemaker, "the first feast is to be commemorated two days after the nativity (which itself falls on 24 December or 6 January according to the different manuscripts), and the second and third are on 15 May and 13 August respectively" (Stephen Shoemaker, "Apocrypha and Liturgy in the Fourth Century: The Case of the 'Six Books' Dormition Apocryphon," in *Jewish and Christian Scriptures: The Function of 'Canonical' and 'Non-canonical' Religious Texts*, ed. J. Charlesworth and L. McDonald [London: T&T Clark, 2010], 156).

56. Wright, "Departure," 152–54; cf. Smith Lewis, *Apocrypha Syriaca*, 59–62.

57. Wright, "Departure," 153; cf. Smith Lewis, *Apocrypha Syriaca*, 61.

58. Shoemaker, *Mary in Early Christian Faith*, 144.

59. See note 7 above; Shoemaker, "Apocrypha and Liturgy," 155; idem, "'Between Scripture and Tradition': The Marian Apocrypha of Early Christianity," in *The Reception and Interpretation of the Bible in Late Antiquity*, ed. L. DiTommaso and L. Turescu, Bible in Ancient Christianity 6 (Leiden: Brill, 2008), 502, 504.

3.4 The Veneration of Mary before the Council of Ephesus

In 431 CE, the Council of Ephesus officially recognized Mary as *theotokos*, "the bearer of God." Generations of scholarship have marked the council's recognition as the beginning of Christian devotion to Mary. A central contribution of Shoemaker's extensive work on the history of Marian veneration has been to demonstrate that this is incorrect. Christian veneration of Mary is much older than the fifth century, though not always existing in orthodox communities. The council's recognition of Mary as the *theotokos* should be understood as a consequence of this preexisting devotion to the Virgin, rather than its cause.[60]

According to Shoemaker, "there is practically no evidence of any Christian devotion to Mary prior to 150 CE (or, for that matter, to any other figure besides Jesus)."[61] The lasting legacy of the New Testament writings is simply to affirm Mary's status as a virgin.[62] Second-century fathers, such as Justin Martyr and Irenaeus, add to her virginity a conception of Mary as a new Eve, who reverses the disobedience of Adam's partner.[63] Also in the late second century, there emerges a remarkable orthodox biography of Mary, the Protevangelium of James.[64] This text stands out among other writings of the second century for its depiction of Mary as the ever-virgin, possessing an unparalleled purity and holiness.[65] Such a presentation is certainly intended to inspire orthodox devotion to the Virgin.[66]

Following the Protevangelium of James, devotion to Mary takes a heterodox turn in the third century. Christians who believe that salvation could be found through Jesus's secret teachings regarding a spiritual realm enlist Mary as their mediator of esoteric knowledge. Texts with such a portrayal of the Virgin include the Book of Mary's Repose and possibly the Gospel of Mary.[67] This heterodox adoption of Mary may account for the lack of development in Mariology among the third-century fathers, and in the case of Tertullian, outright opposition to the Virgin.[68]

The Six Books could represent a fourth-century orthodox response to earlier heterodox narratives. The Six Books certainly evidences that explicit devotion to Mary and an established liturgy were in place among orthodox Christians well before the Council of Ephesus. In fact, there is much more explicit evidence of Marian devotion among more popular (mostly non-textual) sources, which predate the Council of Ephesus. These include shrines and churches dedicated to Mary, art in Roman catacombs, depictions on

---

60. For general histories of Mariology in the patristic period, see H. C. Graef, *Mary: A History of Doctrine and Devotion* (New York: Sheed and Ward, 1963, 1965; repr., Notre Dame, IN: Christian Classics, 2009); B. Reynolds, *Gateway to Heaven: Marian Doctrine and Devotion, Image and Typology in the Patristic and Medieval Periods* (Hyde Park, NY: New City Press, 2012).

61. Shoemaker, *Mary in Early Christian Faith*, 3.

62. For a discussion of the variety and development in Late-Antique concepts of virginity, see J. Kelto Lillis, "Virgin Territory: Configuring Female Virginity in Early Christianity" (PhD diss., Duke University, 2017).

63. Lillis, "Virgin Territory," 44–47. Shoemaker states that "with these two thinkers we see the first significant moves toward developing Mary as a figure who plays a role in her own right within the drama of human salvation" (44–45).

64. See Eric M. Vanden Eykel's essay in this volume (ch. 9).

65. Shoemaker, *Mary in Early Christian Faith*, 53–61.

66. According to Shoemaker, "this first Marian biography unquestionably marks the beginnings of Marian piety in ancient Christianity . . . most scholars are agreed that its aim is first and foremost to glorify the Virgin Mary" (*Mary in Early Christian Faith*, 54).

67. Shoemaker, *Mary in Early Christian Faith*, 100–29. Shoemaker argues for the possibility that Mary of Nazareth should be the referent of "Mary" in the Gospel of Mary and in several other early Christian apocrypha (75–95). Cf. Shoemaker, "From Mother of Mysteries to Mother of the Church: The Institutionalization of the Dormition Apocrypha," *Apocrypha* 22 (2011): 14–28.

68. Shoemaker, *Mary in Early Christian Faith*, 66–68.

tombstones and sarcophagi, the woman at the well from the Dura-Europos house, and the *Sub tuum praesidium* papyrus, a third-century amulet requesting protection from the *theotokos*.[69] In addition to the devotion and liturgy in the Six Books, these popular artifacts have encouraged the growing realization among scholars that the *lex orandi* of the populous gave rise to the *lex credendi* of the Third Council, and not vice-versa.[70]

4. KEY PASSAGES FOR NEW TESTAMENT STUDIES AND THEIR SIGNIFICANCE

The earliest New Testament texts are those of Paul, written roughly between 50–60 CE.[71] Paul has very little to say about Mary. His single reference to her comes in Galatians 4:4, where he recalls how when "the fullness of time had come, God sent his Son, born of a woman, born under the law" (NRSV). Paul's brief reference to this unnamed woman functions to ensure the inherited humanity of the Son of God.[72]

The Gospel of Mark was probably written sometime shortly after 70 CE. Although not explicit, Mark indicates his awareness of the virgin-birth tradition. In Mark 6:3 (Matt 13:55; Luke 4:22), while Jesus teaches in his hometown, his hearers question him saying, "'Is not this the carpenter, the son of Mary?' ... And they took offense at him." Scholars have frequently noted how Mark uses the negative comments of Jesus's opponents to ironically declare what Mark's readers believe to be true about him; for example, in Mark 15:18 the mocking soldiers salute him, "Hail, King of the Jews!" (NRSV). Similarly, in Mark 6:3, by referring to Jesus as the "son of Mary," Jesus's hometown opponents are shown to engage rumors of Jesus's illegitimate birth, but the readers of Mark's Gospel know that Jesus is the son of the Virgin Mary, rather than Joseph, because his true father is God.

Mary's second appearance in Mark's Gospel comes in 3:20–35. Here Jesus's family attempts to restrain him in response to claims that "he has gone out of his mind" (3:21). Shortly thereafter, Jesus is told, "Your mother and your brothers and sisters are outside, asking for you." Jesus replies, "Who are my mother and my brothers? ... Whoever does the will of God is my brother and sister and mother" (3:32–35 NRSV; cf. Matt 12:47–50; Luke 8:19–21). This passage suggests that Jesus's family, including his mother, are outsiders to his public ministry. It is noteworthy that Mark's Gospel also portrays the Twelve as outsiders (Mark 8:31–33; 9:30–32; 10:32–37). Only the Roman centurion shows himself to be a true insider (15:39).

The Gospel of Matthew expands on both elements found in Mark 6:3: the accusation of Jesus's illegitimate birth, and the implicit message that Jesus's true father is not Joseph. Regarding the accusation, Matthew's Gospel opens with a genealogy tracing Jesus's lineage from Abraham. Scholars have frequently noted that in addition to Mary, four other women appear in the genealogy: Tamar, Rahab, Ruth, and "the wife of Uriah" (Matt 1:3, 5, 6). Each of these women were known for questionable sexual activities. It is most likely that

---

69. Shoemaker, *Mary in Early Christian Faith*, 17–20, 68–73, 194–203. On the woman at the well, see M. Peppard, *The World's Oldest Church: Bible, Art, and Ritual at Dura-Europos, Syria* (New Haven: Yale University Press, 2016), 155–201.

70. Shoemaker, *Mary in Early Christian Faith*, 228.

71. For a general introduction to Mary in the New Testament, see R. E. Brown et al., *Mary in the New Testament: A Collaborative Assessment by Protestant and Roman Catholic Scholars* (Philadelphia: Fortress, 1978); B. R. Gaventa, *Mary: Glimpses of the Mother of Jesus*, Studies on Personalities of the New Testament (Columbia, SC: University of South Carolina Press, 1995); Shoemaker, *Mary in Early Christian Faith*, 30–39.

72. It is dangerous to read too much into Paul's single impersonal reference to Mary. He may have known much more than he had occasion to mention in his extant writings. Paul also does not say much about Jesus of Nazareth, outside of his death and resurrection, but few would doubt that he knew much more, given his interactions with Jesus's disciples.

the author of Matthew has included these women to establish a solidarity with Mary, who is accused of illicit sexual activity.

Regarding Jesus's true father, the Gospel of Matthew adds to Mark's implicit suggestion of Mary's virginity a birth narrative where Mary is explicitly a virgin who is impregnated by God's own doing (Matt 1:18–25). Other than being impregnated from the Holy Spirit, Mary does not play an active role in Matthew's birth narrative.

The Gospel of Luke greatly expands Mary's role in the birth and childhood narrative. Luke focuses directly on Mary's active obedience to the angelic annunciation that she, as a virgin, will give birth to the Son of God: "Here am I, the servant of the Lord; let it be with me according to your word" (Luke 1:38 NRSV). When Mary visits Elizabeth, she declares to Mary, "Blessed are you among women, and blessed is the fruit of your womb" (v. 42). Luke gives Mary a prophetic voice in the Magnificat (vv. 46–55). A man named Simeon informs Mary, presumably in reference to Jesus's death, that "a sword will pierce your own soul" (2:35). When the adolescent Jesus is lost and then found at the temple, in his Father's house, Luke says that "his mother treasured all these things in her heart" (v. 51). All this conveys that in Luke's Gospel Mary is an insider to what God is doing through Jesus, and this leads the author to redact Mark's more negative portrayals—contrast Mark 3:31–35 with Luke 8:19–21.[73] This is further confirmed when in Luke's second volume, the Acts of the Apostles, we find Mary alongside the disciples praying in anticipation of the Holy Spirit (Acts 1:14).

Like Luke and Acts, the Gospel of John portrays Mary as an insider to Jesus's ministry. Both she and his brothers are included with the disciples as Jesus begins his ministry (John 2:12). At the wedding of Cana, it is Mary who actively presses Jesus to get his ministry going (vv. 1–11). At the conclusion of Jesus's life, Mary is there at the cross, and while dying, Jesus ensures that she will be cared for by the beloved disciple (19:25–27). The Gospel of John's depiction of Mary's presence at the beginning and end of Jesus's ministry functions as a merism, indicating that she has been there the whole time.

In contrast to Mark and Matthew, where Mary is simply a pregnant virgin and possibly an outsider to Jesus's ministry, Luke and John portray her as actively obedient to the divine instruction that she bear God's son. She is a prophetess, beloved of Jesus, and an active participant in his public ministry. The Gospels of Luke and John must be considered foundational for the late-antique devotion to the Virgin Mary expressed in the Six Books and at the Council of Ephesus.

Given that scholars generally order the above sources chronologically from Paul to Mark to Matthew to Luke to John, it is possible that the New Testament writings witness to the temporal development of Mary from a nameless woman in Paul, to a virgin in Mark and Matthew, to an active follower of Jesus in Luke and John. However, Shoemaker notes another possibility, which is sometimes suggested by scholars. He points out that the negative portrayal of Mary and the other disciples in Mark, which is a gospel in the Pauline sphere, may be symptomatic of the rift between Paul and the members of Jesus's family.[74]

---

73. Some have seen a negative portrayal of Mary in Luke 11:27–28 when a woman declares to Jesus, "Blessed is the womb that bore you and the breasts that nursed you!" Jesus replies, "Blessed rather are those who hear the word of God and obey it" (NRSV). However, J. A. McGuckin correctly observes that this passage promotes Mary, who is not blessed simply because she bore and nursed Jesus but because she is obedient to God, as emphasized in Luke 1 ("The Early Cult of Mary and Inter-Religious Contexts in the Fifth Century Church," in *The Origins of the Cult of the Virgin*, ed. C. Maunder [London: Burns & Oates, 2008], 21n11).

74. Shoemaker, *Mary in Early Christian Faith*, 39–43. On Mark as a Gospel in the Pauline sphere, see, e.g., J. Marcus, "Mark—Interpreter of Paul," *NTS* 46 (2000): 473–87.

James is at the very least a close relation to Jesus and was the leader of the early Jerusalem church. It is well known that James and Paul have conflicting ideas about law observance within a gentile mission (Gal 1:13–2:14). Therefore, Paul struggles with a church led by a member of Jesus's family. This struggle with Jesus's kin and the other Jerusalem apostles may be at the root of the negative portrayals of Mary and the disciples in the Pauline Gospel of Mark. It may simply be Markan redaction, rather than some earlier Marian traditions, that produces the tensions between Jesus and his family in that Gospel. If correct, this explanation would invalidate the perspective of chronological development of Marian doctrine in the New Testament, and it would open the possibility that the lofty traditions of Mary found, for example, in Luke's Gospel are themselves part of the earliest recoverable traditions about the Virgin.

5. BIBLIOGRAPHY

Brown, R. E. et al. *Mary in the New Testament: A Collaborative Assessment by Protestant and Roman Catholic Scholars*. Philadelphia: Fortress, 1978.

Gaventa, B. R. *Mary: Glimpses of the Mother of Jesus*. Studies on Personalities of the New Testament. Columbia, SC: University of South Carolina Press, 1995.

Graef, H. C. *Mary: A History of Doctrine and Devotion*. New York: Sheed and Ward, 1963, 1965. Repr., Notre Dame, IN: Christian Classics, 2009.

Peppard, M. *The World's Oldest Church: Bible, Art, and Ritual at Dura-Europos, Syria*. New Haven: Yale University Press, 2016.

Reynolds, B. *Gateway to Heaven: Marian Doctrine and Devotion, Image and Typology in the Patristic and Medieval Periods*. Hyde Park, NY: New City Press, 2012.

Shoemaker, Stephen J. *Ancient Traditions of the Virgin Mary's Dormition and Assumption*. Oxford Early Christian Studies. Oxford: Oxford University Press, 2002.

———. "Epiphanius of Salamis, the Kollyridians, and the Early Dormition Narratives: The Cult of the Virgin in the Fourth Century." *JECS* 16 (2008): 371–401.

———. "'Let Us Go and Burn Her Body': The Image of the Jews in the Early Dormition Traditions." *Church History* 68 (1999): 775–823.

———. *Mary in Early Christian Faith and Devotion*. New Haven: Yale University Press, 2016.

———. "A Peculiar Version of the *Inventio Crucis* in the Early Syriac Dormition Traditions." *Studia Patristica* 41 (2006): 75–81.

Smith Lewis, Agnes. *Apocrypha Syriaca*. Studia Sinaitica 11. London: C. J. Clay, 1902.

Wright, William. "The Departure of My Lady Mary from This World." *The Journal of Sacred Literature and Biblical Record* 7 (1865): 129–60.

CHAPTER 19

THE PSEUDO-CLEMENTINES

F. STANLEY JONES

1. INTRODUCTION

The body of the Pseudo-Clementines opens with the words, "I, Clement, a fellow-citizen of the Romans" and proceeds with a detailed autobiographical account of Clement's life and travels with the apostle Peter. This overt assertion of authorship by Clement I of Rome has not been accepted by modern scholars, though they have distinguished this set of writings as "the Pseudo-Clementines" in a preferred sense and have thereby set them somewhat apart from other spurious writings ascribed to Clement (such as 2 Clement, the Letters to the Virgins, and the Apostolic Constitutions).

The heart of the Pseudo-Clementines is an entertaining early Christian novel titled the Circuits of Peter (*Periodoi Petrou*). It has survived to the modern world only in rewritten forms, not in its original. The most prominent of these revamped versions are the *Klementia* and the Recognition. The *Klementia* is often called the "Homilies," after one of its main components, twenty numbered books, the last nineteen of which are each entitled a "homily" in the Greek manuscripts. But the first book of the *Klementia* opens with three other writings—namely, the Letter of Peter (to James), the Declaration, and the Letter of Clement (to James). Two Greek manuscripts have preserved the *Klementia*, which originated about 320 CE. The Recognition, often called the "Recognitions," dates to roughly the same time, though no known manuscript has retained its original Greek. Instead, ancient Syriac and Latin translations (fourth and early fifth centuries) from the Greek provide access to the Recognition. It was Rufinus's Latin version of the Recognition that alone was known and popular throughout the medieval period in the West (well over a hundred manuscripts survive).

The *Klementia* and the Recognition have a good deal of material in common, sometimes sharing passages verbatim for pages at a time. After much study and debate, scholars have now largely reached the consensus that the *Klementia* and the Recognition must each independently have used the earlier original form of the novel, which was composed about 220 CE and was known to early Christian authors such as Origen under the title "Circuits of Peter" in fourteen books. It seems that a century later, at the time of the christological debates just prior to the Council of Nicaea (325 CE), competing parties in and around Antioch got their hands on the Circuits of Peter and reworked it to support their christological and theological views (hence the *Klementia* and the Recognition). Scholars sometimes call the Circuits of Peter (the recovered title of the original novel) the *Grundschrift* or "basic writing." An important indicator for the date of the Circuits of Peter is the statement in Recognition 1.45.3 that the distinctive name for "king" among the "Parthians" is "Arsac," because the Parthian dynasty of the Arsacids was overthrown and replaced by the

Sassanids in the mid-220s CE; thus, the Circuits of Peter was probably written before this political revolution.

The Pseudo-Clementines fit only somewhat awkwardly in the category of New Testament apocrypha. On the one hand, they are the sole preserved ancient Christian novel and, in keeping with novels, are somewhat too lengthy to be included in standard collections of New Testament apocrypha. On the other hand, they have been excluded from the modern notion of the corpus of the "apostolic fathers," though they were originally included in the first, seventeenth-century collection that bore this name.[1] The Pseudo-Clementines nevertheless fascinate students of early Christianity because they seem to retain intact early Jewish-Christian perspectives that are found elsewhere only in fragments. In particular, expressly anti-Pauline material in the Pseudo-Clementines has led scholars to believe that the Pseudo-Clementines provide an extraordinary vista onto the forgotten Jewish-Christian wing of early Christianity. And, indeed, the Circuits of Peter can legitimately be viewed as the greatest surviving repository of Jewish-Christian traditions from the first two centuries in Syria.

The Circuits of Peter was composed by a gifted Syrian Greek-speaking Jewish Christian to counter the gentile Christianity that was becoming the dominant form of the faith throughout the Roman Empire. With knowledge of contemporary popular Greek novels, the author of the Circuits of Peter created an intricate story to present the originally intended type of Christian belief and practice on the lips of Peter himself, Jesus's most eminent disciple. The novel-genre allowed the author to "make believe" in a realistic manner and thus to illustrate how Christians should actually act, think, and believe. Again here, the Circuits of Peter differs from apocryphal Acts of the apostles with their frequent use of apostolic miracles or talking animals. The characters in the Circuits of Peter, in contrast, are true humans confronted with the facts and realities of the actual world (in realistic make-believe). While it has been suggested that the Circuits of Peter has violated its own criterion of truth by trying to convince with an entirely fictitious story,[2] this claim overlooks the fact that, according to the novel, "hearing" (and not seeing) is the mode for true Christian conviction.[3] Thus, intimating this recurrent theme in the novel, Clement states that after Peter's first instructions to him, their "truth was more manifest to the ears than things seen by the eyes" (Ps.-Clem., *Hom.* 1.20.1, par. Ps.-Clem., *Rec.* 1.17.1 Syriac; all translations in this chapter are my own, except when otherwise indicated).

2. SUMMARY OF CONTENT

The Circuits of Peter began with the three disjointed pieces that are now found at the beginning of the *Klementia*: the Letter of Peter (to James), the Declaration (Pertaining to Those Who Receive the Books), and the Letter of Clement (to James). These introductory writings seem to imitate a convention of attaching "documents" at the beginning of a novel to lend it a sense of verisimilitude, but also to prepare the reader for some extraordinary content. The Greek novel *The Wonders beyond Thule* did something similar, providing the

---

1. Jean Baptiste Cotelier, ed., *Ss. Patrum Qui Temporibus Apostolicis Floruerunt; Barnabæ, Clementis, Hermæ, Ignatii, Polycarpi; Opera Edita et Inedita, Vera et Suppositicia. Unà cum Clementis, Ignatii, Polycarpi Actis atque Martyriis*, 2 vols. (Paris: Typis Petri le Petit, 1672), 1:390–746.

2. Étienne Barilier, "Le revanche de Simon le Magicien," in *Nouvelles intrigues pseudo-clémentines*, ed. F. Amsler et al., Publications de l'Institut Romand des Sciences Bibliques 6 (Lausanne: Éditions du Zèbre, 2008), 21.

3. Nicole Kelley, "What Is the Value of Sense Perception in the Pseudo-Clementine Romance?," in Amsler et al., *Nouvelles intrigues pseudo-clémentines*, 364–66.

story via several layers of one report inside another report inside yet others. For the Circuits of Peter, these introductory pieces entice the reader with the possibility of access to information from the earliest stages of Christianity, formally declared to have been kept secret by the Jerusalem elders under James their bishop, the brother of Jesus.[4] Here is a sample of what Peter writes to James:

> Since I know that you, my brother, eagerly seek the common good for all of us, I request and beg you to share the books of my sermons that I am sending to you with no one of those from the gentiles nor with one of the same race before testing, but if someone should be found who has been proven worthy, then to pass on to him according to the discipline by which Moses also passed on to the seventy who inherited his chair. [...] For if this is not done, our word of truth will be torn apart into many opinions. Now I know this, not as one who is a prophet, but as one who already sees the beginning of the evil itself. (Letter of Peter 1.2; 2.2)

In the Declaration, James is said to have administered a bloodcurdling oath to the presbyters for the preservation of the books. Then, it is stated:

> After James had said these things, the presbyters fell into agony and turned pale. Thus, when James saw that they had become exceedingly afraid, he said, "Listen to me, brothers and fellow servants! If we furnish the books to all at random and these are falsified by certain bold men or are distorted through interpretations, as you have heard that certain ones have already done, then there will be everlasting deception even for those who really seek the truth. Therefore, it is better for them [sc., the books] to be among us and to pass along [the books] with all aforementioned care to those who wish to live and to save others. But, if someone does otherwise after having made such a deposition, he will reasonably be subjected to eternal punishment. For by what reason should he not be destroyed who has become the cause of the destruction of others?" (Declaration 5)

After this enticing introduction, the Letter of Clement notifies James, as Peter had requested, that Peter has now been martyred in Rome. Reporting first on his ordination as bishop by Peter before his death, Clement indicates that Peter had also asked him to send James the following autobiographical recapitulation, starting from Clement's childhood through how he came to leave Rome and to accompany Peter on his mission in Syria on his way to Rome. Clement notes here that Peter's discourses have already been recorded in greater detail and periodically sent back to James, the bishop in Jerusalem (Letter of Clement 20).

The actual "autobiographical" report then opens with a description of the young noble Clement (a relative of the emperor) in Rome as he searches among the philosophical teachers after some meaning for life, but comes away disappointed and depressed. Eventually, Barnabas arrives in the capital, apparently as part of Jesus's mission of the seventy, and is ridiculed by the philosophers, though he garners Clement's concurrence and protection. Barnabas soon departs for home, while Clement vows to follow presently in order to learn more. Clement later arrives in Caesarea and chances upon Peter there, who has heard about Clement's hospitality toward Barnabas. Through an initial discussion, Peter is able to alleviate Clement's philosophical quandaries, so Clement decides to travel in Peter's company.

---

4. Patricia A. Duncan, *Novel Hermeneutics in the Greek Pseudo-Clementine Romance*, WUNT 395 (Tübingen: Mohr Siebeck, 2017), 38.

Peter, meanwhile, is slated to hold a public debate with Simon Magus, a formidable foe with extensive education and documented competencies in magic. The novel proceeds with morning preparatory discussions among Peter and his adherents followed by rather intense debates with Simon. Differing from what is found in most other apocryphal Acts, these discussions and debates are largely genuine intellectual inquiries guided by order of thought and logic (and never resolved by miracles). Topics include whether there is one god or more, the nature and origin of evil, and whether the soul is immortal.

After three days of debate, Simon finds himself cornered and flees the scene up the coast toward Antioch. Peter sets up a church in Caesarea and, after a while, follows in pursuit to preach and convert in the cities in the wake of Simon's destructive path. At the planned longer stopover in Tripolis, one sees exactly how the author thinks the Christian message should be presented to gentiles. The overarching theme of Peter's discourses is proper piety toward God (*theosebeia*). Topics include the origin of sin and evil, the nature of demons and their involvement in the worship of idols, whether it is proper to abandon the religion of one's ancestors, the immortality of the soul, and baptism and purity. At the end of the proclamation in Tripolis, Clement fasts and is baptized.

As Peter and his followers proceed up the coast toward Antioch, Peter learns that Clement had lost touch with his parents and siblings when he was a boy. Clement states that he has not seen his father for twenty years; by combining this number with other chronological indications here, the inquisitive reader can figure out that Clement is now thirty-two years old. The story continues through a set of vivid recognition-scenes, in which members of Clement's lost family are gradually recovered. As the details of the story progressively disclose, Clement's baptism has apparently broken the astrological hold of a bad horoscope on the fate of the family. First, Clement's mother is discovered as an abject beggar outside a famous temple of Aphrodite on the island Arados, which had been featured for a (divinely influenced) "recognition" in another Greek novel (Chariton, *Chaer.* 7.5.1–8.1.17). Later, Clement's father is found as an elderly laborer near the coast. This encounter unleashes detailed discussions with the father on Greek philosophy, astrology, free will, cosmology, and mythology. Since these topics are beyond Peter's dignity and immediate competencies, Clement and his older brothers (twins also recovered along the way) bring their extensive education to bear in the considerations. Once all these intellectual issues are resolved, Clement's father is baptized, and the story closes.

3. INTERPRETIVE ISSUES
3.1 Circuits of Peter

The Circuits of Peter is an elaborate and skillfully constructed novel that deals with numerous intellectual and theological issues in impressive and entertaining detail. After the initial instruction of Clement, there are three cycles to the presentation. The first cycle is the debate with Simon, who largely represents Marcionite views.[5] The second cycle is Peter's proclamation to fairly generic pagans in Tripolis. The third cycle consists of the discussions with the father, who may be said to represent the mature, educated pagan. As a whole, the Circuits of Peter enunciates an understanding of the world as a realm established by God to yield a selection of humans proven by free will to be worthy friends for his Son (*Rec.* 3.26.2–4; 3.52.2–3 par. *Hom.* 19.21.3). On the topic of evil that the Marcionites highlighted, the Circuits of Peter asserts that there is no evil in substance (*Rec.* 4.23.3 par.

---

5. F. Stanley Jones, *Pseudoclementina Elchasaiticaque inter Judaeochristiana: Collected Studies*, OLA 203 (Leuven: Peeters, 2012), 161–67.

Hom. 20.8) but only as a part of this good plan. The Circuits of Peter seems to have leaned here on the Aristotelian concept of "accident" (*symbebēkos*) and combined it with the Greek philosophical notion of "disposition" (*prohairesis*). It was doubtless in view of Marcionite assertions that the Circuits let Peter take the blamelessness of God the creator as the starting point for his teaching (*Rec.* 4.8 par. *Hom.* 8.9). The human has been endowed with the ability to choose between "two kingdoms," the kingdom of the present age or the kingdom of the eternal age to come (*Rec.* 1.24.5; 3.52 par. *Hom.* 20.2–3; 15.7.4–6). In this strong emphasis on human free will and in the terminology and concepts involved, the Circuits of Peter is indebted to the writings of Justin Martyr and to the dialogue *The Book of the Laws of the Countries* that features the Syrian Christian philosopher Bardaisan; the Circuits of Peter thereby participates in a significant (and largely unstudied) philosophical advancement by the early Christians.

The Circuits of Peter simultaneously promotes a distinctly Jewish-Christian version of Christianity to correct what it characterizes as the "seed of tares" or "false gospel" that had gained currency and is apparently connected with Paul (*Rec.* 3.61.2 par. *Hom.* 2.17.4). Among these Jewish-Christian features is a form of the apostolic decree that is usually thought to have reached the author independently of the canonical Acts 15 (*Rec.* 4.36.4 par. *Hom.* 7.8.1), and the insistence throughout the novel that the baptized should not share a table with the unbaptized (e.g., *Rec.* 7.29.3 par. *Hom.* 13.4.3). Baptism occurs, after a fast, under the "thrice blessed invocation" and in "living water," which the author specifies to mean a "fountain, river, or sea" (*Rec.* 4.32.2 par. *Hom.* 9.19.4). It is after baptism that a meal or thanksgiving/Eucharist is mentioned, which initiates into the common table and seems to have consisted of bread and salt followed by praise of God (*Rec.* 6.15.4 par. *Hom.* 11.36.2; cf. *Hom.* 14.1.4 par. *Rec.* 7.38.1–2). While Peter states that his meals involve only bread, olives, and herbs (*Rec.* 7.6.4 par. *Hom.* 12.6.4), strict religious vegetarian beliefs do not seem to be promoted by the Circuits of Peter (*Rec.* 9.6.6 par. *Hom.* 15.7.6), though they do appear in the *Klementia* (*Hom.* 8.15.2–16.2; 3.45.2). Besides the avoidance of intercourse with a menstruating woman, which the Circuits of Peter declares to be "the law of God" (*Rec.* 6.10.5 par. *Hom.* 11.28.1), "washing the body" (*Rec.* 6.11.1 par. *Hom.* 11.28.2) is also prominent in the novel. Though the precise nature and meaning of these baths are not completely clear (they occur before morning prayer and before meals), the author apparently associates them with the "Pharisaic" tradition, because it is at this point that the author insists that Jesus did not rebuke all the Pharisees but only some of them, namely, the hypocrites among them (*Rec.* 6.11.2–3 par. *Hom.* 11.28.4–29.2)—a unicum in the preserved ancient Christian tradition and further evidence of the author's Jewish Christianity.

This distinctive attitude toward the Pharisees raises the question of the type of Judaism that was known to the basic writer. This issue has become more prominent, particularly in the light of recent research into ancient Judaism that has cast doubt on the older view that rabbinic Judaism became dominant soon after the Jewish wars against Rome. This somewhat dated perspective has been turned on its head, and the rabbis are now often suggested to have been originally a small enclave that only very gradually established their tenets in broader swaths of Judaism.[6] In this light, the significance of the Circuits of Peter in this debate is that it may well witness to early rabbinization or at least to its own proximity to the rabbinic circle. Beyond its approbation of the Pharisees, the Circuits displays distinctive similarities to rabbinic tradition also in its denial of the substantial existence of

---

6. Annette Yoshiko Reed, *Jewish-Christianity and the History of Judaism: Collected Essays*, TSAJ 171 (Tübingen: Mohr Siebeck, 2018), 295–97.

evil. These and other items, such as the notion of the obscurity of Scripture and the consequent need for a tradition of interpretation, or the concept of gentile impurity and its rationale, are open for further investigation for the history of Judaism as well as for the Jewish
Christianity of the Circuits. For a self-designation, the Circuits of Peter avoids making a
direct claim to the label "Jew" and shows instead a preference for the term "worshiper of
God" (*theosebēs*), as Recognition 5.34.1–2 par. Homily 11.16.1 indicate, where this *tertium
quid* stands not between Hebrews and gentiles but rather between non-Jesus-believing
Hebrews/Jews and Jesus-believing gentiles (*Rec.* 4.5.1–9 par. *Hom.* 8.5.1–7.5).

In any event, the Jewish-Christian slant of the Circuits, along with the increasing
marginalization of Jewish Christians (what the Circuits had attempted to reverse), likely
contributed to the disappearance of this Christian novel, perhaps the first and last, in its
initial form. But this disappearance did not happen before the power of the original so
captured two later authors that they decided to revise and rewrite the tale to better suit
their contemporaries. Their versions were apparently successful enough to help eclipse
the prototype.

3.2 Recognition

The author of the Recognition largely followed the outline of the original Circuits of
Peter, though in the interest of even greater order, the initial instruction of Clement was collected and presented before the preparation for the debate with Simon. The author's marked
concern for order is also probably responsible for the omission of the Letter of Peter and the
Declaration, which jarred with the conceptual and chronological framework of the remaining material. This author was apparently a celibate ascetic who variously tones down the
Jewish-Christian and pro-family material, evidently omitting Peter's rather intimate encomium of the temperate wife/woman preserved via Homily 13.14.2–21.3. The author of the
Recognition also shows little interest in actual debate, urging instead simple obedience to the
truth expressed in deeds, not inquiry (*Rec.* 2.24.1–4; 2.21.5–6; 3.37). There is, furthermore,
a proper order in which the truth should be presented and learned (*Rec.* 3.32.4–7; 3.34);
discussion and argument about the details can only mislead (*Rec.* 8.60–61). Accordingly, the
Recognition places a long christological exposition directly on the lips of Peter, obviously to
resolve the debate around the time of the Nicene Council (*Rec.* 3.2–11, left out by Rufinus
but translated into Latin by a later hand and included in one group of Latin manuscripts;
the Syriac translator toned down the "Arian" elements for the Syriac rendering):

> The only begotten himself is not unoriginate, but he shows through himself the whole power
> of the unoriginate as it is in kind and size with respect to deity. Now by those who have not
> diligently inquired he has been supposed to be unoriginate, but by those where the fear of
> God precedes the investigation, not only do they refuse to say such a thing but they guard
> against even thinking [it]. While therefore there should be one unoriginate and one begotten,
> it is not possible for the Holy Spirit to be called Son or First-Born (for it was made through
> something made). But it is numbered below the Father and the Son, as if the first perfect seal
> of the second power. (*Rec.* 3.11.8–10 Latin)

Since it was this rewriting of the novel that reached the West through Rufinus's (further
homogenized) early Latin translation, the Pseudo-Clementines got a reputation here for
being a rather tedious set of sermons cloaked in the form of a novel, even though Rufinus
tried to spice up his version by tacking on at the end a racy story about Clement's father
drawn from the finale of the *Klementia* (see below; failure to recognize that Rufinus

made this addition created a fair amount of havoc in older research). One further reason that the Recognition strikes the modern reader as tiresome is that it preserves the prolix anti-Marcionite argument with Simon largely intact, while the original Marcionite threat (belief in a previously "unknown" God beyond the creator of the world) had since subsided into oblivion. Few readers find the strength to plod through this material to reach greener pastures on the other side and finally the pleasant fields of the family reunifications.

3.3 Klementia

The author of the *Klementia*, in contrast, modified and rearranged the original novel in quite radical ways. In this version, for example, Simon comes back from Antioch to debate Peter for a second time in Laodicea (*Hom.* 16–19; it is here that the author of *Klementia* transports and largely reframes the anti-Marcionite discussion with Simon into a base for the presentation of a *miahypostatic* [one substantial existence] theology and Christology,[7] the opposite end of the spectrum from the Arian position). The Klementinist also omits the long discussion of fate with the father and instead introduces piquant extraordinary figures (such as Appion, the infamous opponent of the Jews already countered by Josephus, and Annubion, the author of a popular astrological treatise) and fantastic elements (e.g., Simon transforms the face of the father to look like Simon's own—only Peter can see through the magical spell). Indeed, this author converts the idealistic Circuits of Peter into a parody, a move also known among the Greek novelists. In this presentation, for example, Peter and Clement can engage in lying and subterfuge (e.g., with the face of Simon, the father is sent by Peter back to Antioch to act as if he is Simon, now repenting of his misdeeds), something quite foreign to the Circuits of Peter. The doubling of the "p" in Appion and the "n" in Annubion is also apparently another piece of ancient humor, triggered perhaps by the Circuit of Peter's name for Clement's mother, Mattidia.

More outrageously, the Klementinist presents a detailed theory that the devil was able to insert passages into the Old Testament in order to make people think that there is more than one God and that the storied righteous figures devoted to God were sinners:

> For the scriptures received many false things against God in this manner: While the prophet Moses, according to the intent of God, handed over the law together with its explanations to the select seventy so that they might inform those of the people who wished, not much later when the law was written down, it received certain and false things against the sole God who had made heaven and earth and all in them; the evil one dared to do this for a certain righteous reason. And this happened for the reason and with the decision that these should be disclosed: those who dare to consider it pleasant to hear things written against God and those who through love for Him not only do not believe the things said against Him but also do not endure to listen to them at all, even if they should happen to be true, judging it safer to run the risk regarding correct belief than to live with a bad conscience based on blasphemous statements. (*Hom.* 2.38)

Among these malicious interpolations are the passages that assert that God was ignorant (*Hom.* 2.48–50), that Adam was a sinner, that Noah was a drunk, that Abraham and

---

7. This theological tradition, which employed Neo-Pythagorean numerology, is what stands behind the Klementinist's striking notion of the expanding body of God (*Hom.* 17.7–10; 16.12; 19.9–13; 20.5–8) that was recently pondered by Christoph Markschies, *God's Body: Jewish, Christian, and Pagan Images of God*, trans. A. Edmonds (Waco, TX: Baylor University Press, 2019), 198–211, without identification of this theological source.

Jacob each had more than one wife at a time, and that Moses was a murderer (*Hom.* 2.52). Christ, creation, and reason teach how to spot and discard such passages.[8] To support this theory, the author spells out further facts:

> The law of God was given through Moses to the seventy wise men to hand down without writing in order that it might be able to govern through transmission. After Moses was taken up, it was written down, though not by Moses. For in the law it is written, "And Moses died, and they buried him near the house of Phogor, and to this day no one knows his grave." How could it be that Moses, who had died, wrote, "Moses died"? Now, in the time after Moses (around five hundred years or more), it is found lying in the temple that had been built, and after around another five hundred years it existed and was destroyed by fire at the time of Nebuchadnezzar. Though written after Moses and destroyed many times, it has thus acknowledged the forethought of Moses that he did not write it because he foresaw its obliteration. But those who wrote, convicted of ignorance for not knowing its destruction, were not prophets. (*Hom.* 3.47; cf. 2.38)

This tangy theory and its explication are what the Klementinist used to replace the already outdated anti-Marcionite disputation with Simon. As a pinnacle of comic irony, the Klementinist allows Simon to protest facetiously: "Far be it from me and from those who love me to listen to your words! As long as I did not know that you think such things about the Scriptures, I endured and discussed. But now I going to distance myself" (*Hom.* 18.21.1–2).

The author also inserts a long episode in which Clement faces off with Appion, the somewhat risqué dispute with Appion in Homilies 4–6. In a retrospect here, one encounters a quite different version of Clement's earlier life in Rome. Appion, it is said, had been a friend of Clement's father and had incorrectly diagnosed Clement's philosophical malaise as love-sickness. To help Clement, Appion had composed at the time an encomium of adultery in the form of a letter to Clement's supposed secret love. Clement still has this letter and reads it aloud, surely one of the most salacious passages in early Christian literature:

> The lover to the beloved (anonymously owing to the laws by senseless humans) upon the injunctions of Eros, the oldest child of all. Greetings! I know that you are devoted to philosophy and that on account of virtue you emulate the life of superior people. Yet who but the gods would be the superior ones among all beings and who but the philosophers among humans? For these alone know which sort of deeds are by nature good or bad and which sort are thought so by the arbitrary determination of laws, though they are not. For example, so-called fornication is a deed that some consider to be evil, although it is good in every respect. For at the injunctions of Eros, it issues into the fecundity of life. But Eros is the oldest of all gods. For without Eros, it is impossible for there to be mixture or birth of elements, of gods, of humans, of irrational animals, or of all other things. For we are all instruments of Eros. Now he, being the artificer through us, dwelling in the souls of everything that is begotten, is mind. Hence, it is not when we wish but rather when we have been commanded by him that we desire to do his will. But if, when we desire through his will, we attempt for the sake of so-called temperance to restrain passion, how will we not be committing the greatest sins since we are acting against the eldest of all, both of gods and humans? (*Hom.* 5.10)

---

8. Jones, *Pseudoclementina Elchasaiticaque*, 167–70. See also Donald H. Carlson, *Jewish Christian Interpretation of the Pentateuch in the Pseudo-Clementine Homilies* (Minneapolis: Fortress, 2013).

The letter continues with a lengthy alphabetical list of the loves of Zeus (transported here from the Circuit of Peter's mythological discourse) and precedents among the philosophers before it closes:

> I know that these things seem frightful and shameful to those uninitiated into the truth, though not to the gods of the Greeks and to the philosophers, nor to the mysteries of Dionysus and Demeter. But beyond all these, lest I waste time relating the lives of all the gods and philosophers, may there be two great guardians for you: from the gods, Zeus, and from wise men, Socrates. Understand and attend to the other matters that I have called to mind in writing you, lest you grieve your lover. For one who has done what is contrary to the gods and love will be judged impious and will suffer the appropriate punishment. But if you make yourself available to every lover, as an imitator of the gods you will chance upon their kindness. As regards the rest, most beloved, when you have thought about the mysteries I have revealed to you, indicate to me in writing your wish. Farewell from me! (*Hom.* 5.19)

In the classic style of the parodist, the Klementinist explains that this incident was all a ruse Clement used to expose the corruption of Appion. Clement himself, it is said, wrote the supposed response to the letter and opened with the words, "I am amazed at how you have praised me for wisdom yet you have written to me as if to a fool" (*Hom.* 5.21.1). When Appion heard the response, he condemned the woman for having been corrupted by a Jew, but Clement confessed to the ploy and declared that he had written the response and that he was the one who had been influenced by a Jewish merchant (another element conspicuously disharmonius with the Circuit of Peter's story of Clement).

Along these lines, the Klementinist later floats the remarkable idea that God himself hid Jesus from the Jews, who therefore are saved without recognition of Jesus:

> Jesus is hidden from the Hebrews who have taken Moses as a teacher, but Moses is hidden from those who have believed Jesus. For since there is one teaching through both, God accepts the one who has believed one of these. But believing a teacher occurs for the sake of doing the things spoken by God. Since this is so, our Lord himself says, "I praise you, Father of heaven and of earth, because you have hidden these things from the wise presbyters and you have revealed them to nursing babes." Thus, God himself hid the teacher from those who already knew what to do, but revealed [him] to those who did not know what to do. Therefore, because of the one who hid, neither are Hebrews condemned for their ignorance of Jesus, if doing the things of Moses they do not hate the one they have not recognized, nor again are the ones from the nations condemned who, because of the revealer, have not recognized Moses, if they too do the things spoken through Jesus and do not hate the one they have not recognized. (*Hom.* 8.6.1–7.2)

The Klementinist goes so far as to say, "You have been commanded to honor also the chair of Moses even if those seated are considered sinners" (*Hom.* 3.70.2).

These moves and others show that the Klementinist was an agile and highly educated writer with a creative, slightly wicked, flair. Past scholarship tended to assign these bizarre (if enlightened) theories to an old, aberrant form of Jewish Christianity, often called Ebionism, but it has become apparent that they are rather to be attributed to the learned wit of the Klementinist. Thus, for example, there is not a single trace of the doctrine of spurious Old Testament interpolations in the Recognition. Not much later than the Klementinist, John Chrysostom polemicizes as bishop of Antioch against "Judaizers" in that city, and it may well be that the Klementinist should be understood, at least partially, in the light of that context, to which the Apostolic Constitutions might also witness.[9] In any event, the Klementinist wrote at a time when other well-educated individuals, often called "sophists," were entering and impacting ecclesial discussions and debates. Should one be surprised that the Klementinist condemns "the entirety of the learning [*paideia*] of the Greeks" as "the worst creation of an evil demon" (*Hom.* 4.12.1)?

3.4 *Kerygmata Petrou*

Nevertheless, the hope of finding early Jewish-Christian traditions in a larger setting, rather than in fragments as elsewhere, has driven much of the interest in the Pseudo-Clementines. But the isolation of the Jewish-Christian elements in the Pseudo-Clementines has proven difficult and has led to some infamous wild-goose chases that have seriously marred the history of their investigation. The most outstanding of these quests was the supposition that the original set of Peter's sermons, referred to in the Circuits of Peter as having been periodically sent to James, could be recovered, particularly through the use of a list of the contents of such books in Recognition 3.75. This supposed source, called the *Kerygmata Petrou* ("Sermons of Peter"), was usually imagined to have contained the outlandish theories of the *Klementia* mentioned above, such as the notion that spurious pericopes (passages) were strewn by the devil throughout the Old Testament. However, the postulation of this *Kerygmata Petrou* source has fairly recently been abandoned as a mirage,[10] just another example of the novelistic "layering" of material and information, while the awareness has increased that the fantastic theories actually line up with the profile of the Klementinist.[11] More attention must be paid to the Circuits and the preserved versions, the Recognition and the *Klementia*, whenever such sources are postulated.

3.5 Conclusion

In general, the redaction-critical phase of New Testament scholarship has not been mirrored in Pseudo-Clementine studies; source-critical speculation about the supposed *Kerygmata Petrou* dominated Pseudo-Clementine research through this period. So there is still much room and need for determination of redaction in the Recognition and the *Klementia* and then systematization into profiles for these early fourth-century authors in their historical contexts. Furthermore, the old Syriac translation of the Recognition can no longer be neglected in blind preference for the Latin whenever one talks about the Recognition. Fortunately, a modern language translation (English) of the ancient Syriac has finally been produced.[12]

Hampering the pursuit of redaction criticism with respect to the Pseudo-Clementines is

9. James Carleton Paget, *Jews, Christians and Jewish Christians in Antiquity*, WUNT 251 (Tübingen: Mohr Siebeck, 2010), 487–88.

10. The research is documented in Jones, *Pseudoclementina Elchasaiticaque*, 22–24. The postulation of this source has been abandoned also by Han J. W. Drijvers, "Adam and the True Prophet in the Pseudo-Clementines," in *Loyalitätskonflikte in der Religionsgeschichte: Festschrift für Carsten Colpe*, ed. C. Elsas and H. Kippenberg (Wurzburg: Königshausen & Neumann, 1990), 321; Luigi Cirillo, "Courants judéo-chrétiens," in *Le nouveau peuple (des origines à 250)*, ed. L. Pietri, vol. 1 of *Histoire du christianisme*, ed. J.-M. Mayeur et al. (Paris: Desclée, 2000), 322; as well as others.

11. Jones, *Pseudoclementina Elchasaiticaque*, 36–37.

12. F. Stanley Jones, trans., *The Syriac "Pseudo-Clementines": An Early Version of the First Christian Novel*, Apocryphes 14 (Turnhout: Brepols, 2014).

also the absence of a synopsis of the Recognition and the *Klementia*. This situation is comparable to the study of the Gospels before the production of synopses or to the study of Q before independent Q-synopses were published. The individual scholar is thus left to try to find, isolate, and compare the parallel material, though the current standard editions do at least list the most important parallels in their notes. The absence of a Pseudo-Clementine synopsis in either the original languages or in translation has also kept the Circuits from substantially entering the sight of scholars.[13]

Another pressing need is for the Circuits of Peter to be understood in the context of other Greek novels of the time.[14] Indeed, the Circuits of Peter belongs as a full member of this group, though classics scholars, too, have been slow to recognize this insight and still cling to the hackneyed source-critical theory that the novel derives *in toto* from some speculatively postulated source.[15] Furthermore, since the theology of the Circuits is presented as a philosophy and is in dialogue with the philosophical discussions of its time, the Circuits must be read within this frame of reference, which is only being gradually reconstructed and understood.[16] The Pseudo-Clementines themselves actually contain elements from the ancient philosophical debate that are not preserved elsewhere—for example, fragments of the Orphic theogony that have long formed a not unsubstantial part in collections of "Orphic fragments."[17] In other words, the identity of the author of the Circuits of Peter needs to be explored in the environment of the entirety of third-century Syria, including not just other varieties of Christians but also varieties of Jews and pagans.

A good example of the progressing state of research into the Pseudo-Clementines is the understanding of the central Pseudo-Clementine figure, the True Prophet. The True Prophet features throughout all levels of the Pseudo-Clementines as the ultimate source of knowledge about God and his will, the world, scriptures, and the nature of the human. The True Prophet alone truly knows the past, the present, and the future, and only he can guide humans to eternal life. While it has often been thought that this figure must represent old Jewish-Christian tradition, it has started to appear more likely that the figure as such is a creation by the basic writer (the Circuits), who needs an anchor for knowledge in the context of early third-century Greek philosophical debates.[18]

---

13. Students of the classics also seem less comfortable with the Pseudo-Clementine source-critical situation (the evidence for a basic writing and the necessity of reconstructing it or bearing it in mind when dealing with the *Klementia* or the Recognition) than theological students with their exposure to the Synoptic problem.

14. Jan N. Bremmer, "*Pseudo-Clementines*: Texts, Dates, Places, Authors and Magic," in *Maidens, Magic and Martyrs in Early Christianity: Collected Essays I*, WUNT 379 (Tübingen: Mohr Siebeck, 2017), 242.

15. Documentation and evaluation in Jones, *Pseudoclementina Elchasaiticaque*, 114–37.

16. See Reed, *Jewish-Christianity and the History of Judaism*, 81–84; György Geréby, "Reasons and Arguments in the *Clementina*," in Amsler et al., *Nouvelles intrigues pseudo-clémentines*, 211–22; Jonathan Barnes, "[Clément] et la philosophie," in Amsler et al., *Nouvelles intrigues pseudo-clémentines*, 283–302; Christoph Jedan, "Faustus: Epicurean and Stoic? On the Philosophical Sources of the *Pseudo-Clementines*," in *The "Pseudo-Clementines"*, ed. Jan N. Bremmer, Studies on Early Christian Apocrypha 10 (Louvain: Peeters, 2010), 142–56.

17. See the references and discussion in Alberto Bernabé, "La teogonía órfica citada en las *Pseudoclementina*," *Adamantius* 14 (2008): 79–99; Lautaro Roig Lanzillotta, "Orphic Cosmogonies in the *Pseudo-Clementines*? Textual Relationship, Character and Sources of *Homilies* 6.3–13 and *Recognitions* 10.17–19.30," in Bremmer, *"Pseudo-Clementines"*, 115–41; Fabienne Jourdan, *Orphée et les chrétiens: La réception du mythe d'Orphée dans la littérature chrétienne grecque des cinq premiers siècles*, 2 vols., Anagôgè 4–5 (Paris: Belles Lettres, 2010–11), 2:34–64, 273–336; F. Stanley Jones, "The Orphic Cosmo-Theogony in the *Pseudo-Clementines*," in *Les polémiques religieuses du Ier au IVe siècle de notre ère: Hommage à Bernard Pouderon*, ed. G. Bady and D. Cuny, ThH 128 (Paris: Beauchesne, 2019), 71–82.

18. Jones, *Pseudoclementina Elchasaiticaque*, 486–89.

4. KEY PASSAGES FOR NEW TESTAMENT AND EARLY CHRISTIAN STUDIES AND THEIR SIGNIFICANCE

Exposition of the sayings of Jesus in a real-life scenario finds an excellent forum in the Circuits of Peter with its spirit of realistic make-believe. Jesus's dictums that one should follow despite one's relatives pose a special challenge for the Circuits, where the family is of paramount importance. The Circuits of Peter interprets these sayings to the effect that one should follow and leave home only if one does not have dependent parents, a spouse, or children who would suffer from the separation (*Rec.* 3.72.2; 7.5.5–6 par. *Hom.* 12.5.5–6). Indeed, the careful construction of the entire novel is an illustration of this interpretation insofar as it opens with a Clement who has lost his family and thus can "piously" follow Peter on the road (*Rec.* 7.5.6 par. *Hom.* 12.5.7). Peter himself is free to travel with his wife because he and his brother Andrew were orphans (*Rec.* 7.6.7 par. *Hom.* 12.6.7). Other "hard" sayings of Jesus are similarly taken up and explained as to how they are to be understood and applied (e.g., what did Jesus actually intend when he blessed the poor?).

The image of Peter in the Circuits is similarly fascinating and unique. On the one hand, the Circuits displays no awareness of the flawed Peter of the canonical Gospels, who usually participated in misunderstandings with the other disciples and who even denied Jesus. On the other hand, the Peter of the Circuits is not the miracle-working apostle known from the apocryphal Acts of the apostles. Instead, Peter is the chosen "realistic" anthropological vessel for the author to display not only proper Christian behavior but also the limits of human capabilities, even under the best of divine guidance, especially given Peter's physical time as Jesus's direct student. Peter is the most esteemed disciple of Jesus (*Rec.* 1.12.2 par. *Hom.* 1.15.2) and thus greatest in the wisdom of God (*Rec.* 1.12.6 par. *Hom.* 1.15.6; cf. also *Rec.* 7.7.1 par. *Hom.* 12.7.1: everyone is inferior to him). But Peter cannot see through the fibs and false names that Clement's (unrecognized) mother initially provides (*Rec.* 7.19.5–20.1 par. *Hom.* 12.19.5–20.1); similarly, he can only pray that God might heal the sick (*Rec.* 7.23.6 par. *Hom.* 12.23.6) and that he might have success in his debate with Simon (*Rec.* 2.19.5–6 par. *Hom.* 3.29.3–4), where he might appear to be defeated (*Rec.* 1.17.6 par. *Hom.* 1.20.6). Every word, reaction, habit, and mannerism of Peter is accordingly infused with the greatest possible significance. Peter serves both as a locus for Christian anthropology and as a realistic paragon for Christian life. It is noteworthy that at the time when Christian teachers generally spurned laughter as a proper form of Christian behavior (e.g., Clement of Alexandria, *Paed.* 2.5), the Circuits of Peter presents a Peter who is at times genuinely jovial and can even laugh in a good-hearted manner (e.g., *Rec.* 7.6.1 par. *Hom.* 12.6.1; *Rec.* 7.36.2 par. *Hom.* 13.11.2). This carefully constructed Peter of the Circuits, however, is thrown overboard by the Klementinist, who allows Peter to prevaricate (*Hom.* 20.21.3–5), heal readily (e.g., *Hom.* 7.12.1), claim to be able to overthrow entire cities (*Hom.* 7.9.5), and alone see through Simon's magical spells (*Hom.* 20.12.7).

Less prominent but nevertheless noteworthy is the particular image of Jesus presented in the Circuits of Peter. Jesus, the Son of God sent by the Father, is said to have appeared, started preaching in the spring, and been active, apparently for one year, in Judea during the reign of Tiberius Caesar (*Rec.* 1.6.1–2 par. *Hom.* 1.6.1–2; *Rec.* 1.7.3 par. *Hom.* 1.7.2; *Rec.* 1.12.2 par. *Hom.* 1.15.2), with Galilee never mentioned in the Pseudo-Clementines. It is asserted that the Son came for the salvation of the entire world and was noble above all, though he submitted himself to slavery (*Rec.* 7.7.5 par. *Hom.* 12.7.5); it was to the Jews that he proclaimed the kingdom of God for all who should correct their manner of life (*Rec.* 1.6.2 par. *Hom.* 1.6.2). Besides his rebuke of some Pharisees mentioned above, Jesus taught that unless one should be regenerated from living water, one cannot enter the kingdom of heaven (*Rec.* 6.9.2 par. *Hom.* 11.26.2). While Jesus healed lepers noteworthily at seeing-distance from afar (*Rec.* 1.6.4 par. *Hom.* 1.6.4), Jesus performed these and other miracles in order that he should be believed (*Rec.* 1.6.3 par. *Hom.* 1.6.3; *Rec.* 3.60.2 par. *Hom.* 2.34.2–3), and, accordingly, meetings were convened at various places to discuss who was the one who had appeared and what he wanted to say (*Rec.* 1.7.1 par. *Hom.* 1.6.6). Finally, the Circuits of Peter affirms that Jesus prayed to the Father to forgive his murderers in their ignorance of their deed (*Rec.* 6.5.5 par. *Hom.* 11.20.4). The attentive student may sense in this image of Jesus possible correspondences with Marcionite views, and below it will be seen that the baptism of Jesus by John was omitted just as it apparently was in Marcion's Gospel.

Other figures in the Circuits also serve as ideals. Clement is the model young cultured pagan convert. His father, as indicated, represents the mature educated pagan, who must carefully inquire before changing religious loyalties. Women, in contrast, seem more open to conversion on the basis of emotions, as is Clement's mother, for whom "temperance" (*sōphrosynē*, sometimes translated as "chastity") is the paramount virtue (*Rec.* 7.30 par. *Hom.* 13.5; cf. *Rec.* 7.36.1 par. *Hom.* 13.11.1–2). This image of women is shared to a good extent with the contemporary Greek novels, where the term *sōphrosynē* is also common and usually carries a sexual overtone, but the mood of the empire at the time similarly played into the hand of the Circuits and its pro-family message. Indeed, the names of the father and the twins (all variants on the root "Faustus") recall that most divine imperial wife of the times, Faustina, who was featured in the Roman forum and on coins and celebrated with her husband, Marcus Aurelius, as the ideal married couple; an altar with their statues was set up as a place for marriage ceremonies. Children were depicted on coins of her felicitous time, and twins in the time of her daughter, Faustina the Younger. Regarding Clement's mother Mattidia, it may be noted that Hadrian explicitly praised his mother-in-law, Trajan's niece, Matidia, for being "most chaste" in an obituary engraved at Tibur (*CIL* XIV 3579, line 24). The Circuits of Peter's adoption and employment of this term "temperance" (*sōphrosynē*) as a paramount virtue for the duration of human life marks a significant advance. It is not an accident that the body of the novel opens with Clement's declaration that he has been able to live "temperately" from the early days of his youth (*Rec.* 1.1.1 par. *Hom.* 1.1.1).

The anti-Paulinism of the Circuits of Peter has been of special interest for New Testament scholars in search of information on the opponents mentioned in Paul's letters. It is found at the very beginning of the novel in the Letter of Peter 2.3–4 where Peter complains to James:

> Certain of those from the gentiles rejected the lawful proclamation by me after having accepted a certain lawless and foolish teaching of the hostile person. And even while I am alive, they have begun with these things in order to transform by certain subtle interpretations my words into the abolition of the law, as if I myself think thus but do not preach with openness. Be away with this!

The reference to Paul's charge of Peter with "hypocrisy" in Galatians 2:13–14 is apparent, while the designation of Paul as "the hostile person" likely derives from Jesus's parable of the tares, in which an "enemy" or "hostile person" had corrupted the good seed with tares (cf. Matt 13:24–30).

Homily 17.13–20 is another locus for Pseudo-Clementine anti-Paulinism. Here Peter argues against Simon:

Now if our Jesus, having appeared, became known also to you through a vision and spoke to you as one angered at an opponent, then he spoke through visions and dreams or even through revelations that are from without. But is anyone able to become skilled for teaching on account of a vision? And if you say, "It is possible," why did the teacher remain and speak to the vigilant for a whole year? And how should we believe you that he even appeared to you? And how did he even appear to you when you think what is contrary to his teaching? Yet if you were visited by him and having been instructed became an apostle, preach his sayings, expound his matters, love his apostles, and do not fight with me who conversed with him. For opposed to a firm rock, which I am, the foundation of the church, you have withstood me. If you did not lie in opposition, you would not defame me and revile my proclamation to the effect that I do not believe what I myself heard from the Lord while in his presence, that is, as if I have been condemned though I am held in good repute. Yet if you call me "condemned," you condemn the God who revealed Christ to me and you debase the one who blessed me upon the revelation. But if you truly wish to aid the truth, learn first from us what we learned from him and having become a disciple of the truth become our fellow worker. (*Hom.* 17.19)

The reference to Galatians 2:11 ("When Cephas came to Antioch, I opposed him to his face, because he stood self-condemned" [NRSV]) seems apparent. Yet this passage is couched in a larger discussion of the origin of divine knowledge that is a recurrent theme in the Pseudo-Clementines. Here, the power of dreams and visions to convey the truth generally is disputed. As Peter states in Homily 17.15.3, "Who is righteous if he needs a vision to learn what it is necessary to learn and to do what it is necessary to do?" Or again Homily 17.18.4: "When something is revealed from the outside through visions and dreams, it seems that it is not of a revelation but rather of wrath." Thus, the Pseudo-Clementines again show involvement in a debate that was current not only among Christians of the time, such as visionary "gnostics" who in part referred to Paul's vision as having imparted knowledge superior to that of the original apostles, but also among contemporary philosophers such as Numenius of Apamea and Plotinus, who sought a vision of the divine. Yet precisely here the Circuits or the *Klementia* is developing its own views when, in a remarkable passage, it attempts to explain exactly how it happened that Peter was able to respond, "You are the Son of the living God," when Jesus asked him who he thought he was (*Hom.* 17.18.1–3):

For the Son was revealed by the Father even to me in this manner. Thus, I know what the power of revelation is, having learned it by myself. For when the Lord said, who do they say him to be? and when I heard others saying him to be different things, it came upon my heart. I do not know how I said, "You are the Son of the living God." Now he who blessed me made known to me that the one who revealed was the Father, and hence I learned that to learn of one's own, without visions and dreams, is revelation. And truly it is so. For all the truth is seminally in what has been placed in us from God, but it is guarded and revealed by the hand of God who operates as One knowing what each has deserved.

The Pseudo-Clementines are thus working on a theory of knowledge (epistemology) throughout the novel, so the temptation to see passages such as this as pure remnants of anti-Paulinism from the time of Paul can lead to oversimplification.

In general, the Circuits of Peter's relationship to the New Testament writings is loose. As just seen, the letters of Paul are employed in a remarkable inverse way as documentation of early depravity. The Circuits of Peter's information on Peter and Simon derives from the Acts of Peter rather than from the canonical Acts, of which the Circuits shows no knowledge. Likewise unusual, the Circuits displays a negative view of John the Baptist, making him the negative forerunner of Jesus just as Simon is of Peter (*Hom.* 2.17.2–3).[19] This perspective can be explained only by distance from the Synoptic Gospels; surprising, perhaps, is that a negative view of John the Baptist was shared with the Circuits' main bugbear, the ascetic Marcionites, whose gospel also left out the baptism of Jesus by John. In this vein, the Circuits has a set of distinctive sayings of Jesus that have parallels with sources outside the New Testament, particularly with Justin Martyr, and they have long attracted attention. Suggestions of origin in a common source of testimonies or in a noncanonical Gospel are noteworthy. But the solution to the conundrum seems to lie rather in the insight that the Circuits admired and employed Justin as a reliable source for sayings of Jesus and more particularly for anti-Marcionite expositions.[20] Less unexpected in view of these observations is that the Circuits contains positive evidence for the employment of the earlier, somewhat esoteric, Jewish-Christian Book of Elchasai, a neglected church order from 116–17 CE.[21] This dependency is evident, for example, in the oath that prospective recipients of Peter's books of sermons should take. They should call to witness heaven, earth, water, and air, and invoke ether and then partake of bread and salt (Declaration 4). This description bears distinctive similarities with the elements in the oath for prospective service as summarized by Epiphanius from the Book of Elchasai: salt, water, earth, bread, heaven, ether, and wind (*Pan.* 19.1.6).

The major premise of the Circuits is that a false gospel has been spread that it (and its Peter) must follow to correct (*Rec.* 3.61.2 par. *Hom.* 2.17.3–4). Peter also warns the new church in Tripolis against accepting any teacher, apostle, or prophet who does not bring testimonies from Jerusalem and James the brother of the Lord (*Rec.* 4.25.1–2 par. *Hom.* 11.35.4). The incarnation of this false gospel for the basic writer is apparently the existing gentile church, with the epitome of this false direction found in the Marcionite churches with their rejection of the creator God and of this world, particularly marriage and family. Accordingly, if Paul is an object of the Circuits' criticism, then it is primarily the Marcionite Paul whom the Circuits has in view. The Circuits' use of the writings of Justin Martyr is thus apparently due in no small part to the fact that Justin wrote a treatise against Marcion. Further evidence that the usual sayings of Jesus were adopted from Justin is found in the observation that the Circuits simultaneously took over the original anti-Marcionite arguments in which the sayings were couched in Justin. Finally, the Circuits allows Peter to enunciate the theory that the false gospel will be promulgated before the destruction of the temple, which will then signal the time for the true gospel (to the gentiles) to be made known (*Rec.* 1.64.2 par. *Hom.* 2.17.4 par. *Rec.* 3.61.2 Syriac).

One special source of the Circuits that has emerged with increasing clarity in recent scholarship is Peter's review of the history of the world and the early church for Clement in Recognition 1.27–71. This fascinating material differs in distinctive ways from the rest of the Circuits and thus evidently derives from a separate, preexisting source. For example,

---

19. F. Stanley Jones, "John the Baptist and His Disciples in the Pseudo-Clementines: A Historical Appraisal," in *Rediscovering the Apocryphal Continent: New Perspectives on Early Christian and Late Antique Apocryphal Texts and Traditions*, ed. P. Piovanelli and T. Burke, WUNT 349 (Tübingen: Mohr Siebeck, 2015), 317–35; Joel Marcus, *John the Baptist in History and Theology*, Studies on Personalities of the New Testament (Columbia, SC: University of South Carolina Press, 2018), 14–18.

20. F. Stanley Jones, "The Distinctive Sayings of Jesus Shared by Justin and the *Pseudo-Clementines*," in *Forbidden Texts on the Western Frontier: The Christian Apocrypha in North American Perspectives*, ed. T. Burke (Eugene, OR: Wipf and Stock, 2015), 200–217.

21. See Jones, *Pseudoclementina Elchasaiticaque*, 371–97, for a translation and analysis.

this material presupposes that seven years have passed since the death of Jesus, whereas the account in the Circuits begins while Jesus is still alive and continues during the year after the crucifixion. In contrast to the Circuits, Recognition 1.27–71 presents a sort of anti-Acts of the Apostles and lays the blame for the non-conversion of "the [Jewish] people" squarely at Paul's feet. At the temple, after James the brother of Jesus has spoken for seven days and has ultimately convinced "the entire people and the high priest to proceed to baptism" (*Rec.* 1.69.8), "the hostile person" intrudes, starts a violent riot, and so halts the entire process:

> In seven full days, he [i.e., James the brother of Jesus] persuaded all the people together with the high priest so that they should immediately make haste to proceed to baptism. Then a certain person who was the enemy entered the temple near the altar with a few others, while he cried out and said, "What are you doing, O people, the children of Israel? How have you been carried off so quickly by wretched men who have strayed after a magician?" He said things such as those, he listened to things against them, and when he was overcome by James the bishop, he began to create a great commotion so that the matters that were rightly being said in calmness would not be put to the test and not be understood and believed. For this purpose, he let forth an outcry over the foolishness and feebleness of the priests and reproached them. He said, "Why are you delaying? Why are you not immediately seizing all those who are with him?" When he had said those things, he rose first, seized a firebrand from the altar, and began to smite with it. Then, when the rest of the priests saw him, they also followed his example. In the great flight that thus ensued, some fell upon others and others were smitten. There were not a few who died so that much blood poured forth from those who had been killed. Now the enemy threw James from the top of the stairs. Since he fell and was as if dead, he did not smite him a second time. (*Rec.* 1.69.8–70.8 Syriac)

It seems likely that the source originally described here the death of James at the hands of "the enemy," but the basic writer altered the story since a living James was needed for the framework of the Circuits. While "the hostile person" is again not explicitly named, the ensuing account of his departure for Damascus with letters from the priests to destroy the believers leaves little room for doubt about who is intended:

> That hostile person had received a commission from Caiaphas the high priest to persecute all who believed in Jesus and to go to Damascus with his letters so that even there, when he had gained the help of the nonbelievers, he might bring destruction on the believers. (*Rec.* 1.71.3–4 Latin; cf. Acts 9:1–2; 22:4–5; 26:10–11)

Recognition 1.27–71 thus contains a variety of anti-Paulinism different from the form found in the Circuits of Peter. Here, the anti-Paulinism does not seem to be wrapped up with the polemic against the Marcionites. As such, this anti-Paulinism may preserve purer elements of an older Jewish-Christian critique of Paul; it is not impossible that these traditions derive ultimately from the lifetime of Paul. While Paul himself briefly mentions his violence against the church (Gal 1:13), the Recognition 1-source (a common shorthand designation of the postulated source behind the old material in Recognition 1.27–71) supplies some concrete imagery for this violence and likely asserts that Paul actually killed James the brother of Jesus by shoving him down a flight of stairs. The reference to stairs here along with a few other details has led some scholars to associate the Recognition 1-source with a Jewish-Christian writing called the Ascents of James and summarized by Epiphanius (*Pan.*

30.16.6–9), but the Ascents of James contains yet another distinct variety of anti-Paulinism in which it is alleged that Paul was born a Greek, converted to Judaism only in order to marry a priest's daughter who had caught his eye, and, when he was unsuccessful in this proposal, got mad and wrote against circumcision and the law. Another branch of research has focused on the similarities between the Recognition 1-source and other accounts of James's martyrdom, particularly as found in Hegesippus (preserved in Eusebius, *Hist. eccl.* 2.23.4–18), Clement of Alexandria, *Hypotyposes* 7 (preserved in Eusebius, *Hist. eccl.* 2.1.5), and the second part of the fairly recently recovered Second Revelation of James (NHC V 4 61.12–63.33). While scholarship has often fallen prey to positing an ill-defined lost source as an undescriptive blanket explanation for the similarities, detailed consideration of the texts leads to the more plausible solution that Hegesippus's account lies at the root of the others.[22] This solution implies that the Recognition 1-source is responsible for the insertion of Paul into the account, which seems likely, even following other source-critical theories.

Though it is also most probable that the author of this Recognition 1-source employed the canonical Acts of the Apostles (again in contrast to the Circuits), scholars are nagged by the possibility that the author might have instead had access to information also used by Luke. If this was the case, the consequences for the interpretation of Acts would be enormous. But even if the author is simply writing a counterhistory to Acts (as seems most likely), the significance of the material is still great. In this case, Recognition 1.27–71 presents the earliest extensive commentary to the canonical Acts. Again, while there is no evidence that the Circuits used a Jewish-Christian Gospel, it is clear that the source of Recognition 1.27–71 used the Gospel of the Ebionites and may contain numerous otherwise undocumented refractions of this Gospel. The Recognition 1-source shares with the Gospel of the Ebionites the view that the mission of Jesus was, above all, to proclaim the end of sacrifices (*Rec.* 1.39.1; 1.54.1). The likely date of the source of Recognition 1.27–71 around 200 CE provides an important anchor for discussion of the Gospel of the Ebionites.

Another intriguing element of the source behind Recognition 1.27–71 is a list and description of Jewish sects in Recognition 1.54—a neglected early heresiological catalogue apparently of Jewish provenance. Beyond information on the Sadducees ("they say it is not appropriate to worship God in the prospect of a reward") and Samaritans ("they worship Mount Gerizim") reflected elsewhere only in Jewish texts outside the New Testament,[23] the list contains a description of the disciples of John the Baptist that likely derives from Baptist tradition. This passage is essentially the only early Christian text that straightforwardly speaks of John's disciples and their beliefs after the death of Jesus, and it often plays a central role in support of the interpretation of the prologue of the Gospel of John as an affront to disciples of John the Baptist. According to the Syriac version of Recognition 1.54.8, the disciples of John "spoke to their teacher as if he was concealed"; this seems to mean that the disciples of John thought that John was still alive after his death, which would imply a quite significant precedent for the resurrection of Jesus.[24]

Finally, the Recognition 1-source promotes an attitude toward Jerusalem and the land that is not found elsewhere in the early Christian tradition in this detail.[25] This source asserts that the believers, in contrast to others, will not be driven from the land, carefully

---

22. Jones, *Pseudoclementina Elchasaiticaque*, 291–305, with review of the literature, and Jones, *Pseudoclementina Elchasaiticaque*, 456–66, on the origin of Hegesippus's report.

23. Jones, *Pseudoclementina Elchasaiticaque*, 267–79, 521–22.

24. Jones, "John the Baptist and His Disciples in the Pseudo-Clementines."

25. Jones, *Pseudoclementina Elchasaiticaque*, 257–66.

defined as "Judea," when the war comes (*Rec.* 1.37.2 Syriac; 1.39.3), a statement that Rufinus could not stomach to translate without modification and spiritualization. Here, too, Jerusalem is a "holy place" or "holy city" that will host abundance at the resurrection of the dead, apparently without a temple and certainly without sacrifices. These Jewish-Christian perspectives seem indeed to provide significant insights into the primitive Jewish-Christian underbelly of the gentile Christian New Testament. The letters of Paul, for example, hint that the Jewish Christians purposely chose and promoted Jerusalem as the center of the church, but Paul does not readily disclose their theological reasoning for this decision, which must have run very deep. Since these Pseudo-Clementine texts are consistently overlooked in surveys of early Christian attitudes to the land, which are thought to reflect decisive earthly detachment and to have been spiritualized, one senses here the clear need for New Testament scholars to broaden their perspectives to include serious consideration of texts such as the Pseudo-Clementines.

The reception-history of the Pseudo-Clementines, particularly in the West, is a vast field that comprises also early vernacular renditions of Rufinus's Latin into languages such as Anglo-Norman and Icelandic. Of particular impact has been the specific strain of Pseudo-Clementine influence on the Faust-legend and its descendants. It is the Circuits of Peter that is responsible for turning the Simon Magus of the Acts of Peter into a highly educated and articulate villain; Recognition 3.49 begins the psychological exploration of Simon's "delusion" that extends into Goethe's *Faust* and on to modern cinematic presentations of extraordinarily learned and refined figures who have gotten onto the wrong path (and thus are villains, the origins of whose manias merit detailed examination). The East, too, has a broad reception-history of the Pseudo-Clementines that includes works in Greek, Syriac, Armenian, Ethiopic, Arabic, Georgian, and Slavonic. The Martyrdom of Clement, in contrast, was originally composed in Latin, perhaps in the early fifth century, and displays only vague awareness of the Pseudo-Clementine novel.[26]

Somewhat surprisingly, the Pseudo-Clementines played a critical role in the birth of the modern discipline of New Testament and early Christian studies. Though it is often thought that this advancement occurred with Ferdinand Christian Baur around 1830, who did indeed draw on the Pseudo-Clementines as a pivotal witness to earliest Christianity, in fact the birth of the modern discipline took place over a century beforehand. John Toland (1670–1722) not only published lists of apostolic apocrypha that led to their first collection by J. A. Fabricius (1703), but he also drew heavily on the Pseudo-Clementines to introduce the term and the concept of "Jewish Christianity." With this postulation of Jewish Christianity as the earliest variety of Christianity, which was later declared heretical by gentile Christianity, along with the insistence that noncanonical sources must be treated on the same level as canonical writings in historical reconstruction, Toland initiated the debate over Christian origins that continues to this day.[27]

In sum, the Pseudo-Clementines present a remarkable apocryphon in terms of both genre and content as well as in terms of their relevance for the study of the New Testament. There is much room for work and progress in the study of these writings, though the challenges posed thereby are real and considerable.

---

26. John C. Buckingham III, *"Passio Sancti Clementis*: A New Critical Edition with English Translation" (MA thesis, California State University, Long Beach, 2018).

27. Carleton Paget, *Jews, Christians and Jewish Christians in Antiquity*, 290–97; F. Stanley Jones, ed., *The Rediscovery of Jewish Christianity: From Toland to Baur*, SBL History of Biblical Studies 5 (Atlanta: SBL Press, 2012); Reed, *Jewish-Christianity and the History of Judaism*, 260–69.

5. BIBLIOGRAPHY

5.1 Current Editions

Frankenberg, Wilhelm. *Die syrischen Clementinen mit griechischem Paralleltext: Eine Vorarbeit zu dem literargeschichtlichen Problem der Sammlung.* TUGAL 48.3. Leipzig: Hinrichs, 1937.

Rehm, Bernhard, ed. *Die Pseudoklementinen I: Homilien.* Edited by Georg Strecker. 3rd ed. GCS. Berlin: Akademie, 1992.

———. *Die Pseudoklementinen II: Rekognitionen in Rufins Übersetzung.* Edited by Georg Strecker. 2nd ed. GCS. Berlin: Akademie, 1994.

5.2 Concordance

Strecker, Georg. *Die Pseudoklementinen III: Konkordanz zu den Pseudoklementinen.* 2 vols. GCS. Berlin: Akademie, 1986–89.

5.3 English Translations

Jones, F. Stanley. *An Ancient Jewish Christian Source on the History of Christianity: Pseudo-Clementine "Recognitions" 1.27–71.* SBLTT 37, Christian Apocrypha Series 2. Atlanta: Scholars Press, 1995.

———, trans. *The Syriac "Pseudo-Clementines": An Early Version of the First Christian Novel.* Apocryphes 14. Turnhout: Brepols, 2014.

Smith, Thomas, Peter Peterson, and James Donaldson, trans. "Pseudo-Clementine Literature." Pages 67–346 in vol. 8 of *The Ante-Nicene Fathers: Translations of the Writings of the Fathers down to A.D. 325.* Edited by Alexander Roberts and James Donaldson. 10 vols. Repr., Grand Rapids: Eerdmans, 1978.

5.4 Studies

Amsler, Frédéric, et al., eds. *Nouvelles intrigues pseudo-clémentines.* Publications de l'Institut romand des sciences bibliques 6. Lausanne: Éditions du Zèbre, 2008.

Bremmer, Jan N., ed. *The "Pseudo-Clementines."* Studies on Early Christian Apocrypha 10. Leuven: Peeters, 2010.

Jones, F. Stanley. *Pseudoclementina Elchasaiticaque inter Judaeochristiana: Collected Studies.* OLA 203. Leuven: Peeters, 2012.

PART 3

APOCRYPHAL EPISTLES

CHAPTER 20

JESUS'S LETTER TO ABGAR

WILLIAM ADLER

1. INTRODUCTION

In the first book of his *Ecclesiastical History*, Eusebius of Caesarea (263–339 CE) recounts the foundation of Christianity in Edessa, the capital city of Osrhoene, a Syrian kingdom located today in southeastern Turkey. The Christian mission to Edessa, he writes, originated in a letter sent to Jesus via courier from the city's king, Abgar V Ukkama (died 40 CE). In his written reply to the king's appeal for relief from an otherwise incurable disease, Jesus promised that, after completing his earthly ministry, he would send an apostle to relieve his suffering. After he arrived in Edessa, Thaddaeus, the apostle appointed for this work, healed the king and, on the following day, proclaimed the Christian gospel to the assembled citizenry.[1]

For Eusebius, the exchange of letters between Abgar and Jesus offered a uniquely valuable witness to the beginnings of Christianity there. Later iterations of the tradition enlarged upon this theme, describing at greater length the circumstances preceding the interactions between the two men, the subsequent conversion of Abgar and his kingdom, and the establishment of churches there. As one of the few surviving documents claiming direct authorship from Jesus himself, the letter to Abgar also proved to be an object of intense interest in its own right. Edessa, home to the original copy of the letter, soon became a destination for religious pilgrims. Legends about the miraculous properties of what came to be revered as a precious relic from Jesus's earthly ministry only added to the letter's mystique.[2]

---

1. Eusebius, *Hist. eccl.* 1.13.

2. For a collection of the more important witnesses to the tradition, see Martin Illert, *Doctrina Addai; De imagine Edessena = Die Abgarlegende; Das Christusbild von Edessa*, Fontes Christiani 45 (Turnhout: Brepols, 2007). Recent surveys and studies of the Jesus/Abgar legend include Sebastian Brock, "Eusebius and Syriac Christianity," in *Eusebius, Christianity and Judaism*, ed. H. Attridge and G. Hata (Detroit: Wayne State University Press, 1992), 212–34; James Corke-Webster, "A Man for the Times: Jesus and the Abgar Correspondence in Eusebius of Caesarea's Ecclesiastical History," *HTR* 110.4 (2017): 563–87; Hendrik Jan Willem Drijvers, "The Abgar Legend," in *NTApoc* 1:492–500; Alexander Mirkovic, *Prelude to Constantine: The Abgar Tradition in Early Christianity*, Arbeiten zur Religion und Geschichte des Urchristentums 15 (Frankfurt am Main: Peter Lang, 2004); Steven K. Ross, *Roman Edessa: Politics and Culture on the Eastern Fringes of the Roman Empire, 114–242 CE* (London: Routledge, 2001), 131–36; David G. K. Taylor, "The Coming of Christianity to Mesopotamia," in *The Syriac World*, ed. D. King (London: Routledge, 2019), 68–87, esp. pp. 72–77; Alberto Camplani, "Traditions of Christian Foundation in Edessa Between Myth and History," *SMSR* 75.1 (2009): 251–78. For useful older studies, see further Ernst von Dobschütz, "Der Briefwechsel zwischen Abgar und Jesus," *ZWT* 43 (1900): 422–86; Richard Adelbert Lipsius, *Die edessenische Abgar-Sage kritisch untersucht* (Braunschweig: Schwetschke, 1880); L. Joseph Tixeront, *Les origines de l'église d'Édesse et la légende d'Abgar: Étude critique suivie de deux textes orientaux inédits* (Paris: Maisonneuve et Ch. Leclerc, 1888).

1.1 Authorship

In the absence of corroborating evidence for the existence of a Christian community in Edessa before the end of the second century, Jesus's letter to Abgar Ukkama is generally regarded as a later literary fabrication intended to establish the apostolic origins of Edessene Christianity. Although responsibility for its composition has been variously assigned to Julius Africanus (ca. 160–240 CE), the Edessene bishop Kûnê (early fourth century), or even Eusebius himself, the question of authorship remains unsettled.

1.2 Language

The original language of Jesus's letter to Abgar was probably Syriac, a dialect of Aramaic first appearing in Edessa of the first century CE. In his *Ecclesiastical History*, Eusebius characterizes his Greek text of the letters as a "literal [πρὸς λέξιν]" translation of documents composed in the "language of the Syrians [ἐκ τῆς Σύρων φωνῆς]."[3] The earliest Syriac version of the letter is found in the *Doctrina Addai*, a Syriac-Christian work dating to the late fourth or early fifth century CE.[4]

1.3 Provenance

The evidence points conclusively to Edessa. According to Eusebius, the original copy of Jesus's letters was stored in the royal archives of Edessa.[5] In the account of her pilgrimage to holy places in the East in the late fourth century, Egeria recalls traveling to Edessa, seeing the letter, and learning about its history from the local bishop acting as her guide.[6] In the *Doctrina Addai*, the exchange of letters between Jesus and Abgar forms one part of a much larger account of the inner workings of the Edessene court, the evangelization of the kingdom by the apostle Addai, and the founding of churches in the city.

1.4 Text

Eusebius's Greek text is the oldest witness to the text of Jesus's letter to Abgar. As he does elsewhere, Eusebius appears to have transcribed his source material faithfully. Semitizing calques in his text recall the Syriac original from which it was translated. Eusebius also leaves untouched notices at odds with his own stated testimony on the same matters.[7] Editorial restraint like this should put to rest the charge that Eusebius either doctored the documents for his own ends, or, even more extreme, simply fabricated the whole story. In the Latin-speaking West, knowledge of the letter was mediated chiefly through Rufinus's

---

3. Eusebius, *Hist. eccl.* 1.13.22.

4. For Syriac text and English translation of the *Doctrina Addai*, see George Howard, ed. and trans., *The Teaching of Addai*, Early Christian Literature Series; Texts and Translations 16 (Chico, CA: Scholars Press, 1981). Howard's Syriac text is based on the older edition and English translation by George Phillips, *The Doctrine of Addai, the Apostle* (London: Trübner, 1876). Chapter numbers follow M. Illert's German translation in *Doctrina Addai; De imagine Edessena*, Fontes Christiani 45 (Turnhout: Brepols, 2007), 132–76. The English translation of the text of the *Doctrina Addai* is based on Howard's edition.

5. Eusebius, *Hist. eccl.* 1.13.5.

6. For an edition of the Latin text of Egeria's diary, see P. Geyer and O. Cuntz, eds., *Itinerarium Egeriae seu Peregrinatio ad loca sancta / Aetheria (Egeria)*, CCSL 175 (Turnhout: Brepols, 1965), 37–90. For a recent English translation, see Anne McGowan and Paul F. Bradshaw, *The Pilgrimage of Egeria: A New Translation of the Itinerarium Egeriae with Introduction and Commentary* (Collegeville, MN: Liturgical Press, 2018).

7. Unlike Eusebius's own characterization of Abgar as a "king," the heading of Jesus's letter to the king refers to him as a "toparch" (*Hist. eccl.* 1.13.5; cf. 1.13.2). A chronological notice at the conclusion of the narrative dates Thaddaeus's mission to Edessa in the "three hundred and fortieth year," according to the Seleucid era (*Hist. eccl.* 1.13.22). Although this date (= 31 CE) presupposes a one-year duration for Jesus's ministry, Eusebius felt no need to bring the chronology into conformity with his own assignment of three years to his ministry.

Latin translation of the *Ecclesiastical History*. Syriac versions of the letter are preserved both in the *Doctrina Addai* and in a later work known as the Acts of Thaddaeus. Translations of the letter and the accompanying legend into Armenian, Coptic, Arabic, and Ethiopic largely derive from either the Syriac version or Eusebius's Greek text.[8]

Egeria's diary attests variant readings in the letter at a relatively early date in the letter's textual history.[9] One of the more notable variants appears at the end of Jesus's letter. The version of the letter first recorded in the *Doctrina Addai* concludes with a blessing of Edessa and the following passage: "May no enemy ever prevail against the city."[10] Although lacking in the Greek text known to Eusebius, Jesus's promise to protect the city became the basis for the widespread belief that the letter possessed the power to deter adversaries.

1.5 Genre

The preservation of the letter in differing historical and literary contexts precludes classification according to a single genre. Eusebius's account of Abgar's dealings with Jesus and Thaddaeus displays the characteristic features of a popular literary genre of the Hellenistic age known as the "court tale."[11] Along with the accompanying description of the establishment of the Edessene church, the letter has also been characterized as an example of a "genealogical myth," intended to "trace the origin of a community back to a mythical or divine ancestor."[12] Venerated on its own as a religious artifact containing the written words of Jesus, the letter represents a prototype of the so-called "heavenly letter," examples of which are plentiful in the Middle Ages.[13] Unlike later examples of the genre, however, the letter to Abgar was said to issue from his earthly ministry, not after his death and resurrection.

2. SUMMARY OF CONTENT

Since it would be impractical to treat the Jesus/Abgar legend in all its many and varied permutations, the following summaries are limited to the three earliest witnesses: Eusebius's *Ecclesiastical History*, the *Doctrina Addai*, and the *Itinerarium Egeriae*.

2.1 The Jesus/Abgar Correspondence in Eusebius's *Ecclesiastical History*

According to Eusebius, masses of people from faraway lands "recognized the signs of divinity in reports they had heard about [Jesus's] ability to cure diseases beyond the powers of human skill to cure." One of them was king Abgar, "perishing from terrible suffering

---

8. For the Armenian version, see Moses of Chorene, *History of the Armenians*, 2.30–33, in Robert W. Thomson, trans., *Moses Khorenats'i, History of the Armenians* (Cambridge: Harvard University Press, 1978). For discussion of the sources of Moses's account of Abgar's reign, see Thomson's introduction, pp. 34, 39–40. For the dissemination of the legend in Ethiopic, see Getatchew Haile, "The Legend of Abgar in Ethiopic Tradition," *OCP* 55 (1989): 375–410. For the Arabic version, see R. J. H. Gottheil, "An Arabic Version of the Abgar Legend," *Hebraica* 7 (1890–91): 268–77. See further Tomasz Polanski, "Translation, Amplification, Paraphrase: Some Comments on the Syriac, Greek and Coptic Versions of the Abgar Letter," *Collectanea Christiana Orientalia* 13 (2016): 159–210.

9. See below in sec. 3, "Interpretive Issues."

10. *Doct. Addai* 5. For discussion, see further Polanski, "Translation, Amplification, Paraphrase," 184–86.

11. See Mirkovic, *Prelude to Constantine*, 143–45.

12. See Ross, *Roman Edessa*, 135; Camplani, "Traditions of Christian Foundation in Edessa," 252.

13. Don C. Skemer, *Binding Words: Textual Amulets in the Middle Ages* (University Park, PA: Pennsylvania State University Press, 2006), 96–105; Rosanne Hebing, "The Textual Tradition of Heavenly Letter Charms in Anglo-Saxon Manuscripts," in László Sándor Chardonnens and Bryan Carella, eds., *Secular Learning in Anglo-Saxon England*, Amsterdamer Beiträge zur älteren Germanistik (Leiden: Brill, 2012), 208–9.

in his body."[14] But instead of undertaking the journey to Judea himself, the king chose to compose a letter to Jesus, delivered to him by a courier named Ananias. Jesus's power to heal without "drugs or plants," Abgar writes in his letter, demanded one of two conclusions: either Jesus was "God who descended from heaven to do these things," or he was the "son of God." For this reason, he pleads with Jesus "to hasten to me and heal the suffering which I have."[15] Having learned that Jesus's adversaries were mocking him and planning to do him harm, the king also offers him sanctuary in his kingdom.

While commending Abgar for the depth of his belief, Jesus tells him in his written reply that he would only be able to satisfy his request after he was taken up by "the one who sent me." At that time, the disciple whom Jesus promised to send to the king would not only heal Abgar's suffering but would also "give life to you and those with you."[16] Thaddaeus, the man later assigned to the mission by the "divinely moved" apostle Thomas, was one of the seventy emissaries whom Jesus instructed to carry out missions on his behalf (cf. Luke 10:1).

Eusebius calls Thaddaeus the "herald and evangelist of the teaching about Christ, through whom all the terms of our Savior's promise received fulfilment."[17] When he arrives in Edessa and begins to perform "great and wonderful deeds," Abgar suspects that he was the disciple whom Jesus had promised to send to heal his suffering.[18] Thaddaeus for his part fulfills this portion of the mission as soon as he appears in Abgar's court, laying his hand on the king and healing his disease. In response to the king's request for additional instruction about the "coming of Jesus, how it happened . . . and by what power he did these things of which I have heard," Thaddaeus asks Abgar to summon the entire citizenry on the following day. At this public assembly, Thaddaeus proclaims what he had described to Abgar the night before as the "word of life."[19]

2.2 The *Doctrina Addai*

In the Syriac *Doctrina Addai*, the recitation of events preceding and following the exchange of letters between Jesus and Abgar is far more detailed. If any single character can be said to play the leading role in the unfolding drama, it is Addai himself, the apostle to Edessa earlier identified by Eusebius as Thaddaeus. Unlike Eusebius's account of Thaddaeus's work in the city, the *Doctrina* continues on after Addai's public proclamation of the Christian kerygma to the Edessene citizenry. He then baptizes king Abgar and the citizenry, preaches at length against the folly of idolatry, establishes churches in Edessa, and ordains priests and deacons.

One other figure assuming a central role in the story is the court scribe Hanan, known earlier to Eusebius as Ananias. Following an extended stay with the governor of Mesopotamia, he joins crowds of people from distant lands who had heard of Jesus's ministry and were traveling to Jerusalem to witness his wondrous deeds for themselves. When Hanan returns to Edessa after a ten-day sojourn in Jerusalem, he informs the

---

14. Eusebius, *Hist. eccl.* 1.13.1–2. Although Eusebius does not disclose the nature of his ailment, sources of a much later date describe it as either gout or leprosy. The English translation of Eusebius's *Ecclesiastical History* is based on Kirsopp Lake, trans., *The Ecclesiastical History*, LCL (Cambridge: Harvard University Press; London: W. Heinemann, 1965).

15. Eusebius, *Hist. eccl.* 1.13.7.

16. Eusebius, *Hist. eccl.* 1.13.9.

17. Eusebius, *Hist. eccl.* 1.13.4. The only Thaddaeus mentioned in the NT Gospels is one of the twelve apostles (cf. Mark 3:18; Matt 10:3).

18. Eusebius, *Hist. eccl.* 1.13.13.

19. Eusebius, *Hist. eccl.* 1.13.15–21.

king of "everything which they had seen and everything which the Messiah had done in Jerusalem."[20] At the king's bidding, Hanan once again departs for Jerusalem with the letter from the king appealing to Jesus for relief from his ailment. Hanan finds Jesus staying at the home of the high priest. In addition to recording his response to the king's appeal, Hanan also paints Jesus's image. Upon his arrival in Edessa, Hanan thereupon reports to the king "everything which he had heard from Jesus."[21]

In addition to enlarging the roles of Hanan and Addai, the *Doctrina* also introduces into the narrative figures previously unmentioned in Eusebius's account. These include Aggai and Palut, the men whom Addai designates as his successors to lead the church of Edessa. As he is nearing death, Addai selects the silk-maker Aggai as "leader and ruler in his place," appoints the deacon Palut as presbyter, and offers his final admonitions.[22] Years later, and after ordaining priests and leaders throughout the churches of Mesopotamia, Aggai suffered martyrdom at the hands of one of Abgar's rebellious sons. Because his sudden death prevented Aggai from laying hands on a successor, Palut traveled to Antioch for consecration as bishop by Serapion, the bishop of Antioch at the time.

2.3 The *Itinerarium Egeriae*

In her diary, Egeria recalls how, during her stay in Edessa, the bishop acting as her guide showed her the city's copy of the letter, recited the words contained in it, and helped to fill in the account with some local traditions about its history. Although Egeria does not reproduce the contents of a copy of the letter given to her at the time of her departure, she does observe that Edessa's text of Jesus's letter was "fuller" (*amplius*) than the version of the letter with which she was already familiar.[23] One other significant feature of her testimony has to do with the identity of the apostle appointed to evangelize Edessa. According to Eusebius, Thaddaeus was sent to Edessa by the apostle Thomas. Egeria's own account of events credits Thomas himself with carrying out the mission.[24]

3. INTERPRETIVE ISSUES

While sharing common features, the versions of the Jesus/Abgar legend recounted in Eusebius, the diary of Egeria, and the *Doctrina Addai* were composed at different times and under different circumstances. In order to understand the origins and development of the legend, it is thus necessary to treat their reports as witnesses to separate stages in the development of what is by any measure a highly dynamic and fluid tradition.

3.1 Stage One: The Jesus/Abgar "Court Tale" as a Witness to Church/State Relations in Edessa of the Late Second Century

Modern conjectures about the source of Eusebius's copy of Jesus's letter to Abgar fall broadly into two camps. One widely held theory traced it to the reign of Abgar the Great (177–212 CE). A competing theory first proposed by Walter Bauer located its origins in Syriac orthodox Christianity of the early fourth century. Bauer maintained that the earliest Christian communities of Edessa consisted of groups later condemned as heresies, notably Marcionites, Manichaeans, and followers of Bardaisan. In order to establish the apostolic origins of a form of Christianity arriving in Edessa only later, a partisan of the orthodox

20. *Doct. Addai* 2.
21. *Doct. Addai* 6.
22. *Doct. Addai* 77.
23. Egeria, *Itinerarium* 19.19.
24. Egeria, *Itinerarium* 17.1. According to Egeria, Edessa also held the relics of Thomas.

church of the early fourth century fabricated the exchange of letters between Jesus and Abgar and the accompanying account of Thaddaeus's mission.[25] The figure behind the imposture was Kûnê, a contemporary of Eusebius and the bishop who "organized orthodoxy in Edessa in an ecclesiastical manner." By publishing a Greek version of the forged documents that the bishop provided to him, Eusebius found himself an unwitting participant in the fraud.[26]

If, as Bauer maintained, Eusebius's version of the Jesus/Abgar legend was intended to demonstrate that orthodoxy was established "with an apostolic seal" in Edessa long before heresies made their first appearance in the city, we would expect to find a more targeted refutation of the various forms of Christianity which, in Bauer's view, preceded its arrival in Edessa. We might also have expected an explanation of the means by which Thaddaeus's teachings and authority were transferred to a designated successor and instrument of orthodox teaching. While later versions of the Jesus/Abgar legend do address these matters, the version of the tradition known to Eusebius has almost nothing to contribute on either subject.

Nor is there any reason to suppose from Eusebius's report that he acquired his knowledge of the letter from a forged document provided to him by an Edessene bishop and contemporary. From Eusebius's statement that his text of the Jesus/Abgar correspondence derived from Syriac documents preserved in the archives of Edessa, we need not draw the improbable inference that Eusebius traveled to Edessa, discovered the letters in its archives, and somehow arranged for their translation into Greek. An admittedly enigmatic statement that they were "removed for us" from the archives when Edessa "was being ruled by a king [τὸ τηνικάδε βασιλευομένην πόλιν]" at least raises the possibility that Eusebius did not know of the correspondence firsthand, depending instead on a source composed at a time when Edessa was not yet a Roman province.[27]

According to the Roman historian Cassius Dio, the last king of Edessa was Abgar VIII the Great, a ruler whose ill-conceived efforts to curry favor with Rome were said to have ended disastrously with his removal from office and the dissolution of his kingdom.[28] Christian witnesses, two of whom had direct connections with Abgar, portray the king in a far more favorable light. One of them was Julius Africanus, a well-traveled Christian scholar, antiquarian, and guest in the king's court. In his chronicle, Africanus describes Abgar the Great as a "holy man."[29] According to the Armenian historian Moses of Chorene, the last book of Africanus's chronicle also contained source material extracted from documents that he had discovered in the city archives.[30] Reports like this were the reason why Grabe went so far as to assign the origins of the letter to Africanus himself.[31]

25. Walter Bauer, *Orthodoxy and Heresy in Earliest Christianity*, 2nd ed. (Philadelphia: Fortress, 1979), 1–43.

26. Bauer, *Orthodoxy and Heresy*, 33–43. For later adaptations and revisions of Bauer's proposal, see, e.g., Hendrik Jan Willem Drijvers, "Addai und Mani, Christentum und Manichäismus im dritten Jahrhundert," *OCA* 221 (1983): 171–85; Helmut Koester, "GNOMAI DIAPHOROI: On the Origin and Nature of Diversification in the History of Early Christianity," *HTR* 58 (1965): 279–318, esp. 290–306.

27. Eusebius, *Hist. eccl.* 1.13.5. For proponents of the theory that Eusebius learned about the documents from an earlier source, see Johann Ernst Grabe, *Spicilegium SS: Patrum ut et haereticorum saeculi I–III*, vol. 1 (Oxford: E. Theatro Sheldoniano, 1700), 314; Theodor Zahn, *Forschungen zur Geschichte des neutestamentlichen Kanons und der altkirchlichen Literatur*, vol. 1 (Erlangen: Deichert, 1881), 352–56.

28. Cf. Cassius Dio, *Roman History* 77[78].12.1a–1,2.

29. Africanus, *Chronographiae* F96, in Martin Wallraff et al., eds., *Iulius Africanus: Chronographiae: The Extant Fragments*, GCS 15 (Berlin: de Gruyter, 2007); see also Epiphanius, *Pan.* 338.10, who calls Abgar "a most holy and learned man [ἀνδρὶ ὁσιωτάτῳ καὶ λογιωτάτῳ]."

30. Moses of Chorene, *History of Armenia* 2.10.

31. Grabe, *Spicilegium S: Patrum ut et haereticorum saeculi I–III*, 314.

In his own study of the subject, F. C. Burkitt understood the Jesus/Abgar legend as part of a broader official campaign to legitimate Abgar the Great's conversion to Christianity by tracing the conversion of the Edessene royal house back to the reign of his ancestor Abgar V.[32] One problem with Burkitt's proposal has to do with Abgar the Great's alleged Christian identity. It is true that the king was welcoming to prominent Christians of his day, including Africanus and Bardaisan, the latter a fixture in the king's court. The evidence for Abgar's own Christian identification is, however, far less certain. Even if he were a Christian, Abgar does not seem to have taken any public measures to promote the recognition of Christianity as the state religion. Coins and official documents issued during his reign, for example, reveal no change in the religious face of the kingdom.[33]

Nor does the "charter-myth" explanation accurately reflect Eusebius's own record of the circumstances of Thaddaeus's mission to Edessa. A story intended to memorialize the early conversion of the kingdom would ideally include a description of some official act to mark the occasion. But Eusebius's account says nothing either about the baptism of Abgar V or of the assembled citizenry of Edessa. Instead, it concludes rather abruptly with Thaddaeus's public proclamation of the Christian kerygma. To understand the purpose of Eusebius's "court tale," we thus need to look elsewhere.

Part of the appeal of the Hellenistic court-tale genre was that it offered a platform from which to explore the dynamics of relations between a king and his clients. In exchange for receiving a service or commodity, the king would offer the subject something of comparable value. While typically commending the magnanimity and virtue of the king, the description of the relationship that developed between the two parties might also challenge conventions governing asymmetrical interactions between royalty and people of lower social standing, among them merchants, scribes, scholars, and foreign visitors. Josephus's account of the conversion of the kingdom of Adiabene to Judaism is illustrative. According to Josephus, Izates (ca. 1–55 CE), the son of King Monobazos, became interested in Judaism when, while dwelling abroad, he learned about its doctrines from a Jewish merchant named Ananias. After returning home and assuming the throne, Izates discovered that his mother Helena, the queen of Adiabene, had previously converted to Judaism. Although Helena and Ananias advised against his formal conversion to Judaism through circumcision, a learned Jew from Galilee named Eleazar subsequently persuaded him to do so.[34]

How or if Josephus's report of Izates's conversion to Judaism served as a model for the story about Abgar's conversion to Christianity remains unclear.[35] What we can say is that, like other examples of the genre, Eusebius's portrayal of Jesus's and Thaddaeus's interactions with the king is multilayered. Upon learning of Jesus's fame as a healer, Abgar, a "celebrated monarch of the nations beyond the Euphrates," became his "suppliant [ἱκέτης]."[36] The king shows equal deference to Thaddaeus during the apostle's stay in

---

32. Francis Crawford Burkitt, *Early Eastern Christianity* (John Murray: London, 1904), 11–38, esp. pp. 26–38; see further L. W. Barnard, "The Origins and Emergence of the Church in Edessa during the First Two Centuries A.D.," *VC* 22.3 (1968): 161–75, esp. p. 162.

33. See Taylor, "Coming of Christianity to Edessa," 73; Ross, *Roman Edessa*, 133–36; J. B. Segal, *Edessa: "The Blessed City"* (Oxford: Oxford University Press, 1970), 70–71. For doubts about Abgar the Great's conversion to Christianity, see further Bauer, *Orthodoxy and Heresy*, 4–7; Fergus Millar, *The Roman Near East, 31 B.C.–A.D. 337* (Cambridge: Harvard University Press, 1993), 475–76. Burkitt seems to have sensed the problem, referring in one place to Abgar the Great as "half a Christian" (*Early Eastern Christianity*, 27).

34. Josephus, *Antiquities* 20.2.

35. For discussion, see Robert Murray, *Symbols of Church and Kingdom: A Study in Early Syriac Tradition* (Cambridge: Cambridge University Press, 1975), 8–9; Segal, *Edessa*, 66–69; Mirkovic, *Prelude to Constantine*, 141–43.

36. Eusebius, *Hist. eccl.* 1.13.2.

Edessa. In the Hellenistic East of the second century, a foreign visitor arriving in the court of a king would customarily perform an act of *proskynēsis*, that is, ritual prostration. The custom is upended when Thaddaeus arrives at Abgar's court. Since Abgar was the only one to behold a great vision in the apostle's face, his courtiers are at a loss when it is the king, not Thaddaeus, who prostrates himself. And after he is healed, the king accedes without hesitation to Thaddaeus's request to summon the citizenry on the day after their meeting.[37]

But despite these displays of devotion and royal largesse, both Jesus and Thaddaeus are always careful to maintain their distance and independence from the king. In all their interactions with the king, the prerogatives of royalty are subordinate to a higher calling. Because of the demands of his ministry, Jesus declines Abgar's offer of sanctuary in a city described by the king as "small but venerable" and "sufficient for the both of us."[38] Upon his arrival in Edessa, Thaddaeus does not immediately appear at the royal court, electing instead to heal others first and to remain in the home of Tobias. When Tobias tells him that the king had sent for him, Thaddaeus agrees to meet with him, but not because of the king's bidding but because he had "been miraculously sent to him."[39] During their meeting, Thaddaeus continues to assert his autonomy as an apostle divinely appointed for his mission. Before laying hands on Abgar, Thaddaeus demands further assurances of the king's faith. He later denies the king's request for private instruction in the Christian kerygma, telling him instead that he would "remain silent" until he could speak publicly to the Edessene citizenry. After doing so, he rejects the king's offer of compensation with gold and plate. "If we have left our own things," he tells the king, "how shall we take those of others?"[40] If there is any underlying political message in Eusebius's story, it is not to document the establishment of a "state church" in the city but rather to affirm Christianity's autonomy and independence from the very moment of its arrival there.

The other notable feature of Eusebius's court history is its alleged origins. For Eusebius, preservation of the original copies in the "public documents" stored in the archives of Edessa guaranteed the validity of the two letters and the accompanying story of Thaddaeus's mission.[41] Given the reputation of civic archives in late antiquity, that endorsement carried real weight. It conferred upon the letters an official state sanction, at the same as it reassured readers of the care with which they were composed and maintained. Careful oversight and severe penalties for destroying, stealing, or altering records maintained in state archives promoted a widespread, albeit not altogether warranted, impression that they were less exposed to the physical deterioration and tampering suffered by documents preserved under less exacting conditions.[42]

In the Hellenistic age, city archives stored royal edicts and correspondence, tax records, private contracts, and other official business of a bureaucracy. Edessa took the additional step of including documents more commonly segregated in a temple archive. Gathering sacred and secular documents together in a single location and entrusting their administration to a single state-appointed overseer helped curb the autonomy of temple priests and other religious officials.[43] At least in the case of the Jesus/Abgar correspondence and

---

37. Eusebius, *Hist. eccl.* 1.13.14.
38. Eusebius, *Hist. eccl.* 1.13.8–9.
39. Eusebius, *Hist. eccl.* 1.13.13.
40. Eusebius, *Hist. eccl.* 1.13.20–21.
41. Eusebius, *Hist. eccl.* 1.13.5.
42. See further William Adler, "Christians and the Public Archive," in Eric F. Mason, ed., *A Teacher for All Generations: Essays in Honor of James C. VanderKam*, 2 vols. (Leiden: Brill, 2012), 2:917–37.
43. See Moses of Chorene, *History of the Armenians* 2.27. For discussion of Moses's testimony, see Giusto Traina, "Archivi armenie mesopotamici: La testimonianza di Movsēs Xorenac'i," in *Archives et sceaux du*

the record of Thaddaeus's subsequent mission, the policy helped to integrate a defining moment in the history of the Christian community of Edessa into the official record of the Edessene state.

For its part, Edessa could now boast possession of an artifact from its past. In the Hellenistic Near East of the second century, fascination with relics and other memorials from antiquity was apparently so pervasive that the author of *De dea Syria* (generally believed to be the satirist Lucian of Samosata) found it a target for derision. He ridicules the willingness of sightseers to be taken in by even the most far-fetched stories about some artifact or natural wonder surviving from a city's heroic age.[44] Thanks to local legends told about them, biblical artifacts and sites had also become objects of international curiosity and destinations for religious tourists, among them Noah's ark, the terebinth tree of Hebron, and the Dead Sea.

By that time, Edessa also had its own stock of relics. Presumably during his stay there, Africanus had learned that the kingdom was once the site of the shepherd's tent of the patriarch Jacob.[45] With its possession of the original correspondence between Abgar and Jesus, Edessa could now claim another ancient reminder of the city's illustrious past. The Christian community of Edessa also stood to benefit. The preservation of the letters in the public archive incorporated Christianity into the kingdom's documentation of its past, creating at the same time a set of guidelines for future interactions between church and state.

3.2 Stage Two: The Jesus/Abgar Legend and the Creation of an Edessene State Church

Although the *Doctrina*'s expanded narration of the Jesus/Abgar legend may have drawn on sources predating Eusebius, its closer attention both to church-state relations and to the process by which Christianity created a permanent institutional presence in the kingdom is best treated as a secondary stage in the development of the tradition.[46] The author's interest in these matters is unmistakable in his treatment of a subject about which Eusebius was previously silent: Addai's work in the city after proclaiming the gospel to the assembled citizenry.

In its report of Addai's ministry, the *Doctrina* preempts any assumption that his initial rejection of payment from the king meant that the establishment of the church in Edessa took place without material assistance from the state. According to the *Doctrina*, the affairs of church and state were intermingled from the very outset. Addai may have declined the king's offer of payment. But the power of his teaching and his signs and wonders inspired Abgar to underwrite the building of a church in the city and offer its teachers "large gifts, so that they might have no other work in addition to the ministry."[47] Addai's own success at noncoercive conversion of Jews and pagans in the city would also serve as a model for the kingdom's future dealings with unbelievers. Since the message of the gospel

---

monde hellénistique (= *Archivi e sigilli nel mondo ellenistico*), ed. M.-F. Boussac and A. Invernizzi, Bulletin de Correspondance Hellénique, Supplément 29 (Athens: Ecole Française d'Athènes, 1996), 49–63.

44. See further Graham Anderson, *Studies in Lucian's Comic Fiction*, Mnemosyne Supplements 43 (Leiden: Brill, 1976), 68–82.

45. *Chronographiae* F29. According to Africanus, the relic was destroyed by a thunderbolt around the time of the reign of the Roman emperor Antoninus.

46. For studies of the *Doctrina*, its sources, and its relationship with Eusebius's account, see Illert, *Doctrina Addai*, 29–44; Brock, "Eusebius and Syriac Christianity," 212–34; Mirkovic, *Prelude to Constantine*, 31–53; Alain Desreumaux, "La *Doctrina Addai*: le chroniqueur et ses documents," *Apocrypha* 1 (1990): 249–81; Ilaria L. Ramelli, "Possible Historical Traces in the *Doctrina Addai*," *Hug* 9.1 (2006): 51–127; Sidney H. Griffith, "The *Doctrina Addai* as a Paradigm of Christian Thought in Edessa in the Fifth Century," *Hug* 6 (2003): 269–92.

47. *Doct. Addai* 65.

was persuasive enough, "neither Abgar the king, nor Addai the Apostle pressed any man by force to believe."[48]

Lacking reliable source material for Christian Edessa of the first century, the *Doctrina*'s account of the practices and beliefs first instituted by Addai had to draw on material from a later and better-documented period in the church's history. In his quest to trace an unbroken chain of episcopal authority extending from Edessa to Rome, the author apparently decided to retroject the names of historical figures from a much later time. According to the *Doctrina*, the bishop of Antioch who consecrated Palut was Serapion, himself ordained by Zephyrinus, bishop of Rome "from the succession of the hand of the priesthood of Simon Cephas." From other sources, we know that, while Serapion and Zephyrinus were indeed contemporaries, they did not assume the office of bishop until the late second century.[49] The *Doctrina*'s reconstruction of worship practices in Christian Edessa of the early first century is equally improbable. Believers attending the churches founded by Addai and Abgar are said to have heard readings both from the Old and New Testaments, and from Tatian's *Diatessaron*, the latter a gospel harmony composed in the middle of the second century.[50]

The result of these efforts was an idealized, albeit historically flawed, vision of a church not fundamentally different from Edessene Christianity of the author's own day. The *Doctrina*'s picture of the Edessene state of the early first century is equally idealized, especially in its description of the flow of information between the kingdom and Jerusalem. Apart from a vaguely worded observation that King Abgar "had heard much" of Jesus's name and miracles, Eusebius's earlier treatment of this subject offers little insight into how the king first learned about Jesus's healing ministry.[51] Nor did Eusebius explain how Thaddaeus's preaching and activities in Edessa were recorded and archived. Most importantly, Eusebius failed to clarify a matter that by the end of the fourth century was no longer purely technical: How did Jesus compose his response to the king's appeal, through dictation or in his own hand?

All these matters are treated at far greater length in the *Doctrina*'s report of the kingdom's official dealings with Jesus and Addai. No longer the unremarkable and nondescript courier mentioned in passing by Eusebius, Hanan is now both an accomplished artist and Edessa's *tabularius*, a high-ranking official charged with the oversight of the public archives and written exchanges between Abgar and foreign powers. When he returns to Edessa after his first sojourn in Jerusalem, Hanan reads his carefully recorded testimony of "everything which they had seen and everything which the Messiah had done in Jerusalem." Hearing Hanan's words was virtually the same as seeing Jesus's wonders firsthand. Upon receiving them, Abgar and his courtiers were "speechless and astonished."[52]

In this way, the *Doctrina*'s account of Hanan's report to the king did more than simply explain to readers how Abgar first learned about Jesus's fame as healer. It also introduced a theme running through the entire narrative: Edessa as "scribal culture." When Hanan later communicates Jesus's response to the king's petition, he again proves himself worthy of

48. *Doct. Addai* 67.
49. *Doct. Addai* 102. Cf. Eusebius, *Hist. eccl.* 6.12.
50. On the use of the New Testament in the *Doctrina*, see Alain Desreumaux, "Das Neue Testament in der *Doctrina Addaï*," in *Christian Apocrypha: Receptions of the New Testament in Ancient Christian Apocrypha*, ed. J.-M. Roessli and T. Nicklas, Novum Testamentum Patristicum 26 (Göttingen: Vandenhoeck & Ruprecht, 2014), 233–48.
51. Eusebius, *Hist. eccl.* 1.13.2.
52. *Doct. Addai* 2–3. See further Corke-Webster, *Man for the Times*, 571–73.

his epithet "faithful scribe."[53] Because everything that Jesus had spoken to him "had been placed in writing," the king and his courtiers could have unqualified confidence in the accuracy of the text of Jesus's letter that Hanan read to them when he returned to the city.

The *Doctrina*'s description of the official record made of Addai's mission is equally attentive to the technicalities of the production and preservation of state documents. Eusebius's own rather sketchy description of the composition and origin of this report states only that his record of Thaddaeus's mission was translated from a document "appended in the Syriac" to the letters of Jesus and Abgar.[54] A work as focused as the *Doctrina* on the inner workings of Edessa's archive culture could hardly have settled for such imprecision. According to its author, the royal scribe Labubna recorded the details of Addai's ministry "from the beginning to the end." In doing so, Labubna was only acting in conformity with the accepted convention both in Edessa and "all kingdoms" of chronicling everything commanded by the king and said in his presence.[55]

In his capacity as overseer of the civic archives, Hanan then notarized the document and saw to its placement "among the records of the writings of the kings, where are put the commands and laws, and the contracts of those who buy and sell." To a modern reader, this might sound like rather routine handling of a record of such momentous events. But that was the whole point. In Edessa, everything was done, as it were, "by the book." According to the *Doctrina*, the acts of Addai received the same attention accorded to all official records, no more, no less. This was because every official document, from commercial contracts to royal edicts, was handled "with care, without any negligence."[56]

Resolution of ambiguities in the received tradition has also shaped the *Doctrina*'s report of Abgar's interactions with Rome. Rome is at best a distant presence in Eusebius's own version of events. When the apostle Thaddaeus arrives at the king's palace, Abgar reaffirms his faith by assuring him that, were it not for Rome, he would have taken an army to Judea and "destroyed the Jews who crucified Jesus."[57] The king's respect for Roman sovereignty is a theme put to far greater use in the *Doctrina*. After first learning from Hanan about Jesus's healing ministry, Abgar's immediate impulse is to travel to Palestine and witness for himself what Hanan had seen and written about him. But a foreign king crossing over into a Roman province was bound to stir up suspicion, even hostility. A letter to Jesus would have to suffice in its place. With this explanation, the *Doctrina* was once again able to address a question remaining from the older tradition: If reports of Jesus's miraculous cures had persuaded the king of his divinity, why, unlike other believers from distant lands, did Abgar choose not to travel to Judea in search of relief from his suffering? Rome was standing in his way.[58]

A similar justification underlies the *Doctrina*'s subsequent report of the king's interactions with the Roman emperor Tiberius. After learning from Addai about the circumstances of Jesus's unlawful death, Abgar suppresses his initial instinct to take matters into his own hands. He decides instead to write a letter to Tiberius, urging him to enforce the necessary legal measures against those responsible for Jesus's crucifixion. The emperor's highly appreciative reply commends the king for tempering his pursuit of justice with loyalty to Rome and respect for its treaties with Edessene kings. Tiberius also reassures the king of his

---

53. For this description of Hanan, see *Doct. Addai* 1.
54. Eusebius, *Hist. eccl.* 1.13.11.
55. *Doct. Addai* 103.
56. *Doct. Addai* 103.
57. Eusebius, *Hist. eccl.* 1.13.16.
58. *Doct. Addai* 3.

own commitment to the rule of law. He had already removed Pontius Pilate for appeasing those demanding Jesus's crucifixion. As soon as he had put down an uprising in Spain, the emperor planned to punish the other guilty parties as well. Tiberius even expresses a reverence for Jesus rivaling Abgar's own belief. Especially after Jesus's fellow countrymen had witnessed firsthand everything Jesus had done, he tells Abgar, they should have honored and worshiped Jesus, not put him to death. Even if it meant magnifying Jewish complicity in Jesus's death, Abgar's ongoing deference to Roman jurisdiction now made it possible for the author to confirm a friendship between the king and his Roman counterpart born of a joint commitment to justice, mutual respect for treaties, and even shared religious leanings.[59]

3.3 Stage Three: The "Performative" Function of Jesus's Letter to Abgar

By the end of the fourth century, religious tourists like Egeria could learn about the contents and story of Jesus's letter not as part of a written narrative but as orally "performed" by local experts. In her diary, Egeria recalled how her guide enriched the whole experience by showing her a marble statue of the king "having a sheen as if made of pearl" and pointing out the gate through which the scribe Ananias gained entrance to the city. When the guide arrived at the gate, he recited a prayer, read the letters to her out loud, and then recited another prayer.[60]

As he was escorting Egeria through Abgar's palace, her guide also described an earlier performance with the letter, in this case to thwart an enemy onslaught. When Persian forces were advancing on the city, King Abgar brandished a copy of the letter before them, appealing at the same time to Jesus to remember what he had written in his letter: "Lord Jesus, you promised that no enemy would enter this city. But look, at this moment the Persians are attacking us." A great darkness suddenly enveloped the Persians, preventing them from finding their way into the city. After God foiled their attempts to deprive Edessa of its sources of water, the Persians repeatedly tried and failed to enter the city. As often as they attacked, Abgar drove them away by holding up the letter before them.[61]

In his earlier account, Eusebius had nothing to say about Abgar's confrontation with the Persians or about any other application of the miraculous powers of the letter. When the apostle Thaddaeus healed king Abgar and the other citizens of Edessa, he did so, Eusebius writes, "in the power of God [ἐν δυνάμει θεοῦ]," not through the agency of the words recorded in his letter.[62] The *Doctrina Addai* holds to much the same view. Although its version of the letter does include the wish that "no enemy ever again rule over the city," there is nothing to suggest that the words dictated to Hanan possessed the power ascribed to them by Egeria's guide and by later sources. It is true that Hanan recorded the words of Jesus's letter with painstaking care. But this was no different from the treatment given any official document destined for conservation in the state archive.

59. *Doct. Addai* 74–75. See further, Ilaria L. E. Ramelli, "The Possible Origin of the Abgar-Addai Legend: Abgar the Black and Emperor Tiberius," *Hug* 16.2 (2013): 325–41. For the author's interest in establishing the Christian leanings of Roman royalty before Constantine, see also chs. 16–32. In this section, Addai reports how Protonice, the wife of the emperor Claudius, became a believer in Christ after witnessing firsthand the wondrous acts he performed in Rome. During her subsequent pilgrimage to Jerusalem, she discovered the wood of the cross and experienced firsthand its miraculous powers when it restored her daughter to life. The story closely parallels legends about the discoveries of Helena, the mother of Constantine. For discussion, see H. J. W. Drijvers, "The Protonike Legend, the *Doctrina Addai* and Bishop Rabbula of Edessa," *VC* 51.3 (1997): 298–315, esp. pp. 302–5.
60. Egeria, *Itinerarium* 19.1–17.
61. Egeria, *Itinerarium* 19.8–13.
62. Eusebius, *Hist. eccl.* 1.13.12.

For both Eusebius and the *Doctrina*, the significance of Jesus's letter was mainly as testimony to a decisive moment in the founding of the Edessene church. But given the prominence of biblical relics in Christian popular piety of late antiquity, it is hardly surprising that other witnesses value this artifact from Jesus's ministry differently. Already in the first century, religious tourists to Mount Ararat were said by Josephus to have removed pieces of Noah's ark for use as amulets.[63] Christian interest in biblical relics received an added boost from stories told about Helena, the mother of Constantine, and her discovery of the remains of the true cross during her pilgrimage to the Holy Land.[64]

What made Edessa's copy of the letter of Abgar an artifact of exceptional character was that, unlike the wood of the cross or the remains of Noah's ark, it contained writing. In antiquity and the Middle Ages, words—whether in prayers, curses, exorcisms, or divine utterances—were thought to possess supernatural agency when written or uttered. Because the efficacy of the very words of Jesus's letter was not bound to the material object on which they were written, they became what Skemer calls "a renewable resource of divine power," transferable to other media and settings.[65]

That belief may explain why, at the time of her departure, Egeria's guide gave her a copy of the letter to take with her on the long and dangerous journey back to Spain.[66] It also accounts for the wide dissemination of copies of the letter in late antiquity and the Middle Ages. In the form of an amulet, it was used to shield the location where it was located, to ward off diseases and unclean spirits, and to protect travelers.[67] Additions to the text of the letter enhanced its power to deter enemies. A copy of Jesus's letter preserved in a collection of Coptic apotropaic texts concludes with a confirmation of its capacity to ward off demonic agents. Wherever the copy of the letter was affixed, "no power of the adversary or unclean spirit will be able to approach." Nor is there any question here about who physically composed the letter. "I am the one who commands, and I am the one who speaks," Jesus says. "I myself wrote these words."[68]

One of the more widely attested additions to the text of Jesus's letter soon earned the critical scrutiny of scholars and professional historians. In his *De bello Persico*, Procopius, a Byzantine historian of the sixth century, observed that "instead of any other defense [ἀντ' ἄλλου τοῦ φυλακτηρίου]," Edessa's citizens inscribed a copy of the letter on the gates of the city as a shield against enemies. They did so, he writes, with the confidence that Jesus would always remain true to his promise that Edessa would "never be liable to capture by

63. See Josephus, *Ant.* 1.3.6 (quoting from the Babylonian historian Berossus).

64. See Barbara Baert, *A Heritage of Holy Wood: The Legend of the True Cross in Text and Image*, Cultures, Beliefs and Traditions: Medieval and Early Modern 22 (Leiden: Brill, 2004). On Egeria's own observations about the wood of the cross, see *Itinerarium* 48.

65. Skemer, *Binding Words*, 97. Skemer also suggests that the extraordinary power ascribed to Jesus's letter may reflect an enduring ancient Near Eastern idea that letters from the gods could confer magical powers.

66. Egeria, *Itinerarium* 19.18.

67. For the use of Jesus's letter in inscriptions and amulets, see Skemer, *Binding Words*, 96–99; T. de Bruyn, *Making Amulets Christian: Artefacts, Scribes, and Contexts* (Oxford: Oxford University Press, 2017), 153–57; Terry G. Wilfong and Kevin P. Sullivan, "The Reply of Jesus to King Abgar: A Coptic New Testament Apocryphon Reconsidered (P. Mich. Inv. 6213)," *Bulletin of the American Society of Papyrologists* 42.1 (2005): 107–23; Andrew Mark Henry, "Apotropaic Autographs: Orality and Materiality in the Abgar-Jesus Inscriptions," *Archiv für Religionsgeschichte* 17.1 (2016): 165–85; J. Gregory Given, "Utility and Variance in Late Antique Witnesses to the Abgar-Jesus Correspondence," *Archiv für Religionsgeschichte* 17.1 (2016): 187–222.

68. Marvin W. Meyer and Richard Smith, eds., *Ancient Christian Magic: Coptic Texts of Ritual Power* (San Francisco: Harper San Francisco, 1994), 320–21. See further Wilfong and Sullivan, "Reply of Jesus to King Abgar," 121.

the barbarians."[69] But since Jesus's pledge to protect the city was lacking in earlier versions of the letter, Procopius doubted whether he had actually ever uttered these words. Even so, Procopius was willing to grant the possibility that Jesus chose to honor the promise anyway. Otherwise, the citizens of the city would have lost faith in him.[70]

In his *Ecclesiastical History*, Evagrius (sixth century CE) was even more measured in his assessment of the efficacy of the inscription as a palladium against enemies. When the Persian king Chosroes decided to lay siege to Edessa, he writes, he did so in order to shatter its trust in Jesus's promise that the "city would never fall into the power of an enemy."[71] But Evagrius was more emphatic than Procopius in pressing the implications of the absence of the promise in earlier witnesses to the text of the letter. Anyone familiar with Eusebius's *Ecclesiastical History*, Evagrius writes, will immediately recognize that his "verbatim [πρὸς λέξιν]" copy of Jesus's letter lacked any guarantee to protect the city against its enemies. Nor was Evagrius willing to entertain Procopius's conjecture that Jesus might have somehow felt constrained to honor a promise that he never actually uttered. The power of the letter originated not in its binding words but in the expression of faith signified by its inscription on the gates of the city—a faith that "when realized, brings about the accomplishment of the prediction."[72]

One further consequence of the proliferation of legends about the unique powers of Jesus's letter was the introduction of legends about other healing relics into the Jesus/Abgar tradition, most notably the portrait of Jesus painted by Hanan the scribe and brought back to Edessa from Jerusalem. During her visit to the city, Egeria makes no mention in her diary about the portrait. The *Doctrina Addai*, the earliest witness to this tradition, states, without further elaboration, that Abgar admired Hanan's handiwork and placed it "with great honor" in one of his palaces. That description of the creation, reception, and conservation of Hanan's portrait of Jesus is far more understated than later iterations of the legend.[73] According to the Acts of Thaddaeus (ca. sixth century CE), Jesus himself, not Hanan, produced the portrait. After conveying Abgar's letter to Jesus, Hanan began to "look at him carefully," as if preparing to paint his portrait. Sensing Hanan's frustration at his inability "to fix him in his mind," Jesus asked for a linen cloth with which to clean himself. He wiped his face on the cloth, leaving on it an imprint of his face. When the apostle Addai later arrived in Edessa, he found its king no longer in need of his assistance. Abgar had already been restored to health after he beheld the image of Jesus impressed on the towel, fell down, and adored it.[74]

In this narrative, the power of Jesus's image, now no longer an artifact of human hands, has preempted Addai's role as the apostle whom Jesus vowed to send to Edessa and heal

---

69. Procopius, *De bellis* 2.12.25, in Gerhard Wirth, ed., *Procopii Caesariensis opera omnia*, vols. 1–2 (Leipzig: Teubner, 1962–63). Since the word φυλακτήριον often applies to amulets, Procopius could be referring to other apotropaic defenses of the city.

70. Procopius, *De bellis* 2.12.29. Cf. Andrew Palmer, "Procopius and Edessa," *Antiquite tardive* 8 (2000): 127–36: "Procopius is cynical enough to accuse former generations of pious fraud, yet credulous enough to imagine that this fraud, by its very success, may effectively have forced the hand of the One who decides the outcome of all wars" (127).

71. Evagrius Scholasticus, *Historia ecclesiastica* 4.27, in Joseph Bidez and Leon Parmentier, eds., *The Ecclesiastical History of Evagrius with the Scholia* (London: Methuen, 1898); cf. Procopius, *De bellis* 2.12.6–7, 31; 2.26.2.

72. Evagrius, *Hist. eccl.* 4.27.

73. See Ernst von Dobschütz, *Christusbilder: Untersuchungen zur christlichen Legende*, TU 18 (Leipzig: Hinrichs, 1899), 102–96. For recent study of the development of the tradition, see Mark Guscin, *The Image of Edessa* (Leiden: Brill, 2009).

74. Acts of Thaddaeus 3–4 (Illert, *Doctrina Addai*, 246).

the king.[75] In much the same way, a story recounted by the historian Evagrius about the image's military applications overshadowed the apotropaic powers imputed to Jesus's letter to the king. Although doubting the efficacy of a textually adulterated version of Jesus's letter engraved on the gates of Edessa, Evagrius had no such misgivings about what he calls "the divinely wrought image [τὴν θεότευκτον εἰκόνα] . . . which Christ our God sent to Abgar on his desiring to see him." During their siege of Edessa, Evagrius writes, the Persians devised a plan to scale the city walls by means of a moveable mound. After failing in their attempts to ignite the timber supporting the mound, the Edessenes enlisted the aid of the image. Water previously poured on the image and then sprinkled on the timber caused the wood to burst into flames and ultimately consume the mound. Unable to extinguish the fire, Chosroes and his army had no choice but to call off the siege.[76]

3.4 The Contested Standing of the Jesus/Abgar Correspondence

When, in his *Ecclesiastical History*, Eusebius identified the authoritative writings that comprised the New Testament of his own day, he described them as "true and genuine and commonly accepted according to ecclesiastical tradition."[77] Eusebius could hardly have made such a claim about two letters that he was introducing to readers for the first time. But their lack of recognition in churches in no way cast doubt on their reliability. The existence of original copies of a written exchange between Jesus and the "most famous of the rulers of the peoples beyond the Euphrates" represented what he calls "documentary evidence [ἀνάγραπτον τὴν μαρτυρίαν]" for the apostolic origins of the church in Edessa.[78]

Because the letters were chiefly of historical value, Eusebius could treat them as truthful without having to provide guidance on the way they should be received and read in the churches. The first official pronouncement on this matter appears in the *Decretum Gelasianum de libris recipiendis et non recipiendis* (ca. sixth century CE). In the decretal, the Jesus/Abgar correspondence now found itself consigned to a long catalogue of works designated as apocrypha.[79] Conceivably, the author may have found the representation of King Abgar as a Christian convert irreconcilable with the generally accepted view that Constantine the Great was the first Christian ruler.[80] Concerns about the widening use of Jesus's letter as an apotropaic may also have contributed to its rejection. Starting in the late fourth century, church fathers and councils were beginning to express alarm at the use of amulets and other devices repudiated in the Council of Laodicea as "chains for the soul [δεσμωτήρια τῶν ψυχῶν]."[81]

But behind the *Decretum*'s repudiation of a letter once held in such high regard lay another and more fundamental imperative. None of the New Testament Gospels claimed

---

75. See Averil Cameron, "The History of the Image of Edessa: The Telling of a Story," in *Okeanos: Essays Presented to Ihor Ševčenko on His Sixtieth Birthday by His Colleagues and Students*, ed. C. Mango, O. Pritsak, and U. Pasicznyk, Harvard Ukrainian Studies 7 (Cambridge: Harvard Ukrainian Research Institute, 1984), 82–83.

76. Evagrius, *Hist. eccl.* 4.27.

77. Eusebius, *Hist. eccl.* 3.15.6.

78. Eusebius, *Hist. eccl.* 1.13.5.

79. Ernst von Dobschütz, ed., *Das Decretum Gelasianum de libris recipiendis et non recipiendis*, TU 38 (Leipzig: Hinrichs, 1912), 5.8.1–2 (p. 57, lines 328–29).

80. For Abgar V as forerunner of Constantine, see Mirkovic, *Prelude to Constantine*; Andrew N. Palmer, "King Abgar of Edessa, Eusebius and Constantine," in *The Sacred Centre as the Focus of Political Interest*, ed. H. Bakker, Groningen Oriental Studies 6 (Leiden: Brill, 1992), 3–29.

81. Council of Laodicea, canon 36, in *Les Canons Des Synodes Particuliers (IVe–IXe s.)*, vol. 1 part 2 of *Discipline générale antique*, ed. P.-P. Ioannou (Rome: Tipografia Italo-Orientale "S. Nilo," 1962), 145. See further de Bruyn, *Making Amulets Christian*, 17–42.

direct authorship by Jesus, either directly or by dictation. Nor could any of the churches boast possession of the original copy of any of the Gospels. How then would they measure up against a letter said to be a genuine and carefully preserved artifact from Jesus's ministry, containing his original words, and composed either in his own hand, or, if not that, at least by a trained scribe?

By the end of the fourth century, Christian writers in the Latin-speaking West were becoming aware of the existence of other writings making equally impressive claims about authorship but lacking the canonical authority of the New Testament Gospels. "Despite what the ravings in a good many apocryphal books contend," Jerome writes in his *Commentary on Ezekiel*, Jesus "has left us no book of his teaching."[82] His contemporary Augustine had arrived at much the same conclusion. Augustine recognized that the absence of writings from Jesus himself gave ammunition to sceptics about the credibility of the testimony of the Gospels about him. But Augustine was certain that, had Jesus written something, the evangelists and the churches would have known about it.[83] The framing of the discussion in the language of "canonical versus apocryphal" did not bode well for the official reception of any letter claiming direct authorship by Jesus yet lacking the authority of those books described by Augustine as "acknowledged and regarded as of supreme authority in the Church."[84]

4. KEY PASSAGES FOR NEW TESTAMENT STUDIES AND THEIR SIGNIFICANCE

In the New Testament Gospels, Jesus sometimes commends the faith of outsiders and those who had not witnessed his works directly. When Thomas finally confesses Jesus's divinity in the Gospel of John, Jesus asks him, "Have you believed because you have seen me? Blessed are those who have not seen and yet have come to believe" (John 20:29 NRSV). In Luke's Gospel, a Samaritan, one of ten lepers whom Jesus had healed, is the only one to turn back to praise God and give thanks to him. "But the other nine, where are they?" Jesus asks. "Was none of them found to return and give praise to God except this foreigner?" (Luke 17:17–18 NRSV). Earlier in his Gospel, Luke recalls another "foreigner," a Roman centurion with a servant "whom he valued highly, and who was ill and close to death" (Luke 7:2 NRSV). Having heard of Jesus's healing ministry, the centurion sent to him elders of the Jews to petition Jesus to restore his servant to health. As he was approaching the centurion's home, Jesus received a second message from him. Feeling unworthy to receive Jesus into his home, the centurion asked Jesus to heal his servant from afar, by his word alone. Upon hearing this, Jesus marveled at the centurion's faith, surpassing anything he had encountered among his own people. "Not even in Israel," Jesus tells the crowds following him, "have I found such faith" (Luke 7:9 NRSV).

Like the centurion, Abgar was also a foreigner from a distant land whose belief in Jesus was grounded in his reputation as a healer. For Jesus, Abgar's confession of belief confirmed what had been foretold of him in Jewish Scriptures: "Those who have seen me will not believe on me, and . . . those who have not seen me will believe and live."[85] But

---

82. Jerome, *Comm. Ezech.* 13.44.29, as found in *Sancti Hieronymi presbyteri Commentariorum in Hiezechielem libri XIV*, ed. F. Glorie, CCSL 75 (Turnhout: Brepols, 1964), 668–69.

83. Cf. Augustine, *Cons.* 1.7.11, in *Sancti Aureli Augustini De consensu evangelistarum libri IV*, ed. F. Weihrich, CSEL 43 (Vienna: Tempsky, 1904).

84. Augustine, *Contra Faustum Manichaeum* 28.2, in *De utilitate credendi, De duabus animabus, Contra Fortunatum Manichaeum, Contra Adimantum, Contra epistulam fundamenti, Contra Faustum Manichaeum*, ed. J. Zycha, CSEL 25/1 (Vienna: Tempsky, 1891).

85. Eusebius, *Hist. eccl.* 1.13.10.

unlike the Roman centurion, whose servant Jesus heals virtually at the very moment of his request, Abgar is not immediately rewarded for his belief. This was because the source of Abgar's faith—namely, Jesus's miraculous healings—was but one feature of a larger mission, much of it still to be accomplished. After that, the disciple whom Jesus promised to send to the king would not only heal Abgar's suffering but would also "give life to you and those with you."[86]

The subsequent fulfillment of his promise unfolds in stages. When Thaddaeus arrives in Edessa, the king recognizes him as the disciple of whom Jesus had spoken. But he does so purely on the basis of the first half of Jesus's promise: to "send to you one of my disciples to heal your suffering."[87] Thaddaeus for his part fulfills this part of the mission as soon as he appears in Abgar's court. He reminds Abgar that his great faith was the reason why Jesus had sent him to the king. After Abgar reaffirms his faith to him, Thaddaeus then lays his hand on the king and heals his disease.

But the interaction between the two men does not end there. In response to the king's request for additional instruction about the "coming of Jesus, how it happened . . . and by what power he did these things of which I have heard," Thaddaeus asks Abgar to summon the entire citizenry on the following day. It is then that Abgar understands the meaning of the second half of Jesus's promise: "To give life to you and those with you." At this public assembly, Thaddaeus proclaims in full what he had described to Abgar the night before as the "word of life."[88] In the apostle's recitation of the essentials of the Christian kerygma, Jesus's healing ministry is now only one, and hardly the defining, part of a much broader mission. Through this culminating event in Thaddaeus's ministry, the king comes to learn that belief in Jesus was far more than a confession of his divinity based on his working of wonders.

Although Thaddaeus's proclamation of the gospel to the king and his subjects may appear at first to be a rather inconclusive ending to his ministry in Edessa, it makes a fitting climax to Eusebius's version of the Jesus/Abgar legend. This is a story of King Abgar's spiritual development, not a preamble to the founding of the Edessene church or to its recognition as the state church. In its long and complex development, elaborations of the Jesus/Abgar legend introduced new themes and traditions. And the meaning ascribed to the word "belief" was equally variable. But whether it was Abgar's developing understanding of the word, or Edessa's confidence in the binding power of Jesus's written promise to protect the city, the faith of Abgar and his subjects continued to excite the admiration of readers, well after Jesus's letter to the king had been condemned as apocryphal. Before offering his readers what appears to be a summary of Eusebius's account, Haimo (or Haymo) Auxerre (ninth century) declined to render a definitive judgment on its historical veracity. "I do not know," he writes, "whether the legend is apocryphal; only God knows." Even so, he considered the story worth retelling, if only for the depth of its piety and faith.[89]

5. BIBLIOGRAPHY

Bauer, Walter. *Orthodoxy and Heresy in Earliest Christianity*. 2nd ed. Philadelphia: Fortress, 1979.

Brock, Sebastian. "Eusebius and Syriac Christianity." Pages 212–34 in *Eusebius, Christianity and Judaism*. Edited by Harry A. Attridge and Gohei Hata. Detroit: Wayne State University Press, 1992.

Burkitt, Francis Crawford. *Early Eastern Christianity*. John Murray: London, 1904.

---

86. Eusebius, *Hist. eccl.* 1.13.9.

87. Eusebius, *Hist. eccl.* 1.13.10.

88. Eusebius, *Hist. eccl.* 1.13.15–21.

89. Haymo of Auxerre, *Enchiridion, de Christianarum rerum historia* (Haganoae: Per Ioannem Secerium, 1531), 2.4.

Corke-Webster, James. "A Man for the Times: Jesus and the Abgar Correspondence in Eusebius of Caesarea's Ecclesiastical History." *HTR* 110.4 (2017): 563–87.

Desreumaux, Alain, Andrew Palmer, and Robert Beylot. *Histoire du roi Abgar et de Jésus*. Paris: Brepols, 1993.

Dobschütz, Ernst von. "Der Briefwechsel zwischen Abgar und Jesus." *ZWT* 43 (1900): 422–86.

Drijvers, Hendrik Jan Willem. "The Abgar Legend." Pages 492–500 in *NTApoc*.

Illert, Martin. *Doctrina Addai; De imagine Edessena = Die Abgarlegende; Das Christusbild von Edessa*. Fontes Christiani 45. Turnhout: Brepols, 2007.

Mirkovic, Alexander. *Prelude to Constantine*. Arbeiten zur Religion und Geschichte des Urchristentums 15. Frankfurt am Main: Peter Lang, 2004.

Polanski, Tomasz. "Translation, Amplification, Paraphrase: Some Comments on the Syriac, Greek and Coptic Versions of the Abgar Letter." *Collectanea Christiana Orientalia* 13 (2016): 159–210.

Tixeront, L. Joseph. *Les origines de l'église d'Édesse et la légende d'Abgar: Étude critique suivie de deux textes orientaux inédits*. Paris: Maisonneuve et Ch. Leclerc, 1888.

CHAPTER 21

CORRESPONDENCE OF PAUL AND SENECA

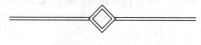

ANDREW GREGORY

1. INTRODUCTION

1.1 Overview

The correspondence of Paul and Seneca consists of fourteen very short pseudonymous letters, all written in Latin.[1] Eight are from Seneca to Paul. Six are from Paul to Seneca. They are now almost universally understood to be pseudepigraphical writings from late antiquity, but prior to the Renaissance they were accepted as authentic, first-century letters. Interestingly, they circulated with the works of Seneca, not with the letters of Paul, and are not found in any biblical manuscript. This suggests that although they were regarded as authentic they were not regarded as Scripture or as inspired.

Unlike Paul's Letter to the Laodiceans and 3 Corinthians, these letters do not address an apparent lacuna in the canonical collection of his writings (cf. Col 4:16), nor do they dovetail neatly with any of the letters attributed to him (cf. 1 and 2 Cor). They differ from other letters attributed to Paul both because of their subject matter and because they reflect a relationship between Paul and someone who was not also a follower of Christ. This makes it difficult to relate them directly to the letters of Paul found in the New Testament and underlines the particular importance of trying to approach this correspondence on its own terms and not to force it into an artificial dialogue with Paul's canonical correspondence.

It is possible, however, to note a number of passages in the New Testament that could have encouraged a Christian to entertain the idea that Paul and Seneca might have met. Luke records that Paul appeared before Gallio (Acts 18:12–16), who was Seneca's brother, and he notes that Paul enjoyed some degree of freedom when under house arrest in Rome (Acts 28:30–32), where he was guarded by a Roman soldier (v. 16). Paul also refers to a period of imprisonment during which he sends greetings from members of Caesar's household (Phil 4:22), and he claims that his circumstances were known to the whole Praetorian Guard (Phil 1:12–13). The Praetorian Guard was at one point commanded by Burrus, once a close ally at court of Seneca, so anyone who knew this and was familiar with Philippians could have connected Paul with Seneca via Burrus, just as anyone familiar with Acts and so inclined could have connected Paul with Seneca through Gallio. Of course, none of these texts gives any good historical reason to suggest that among those whom Paul met in Rome was anyone of the standing of Seneca, a tutor and adviser to Emperor Nero, and Paul

---

1. English translations include those in J. K. Elliott, *The Apocryphal New Testament*, rev. ed. (Oxford: Clarendon, 1999), and in *NTApoc* 2:46–53. The best critical edition of the Latin is found in Laura Bocciolini Palagi, *Il carteggio apocrifo di Seneca e san Paolo: introduzione, testo, commento* (Firenze: L. S. Olschki, 1978), and reprinted with a shorter introduction and commentary in idem, *Epistolario apocrifo di Seneca e san Paolo* (Firenze: Nardini, 1985).

appeared before Gallio as a prisoner, not as a friend. But it is not out of the question that knowledge of such texts could help to explain how someone came to compose—or cause someone else to compose—the correspondence of Seneca and Paul.

1.2 The Integrity and Development of the Collection

It seems likely that two letters, 11 and 14 (which need not have been written by the same author, or at the same time), were not part of the original collection. One reason for this, which points to both letters as interpolations, concerns differences between the subject matter of letters 11 and 14 and the subject matter of the rest of the correspondence. If we remove these two letters, the remainder work together as a short but unified corpus that presents Seneca and Paul as friends, and allows the former to make some constructive criticism of the latter's style, while praising the nobility of his ethical teaching. Letter 11 makes no contribution to this conceit, but concerns itself instead with the fire of Rome and the resulting persecution of Christians and Jews. Letter 14 could contribute to the collection's depiction of the relationship between Seneca and Paul, but it goes beyond the others in that it has Paul encourage Seneca to act as an advocate for the Christian faith. This may link it to the later tradition that claimed that Seneca was a Christian (a tradition that this letter may have encouraged), but it differentiates it from the rest of the present collection, in which Paul is much more restrained and in which the emphasis is on Seneca's regard for Paul rather than on any attempt by Paul to enlist Seneca in support of his work.

A second reason, which applies more clearly to letter 11 than to letter 14, is that a twelve-letter collection works perfectly well, and arguably much better, than the fourteen-letter collection that we have today. Letters 1 to 10 read as part of a coherent, ordered correspondence that would continue naturally from 10 to 12 and then to 13, were it not for the insertion of letter 11, which breaks the flow of the correspondence and appears out of place. It is not possible to argue that letter 14 interrupts the flow of the preceding correspondence, since it comes last. Yet its presence does mean that the correspondence does not come to an end with Seneca's praise of Paul's teaching and his wish that he would learn from him and comply with pure Latin style; this seems a much more fitting and satisfactory conclusion to the correspondence than does the content of letter 14.

Nevertheless, it does seem that someone went to some length to integrate letters 11 and 14 into the collection. This is because in most manuscripts some or all of letters 10 to 14 (unlike letters 1 to 9) end with a date. The inclusion of these dates implies that these letters are to be read as part of an ordered sequence (even if some of the dates are out of sequence with the ordering of the letters), and it is reasonable to infer that this was intended by the person who inserted them. The widespread presence of these dates in the manuscript tradition raises the question of whether or for how long the collection may have circulated with only twelve or thirteen letters,[2] if we may be confident that these dates were added at an early stage as a way of trying to integrate either letter 11 or letter 14 or both letters into the collection. The fact that modern scholars with ready access to reference books can identify the clash between the sequence of dates given at the end of certain letters and the literary ordering of the letters within the collection does not mean that this discrepancy would have been readily apparent to earlier readers, since the dates are given by reference to who was consul at the time. This was a common way for Roman authors to date their work, but not all readers, especially in a period long after the date when a text was said to have

---

2. On which see further below on p. 365 for one hypothesis that would allow all the letters to have been written in the same context, but by different authors.

been written, would be able immediately to identify the year that was meant or to know which consuls held office earlier or later than others. If the dates were entered to provide verisimilitude, or are an attempt to integrate further letters into an existing collection, it would not be surprising if a later author was not accurate in every aspect of the chronology that he seeks to establish.[3]

Turning from the internal evidence of the text of the letters to the evidence of the manuscripts in which they were transmitted, we find that most manuscripts (which usually also contain Seneca's *Letters to Lucilius*, together with Jerome's entry on Seneca in his *On Famous Men*) contain a fourteen-letter version of the correspondence.[4] It therefore seems likely that most of its readers encountered it in this form, at least from the tenth century onward, although the correspondence likely circulated in more than one version before the fourteen-letter collection prevailed. However, we cannot determine from this whether any of the letters were written at a later time or by a different author than the others. Nor, as we shall see, is the evidence of earlier authors who refer to these writings decisive on this point.

1.3 Date and External Attestation

Our earliest external evidence for these letters is Jerome if, as seems likely, his reference to letters of Seneca and Paul is to some or all of those known to us. This means that they must have been in circulation by 392–93 CE, when Jerome completed his *On Famous Men* (*De viris illustribus*), which contains an entry on Seneca. There he states that he included Seneca because of his correspondence with Paul (*Vir. ill.* 12.1). He makes no reference to Seneca as a convert to Christianity or as an ambassador for it, which may suggest that he was unaware of the content of letter 14 or of any tradition that Seneca had converted to Christianity. This could mean that the collection known to Jerome did not yet contain letter 14. But it could also mean that he knew of the collection only indirectly and was unfamiliar with some or most of its content. The only point in his entry on Seneca that appears to reflect any knowledge of the content of any of these letters is Jerome's note that Seneca (whom he identifies as the most influential person of his time) said that he wished to have the same position among his own people that Paul had among the Christians, which appears to be a reference to letter 12. Nothing that Jerome says sheds any light on whether he was aware of the content of letters 11 or 13. The same is true of Augustine, who refers in passing to Seneca as a contemporary of the apostles and notes that he wrote letters to Paul (*Letters* 153.14, usually dated 413–14 CE).

The fact that Lactantius refers to Seneca (*Inst.* 6.24.13–14, published in 325 CE) and suggests that Seneca would have become a true worshiper of God had he received Christian instruction, but is unaware of his correspondence with Paul, may provide a *terminus a quo* for the composition of the letters. However, this cannot be decisive, since it is possible that

---

3. It is possible, as Claude W. Barlow observes (*Epistolae Senecae ad Paulum et Pauli ad Senecam (quae vocantur)* [Horn, Austria: American Academy in Rome, 1938], 83), that the author would have taken the names of the consuls from one of the many chronologies that were in circulation in late antiquity.

4. A significant exception is the manuscript usually denoted by the siglum P, which may be dated to the tenth century. It was probably copied from a different exemplar than the other manuscripts, so it is the sole surviving witness to a second branch of the manuscript tradition. It omits letters 13 and 14 but includes 11, and has partial dates for 10, 11, and 12. It also presents some of the letters that it includes in a different order from that of the other manuscripts. P is clearly evidence for a twelve-letter version of the correspondence in the tenth century, but it may also suggest that there were twelve letters in the manuscript from which it was copied, which Barlow dates to the fifth or sixth century. For further information on the manuscripts, see Barlow, *Epistolae*, 8–69; and Bocciolini Palagi, *Il carteggio apocrifo di Seneca e san Paolo*, 61–66; idem, *Epistolario apocrifo di Seneca e san Paolo*, 45–47.

some or all of the letters were written at an earlier date, and that Lactantius was simply unaware of them.

Internal evidence, based on the Latin style of the letters, has also played an important part in attempts to date them. Renaissance humanists noted that the style of the letters was greatly inferior to the much more polished Latin of Seneca's genuine work and that the texts attributed to Paul were very different from his authentic writings[5] (although of course these letters are presented in a context that is very different from the setting of New Testament letters attributed to Paul). Their arguments were widely accepted as decisive and have been built on by twentieth-century scholars whose analysis of the style of the correspondence has led them to suggest a date in the fourth century.[6]

This has not stopped some scholars from claiming that the letters are genuine first-century texts,[7] although a fourth-century date remains the view of the overwhelming majority. One scholar who questions this consensus is Ilaria Ramelli, who proposes a theoretical date from the first century to the third, and favors before 180 CE.[8] She presents a number of arguments in favor of this earlier dating. One is based on her analysis of the use of earlier Pauline letters in the original version of the correspondence (i.e., excluding letters 11 and 14), in which she finds no knowledge of deutero-Pauline texts, but only those that are today widely recognized as having been written by Paul himself and that may have been included in the earliest collection of his letters. She argues that it is impossible to think that a fourth-century or even third-century forger could have differentiated between Pauline and deutero-Pauline writings in this way, for which reason she claims that her findings support an earlier date.[9] She also notes that in letter 7 Seneca refers only to letters of Paul that were likely written before the fictive setting of the correspondence (i.e., 58–62 CE, except for letter 11, which is dated 64 CE), and she argues that this, too, supports an early date for the letters that belonged to the original twelve-letter collection.[10] A third argument for a date in the middle or late second century is based on possible links between the correspondence and Marcionism.[11]

Ramelli's arguments about the use in the correspondence of genuine Pauline letters are intriguing, but they rest on a very slender evidential base, since the short length of the letters makes it difficult to reach any firm conclusions about which earlier letters they may or may not draw on. Even if they do draw only on undisputed Pauline letters, that could be because those undisputed writings were the most widely used of Paul's letters, not because the author of the apocryphal correspondence of Seneca and of Paul was using a collection

---

5. Harry M. Hine, "Seneca and Paul: The First Two Thousand Years," in *Paul and Seneca in Dialogue*, ed. J. Dodson and D. Briones, Ancient Philosophy and Religion 2 (Leiden: Brill, 2017), 32–33.

6. The most important was Edmond Liénard, whose demonstration of extensive similarities between this correspondence and the letters of Symmachus is widely regarded as decisive (Edmond Liénard, "Sur la correspondence apocryphe de Sénèque et de Saint-Paul," *RBPH* 11 (1932): 5–23.

7. For bibliography and discussion, see Hine, "Seneca and Paul," 33–34.

8. Ilaria L. E. Ramelli, "A Pseudepigraphon inside a Pseudepigraphon? The Seneca-Paul Correspondence and the Letters Added Afterwards," *JSP* 23.4 (2014): 288–89.

9. Ilaria L. E. Ramelli, "The Pseudepigraphical Correspondence between Seneca and Paul: A Reassessment," in *Paul and Pseudepigraphy*, ed. S. Porter and G. Fewster, Pauline Studies 8 (Leiden: Brill, 2013), 330–32; idem, "Pseudepigraphon inside a Pseudepigraphon," 268–86.

10. Ramelli, "Pseudepigraphical Correspondence," 332–33, cf. "Pseudepigraphon inside a Pseudepigraphon," 278–80.

11. Ilaria L. E. Ramelli, "Paul's Problematic Relation to Judaism in the Seneca-Paul Original Correspondence (Second Century CE)," in *The Early Reception of Paul the Second Temple Jew*, ed. I. Oliver and G. Boccaccini, LSTS 92 (London: Bloomsbury T&T Clark, 2019), 220–35.

of letters that originated within the lifetime of the apostle.[12] Further, we do not know for how long such early collections remained in circulation, even if we think it arguable or likely that they existed, so Ramelli's hypothesis is not only unnecessary but also precarious. Her observation that the letters of Paul that Seneca names in letter 7 were likely earlier than the fictive date of that letter is astute, but hardly probative of her case, and alleged affinities with Marcionism can often be explained in different ways.

1.4 Occasion, Genre, and Purpose

Everything that we may claim to know about these letters depends on what we may deduce from their text, since everything else is so uncertain. Two proposals for the specific context in which the correspondence was written, and for its literary genre, may be noted.

One setting that has been proposed is a school of rhetoric, in which a student was set the task of writing some letters in the character of a historical person: "An exercise on a fictitious subject assigned by the teacher."[13] The interest that the correspondence shows in rhetorical style rather than theological or philosophical ideas, together with the less than always elegant Latin in which it is written, as Barlow has noted, would support this hypothesis that the work was a rhetorical exercise.[14] Further, he observes, it is possible that two or three scholars, working in the same school, might have been set the same text, possibly in competition with each other. If so, "This hypothesis has the additional value that it will give a satisfactory explanation for the numerous inconsistencies in the letters, such as the varying attitude towards Nero, the slight emphasis upon Christianity except in 14, and the differences in vocabulary."[15]

A second proposal, which may not be incompatible with the suggestion that these letters were a school exercise, is that they should be considered an example of an epistolary novel (or, given their brevity, an epistolary novella or short story). Epistolary novels were collections of pseudepigraphic letters that used the epistolary form to narrate a series of events in the life of the historical figure whose life or accomplishments the letters are intended to celebrate. The best-known of these ancient epistolary novels is the *Letters of Chion*, but there are nine collections that survive, all in Greek, five of which may be attributed to philosophers or cover themes in popular philosophy.[16] Their subject matter is in some ways

---

12. This appears to be the reason why Ramelli thinks that the author was able to use only genuine letters by Paul, and not those later attributed to him. This may be seen most clearly in Ramelli, "Paul's Problematic Relation to Judaism," 232. See also idem, "Pseudepigraphon inside a Pseudepigraphon," 279–80, where she appeals to the work of David Trobisch in support of her claim that a collection of Paul's letters was already circulating in 58–62 CE.

13. Barlow, *Epistolae*, 91–92, quotation on 92. Basic compositional exercises, known as progymnasmata (Greek: προγυμνάσματα, Latin: *prae-exercitamina*) were a key component in a basic education in rhetoric. For brief discussions, with further bibliography, see Donald M. Russell, "Progymnasmata," in *The Oxford Classical Dictionary*, 4th ed., ed. S. Hornblower, A. Spawforth, and E. Eidinow (Oxford: Oxford University Press, 2012), 1216. At greater length, George A. Kennedy, *Progymnasmata: Greek Textbooks of Prose Composition and Rhetoric*, WGRW 10 (Leiden: Brill; Atlanta: SBL, 2003). See also Abraham J. Malherbe, "'Seneca' on Paul as Letter Writer," in *The Future of Early Christianity*, ed. B. Pearson, FS for H. Koester (Minneapolis: Fortress, 1991), 414–21, who notes the author's familiarity with epistolary conventions and possibly also with collections of published correspondence; see also Alfons Fürst, "Pseudepigraphie und Apostolizität im apokryphen Briefwechsel zwischen Seneca und Paulus," *JAC* 41 (1998): 88–94.

14. Barlow, *Epistolae*, 91.

15. Barlow, *Epistolae*, 92.

16. The five attributed to philosophers are as follows: *The Letters of Plato, The Letters of Socrates, The Letters of the Seven Wise Men,* and *The Letters of Chion*. For a discussion of all nine collections, with particular reference to *The Letters of Chion,* see Niklas Holzberg, "Novel-Like Works of Extended Prose Fiction II

comparable to the letters of Seneca and Paul, but there are also some differences. The other collections are not only longer, but they are written in Greek, and most of the letters in them are authored by the person whose life they illuminate, whereas the Latin letters of Seneca and Paul are split almost evenly between the two named authors. If the latter are to be understood as a Christian appropriation of the epistolary novel, it must be recognized that they are at most a very attenuated example of the genre. This raises the question of whether their form may be explained simply by the knowledge that the historical Seneca and the historical Paul each wrote letters (although not to each other!), without the need to appeal to any familiarity with the epistolary novel or the portrayal of philosophers in collections such as the *Letters of Chion*.

Such considerations suggest that there may be a stronger case for seeing these letters as the product of a school exercise rather than an attempt at an epistolary novel, yet the two proposals are not altogether incompatible, and may be combined in a way that gives more weight to one proposal but does not exclude the other; a student in a school may have been instructed to model his work on an epistolary novel. Readers who place significant weight on the unevenness of the Latin style may wish to emphasize the school setting over any claim to mastery of a particular genre. Readers who follow Richard Pervo in noting the degree of restraint shown by the author,[17] and see that restraint as a mark of a psychological sophistication that appears greater than the author's capacity to produce elegantly written Latin, may wish to foreground the claim that the correspondence may be considered an epistolary novella, granting that not everyone with good ideas can succeed in expressing them as well or as consistently as others might wish.

2. SUMMARY OF CONTENT

The letters are very brief; the combined length of all fourteen is less than that of Colossians, or less than 15 percent of the length of the Gospel according to Mark. We might think of most of them as more like postcards than as epistles. Twelve letters portray a friendly relationship between Seneca and Paul and reflect a number of epistolary conventions;[18] their authors exchange pleasantries in such a way as to convey the impression of a warm and established relationship between them. That relationship is based on mutual admiration or flattery, but it is of sufficient strength to allow Seneca to criticize Paul for his poor Latin style and to send him a book intended to help him to improve it. In one letter Seneca writes to Paul about the aftermath of the great fire of Rome, and in another Paul encourages Seneca to become a herald of Jesus Christ.

Three key themes may be noted. The first may be labeled social anxiety and literary self-consciousness; the two issues are inextricably linked, so it seems better to consider them as two aspects of the same concern and not as two separate themes. This concern helps to explain why an unknown author might have written the twelve letters that together comprised the original ordered collection with its developing portrayal of the relationship between Seneca and Paul. Two other themes may be noted, one from each of the two

---

E. Letters: Chion," in *The Novel in the Ancient World*, ed. G. Schmeling, Mnemosyne Supplements 159 (Leiden: Brill, 1996), 645–53. Other introductions to the genre include Niklas Holzberg, *The Ancient Novel: An Introduction* (London: Routledge, 1995), 19–21; Patricia Rosenmeyer, "The Epistolary Novel," in *Greek Fiction: The Greek Novel in Context*, ed. J. Morgan and R. Stoneman (London: Routledge, 1994), 146–65; and, at greater length, idem, *Ancient Epistolary Fictions: The Letter in Greek Literature* (Cambridge: Cambridge University Press, 2008).

17. Richard I. Pervo, *The Making of Paul: Constructions of the Apostle in Early Christianity* (Minneapolis: Fortress, 2010), 110, 112.

18. On which, see below in footnote 20.

letters that were probably added at a later date. The first of these is the apparently ongoing and deep-seated Christian fear of persecution, which is reflected in letter 11. The second, found in letter 14, is an interest in portraying Seneca as a potential ambassador for or possibly even as a convert to Christianity.

Questions about how to address all three of these themes are bound up inextricably with the major interpretive issues that these letters present, so in the following section I address each of these issues or themes at greater length. As will become clear, the major interpretive issues in these texts arise from the identification of their key themes, and views reached on the interpretive issues determine how we may best understand the significance of the three key themes.

3. INTERPRETIVE ISSUES
3.1 Social Anxiety and Literary Self-Consciousness

Unlike the genuine letters of Seneca and Paul respectively, the fictional correspondence between them tells us very little about the theological or philosophical or ethical beliefs of either author.[19] But they make no claim to do that, so it seems unfair to dismiss or to disregard them for that reason. If we focus instead on what they do convey, we find in the main a series of polite conventional greetings, shaped by epistolary conventions,[20] which reflect a respectful literary and philosophical friendship. Thus the letters show that Seneca not only accepted Paul as a member of his circle of friends but was willing to recognize the value of his ethical teaching, even if he questioned (and hoped to help improve) the quality of his written style. By doing this, the letters address the situation of Christians who were anxious about their place in Roman society and aware that educated people had criticized the writings that they regarded as Scripture and therefore as central to their faith. Tackling these issues appears to be the primary purpose of the letters. They demonstrate Seneca's admiration for and acceptance of Paul, and they give him an opportunity to offer some constructive criticism to Paul in order to help him better convey the ideas that Seneca considers worthy of praise and wider circulation. In this way they address the social anxiety and literary self-consciousness of Christians concerned that educated pagan Romans could not possibly take seriously the Christian faith because they could not take seriously some or all the Christian texts that convey the claims on which that faith is founded.

The correspondence assumes that Paul is resident in Rome and free to communicate with other people. This setting reflects the depiction of Paul at the end of the canonical Acts of the Apostles (28:16–31), and also that of the Martyrdom of Paul, the last section of the noncanonical Acts of Paul, although neither text makes any reference to Seneca.[21] Elements of local color are provided by Seneca's reference to meeting for leisurely discussions in the gardens of Sallust, a famous Roman pleasure garden. Seneca's reference to his companion Lucilius (to whom the genuine letters of the historical Seneca were dedicated) contributes to verisimilitude (letter 1; note also Paul's address to Seneca and Lucilius in letter 6), as does Seneca's address of one of his letters to Paul and to Theophilus (letter 7; cf. Luke 1:3; Acts

---

19. Thus Alfons Fürst observes, "The substance of the stylistically dreadful concoction is meager, having nothing to do with either the philosophy of Seneca or the theology of Paul" (Alfons Fürst, "Seneca and Paul, Correspondence between," in *Religion Past and Present*, vol. 11, ed. H. Betz et al. (Leiden: Brill, 2012), 614.

20. For a list and discussion of conventional features, see Malherbe, "'Seneca' on Paul," 418–21; and Fürst, "Pseudepigraphie und Apostolizität," 88–92.

21. A later Latin narrative, *The Martyrdom of Paul the Apostle Written by Linus*, expands on the Greek Martyrdom and includes an account of Seneca's admiration for Paul. Its author likely drew on the Letters of Seneca and Paul. For an introduction, text, and translation see David Eastman, *The Ancient Martyrdom Accounts of Peter and Paul*, WGRW 39 (Atlanta: SBL, 2015), 139–69.

1:1). A similar concern for vivid detail and verisimilitude (and also "human interest") likely explains why Seneca asks Paul whether he is concerned about encountering the displeasure of the empress (*Domina*), since he had withdrawn from his former religious allegiances and community and converted to another (letter 5: *quod a ritu et secta veteri recesseris et aliorsum converteris*). Seneca is evidently referring to Poppaea, Nero's second wife, who was said to have Jewish sympathies (Tacitus, *Ann.* 16.6, Josephus, *Ant.* 20.195), although both Tacitus and Josephus depict those sympathies as political rather than religious.

The start of the correspondence shows that Paul and Seneca are already well-known to each other: Seneca regrets that Paul had not been present at his conversation with Lucilius the preceding day, although he notes that some of the followers of Paul's teaching were there. Seneca's reference to the subject matter of that conversation as concerning "apocrypha" and other matters (*de apocrifis et aliis rebus*) is intriguing. In all likelihood "apocrypha" means something like confidences, private matters or secrets, and is intended to emphasize the level of intimacy between the two men and the bonds that their shared confidences create. If this is correct, and the secrets are confidences shared by friends, there is no need to appeal to any concept of a secret or hidden gnostic tradition, as found in some early Christian texts, which refer to secret or hidden knowledge available only to those with the ability to interpret a meaning hidden in a text, or to those who are members of a small and elite religious group who claim to possess esoteric knowledge that others do not. Nor is there any need to appeal to a similar conceptual background to explain the opening of letter 14, which refers to things revealed to only a few people (and is likely by a different author than the author of letter 1).[22]

An alternative, although less likely, explanation is that the word "apocrypha" is to be understood in its late and technical Christian sense of referring to books that were deemed either heretical or noncanonical or both. Examples of such use can be found in the fourth-century Greek authors Eusebius of Caesarea (*Hist. eccl.* 4.22.9) and Athanasius (*Ep. fest.* 39), and in the Latin letters of Jerome (*Epist.* 78.20; 96.20). However, it is not until the Gelasian Decree (written in Latin, perhaps in the late fifth or sixth century) that we find "apocrypha" clearly used to refer to all books that are not to be included in the biblical canon. This later use contrasts with its earlier use in Christian texts of the second and third centuries where the term "apocryphal" is used to mean "secret" or "hidden" and can be understood in a positive or negative sense. If the term "apocrypha" were used in this letter to refer to noncanonical texts, it would be a clumsy and accidental anachronism, since the term did not have that meaning in the first century. Yet it could have been included as a joke, the anachronism notwithstanding. Such a playful or ironic use of the term in a correspondence that its author knew could itself rightly be considered apocryphal might be found appealing to a postmodern reader, but a late antique text is an unlikely setting for a literary conceit that may depend on the sensibilities of a much later age.

In the correspondence that follows, Seneca expresses his admiration for Paul. He affirms him as a Roman citizen as Luke had presented him (letter 12; cf. Acts 16:37–38; 22:25–29; 23:27; 25:11–12), and he praises the quality of his moral insight and teaching (letters 1 and 7). As Pervo observes, "The author shows that Paul was accepted into the friendly circle of those who stood at the very apex of Roman imperial society."[23] Yet Seneca's admiration for Paul was not unqualified, and it is his criticism of Paul's Latin style that stands at the heart of the correspondence. Seven letters touch on the question of style, and the issue is

---

22. Others take a different view. In support of a "gnosticizing" interpretation, see Fürst, "Pseudepigraphie und Apostolizität," 36n1; 62–63nn204, 206, 208.

23. Pervo, *Making of Paul*, 110.

addressed most clearly in letters 7 and 13. In the former, Seneca praises Paul's ideas but wants to improve his Latin style, and even the emperor is said to have admired Paul's ideas, but to have asked how an uneducated person could have had them. Seneca's reply reflects or repeats what Christian apologists had written elsewhere in response to similar questions: that the gods are accustomed to speak through the mouths of simple people and not through those who pride themselves on their learning.[24] But even if Paul's teaching was good enough for Seneca and good enough for the emperor, that was not the end of the matter. So in letter 13, his last to Paul, and possibly the last of the correspondence in its original form, Seneca encourages Paul to work on his style:

> *Allegorice et aenegmatice multa a te usquequaque [opera] colliguntur et ideo rerum tanta vis et muneris tibi tributa non ornamento verborum, sed cultu quodam decoranda est. Nec vereare, quod saepius dixisse retineo, multos qui talia adfectent sensus corrumpere, rerum virtutes evirare. Certum mihi velim concedas latinati morem gerere, honestis vocibus et speciem adhibere, ut generosi muneris concessio digne a te possit expediri. Bene vale. Data pridie Non. Iul. Lu<r>cone et Sabino consulibus.*[25]

On every occasion you bring together many writings in an allegorical and enigmatic way, and for that reason you must adorn not with verbal embellishment but with a measure of refinement that great power which has been bestowed upon you and upon your office. And do not be afraid, as I remember that I have very often said, that many who affect such things corrupt the thought and emasculate the force of their subject-matter. Of course I would like you to agree to adopt a true Latin style, giving a good impression through a carefully considered choice of words, so that you may make fitting use of the great office that has been entrusted to you. Go well. Written 6 July, in the consulship of Lurco and of Sabinus.[26]

By having Seneca address the problem, the author acknowledges that Paul's letters, and perhaps also other New Testament texts, did not live up to the literary standards of the Roman elite. And in addressing the point, he seeks to neutralize its force, for he suggests that their poor style was no reason to reject either those writings or the noble teaching that they contained. Few educated Romans who were not already Christians or sympathetic to Christian faith may have read or heard these letters for themselves. But apologetic writings are often directed more at insiders than outsiders to Christian faith, and these letters address and answer a difficulty that many Christians may have felt for themselves, and for which they would have been grateful for an encouraging answer. If Paul's letters were good enough for Seneca,[27] and good even for an emperor, they could be good enough for them as well, even if their Latin left much to be desired.

3.2 Nero and the Fear of Persecution: Letter 11

As noted above, there is good reason to believe that letter 11 is an interpolation, since it interrupts the flow of the correspondence in which it is inserted and because its style is

---

24. So Origen, *Cels.* 1.62; Lactantius, *Inst.* 6.21; Arnobius of Sicca, *The Case Against the Pagans* 1.58. Note also the discussion of the issue in Graeme W. Clarke's introduction in his translation of *The Octavius of Marcus Felix*, Ancient Christian Writers 39 (New York: Paulist, 1974), 18–22, for which reference I am indebted to Malherbe, "'Seneca' on Paul," 414n3.

25. Text from Bocciolini Palagi, *Il carteggio apocrifo di Seneca e san Paolo*, 73–74.

26. Translation mine.

27. Pervo, *Making of Paul*, 115.

different from that of the other letters. Two other factors are incongruous. The first is that the letter is dated March 64 CE, but it refers to the great fire of Rome that took place in July 64 CE. This is the only place in the correspondence that we can identify as a straight-forward mistake, although there are various points in different letters that stretch our credulity. Perhaps the most significant of these is the way in which this letter has Seneca refer obliquely to Emperor Nero, who is presumably the person to whom he refers not by name but as "that villain" or "that layabout" (*Grassator iste*), and whom he appears to blame for the fire (although what he is saying is somewhat unclear, which also distinguishes this letter from others in the collection). Seneca had been tutor to Nero, and was his adviser and confidant from 54 to early 62 CE. He was out of favor from 62, and committed suicide in 65 at the emperor's behest, yet it is all but inconceivable that he would ever have written so disparagingly of Nero in this clumsy and open way.[28]

Rather, the letter reflects the virulent disdain with which Nero was remembered by the Roman elite as well as by Christians. Both Tacitus and Suetonius, writing in the early second century, portray (or perhaps caricature) him as a villainous tyrant, but they appear to build on earlier traditions. Although he had initially been considered an excellent ruler, Nero lost the support of the Roman elite after the great fire of Rome, from which he profited greatly, sometimes at their expense, and shortly before his death the Roman Senate declared him a public enemy. The play *Octavia*, sometimes attributed to Seneca, is most likely a post-Neronian text that may be taken as evidence for how Nero was viewed not long after his death.[29] It, too, blames him for the great fire of Rome; compared to its invective the criticism voiced in letter 11 is remarkably mild.

In addition to reflecting elite Roman disdain for Nero (which may have helped late antique pagan Romans who read the correspondence to relate to Christians, since on this point they were agreed), the letter is also a valuable witness to early Christian perceptions of persecution, and perhaps to the importance of Nero in Christian collective memory of that persecution. Whether the letter was written in the fourth century or at a later date, its author will almost certainly have been aware of the systematic and targeted (albeit short-lived) per-secution of Christians by Valerian and Diocletian, and also the persecution of Christians under Decius. He may also have been aware of a range of Christian texts that either recount the martyrdoms of apostles and other Christians, or that otherwise reflected (and possibly heightened and perpetuated) Christian perceptions that they were a persecuted group.

Its author's choice to write about Nero and his persecution of Christians as a tactic to divert from himself any blame for the great fire of Rome may perhaps be taken as a coded way of referring to or standing for any or all Roman persecution of the Christians, and Seneca's reference to others whose rule had to be endured might be taken to support this reading of the letter. However, it is not the only way. Since Seneca knew Nero, and since early tradition blamed Nero for the martyrdom of Paul, it may be only natural that the author of the letter would refer to Nero in any discussion of Christian persecution at the hands of the Roman authorities, for it adds some color and vivid human interest

---

28. The historical Seneca was not blind to the faults of Nero, nor unprepared to address them, but he did so in a much more sophisticated way than did the author of this pseudonymous letter. On Seneca's relationship to Nero, see Susanna Braund, ed., *Seneca: De Clementia* (Oxford: Oxford University Press, 2009), 2–4. On the extent of his criticism of the emperor, see Victoria Rimell, "Seneca and Neronian Rome: In the Mirror of Time," in *The Cambridge Companion to Seneca*, ed. S. Bartsch and A. Schiesaro (Cambridge: Cambridge University Press, 2015), 131–32.

29. See Gareth Williams, "Nero, Seneca and Stoicism in the Octavia" in *Reflections of Nero: Culture, History and Representation*, ed. J. Elsner and J. Masters (London: Duckworth, 1994), 178–91, with comments about dating on 191.

to the correspondence. Yet the author of the letter did not have to refer to persecution at all, so the fact that he did may point to the enormous shadow that the fear of persecution still cast, even in the period after Constantine, and to the particular fear associated with Christian traditions about Nero. Christians were presumably aware from an early date of the execution of some of their number, as recorded by Tacitus.[30] Tertullian refers by name to Nero as a persecutor (*Apol.* 5.3), and the Martyrdom of Paul associates him explicitly with the death of Paul, but his involvement may also be implied obliquely in earlier references to Paul's death. These include 1 Clement, a Christian text written in Greek from Rome and usually dated to the late first or early second century, in which Paul was said to have died "having borne witness before the rulers" (1 Clem. 5.7), and other texts that place Paul's death in Rome.

The letter begins with Seneca expressing his regret that Christians are repeatedly punished despite being innocent, and that the non-Christian populace think them guilty and responsible for every misfortune that befalls them. He addresses these innocent Christians as "you," using the second person and so distinguishing himself from them, but when he echoes Stoic sentiment and refers to the necessity of patient endurance until death brings release, he writes in the second-person plural: "Let us endure it calmly." This may be a clumsy transition from the second person to the first because the author of this letter is eager to identify Seneca as a Christian. It seems more likely, however, that he wishes to say that Christians and non-Christians alike should respond to adversity in a similar way, and that this is the point of listing a series of rulers whom he says others had to endure.

The main concern of the letter is not how to endure adversity, understood in generic terms, but the persecution of Christians, and Seneca sounds remarkably like a Christian apologist. His reference to the whole people (*vulgus*) finding the Christians cruel and liable to guilt and responsible for every misfortune in the city may be compared with Tacitus's account of the Christians as a people whom the populace hated on account of their abominations. But Seneca's statement that the populace blamed every misfortune in the city on the Christians is closer to Tertullian's claim in his *Apology* 40.2 that Christians were blamed if the Tiber flooded or if the Nile did not, or if there was a drought or an earthquake or famine or plague. Whether the author of this letter was writing an exercise in school or setting out to produce an epistolary novella, it seems likely that he drew on earlier traditions about the fire and its consequences for the Christians in Rome.

Seneca's reference to both Christians and Jews being punished for the fire is of interest. It is in some tension with other references in the correspondence that seem to imply knowledge of tension between Christians and Jews, but they are almost certainly the work of another author. This leaves open the possibility that the claim that both Christians and Jews were punished originates with the author of this letter. We cannot exclude the possibility that he was drawing on an otherwise unknown source, which may also have been the source for his statement about the precise extent of the fire, but it is more likely that he has added these details in order to provide some color to his narrative.

3.3 Seneca as One of Us: Letter 14

Although most likely an interpolation, letter 14 is of interest because it is the only letter in the collection in which Paul is portrayed as seeking to share his faith with Seneca and

---

30. The historical basis of Tacitus's report of Nero's execution of Christians has recently been questioned, but most scholars continue to believe that it remains a credible account and not a Christian invention that Tacitus repeated.

as asking Seneca to speak or to act as a follower of Jesus (*novum auctorem Christi Iesu*). This explicit reference to Christian faith and Paul's request to Seneca jars with the rest of the correspondence, in which Seneca is the senior partner and instructs or advises Paul on the need to improve his written Latin style. This incongruity between this letter and those that precede it supports the likelihood that letter 14 was not originally part of the correspondence, but it is unclear when it may have been added.[31]

Paul's appeal to Seneca to speak or to act as a follower of Jesus serves also to distance the letter from other late antique references to Seneca, none of which suggests that he was a Christian or sympathetic to Christianity. Famously, Tertullian referred to Seneca as *saepe noster* (*De anima* 21), which may be translated as "often ours" or even "often on our side." However, by this he meant that Seneca often offered arguments that were useful and congenial to Christians, not that Seneca was a Christian, and other Christian apologists also drew on Seneca's critique of what he saw as false or superstitious pagan religious practices.[32]

Lactantius, as noted above, thought that Seneca would have been a true worshiper of God had he received Christian instruction, but this underlines the fact that he makes no suggestion that Seneca was a Christian. Neither, as we have seen, did Jerome. The same is true of Augustine, who only once refers to the correspondence (*Letters* 153.14) and who notes elsewhere that Seneca neither praised nor criticized the Christians (*Civ.* 6.11). This clearly suggests that Augustine assumed that Seneca may have been aware of followers of Jesus, but Augustine speculates that, had he known of them, his inclination would have made him more likely to criticize than to endorse their views. The author of the (fifth or sixth century?) Martyrdom of Paul, ascribed to Linus, appears to be familiar with at least the existence of the correspondence, for he refers to a friendship and letters between Paul and an unnamed teacher of the emperor and notes that the unnamed tutor saw "divine knowledge" (*divinam scientiam*) in Paul (Pseudo-Linus, *Martyrdom of Paul* 1). However, he does not suggest that this teacher was either a Christian or an advocate of the Christian faith, so if he were aware of letter 14 he makes no discernible reference to it.

It is not in fact until the fourteenth century that the legend of Seneca's conversion to Christianity is first attested, when Giovanni Colona argued for it in his *On Famous Men*, but the claim never gained universal acceptance.[33] Given that letter 14 was well-established in the manuscript tradition before the legend is recorded, it seems likely that the former contributed to the latter, but this tells us nothing about when letter 14 was composed or how its earliest readers responded to the apparent failure of Paul's appeal. What the legend shows, however, is that the attraction of co-opting a prominent Roman author as a convert or sympathizer to Christianity was as attractive to at least some Renaissance humanists and other Christians as it had been to whoever composed letter 14.

4. KEY PASSAGES FOR NEW TESTAMENT AND EARLY CHRISTIAN STUDIES AND THEIR SIGNIFICANCE

The letters of Seneca and Paul have no direct points of contact with any of the texts found in the New Testament, although they feature Paul as a letter writer, and they reflect the circumstances of his house arrest in Rome as portrayed in the Acts of the Apostles.

This does not mean, however, that they are of no use or no interest to readers whose

---

31. See above, in sec. 1.2.
32. See Chiara Torre, "Seneca and the Christian Tradition," in Bartsch and Schiesaro, *Cambridge Companion to Seneca*, 269–70.
33. On the medieval evidence, and for further bibliography, see Hine, "Seneca and Paul," 30–31.

primary interest is in the early Christian writings that came to be included in the New Testament. When understood on their own terms, these letters cast valuable light on the Latin-speaking western part of the late antique Roman world as it was experienced by Christians who were conscious of the inelegant style and lack of literary sophistication of their sacred books, and who wanted to be able to present and commend those books in a positive way. They wanted to do this first for themselves, yet possibly also for others who did not share their faith and may have been aware of criticism of their sacred books. The Roman author Seneca is shown to admire Paul's teaching, as also does Emperor Nero, and Seneca is said to have read and taken seriously the letters of Paul. This conceit is used in an attempt to assure Christian readers that they need not be embarrassed by the literary quality of their Scriptures; books that were worth the attention of Seneca are surely worth the attention of other educated people, too, even if their Latin style requires improvement. Thus, in what was likely its original twelve-letter form, the correspondence offers comfort to Christians experiencing social anxiety and literary self-consciousness as a result of pagan criticism of their faith and the Scripture in which its central claims are made. It indicates how some or all of the New Testament books may have been received at a particular point in the corpus's translation and transmission, even if it sheds no direct light on the social or historical setting in which it may have been written.

Two other letters, likely added later, also shed light on Christian concerns in late antiquity. In one we see reflected an ongoing discourse about Christian fears of persecution, even after the threat had apparently receded. In the other we find what appears to be the desire that Christian faith be embraced and expounded by people of the standing in society that Seneca had once enjoyed before he, like Paul, fell afoul of Emperor Nero.

If the correspondence also shows how an ancient author could develop a narrative based on only a small number of details in earlier texts, it may raise questions about whether other early Christian authors may have done the same.

5. BIBLIOGRAPHY

Barlow, Claude W. *Epistolae Senecae ad Paulum et Pauli ad Senecam (quae vocantur)*. Horn, Austria: American Academy in Rome, 1938.

Bocciolini Palagi, Laura. *Il carteggio apocrifo di Seneca e san Paolo: introduzione, testo, commento*. Firenze: L. S. Olschki, 1978.

Bonar, Chance. "Epistles of Paul and Seneca." e-Clavis: Christian Apocrypha. www.nasscal.com/e-clavis -christian-apocrypha/epistles-of-paul-and-seneca/.

Elliott, J. K. *The Apocryphal New Testament*. Rev. ed. Oxford: Clarendon, 1999.

Hine, Harry M. "Seneca and Paul: The First Two Thousand Years." Pages 22–48 in *Paul and Seneca in Dialogue*. Edited by Joseph R. Dodson and David E. Briones. Ancient Philosophy and Religion 2. Leiden: Brill, 2017.

Malherbe, Abraham J. "'Seneca' on Paul as Letter Writer." Pages 414–21 in *The Future of Early Christianity*. Edited by Birger A. Pearson. FS for H. Koester. Minneapolis: Fortress, 1991.

Pervo, Richard I. *The Making of Paul: Constructions of the Apostle in Early Christianity*. Minneapolis: Fortress, 2010.

Ramelli, Ilaria L. E. "The Pseudepigraphical Correspondence between Seneca and Paul: A Reassessment." Pages 319–36 in *Paul and Pseudepigraphy*. Edited by Stanley E. Porter and Gregory P. Fewster. Pauline Studies 8. Leiden: Brill, 2013.

———. "A Pseudepigraphon inside a Pseudepigraphon? The Seneca-Paul Correspondence and the Letters Added Afterwards." *JSP* 23.4 (2014): 259–89.

Römer, Cornelia. "The Correspondence between Seneca and Paul." *NTApoc* 2:46–53.

Rosenmeyer, Patricia. "The Epistolary Novel." Pages 146–65 in *Greek Fiction: The Greek Novel in Context*. Edited by J. R. Morgan and Richard Stoneman. London: Routledge, 1994.

Russell, Donald M. "Progymnasmata." Page 1216 in *The Oxford Classical Dictionary*. 4th ed. Edited by S. Hornblower, A. Spawforth, and E. Eidinow. Oxford: Oxford University Press, 2012.

CHAPTER 22

THE APOCRYPHAL EPISTLE TO THE LAODICEANS

PHILIP L. TITE

1. INTRODUCTION

The apocryphal Epistle to the Laodiceans is a short letter written in the name of Paul to the Christian congregation in Laodicea, a city in the Lycus Valley located in Phrygia of Asia Minor. Although the letter addresses the Laodicean Christians, there is no evidence to support any historical connection between this apocryphal letter and the city of Laodicea. This pseudonymous letter was likely written in the second or third century, either in Latin or Greek, and survives in approximately one hundred manuscripts in Latin as well as several vernacular translations in the medieval West. In the Western Church, the Epistle to the Laodiceans enjoyed popularity as an authentic Pauline letter up to the Protestant Reformation and the Council of Trent, whereas in the Eastern Church it was rejected early on as a forgery. The Epistle to the Laodiceans is dependent on Philippians, while also demonstrating knowledge of Galatians and Colossians.

The second century witnessed a widespread fascination with the apostle Paul, resulting in not only the collecting, editing, and circulation of his letters from the 50s and 60s CE but also the production of several narratives sharing the exploits of this famed apostle—including not only the canonical Acts but several apocryphal Acts and narrative legends, notably the Acts of Paul (incorporating the Martyrdom of Paul and the Acts of Paul and Thecla) and several independent apocalypses of Paul. A Prayer of the Apostle Paul emerged by the end of the second century, likely from the rich theological and ritualized context of Valentinian Christianity. The first New Testament canon that arose from Marcionite circles centered on Paul (i.e., edited or variant renditions of the Gospel of Luke and of several Pauline letters; cf. Irenaeus, *Haer.* 1.27.2), and by the 180s Irenaeus recognized the core canon to include the four canonical Gospels and the letters of Paul. To speak of second-century "Christianities" is to speak of competing efforts at theologizing Paul, notably within a rich literary production in the Pauline tradition.[1]

During this period of energetic fascination with Paul, a rich epistolary tradition arose. By the turn of the century, his authentic letters were being edited, merged together to form composite letters, or interpolated to fit late first and early second-century theological and

---

1. On the second-century reception of Paul, see Michael F. Bird and Joseph R. Dodson, eds., *Paul in the Second Century*, LNTS 412 (London: Continuum, 2011); Calvin J. Roetzel, "Paul in the Second Century," in *The Cambridge Companion to Paul*, ed. J. D. G. Dunn (Cambridge: Cambridge University Press, 2003), 227–41; Judith M. Lieu, "The Battle for Paul in the Second Century," *ITQ* 75.1 (2010): 3–14; and William Arnal, "The Collection and Synthesis of 'Tradition' and the Second-Century Invention of Christianity," *MTSR* 23 (2011): 193–215.

social interests. Scholarship continues to debate how extensive such redactional activity impacted the canonical form of these letters. Beyond reworking Paul's epistolary production into new products, other second-century Christians created fictional letters to embellish and adjust Paul's life and teaching to advance theological, social, and ritual concerns debated from the second century onward. Some of these pseudonymous letters found their way into the nascent New Testament canon, and scholars continue to debate the authenticity of several of these letters (Colossians, 2 Thessalonians, Ephesians, and the Pastoral Epistles). However, there were several letters produced in early Christians circles that remain outside the modern New Testament canon even though prized by many Christians for centuries and perhaps viewed as authentic Scriptures by some. Scholars are only now beginning to focus on these so-called apocryphal letters as well as Pauline agrapha, along with later apocryphal Acts in the Pauline tradition. Of the apocryphal letters of Paul, there are possibly seven such letters or letter collections, with two of them discussed together below:

1. **3 Corinthians**. These are letters to and from Paul, embedded in the Acts of Paul with a narrative framework. This Corinthian correspondence may have circulated as an independent Pauline tradition later incorporated into the aggregate Acts of Paul by the end of the second century. These letters portray Paul as the defender of orthodoxy, especially in conjunction with the New Testament Gospels, against heresy or false teachers.

2. **The Correspondence of Paul and Seneca**. This work is a series of short letters between Paul and the famed first-century philosopher Seneca; though a much later production, likely emerging in the fourth century, this collection illustrates an attempt to portray Paul as a philosophical figure and thus an embodiment of both *Romanitas* and *Christianitas*.

3. References in the Muratorian Canon to Paul's **Letter to the Alexandrians** and **Letter to the Laodiceans**. These are both related to the Marcionite Church. The Letter to the Alexandrians is no longer extant, and the Letter to the Laodiceans is likely not the Latin letter by similar name discussed in the present chapter. Based on the brief mention in the Muratorian Canon, these letters likely advanced Marcionite teaching in the name of Paul.[2]

4. Perhaps a **Letter to the Macedonians**. It is mentioned in Clement of Alexandria, *Protrepticus* 9, though this could be an alternative name for the canonical letter to the Philippians.

5. Possibly the (no longer extant) **Apocryphal Pauline Letter by Themiso**. In Eusebius's *Ecclesiastical History* 5.18.5 we find a mention of a "catholic letter" by Themiso written in imitation of "the apostle." The "imitation" may indicate that this is a letter written in Paul's name or that Themiso modeled a letter on the Pauline structure, but we know nothing further about this letter.[3]

6. Finally, there is the Latin **Epistle to the Laodiceans**. This has survived not only in several Latin manuscripts (the most important being Codex Fuldensis dated to 546 CE as well as referenced in the Vulgate) but also in various medieval translations from Western Europe. This epistle is the subject of the present chapter.

---

2. Theodore Zahn, *Geschichte des Neutestamentlichen Kanons*, vol. 3 (Erlangen: Deichert, 1890), 586–92, attempted to reconstruct the Letter to the Alexandrians from an eight-century lectionary, but more likely this apocryphal letter is simply lost.

3. See the discussion of the Apocryphal Pauline Letter by Themiso in Geoffrey S. Smith, *Guilt by Association: Heresy Catalogues in Early Christianity* (Oxford: Oxford University Press, 2015), 24–25.

1.1 Search for Laodiceans

The Epistle to the Laodiceans is one of the most neglected of the apocryphal Pauline works, often treated in scholarship as a poorly constructed fabrication that simply lifts phrases from Paul's authentic letters to construct a random set of verses with no purpose beyond filling the gap of the missing letter mentioned in Colossians 4:16. At the close of Colossians, Paul (or the person writing in Paul's name) instructs the Church at Colossae: "And when this letter has been read among you, have it read also in the church of the Laodiceans; and see that you read also the letter from Laodicea" (NRSV).

A lost "letter from Laodicea" has surprised exegetes (both ancient and modern). How is it possible that an authentic letter from Paul would not have been preserved?[4] There have been several attempts to explain this missing Laodicean letter from the Pauline corpus. One option is to claim that Paul did not write a letter to the Laodiceans, but rather that he is recommending a letter that was produced by the Laodicean community. This reading takes the preposition *ek* ("from") as indicating authorial source (i.e., written *by* the Laodiceans, likely *to* Paul either as prompting Paul's letter or as a response to Paul's letter to Colossae) rather than as indicating the transmission of an otherwise unknown letter written *by* Paul *to* Laodicea (i.e., *ek* could be translated as "via Laodicea," marking a letter transmitted either to Colossae via Laodicea or from Laodicea to Colossae via Paul). If the letter from Laodicea was not written by Paul, then there is no lost Pauline letter, just a lost letter *to* Paul (such as we have in the Corinthian correspondence). It has also been suggested that this letter was written not by Paul but by a colleague such as Epaphras.[5] Another option is to claim that the letter to the Laodiceans should be identified with another extant letter that can be attributed to Paul. Several candidates have been suggested, including Philemon and Hebrews, but the most popular candidate is Ephesians.[6] It is well-known that the *adscriptio* in Ephesians 1:1 ("the saints who are *in Ephesus*," NRSV) is not original to the letter. This lacuna opens the door for identifying alternative recipients or even treating Ephesians as a circular letter written to various communities.[7] As early as the second century, Marcion identified Laodiceans as Ephesians (Tertullian, *Marc.* 5.17.1). A third option is to claim that the letter to the Laodiceans is not lost but has been incorporated into a composite letter. Marie-Émile Boismard argues that canonical Colossians is a composite

---

4. There are indications that Paul's epistolary output has not been fully preserved. Letters of Paul, no longer extant, are mentioned in 1 Cor 5:9 and 2 Cor 2:4. Similar to Ep. Lao., the search for these "lost" Pauline letters has been driven by the assumption that a letter from Paul would have been preserved. Thus, various attempts have been made to find these letters. Paul's missing "painful letter" in 2 Cor 2:4, for instance, has been resolved by means of partition hypothesis of 2 Corinthians, notably identifying chs. 10 to 13 as this letter. While identifying 2 Cor. 10–13 as a separate letter, the mention of a prior letter in 1 Corinthians is likely in reference to a now lost letter arising from the rich correspondence between Paul and his community in Corinth.

5. See the discussion on these exegetical possibilities, with the suggestion of Epaphras as author of the lost letter mentioned in Col 4:16, in Charles P. Anderson, "Who Wrote 'The Epistle from Laodicea'?," *JBL* 85.4 (1966): 436–40. Cf. Anderson, "Epistle to the Laodiceans," *ABD* 4:231–33. See also the geographic explanation for a lost Pauline letter to or from Laodicea in Lucetta Mowry, "The Early Circulation of Paul's Letters," *JBL* 63 (1944): 84n27.

6. On identifying Hebrews as Laodiceans, see Leon Hermann, "L'Épitre aux Laodicéens (Laodicéens et l'apologie aux Hébreux)," *Cahiers du Cercle Ernest Renan* 58.2 (1968): 1–16, and in identifying Philemon with Laodiceans see John Knox, *Philemon Among the Letters of Paul: A New View of Its Place and Importance*, rev. ed. (New York: Abingdon, 1959), 38–47; Knox, *Marcion and the New Testament: An Essay in the Early History of the Canon* (Chicago: University of Chicago Press, 1942), 40–41; cf. E. J. Goodspeed, *New Solutions of New Testament Problems* (Chicago: University of Chicago Press, 1935), 18; idem, *The Meaning of Ephesians* (Chicago: University of Chicago Press, 1937), 7.

7. See also Richard Batey, "The Destination of Ephesians," *JBL* 82.1 (1963): 101, who argued that Ephesians was a circular letter to churches in Asia Minor, thereby explaining why Marcion identified it with Laodiceans (cf. John Rutherford, "St. Paul's Epistle to the Laodiceans," *ExpT* 19.7 [1908]: 311–14).

letter merging both Laodiceans and Colossians into one letter.[8] Despite all these efforts, it seems most likely that Colossians 4:16 refers to a lost letter written either by Paul or by the Laodicean community.

In antiquity, early Christians also struggled with these questions regarding a lost letter to or from the Laodiceans. Marcion, of course, identified Ephesians as the letter to the Laodiceans. Other Christians creatively produced pseudonymous works to fill in the gap of Colossians 4:16. We have evidence of at least two such efforts. The Muratorian Canon (lines 63–67) mentions that "there is current also (an epistle) to the Laodiceans, another to the Alexandrians, forged in Paul's name for the sect of Marcion, and several others, which cannot be received in the catholic Church; for it will not do to mix gall with honey."[9] This mention of Laodiceans is problematic given the uncertainty in dating the Muratorian Canon.[10] If taken as produced about 200 CE, then it likely connects the two pseudo-Pauline letters to the Marcionite church. However, if dated to the fourth century or later, possibly as late as the eighth or ninth century, as a poor Latin translation of an original Greek text, then the fragment is problematic for two reasons. First, does it accurately present and describe a now lost letter that circulated several centuries earlier? In other words, how far can we trust the Muratorian Canon as a fourth- or an eighth-century fragment in reconstructing second-century Christianity? Second, does the mention of "the sect of Marcion" refer to the Marcionite church that flourished in the second century, or is the mention of Marcion an eponymous device referring to "heresy" in general? Long after the Marcionite and Valentinian movements died out, both heresiarchs were evoked to taint opponents and movements as heretical regardless of any historical or theological connection with these earlier movements. Thus, the Muratorian Canon may be useless in connecting Laodiceans to the Marcionites. However, if the Muratorian Canon is dated to the beginning of the third century, then it may indeed refer to two pseudo-Pauline letters in connection with Marcion, one to the Laodiceans and one to the Alexandrians. With the earlier date, we may have an instance of Colossians 4:16 serving to inspire a fictional Pauline letter to the Laodiceans. Such a letter, therefore, would need to be included in our reconstruction of the battle over Paul within the Marcionite controversy.

The other known effort to "fill the gap" of Colossians 4:16 is the extant Latin Epistle to the Laodiceans. At some point in the second or third century, an anonymous individual composed a short letter in the name of Paul directed at the church in Laodicea, largely drawing on material from Galatians, Colossians, and especially Philippians. Awareness of Colossians 4:16 is obvious given Epistle to the Laodiceans 18, which inverts the directions in Colossians: "And see that this letter is read to the Colossians and that of the Colossians among you."[11] J. B. Lightfoot argued that our copy of the Epistle to the Laodiceans was translated from a now lost Greek original (and he offers a retroversion, translating the Latin

---

8. Marie-Émile Boismard, "Paul's Letter to the Laodiceans," in *The Pauline Canon*, ed. S. Porter, Pauline Studies 1 (Leiden: Brill, 2004), 45–57; idem, *La Letter de Saint Paul aux Laodicéens: Retrouvée et commentée*, Cahier de la Revue Biblique 42 (Paris: J. Gabalda, 1999).

9. Wilhelm Schneemelcher, "The Canon Muratori," *NTApoc* 1:36.

10. A helpful overview of the interpretative problems surrounding the Muratorian Canon is offered by Edmon L. Gallagher and John D. Meade, *The Biblical Canon Lists from Early Christianity: Texts and Analysis* (Oxford: Oxford University Press, 2017), 175–83 (with Latin text and English translation on pp. 178–82). For further discussion, with a suggested eighth or ninth century dating, dating the fragment to the time when the codex was produced, see Clare K. Rothschild, "The Muratorian Fragment as Roman Fake," *NovT* 60 (2018): 55–82. Note also the counter to Rothschild's late dating by Christophe Guignard, "The Muratorian Fragment as a Late Antique Fake? A Response to C. K. Rothschild," *Revue des Sciences Religieuses* 93.1–2 (2019): 73–90.

11. All translations of Ep. Lao. are mine.

back to the Greek).[12] Although many scholars have accepted Lightfoot's hypothesis of an underlying Greek letter, there is no manuscript evidence of a Greek original, and furthermore any awkward constructions in the Latin need not point to a translation of a Greek version of the Epistle to the Laodiceans.[13] Rather, such grammatical difficulties could be explained as resulting from direct translation from the Greek Pauline source material. The earliest mention of our letter comes from the fourth century,[14] while the earliest and best manuscript evidence for the Epistle to the Laodiceans is Codex Fuldensis (546 CE).[15] This apocryphal letter has been rejected in the Eastern Church since the Second Council of Nicea (787 CE). In the Western Church, the Epistle to the Laodiceans continued to be prized, often included in lists of Paul's letters as if canonical, and translated into several medieval languages. It also is mentioned in the Vulgate. The Epistle to the Laodiceans was fully excluded from the New Testament canon with the Protestant Reformation and the Council of Trent in the sixteenth century. Since the letter's exclusion from the New Testament canon, it has been largely neglected until recently.

2. SUMMARY OF CONTENT

The Epistle to the Laodiceans is a short letter addressed to the church at Laodicea by the apostle Paul. The letter addresses a concern over false teachers in Laodicea and exhorts the recipients to remain true to the "gospel truth" taught by Paul and his coworkers. The letter is clearly a pseudonymous letter that demonstrates a close familiarity with Philippians, Galatians, and Colossians. This letter has been identified as a paraenetic letter—a letter of "moral exhortation"—following the fivefold structure of a Pauline letter: prescript, thanksgiving, letter-body, paraenetic section, letter-closing.[16] The letter is structured as follows:

Prescript (vv. 1–2)
Thanksgiving (v. 3)—Remaining steadfast with eschatological benefit
Letter-Body (vv. 4–9)
    Body-Opening (v. 4)—The true gospel and threat of false teachers
    Body-Middle (vv. 5–8)
        Section A: Community Situation—Challenges to Paul's gospel (v. 5)

---

12. J. B. Lightfoot, *St. Paul's Epistles to the Colossians and to Philemon*, rev. ed. (Grand Rapids: Zondervan, 1978 [1879]), 274–300, with Greek text on pages 293–94. The Greek is reprinted in Adolf von Harnack, "Der apokryphe Brief des Apostels Paulus an die Laodicener, eine Marcionitische Fälschung aus der 2. Hälfte des 2. Jahrhunderts," *Sitzungsberichte der preussischen Akademie der Wissenschaften, Jahrgang 1923: Philosophisch-historische Klasse* (Berlin: Verlage der Akademie der Wissenschaften/de Gruyter, 1923), 238. See also the earlier Greek retroversion by Elias Hutter, *Polyglott New Testament* (Nuremberg, 1599), which is reproduced in Rudolph Anger, *Ueber den Laodiceans: Eine biblischkritische Untersuchung* (Leipzig: Gebhardt and Reisland, 1843), 172.

13. The possibility of Ep. Lao. being a Latin letter depending on Greek Pauline letters rather than a translation of a Greek version of Ep. Lao. is explored in Philip L. Tite, *The Apocryphal Epistle to the Laodiceans: An Epistolary and Rhetorical Analysis*, TENTS 7 (Leiden: Brill, 2012), 130–32.

14. See the discussion in Luigi Firpo, *Apocrifi del Nuovo Testamento*, Classici delle Religioni (Torino: UTET, 1971), 1720–23; and Mario Erbetta, "La Lettera ai Laodiceni (160–190?)," in *Gli Apocrifi del Nuovo Testamento*, vol. 3 of *Lettere e Apocalissi* (Milan: Marietti, 1981), 63–67.

15. See *Codex Fuldensis: Novum Testamentum Latine Interprete Hieronymo, ex manuscript Victoris Capuani*, ed. E. Ranke (Marburg: Sumptibus N. G. Elwerti Bibliopolae Academici, 1868).

16. Tite, *Apocryphal Epistle to the Laodiceans*; idem, "Dusting Off a Pseudo-Historical Letter: Re-Thinking the Epistolary Aspects of the Apocryphal Epistle to the Laodiceans," in *Paul and Pseudepigraphy*, ed. S. Porter and G. Fewster, Pauline Studies 8 (Leiden: Brill, 2013), 289–318; and idem, "Epistle to the Laodiceans," e-Clavis: Christian Apocrypha, www.nasscal.com/e-clavis-christian-apocrypha/epistle-to-the-laodiceans/. See also Richard I. Pervo, *The Making of Paul: Constructions of the Apostle in Early Christianity* (Minneapolis: Fortress, 2010), 105–9, esp. 107–8.

Section B: Paul's Situation—Paul's suffering in Christ (vv. 6–8)
Body-Closing (v. 9)—Divine mercy and community unity
Paraenesis ("Moral Exhortation") (vv. 10–16)
   A General Exhortation to the Laodiceans (vv. 10–12)
     B Specific Exhortation—Threat of false teachers (v. 13)
   A' General Exhortation to the Laodiceans (vv. 14–16)
Letter-Closing (vv. 17/18–20)

As paraenesis ("moral exhortation"), the Epistle to the Laodiceans exhorts the recipients to continue following the moral path that they have been on. Paraenesis, as persuasive discourse, does not try to convert the recipients to a new path, nor does it function as a corrective to inappropriate behavior or beliefs, but rather it reminds the recipients of their adherence to the path of virtue in order to encourage them to continue along that path.[17] The Epistle to the Laodiceans is rhetorically designed along such lines, drawing upon the first-century figure of Paul to create a fictional correspondence to the church in Laodicea in order to enjoin or urge this unknown second-century Christian community to be on their guard against false teaching. The content of such false teaching is unknown. There is nothing in the letter, for example, that links the letter to—either standing in support of or in opposition to—the Marcionite movement.[18]

As with other ancient letters, the Epistle to the Laodiceans opens with a prescript following the A (sender) to B (recipients) greetings structure that we find in all of Paul's undisputed letters. This formulaic structure is modified in ancient letters to suit the occasion of the letter.[19] These modifications establish the tone of the letter, the relationship between the sender and receiver, and sometimes foreshadow key themes in the letter.[20] The Epistle to the Laodiceans's prescript (vv. 1–2) likely follows Galatians 1:1–2, though with notable variances in the expansions (specifically dropping any mention of coworkers). It limits the identification of the sender to Paul, giving him the title of apostle, while noting the divine source of his authority. In the undisputed letters, Paul's apostolic credentials

---

17. For a further discussion of paraenesis, see below. A helpful overview of paraenesis in early Christian literature, with a comprehensive overview of the history of scholarship on paraenesis, is Tite, *Valentinian Ethics and Paraenetic Discourse: Determining the Social Function of Moral Exhortation in Valentinian Christianity*, NHMS 67 (Leiden: Brill, 2009), esp. 56–133.

18. Contra Harnack, Quispel, and Ehrman. See Harnack, "Der apokryphe Brief des Apostels Paulus"; idem, *Apocrypha, IV. Die apokrphen Briefe des Paulus an die Laodicener und Korinther*, Kleine Texte für theologische Vorlesungen und Übungen 12 (Bonn: A. Marcus und E. Weber's, 1905); idem, *Marcion, das Evangelium vom fremden Gott*, 2nd ed. (Leipzig, 1924), esp. appendix 3; see in English translation *Marcion: The Gospel of the Alien God*, trans. J. Steely and L. Bierma (Durham, NC: Labyrinth, 1990), though this edition lacks the appendices; Gilles Quispel, "De Brief aan de Laodicensen een Marcionitische vervalsing," *Nederlands Theologisch Tijdschrift* 5 (1950/51): 43–46 (ET: "The Epistle to the Laodiceans: A Marcionite Forgery," in *Gnostica, Judaica, Catholica: Collected Essays of Gilles Quispel*, ed. J. van Oort, NHMS 55 [Leiden: Brill, 2008], 689–93); Bart Ehrman, *Lost Scriptures: Books That Did Not Make It into the New Testament* (Oxford: Oxford University Press, 2003), 165, and repeated in Ehrman, *Lost Christianities: The Battles for Scripture and the Faiths We Never Knew* (Oxford: Oxford University Press, 2003), xiii, 213–15.

19. Examples of such modifications to a prescript include P.Mich. 9.466 ("Julius Apollinarios to his dearest father, Julius Sabinus, very many greetings") and P.Tebt. 2.410 ("Hermias to his dearest Akousilaos many greetings," which personalizes the external address: "To Akousilaos, toparch of Tebtunis").

20. Tite, "How to Begin, and Why? Diverse Functions of the Pauline Prescript within a Greco-Roman Context," in *Paul and the Ancient Letter Form*, ed. S. Porter and S. Adams, Pauline Studies 6 (Leiden: Brill, 2010), 57–99. See also idem, "The Compositional Function of the Petrine Prescript: A Look at 1 Pet 1:1–3," *JETS* 39 (1996): 47–56, and idem, *Compositional Transitions in 1 Peter: An Analysis of the Letter-Opening* (San Francisco: International Scholars Publications, 1997). This approach to the prescript is applied to Ep. Lao. in Tite, *Apocryphal Epistle to the Laodiceans*, 19–28.

are given in letters where he needs to assert his authority.[21] In the disputed letters, such as in the Epistle to the Laodiceans (so also 1 and 2 Timothy, Ephesians, and Colossians; but not 3 Corinthians, Titus, or 2 Thessalonians), the apostolic credentials offer authority to the pseudonymous letter, thereby elevating the voice of "Paul" in the letter above that of the "false" teachers rejected by the letter. The admonishing tone of Galatians is completely dropped in Laodiceans, especially in the description of the recipients. The recipients are described using fictive kinship terminology ("brethren"). Such kinship language is used by Paul to reinforce positive relations, and such is the function of familial language in this letter.[22] The prescript establishes a positive relationship between Paul and the Laodicean Christians, while stressing the authority of the apostle.

The thanksgiving (v. 3) follows standard Pauline formulas.[23] Ancient letters often included a health-wish clause, sometimes framed with a thanksgiving for the well-being of the recipient. Peter Arzt-Grabner identifies three types of clauses from which the Pauline thanksgiving is built: (1) a prayer on behalf of the recipient; (2) an affirmation of remembrance (reminding the recipient that despite the distance between them, the sender remembers them); and (3) a thanksgiving (e.g., giving thanks to a deity due to the health of the recipient). These clauses may include a report on the condition of the sender.[24] Raymond Collins has identified five elements in Paul's thanksgivings, and we can apply the first three of these to the Epistle to the Laodiceans: (1) an expression of thanks ("I give thanks"); (2) the recipient of the thanks ("to Christ"); (3) a temporal adverb (reflected by the Laodiceans remaining "steadfast" and "persevering"); (4) the motivation for writing; and (5) an explanatory clause.[25] The Pauline thanksgiving builds a triadic relationship between Paul, his community (in this case the church in Laodicea), and the divine (God or Christ). The well-being and health of the community is determined by the health of this triadic relationship (e.g., in 1 Thessalonians, Philippians, and Laodiceans), while a breach in one of these relations results in an unhealthy community in need of correction (e.g., Galatians and possibly the Corinthian correspondence). The thanksgiving in Laodiceans advances the positive relations established in the prescript, adding an eschatological finale that situates the Laodicean Christians on an eschatological journey that will result in the fulfillment of divine promises if they remain steadfast.

The letter-body of the Epistle to the Laodiceans (vv. 4–9) follows ancient letter conventions of a body-opening, body-middle, and body-closing.[26] The body-opening (v. 4)

---

21. Tite, "How to Begin, and Why?," 66.

22. Two noteworthy studies of the use of familial language are Reidar Aasgaard, *"My Beloved Brothers and Sisters!": Christian Siblingship in Paul*, Early Christianity in Content (London: Continuum, 2004), 306–7, and Philip A. Harland, "Familial Dimensions of Group Identity: 'Brothers' (ΑΔΕΛΦΟΙ) in Associations of the Greek East," *JBL* 124 (2005): 491–513.

23. Tite, *Apocryphal Epistle to the Laodiceans*, 29–41.

24. Peter Arzt-Grabner, "Paul's Letter Thanksgiving," in Porter and Adams, *Paul and the Ancient Letter Form*, 129–58. See also idem, "The Epistolary Introductory Thanksgiving in the Papyri and in Paul," *NovT* 36 (1994): 29–49; cf. Jeffrey T. Reed, "Are Paul's Thanksgivings 'Epistolary'?," *JSNT* 61 (1996): 87–99.

25. Raymond F. Collins, "A Significant Decade: The Trajectory of the Hellenistic Epistolary Thanksgiving," in Porter and Adams, *Paul and the Ancient Letter Form*, 159–84. See also L. Ann Jervis, *The Purpose of Romans: A Comparative Letter Structure Investigation*, JSNTSup 55 (Sheffield: Sheffield Academic Press, 1991), 86–109.

26. Troy W. Martin, "Investigating the Pauline Letter Body: Issues, Methods, and Approaches," in Porter and Adams, *Paul and the Ancient Letter Form*, 185–212; idem, *Metaphor and Composition in 1 Peter*, SBLDS 131 (Atlanta: Scholars Press, 1992), 69–77. Martin's work builds on the tripartite letter structure of the body middle established by John L. White, "New Testament Epistolary Literature in the Framework of Ancient Epistolography," *ANRW* 25.2:1730–56; idem, *The Form and Function of the Greek Letter*, SBLDS 2 (Missoula, MT: Scholars Press, 1972); and idem, "Introduction to the Formulae in the Body of the Pauline Letter," *JBL* 40 (1971): 91–97.

sets forth the motivation for writing, specifically the threat of false teachers who strive to dissuade the recipients from what the letter writer sees as the "true gospel" (perhaps a particular understanding of Paul's teaching and legacy in competition with alternative understandings). The body-closing (v. 9) effectively closes the epistolary occasion by stressing the "mercy [at] work in you," with the result of having "the same love and be[ing] like-minded." The body-middle (vv. 5–8), as with other Pauline letters, does not follow epistolary conventions and thus must be studied using other structural mechanisms.[27] In the case of Laodiceans, there are two possible structures that have been identified:[28] (1) a twofold structure presenting the condition of the community (vv. 4–5; suffering due to false teachers), and the suffering of Paul as exemplar for the community (vv. 6–9); and (2) a chiastic structure of:

> A (v. 4 beware those who would undermine the "true gospel")
>   B (v. 5 those from Paul further the "truth of the gospel")
>   C (v. 6 suffering of Paul)
>   B' (v. 7 prayers of the Laodiceans administered by the Holy Spirit)
> A' (v. 9 Christ's mercy at work in the community and being of like mind/love).

Both structures place emphasis on the role of Paul as a moral example for the community to emulate. Such emulation of the apostle is based on the positive relationship between Paul and the Laodiceans. An eschatological promise concludes the body-middle, as it did the thanksgiving, by presenting an assurance of divine mercy.

While the letter-body of the Epistle to the Laodiceans encourages the recipients to stay firm in their eschatological journey, that encouragement is described rather than exhorted. It is in the paraenesis section (vv. 10–16) that the letter writer directly exhorts the community.[29] The paraenesis is designed with three sections, with the first and third framing the central focus of the double exhortation of the middle section. Verses 10–12 mirror verses 14–16 with typical paraenetic conventions: a reminding (vv. 10a//16a); static commands (vv. 10b//14b; 16b); dynamic commands (vv. 10c//12); and motivation (vv. 10d//16c). At the center (v. 13) is a twofold exhortation that embodies the main theme of the letter: "And as for the rest, beloved, *rejoice* in Christ and *be wary* of those who are out for sordid gain." Here we find the positive (persuasion) and negative (dissuasion) sides of the letter's moral exhortation. The "truth" of "Paul's" gospel, which the community is to continue following and rejoice in, is set in antithesis to the threat of false teachers.

The motivation of the false teachers fits the ancient trope of the charlatan. In ancient discussions of the charlatan, the validity of the teaching is tied to the validity of the teacher or philosopher.[30] What marks a charlatan is the lack of the would-be philosopher's moral character matching their teaching. Charlatans were presented in antiquity as seeking wealth, sexual gratification, or a legacy rather than seeking truth. In Laodiceans, the charlatan motif is tied to seeking "sordid gain" and builds on v. 4's "deceptive discourse" that

---

27. Martin, *Metaphor*, 74–75.

28. Tite, *Apocryphal Epistle to the Laodiceans*, 48–55.

29. The paraenesis section is a unique Pauline innovation in letter writing, though it does have some ancient precedents. Often letters would close with a call to respond to the request or to encourage a given virtue. We see such a closing "call to response" in P.Amh. 2.133 ("I urge you to write to me about your health"; my translation). More developed hortatory sections, similar to what we see in Paul, are found in a few letters, notably P.Oxy. 42.3069.

30. See Lucian, *Pisc.*; *Alex.*; and *Peregr.*; in Christian circles see 1 Cor 2:17; 1 Thess 2:1–6; Titus 1:11–12; 1 Pet 5:1–2; Herm. Mand. 11.12; Did. 11–12; and notably the presentation of Marcus the Magician in Irenaeus, *Haer.* 1.13.3.

attempts to undermine the "true gospel." Building on the letter-body, the paraenesis effectively sets in contrast the self-giving (and thus legitimate) work of Paul and his coworkers with the selfish (and thus illegitimate) work of false teachers, with, once again, an eschatological promise (vv. 3, 8, 10) for those who hold firm on their eschatological journey. The author of the Epistle to the Laodiceans sets up a contrast between the true teacher (Paul) and false teachers. While false teachers lack moral character, Paul embodies the teaching of the true gospel by his suffering in Christ and for the benefit of the community. This contrast in moral character reinforces the author's argument that Paul declares the true gospel and has done so from the founding of the community (vv. 6–9). Thus, to "hold fast" and "to remain firm" (vv. 10, 14), as an act of rejoicing "in Christ" (v. 13a), is to continue holding to the teaching ("true gospel") that Paul initially gave them. Note the parallels of "in Christ" in verse 13 and "in Christ" in verses 6, 8. To "suffer" in Christ (i.e., Paul's condition) enables the Laodicean Christians to "rejoice" in Christ. The paraenesis links the direct exhortation of the letter to the moral example of Paul in the letter body.

The letter closes (vv. 17/18–20) with a direct reworking of Colossians 4:16. The closing ends with (in some manuscripts) a greeting and holy kiss (v. 17). The early Christian holy kiss reinforced or demonstrated the shared group identity between community members.[31] The letter writer's closing with a "greeting from the saints" and instructions to pass the letter along to the Colossians and to read the letter from the Colossians may emphasize the validity of the teachings of Paul. Paul and his coworkers are positioned within the universal Christian church that the Laodiceans, if they remain steadfast, will continue to be part of as a larger and authentic network of Christian communities. Implicitly, the false teachers are excluded from such universal communion of the faith; they remain a separate, isolated threat with inauthentic teaching. Paul's teaching is authenticated once again by stressing the apostle's moral character, now by means of his standing in the universal church. The moral character and teaching of the philosopher are, once again, linked. As the epistolary "leave taking" section of the letter, the closing reinforces the moral exhortation of the letter while simultaneously highlighting again the positive relations between letter writer and recipients.

3. INTERPRETIVE ISSUES
3.1 History of Scholarship

Scholarly treatment of the Epistle to the Laodiceans can be divided into three general approaches: the dismissal approach, the derivative-value approach, and recent approaches demonstrating greater appreciation for the letter. All three approaches can be found in current scholarship.

The dominant approach has been the *dismissal approach*. Modern scholarship has almost universally ignored the Epistle to the Laodiceans as merely a clumsy forgery that is not worth studying. This pseudonymous letter is often described as an inept forgery comprised of lifted phrases from the authentic letters of Paul woven together randomly to "fill the gap" of a missing letter mentioned in Colossians 4:16. Scholars have referred to

---

31. For an insightful analysis of letter closings, see Jeffrey A. D. Weima, "Sincerely, Paul: The Significance of the Pauline Letter Closings," in Porter and Adams, *Paul and the Ancient Letter Form*, 305–45; idem, *Neglected Endings: The Significance of the Pauline Letter Closings*, JSNTSup 101 (Sheffield: JSOT Press, 1994). On the Christian "kiss of peace," see Weima, "Sincerely," 331; and Stephen Benko, "The Kiss," in *Pagan Rome and the Early Christians* (Bloomington, IN: Indiana University Press, 1984), 79–102, especially 98: "[The kiss] could be simply an expression of friendship and good will, but among Christians it assumed a deeper meaning; it symbolized the unity, the belonging together of Christians, in the church of Jesus Christ." This kiss in Ep. Lao. 17 is qualified as a "holy kiss," a qualification that may stand in contrast to inappropriate kisses initiated by charlatans, such as we find in Lucian, *Alex.* 41–42.

Laodiceans as a mere rhapsody, a cento, a catena, a patchwork, or a pastiche thoughtlessly thrown together with no theological point or compositional logic. The letter is often read as a harmless and theologically bland work. Wilhelm Schneemelcher, in what is arguably the standard English collection of early NT apocrypha, openly declares that there is no value in studying Laodiceans: "Too much honour is done the author of this paltry and carelessly compiled concoction when we judge him by the yardstick of ancient literary practices."[32] Schneemelcher echoes the view of earlier scholars such as M. R. James, who judged the letter "wholly uninteresting," John Eadie, who saw the letter as a "brief and tasteless forgery," and Adolf Jülicher, who also saw it as "short, unimportant and colourless."[33] More recent scholarship has perpetuated the dismissal approach. John Drane views Laodiceans as a late production, declaring that it "contains no real substance, and consists of a series of bits and pieces from Paul's other letters strung together in an aimless way."[34] Similarly, J. Albert Harrill describes the letter as "a banal pastiche" written both to supply the missing letter of Colossians 4:16 and, clearly under the influence of Bart Ehrman, to counter an earlier forgery that was deemed heretical.[35] Neil Elliott describes the Epistle to the Laodiceans as arising from the hand of a third- or fourth-century Christian, under the influence of Colossians 4:16, a letter that is produced "by patching together phrases from the available letters of Paul."[36] And James Charlesworth ponders the inclusion of the Epistle to the Laodiceans in the canon prior to the Reformation: "The reception into the canon of this pastiche is inexplicable, given its inelegance."[37]

---

32. Wilhelm Schneemelcher, "The Epistle to the Laodiceans," *NTApoc* 2:44.

33. M. R. James, *New Testament Apocrypha* (Oxford: Clarendon, 1924; repr., Berkeley: Apocryphile Press, 2004), 478; John Eadie, *A Commentary on the Greek Text of the Epistle of Paul to the Ephesians*, 2nd ed. (New York: Robert Carter, 1861), xxiv; Adolf Jülicher, *An Introduction to the New Testament*, trans. J. P. Ward (London: Smith, Elder, & Co., 1904), 544. This dismissive attitude to Ep. Lao. appears in most treatments of the letter. See, e.g., Lightfoot, *Colossians*, 300; John David Michaelis, *Introduction to the New Testament*, vol. 4, 4th ed., trans. H. Marsh (London: F. C. & J. Rivington, 1822), 127; E. C. Blackman, *Marcion and His Influence* (London: SPCK, 1948), 61–62; Leander E. Keck, *Paul and His Letters*, 2nd ed. (Philadelphia: Fortress, 1988), 17; Charles H. Cosgrove, "Laodiceans, Epistle to the," in *Mercer Dictionary of the Bible*, ed. W. Mills (Macon, GA: Mercer University Press, 1990), 500; Duane F. Watson, "Laodiceans, Letter to the," in *Eerdmans Dictionary of the Bible*, ed. D. Freedman (Grand Rapids: Eerdmans, 2000), 790; Claudio Moreschini and Enrico Norelli, *Early Christian Greek and Latin Literature: A Literary History*, 2 vols., trans. M. O'Connell (Peabody, MA: Hendrickson, 2005), 1:29; Enrico Norelli, "La Lettre aux Laodicéens: essai d'interprétation," in *Il Mosaico della Basilica di S. Colombano in Bobbio e altri studi dal II al XX secolo*, ed. F. Nuvolone, Archivum Bobbiense 23 (Bobbio, 2002), 45–90; Wayne A. Meeks and John T. Fitzgerald, *The Writings of Paul: Annotated Texts, Reception and Criticism*, 2nd ed., Norton Classical Edition (New York: W. W. Norton, 2007), 141–48, esp. 142; Raymond F. Collins, *Introduction to the New Testament* (New York: Doubleday, 1987), 31; Bruce M. Metzger, *The Canon of the New Testament: Its Origins, Development, and Significance* (Oxford: Clarendon, 1987), 182–83; and David B. Capes, Rodney Reeves, and E. Randolph Richards, *Rediscovering Paul: An Introduction to His World, Letters and Theology* (Downers Grove, IL: InterVarsity Press, 2011), 291–92.

34. John Drane, *Introducing the New Testament*, 3rd ed. (Oxford: Lion Hudson, 2010), 338.

35. J. Albert Harrill, *Paul the Apostle: His Life and Legacy in Their Roman Context* (Cambridge: Cambridge University Press, 2012), 6.

36. Neil Elliott, "Situating the Apostle Paul in His Day and Engaging His Legacy in Our Own," in *The Letters and Legacy of Paul*, Fortress Commentary on the Bible Study Edition, ed. M. Aymer, C. Kittredge, and D. Sánchez (Minneapolis: Fortress, 2016), 379–80. So also, Brandon W. Hawk, *Apocrypha for Beginners: A Guide to Understanding and Exploring Scriptures Beyond the Bible* (Emeryville, CA: Rockbridge, 2021), 110. Similarly, Laura Salah Nasrallah, *Archaeology and the Letters of Paul* (Oxford: Oxford University Press, 2019), 2, merely lists Ep. Lao. and 3 Cor. as examples of letters "spawned" by Paul's own epistolary activity—as a kind of "thinking with Paul." Nasrallah's dismissive treatment, however, is more directed at 3 Cor., which is described as "stunningly boring."

37. James H. Charlesworth, "Preface: The Fluid Borders of the Canon and 'Apocrypha,'" in *Sacra Scriptura: How "Non-Canonical" Texts Functioned in Early Judaism and Early Christianity*, ed. J. Charlesworth, L. McDonald, and B. Jurgens (London: Bloomsbury, 2014), xxii (for full discussion, see xiii–xxv, especially xx–xxii where Charlesworth focuses on Ep. Lao.). Charlesworth also describes Ep. Lao. as "a poor forgery that

Although the dismissal approach has dominated scholarship, there have been some scholars who have studied the Epistle to the Laodiceans more closely in what we could call the *derivative-value approach*. This approach treats Laodiceans as a valuable histori-cal source for scholarship, but only in so far as it contributes to other scholarly interests. The Epistle to the Laodiceans itself is of no value but carries value in that other, more significant research questions may be advanced by using it. There have been three areas of research where Laodiceans has carried derivative value. The first is a connection to the Marcionite church, which flourished in the second century as a major form of Christianity. The Muratorian Canon mentions two Pauline letters written "in regard to" the Marcionite "heresy" (i.e., the Letter to the Laodiceans and the Letter to the Alexandrians). The Latin can be read either as written to "advance" Marcionite Christianity or more neutrally as "regarding" Marcionism. Adolf von Harnack followed the former reading, advancing the position that the Latin Epistle to the Laodiceans arose from Marcionite circles and demonstrates Marcionite redactional tendencies.[38] Harnack's reading was advanced by Gilles Quispel,[39] and though rejected by most scholars, occasionally finds support (e.g., in Obolensky's treatment of Paulicianism).[40] A variant of the Marcionite hypothesis has been advanced by Ehrman, who argues that the Epistle to the Laodiceans, being so dull and unimaginative, was written to counter the Marcionite letter mentioned in the Muratorian Canon.[41] Ehrman's interpretation was advanced earlier by Karl Pink, Luigo Firpo, and Donald Penny.[42] E. C. Blackman, however, suggested that "the forger used Marcionite texts, but was himself orthodox, and made his compilation at a time when the Marcionite danger was past."[43] The Marcionite hypothesis, however, has largely been rejected in scholarship. Not only did Marcion identify Ephesians as the Laodiceans mentioned in Colossians 4:16, but, more importantly, there is nothing in the Latin letter to suggest a Marcionite connection. As a result, nearly every scholar today rejects the Marcionite hypothesis in any form.

The second area of research where the Epistle to the Laodiceans carries derivative value is in the assessment of the authorship of the disputed Pauline letters (Ephesians, Colossians, 2 Thessalonians, and the Pastoral Epistles). The most extensive treatment of the Epistle to the Laodiceans from this perspective is Gregory MaGee's recent argument for Paul's authorship of Colossians and Ephesians. MaGee uses the noncanonical Pauline letters, including the Epistle to the Laodiceans, to establish criteria to test whether the disputed

---

plagiarizes some of Paul's authentic letters" (xx) and approvingly cites Eldon Jay Epp, who refers to the letter as "the greatest puzzle" with regard to the biblical canon (xx), as well as Bruce M. Metzger, who called Ep. Lao. "a pedestrian patchwork" (xxii). See Epp, "Issues in the Interrelation of New Testament Textual Criticism and Canon," in *The Canon Debate*, ed. L. McDonald and J. Sanders (Peabody, MA: Hendrickson, 2002), 483–515, esp. 494–95, and Metzger, *Canon*, 183, with full discussion on 182–83 and, in discussing Ep. Lao.'s final exclu-sion from the biblical canon, 239–47.

38. Harnack, "Der apokryphe Brief des Apostels Paulus," esp. 239–45; idem, *Apocrypha*, 1–6; idem, *Marcion*, appendix 3. An earlier identification of the Latin letter with Marcion was made by Samuel Prideaux Tregelles, *Canon Muratorianus: The Earliest Catalogue of the Books of the New Testament* (Oxford: Clarendon, 1867), 47. See also Alfred Barry, "Ephesians," in *Galatians, Ephesians, and Philippians*, ed. C. Elliott (London: Cassell, Petter, Galpin, 1879), 126.

39. Quispel, "De Brief aan de Laodicensen een Marcionitische vervalsing."

40. Dmitri Obolensky, *The Bogomils: A Study in Balkan Neo-Manichaeism* (Cambridge: Cambridge University Press, 1948), 39, 47, who argues that the Paulicians made use of the apocryphal epistle to the Laodiceans.

41. Ehrman, *Lost Scriptures*, 165; idem, *Lost Christianities*, xiii, 213–15.

42. Karl Pink, "Die Pseudo-Paulinischen Briefe II: (2) Der Laodizenerbrief," *Biblica* 6 (1925): 179–93, esp. 192; Firpo, *Apocrifi del Nuovo Testamento*, 1722; Donald N. Penny, "The Pseudo-Pauline Letters of the First Two Centuries" (PhD diss., Emory University, 1979), 330.

43. Blackman, *Marcion and His Influence*, 62.

letters are also pseudonymous works.[44] The Epistle to the Laodiceans is used similarly by William Moorehead and Donald Penny to argue for Paul's authorship of the Pastorals and, more recently, by Raymond Collins regarding Ephesians.[45] A similar use of Laodiceans arises in James Kelhoffer's study of the longer ending of the Gospel of Mark, where he uses the letter as an analogy to elucidate Mark's longer ending.[46] The central focus in these studies is not the Epistle to the Laodiceans. Rather than advancing our understanding of the Epistle to the Laodiceans, these studies utilize the letter to advance other research goals.

A third area of research where the Epistle to the Laodiceans has been used is the debate between Philip Sellew and Paul Holloway in the late 1990s over partition readings of Philippians.[47] Sellew observed that the Epistle to the Laodiceans only demonstrates knowledge of certain parts of Philippians, parts that constitute the so-called Letter B hypothesis. The Epistle to the Laodiceans clearly draws on Philippians and follows the order in Philippians, but only of Philippians 1:1–3:1, 4:4–9, and 4:21–23. Sellew treats the Epistle of the Laodiceans as an external witness to an earlier, shorter version of Philippians (letter B). Holloway, however, attempted to counter this partition reading of Philippians, though Sellew's response effectively countered Holloway's arguments. Although Sellew's study is fascinating and insightful for our understanding of Laodiceans (see my discussion below), this debate is centered on exegetical matters pertaining to Philippians, not Laodiceans. Once again, the Epistle to the Laodiceans is only valuable in so far as it elucidates other research interests.

Beyond these three areas of derivative-value research could be added Régis Burnet's treatment of the Epistle to the Laodiceans, where the letter is viewed as more of an artifact that illustrates the significance of "Paul" as an apostolic figure in second-century Christianity rather than as a letter with intrinsic research value.[48] Burnet sees more value in the existence of the Epistle to the Laodiceans as an *object* rather than in the *message* embedded in the text.[49] Similarly, there have been numerous treatments of Laodiceans, though often in brief mentions of the letter, in broader discussions of the formation of the New Testament canon or in discussions of manuscript traditions, transmission, and medieval translations of Laodiceans.[50]

---

44. Gregory S. MaGee, *Portrait of an Apostle: A Case for Paul's Authorship of Colossians and Ephesians* (Eugene, OR: Pickwick, 2013), especially ch. 3.

45. Penny, "Pseudo-Pauline Letters"; William G. Moorehead, *Outline Studies in the New Testament: Philippians to Hebrews* (London: Fleming H. Revell, 1905), 136–37; and Collins, *Letters That Paul Did Not Write*, 150–51.

46. James A. Kelhoffer, *Miracle and Mission: The Authentication of Missionaries and Their Message in the Longer Ending of Mark*, WUNT 2.112 (Tübingen: Mohr Siebeck, 2000), 150–51.

47. Philip Sellew, "*Laodiceans* and the Philippians Fragments Hypothesis," *HTR* 87 (1994): 17–28. See the counter by Paul A. Holloway, "The Apocryphal *Epistle to the Laodiceans* and the Partitioning of Philippians," *HTR* 91 (1998): 321–25; Holloway, *Consolation in Philippians: Philosophical Sources and Rhetorical Strategy* (Cambridge: Cambridge University Press, 2001), 9–11. Holloway's defense of the unity of Philippians against the partitionist case vis-à-vis Ep. Lao. is persuasively refuted by Sellew, "*Laodiceans* and Philippians Revisited: A Response to Paul Holloway," *HTR* 91 (1998): 327–29.

48. Régis Burnet, "Pourquoi avoir écrit l'insipide épître aux Laodicéens?," *NTS* 48 (2002): 132–41.

49. Burnet, "Laodicéens," 141.

50. Helpful discussions of the manuscript and transmission history of Ep. Lao., as well as patristic testimonies for it, include Lightfoot, *Colossians*, 282–84; Leon Vouaux, *Les Actes de Paul et ses letters apocryphes: Introduction, texts, traduction et commentaire*, Les Apocryphes du Nouveau Testament (Paris: Librairie Letouzet et Ané, 1913), 315–26; Harnack, "Der apokryphe Brief des Apostels Paulus," 235–36; idem, *Apocrypha*, 2–3; Firpo, *Apocrifi del Nuovo Testamento*, 1720–23; and Erbetta, "La Lettera ai Laodiceni." See also E. J. Goodspeed, "A Toledo Manuscript of Laodiceans," *JBL* 23.1 (1904): 76–78; idem, "The Madrid MS of Laodiceans," *American Journal of Theology* 8 (1904): 536–38; Thomas W. Mackay, "Content and Style in Two Pseudo-Pauline Epistles (3 Corinthians and the Epistle to the Laodiceans)," in *Apocryphal Writings and the*

In recent years, a third major approach to the Epistle to the Laodiceans has emerged, the *appreciative approach*. This approach is typified by scholars treating the letter as holding intrinsic value, as an early Christian text worth studying in its own right rather than as merely part of a broader research project. Rather than seeing the letter as randomly lifted phrases from Paul's letters with no theological point, scholars increasingly are studying Laodiceans through literary and rhetorical lenses that elucidate an internal logic and intentional purpose for this pseudonymous letter. Three key studies are worth noting. An epistolary appreciation for Laodiceans, arising in the brief treatment by Richard Pervo, views this letter as presenting a modest and conservative "Paul" from the hand of a vigorous Paulinist in the first half of the third century.[51] Philip Tite offers the most substantial epistolary analysis of Laodiceans to date.[52] Tite's comprehensive analysis argues that the letter follows the fivefold Pauline letter structure (both drawing on and innovating within the Pauline epistolary tradition),[53] fits the paraenetic genre, and stresses Paul as a moral exemplar for the recipients in the face of false teachers (perceiving the letter as evoking the charlatan trope).[54] The letter is identified as possibly composed in the early second century, largely due to the use of the charlatan trope. More recently, Bruce Longenecker and Scott Ryan have attempted to identify a complex chiastic structure in Laodiceans, with the interpretative weight falling on verses 6–8.[55] Although Longenecker and Ryan's work demonstrates a welcomed appreciation for the structural and thematic coherence of this letter, their literary approach is problematic in that it fails to locate the chiastic elements within Pauline epistolary structures. More plausible is the use of chiasm to structure the letter body rather than the entire letter.[56] Recent responses to the appreciative approach have been positive.[57] These various studies bode well for future scholarship on the Epistle to the Laodiceans and the apocryphal Paul.

Latter-Day Saints, ed. C. Wilfred Griggs, Religious Studies Monograph Series 13 (Salt Lake: Brigham Young University, 1986); Metzger, *Canon*, 239–40; and Thomas N. Hall, "Aelfric and the Epistle to the Laodiceans," in *Apocryphal Texts and Traditions in Anglo-Saxon England*, ed. K. Powell and D. Scragg (Cambridge: D. S. Brewer, 2003), 65–84. Among more recent treatments, Backus is especially noteworthy: Irena Backus, *Historical Method and Confessional Identity in the Era of the Reformation (1378–1615)*, Studies in Medieval and Reformation Thought 94 (Leiden: Brill, 2003), 276–86; idem, "New Testament Apocryphal Writings: Jacques Lefèvre d'Etaples and His Epigones," *Renaissance Quarterly* 51 (1998): 1169–98. See also Gregory Fewster, "Archiving Paul: Manuscripts, Religion, and the Editorial Shaping of Ancient Letter Collections," *Archivaria* 81 (2016): 101–28, esp. 124–25.

51. Pervo, *Making of Paul*, 105–9.

52. Tite, *Apocryphal Epistle to the Laodiceans*; idem, "Dusting Off a Pseudo-Historical Letter"; idem, "Epistle to the Laodiceans."

53. Epistolary treatments of Ep. Lao. are also offered by Penny, "Pseudo-Pauline Letters," and Vouaux, *Les Actes de Paul et ses letters apocryphes*, though neither breaks with the dismissal approach as do Pervo and Tite.

54. Similarly, see Lewis R. Donelson, *Pseudepigraphy and Ethical Argument in the Pastoral Epistles* (Tübingen: Mohr Siebeck, 1986), 42–43. Donelson does not offer a detailed analysis of the letter; however, he does make a helpful suggestion about the themes of the letter. Specifically, for Donelson, Ep. Lao. counters heterodoxy using two major admonitions: "Beware of heretics and devote yourself to the ethical life" (43).

55. Bruce W. Longenecker and Scott C. Ryan, "Presenting the Pauline Voice: An Appreciation of the *Letter to the Laodiceans*," *NTS* 62 (2016): 136–48.

56. Tite, *Apocryphal Epistle to the Laodiceans*, 52–55; idem, "Dusting Off a Pseudo-Historical Letter," 301–2.

57. Smith, *Guilt by Association*, 24–25, with Smith insightfully locating Ep. Lao. within early Christian pseudepigraphic treatments of Paul in the early second century; Trevor W. Thompson, "Epistles, Apocryphal," in *Encyclopedia of the Bible and Its Reception*, vol. 7, ed. H. Klauck et al. (Berlin: de Gruyter, 2013), 1084–86; and Andrew Gregory, "Non-Canonical Epistles and Related Literature," in *The Oxford Handbook of Early Christian Apocrypha*, ed. A. Gregory and C. Tuckett (Oxford: Oxford University Press, 2015), 90–114, esp. 97–98.

3.2 Dating the Text

The Epistle to the Laodiceans can be dated from the second to sixth century. Attempts to locate this letter chronologically have been fraught with methodological difficulties, given limited external and internal clues. The earliest Latin manuscript is Codex Fuldensis dated to 546 CE, which serves as the *terminus ante quem*. The *terminus post quem* for Laodiceans is less certain. Given the letter's knowledge of Galatians, Colossians, and some version of Philippians, the date of composition should fall to after the circulation of a Pauline corpus. When Paul's letters began to circulate as a collection is unclear, though certainly this collection emerged by the beginning of the second century (though there is nothing to indicate that Paul's letters could not have circulated earlier in the first century or even during Paul's lifetime). The date for the *terminus ante quem* could be narrowed to the fourth century due to a brief mention by Jerome (*Vir. ill.* 5), where he claims that everyone rejects Laodiceans. It is unclear, however, if Jerome had our letter in mind or one of the other letters known as Laodiceans. For those arguing for 200 CE as the *terminus ante quem*, the Muratorian Canon, if dated to about 200 CE, serves as the anchor for such chronology. However, the Muratorian Canon is not helpful—not only is its dating contested, but it is unlikely that the Laodiceans mentioned is the same letter. Internal evidence is also vague, though it does raise new possibilities. Pervo dated the letter to about 200 to 250 CE, given the Trinitarian theology discernable in the letter.[58] Tite argues for a possible date range of the first half of the second century, given both the charlatan motif and the possible use of an earlier version of Philippians.[59] Smith supports this earlier date, given the early second-century use of pseudonymous epistles to transform Paul into a polemical voice to keep "the Christian community safe from the perceived threat of heretical teachers and teachings."[60] The Epistle to the Laodiceans is one of several works that fit into Smith's *Corpus Polemicum* (including 1 and 2 Timothy, Titus, Laodiceans, and 3 Corinthians). The epistolary form soon gave way to catalogues of heresies by the mid-second century, notably with Justin Martyr's *Syntagma against All Heresies*.[61] Consequently, the letter can be dated to the second or third century, with good reasons to locate it in the first half of the second century.

3.3 Provenance and Transmission

We do not know where this apocryphal letter was produced. There is nothing in the letter or in Christian tradition to identify the Epistle to the Laodiceans with the city of Laodicea or even Asia Minor. The addressees could be as fictional as its authorship, possibly building on the "lost letter" in Colossians 4:16 or even the rich plethora of "Laodicean" letters in early Christian thought (e.g., Col. 4:16; Muratorian Canon; Marcion's Ephesians; and the letter to the church of Laodicea in Rev 3:14–22—none of which are related to the Epistle to the Laodiceans).

The original language of the letter is also a disputed factor. Lightfoot and Hutter proposed that the Latin version is a translation of an original Greek letter.[62] As Thomas MacKay indicates, seeing the Latin as an awkward translation of a Greek letter is based

---

58. Pervo, *Making of Paul*, 106; Tite, *Apocryphal Epistle to the Laodiceans*, 94–99. See below for a further discussion of Trinitarianism in the letter.

59. Tite, *Apocryphal Epistle to the Laodiceans*, 129–33.

60. Smith, *Guilt by Association*, 25.

61. Smith, *Guilt by Association*, 21–27, 35–43, 49–86.

62. Lightfoot, *Colossians*, 274–300, with Greek translation on 293–94; Hutter, *Polyglott New Testament*, 2:526–27.

on two major arguments.[63] The first argument is the rejection of the letter in the Eastern church by 787 CE, resulting in no Greek manuscripts of our letter, with the continued transmission of the letter in the Western church until the sixteenth century. This argument is more an explanation for the lack of Greek manuscript witnesses than it is an argument for an early, Eastern Greek letter transmitted to the West. Second, the poor Latin is understood as an awkward translation from the Greek. The problem here is that there is no need for a Greek intermediary letter between Philippians and the Latin Epistle to the Laodiceans. The translation process could be more directly taken from an earlier version of Philippians, to build on Sellew's insightful study. The original language is important, however, as a Latin original could push this letter into the third century, though it could also have emerged in the second century, and allow it to be located as either a Western or Eastern production. A Greek original would more confidently limit the date to the second century and see the letter as originally produced in the East with subsequent transmission to the West.

The letter was widely transmitted in the Western church in late antiquity and throughout the medieval period. The letter was translated in a wide range of vernacular European languages and continued to be prized as a Pauline letter. The existence of Arabic and Slavonic translations, drawing from the Latin text, indicates that the Epistle to the Laodiceans continued to circulate in Eastern Christian regions even if beyond the Greek Byzantine context.[64] We also have no idea of the historical context from which this letter emerged nor the occasion prompting its composition. The best we can do is to explore the narrative world created by the text rather than the historical situation addressed by the text.

3.4 Genre and Rhetorical Elements in the Letter

The Epistle to the Laodiceans has been identified as a paraenetic letter that follows the fivefold Pauline letter structure. Paraenesis, as "moral exhortation," was the discourse of persuading or dissuading a given course of action.[65] Although older New Testament scholarship, largely under the influence of Martin Dibelius's work on James, treated moral exhortation in Paul's letters as stereotypical moral advice with no connection to the letter's occasion, more recent scholarship has broken new ground in appreciating the social and rhetorical functions of hortatory elements in early Christian texts.[66] The most significant work emerged from two collections of essays, one in the early 1990s under the leadership of Leo Perdue (the *Semeia* group) and the other in the early 2000s under the leadership of Troels Engberg-Pedersen and James Starr (the Lund-Oslo group).[67] Both stressed the social

---

63. Mackay, "Content and Style," 215–40.

64. On the Slavonic translation, see Aurelio de Santos Otero, *Die handschriftliche Überlieferung der altslavischen Apokryphen*, vol. 1 (Berlin: de Gruyter, 1978), 147–48; for the Arabic translation, see B. Carra de Vaux, "L'Épitre aux Laodiceans en arabe," *RB* 6 (1896): 221–26.

65. Ps.-Libanius's definition of paraenesis is apt: "The paraenetic style is that in which we exhort someone by urging him to pursue something or to avoid something. Paraenesis is divided into two parts, encouragement and dissuasion" (*Epistolary Styles*; cited from Stanley K. Stowers, *Letter Writing in Greco-Roman Antiquity*, Library of Early Christianity [Philadelphia: Westminster, 1986], 94).

66. Martin Dibelius, *James: A Commentary on the Epistle of James*, trans. M. Williams, Hermeneia (Philadelphia: Fortress, 1976). See also David Bradley, "Topos as a Form in the Pauline Paraenesis," *JBL* 73 (1953): 238–46.

67. Leo G. Perdue, "The Social Character of Paraenesis and Paraenetic Literature," *Semeia* 50 (1990): 5–38. Other contributors to this thematic issue on "Paraenesis: Act and Form" include John G. Gammie, Raymond Van Leeuwen, Amy-Jill Levine, James G. Williams, Jerome D. Quinn, Harold W. Attridge, James M. Reese, Claudia V. Camp, and Vernon K. Robbins. The *Semeia* group broke new ground in exploring the forms and

and conceptual aspects of paraenesis as enjoining the recipients to continue to hold to the moral path they are currently on. Perdue stressed the liminal aspects of paraenesis, often as instruction given from an aged or revered figure to someone entering a new stage in life, whereas the Lund-Oslo group demonstrated that moral exhortation is a call to remember what is known rather than to embrace a new worldview—indeed, the effectiveness of the exhortation rests on the assumption of a shared worldview between the preceptor and the audience (and in this sense, paraenesis is distinguished from protrepsis [i.e., the call to embrace a new or different moral path or worldview]). Although sections of a text can be paraenetic (notably within the Pauline letter structure), Abraham Malherbe and Troy Martin have both demonstrated that entire texts—notably 1 Thessalonians and 1 Peter—can fit a paraenetic genre.[68]

The Epistle to the Laodiceans fits the paraenetic genre. It speaks to (fictive) recipients that are already adhering to Paul's teaching but face the threat of alternative or false teaching. Paul writes to the Laodicean Christians to encourage them to hold fast to the "truth" that Paul preached to them. It is notable that the letter does not address the dissidents directly, nor does it call for reconciliation between factions in Laodicea. Rather, the letter affirms the truthfulness of Paul's teaching—as the "true gospel"—and encourages the Laodicean Christians to continue adhering to that teaching by resisting false teaching. This rhetorical technique is accomplished by evoking a universal identification with the universal church, while reinforcing the positive relations between Paul and the Laodiceans. Such social affinity isolates the false teachers or dissidents (who are left vague as to their identity and teaching), thereby delegitimizing alternative or "heretical" teaching while legitimizing the "Paul" constructed by this letter.

The letter is built around two kinds of moral exempla: a positive example and a negative example. Such binaries are not atypical in moral discourse and often arise in paraenesis.[69] In the Epistle to the Laodiceans, Paul serves as the positive example (notably vv. 6–9). His suffering and reward for endurance serve as a model for the Laodiceans as they continue to hold fast to the true gospel that Paul proclaimed to them. In contrast, false teachers are presented through the trope of the charlatan. Their motives are immoral—they are "out for sordid gain" (v. 13)—and thus they are not legitimate models for the Laodiceans to emulate. The binary of Paul and the false teachers articulates the moral character that is to be attached to the gospel and to the eschatological promise of eternal life (vv. 4–5). The use of significant historical or legendary figures was common in paraenesis. Ps.-Crates's letter to Patrocles, a fictional letter that circulated in second-century Cynic circles, offers an excellent example. Patrocles is exhorted to emulate Diogenes, the famed founder of Cynicism, rather than Odysseus, for Diogenes "delivered many from evil to virtue" and his influence continues "after he died through the teachings he left behind for us."[70] For second-century

---

social functions of paraenesis in Second Temple Judaism and early Christianity. Troy Martin's seminal work on paraenesis in 1 Peter is heavily indebted to this group of scholars. The Lund-Oslo group's work emerged over two conferences held in Lund, Sweden (August 25–27, 2000) and Oslo, Norway (August 24–26, 2001) and collected in Troels Engberg-Pedersen and James M. Starr, eds., *Early Christian Paraenesis in Context* (Berlin: de Gruyter, 2004).

68. Martin, *Metaphor*; Abraham J. Malherbe, "Exhortation in First Thessalonians," *NovT* 25 (1983): 238–56.

69. See Tite, *Valentinian Ethics*, 147–64. See Aristotle, *Rhet.* 2.10.11: "Emulation therefore is virtuous and characteristic of virtuous men, whereas envy is base and characteristic of base men; for the one, owing to emulation, fits himself to obtain such goods, while the object of the other, owing to envy, is to prevent his neighbour possessing them" (Freese, LCL).

70. Ps.-Crates, *Epistle* 19. Translation by Ronald F. Hock in *The Cynic Epistles: A Study Edition*, ed. A. Malherbe, SBLSBS 12 (Missoula, MT: Scholars Press, 1977; repr., Atlanta: SBL Press, 2006), 69. On the

Christians, Paul serves just this role as a famed figure to emulate. As part of a fluid *Corpus Polemicum*, the Epistle to the Laodiceans is one example of an early Christian historical-fictional letter designed to tap into the continued influence and authority of Paul from the first century to speak to Christians in the second century (using the figure of Paul to draw boundaries of a perceived true Christian identity from false teaching). Like Diogenes, Paul serves as a focal point for remaining on the correct moral path, while warning the recipients of the threat of alternative (negative) examples.

3.5 Theological Motifs

The main theological motif of the Epistle to the Laodiceans is eschatology, to which all other theological ideas lend support. An "end time" promise of eternal life arises throughout the letter (vv. 3, 5, 7, 10, and possibly 16 if "peace will be with you" is read eschatologically). Laodiceans follows the typical Pauline eschatological model of the "already/not yet" in order to encourage the recipients to remain firm on the path they are on. What they have must be preserved in the face of false teaching in order to attain their eschatological reward upon successfully completing their eschatological journey during this liminal period leading to the end of the earthly age.[71]

Laodiceans also includes a slight ecclesiology, where Paul situates the Laodicean Christians within a universal ecclesia. Not only does the Laodicean church belong to the Pauline mission due to the work of Paul and his coworkers (see v. 5), but they have a shared network connection with the church in Colossae (v. 20). Implied is the exclusion of the false teachers from the universal church. Such a rhetorical positioning of the Laodiceans within a broader catholic church effectively serves the polemical function of the pseudo-Pauline letters identified by Smith as comprising an early second-century *Corpus Polemicum*.

Trinitarian theology also has been identified in the Epistle to the Laodiceans.[72] The Father, Christ, and the Holy Spirit are distinct divine persons with various functions in the life of the Laodicean community. It is the Holy Spirit who works within the community, Christ who is the reason for Paul's (and by extension the community's) suffering, and the Father to whom prayers are directed for future benefits. There is a vaguely articulated past (Christ), present (Spirit), and future (Father) assignment of divine functions—with all three members of the Trinity bringing the Christian community to eschatological fulfillment. Although all three members of the Trinity hold distinct personhood in the letter, there are no indications of debates over the tension between distinct personhood and shared essence, such as we find in Tertullian (*Prax.* 13: "three persons, one substance"), nor does Laodiceans articulate or counter subordinationist or modalist theologies. The Holy Spirit's "administrative" function (v. 7), however, does parallel Origen's functional view of the Spirit.[73] This undeveloped Trinitarian theology could be due to the simple theology in Laodiceans or to the secondary role that Trinitarianism and ecclesiology play to eschatology in the letter, or it could be an indication that Laodiceans was composed prior to these theological debates erupting in the third century.

---

emulation of legendary figures within Cynicism, see Donald R. Dudley, *A History of Cynicism: From Diogenes to the 6th Century AD*, 2nd ed., ed. M. Griffin (London: Methuen, 2003), 198–201. Even twenty years later, the Lund-Oslo group's work remains the standard framework for the study of early Christian paraenesis.

71. For a helpful overview of Pauline eschatology and its application to the letter, see Tite, *Apocryphal Epistle to Laodiceans*, 83–91.

72. Pervo, *Making of Paul*, 106, 109; Tite, *Apocryphal Epistle to the Laodiceans*, 94–99.

73. See Tite, "The Holy Spirit's Role in Origen's Trinitarian System: A Comparison with Valentinian Pneumatology," *Theoforum* 32 (2001): 131–64, esp. 152–57.

Other themes in the Epistle to the Laodiceans include martyrdom and suffering linked to life and achieved through communal unity. As a pseudonymous work written, at the earliest, nearly a century after Paul's death, verse 8's "For my life is in Christ and so to die is joy (to me)" may have evoked for a second- or third-century audience the martyrdom traditions circulated about Paul at the beginning of the second century (e.g., 1 Clem. 5; cf. Ign. *Rom.* 4.3) and which eventually formed into the martyrdom account incorporated into the Acts of Paul. "Life" is a key concept in Laodiceans, where suffering leads to eternal life if the Christian endures and remains firm in the truth. Thus, just as Paul suffered and attained the eschatological promise, so also will the Laodiceans (as narrative stand-ins for the second-century recipients) if they follow Paul's example by remaining united (i.e., "have the same love and be likeminded"; v. 9).

4. KEY PASSAGES FOR NEW TESTAMENT STUDIES AND THEIR SIGNIFICANCE

There is a direct literary relationship between the Epistle to the Laodiceans and several of the New Testament letters attributed to Paul, specifically Colossians, Galatians, and most importantly Philippians. The letter is the product of a period when the figure of Paul was being shaped in various ways to establish competing Christian identities. Such efforts occurred through Pauline works that found a place within the New Testament and those that remained outside the canon, or, like Laodiceans, seemed to fluidly reside within and without the canon until finally excluded.

Colossians is evoked, and inverted, in the letter-closing:

Colossians 4:16	Epistle to the Laodiceans 20
"And when this letter has been read among you, have it read also in the church of the Laodiceans; and see that you read also the letter from Laodicea." (NRSV)	"And see that this letter is read to the Colossians and that of the Colossians among you."

Dependency on Colossians is widely assumed. Laodiceans simply closes by reversing the instructions to exchange letters, thereby filling the "gap" created by the missing letter. Although scholarship treats Colossians as the inspiration for the pseudonymous letter to Laodicea, the exact relationship between Colossians and Laodiceans has not been adequately explored. Discussions often ignore the disputed authorship of Colossians and thus ignore that both letters may be interlinked pseudonymous letters.

There are several possible relations between the two letters: (1) Colossians is an authentic letter coming from the hand of Paul, and Laodiceans uses Colossians to construct a pseudonymous device; (2) Colossians is pseudonymous, but has been received by the author of Laodiceans as authentic and treated as such; (3) Colossians and Laodiceans are both pseudonymous letters and were designed to support each other as authentic Pauline epistles; or (4) Laodiceans was authentic or received as authentic and used by the author of Colossians to create a pseudonymous device. All four are problematic. There is little shared overlap in content or concepts beyond the closing instructions in Colossians 4:16 and the Epistle to the Laodiceans 20. Although the suffering of Paul and the threat of false teaching or philosophy arises in both letters, the themes are developed distinctly. If these closing instructions were not present, there would be no basis for relating these two letters.

A similar problem arises with Galatians as with Colossians, even though Paul's authorship of Galatians is undisputed. The overlap is found at the beginning, rather than the end, of both letters:

Galatians 1:1–5	The Epistle to the Laodiceans 1–2
"Paul an apostle—sent neither by human commission nor from human authorities, but through Jesus Christ and God the Father, who raised him from the dead— and all the members of God's family, who are with me, to the churches of Galatia: Grace to you and peace from God our Father and the Lord Jesus Christ, who gave himself for our sins to set us free from the present evil age, according to the will of our God and Father, to whom be the glory forever and ever. Amen." (NRSV)	"Paul, an apostle not from mortals nor through mortals, but through Jesus Christ, to the brethren who are in Laodicea. Grace to you and peace from God the Father and the Lord Jesus Christ."

There are significant overlaps between the two prescripts, though some elements are formulaic conventions and need not rely on literary dependency. More significant is "not from mortals nor through mortals, but through Jesus Christ." This expansion on the A to B greeting formula in both letters suggests familiarity between them. All other overlaps indicate that Laodiceans follows the normal Pauline epistolary style. If Laodiceans is using Galatians, then the author has framed the expansion into a distinctly unique epistolary context that diverges from Galatians and thus uses the expansion to address a different social situation than found in Galatians. In Galatians, Paul asserts his authority as an apostle to reprimand the Galatian Christians. In Laodiceans Paul's authority is not threatened and the declaration of apostleship is used to reinforce—not to reestablish—the positive relations already existing between the letter writer and the Christian community. The lack of a thanksgiving in Galatians and the very positive view of the community in the Epistle to the Laodiceans's thanksgiving further distances the two letters. Beyond the prescript, there are no other parallels between these two letters.

The main source for Laodiceans is Philippians. Sellew has argued persuasively that Laodiceans demonstrates knowledge of only those sections of Philippians identified as letter B (1:1–3:1; 4:4–9, 21–23), with notable differences (e.g., the prescript and thanksgiving). Sellew offers the following breakdown of parallels between letter B and Laodiceans:[74]

The Epistle to the Laodiceans	Philippians
6	1:13, 18
7	1:19–20
8	1:21
9	2:2
10	2:12
11	2:13
14	4:6
15	4:8
16	4:9
18	4:22
19	4:23

74. Sellew, "*Laodiceans* and the Philippians Fragments Hypothesis," 28.

In addition, Laodiceans may have used Philippians at other points, though some of these parallels are debatable (v. 5 = Phil 1:12; v. 12 = 2:14; v. 13 = 3:1). Sellew's parallels in the letter-opening (vv. 2–3 = Phil 1:2–3) are unlikely, given the standard formula used in both the greeting section of the prescript and the opening of the thanksgivings.

Sellew demonstrates that if Laodiceans is using Philippians, then it is using a version of Philippians that is a much-abbreviated version from canonical Philippians, that is, letter B. Such a conclusion supports the partition reading of Philippians. However, if we look closer at the parallels, then it becomes clear that the version of Philippians present in, or used by, Laodiceans is much simpler than the letter B embedded in canonical Philippians. The relationship of Laodiceans to Philippians and especially to letter B, therefore, needs to be addressed. There are several possibilities:

1. The Epistle to the Laodiceans carefully abbreviates letter B, removing possible historical markers as well as softening the Pauline themes in letter B;
2. Letter B was redacted when merged with letters A and C to form canonical Philippians; or
3. Letter B has expanded on an even more primitive version of letter B that is discernable in Laodiceans.

Most likely we are seeing either option 2 or 3, with perhaps some elements of option 1 (e.g., eliminating specifics about Paul's imprisonment in Phil 1:13). The differences between the two letters are best understood as expansions on letter B embedded in Laodiceans rather than abbreviations of Philippians, with the caveat of further redactional work by Laodiceans on sections of letter B (notably the use of Galatians and Colossians as well as the elimination of elements specific to Philippians). Consequently, the letter-B version of Philippians found in Laodiceans may be more primitive, and thus more likely to go back to Paul, than what we find in canonical Philippians. Such a line of reasoning results in the possibility that Laodiceans, not as a letter to Laodicea but as an edited version of one of Paul's letters to Philippi, may be more authentically Pauline than canonical Philippians.

However, even if we treat Laodiceans as purely pseudonymous and dependent on the New Testament Pauline letters—and certainly Laodiceans is a product of emerging Christian communities from at least the second century as they refashioned Paul to serve their own literary imagination and communal concerns—this apocryphal letter offers a valuable testimony to the creative excitement that erupted around the figure of Paul in the early church. The second and third centuries were formative periods where Christian identity was being fashioned, contested, authenticated, and diffused throughout the Mediterranean world via a growing network of Christian communities. The Epistle to the Laodiceans was part of that process, offering one more unique portrayal of this famed apostle. It was a short apocryphal letter that was cherished by Christians for centuries, at least in the West, until it fell into a state of neglect in modern times. The renewed scholarly interest in this delightful apocryphal letter offers us a fresh opportunity to explore anew the legacy of Paul in late antiquity and medieval Christianity.

5. BIBLIOGRAPHY

Backus, Irena. "Lettre de Paul aux Laodicéens." Pages 1089–97 of vol. 2 of *Écrits apocryphes chrétiens*. Edited by Pierre Geoltrain and Jean-Daniel Kaestli. Bibliothèque de la Pléiade 443. Paris: Gallimard, 2005.

Burnet, Régis. "Pourquoi avoir écrit l'insipide épître aux Laodicéens?" *NTS* 48 (2002): 132–41.

Hall, Thomas N. "Aelfric and the Epistle to the Laodiceans." Pages 65–84 in *Apocryphal Texts and Traditions in Anglo-Saxon England*. Edited by Kathryn Powell and Donald Scragg. Cambridge: D. S. Brewer, 2003.

Longenecker, Bruce W., and Scott C. Ryan. "Presenting the Pauline Voice: An Appreciation of the *Letter to the Laodiceans*." *NTS* 62 (2016): 136–48.

Mackay, Thomas W. "Content and Style in Two Pseudo-Pauline Epistles (3 Corinthians and the Epistle to the Laodiceans)." Pages 215–40 in *Apocryphal Writings and the Latter-Day Saints*. Edited by C. Wilfred Griggs. Religious Studies Monograph Series 13. Salt Lake: Brigham Young University, 1986.

Pervo, Richard I. *The Making of Paul: Constructions of the Apostle in Early Christianity*. Minneapolis: Fortress, 2010.

Schneemelcher, Wilhelm. "The Epistle to the Laodiceans." *NTApoc* 2:44–46.

Sellew, Philip. "Laodiceans and the Philippians Fragments Hypothesis." *HTR* 87 (1994): 17–28.

Tite, Philip L. *The Apocryphal Epistle to the Laodiceans: An Epistolary and Rhetorical Analysis*. TENTS 7. Leiden: Brill, 2012.

———. "Dusting Off a Pseudo-Historical Letter: Re-Thinking the Epistolary Aspects of the Apocryphal Epistle to the Laodiceans." Pages 289–318 in *Paul and Pseudepigraphy*. Edited by Stanley E. Porter and Gregory P. Fewster. Pauline Studies 8. Leiden: Brill, 2013.

———. "Epistle to the Laodiceans." e-Clavis: Christian Apocrypha. www.nasscal.com/e-clavis-christian-apocrypha/epistle-to-the-laodiceans/.

CHAPTER 23

EPISTULA APOSTOLORUM

FLORENCE GANTENBEIN

1. INTRODUCTION

The *Epistula Apostolorum*, or the "Epistle of the Apostles" (henceforth *EpAp* in the notes), is an early Christian gospel text stylized as a circular letter of the eleven disciples to the universal church. It gives an account of Jesus's life and ministry with a particular focus on his post-resurrection teaching. While the second-century text has circulated in late antiquity in at least four languages (Greek, Coptic, Latin, and Ethiopic), no references to *Epistula Apostolorum* have been identified in extant patristic writings so far. Despite the text's continuous transmission in the Ethiopian Orthodox Church, scholarship only became aware of the work at the beginning of the twentieth century.

1.1 Authorship and Intention

The *Epistula Apostolorum* presents itself as the revelation of Jesus Christ, transmitted in epistolary form by the apostolic collective headed by John. This "apostolic" account of Christ's life and teaching aims at the instruction and assurance of Christians challenged by diverging teachings as well as moral and social differential within their communities. While research on the identity of *Epistula Apostolorum*'s author is still scarce, the text was evidently written in Greek by a second-century Christian, presumably in Asia Minor, who was familiar with traditions preserved in the Septuagint and in the emerging New Testament collection.[1]

1.2 Genre

The *Epistula Apostolorum* features a range of genres. First, it participates in the gospel genre by bridging the subgenres of narrative and dialogue gospels.[2] As a narrative gospel, *Epistula Apostolorum* retells Jesus's life from birth to ascension, including his childhood, ministry, death, and resurrection. Occasionally, the text relates Christ's preexistent activities, such as his interaction with Israel's forefathers and prophets or his descent through the heavens down to earth.[3] Contrary to most narrative gospels, *Epistula Apostolorum*

---

1. The author does not necessarily need to be familiar with NT writings but with the early Christian traditions transmitted in them. For more details, see sec. 4 below.

2. This article follows the definition of *gospel* offered by Gregory and Tuckett: "'Gospels' make at least some claim to give direct reports of the life and/or teaching of Jesus" (Andrew Gregory and Christopher Tuckett, "Series Preface," in *The Gospel of Mary*, ed. C. Tuckett, Oxford Early Christian Gospel Texts [Oxford: Oxford University Press, 2007], v–xi [vi–vii]). Gregory and Tuckett list four subgenres: "narrative gospels," "sayings gospels," "infancy gospels," and "resurrection dialogues/discourses" (ix). In this article, the latter category is replaced by "dialogue gospels" to highlight its gospel dimension.

3. For a detailed evaluation of *EpAp* as a narrative gospel, see Francis Watson, "On the Miracle Catena in

contextualizes a substantial proportion of its content after Jesus's death and resurrection—namely, in a sizeable dialogue between the risen Christ and his disciples. This shift of emphasis toward Christ's post-resurrection teaching as well as *Epistula Apostolorum*'s prevalent dialogue format are literary characteristics commonly associated with dialogue gospels.[4] Secondly, the work is stylized as an epistle of the eleven disciples. Although the text's explicit epistolary elements are fragmentary and restricted to *Epistula Apostolorum* 1–2 and 6–8,[5] its conceptualization as an apostolic letter is crucial for the work's self-presentation as an apostolic witness of Christ. Accordingly, the text's epistolary character has been foregrounded in Schmidt's denotation of the text as *"Epistula Apostolorum."*[6]

Due to its versatility, *Epistula Apostolorum* has acquired several generic labels over time, each depending on the respective scholarly focus. While the work used to be described as a *resurrection discourse* (Tuckett and Gregory)[7] or a *revelation dialogue* (Hills),[8] recent research tends to emphasize its gospel qualities by referring to it as a *dialogue gospel* (Hartenstein; Parkhouse)[9] or even as an *apostolic gospel* (Watson).[10]

1.3 Date of Composition

The *Epistula Apostolorum* is commonly dated to either the first or the second half of the second century CE. Since no references to it have been identified in surviving early Christian literature so far, dating relies on text-immanent evidence. A second-century origin of *Epistula Apostolorum* is indicated by three major observations. First, while the author displays knowledge of Matthew, Luke, and John, there is a "degree of freedom in his handling of the gospel material which is not untypical of second-century authors."[11] At the same time, the author's use of early Christian tradition is not yet informed by a divide into "canonical" and "noncanonical" material but rather by the integration of (later to become) "apocryphal" traditions, such as an account of Jesus's first day at school (*EpAp* 4.1–2) or Christ's descent to earth in angelic form (*EpAp* 13.1–14.5). Second, *Epistula Apostolorum* builds upon apostolic authority and elaborates on church ministry without assuming a differentiated ecclesiastical structure. Third, several of the work's theological characteristics point toward a relatively early date of composition, such as its imminent eschatological expectation, its emphasis on Christ's bodily resurrection, the form and content of its creedal statements, as well as the address of Jewish and gentile Christians as part of the same *ecclesia*.

Epistula Apostolorum 4–5," in *Gospels and Gospel Traditions in the Second Century: Experiments in Reception*, ed. J. Schröter, T. Nicklas, and J. Verheyden, BZNW 235 (Berlin: de Gruyter, 2019), 107–27.

4. On dialogue gospels, see Sarah Parkhouse, *Eschatology and the Saviour: The Gospel of Mary among Early Christian Dialogue Gospels*, SNTSMS 176 (Cambridge: Cambridge University Press, 2019), 1–68.

5. In this article, *EpAp*'s English translation and chapter/verse enumeration are taken from Francis Watson, *An Apostolic Gospel: The "Epistula Apostolorum" in Literary Context*, SNTSMS 179 (Cambridge: Cambridge University Press, 2020), 42–77.

6. Carl Schmidt (with Isaak Wajnberg), *Gespräche Jesu mit seinen Jüngern nach der Auferstehung: Ein katholisch-apostolisches Sendschreiben des 2. Jahrhunderts* (Leipzig: J. C. Hinrichs, 1919; repr., Hildesheim: Georg Olms, 1967).

7. Tuckett and Gregory, "Series Preface," ix.

8. Julian V. Hills, *Tradition and Composition in the Epistula Apostolorum*, 2nd ed., Harvard Theological Studies 57 (Minneapolis: Fortress, 2008), 27.

9. Judith Hartenstein, *Die zweite Lehre: Erscheinungen des Auferstandenen als Rahmenerzählungen früh-christlicher Dialoge*, TUGAL 146 (Berlin: Akademie, 2000), 97–126; Parkhouse, *Eschatology and the Saviour*, 13–125.

10. See Watson's title of his study on and translation of *EpAp*, *An Apostolic Gospel: The "Epistula Apostolorum" in Literary Context*.

11. Darrell D. Hannah, "The Four-Gospel 'Canon' in the Epistula Apostolorum," *JTS* 59 (2008): 598–633 (606).

Within the second century CE, a potential *terminus ante quem* for *Epistula Apostolorum*'s time of composition is provided by its announcement of Christ's parousia. Unfortunately, the prediction "has proved disappointingly slippery"[12] since at least three decisive factors must be considered. To begin with, the work's textual tradition has preserved two diverging figures. While the sole Coptic manuscript predicts Christ's return after the completion of 120 "parts,"[13] the Ethiopic tradition unanimously offers 150 years (*EpAp* 17.2):

And we said to him, "Lord, after how many years will these things be?" He said to us,

> *Cop.* "When the hundredth part and the twentieth part are completed,
> *Eth.* "When the hundred and fiftieth year is completed,

between Pentecost and the Feast of Unleavened Bread, the coming of my Father will take place."[14]

Since both figures predict the parousia for the second century CE, and the Ethiopic textual tradition offers no variations, the alteration of the original figure presumably occurred in the early Greek transmission of the text. While one or both of the current figures might stem from transcriptional errors, the higher figure might also manifest a correction of the lower one—either based on the availability of more accurate chronological information[15] or due to the nonoccurrence of the parousia, that is, when Christ had not returned after 120 years (*Cop.*), the time frame was extended for another thirty years (*Eth.*). Aside from preferences for either of the two figures, the starting point for a date calculation needs to be determined, for which Christ's incarnation and ascension have been suggested. Starting from Christ's incarnation, the text would predict the parousia either around 120 CE (*Cop.*) or 150 CE (*Eth.*). Starting from Christ's ascension (ca. 30 CE), the prediction amounts to 30 + 120 = 150 CE (*Cop.*) or 30 + 150 = 180 CE (*Eth.*) respectively. Since Christ announces the parousia between his resurrection and ascension, the latter alternative (150/180 CE) seems more plausible and is followed by most scholars.[16] Finally, *Epistula Apostolorum* presumably granted its recipients some preparation time before Christ's return. In consideration of the text's imminent eschatological expectation, most scholars assume that *Epistula Apostolorum* notified its recipients a decade in advance of the parousia. Thus, starting from Christ's ascension, dating is dependent on the preference of either the Coptic or the Ethiopic figure minus a decade. Accordingly, the work is commonly dated to either the 140s CE (*Cop.*; see Hill; Hannah)[17] or the 170s CE (*Eth.*; see Watson; Pérès; Kiel).[18]

---

12. Charles E. Hill, "The Epistula Apostolorum: An Asian Tract from the Time of Polycarp," *JECS* 7 (1999): 1–53 (4).

13. For a discussion of the Coptic usage of "parts," see Watson, *Apostolic Gospel*, 239.

14. Christ explains the parousia as his and the Father's return: "I am wholly in my Father and my Father is in me" (*EpAp* 17.4).

15. According to Watson, "It is also possible that both the original figure and its correction originated at much the same time" (*Apostolic Gospel*, 8). The higher figure (the Ethiopic's "150") does not necessarily indicate a delayed parousia but might be based on the availability of more accurate chronological information. This allows for an assumption of the Coptic's "120" as the original Greek figure while still dating *EpAp* in accordance with the higher figure. Consequently, Christ's return was anticipated in 180 CE, and *EpAp*'s composition can be dated in the 170s CE.

16. It was mainly Manfred Hornschuh who evaluated a starting point at Christ's incarnation and thus a composition date shortly before 120 CE; see his *Studien zur Epistula Apostolorum*, PTS 5 (Berlin: de Gruyter, 1965), 116–19.

17. Hill, "Asian Tract," 39–53; Hannah, "Four-Gospel," 628–32.

18. Watson, *Apostolic Gospel*, 8–11; Nikolai Kiel, "Auferstehung des Fleisches in der Epistula Apostolorum,"

In view of this relatively open result, scholars have further suggested correlating *Epistula Apostolorum*'s description of the end times to historical events. In *Epistula Apostolorum* 34–35, Jesus predicts a sequence of earthquake, drought, and plague that results in the persecution of Christians. Hill, who prefers the Coptic figure (120), points to the high probability of such a disastrous confluence in second-century Asia Minor. Based on several local earthquakes in the 140s CE, he suggests a date of composition between 142–49 CE.[19] Watson, who prefers the Ethiopic figure (150), identifies the text's description of a severe epidemic with the Antonine Plague in 165–180 CE, thus dating *Epistula Apostolorum* around 170 CE.[20]

1.4 Provenance

Egypt, Syria, and Asia Minor have been discussed as possible origins of *Epistula Apostolorum*. The proposal for an Egyptian origin is primarily based on the work's alleged "anti-gnostic" orientation that was further associated with Hellenistic Jewish-Christianity in Alexandria. Additionally, *Epistula Apostolorum*'s dialogue format and post-resurrection focus have been linked to dialogue gospels circulating in Egypt, such as the Gospel of Mary, the Apocryphon of James, and the First Apocalypse of James. While popular in twentieth-century research, the Egypt-hypothesis has been compellingly challenged by recent scholarship.[21] Regarding a Syrian origin, Pérès has argued that the work displays parallels to the presumably third-century Anaphora of Addai and Mari, which is linked to Edessa in Syriac Osroene. Also, he points to a passage in *Epistula Apostolorum* in which the coming of a new Jerusalem is associated with Roman Syria (*EpAp* 33.5).[22] Kiel further interprets *Epistula Apostolorum* 33.2 as associating the founding of the church with Damascus.[23]

While the arguments for Syria are not unreasonable, they are less compelling than the case for an Asian background. The latter is suggested by *Epistula Apostolorum*'s strong links to the Johannine tradition, evident in its parallels to the Fourth Gospel,[24] the primacy of John among the disciples (*EpAp* 2.1), and the reference to Cerinthus (1.1; 7.1), presumably an Asian Christian teacher traditionally associated with John and located in Ephesus.[25] Further, *Epistula Apostolorum*'s description of weather conditions (e.g., winter rain, mist, frost, and hail in *EpAp* 3.8) as well as the confluence of earthquake, drought, plague, and persecution (chs. 34–36) largely correspond with Asia Minor's climatic, geological, and social circumstances during the second century CE.[26] Finally, Christ's

---

VC 74 (2020): 165–98 (174n27); Jacques-Noël Pérès, "Das lebendige Wort: Zu einem Agraphon in der *Epistula Apostolorum*," in *Christian Apocrypha: Receptions of the New Testament in Ancient Christian Apocrypha*, ed. J.-M. Roessli and T. Nicklas, Novum Testamentum Patristicum 29 (Göttingen: Vandenhoeck & Ruprecht, 2014), 125–32 (125). For an evaluation of *EpAp*'s composition around 160–170 CE, see Schmidt, *Gespräche*, 370–402.

19. Hill is unsure whether to start calculating at Christ's birth or ascension and thus also offers support for a dating prior to 120 CE ("Asian Tract," 47–52).

20. Watson, *Apostolic Gospel*, 9–11.

21. Egypt was advocated by Hornschuh, *Studien*, 99–115; and Caspar D. G. Müller, "Die Epistula Apostolorum: Einleitung und Übersetzung," in *Evangelien und Verwandtes*, vol. 1 of *Antike christliche Apokryphen in deutscher Übersetzung*, ed. C. Markschies and J. Schröter, 7th ed., 2 vols. (Tübingen: Mohr Siebeck, 2012), 1062–92. For a critique, see Hill, "Asian Tract," 6–18.

22. Jacques-Noël Pérès, "Paul et la Syrie comme nouvelle Jérusalem dans l'Épître des apôtres," in *Pierre Geoltrain ou comment «faire l'histoire» des religions?*, ed. S. Mimouni and I. Ullern-Weité, BEHER 128 (Turnhout: Brepols, 2006), 239–45.

23. Kiel, "Auferstehung," 191n83.

24. For details, see sec. 4 below.

25. See Irenaeus, *Haer.* 3.3.4. For more details on Cerinthus, see sec. 3 below.

26. Hill, "Asian Tract," 15.

instruction to "celebrate the memorial of my death when the Feast of the Pascha comes" (15.1) might indicate a Quartodeciman practice—that is, the celebration of Easter on Nissan 14, the date of the Jewish Passover feast, which was particularly prominent among Christians in Asia Minor and Syria. As potential locations within Asia Minor, Ephesus (Schmidt; Watson)[27] and Smyrna (Hill)[28] have been suggested. Although none of the above arguments makes a clear case by itself, the combined evidence is strongest for an Asian provenance of *Epistula Apostolorum*.[29]

1.5 Language and Manuscripts

While the original Greek version of *Epistula Apostolorum* is lost, the text has been preserved in a Coptic and several Ethiopic manuscripts as well as in a Latin fragment. The oldest extant version of the work is found in a fourth- or fifth-century Coptic manuscript.[30] Written in the Akhmimic dialect, it covers around 60 percent of *Epistula Apostolorum* while "30 out of (probably) 68 pages are entirely or almost entirely missing. All extant pages have suffered more or less significant damage."[31] Consequently, the Coptic version lacks the opening (*EpAp* 1.1–6.3) and close (49.1–51.5), as well as crucial passages in between, such as Christ's first commissioning of his disciples (18.5b–19.8), a part within the discourse on the resurrection of the flesh (21.3b–22.3b), as well as the prediction of Paul and the end times (31.1–38.3a). The surviving pagination in the Coptic manuscript suggests an almost identical length of its version of *Epistula Apostolorum* compared to the ones preserved in the Ethiopic textual tradition. Several complete versions of the work are preserved in more than sixteen Ethiopic (Ge'ez) manuscripts dated from the fifteenth to the nineteenth centuries CE.[32] While the Ethiopic text of *Epistula Apostolorum* was assumed to have been translated from an Arabic or Coptic *Vorlage*, recent research suggests that it was originally translated directly from Greek.[33] Due to the age of the Coptic manuscript, it is generally prioritized over Ethiopic variants, yet the close agreement between the Ethiopic and the Coptic in extant passages allows for complementing the lacunae in the damaged Coptic text with Ethiopic variants.[34] The fragment discovered in a fifth- or sixth-century Latin palimpsest codex preserved only a small part of *Epistula Apostolorum* that "amounts to a single leaf with eighteen short lines (approximately twenty characters per line) in two columns on each side."[35] The preserved Latin heading *epistula* was another reason for Schmidt's designation of the text.

In most Ethiopic manuscripts, *Epistula Apostolorum* is accompanied by two other

27. Schmidt, *Gespräche*, 361–70; Watson, *Apostolic Gospel*, 7.

28. Hill, "Asian Tract," 29–39.

29. Suggested by Schmidt, *Gespräche*, 361–402; Hill, "Asian Tract," 19–39; Watson, *Apostolic Gospel*, 7; Alistair Stewart-Sykes, "The Asian Context of the New Prophecy and of Epistula Apostolorum," *VC* 51 (1997): 416–38.

30. IFAO Copte inv. 413–433, Bibliothèque nationale, Paris, ed. Schmidt.

31. Watson, *Apostolic Gospel*, 42n1.

32. For an annotated list of the Ethiopic manuscripts and more details on the Coptic and Ethiopic agreement, see Julian V. Hills, *The Epistle of the Apostles* (Santa Rosa, CA: Polebridge, 2009), 5–12; Watson, *Apostolic Gospel*, 37–43.

33. See Darrell D. Hannah, "The Vorlage of the Ethiopic Version of the Epistula Apostolorum: Greek or Arabic?," in *Beyond Canon: Early Christianity and the Ethiopic Textual Tradition*, ed. F. Watson, M. Gebreananaye, and L. Williams, LNTS 643 (London: T&T Clark, 2020), 97–116.

34. This has only been realized in a minority of translations, most recently by Watson, *Apostolic Gospel*, 42–77.

35. Hills, *Epistle*, 12. The name of the codex is Codex Vindobonensis 16. The Latin fragment preserved *EpAp* 12.1; 13.1–2; 13.3–5; and 17.2–5.

writings—namely, the *Testamentum Domini* and the *Galilean Discourse* (GD).[36] The manuscripts usually open with an Ethiopic version of *Testamentum Domini*, a presumably mid-fourth century church-order manual set in a post-resurrection context, followed by *Galilean Discourse*, an apocalyptic text located in Galilee in which the risen Christ pronounces signs and trials of the end times. The latter most likely originated in an Ethiopic setting and was presumably composed as an introduction to *Epistula Apostolorum*, on which it is dependent (cf. *GD* 4.1–16 and *EpAp* 34.3–36.7).[37] In line with the Ethiopic manuscript tradition, Guerrier initially translated *Galilean Discourse* as an integral part of *Epistula Apostolorum*, with the result that the chapter enumeration of *Galilean Discourse* (1–11) continues in *Epistula Apostolorum* (12–62).[38] Schmidt subsequently separated the writings and reset the numbering for *Epistula Apostolorum*. From Schmidt and Wajnberg's German translation (1919) onward, *Epistula Apostolorum* has been divided into fifty-one chapters. Nevertheless, Guerrier's initial chapter enumeration has survived in brackets in most translations—for example, *Epistula Apostolorum* 1(12)—although *Galilean Discourse* is usually not displayed anymore. A subsequent verse enumeration was introduced by Hills, who translated *Epistula Apostolorum* into English directly from Coptic and Ethiopic (2009),[39] followed by Watson's translation (2020),[40] which is further supplemented by a critical apparatus in English indicating variations between the Coptic and the Ethiopic as well as within the Ethiopic textual traditions.

2. SUMMARY OF CONTENT

The *Epistula Apostolorum* is roughly separated into two sections by the death and resurrection of Jesus Christ. The first section (1–8) is framed by epistolary elements (1–2; 6–8) and summarizes Jesus's life and ministry (3–5). In a longer second section (9–51), the disciples relate their encounter with the risen Christ (9–12), followed by an extensive conversation about mission and eschatological matters (13–50) before the work closes with an ascension narrative (51).

Account of Jesus's Life and Ministry	
1–2	Prescript
3	Confession of Faith
4–5	Jesus's Ministry (Miracle Catena)
6–8	Recapitulation: Reason for Writing
Encounter and Dialogue with the Risen Christ	
9–12	Easter Narrative
13–50	Revelatory Dialogue
51	Ascension Narrative

FIGURE 23.1: Outline of *Epistula Apostolorum*

---

36. The name *"Galilean Discourse"* was introduced by Watson (*Apostolic Gospel*, 266).

37. For more details as well as a recent translation of *GD*, see Watson, *Apostolic Gospel*, 265–75.

38. In 1912, Louis Guerrier (with Sylvain Grébaut) was the first to publish the (rediscovered) Ethiopic text of *GD* + *EpAp*, accompanied by a translation into French; see *Le Testament en Galilée de Notre-Seigneur Jésus-Christ*, Patrologia Orientalis (Paris: Firmin-Didot, 1912; repr., Turnhout: Brepols, 2003).

39. Hills, *Epistle*. All previous English translations have been based on German or French translations of *EpAp*.

40. Watson, *Apostolic Gospel*.

Prescript (1–2)

The *Epistula Apostolorum* opens as an epistle of the eleven disciples to the universal church. The prescript is headed by the following content's declaration as revelation of Christ, similar in form to Revelation 1:1. The disciples warn against the misleading activities of the "false apostles" Simon and Cerinthus (1.2), and by contrast pronounce their own testimony of Christ to strengthen their recipients. The opening is worth quoting in full:

> What Jesus Christ revealed to his disciples and to all: on account of Simon and Cerinthus the false apostles this has been written, so that no one should associate with them, for there is in them a venom by which they kill people; so that you may be strong and not waver or be disturbed or depart from what you have heard, the word of the gospel. What we have heard and remembered and written for the whole world we entrust to you, our sons and daughters, in joy. In the name of God, ruler of the whole world, and of Jesus Christ, grace be multiplied to you.
>
> John and Thomas and Peter and Andrew and James and Philip and Bartholomew and Matthew and Nathanael and Judas the Zealot and Cephas to the churches of the east and the west, to those in the north and the south: proclaiming and declaring to you our Lord Jesus Christ, as we heard so have we written; and we touched him after he rose from the dead, when he revealed to us what is great and wonderful and true. (*EpAp* 1.1–2.3)

Confession of Faith (3)

The subsequent confession of faith declares Christ's authority in the present, God's creation and revelation, and Christ's incarnation. Rooted in and framed by the disciples' faithful testimony ("This we declare," 3.1; "as we saw," 3.13), Christ is denoted as "Lord and Saviour" (3.1), "God, the Son of God" (3.1), and "the Word" (3.13), "who was sent from God" (3.2), "is above all authorities" (3.3), and "sits above the Cherubim at the right hand of the throne of the Father" (3.4). The hymn-like passage also briefly refers to the Holy Spirit ("the Word became flesh of Mary, carried in her womb through the Holy Spirit," 3.13) and to God the Father ("ruler of the whole world, maker of every name that is named," 3.2). The confession's central statements regarding creation (3.5–10) indicate no clear referent, thus allowing for a reading of either the Father or the Son as agent of creation. The following statements about revelation presumably refer to Christ as the one who "spoke with the forefathers and prophets in parables and in truth" (3.11) and "whom the apostles preached and the disciples touched" (3.12).[41] The confession's final statement declares the incarnation and birth of the Word (ܟܐ [*kal*], presumably λόγος [*logos*]), initializing the subsequent account of Jesus's ministry:

> And God the Son of God do we confess, the Word who became flesh of Mary, carried in her womb through the Holy Spirit. And not by the desire of the flesh but by the will of God was he born; and he was swaddled in Bethlehem and manifested and nourished and grew up, as we saw. (*EpAp* 3.13–15)

Jesus's Ministry, or the Miracle Catena (4–5)

After having declared their faith in the preexistent Christ and his incarnation, the disciples focus on "the things he did as we watched him" (8.2). The following miracle

---

41. For a discussion of *EpAp* 3.5–12, see sec. 3 below.

catena contains seven miracle stories that are paralleled in other early Christian gospel texts:[42]

1. Jesus's alphabet lesson (*EpAp* 4.1–3; see Inf. Gos. Thom. 6; 14; also Irenaeus, *Haer.* 1.20.1)
2. Water into wine (*EpAp* 5.1; see John 2:1–12)
3. The hemorrhaging woman (*EpAp* 5.3–8; see Matt 9:20–22; Mark 5:25–34; Luke 8:43–48)
4. Legion (*EpAp* 5.10–12; see Matt 8:28–34; Mark 5:1–20; Luke 8:26–39)
5. Walking on water (*EpAp* 5.13; see Matt 14:22–33; Mark 6:45–52; John 6:16–21)
6. The coins in the fish's mouth (*EpAp* 5.14–16; see Matt 17:24–27)
7. The feeding of the five thousand (*EpAp* 5.17–21; see Matt 14:13–21; Mark 6:30–44; Luke 9:10–17; John 6:1–15)

In between these stories, the disciples present two short summaries of Jesus's healing ministry: "The dead he raised, and paralytics he made to walk, and the man whose hand was withered he restored" (5.2) and "the deaf he made to hear and the blind to see and those with demons he exorcized and those with leprosy he cleansed" (5.9). Regarding Jesus's feeding of the five thousand, the disciples offer an interpretation of the five loaves as a minimal *regula fidei*:

> If we ask and say, "What do these five loaves mean?" they are an image of our faith as true Christians; that is, in the Father, ruler of the whole world, and in Jesus Christ and in the Holy Spirit and in the holy church and in the forgiveness of sins. (*EpAp* 5.20–21)

Recapitulation: Reason for Writing (6–8)

The miracle catena concludes with an exhortation and a recapitulation of *Epistula Apostolorum*'s reason for writing (6–8) that corresponds with the text's opening (1.1–6). The recipients are reminded to "be strong and not [to] waver" (6.3) by holding on to the presented account of Christ. The following warning against Cerinthus and Simon,[43] who are identified by the disciples as their reason for writing, primarily serves as a rhetorical means to enhance *Epistula Apostolorum*'s significance. In contrast to the deadly "venom" (1.2) of these "enemies of our Lord Jesus Christ" (7.2), the work depicts the disciples as trustworthy witnesses to Christ.[44]

Overall, the first section of *Epistula Apostolorum* (1–8) establishes the authority of the text's source of revelation, Jesus Christ, and legitimizes his chosen medium of transmission, the apostles. Accordingly, the confession of faith does not only instruct the work's recipients about Christ's authority, preexistence, and incarnation but also portrays the disciples' faith. Likewise, the miracle catena outlines Jesus's redeeming ministry while demonstrating the apostles' crucial role as eyewitnesses. Thus, by the end of chapter eight, the recipients are both reminded of Christ's authority and ministry as well as confirmed in their trust in the apostles' testimony.

---

42. The following list is adapted from Watson's detailed evaluation of *EpAp* 4–5, see Watson, "Miracle Catena," 107.

43. While 1.2 refers to "Simon and Cerinthus," 7.1 mentions them in reverse order, i.e., "Cerinthus and Simon."

44. For a detailed evaluation of the significance of Cerinthus and Simon, see sec. 3 below.

Easter Narrative (9–12)

The Easter narrative is anticipated in *Epistula Apostolorum's* prescript (2.3) and opens with a resuming notice of Christ's crucifixion: "This we confess, that the Lord was crucified by Pontius Pilate" (9.1). It proceeds with Mary, Martha, and Mary Magdalene's discovery of the empty tomb and their ensuing encounter with the risen Christ.[45] Although he commissions them to proclaim the good news of his resurrection to their brothers ("Come, the Teacher has risen from the dead!" 10.2), the male disciples reject the women's proclamation twice ("What do you want with us, O woman? One who died and is buried, can he live?" 10.4, 8). Their doubt even prevails when Christ approaches them ("We thought it was a phantasm," 11.3) as well as throughout his attempt to verbally convince them ("Come, fear not, I am your teacher whom you, Peter, denied three times, and now do you deny again?" 11.4). Only the touch of his body leads the disciples to believe "that he had truly risen in flesh" (12.1). At their recognition, Jesus sets in with his revelatory speech:

> Rise and I will reveal to you what is above the heavens and what is in the heavens and your rest in the kingdom of the heavens. For my Father gave me authority to take you up and those who believe in me. (*EpAp* 12.3b–4)

The Easter narrative foregrounds the (male) disciples' collective overcoming of their disbelief in Christ's (bodily) resurrection.[46] The risen Christ is identified with the crucified Jesus ("Peter, put your fingers into the nail-marks of my hands; and you, Thomas, put your fingers into the spear wounds in my side," 11.7), and his physical appearance is examined ("and you, Andrew, look at my feet and see if they are not in contact with the ground," 11.7). His corporeality is underscored by his adherence to physical law. For instance, Christ walks with the women from his tomb to the gathering of the disciples instead of suddenly appearing in an enclosed space (cf. John 20:19, 26). The issue of bodily resurrection continues to intrigue the disciples in their following conversation with Jesus.

Revelatory Dialogue (13–50)

The text's central dialogue sets in with the following remark: "And what he revealed are these things that he said to us" (13.1). In a series of questions and answers, Jesus prepares his disciples for their impending mission. The apostolic collective is instructed to preach and teach the hope of the heavenly kingdom to Israel and the gentiles in accordance with the Scriptures and supported by Paul. The dialogue further examines eschatological issues and provides additional revelatory material on Christ's past actions and future events. The dialogic form of *Epistula Apostolorum's* central piece entails fluid transitions between single themes and, in some cases, leads to the resumption of previously discussed topics. Nevertheless, the conversation can be divided into five thematic blocks with individual subsections:

---

45. The Ethiopic reads, "Sarah and Martha and Mary Magdalene," while the Coptic reads, "Mary and the one of Martha and Mary Magdalene." Watson argues for "Mary and Martha and Mary Magdalene" as the original names; see Francis Watson, "A Gospel of the Eleven: The Epistula Apostolorum and the Johannine Tradition," in *Connecting Gospels: Beyond the Canonical/Non-Canonical Divide*, ed. F. Watson and S. Parkhouse (Oxford: Oxford University Press, 2018), 190–215 (208–9). Cf. Hannah, who suggests "Salome and Martha and Mary Magdalene" ("Four-Gospel," 616–22).

46. Hartenstein, *Zweite Lehre*, 122. For a detailed evaluation of *EpAp*'s Easter narrative, see 119–26.

Christology, Eschatology, and Instructions for the Interim	
13.1–14.8	Christ's Descent and Incarnation
15.1–9	Memorial of Christ's Death (*Easter*)
16.1–17.4	Parousia
17.5–19.16	The Interim: Commission and Hope
19.17–25.9	Resurrection of the Flesh
26.1–29.4	Day of Judgment
Mission	
29.5–30.5	Proclamation to Israel, and the Gentiles
31.1–33.9	Paul, Preacher to the Gentiles
End Times	
34.1–38.7	Signs and Trials of the End Times
39.1–40.4	Divine Justice
Ministry	
40.5–42.8	Threefold Ministry
42.9–45.8	Parable of the Ten Virgins
Church Discipline	
46.1–49.3	Mutual Rebuke
49.4–50.11	Division among Christians

FIG. 23.2: Outline of *Epistula Apostolorum*'s Dialogue

Themes[47]

A major objective of the dialogue is the clarification of christological and eschatological issues. Of particular interest to the disciples is the *when* and *how* of Christ's parousia, the resurrection of the flesh, and the signs and trials of the end times. In correspondence with the disciples' questions, Jesus predicts his return in 120/150 years (17.2), confirms the resurrection of the flesh (19.17–25.9), and gives a detailed outline of the end times (34.1–38.7). Throughout *Epistula Apostolorum*, Jesus repeatedly attempts to inculcate enduring faithfulness in his disciples by announcing the severity of divine justice and the punishment of disobedient Christians. Among the latter, Jesus particularly criticizes Christians who diverge from his teaching (29.1–4; 37.4; 50.8) and/or possess great wealth (37.5; 38.1; 42.6; 46.1–2). Further, he clarifies that faith in him and in the Father only serves as the prerequisite for resurrection, which is followed by a judgment according to works that separates obedient Christians from disobedient ones and assigns to them eternal rest or punishment respectively (26.1–29.4).

Aside from the recurring commission to "preach and teach" (19.1–5; 30.1–5; 41.1; 46.1), other minor instructions concern the annual celebration of Easter (15.1–9) and the disciples' threefold ministry as fathers, servants, and teachers. As such, they will baptize,

---

47. Due to the dialogue format, the following summary is thematically structured and follows the above-presented consecutive outline only loosely.

teach, and discipline believers (40.5–42.8). Church discipline, however, is equally to be enacted by all community members (46.1–49.3).

Throughout the conversation, Jesus reveals past and future events. He begins his revelatory speech with an account of his hidden descent in angelic form through multiple heavens down to earth, where he appeared to Mary in the likeness of the archangel Gabriel and incarnated himself (13.1–14.8). Further, he predicts the imprisonment of a disciple during the Feast of the Pascha (Easter) and his miraculous release for the duration of the paschal vigil (15.1–9; see Acts 12:1–19). Christ also recounts his descent to "the place of Lazarus" to proclaim salvation to the "fathers and the prophets" (27.1–28.5) and predicts the conversion of Paul and his gentile mission (31.1–33.9). In a final parable, Christ illustrates the significance of obedience and the severity of divine justice with the wise and foolish virgins' fate (42.9–45.8).

The disciples actively engage in the conversation, always as a collective. Their initial concern at the continuation and proclamation of Christ's ministry steadily gives way to the confident certainty of his enduring presence among them ("It is you who will preach through us," 41.2). Despite frequent expressions of gratitude and astonishment regarding Christ's revelation, the disciples continuously ask questions and scrutinize his statements. In particular, they criticize the announced trials for the elect (36.1–12) and repeatedly appeal to Christ's might to save the unrighteous from their dreadful fate ("Lord, it is in your power not to allow these things to befall them!" 39.1; see also 45.7). When faced with Jesus's annoyance at their ceaseless inquiry, the disciples justify it as an inevitable part of their training:

> Again we said to him, "Lord, it is necessary for us to question you, for you command us to preach; so that we ourselves may know with certainty through you and be useful preachers, and [that] those who will teach through us may believe in you. That is why we question you so much!" (*EpAp* 23.1–3)

Jesus assures them of his favor:

> I indeed know that in faith and with your whole heart you ask of me—therefore I rejoice over you! Truly I say to you, I am glad, and my Father who is in me, that you ask me, for your shamelessness brings me joy and gives you life. (*EpAp* 25.2b–3)

Ascension Narrative (51)

At the end of the dialogue, Jesus reminds the disciples of his ascension "on the third day, at the third hour" (51.1), which immediately occurs.[48] Jesus ascends into a bright cloud, accompanied by thunder, lightning, and an earthquake. Angels greet him by saying, "Gather us, O priest, into the light of glory!" (51.3). The angels address Christ's heavenly priesthood, a task that he assigned to the archangels during his time on earth (see 13.5). Jesus leaves his disciples with his peace, and *Epistula Apostolorum* ends with a reference to his authority ("In the name of our Lord Jesus Christ," 51.5) that corresponds with the text's opening (1.1).

---

48. The disciples' encounter and dialogue with the risen Christ as well as the latter's ascension take place on the same day, i.e., the "third day." For more details, see Hartenstein, *Zweite Lehre*, 107n64; Watson, *Apostolic Gospel*, 120.

3. INTERPRETIVE ISSUES

3.1 Agent of Creation

In *Epistula Apostolorum*'s confession of faith (3.1–15), the disciples declare the divine act of creation without specifying its agent (3.5–10). Consequently, the passage can be read as referring either to the Father or to the Son as creator. The ambiguity arises from the consistent use of the Ethiopic relative pronoun ñ (za-), which, translated as "who," introduces most creedal statements. Although the Son is the main subject of the confession's opening (3.1–4), the same section ends on a mention of the Father (3.4), with the result that the following relative clauses could refer to either one.

1	This we declare, that our Lord and Saviour Jesus Christ is God, the Son of God,
2	who was sent from God, ruler of the whole world, maker of every name that is named;
3	who is above all authorities, Lord of lords and King of kings, Power of the heavenly powers;
4	who sits above the Cherubim at the right hand of the throne of the Father;
5	who by his word commanded the heavens and founded the earth and what is in it, . . .
10	who made humankind in his image and likeness;
11	who spoke with the forefathers and prophets in parables and in truth;
12	whom the apostles preached and the disciples touched.
13	And God the Son of God do we confess, the Word who became flesh of Mary, carried in her womb through the Holy Spirit.

FIG. 23.3: Confession of Faith (*EpAp* 3.1–15)

3.1.1 Christ as Creator

The explicit subject of the confession's opening (3.1–4) and close (3.13–15) is Christ. Against the backdrop of the work's Christology, two further verses can be read as implicitly referring to the Son—namely, the passage on divine-human interaction in 3.11–12.[49] Since no change of subject is indicated within the remaining passage (3.5–10), syntax suggests a christological reading of the entire confession.[50] This reading entails a Christocentric focus of the confession that declares Christ's rank in the present (3.1–4), his preexistent role as creator and communicator (3.5–12), as well as his incarnation (3.13–15).

3.1.2 Father as Creator

In light of the Father's mention at the end of 3.4, all subsequent relative clauses might syntactically refer to him instead of Christ (3.5–10). This alternative reading is in line with the Father's attribution in 3.2 as "ruler of the whole world, maker of every name that is named," for which most Ethiopic manuscripts supplement "maker" with "creator." Further support is provided by the phrase "by his word" in the passage's opening (3.5). Since the Ethiopic term used for "word" (ቃል [*kal*]; presumably λόγος [*logos*]) is subsequently applied to indicate the divine Word (3.13), it is possible to read 3.4–3.5 as "the Father, who by his Word commanded the heavens." A major obstacle to this reading is the above mentioned Christ-centered focus of 3.11–12, particularly the disciples' touch. Aware of this issue,

---

49. *EpAp* refers to Christ's interaction with the forefathers and prophets (19.28; 27.1; 28.3), his speaking in parables (32.3; 42.9–45.8), the disciples' proclamation (2.3; 3.1; 8.1–2; etc.) and touching of Christ (2.3; 12.1).
50. See Watson, "Miracle Catena," 109.

some translations emended the text in 3.12 to adapt it in favor of the Father.[51] This reading evokes an almost Trinitarian form of the confession by declaring the Son (3.1–4), the Father (3.5–12), and the Holy Spirit's limited assistance in the Son's incarnation (3.13–15).

The equal plausibility of both readings suggests a remaining ambiguity within the divine, which is in line with *Epistula Apostolorum*'s recurrent emphasis on the unity of Father and Son. A similar case of ambiguity is Christ's announcement of his own parousia as "the coming of my Father" (17.2), leading to the confusion of the disciples:

> And we said to him, "Just now did you not say to us, 'I will come'? So how can you say to us, 'The one who sent me will come'?" Then he said to us, "I am wholly in my Father and my Father is in me." (*EpAp* 17.3–4)

Occasionally, Christ also refers to "his commandments" (24.5; 27.3–4; 29.1; et al.) as the "commandments of my Father" (26.2, 5; 42.6) and asserts that the intercession of believers is addressable to Father and Son (40.1–4). Thus, although *Epistula Apostolorum* distinguishes between Father, Son, and Holy Spirit (5.20), the desire of post-Nicene interpreters to articulate a precise inner-Trinitarian task differentiation has presumably not been a primary issue to *Epistula Apostolorum*'s second-century author.

3.2 An Anti-Gnostic Orientation?

In twentieth-century research, *Epistula Apostolorum* was predominantly read against the backdrop of the church's alleged struggle against Gnosticism. Accordingly, the text had either to display gnostic influences or to explicitly confront them.[52] A majority of scholars placed *Epistula Apostolorum* on the "proto-orthodox" side of the dichotomy and classified it as "an orthodox defense against gnostic Christianity."[53] While the debate on an accurate definition of "Gnosis" and "Gnosticism" is still ongoing,[54] *Epistula Apostolorum* was commonly denoted "anti-gnostic" on grounds of its warning against Simon and Cerinthus, its prediction of rival teachings, and its participation in the genre of dialogue gospels. The latter argument stemmed from the assumption of the author's attempt to silence gnostic Christians by appropriating their allegedly preferred genre (i.e., "gnostic dialogues").[55]

---

51. See Müller's translation: "der durch die Patriarchen und Propheten in Bildern geredet hat und in Wahrheit durch den, den die Apostel verkündigt und die Jünger betastet haben" (who spoke in parables through the patriarchs and prophets and in truth through him whom the apostles declared and the disciples touched) in "Epistula," 1066. The second *durch* ("through") is an emendation of the text and has no basis in the Ethiopic manuscripts.

52. For the assumption of gnostic influences in *EpAp*, see primarily Hornschuh, *Studien*, 35, 120; Hartenstein, *Zweite Lehre*, 106; Kiel, "Auferstehung," 190.

53. Julian V. Hills, "Apostles, Epistles of," *ABD* 1:311–12 (312). See Schmidt: "Die Epistola apostolorum ist von einem Vertreter der Großkirche behufs Bekämpfung der gnostischen Häresie, speziell des Doketismus verfaßt" (*Gespräche*, 402). In 1990 (repr., 2008), Hills stated that "here, then, is a writing that breathes the spirit of the emerging 'Catholic' (or 'Great') church vs. 'Gnostic' church debate" (*Tradition*, 2–3).

54. This article is based on Christoph Markschies' eight components of Gnosticism: (1) a supreme God; (2) additional divine/intermediary figures; (3) world and matter as evil; (4) separate creator god who is ignorant and/or evil; (5) mythological drama of a divine spark that slumbers in members of a certain class; (6) "knowledge" (gnosis) about this state brought by a redeemer figure; (7) redemption as "knowledge" about the divine spark; (8) tendency toward dualism in concept of God and human. See "Gnosis/Gnostizismus," *RGG* 3:1045–53.

55. See Hornschuh: "So griff man zu den von den Gegnern geschmiedeten Waffen, indem man ebenfalls apokryphe Offenbarungsliteratur schuf, um sich zum Kampf gegen sie zu wappnen" (*Studien*, 7). For a compelling criticism on associating dialogue gospels with Gnosticism, see Parkhouse, *Eschatology and the Saviour*, 13–67.

Occasionally, *Epistula Apostolorum*'s parable of the ten virgins served as further evidence for the text's "anti-gnostic" orientation. In line with earlier research's common view that a gnostic Christology necessarily is a docetic one, an "anti-docetic" orientation was further attributed to *Epistula Apostolorum*'s Christology, supported by the warning against Cerinthus as well as the text's emphasis on the resurrection of the flesh.[56] Thus, the work has frequently been characterized as an "anti-gnostic" and "anti-docetic" writing.[57]

Although recent research has become more cautious to (re)construct gnostic opponents within *Epistula Apostolorum*'s context, the work is still widely referred to as containing "a strong anti-docetic tenor."[58] In view of a refined understanding of Gnosticism as well as the "elusive phenomenon"[59] of docetic claims, the assumption of *Epistula Apostolorum*'s explicit "anti-gnostic" and "anti-docetic" orientation has become questionable. Thus, the assumption's main arguments need to be revaluated, particularly the significance of Simon and Cerinthus, *Epistula Apostolorum*'s criticism of diverging teachings, and its emphasis on Christ's corporeality.

3.2.1 The Significance of Simon and Cerinthus

Simon and Cerinthus, two controversial figures of early Christianity, are mentioned twice in *Epistula Apostolorum*'s first part (1.2; 7.1). However, the warning against these paradigmatic "nonorthodox" figures primarily serves as a rhetorical device and not as discrediting specific gnostic groups.

Simon Magus is first introduced in canonical Acts (8:9–24) as a magician in Samaria, who, after being baptized by Philip, was rebuked by Peter and John while attempting to acquire the disciples' endorsement by purchase. Starting with Justin (*1 Apol.* 26.1–3), subsequent Christian writers such as Irenaeus identified Simon as "source and root" of all heresies and "falsely so-called knowledge" (i.e., "gnosis"; *Haer.* 1.22.2–4; 23) and traced the Simonians back to him. In the second-century Acts of Peter, the antagonism between Peter and Simon is further developed and concludes with the apostle's triumph over Simon in Rome. Cerinthus, on the other hand, lived as a Christian teacher in Asia Minor around 100 CE and was potentially opposed by the Johannine circle. He is initially referred to by Irenaeus (*Haer.* 1.26.1; 3.3.4; 11.1), who ascribed to him a protological dualism and a Christology in which the divine Christ is united with the human Jesus at baptism and departs from him by the time of his suffering. Irenaeus further retells an encounter between John the disciple and Cerinthus in an Ephesian bathhouse, which John left exclaiming, "Let us fly, lest even the bathhouse fall down, because Cerinthus, the enemy of the truth, is within" (*Haer.* 3.3.4).

In historical terms, little can be said about Simon and Cerinthus or their respective

---

56. According to Winrich Löhr, "Doketismus," *RGG* 2:925–27, the word *docetic* (Greek: δοκέω, "to appear") is a relatively open term to describe different kinds of christological claims that attempt to limit the reality and/or significance of Jesus Christ's human nature, either by ascribing certain qualities to his body, or by declaring his suffering and death as only apparent, or by separating Jesus's humanity, including his life, passion, and death, from the Savior's true identity.

57. For an "anti-gnostic" and/or "docetic" orientation, see Schmidt, *Gespräche*, 402; Hornschuh, *Studien*, 120; Hill, "Asian Tract," 1; Müller, "Epistula," 1064; Hartenstein, *Zweite Lehre*, 106; Kiel, "Auferstehung," 165–98. For a critique, see Watson, *Apostolic Gospel*, 117–21; Parkhouse, *Eschatology and the Saviour*, 3–4, 46–47.

58. Recently by Paul Parvis, "Epistula Apostolorum," in *From Thomas to Tertullian: Christian Literary Receptions of Jesus in the Second and Third Centuries CE*, ed. J. Schröter and C. Jacobi, vol. 2 of *The Reception of Jesus in the First Three Centuries*, ed. C. Keith et al. (London: T&T Clark, 2020), 215.

59. For the term, see Joseph Verheyden et al., eds., *Docetism in the Early Church: The Quest for an Elusive Phenomenon*, WUNT 402 (Tübingen: Mohr Siebeck, 2018).

teachings. While the mention of Simon merely indicates *Epistula Apostolorum*'s participation in a particular early Christian tradition that regarded him as the archetypal opponent of the apostles, the reference to the "local Asian heretic" might indicate a connection of the work to the Johannine tradition in Ephesus. A further classification of *Epistula Apostolorum*'s Christology as "anti-docetic" solely based on Irenaeus's relatively late description of Cerinthus's theology (ca. 180 CE) is speculative and bears the danger of anachronism. Apart from the work's general notion that both figures "pervert . . . Jesus Christ" (7.2), there is no evidence to assume a docetic Christology regarding *Epistula Apostolorum*'s Cerinthus.[60]

Conversely, more can be said regarding Simon and Cerinthus's function as arch-heretics and paradigmatical opponents of the apostles. While *Epistula Apostolorum* is silent about their teaching and does not attempt to differentiate between these temporally and geographically separated figures, it emphatically denounces them as "false apostles" (1.1) and "enemies of our Lord Jesus Christ" (7.2) that "go around the world" (7.1) and "pervert the words and the work, that is, Jesus Christ" (7.2). The apostles warn against their "venom by which they kill people" (1.2) and associate them with "death and a great defilement of corruption" (7.3). After 7.1–4, Simon and Cerinthus are not mentioned again and thus not linked to the subsequent (and equally cursory) criticism of diverging teachings. The text's fictional pairing of both figures was presumably inspired by early Christianity's association of Simon and Cerinthus with the apostles Peter and John, who play a prominent role in *Epistula Apostolorum* (2.1; 11.4, 7). The strategic placing of warnings against Simon and Cerinthus in the opening (1.2) and at one of the text's main transition points (7.1–4) promotes the rhetorical usage of these figures as archetypal yet successfully combatted antagonists of the disciples.

3.2.2 The Prediction of Other Teachings

Within *Epistula Apostolorum*'s dialogue, Christ issues three warnings against diverging teachings and their disastrous moral impact on believers (29.1–4; 37.4; 50.8). While the specific content of those teachings is not spelled out, they are characterized as "teachings other than what is written" that are taught "with different words" by "those who transgress my commandments" (29.1), "follow evil" (37.4), and "desire their own glory" (50.8; see also 29.1). Consequently, these teachings evoke disobedience, partiality, bribery, and vice among Christians, to the point that some believers are being led astray (29.1). Although *Epistula Apostolorum* reckons with the prospect of alternative teachings, it neither provides any details about doctrinal divergences nor explicitly refers to specific theological positions or groups, but instead warns against any teaching that diverges from its own words, that is, Christ's words. A characterization of the work as distinctively "anti-gnostic" or "anti-docetic" based on its prediction of diverging teachings is not substantiated.

3.2.3 Emphasis on the Flesh

The *Epistula Apostolorum*'s recurrent emphasis on Christ's bodily nature, death, and resurrection constitutes a possible argument in favor of an anti-docetic orientation.[61] Throughout *Epistula Apostolorum*, Christ is referred to as "the Word who became flesh

---

60. In current scholarship, Cerinthus is described as a (pre-)gnostic Christian (see, Barbara Aland, *Die Gnosis* [Stuttgart: Reclam, 2014], 162–63) or even as potentially situated in a Jewish-Christian framework (see Christoph Markschies, "Kerinth: Wer war er und was lehrte er?," *JAC* [1998]: 68–69).

61. For further studies, see Horacio E. Lona, *Über die Auferstehung des Fleisches: Studien zur frühchristlichen Eschatologie*, BZNW 66 (Berlin: de Gruyter, 1993), 79–90; and Kiel, "Auferstehung," 165–98.

of Mary" (3.13; also 14.5–8; 39.12), who was "carried in her womb" (3.13), "swaddled in Bethlehem," was "nourished" and "grew up" (3.15). Later on, he "suffered" (39.12), was "crucified by Pontius Pilate" (9.1), "buried in a place called 'The Skull'" (9.1), and is "truly risen in flesh" (12.1), as testified by the disciples' touch (11.7–8; 12.1). Starting from his incarnation and enduring death and resurrection, Christ's corporeality is evidently a crucial component of *Epistula Apostolorum*'s theological landscape. At the same time, the emphasis on Christ's flesh is closely connected to the text's soteriology. Christ's resurrection foreshadows and guarantees the bodily resurrection of all believers and their incorruptible state of being. Accordingly, the discourse on the resurrection of the flesh (19.17–25.9), while being based on Christ's resurrection, focuses on the clarification of the believers' resurrected state. Thus, the discourse is not aimed at a potential christological debate but tackles the eschatological issues present among the disciples:

> Truly I say to you, as my Father raised me from the dead, so you too will rise and they will take you up above the heavens to the place of which I spoke to you in the beginning, to the place prepared for you by the one who sent me. (. . .) For this is why I came, so that you who were born in flesh might be raised in your flesh as in a second birth, a garment that will not perish, with all who hope and believe in the one who sent me. (*EpAp* 21.1–3; see also 39.12–13)

While the text's emphasis on Christ's corporeality is primarily instructive for its soteriology, it is self-evidently also incompatible with any so-called docetic claims. However, the assumption of a christological controversy within *Epistula Apostolorum*'s context lacks any evidence of an explicit attack on docetic claims or a reference to a specific group of docetic opponents. Thus, to classify *Epistula Apostolorum* as an "anti-docetic" document solely based on its interest in Christ's enduring humanity as well as the salvation of the flesh remains questionable.

3.2.4 Preliminary Conclusion

In view of the above-mentioned arguments, a hasty characterization of *Epistula Apostolorum* as "anti- . . ." seems unsubstantiated. The "heretic" figures and false teachings referred to throughout the text are ultimately *fictional* opponents, who do not represent any specific theological perspectives but rather exemplify general divergences from *Epistula Apostolorum*'s position and thus from Christ's initial teaching. In this way, the warnings serve as rhetorical means to enhance the text's own claim of apostolic authority based on its (equally fictional) apostolic authorship. While the theological reasons behind *Epistula Apostolorum*'s emphasis on Christ's corporeality remain open for further interpretation, its christological statements are not polemically motivated since the text nowhere attacks nor directly rejects christological claims that heresiologists might later describe as docetic. Thus, instead of classifying *Epistula Apostolorum* as "anti-docetic," it could rather be described as a second-century outline of Christian faith that is based on a strong apostolic claim and displays a particular interest in the eternal fate of the human body.[62]

---

62. *EpAp*'s interpretation as gnostic/docetic or anti-gnostic/anti-docetic mirrors a similar development in Johannine research. On this, see Jörg Frey, "'Docetic-like' Christologies and the Polymorphy of Christ: A Plea for Further Consideration of Diversity in the Discussion of 'Docetism,'" in *Docetism in the Early Church: The Quest for an Elusive Phenomenon*, ed. J. Verheyden et al., WUNT 402 (Tübingen: Mohr Siebeck, 2018), 27–50.

3.3 Parable of the Ten Virgins

Christ exemplifies the significance of enduring obedience in *Epistula Apostolorum*'s parable of the ten virgins (42.9–45.8). The parable is reminiscent of the Matthean version (Matt 25:1–13) and represents *Epistula Apostolorum*'s engagement with and contribution to early Christianity's parable tradition. Based on the text's classification as "anti-gnostic," scholars have identified the foolish virgins with the work's alleged gnostic opponents. The presented difficulties of such a reading as well as the parable's detailed study within *Epistula Apostolorum* make such an interpretation questionable.

3.3.1 Content

In an instruction to follow his example, Jesus compares the disciples' reward for their ministry with the entry of five wise virgins into the wedding-chamber. At the same time, he recounts the exclusion of five foolish virgins who "were unable to watch but slept" (43.2) and thus "did not fulfil my commandments" (44.1). The wise sisters, called "Faith, Love, Grace, Peace, and Hope" (43.6), are identified by Jesus as "guides among those who believe in me" (43.7). The foolish virgins are also named after virtues—namely, "Knowledge, Wisdom, Obedience, Patience, and Mercy" (43.16), signifying those "that slept among those who believe and confess me" (43.17). While all virgins are "daughters of God the Father" (45.6) and bear virtuous names, the foolish sisters await a dreadful fate of torture and punishment. From the beginning, the disciples are deeply concerned about the foolish virgins and begin to intercede on their behalf. Jesus, however, represented by the bridegroom, confirms their eternal exclusion ("Whoever is shut out is shut out," 43.14).

3.3.2 Interpretation

The parable follows the basic story line of so-called watching-parables[63] and is related to the Matthean version of the parable (Matt 25:1–13). Although knowledge of Matthew is assumed for *Epistula Apostolorum* in general, there is no apparent literary dependency concerning the parable. Frequently, the two versions diverge distinctively, as for instance on the significance of sleep. While all virgins fall asleep in Matthew, sleep is the main indicator for foolishness in *Epistula Apostolorum*. Further, *Epistula Apostolorum*'s virgins bear names that are crucial for the parable's interpretation. Against the backdrop of the work's alleged anti-gnostic orientation, the foolish virgins' virtuous names have been interpreted as signifying virtues prominent among gnostic Christians (e.g., "Knowledge," presumably γνῶσις [*gnōsis*]).[64] Occasionally, such a reading has been supplemented by alleged parallels to the Valentinian Sophia-Myth[65] or a Valentinian interpretation of the Matthean parable.[66] According to all these readings, *Epistula Apostolorum*'s parable aims at criticizing and condemning gnostic Christians. However, a negative and/or gnostic characterization of traditional Christian virtues such as knowledge, wisdom, obedience, mercy, and patience is questionable, especially given the work's emphasis on obedience.

Alternatively, the virgins' names can be read as representing virtues that are active in the wise sisters (i.e., awake) and lacking in the foolish ones (i.e., asleep).[67] Thus, the virgins' foolishness manifests itself not in their knowledge and obedience but, to the contrary, in their ignorance and disobedience, etc. In line with the Matthean parable, the virgins'

---

63. Other watching-parables are found in Matt 24:42–25, 30; Mark 13:33–37; Luke 12:35–40, 41, 48.
64. Hartenstein, *Zweite Lehre*, 103–5; Kiel, "Auferstehung," 196–97.
65. Hornschuh, *Studien*, 21–29.
66. Kiel, "Auferstehung," 197n101.
67. Such a reading is, e.g., applied by Hills, *Tradition*, 146–68, and Watson, *Apostolic Gospel*, 209–12.

foolishness signifies disobedience toward Christ's commandments that results in eternal perdition. According to this reading, foolish Christians live in contradiction to their virtuous names, a prevalent point of criticism throughout *Epistula Apostolorum*:

> But if anyone believes in me and does not do my commandments, after confessing my name, he receives no benefit at all and has run his course in vain. For such people will incur loss and punishment, because they have transgressed my commandments. (*EpAp* 27.3–4; see 36.10; 39.8–10).

The disciples' sorrow at the fate of disobedient Christians and their intercession on their behalf is informed by a concern about the inevitable eschatological divide within Christian communities. In this way, *Epistula Apostolorum*'s parable of the ten virgins addresses the limitation of intercession and reminds its recipients of the significance of enduring obedience.

4. KEY PASSAGES FOR NEW TESTAMENT STUDIES AND THEIR SIGNIFICANCE

The *Epistula Apostolorum* is in close relation with oral and written Jewish and Christian traditions circulating in the second century CE. While it applies a christological reading to the Septuagint and presents a "proto-orthodox" outline of Christian faith that has much in common with (later to become) New Testament writings, the text also participates in traditions that have subsequently been identified as noncanonical. Most of *Epistula Apostolorum*'s "apocryphal material" has parallels in other noncanonical writings, such as the account of Jesus's first day at school (*EpAp* 4.1–3; see Inf. Gos. Thom. 6; 14) or Christ's metamorphosis in his descent through the heavens (*EpAp* 13.1–14.8; see Mart. Ascen. Isa. 10.7–11.32). Further, the work assumes a particular clarity for Christ's post-resurrection teaching, so that the risen Christ is confronted with the disciples' complaint when attempting to speak in parables ("And we said to him, 'Lord, you are again speaking with us in parables!'" 32.3).[68] This focus on post-resurrection revelation is particularly prominent among dialogue gospels (Gospel of Mary, Apocryphon of James, et al.). Finally, *Epistula Apostolorum* deals with the concern of the righteous for the unrighteous by evaluating the power of intercession (see 4 Ezra 7).[69] Aside from these parallels to early Jewish and Christian texts, some of *Epistula Apostolorum*'s passages are of interest to early Christian liturgical studies, such as its description of a paschal vigil (15.1–7),[70] its confession of faith (3.1–15), and its *regula fidei* (5.17–21).

4.1 Canonical Context

With regard to Old Testament writings, *Epistula Apostolorum* generally views Israel's prophecy as fulfilled in Christ and depicts his interaction with the forefathers and prophets "in parables and in truth" (3.11).[71] In particular, *Epistula Apostolorum* quotes Psalm 3 LXX in the context of Christ's resurrection (*EpAp* 19.20–27) and applies a prophetic statement to the end times that is derived from Psalms 13:3 and 49:18–20 LXX (*EpAp* 35.6–8).[72] Frequently, the author uses prophetic sayings to underscore a particular argument

---

68. However, the disciples tolerate the subsequent parable of the ten virgins (*EpAp* 42.9–45.8).
69. For an extensive evaluation of *EpAp* in literary context, see Watson, *Apostolic Gospel*, 81–202.
70. See Harald Buchinger, "Liturgy and Early Christian Apocrypha," in *The Oxford Handbook of Early Christian Apocrypha*, ed. A. Gregory and C. Tuckett (Oxford: Oxford University Press, 2015), 361–77.
71. *EpAp* 19.19, 28; 31.10.
72. See Rom 3:13–18. For a discussion, see Watson, *Apostolic Gospel*, 254–55.

or predict an event. While the Scriptures are of enduring significance,[73] the sources of individual sayings remain mostly obscure and might be traced back to noncanonical, early Jewish/Christian traditions or even to *Epistula Apostolorum*'s author himself.[74]

With regard to New Testament writings, *Epistula Apostolorum* applies a similar narrative framework as the canonical Gospels but also decidedly expands on traditions that are hardly covered or left out by them. This is particularly striking in its account of Christ's descent through the heavens (13.1–6), his self-incarnation (14.1–8), his descent into hell (27.1–28.5), and his post-resurrection teaching (13.1–50.11), including his commissioning of the disciples, his instructions for Christian life during his absence, as well as his prediction of Paul and the gentile mission. While the author of *Epistula Apostolorum* most likely knew Matthew, Luke, and John, the case for Mark remains unclear, as evidence is scarce.[75] Most parallels to the canonical Gospels are found in *Epistula Apostolorum*'s miracle catena (4–5) and in its annunciation (14), Easter (9–12), and ascension narratives (51). While its linguistic matrix features a strong Johannine influence,[76] the text also displays an adaption of several Matthean themes, such as the Great Commission (Matt 28:16–20; *EpAp* 19.1–5; 30.1–5; 41.1; 46.1), the parable of the ten virgins (Matt 25:1–11; *EpAp* 42.9–45.8), and church discipline (Matt 18:15–17; *EpAp* 48.1–3). Regarding narrative material, the text frequently contains parallels to Luke-Acts, such as Gabriel's announcement to Mary (Luke 1:26–38; *EpAp* 14.1), Christ's birth (and "swaddling") in Bethlehem (Luke 2:1–7; *EpAp* 3.13), his ascension (Luke 24:50–53; *EpAp* 51.1–5), and Peter's imprisonment (Acts 12:1–19; *EpAp* 15.1–7). While Luke-Acts recounts the continuation of Jesus's teaching after his resurrection (Luke 24:27, 45–48; particularly Acts 1:3), *Epistula Apostolorum* expands on it.

The *Epistula Apostolorum*'s free handling of material preserved in the canonical Gospels is exemplified in its critical modification of certain traditions. In 14.1–4, Jesus invokes the common assumption that Gabriel appeared to Mary (see Luke 1:26), yet he clarifies that it was he who encountered her in Gabriel's form. Similarly, Christ alters the dominical saying preserved in Matthew 23:8:

> Then he answered us, saying, "Will you not all be fathers? Will you not all be teachers?"
>
> We said to him, "Lord, you said to us, 'Do not call anyone your father on earth, for there is one who is your Father who is in heaven and your teacher.' Why do you now say to us, 'You will be fathers of many children, and servants and teachers'?"
>
> And he answered and said to us, "It is as you have said. For truly I say to you, whoever hears you and believes in me will receive [from y]ou the light of the seal throu[gh me]. You will [be fath]ers and servants and teachers." (*EpAp* 41.3–7)

---

73. The disciples are commissioned to provide continuous guidance in the Scriptures (31.10). *EpAp*'s usage of the term "Scriptures" presumably includes the LXX (see Pss 3; 13; 49).

74. See *EpAp* 11.8; 33.5; 35.2–9; 43.3; 47.6; 49.2. On *EpAp* 11.8, see Pérès, "Das lebendige Wort," 126–32.

75. Cf. Hannah's argument for *EpAp*'s knowledge of Mark in "Four-Gospel," 622. He primarily suggests a dependency of the opening of *EpAp*'s Easter narrative (9.2–4) on Mark 16:1, namely, in the shared features of the women's intention to anoint Jesus's body with oil as well as the presence of Salome. However, the name "Salome" is an emendation of "Sarah" (Ethiopic) by Hannah. For an evaluation of *EpAp*'s knowledge of all canonical Gospels, see Hannah, "Four-Gospel," 608–25. By dating *EpAp* to the 140s, Hannah recognizes *EpAp* as an early witness to the fourfold Gospel (598).

76. For instance, "the Father who sent me" (*EpAp* 39.6; John 12:49 et al.), "he/the one who sent me" (*EpAp* 34.7; John 7:29; 8:29 et al.), "the Word who became flesh" (*EpAp* 3.13; John 1:14); further thematical parallels, such as the unity of Father and Son (*EpAp* 17.4; John 10:30), the image of the shepherd and his flock (*EpAp* 44.1; John 10:1–18), the miracle at Cana (*EpAp* 5.1; John 2:1–12), the new commandment (*EpAp* 18.5; John 13:34), etc. For extensive lists of *EpAp*'s parallels to all canonical Gospels, see Hannah, "Four-Gospel," 610–25.

A striking case of divergence from certain early Jewish/Christian traditions is Jesus's reasoning about humanity's free will, in which he applies a positive reading of Adam:[77]

> Then he said, "I will answer them, saying: 'Adam was given the power to choose one of the two. And he chose the light and stretched out his hand for it, but the darkness he rejected and cast it from him. So all people have the power to believe in the light, which is the life of the Father who sent me.'" (*EpAp* 39.4–5)

4.2 The Twelfth Disciple

Contrary to the canonical Gospels, *Epistula Apostolorum* unambiguously states its authorship. By claiming the authority of the apostolic collective, the work depicts the eleven disciples as literate and even as literary authors.[78] The text thus shares in the apostolic-authorization process of early Christian writings, including gospel texts.[79] While the work's prescript lists eleven disciples (2.1), "the number of apostles is restored from eleven to twelve by the inclusion of Paul."[80] Paul is introduced in *Epistula Apostolorum* 31–33 as a "Jew, circumcised by the commandment of the law" (31.1) and "an elect vessel and a wall that shall not fall . . . a preacher to the Gentiles" (31.8–9). According to *Epistula Apostolorum*, he leaves his Cilician homeland to stay in Damascus and is neither associated with Jerusalem (cf. Acts 8:1; 9:26–30 et al.; Gal 1:18) nor successful in his "evil intention" (*EpAp* 33.7) to persecute the church. Instead, *Epistula Apostolorum* depicts Paul as a "would-be persecutor."[81] Paul loses his eyesight in his encounter with Christ (see Acts 9:1–19) and is subsequently taught by the eleven disciples:

> And every word that I have spoken to you and that you write about me, that I am the Word of the Father and the Father is in me, you also must pass on to that man, as is fitting for you. Teach him and remind him what is said in the scriptures about me and is now fulfilled, and then he will be the salvation of the Gentiles. (*EpAp* 31.11–12)

In its high esteem for the disciples, *Epistula Apostolorum* portrays them not only as authors but also as scribes and teachers. By highlighting their active engagement in Paul's conversion and training, the text implies that not only Paul but all subsequent "fathers, teachers, and servants" (see 41.7) should be taught in the apostolic testimony of Christ according to the *Epistula Apostolorum*.

5. BIBLIOGRAPHY

Hannah, Darrell D. "The Four-Gospel 'Canon' in the *Epistula Apostolorum*." *JTS* 59 (2008): 598–633.
Hartenstein, Judith. *Die zweite Lehre: Erscheinungen des Auferstandenen als Rahmenerzählungen frühchristlicher Dialoge*. TUGAL 146. Berlin: Akademie, 2000.
Hill, Charles E. "The Epistula Apostolorum: An Asian Tract from the Time of Polycarp." *JECS* 7 (1999): 1–53.

---

77. For further discussion, see Watson, *Apostolic Gospel*, 206–8.

78. See also *EpAp* 31.11. On the disciples' depiction as authors, see Julia D. Lindenlaub, "The Gospel of John as Model for Literate Authors and their Texts in Epistula Apostolorum and Apocryphon of James (NHC 1,2)," *JSNT* 43 (2020): 3–27.

79. See Justin's reference to gospel literature as "memoirs of his apostles" (*Dial.* 100.4. et al.).

80. Watson, *Apostolic Gospel*, 218. For a detailed evaluation on Paul, see Francis Watson, "The Conversion of Paul: A New Perspective (Epistula Apostolorum 31–33)," in *Receptions of Paul in Early Christianity: The Person of Paul and His Writings through the Eyes of his Early Interpreters*, ed. J. Schröter, S. Butticaz and A. Dettwiler, BZNW 234 (Berlin: de Gruyter, 2018), 195–211.

81. Watson, *Apostolic Gospel*, 179.

Hills, Julian V. *Tradition and Composition in the Epistula Apostolorum*. 2nd ed. HTS 57. Minneapolis: Fortress, 2008.

Kiel, Nikolai. "Auferstehung des Fleisches in der Epistula Apostolorum." *VC* 74 (2020): 165–98.

Lindenlaub, Julia D. "The Gospel of John as Model for Literate Authors and Their Texts in Epistula Apostolorum and Apocryphon of James (NHC 1,2)." *JSNT* 43 (2020): 3–27.

Schmidt, Carl (with Isaak Wajnberg). *Gespräche Jesu mit seinen Jüngern nach der Auferstehung: Ein katholisch-apostolisches Sendschreiben des 2. Jahrhunderts*. Leipzig: J. C. Hinrichs, 1919. Repr., Hildesheim: Georg Olms, 1967.

Stewart-Sykes, Alistair. "The Asian Context of the New Prophecy and of Epistula Apostolorum." *VC* 51 (1997): 416–38.

Watson, Francis. *An Apostolic Gospel: The "Epistula Apostolorum" in Literary Context*. SNTSMS 179. Cambridge: Cambridge University Press, 2020.

———. "The Conversion of Paul: A New Perspective (*Epistula Apostolorum* 31–33)." Pages 195–211 in *Receptions of Paul in Early Christianity: The Person of Paul and His Writings through the Eyes of His Early Interpreters*. Edited by Jens Schröter, Simon Butticaz, and Andreas Dettwiler. BZNW 234. Berlin: de Gruyter, 2018.

———. "A Gospel of the Eleven: The *Epistula Apostolorum* and the Johannine Tradition." Pages 189–215 in *Connecting Gospels: Beyond the Canonical/Non-Canonical Divide*. Edited by Francis Watson and Sarah Parkhouse. Oxford: Oxford University Press, 2018.

———. "On the Miracle Catena in *Epistula Apostolorum* 4–5." Pages 107–27 in *Gospels and Gospel Traditions in the Second Century: Experiments in Reception*. Edited by Jens Schröter, Tobias Nicklas, and Joseph Verheyden. BZNW 235. Berlin: de Gruyter, 2019.

CHAPTER 24

SUNDAY LETTER

JON C. LAANSMA

1. INTRODUCTION

This document,[1] as herein summarized, contains within it a letter—aptly described as a "chain letter" and probably the first one documented[2]—purporting to have been personally written by God the Father in the voice of Christ, sent to the bishop in Rome, primarily commanding strict observance of Sunday and other rites, and pronouncing blessings and woes connected to the reading and distribution of the letter itself. Whatever the sincerity of the beliefs informing the document's intentions, it trades on the piety of a distant audience that would accept the possibility of such a miraculous letter and that could not confirm or disprove its claims about its source, appearance, and authority. Evidently originating in the epochal transition from earlier Lord's Day customs to Sabbatarianism, the letter both echoed and, through its claim to be a direct proclamation of Christ, contributed to this development.

Indirectly attested at least as early as the end of the sixth century CE (further on its provenance and reception history under sec. 3 below), the document has spread in revised forms in the centuries since. There must have been a first such text, and efforts have been made to sift through proposed earliest redactions, but in the course of its history the Sunday Letter became as much a seminal idea that found ever renewed expression as it was a manuscript tradition stemming from a single original like one of Paul's letters. For the sake of discussion, we will speak of it as a prototype. The constant of these letters is strict observance of Sunday, though otherwise the versions can vary somewhat freely. For instance, most versions begin with some sort of account of the letter's discovery: It was brought to earth by the archangel Michael; it had fallen on the altar at Jerusalem, Rome, Constantinople, or on Mont Saint-Michel; it was found at the foot of Jesus's cross, having originated in Mesopotamia; it was hidden under a stone that no one could move until a very young child did so; it was hanging in the air and could be copied but not caught.[3]

---

1. The document is discussed by others under several names, including *Letter(s) from Heaven*; *Epistle of Christ from Heaven*; *Leaflets from Heaven*; *Letter on the Observance of the Lord's Day*; *Scrolls from Heaven*; *Heavenly Letter*; *Carta Dominica*. In this chapter it will be referred to as the Sunday Letter.

2. Calogero A. Miceli, "Epistle of Christ from Heaven," e-Clavis: Christian Apocrypha, www.nasscal .com/e-clavis-christian-apocrypha/epistle-of-christ-from-heaven/.

3. Per Beskow, *Strange Tales about Jesus: A Survey of Unfamiliar Gospels* (Philadelphia: Fortress, 1983), 26–27; Edgar J. Goodspeed, *Strange New Gospels* (Chicago: University of Chicago Press, 1931), 100–101; Dorothy Haines, *Sunday Observance and the Sunday Letter in Anglo-Saxon England*, Anglo-Saxon Texts 8 (Cambridge: D. S. Brewer, 2010), 44, 46, 52, 57.

Calogero A. Miceli,[4] summarizing the work of Irena Backus,[5] Mario Erbetta,[6] Maximilian Bittner,[7] and Michel van Esbroeck,[8] states that the "dizzying number of languages" and "countless forms" of the letter make reconstruction of an "original" impracticable. Eastern and Western traditions of the text represent the most primitive version and later redactions respectively. The original language may have been Greek, but this is also uncertain. The two earliest Greek manuscripts both date to the fifteenth century and "are believed to represent the earliest redaction of the text."[9] Miceli provides an English translation of Paris gr. 929 (fifteenth century CE),[10] the same manuscript utilized by most others; it is this, including the chapter and versification system, that serves as the basis of the following summary, with the understanding that this cannot be identified in all its details with the earliest form.

2. SUMMARY OF CONTENT

The document (Paris gr. 929) opens with a brief description of the miraculous appearance of the letter to the bishop, the high priest in the basilica in Rome. Peter, described as the first leader of the church, appears to the bishop in a dream, directing him to see the letter that has descended from heaven and hovers in the air in the sanctuary of the basilica. The letter descends to the hands of the bishop. The contents of the letter follow.

The letter proper, composed entirely in the voice of the Lord but personally inscribed by his Father, begins by upbraiding humanity for being unrepentant in the face of earlier judgments he sent "for the sake of the holy Sunday." If it had not been for the intercessions of Mary, angels, and saints he would have destroyed yet more of humanity. There follows, not entirely coherently, a description of the historical importance of Sunday and threatened punishment for its violation, a further elaboration of the form of the judgments (*Strafwunder*) that are about to come if this call to observe Sunday is not observed, affirmations of the authenticity of the letter, and mentions of various other sins. Other elements include the requirement that the letter be read, blessings on priests who read the letter publicly and send copies of it elsewhere, and woes on those who do not (at one point a curse is pronounced on anyone who doubts the letter's authenticity). The self-styled dominical letter itself closes with the speaker's self-identification as "I, God," and "I, Christ," reminders of his omniscience, a threat to reveal secrets, a command to confess to his priests, and a blessing on those who honor Sunday.

The final passage of the document is a summons from the "Pope of Rome," addressed to various classes of people, to honor Sunday and other festivals in the hope of finding compassion on the day of judgment.

---

4. "The Epistle of Christ from Heaven: A New Translation and Introduction," in vol. 1 of *New Testament Apocrypha: More Noncanonical Scriptures*, ed. T. Burke and B. Landau (Grand Rapids: Eerdmans, 2016), 455–63 (456–58).

5. "Lettre de Jésus-Christ sur le dimanche," in vol. 2 of *Écrits apocryphes chrétiens*, ed. P. Geoltrain and J.-D. Kaestli, Bibliothèque de la Pléiade 443 (Paris: Gallimard, 2005), 1101–19.

6. "Lettera della Domenica," in *Lettere e apocalissi*, vol. 3 of *Gli Apocrifi del Nuovo Testamento*, ed. M. Erbetta (Turin: Marietti, 1969), 113–18.

7. "Der vom Himmel gefallene Brief in seinen morgenländischen Versionen und Rezensionen," *Denkschriften der kaiserlichen Akademie der Wissenschaften: Philosophisch-historische Klasse* 51 (1906): 1–240.

8. "La lettre sur le dimanche, descendue du ciel," *Analecta Bollandiana* 107 (1989): 267–84.

9. Miceli, "Epistle of Christ," 456–57.

10. For the manuscript, see "Paris, Bibliothèque nationale de France, gr. 929," North American Society of Christian Apocryphal Literature (NASSCAL), www.nasscal.com/manuscripta-apocryphorum/paris-bibliotheque-nationale-de-france-gr-929/.

Returning to the contents of the self-styled dominical letter itself, though the overarching concern is with the observance of Sunday, there are scattered allusions to the neglect of widows, orphans, and beggars, the failure to honor one's godfather and his children, the failure to fast on Wednesdays and Fridays, lists of vices (e.g., liars, murderers, atheists), along with assorted other sins, such as speaking to others during the divine service, disbelieving the Scriptures, depriving laborers of wages, and more. It is not clear if all of these are viewed as organically bound up with Sunday observance or if they are included as characterizations of the general wickedness of a generation that would dishonor Sunday and not live in fear of the day of judgment. It would seem that the wider concern is to reinforce respect for the institutions of the priesthood, the divine service, and related ecclesial structures.

The letter traces the roots of Sunday observance along with the Wednesday and Friday fasts to the creation account of Genesis 1 and the resurrection of Christ. Through the incorporation of the so-called "Sunday Lists,"[11] it then catalogs major Old Testament events that were to have occurred on Sunday: Christ's visit to Abraham (Gen 18:1–8) and his appearance to Moses on Sinai (Exod 24:12). Other events belong to the same list: Gabriel's appearance to Mary, Jesus's baptism, and the future judgment. Thus readers are made aware of the gravity of Sunday's observance and the seriousness of the sanctions.

3. INTERPRETIVE ISSUES

Lurking behind any literary work is the question of genre. The Sunday Letter borrows from apocalypticism, employs prophetic and sermonic tones, and arrogates to itself legislative authority,[12] but at bottom it is an epistle, a formal letter. Whatever one decides about pseudonymous (i.e., falsely claimed authorship, without or against the named person's authorization) epistles in the apostolic period and New Testament writings[13]—whether they exist in the New Testament canon, whether they intended to deceive, and so on— there are certainly later examples.[14] Other apocryphal letters supposed to have been written by Jesus himself, otherwise unrelated to the Sunday Letter, are noted by Miceli. There is a letter from the earthly Jesus included in the Abgar Correspondence,[15] another which Jesus writes from the cross, mentioned in Narrative of Joseph of Arimethea 3:4,[16] and the *Epistula Apostolorum*,[17] which describes itself as a letter from the ascended Jesus, though it is in substance a letter from the apostles. The Sunday Letter for its part does not purport to be a recovered or preserved artifact of some earlier figure and setting but to be a contemporaneous, direct, written utterance of Jesus, and nothing about it suggests that it was intended as an "innocent fiction"; either it is an outright deception or it is genuine.

Setting and reception history can also shed some light on the letter. In the earliest period of the Sunday Letter's history, a growing Sabbatarianism—popular and then official—fueled the Sunday Letter's spread, as indicated below. The claim to direct divine authorship (2.31–32, 51–56), the dire threats of judgment, and the blessings and woes

---

11. Clare A. Lees, "The 'Sunday Letter' and the 'Sunday Lists,'" *Anglo-Saxon England* 14 (1985): 129–51.

12. Miceli, "Epistle of Christ," 455, referring to van Esbroeck, "La lettre sur le dimanche," 267.

13. Terry L. Wilder, *Pseudonymity, the New Testament, and Deception: An Inquiry into Intention and Reception* (Lanham, MD: University Press of America, 2004).

14. E.g., *NTApoc* 2:28–74, 254–56; Goodspeed, *Strange New Gospels*.

15. See ch. 20 of the present volume; see also *NTApoc* 1:492–500.

16. Bart D. Ehrman and Zlatko Pleše, *The Apocryphal Gospels* (Oxford: Oxford University Press, 2011), 572–85.

17. See ch. 23 of the present volume; see also *NTApoc* 1:249–84. The work possibly originates from the second century CE.

connected to the letter's reading and dissemination (2.34, 47–48; contrast Rev 1:3; 22:7) further explain this history, as also the way it would have served as a vehicle for whatever a copyist wished to append. Scanning more recent centuries, Beskow refers to the existence of many and varied "letters from heaven," constantly emerging, which have as their "oldest and most original form" what he terms "Sunday letters"; "they exist in more than twenty European and Oriental languages, they exist in innumerable variants, they extend from India to Iceland and can be traced to Egyptian, Babylonian, and Chinese sources." Distant relatives of these letters (taking the form of a *Schutzbrief*) were carried by German soldiers as amulets during World War I.[18] Edgar Goodspeed, after mentioning other types of epistolary forgeries—"Letters of Pontius Pilate," "Letters from Pontius Pilate's Wife," among others, all quite modern works passed off as copies of ancient texts—refers to a "Letter of Jesus Christ" with contents generally like the manuscript summarized above and said to have been found under a stone near Iconium; it had been published in the *Chicago Evening Post* and seemed to Goodspeed to have originated in England some forty years prior to 1931.[19] Beskow and Goodspeed's observations about this later history, before circling back to the beginnings of such a letter, would seem to carry the point that the spirits of superstition that reveal themselves through much of this proliferation will also likely explain the original conceit, and in this case there is reason to agree.

The earliest known report of such a letter—known only indirectly through the response to the report—dates from the sixth century CE on the island of Ibiza off of Spain. The bishop of the island, Vincent, read, evidently believed, and copied the Sunday Letter; when it was received from him by Bishop Licinian of Cartagena in Spain, the latter denounced it in his extant *Epistola ad Licinianum Vincentium*.[20] The other earliest references to the Sunday Letter's existence are the Lateran Council of 745, condemning such letters, and a letter of Ecgred, bishop of Lindisfarne, dated to the 830s.[21] Whether or not the earliest of these brings us within decades of the letter's actual origin is a matter of speculation only. Partial precedents have been connected to a Coptic fragment possibly of African provenance,[22] but besides the evidence just noted from sixth-century Spain, the writings of ecclesiastics in Spain and southern Gaul in the sixth century contain parallels to ideas in the Sunday Letter, and the spreading Sabbatarian views of that region at that time could easily have given impetus to such an effort as this letter;[23] the effort of this period to compel compliance with Sunday regulations is not much in evidence prior to the sixth century. Dorothy Haines comments, "Such an environment seems fertile ground for an apocryphal letter written in support of a growing [Sabbatarian] movement against more traditional views of Sunday. Its extreme rhetoric and bold claim to divine authorship reflect the uncertainty of the time."[24] Again, Haines states that in the absence of an authoritative theological rationale or an ecclesiastical pronouncement, "our writer saw himself as providing divine confirmation of practices which, though not required by the fathers, were in the process of becoming obligatory."[25] Dated to this period, the Sunday Letter is "the oldest document in the Western Church setting forth, in mythological form, a theory

---

18. Beskow, *Strange Tales*, 26; cf. Lees, "Sunday Letter," 129n1; Haines, *Sunday Observance*, 62.

19. Goodspeed, *Strange New Gospels*, 99–100; Beskow, *Strange Tales*.

20. Miceli, "Epistle of Christ," 457; cf. PL 72:689–700.

21. Cf. Haines, *Sunday Observance*, 39.

22. Haines, *Sunday Observance*, 54, tentatively.

23. Robert Priebsch, *Letter from Heaven on the Observance of the Lord's Day* (Oxford: Basil Blackwell, 1936); likewise Beskow, *Strange Tales*, 28; Haines, *Sunday Observance*, 54–57.

24. Haines, *Sunday Observance*, 56.

25. Haines, *Sunday Observance*, 36.

which teaches the substitution of the Lord's day for the Jewish Sabbath and does so not in any hesitant manner as did the Council of Macon [585 CE] but clearly and unmistakably."[26]

As to possible literary sources behind the Sunday Letter, the distinct tradition of the "Sunday Lists"—catalogs of biblical and other world events to have occurred on Sunday, establishing the importance of the day—has been mentioned.[27] A sixth- or seventh-century sermon of Eusebius of Alexandria and a sermon (somewhat doubtfully) ascribed to Ephrem the Syrian (d. 373 CE) are mentioned as possible sources, only to be discounted by Haines.[28] The African precedent noted above could be included here. There are parallels with Apocalypse of Paul (= Vis. Paul)[29] and Apocalypse of Mary (= Apoc. Vir.);[30] influence from these is "possible but uncertain."[31] Myths of books and other objects passing into human hands will be noted below, again to be discounted as recognizable influences. There are too many unknowns on every side to establish definite lines. The single clearest literary source is Scripture.

Among attempts to reconstruct the earliest history of the Sunday Letter, Robert Priebsch painstakingly orders the manuscripts available to him into redactions I, II, III, and IV and tracks the spread of the first from its probable origin, presumably by the hand of a cleric, in northeast Spain or southern Gaul "shortly before 584," via the condemnation of such letters at the Lateran Council of 745, unchecked into Britain somewhat earlier than the eleventh century.[32] He notes ninth-century evidence of its appearance in Ireland and then also Iceland, where it (or possibly his redaction III) is indirectly attested as early as the twelfth or thirteenth century (if not even the tenth century); there is some additional indication that by the early twelfth century it "had spread [in more than one redaction] over the whole globe then known to men."[33] Haines, in her close study of the Sunday Letter in Anglo-Saxon England, notes the possibility that it could have arrived in Ireland as early as the sixth century, but in any event it had passed from Ireland to England sometime before the 830s CE. She observes that Ireland proved particularly receptive to the Sunday Letter due to a regard for the Mosaic law, the activity of ascetic groups, and a rising Sabbatarianism in search of a theological rationale.[34] Both Priebsch and Haines observe how the letter is adapted to these changing contexts. For further reception history and comparisons to other texts, see Beskow; Goodspeed; Miceli.

A few matters of interpretation merit mention: The voice of Christ is one with that of his Father, he identifies himself straightforwardly as the creator of the heavens and earth, he is credited with the Old Testament works of God in judging the Egyptians, and he closes simply as, "I, God" (2.52). Soteriologically, the closing paragraph of the document in the wording of the archbishop promises "peace" in the present world and declares that "humans

---

26. Priebsch, *Letter from Heaven*, 29.

27. Lees, "Sunday Letter," studies the evolution of these lists; cf. also Haines, *Sunday Observance*, 59–60; Richard Bauckham, "Sabbath and Sunday in the Post-Apostolic Church," in *From Sabbath to Lord's Day: A Biblical, Historical, and Theological Investigation*, ed. D. A. Carson (Grand Rapids: Zondervan, 1982), 280; idem, "Sabbath and Sunday in the Medieval Church in the West," in Carson, *From Sabbath to Lord's Day*, 304.

28. Haines, *Sunday Observance*, 56–57.

29. See *NTApoc* 2:712–48.

30. Tony Burke and Brent Landau, eds., *New Testament Apocrypha: More Noncanonical Scriptures*, 2 vols. (Grand Rapids: Eerdmans, 2016), 1:492–509; cf. also *Liber Requiei Mariae* 100; for a translation of the latter, see Stephen J. Shoemaker, *Ancient Traditions of the Virgin: Mary's Dormition and Assumption*, Oxford Early Christian Studies (Oxford: Oxford University Press, 2002), 290–350.

31. Haines, *Sunday Observance*, 61.

32. Priebsch, *Letter from Heaven*, 33.

33. Priebsch, *Letter from Heaven*, 18.

34. Haines, *Sunday Observance*, 36–43, 50, 52.

have nothing without pure love," but the document (Paris gr. 929) as a whole says nothing of faith in the Pauline vein (including 2.28, 37, 40), while the Gospel is straightforwardly identified as "my law" (2.7)—in direct parallel with the law given through Moses—and the document's entire message is one of reward for obedience and swift, severe punishment for disobedience. Notable by their absence (at least in Paris gr. 929) are motives of material gain and the like. Rather, the care of widows, orphans, beggars, and laborers is commanded, along with the honor due priests and godparents. Righteousness of life in general is what is sought. The word σταυροπάτης, "one who tramples on the cross" (2.16, 28), one of the many sins condemned, finds nine occurrences (the earliest in the fourth or fifth century CE; the rest are ninth century and later) in the full *TLG* corpus (which does not include the Sunday Letter) and is of uncertain significance (cf. Heb 6:6; 10:29); E. A. Sophocles suggests as a definition, "one who swears falsely by the cross, perjurer."[35]

4. KEY PASSAGES FOR NEW TESTAMENT STUDIES AND THEIR SIGNIFICANCE

The Sunday Letter is laced with allusions to and echoes of both the Old Testament (e.g., Gen 1:1–5, 26–27; Num 18:12; Ps 86:10; Isa 5:8; Jer 22:13; Joel 2:19) and the New Testament (e.g., Matt 16:18–19; 23:13; Mark 13:31; Luke 1:26–38; Jas 5:4; Rev 4:6, 8), along with other apocryphal texts (Apoc. Vir.; *Liber Requiei*; Vis. Paul; Apoc. Pet.). In the main, however, these are gilding more than the substance of the letter's message. The letter's claim of divine authorship is incredible, but it is useful to consider both this and other major themes against the backdrop of the New Testament and its history. With respect to the following selections, different interpretive communities and traditions will assess in their own way where the Scriptures forbid, discourage, permit, anticipate, or demand what developed only later.

By way of lending further perspective to what it is we are dealing with here, and thinking of the form of a heavenly letter authored by the Father in Christ's voice, one can note that New Testament scholars have debated whether the earliest church distinguished sayings of the pre-Easter Jesus from prophetic, inspirational sayings of the risen Jesus, and, as a distinct question, the degree to which the latter may feature as sayings of Jesus in the canonical Gospels.[36] There exist later, apocryphal records of dialogues of the risen Jesus with his disciples, especially set within the period prior to his ascension.[37] There also exist (see above) apocryphal letters ascribed to the pre-Easter Jesus, Jesus on the cross, and the risen Jesus. It is in the last group that the Sunday Letter belongs, first, as an unmediated (vs. prophetically mediated) writing of Jesus himself, and second, as a contemporaneous, newly uttered declaration in written form.

Do the Scriptures exclude the possibility of such as this? To begin with, there is the medium: a physical text fallen from heaven. Priebsch alludes to several Jewish, Christian, and pagan legends of books and other objects passing from above into human hands but sees no reason to think that these influenced the author of the Sunday Letter (whether or

---

35. *Greek Lexicon of the Roman and Byzantine Periods from B.C. 146 to A.D. 1100* (New York: Scribner's, 1900), 1007.

36. David Hill, *New Testament Prophecy*, New Foundations Theological Library (Atlanta: John Knox, 1979); M. Eugene Boring, *The Continuing Voice of Jesus: Christian Prophecy and the Gospel Tradition* (Louisville: Westminster John Knox, 1991). A collection of noncanonical sayings of Jesus, regardless of derivation, is provided by William D. Stroker, *Extracanonical Sayings of Jesus*, SBL Resources for Biblical Study 18 (Atlanta: Scholars Press, 1989). A pruned down list of "agrapha"—sayings defensibly ascribed to the pre-Easter Jesus that are not contained in the canonical Gospels, exclusive of, e.g., sayings ascribed to or derived from the risen Christ—is provided by Otfried Hofius in *NTApoc* 1:88–91.

37. *NTApoc* 1:228–353.

not such influenced later versions).[38] The Scriptures themselves, Old Testament and New Testament together, know of divine writing on earthly objects (e.g., Exod 31:18; 32:16; Dan 5:5), or visions of heavenly scrolls passing into human hands (e.g., Ezek 2:8–3:3; Rev 10:8–10), but not of heavenly scrolls or books actually passing into earthly hands (Exod 24:12?).

As for the contents of the heavenly letter, certainly the Gospels record a number of sayings of Jesus following his resurrection and before his ascension (e.g., Matt 28:18–20; Luke 24:36–49; John 21:22–23; that John 20:17 means that Jesus ascended before the encounter with Thomas in v. 27 is doubtful, but scholars take differing views of this verse), but the New Testament's only recorded words of the *ascended* Christ outside of the book of Revelation (e.g., Rev 1:17–3:22; 16:15)[39] are those to Paul and Ananias upon Paul's conversion (Acts 9:4–6, 10–16; 22:7–8; 26:14–18), and to Paul at other points in his ministry (Acts 18:9–10; 22:17–21; 23:11; 2 Cor 12:9). The words to Peter in connection with Cornelius also belong here (Acts 10:13–15; 11:7–9). All of these, outside of Revelation, are comprised of visions, dreams, or a heavenly voice (not tangible epistles) and relate to the earliest mission (rather than church government and liturgy). In Revelation 1:17–3:22 (cf. 1:11), the ascended Lord verbally dictates letters to be written down, the contents of which do concern church life. The warning of Revelation 22:18–19 refers to the words of that book, guarding them against the tampering of false prophets, rather than referring to further prophetic activity in general. In John 16:12, contextually the reference is not to new acts of speech that relativize or replace what has been given in Jesus but to the Spirit's role in clarifying and guiding in the singular revelation already given in Jesus (cf. 14:26; 16:25), yet it remains that Jesus asserts that he still has much "to say" (λέγειν) following his ascension (cf. Acts 1:1). Elsewhere, the Spirit is the "Spirit of Jesus" (Acts 16:6–7; cf. Rom 8:9; Gal 4:6), so that pronouncements of/in the Spirit could be construed as sayings of the ascended Jesus. The New Testament warns in general against some speaking falsely or without legitimacy in Jesus's name (e.g., Matt 7:22; 24:5; Luke 21:8) and cautions that spirits must be tested (1 John 4:1; see also 1 Cor 12:10; 14:29; 1 Thess 5:1–22; cf. Rom 12:6; 1 Cor 2:6–16; 12:1–3; 14:37–38; 2 Thess 2:1–2).

How to assess the letter's central concern with Sunday observance—a day that this letter (Paris gr. 929) stipulates officially begins at 3:00pm on Saturday and continues until dawn on Monday, the nonobservance of which in all the ways the letter prescribes results in terrible judgments on humanity—is a question that roots into the historical and theological questions of the origin of the observance of the Lord's Day (Sunday) during the apostolic period, vexed questions in their own right. In fact, when we turn to the New Testament for these roots, we find only a small group of passages that can at best be interpreted as hints (and not without justified disagreements), not positive evidence, of an early custom—with a variety of qualifications quickly following. The key passages from a historical perspective are Luke 24:1; John 20:1, 19; Acts 20:7; 1 Corinthians 16:2; Revelation 1:10 (for early post-NT texts, note Did. 14.1; Ign. *Magn.* 9.1; Barn. 15.9; Justin Martyr, *1 Apol.* 67; Gos. Pet. 35; 50; Pliny *Ep.* 10.96); a theological angle is afforded by Romans 14:5–6; Galatians 4:8–11; Colossians 2:16; and also, among others, Matthew 11:28–12:14; John 5:17; 7:23; and Hebrews 3:7–4:11.[40] In general, the New Testament's

---

38. Priebsch, *Letter from Heaven*, 30–31.

39. For a broad treatment of prophecy and sayings of Jesus in the apocalypse, see David E. Aune, *Prophecy in Early Christianity and the Ancient Mediterranean World* (Grand Rapids: Eerdmans, 1983), 274–88; Louis A. Vos, *The Synoptic Traditions in the Apocalypse* (Kampen: Kok, 1965).

40. See Carson, *From Sabbath to Lord's Day*; Willy Rordorf, *Sunday: The History of the Day of Rest and*

hints are that Lord's Day observance arose as an early, nonmandatory custom in at least some Christian churches, apparently in correlation with the day of Christ's resurrection; that it was not thought of as a Sabbath or in terms of Sabbath law (including a one-in-seven principle); that (Saturday) Sabbath observance according to Jewish customs may have continued among some churches alongside Sunday Christian gatherings, while being discontinued or never initiated among others; that Christians probably met other days for gatherings as also on Sunday, in whatever way Sunday was demarcated; and that how the day was both marked out and observed (possibly morning and/or evening from an early date, probably incorporating the Eucharist if in the evening) will have varied. Naturally, Sunday would have been a day of regular work. Nothing in the New Testament evidence verbally supports the formalized picture of Sunday that is projected by the Sunday Letter.

In his surveys of the postapostolic period through the Protestant tradition, Richard Bauckham finds no evidence that Sunday was regarded as a day of rest in the second century, though the regard for Sunday as a festival might have led to the desire that it be a work-free day;[41] Sabbath and Sunday were in that century infrequently compared, though there were hints toward a correlation of them. The Old Testament Sabbath command was interpreted metaphorically or eschatologically rather than transferred to Sunday. The legislation of Constantine (321 CE) is the earliest clear reference to Sunday as a work-free day, in the interest of Sunday observance and without a theological, let alone specifically Sabbatarian, rationale.[42] The first known transference of Sabbath to Sunday is Eusebius of Caesarea's commentary on Psalm 91 (dated to after 330 CE).[43] True Sabbatarianism was, however, "a medieval, not a patristic, development,"[44] and was not a theological development in the first place; it "grew from below, from popular sentiment, and was imposed from above, by legislation. It was a long time before the theologians provided much more than a means of accommodating it."[45] The greatest impetus may have been the Christianization of Germanic tribes, who saw a similarity between their own taboo-days and the Sabbath.[46] Among the key markers of sixth-century Sabbatarianism noted by Bauckham is the Sunday Letter itself,[47] which both grew out of and fueled this development. Bauckham summarizes that "medieval Sabbatarianism grew in the context of theocratic kingship and of church discipline of an increasingly juridical character. Its legalistic quality derives less from its Old Testament model than from its origin in attempt to legislate for a Christian society. The laws for Sunday rest had a minimum of genuinely ethical content and existed for several centuries as rules in search of a theological context and justified by a divine authority curiously difficult to locate."[48] The Sabbatarian doctrine was accepted unanimously among the scholastics, reversed somewhat by the Reformers, and then renewed among Puritans and in English, Scottish, and American Protestantism.[49]

Prescribed Christian fasts for Wednesday and Friday are unknown from the New

Worship in the Earliest Centuries of the Christian Church, trans. A. Graham (Philadelphia: Westminster, 1968); Jon C. Laansma, "Lord's Day," in *Dictionary of Later New Testament and its Developments*, ed. R. Martin and P. Davids (Downers Grove, IL: InterVarsity Press, 1997), 679–86.

41. Bauckham, "Sabbath and Sunday in the Post-Apostolic Church," 274–75.

42. Bauckham, "Sabbath and Sunday in the Post-Apostolic Church," 280–81.

43. Bauckham, "Sabbath and Sunday in the Post-Apostolic Church," 282.

44. Bauckham, "Sabbath and Sunday in the Post-Apostolic Church," 287.

45. Bauckham, "Sabbath and Sunday in the Medieval Church," 302.

46. Bauckham, "Sabbath and Sunday in the Medieval Church," 303.

47. Bauckham, "Sabbath and Sunday in the Medieval Church," 303.

48. Bauckham, "Sabbath and Sunday in the Medieval Church," 303.

49. Richard Bauckham, "Sabbath and Sunday in the Protestant Tradition," in Carson, *From Sabbath to Lord's Day*, 312.

Testament, though the general practice of fasting (Matt 4:2; 6:16–18; 9:15; Acts 13:2–3; 14:23; cf. Luke 2:37; 18:12; Acts 27:9) and, in certain cases, regular hours of prayer (Acts 3:1; 10:3, 9, 30) are attested. At this stage, these practices would be matters of liberty and conscience. As early as Didache 8.1 (late first or early second century), however, the regularized, though still nonobligatory, practice of Wednesday and Friday fasts is attested; the Didache merely posits these days over against "the hypocrites" (an allusion to the Jews) who fast on Monday and Thursday, without supplying the rationale for the choice of the Wednesday and Friday. Later tradition supplied a rationale corresponding to the arrest and death of Christ and considered these fasts mandatory.[50]

Other post-New Testament ecclesial developments are contained incidentally within the letter: Peter as the first leader of the church of Rome, Christian priests and monks, godparents, angels' celebration of the church's liturgy, and the intercession of deceased saints and Christ's "immaculate mother."[51]

5. BIBLIOGRAPHY

Bauckham, Richard. "Sabbath and Sunday in the Medieval Church in the West." Pages 299–309 in *From Sabbath to Lord's Day: A Biblical, Historical, and Theological Investigation*. Edited by D. A. Carson. Grand Rapids: Zondervan, 1982.

———. "Sabbath and Sunday in the Post-Apostolic Church." Pages 251–98 in *From Sabbath to Lord's Day: A Biblical, Historical, and Theological Investigation*. Edited by D. A. Carson. Grand Rapids: Zondervan, 1982.

———. "Sabbath and Sunday in the Protestant Tradition." Pages 311–41 in *From Sabbath to Lord's Day: A Biblical, Historical, and Theological Investigation*. Edited by D. A. Carson. Grand Rapids: Zondervan, 1982.

Beskow, Per. *Strange Tales about Jesus: A Survey of Unfamiliar Gospels*. Philadelphia: Fortress, 1983.

Burke, Tony, and Brent Landau, eds. *New Testament Apocrypha: More Noncanonical Scriptures*. 2 vols. Grand Rapids: Eerdmans, 2016.

Goodspeed, Edgar J. *Strange New Gospels*. Chicago: University of Chicago Press, 1931.

Haines, Dorothy, ed. *Sunday Observance and the Sunday Letter in Anglo-Saxon England*. Anglo-Saxon Texts 8. Cambridge: D. S. Brewer, 2010.

Laansma, Jon C. "Lord's Day." Pages 679–86 in *Dictionary of Later New Testament and Its Developments*. Edited by Ralph P. Martin and Peter H. Davids. Downers Grove, IL: InterVarsity Press, 1997.

Lees, Clare A. "The 'Sunday Letter' and the 'Sunday Lists.'" *Anglo-Saxon England* 14 (1985): 129–51.

Miceli, Calogero A. "Epistle of Christ from Heaven." e-Clavis: Christian Apocrypha. www.nasscal.com/e-clavis-christian-apocrypha/epistle-of-christ-from-heaven/.

———. "The Epistle of Christ from Heaven: A New Translation and Introduction." Pages 455–63 in vol. 1 of *New Testament Apocrypha: More Noncanonical Scriptures*. Edited by Tony Burke and Brent Landau. Grand Rapids: Eerdmans, 2016.

Priebsch, Robert. *Letter from Heaven on the Observance of the Lord's Day*. Oxford: Basil Blackwell, 1936.

---

50. Kurt Niederwimmer, *The Didache*, ed. H. Attridge, trans. L. Maloney, Hermeneia (Minneapolis: Fortress, 1998), 131–33.

51. These last are early additions to the Sunday Letter according to Haines (*Sunday Observance*, 46).

PART 4

APOCRYPHAL APOCALYPSES

CHAPTER 25

APOCALYPSE OF PAUL

JAN N. BREMMER

1. INTRODUCTION

The Jewish and Christian apocalyptic literature about the fate of the dead, which supplemented the meagre information on the afterlife in the New Testament, has never ceased to fascinate theologians, artists, and writers as well as the general public. Despite the fact that virtually all of these apocalyptic writings have been stamped apocryphal, the genre exercised a thorough influence on European thought that extended beyond antiquity and the Middle Ages into modernity. Among the early Christian apocalypses, the Apocalypse of Paul, also known as the *Visio Pauli*, occupies a special position because of its exceptional popularity, witnessed by its many translations, albeit often only partially, in the vernacular languages,[1] but also in many Oriental ones, such as Arabic, Armenian, Coptic, Georgian, and Syriac.[2] Its description of the visit of the apostle Paul to hell and paradise was extremely popular, and its rich history of reception probably even extended to an influence on Dante's *Divina commedia*, although perhaps only indirectly.[3] Despite this popularity, or perhaps because of it, there are still many problems concerning its text, authorship, date, provenance, intended readership, and place in the genre of apocalypses (see sec. 3 below). In any case, it should not be confused with another Apocalypse of Paul, which was found among the Nag Hammadi codices. That treatise is the product of an anonymous author with "gnostic" sympathies and has no connections with the later Apocalypse of Paul.[4]

---

1. See, most recently, Lenka Jiroušková, *Die Visio Pauli: Wege und Wandlungen einer orientalischen Apokryphe im lateinischen Mittelalter unter Einschluß der alttschechischen und deutschsprachigen Textzeugen* (Leiden: Brill, 2006); Peter Dinzelbacher, *Von der Welt durch die Hölle zum Paradies—das mittelalterliche Jenseits* (Paderborn: Schöningh, 2007), 165–80 (the *Visio Pauli* in the Middle Ages); Julia Zimmermann, "Die Tiroler Predigtsammlung und ihre *Visio Pauli* (mit Edition des Predigttextes)," in *Mertens lessen: Exemplarische Lektüren für Volker Mertens zum 75. Geburtstag*, ed. M. Costard et al. (Göttingen: Vandenhoeck & Ruprecht, 2012), 9–30; Nikolaos H. Trunte, *Reiseführer durch das Jenseits: Die Apokalypse des Paulus in der Slavia Orthodoxa* (Munich: Peter Lang, 2013). For the *Forschungsgeschichte*, see Pierluigi Piovanelli, *Apocryphités* (Turnhout: Brepols, 2016), 380–88.

2. Cf. Piovanelli, *Apocryphités*, 371–79.

3. For this much-disputed question, see, most recently, Gerhard Regn, "Die Apokalypse im irdischen Paradies: Offenbarung, Allegorie und Dichtung in Dantes Commedia," in *Autorschaft und Autorisierungsstrategien in apokalyptischen Texten*, ed. J. Frey et al. (Tübingen: Mohr Siebeck, 2019), 391–412.

4. Cf. Dylan Burns, "Is the Apocalypse of Paul a Valentinian Apocalypse? Pseudepigraphy and Group Definition in NHC V,2," in *Die Nag-Hammadi-Schriften in der Literatur- und Theologiegeschichte des frühen Christentums*, ed. J. Schröter and K. Schwarz (Tübingen: Mohr Siebeck, 2017), 97–112.

1.1 Text

The original Greek text has been lost, and what survived is only an abbreviated version based on two manuscripts of the thirteenth and fifteenth centuries,[5] even though the compilers of Middle Byzantine apocalypses still had access to a fuller version, as appears from similarities with the long Latin versions,[6] the original of which was probably composed in Rome at the end of the sixth century.[7] From this original translation, which has not survived, we have a number of versions, of which a Paris manuscript of the late first millennium probably has the longest and best text.[8] However, a strong case has also been for the importance of the Coptic translation, which has survived in a manuscript dated to 960 CE, but of which the original is undoubtedly somewhat older and much closer to the Latin versions than the Syriac and Greek texts.[9] We will base our contribution mainly on the Paris text, which, together with three other long Latin versions, has been exemplarily edited by Hilhorst and Silverstein,[10] but also on the Coptic translation (henceforth: C), which is presently being prepared for a new critical edition, translation, and commentary.[11] However, I will also pay more attention than is usual to the Arnhem Latin text (= L⁴), dating from the early fifteenth century, as it sometimes better preserves readings than the Paris version (L¹). It seems reasonable to suppose that when the Latin and Coptic texts agree, we come close to the lost Greek original.

1.2 Authorship

There is, unfortunately, nothing known about the authorship of the Apocalypse of Paul. Like most apocalypses, it is a pseudepigraphical writing, the name of whose author is absent in order not to disturb the illusion that it is the apostle Paul who is speaking. Evidently, its author did not consider his institutional or social affiliations sufficiently imposing to lend his own name to his teaching about the postmortem fate of the souls as inspired by Paul's mention of his visit to the third heaven (see 2 Cor 12:2). In chapter 46

---

5. Constantinus Tischendorf, *Apocalypses Apocryphae: Mosis, Esdrae, Pauli, Iohannis, item Mariae Dormitio, additis evangeliorum et actuum apocryphorum supplementis* (Leipzig: Mendelssohn, 1866; repr., Hildesheim: Olms, 1966), xiv–xviii, 34–69; Bernard Bouvier and François Bovon, "Prière et Apocalypse de Paul: Un fragment grec inédit conservé au Sinaï: Introduction, texte, traduction et notes," *Apocrypha* 15 (2004): 9–30; Piovanelli, *Apocryphités*, 427–34, rightly concludes that this text has made some use of Apoc. Paul, but at quite a distance; for a German translation and commentary, see Jan Dochhorn, "Gebet und Apokalypse des Paulus," www.academia.edu/40671822/Gebet_und_Apokalypse_des_Paulus. For a recent introduction and German translation of this late Greek apocalypse, see Hans-Josef Klauck, *Die apokryphe Bibel* (Tübingen: Mohr Siebeck, 2008), 157–98.

6. As noted by Jane Baun, *Tales from Another Byzantium: Celestial Journey and Local Community in the Medieval Greek Apocrypha* (Cambridge: Cambridge University Press, 2007), 79–81.

7. J. N. Bremmer, *Maidens, Magic and Martyrs in Early Christianity* (Tübingen: Mohr Siebeck, 2017), 299–302.

8. For the various Latin versions and their relationships, see Claudio Zamagni, *Recherches sur le Nouveau Testament et les apocryphes chrétiens* (Rimini: Guaraldi, 2017), 351–71.

9. Lautaro Roig Lanzillotta, "The Coptic *Apocalypse of Paul* in Ms Or 7023," in *The Visio Pauli and the Gnostic Apocalypse of Paul*, ed. J. Bremmer and I. Czachesz (Leuven: Peeters, 2007), 158–97; Alin Suciu, *The Berlin-Strasbourg Apocryphon: A Coptic Apostolic Memoir* (Tübingen: Mohr Siebeck, 2017), 113, mentions the discovery of two small fragments of a different manuscript with an account in the third-person singular, which he hopes to publish in the near future.

10. Theodor Silverstein and Anthony Hilhorst, *Apocalypse of Paul: A New Critical Edition of Three Long Latin Versions* (Geneva: Patrick Cramer, 1997); Marie-Françoise Damongeot-Bourdat, "Un nouveau manuscrit de l'Apocalypse de Paul (Paris, BnF, nouv. acq. lat. 2676)," *Bulletin du Cange* 67 (2009): 29–64; Rossana Guglielmetti, "Deux témoins inédits de la *Visio Pauli*," *Apocrypha* 26 (2015): 57–78.

11. I am very grateful to Lautaro Roig Lanzillotta and Jacques van der Vliet for allowing me to use their forthcoming translation. For the Coptic text and translation, see for now Ernest A. Wallis Budge, *Miscellaneous Coptic Texts in the Dialect of Upper Egypt* (London: British Museum, 1915), 534–74, 1043–84.

we find an important indication of the intentions of the author. In a passage of the Coptic translation, which is not found in the Latin versions, we read: "As for him who will read it with faith, the written record of his sins will be torn, and whoever will listen to it and observe the commandments of my son, my son will bless them in this world and show mercy to them on the day of their visitation." Roig Lanzillotta argues that this "emphasis on the importance of writing, reading and transmitting the vision of Paul was intended as a writer's self-legitimization comparable to the introduction to the Tarsus text."[12] This seems hardly persuasive, as the Tarsus introduction much more strongly emphasizes the authorship of Paul. In this case, as somewhat later in the Coptic text (C 64), the point at issue is the status of the text as a canonical one that should be required reading in the churches.

1.3 Provenance and Intended Readership

The ancient Roman church historian Sozomen (*Hist. eccl.* 7.9.10) notes that "most monks praise" the Apocalypse of Paul, and the oldest Latin references also come from a monastic milieu.[13] As the text actually does refer to ascetics and monks (§ 2), the monastic milieu of late antique Egypt seems to be its most likely place of origin and its intended readership.[14] An Egyptian origin is also supported by a passage in the Coptic version that has not yet been adduced in this connection. Immediately after its surviving beginning (= L[1] 16), it describes the "Powers of Darkness."[15] This section appears only in the Coptic translation, but it may well have been part of the original Greek version, as it is very difficult to ascertain that it is an interpolation.[16] One group of the Powers is there described as having "crocodile faces," probably another reference to Egypt. Thus, the original Greek version will have been produced in Egypt around 400 CE, and the Latin translation will have been made at the end of the sixth century, as is also suggested by the converging references to its text in the *Regula Magistri*,[17] Caesarius of Arles,[18] and the *Decretum Gelasianum* (5.5.1).[19]

1.4 Date

The received opinion has long been that the original version of the Apocalypse of Paul was written in Greek, perhaps even in the second century, as it was supposed to be mentioned by Origen. The supporting testimony for this idea derived from the thirteenth-century Syrian scholar Barhebraeus, but his information was evidently not based on firsthand knowledge, and clear indications suggest that our text derives from the period around 400 CE.[20]

The actual date must be close to 400 CE, as the Prologue tells us:

(1) In the consulate of Theodosius Augustus the Younger and Cynegius (AD 388), in that time there lived a *honoratus* in Tarsus in the house that once had belonged to Saint Paul.

---

12. Roig Lanzillotta, "Coptic *Apocalypse of Paul*," 176.

13. Catherine Paupert, "Présence des apocryphes dans la littérature monastique occidentale ancienne," *Apocrypha* 4 (1993): 115–17, 119.

14. As was already concluded by Roger Casey, "Apocalypse of Paul," *JTS* 34 (1933): 26.

15. Translations are mine unless otherwise noted.

16. See the text and discussion by Roig Lanzillotta, "Coptic Apocalypse of Paul," 171–74.

17. Adalbert de Vogüé, *La Règle du Maître*, 2 vols. (Paris: Cerf, 1964), 2:188–90, 350–51, 506.

18. Benedikt Fischer, "Impedimenta mundi fecerunt eos miseros," *VC* 5 (1951): 84–87.

19. See also Silverstein and Hilhorst, *Apocalypse of Paul*, 12.

20. Piovanelli, *Apocryphités*, 367–404; Bremmer, *Maidens, Magic and Martyrs*, 298–301. This was, in fact, already noted by Montague R. James, *The Apocryphal New Testament* (Oxford: Oxford University Press, 1924), 525.

An angel appeared in the night and told him in a revelation that he should destroy the foundations of the house and make public what he found. He thought, however, that these were delusions.

(2) When the angel came for the third time, he whipped him and compelled him to destroy the foundations. And, when digging, the man found a marble box inscribed on the sides. In it were the revelation of Saint Paul and his sandals, in which he used to walk when teaching the word of God. But he feared to open that box and gave it to a judge. Having accepted it, the judge sent it as it was, sealed with lead, to the Emperor Theodosius, fearing that it was something else (other than the *Apocalypse*). When he had accepted it, the Emperor opened it and found the revelation of Saint Paul. He sent a copy to Jerusalem and kept the original.

Now we know that Theodosius I ruled from 379 to 395 CE and that Cynegius died in 388 CE. The latter was a great friend of monks and ascetics, and we may reasonably assume that for the author his name was still one of living memory. This puts the date around 400 CE, the more so as Augustine refers to this work in his *Tractates on the Gospel of John* (98.8) of 416 CE in negative terms, thus establishing a *terminus ante quem*. The late date is also clear from various references to monks in our text, which can hardly date from before the fourth century.[21] Given these references and the mention of Cynegius as well as the presence of apocalypses in Egypt at the time, an Egyptian origin seems likely. This would be even more the case if we can accept a passage in the Coptic translation that mentions among the "Powers of Darkness" some with "crocodile faces" (C 16) as authentic.

2. SUMMARY OF CONTENT

Let us now turn to its contents.[22] The Apocalypse of Paul starts with the familiar but still intriguing words of Paul in 2 Corinthians (12:1–5) that he was caught up into the third heaven and into paradise, but in part 2 (Apoc. Paul 3–6) the text rather abruptly changes to an appeal of the sun, moon, stars, sea, and earth to God about the sins of humankind. They want to act against all the transgressions, fornications, and murders they see, but God tells them that he has patience with the human race until they convert and repent. The appeal culminates in the voice of the earth complaining that it has to bear the "fornications, adulteries, murders, thefts, perjuries, magic, crimes and all the evil they do" (6). Yet even the earth has to be patient. These first chapters sound the theme of sins and repentance, and we will later see to what extent these themes recur in our text.

After the elements of the cosmos, part 3 (Apoc. Paul 7–10) shifts our attention to angels. Drawing on rich Jewish angelic lore, the author lets us hear of guardian angels of every man and woman, as "man is the image of God," of angels coming to worship God but also telling him what humans have done, good or evil. Asked what they have done, they interestingly tell that they have come from "those who have renounced this world for the sake of your holy name, wandering as strangers in the caves of the rocks, weeping every hour in which they inhabit the earth, and hungering and thirsting because of your name" (9). After these angels, others come who relate about the sinners and wonder why they

---

21. These references are not specific enough, though, to connect them with the Pachomian community, contra Emiliano Fiori, "The Reactivation of the Apocalyptic Genre in Early Egyptian Monasticism: The Apocalypse of Paul," in *Wissen in Bewegung: Institution-Iteration-Transfer*, ed. E. Cancik-Kirschbaum and A. Traninger (Wiesbaden: Harrassowitz, 2015), 307–22, and idem, "Death and Judgment in the *Apocalypse of Paul*: Old Imagery and Monastic Reinvention," *ZAC* 20 (2016): 92–108.

22. For the contents and a comparison to the gnostic Apocalypse of Paul, see also Jacques van der Vliet, *Paulus als ruimtereiziger: Koptische visioenen van de heilige Paulus* (Nijmegen: Radboud Universiteit, 2020).

would care about them. But like with the elements, God tells them to go on ministering to the sinners until they convert and repent (10).

Having heard about the angels, part 4 (Apoc. Paul 11–18) introduces an angel who tells Paul to follow him, as he will show him the place where the righteous will be after their death as well as the bottomless pit that awaits the souls of sinners. Paul does as he is told, and the angel takes him into heaven, where he sees the firmament and the powers, without us being told where the firmament is situated and what these powers are, although we also hear of the "firmament of heaven." Apparently, we are to imagine that Paul looks down, as in the next chapter (12) he looks up to see wonderful angels. The firmament contains evils, such as oblivion, slander, fornication, madness, insolence, and the princes of vices.

It is fitting that among these vices there are horrifying angels, "without mercy, having no pity, whose face was full of madness, and their teeth sticking out of their mouth; their eyes shone like the morning star of the east, and sparks of fire went out from the hairs of their head or from their mouth" (11). Understandably, Paul asks the angel, "Who are these, Lord?" And the angel said to him: "*These* are those who are destined for the souls of the impious in the hour of their need, who did not believe that they had the Lord as their helper nor have hoped in him" (11). Paul asks the angel for information, and the latter functions as the *angelus interpres*—that is, the angel who interprets what he sees, who also uses the demonstrative pronouns, which are typical of the tours of hell.[23]

After the horrifying angels, Paul next looks up and sees the opposite: angels with shining faces, their loins clad with golden girdles (cf. Dan 10:5), with palms in their hands, full of gentleness and mercy. The latter qualities must have appealed to the contemporary readers, as justice became increasingly severe in late antiquity. As with the "bad" angels, Paul asks who they are, and the angel answers with the characteristic demonstrative pronouns: "*these* are the angels of justice," who will guide the souls of the righteous who did believe in the Lord as their helper. The angel also explains that both categories, sinners and righteous, go along the same road to God, but the righteous will have a helper (Apoc. Paul 12).

Paul then sees how the soul of the righteous leaves its body, but he also hears that it will have to return at the resurrection. The soul is brought up to God, who sees no evil in him and hands him to Michael to be brought to the "paradise of exultation" (Apoc. Paul 14). It is different with the soul of the sinner, who is also brought before God. The Coptic translation tells us that he is brought up by the powers of darkness, of which it gives a detailed description, going from "faces of lions, dressed in iron armor, glowing with fire, with piercing swords in their hands" to some who are "crocodile faced, with great swords in their hands, cutting up the limbs of the soul secretly" (C 16). Roig Lanzillotta has made a reasonable case that this description belonged to the original text, even if it looks somewhat amplified in comparison to the rest of the Apocalypse of Paul.[24] This is the more likely since, as we saw, our text already mentioned "powers" without further identifying them. God rejects the sinner and orders him to be "delivered unto the angel Tartarouchos who is set over the punishments." This angel also appears in the Ethiopic version of the Apocalypse of Peter (13E) and is a nice example of the influence of the latter on the Apocalypse of Paul (15–16).

After the examples of the treatment of the souls of the righteous and the sinners, we get a sinner who denies having sinned. His guardian angel wants to read all his sins from his record, but God orders his victims to be brought before him, and the sinner confesses to

23. Martha Himmelfarb, *Tours of Hell* (Philadelphia: University of Pennsylvania Press, 1981), 45–56.
24. Roig Lanzillotta, "Coptic *Apocalypse of Paul*," 170–74.

have killed the one and to have committed adultery with the other. He is also handed to Tartarouchos and is to be imprisoned in the lower prison until the day of the resurrection (Apoc. Paul 17–18).

Having seen the fate of the good, the bad, and the ugly, in part 5 (Apoc. Paul 19–30) Paul is taken by an angel to paradise, the entrance of which is in the third heaven—obviously a reference to Paul's own description with which the Apocalypse of Paul starts, but paradise is also in the third heaven in 2 Enoch (8; 20). In Genesis, there is no mention of walls, but they are clearly presupposed, since an angel guards the way to the tree of life (Gen 3:24), and walls are also mentioned in the Apocalypse of Moses (17.1) and other early Christian and Jewish writings.[25] Having entered paradise, Paul is greeted by an old man, whom the angel identifies as "Enoch, the scribe of righteousness," although in 2 Enoch 8.1 Enoch is in the third heaven but not in paradise. Paul also sees Elijah, and indeed, both Enoch and Elijah are alluded to as being in paradise in 1 Enoch (1 En. 89.52). Elijah tells Paul that only a very few people are allowed into paradise (Apoc. Paul 20), which stresses the uniqueness of Paul's vision.

After this quick visit to paradise, Paul is led back by the angel to the very beginning of heaven, its gates. The angel explains that this is the land of promise, or, probably more original, the land of inheritance in the Coptic version, as the name is explained with a reference to the meek that will inherit the earth (Matt 5:4). It is this land where Christ will come back at the end of time (Apoc. Paul 21). Most Latin versions do not properly inform us where this land is, but the Coptic version (C 22) suggests that it is in the east, as does the Arnhem Latin text, which is also the only one of the Latin versions that has the name of Elijah in chapter 20.

The land contains a river flowing with milk and honey and trees with many fruits. This land will be nicer for the ascetics and virgins, thus once again pointing to an ascetic milieu of composition. From there, Paul goes to a river that is even whiter than milk. This is Lake Acherousia, in which the archangel Michael will purify repentant sinners before letting them enter the land of inheritance (Apoc. Paul 23).

Paul continues his journey on a boat full of precious metals and stones with a thousand angels from Lake Acherousia to the city of Christ, which presumably is situated at the far east (C and Arnhem). Here, he sees four rivers: "To the west of the city, it was a river of honey; to the south of the city, a river of milk; to the east of the city, a river of wine; to the north of the city, a river of oil" (C and Arnhem 23, the cardinal points not in Paris [L¹]). This is where the righteous will be abundantly rewarded (Apoc. Paul 23). The presence of honey, milk, wine, and oil in paradise first occurs in 2 Enoch where we read: "And two streams come forth, one a source of honey and milk, and a source which produces oil and wine" (8.5),[26] and the reversed order of honey and milk, instead of the proverbial order milk and honey, occurs here also for the first time.

The apostle now enters a city that is rather similar to the heavenly Jerusalem, and which is indeed called the city of Jerusalem (Apoc. Paul 29). At the entrance of the city gate, Paul sees trees without fruit and people crying among them whenever they see somebody actually entering the city. These, as the angel explains, are those ascetics who did not contain their pride and boastfulness. They will enter the city at Christ's advent but will never enjoy

---

25. Jan N. Bremmer, "The Birth of Paradise: To Early Christianity via Greece, Persia and Israel," in *The Cosmography of Paradise: The Other World from Ancient Mesopotamia to Medieval Europe*, ed. A. Scafi (London: Warburg Institute, 2016), 17.

26. F. I. Andersen, "2 Enoch," in *The Old Testament Pseudepigrapha*, 2 vols., ed. J. H. Charlesworth (Garden City, NY: Doubleday, 1983–1985), 1:116.

the same freedom as those who always served God in humility (24). Paul now proceeds counterclockwise:[27] from the river of honey in the west, where he sees major and minor prophets who will welcome the martyrs there (25), to the river of milk in the south, where the children murdered by Herod will receive those who have remained chaste all their life (26), to the river of wine in the east where the patriarchs will welcome those who have been hospitable (27), and ending at the river of oil at the north, where he sees the people who were not hypocrites chanting and singing for God (28).[28]

So far, we have heard of twelve gates (Apoc. Paul 23), but it now appears that there are twelve walls, the one higher than the other, with the twelfth being the highest. This wall encompasses the very center of the city of Christ. It is only here that the completely blameless will be received. In this part, there are fabulous empty golden thrones. The feature was apparently too unusual for the scribes of texts Paris (L[1]) and Escorial so that they let people sit on the thrones, but those of St. Gallen and Arnhem, like the Coptic text, rightly leave the thrones empty. There is also an altar in the center where David is playing a golden harp with a golden psaltery in his hand. And those present respond with "alleluia!" (Apoc. Paul 29). Undoubtedly, it is David because the psalms were by far the most popular part of the Bible in Egypt, as witnessed by the papyri.[29] Somewhat surprisingly, Paul asks what "alleluia" means. The answer stresses that all people should repeat it, except those who are rather old or ill (30).

In part 6 (Apoc. Paul 31–44), after the visit to the city of Christ, we move back westward, as the angel guides Paul out of the city, beyond Lake Acherousia and the river of milk and honey and over the ocean (31). The Coptic version (C 31) has Paul back in heaven, but this is not mentioned by the Latin ones and is perhaps a misunderstanding of the statement in the text that the ocean bears the foundations of heaven. The Latin versions just let the angel ask Paul if he understands where he is, which seems more likely in the context. After an affirmative answer, they proceed further westward to the setting of the sun and cross the ocean to a place where it is gloomy and dark. Here, the Coptic version (C 31) has a passage lacking in the Latin versions, which shows the love of the author for numbers, but it also mentions pits and holes, which do occur later in the Latin versions (32; 37; 38). It is not impossible that the reason for its omission is the fact that the text perhaps twice says, "And I saw," which made the Latin translator jump straight to the second case of "And I saw." If original, as persuasively argued by Roig Lanzillotta,[30] it is a kind of summary view of hell as a place before coming to a detailed survey of the sinners and their punishments.

Paul then sees "a river of fire burning with heat, and in it was a multitude of men and women immersed up to the knees, and other men up to the navel; others even up to the lips and others up to their hair" (Apoc. Paul 31). These men and women are the first in a series of sinners and their punishments, which are now explained in considerable detail (31–44). Naturally, Paul asks the angel who these are in this river of fire. The angel answers: "These are those who are neither warm nor cold, neither are they found in the number of the righteous nor in the number of the impious." I have cited here the version of the Arnhem text, which is supported by the Coptic version, as likely better than the Paris version, for it

---

27. Roig Lanzillotta, "Coptic *Apocalypse of Paul*," 184–85.

28. For the rivers, see Jacques van Ruiten, "The Four Rivers of Eden in the *Apocalypse of Paul* (*Visio Pauli*): The Intertextual Relationship of Genesis 2.10–14 and the *Apocalypse of Paul* 23," in Bremmer and Czachesz, *Visio Pauli*, 50–76.

29. David G. Martinez, "The Papyri and Early Christianity," in *The Oxford Handbook of Papyrology*, ed. R. Bagnall (Oxford: Oxford University Press, 2009), 591.

30. Roig Lanzillotta, "Coptic *Apocalypse of Paul*," 185–87.

preserves the typical structure of the "tour of hell" questions, such as "Who are these?" answered by "These are those who . . . ."

After the explanation of the various sins of those in the river, the Coptic version (C 32) continues with "the (region) west of the river of fire, too, was allotted to various kinds of punishments and was full of men and women before whom the river of fire was flowing." This version seems more original than the Latin Paris version, which reads: "I saw on the north side a place of varying and diverse torments, full of men and women, and a river of fire flowed down upon it." So far, we have been going westward, and it seems more logical, if we can trust our original author to be that, to proceed in that direction than suddenly to turn to the north. Apparently, we now have reached the outer westward limit, with the worst sinners and punishments.

In this place, Paul sees bottomless pits filled by those who did not trust in the Lord (Apoc. Paul 32). Paul laments at the fate of humankind but is berated by the angel as willing to be more compassionate than God himself (33). The apostle now sees "an old man who had been brought by dragging him along and he was immersed up to his knees" (C 34). The punishing angel Tartarouchos, whom we already met above, tears out his entrails with an iron trident because he was eating, drinking, and whoring when performing the Eucharist. In the Coptic version, the angel is called Aftemelouchos, a name which is also found in the Greek version (Temelouchos). It seems that the Latin version here has simplified the name of the angels, as it has also omitted this name in chapter 40, where it is present in the Coptic version.[31]

The next sinner seen by Paul is an old bishop whom four angels "immersed up to his knees in the river of fire while flashes of fire struck his face like whirlwinds and he was not allowed at all to say: 'Have pity upon me!'" (C 35). The bishop had not given righteous judgments nor cared for widows and orphans (35), an important issue in early Christianity and one of its Jewish legacies.[32]

Subsequently, Paul sees two clergymen, a deacon and a reader. The former was a fornicator and consumed the offerings, which he presumably was supposed to share out. The latter taught the people but did not obey his own teachings. It is probably not incidental that his tongue was cut out and his lips were cut off, as these were the organs of his teaching: in other words, a typical measure-for-measure punishment (36).

In the following chapters, Paul sees a whole spectrum of sinners, running from those who had overcharged interest and slandered within the church (Apoc. Paul 37), to sorcerers and adulterous men and women (38), to girls who had lost their virginity, men and women who had not taken care of widows and orphans, and those who had broken the fasts (39). The Coptic version (C 39) adds: "I saw other men and other women who were hanging from the hair of their head, while huge torches of fire were burning under their face and snakes were glued to their body, devouring them." The torches are also mentioned by the Latin version of St. Gallen, but not the snakes, which perhaps have been added in this passage, although similar snakes are mentioned later (40). In any case, these adulterous sinners adorned themselves with unguents when they went to church. The latter detail is omitted in the Latin versions, but it seems to belong to the original. Apparently, the place of transgression, the church, is important here,[33] as adultery as such has been mentioned

---

31. For the names, see Jean-Marc Rosenstiehl, "Tartarouchos-Temelouchos: Contribution à l'étude de l'Apocalypse apocryphe de Paul," in *Deuxième Journée d'Études Coptes* (Louvain: Peeters, 1986), 29–56, somewhat corrected and supplemented by Bremmer, *Maidens, Magic and Martyrs*, 275–76.

32. Bremmer, *Maidens, Magic and Martyrs*, 43–64.

33. This is not considered by Roig Lanzillotta, "Coptic *Apocalypse of Paul*," 189.

before (38). Interestingly, the Latin versions conclude with a view of males who have committed homosexual acts, whereas this detail is lacking in the Eastern versions. Was it added later or omitted in the East? The case seems hard to resolve.

The somewhat monotonous and depressing row of sinners is continued with those who had dispensed alms (not in the Coptic) but had not known God, with women, as well as their complicit males, who had performed abortions to get rid of the results of their adulteries, and with monks who had not cared for widows and orphans, strangers and foreigners (Apoc. Paul 40). Here, it is noteworthy that the Coptic version sometimes adds an explanation. Thus, it is added of the angel who presides over the punishments: "That is Aftimelouchos." And about the women who performed abortions it is said that they did so even though they were "having the name of God," but to which the Coptic version adds: "to wit 'Christian'" (C 40). Consequently, it cannot be excluded that the Coptic version has also added explanations elsewhere.

Although neither the Latin nor the Coptic version are wholly clear at this point, in the last two chapters describing his tour of hell, Paul first seems to go further to the west, as is stated by the Syriac version, and, finally as it seems, to the northwest, apparently as the most terrible place to be for punished sinners. But the sins are now clearly of a different order. First, he is led to an extremely smelly pit full of fire in which people simply disappear never to be heard of again. This is the place for those who denied the incarnation of Christ, the virgin birth of Mary, and the transubstantiation of the Eucharist (Apoc. Paul 41). Further away, in a place characterized by extreme cold and snow, Paul notices those who denied the resurrection of Christ and the raising of the flesh (42). Strangely, there is also a worm with a size of one cubit but with two heads, which is clearly a not wholly fitting adaptation of Isaiah 66:24.

Seeing these extreme punishments, the apostle weeps, which makes the sinners ask for mercy. In response, the archangel Michael descends from heaven together with the host of angels and berates the sinners for their lack of repentance. These weep deeply and again appeal for mercy, joined by Paul (Apoc. Paul 43). This concerted effort makes Christ descend from heaven, and eventually he succumbs to the pleas of Michael, the angels, and Paul and gives them respite on Sundays, a day and a night, forever (44),[34] but the Coptic version adds "as well as the fifty days following the resurrection, when I rose from among the dead" (C 44). The Coptic mention of Easter is perhaps supported by the fact that Prudentius in his *Cathemerinon* (5.125–36) also mentions Easter as a day of respite for the damned.[35] However, the addition of fifty days does not appear in the Latin, Greek, Syriac,[36] or Armenian versions; therefore, it seems to be a Coptic addition.[37] The importance of Sunday as a day of rest starts to emerge only with Constantine and is an important argument for the late fourth-century date of the original Apocalypse of Paul.[38]

After this *moment suprême* in Paul's visit to hell, we turn again to paradise in part 7

---

34. Like many before him, Richard Bauckham, *The Fate of the Dead* (Leiden: Brill, 1998), 141, ascribes the idea of the respite on Sunday to Jewish influence, but the evidence is late, and influence from Christianity seems more likely; cf. Bremmer, *Maidens, Magic and Martyrs*, 311–12.

35. Sebastian Merkle, "Die Sabbatruhe in der Hölle: Ein Beitrag zur Prudentius-Erklärung und zur Geschichte der Apokryphen," *Römische Quartalsschrift* 9 (1895): 489–505.

36. Note that one Arabic version also derives from a Syriac text; see Alessandro Bausi, "A First Evaluation of the Arabic Version of the Apocalypse of Paul," *Parole de l'Orient* 24 (1999): 131–64.

37. Contra Roig Lanzillotta, "Coptic *Apocalypse of Paul*," 193.

38. Klaus M. Girardet, "Vom Sonnen-Tag zum Sonntag: Der *dies solis* in Gesetzgebung und Politik Konstantins d. Gr.," in idem, *Kaisertum, Religionspolitik und das Recht von Staat und Kirche in der Spätantike* (Bonn: Habelt, 2009), 177–215.

(Apoc. Paul 45–51). But whereas in the earlier visit paradise is mentioned without further explanation (20), we are here explicitly referred to Genesis, as the angel says to Paul, "This is the Paradise, in which Adam and his wife erred."[39] *The* characteristic of paradise apparently is its rivers, as the angel points to the four rivers of paradise, which are enumerated in the order of Genesis 2:10–14, but of which the geographical location is elaborated. The Coptic version adds about the Gihon that it is "the one that surrounds the entire land of the Kushites" (Apoc. Paul C 45), whereas the Latin version has that it "runs through the whole land of Egypt and Ethiopia." It seems likely that the Coptic here has changed the text to incorporate the then still existing kingdom of Kush (Cush).[40] The rivers originate from a tree, which is neither the tree of life nor the tree of knowledge, which are also shown to Paul. However, the tree of the rivers is the one above which the Spirit of God rests since the creation—a detail that seems without parallel in the preceding literature (45).[41]

Paul then meets a number of persons, starting with Mary, who receives a surprising amount of attention here. Next, he sees Abraham, Isaac, and Jacob, and the twelve patriarchs, of whom Joseph stresses that suffering for the Lord will be rewarded multiple times (Apoc. Paul 47). Paul then sees Moses, who tells the apostle that during the crucifixion of Jesus by the Jews, Michael, the angels, and all the just wept and told Moses to see what his people (the Jews) had done.[42] That is why he, Paul, according to Moses, was blessed, just like the people who had believed his word (48). The anti-Jewish sentiment is unique in the Apocalypse of Paul and not thematized. It is hard to contextualize the passage, the more so as our contemporary sources hardly mention an attraction of Judaism to Egyptian Christians, unlike, for example, in Antioch or North Africa.[43] After Moses, Paul will meet other saints, such as the major prophets, Lot, Job (49), Noah (50), and finally Elijah and Elisha, who all in their own ways prayed for the unjust and exhorted them to repent. And precisely when Elijah says that God will send rain when he prays for it, our text stops (51).

This is obviously not a satisfactory ending, and the Coptic version is the only one of all the various translations to continue at considerable length, although it lacks parts of chapters 49–51. Paul will still meet Enoch (Apoc. Paul C 52), Zechariah, and his son John, who seem to be out of place in this early Old Testament company, as well as Abel (C 53), all of them stressing that they were killed for the sake of God, thus sounding the theme of martyrdom that recurs throughout the Apocalypse of Paul. The row of patriarchal figures is fittingly concluded with Adam, who says to Paul, "Be victorious, O Paul, beloved of God, who made many believe in God and repent, even as I myself repented and received my glory from the merciful, compassionate one" (C 54).

After these meetings, Paul is seized in a cloud and taken to the third heaven. Here, an angel orders him not to reveal what he will see, but Paul immediately disobeys this command and tells us all about heaven (Apoc. Paul C 55), after which he is taken to paradise,

39. Albert L. A. Hogeterp, "The Relation between Body and Soul in the *Apocalypse of Paul*," in Bremmer and Czachesz, *Visio Pauli*, 114, wrongly states that Paul met Adam and Eve.

40. Derek A. Welsby, *The Kingdom of Kush: The Napatan and Meroitic Empires* (London: Markus Wiener, 1996); see also Kevin Burrell, *Cushites in the Hebrew Bible: Negotiating Ethnic Identity in the Past and Present* (Leiden: Brill, 2020).

41. See also the detailed discussion of this chapter by Anthony Hilhorst, "A Visit to Paradise: *Apocalypse of Paul* 45 and Its Background," in *Paradise Interpreted*, ed. E. Noort and G. Luttikhuizen (Leiden: Brill, 2002), 128–39.

42. The Coptic version inserts Gabriel after Michael. In the Greek version, Gabriel replaces Michael, but he is absent from other traditions and seems, once again, to be a Coptic addition.

43. Wolfgang Kinzig, "Juden und Christen in der Antike: Trennungen, Transformationen, Kontinuitäten und Annäherungen," in *Among Jews, Gentiles and Christians in Antiquity and the Middle Ages*, ed. R. Hvalvik and J. Kaufman (Trondheim: Tapir, 2011), 129–56.

where he is told that the saints are living until the day of judgment; here a throne is wait-ing for him (C 56). Strangely, the angel then takes him to the celestial paradise, which is described in great detail with a surprising attention to the trees in it (C 57–58), which reflects the prominence of trees in the ancient *paradeisoi*.[44] Here, Paul is again shown his throne and the crowns awaiting him and his fellow apostles (C 59–60), as well as David who plays on the kithara (61). In a different place in this holy land, Paul also sees the mar-tyrs (C 62). Then, he is lifted to the Mount of Olives where he meets his fellow apostles, who charge Mark and Timothy to write down Paul's holy revelation (C 63). Finally, Christ appears and tells that to everyone who writes down the revelation, "(he) will not show him Hell nor its bitter weeping up to the second generation of his offspring. And whoever will read it in faith, I will bless him, together with his household." Moreover, Christ orders it to be read only on holy days, presumably Sundays, so that, we may conclude, its status will be like the canonical Revelation of John. Peter and Paul are told that they will finish their course on the fifth of Epiphi (29 June), the traditional date for the celebration of their mar-tyrdoms since the fourth century.[45] The Apocalypse of Paul is concluded with the sending out of the apostles to the areas assigned to them to preach the gospel of the kingdom of heaven (C 64).

3. INTERPRETIVE ISSUES
3.1 Genre and Place in the Tradition

To what genre should we assign the Apocalypse of Paul, and what is its place in the genre? The revelations to Paul clearly locate our writing in the genre of the apocalypses. Yet within this genre, it belongs to those apocalypses that concentrate on what Martha Himmelfarb has called the "tours of hell," which, as she has shown, are characterized by the combination of an *angelus interpres* (i.e., an angel or another supernatural figure who explains to the protagonist what he sees in hell and paradise), the usage of demonstrative pronouns when answering questions about sinners, as in chapter 11: *qui sunt isti . . . Hii sunt* ("Who are *these*? . . . *These* are"), and representations of punishments, often according to the measure-for-measure principle.[46]

The oldest surviving Christian apocalypse with a tour of hell, the Apocalypse of Peter, which was probably written in Alexandria in the middle of the second century,[47] started a long Christian tradition of describing punishment in hell after death and, albeit to a much less detailed extent, the splendor of heaven, although still clearly based on Jewish models. The Apocalypse of Peter was followed by a series of apocalypses well into the fourth cen-tury, such as the Apocalypse of Elijah and Apocalypse of Zephaniah, both unfortunately surviving only fragmentarily but almost certainly still preserving elements of the Jewish tradition. In the end, though, the reliance on Jewish models, the stress on persecution,

---

44. For the ancient *paradeisoi* and their trees, see, most recently, Bremmer, "The Birth of Paradise"; William Malandra, "Artaxerxes' 'Paradise,'" *Dabir* 6 (2018): 67–71; and, highly informative, Christopher Tuplin, "Paradise Revisited," in *L'Orient est son Jardin: Hommage à Rémy Boucharlat*, ed. S. Gondet and E. Haerinck (Leuven: Peeters, 2018), 477–501.

45. For this date of their martyrdom, see David L. Eastman, *Paul the Martyr* (Atlanta: Society of Biblical Literature, 2011), 22–23.

46. Himmelfarb, *Tours of Hell*.

47. See, most recently, Eric J. Beck, *Justice and Mercy in the Apocalypse of Peter: A New Translation and Analysis of the Purpose of the Text* (Tübingen: Mohr Siebeck, 2019); Jan N. Bremmer, "The *Apocalypse of Peter* as the First Christian Martyr Text: Its Date, Provenance and Relationship with *2 Peter*," in *Second Peter and the Apocalypse of Peter: Towards a New Perspective*, ed. J. Frey, M. den Dulk, J. van der Watt, BibInt 174 (Leiden: Brill, 2019), 75–98.

and probably their heterodox aura made earlier apocalypses look old-fashioned or no longer acceptable, and in due time they were no longer copied. This was not the case with the Apocalypse of Paul, which was also the last major ancient apocalypse and the most popular medieval one.

3.2 Greek and Jewish Traditions

Given that the New Testament is very reticent with information about the life hereafter, it is not surprising that the early Christians filled this void with other traditions that were more forthcoming with details. Naturally, the early Christians took recourse to Jewish accounts of the afterlife, as we noted above, but these had been developed in dialogue with Greek traditions, probably especially in Alexandria, where Orphic traditions, which were particularly detailed about the underworld, were available.[48] Let me mention here just some examples of these influences, which could easily be elaborated.

Let us start with a Jewish example. When Paul has entered the city that is similar to the heavenly Jerusalem, he sees golden thrones near the gates of the twelve walls. Evidently, paradise is walled, and the entrance is by a golden gate, one of the many reminiscences to the canonical book of Revelation in the Apocalypse of Paul (see sec. 4 below), although more in allusions than straight quotations.[49] The thrones were occupied by twelve men, with diadems and jewels. But within the circle of these thrones there was another row of empty thrones. Hilhorst plausibly sees this emptiness as a Jewish motif, as in the Testament of Job, Job tells his friends that he has a throne in heaven waiting for him (33.2–5; 41.4).[50] In our case, it is stipulated that the thrones are destined for the uneducated ascetics who will be honored because of their simplicity. Apparently, the author has in mind the uneducated monks, who presumably constituted the majority of the ascetics (see also below on the intended readership).

Regarding Greek motifs, some are obvious. Like the Apocalypse of Peter, the Apocalypse of Paul has a reference to Lake Acherousia (Apoc. Paul 22–23) and to the river of fire (31), which eventually derives from Plato's *Phaedo* (114A), but it is a device of the author of the Apocalypse of Paul to let the fire reach different parts of the body depending on the seriousness of the crime. The choice of fire coming to the lips is explained as being suitable for those that slandered within the church of God. The punishment cannot be incidental. The Apocalypse of Peter contains many punishments that are based on the principle of measure-for-measure,[51] and the Apocalypse of Paul is clearly a tributary of this tradition.

If the lake and the river eventually go back to Homer, a later Greek tradition can be found regarding the gate of the third heaven, where Paul sees two golden pillars with golden letters, which record the names of the righteous (Apoc. Paul 19). Here we have a development of an Orphic theme, as in Orphism we first find the idea of a book with the names of the elect and the damned.[52] Another Orphic heritage we probably see when Paul looks at the soul of a sinner who was met by evils, such as oblivion, slander, fornication, madness, insolence, and the princes of vices. In this enumeration, oblivion is rather uncommon as a vice. We may wonder if this is not also a survival of the Greek tradition, as forgetfulness is mentioned in the so-called Orphic Gold Leaves, which serve as a sort of passport to the underworld.[53]

48. Bremmer, *Maidens, Magic and Martyrs*, 269–80.

49. Cf. Zamagni, *Recherches sur le Nouveau Testament*, 313–24.

50. Anthony Hilhorst, "The *Apocalypse of Paul*: Previous History and Afterlife," in Bremmer and Czachesz, *Visio Pauli*, 12.

51. Bremmer, *Maidens, Magic and Martyrs*, 286.

52. Albrecht Dieterich, *Nekuia*, 2nd ed. (Leipzig: Hinrichs, 1913), 126–27.

53. Jan N. Bremmer, *The World of Greek Religion and Mythology* (Tübingen: Mohr Siebeck, 2019), 202–3.

Another motif derived from the Greek tradition we find when Paul sees the souls of a righteous person and a sinner leaving their bodies. This interest in the soul leaving the body at the moment of death was gradually developing at this stage in early Christianity. It was not original to the earliest Christians, who, like the Jews, did not have a dualistic view of the body. Yet we can already see an interest in the soul in later second-century apocalypses, such as those of Ezra and Abraham (assuming their early dates, which are not wholly certain), even though the dualistic view is not accepted wholeheartedly.[54] In the Apocalypse of Paul, we can observe a contrast between those dying righteous and sinners and Paul himself, as he visits heaven "in the flesh," whereas the former only go to the afterlife in the shape of a soul.

3.3 Christian Motifs

In his second visit to paradise, Paul also sees Mary (Apoc. Paul 46), but it is a complicated question to what extent the Apocalypse of Paul is dependent on earlier Mary traditions, such as found in the Obsequies (Apocalypse) of the Virgin Mary, which is also known as the Book of Mary's Repose. Richard Bauckham, followed by Stephen Shoemaker, has argued that the latter might be prior to the former, given that Paul sees four individual clerical sinners (Apoc. Paul 34–36), which seems to suggest a particular source. Moreover, the Obsequies has a respite of three hours, which Bauckham considers more original than the one of one day.[55] Evidently these arguments are inconclusive, as he admits, and the sudden outburst of quite extensive Marian material around 500 CE makes me rather reticent to claim the influence of a much earlier Marian apocalypse, which cannot be properly located and is also hard to date, although an early date is not necessarily implausible. In any case, the prominent position of Mary is surely striking and in need of further exploration.

The Apocalypse of Paul can also be investigated as to what it has to say about institutional features of its readership. Some of the sins it mentions were considered sins in earlier apocalypses as well, such as same-sex relations or neglecting widows and orphans, but some are clearly new and show that the Apocalypse of Paul had innovated in its enumerations of sins. For example, its monastic milieu, as sketched above in the introduction, is clearly reflected in some of the sins, such as the breaking of the fast before the appointed hour (Apoc. Paul 39), just as the mention of communal psalm singing (29–30) points to the communities of monks. And when the angel explains why men and women were dressed in rags full of tar and sulphur, with snakes around them, he says, "They are those who seemed to renounce the world by wearing our raiment," but then miserably failed in charity (40), the reference is clearly to the white habit of the monks, which reflects that of the angels, the *angelikon schēma*.[56]

But we need not stay in a monastic milieu. When Paul sees an old man being terribly

---

54. Françoise Mirguet, "They Visited Heaven and Refused to Die: Anxieties of Discontinuity in the *Testament of Abraham* and in Ezra Traditions," in *Figures of Ezra*, ed. J. Bremmer et al. (Leuven: Peeters, 2016), 277–304. For the body/soul-problem in Apoc. Paul, see Thomas J. Kraus, "'Körper,' 'Fleisch,' 'Seele' und 'Geist' in der *Apokalypse des Paulus/Visio Pauli*: Was Ist der Mensch?," in *Der voũς bei Paulus im Horizont griechischer und hellenistisch-jüdischer Anthropologie*, ed. J. Frey and M. Nägele (Tübingen: Mohr Siebeck, 2021), 239–58, and "Being *in corpore/carne* and *extra corpus*: Some Interrelations within the *Apocalypsis Pauli/Visio Pauli*," in *Dreams, Visions, Imaginations: Jewish, Christian and Gnostic Views of the World to Come*, ed. T. Nicklas and J. Schröter (Berlin: de Gruyter, 2020), 412–32.

55. Bauckham, *Fate of the Dead*, 340–46; Stephen J. Shoemaker, *The Dormition and Assumption Apocrypha* (Leuven: Peeters, 2018), 325, 329.

56. *Historia Monachorum* 2.12; 8.19; Theodorus, *Vita Theodosii* 71.23. See Georg Schmelz, *Kirchliche Amtsträger im spätantiken Ägypten nach den Aussagen der griechischen und koptischen Papyri und Ostraka* (Munich: Saur, 2002), 114.

tortured by angels, he is told that he ate, drank, and fornicated during the Eucharist (34). The scene is a striking illustration of the sanctity of the Eucharist, which we already start to find in the second century, but its growing importance is illustrated by the fact that sometimes, as time went on, even silver plates and cups were used for its administration (34).[57]

3.4 Original End

The fact that the Coptic version has a longer end than the Latin versions raises the question of the nature of the original end of the Apocalypse of Paul. In his discussion, Roig Lanzillotta does not really enter into a detailed discussion of this problem, although he seems to think that the end of the Coptic version is the original one. The question was already discussed by Robert Casey (1897–1957) in his learned and still valuable study.[58] He rightly first looked at the endings of the other versions in the East and West and noted that the Armenian versions all end at chapter 44, as does the Ethiopic Apocalypse of the Virgin, which is highly dependent on the Apocalypse of Paul,[59] whereas the Paris Latin text (L[1]) as well as the Greek, Russian,[60] and Syriac versions all end the main text with Elijah and Elisha (51), Thus, I would conclude that at a relatively early stage, the manuscript of the Apocalypse of Paul had lost the last pages. Moreover, given that it was not considered canonical, it will have been rarely copied, since, if there would have been many copies, it would have been hard to explain why the same loss had occurred at the very end both in texts from the East and the West.

On the other hand, a complete copy must have survived in Egypt, which is not that surprising given the Egyptian interest in apocalypses. Yet there are important arguments to consider the Coptic ending a later addition. First, the beginning of the Coptic version must have started on the Mount of Olives,[61] which presupposes that the beginning as related in the Paris Latin version would have been a later insertion. Casey could believe that, as he thought that the Apocalypse of Paul had already been referred to by Origen, which would give ample time for the replacement. However, when we accept the roughly 400 CE date, we should note that Sozomen still knows the episode of the discovery (*Hist. eccl.* 7.19.10–11), and given that he wrote sometime between 439 and 450 CE,[62] it is highly improbable that the beginning was already changed during the very reign of Theodosius II (408–450 CE), the uncle of Theodosius I.

Second, there are stylistic features that set the Coptic ending apart from the preceding chapters. Whereas until the end the pace of traveling by Paul is fairly measured, we now hear that he is lifted up to the third heaven (Apoc. Paul C 55), taken to paradise (C 56), the celestial paradise (C 58), a place reserved for martyrs within the celestial paradise (C 62), and the Mount of Olives (C 63). Moreover, whereas in the earlier chapters the apostle is

---

57. Jan N. Bremmer, "Eucharist and *Agapê* in the Later Second Century: The Case of the Older Apocryphal Acts and the Pagan Novel," in *Rituals in Early Christianity: New Perspectives on Tradition and Transformation*, ed. A. Geljon and N. Vos (Leiden: Brill, 2020), 69–105.

58. Casey, "Apocalypse of Paul," 25.

59. For this apocalypse, see Bauckham, *Fate of the Dead*, 338–40; Shoemaker, *The Dormition and Assumption Apocypha*, 192, who suggests that Apoc. Paul depends on an earlier Marian tradition.

60. For the Russian text, see Julian Petlov, *Altslavische Eschatologie* (Tübingen: Narr Francke Attempto, 2016), 155–62.

61. As shown by Casey, "Apocalypse of Paul," 25; Roig Lanzillotta, "Coptic *Apocalypse of Paul*," 195–96.

62. Peter Van Nuffelen, *Un héritage de paix et de piété: étude sur les histoires ecclésiastiques de Socrate et de Sozomène* (Leuven: Peeters, 2004), 59–61, who has convincingly refuted the traditionally accepted *terminus ante quem* of 443 CE.

just called "Paul" (20; 46; 47), "brother Paul" (48–49) or "Paul, Beloved" ("of God": 20; 41; 43–44; 46 ["of God, angels, and men"]; 47; C 51; 53–55; but in 57: "of God and men"), in the Coptic ending he is suddenly called "excellent letter-carrier," "mediator of the covenant," "gable and foundation of the Church," and "my chosen one" (C 64).[63] These two features strongly suggest that the Coptic version was written by a different author from the preceding chapters.

Alin Suciu has recently shown that the ending contains two passages taken from the Book of Bartholomew,[64] which Westerhoff and van Minnen have reasonably dated to the eighth or ninth century.[65] As the Coptic manuscript dates to 960 CE, we may think of a date in the eighth century, but in any case later than the original date of the Apocalypse of Paul. As Suciu notes,[66] the expression "holy members" in the Coptic ending points to a monastic milieu for the addition, which seems perfectly in line with the originally intended readership (cf. sec. 1 above).

The conclusion of a later Coptic ending has, of course, also implications for our understanding of the Apocalypse of Paul. James thought that everything after chapter 44 "is an otiose appendix" and that "the climax of the Apocalypse is reached when the Sunday is granted as a day of rest from torment. Paul has seen Paradise and Hell, and there is no more for him to do."[67] Roig Lanzillotta has objected that such a conclusion "is only valid if based on the *a priori* argument that the goal of the text was indeed the granting of respite."[68] Yet this argument does not consider those readers' responses that we can see. We know that the St. Gallen and Arnhem Latin versions end at chapter 44, as do three Armenian versions (A[1], A[3], A[4]), being all independent of one another, which seems to suggest that some Greek versions also ended at chapter 44, as certainly does the Ethiopic Apocalypse of the Virgin. The state of the manuscripts thus shows that at least a number of readers considered the respite to be the climax of the Apocalypse of Paul. This is not implausible, as the dogmatic transgressions are clearly the climax of the sins, and the respite is the response to these transgressions and the pleas of their sinners. However, the author could hardly have ended his apocalypse with Paul in hell, so he added a visit to paradise. That does not mean that the author wrote the Apocalypse of Paul to focus solely on the problem of respite, but it certainly shows that respite was a highly important theme that the author wanted to stress in his eschatological work.

4. KEY PASSAGES FOR NEW TESTAMENT STUDIES AND THEIR SIGNIFICANCE

Even though Paul is one of the most important figures of the New Testament and is the protagonist of the Apocalypse of Paul, the actual influence of the New Testament and specifically Paul's epistles on the work is perhaps less than one would have expected. The question of the influence of Paul has been repeatedly posed from various angles.

---

63. The difference is noted by Thomas J. Kraus, "Apocalipsis Pauli/Visio Pauli—*Warum eigentlich Paulus?*," in *Receptions of Paul in Early Christianity*, ed. J. Schröter et al. (Berlin: de Gruyter, 2018), 595–96 (which I somewhat supplement), but more fully elaborated in idem, "Wieviel 'Paulus' ist in der *Apokalypse des Paulus/ Visio Pauli*? Eine Apokalypse und ihr Protagonist," in Frey et al., *Autorschaft und Autorisierungsstrategien*, 355–59.

64. Suciu, Berlin-Strasbourg Apocryphon, 113–14.

65. Matthias Westerhoff, *Auferstehung und Jenseits im koptischen "Buch der Auferstehung Jesu Christi, unseres Herrn"* (Wiesbaden: Harrassowitz, 1999), 227; see P. van Minnen's review of this work in *Bulletin of the American Society of Papyrologists* 45 (2008): 280–81.

66. Suciu, *Berlin-Strasbourg Apocryphon*, 120.

67. James, *Apocryphal New Testament*, 555.

68. Roig Lanzillotta, "Coptic *Apocalypse of Paul*," 195.

An investigation into the descriptions of the beyond has to conclude that the historical Paul had virtually nothing to contribute to these descriptions except for the ascent to the third heaven.[69] And indeed, the next investigation notes that the Apocalypse of Paul does not contain any clear citations or identifiable allusions to the *Corpus Paulinum*. Instead, it observes that we can see a development away from Paul, who promises all the faithful to be in the house of Christ, to only a small elite of ascetics/monks. In fact, in chapters 11–18 we lack any mention of a conversion or saving through Christ, but man becomes justified by his works and his efforts. The result of this development in thinking appears in chapters 19–30, where we can observe a certain hierarchy that promises larger rewards for higher ascetic efforts instead of equal salvation for all.[70] The next chapters (31–44) show another development away from Paul, as we now no longer hear of a living faith in Christ but of specific dogmas, such as the incarnation (see sec. 2 above). Finally, in the part about paradise (45–51), there is a focus on orthodoxy and proper works, and we hear nothing of Paul's Jewish origin when the Jews are being berated. On the whole, then, Paul is pictured as an important saint of the Christian tradition, but his thought plays no role for the author.[71]

It is unsurprising, then, that the latest study of the influence of Paul returns to the passage in 2 Corinthians 12:2–5, which seems to have been the starting point of the Apocalypse of Paul:[72]

> I know a person in Christ who fourteen years ago was caught up to the third heaven—whether in the body or out of the body I do not know; God knows. And I know that such a person—whether in the body or out of the body I do not know; God knows—was caught up into Paradise and heard things that are not to be told, that no mortal is permitted to repeat. On behalf of such a one I will boast, but on my own behalf I will not boast, except of my weaknesses. (NRSV)

These words have received much attention in recent decades.[73] None of these studies, though, really help us much in understanding the Apocalypse of Paul. Still, verses 2–4 open the Apocalypse of Paul in the Latin Paris version, and the third heaven returns at various moments in the work, in chapters 11 (but only in the Syriac version), 19 (in all four Latin long versions), and 21 (only in the Paris version). In all these passages, the author has nothing really to add to Paul's own description. As the third heaven is connected with paradise in a number of Jewish writings,[74] it is perhaps unsurprising that the author of the Apocalypse of Paul also uses the third heaven as an entry into paradise (19).

Regarding the prohibition to tell what he had seen, the Apocalypse of Paul somewhat expands on this by telling that when in paradise and having met Enoch, Paul was told

---

69. Ernst Dassmann, "Paulus in der 'Visio sancti Pauli,'" in *Jenseitsvorstellungen in Antike und Christentum*, ed. T. Klauser et al. (Münster: Aschendorff, 1982), 124–28.

70. This development is elaborated by Kirsty Copeland, "'The Holy Contest': Competition for the Best Afterlife in the *Apocalypse of Paul* and Late Antique Egypt," in *Other Worlds and Their Relation to This World: Early Jewish and Ancient Christian Traditions*, ed. T. Nicklas et al. (Leiden: Brill, 2010), 189–207.

71. So Tobias Nicklas, "Gute Werke, rechter Glaube: Paulusrezeption in der *Apokalypse des Paulus*?," in *Ancient Perspectives on Paul*, ed. T. Nicklas et al. (Göttingen: Vandenhoeck & Ruprecht, 2013), 150–69.

72. Kraus, "Wieviel 'Paulus'?"

73. Most recently, Maximilian Benz, *Gesicht und Schrift: Die Erzählung von Jenseitsreisen in Antike und Mittelalter* (Berlin: de Gruyter, 2013), 13–23; Charlotte Touati, "Das Schweigen sprechen lassen: Von 2 Kor 12,2–4 zu den apokryphen Apokalypsen," in *Christian Apocrypha: Receptions of the New Testament in Ancient Christian Apocrypha*, ed. J.-M. Roessli and T. Nicklas (Göttingen: Vandenhoeck & Ruprecht, 2014), 301–12.

74. Kraus, "Wieviel 'Paulus'?," 351–52, who compares 2 Enoch, the Apocalypse of Moses, 3 Baruch, and Gedula Moshe.

by the angel not to relate both what he had seen and heard (Paris [L¹] 21 and, in slightly different ways, in the other long versions). It is clear that the author at this point quotes Paul's ἄρρητα ῥήματα, "things that are not to be told" (2 Cor 12:4 NRSV), but it is only in the prologue that the Latin Paris version has the translation *archana verba*, whereas at this point in the Apocalypse of Paul we have the circumscription *verba que non liceat omini loqui* (21: "words which it is not permitted to tell a mortal"). Basically, this is all we can say about the influence of Paul on the Apocalypse of Paul. Given this real absence of substantial derivations from Paul, it cannot be wholly surprising that later authors simply exchanged Paul for the Virgin as the protagonist of their new apocalypse but otherwise kept much of the contents of the Apocalypse of Paul, as happened in the case of the Ethiopic Apocalypse of the Virgin, the Greek Apocalypse of the Theotokos, and the Greek Apocalypse of Anastasia, as well as other apocalypses.[75]

Yet the disappointing absence of Paul does not mean that no other books of the New Testament had impacted our author. Of course, the prologue (with the discovery of the Tarsus manuscript) refers to Paul's self-identification as a Jew from Tarsus in Cilicia (Acts 22:3). The repeated expression "Jesus whom you proclaim" (Paris 21; 46; 48) is undoubtedly quoting Paul's words in Acts: "Jesus, whom I am proclaiming to you" (Acts 17:3), and there are other snippets that look like they are being taken from the Gospels and Acts. However, from a more narrative point of view, the author seems to have concentrated on the killing of the children by King Herod and the passion of Christ in the Gospels as well as the New Jerusalem from the Book of Revelation.

Regarding the killing of the children of Bethlehem, Paul sees them during his first visit to paradise (Apoc. Paul 26) at the river of milk, as we already saw (see sec. 2 above). Unlike what one would perhaps expect, the children are seen as the prototypical chaste ones, and all those who kept their chastity will be brought to them by Michael after they have left their bodies. It is noteworthy that in the long Latin version of the Vision of Ezra, Ezra sees Herod sitting on a fiery seat on account of his murder of the infants of Bethlehem (Vision of Ezra 37). The reference must be old, as we find the same punishment in the Greek Apocalypse of Ezra (4.9–12), which suggests that it belonged to the *Urtext* of this apocalypse.[76] Apparently, the story of the murder made a deep impression on the early Jesus-followers and was retold in a number of later apocalypses, even though the theme here has received a rather different focus.

The passion of Christ comes to the fore at the moment that Paul is visiting the worst sinners, those who have failed to believe the most important dogmas (Apoc. Paul 44). These entreat the archangel Michael, who berates them and tells them to weep together with him, the angels and the "very beloved Paul" (43). When this happens, a voice asks them why they were entreating, and they answer that it is because of his "great goodness toward mankind." The voice is speaking after the mention of the twenty-four elders and the four beasts worshiping God, but not with a description of God himself, who is rarely described in the ancient apocalypses. But it is the Son of God who now descends from heaven with a crown on his head.

As in Apocalypse of Paul 14, we hear no more than his voice, which asks them what they have done to deserve his mercy. We then get a series of specific details from the passion episode: the crown of thorns (Matt 27:29; Mark 15:17; John 19:2), punches on his cheeks (John 19:3), vinegar (instead of the wine in the Gospels) mixed with gall (Matt 27:34;

---

75. Bauckham, *Fate of the Dead*, 332–62; Baun, *Tales from Another Byzantium*, 78–109.
76. Himmelfarb, *Tours of Hell*, 125, notes the transformation of the theme in later apocalypses.

John 19:28–29), and the piercing of his side with a lance (John 19:34). Later, in the anti-Jewish passage (Apoc. Paul 48), we hear that Jesus hangs on the cross without further details from the passion. Looking at the relevant texts, we see that the main sources for the passion and the killing of the children of Bethlehem are Matthew and John, which were indeed the most popular Gospels in Egypt.[77]

The most influential book of the New Testament, though, is the book of Revelation. Its picture of the New Jerusalem was an important source of inspiration for the author of the Apocalypse of Paul.[78] This is particularly manifest in the passages about heaven and the celestial court. When Paul is brought to heaven by the angel, he looks up and sees "angels whose face shone as the sun, their loins girded with golden girdles, having palms in their hands and the sign of God, dressed in garments on which was written the name of the Son of God" (Apoc. Paul 12). The passage is clearly a pastiche of various verses of Revelation. The shining of the face is mentioned in Revelation 1:16 and 10:1, the garments in 15:6, the palms in 7:9, and the name of God in 3:12 and 22:4. Evidently, our author knew the book of Revelation by heart. This is also clear from the continuation of our passage, when Paul looks down on earth and sees a just person at the moment of his death, whose soul is carried into heaven before God. In reaction, we read that "thereafter I heard the voices of thousands of thousands of angels, archangels and cherubim and the 24 elders saying hymns and glorifying the Lord, shouting: 'You are just, O Lord, and Your judgments are just, and there is no respect of persons with You, but You reward every man according to Your judgment'" (Apoc. Paul 14). Again, the great number recurs in Revelation 5:11, the twenty-four elders are mentioned frequently (Rev 4:10; 5:8; 11:16; 19:4), and God's judgment is twice called "true and just" (Rev 16:7; 19:2 NRSV).

Finally, after Paul was weeping and asking God for mercy (Apoc. Paul 43), he saw heaven moving like a tree shaken by the wind. "Suddenly, they threw themselves on their faces before the sight of his throne. And I saw the 24 elders and the four animals adoring God, and I saw an altar and veil and throne, and all were rejoicing. And the smoke of a good smell rose near the altar of the throne of God" (44). Again, the allusions to Revelation are unmistakable: the twenty-four elders we have just met; the four animals are sometimes mentioned together with them or separately (5:8; 15:7; 19:4); the altar is not unusual (6:9; 16:7); and the smoke is not unknown either (15:8).

With these examples we have come to the end of our discussion. The Apocalypse of Paul only has a relatively small amount of material that is directly relevant to the New Testament. This is understandable. With the early Christians expecting the speedy return of Jesus, there was no need for thoughts about the fate of the just or the unjust. Consequently, the New Testament only gave very limited information about the life hereafter. As time went on, needs changed, and the faithful became increasingly curious about their fate after death; in addition, the idea of a heavenly Jerusalem as we have it in Revelation, where everybody has the same access to God/the Lamb must have become problematic in an increasingly hierarchical church and society. In response to their curiosity, later authors mined the New Testament and their Jewish tradition. It is a sign of our *diesseitige* times that such apocalypses today are looked at as sources for our knowledge of early Christianity or as sources for later literary compositions, like Dante's *Divina commedia*, instead of informing us about what is awaiting us after death. Many of us no longer believe in the existence of such cosmologies and their focus on judgment. However

---

77. Martinez, "Papyri and Early Christianity," 591.
78. Cf. Hilhorst, *"Apocalypse of Paul*: Previous History and Afterlife," 16.

apocalyptic our modern world sometimes may be, such as with the terrible bushfires in Australia and the COVID-19 pandemic, both occurring when writing this contribution, the time of the ancient apocalypses with their terrible fires of hell is irrevocably a thing of the past.[79]

5. BIBLIOGRAPHY

For a very detailed bibliography of the Apocalypse of Paul and its various translations in the East and West, see Jan N. Bremmer and Istvan Czachesz , eds., *The Visio Pauli and the Gnostic Apocalypse of Paul* (Leuven: Peeters, 2007), 211–36. Below, I list only those writings that have appeared afterward or that were missed in that bibliography.

Baun, Jane. *Tales from Another Byzantium: Celestial Journey and Local Community in the Medieval Greek Apocrypha*. Cambridge: Cambridge University Press, 2007.

Bremmer, Jan N. "Christian Hell: From the *Apocalypse of Peter* to the *Apocalypse of Paul*." *Numen* 56 (2009): 298–325. Updated on pages 295–312 of Jan N. Bremmer, *Maidens, Magic and Martyrs in Early Christianity*. Tübingen: Mohr Siebeck, 2017.

Bullita, Dario. *Páls leizla: The Vision of St Paul*. London: Viking Society for Northern Research, 2017. Norse translation.

Copeland, Kirsti. "'The Holy Contest': Competition for the Best Afterlife in the *Apocalypse of Paul* and Late Antique Egypt." Pages 189–207 in *Other Worlds and Their Relation to This World: Early Jewish and Ancient Christian Traditions*. Edited by Tobias Nicklas et al. Leiden: Brill, 2010.

Di Paolo Healy, Antonette. *The Old English Vision of St. Paul*. Cambridge, MA: Mediaeval Academy of America, 1978.

Meyer, Paul. "La descente de Saint Paul en enfer: poème français composé en Angleterre." *Romania* 24 (1895): 357–75, 589–91.

Micha, Alexandre. "Les Visions de saint Paul en vers." Pages 963–69 of vol. 2 of *Et c'est la fin pour quoy sommes ensemble: Hommage à Jean Dufournet*. Edited by Jean-Claude Aubailly. 3 vols. Paris: Champion, 1993.

Nicklas, Tobias. "Gute Werke, rechter Glaube: Paulusrezeption in der *Apokalypse des Paulus*?" Pages 150–69 in *Ancient Perspectives on Paul*. Edited by Tobias Nicklas et al. Göttingen: Vandenhoeck & Ruprecht, 2013.

Piovanelli, Pierluigi. *Apocryphités*. Turnhout: Brepols, 2016. See pp. 365–434.

Seymour, John D. "Irish Versions of the Vision of St. Paul." *JTS* 24 (1922): 54–59.

Williams, J. E. Caerwyn. "Irish Translations of Visio Sancti Pauli." *Éigse* 6 (1948–52): 127–34.

79. This contribution was written in the inspiring environment of the Centre for Advanced Studies "Beyond Canon" of the University of Regensburg, Germany. An abbreviated version was presented at a symposium in honor of Jacques van der Vliet in Nijmegen on January 24, 2020. I am most grateful to Tobias Nicklas and the Nijmegen audience for comments, and to Charlotte von Schelling for her careful correction of my English.

CHAPTER 26

APOCALYPSE OF PETER (GREEK)

DAN BATOVICI

1. INTRODUCTION

The Apocalypse of Peter is one of the oldest Judeo-Christian apocalyptic books, composed around the middle of the second century,[1] narrating the second coming of Christ, the eschatological conflagration, a catalogue of torments in a tour of hell, and a description of paradise in a succession of visions offered to Peter. This apocalypse poses several problems for the modern reader, the first difficulty being the fact that there are several ancient texts that are referred to today as the Apocalypse of Peter, with no connection of contents between them: a) the Coptic Apocalypse of Peter (or Revelation of Peter) found in the Nag Hammadi codex VII (NHC VII, 3), probably originally composed in Greek;[2] b) the so-called Arabic Apocalypse of Peter, otherwise a modern collection named the Book of the Rolls in manuscript Mingana Syr. 70, written in Syriac script;[3] and c) the early Christian Apocalypse of Peter, composed in Greek but surviving for the most part in Ethiopic. The subject matter of this chapter is this last-mentioned text, the apocalyptic text that was composed and was known under this title in early Christianity.

1.1 Language

A riddle that has shaped the history of research devoted to this apocalypse is posed by its textual integrity. While it was composed in Greek, there are precious few extant Greek fragments with only small sections, and the complete text is only preserved in Ethiopic, itself presumably translated from a now lost Arabic version. Only one Greek witness, the so-called Akhmîm codex, spans over several pages. However, since the quotations from the Apocalypse of Peter preserved by early Greek fathers confirm the Ethiopic text and not that of the Akhmîm Codex, it becomes evident that the latter is a different recension and therefore an edited text, secondary to the one preserved in Ethiopic. As a result, this book is sometimes referred to as the "Greek (Ethiopic) Apocalypse of Peter" in scholarly literature.

---

1. "At present there is a general consensus that it must date from the last decades of the first half of the second century AD, given its mention by Clement of Alexandria" (Jan N. Bremmer, "Orphic, Roman, Jewish and Christian Tours of Hell: Observations on the Apocalypse of Peter," in *Other Worlds and Their Relation to This World: Early Jewish and Ancient Christian Traditions*, ed. by T. Nicklas et al., JSJSup 143 [Leiden: Brill, 2010], 309).
2. On which, see *The Coptic Apocalypse of Peter (Nag-Hammadi-Codex VII,3)*, TU 144 (Berlin: de Gruyter, 2012). Besides this Coptic version, there are several Arabic Apocalypses or Revelations of Peter, with no connection to the book discussed here.
3. Alphonse Mingana, "Apocalypse of Peter," in *Woodbrooke Studies*, vol. 3, fasc. 6 (Cambridge: Heffer and Sons, 1931), 93–449. Alin Suciu is currently editing yet another Arabic text that is a revelation to Peter.

1.2 Date

While problems of dating and provenance are rather common for most early Christian writings, in the case of the Apocalypse of Peter they are aggravated by the fact that we do not have access today to the original text in Greek in its entirety. Even the more complete Ethiopic translation is tertiary, presumably made after a now lost Arabic translation. In an important article, in many ways programmatic for the study of the Apocalypse of Peter, Richard Bauckham argued for a date during the Bar Kokhba revolt (132–135 CE).[4] Subsequent scholarship, however, found this to be too clear-cut of an identification and therefore unconvincing.[5] There seems to be consensus now on this matter, favoring a date around the middle of the second century,[6] but as we will see, the question of the relative chronology compared to 2 Peter remains open, further complicating the issue. In a recent discussion, for instance, Jan Bremmer emphasizes the fact that the apocalypse reflects a context in which the term for martyrs is already coined, and they are "ascribed the power of intercession"; he argues that "it is very improbable that we should locate those developments very early" and that "the most likely date of composition of our Apocalypse is around AD 150."[7]

1.3 Provenance

If the facts that there are early Greek papyri of the Apocalypse of Peter and that early Greek patristic authors quote from it seem to suggest that it was composed in Greek, the provenance proves far more complicated to establish. Several suggestions have been made regarding the context of its composition: Palestine,[8] Syria,[9] Rome,[10] and, presently gaining momentum, Egypt and in particular Alexandria.[11] Ultimately, in the absence of clear pointers for one or another hypothesis, this is a matter of establishing degrees of likelihood, and we might have to settle for not being able to establish the provenance in a conclusive manner.

---

4. Richard Bauckham, "The Apocalypse of Peter: A Jewish Christian Apocalypse," *Apocrypha* 5 (1994), 7–111, esp. 24–43.

5. See, for instance, Eibert Tigchelaar, "Is the Liar Bar Kokhba? Considering the Date and Provenance of the Greek (Ethiopic) Apocalypse of Peter," in *The Apocalypse of Peter*, ed. J. Bremmer and I. Czachesz, Studies on Early Christian Apocrypha 7 (Leuven: Peeters, 2003), 63–77; T. J. Kraus, "Die griechische Petrus-Apokalypse und ihre Relation zu ausgewählten Überlieferungsträgern apokalyptischer Stoffe," *Apocrypha* 14 (2003): 94; L. J. Lietaert Peerbolte, *The Antecedents of Antichrist: A Traditio-Historical Study of the Earliest Christian Views on Eschatological Opponents*, JSJSup 49 (Leiden: Brill, 1996), 56–61; P. van Minnen, "The Greek Apocalypse of Peter," in Bremmer and Czachesz, *Apocalypse of Peter*, 29.

6. Bremmer, "Orphic, Roman, Jewish and Christian Tours of Hell," 309.

7. Jan N. Bremmer, "The *Apocalypse of Peter* as the First Christian Martyr Text: Its Date, Provenance and Relationship with *2 Peter*," in *Second Peter and the Apocalypse of Peter: Towards a New Perspective*, ed. J. Frey, M. den Dulk, J. van der Watt, BibInt 174 (Leiden: Brill, 2019), 91.

8. Bauckham, "Apocalypse of Peter," 24–43. Bauckham's argument on the dating of the Apoc. Pet. is intrinsically linked to a Palestinian provenance through the identification of the liar of Apoc. 2.10 with Bar Kokhba.

9. Enrico Norelli, "L'adversaire eschatologique dans l'Apocalypse de Pierre," in *Les forces du bien et du mal dans les premiers siècles de l'église*, ed. Y.-M. Blanchard, B. Pouderon, and M. Scopello, Théologie historique 118 (Paris: Beauchesne, 2011), 317.

10. Van Minnen, "Greek Apocalypse of Peter," 29–30.

11. Bremmer, "*Apocalypse of Peter* as the First Christian Martyr Text," 85; Tobias Nicklas, "Petrus-Diskurse in Alexandria: Eine Fortführung der Gedanken von Jörg Frey," in Frey, den Dulk, and van der Watt, *2 Peter and the Apocalypse of Peter*, 99–127; Kraus, "Die griechische Petrus-Apokalypse," 94–95; Tobias Nicklas, "Jewish, Christian, Greek? The *Apocalypse of Peter* as a Witness of Early 2nd-Cent. Christianity in Alexandria," in *Beyond Conflicts: Cultural and Religious Cohabitations in Alexandria and Egypt Between the 1st and the 6th Century CE*, ed. L. Arcari, Studien und Texte zu Antike und Christentum 103 (Tübingen: Mohr Siebeck, 2017), 27–46.

1.4 Genre

In a pivotal essay on early Christian apocalypses, Adela Yarbro Collins places the Apocalypse of Peter in the category of "apocalypses of cosmic and/or political eschatology with neither historical review nor otherworldly journey" together with, for instance, Revelation and the Shepherd of Hermas.[12] Several elements of the genre are therein: visions through and dialogue with an otherworldly mediator, the judgment of sinners, and the notion of afterlife. However, an important difference is that, unlike Revelation, which is described from this perspective as an apocalypse that expects cosmic destruction as well as cosmic renewal, the Apocalypse of Peter and the Shepherd of Hermas are described as apocalypses that "predict cosmic destruction, but contain no indication of cosmic transformation."[13]

1.5 Text

The Apocalypse of Peter comes with a host of textual problems, the most obvious being the fact mentioned already that it is not completely preserved in its original language,[14] which in turn makes for a very interesting manuscript reception history. There are two Greek manuscripts that preserve parts of the text of the Apocalypse of Peter. One is the highly fragmentary remnant of a miniature parchment codex of the fifth century stemming from Egypt. Only two scraps survive of this codex, which are today housed in different libraries,[15] adding up to around 150 words.

A very interesting reception-historical artifact is the so-called Akhmîm Codex (P.Cair. 10759), found in ancient Panopolis in Upper Egypt during an archaeological dig lead by a French team in the winter of 1886–1887. The codex contains two Petrine apocryphal writings among other writings: 1 Enoch, the Gospel of Peter, the Apocalypse of Peter, and a fragment of the Martyrdom of Julian of Anazarbus. Given that the codex is "in fact made up of several parchment manuscripts and the leftover of other parchment manuscripts,"[16] the two Petrine writings are dated palaeographically to the end of the sixth century and the other texts to the first half of the seventh century.[17] Interestingly, although both texts are written by the same scribe, the Apocalypse of Peter was sewn upside-down and back-to-front after the Gospel of Peter in the manuscript, meaning that the last leaf of the Gospel was followed, after a blank leaf, by the upside-down last page of the Apocalypse of Peter.[18] The discovery of the manuscript opened the attractive possibility of having access to

---

12. Adela Yarbro Collins, "The Early Christian Apocalypses," in *Apocalypse: The Morphology of a Genre*, ed. J. Collins, thematic issue of (the then journal) *Semeia* 14 (1979): 61–121, esp. 63–64.

13. Yarbro Collins, "Early Christian Apocalypses," 64.

14. An overview of the textual tradition is available in Paolo Marrassini, "Peter, Apocalypse of," in *Encyclopaedia Aethiopica*, vol. 4, ed. S. Uhlig and A. Bausi (Wiesbaden: Harrassowitz, 2010), 135b–137a.

15. Bodl. Ms Gr. tb. f. 4 [P] hosted in the Bodleian Library in Oxford and P.Vindob. G 39756 hosted in the Vienna National Library.

16. Van Minnen, "Greek *Apocalypse of Peter*," 10.

17. Van Minnen, "Greek Apocalypse of Peter," 20–24. But see, e.g., T. J. Kraus and T. Nicklas, *Das Petrusevangelium und die Petrusapokalypse: Die griechischen Fragmente mit deutscher und englischer Übersetzung*, GCS NF 11/Neutestamentliche Apokryphen 1 (Berlin: de Gruyter, 2004), 29, who seem to date it to the early seventh century. Also, Paul Foster, *The Gospel of Peter: Introduction, Critical Edition and Commentary*, TENTS 4 (Leiden: Brill, 2010), 56: "While without the actual manuscript it is impossible to come to firm conclusion, it does appear that a date of the late 6th to the early 9th century provides a highly probable period for the composition of the text."

18. The codex is now dismembered, but initially opened with a decorative front page displaying three crosses together with an α and an ω in a rectangle; the Gos. Pet. was then on pages 2–10 followed by two blank pages (11–12) and then the Apoc. Pet. on pages 13–19 upside down, so that its first page is on page 19 of the codex, and its last on page 13 of the codex.

several pages of the Apocalypse of Peter in the original language, but scholars soon realized that the text on the miniature codex fragments is much closer to the Ethiopic text than to that of the Akhmîm Codex, the latter being now considered more often than not to have an abbreviated and revised text, showing differences in the order of the narrative, and therefore to be a secondary recension or even a separate apocryphon in its own right.

The implication of this fact is that, in a paradoxical manner, the closest witness to the Greek original text remains the Ethiopic translation. The Ethiopic, however, presents us with further problems, not least because it is based not on the Greek but on an Arabic intermediary. To begin with, the Ethiopic text of the Apocalypse of Peter does not have this title in the two extant Ethiopic manuscripts. Instead, it is embedded in a larger "eschatological dossier with the treatise entitled 'The Second Coming of Christ and Resurrection of the Dead' whose first part has been identified as the Ethiopic version of the A[pocalypse of] P[eter] proper."[19] Indeed, what is normally identified as the ending of the Apocalypse of Peter in Ethiopic is simply a shift in the narrative within an otherwise continuous text.[20] Moreover, an updated critical edition of the Ethiopic text is still lacking,[21] which remains an important desideratum, considering that this is in various ways the most important version of the book. Complicating things further, a recent scholarly contribution has shown the relationship between each separate Greek witness and the Ethiopic text to be more complex than previously thought, with alternating priority: in this reconstruction, the Ethiopic text is taken as the base, and then the Greek text of either the miniature codex or the Akhmîm Codex are argued alternatively to preserve a better text,[22] resulting in a composite work.

2. SUMMARY OF CONTENT

Modern scholarship divides the Apocalypse of Peter into seventeen sections, each summarized below.[23] Put briefly, after the prologue that introduces Jesus and Peter, the narrative presents successively the second coming of Christ (1–2), an introduction to the resurrection of the dead (3), the cosmic conflagration (4–6), the so-called tour of hell (7–14), the transfiguration and prejudgment paradise (15–16), and a conclusion (17).

The prologue briefly introduces the main characters, Christ and Peter, and the contents of the book as "the second coming of Christ and the resurrection of the dead" that the former will be describing to the latter. Setting the tone of this peculiar early Christian text, the dead are referred to in the prologue as those "who die for their sins because they

---

19. Marrassini, "Peter, Apocalypse of," 135b.

20. Bauckham, "Jewish Christian Apocalypse," 10: "The section of the Ethiopic work which is the ancient *Apocalypse of Peter* can be distinguished from the rest with no difficulty. Whereas the *Apocalypse of Peter* itself is written as though by Peter in the first person, the latter continuation begins by introducing Peter's disciple Clement, who writes in the first person and reports what Peter said to him (according to a literary convention of the later Pseudo-Clementine literature)."

21. Alessandro Bausi, "Towards a Re-Edition of the Ethiopic Dossier of the *Apocalypse of Peter*: A Few Remarks on the Ethiopic Manuscript Witnesses," *Apocrypha* 27 (2016): 179–96.

22. Eric J. Beck, *Justice and Mercy in the Apocalypse of Peter: A New Translation and Analysis of the Purpose of the Text*, WUNT 427 (Tübingen: Mohr Siebeck, 2019), 76–92.

23. This description follows the text translated in Eric J. Beck, *Justice and Mercy in the Apocalypse of Peter*, 66–73, which offers a composite translation in as much as he translates not only the Ethiopic text (the most complete form), but also in parallel the Greek text, which is fragmentary and somewhat different from the Ethiopic text. The book is a close version of Beck's PhD thesis, defended at the University of Edinburgh in 2018; the whole thesis, including the new translation of the Apocalypse of Peter, is available online in Open Access at https://era.ed.ac.uk/bitstream/handle/1842/35442/Beck2019.pdf (with the title "Perceiving the Mystery of the Merciful Son of God: An Analysis of the Purpose of the Apocalypse of Peter").

did not observe the commandment of God." Jesus is described here as the "Son of God, the merciful and lover of mercy," whose mystery Peter (and with him the reader) is meant to contemplate by reflecting on the contents of the revelation that is offered to him.

Section 1. In the opening of the narrative, Jesus's followers approach him on the Mount of Olives, requesting details about the signs of his second coming for the purpose of edifying their own following, in order that the church they will establish might recognize his return. Jesus's response offers a word of caution (false messiahs will precede him and should be avoided), mentions lightnings from the east as visible announcements, and describes himself coming on a cloud from heaven in glory, preceded by the sign of the cross, accompanied by angels and gifted by the Father with a crown to judge the living and the dead.

Section 2. Jesus then turns to his interlocutors and asks them to be mindful of the lesson offered by the fig tree. With a rhetorical device recurrent in apocalyptic literature, Peter confesses his lack of understanding and asks for an explanation of the fig allegory. The fig tree that does not bear fruit and is in danger of peril is the house of Israel. Being in danger of being uprooted, it is weeded and cared for, and it starts to bud, but at that moment a false messiah emerges, who will cause many to fall and stray away. Those who resist him will be met by violence and will become praised martyrs.

Section 3. Peter is then offered a vision of the separation of the souls on the last day, though at this point the text only mentions the sufferings and the rooting out of sinners, and the sorrow of the righteous together with the angels and Christ at the sight of their torments. Peter, too, is moved by this sight, yet his request that he be allowed to describe this vision to others is first met with a rebuke before further visions of the torments are announced, which is another trope in apocalyptic literature in the dialogues between the seer and the otherworldly mediator.

Section 4. This section marks the start of the description of the eschatological vision received by Peter. On the day of punishment, all humanity will be gathered before God the Father, including those in Gehenna, presumably in body, given that the animals and birds are required to return the human flesh they would have consumed. God is consequently described as the one for whom nothing is impossible. A new parable of the seed is put forth: the dead are like seeds in that they are soulless when put in the ground, yet God will raise them in the day of judgment and punishment according to the qualities they had when they were buried.

Section 5. The day of judgment is then described as a blaze of fire and darkness that will cover the world under heaven, consuming the stars and the oceans. The transformation of the water into fire causes the firmaments of heaven to be undone. The souls of the dead, too, will become fire at God's command, leading to the dissolving of all creation. Living humans will try to flee, uprooted and chased by the rivers of fire, but to no avail.

Section 6. Visible to all will be the returned Jesus in glory on a bright cloud, the accompanying angels, and his throne at the right hand of the Father who places a crown on his head. The nations will weep at this sight and will be commanded by God to pass through the river of fire with their deeds before them. The chosen righteous will not be consumed by the fire, but the "wicked, sinners and hypocrites" will endure fire in the pit of darkness as punishment for their transgressions. God's angel Uriel will summon the remaining transgressing souls for the eternal fiery pit.

Section 7. This section introduces Peter (and the reader) to the so-called "tour of hell," containing a series of graphic torments associated with a corresponding series of perceived transgressions. First described are the blasphemers, who will be hung by their tongues above the fire. Elsewhere in a large, full pit will be placed on fire "those who have rejected righteousness." Women causing fornication are hung by their necks and hair, and the men that join in fornication are hung by their thighs, over the fire. Murderers and their associates will be put in a fire pit with biting venomous animals, while their torments are shown to the souls of their victims, brought near the pit by the angel Ezrael.

Section 8. In yet another pit, filled with "judgment and horror and excreta," will be women who killed their children. They will be sunk up to their neck, and the lost children will watch the torment from nearby, from "a place of delight," given into the care of an angel. The women's breast will produce rotting milk, and out of it "flesh-eating animals" will emerge that will eternally punish them and their husbands.

Section 9. Persecutors (both men and women) of the righteous will be consumed by fire up to their waist and thrown into the darkness, where they will endure flogging while "their entrails will be eaten by sleepless worms." Blasphemers (men and women) will chew on their own lips and their eyes will be gouged with red hot iron. Opposite them, perjurers are chewing on their tongues, with fire in their mouths. The uncompassionate rich who neglected the orphans and widows will be dressed in poor clothes and rolled over stones that are "sharper than swords or any skewer."

Section 10. In a place nearby full of excreta, men and women will be sunk to their knees for taking usury. Men who behave as women and women who slept with each other will be thrown repeatedly from a great cliff, without rest. Those who followed false idols will self-flog in front of a fire burning their idols, and those who followed demons will burn in this fire.

Section 11. For those who disrespect and abandon their parents, there will be a very high place brimming with overflowing fire, which they will have to climb and descend repeatedly in eternal punishment. The angel Ezrael again will bring around children and virgins to witness the torments of "those who believe in their error," who disobey parents, elders, and ancestors altogether and are hung prey to "flesh-eating" birds. Moreover, ten young women who did not preserve their virginity for marriage will be clothed in darkness that will consume their flesh, while the disobeying slaves, men and women, will be punished to chew on their tongues without rest.

Section 12. Those who only claim to be righteous without being so will be blind and deaf and bound to stumble and fall on burning coals. Ezrael will collect them (or the following group) from the fire and redeliver them to their punishment. Sorcerers and sorceresses will be attached to a wheel of fire, through the permanent rotation of which they will descend into the river of fire.

Section 13. At this point, the elect and the righteous of Christ are introduced, carried by the hands of the angels, to witness the various torments of the transgressors. The transgressors themselves will cry out for mercy, as they will now have understood that they did wrong, but they will be met with the rebuke of the angel of Tartarus and "more punishment," causing them to recognize that the judgment is just and fair.

Section 14. Jesus then states that he will grant to his elect baptism toward salvation as well as whatever they might ask of him, taking them to rejoice with the patriarchs in his eternal kingdom. Peter, for whose benefit were both the vision and its explanation, is now sent to "the city that rules the west," where his demise will be the beginning of the eventual destruction of Hades. In the meantime, Peter should also pass on the new knowledge he was imparted in this vision.

Section 15. This section marks a narrative shift toward the significantly briefer presentation of the prejudgment paradise, which begins with Jesus taking his twelve disciples with him up on the mountain to pray. They request to be shown a righteous person that passed away, and later on as they are praying they see two radiant men next to Jesus, too bright to look at and indescribably glorious and beautiful. They are described nonetheless as "whiter than snow and redder than any rose" with curly splendid hair, "as though it were a crown woven of spikenard and many colored flowers, or as a rainbow in the sky."

Section 16. Jesus explains to the perplexed disciples that these are their righteous brothers, and Peter confesses that they are all amazed at the glory of their appearance. This starts a new vision, offered to Peter alone of an otherworldly place "exceedingly bright with light," where under a sunny sky luxuriant, unfading flowers grow fragrant along with "blessed fruit" bearing "beautifully blooming and imperishable" plants. Those who are dwelling there have angelic appearance, with radiant clothes that match their surroundings, and angels above them. Jesus further explains this to be "the place of your high priests, the righteous people." Peter offers to build three tabernacles for Jesus, Moses, and Elijah, yet Jesus scolds him again for his lack of understanding and shows him a tabernacle already made there by the "heavenly father."

Section 17. In conclusion, Peter hears a voice from heaven saying, "This is my son whom I love, and I have delighted in my commandment." Jesus, Moses, and Elijah are then carried away by a great white cloud, leaving Peter terrified. The sky is open, and he and the other disciples see people welcoming the three, before their departing "into the second heaven." The sky then closes, and the disciples pray and descend "from the mountain while praising God who has written the names of the righteous in the book of life in the heavens."

3. INTERPRETIVE ISSUES
3.1 Literary Sources and New Testament Parallels

The fact that the largest part of the Apocalypse of Peter has only survived in Ethiopic impacts the scholarly assessment of its sources, composition, and provenance. For instance, it is often difficult to establish with certainty for virtually any early apocryphal text for which we have a Greek text whether or not it used a New Testament book to which it bears resemblance, given the possibility that they both draw on a common source (rather than on one another). When we have a text that has mainly survived in Ethiopic, these types of problems are aggravated, as it is more complicated to compare texts in different languages with the same level of confidence.

On two occasions, in 4.7–8 and 17.4–5, the Apocalypse of Peter describes the events it narrates as the confirmation of what has been written in Scripture. In these cases, the author seems to quote from or refer to Ezekiel 37 in 4.7–8, and twice from Psalm 23 (LXX) in 17.4–5. However, since these books are not named in any way other than "Scripture," it remains unclear (especially in the case of Ezekiel) whether the author used them directly or through intermediaries.[24]

Furthermore, given that this is a very early apocryphon, the question of the use of New Testament books is even more complicated. While there seem to be parallels to Matthew's parable of the fig tree (Matt 24) in sections 1 and 2,[25] as well as to Matthew's account of

---

24. Beck, *Justice and Mercy in the Apocalypse of Peter*, 143, and the more developed discussion in D. D. Buchholz, *Your Eyes Will Be Opened: A Study of the Greek (Ethiopic) Apocalypse of Peter*, SBLDS 97 (Atlanta: Scholars Press, 1988), 295–96, 374.

25. See, e.g., Richard Bauckham, "The Two Fig Tree Parables in the Apocalypse of Peter," *JBL* 104.2 (1985): 269–87, who argues at 273 that "it is clear that the Apocalypse of Peter is here dependent not simply on the synoptic apocalypse, but on the specifically Matthean redaction of the synoptic apocalypse." For this view, see also É. Massaux, *Influence de l'Évangile de saint Matthieu sur la littérature chrétienne avant saint Irénée* (Louvain: PUL, 1950), 248–58.

the transfiguration (Matt 17:1–7) in section 15 and 16, Robert Helmer has argued that the First Gospel is not necessarily a source for the Apocalypse of Peter, or at least not in the form that we know today. He shows, for instance, that in the case of the ascension narrative "the major difference is that in Apoc. Pet. it is not Jesus who is transfigured, but rather Moses and Elijah."[26] He further suggests that the shared use of Synoptic material remains possible. In other words, in his view the author of the Apocalypse of Peter is more likely to have used the material that Matthew used in the composition of the Gospel rather than the finished Gospel as we know it today.[27]

Even more thorny is the question of the exact relationship between the Apocalypse of Peter and 2 Peter and their relative chronology. Bauckham initially had documented in detail the received view and argued based on a broader sample of possible parallels that at least some of them indicate that the Apocalypse of Peter used 2 Peter.[28] More recently, however, Wolfgang Grünstäudl argued that, on the contrary, 2 Peter is dependent on Matthew and the Apocalypse of Peter,[29] followed in this most notably by Jörg Frey.[30] Frey further developed this view in an even more recent collective volume, in which several scholars interact in various ways with his argument that reading 2 Peter with the Apocalypse of Peter as background has the advantage of better explaining several passages of the letter, e.g., 2 Peter 3:5–13.[31] In the same volume, the view that 2 Peter used the Apocalypse of Peter instead of the other way around, supported by Grünstäudl and Frey, is found convincing by Bremmer, Nicklas, and Hultin,[32] but less so by Ruf, Foster, and Bauckham.[33] The latter three scholars argue from different perspectives that the argument for 2 Peter's dependence on the Apocalypse of Peter is ultimately inconclusive and that the direction of dependence remains therefore an open question.

3.2 The Purpose of the Apocalypse of Peter

The fact that this book uses a series of tropes common to apocalyptic literature, including rhetorical devices such as Peter's repeatedly confessed lack of understanding and Jesus's rebuke in their dialogue (before essentially granting him what he has requested), suggests that it was composed with a rhetorical aim in mind.[34] The same goes for the placement

---

26. Robert C. Helmer, *"That We May Know and Understand": Gospel Tradition in the Apocalypse of Peter* (PhD diss., Marquette University, 1998), 136.

27. Helmer, *Gospel Tradition in the Apocalypse of Peter*, 155.

28. Richard Bauckham, "2 Peter and the Apocalypse of Peter," in his *The Fate of the Dead: Studies on the Jewish and Christian Apocalypses*, NovTSup 93 (Leiden: Brill, 1998), 291–303.

29. Wolfgang Grünstäudl, *Petrus Alexandrinus: Studien zum historischen und theologischen Ort des zweiten Petrusbriefes*, WUNT 2.353 (Tübingen: Mohr Siebeck, 2013), 118–41.

30. Jörg Frey, *Der Brief des Judas und der zweite Brief des Petrus*, THKNT 15/II (Leipzig: Evangelische Verlagsanstalt, 2015), 170–73.

31. Jörg Frey, "Second Peter in New Perspective," in *2 Peter and the Apocalypse of Peter: Towards a New Perspective*, ed. J. Frey, M. den Dulk, and J. van der Watt, BibInt 174 (Leiden: Brill, 2019), 7–74.

32. Bremmer, "*Apocalypse of Peter* as the First Christian Martyr Text," 75–98, Nicklas, "Petrus-Diskurse in Alexandria," 99–127, and Jeremy Hultin, "Reading 2 Peter 3 in the Light of the *Apocalypse of Peter* and the *Sibylline Oracles*," in Frey, den Dulk, and van der Watt, *2 Peter and the Apocalypse of Peter*, 160–95.

33. Martin G. Ruf, "'In Aegyptum, ut denuo disseratur de me,'" 196–216; Paul Foster, "Does the Apocalypse of Peter Help to Determine the Date of 2 Peter?," 217–60; and Richard Bauckham, "2 Peter and the Apocalypse of Peter Revisited: A Response to Jörg Frey," 261–81, all in Frey, den Dulk, and van der Watt, *2 Peter and the Apocalypse of Peter*. Notably, Bauckham's article reconsiders the evidence and qualifies the results reached in his earlier article, arguing now that the data is unclear with regard to the direction of dependence.

34. For a discussion of this and other early Christian apocalypses from this perspective, see Greg Carey, "Early Christian Apocalyptic Rhetoric," in *The Oxford Handbook of Apocalyptic Literature*, ed. J. Collins (Oxford: Oxford University Press, 2014), 218–34. For a study of the use of "tours of hell" imagery and rhetoric

of the whole work under the name and authority of Peter and, in a different way, for the emphasis on individual punishment.[35] Scholars have tried therefore to better describe the purpose of the Apocalypse of Peter, reaching varying conclusions.[36] The most intuitive one would be the notion that the book is written as a reprimand for bad behavior and transgression, to convince the reader to better his or her ways. In this sense, the list of torments could be construed as intended to straighten one's behavior by pressing the idea that there are consequences (compensation or torment) for one's actions.

But other explanations for the purpose of the text have been put forth as well,[37] especially by Lautaro Roig Lanzilotta and Eric Beck. Roig Lanzillotta addresses the question of whether the Apocalypse of Peter presupposes a justice that is compensatory (the better you do, the more you receive), or one that is vindictive in nature, exalting the "triumph of justice."[38] He proposes two possible interpretations: (1) the Apocalypse of Peter "considered punishment and suffering as strictly necessary in order to provide the expiation of guilt"; or (2) "Peter's compassion intended to reject altogether the idea that *any* man deserves eternal suffering."[39]

More recently, Beck takes a different route, as he sets to understand the Apocalypse of Peter among other writings (composed in and around the first three centuries, Greek, Jewish, and Christian) that contain descriptions of torments in the afterlife. He focuses specifically on the relationship between the account of torments and the broader narrative in which it is framed and includes, among others, episodes from Plutarch and Lucian, the Testament of Isaac, the Greek Apocalypse of Ezra, the Acts of Thomas, and the Apocalypse of Paul. Beck shows that although in most cases the function of the torment accounts is to serve as a cautionary tale, at least some can serve different purposes, as in the case of "Plutarch's *On the Daimonion of Socrates* [that] uses an afterlife torment to prove a philosophical point."[40] He then turns to analyze the purpose of the Apocalypse of Peter by setting the tour of hell against the background formed by the narrative framework in the rest of the book and argues extensively that the "primary purpose of the Apocalypse of Peter is to encourage the righteous to show compassion to the wicked."[41]

Finally, in the latest proposal to date regarding the purpose of the Apocalypse of Peter, Enrico Norelli argues, based on a complex textual analysis, that the intercession of the righteous on behalf of the tormented sinners in section 13 suggests that, despite the extended description of the torments to come, the apocalypse projects the saving activity of Jesus as one that envisages universal salvation after the last judgment.[42]

---

in early Christian instruction, see Meghan Henning, *Educating Early Christians through the Rhetoric of Hell*, WUNT 2.382 (Tübingen: Mohr Siebeck, 2014).

35. Carey, "Early Christian Apocalyptic Rhetoric," 227–28.

36. See especially the literature survey in Beck, *Justice and Mercy in the Apocalypse of Peter*, 14–18.

37. E.g., Michael J. Gilmour, "Delighting in the Suffering of Others: Early Christian *Schadenfreunde* and the Function of the Apocalypse of Peter," *BBR* 16.1 (2006): 129–39, argues that "the Apocalypse of Peter is . . . an apologetic intended to relieve readers of their guilty consciences" (138) in a context in which the members of the intended audience under the duress of persecution might have felt guilt for "finding pleasure in the expectation that the wicked would be punished" (129). For a critique, see Beck, *Justice and Mercy in the Apocalypse of Peter*, 16.

38. Lautaro Roig Lanzillotta, "Does Punishment Reward the Righteous? The Justice Pattern Underlying the *Apocalypse of Peter*," in Bremmer and Czachesz, *Apocalypse of Peter*, 127–57, at 131–32.

39. Roig Lanzillotta, "Does Punishment Reward the Righteous?," 155.

40. Beck, *Justice and Mercy in the Apocalypse of Peter*, 53.

41. Beck, *Justice and Mercy in the Apocalypse of Peter*, 16.

42. Enrico Norelli, "*L'Apocalisse di Pietro* come apocalisse cristiana," *Rivista di storia del Cristianesimo* 17.1 (2020): 111–84, esp. 138–75.

3.3 The Patristic Reception

The Apocalypse of Peter is quoted or mentioned by name by authors such as Clement of Alexandria and Eusebius of Caesarea. Interestingly, it also featured in the so-called Muratorian Canon, and sections of it are used in the second book of the Sibylline Oracles.

Clement of Alexandria is reported by Eusebius of Caesarea in *Ecclesiastical History* 6.14 to have included, in his now lost book *Hypotyposes*, abridged accounts of Scripture as well as of the Epistle of Barnabas and the Apocalypse of Peter, although the nature of these abridged accounts is not clear, with some scholars suggesting that it might have been a series of commentaries. Clement quotes from the Apocalypse of Peter in his *Eclogae propheticae*. This is a work that comments on excerpts from prophetic sayings, preserved only in quotations in subsequent patristic authors, which some scholars consider to be a remnant of the lost *Hypotyposes*.[43] Overall, in the surviving fragments "Clement used it [the Apocalypse of Peter] as scripture and drew theological conclusions from it,"[44] although the question of whether he considered it Scripture depends on one's definition of Scripture. If one means by it a clear-cut collection as that in a United Bible Society's volume for the New Testament, then this is not what we have in Clement. However, if one rather thinks of an important early Christian book that Clement used among others, this fits the data easier. Clement was active in the second half of the second and the beginning of the third century, therefore before the fourth-century production of closed New Testament lists, and he himself does not produce a list of accepted books. He just used a range of early Christian books as in some ways authoritative, before the discussion of what books should be kept on the first tier of books occurred.[45]

On the other hand, Eusebius of Caesarea, active around the turn of the fourth century, does make an attempt at systematizing and organizing the early Christian literature on tiers in *Ecclesiastical History* 3.25.1–7,[46] apparently from the perspective of their reception so far: (1) books that are known and accepted by all; (2) books that are known to most but have met some resistance, being contested by some; (3) books that are not only contested but are also pseudepigraphical; and (4) books that are pseudepigraphical in the sense that they are intentional forgeries that should be avoided. It is only the fourth group of books that is completely rejected as harmful. The first group contains most of what we know as the New Testament, and the second contains books of our New Testament that were suspected in antiquity to have not been written by the apostles to which they were ascribed, like James, Jude, 2 Peter, and 2 and 3 John. The third category includes the Apocalypse of Peter (with the Shepherd of Hermas, the Didache, and Barnabas, as well as the book of Revelation), which is described as pseudepigraphical and disputed, but known to most. While these books are put clearly outside the first tier of books, they form nonetheless a group of books that are in use and that are distinct from the fourth category of books. This fourth group of books alone are rejected as pseudepigraphical books, which are proclaimed or published by the heretics under the names of the apostles.

A peculiar document is also the so-called Muratorian Canon or Fragment, which

---

43. Bogdan G. Bucur, *Angelomorphic Pneumatology: Clement of Alexandria and Other Early Christian Witnesses*, VCSup 95 (Leiden: Brill, 2009), 5–11.

44. Buchholz, *Your Eyes Will Be Opened*, 29.

45. For a survey, see J. A. Brooks, "Clement of Alexandria as a Witness to the Development of the New Testament Canon," *Second Century* 9.1 (1992): 41–55.

46. For a recent introduction to Eusebius's list of books, see Edmond L. Gallagher and John D. Meade, *The Biblical Canons Lists from Early Christianity: Texts and Analysis* (Oxford: Oxford University Press, 2017), 100–110.

contains a list of books that assigns status to each of them in a prescriptive manner. Scholars debate whether it is to be dated to the second or the fourth century, as well as the extent to which it is relevant for the broader Christianity of either of those centuries,[47] but it is of interest here nonetheless, as it claims that the Apocalypse of Peter was received along with Revelation by most of those known to the author of the fragment, even though it is disputed by some: "We receive only the apocalypse of John and Peter, though some of us are not willing that the latter be read in the church."[48] As far as the context goes, the two apocalyptic titles appear after a series of accepted books (Jude, 1 and 2 John, and the Wisdom of Solomon) that follows one of completely rejected books (the epistles to the Laodiceans and one to the Alexandrians). Revelation and the Apocalypse of Peter are then said to be received, and it is further said that some would not read at least the latter in the church. Like Eusebius, the Muratorian Fragment envisages the Apocalypse of Peter as a secondary text (compared to the first tier of books), but not one among those that are completely to be rejected as harmful. We see therefore in the Apocalypse of Peter a peculiar text, which was copied and read in early Christianity, sometimes in churches, projected as a secondary text, and used for theological reasoning.

4. KEY PASSAGES FOR NEW TESTAMENT STUDIES AND THEIR SIGNIFICANCE

The number of characters from the New Testament that make an appearance in the Apocalypse of Peter is limited to Peter, Jesus, and his followers. In this apocalypse, Jesus is the otherworldly mediator who conveys to Peter and the other followers the vision of hell and paradise and provides explanations about them. He is only named "Jesus" once, toward the end of the book, during the vision of paradise: "My Lord, Jesus Christ" (16.6). In the prologue he is designated "Christ" and the "Son of God" (and in 17.1, the voice of God describes him as "my son whom I love") and elsewhere occasionally "master" (2.4) and "savior" (3.5), but for the most part "Lord" (1.4; 3.4; 15.1; 16.1–3; 17.2).

Peter is mentioned from the prologue as the receiver of the revelation about Christ's second coming and remains in dialogue with Jesus throughout, which seems to be his main character trait. Peter is the one who asks for the explanation of the fig-tree allegory (2.2) and then seeks permission to proclaim Jesus's words about the tormented souls (3.4). Later on he will ask for details about the place of the righteous (16.1), which will lead to the vision of paradise, and he will also offer to build three tabernacles for Jesus, Moses, and Elijah (16.7). On three of these occasions, Peter is rebuked by Jesus for a clumsy question (2.4; 3.5–7; and 16.8–9), but he is nonetheless granted an explanation about the fig-tree allegory (2.5–13) that leads to the first prefiguration of the post-judgment torments (3.1–3), is tasked with proclaiming the contents of the vision into the world as he had asked (14.5), and is offered an explanation of the tabernacle (16.9). Given this, Jesus's rebuke of Peter in the Apocalypse of Peter is unlikely to indicate a low view of the apostle; rather, it is the common trope found in apocalyptic literature where, during the dialogue between the seer and the otherworldly mediator, the scolding for otherwise innocuous questions and requests is used as a rhetorical device for stressing a point or for providing an explanation and therefore for advancing the plot.

Finally, other disciples are also mentioned, even though generically as "followers" (1.1)

---

47. A recent introduction and survey of scholarly debates around the problems posed by the Muratorian Fragment is available in Gallagher and Meade, *Biblical Canon Lists*, 175–83.

48. Bruce M. Metzger, *The Canon of the New Testament: Its Origin, Development, and Significance* (Oxford: Clarendon, 1987), 307.

and throughout as "we" and "us." On one occasion alone are they named "the twelve," toward the end of the book (15.1), in a phrase that has survived only in the redacted version of the Akhmîm Codex, which in turn might suggest that this is a later edit, meant to render clearer the somewhat vague "followers." Their presence in the narrative is intertwined with that of Peter. Occasionally, even the narrator's voice—normally "I, Peter"—shifts to "we, the twelve" in 15.1, before switching back to Peter in 16.1. Incidentally, the opening section is formulated almost entirely in the first-person plural: "we worshiped" (1.1), "we asked him" (1.2), "we will proclaim" (1.3), "our Lord answered us, saying to us" (1.4). Peter picks up the conversation in 2.1 for the rest of the book, except the few occasions when a generic "we" that includes him is used.

As mentioned earlier, the Apocalypse of Peter has parallels to Matthew's parable of the fig tree (Matt 24) in sections 1 and 2, to Matthew's account of the transfiguration (Matt 17:1–7) in sections 15 and 16, as well as to 2 Peter 1:16–18 in the transfiguration account in sections 15–17 and to 2 Peter 1:4–14 regarding the prophecy of Peter's death in section 14. However, given the early date of this apocalypse and the significant differences between these accounts, the situation is not as straightforward as we might be inclined to see it. Indeed, as shown, scholars have argued that perhaps 2 Peter used the Apocalypse of Peter (Grünstäudl and Frey) rather than the other way around, and that the author of the apocalypse might have used Matthew's sources rather than Matthew's text as we know it (Helmer).

Perhaps the most interesting thing about the Apocalypse of Peter is the way in which it differs from apocryphal texts that have been composed later (like the Acts of Thomas, dated around the middle of the third century [see ch. 17 in this volume]), where it is more or less clear that if they display parallels to a New Testament book, it is probably safe to assume that the canonical book had been used in the composition of the apocryphal writing. Yet the Apocalypse of Peter is one of the earliest apocryphal texts, to the point that it might have preceded one of the New Testament texts (2 Peter) and perused the sources behind another (Matthew). This pushes us to try to imagine a time in which not all the New Testament was written and when the traditions that preceded it and informed it were perhaps still available for other authors.

To conclude, the fact that the Apocalypse of Peter has survived mostly in Ethiopic means that it is probably the least studied among the first stratum of apocrypha.[49] It is among the first texts to mention martyrs by name, and which "ascribed the power of intercession to those martyrs, making our Apocalypse the first martyr text of early Christianity,"[50] predating what will prove then to be a very productive genre in early and late-antique Christianity. Its brand of apocalyptic is very ancient as well, of a markedly different character than that of Revelation, intent on leading its readers away from transgression and possibly toward showing compassion to the torment of transgressors, and for that it found a remarkable readership as reflected in its earliest reception.

5. BIBLIOGRAPHY

Bauckham, Richard. *The Fate of the Dead: Studies on the Jewish and Christian Apocalypses.* NovTSup 93. Leiden: Brill, 1998.

Bausi, Alessandro. "Towards a Re-Edition of the Ethiopic Dossier of the *Apocalypse of Peter*: A Few Remarks on the Ethiopic Manuscript Witnesses." *Apocrypha* 27 (2016): 179–96.

---

49. Bauckham's often quoted statement that the Apocalypse of Peter "is probably the most neglected of all Christian works written before 150 CE" still stands (Bauckham, "Apocalypse of Peter," 7).

50. Bremmer, *"Apocalypse of Peter* as the First Christian Martyr Text," 91.

Beck, Eric J. *Justice and Mercy in the Apocalypse of Peter: A New Translation and Analysis of the Purpose of the Text.* WUNT 427. Tübingen: Mohr Siebeck, 2019.

Bremmer, Jan N. "Orphic, Roman, Jewish and Christian Tours of Hell: Observations on the Apocalypse of Peter." Pages 305–21 in *Other Worlds and Their Relation to This World: Early Jewish and Ancient Christian Traditions.* Edited by T. Nicklas et al. JSJSup 143. Leiden: Brill, 2010.

Bremmer, Jan N., and István Czachesz, eds. *The Apocalypse of Peter.* Studies on Early Christian Apocrypha 7. Leuven: Peeters, 2003.

Buchholz, D. D. *Your Eyes Will Be Opened: A Study of the Greek (Ethiopic) Apocalypse of Peter.* SBLDS 97. Atlanta: Scholars Press, 1988.

Frey, Jörg, Matthijs den Dulk, and Jan G. van der Watt, eds. *2 Peter and the Apocalypse of Peter: Towards a New Perspective.* BibInt 174. Leiden: Brill, 2019.

Grünstäudl, Wolfgang. *Petrus Alexandrinus: Studien zum historischen und theologischen Ort des zweiten Petrusbriefes.* WUNT 2.353. Tübingen: Mohr Siebeck, 2013.

Helmer, Robert C. *"That We May Know and Understand": Gospel Tradition in the Apocalypse of Peter.* PhD diss., Marquette University, 1998.

Kraus, Thomas J., and Tobias Nicklas. *Das Petrusevangelium und die Petrusapokalypse: Die griechischen Fragmente mit deutscher und englischer Übersetzung.* GCS NF 11/Neutestamentliche Apokryphen I. Berlin: de Gruyter, 2004.

Nicklas, Tobias. "Jewish, Christian, Greek? The *Apocalypse of Peter* as a Witness of Early 2nd-Cent. Christianity in Alexandria." Pages 27–46 in *Beyond Conflicts: Cultural and Religious Cohabitations in Alexandria and Egypt Between the 1st and the 6th Century CE.* Edited by Luca Arcari. Studien und Texte zu Antike und Christentum 103. Tübingen: Mohr Siebeck, 2017.

Norelli, Enrico. "L'adversaire eschatologique dans l'Apocalypse de Pierre." Pages 291–317 in *Les forces du bien et du mal dans les premiers siècles de l'ėglise.* Edited by Yves-Marie Blanchard, Bernard Pouderon, and Maddalena Scopello. Théologie historique 118. Paris: Beauchesne, 2011.

CHAPTER 27

APOCALYPSE OF THOMAS

MARY JULIA JETT

1. INTRODUCTION

On the surface, the Apocalypse of Thomas creates a deceptively simple picture. Whereas other apocalypses are associated with dreams, visions, and experience, in the Apocalypse of Thomas the Son merely asks Thomas to listen to a seemingly orderly account of the end of the world. A seven-day week concludes the world, and different signs mark each day. Darkness and smoke follow the openings of heaven and earth. Each day involves more darkness than light, repeated exclamations of fear, and a rhythmic refrain that "these are the signs of the *n*th day."[1] However, if such a clean and organized exchange of information occurred, its transmission commenced with centuries of deafening silence, followed by a cloud of medieval European variations. The result is an anomaly in text, content, and context that is anything but simple.

The complexity begins at the opening of the Apocalypse of Thomas. Some manuscripts include a retelling of history or future prophecy of kings,[2] while others add the arrival of the antichrist to that retelling.[3] Some lead with only a general summary of the usual societal failures, while other variations contain what many believe to be clues of its historical origin.[4] Some versions only have the seven days of doom, while many others include an eighth day with the resurrection of the dead and the return of the Son of Man.[5] A limited few other versions depict the burning of the world and the final abyss. No version is definitively

---

1. Cf. Gen 1.

2. "V," Verona, Biblioteca Capitolare, I (1), fols. 403v, 404v, transcribed in M. R. James, "Notes on Apocrypha," *JTS* 11 (1910): 288–91; "W," Würzburg, Universitätsbibliothek, M.p.th.f. 28, fols. 57r–58v, transcribed in Charles Wright, "The Apocalypse of Thomas: Some New Latin Texts and their Significance for the Old English Versions," in *Apocryphal Texts and Traditions in Anglo-Saxon England*, ed. K. Powell and D. Scragg (Cambridge: D. S. Brewer, 2003), 27–64; "P," Vatican, Biblioteca Apostolica Vaticana, Pal. lat. 220, fols. 48v–53r, and transcribed in Tomás O'Sullivan, "The Apocalypse of Thomas," in *The End and Beyond: Medieval Irish Eschatology* (Aberystwyth: Celtic Studies, 2014), 567–92.

3. "C," Kassel, Universitätsbibliothek Kassel, Landesbibliothek und Murhardsche Bibliothek der Stadt Kassel, 4°Ms. Theol. 10, fol. 135r–38v, transcribed in Charles Wright, "6 Ezra and the Apocalypse of Thomas: With a Previously Unedited 'Interpolated' Text of Thomas," *Apocrypha* 26 (2015): 9–55; "M," Munich, Bayerische Staatsbibliothek, Clm. 4585, fols. 65v–67v, transcribed in Friedrich Wilhelm, *Deutsche Legenden und Legendare: Texte und Untersuchungen zu ihrer Geschichte im Mittelalter* (Leipzig: J. C. Hinrichs, 1907), 40–42.

4. "N," Naples, Biblioteca Nazionale Vittorio Emanuele III, lat. 2 (Vindob. 16), fol. 60; Munich, "B," Bayerische Staatsbibliothek, Clm. 4563, fol. 40. For a composite version of both, see Pius Bihlmeyer, "Un Texte non interpolé de l'Apocalypse de Thomas," *Revue bénédictine* 28 (1911): 270–82 (using B and N); Edmund Hauler, "Zu den neuen lateinischen Bruchstücken der Thomasapokalypse und eines apostolischen Sendschreibens im Codex Vind. Nr. 16," *Wiener Studien* 30 (1908): 308–40.

5. Several abbreviated versions only included the days of doom. Cf. Charles Wright, "*The Apocalypse of Thomas*: Some New Latin Texts and Their Significance for the Old English Versions," in Powell and Scragg, *Apocryphal Texts and Traditions in Anglo-Saxon England*, 27–64.

agreed to be the oldest or most authoritative, and no known manuscript has a complete text of any variant.[6] Versions emerged from barely legible palimpsests, fragments among codices, and compositions with altogether different texts flowing in between Apocalypse of Thomas's neatly structured days.[7] Any full rendition of the Apocalypse of Thomas is a composition of some combination of manuscripts ranging from a small fifth-century fragment to a fuller version a millennium later.[8]

Aside from fragments in early Latin manuscripts, the Apocalypse of Thomas is referenced primarily in medieval homilies. The fullest and earliest known interpretations reside amid Anglo-Saxon,[9] Old English,[10] and Irish homilies[11] with ever more detailed and, at times, reconstructed days of doom. Although medieval scholars postulate a third-century Greek or fifth-century Latin origin, the Apocalypse of Thomas is rarely, if ever, mentioned in more ancient texts.[12] Generally, New Testament and early Christian historians render the Apocalypse of Thomas to the abyss of footnotes on the canonical book of Revelation or as a fruit of Gnosticism, though it may have no definitive connection to either.[13]

Limited scholarship and understanding of the Apocalypse of Thomas are understandable. For most of the modern era, few even knew its existence. In some manuscripts of the Pseudo-Gelasian Decrees (ca. 400–800 CE), *Revelatio quae appelatur Thomae* is listed among an array of other apocryphal Acts, Gospels, and Apocalypses.[14] Those who studied and debated the list's authenticity found references to many of its forbidden books in Jerome and others, though the inclusion of the Apocalypse of Thomas is rare, and no version described its content.[15]

---

6. For a discussion of the shorter version as the oldest, with parts of the longer version as interpolations, see A. de Santos Otero, "Apocalypse of Thomas," *NTApoc* 2:748–52. For a discussion of the longer version, see Marcel Dando, "L'Apocalypse de Thomas," *Cahiers d'Études Cathares* 28 (1977): 42n19, discussed but not completely accepted in Charles D. Wright, "Rewriting (and Re-editing) the Apocalypse of Thomas," in *Écritures et réécritures: la reprise interprétative des traditions fondatrices par la littérature biblique et extrabiblique* (Leuven: Peeters, 2012), 446–47.

7. Cf. Wright, "*Apocalypse of Thomas.*"

8. For the most recent detailing of manuscripts, see Matthias Geigenfeind, "The Apocalypse of Thomas: A New Translation and Introduction," in *New Testament Apocrypha: More Noncanonical Scriptures*, vol. 2 (Grand Rapids: Eerdmans, 2020), 581–82. The oldest fragment is on a fifth-century palimpsest, and the last is an abbreviated version, Munich, Bayerische Staatsbibliothek, Clm. 8439, fol. 191.

9. Charles D. Wright, "Vercelli Homily XV and the Apocalypse of Thomas," in *New Readings in the Vercelli Book* (Toronto: University of Toronto Press, 2009), 150–84.

10. Cf. Charles W. Dunn, "Rev. of Heist, The Fifteen Signs before Doomsday," *Journal of American Folklore* 71 (1958): 189; Milton McCormick Gatch, "Two Uses of Apocrypha in Old English Homilies," *Church History* 33.4 (1964): 379–91; Mary Swan, "The *Apocalypse of Thomas* in Old English Homilies," *Leeds Studies in English* 29 (1998): 333–46; Max Förster, "A New Version of the Apocalypse of Thomas in Old English," *Anglia* 73 (1955): 6–36.

11. Martin McNamara, "The (Fifteen) Signs before Doomsday in Irish Tradition," *Warszawskie Studia Teologiczne* 20.2 (2007): 223–54.

12. Cf. Gatch, "Two Uses of Apocrypha," 382 (third-century Greek); de Santos Otero, "Apocalypse of Thomas," 799 (the Latin variants "point to different versions of an original Greek text").

13. E.g., Daniel Cameron writes, "The *Apocalypse of Thomas* appears to simply be a reflection of the book of Revelation and not original material" (Daniel J. Cameron, "Apocalypse of Thomas," ed. John D. Barry et al., *The Lexham Bible Dictionary* [Bellingham, WA: Lexham, 2016], with no citation or discussion). See also Brian Daley, "Early Christian Theology," *Encyclopedia of Apocalypticism*, vol. 2 (New York: Continuum, 2000), 37; David M. Scholar, "Apocalypse of Thomas," *Encyclopedia of Early Christianity* (New York: Taylor & Francis, 1999), 73 (includes a brief paragraph referring to a seven-day sequence condemned as Manichaen and Priscillianist); James H. Charlesworth, *The Beloved Disciple: Whose Witness Validates the Gospel of John?* (Valley Forge, PA: Trinity Press International, 1995), 380 (authorship intended to reference Thomas, a follower of Mani); R. F. Collins, "Thomas," *ABD* 6:529 (briefly states that Apoc. Thom. and the Coptic Gospel of Thomas are both secret revelations).

14. *Decretum Gelasianum* 5.5.2. For notes on manuscript variations with or without Apoc. Thom., see Ernst von Dobschütz, *Das Decretum Gelasianum de libris recipiendi* (Leipzig: J. C. Hinrichs, 1912), 295–96; 301n3.

15. For a discussion of the various apocalyptic declarations of the fourth and fifth centuries as well as a later

The seemingly benign and orderly Apocalypse of Thomas remained so mysterious that in the early twentieth century the first two scholars who transcribed fragments also misidentified them. One thought a scribal error led to the phrase "Audi Thomae" in a Merovingian text, and Joseph Bick identified a similar version as the Epistle of the Apostles.[16] However, before long, these and a handful of fragments were identified as dispersed and diverse traditions of the Apocalypse of Thomas.[17] Most recently, Charles Wright and others found more Latin variants and Anglo-Saxon and Irish texts.[18]

Over the past century, these various texts were categorized into three versions: long versions, which include a detailed historical prophecy, mention of the antichrist, and, in some versions, an abyss at the end (LV = long version); short versions that have a shorter introduction and no abyss (SV = short version); and abbreviated versions that only address the listing of days of the end of the world.[19]

2. SUMMARY OF CONTENT

One century apart, Ernst von Dobschütz and then Charles Wright began work on a critical edition of the Apocalypse of Thomas.[20] To date, neither is published, and transcriptions of the various manuscripts span a half dozen book chapters and articles.[21] The most widely available and cited English translation by M. R. James relies on limited and abbreviated manuscripts, which conclude the LV after day six.[22] The most recent English translation by Matthias Geigenfeind draws together several notes on manuscript differences in the LV and SV and provides the most detail with versification from the French translation.[23] Unless otherwise noted, the following summary corresponds with Geigenfeind's composition, notes, and translation.

Opening Line (SV/LV)

At the beginning, Thomas asks no questions but is merely told to listen, although some versions omit his name entirely or change the recipient.[24] Here, the speaker is identified either as "father of all spirits" (SV1)[25] or various iterations of the Son of the Father (SV/LV).

---

dating of the *Decretum*, see Els Rose, *Ritual Memory: The Apocryphal Acts and Liturgical Commemoration in the Early Medieval West (c.500–1215)* (Leiden: Brill, 2009), 25–26.

16. Wilhelm, *Deutsche Legenden und Legendare*, 40, and discussed in detail in Geigenfeind, "Apocalypse of Thomas," 592; J. Bick, "Wiener Palimpseste I," *Sitzungsberichte der Wiener Akademie der Wissenschaften* 159.7 (1908): 97–8; and identified as Apoc. Thom. in Hauler, "Zu den neuen lateinischen Bruchstücken der Thomasapokalypse."

17. For a history of these sources and discoveries, see Wright, "Rewriting."

18. Wright, "6 Ezra," 9–55; W. W. Heist, *The Fifteen Signs before Doomsday* (East Lansing: Michigan State College Press, 1952), 1–21.

19. For details on the variants in the manuscripts as well as a translation that notes these differences, see Geigenfeind, "Apocalypse of Thomas," 580–604. For examples and histories of many of the abbreviated versions, see Wright, "*Apocalypse of Thomas*."

20. Wright, "Vercelli Homily XV," 150n2.

21. See manuscript notes above.

22. M. R. James, "The Apocalypse of Thomas," in *The Apocryphal New Testament: Being the Apocryphal Gospels, Acts, Epistles, and Apocalypses* (Oxford: Clarendon, 1924), 555–62, with translations of M and N/V.

23. Robert Faerber, "Apocalypse de Thomas," in *Écrits apocryphes chrétiens*, vol. 2 (Paris: Gallimards, 2005), 1019–43, as applied in Geigenfeind, "Apocalypse of Thomas."

24. "Gregory" is the recipient in H, "Augustine" in E, and a name is omitted entirely from several of the abbreviated versions in Wright, "New Latin."

25. Cf. Eusebius, *Comm. Isa.* 63.15–16. Notably, Eusebius uses this phrase and then, akin to Apoc. Thom.'s day 8, describes souls as made in God's image. See also Num 16:22; 27:16 (Heb.; Vulgate; LXX); Rev 22:6 ("God of the spirits of the prophets," NRSV). See also Jub. 10.3; 1 En. 37.2; Philo, *Somn.* 2.273.

Hiddenness (Beginning of the SV and Conclusion of the LV)

Both versions contain references to "hiddenness" from all people. Toward the start of SV, the Son of God says, "I will tell you openly what is not revealed openly to (all) people," though the time of the events remains hidden even from the princes of angels.[26] LV 28 summarizes the message at the end as "the book hidden in the nations of the world." He tells Thomas to describe the hidden things to the saints who should keep it hidden in themselves, according to some manuscripts.[27]

Description of the Priests and the Kings (LV)

The story begins with the priesthood in disarray. Divided priests "sacrifice with a deceitful mind," and God's house is abandoned by God and the people. Poll taxes again are sent to Caesar, condemnation befalls leaders, and "a great disturbance goes throughout all the people." Everything falls apart. Abandoned in the wilderness, the house of God now houses spiders, cobwebs, and a defiled altar.[28] Joylessness, corruption of the priesthood and temple, and favoritism all transpire before a description of the kings and the arrival of the antichrist.

LV 5 Suddenly, near the end time, a king will arise who is a lover of the law. This king rules for a short time, leaving two sons. The first son's name begins with the first letter of the alphabet and will die before the second, whose name begins with the eighth letter (*primus prima litera nuncupabitur, secundus octava*).

LV 6 Thereafter, two oppressive princes arise with southern famine, war, and exile.

LV 7 A cunning king commands the creation and worship of a golden image.[29] In some versions, this is a golden image of Caesar. Thereafter, martyrdom, zeal, and faith come to the people of God. In varying ways in different fragments, fire, mountains, and sweetness symbolize comfort, and all concludes after a particular, unidentified number of martyrs. Geigenfeind translates this as "the number of the saints are accomplished."

LV 8 After some time, a lover of law from the East provides for the house of God, the widows, the needy, and a royal status for the priests. This royal status is described as a *donum*, which often means "house," though some argue could mean "gift."[30]

LV 9 King from the south rules for a short time with a Roman military debt requiring the powerful to share "with the same king."

LV 10 Grain is abundant, but inflation devalues gold and silver, leading to scarcity.

LV 11 No ships arrive, and the rulers and the wealthy are troubled. Some versions describe an inhibition to speak during this time, as well as the premature aging of young boys.

LV 12 Another cunning king rules for a short time but with "all manner of evils"[31] and all of humanity's death from Babylon in the north to Tyre in the south.[32]

---

26. SV 2.

27. In P but not C. See Geigenfeind, "Apocalypse of Thomas," 604a.

28. The similar metaphors of spiderwebs and altars covered in thick grass is used of pagan temples under a non-pagan emperor in Chrysostom, *De Babyla contra Julianum et gentiles* 41, commonly found in English translations as *Discourse on Blessed Babylas and Against the Greeks*. Much of this section interprets the Letter of Jeremiah 6:10ff to describe the failings of pagan temple worship.

29. Cf. Dan 3.

30. Geigenfeind, "Apocalypse of Thomas," 593.

31. Cf. Matt 5:11.

32. Cf. Ezek 26:7–21.

Most commentators attribute this to a fifth-century Western Roman perspective, based primarily on the two sons in LV 5.[33] Taking the reference of sons with the first and eighth letter, those who consider the Apocalypse of Thomas to be a Latin source identify the sons as Arcadius and Honorius ("A" and "H"). If viewed as a Greek source, Arcadius and Theodosius II (*alpha* and *theta*) are the sons.[34] Both interpretations allow for a father who loved the law with a relatively short reign. Some then view the introduction as a later interpolation of an earlier, now lost version, while others view the entirety of the Apocalypse of Thomas to be a Latin, fifth-century creation. For either language or compositional theory, caution may be warranted, as many kings named their offspring with the first and eighth letters, and the text itself may not fit one historical reign.

For example, the Apocalypse of Thomas's prophecies also correspond with a dynasty often associated with Daniel 11.[35] Many believed that peace and a secure place for Jews would come when the supportive king of the north, Antiochus II Theos (286–246 BCE) left his first wife, Laodice, to marry Berenice, the daughter of Ptolemy II, the king of the south.[36] However, the union did not endure. Antiochus II would have a child, Antiochus, with Berenice, only to return to Laodice and have two more sons, the youngest of which was also named Antiochus, known also as "the hawk" (*Hierex*).[37] In 246 BCE, when Antiochus II died, the two rival widows and their dynastic relatives went to war, leading to the death of the first wife and the eldest Antiochus offspring.[38] In this period of short-lived reigns and warring relatives, "A" is the oldest who is outlived, briefly, by "(A)H."[39]

Later, Herod the Great and his children Alexander, Aristobulus III, Herod Antipater, and Herod Archelaus also may apply.[40] Both "A" and "H" are actually common letters to start names in the Archimedean, Hasmonean, and Herodian dynasties, and less specific clues fill the rest of the LV's introduction.[41]

Like many ancient dynasties, these monarchal lineages included famine, war, emperor worship, martyrdom, and military debt. Many brought recognition and even royal titles for priests, resources for the house of God, and care for widows.[42] Several centuries later, Christian authors accredit Constantine with similar praise, as well as his fifth-century offspring. Whether due to revisions of a long-lost original version or an ancient divine

---

33. Cf. Hauler, "Zu den neuen lateinischen Bruchstücken der Thomasapokalypse"; Tobias Nicklas, "The Interpretation of World History in the Long Form of the Apocalypse of Thomas (Codex Palatinus: 2–10)," *Ephemerides Theologicae Lovanienses* 94.2 (2018): 257–74.

34. For the Greek theory, which is less often cited, see Dando, "L'Apocalypse de Thomas."

35. For Antiochus II's reputation for supporting Jewish leaders and society, see Josephus, *Ant.* 12; Peter Schäfer, *The History of the Jews in the Greco-Roman World* (London: Routledge, 1983), 32.

36. Cf. Louis F. Hartman and Alexander A. Di Lella, *The Book of Daniel: A New Translation with Notes and Commentary on Chapters 1–9*, Anchor Yale Bible 23 (New Haven: Yale University Press, 2008), 286ff.

37. Paul Kosmin, *The Land of the Elephant Kings* (Cambridge: Harvard University Press, 2014), 19.

38. Kosmin, *Land of the Elephant Kings*, 19. Many also see a parallel between the death of Berenice and Dan 11:6. Cf. Hartman and Di Lella, *Book of Daniel*, 286.

39. Then, Laodice's children struggled over control, with Antiochus Hierex usurping his older brother in the "War of the Brothers" (Kosmin, *Land of the Elephant Kings*, 19–20).

40. Cf. Herod the Great's children with Mariamne I, Alexander (ca. 35–7 BCE) and Aristobulus IV (31–7 BCE), who were assassinated.

41. The Persian dynasty began with Achaemenes or in Old Persian *Hakhamanes*. "A" and "H" are the first and eighth letters in the Persian alphabet as well. The dueling of the Hasmoneans Aristobulus II and Hyrcanus II includes the eldest's death first and the short reign of the youngest. However, in that case Hyrcanus II was the eldest (i.e., "H" before "A"). Cf. Kenneth Atkinson, *A History of the Hasmonean State: Josephus and Beyond* (London: Bloomsbury), 134–65. Thereafter, Antipas appoints his two sons.

42. Cf. Ezra 4–5. See also Martha Roth, "The Neo-Babylonian Widow," *Journal for Cuneiform Studies* 43–45.1 (1991–1993): 1–26. This includes a text ascribed to Darius and the temple's responsibility to care for widows, where the king delegates care for widows to temple authorities.

revelation designed to reach past any particular context, LV's introduction seems to apply to multiple historical situations and provides shaky basis for dating the Apocalypse of Thomas.

Another interpretative possibility sets aside any historical connection at all. Instead of serving as markers of particular kings, the numbered letters may reflect the completion of a cycle repeated throughout the text. In the LV, seven leaders are accompanied by seven signs before the eighth set of signs reveals the antichrist's arrival, and in both the SV and LV seven days of signs precede the eighth day's signs of the arrival of the Son.[43] References to the first and eighth are more than a passing historical reference. It may be a structural symbol that flows throughout the entirety of the text.

Arrival of the Antichrist (LV)

After the description of the cunning king's wickedness and violence from east to west, the LV continues with the signs of the antichrist's arrival. After he "draws near," waters turn to dust and blood, heaven moves, stars fall to the earth, and the sun is reduced to half of the moon, which fails altogether.[44] At this time, woes are then declared (LV 14). Particular woes vary across manuscripts, but versions blend common prophetic descriptions of the end with common immoral behaviors. Lists include those who build houses in which they won't live,[45] marry only to bear children who will see famine and captivity,[46] join houses or fields together only to see them burn,[47] and those who do not care for the poor, hungry, or thirsty, who are condemned to fire.[48]

The Days (LV & SV)

Hereafter, the most popular component of the Apocalypse of Thomas begins. Each day concludes with the refrain, "These are the signs of the [first, second, third, etc.] day."

Day 1 (SV 5/LV 18). Thunder, lightning, and a rain of blood follow a mighty voice in heaven and a cloud of blood from the north. The LV calls this the day of the "Last Judgment."

Day 2 (SV 6/LV 19). The firmament of heaven and earth are shaken out of place, and the gates of heaven open toward the east with smoke from a great fire bursting forth, covering heaven until evening.

Day 3 (SV 7/LV 20). Voices come from heaven, and roaring comes from the "abysses of the earth from the four corners of the world."[49] The LV says that heaven rolls up like a scroll to vanish, while the SV describes the opening of the "pinnacles of the firmament of heaven." Both state that fumes and a stench of brimstone continue until the tenth hour. All then conclude the end is near and that soon they will perish.

---

43. Albeit in a different eschatological order and context, Rev 17:9b–11 also describes seven kings with the arrival of the beast.

44. Cf. 1 En. 73 (similar reduction in the power of the sun); Matt 24:29 (stars falling, but the sun failing altogether); Dan 8:10 (stars falling); Rev 9:1 (a star falls). It is unclear what the sun being reduced to half of the moon means (brightness, etc.), but the idea of a reduction of the sun, generally, is also found in the Persian apocalyptic text *Bahman Yašt* II.31.

45. Cf. Deut 28:30; Zeph 1:13.

46. Cf. Deut 28:41; 2 Esd 16:46.

47. Cf. Isa 5:8–10; Jer 7:20.

48. Cf. Tg. Ps.-J. Gen 18:20; Tertullian, *Marc.* 4.14.

49. Cf. 1QH^a XI. The echo is distant, but several parts of the "Thanksgiving Hymn" use the same imagery that is found in the later Apoc. Thom. Satan reaches all sides of the world, bases of mountains blaze, and the conclusion of the terrors and destructions—a war of heavenly warriors—scourge the earth before its destruction.

Day 4 (SV 8/LV 21). At the first hour, the land speaks from the east, and the abyss roars before an earthquake shakes the whole earth, causing the heathens' idols and the earth's buildings to fall.[50]

Day 5 (SV 9/LV 22). At the sixth hour, sudden thunder from heaven precedes the covering of the powers of light and the sun. The darkness lasts until evening, and the nations despise the world.

Day 6 (LV 10/SV 23). At the fourth hour, a great voice comes from heaven. Heaven then is slit from east to west with angels looking down. When people on earth look, they flee and hide in tombs. The people declare, "Would that the earth swallow us! Such things are happening as never happened since this world was created!"

Day 7 (SV 11/LV 24). At the second hour (or in one version, the eighth hour), voices come from the four corners of heaven, and holy angels fill the shaken air to make war among themselves. The angels are holy in SV, but in many LV they are unjust (*iniquorum*). Angels then seek out the elect to spare them from the destruction of the world. The SV says the hour is drawing near, while the LV says it arrived.

Day 8 (SV 12/LV 25). At the sixth hour, a gentle and pleasant voice comes from the east in notable contrast to the loud voices of days past. An angel, specifically the "angel of peace" in some LV, holds power over the other angels, and all go out on chariots of clouds or in light. They liberate the elect and then "rejoice in the destruction of the world."

Resurrection and the Son of Man

Both versions describe Christ's arrival from above with the light of the Father and the angels' power and honor. This and imagery throughout this section echoes Psalm 104 (103):1–6.[51]

> You are clothed with honor and majesty,
>> wrapped in light as with a garment.
> You stretch out the heavens like a tent,
>> you set the beams of your chambers on the waters,
> you make the clouds your chariot,
>> you ride on the wings of the wind,
> you make the winds your messengers,
>> fire and flame your ministers.[52]

Upon his arrival, the fiery fence enclosing paradise moves to consume the world perpetually instead. No longer fenced in, the souls and the spirits of the saints come forth to reclaim their bodies. Each declares, "Here my body is set aside," and an earthquake shatters the mountains and rocks. In the LV, this earthquake also loosens the tombs. Again, both versions describe the spirits returning to their vessels and the rising of the saints who fell asleep. Their bodies change into the likeness and image of the angels and the holy Father. Then, angels clothe them with the garment of eternal life, composed of a cloud of light from the highest heaven. Like the clouds that covered the heavens before, these clouds

---

50. Of idols to Babylon, see Isa 21:9; Jer 51:7. Of the destruction of Israel, see Lev 26:30; Ezek 6:2.

51. This variance in Psalm numbering is found in both the LXX and Vulgate. Since Apoc. Thom. likely draws on the Greek or Latin versions of the Old Testament, the alternative numbering is provided.

52. This translation is taken from the NRSV. Aside from the alternative numbering, the *BHS*, Vulgate, and LXX have no significant variants. As noted above, this passage continues with several creation promises reversed in Apoc. Thom.

cover the faithful spirits (LV saints) before they ascend to heaven in light to rejoice in heaven. Before the resurrection, angels and the elect rejoice at the destruction of the world, but at the end of day 8, the angels and saints rejoice in the presence of the Father in heaven.

Abyss

After the departure of the elect, fire covers the globe from east to west, "eliminating decay and crudeness." The unjust angels lead away "the spirits of the souls of the whole world" to return to the "abyss of darkness, into Satan's perpetual darkness, where there is a perpetual fire in place of darkness." "The souls of the whole world" undergo torment and howl like cattle, since their spirit leaves them to return "in the light of the Father."

3. INTERPRETIVE ISSUES
3.1 Medieval Homilies

At times medieval manuscripts will remove a reference to Thomas altogether, perhaps because of an awareness of the prohibition in some versions of the Pseudo-Gelasian decrees or fear of a lackluster reception of noncanonical apostolic authorities.[53] However, with or without Thomas's name, the ordering and imagery took hold of the Latin medieval imagination for primarily two reasons: the timing of the end of the world and the organized imagery of destruction.

For example, in an eighth-century manuscript of fifth-century Hydatius's notes on Jerome's fourth-century expansion and translation of Eusebius,[54] there is added the earliest known description of the Apocalypse of Thomas:

> In a certain apocryphal book that is claimed to be by the Apostle Thomas it is written that the Lord Jesus had said to him that the period of time from his ascension into heaven until his second coming encompassed nine jubilees, which you who read this will find marked out every fifty years from this point. For a single jubilee is fifty years.[55]

Though no known manuscripts describe the ascension or mention the jubilees, several versions show marks of adjustment to a timed millennial schema. The fragmentary variants in the number, ordering, and content of the days may reflect the varied apocalyptic calculations of its medieval transmitters. In both modern and medieval interpretations, LV provides the most evidence of the world's imminent end, and LV includes the most wide and varied textual tradition.[56] In the early fifth- and ninth-century fragments, the identification of particular kings (first and eighth lettered sons), and the ordering of the events and days thereafter, lead these same interpreters to see a concern with the end of the world on or around the year 1000.

---

53. Wright, "New Latin," 41–46. See the introduction for a discussion of the Pseudo-Gelasian decrees, and Apoc. Thom.'s inclusion in some of the prohibited text lists.

54. This is an ascription added to Jerome's fourth-century Chronicon, perhaps by fifth-century Hydatius. Some date the reference to the fourth century itself, though more likely it is an addition of the chronicler Hydatius. See Carolus Frick, "Die Thomasapokalypse," *ZNW* 9 (1908): 172–73. Cf. Wright, "Some New Latin Texts," 47.

55. As translated in R. W. Burgess, *The Chronicle of Hydatius and the Consularia Constantinopolitana: Two Contemporary Accounts of the Final Years of the Roman Empire* (Oxford: Oxford University, 1993), 32. Burgess argues that this was an addition of Hydatius.

56. See Richard Landes, "The Fear of an Apocalyptic Year 1000: Augustinian Historiography Medieval and Modern," *Speculum* 75 (2000): 123–30, and described with particular attention to Apoc. Thom. in Wright, "New Latin," 47.

Every other SV and a wide array of abbreviated versions come after 1000 CE.[57] When Christ did not hasten to return so soon, some revisions may reflect efforts to continue the tradition of the Apocalypse of Thomas, even as the world continued. One manuscript shows the so-called *ex eventu* prophecy crossed out, perhaps half-heartedly.[58] Many other abbreviated versions extract the days of the end to attach and rearrange them to modify calculations or adjust the dawn of the timing of the new millennium and the symbolic order.[59]

Modifications also allowed for moralistic and liturgical recontextualizations of the destruction. Medieval homilists drew out and expanded the most fearful portions, lobbed off the rest, and combined what remained with more fearful starts and conclusions.[60] Unlike fuller compositions of the Apocalypse of Thomas, the day of judgment encouraged people to both fear and prepare, even though no known manuscript is concerned about people's preparedness. Where the Apocalypse of Thomas manuscripts give no opportunity for repentance, change, or even the ability to determine one's place at the end, these medieval homilies added and emphasized aspects of human agency.

These modifications created homilies for an array of occasions.[61] Some seized the terrifying imagery of destruction to temper the joy of Easter.[62] Others used the description of the end of all creation to celebrate Rogation Sunday's celebration of creation.[63] On the same day that processions bless the fields, crops, and residences, "woe" is declared for those who toil on the land and build houses in a homily using the Apocalypse of Thomas. Still others modified the LV kings' narrative to condemn the ecclesiastical reforms of their own times. In traditions that range from a few to fifteen days, days of destruction served as ways of placing blame and inspiring preventative behavior in their contemporary settings.

A vast majority of Apocalypse of Thomas scholarship focuses on these medieval homiletical uses, and consequently depictions of doom and predictions of the end fill many reference summaries of the text. However, in most LV and SV the eighth day is nearly as long as the other seven combined, and many of the abbreviated versions of these homilies omit those sections altogether.

3.2 Early Christian and Patristic Calculations: The Eighth Day

Using whatever dating, the Apocalypse of Thomas was not the first to describe seven segments of time and the world's end.[64] For example, 4 Ezra (2 Esdras) 7 describes seven days of silence before the end, 1 Enoch describes seven weeks, and Daniel 9 describes seven weeks and years.[65] Thereafter, early Christian and early medieval calculations depicted the end of the world with calculations of the last seven generations, years, weeks, or millennia.[66] These authors described this seven-based cosmic deconstruction with an array

---

57. Cf. Wright, "Apocalypse of Thomas," 43–45.

58. Wright, "New Latin," 63.

59. Cf. Wright, "New Latin," 51–64, with transcriptions of these versions.

60. Wright, "New Latin," 51–64.

61. For a good summary of the liturgical context and content of these homilies, see Milton McCormick Gatch, "Two Uses of Apocrypha in Old English Homilies," *Church History* 33.4 (1964): 379–91.

62. Corpus-Hatton sermon as described by Gatch, "Two Uses," 381–82.

63. Bickling VII, as described by Gatch, "Two Uses," 382.

64. Contra Bihlmeyer, "Texte non interpolé de l'Apocalypse de Thomas," 276.

65. Cf. Loren Stuckenbruck, "The Apocalypse of Weeks," in *Four Kingdom Motifs Before and Beyond the Book of Daniel* (Leiden: Brill, 2020), 81–95. Also worth noting, the Persian apocalypse *Bahman Yašt* includes seven ages, a wealthy man's descent into hell, and the poor's arrival in paradise. See *Bahman Yašt* 2.1–22. This is followed by the signs announcing the end of Zoroaster's millennium.

66. Cf. O. P. Nicholson, "The Source of the Dates in Lactantius' 'Divine Institutes,'" *JTS* 36.2 (1985): 291–310.

of symbols drawn from seemingly unrelated biblical sevens (the day of rest at the end of creation, the feast of the unleavened bread, the days before circumcision on the eighth day, etc.).[67] With variations similar to the varied traditions of the Apocalypse of Thomas, early Christian and medieval interpreters varied in declaring an end after the sixth, seventh, or eighth days.[68] Some of these differences are tied to differences in the calculation and interpretation of the Sabbath. For some, the resurrection overtook any semblance of Sabbath tradition, while others saw it as a day of divine rest, albeit with rest allegorically interpreted.[69] These differences applied to their weekly liturgical observances of the cosmic reconstruction of each week around the resurrection as well as the calculations of eschatological thought that hung on the construction of those seven phases.[70] Consequently, some saw a seventh year of Sabbath before the eighth and eternal day, and some saw the seventh day immediately usher in the reign of God.[71] With the Apocalypse of Thomas's renowned "seven days," this is a tempting parallel except for an absence of either peace or completion at the end of either the sixth or seventh days.

Depending on the manuscript, holy or unholy angels war against themselves on the seventh day.[72] On a day reserved for rest, appointed for triumph (or at the least whatever comes in the wake of the end of the world), the Apocalypse of Thomas describes some sort of angelic infighting. One interesting resonance is found in the Mishnah's Megillah 17b and its structure of the seven days before the return of David. Days one through five differ, but on the seventh day wars take place followed by the return of David on the eighth.[73] Another possibility may be a concept of a Sabbath through liberation. The prophet Isaiah ties the Sabbath to the end times with the concept of joyfulness, and celebrations like Passover denote a similar liberating concept.[74]

Aside from war, most versions of the Apocalypse of Thomas take cosmic-week events of the sixth and seventh days and move them all to the eighth day. Only in the oldest SV manuscript does the text declare Christ's arrival at the end of the sixth day, and this puts that text in close connection to many constructions of the cosmic week.[75] In every other version, the eighth day describes the reigning angelic retrieval of the elect, joy in the destruction of the world, the arrival of the Son, the resurrection of the dead, and the joy at their arrival in

---

67. For circumcision as imagery, see Justin, *Dial.* 24; Cyprian, *Ep.* 58.4; Methodius, *Symp.* 7.6. For the Feast of Tabernacles, see 2 Chr 7:9; Methodius, *Symp.* 9.1. Some variations emerge if the author believes circumcision happens on the eighth day or on the Sabbath. See also Victorinus, *Creation of the World*.

68. Cf. Brain Dailey, *The Hope of the Early Church: A Handbook of Patristic Eschatology* (Cambridge: Cambridge University Press, 1991), 11, 61.

69. Cf. Robert Johnson, "The Sabbath as Metaphor in the Second Century C.E.," *Andrews University Seminary Studies* 49.2 (2011): 321–25.

70. Cf. Mario Baghos, "St. Basil's Eschatological Vision: Aspects of the Recapitulation of History and the 'Eighth Day,'" *Phronema* 25 (2018): 85–103; Alexander Schmemann, "On the Origins of Worship on Sunday: The Mystery of the Eighth Day," in *Introduction to Liturgical Theology* (Crestwood: St. Vladimir, 1975), 59–70.

71. Cf. Barn. 15; Origen, *Hom. Num.* 23.3 (translated by Rufinus and at least in part reflective of a fourth-century Latin view); Augustine, *Civ.* 22.30 (who renders seven days as five ages from Scripture with two unidentified ages to come); Andrew of Caesarea, *Com. Apoc.* 7.19. See also 2 En. 32.

72. Cf. LV 3 and the priests who fail to have peace among themselves. See also 2 Macc 2:32–38 when the king goes to war on the Sabbath but people refuse to fight.

73. Cf. Samuele Bacchiocchi, "Sabbatical Typologies of Messianic Redemption," *JSJ* 17.2 (1986):153–76.

74. Isa 58:13; 66:11, as interpreted by Theodore Friedman, "The Sabbath: Anticipation of Redemption," *Judaism* 16.4 (1967): 445.

75. Though this could possibly be related to an older Christian conception of the timing of the last seven phases, Geigenfeind uses this as evidence of the opposite. He argues that Christ on the eighth day is the oldest form because it fits the "stereotypical structure" and "fits much better as the culmination of the apocalyptic events that are presented as signs that lead up to the second coming" (Geigenfeind, "Apocalypse of Thomas," 564).

heaven. Unlike the construction of many cosmic weeks, destruction comes amid the saving acts on the day typically marked for eternal goodness.

3.3 Priscillianism, Manichaeism, and Gnosticism

Some argue that the entire introduction to the LV is a fifth-century interpolation.[76] This relies, in part, on the historical identification of the sons "A" and "H" discussed above. This theory also presumes a connection between this introduction and fifth-century heretical groups, in particular Priscillianism.[77] Indeed, during the fifth century, priests were at conflict with one another, and ascetics called into question the purity of the leadership who opposed them. However, this sort of conflict is common enough and is reflected throughout the Old Testament, the New Testament, and Christian history to the present day.[78] Some note that this may be an intentional reversal of the apocalyptic hope of "peace among yourselves" in the New Testament or is part of the divisions associated with the presence of the antichrist.[79] In the context of the Apocalypse of Thomas, these priests who fail to keep peace among themselves may even echo the angels who fight among themselves in the work's day seven (SV 11/LV 24).

The Apocalypse of Thomas includes no specifics regarding the priests' dispute, and any particular devotional practices are clouded in symbol if referenced at all.[80] Most commonly, those who see this as a Priscillian source note a condemnation of marriage amongst the "woes" in the LV introduction.[81] Priscillianists were deeply concerned with purity, and one means of achieving this purity was to abhor sexual relations, including those within marriage. Though many early and patristic Christians endorsed chastity and virginity, the Priscillianists (and Manichaeans) were condemned for many things, including the condemnation of marriage and procreation.[82] However, the Apocalypse of Thomas is not as clear about the condemnation of any particular practice.

The particular "woes" vary in different manuscripts, but woe to those who marry and give birth sometimes falls between the seemingly ordinary parts of life (building houses, farming) and the obviously bad moral choices (refusing to care for the poor). Amid the first group, some manuscripts include a "woe" for those who marry and bear children because "they will beget sons to famine and captivity" (LV 14). Unlike a condemnation of someone

---

76. Cf. Sylvain Jean Gabriel Sanchez, "L'usage de l'Apocalypse de Thomas au sein des Priscillianistes," in *Parcs et jardins au Moyen Age et à la Renaissance: L'Apocalypse* (Valenciennes: Presses Universitaires de Valenciennes, 2009), 259–69. See a critique of this view in Wright, "6 Ezra."

77. In addition to the content above, early theories were also based on the inclusion of the LV among a set of sermons, all thought to be used by Priscillians. This is no longer the prevailing theory of the manuscript collection. For the original theory of the "K" manuscript, see Donatien De Bruyne, "Fragments Retrouvés d'Apocryphes Priscillianistes," *Revue bénédictine* 24.3 (1907): 318–35, and its critique in Wright, "6 Ezra," 34–36.

78. Cf. Herm. Sim. 8.7.1–2; Eusebius, *Vit. Const.* 2.71; Ps.-Dionysius, *Eccl. Hier.* 3.

79. Cf. Wright, "6 Ezra," 35n74. This wording "peace among yourselves" is also the admonition at the conclusion of 1 Thess 5:12 (NRSV).

80. Sanchez suggests that Apoc. Thom.'s mountains "dripping with sweetness" alludes to mountain retreats of Priscillianists ("L'usage de l'Apocalypse de Thomas," 265). However, mountain retreats are common for many religious devotees, and fleeing to the mountains takes place in the latter days of Apoc. Thom. and seems to echo Joel 3:18 and Amos 9:13. For a discussion of the biblical parallels, see Wright, "6 Ezra," 36.

81. Sanchez, "L'usage de l'Apocalypse de Thomas," 265.

82. Several sources on Apoc. Thom. cite the Council of Braga (561 CE) for this condemnation, which explicitly named Priscillian as well as Mani. However, 161 years before, a similar declaration is found in the First Council of Toledo's Canon 16 (400 CE). Cf. Virginia Burrus, *The Making of a Heretic: Gender, Authority, and the Priscillianist Controversy* (Berkeley: University of California, 1995), 114; Alberto Ferriero, "Priscillian and Nicolaitism," *VC* 58.2 (1998): 382–92. Burrus's book does an excellent job of outlining many of the groups who forsook marriage and offspring, well before and after Priscillian.

for marriage, the harm befalls the sons in captivity. In the context of the LV's introductory history of corruption and destruction, someone born at the end of that history likely would experience famine and captivity. Both are stated consequences of cunning kings and the arrival of the antichrist.

The condemnation of offspring to famine and captivity is found in the Old Testament, the New Testament, and other, apocryphal works.[83] Where the LV of the Apocalpyse of Thomas begins with this woe of offspring and concludes with humanity made into angels on the seventh day, the Synoptic Gospels bind both points together.

> *In resurrectione enim neque nubent neque nubentur sed sunt sicut angeli Dei in caelo.* (Matt 22:30 Vulgate; cf. Mark 12:25; Luke 20:24–26)

> In the resurrection they shall neither marry nor are given in marriage, but are like the angels of God in heaven. (NRSV)

Perhaps more significant to issues of Priscillianism, the Apocalypse of Thomas reaches a very different conclusion about the connection between marriage, the resurrection, and angelic transformation. Yes, Gnostics, Manichaeans, Valentinians, Priscillians, and an array of others eschewed marriage and a host of other material attachments, but their issue was not about the particularities of practice. They sought divestment of the physical body and existence.[84] Their quest for the divine image was intimately tied to the desired escape from the lesser realm of materiality. Both in the present moment and in the world to come, materialism is a curse from which one seeks to be liberated and consequently access the divine.[85] However, the Apocalypse of Thomas describes the exact opposite.

In the seventh and eighth days, salvation comes forth through the physical body and physical interaction. Descriptions of light draw on biblical imagery of the Old Testament arrival of God and human interactions with the divine, as well as the New Testament's description of baptism.[86] Though Priscillians and others use these verses to explain the superiority of light over matter, the Apocalypse of Thomas uses them to describe the union of the divine and the material. On day 8, the Son and the angels arrive (with imagery from Psalm 104[103]) and the resurrection reunites the soul and spirit with each person's original vessel.[87] In the Apocalypse of Thomas, that body continues in the redemptive process through angelic vestiture and physical transport to heaven.

While a Priscillian may find comfort in references to celibacy or ecclesiastical conflict,

---

83. Cf. Deut 28:41; 2 Esd 16.46; Matt 24:19; Mark 13:17; Luke 21:23. See also Jer 15:2. The 2 Esdras use is discussed in detail in Wright, "6 Ezra."

84. Cf. Werner Sundermann, "The Manichaean View of the Resurrection of the Body," *Bulletin of the Asia Institute* 10 (1996): 187–94.

85. Sanchez, "L'usage de l'Apocalypse de Thomas," 266, explicitly cites the Priscillian tradition's use of Matt 22:30 and its "like the angels of God" in *De parabolis Solomonis* as evidence of its heretical marriage practices.

86. Cf. Zech 3:1–6; Gal 3:27; Rev 10:1–2. See also this same imagery ascribed to martyrs, the baptized, and Constantine. Cf. Chrysostom, *Mart.* 10; Augustine, *Enarrat. Ps.* 105.1.

87. Though also concerned with the spiritual over the physical, the Valentinians may provide a closer parallel with both tripartite views of human composition, commentaries on Genesis, a preexistent Adam, and the goal of returning to the original state of creation in Genesis. Cf. Ismo Dunderberg, "Gnostic Interpretations of Genesis," in *The Oxford Handbook of the Reception History of the Bible* (Oxford: Oxford University Press, 2011), 385–89. See also on the interchangeable use of "spirit" and "soul" in the Gos. Thom., see Ivan Miroshnikov, *The Gospel of Thomas and Plato* (Leiden: Brill, 2018), 115.

few would accept the Apocalypse of Thomas's reversal of the bodily curse into the key tool for liberation and deification. The same Council that condemned Priscillian (and Manichean) opposition to procreation also condemned their belief that the creation of flesh took place through evil angels and not God.[88] Instead, in the Apocalypse of Thomas the bodily resurrection is followed by a transformation into the image of the Father and the angels with wording strikingly similar to Genesis 1:26: "Let us make humankind in our image."

3.4 Syrian and Syriac Origins

A less considered Apocalypse of Thomas origin story may explain an eighth day with both eternal garments and a universal, physical resurrection. Some note a possible Syrian origin, and both Persian Zoroastrianism and Syriac Christianity utilize many of these symbols, including a particular emphasis on the resurrection of the physical body.[89] For example, in the fourth century, Aphrahat the Persian sage engages with someone questioning the need for the bodily resurrection. With symbolism and imagery strikingly similar to the Apocalypse of Thomas, he explains both the waking of the soul and a resurrection with the return to each original body.[90] At the time of the resurrection, the earthly is swallowed up by the heavenly, but that which is not transformed will be called earthly.[91] Those who are transformed will be lifted up, and as he explains later, they will wear garments of light forever.[92] Those who lack the divine spirit or from whom the spirit fled will remain on earth in a natural state.[93] Without this spirit, they remain on earth due to the weight of their bodies, and they will return to Sheol.[94] This resembles the Apocalypse of Thomas in the abyss of the eighth day.

Garment metaphors,[95] constructions of spirit, soul, and body of the righteous, and most especially a deep concern for the physical resurrection are all commonplace references in Syriac Christianity, which seem to complicate interpretations of the Apocalypse of Thomas.[96] Transmission history shows that the delivery of these ideas to Northern Europe is just as possible in the Syriac tradition as the Latin. Some of the same Irish, Anglo-Saxon, and Old English sermon collections containing the Apocalypse of Thomas also cite established Syriac sources.[97]

---

88. Cf. The Council of Braga, Canon 13. See also Alberto Ferreiro, "Pope Leo I the Great, Turibius of Astorga, and Priscillianism," in *Epistolae Plenae* (Leiden: Brill, 2020), 73–116.

89. The earliest reference to this is made in passing. See Frick, "Thomas Apocalypse," 173n24. A more developed theory of these origins is found in Dando, "L'Apocalypse de Thomas." See also discussions of the apocalyptic collection *Bahman Yašt* in Anders Hultgård, "Persian Apocalypticism," in *The Origins of Apocalypticism in Judaism and Christianity*, ed. John J. Collins, vol. 1 of *The Encyclopedia of Apocalypticism* (New York: Continuum, 2000), 39–83.

90. Aphrahat, *Dem.* 8.3.

91. Aphrahat, *Dem.* 8.5. Cf. *Dem.* 6.14. Cf. 2 Cor 5:3–4.

92. Cf. Ephrem, *Hymns on the Nativity* 1; 37; and 51.

93. Aphrahat, *Dem.* 8.23.

94. Aphrahat, *Dem.* 6.18.

95. Cf. Aphrahat, *Dem.* 9.4 (wear Christ like a coat).

96. Cf. Francis Young, "Body and Soul: Union in Creation, Reunion at Resurrection," *The Garb of Being: Embodiment and the Pursuit of Holiness in Late Ancient Christianity* (New York: Fordham, 2020), 15–34; J. Edward Walters, "Sleep of the Soul and Resurrection of the Body: Aphrahat's Anthropology in Context," *Hug* 22.2 (2019): 433–65.

97. Cf. Jane Stevenson, "Ephraim the Syrian in Anglo-Saxon England," *Hug* 1.2 (1998): 253–72; Katayoun Torabi, "Asceticism in Old English and Syriac Soul Body Narratives," *Humanities* 9.3 (2020): 100–114, describing connections to the Vercelli sermon referenced above.

4. KEY PASSAGES FOR NEW TESTAMENT STUDIES AND THEIR SIGNIFICANCE
4.1 Revelation

Most modern discussion of the Apocalypse of Thomas assumes a connection with the book of Revelation, but this connection should be made with caution.[98] Where an image appears in both, many times a third source shares the symbolism on a deeper level. Both mention an abyss, but in the Apocalypse of Thomas this is simply the earth at the end, not a prison holding-cell for Satan (Rev 9:1–2; 20:1–3). Both mention multiples of seven, though as discussed above many other iterations of seven may inform the Apocalypse of Thomas.[99] The descent of the son of man on a cloud, the four corners of the world, the four corners of heaven, the use of the number seven,[100] clouds as clothing and transportation methods,[101] earthquakes, wars, and loud, heaven-based voices[102] are found in both. However, in almost every instance, these images can be found elsewhere in canonical texts with a similar or closer context and meaning.[103] At times, for example, Revelation draws on Daniel, and Apocalypse of Thomas may be drawing directly from Daniel or a different intermediary altogether.[104]

One significant difference is the role and fate of the antichrist and Satan. War does transpire on the seventh day, though it is almost always a war among similar angels (holy or unjust, depending on the version).[105] LV's abyss has no triumph over Satan, but merely an abandonment of some souls to an eternal existence in torment.[106] Evil is never vanquished, and even more, nothing new ever transpires. No new earth, new heaven, new reign, new church, or new hope comes about. Instead, the celebration seems based entirely on destruction and a reversal of creation to its original or perfect state. No new fire consumes the world, but the fire guarding paradise is reversed (cf. Gen 3:24).[107] Where domes separated the heavens and lights separated the days, each of these boundaries is broken, removed, or shaken. Resurrection brings together the body, the spirit, and the soul, and that creation is made into the likeness and image of the divine (Gen 1:26).[108] Humanity returns to the perfect state at the beginning, with no glimpse of power or reigning

---

98. For a critical consideration of past scholarship assuming this connection, see Tobias Nicklas, "Die apokryphe Thomasapokalypse und ihre Rezeption der Offenbarung des Johannes," in *Die Johannesapokalypse: Kontexte-Konzepte-Rezeption* (Tübingen: Mohr Siebeck, 2012), 683–708.

99. Cf. Nicklas, "Die apokryphe Thomasapokalypse und ihre Rezeption," 690–92. See also Jack Sanders, "Whence the First Millennium? The Sources behind Revelation 20," *NTS* 50.3 (2004): 444–56. Sanders finds a connection between the thousand-year schema in Revelation and the seven-day cosmic week in Apoc. Thom. and elsewhere.

100. Cf. Bihlmeyer, "Texte non interpolé de l'Apocalypse de Thomas," 276n10. For other uses of "seven," see 2 Bar 28; Sib. Or. 2.311; 8.357, as well as the myriad of laws in the Pentateuch based on seven days.

101. Rev 10:1 (angel wrapped in a cloud); 11:12 (two prophets taken up before an earthquake).

102. Apoc. Thom. also notes gentle voices, perhaps like Rev 14:2 but also like Gen 21:17; Deut 4:36; 1 Kgs. 19:12; Dan 4:36; Sir 46:17; Matt 3:17; Mark 1:1; Luke 3:22; John 12:28; Acts 11:9; 2 Pet 1:18; Rev 10:4; 14:2, 13–14. Cf. Nicklas, "Die apokryphe Thomasapokalypse und ihre Rezeption," 704.

103. Nicklas, "Die apokryphe Thomasapokalypse und ihre Rezeption," 690–92.

104. Cf. Nicklas, "Die apokryphe Thomasapokalypse und ihre Rezeption," 690–92. See also James, *Apocryphal New Testament*, 562, where he argues that the LV history resembles Daniel, and the ordered days resemble Revelation. However, much of latter part of Apoc. Thom. may also resemble Dan 12.

105. Manuscripts W, R, and H have "unjust" (*iniquorum*), C has the corrupt *inque*. P has "a multitude of angels." Abbrev. T has "with a choir of angels," and E and O have "four choirs of angels," as noted by Geigenfeind, "Apocalypse of Thomas," 594.

106. Cf. Origen, *Comm. John* 13.30, which equates the abyss with Satan himself.

107. Cf. St. Simeon the New Theologian, *On the Mystical Life* 1.1.1, describing how the garden of Eden was created as an image of the eighth day. I note this to show an array of possible influences and traditions beyond the more common connections of Spain and Northern Italy.

108. Gen 2:7 is commonly used to explain and support the tripartite view of a person. Adam is given a body, a spirit, and a soul, and this exegesis may lie behind this reference as well. Cf. Lautaro Roig Lanzillotta,

thereafter. In the LV's conclusion, the earth's final state resembles its original condition. Both are a dark abyss (Gen 1:1), with fire to consume any corruption. Spirits return to the Father, and on the last day all that is put in place at creation is shaken loose to return to its prior state. The first day of creation and the eighth day of the world are strikingly the same on earth.[109]

4.2 Second Peter 3

Second Peter 3 confronts scoffers who question, "Where is the promise of his coming? For ever since our ancestors died [lit. "fell asleep"], all things continue as they were from the beginning of creation" (2 Pet 3:3–4 NRSV). Peter uses this question to explain the destructive chaos with water at the start of the world and the destructive fire that will come at the end (vv. 5–7). A similar phrase is a declaration of terror at the end of the sixth day in the Apocalypse of Thomas: "Such things are happening as never happened since this world was created."[110] Here the phrase comes at the traditional cosmic-week conclusion, after the people flee to hide in the mountains on the eve of the battle of angels and the final judgments. A similar phrase is used in Mark 13:19 amid apocalyptic destruction.[111]

4.3 Matthew and Mark

The Synoptic Gospels may provide a closer comparative framework for the Apocalypse of Thomas. As discussed above, both describe the resurrected like angels in heaven (Matt 22:30; Mark 12:25), but the parallels may also be found in the LV's descriptions of societies' failings. The failings of the priest and temple echo many of Matthew and Mark's condemnations of the Pharisees and scribes. Boundaries are established in the house of God (cf. Matt 23:13), and God will not look on their sacrifices, leaving the house desolate (Matt 23:37–39; Luke 13:34–35).[112]

> In those days, when Antichrist already draws near, these are the signs. Woe to those who dwell on earth; in those days the pains of great travail will come upon them. Woe to those who build, for they will not inhabit. Woe to those who break up the fallow, for they will labor without cause. Woe to those who make marriages, for they will beget sons to famine and captivity. (Apoc. Thom. [LV])[113]

> But when you see the desolating sacrilege set up where it ought not to be (let the reader understand), then those in Judea must flee to the mountains; the one on the housetop must not go down or enter the house to take anything away; the one in the field must not turn back to get a coat. Woe to those who are pregnant and to those who are nursing infants in those days! (Mark 13:14–17 NRSV)

"Anthropological Views in Nag Hammadi: The Bipartite and Tripartite Conceptions of Human Being," in *Dust of the Ground and Breath of Life (Gen 2:7)* (Leiden: Brill, 2016), 136–53. Cf. 1 Thess 5:23; Heb 4:12.

109. Some interpretations of the eighth day declare it superior to the first, while others describe it more like a return. Cf. 1 En. 91; 2 En. 33; Justin, *Dial.* 138. See also Schmemann, "On the Origins of Worship."

110. As translated in Geigenfeind, "Apocalypse of Thomas," 600. In LV manuscripts at the end of the seventh day, people of the nations say that the hour of their destruction has arrived (LV 24).

111. See also 2 Esd 6:38 that begins with a description of creation, before using similar woes with the world's destruction. Cf. Wright, "6 Ezra."

112. Perhaps coincidentally, the priests pay taxes; cf. Matt 22:15–22; Mark 12:13–17. Also note the common imagery on the fourth day of buildings falling down; cf. SV 8/LV 21; Matt 24:1–2; Mark 13:1–2; Luke 21:5–6.

113. Geigenfeind, "Apocalypse of Thomas," 594.

The woes may share a step in between the use of similar forms in 6 Ezra, but the Apocalypse of Thomas continues on to depict a similar arrival of the Son of Man as found in Mark and Matthew:[114]

> Then they will see "the Son of Man coming in clouds" with great power and glory. Then he will send out the angels, and gather his elect from the four winds, from the ends of the earth to the ends of heaven. (Mark 13:24–27 NRSV; cf. Matt 24:30–31)

> Then they all will behold me coming down from the clouds of the light of my Father with power and the light of the holy angels. (Apoc. Thom. 26 [LV]; cf. SV 13)[115]

However, in the Apocalypse of Thomas another divine power retrieves the elect before the Son arrives on clouds. Angels protect and collect on both the end of the sixth day and the start of the seventh. Except in the one manuscript that places the Son's arrival at the end of the sixth day, the dramatic scene reminiscent of Daniel 7:13 does not declare a reign, triumph, or any discernible action on earth. It precedes the resurrection, the vestiture with garments of eternal life, and the lifting up to join the choir of angels offering heavenly worship. Unlike both the Synoptics and Revelation, the Son seems to take on no clear judge or kingly role.

Both the first angelic retrieval efforts and those that follow the resurrection focus more on retrieval than either triumph or redemption. Where Matthew 25 judges nations and appoints people heirs of the divine kingdom, the Apocalypse of Thomas's eighth day includes no nationalistic language. The destruction of the earth seems to destroy any applicable hierarchy, any distributable power, and consequently all divisions cease, and all power consolidates into the Father. The Father collects all that is his and all that may be brought up to heaven. In the LV, everything else reverts to the terrifying state of the beginning, save the transformation of the chaotic waters into the destructive fire (Gen 1; 2 Pet 3).

4.4 The Tradition of Thomas

In almost every way, the Apocalypse of Thomas is considered an outlier if thought part of the Thomas tradition at all.[116] Thomas is known as the missionary to the southernmost east of Roman Christianity, but the most substantial testimony of the Apocalypse of Thomas comes from the northernmost west almost a thousand years later. Few observe a substantive connection between either the known Thomas traditions or their subsequent condemnations.[117] In many ways, both references to hiddenness and even Thomas's name feel almost like an afterthought.

Yet, perhaps coincidentally Apocalypse of Thomas is consistent with Thomas and his conversations in the Gospel of John. Thomas's four references in John relate to death and resurrection (John 11:16), the way to the Father (14:5), the tangible interaction with the risen body (20:24–28), and John's description of the third resurrection appearance (21:2).

---

114. Cf. Wright, "6 Ezra."

115. Geigenfeind, "Apocalypse of Thomas," 603.

116. Cf. Simon Gathercole, *The Gospel of Thomas: Introduction and Commentary* (Leiden: Brill, 2014), 35–90, including transcriptions and translations of "Named Testimonia to *Thomas*," and "Early References to the Contents of *Thomas*," which Gathercole suggests may apply to a different Thomas text, including Apoc. Thom. (p. 60).

117. Almost no texts about Thomas traditions make a substantive reference to Apoc. Thom. Cf. Thomaskutty, *Saint Thomas the Apostle*, 6nn32–33.

Likely without intention, these issues are all shaped into the eighth day of the resurrection in the Apocalypse of Thomas.

In conclusion, the Apocalypse of Thomas combines ideas of creation and destruction with possible connections spanning every border of the Roman Empire and beyond. Relationships of its content are as elusive as its origin. The work can transform symbols, hopes, dreams, and historical prophecies into such an array of meanings that the quest for the original may be futile, at least at this point. Instead of the traditional assumptions that the work is of heretical origins or that it simply rephrases or recycles Revelation, the Apocalypse of Thomas warrants more consideration and connection with other early and patristic Christian traditions.

Aside from the complex manuscript traditions, the composition is more in sync with reformulations of Old Testament imagery in Persian-Syriac Christianity, albeit filtered through medieval Latin, Anglo-Saxon, and Irish interpretive and homiletical concerns. In its current forms, the Apocalypse of Thomas seems to fit everywhere and nowhere at once. These complexities complicate, frustrate, and at times entirely halt the use or study of the work for many. However, its shaping and reshaping of biblical tradition may provide a glimpse into several different interpretative traditions and perhaps an original, now lost, reshaping of creation, the Synoptics, and a hopeful act of renewing destruction.

5. BIBLIOGRAPHY

Bihlmeyer, Pius. "Un Texte non interpolé de l'Apocalypse de Thomas." *Revue bénédictine* 28 (1911): 270–82.
Dando, Marcel. "L'Apocalypse de Thomas." *Cahiers d'Études Cathares* 28 (1977): 3–58.
Frick, Carolus. "Die Thomasapokalypse." *ZNW* 9 (1908): 172–73.
Geigenfeind, Matthias. "The Apocalypse of Thomas." Pages 580–604 in vol. 2 of *New Testament Apocrypha: More Noncanonical Scriptures*. Edited by Tony Burke. Grand Rapids: Eerdmans, 2020.
———. "Audi Thomas, . . . Audi a me signa quae futura sunt in fine huius saeculi—Zum Textbestand und zur Überlieferung der apokryphen Thomas-Apokalypse." *ZAC* 20 (2016): 147–81.
James, Montague Rhodes. "The Revelatio Thomas Again." *JTS* 11 (1910): 569.
Nicklas, Tobias. "Die apokryphe Thomasapokalypse und ihre Rezeption der Offenbarung des Johannes." Pages 683–708 in *Die Johannesapokalypse: Kontexte-Konzepte-Rezeption*. Edited by Jörg Frey, James A. Kelhoffer, and Franz Tóth. Tübingen: Mohr Siebeck, 2012.
Sanchez, Sylvain Jean Gabriel. "L'usage de l'Apocalypse de Thomas au sein des Priscillianistes." Pages 259–69 in *Parcs et jardins au Moyen Age et à la Renaissance: L'Apocalypse*. Edited by C. Ridoux. Recherches valenciennoises 28. Valenciennes: Presses Universitaires de Valenciennes, 2009.
Santos Otero, Aurelio de. "Apocalypse of Thomas." Pages in *NTApoc* 2:748–52.
Seymour, John D. "The Signs of Doomsday in the Saltair na Rann." *Proceedings of the Royal Irish Academy* C 36 (1923): 154–63.
Swan, Mary. "The Apocalypse of Thomas in Old English." *Leeds Studies in English* 29 (1998): 333–46.
Wilhelm, Friedrich. *Deutsche Legenden und Legendare: Texte und Untersuchungen zu ihrer Geschichte im Mittelalter*. Leipzig: J. C. Hinrichs, 1907
Wright, Charles D. "Rewriting (and Re-editing) the Apocalypse of Thomas." Pages 441–54 in *Écritures et réécritures: la reprise interprétative des traditions fondatrices par la littérature biblique et extra-biblique*. Edited by Claire Clivaz et al. Leuven: Peeters, 2012.
———. "Vercelli Homily XV and the Apocalypse of Thomas." Pages 150–84 in *New Readings in the Vercelli Book*. Edited by Samantha Zacher and Andy Orchard. Toronto Anglo-Saxon Series 4. Toronto: University of Toronto Press, 2009.

CHAPTER 28

FIRST APOCRYPHAL APOCALYPSE OF JOHN

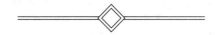

ROBYN J. WHITAKER

1. INTRODUCTION

The First Apocryphal Apocalypse of John is a postbiblical Christian text that narrates a conversation between the apostle John and the resurrected Jesus about the nature of resurrection life, Jesus's second coming, and the final judgment. The conversation begins on Mount Tabor after Jesus's ascension, and the dominant concern is what is going to happen now that Jesus is risen and ascended. Frequent questions punctuate the text: What will happen? When will this happen? What are you going to do next? Of notable interest is the role and character of the antichrist, who is vividly described in chapter seven.

Readers may have encountered this text under one of the other titles that is used to refer to it: Apocalypse of John the Theologian, Second Apocalypse of John, or Apocryphal Apocalypse of John. In keeping with the standard tradition, we will be referring to it here as the First Apocryphal Apocalypse of John, abbreviated as 1 Apocr. Apoc. John.

1.1 Authorship

The First Apocryphal Apocalypse of John presents its author as "John," the disciple of Jesus, who writes a first-person account of his conversations with Jesus following his ascension. By attributing the text to the apostle John, sometimes known as John the Theologian, the author connects this later work with the authority and tradition of the apostle John who is credited in early Christian tradition with writing the Gospel of John, the epistles attributed to John, and the Apocalypse (book of Revelation).[1]

In contrast to church tradition, there is strong scholarly agreement that the Gospel, the epistles, and the Apocalypse all attributed to "John" in the New Testament, were actually written by different authors.[2] Authorship of the Gospel is most strongly tied to the apostle John, son of Zebedee, although many contemporary scholars challenge this traditional designation, pointing out that that the Gospel itself does not claim such authorship but rather refers to the author as "the disciple whom Jesus loved" (John 21:20) or to John in the third person (19:35). The author of the book of Revelation remains a mystery, and there is little agreement as to the author's identity. Craig Koester reflects the general view when he suggests that the author of Revelation was "probably an early Christian prophet who

---

1. See Irenaeus, *Haer.* 3.1.1 (who identifies the writer of John's Gospel as the disciple John who reclined on Jesus's breast), and 3.15.5, where he says this same John wrote 1 and 2 John. Eusebius suggests a different transmission in *Hist. eccl.* 3.39.1–7, distinguishing between the apostle John and his disciples and later presbyters. The author of 2 John identifies himself as "the presbyter."

2. For a short summary of Johannine authorship, see M. E. Boring, *An Introduction to the New Testament: History, Literature, Theology* (Louisville: Westminster John Knox, 2012), 628–31.

knew several types of early Christian traditions but was not directly acquainted with John's gospel or epistles."[3]

Despite these historical complexities, a Johannine corpus emerged—a group of texts associated with John, son of Zebedee, and with a Christian community located in and around Ephesus, in Asia Minor. It is to this tradition that this later author appeals by using the pseudonym John, placing his text within the Johannine tradition.

1.2 Language and Text

The First Apocryphal Apocalypse of John is a Greek-language text sharing similar vocabulary to the New Testament and particularly the book of Revelation. A critical edition of the Greek text by Tischendorf is based on two manuscripts from Paris, three from Venice, and Birch's 1804 edition based on Vatican and Viennese manuscripts.[4]

The earliest explicit attestation to this text is in the scholia to the grammar of Dionysius of Thrace, dating to the ninth century CE. While composed in Greek, there are several extant translations. In the eighteenth century, Joseph Simonius Assemani recorded he found an "apocalypsim Iohannis apostoli" in Arabic in three manuscripts.[5] A thirteenth-century Arabic manuscript can be found in St. Catherine's Monastery.[6] Other versions exist in Armenian, Syriac (Karshuni), and Slavonic.[7] It is preserved in over twenty manuscripts and several translations.

1.3 Date

The precise date of the First Apocryphal Apocalypse of John is difficult to establish with any certainty, but it was feasibly composed sometime between the fifth and eighth centuries CE. The text itself quotes from both the Old and New Testaments and may also be dependent on "question and answer" texts, such as that of Ephrem the Syrian dating to the third century CE.[8] John Court argues for a date no earlier than the fourth century CE on this basis, but acknowledges that its use of the Psalms as prophecy is typical of patristic usage and may be an argument for placing it in the fifth century.[9]

At the heart of the debate about dating this text is a sentence in chapter thirteen that refers to a venerated scepter: "Then I will command the great and venerated scepter [τὸ μέγα καὶ σεβάσμιον σκῆπτρον] be raised up."[10] While this could refer to the discovery of the True Cross in 326 CE,[11] Alice Whealey argues it more plausibly reflects Byzantine

---

3. Craig Koester, *Revelation* (New Haven: Yale University Press, 2014), 65. See pages 65–68 for a discussion of possible authors for Revelation.

4. Constantin Tischendorf, *Apocalypses Apocryphae: Mosis, Esdrae, Pauli, Iohannis, Item Mariae Dormitio* (Leipzig: Mendelssohn, 1866), 70–94. An English translation of Tischendorf's edition can be found in John M. Court, *The Book of Revelation and the Johannine Apocalyptic Tradition*, JSNTSup 190 (Sheffield: Sheffield Academic Press, 2000), 32–47, and there is also a reader's edition with translation in Rick Brannon, *The First Apocryphal Apocalypse of John: A Greek Reader* (Bellingham, WA: Appian Way, 2017).

5. See Court, *Book of Revelation*, 30.

6. Mount Sinai, St. Catherine's Monastery, ar. 485, fols. 1ʳ–13ᵛ (13th cent.).

7. Details of these can be found at Rick Brannan, "1 Apocryphal Apocalypse of John." e-Clavis: Christian Apocrypha, www.nasscal.com/e-clavis-christian-apocrypha/1-apocryphal-apocalypse-of-john/.

8. Court, *Book of Revelation*, 25.

9. Court, *Book of Revelation*, 25.

10. Translations are my own unless otherwise stated.

11. This is the view favored by Court and critiqued by Whealey. The "True Cross" refers to the supposed discovery of the actual cross on which Jesus was crucified by Empress Helena in 326 CE. This discovery is referred to by Cyril of Jerusalem in his *Letter to Emperor Constantius* (3) and is associated with a number of miracles in antiquity. However, several later texts also refer to a "true cross" and are not necessarily referring

Christianity and specifically the iconoclasm of the 720s through to 843 CE.[12] Part of her argument is that the reference to the taking up of icons (ἁγίας εἰκόνας), along with anti-imperial sentiment in chapter 24, reflects the tension between the church and the emperors who banned religious images during this period.[13] A possible reference to the First Apocryphal Apocalypse of John in the ninth-century scholion of Dionysius of Thrace gives us an end date, but additional work remains to narrow the date any further.

1.4 Genre

In Christian tradition, the First Apocryphal Apocalypse of John sits alongside other apocryphal texts that utilize and extend the biblical tradition. As the title suggests, and because it shares some characters and motifs with the book of Revelation, it might appear straightforward to consider this text as an apocalypse in keeping with the genre definition outlined by John Collins.[14] Unlike Revelation and many other apocalypses, such as the Apocalypse of Peter, this text does not emphasize heavenly tours or visionary experiences. Apart from an initial experience of being carried within sight of heaven to see a book, what is revealed about the afterlife is communicated exclusively through a dialogue between the risen Jesus and "righteous" John.

Scholars have pointed out the similarity between the First Apocryphal Apocalypse of John and Byzantine dialogues based on Hellenistic *Erotapokriseis*.[15] Referred to by scholars as an "apocryphal revelation dialogue" or "revelation dialogues,"[16] these texts show a remarkable similarity of form and shared characteristics across a range of languages and theological positions that use a similar question-and-answer style. Whether this literary form should be considered a genre in its own right is a matter of some debate.

I find the designation of Péter Tóth helpful in drawing these two strands, the biblical and the Hellenistic, together. He suggests that the First Apocryphal Apocalypse of John be considered an "apocryphal revelation dialogue," noting its place in the Christian apocryphal tradition as well as its question-and-answer format that sits within a wider Byzantine textual tradition.[17]

2. SUMMARY OF CONTENT

The text of the First Apocryphal Apocalypse of John has traditionally been divided into twenty-eight chapters. Some of these are rather short, not more than a sentence or two, whereas others are longer. There are no further verses or subdivisions.

The scene is set in chapters 1–4, where John is taken to look into heaven and attain knowledge of the things to come. Chapters 5–27 constitute the dialogue proper, where

---

to the historical discovery (see Alice Whealey, "The Apocryphal Apocalypse of John: A Byzantine Apocalypse from the Early Islamic Period," *JTS* 53.2 [2002]: 539).

12. Whealey, "Apocryphal Apocalypse of John," 534.

13. Whealey, "Apocryphal Apocalypse of John," 535.

14. "An apocalypse is a genre of revelatory literature within a narrative framework, in which a revelation is mediated by an otherworldly being to a human recipient, disclosing a transcendent reality which is both temporal, insofar as it envisages eschatological salvation, and spatial insofar as it involves another, supernatural world" (John J. Collins, "Towards the Morphology of a Genre," *Semeia* 14 [1979]: 9).

15. See Jean-Daniel Kaestli, "La figure de l'antichrist dans l'Apocalypse de Saint Jean le Théologien," (Première Apocalypse Apocryphe de Jean)," in *Les forces du bien et du mal dans les premiers diècles de l'église*, ed. J.-M. Blanchard, B. Pouderon, and M. Scopello (Paris: Beauchesne, 2011), 278–79.

16. Pheme Perkins, *The Gnostic Dialogue: The Early Church and the Crisis of Gnosticism* (New York: Paulist, 1980), 26–28.

17. Péter Tóth, "New Wine in Old Wineskin: Byzantine Reuses of the Apocryphal Revelation Dialogue," in *Dialogues and Debate from Late Antiquity to Late Byzantium* (New York: Routledge, 2017), 78.

John asks questions and the risen Jesus speaks in response. Chapter 28 concludes the dialogue with a commission to pass on these teachings and ends with a series of doxologies.

Throughout the dialogue proper, the narrative can be further grouped into a number of themes: concerns about the timing of events (ch. 5), concerns about the fate of evil and the antichrist (chs. 6–8), concerns about the nature of human bodies in the afterlife (chs. 9–12), the ascension of all life from earth (chs. 13–14), the cleansing of the earth (chs. 14–17), the appearance of the Lamb and the opening of the heavenly book (chs. 18–19), judgment (chs. 20–24), and the nature of the righteous and paradise (chs. 25–27). These are described in more detail below.

The First Apocryphal Apocalypse of John begins its narrative on Mt. Tabor, the traditional site of Jesus's transfiguration, sometime after Jesus's ascension. What follows, therefore, is an account of a conversation with the resurrected and ascended Christ. Jesus appears in "undefiled divinity," but his appearance is not described. This is somewhat surprising, but has the effect of focusing the reader on what is said rather than what is seen. The impact on John, however, is similar to an epiphanic encounter, as he is unable to stand before Jesus and falls to the ground to pray.

John speaks first, addressing Jesus as "Lord, my God." After affirming that he is one of God's servants, John immediately launches into a question, the first of many in this text. This first question, however, is one that governs the entire text, while more specific questions will follow. John wants to know what will happen when Jesus returns to earth and how the entire cosmos will be affected. This, in essence, is the subject of the text. What will happen at the end when Jesus returns, and what will it look like?

Jesus does not answer right away. Chapter 2 continues to set the scene and describes John praying for seven days, a suitably biblical amount of time. This period ends with him seeing a light-filled cloud and being taken up by God to the heavenly realm. John doesn't enter heaven specifically. He is placed "before heaven" and therefore can see into it when it opens. The invitation from God is to "look up and come to know," emphasizing the importance of knowledge for this author. When heaven is opened, John sees incense billowing out from "a great sacrifice," most likely a reference to Jesus's death on the cross since it is in the singular. Light also shines forth from heaven, another symbol of divine presence.

Chapters 3 and 4 continue the pattern begun in chapter 2: a divine command to see and a report on what is seen. The author begins by reiterating the previous divine command to look and know. This time John is told to "observe" using a verb (θεωρέω) typically used to describe watching a spectacle or being sent to consult an oracle. That is, John is told to observe in order to know or learn something. Here John is addressed for the first time as "righteous John" (δίκαιε Ἰωάννη), a title that is frequently used for him in the dialogue that follows.

While his first glimpse into heaven revealed the signs of a sacrifice and light, in chapter 4 John sees a book in heaven. It is not a normal book. It is the size of seven mountains and is sealed with seven seals, a number that indicates completeness or perfection. Hence this book is unfathomably large and perfectly sealed up, yet John demands that God reveal the contents of the book to him. God responds by affirming the importance of the book: it contains things pertaining to heaven, earth, and the abyss, as well as about the judgment and righteousness of humanity.

With the scene set in chapters 1 to 4, chapter 5 marks the beginning of the dialogue proper that will continue until the end of chapter 27. John asks the risen Jesus his first specific questions: What will happen, and when will it occur? The main concern here is the timing of "these things," presumably the contents of the book and therefore matters pertaining to the end of the cosmos and judgment. The answer is that a time of abundance and plenty will precede a time of extreme famine when no grain or wine will be found on earth.

The subject shifts abruptly to the antichrist in chapters 6 through 8. In response to a further question about what will happen next, Jesus replies that the antichrist will appear, one known as "the denier." His monstrous nature is revealed in a vivid description of him as dark with sharp arrow-like hair, one eye like a lion and the other like a star, a large mouth, huge teeth, big feet, and hands like sickles. This is the most detailed description of the antichrist in ancient literature and is one of the things for which the First Apocryphal Apocalypse of John is known.

The appearance of the antichrist is followed by divine action that turns the sky bronze and hides the rain. Chapter 8 states that the antichrist will be on the earth for three years, followed by a theological statement that softens this time of tribulation and indicates these time periods are symbolic rather than literal: three years will be like a mere moment in God's time. The author quotes the Psalms as evidence for God's ability to drive out the antichrist and cut short his time through the prophetic actions of Enoch and Elijah.

Chapters 9 through 12 concern the form of resurrected humans. A rather bleak declaration begins this section of the text. The risen Jesus declares that all humanity will die, and no one will survive on earth. This mass death precedes a mass resurrection. Angels will blow the heavenly ram's horns, and the trumpet-like sound will rouse the dead.

Chapter 10 introduces a more specific question from John: "In what form will they rise?" The form, age, and appearance of humans in post-resurrection life is a major preoccupation of the text. Chapter 10 addresses the matter of age—all humans will be raised as thirty-year-olds.[18] No explanation is offered or reaction narrated. Chapter 11 then addresses the issue of race and gender. Again, there is radical uniformity imagined in the afterlife. Jesus declares to John that "all will rise with the same appearance." Differences in gender, age, and skin color are no longer. In what is arguably a departure from Pauline theology,[19] this author adds that humans will be bodiless (ἀσώματος) in the resurrection, citing Jesus's teaching in Matthew 22:30 that there is no marriage in the resurrection to support this idea.

The homogeneous nature of resurrected life prompts a follow-up question in chapter 12: Will humans be able to recognize each other? Now a differentiation between the righteous and the unrighteous is introduced into the text. The righteous will be able to recognize their friends and family members, but "sinners" will not be able to recognize people they knew on earth. It seems that one of the punishments for the unrighteous is the inability to know their loved ones or be known by them, implying a state of alienation in the afterlife. A more cryptic answer is offered in response to John's question about whether humans will have any memory of earthly life. Jesus quotes "the prophet David" (Pss 103 and 146) to say that such thoughts and memories will perish like dust and wind.

The narrative shifts away from the features of human resurrected life to a "what next?" question in chapter 13. The subject here is the place of the church and the future fate of its artifacts. Jesus declares he will send angels to take up everything precious from earth. These precious things include holy images, crosses, sacred books, and the "venerated scepter" before which all angels will prostrate themselves. As mentioned above, this specific

---

18. Court suggests that thirty would have been considered the age of peak maturity (Court, *Book of Revelation*, 53).

19. See 1 Cor 15:35–49. In 15:40 Paul differentiates "heavenly bodies" (σῶμα) from "earthly bodies," but does not talk about being bodiless (ἀσώματος).

reference is particularly interesting for dating the text: the long list of ecclesial iconography and apparatus reflects a period of history in which there is a well-established, potentially wealthy church.

The destination of these ecclesial items is "the clouds," and it is to that destination humans now go likewise. Jesus declares that following the taking up of the great cross, every human being will be carried away into the clouds. While Paul's teaching in 1 Thessalonians 4:17 is explicitly cited—that "we will be caught up in the clouds to meet the Lord in the air"—the author has expanded Paul's teaching to include all humans. Additionally, every evil spirit or demon, including those in the abyss, will emerge and be gathered up with the antichrist on the clouds. In other words, this author imagines all life-forms, both good and evil, will be taken up from earth into the sky.

The reason for the taking up of all life is explained in chapter 14. God's angels are sent to earth to destroy everything. What is described here is total and utter annihilation of the natural world. The earth is burnt up to an astonishing depth of 8,500 measures,[20] rocks are reduced to dust, and all nonhuman life is destroyed. In a concise, chilling summary of these events, the chapter ends with "the earth will be motionless."

Chapters 14 to 17 describe the devastating destruction that awaits the entire cosmos. Each step in the process toward the final judgment is prompted by a question from John: "What are you going to do next?" Whereas chapter 14 envisages the depth and breadth of destruction, a theological element enters the equation in chapters 15 and 16 with a reference to sin and cleansing. Four winds winnow the earth, and the Lord also winnows sin from the earth, leaving it looking like "a piece of papyrus." The author cites part of Psalm 51:7 where the psalmist speaks of purging and cleansing, as well as Isaiah's vision of God transforming the earth's landscape to ready it for salvation (Isa 40:4–5).

The reason for the purging of the earth becomes clear in chapter 16, as Jesus declares, "I am about to descend to earth." The earth must be cleansed of all sin to be ready for Jesus's return. The author depicts a worship scene gathered around Jesus as he returns to earth, one that includes fragrance, the return of the venerated scepter, and thousands of angels who worship it. Why the angels worship the cross instead of Jesus himself does not seem to be a problem for this author.

There is a cryptic reference to "the sign of the Son of Man appearing" in chapter 16 embedded in a quotation from Matthew 24:30. In Matthew 24, "the sign of the Son of Man" is seen by humans on earth who mourn upon seeing it. It precedes the angels gathering the elect from the earth. In the First Apocryphal Apocalypse of John, the timing of events differs. The sign is viewed at a distance by "the Evildoer" and his followers from their location in the clouds, prompting them to gnash their teeth. The precise identity of this Evildoer is unclear, but it is worth noting the play on words here that casts him as John's opposite. Where John has been called "righteous John," using δίκαιε throughout, this figure is ὁ τῆς ἀδικαίας ἐργάτης, literally, the one doing unrighteous works.

At the realization that this Evildoer has lost control of the earth and been defeated by Jesus, the unclean spirits turn on him, questioning his power and claiming they have been deceived. It is likely that the tradition of fallen angels is at play here, as these spirits complain that they "fell from glory" and left the presence of the coming judge in order to follow the Evildoer.

Chapter 17 begins with another "what next?" that introduces the final stage of events that precede judgment. An angel addresses the earth, calling it to "regain your strength."

---

20. Court suggests this is equivalent to about 4,650 yards (= 4,250 meters); see Court, *Book of Revelation*, 55.

This results in something like an enormous earthquake that reaches the depths of the abyss and the heights of heaven. In other words, the entire cosmos shakes, and now even God's angels are terrified and confused. Their fear is justified, as this shaking tears apart the heavens, causing all the angels to descend to earth along with all the ecclesial treasures that were taken up in chapter 13. The climax is reached when the heavenly Jerusalem descends to earth, dressed as a bride, and the Lord's throne with it. As the entirety of heaven and everything that was taken up is now relocated on the earth, Jesus is worshiped by "every knee in heaven, on earth, and under the sky." Heaven has been emptied, and God now dwells on earth, much like the final vision in the book of Revelation (Rev 21–22).

Notable here is that the antichrist, the evil spirits, and all humans are also returned to earth in this cosmic shake-up. They have not yet been judged, and, much like the ecclesial items, their removal from the earth functioned to protect them from the cleansing of the earth that preceded divine descent.

In chapter 18, John's response to the removal of all things from the heavenly realm is reflected in his question, "What will become of the heavens, the sun, the moon, and stars?" He is told to observe, and what he sees is a lamb with seven eyes and seven horns, much like the lamb in Revelation 5. The lamb's role is to open the huge, sealed book that John saw early on.

Chapter 19 narrates the result of the book's seals being opened. After the first seal, stars fall from the heavens. After the second, the moon is hidden away. Sunlight and all light vanishes after the third seal is opened, and the heavens dissolve entirely after the fourth. These first four seals therefore account for the disappearance of the heavenly realm. The fifth seal takes the reader's focus back to earth as it reveals the earth being torn open to expose "places of judgment" throughout the earth. The sixth seal shows half the sea ceasing to exist, and finally the seventh seal uncovers the underworld. While there is a narrative logic in the sequence of events, the cosmology is not consistent throughout.

Who will be judged and in what order is the subject of chapters 20 through 24. Unclean spirits and the adversary are questioned and judged first. Their punishment is banishment to the outer darkness, a place associated with watery depths. John is curious about where such a place is, to which Jesus replies that it lies at such a distance below Hades that a large stone would drop for twenty years before it reached that place.

The first humans to be judged are the Greeks and other non-Hebrew nations. This is described in chapter 21, where judgment again includes questioning or interrogation. Details about the nature of the interrogation are not given, but these people are described as believing in idols and the sun or those who reject the resurrection and the Trinity. In other words, their doctrine condemns them rather than their deeds. They too are condemned to the underworld, again referred to using the term Hades. The author quotes the psalmist twice, grounding this vision in a biblical tradition: "Let the sinners turn away to Sheol" (cf. Ps 9:17) and "like sheep they are appointed for Sheol" (cf. Ps 49:14).

Chapter 22 describes the questioning and judgment of the Hebrew people. Anti-Jewish sentiment is expressed through the charge that they are responsible for "nailing Jesus to the tree like a criminal." Their punishment is banishment to Tartarus, another name for the realm of the dead or the underworld, although less common in the New Testament than Gehenna, the abyss, or Hades.[21] It is unclear whether the author imagines this to be the

---

21. 2 Peter 2:4 uses a verb form (ταρταρόω) to describe sinners being chained in darkness as a punishment. It does not appear elsewhere in the New Testament. In later classical Greek texts, Tartarus is a term for the nether world.

same place as Hades and therefore the same locale as the unclean spirits and other nations, or whether he is attempting to differentiate fates in his use of different terms.

Believers who have been baptized are the next to face questioning and judgment. Chapter 23 calls these baptized ones a "race" (γένος) of Christians, paralleling the earlier race of Hebrews. Where the previous three cohorts have shared a common fate, Christians are separated out and designated as either righteous or sinners. The righteous are those who come at the Lord's command. These are gathered by the angels and placed at the right hand of Jesus. Quoting Matthew, the author says they "will shine like the sun" (Matt 13:43 NRSV). By contrast, the sinners are described as left in darkness, yet seem to be left on the earth rather than assigned to Hades or Tartarus like previous sinners. This suggests they have higher status as baptized believers, even if they are not quite righteous.

The fate of these less righteous Christians is John's concern in chapter 24. Is there one kind of punishment for them all, he asks? Jesus's response privileges the poor who "shall not perish forever" (cf. Ps 9:18). Conversely, kings, priests, patriarchs, and others with power and wealth are "demoted as slaves and cry like babies," a fate that denotes a dramatic reduction in power and status. The work envisages proportional punishments for each individual error. Some will go to a river of fire, others to an ever-moving worm, punishments associated with Gehenna (cf. Mark 9:48).

The First Apocryphal Apocalypse of John shifts its focus to the location of the righteous in chapter 25. John wants to know where they will live. What is outlined here is a vision of the whole earth (cosmos) becoming paradise. This will be the dwelling place for both resurrected, righteous humans and the angels. Paradise is not described in any detail and lacks the elements associated with the traditional idea of paradise as a walled garden.[22] Neither is there reference to a tree of life or even to God. Perhaps the author assumes the earlier vision of God's throne and Jerusalem descending (ch. 17) establishes those things on earth and thus as part of paradise.

Chapter 26 addresses the number of the angels and John's concern that they outnumber humans in this new world. Jesus's response cites Deuteronomy 32:8 (LXX) to assert that the number of people and angels are exactly equal, as they are bound together.

Chapter 27 opens with another "what next" question. John wants everything revealed, including the nature of this new world. What is revealed is that the world will be free of all pain, suffering, animosity, death, and evil. A long list of vices are listed as absent from this new earth. Daylight is continuous, and all humans become like the angels because they are so virtuous.

The First Apocryphal Apocalypse of John comes to its conclusion in chapter 28. John has asked his last question, and now the risen Jesus addresses him. John is charged to consider (behold) what he has heard and pass it on to faithful people, so that it may be taught to others. What has been revealed through the dialogue is to be treated with respect, not contempt.

John's account ends with his return to Mt. Tabor. He describes being carried down on a cloud and deposited back where he started. There the divine voice speaks a series of doxologies. The first one is general—"Blessed [μακάριος] are they who observe justice, who do righteousness in every moment." Then the Lord utters a blessing on any house where such an attitude prevails and states, "If someone loves me, he keeps my words" (a paraphrase of John 14:23). The text ends with a final doxology to "Christ Jesus our Lord": "To him be glory forever, Amen."

---

22. See, e.g., Gen 2:8ff.; Isa 51:3; Ezek 36:35; 2 Esdras 8:52.

3. INTERPRETIVE ISSUES

In some ways, the interpretation of the First Apocryphal Apocalypse of John is linguistically straightforward since the Greek text of the work is written in similar Greek to the New Testament. What complicates interpretation is the lack of historical or geographical markers, which makes dating and locating this text very imprecise. Additionally, the nature of its genre opens possibilities for interpretation that go well beyond treating it as another apocalypse in the biblical tradition or reading it as an "imitation" of Revelation.[23]

3.1 Relationship to Other Ancient Christian Texts

One of the interesting questions that arises when it comes to interpreting the First Apocryphal Apocalypse of John is its relationship to other ancient Christian literature. Against which body of literature should we be reading this text? Apocalypses? Gnostic dialogues? Hellenistic dialogues? Johannine literature? And how does the genre affect interpretation? Traditionally, the work has been grouped with other Johannine literature due to the author's chosen pseudonym and its use of Revelation. This places it alongside gospels and apocalypses, for the most part,[24] when it may be more appropriate to consider it alongside other revelation dialogues.

One of the markers of a revelation dialogue is the setting. Numerous ancient texts set their revelatory dialogue on a mountain after the resurrection, much like the First Apocryphal Apocalypse of John 1. For example, the Letter of Peter to Philip depicts the disciples going up the Mount of Olives to seek understanding and revelation. The Apocryphon of John portrays John going to a "mountainous place" where he encounters the Savior in his glorified form.[25] Like the First Apocryphal Apocalypse of John, both texts are concerned with questions about soteriology.

Going beyond the Johannine tradition, we find numerous other revelatory dialogues that similarly depict special knowledge being revealed by the risen Christ to an interlocutor or group of interlocutors.[26] Two examples may suffice. The first is a sixth-century CE text, Ammonios, by Bishop Zacharias, which is a polemic against the teaching of a fifth-century philosopher, Ammonios. It is written in question-and-answer style to refute his teaching. In this sense it is similar to the much earlier text attributed to Justin Martyr, Ps.-Justin's *Quaestiones et Responsiones ad Orthodoxos*, which also seeks to refute incorrect teaching. Papadoyannakis writes that there "is a striking overlap in the range of concerns that are addressed in these works (demonology, resurrection, eschatology, cosmology, theodicy)."[27]

While the most familiar early dialogue texts for Christians are usually those found in the Nag Hammadi corpus and associated with Gnosticism,[28] there were of course Egyptian, Hellenistic, and classical precedents for this revelation-dialogue text type, notably of a philosophical nature. Christians adopted this form fairly early on as a means

---

23. Court, *Book of Revelation*, 23, uses the language of imitation in his treatment of 1 Apocr. Apoc. John.

24. There are other texts using the pseudonym John that are of a dialogue style. For example, fragments of the *Dialogue between Jesus and John* date to the fourth or fifth century CE. See *NTApoc* 1:332.

25. The Apocryphon of John is a gnostic dialogue text dating to the second century CE, used by Irenaeus in his account on the gnostics (Irenaeus, *Haer.* 1.27). Set after the resurrection on the Mount of Olives, it is a visionary narrative wherein Christ, in the role of revealer, discloses divine knowledge through a dialogue. Topics include the nature of salvation and the perfection of humans through the spirit.

26. E.g., (First) Apocalypse of James; Dialogue of the Savior.

27. Yannis Papadoyannakis, "Instruction by Question and Answer: The Case of Late Antique and Byzantine *Erotapokriseis*," in *Greek Literature in Late Antiquity: Dynamism, Didacticism, Classicism*, ed. S. Johnson (Burlington, VT: Ashgate, 2006), 98.

28. The *Corpus Hermeticum* includes some of the texts in the Nag Hammadi Library, but also includes texts that predate Gnosticism.

by which to teach and argue for orthodox theology or to refute heresy.[29] The popularity of this genre burgeoned in the Byzantine era, spawning a range of question-and-answer type texts known as *erotapokriseis* (*quaestiones* in Latin). This popular style was used for a broad range of subject matter over many centuries, and more scholarly work remains to be done on these texts.[30] What we can say is that while the subject matter of *erotapokriseis* might differ wildly, they tend to have both a didactic and polemical function. The implications of this are addressed below.

3.2 Reading the First Apocryphal Apocalypse of John as *Erotapokriseis*

"In late antiquity, the dialogue form was seen as a suitable vehicle for carrying out the wars of sectarian rivalry among Christians and was put to use in apologetic and polemical efforts as well as in prophylactic and catechetical exercises," writes Richard Lim.[31] We see evidence of doctrinal concerns as well as polemics at several points in the First Apocryphal Apocalypse of John.

Doctrinal issues come to the fore in the discussion of heretics in chapter 22, a section which reveals the first group of humans to face judgment. Greeks are judged first and portrayed as idolaters. They are clustered together with "heretics," a group defined as those who do not believe in the resurrection and do not confess "Father, Son, and Holy Spirit." The language of confession (ὁμολογέω) is technical, denoting that a creedal formula lies behind the text.

As the group judged first, being labeled a heretic and being associated with the Greeks demonstrates the strong level of polemic toward other Christians who do not conform to these two tenants of what, by this time, was considered orthodox Christian faith: belief in the Trinity and the resurrection of Jesus. Any other shared beliefs are swept aside, and those with alternate theology are condemned to Sheol (ch. 21). To put this criticism in perspective, one could compare it to the way this author speaks of the Jews. For him, the "Hebrew race" is responsible for Jesus's death and therefore deserves condemnation in what is very clearly an anti-Semitic stance (ch. 22). Yet Christians who deny the Trinity or resurrection are worse.

We see another strong polemical stance in the chapter on the fate of the powerful (ch. 24). John asks what kind of punishment awaits kings, high priests, priests, patriarchs, the rich and the poor, and slave and free. The risen Lord affirms God's preference for the poor, announcing that they will not perish. By contrast, those with wealth and power face some of the more vivid punishments in the book. Instead of simply being banished to Sheol or Tartarus, this group is "demoted as slaves" and will "cry like babies," indicating a loss of status and degradation are in mind. Unlike previous categories of humans, these humans face proportional punishment, suggesting that specific leaders may be in mind.

The personal, humiliating nature of the fate of the leaders may well reflect the early iconoclastic clashes of the Byzantine era.[32] The author's vindictiveness toward these imperial and ecclesial leaders is evident in the final aspect of their punishment: some will go to a "fiery river," others to a "sleepless worm," and others still to a "seven-mouthed punishment pit" (ch. 24). No other group's fate is narrated in such specific language, nor are any other punishments so personal. The dialogical nature of the text becomes a vehicle for a polemic

29. E.g., Ps.-Justin, *Quaestiones et responsiones ad orthodoxos* (2nd cent.).
30. Papadoyannakis, "Instruction by Question and Answer," 91–92.
31. Richard Lim, "Theodoret of Cyrus and Speakers in Greek Dialogues," *Journal of Hellenic Studies* 111 (1991): 182.
32. Whealey, "Apocryphal Apocalypse of John," 534.

against certain specific people, a view that is imbued with divine authority when placed in the mouth of the risen Jesus.

While there is clearly a strong polemical element to this text, *erotapokriseis* also serve a didactic or pedagogical function. The small pieces of information that are disseminated in this question-and-answer style potentially make the information more digestible. For example, when revealing the nature of resurrection bodies, the text moves through age, race, gender, and finally questions of recognition and memory. That is, it moves from something tangible to something more esoteric and profound (the place of memory in eternity). The questions function to guide the hearer and step them through a learning process.

The question as to why this author is so interested in resurrected bodies and why his solution is to reveal a homogenous, angelic, nonbodily future form is not one that is resolved in the text. For all its potential problems, it offers a theologically egalitarian view of the afterlife, where the things that denote status or division, such as age, gender, and ethnicity, are removed. This is in keeping with the imagined demise of ecclesial and imperial rulers (ch. 24), suggesting this author reflects the views of a person of ordinary status rather than the leadership.

In terms of moral exhortation, the revelation that all nonbelievers and heretics will be cast into Hades invokes fear in the reader and offers encouragement to remain faithful. This is reinforced in the promise that virtuous humans will become like angels (ch. 27). Remaining virtuous and faithful will reap reward. Comfort is offered in the disclosure that three years of human time will be made to feel like three seconds by God (ch. 8) and in the promise that the New Jerusalem will be free of all kinds of vices and sins (ch. 27).

Theologically, the First Apocryphal Apocalypse of John teaches readers that God is in control and has a plan for the end of the cosmos. Christians are taught to remain righteous in their living and orthodox in their views. Readers are also schooled to see that ecclesial objects are precious to God and worthy of being saved.

4. KEY PASSAGES FOR NEW TESTAMENT STUDIES AND THEIR SIGNIFICANCE

The lateness of the First Apocryphal Apocalypse of John means its significance for understanding the New Testament or contributing to New Testament interpretation is limited.[33] It is, however, typically considered important for its use of Revelation and thus as a form of reception history. This will be discussed below. Several other characters and passages are also important for understanding how ancient Christians interpreted, extended, and utilized the New Testament, which in turn can help place the theological developments of the New Testament in a wider context. Below we examine this text's use of Scripture as well as two key themes: the antichrist and the rapture. Lastly, we turn to its reliance on Revelation.

4.1 Use of Scripture

The First Apocryphal Apocalypse of John explicitly cites the Bible numerous times throughout. These overt uses are usually marked and introduced by a reference to the writer. When quoting a psalm, for example, the author uses an introductory phrase such as "just as the prophet said" (ch. 8) or "as David foretold" (ch. 9). When the Gospels are quoted, they are treated as Jesus's actual words and placed in the mouth of the risen Jesus with a phrase like "just as I told you" (ch. 11). Along with the Psalms and the Gospels, this author also quotes Paul (Rom; 1 Cor; 1 Thess) and Isaiah.

---

33. Craig Evans, *Ancient Texts for New Testament Studies* (Grand Rapids: Baker Academic, 2005), 257. Evans argues this is the case for most of the New Testament Apocrypha and Pseudepigrapha.

Two patterns emerge that are of interest. Firstly, when quoting the Gospels, the First Apocryphal Apocalypse of John demonstrates a clear preference for Matthew over the other Synoptic Gospels. In some cases, the author quotes a verse exclusive to Matthew (e.g. Matt 7:6; see 1 Apocr. Apoc. John 28). In other cases, however, the author has chosen the Matthean text where parallels exist in Mark and Luke. This can be seen in chapter 11, where the phrasing reflects the text of Matthew 22:30 rather than parallel versions of a similar saying in the other Synoptic Gospels. We can only speculate as to why this author exhibits a preference for Matthew. Perhaps it is simply that Matthew was first in the New Testament canon and assumed to be the oldest of the Synoptics around this time. Matthew's Gospel was enormously popular among patristic exegetes as well as in the early church's lectionaries. It is also feasible that Matthew's attention to eschatology and his dramatic depictions of future judgment appealed to this author, given the subject matter of the text.[34]

The author's use of the Psalms is also of interest. The Psalms are the most frequently cited biblical texts in the First Apocryphal Apocalypse of John and are quoted almost twice as often as all other biblical texts combined. Treated as a form of prophecy, quotes from the Psalms imbue the text with biblical authority and offer support for this particular vision of the end. While reading the Psalms as prophecy may seem foreign to some modern readers, this interpretive lens begins in the Old Testament. Later prophets such as Malachi quote or allude to the Psalms in their portrayal of the end.[35] Treating the Psalms as prophecy was also common in the patristic era,[36] and the Psalms are frequently quoted or alluded to by the writers of the New Testament.

4.2 The Antichrist

In the New Testament, the term "antichrist" (ἀντίχριστος) only occurs in the first and second epistles of John (1 John 2:18 [twice], 22; 4:3; 2 John 7). This character is described as one who lies and who denies Jesus is the Christ, literally, he is the one who is against or anti-Christ. He is, most likely, a human opponent. Denying Jesus as Messiah is the key charge in three of these passages (1 John 2:22; 4:3; 2 John 7), along with this person's capacity for deception.[37] None of the New Testament passages describe the physical attributes of this antichrist figure.

The antichrist is named as such three times in First Apocryphal Apocalypse of John (chs. 6–7; 13; 17). He first appears in chapter 6, where he is called "the Denier," and then he is vividly described in chapter 7. The author writes:

> The appearance of his face is dark; the hairs of his head are sharp like darts; his eyebrows like a field; his right eye like the star which rises in the morning, and the other like a lion's; his mouth one cubit wide; his teeth a span in length; his fingers like sickles; the print of his feet of two spans; and on his brow an inscription, "Antichrist." He shall be exalted as far as the heaven and shall descend even to Hades, making false displays. (1 Apocr. Apoc. John 7)

---

34. E.g., see Matt 25:30–46.

35. E.g., Mal 4:1 imagines a future when evildoers will burn up "like an oven," a phrase found in Ps 29:1.

36. Court, *Book of Revelation*, 25.

37. The term "antichrist" does not appear in Revelation, although arguably the concept lies behind that text's presentation of the beast in Rev 12–13. There, too, deception is a key quality not only of the dragon or beast (Rev 12:9; 13:14; 19:2; 20:3, 8, 10) but also of others who oppose Christ, such as Rome (18:23), or teach alternate theologies, such as the false teachers (2:20). See Wilhelm Bousset, *The Antichrist Legend: A Chapter in Christian and Jewish Folklore* (London: Hutchinson, 1896), 201, and Kaestli, "La figure de l'antichrist dans l'Apocalypse," 284.

His sharp teeth and the size of his limbs make this figure grotesque, wild, and frightening. It depicts him as a more-than-human opponent, turning him into a kind of monstrous beast much like the beast of Revelation 13. That beast also has large feet, spikes on its head in the form of horns, and the attributes of a lion, although in its case it is his mouth (Rev 13:2).[38] To these types of attributes, the author of 1 Apocr. Apoc. John has added a darkened face and scythe-like fingers.

Despite the fear such a figure might have aroused in readers, the work depicts God as very much in control of the antichrist throughout the text. In chapter 7 (quoted above), the antichrist is lifted up to heaven by God, an idea that is expanded in chapter 13, where all evil and unclean beings are taken up from the earth. There the antichrist is described as the "devil's servant," although no further physical description is offered. His return is narrated in chapter 17, when everything is brought back to earth at the divine command—humans, unclean spirits, and the antichrist. In this scene, Jesus declares "all will appear naked and prostrate" before him, indicating his dominion over evil and subjugation of it. Lastly, the antichrist is not named, but he is implied as one of the wicked who are banished to the outer darkness and confined to watery depths (ch. 20).

The Greek Apocalypse of Ezra comes closest to the First Apocryphal Apocalypse of John in offering a detailed description of the antichrist:

> And he said to me: "The form of his countenance is like that of a wild beast; his right eye like the star that rises in the morning, and the other without motion; his mouth one cubit; his teeth a span long; his fingers like scythes; the track of his feet of two spans; and on his face an inscription, Antichrist. He has been exalted to heaven; he will go down to Hades." (Apoc. Ezra 4.29–32)

There is a striking overlap with several facets of the description in the First Apocryphal Apocalypse of John. The description of the antichrist's hands as like sickles ("scythes") is almost identical, as too are the descriptions of his feet and right eye. Both texts picture his name being inscribed on his forehead or face as well as describe his exaltation to heaven and descent to Hades. Both also ultimately assign him to the outer darkness. Which text may have influenced or predated the other is difficult to determine, given the indeterminate date of the Apocalypse of Ezra.[39]

What both these apocryphal apocalypses demonstrate, however, is a tradition in which interest in the appearance and nature of the antichrist continues and develops.[40] The detail of the antichrist's appearance in these texts parallels the increasingly vivid depictions of the punishments in hell described in texts like the Apocalypse of Peter and the Apocalypse of Paul. These texts use *ekphrasis*, a rhetorical technique that utilizes the imagination to appeal to fear and teach moral formation.[41] This interest in vividly portraying negative aspects of the afterlife as a warning not to sin does, of course, continue into the medieval period.

---

38. Irenaeus also associates the antichrist with a lion (*Haer.* 3.23.7).

39. Apocalypse of Ezra is usually dated in the general period between the second and ninth centuries CE.

40. The number of variants for this chapter in Tischendorf's edition indicates the variety and interest in describing the antichrist. See Tischendorf, *Apocalypses Apocryphae*, 74.

41. Meghan Henning, "Eternal Punishment as Paideia: The Ekphrasis of Hell in the Apocalypse of Peter and the Apocalypse of Paul," *BR* 58 (2013): 29–48.

4.3 The Rapture

The so-called rapture is radically reconfigured in the First Apocryphal Apocalypse of John. Instead of being a reward for the righteous, removal from the earth is a way to keep everyone, both good and evil, safe until the earth is cleansed and the book of judgment is opened.

In chapter 13, Jesus explains that the ecclesial and holy items will be taken up (αἴρω) with the clouds into the air. Humans, too, will be taken up on the clouds. The author explicitly quotes part of 1 Thessalonians 4:17, in the exact Greek of the New Testament, yet uses it differently to support the notion that all humanity will meet the Lord "in the air."[42] In its original setting, this well-known Pauline passage portrays God descending to earth and righteous, living Christians being "snatched up" to be with Jesus at the end of time.[43] Contemporary Christians who espouse a pretribulation rapture interpret this event as a reward for faithful Christians who will avoid a time of tribulation on earth. Interestingly, the ancient author of the First Apocryphal Apocalypse of John does not interpret 1 Thessalonians 4:17 in this way, or at least feels free to adapt this Pauline tradition. Instead of believers exclusively being taken up to the sky, this author depicts the whole of humanity, important church paraphernalia, as well as the antichrist and evil spirits all being taken up to the clouds. As an insight into how some early Christians interpreted 1 Thessalonians 4, this text is evidence for a diversity of views about the order and nature of events at the end of time. The point here is that they are protected while the earth is cleansed and preserved to face judgment on God's terms.

4.4 Similarity to Revelation

John Court claims that the First Apocryphal Apocalypse of John "imitates the canonical book of Revelation."[44] Other scholars have claimed it may be an attempt to complete Revelation by filling in some gaps.[45] While both positions are a little overstated, it is certain that this author is very familiar with Revelation and that he adapts and extends images from it. In this sense, his use of Revelation is in keeping with that of Paul's Thessalonian correspondence (discussed above).

The first clear indication that Revelation has influenced this author's theology occurs in chapter 2 when John sees a large, sealed book in heaven. The book's seven seals are much like those in Revelation 5:1 as is its location in heaven. In Revelation, the content of the book is not known until it is opened. In the First Apocryphal Apocalypse of John, however, the divine voice declares that the book contains knowledge of "heaven, earth, and the abyss, and judgments on the whole of human nature and righteousness." These are essentially all the things John wants to know about. Whereas in Revelation the Lamb, the only one worthy to open the book, appears almost immediately, in the First Apocryphal Apocalypse of John there is a delay while Jesus answers some of John's other questions related to the nature of resurrected bodies.

---

42. Cf. Matt 24:31 for a similar idea of the "elect" being taken up by the Son of Man.

43. Paul may well be drawing upon Ps 47:5 (LXX Ps 46:6) in 1 Thess 4:16–17, in which case he has taken a psalm about God and applied it to Jesus, indicating a very early, high Christology. That Jesus would descend the same way he ascended is also found in Acts 1:11. See Evans, *Ancient Texts for New Testament Studies*, 338.

44. Court, *Book of Revelation*, 23.

45. Heinrich Weinel, "Die spätere christliche Apokalyptik," in *EYXAPIΣTHRION: Studien zur Literatur des Alten und des Neuen Testaments*, ed. H. Schmidt, FRLANT 36 (Göttingen: Vandenhoek & Ruprecht, 1923), 149.

The Lamb appears in chapter 18 in response to John's question about what will happen to the heavenly realm. John is told to "look," and he sees a lamb with seven eyes and seven horns, a descriptor that matches the lamb in Revelation (Rev 5:6). The precise sequence differs from that of Revelation and there is far less dramatic tension.[46] Also missing from the First Apocryphal Apocalypse of John is worship of the Lamb, something which is a major theme in Revelation 5 and establishes his identity as Christ and ruler. The First Apocryphal Apocalypse of John does not conflate the risen Jesus with this lamb but rather treats the lamb as another character whose only task is to open the seals. As such, this later use of the lamb tradition lacks the theological significance and drama of the original.

What occurs at the opening of each seal is narrated in a concise and dispassionate manner in chapter 19. In Revelation, the seven seals release a series of judgments that are narrated in great detail over many chapters, thus forming the bulk of the text. This tradition has been remarkably condensed in the First Apocryphal Apocalypse of John, where it simply functions to explain the disappearance of heaven and heavenly bodies (sun, moon, stars) and the appearance of places of judgment and punishment on earth (ch. 19). As such, it is a narrative device that allows the author to move to specific questions about who will be judged and in what order.

The author comes closest to quoting Revelation directly in the penultimate chapter (ch. 27), where he uses three phrases from Revelation 21 to describe paradise: there will be "no pain" (21:4), "no death" (v. 4), and "no night" (v. 25). Each of these is obviously very short, and while the vocabulary is the same, the word order is not, indicating the author may be citing from memory or using a similar refrain. The wider context, however, makes it probable that Revelation 21 is in the author's mind here. To Revelation's depiction of the New Jerusalem this author has added several elements, notably extending the list of vices that are not present in the eschaton. For example, money worries, malicious thoughts, and hatred of brother are just three of several failings added to Revelation's more conventional list of idolaters, sorcerers, murderers, and fornicators.

Other traces of Revelation's vision are apparent in the name of the evil one being on his forehead (ch. 7), four great winds that sweep the earth (ch. 15), many-eyed creatures (ch. 17), and Jerusalem dressed as a bride (ch. 17). None of these motifs are expanded or appear to play a particularly vital role in the First Apocryphal Apocalypse of John. Their inclusion suggests that Revelation's vision of judgment and the end is dominant enough for this author that it cannot be ignored. He is not, however, at pains to simply repeat Revelation but rather uses its themes and language as a common point of reference. Indeed, the concise nature of material in common with Revelation highlights that the foremost concerns of this author are on the nature of resurrected bodies and the order and result of judgment. Far more attention and time is given to these themes in the text. The only biblical traditions on which this author has expanded are those mentioned above: the appearance of the antichrist and the notion that all life is "raptured" or taken up to the clouds before being returned to earth for final judgment.

In conclusion, the First Apocryphal Apocalypse of John is an important, late Christian, early Byzantine text that gives insight into later Christian use of Scripture, conveys ideas about resurrection life, and shows a development of the antichrist tradition and a concern for orthodox expressions of Christianity. Through a question-and-answer style, revelatory

---

46. In Rev 5 the scene is full of emotion, and John cries when he thinks no one is able to open the book and see its contents.

dialogue, this text extends and develops New Testament ideas and teachings, interpreting them for a later time and place.

5. BIBLIOGRAPHY

Brannan, Rick. "1 Apocryphal Apocalypse of John." e-Clavis: Christian Apocrypha. www.nasscal.com/e-clavis -christian-apocrypha/1-apocryphal-apocalypse-of-john/.

———. *The First Apocryphal Apocalypse of John: A Greek Reader.* Appian Way Greek Readers. Bellingham, WA: Appian Way, 2017.

Court, John M. *The Book of Revelation and the Johannine Apocalyptic Tradition.* Sheffield: Sheffield Academic Press, 2000.

Kaestli, Jean-Daniel. "La figure de l'antichrist dans l'Apocalypse de Saint Jean le Théologien (Première Apocalypse Apocryphe de Jean)." Pages 277–90 in *Les forces du bien et du mal dans les premiers siècles de l'église.* Edited by J.-M. Blanchard, B. Pouderon, and M. Scopello. Théologie historique 118. Paris: Beauchesne, 2011.

Papadoyannakis, Yannis. "Instruction by Question and Answer: The Case of Late Antique and Byzantine Erotapokriseis." Pages 91–106 in *Greek Literature in Late Antiquity: Dynamism, Didacticism, Classicism.* Edited by Scott F. Johnson. Burlington, VT: Ashgate, 2006.

Tischendorf, Constantinus. Pages 70–94 of *Apocalypses Apocryphae: Mosis, Esdrae, Pauli, Iohannis, Item Mariae Dormitio.* Leipzig: Mendelssohn, 1866.

Tóth, Péter. "New Wine in Old Wineskin: Byzantine Reuses of the Apocryphal Revelation Dialogue." Pages 77–93 in *Dialogues and Debate from Late Antiquity to Late Byzantium.* New York: Routledge, 2017.

Volgers, A., and Claudio Zamagni, eds. *Erotapokriseis: Early Christian Question-and-Answer Literature in Context.* Contributions to Biblical Exegesis and Theology 37. Leuven: Peeters, 2004.

Weinel, Heinrich. "Die spätere christliche Apokalyptik." Pages 141–73 in *EYXAPIΣTHRION: Studien zur Literatur des Alten und des Neuen Testaments.* Edited by H. Schmidt. FRLANT 36. Göttingen: Vandenhoek & Ruprecht, 1923.

Whealey, Alice. "The Apocryphal Apocalypse of John: A Byzantine Apocalypse from the Early Islamic Period." *JTS* 53.2 (2002): 533–40.

CONCLUSION

CONCLUSION

CHAPTER 29

NEW TESTAMENT APOCRYPHA: INTRODUCTION AND CRITIQUE OF A MODERN CATEGORY

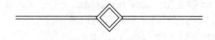

DALE B. MARTIN

The title *New Testament Apocrypha*—or as people may also encounter it, the *Apocryphal New Testament*—is sometimes confusing. The different parts of the phrase don't mean what the phrase looks like it should mean. And the phrase does not mean what most people may think it means. So let's take it apart.

Apocryphal to many people will mean "something that people may suppose to be true or historical but is not." As in: "I believe that old story about Professor Smith and his umbrella is apocryphal." In that context, the meaning is that a story has circulated as true but really isn't, or at least is doubtful. In this very common use, *apocryphal* just means "fictional" or "false," even if there is no nefarious intention implied in the telling.

But the most basic meaning of *apocryphal* comes from the Greek word *apokryphos* (ἀπόκρυφος), which means "something hidden." Probably the most common occurrence of the word people may now encounter is in the neuter form, *apocryphon*; or the neuter plural form, *apocrypha*. Etymologically, the word may be broken down into the Greek *kryphon*, "hidden," and *apo*, "away." So something that is "apocryphal" is something that has been "hidden away." When referring to a piece of knowledge or writing, the meaning is that something is esoteric, something meant to be hidden and exposed to only a select few. In the ancient world, perhaps even more so than in the modern, knowledge was considered "special" or "esoteric" if it was available only to a few people. This is probably the meaning of the term at the beginning of the Gospel of Thomas, which announces itself as "the hidden sayings of the living Jesus, which Didymus Judas Thomas recorded."[1] The author or editor is certainly not implying that the book is dangerous or false, only that it may contain teachings that are appropriate only for "certain ears."

It is difficult to say, for example, what Clement of Alexandria (who lived and wrote around the year 200 CE) had in mind when he mentions "hidden books" (βίβλοι

---

1. One may consult, for English translation, Bentley Layton, ed., *The Gnostic Scriptures: A New Translation with Annotations and Introductions by Bentley Layton* (Garden City, NY: Doubleday, 1987), 380. Layton's text uses the word "obscure," but a footnote indicates that the word may also be translated as "hidden." In this, Gos. Thom. saying 1, the word "hidden," taken to be from the Greek for "apocryphal," has been supplied by the editor, given a lacuna in the manuscript evidence. But in Gos. Thom. saying 5, different versions of some Greek for "hidden" (including a form of *apocrypha*) are discernable in the manuscripts. So the editor's understanding that the Gos. Thomas announced itself as "hidden" or "esoteric," using some form of the word *apocryphal*, is defensible.

ἀπόκρυφοι) claimed by followers of "Prodicus" to be in their possession (*Stromata* 1.15.69.6). Clement apparently considers the content of these books as derived from Zoroaster, the Persian *magos*. And he calls the group a "sect," using the term *hairesis*, that took its inspiration from a "Prodicus." Some translators render that word as "heresy," but since this seems to be a reference to followers of a philosopher (if "Prodicus" is intended to be the Stoic philosopher, which is likely), Clement could mean only the "school" or "sect" of philosophy that took Prodicus to be their leader. We may note also that Clement himself can praise the use of esoteric knowledge, passed along orally and only to more initiated persons (see ch. 12 of the same first book of Clement's *Stromata*).

But other Christian authors use the term against Christians they consider "false" or "heretical," and include those Christians' books also in their condemnations. Around 200 CE, Irenaeus condemns Christians he considered heretics, calling them "Marcosians." He accuses them of creating their own "apocryphal" and "forged" books, so Irenaeus could equate an "apocryphal" book with a "forgery" (Irenaeus, *Haer.* 1.20.1; the word for "forgery" is νόθος). Around the same time, the Latin author Tertullian equates *apocrypha* with *falsa* (*De pudicitia* 10.12). So, for some Christian authors, *apocryphal* became synonymous with *false*. But we must remember that the equation was not assumed by all people, even by all Christian authors.

Although *apocrypha* would often be taken to refer to hidden, esoteric, or false documents, that is not at all the meaning of the term when found in the title *New Testament Apocrypha*. The phrase has a complicated and rather confusing history that needs to be explained.

Any reference to *New Testament Apocrypha* is dependent on the much older and more established title, *the Apocrypha*. And we should put emphasis on *the*, because for many centuries there was no recognition of *New Testament Apocrypha* as opposed to *Old Testament Apocrypha*. There was only *the Apocrypha*, which referred to a collection of documents that were published as part of many Christian Bibles, but often separated from the Old Testament and the New Testament. The explanation of the term *the Apocrypha* is itself dependent on the creation of the Christian canon of Scripture, which took centuries to come about. This is not the place to provide a complete "history of the canon" or the history of how the Christian Bible became completed, collected, and published together.[2] But I can provide a very brief history.

From an early period of Christian history, say from around 50 to 100 CE, some letters of Paul were being circulated in collections. We may imagine that some churches to whom he sent letters made copies of those letters, grouped them with letters they collected from other churches, and sent them around in what we may imagine to have been pamphlets, all hand-copied and hand-circulated, of course, since the printing press had not yet been invented. Later, in the second century, some Christians began also circulating copies they made of the earliest Gospels, which were certainly Mark (the earliest, from around 70 CE), and Matthew and Luke (both of which used Mark as a source for their own Gospels, and so must have post-dated Mark). Later, the Gospel we know as John probably was composed

---

2. A modern classic of the history of the canon is Hans von Campenhausen, *The Formation of the Christian Bible* (Philadelphia: Fortress, 1972). For more recent, and varied, discussions, see Einar Thomassen, ed., *Canon and Canonicity: The Formation and Use of Scripture* (Copenhagen: Museum Tusculanum, 2010). My own account of the creation of the canon and its meaning may be found in Dale B. Martin, *New Testament History and Literature* (New Haven: Yale University Press, 2012), 15–33. For a more theological, rather than simply historical, account of the canon, see idem, *Biblical Truths: The Meaning of Scripture in the Twenty-First Century* (New Haven: Yale University Press, 2017), 71–110.

and circulated around the years 90 to 110, or perhaps even later.[3] There was no attempt at this early date to proclaim that these, and only these, documents were "holy," or "Scripture," or, even less likely, "the New Testament." They were just texts that some Christians took to be important for the story of Jesus, Paul, and the beginnings of the Jesus movement.

It was only in the late second century, say around the year 200 CE, that "our" four Gospels became better established as Christian "Scripture," along with several letters by Paul, in addition to other letters claiming to be by Paul.[4] Only gradually, and later, did other writings (Hebrews; James; 1 and 2 Peter; 1, 2, and 3 John; Jude; and Revelation) become accepted as "Scripture," usually meaning that they were permitted for public reading in the liturgies of churches. But the "canon" of the New Testament took centuries to be established and accepted by at least many churches.

There was no one ecumenical council of the entire Christian church that finalized, forever and for everyone, what counted as "the New Testament." Even today, some churches among what we may call Eastern forms of Christianity do not allow the book of Revelation to be read in their public liturgy. We can generally say, however, that the canon of the Bible, at least for most Christians, became more settled in the fourth to sixth centuries CE. But that represents a long and controversial process of church deliberation, among many different churches and church leaders, we should add, about what should constitute the "canon" of the "Bible" for Christians.

That last sentence introduces the issue of what we mean by *canon*. The word comes from, very early, a Semitic word for a "reed," something that was used for measuring things. It was taken into Greek to mean a measuring stick, or, eventually, any kind of norm or standard. So *canon* could refer to any series of values or standards to which something else could be compared. It could be used to speak of a "norm" or "criterion" of philosophy: what should be counted as "normal philosophical values."[5] From those common uses of the term *canon*, Christians eventually developed the idea that a *canon* could be a list of books that should be allowed to be read in the liturgy of the church. That is, they began to equate *canon* to "liturgically approved Scripture."[6] Thus, in many ancient manuscripts we find lists of books that are "approved" compared with other books that are "allowed" for private (but not public) reading, and contrasted with other books that are "forbidden" or considered misleading or heretical. Here, in these so-called canon lists of ancient Christian manuscripts, we find the beginnings of the later Christian equation of "canon" with "the Bible."

From an early period, there were some books, however, that occupied something like a middle ground between "canon" and "not permitted." These were texts composed almost certainly by Jews, and often by Greek-speaking Jews, in the years of the Second Temple period, say from around 350 BCE to 70 CE. The books were sometimes certainly composed originally in Hebrew or Aramaic—such as, for example, Tobit. Others seem to have been

---

3. These Gospels were written and circulated probably without any names attached. The names Matthew, Mark, Luke, and John were added to the text only in the second century, and probably the late second century, close to the year 200 CE.

4. Critical scholars are convinced that only seven of the New Testament letters claiming to be by Paul were actually written by him (Romans, 1 and 2 Corinthians, Galatians, Philippians, 1 Thessalonians, and Philemon). The others were written, we think, by later disciples of Paul, often using his own letters as models for their own creations in his name.

5. See 4 Macc 7.21; Epictetus, *Diatribai (Dissertationes)* 2.11.24.

6. It should be noted that Christianity never did completely equate *canon* with Scripture, at least not until the modern period and mainly with Protestantism. *Scripture* could refer to all kinds of holy writings. But *canon* came to refer to a closed list or category of "these and only these writings." For a more nuanced comparison of the categories of canon and Scripture, see Martin, *Biblical Truths*, 75–78.

originally composed in Greek, though probably by Jews—such as the Wisdom of Solomon. Indeed, the book known variously as Sirach, Ecclesiasticus, or the Wisdom of Jesus Son of Sirach, was obviously composed in Hebrew sometime before 180 BCE, translated by the author's grandson sometime after 132 BCE, into Greek, and survives in versions and fragments in different languages. At any rate, by the time Christians started putting together their collections of what they considered the canon, or Scripture, these specific books (as opposed to those books that eventually came to make up rabbinic Scripture or the Protestant Old Testament) survived not in Hebrew or Aramaic, for the most part, but in Greek or Greek translations. Christians, including apparently Jewish Christians, did not seem to find that a problem. So these texts were considered part of the Christian Bible by Roman Catholics and Eastern Orthodox churches, along with many other branches of Christianity. They were usually just interspersed with other documents of the Old Testament, whether as books of "history," "prophecy," "writings," or whatever genre.

For example, in older Bibles, the books of Tobit and Judith were included simply after the "historical books" of Ezra and Nehemiah and before the book of Esther. Then, after Esther, one would find the books of 1 and 2 Maccabees. It was mainly in the Protestant Reformation, led especially by Martin Luther and John Calvin, that these books—that may have been written in Hebrew or Aramaic but that survived almost exclusively in Greek translations—became questionable for inclusion in the Old Testament. So they were excluded by most Protestant churches from the Old Testament entirely, or sometimes placed in a special place, between the Old Testament and the New Testament or in an appendix, in Protestant Bibles. These books are not, and have never been, really "hidden" or completely "forbidden." They were just considered by Protestants as not having the same status as the Old Testament or the New Testament.

One can easily find these books, and lists of them, in many modern Bibles, especially "study" Bibles designed for seminary or academic study of the Bible and the history of the Bible. In *The New Oxford Annotated Bible: New Revised Standard Version with the Apocrypha*,[7] some eighteen or so such books are included, but one can find different lists in different Bibles.[8] These books are variously called *the Apocrypha* or the *deuterocanonical books*. The term *deuterocanonical* just means "of secondary status to the undisputed canonical books" of the Old Testament.

To sum up a long history with an overly simplistic explanation: the collection of texts included in some modern Bibles as the Apocrypha came about because Protestants decided that their Bibles should contain, as the Old Testament, only those books that survived in Hebrew or Aramaic, and that the Jewish books that survived mostly or entirely in Greek should have a secondary status. So they left those books out of their Old Testament and included them in a special section of their Bibles called the Apocrypha.

But we must be clear about the history, especially because the word *apocrypha* can be misunderstood. The Apocrypha designated books and fragments of books that had never been really "hidden" to any significant extent by the church or anyone else. There was no conspiracy entertained to keep these texts out of the hands of ordinary Christians.

---

7. Michael D. Coogan et al., eds., *The New Oxford Annotated Bible: New Revised Standard Version with the Apocrypha*, 3rd ed. (New York: Oxford University Press, 2001).

8. I say "some eighteen or so such books" because it depends on how one counts them. Some texts included in collections of the Apocrypha are actually just partial books; for example, the additions to Old Testament books such as Daniel or Esther. Some lists of the Apocrypha include Psalm 151, which in older Bibles followed Psalm 150, but which is not included in most Protestant Bibles. And different collections of the Apocrypha in modern Bibles do not all include the same texts. So the numbering of them cannot be stated exactly.

Nor were these texts considered by most Christians, including many Protestants, to be "heretical" or any more "false" than any part of the Bible. The term designated texts that were eventually excluded from most *Protestant* Bibles because they were written or survived in Greek rather than Hebrew. So for most of Christian history, including most of Protestant history, there was nothing nefarious or conspiratorial about the existence of the Apocrypha. In Roman Catholic, Eastern Orthodox, and Anglican Churches, one may hear passages of these texts still read as part of the public liturgy. The texts that are now called the Apocrypha have existed since ancient times, were recognized for most of history as part of the Christian Bible, were recommended for reading both in public liturgy and for private edification, and during the Protestant Reformation became a collection of ancient texts included in some Bibles, though often as a separate section or an appendix.

This is important for our purposes here, because the texts often published as New Testament Apocrypha never existed before the modern period in any of those senses. There never was a collection of New Testament Apocrypha in the ancient or medieval worlds. Such documents, however we want to count them (and as we will see that is controversial and unsettled), were never recognized, even until now, as a genre or body of literature. And these documents never had any extensive presence or importance in Christian churches or in any major denomination. *New Testament Apocrypha* does not refer to a recognized body of literature, did not evolve historically or liturgically in the Christian church, and is an invention of scholars of the modern world. The term *New Testament Apocrypha* is certainly dependent on the existence, for centuries, of the category of "the Apocrypha." But it is an artificially created, modern category that has none of the more ancient, organic, or liturgical characteristics of *the* Apocrypha.

So where and when did the name *New Testament Apocrypha* come about? One of the most important modern publications of apocryphal New Testament texts traces the beginning of the concept (of New Testament Apocrypha, though not the phrase itself) to a "Latin lives of apostles" published in 1531 by Friedrich Nausea (yes, that is apparently a translation of his name, or at least his nickname).[9] The editors say that this collection "may be recognized as the first attempt at a collection of apocryphal literature" (they mean *New Testament* apocryphal literature, since of course *the* Apocrypha had existed from long before, both in concept and in name). But the editors' designation is clearly an anachronistic retrojection. The publication presents itself simply as a collection of "popular"—that is, noncanonical—Christian stories about the apostles. To call it an early collection of "New Testament apocryphal literature" is simply inaccurate. The category at the time probably did not exist.

Hennecke-Schneemelcher, one of the most important modern discussions and collections of "New Testament Apocrypha" in both German and English, then mentions an early collection of texts that actually uses, in Latin, the term *apocrypha* for its contents: Michael Neander, *Apocrypha, hoc est, narrationes de Christo, Maria, Josepho, cognatione et familia Christi, extra biblia etc.*, published in Basel in 1564.[10] We should note that the term *apocrypha* is used, but not the term *New Testament Apocrypha*. And the term is glossed as stories of Christ, Mary, Joseph, and Christ's *familia* that are *extra biblia*—that is, not found in the Bible. Hennecke-Schneemelcher adds that the purpose of this book was to provide the humanist with material to be used in educating his pupils.[11] In other words,

---

9. *NTApoc* 1:66. The title of the Latin work referred to was *Anonymi Philalethi Eusebiani In vitas, miracula, passionesque apostolorum rhapsodiae, antehac typis haudquaquam excusae.-"A la fin."*
10. *NTApoc* 1:66.
11. *NTApoc* 1:66.

this collection was a scholarly category for educational purposes. It was not created, at least according to Hennecke-Schneemelcher, for liturgical purposes.

The first book mentioned by Hennecke-Schneemelcher that actually uses the term *New Testament Apocrypha* is Johann Albert Fabricius, *Codex Apocryphus Novi Testamenti* (1703), in three volumes.[12] The first volume offers Latin versions of noncanonical Gospels and fragments of texts it calls Gospels, including some epistles of Pilate and others. The second volume presents mainly Acts, Epistles, and Apocalypses. And the third expands to include all kinds of other texts, including liturgical documents and the Shepherd of Hermas (now included in "the Apostolic Fathers") and other rather random texts.

The real interest and publication of "New Testament Apocrypha" texts increased in the nineteenth century. So we have Johann Karl Thilo, *Codex apocryphus Novi Testamenti* (Leipzig: Vogel, 1832). Thereafter occur the several important publications by that paragon of nineteenth-century scholarship of biblical and early Christian history, Constantine Tischendorf, publications that took place in 1851, 1852, 1866, and 1876.[13] The editing and publishing of "New Testament Apocrypha" texts then really took off in the twentieth century, as any internet or library search can demonstrate.

What is truly interesting is that a survey of those modern publications of "New Testament Apocrypha" shows just how problematic and disputable the very category or genre is. I have already referred to the twentieth-century collection of "New Testament Apocrypha" by Edgar Hennecke, later edited by Wilhelm Schneemelcher, and translated by R. McL. Wilson, published in German first in 1904. Its several editions, translations, and publications did much to define the topic for twentieth- and twenty-first-century scholarship. The several editions and their introductions may be used to study the confusion surrounding the entire topic.

For example, in the general introduction to the third edition (in vol. 1 of the English translation of 1963, p. 19), Schneemelcher notes, "The concept 'New Testament Apocrypha' was probably formed on the analogy of that of the 'Old Testament Apocrypha.'" This is misleading in two ways. First, there is no "probably" about it. It is obvious that the term *New Testament Apocrypha* would never have existed had scholars not already had a centuries-old term of *the Apocrypha* to refer to "biblical" writings that were of some disputed canonicity. Second, the term *Old Testament Apocrypha* was not a concept either until later contrasted with *New Testament Apocrypha*. Throughout most of history, the term *the Apocrypha* was taken to refer to a body of texts included as "biblical" by some Christians and accepted only as "deuterocanonical" or rejected as noncanonical by other Christians. They didn't call the latter texts *Old Testament Apocrypha*. They just called them *the Apocrypha* if they used the term at all. In fact, the term *Old Testament Apocrypha* is derivative from *New Testament Apocrypha*, which itself was derivative of the older, traditional term *the Apocrypha*. Scholars created, mainly in the nineteenth century, *New Testament Apocrypha*. And then, even later, the term *Old Testament Apocrypha* was invented for what had always been simply *the Apocrypha*.

But once scholars invented the category of *New Testament Apocrypha*, they had to decide what to include in the category. Probably the most conservative requirements would

---

12. I am depending on the history of the discipline from Hennecke-Schneemelcher (*NTApoc* 1:66). The subject could doubtless be improved by new research and bibliographical examination. But my purpose here is not to advance original research into the history of the term *New Testament Apocrypha* but simply to illustrate that it is a modern and constructed category that cannot be traced even to the medieval period, much less the ancient.

13. *NTApoc* 1:67.

be that these would be books that resembled those books actually in the New Testament, which is to say books that looked like one of the four genres of the New Testament: Gospels, Acts (usually of apostles), Letters or Epistles (again usually of apostles or leaders of early Christian churches), and Revelation (or to use the term derived more directly from the Greek, "Apocalypses"). The other criteria might be that these books were ancient and could conceivably have been included in the New Testament canon.

The only document from early Christianity that clearly meets these criteria is the Gospel of Thomas. Most scholars agree that it probably was composed in the second century, maybe even in the first century. So it is at least contemporaneous with the four canonical Gospels. One of the problems with the criteria, though, is that the Gospel of Thomas doesn't present a narrative of the life and ministry of Jesus. It looks mainly like a collection of sayings of Jesus passed on to his disciples, perhaps even after his resurrection. So it does not really look, generically, like the four canonical Gospels after all, which all include sections of Jesus's teachings but also narrative accounts of his life, death, and resurrection. But even though the Gospel of Thomas appears very different from the four canonical Gospels, it was certainly early enough that churches, had they wanted to do so, could have included it among those other Gospels they allowed to be read in church as part of the liturgy.

Few of the other texts that are often included among the *New Testament Apocrypha* meet these limited criteria (of being both early and "like" the canonical genres). And some are very much outside those boundaries. Some scholarly collections, including Hennecke-Schneemelcher, include letters that look nothing like the letters of our New Testament. Editors regularly, for example, include the *Epistula Apostolorum*, an "epistle" sent out by all the apostles.[14] It is actually of a genre (known from other sources in the ancient world) that is not one of the New Testament proper. It is in the form of a letter from the apostles as a group, but it mainly consists of a dialogue between the raised Jesus and the apostles. It is a "group authorized" letter that contains a dialogue reported to the churches by the apostles—a dialogue they had with Jesus after his resurrection. This is certainly a kind of early Christian literature, but it is not "New Testament" in genre or orientation. Nor was it supposed to be "hidden." What could make this document either "apocryphal" or "New Testament" is not at all obvious.

Another document included by Hennecke-Schneemelcher is *The Two Books of Jeu*. This is, in the words of the editors, "a didactic treatise in the form of a revelation."[15] That is entirely correct. But that also means it is not a Gospel in any sense that should be derived from the New Testament. It is a different kind of early Christian genre of literature, familiar to scholars and valuable in itself, but one that can hardly be adequately called *New Testament Apocrypha*. It is "a didactic treatise in the form of a revelation," as the editors themselves describe it.

Another genre that editors often include as New Testament Gospel Apocrypha are simply "sayings" of Jesus or random stories about him derived from different sources. Hennecke-Schneemelcher have one section called "Isolated Sayings of the Lord,"[16] which include simply sayings of or about Jesus gleaned from different ancient sources, such as church fathers. Or "Fragments of Unknown Gospels."[17] There is no scholarly reason to call these *Gospels* (they are not narratives that resemble the Gospels of the New Testament),

---

14. See the discussion at *NTApoc* 1:249–84.
15. *NTApoc* 1:370.
16. *NTApoc* 1:88–91.
17. *NTApoc* 1:92–109.

and there is little reason to believe they are all Gospels. The genre or category of New Testament Apocrypha has been stretched to be without meaning.

Another famous collection of the apocryphal New Testament may be used also to illustrate these problems of classification. The volume by J. K. Elliott titled *The Apocryphal New Testament: A Collection of Apocryphal Christian Literature in an English Translation* (Oxford: Clarendon, 1993), is a reworking of W. Hone's *The Apocryphal New Testament* (London: William Hone, 1820). Elliott admits that the very title of the collection is something of a problem. He admits that most of the books included were not "hidden" or "secret," though a few claim to have been. And the "more normal" meaning of *apocryphal* as "spurious, fictitious, or false" would apply to these texts no more than to most books of the New Testament.[18]

Moreover, the genres of many of these texts don't resemble those of the New Testament. "Many of the texts translated here have no obvious link with the genres of literature to be found in the canonical New Testament."[19] In particular, Elliott cites the Epistle of the Apostles (*Epistula Apostolorum*), which we have already encountered, as nothing like a letter of the canon but rather of a genre of "dialogues of the risen Jesus." Several other documents in the section designated "apocryphal Gospels" are not like the canonical Gospels at all.[20] The different "quotations" of or about Jesus or his family are placed under the rubric of "agrapha"—the literal meaning of which is "unwritten," though of course they *were* written or we wouldn't have them at all. They are just sayings attributed to Jesus that we do not have in our canonical Gospels.[21] Elliott admits that the category, as a category of literary *genre*, makes no sense.

Elliott also admits that many other kinds of early Christian literature that are also noncanonical are usually excluded from books claiming to publish "New Testament Apocrypha," such as the Apostolic Fathers, the texts of the Nag Hammadi Library, texts that "deal with church order and liturgy" (such as the Apostolic Constitutions), "all Rabbinic and Islamic traditions about Jesus" (though, as we will see, some collections do include a few such documents), and "Christian or Christianized books bearing the name of Old Testament worthies," which Elliott assigns to the category "Old Testament pseudepigrapha."[22] What is the rationale for excluding all such documents from his category "New Testament Apocrypha"? Mainly, he explains, just because those texts are available in other editions and translations.

Elliott also addresses another controversial question about the category: Is there a chronological limit? Are only "early" Christian documents, say, from the first few centuries of Christianity—whether Gospels, Acts, Letters, or Apocalypses—to be included? He says no. "One cannot really tie the production of apocryphal texts to a limited period up to, say, the fourth century."[23] This then raises the question as to why one should not include, therefore, later works, such as the *Book of Mormon* (first published in 1830); Kahlil Gibran, *The Prophet* (1923); Nikos Kazantzakis, *The Last Temptation of Christ* (1960); or even Dan Brown, *The Da Vinci Code* (2003)?[24]

---

18. Elliott, *Apocryphal New Testament*, xii.

19. Elliott, *Apocryphal New Testament*, xi.

20. Elliott, *Apocryphal New Testament*, xi.

21. Elliott, *Apocryphal New Testament*, 26.

22. Elliott, *Apocryphal New Testament*, xiii. Perhaps the most well-known publication of Old Testament pseudepigrapha in English translation is James H. Charlesworth, ed., *Old Testament Pseudepigrapha*, 2 vols. (New York: Doubleday, 1983, 1985).

23. Elliott, *Apocryphal New Testament*, x.

24. Joseph Smith, *The Book of Mormon: An Account Written by the Hand of Mormon upon Plates Taken*

So why retain the title *New Testament Apocrypha* even when Elliott recognizes the problems of the designation? Mainly just because, he claims, that is the genre category that many of his readers will already know: "Most readers turning to a book with this title are usually aware of the sort of literature they expect to find within its covers."[25] Having spent a career speaking about such texts and their origins to all kinds of audiences, I would have to disagree. In fact, most people in my experience, both scholars and lay audiences, are regularly confused about the contents or rationale of the category *New Testament Apocrypha*. Why these texts and not others? So far, I've yet to find a scholar to give a rationale or coherent answer.

Other texts often included in collections of *New Testament Apocrypha* have even less claim to the title. The medieval document often called Toledot Yeshu is sometimes called an "apocryphal Gospel of Jesus." But it is actually a medieval Jewish, anti-Christian document that depicts Jesus as the illegitimate son of Mary, a young girl impregnated by a Roman soldier with the name or nickname of "Panther."[26] Jesus performs miracles by means of magic and deceives the people. It is quite a stretch to call this a Gospel, much less something that might have been considered for inclusion in the Christian canon, the New Testament.

This is not at all to say that Toledot Yeshu does not merit study, but it should be studied for its own sake: as a document illustrating the controversies of the "history of religions," especially the debates among Jews and Christians. But to call it *New Testament Apocrypha* misleadingly implies that it is of the same genre classification as the documents of the New Testament, that it may supplement our historical or theological interpretations of the historical Jesus or even the Christ of early Christian faith, or that it could even have conceivably been considered for inclusion in the Christian Bible. None of those claims for the document can be responsibly supported. It should be called, as it is, Jewish narrative fiction that illustrates later Jewish-Christian disputes about Jesus.

This brief survey of what has counted as New Testament Apocrypha in the modern world of publishing is intended to call into question the very category or genre. Many more examples of documents often called New Testament Apocrypha, but with questionable motives or defense, could be cited. But I hope to have illustrated that what is included or what is excluded in such collections ends up seeming rather arbitrary. This observation may be supported by noting how the great Hennecke-Schneemelcher editors characterize one competitor of their own collection. They mention Aurelio de Santos Otero, *Los Evangelios apócrifos, Colección de textos griegos y latinos, versión crítica, estudios introductorios, comentarios e ilustraciones*, Biblioteca de Autores Christianos 148 (Madrid: Editorial Católia, 1956). But then they dismiss it by saying that it "can be no substitute for a scientific edition of the whole of the material."[27] But this statement is indefensible on its face: What *could* or

---

from the Plates of Nephi (Palmyra, NY: E. B. Grandin, 1830); Kahlil Gibran, *The Prophet* (New York: Alfred A. Knopf, 1923); Nikos Kazantzakis, *The Last Temptation of Christ* (New York: Simon and Schuster, 1960); Dan Brown, *The Da Vinci Code* (New York: Doubleday, 2003).

25. Elliott, *Apocryphal New Testament*, xii.

26. The legend of Mary's impregnation by a Roman soldier named "Panther" goes back at least to the second-century anti-Christian author Celsus (fragments of Celsus's book from the second century survive only as cited by the church father Origen in *Contra Celsum* (1.32, 33, and 69), written in the third century. Celsus implies he got the story from some Jewish source. My own belief is that the story arose because the Latin *pantheros* (or *panteros*; meaning "panther") was not an unknown name or nickname for a Roman soldier, and that it is close to the spelling, in Greek, of *parthenos* (παρθένος), meaning "virgin." It would have been an easy way to question Christian teachings about the virgin birth of Jesus by Mary.

27. Edgar Hennecke and Wilhelm Schneemelcher, eds., *New Testament Apocrypha*, 2 vols. (Philadelphia: Westminster, 1963–1965), 1:66. The 1991 revised edition changes the wording and offers a more positive appraisal of de Santos Otero's work (*NTApoc* 1:67).

would count as an edition of "the whole of the material"? As we have seen, what a scholar includes in such a collection could range from ancient to medieval texts, from Christian to Jewish (or Islamic, for that matter) documents, from sayings of church fathers to modern texts such as the *Book of Mormon*. There are simply no criteria by which to determine what would be "the whole of the material" of the modern categorical invention of "New Testament Apocrypha."

But the statement shows that the authors, or at least Schneemelcher by the time he published his own revision of the collection, were working as if there was a "genre" of "New Testament Apocrypha" that they assumed was self-evidently discernible, that a scholar could even speak of some collection that could include "the whole" of "New Testament Apocrypha," and that their two volumes do precisely that, at least better than the publication of de Santos Otero. The claim is self-serving and bogus. But it should encourage scholars to examine, critically, the publishing category of "New Testament Apocrypha" itself.

To review briefly, what is generally *not* included as "New Testament Apocrypha"? Most recent and current editions do not include the collection now known as the Apostolic Fathers; almost all patristic literature of a theological, philosophical, or historical nature except for a few fragments that relate to Jesus and possibly his family; the so-called Nag Hammadi library; general documents addressing issues of liturgy; and modern creations purporting to be by or about Jesus or early Christians, such as the *Book of Mormon* or modern historical novels of Jesus, Paul, or other early Christian characters.

What is included? Practically any document the editor considers to have something to do with Jesus, his family, other early Christian characters, or narratives or sayings on such topics that are not included in the Bible.

I want to emphasize that my comments are not meant to imply that the documents sometimes called *New Testament Apocrypha* are unworthy of study. But we must be clear about why we want to study them. They almost certainly do not provide us with any useful historical material about Jesus, Paul, or other early Christians or Christian history that cannot be found within the New Testament, except perhaps for the Gospel of Thomas, which may well contain forms of sayings of the historical Jesus different from those in our canon and valuable for historical purposes. But all the other early Christian literature would be categorized much more accurately as noncanonical early Christian narrative and sayings. It is simply popular early Christian literature.

And that literature deserves our attention. Much of it provides useful historical information for early Christian debates, Christian imagination, Christian literary creativity, and not least early Christian theology and especially Christology. And much of it is highly entertaining. Once one has read the Infancy Gospel of Thomas, who can forget the delightful story of Jesus making birds out of mud and clay and then happily clapping his hands to make them fly away? Or from the Acts of Andrew, the scene where the ruler Aegeates is straining away in pain on his chamber pot while the apostle Andrew and his companions, unseen, sneak out of the bedroom of Aegeates's wife? So we should cherish and study these documents, and teach them. We just do not need to think that they supplement, in any important way, the New Testament except as representing later Christian literature. They are better represented as early Christian extrabiblical narrative literature than as "New Testament Apocrypha."

So where should we go from here, if we may agree that the label *New Testament Apocrypha* is too misleading for the future? I would suggest two different, but possibly complementary, solutions.

First, we could just use some designation that more correctly signals what kind of literature we are naming. Probably the most succinct but accurate designation would be something like "early Christian noncanonical fiction." This would include all kinds of early Christian literature not found in the Bible, such as gospels, letters, apocalypses, and "acts" about early Christian "apostles" or heroes. In other words, the term would include literary genres that were created to imitate the four genres found in the New Testament. But it would also *not* be intended to include the vast writings of the church fathers, which better fit categories imitating classical philosophical or theological writings. The apologies of Justin Martyr or Tertullian, the writings on "heresy" by Irenaeus, most of the documents that make up what we now call the Apostolic Fathers, all look more like ancient philosophy or other theoretical and apologetic writings than like the documents of the New Testament. Moreover, this term would exclude writings that more resemble ancient historiography (though the Acts of the Apostles *could* be included here) than ancient "fiction" (to use this last term in a somewhat anachronistic sense). This would include ancient Christian literature that imitates the historical writings of, say, Herodotus, Thucydides, or even Josephus, such as the historical accounts of Eusebius or those Christian authors before him on whom he depended. Grouping documents under the rubric of "early Christian noncanonical fiction" at least is more historically accurate and appropriate than the term *New Testament Apocrypha*.

A different solution, however, may be even better. We could do away with any broad, overarching, generic designation and group different documents of this ancient Christian literature into smaller but more accurate and generic categories. We could simply talk about ancient Christian noncanonical gospels, letters, acts, and apocalypses. That strategy of publication would likewise exclude the kinds of philosophical, doctrinal, theological, and historical texts normally *not* included by scholars in what they call *New Testament Apocrypha*. And it would allow for inclusion of ancient Christian literature that imitates New Testament literature but that is not included in the New Testament. That, after all, is what is normally meant by *New Testament Apocrypha*.

In any case, whether scholars continue to use the genre designation *New Testament Apocrypha* or throw it out to come up with other genre designations that are historically more defensible, a critical awareness of the problems of the term *New Testament Apocrypha* is necessary for responsible modern scholarship.

BIBLIOGRAPHY

Burke, Tony, and Brent Landau. *New Testament Apocrypha: More Noncanonical Scripture*. Vol 1. Grand Rapids: Eerdmans, 2016.

Ehrman, Bart D., and Zlatko Pleše, *The Apocryphal Gospels: Texts and Translations*. New York: Oxford University Press, 2011.

Elliott, J. K. *The Apocryphal New Testament: A Collection of Apocryphal Christian Literature in an English Translation*. Oxford: Clarendon, 1993.

Hennecke, Edgar. *Neutestamentliche Apokryphen*. 3rd ed. Edited by Wilhelm Schneemelcher. Tübingen: Mohr Siebeck, 1959. (Originally published in 1904.)

Hennecke, Edgar, and Wilhelm Schneemelcher, eds. *New Testament Apocrypha*. 2 vols. English translation edited by R. McL. Wilson. Philadelphia: Westminster, 1963–1965.

Martin, Dale B. *Biblical Truths: The Meaning of Scripture in the Twenty-First Century*. New Haven: Yale University Press, 2017.

———. *New Testament History and Literature*. New Haven: Yale University Press, 2012.

Thomassen, Einar, ed. *Canon and Canonicity: The Formation and Use of Scripture*. Copenhagen: Museum Tusculanum, 2010.

BIBLIOGRAPHY

CHAPTER 1: AGRAPHA
Primary Sources: Edited Collections of Agrapha

Asin y Palacos, Michael. *Logia et agrapha Domini Jesus apud Moslemicos Scriptores*. Edited by R. Graffin and F. Nau. Patrologia Orientalis 13, 19. Paris: Firmin-Didot, 1919, 1926. Pages 335–441 (vol. 13) and pages 531–624 (vol. 19).

Berger, Klaus, and Christiane Nord. "Agrapha." Pages 1114–202 in *Das Neue Testament und Frühchristliche Schriften*. Frankfurt: Insel, 2005.

Hofius, Otfried. "Isolated Sayings of the Lord." *NTApoc* 1:88–91.

——. "Unknown Sayings of Jesus." Pages 336–60 in *The Gospel and the Gospels*. Edited by Peter Stuhlmacher. Grand Rapid: Eerdmans, 1991.

Jeremias, Joachim. *Unknown Sayings of Jesus*. 2nd English ed. London: SPCK, 1964.

Pesce, Mauro. *Le Parole Dimenticate di Gesù*. Scrittori Greci e Latini. Milan: Fondazione Lorenzo Valla / Arnoldo Mondadore Editore, 2004.

Resch, Alfred. *Agrapha: Aussercanonische Schriftfragmente*. 2nd ed. TU NF 15.3–4. Leipzig: J. C. Hinrichs, 1906. Repr., Darmstadt: Wissenschaftliche Buchgesellschaft, 1976.

Ropes, James Hardy. "Agrapha." Pages 343–52 of the extra volume in *Dictionary of the Bible*. Edited by J. Hastings. Edinburgh: T&T Clark, 1904.

——. *Die Sprüche Jesu: die in den kanonischen Evangelien nicht überliefert sind: eine kritische Bearbeitung des von Alfred Resch gesammelten Materials*. TU 14.2. Leipzig: J. C. Hinrichs, 1896.

Stroker, William D. *Extracanonical Sayings of Jesus*. SBLRBS 18. Atlanta: Scholars Press, 1989.

Secondary Sources

Allison, Dale C. "The Pauline Epistles and the Synoptic Gospels: The Pattern of the Parallels." *NTS* 28 (1982): 1–32.

Bazzana, Giovanni. "'Be Good Moneychangers.' The Role of an Agraphon in a Discursive Fight for the Canon of Scripture." Pages 297–311 in *Invention, Rewriting, Usurpation: Discursive Fights over Religious Traditions in Antiquity*. Edited by J. Ulrich, A.-C. Jacobsen, and D. Brakke. Frankfurt: Peter Lang, 2012.

——. "Replaying Jesus' Sayings in the 'Agrapha': Reflections on the *Neu-Inszenierung* of Jesus' Traditions in the Second Century between 2 *Clement* and Clement of Alexandria." Pages 27–43 in *Gospels and Gospel Traditions in the Second Century: Experiments in Reception*. Edited by J. Schröter, T. Nicklas, and J. Verheyden. BZNW 235. Berlin: de Gruyter, 2019.

Carleton Paget, James. *The Epistle of Barnabas: Outlook and Background*. WUNT 2.64. Tübingen: Mohr Siebeck, 1994.

Dungan, David L. *The Sayings of Jesus in the Churches of Paul*. Oxford: Basil Blackwell; Philadelphia: Fortress, 1971.

Edwards, J. Christopher. *The Gospel According to the Epistle of Barnabas: Jesus Traditions in an Early Christian Polemic*. WUNT 2.503. Tübingen: Mohr Siebeck, 2019.

Gregory, Andrew. "*1 Clement* and the Writings That Later Formed the New Testament." Pages 129–57 in *The Reception of the New Testament in the Apostolic Fathers*. Edited by A. Gregory and C. Tuckett. Oxford: Oxford University Press, 2005.

Hagner, Donald M. *The Use of the Old and New Testaments in Clement of Rome*. NovTSup 32. Leiden: Brill, 1973.

Hartog, Paul. *Polycarp's Epistle to the Philippians and the Martyrdom of Polycarp: Introduction, Text and Commentary*. Oxford Apostolic Fathers. Oxford: Oxford University Press, 2013.

Holmes, Michael. "Polycarp's *Letter to the Philippians* and the Writings That Later Formed the New Testament." Pages 187–228 in *The Reception of the New Testament in the Apostolic Fathers*. Edited by A. Gregory and C. Tuckett. Oxford: Oxford University Press, 2005.

Klauck, Hans-Josef. Pages 6–21 in *Apocryphal Gospels: An Introduction*. London: T&T Clark, 2003.

Knust, Jennifer, and Tommy Wasserman. *To Cast the First Stone: The Transmission of a Gospel Story*. Princeton: Princeton University Press, 2019.

Nicklas, Tobias. "Zur Problematik der so genannten 'Agrapha': Eine Thesenreihe." *Revue Biblique* 113.1 (2006): 78–93.

Norelli, Enrico. "Déchirements et sects: un *agraphon* derrière 1 Corinthiens 11,18–19." Pages 265–85 in *Nuove Testamento: Teologie in Dialogo Culturale*. Edited by N. Ciola and G. Pulcinelli. FS for R. Penna. Supplementi all Rivista Biblica. Bologna: Edizioni Dehoniane Bologna, 2008.

———. "Étude Critique: Une Collection de Paroles de Jésus non comprises dans les Évangiles Canoniques." *Apocrypha* 17 (2006): 223–44.

Roukema, Riemer. "Jesus Tradition in Early Patristic Writings." Pages 2119–47 of vol. 3 in *Handbook for the Study of the Historical Jesus*. Edited by T. Holmén and S. E. Porter. Leiden: Brill, 2010.

Ruwet, J. "Les 'Agrapha' dans les Oeuvres de Clément d'Alexandrie." *Biblica* 30 (1949): 133–60.

Stroker, William D. "Agrapha." *ABD* 1:92–95.

Tuckett, Christopher M. "*2 Clement* and the Writings That Later Formed the New Testament." Pages 252–78 in *The Reception of the New Testament in the Apostolic Fathers*. Edited by A. Gregory and C. Tuckett. Oxford: Oxford University Press, 2005.

———, ed. *2 Clement: Introduction, Text and Commentary*. Oxford Apostolic Fathers. Oxford: Oxford University Press, 2012.

———. "The *Didache* and the Writings That Later Formed the New Testament." Pages 83–127 in *The Reception of the New Testament in the Apostolic Fathers*. Edited by A. Gregory and C. Tuckett. Oxford: Oxford University Press, 2005.

Vos, Johan S. "Das Agraphon 'Seid kundige Geldwechsler!' bei Origenes." Pages 277–302 in *Sayings of Jesus: Canonical and Non-Canonical*. Edited by W. L. Petersen, J. S. Vos, and H. J. de Jonge. FS for T. Baarda. NovTSup 89. Leiden: Brill, 1997.

Walt, Luigi. "Agrapha of Jesus." e-Clavis: Christian Apocrypha. www.nasscal.com/e-clavis-christian-apocrypha/agrapha-of-jesus/.

Wenham, David. "Jesus Tradition in the Letters of the New Testament." Pages 2041–57 of vol. 3 in *Handbook for the Study of the Historical Jesus*. Edited by T. Holmén and S. E. Porter. Leiden: Brill, 2010.

———. *Paul: Follower of Jesus or Founder of Christianity?* Grand Rapids: Eerdmans, 1995.

Young, Stephen E. *Jesus Tradition in the Apostolic Fathers*. WUNT 2.311. Tübingen: Mohr Siebeck, 2011.

CHAPTER 2: GOSPEL FRAGMENTS ON PAPYRUS

Chapa, J. "Uncanonical Gospel?" Pages 1–20 in *The Oxyrhynchus Papyri 76*. Edited by J. Chapa and D. Colomo. Graeco-Roman Memoirs. London: Egyptian Exploration Society, 2011.

Foster, P. "Papyrus Oxyrhynchus X 1224." Pages 59–96 in *Early Christian Manuscripts: Examples of Applied Method and Approach*. Edited by T. J. Kraus and T. Nicklas. Texts and Editions for New Testament Study 5. Leiden: Brill, 2010.

Gronewald, M. "P.Köln VI 255: Unbekanntes Evangelium oder Evangelienharmonie (Fragment aus dem 'Evangelium Egerton')." Pages 136–45 in *Kölner Papyri (P.Köln), Volume VI*. Opladen: Westdeutscher, 1987.

Kraus, T. J. "Other Gospel Fragments." Pages 219–80 in *Gospel Fragments*. Edited by T. J. Kraus, M. J. Kruger, and T. Nicklas. Oxford Early Christian Gospel Texts. Oxford: Oxford University Press, 2009.

———. "*P.Oxy.* V 840—Amulett oder Miniaturkodex? Grundsätzliche und ergänzende Anmerkungen zu zwei Termini." *Zeitschrift für Antikes Christentum* 8 (2005): 485–97. Republished as "*P.Oxy.* V 840—Amulet or Miniature Codex? Principal and Additional Remarks on Two Terms." Pages 47–68 in *Ad fontes: Original Manuscripts and Their Significance for Studying Early Christianity*. By T. J. Kraus. Texts and Editions for New Testament Study 3. Leiden: Brill, 2007.

———. "*P.Vindob.G* 2325: The So-Called Fayûm-Gospel—Re-edition and Some Critical Conclusions." Pages 69–94 in *Ad fontes: Original Manuscripts and Their Significance for Studying Early Christianity*. By T. J. Kraus. Texts and Editions for New Testament Study 3. Leiden: Brill, 2007.

Kraus, T. J., M. J. Kruger, and T. Nicklas, eds. *Gospel Fragments*. Oxford Early Christian Gospel Texts. Oxford: Oxford University Press, 2009.

Kruger, M. J. *The Gospel of the Savior. An Analysis of P.Oxy. 840 and Its Place in the Gospel Traditions of Early Christianity*. Texts and Editions for New Testament Study 1. Leiden: Brill, 2005.

———. "*Papyrus Oxyrhynchus 840*." Pages 123–215 in *Gospel Fragments*. Edited by T. J. Kraus, M. J. Kruger, and T. Nicklas. Oxford Early Christian Gospel Texts. Oxford: Oxford University Press, 2009.

Nicklas, T. "The 'Unknown Gospel' on *Papyrus Egerton* 2 (+ *Papyrus Cologne* 55)." Pages 11–120 in *Gospel Fragments*. Edited by T. J. Kraus, M. J. Kruger, and T. Nicklas. Oxford Early Christian Gospel Texts. Oxford: Oxford University Press, 2009.

Zelyck, L. *The Egerton Gospel (Egerton Papyrus 2 + Papyrus Köln VI 255): Introduction, Critical Edition, and Commentary*. Texts and Editions for New Testament Study 13. Leiden: Brill, 2019.

CHAPTER 3: GOSPEL OF BARNABAS
Primary Sources

Cirillo, Luigi, and Michel Frémaux, eds. *Évangile de Barnabé: Fac-simile, traduction et notes*. 2nd ed. Paris: Éditions Beauchesne, 1999.

———. *Évangile de Barnabé: recherches sur la composition et l'origine.* 1st ed. Paris: Éditions Beauchesne, 1977.

Ragg, Lonsdale, and Laura Ragg, eds. *Gospel of Barnabas.* Oxford: Clarendon, 1907.

Secondary Sources

Blackhirst, R. "*Barnabas* and the Gospels." *Journal of Higher Criticism* 7 (2000): 1–22.

Epalza, Mikel de. "Garcia Gómez und die Autorschaft des Barnabas-Evangeliums." *Religionen im Gespräch* 6 (2000): 10–13.

Giustolisi, Eugenio, and Giuseppe Rizzardi. *Il vangelo di Barnaba: Un vangelo per i musulmani?* Milano: Istituto Propaganda Libraria, 1991.

Hollander, August den, and Ulrich Schmid. "The Gospel of Barnabas, the Diatessaron, and Method." *VC* 61 (2007): 1–20.

Jenkins, Philip. *The Many Faces of Christ: The Thousand-Year Story of the Survival and Influence of the Lost Gospels.* New York: Basic Books, 2015.

Joosten, Jan. "The Date and Provenance of the Gospel of Barnabas." *JTS* 61 (2010): 200–215.

———. "The Gospel of Barnabas and the Diatessaron." *HTR* 95 (2002): 73–96.

———. "Jésus et l'aveugle-né (Jn 9, 1–34) dans l'Évangile de Barnabas et dans le Diatessaron." *RHPR* 80.3 (2000): 359–69.

Leirvik, Oddbjørn. "History as a Literary Weapon: The *Gospel of Barnabas* in Muslim-Christian Polemics." *Studia Theologica* 56.1 (2010): 4–26.

———. *Images of Jesus Christ in Islam.* 2nd ed. London: A&C Black, 2010.

Malcolm, Noel. *Useful Enemies: Islam and the Ottoman Empire in Western Political Thought 1450–1750.* New York: Oxford University Press, 2019.

Pons, Luis F. Bernabé. *El texto morisco del Evangelio de San Bernabé.* Granada: Universidad de Granada, 1998.

Pulcini, Theodore. "In the Shadow of Mount Carmel." *Islam and Christian-Muslim Relations* 12.2 (2001): 191–209.

Reed, Annette Yoshiko. "Muslim Gospel Revealing the 'Christian Truth' Excites the *Da Vinci Code* Set." *Religion Dispatches.* May 22, 2014.

Slomp, Jan. "The Gospel in Dispute." *Islamochristiana* 4.1 (1978): 67–111.

———. "The Gospel of Barnabas in Recent Research." *Islamochristiana* 23 (1997): 81–109.

Sox, David. *The Gospel of Barnabas.* London: Allen & Unwin, 1984.

Toland, John. *Nazarenus, or Jewish, Gentile and Mahometan Christianity.* London: J. Brown, 1718.

Wiegers, Gerald A. "Gospel of Barnabas." In *Encyclopedia of Islam.* 3rd ed. Edited by K. Fleet et al. Leiden: Brill, 2013.

———. "Muhammad as the Messiah." *Biblitheca Orientalis* 52.3/4 (1995): 245–91.

Zahniser, A. H. Mathias. *The Mission and Death of Jesus in Islam and Christianity.* Eugene, OR: Wipf & Stock, 2017.

CHAPTER 4: GOSPEL OF PETER

Augustin, P. *Die Juden im Petrusevangelium: Narratogische Analyse und theologiegeschichtlicke Kontextisierung.* BZNW 214. Berlin: de Gruyter, 2015.

Bouriant, U. "Fragments du texte grec du livre d'Énoch et de quelques écrits attribués à saint Pierre." Pages 93–147 in *Mémoires publiés par les membres de la Mission archéologique française au Caire.* Vol. 9. Paris: Ernest Leroux, 1892.

Brown, R. E. *The Death of the Messiah: From Gethsemane to the Grave.* 2 vols. ABRL. New York: Doubleday, 1994. See esp. vol. 2, appendix 1, pp. 1317–49.

———. "The Gospel of Peter and Canonical Gospel Priority." *NTS* 33 (1987): 321–43.

Cassels, W. R. *The Gospel according to Peter: A Study by the Author of "Supernatural Religion".* London: Longman, Green, and Co., 1894.

Crossan, J. D. "The Cross That Spoke: The Earliest Narrative of the Passion and Resurrection." *Forum* 3 (1987): 3–22.

———. *The Cross That Spoke: The Origins of the Passion Narrative.* San Francisco: Harper & Row, 1988.

———. *Four Other Gospels: Shadows on the Contours of Canon.* New York: Harper & Row, 1985. Repr., Sonoma: Polebridge, 1992. See esp. pp. 85–127.

Denker, J. *Die theologiegeschichtliche Stellung des Petrusevangeliums.* Europäische Hochschulschriften 23/36. Bern: Herbert Lang; Frankfurt: Peter Lang, 1975.

Edwards, R. G. T. "The Theological Gospel of Peter?" *NTS* 63 (2019): 477–95.

Foster, P. "Are There Any Early Fragments of the So-called Gospel of Peter?" *NTS* 52 (2006): 1–28.

———. "The Discovery and Initial Reaction to the So-called Gospel of Peter." Pages 9–30 in *Das Evangelium nach Petrus: Text, Kontexte, Intertexte.* Edited by T. J. Kraus and T. Nicklas. Berlin: de Gruyter, 2007.

———. "The Disputed Early Fragments of the So-called Gospel of Peter—Once Again." *NovT* 49 (2007): 402–6.

———. "The Gospel of Peter." Pages 30–42 in *The Non-Canonical Gospels.* Edited by P. Foster. London: T&T Clark, 2008.

———. *The Gospel of Peter: Introduction, Critical Edition and Commentary.* Leiden: Brill, 2010.

———. "The Gospel of Peter: Directions and Issues in Contemporary Research." *Currents in Biblical Research* 9.3 (2011): 310–38.

———. "Is There a Relationship between the Writings of Justin Martyr and the Gospel of Peter?" Pages 104–12 and 198–200 in *Justin and His Worlds.* Edited by S. Paris and P. Foster. Minneapolis: Fortress, 2007.

———. "Passion Traditions in the *Gospel of Peter.*" Pages 47–68 in *Gelitten Gestorben Auferstanden: Passions- und Ostertraditionen in antiken Christentum.* Edited by T. Nicklas, A. Merkt, and J. Verheyden. WUNT 2.273. Tübingen: Mohr Siebeck, 2011.

———. "P.Oxy. 2949—Its Transcription and Significance: A Response to Thomas Wayment." *JBL* 129 (2010): 173–76.

Gardner-Smith, P. "The Gospel of Peter." *JTS* 27 (1926): 255–71.

Gebhardt, O. von. *Das Evangelium und die Apokalypse des Petrus: Die neuentdeckten Bruchstücke nach einer Photographie der Handschrift zu Gizéh in Lichtdruck herausgegeben.* Leipzig, 1893.

Green, J. B. "The Gospel of Peter: Source for a Pre-canonical Passion Narrative?" *ZNW* 78 (1987): 293–301.

Harnack, A. *Bruchstücke des Evangeliums und der Apokalypse des Petrus.* TU 9.2. J. C. Hinrichs: Leipzig 1893.

Harris, J. R. *A Popular Account of the Newly Recovered Gospel of St Peter.* London: Hodder and Stoughton, 1893.

Henderson, T. P. *The Gospel of Peter and Early Christian Apologetics.* WUNT 2.301. Tübingen: Mohr Siebeck, 2011.

Johnston, J. J. *The Resurrection of Jesus in the Gospel of Peter: A Tradition-Historical Study of the Akhmîm Gospel Fragment.* JCTS 21. London: T&T Clark, 2016.

Kraus, T. J., and T. Nicklas, eds. *Das Evangelium nach Petrus: Text, Kontexte, Intertexte.* Berlin: de Gruyter, 2007.

———. *Das Petrusevangelium and die Petrusapokalypse: Die griechischen Fragmente mit deutscher und englischer Übersetzung.* Berlin: de Gruyter, 2004.

Lods, A. *Evangelii secundum Petrum et Petri Apocalypseos quae supersunt.* Paris : Ernest Leroux, 1892.

Lührmann, D. "Ein neues Fragment des Petrus-evangeliums." Pages 579–81 in *The Synoptic Gospels: Source Criticism and the New Literary Criticism.* BETL 110. Louvain: Peeters, 1993.

———. "POx 2949: EvPt 3–5 in einer Handschrift des 2ten/3ten Jahrhunderts." *ZNW* 77 (1981): 216–26.

———. "POx 4009: Ein neues Fragment des Petrusevangeliums?" *NovT* 35 (1993): 390–410.

Mara, M. G. *Évangile de Pierre: Introduction, Texte Critique, Traduction, Commentaire et Index.* Sources Chrétiennes 201. Paris: Cerf, 1973.

McCant, J. W. "The Gospel of Peter: Doceticism Reconsidered." *NTS* 30 (1984): 258–73.

Nicklas, T. "Die 'Juden' im Petrusevangelium (PCair 10759): ein Testfall." *NTS* 47 (2001): 206–21.

———. "Erzähler und Charakter zugleich: zur literarischen Funktion des 'Petrus' in dem nach ihm benannten Evangelienfragment." *VC* 55 (2001): 318–26.

———. "Ein 'neutestamentliches Apokryphon'? Zum umstrittenen Kanonbezug des sog. Petrusevangeliums." *VC* 56 (2002): 260–72.

Robinson, J. A., and M. R. James. *The Gospel according to Peter, and the Revelation of Peter: Two Lectures on the Newly Recovered Fragments together with the Greek Texts.* London: C. J. Clay and Sons, 1892.

Stillman, M. K. "The Gospel of Peter: A Case for Oral-Only Dependency?" *Ephemerides Theologicae Lovanienses* 73.1 (1997): 114–120.

Swete, H. B. *The Akhmîm Fragment of the Apocryphal Gospel of St Peter.* London, 1893.

———. "The Gospels in the Second Century." *The Interpreter* 4 (1907): 138–55.

Treat, J. C. "The Two Manuscript Witness to the Gospel of Peter." Pages 391–99 in *Society of Biblical Literature 1990 Seminar Papers.* SBLSP 29. Atlanta: Scholars Press, 1990.

Turner, C. H. "The Gospel of Peter." *JTS* 14 (1913): 161–95.

Vaganay, L. *L'Évangile de Pierre.* Études Biblique. 2nd ed. Paris: Gabalda, 1930.

Verheyden, J. "Silent Witness: Mary Magdalene and the Women at the Tomb in the Gospel of Peter." Pages 457–82 in *Resurrection in the New Testament.* Edited by R. Bieringer, V. Koperski, and B. Lataite. BETL 165. Leuven: Peeters, 2002.

CHAPTER 5: INFANCY GOSPEL OF THOMAS

Aasgaard, Reidar. *The Childhood of Jesus: Decoding the Apocryphal Infancy Gospel of Thomas.* Eugene, OR: Cascade, 2009.

———. "How Close Can We Get to Ancient Childhood? Methodological Achievements and New Advances." Pages 321–34 in *Children and Everyday Life in the Roman and Late Antique World.* Edited by C. Laes and V. Vuolanto. London: Routledge, 2017.

———. "The Protevangelium of James and the *Infancy Gospel of Thomas*: Orthodoxy from Above or Heterodoxy from Below?" Pages 75–97 in *The Other Side: Apocryphal Perspectives on Ancient Christian "Orthodoxies".* Edited by T. Nicklas et al. Göttingen: Vandenhoeck & Ruprecht, 2017.

Alexander, Philip. "Jesus and His Mother in the Jewish Anti-Gospel (the *Toledot Yeshu*)." Pages 588–616 in *Infancy Gospels: Stories and Identities.* Edited by C. Clivaz et al. Tübingen: Mohr Siebeck, 2011.

Amsler, Frédéric. "Les *Paidika Iesou*, un nouveau témoin de la rencontre entre judaïsme et christianisme à Antioche au IVe siècle?" Pages 433–58 in *Infancy Gospels: Stories and Identities*. Edited by C. Clivaz et al. Tübingen: Mohr Siebeck, 2011.

Betsworth, Sharon. *Children in Early Christian Narratives*. London: Bloomsbury T&T Clark, 2015.

Betsworth, Sharon, and Julie Faith Parker, eds. *T&T Handbook of Children in the Bible and the Biblical World*. London: T&T Clark, 2019.

Burke, Tony. *De Infantia Iesu Evangelium Thomae, Graece*. CCSA 17. Turnhout: Brepols, 2010.

———. "Infancy Gospel of Thomas." e-Clavis: Christian Apocrypha. www.nasscal.com/e-clavis-christian-apocrypha/infancy-gospel-of-thomas/.

———. *The Syriac Tradition of the Infancy Gospel of Thomas: A Critical Edition and English Translation*. Piscataway, NJ: Gorgias, 2017.

Clivaz, Claire et al., eds. *Infancy Gospels: Stories and Identities*. Tübingen: Mohr Siebeck, 2011.

Cousland, J. R. C. *Holy Terror: Jesus in the Infancy Gospel of Thomas*. London: Bloomsbury T&T Clark, 2018.

Davis, Stephen J. *Christ Child: Cultural Memories of a Young Jesus*. New Haven: Yale University Press, 2014.

Dzon, Mary. *The Quest for the Christ Child in the Later Middle Ages*. Philadelphia: University of Pennsylvania Press, 2017.

Dzon, Mary, and Theresa M. Kenney, eds. *The Christ Child in Medieval Culture*. Toronto: University of Toronto Press, 2012.

Frey, Jörg, and Jens Schröter, eds. *Jesus in apokryphen Evangelienüberlieferungen: Beiträge zu ausserkanonischen Jesusüberlieferungen aus verschiedenen Sprach- und Kulturtraditionen*. Tübingen: Mohr Siebeck, 2010.

Frilingos, Christopher A. *Jesus, Mary, and Joseph: Family Trouble in the Infancy Gospels*. Philadelphia: University of Pennsylvania Press, 2017.

Hägg, Tomas. *The Art of Biography in Antiquity*. Cambridge: Cambridge University Press, 2012.

Horn, Cornelia B., and John W. Martens. *"Let the Little Children Come to Me": Childhood and Children in Early Christianity*. Washington, DC: Catholic University of America Press, 2009.

Horn, Cornelia B., and Robert R. Phenix. "Apocryphal Gospels in Syriac and Related Texts Offering Traditions about Jesus." Pages 527–55 in *Jesus in apokryphen Evangelienüberlieferungen: Beiträge zu ausserkanonischen Jesusüberlieferungen aus verschiedenen Sprach- und Kulturtraditionen*. Edited by J. Frey and J. Schröter. Tübingen: Mohr Siebeck, 2010.

Kaiser, Ursula Ulrike. "Jesus als Kind: Neuere Forschungen zur Jesusüberlieferung in den apokryphen 'Kindheitsevangelien.'" Pages 253–69 in *Jesus in apokryphen Evangelienüberlieferungen: Beiträge zu ausserkanonischen Jesusüberlieferungen aus verschiedenen Sprach- und Kulturtraditionen*. Edited by J. Frey and J. Schröter. Tübingen: Mohr Siebeck, 2010.

———. "Die sogenannte 'Kindheitserzählung des Thomas': Überlegungen zur Darstellung Jesu als Kind, deren Intention und Rezeption." Pages 459–81 in *Infancy Gospels: Stories and Identities*. Edited by C. Clivaz et al. Tübingen: Mohr Siebeck, 2011.

Kurzmann-Penz, Isolde. *Zur literarischen Fiktion von Kindheit: Überlegungen zu den apokryphen Kindheitsevangelien Jesu im Rahmen der antiken Biographie*. Stuttgart: Franz Steiner, 2018.

Schäfer, Peter, Michael Meerson, and Yaacov Deutsch, eds. *Toledot Yeshu ("The Life Story of Jesus") Revisited*. Tübingen: Mohr Siebeck, 2011.

Thomas, Christine M. *The Acts of Peter, Gospel Literature, and the Ancient Novel: Rewriting the Past*. Oxford: Oxford University Press, 2003.

Upson-Saia, Kristi. "Holy Child or Holy Terror? Understanding Jesus' Anger in the Infancy Gospel of Thomas." *Church History* 82.1 (2013): 1–39.

Van Oyen, Geert. "Rereading the Rewriting of the Biblical Traditions in the Infancy Gospel of Thomas (*Paidika*)." Pages 482–505 in *Infancy Gospels: Stories and Identities*. Edited by C. Clivaz et al. Tübingen: Mohr Siebeck, 2011.

Vukovíc, Marijana. *Survival and Success of an Apocryphal Childhood of Jesus: Reception of the* Infancy Gospel of Thomas *in the Middle Ages*. Berlin: de Gruyter, 2022.

CHAPTER 6: JEWISH-CHRISTIAN GOSPELS

Bauckham, Richard. "The Origin of the Ebionites." Pages 162–81 in *The Image of the Judaeo-Christians in Ancient Jewish and Christian Literature*. Edited by P. J. Tomson and D. Lambers-Petry. WUNT 158. Tübingen: Mohr Siebeck, 2003.

Broadhead, Edwin. *Jewish Ways of Following Jesus*. WUNT 266. Tübingen: Mohr Siebeck, 2010.

Carleton Paget, James. "The Definition of the Terms Jewish Christian and Jewish Christianity in the History of Research." Pages 22–52 in *Jewish Believers in Jesus*. Edited by O. Skarsaune and R. Hvalvik. Peabody, MA: Hendrickson, 2007.

Evans, Craig A. "The Jewish Christian Gospel Tradition." Pages 241–77 in *Jewish Believers in Jesus: The Early Centuries*. Edited by O. Skarsaune and R. Hvalvik. Peabody, MA: Hendrickson, 2007.

Frey, Jörg. "Die Fragmente des Ebionäerevangeliums." Pages 607–22 in *Antike christliche Apokryphen in deutscher Übersetzung. I Band: Evangelien und Verwandtes. Teilband I*. Edited by C. Markschies and J. Schröter. Tübingen: Mohr Siebeck, 2012.

———. "Die Fragmente judenchristlicher Evangelien." Pages 560–92 in *Antike christliche Apokryphen in deutscher Übersetzung. I. Band: Evangelien und Verwandtes. Teilband 1.* Edited by C. Markschies and J. Schröter. Tübingen: Mohr Siebeck, 2012.

Gallagher, Edmon L. *Hebrew Scripture in Patristic Biblical Theory: Canon, Language, Text.* VCSup 114. Leiden: Brill, 2012.

Goulder, Michael D. *A Tale of Two Missions.* London: SCM, 1994.

Gregory, Andrew, ed. *The Gospel according to the Hebrews and the Gospel of the Ebionites.* Oxford Early Christian Gospel Texts. Oxford: Oxford University Press, 2017.

———. "Hindrance or Help: Does the Modern Category of 'Jewish-Christian Gospel' Distort Our Understanding of the Texts to Which It Refers?" *JSNT* 28 (2006): 387–413.

Häkkinen, Sakari. "Ebionites." Pages 247–78 in *A Companion to Second-Century Christian "Heretics".* Edited by A. Marjanen and P. Luomanen. VCSup 76. Leiden: Brill, 2005.

Jackson-McCabe, Matt. "What's in a Name? The Problem of 'Jewish Christianity.'" Pages 7–38 in *Jewish Christianity Reconsidered.* Edited by M. Jackson-McCabe. Minneapolis: Fortress, 2007.

Jones, F. Stanley. *An Ancient Jewish-Christian Source on the History of Christianity: Pseudo-Clementine Recognitions 1.27–71.* Society of Biblical Literature Texts and Translations 37; Christian Apocrypha Series 2. Atlanta: Scholars Press, 1995.

Kelly, J. N. D. *Jerome: His Life, Writings, and Controversies.* New York: Harper & Row, 1975.

Klauck, Hans-Josef. *Apocryphal Gospels: An Introduction.* London: T&T Clark, 2003.

Klijn, A. F. J. *Jewish-Christian Gospel Tradition.* VCSup 17. Leiden: Brill, 1992.

Kloppenborg Verbin, John S. *Excavating Q: The History and Setting of the Sayings Gospel.* Minneapolis: Fortress, 2000.

Luomanen, Petri. *Recovering Jewish-Christian Sects and Gospels.* VCSup 110. Leiden: Brill, 2012.

Luz, Ulrich. *Das Evangelium nach Matthäus, Mt 18–25.* EKK 1/3. Zürich: Benziger; Neukirchen-Vluyn: Neukirchener, 1997.

Malina, Bruce J., and Richard L. Rohrbaugh. *Social Science Commentary on the Synoptic Gospels.* Minneapolis: Fortress, 1992.

Marjanen, Antti, ed. *Was There a Gnostic Religion?* Publications of the Finnish Exegetical Society 87. Helsinki: Finnish Exegetical Society, 2005.

Mimouni, Simon C. *Le judéo-christianisme ancien: Essais historiques.* Paris: Cerf, 1998.

Myllykoski, Matti. "'Christian Jews' and 'Jewish Christians': The Jewish Origins of Christianity in English Literature from Elizabeth I to Toland's *Nazarenus.*" Pages 3–41 in *The Rediscovery of Jewish Christianity: From Toland to Baur.* Edited by F. S. Jones. HBS 5. Atlanta: Society of Biblical Literature, 2012.

Petersen, William L. *Tatian's Diatessaron: Its Creation, Dissemination, Significance and History in Scholarship.* VCSup 25. Leiden: Brill, 1994.

Pourkier, Aline. *L' Hérésiologie chez Épiphane de Salamine.* Christianisme Antique 4. Paris: Beauchesne, 1992.

Räisänen, Heikki. *Paul and the Law.* Philadelphia: Fortress, 1986.

Reed, Annette Yoshiko. *Jewish Christianity and the History of Judaism.* TSAJ 171. Tübingen: Mohr Siebeck, 2018.

Robinson, James M. *Jesus according to the Earliest Witness.* Minneapolis: Fortress, 2007.

Skarsaune, Oskar. "Jewish Believers in Jesus in Antiquity: Problems of Definition, Method, and Sources." Pages 3–21 in *Jewish Believers in Jesus.* Edited by O. Skarsaune and R. Hvalvik. Peabody, MA: Hendrickson, 2007.

Vielhauer, Philipp, and Georg Strecker. "Jewish-Christian Gospels." *NTApoc* 1:134–77.

Waitz, Hans. "Die judenchristlichen Evangelien in der altkirchlichen Literatur." Pages 10–17 in *Neutestamentliche Apokryphen.* Edited by E. Hennecke. Tübingen: J. C. B. Mohr, 1924.

CHAPTER 7: THE LEGEND OF APHRODITIAN

Bobrov, Alexander G. *Апокрифическое Сказание Афродитиана в литературе и книжности Древней Руси. Исследование и тексты.* St. Petersburg: Nauka, 1994.

Bratke, Eduard. *Das sogenannte Religionsgespräch am Hof der Sassaniden.* TU NF 4/3. Leipzig: Hinrichs, 1899.

Bringel, Pauline. "Interprétation et réécritures dans la tradition manuscrite du Récit d'Aphroditien." Pages 285–96 in *Entré Actes. Regards croisés en sciences humaines. Réalités et représentations: les pistes de la recherche. Actes du Ier Colloque international des jeunes chercheurs en sciences humaines et sociales de Strasbourg, 10 et 11 mai 2004.* Edited by L. Angard. Strasbourg: Université Marc Bloch, 2005.

Gaster, M. "Die rumänische Version der Legende des Aphroditian." *Byzantinisch-Neugriechische Jahrbücher* 14 (1938): 119–28.

Heyden, Katharina. "Die Christliche Geschichte des Philippos von Side. Mit einem kommentierten Katalog der Fragmente." Pages 209–43 in *Julius Africanus und die christliche Weltchronistik.* Edited by M. Wallraff. TU 157. Berlin: de Gruyter 2006.

———. *Die "Erzählung des Aphroditian": Thema und Variationen einer Legende im Spannungsfeld von Christentum und Heidentum.* Studien und Texte zu Antike und Christentum 53. Tübingen: Mohr Siebeck, 2009.

———. "The Legend of Aphroditianus: A New Translation and Introduction." Pages 3–18 in *New Testament Apocrypha: More Noncanonical Scriptures*. Vol. 1. Edited by T. Burke and B. Landau. Grand Rapids: Eerdmans, 2016.

Monneret de Villard, Ugo. *Le leggende orientali sui magi evangelici*. Studi e Testi 163. Vatican: Biblioteca apostolica vaticana, 1952.

Schwartz, Eduard. "Aphroditianos." PW 1:2788–93.

Usener, Hermann. *Religionsgeschichtliche Untersuchungen: Das Weihnachtsfest*. 2nd ed. Bonn: Friedrich Cohen, 1911.

Veder, William R. "The Slavonic Tale of Aphroditian: Limitations of Manuscript-Centred Textology." *Търновска книжовна школа* 9 (2011): 344–58.

CHAPTER 8: PILATE CYCLE

Bovon, François, and Pierre Geoltrain, eds. *Écrits apocryphes chrétiens*. Vol. 1. Bibliothèque de la Pléiade 442. Paris: Gallimard, 1993.

Cartlidge, David R., and J. Keith Elliott. *Art and the Christian Apocrypha*. London: Routledge, 2001.

Charlesworth, James H., ed. *The Dead Sea Scrolls: Hebrew, Aramaic and Greek Texts*. The Princeton Theological Seminary Dead Sea Scrolls Project. Tübingen: Mohr Siebeck; Louisville: Westminster John Knox, 1994–.

Collins, Nina L. *Jesus, the Sabbath and the Jewish Debate in the First and Second Centuries CE*. LNTS 474. London: Bloomsbury, 2014.

Elliott, J. K. *The Apocryphal Jesus: Legends of the Early Church*. Oxford: Oxford University Press, 1996.

———. *The Apocryphal New Testament*. Oxford: Clarendon, 1993.

Erbetta, Mario. *Gli apocrifi del Nuovo Testamento*. Casale Monferrato: Marietti, 1975.

Geoltrain, Pierre, and Jean-Daniel Kaestli, eds. *Écrits apocryphes chrétiens*. Vol. 2. Bibliothèque de la Pléiade 516. Paris: Gallimard, 2005.

Klauck, Hans-Josef. *Apocryphal Gospels: An Introduction*. London: Continuum T&T Clark, 2003.

Moraldi, Luigi. *Apocrifi del Nuovo Testamento*. Casale Monferrato: Piemme, 1994.

Santos Otero, Aurelio de. *Los evangelios apócrifos*. 6th ed. Madrid: Biblioteca Autori Cristianos, 1963.

Voragine, Jacobus de. *The Golden Legend: Readings on the Saints*. 2 vols. Princeton: Princeton University Press, 1993.

CHAPTER 9: PROTEVANGELIUM OF JAMES
Primary Sources

de Strycker, Émile. *La Forme la plus ancienne du Protévangile de Jacques*. SH 33. Bruxelles: Société des Bollandistes, 1961.

Hock, Ronald F. *The Infancy Gospels of James and Thomas*. Scholars Bible 2. Santa Rosa: Polebridge, 1995.

Vuong, Lily. *The Protevangelium of James*. Early Christian Apocrypha 7. Eugene, OR: Cascade Books, 2019.

Secondary Sources

Aldama, Jose Antonio de. "El Protoevangelio de Santiago y sus problemas." *Ephemerides Mariologicae* 12 (1962): 107–30.

———. "Un nuevo testigo indirecto del Protoevangelio de Santiago." *Studia Patristica* 12 (1975): 79–82.

Allen, John L. "The 'Protevangelium of James' as an 'Historia': The Insufficiency of the 'Infancy Gospel' Category." Pages 508–17 in *Society of Biblical Literature 1991 Seminar Papers*. SBLSP 30. Atlanta: Scholars Press, 1991.

Bovon, François. "The Suspension of Time in Chapter 18 of *Protevangelium Jacobi*." Pages 393–405 in *Future of Early Christianity: Essays in Honor of Helmut Koester*. Edited by B. A. Pearson. Minneapolis: Fortress, 1991.

Cothenet, Édouard. "Le Protévangile de Jacques: Origine, genre et signification d'un premier midrash chrétien sur la nativité de Marie." *ANRW* 25.6:4252–69. Berlin: de Gruyter, 1988.

Daniels, Boyd Lee. "The Greek Manuscript Tradition of the Protevangelium Jacobi." PhD diss., Duke University, 1956.

de Strycker, Émile. "Die griechischen Handschriften des Protevangeliums Iacobi." Pages 577–612 in *Griechische Kodikologie und Textüberlieferung*. Edited by D. Harlfinger. Darmstadt: Wissenschaftliche Buchgesellschaft, 1980.

———. "Le Protévangile de Jacques: Problèmes critiques et exégétiques." Pages 339–59 in *Studia Evangelica 3*. Edited by F. L. Cross. Berlin: Akademie, 1964.

Foskett, Mary F. "The Child Mary in the *Protevangelium of James*." Pages 195–221 in *"Non-canonical" Religious Texts in Early Judaism and Early Christianity*. Edited by L. M. McDonald and J. H. Charlesworth. Jewish and Christian Texts in Contexts and Related Studies 14. London: Bloomsbury T&T Clark, 2012.

———. "Miriam/Mariam/Maria: Literary Genealogy and the Genesis of Mary in the Protevangelium of James." Pages 63–74 in *Mariam, the Magdalen, and the Mother*. Bloomington: Indiana University Press, 2005.

———. *A Virgin Conceived: Mary and Classical Representations of Virginity.* Bloomington: Indiana University Press, 2002.

———. "Virginity as Purity in the Protevangelium of James." Pages 67–76 in *Feminist Companion to Mariology.* Edited by A.-J. Levine. London: T&T Clark, 2005.

Lillis, Julia Kelto. "Paradox in Partu: Verifying Virginity in the *Protevangelium of James.*" *JECS* 24 (2016): 1–28.

Nutzman, Megan. "Mary in the *Protevangelium of James*: A Jewish Woman in the Temple?" *Greek, Roman, and Byzantine Studies* 53 (2013): 551–78.

Smid, H. R. *Protevangelium Jacobi: A Commentary.* Translated by G. E. Van Baaren-Pape. Assen: Van Gorcum, 1965.

Stempvoort, P. A. van. "The Protevangelium Jacobi, the Sources of Its Theme and Style and Their Bearing on Its Date." Pages 410–26 in *Studia Evangelica 3.* Edited by F. L. Cross. Berlin: Akademie, 1964.

Testuz, Michel. *Papyrus Bodmer V: Nativité de Marie.* Geneva: Bibliotheca Bodmeriana, 1958.

Vanden Eykel, Eric M. *"But Their Faces Were All Looking Up": Author and Reader in the Protevangelium of James.* The Reception of Jesus in the First Three Centuries 1. London: Bloomsbury T&T Clark, 2016.

———. "Protevangelium Jacobi." Pages 93–105 in *From Thomas to Tatian: Christian Literary Receptions of Jesus in the Second and Third Centuries CE.* Edited by J. Schröter and C. Jacobi. Vol. 2 of *Reception of Jesus in the First Three Centuries.* Edited by C. L. Keith, H. K. Bond, C. Jacobi, and J. Schröter. London: Bloomsbury T&T Clark, 2019.

Vorster, Willem S. "The Annunciation of the Birth of Jesus in the Protevangelium of James." Pages 33–53 in *A South African Perspective on the New Testament: Essays by South African New Testament Scholars Presented to Bruce Manning Metzger during His Visit to South Africa in 1985.* Leiden: Brill, 1986.

———. "The Protevangelium of James and Intertextuality." Pages 262–75 in *Text and Testimony: Essays in Honor of A. F. J. Klijn.* Edited by T. Baarda, A. Hilhorst, G. P. Luttikhuizen and A. S. van der Woude. Kampen: Kok, 1988.

Vuong, Lily. *Gender and Purity in the Protevangelium of James.* WUNT 2.358. Tubingen: Mohr Siebeck, 2013.

———. "'Let Us Bring Her Up to the Temple of the Lord': Exploring the Boundaries of Jewish and Christian Relations through the Presentation of Mary in the *Protevangelium of James.*" Pages 418–32 in *Infancy Gospels: Stories and Identities.* Edited by C. Clivaz, A. Dettwiler, L. Devillers, and E. Norelli. Tübingen: Mohr Siebeck, 2011.

———. "Purity, Piety, and the Purposes of the *Protevangelium of James.*" Pages 205–21 in *"Non-canonical" Religious Texts in Early Judaism and Early Christianity.* Edited by L. M. McDonald and J. H. Charlesworth. Jewish and Christian Texts in Contexts and Related Studies 14. London: Bloomsbury T&T Clark, 2012.

Zervos, George T. "Prolegomena to a Critical Edition of the Genesis Marias (Protevangelium Jacobi): The Greek Manuscripts." PhD diss., Duke University, 1986.

CHAPTER 10: TOLEDOT YESHU

Ahuvia, Mika, and John G. Gager. "Some Notes on Jesus and His Parents: From the New Testament to the *Toledot Yeshu.*" Pages 997–1119 in *Envisioning Judaism: Studies in Honor of Peter Schäfer on the Occasion of His Seventieth Birthday.* Edited by R. Boustan et al. Tübingen: Mohr Siebeck, 2013.

Barbu, Daniel. "The Case about Jesus: (Counter-)History and Casuistry in *Toledot Yeshu.*" Pages 65–98 in *A Historical Approach to Casuistry: Norms and Exceptions in a Comparative Perspective.* Edited by C. Ginzburg and L. Biasori. London: Bloomsbury, 2018.

Barbu, Daniel, and Yaacov Deutsch, eds. *Toledot Yeshu in Context: Jewish-Christian Polemics in Ancient, Medieval, and Modern History.* Tübingen: Mohr Siebeck, 2020.

Biale, David. "Counter-History and Jewish Polemics against Christianity: The *Sefer Toledot Yeshu* and the *Sefer Zerubavel.*" *Jewish Social Studies* 6.1 (1999): 130–45.

Clivaz, Claire, Andreas Dettwiler, Luc Devillers, and Enrico Norelli, eds. *Infancy Gospels: Stories and Identities.* Tübingen: Mohr Siebeck, 2011.

Cuffel, Alexandra. "Between Epic Entertainment and Polemical Exegesis: Jesus as Antihero in *Toledot Yeshu.*" Pages 155–70 in *Medieval Exegesis and Religious Difference: Commentary, Conflict, and Community in the Premodern Mediterranean.* Edited by R. Szpiech. New York: Fordham University Press, 2015.

Davis, Stephen. *Christ Child: Cultural Memories of a Young Jesus.* New Haven: Yale University Press, 2014.

Deutsch, Yaacov. "New Evidence of Early Versions of *Toldot Yeshu.*" *Tarbiz* 69 (2000): 177–97 (in Hebrew).

Di Segni, Riccardo. "La tradizione delle Toledòth Jeshu: Manoscritti, edizioni a stampa, classificazione." *Rassegna Mensile di Israel* 50 (1984): 83–100.

Goldstein, Miriam. *A Judeo-Arabic Parody of the Life of Jesus: The* Toledot Yeshu *Helene Narrative.* Tübingen: Mohr Siebeck, forthcoming.

———. "Judeo-Arabic Versions of *Toledot Yeshu.*" *Ginzei Qedem* 6 (2010): 9–42.

———. "A Polemical Tale and Its Function in the Jewish Communities of the Mediterranean and the Near East: *Toledot Yeshu* in Judeo-Arabic." *Intellectual History of the Islamicate World* 7 (2019): 192–227.

Gribetz, Sarit Kattan. "Jesus and the Clay Birds: Reading *Toledot Yeshu* in Light of the Infancy Gospels." Pages 1021–48 in *Envisioning Judaism: Studies in Honor of Peter Schäfer on the Occasion of His Seventieth Birthday.* Edited by R. Boustan et al. Tübingen: Mohr Siebeck, 2013.

———. "The Mothers in the Manuscripts: Gender, Motherhood and Power in the *Toledot Yeshu* Narratives." Pages 99–129 in *Toledot Yeshu in Context: Jewish-Christian Polemics in Ancient, Medieval, and Modern History*. Edited by D. Barbu and Y. Deutsch. Tübingen: Mohr Siebeck, 2020.

Hasan-Rokem, Galit. "Polymorphic Helena—*Toledot Yeshu* as a Palimpsest of Religious Narratives and Identities." Pages 101–35 in *Toledot Yeshu ("The Life Story of Jesus") Revisited: A Princeton Conference*. Edited by P. Schäfer, M. Meerson, and Y. Deutsch. Tübingen: Mohr Siebeck, 2011.

Horbury, William. "A Critical Examination of the Toledoth Yeshu." PhD diss., University of Cambridge, 1970.

Karras, Ruth Mazo. "The Aerial Battle in the *Toledot Yeshu* and Sodomy in the Late Middle Ages." *Medieval Encounters* 19 (2013): 493–533.

Krauss, Samuel. *Das Leben Jesu nach jüdischen Quellen*. Berlin: S. Calvary, 1902. Repr., Hildesheim: Olms, 1977 (2006).

Meerson, Michael. "Yeshu the Physician and the Child of Stone: A Glimpse of Progressive Medicine in Jewish-Christian Polemics." *Jewish Studies Quarterly* 20 (2013): 297–314.

Newman, Hillel I. "The Death of Jesus in the 'Toledot Yeshu' Literature." *JTS* 50 (1999): 59–79.

Rosenzweig, Claudia. "The 'History of the Life of Jesus' in a Yiddish Manuscript from the Eighteenth Century (Ms. Jerusalem, NLI, Heb. 8°5622)." Pages 263–316 in *Toledot Yeshu in Context: Jewish-Christian Polemics in Ancient, Medieval, and Modern History*. Tübingen: Mohr Siebeck, 2020.

Schäfer, Peter. "Jesus' Origin, Birth, and Childhood according to the *Toledot Yeshu* and the Talmud." Pages 139–63 in *Judaea-Palaestina, Babylon and Rome: Jews in Antiquity*. Tübingen: Mohr Siebeck, 2012.

Schäfer, Peter, and Michael Meerson, eds. and trans. *Toledot Yeshu: The Life Story of Jesus*. 2 vol. and database. Tübingen: Mohr Siebeck, 2014.

Schäfer, Peter, Michael Meerson, and Yaacov Deutsch, eds. *Toledot Yeshu ("The Life Story of Jesus") Revisited: A Princeton Conference*. Tübingen: Mohr Siebeck, 2011.

Stökl Ben Ezra, Daniel. "An Ancient List of Christian Festivals in *Toledot Yeshu*: Polemics as Indication for Interaction." *HTR* 102.4 (2009): 481–96.

Tartakoff, Paola. "The *Toledot Yeshu* and Jewish-Christian Conflict in the Medieval Crown of Aragon." Pages 297–309 in *Toledot Yeshu Reconsidered*. Edited by P. Schäfer, M. Meerson, and Y. Deutsch. Tübingen: Mohr Siebeck, 2011.

CHAPTER 11: REVELATION OF THE MAGI

Brock, S. P. "An Archaic Syriac Prayer over Baptismal Oil." Pages 3–12 in *StPatr 41: Papers Presented at the Fourteenth International Conference on Patristic Studies Held in Oxford 2003*. Edited by F. Young, M. Edwards, and P. Parvis. Leuven: Peeters, 2006.

Chabot, I.-B. (J.-B.), ed. *Chronicon anonymum pseudo-Dionysianum vulgo dictum I*. CSCO 91, Scriptores Syri 43. Leuven: Peeters, 1927. This is a Syriac critical edition of the Chronicle of Zuqnin.

———, ed. *Incerti auctoris Chronicon Pseudo-Dionysianum vulgo dictum I*. CSCO 121, Scriptores Syri 66. Leuven: Peeters, 1949. This is the Latin translation of the Syriac critical edition listed above.

Chronicle of Zuqnin, Vaticanus Syriacus 162. Scan of the manuscript at https://digi.vatlib.it/view/MSS_Vat .sir.162.

Foster, Paul. "Polymorphic Christology: Its Origins and Development in Early Christianity." *JTS* 58 (2007): 66–99.

Kaestli, Jean-Daniel. "Mapping an Unexplored Second Century Apocryphal Gospel: The *Liber de Nativitate Salvatoris* (CANT 53)." Pages 506–33 in *Infancy Gospels: Stories and Identities*. Edited by C. Clivaz et al. Tübingen: Mohr Siebeck, 2011.

Landau, Brent. "'One Drop of Salvation from the House of Majesty': Universal Revelation, Human Mission and Mythical Geography in the Syriac *Revelation of the Magi*." Pages 83–103 in *The Levant: Crossroads of Late Antiquity: History, Religion and Archaeology*. Edited by E. B. Aitken and J. M. Fossey. Leiden: Brill, 2014.

———. "*The Revelation of the Magi*: A Summary and Introduction." Pages 19–29 in vol. 1 of *New Testament Apocrypha: More Noncanonical Scriptures*. Edited by T. Burke and B. Landau. Grand Rapids: Eerdmans, 2016.

———. *Revelation of the Magi: The Lost Tale of the Wise Men's Journey to Bethlehem*. New York: HarperOne, 2010. Includes English translation, substantially the same as in Landau (2008) below.

———. "The Sages and the Star-Child: An Introduction to the *Revelation of the Magi*, An Ancient Christian Apocryphon." ThD diss., Harvard Divinity School, 2008. Includes Syriac critical edition and English translation. Available from https://utexas.academia.edu/BrentLandau.

Monneret de Villard, Ugo. *Le leggende orientali sui Magi evangelici*. StT 163. Vatican City: Vatican Library, 1952. Includes an Italian translation of the text by Giorgio Levi Della Vida (pp. 27–49).

Reinink, G. J. "Das Land 'Seiris' (Šir) und das Volk der Serer in jüdischen und christlichen Traditionen." *JSJ* 6.1 (1975): 72–85.

Witakowski, Witold. "The Magi in Syriac Tradition." Pages 809–43 in *Malphono w-Rabo d-Malphone: Studies in Honor of Sebastian P. Brock*. Edited by G. Kiraz. Gorgias Eastern Christian Studies. Piscataway, NJ: Gorgias, 2008.

CHAPTER 12: ACTS OF ANDREW

Bremner, Jan N., ed. *The Apocryphal Acts of Andrew*. Studies on the Apocryphal Acts of the Apostles 5. Leuven: Peeters, 2000.

Elliott, J. K. "The Acts of Andrew." Pages 231–302 in *The Apocryphal New Testament: A Collection of Apocryphal Christian Literature in an English Translation*. Oxford: Clarendon, 1993.

MacDonald, Dennis R. *The Acts of Andrew*. Early Christian Apocrypha 1. Santa Rosa, CA: Polebridge, 2005.

———. "*The Acts of Andrew and Matthias* and *The Acts of Andrew*." *Semeia* 38 (1986): 9–26.

———. *The Acts of Andrew and the Acts of Andrew and Matthias in the City of the Cannibals*. SBLTT 33.1. Atlanta: Scholars Press, 1990.

Prieur, Jean-Marc. *Acta Andreae*. 2 vols. CCSA 5–6. Turnhout: Brepols, 1989.

———. "Les Actes apocryphes de l'apôtre André: Présentation des diverses traditions apocryphes et état de la question." *ANRW* 25.6:4383–414. Part 2, *Principat*, 25.6. Edited by H. Temporini and W. Haase. Berlin: de Gruyter, 1988.

———. "Acts of Andrew." *ABD* 1:244–47.

Prieur, Jean-Marc, and Wilhelm Schneemelcher. "The Acts of Andrew." *NTApoc* 2:101–51.

Roig Lanzillotta, Lautaro. "The Acts of Andrew: A New Perspective on the Primitive Text." *Cuadernos de Filología Clásica* 20 (2010): 247–59.

Santos Otero, Aurelio de. "Acta Andreae et Matthiae apud anthropophagos." *NTApoc* 2:443–47.

Snyder, Julia A. "Christ of the Acts of Andrew and Matthias." Pages 247–62 in *Christ of the Sacred Stories*. Edited by P. Dragutinović, T. Nicklas, K. G. Rodenbiker, and V. Tatalović. WUNT 2.453. Tübingen: Mohr Siebeck, 2017.

CHAPTERS 13, 14, 17: ACTS OF JOHN, PAUL, THOMAS
Primary Sources

Bonnet, Maximillian. *Acta Apostolorum Apocrypha*. Edited by R. Lipsius. 3 vols. Leipzig: Mendelssohn, 1889. Repr., Hildesheim: Olms, 1972.

Ferreira, Johan. *The Hymn of the Pearl: The Syriac and Greek Texts with Introduction, Translation, and Notes*. Sydney: St. Paul's, 2002.

Junod, Eric, and Jean-Daniel Kaestli. *Acta Iohannis*. 2 vols. CCSA 1–2. Turnhout: Brepols, 1983.

Klijn, A. J. F. *The Acts of Thomas: Introduction, Text and Commentary*. 2nd ed. Leiden: Brill, 2003.

Poirier, P.-H. *L'Hymne de la Perle des Actes de Thomas: Introduction, Text, Traduction, Commentaire*. Homo Religiosus 8. Louvain: Pierier, 1981.

Wright, W. "The Acts of Judas Thomas (or the Twin) the Apostle." In *Apocryphal Acts of the Apostles Edited from Syrian Manuscripts in the British Museum and Other Libraries*. 2 vols. London: Williams & Norgate, 1871. Repr., Amsterdam: Philo, 1968.

Secondary Literature

Andrade, Nathanael J. *Journey of Christianity to India in Late Antiquity: Networks and the Movement of Culture*. Cambridge: Cambridge University Press, 2018.

Attridge, Harold W. "The Acts of John and the Fourth Gospel." Pages 255–65 in *From Judaism to Christianity: Tradition and Transition: A Festschrift for Thomas Tobin, S.J., on the Occasion of His Sixty-Fifth birthday*. Edited by P. Walters. NovTSup. Leiden: Brill, 2010.

———. *The Acts of Thomas*. Early Christian Apocrypha 3. Salem, OR: Polebridge, 2010.

———. "Intertextuality in the Acts of Thomas." *Semeia* (1999): 87–124.

———. "The Original Language of the Acts of Thomas." Pages 241–50 in *Of Scribes and Scrolls: Studies on the Hebrew Bible, Intertestamental Judaism and Christian Origins*. Edited by H. W. Attridge, J. J. Collins, and T. H. Tobin. College Theology Society Resources in Religion 5. Lanham, MD: University Press of America, 1990.

Barrier, Jeremy W. *The Acts of Paul and Thecla: A Critical Introduction and Commentary*. WUNT 2.270. Tübingen: Mohr Siebeck, 2009.

Bivar, A. D. H. "Gondophares and the Indo-Parthians." Pages 26–36 in *The Age of the Parthians*. Edited by V. S. Curtis and S. Steward. London: Tauris, 2007.

Bremmer, Jan N. "The Acts of Thomas: Place, Date, Women." Pages 74–90 in *The Apocryphal Acts of Thomas*. Edited by J. N. Bremmer. Leuven: Peeters, 2001.

———, ed. *The Apocryphal Acts of John*. Studies on the Apocryphal Acts of the Apostles 1. Kampen: Kok, 1995.

———, ed. *The Apocryphal Acts of Paul and Thecla*. Studies on the Apocryphal Acts of the Apostles 2. Kampen: Kok Pharos, 1996.

Brock, Sebastian. "Thomas Christians." Pages 410–14 in *Gorgias Encyclopedic History of the Syriac Heritage*. Edited by S. Brock et al. Piscataway, NJ: Gorgias, 2011.

Cartlidge, David R. "Transfiguration of Metamorphosis Traditions in the Acts of John, Thomas and Peter." *Semeia* 38 (1986): 53–66.

Cereti, Carlo, Luca Olivieri, and Joseph Vazhuthanapally. "The Problem of the St. Thomas Crosses and Related Questions: Epigraphical Survey and Preliminary Research." *East and West* 52.1 (2002): 285–310.

Culpepper, R. Alan. *John, the Son of Zebedee: The Life of a Legend*. Columbia, SC: University of South Carolina Press, 1994. Repr., Minneapolis: Fortress, 2000. See pp. 187–205.

Davis, Stephen J. *The Cult of Saint Thecla: A Tradition of Women's Piety in Late Antiquity*. Oxford: Oxford University Press, 2001.

Glancy, Jennifer. "Slavery in the *Acts of Thomas*." *Journal of Early Christian History* 2 (2012): 3–21.

Gunther, J. J. "The Meaning and Origin of the Name 'Judas Thomas.'" *Le Museon* 93 (1980): 113–48.

Huxley, George. "Geography in the *Acts of Thomas*." *Greek Roman and Byzantine Studies* 24 (1983): 71–80.

Hylen, Susan E. *Modest Apostle: Thecla and the History of Women in the Early Church*. Oxford: Oxford University Press, 2015.

Johnson, Caroline. "Ritual Epicleses in the Greek Acts of Thomas." Pages 171–200 in *The Apocryphal Acts of the Apostles*. Edited by F. Bovon, A. G. Brock, and C. Matthews. Harvard Divinity School Studies. Cambridge: Harvard University Press, 1999.

Junod, Eric. "Les traits caractéristiques de la théologie des Actes de Jean." *RTP* 26 (1976): 125–45.

———. *L'histoire des Acts apocryphes des apotres du IIIe au IXe siecle: Le cas des Actes de Jean*. Cahiers de la Revue de Théologie et de Philosophie 7. Geneva, Lausanne, and Neuchatel: Revue de Théologie et de Philosophie, 1982.

Kaestli, Jean-Daniel. "Le mystère de la croix de lumière et le Johannisme: Acts de Jean ch 94–102." *Foi et Vie* 86.5 [*Cahier Biblique* 26] (1987): 35–46.

Klauck, Hans-Josef. *The Apocryphal Acts of the Apostles: An Introduction*. Trans. B. McNeil. Waco, TX: Baylor University Press, 2008. See pp. 47–79.

Klijn, A. J. F. "Baptism in the Acts of Thomas." Pages 57–62 in *Studies on Syrian Baptismal Rites*. Edited by J. Vellian. Syrian Churches Series 6. Kottayam: CMS, 1973.

Kolangadan, Joseph. "The Historicity of Apostle Thomas Evangelization in Kerala." *The Harp* 8–9 (1995–1996): 8–9; 305–27.

König, Jason. "Novelistic and Anti-Novelistic Narrative in the *Acts of Thomas* and *Acts of Andrew and Matthias*." Pages 121–50 in *Fiction on the Fringe: Novelistic Writing in the Post-Classical Age*. Edited by K. Grammatiki. Leiden: Brill, 2009.

Kurikilamkatt, James. "The First Port of Disembarkation of the Apostle Thomas in India according to the Acts of Thomas." *Ephrem's Theological Journal* 8 (2004): 3–20.

LaFargue, Michael. *Language and Gnosis: The Opening Scenes of the Acts of Thomas*. Philadelphia: Fortress, 1985.

Lalleman, Pieter J. *The Acts of John: A Two-Stage Initiation into Johannine Gnosticism*. Leuven: Peeters, 1998.

Luttikhuizen, Gerard. "A Gnostic Reading of the Acts of John." Pages 119–52 in *The Apocryphal Acts of John*. Edited by J. N. Bremmer. Kampen: Kok Pharos, 1995.

———. "The Hymn of Judas Thomas, the Apostle, in the Country of the Indians." Pages 101–14 in *The Apocryphal Acts of Thomas*. Edited by J. N. Bremmer. Leuven: Peeters, 2001.

MacDonald, Dennis R., ed. *The Apocryphal Acts of Apostles*. Semeia 38. Atlanta: Scholars Press, 1986.

———. "Jesus and Dionysian Polymorphism in the Acts of John." Pages 97–104 in *Early Christian and Jewish Narrative: The Role of Religion in Shaping Narrative Forms*. Edited by I. Ramelli and J. Perkins. WUNT 348. Tübingen: Mohr Siebeck, 2015.

Marcovich, Miroslav. "The Wedding Hymn of the Acta Thomae." *Illinois Classical Studies* 6 (1981): 367–85.

MacNamara, Martin. *The Apocrypha in the Irish Church*. Dublin: Institute for Advanced Studies, 1975.

McDowell, Sean. *The Fate of the Apostles: Examining the Martyrdom Accounts of the Closest Followers of Jesus*. Farnham: Ashgate, 2015.

McGrath, James F. "History and Fiction in the Acts of Thomas: The State of the Question." *JSP* 17 (2008): 297–311.

McLarty, J. D. *Thecla's Devotion: Narrative, Emotion and Identity in the Acts of Paul and Thecla*. Cambridge, UK: James Clark, 2018.

Morrison, Craig. "The Text of the New Testament in the Acts of Judas Thomas." Pages 187–205 in *The Peshitta: Its Use in Literature and Liturgy. Papers Read at the Third Peshitta Symposium*. Monographs of the Peshitta Institute 15. Leiden: Brill, 2006.

Myers, Susan. "Revisiting Preliminary Issues in the Acts of Thomas." *Apocrypha* 17 (2006): 95–112.

———. *Spirit Epicleses in the Acts of Thomas*. Tübingen: Mohr Siebeck, 2010.

Nedungatt, George. "The Apocryphal Acts of Thomas and Christian Origins in India." *Gregorianum* 92 (2011): 533–57.

———. "India Confused with Other Countries in Antiquity." *Orientalia Christiana Periodica* 76 (2010): 315–37.

———. *The Quest for the Historical Thomas: A Re-reading of the Evidence*. Bangalore: Theological Publications in India, 2008.

Parpola, Simo. "Mesopotamian Precursors of the Hymn of the Pearl." Pages 181–94 in *Mythology and Mythologies: Methodological Approaches to Intercultural Influences*. Edited by R. M. Whiting. Helsinki: Neo-Assyrian Text Corpus Project, 2001.

Pervo, Richard I. *The Acts of Paul: A New Translation with Introduction and Commentary.* Cambridge, UK: James Clarke, 2014.

——. "Johannine Trajectories in the Acts of John." *Apocrypha* 3 (1992): 47–68.

——, with Julian Hills. *The Acts of John.* Early Christian Apocrypha 6. Salem, OR: Polebridge, 2016.

Piovanelli, Pierluigi. "Thomas in Edessa? Another Look at the Original Setting of the Gospel of Thomas." Pages 443–62 in *Myths, Martyrs, and Modernity: Studies in the History of Religions in Honor of Jan Bremmer.* Edited by J. Dijkstra, J. Kroesen, and Y. Kuiper. Leiden: Brill, 2010.

Plümacher, Eckhard. "Apokryphe Apostelakten." PWSup 15 (1978): 11–70.

——. *Geschichte und Geschichten: Aufsätze zur Apostelgeschichte und zu den Johannesakten.* Edited by J. Schröter and R. Brucker. WUNT 170. Tübingen: Mohr Siebeck, 2004.

Poirier, P.-H. "*Évangile de Thomas, Actes de Thomas, Livre de Thomas,* une tradition et ses transformations." *Apocrypha* 7 (1996): 9–26.

——. "Les Actes de Thomas et le Manichéisme." *Apocrypha* 9 (1998): 263–90.

Ramelli, Ilaria. "Early Christian Missions from Alexandria to 'India': Institutional Transformations and Geographical Identifications." *Augustinianum* 51 (2011): 221–31.

Roger, Gary. "On the Road to India with Apollonios of Tyana and Thomas the Apostle." Pages 249–63 in *Greek and Roman Networks in the Mediterranean.* 2nd ed. Edited by I. Malkin et al. London: Routledge, 2009.

Roig Lanzillotta, Lautaro. "A Syriac Original for the Acts of Thomas? The Hypothesis of Syriac Priority Revisited." Pages 105–34 in *Early Christian and Jewish Narrative: The Role of Religion in Shaping Narrative Forms.* Edited by I. Ramelli and J. Perkins. Tübingen: Mohr Siebeck, 2015.

Roldanus, Hans. "Die Eucharistie in den Johannesakten." Pages 72–96 in *The Apocryphal Acts of John.* Edited by J. N. Bremmer. Studies on the Apocryphal Acts of the Apostles 1. Kampen: Kok, 1995.

Rordorf, Willy. "Actes de Paul." Pages 1115–77 of vol. 1 in *Écrits apocryphes chrétiens.* Edited by F. Bovon and P. Geoltrain. Paris: Gallimard, 1997.

Rowhorst, Gerard. "Hymns and Prayers in the Apocryphal Acts of Thomas." Pages 195–212 in *Literature or Liturgy? Early Christian Hymns and Prayers in their Literary and Liturgical Context in Antiquity.* Edited by C. Leonhard and H. Löhr. WUNT 2.363. Tübingen: Mohr Siebeck, 2014.

Schneider, Pierre. "The So-Called Confusion between India and Ethiopia: The Eastern and Southern Edges of the Inhabited World from the Greco-Roman Perspective." Pages 184–202 in *Brill's Companion to Ancient Geography: The Inhabited World in the Greek and Roman Tradition.* Edited by S. Bianchetti et al. Leiden: Brill, 2016.

Sellew, Phillip. "Paul, Acts of," and "Paul, Martyrdom of." *ABD* 5:202–3; 204–5.

——. "Thomas Christianity: Scholars in Quest of a Community." Pages 11–35 in *The Apocryphal Acts of Thomas.* Edited by J. N. Bremmer. Leuven: Peeters, 2001.

Schäferdiek, Kurt. "Acts of John." *NTApoc* 2:152–258.

Schneider, P. G. *The Mystery of the Acts of John: An Interpretation of the Hymn and the Dance in the Light of the Acts' Theology.* San Francisco: Mellen Research University Press, 1991.

Sirker-Wicklaus, Gerlinde. *Untersuchungen zu den Johannes-Akten.* Witterschlick and Bonn: Wohle, 1988.

Snyder, Glenn E. *Acts of Paul.* WUNT 2.352. Tübingen: Mohr Siebeck, 2013.

Spittler, Janet. *Animals in the Apocryphal Acts of the Apostles: The Wild Kingdom of Early Christian Literature.* WUNT 2.247. Tübingen: Mohr Siebeck, 2007.

——. "Christianity at the Edges: Representations of the Ends of the Earth in the Apocryphal Acts of the Apostles." Pages 353–75 in *Rise and Expansion of Christianity in the First Three Centuries of the Common Era.* Edited by C. Rothschild and J. Schröter. WUNT 301. Tübingen: Mohr Siebeck, 2013.

Thomaskutty, Johnson. *Saint Thomas the Apostle, New Testament, Apocrypha and Historical Traditions.* London: Bloomsbury T&T Clark, 2018.

Tissot, Yves. "Les Acts de Thomas: exemple de recueil composite." Pages 223–32 in *Les Actes apocryphes des Apôtres: Christianisme et monde païen.* Edited by F. Bovon et al. Geneva: Labor et Fides, 1981.

Van den Bosch, Lourens P. "India and the Apostolate of St. Thomas." Pages 125–48 in *The Apocryphal Acts of Thomas.* Edited by J. N. Bremmer. Leuven: Peeters, 2001.

CHAPTER 15: ACTS OF PETER
Primary Sources

Bovon, François, and Bertrand Bouvier. "Une fragment grec inédit des actes de Pierre?" *Apocrypha* 17 (2006): 9–54.

Brashler, James, and Douglas M. Parrott. "The Act of Peter." Pages 473–93 in *Nag Hammadi Codices V, 2–5 and VI with Papyrus Berolinensis 8502,1 and 4.* Edited by D. M. Parrott. NHS 11. Coptic Gnostic Library. Leiden: Brill, 1979.

Döhler, Mariatheres. *Acta Petri: Text, Übersetzung und Kommentar zu den Actus Vercellenses.* Berlin: de Gruyter, 2018.

Eastman, David L. *The Ancient Martyrdom Accounts of Peter and Paul.* Writings from the Greco-Roman World 39. Atlanta: SBL Press, 2015.

Elliott, J. K. "The Acts of Peter." Pages 390–430 in *The Apocryphal New Testament: A Collection of Apocryphal Christian Literature in an English Translation Based on M. R. James.* Edited by J. K. Elliott. Oxford: Clarendon, 1993.

LeLoir, Louis. "Martyre de Pierre." Pages 77–86 in *Écrits apocryphes sur les apôtres: traduction de l'edition armenienne de Venise, vol. 1: Pierre, Paul, Andre, Jacques, Jean.* Edited by L. LeLoir. CCSA 3. Turnhout: Brepols, 1986.

Poupon, Gérard, ed. and trans. "Actes de Pierre." Pages 1041–114 of vol. 1 in *Écrits apocryphes chrétiens.* Edited by F. Bovon, P. Geoltrain, and J.-D. Kaestli. Bibliothèque de la Pléiade 442. Paris: Gallimard, 1997.

Schneemelcher, Wilhelm. "The Acts of Peter." *NTApoc* 2:271–321.

Stoops, Robert F., Jr. *The Acts of Peter.* Early Christian Apocrypha 4. Salem, OR: Polebridge, 2012.

Tardieu, Michel. *Écrits gnostiques: Codex de Berlin.* Sources gnostiques et manichéens 1. Paris: Cerf, 1984. Text on pp. 217–22; commentary on pp. 403–10.

Secondary Sources

Baldwin, Matthew C. *Whose Acts of Peter? Text and Historical Context of the Actus Vercellenses.* WUNT 2.196. Tübingen: Mohr-Siebeck, 2005.

Bauckham, Richard J. "The Martyrdom of Peter in Early Christian Literature." *ANRW* 26.1:539–95. Part 2, *Principat,* 26.1. Edited by H. Temporini and W. Haase. New York: de Gruyter, 1992.

Bovon, François, et al., eds. *Les actes apocryphes des apôtres: Christianisme et monde païen.* Publications de la Faculté de Théologie de l'Université de Genève 4. Geneva: Labor et Fides, 1981.

Bovon, François, Ann Graham Brock, and Christopher R. Matthews, eds. *The Apocryphal Acts of the Apostles: Harvard Divinity School Studies.* Religions of the World. Cambridge: Harvard University Center for the Study of World Religions, 1999.

Bremmer, Jan N., ed. *The Apocryphal Acts of Peter: Magic, Miracles and Gnosticism.* Studies on the Apocryphal Acts of the Apostles 3. Louvain: Peeters, 1998.

Cartlidge, David. "Transfigurations of Metamorphosis Traditions in the Acts of John, Thomas and Peter." *Semeia* 38 (1986): 56–66.

Klauck, Hans-Joseph. *The Apocryphal Acts of the Apostles: An Introduction.* Trans. B. McNeil. Waco, TX: Baylor University Press, 2008.

Molinari, Andrea Lorenzo. *"I Never Knew the Man": The Coptic Act of Peter (Papyrus Berolinensis 802,4), Its Independence from the Apocryphal Acts of Peter, Genre and Origins.* Bibliothèque copte de Nag Hammadi; Section Études 5. Quebec: Université Laval, 2000.

Perkins, Judith B. "Healing and Power: The *Acts of Peter.*" Pages 124–41 in *The Suffering Self.* Edited by J. B. Perkins. London: Routledge, 1995.

Poupon, Gérard. "Les 'Actes de Pierre' et leur remaniement." *ANRW* 25.6:4363–82. Part 2, *Principat,* 25.6. Edited by H. Temporini and W. Haase. Berlin: de Gruyter, 1988.

Santos Otero, Aurelio de. "The Pseudo-Titus Epistle." *NTApoc* 2:53–74.

Smith, Jonathan Z. "Birth Upside Down or Right Side Up?" *History of Religion* 9 (1970): 281–303.

Stoops, Robert F., Jr. "The *Acts of Peter* in Intertextual Context." *Semeia* 80 (1997): 57–86.

———. "Christ as Patron in the *Acts of Peter.*" *Semeia* 56 (1991): 143–57.

———. "Patronage in the *Acts of Peter.*" *Semeia* 38 (1986): 91–100.

Thomas, Christine M. *The Acts of Peter, Gospel Literature, and the Ancient Novel: Rewriting the Past.* New York: Oxford University Press, 2003.

Zwierlein, Otto. *Petrus in Rome: Die literarischen Zeugnisse. Mit einer kritischen Edition der Martyrien des Petrus und Paulus auf neuer handschriftliche Grundlage.* 2nd ed. UALG 109. Berlin: de Gruyter, 2010.

CHAPTER 16: ACTS OF PHILIP

Amsler, Frédéric. *Acta Philippi: Commentarius.* CCSA 12. Turnhout: Brepols, 1999.

Amsler, Frédéric, François Bovon, and Bertrand Bouvier. *Actes de l'apôtre Philippe.* Apocryphes 8. Turnhout: Brepols, 1996.

———. "Les Actes de Philippe." Pages 1179–320 in vol. 1 of *Écrits apocryphes chrétiens.* Edited by F. Bovon and P. Geoltrain. Bibliothèque de la Pléiade 442. Paris: Gallimard, 1997.

Bovon, François. "Les Actes de Philippe." *ANRW* 25.6:4431–527. Part 2, *Principat,* 25.6. Edited by H. Temporini and W. Haase. Berlin: de Gruyter, 1988.

———. *New Testament and Christian Apocrypha.* WUNT 237. Tübingen: Mohr Siebeck, 2009.

———. *Studies in Early Christianity.* WUNT 161. Tübingen: Mohr Siebeck, 2003.

Bovon, François, Bertrand Bouvier, and Frédéric Amsler. *Acta Philippi: Textus.* CCSA 11. Turnhout: Brepols, 1999.

Bovon, François, Ann Graham Brock, and Christopher R. Matthews, eds. *The Apocryphal Acts of the Apostles: Harvard Divinity School Studies.* Religions of the World. Cambridge: Harvard University Center for the Study of World Religions, 1999.

Bovon, François, and Christopher R. Matthews. *The Acts of Philip: A New Translation.* Waco, TX: Baylor University Press, 2012.

Lipsius, Richard Adelbert, and Maximilien Bonnet. *Acta Apostolorum Apocrypha*. Vol. 2.2. Leipzig: Mendelssohn, 1903. Repr., Darmstadt: Wissenschaftliche Buchgesellschaft, 1959.

Matthews, Christopher R. *Philip: Apostle and Evangelist. Configurations of a Tradition*. NovTSup 105. Leiden: Brill, 2002.

Zimmermann, Ruben, ed. *Die Wunder der Apostel*. Vol. 2 of *Kompendium der frühchristlichen Wundererzählungen*. Gütersloh: Gütersloher, 2017.

CHAPTER 17: ACTS OF THOMAS

See above on chapter 13.

CHAPTER 18: THE DEPARTURE OF MY LADY MARY FROM THIS WORLD (THE SIX BOOKS DORMITION APOCRYPHON)

Brown, R. E. et al. *Mary in the New Testament: A Collaborative Assessment by Protestant and Roman Catholic Scholars*. Philadelphia: Fortress, 1978.

Gaventa, B. R. *Mary: Glimpses of the Mother of Jesus*. Studies on Personalities of the New Testament. Columbia, SC: University of South Carolina Press, 1995.

Graef, H. C. *Mary: A History of Doctrine and Devotion*. New York: Sheed and Ward, 1963, 1965. Repr., Notre Dame, IN: Christian Classics, 2009.

Peppard, M. *The World's Oldest Church: Bible, Art, and Ritual at Dura-Europos, Syria*. New Haven: Yale University Press, 2016.

Reynolds, B. *Gateway to Heaven: Marian Doctrine and Devotion, Image and Typology in the Patristic and Medieval Periods*. Hyde Park, NY: New City, 2012.

Shoemaker, Stephen J. *Ancient Traditions of the Virgin Mary's Dormition and Assumption*. Oxford Early Christian Studies. Oxford: Oxford University Press, 2002.

———. "Epiphanius of Salamis, the Kollyridians, and the Early Dormition Narratives: The Cult of the Virgin in the Fourth Century." *JECS* 16 (2008): 371–401.

———. "'Let Us Go and Burn Her Body': The Image of the Jews in the Early Dormition Traditions." *Church History* 68 (1999): 775–823.

———. *Mary in Early Christian Faith and Devotion*. New Haven: Yale University Press, 2016.

———. "A Peculiar Version of the *Inventio Crucis* in the Early Syriac Dormition Traditions." *Studia Patristica* 41 (2006): 75–81.

Smith Lewis, Agnes. *Apocrypha Syriaca*. Studia Sinaitica 11. London: C. J. Clay, 1902.

Wright, William. "The Departure of My Lady Mary from This World." *The Journal of Sacred Literature and Biblical Record* 7 (1865): 129–60.

CHAPTER 19: PSEUDO-CLEMENTINES
Primary Sources
Current Editions

Frankenberg, Wilhelm. *Die syrischen Clementinen mit griechischem Paralleltext: Eine Vorarbeit zu dem literargeschichtlichen Problem der Sammlung*. TUGAL 48.3. Leipzig: J. C. Hinrichs, 1937.

Rehm, Bernhard, ed. *Die Pseudoklementinen I: Homilien*. Edited by G. Strecker. 3rd ed. GCS. Berlin: Akademie, 1992.

———. *Die Pseudoklementinen II: Rekognitionen in Rufins Übersetzung*. Edited by G. Strecker. 2nd ed. GCS. Berlin: Akademie, 1994.

Concordance

Strecker, Georg. *Die Pseudoklementinen III: Konkordanz zu den Pseudoklementinen*. 2 vols. GCS. Berlin: Akademie, 1986–89.

English Translations

Jones, F. Stanley. *An Ancient Jewish Christian Source on the History of Christianity: Pseudo-Clementine "Recognitions" 1.27–71*. SBLTT 37. Christian Apocrypha Series 2. Atlanta: Scholars Press, 1995.

———, trans. *The Syriac "Pseudo-Clementines": An Early Version of the First Christian Novel*. Apocryphes 14. Turnhout: Brepols, 2014.

Smith, Thomas, Peter Peterson, and James Donaldson, trans. "Pseudo-Clementine Literature." Pages 67–346 in vol. 8 of *The Ante-Nicene Fathers: Translations of the Writings of the Fathers Down to A.D. 325*. Edited by A. Roberts and J. Donaldson. 10 vols. Repr., Grand Rapids: Eerdmans, 1978.

Foreign Language Translations

Cola, Silvano, trans. *Pseudo-Clemente: I Ritrovamenti (Recognitiones)*. Collana di Testi Patristici 104. Rome: Città Nuova Editrice, 1993.

Geoltrain, Pierre, et al., trans. "Roman pseudo-clémentin." Pages 1173–2003 in *Écrits apocryphes chrétiens II*. Edited by P. Geoltrain and J.-D. Kaestli. Bibliothèque de la Pléiade 516. Paris: Gallimard, 2005.

Vielberg, Meinolf, trans. *Rufinus von Aquileia: Übersetzung der "Pseudoklementinischen Recognitionen" Buch 1 und 2*. Bibliothek der lateinischen Literatur der Spätantike 2.1. Stuttgart: Franz Steiner, 2021.

Wehnert, Jürgen, trans. *Der Klemensroman*. Kleine Bibliothek der antiken jüdischen und christlichen Literatur. Göttingen: Vandenhoeck & Ruprecht, 2015.

Secondary Literature

Amsler, Frédéric, et al., eds. *Nouvelles intrigues pseudo-clémentines: Plots in the Pseudo-Clementine Romance*. Publications de l'Institut romand des sciences bibliques 6. Lausanne: Éditions du Zèbre, 2008.

Bremmer, Jan N., ed. *The "Pseudo-Clementines."* Studies on Early Christian Apocrypha 10. Leuven: Peeters, 2010.

Carleton Paget, James. *Jews, Christians and Jewish Christians in Antiquity*. WUNT 251. Tübingen: Mohr Siebeck, 2010.

Carlson, Donald H. *Jewish Christian Interpretation of the Pentateuch in the Pseudo-Clementine Homilies*. Minneapolis: Fortress, 2013.

Duncan, Patricia A. *Novel Hermeneutics in the Greek Pseudo-Clementine Romance*. WUNT 395. Tübingen: Mohr Siebeck, 2017.

Giménez de Aragón Sierra, Pedro. *Historia de la salvación, Una antigua fuente judeocristiana: Traducción y comentario de "Recognitiones" I, 27–42, 2*. Historia de las ideas religiosas. Madrid: Mino y Davila, 2007.

Jones, F. Stanley. "The Distinctive Sayings of Jesus Shared by Justin and the *Pseudo-Clementines*." Pages 200–217 in *Forbidden Texts on the Western Frontier: The Christian Apocrypha in North American Perspectives*. Edited by T. Burke. Eugene, OR: Wipf & Stock, 2015.

———. "John the Baptist and His Disciples in the Pseudo-Clementines: A Historical Appraisal." Pages 317–35 in *Rediscovering the Apocryphal Continent: New Perspectives on Early Christian and Late Antique Apocryphal Texts and Traditions*. Edited by P. Piovanelli and T. Burke. WUNT 349. Tübingen: Mohr Siebeck, 2015.

———. "The Orphic Cosmo-Theogony in the *Pseudo-Clementines*." Pages 71–82 in *Les polémiques religieuses du Iᵉʳ au IVᵉ siècle de notre ére: Hommage à Bernard Pouderon*. Edited by G. Bady and D. Cuny. Théologie historique 128. Paris: Beauchesne, 2019.

———. *Pseudoclementina Elchasaiticaque inter Judaeochristiana: Collected Studies*. OLA 203. Leuven: Peeters, 2012.

———, ed. *The Rediscovery of Jewish Christianity: From Toland to Baur*. History of Biblical Studies 5. Atlanta: SBL Press, 2012.

Jourdan, Fabienne. *Orphée et les chrétiens: La réception du mythe d'Orphée dans la littérature chrétienne grecque des cinq premiers siècles*. 2 vols. Anagôgê 4–5. Paris: Les Belles Lettres, 2010–2011.

Kelley, Nicole. *Knowledge and Religious Authority in the Pseudo-Clementines: Situating the "Recognitions" in Fourth Century Syria*. WUNT 2.213. Tübingen: Mohr Siebeck, 2006.

Kline, Leslie Lee. *The Sayings of Jesus in the Pseudo-Clementine Homilies*. SBLDS 14. Missoula, MT: Scholars Press, 1975.

Markschies, Christoph. *God's Body: Jewish, Christian, and Pagan Images of God*. Translated by A. J. Edmonds. Waco, TX: Baylor University Press, 2019.

Pouderon, Bernard. *La genèse du roman pseudo-clémentin: Études littéraires et historiques*. CREJ 53. Leuven: Peeters, 2012.

Reed, Annette Yoshiko. *Jewish-Christianity and the History of Judaism: Collected Essays*. TSAJ 171. Tübingen: Mohr Siebeck, 2018.

Strecker, Georg. *Das Judenchristentum in den Pseudoklementinen*. TUGAL 70. 2nd ed. Berlin: Akademie, 1981.

Vielberg, Meinolf. *Klemens in den pseudoklementinischen Rekognitionen: Studien zur literarischen Form des spätantiken Romans*. TUGAL 145. Berlin: Akademie, 2000.

CHAPTER 20: JESUS'S LETTER TO ABGAR

Bauer, Walter. *Orthodoxy and Heresy in Earliest Christianity*. 2nd ed. Philadelphia: Fortress, 1979.

Brock, Sebastian. "Eusebius and Syriac Christianity." Pages 212–34 in *Eusebius, Christianity and Judaism*. Edited by H. A. Attridge and G. Hata. Detroit: Wayne State University Press, 1992.

Burkitt, Francis Crawford. *Early Eastern Christianity*. John Murray: London, 1904.

Corke-Webster, James. "A Man for the Times: Jesus and the Abgar Correspondence in Eusebius of Caesarea's Ecclesiastical History." *HTR* 110.4 (2017): 563–87.

Desreumaux, Alain, Andrew Palmer, and Robert Beylot. *Histoire du roi Abgar et de Jésus*. Paris: Brepols, 1993.

Dobschütz, Ernst von. "Der Briefwechsel zwischen Abgar und Jesus." *ZWT* 43 (1900): 422–86.

Drijvers, Hendrik Jan Willem. "The Abgar Legend." *NTApoc* 1:492–500.

Illert, Martin. *Doctrina Addai; De imagine Edessena = Die Abgarlegende; Das Christusbild von Edessa*. Fontes Christiani 45. Turnhout: Brepols, 2007.

Mirkovic, Alexander. *Prelude to Constantine*. Arbeiten zur Religion und Geschichte des Urchristentums 15. Frankfurt am Main: Peter Lang, 2004.

Polanski, Tomasz. "Translation, Amplification, Paraphrase: Some Comments on the Syriac, Greek and Coptic Versions of the Abgar Letter." *Collectanea Christiana Orientalia* 13 (2016): 159–210.

Tixeront, L. Joseph. *Les origines de l'église d'Édesse et la légende d'Abgar: Étude critique suivie de deux textes orientaux inédits*. Paris: Maisonneuve et Ch. Leclerc, 1888.

CHAPTER 21: CORRESPONDENCE OF PAUL AND SENECA

Barlow, Claude W. *Epistolae Senecae ad Paulum et Pauli ad Senecam (quae vocantur)*. Horn, Austria: American Academy in Rome, 1938.

Bocciolini Palagi, Laura. *Il carteggio apocrifo di Seneca e san Paolo: introduzione, testo, commento*. Firenze: L. S. Olschki, 1978.

Bonar, Chance. "Epistles of Paul and Seneca." e-Clavis: Christian Apocrypha. www.nasscal.com/e-clavis-christian -apocrypha/epistles-of-paul-and-seneca/.

Elliott, J. K. *The Apocryphal New Testament*. Rev. ed. Oxford: Clarendon, 1999.

Hine, Harry M. "Seneca and Paul: The First Two Thousand Years." Pages 22–48 in *Paul and Seneca in Dialogue*. Edited by J. R. Dodson and D. E. Briones. Ancient Philosophy and Religion 2. Leiden: Brill, 2017.

Malherbe, Abraham J. "'Seneca' on Paul as Letter Writer." Pages 414–21 in *The Future of Early Christianity*. Edited by B. A. Pearson. FS for H. Koester. Minneapolis: Fortress, 1991.

Pervo, Richard I. *The Making of Paul: Constructions of the Apostle in Early Christianity*. Minneapolis: Fortress, 2010.

Ramelli, Ilaria L. E. "The Pseudepigraphical Correspondence between Seneca and Paul: A Reassessment." Pages 319–36 in *Paul and Pseudepigraphy*. Edited by S. E. Porter and G. P. Fewster. Pauline Studies 8. Leiden: Brill, 2013.

———. "A Pseudepigraphon inside a Pseudepigraphon? The Seneca-Paul Correspondence and the Letters Added Afterwards." *JSP* 23.4 (2014): 259–89.

Römer, Cornelia. "The Correspondence between Seneca and Paul." *NTApoc* 2:46–53.

Rosenmeyer, Patricia. "The Epistolary Novel." Pages 146–65 in *Greek Fiction: The Greek Novel in Context*. Edited by J. R. Morgan and R. Stoneman. London: Routledge, 1994.

Russell, Donald M. "Progymnasmata." Page 1216 in *The Oxford Classical Dictionary*. 4th ed. Edited by S. Hornblower, A. Spawforth, and E. Eidinow. Oxford: Oxford University Press, 2012.

CHAPTER 22: APOCRYPHAL EPISTLE TO THE LAODICEANS

Anderson, Charles P. "Epistle to the Laodiceans." *ABD* 4:231–33.

Anger, Rudolph. *Ueber den Laodiceans: Eine biblischkritische Untersuchung*. Leipzig: Verlag von Gebhardt & Reisland, 1843.

Backus, Irena. "Lettre de Paul aux Laodicéens." Pages 1089–97 of vol. 2 in *Écrits apocryphes chrétiens*. Edited by P. Geoltrain and J.-D. Kaestli. Paris: Gallimard, 2005.

———. "New Testament Apocryphal Writings: Jacques Lefèvre d'Etaples and His Epigones." *Renaissance Quarterly* 51 (1998): 1169–98.

Burnet, Régis. "Pourquoi avoir écrit l'insipide épître aux Laodicéens?" *NTS* 48 (2002): 132–41.

Carra de Vaux, B. "L'Épitre aux Laodiceans en arabe." *RB* 6 (1896): 221–26.

Cosgrove, Charles H. "Laodiceans, Epistle to the." Page 500 in the *Mercer Dictionary of the Bible*. Edited by W. E. Mills. Macon, GA: Mercer University Press, 1990.

Erbetta, Mario. "La Lettera ai Laodiceni (160–190?)." Pages 63–67 in *Lettere e Apocalissi*, vol. 3 of *Gli Apocrifiji del Nuovo Testamento*. Casa Editrice Marietti, 1981.

Firpo, Luigi. *Apocrifiji del Nuovo Testamento*. Classici delle Religioni. Editrice Torinese, 1971. See pp. 1720–23.

Goodspeed, E. J. "A Toledo Manuscript of Laodiceans." *JBL* 23.1 (1904): 76–78.

———. "The Madrid MS. of Laodiceans." *AJT* 8 (1904): 536–38.

Gregory, Andrew. "Non-Canonical Epistles and Related Literature." Pages 90–114 in *The Oxford Handbook of Early Christian Apocrypha*. Edited by A. Gregory and C. Tuckett. Oxford: Oxford University Press, 2015.

Günther, Matthias. "Laodiceans, Letter to the." Page 326 of vol. 7 in *Religion Past & Present: Encyclopedia of Theology and Religion*. Edited by H. D. Betz, D. S. Browning, B. Janowski, and E. Jüngel. Leiden: Brill, 2009.

Hall, Thomas N. "Aelfric and the Epistle to the Laodiceans." Pages 65–84 in *Apocryphal Texts and Traditions in Anglo-Saxon England*. Edited by K. Powell and D. Scragg. Cambridge: D. S. Brewer, 2003.

Harnack, Adolf von. *Apocrypha, IV. Die apokrphen Briefe des Paulus an die Laodicener und Korinther*. Kleine Texte für theologische Vorlesungen und Übungen 12. Bonn: Marcus and Weber, 1905.

———. "Der apokryphe Brief des Apostels Paulus an die Laodicener, eine Marcionitische Fälschung aus der 2. Hälfte des 2. Jahrhunderts." In *Sitzungsberichte der preussischen Akademie der Wissenschaften, Jahrgang 1923. Philosophisch-historische Klasse*. Berlin: Verlage der Akademie der Wissenschaften/de Gruyter, 1923.

———. *Marcion, das Evangelium vom fremden Gott*. 2nd ed. Leipzig, 1924. See esp. appendix 3. Later translated into English as *Marcion: The Gospel of the Alien God*. Translated by J. E. Steely and L. D. Bierma. Durham, NC: Labyrinth, 1990.

Hermann, Leon. "L'épître aux Laodicéens (Laodicéens et l'apologie aux Hebreux)." *Cahiers du Cercle Ernest Renan* 58.2 (1968): 1–16.

Holloway, Paul A. "The Apocryphal Epistle to the Laodiceans and the Partitioning of Philippians." *HTR* 91 (1998): 321–25.

———. *Consolation in Philippians: Philosophical Sources and Rhetorical Strategy*. Cambridge: Cambridge University Press, 2001.

Hutter, Elias. *Polyglott New Testament*. Nuremberg, 1599.

James, M. R. *New Testament Apocrypha*. Oxford: Clarendon, 1953 (1924). See pp. 478–80.

Longenecker, Bruce W., and Scott C. Ryan. "Presenting the Pauline Voice: An Appreciation of the *Letter to the Laodiceans*." *NTS* 62 (2016): 136–48.

Mackay, Thomas W. "Content and Style in Two Pseudo-Pauline Epistles (3 Corinthians and the Epistle to the Laodiceans)." Pages 215–40 in *Apocryphal Writings and the Latter-Day Saints*. Edited by C. W. Griggs. Religious Studies Monograph Series 13. Salt Lake: Brigham Young University, 1986.

MaGee, Gregory S. *Portrait of an Apostle: A Case for Paul's Authorship of Colossians and Ephesians*. Eugene, OR: Pickwick, 2013.

Meeks, Wayne A., and John T. Fitzgerald. *The Writings of Paul: Annotated Texts, Reception and Criticism*. 2nd ed. New York: W. W. Norton, 2007.

Moreschini, Claudio, and Enrico Norelli. *Early Christian Greek and Latin Literature: A Literary History*. Translated by M. J. O'Connell. Peabody, MA: Hendrickson, 2005. See p. 29.

Norelli, Enrico. "La Lettre aux Laodicéens: essai d'interprétation." Pages 45–90 in *Il Mosaico della Basilica di S. Colombano in Bobbio e altri studi dal II al XX secolo*. Edited by F. G. Nuvolone. Archivum Bobbiense 24. Bobbio, 2002.

Østmoe, Tor Ivar. "Paulus' brev til laodikeerne." Pages 295–98 in *Tidligkristne apokryfer*. Edited by R. Aasgaard. Verdens Hellige Skrifter. Oslo: De norske bokklubbene, 2011.

Penny, Donald N. "The Pseudo-Pauline Letters of the First Two Centuries." PhD diss., Emory University, 1979.

Pervo, Richard I. *The Making of Paul: Constructions of the Apostle in Early Christianity*. Minneapolis: Fortress, 2010.

Pink, Karl. "Die Pseudo-Paulinischen Briefe II: (2) Der Laodizenerbrief." *Biblica* 6 (1925): 179–93.

Quispel, Gilles. "The Epistle to the Laodiceans: A Marcionite Forgery." Pages 689–93 in *Gnostica, Judaica, Catholica: Collected Essays of Gilles Quispel*. Edited by J. van Oort. NHMS 55. Leiden: Brill, 2008.

Ranke, Ernst, ed. *Codex Fuldensis: Novum Testamentum Latine Interprete Hieronymo, ex manuscript Victoris Capuani*. Marburg: Sumptibus N. G. Elwerti Bibliopolae Academici, 1868.

Santos Otero, Aurelio de. *Die handschriftliche Überlieferung der altslavischen Apokryphen*. Berlin: de Gruyter, 1978. See pp. 147–48.

Schneemelcher, Wilhelm. "The Epistle to the Laodiceans." *NTApoc* 2:44–46.

Sellew, Philip. "Laodiceans and Philippians Revisited: A Response to Paul Holloway." *HTR* 91 (1998): 327–29.

———. "Laodiceans and the Philippians Fragments Hypothesis." *HTR* 87 (1994): 17–28.

Smith, Geoffrey S. *Guilt by Association: Heresy Catalogues in Early Christianity*. Oxford: Oxford University Press, 2015.

Tite, Philip L. *The Apocryphal Epistle to the Laodiceans: An Epistolary and Rhetorical Analysis*. TENTS 7. Leiden: Brill, 2012.

———. "Dusting Off a Pseudo-Historical Letter: Re-Thinking the Epistolary Aspects of the Apocryphal Epistle to the Laodiceans." Pages 289–318 in *Paul and Pseudepigraphy*. Edited by S. E. Porter and G. P. Fewster. PAST 8. Leiden: Brill, 2013.

———. "Epistle to the Laodiceans." e-Clavis: Christian Apocrypha. www.nasscal.com/e-clavis-christian -apocrypha/epistle-to-the-laodiceans/.

Thompson, Trevor W. "Epistles, Apocryphal." Pages 1084–86 of vol. 7 in *Encyclopedia of the Bible and Its Reception*. Edited by H. J. Klauck et al. Berlin: de Gruyter, 2013.

Vouaux, Leon. *Les Actes de Paul et ses letters apocryphes: Introduction, texts, traduction et commentaire*. Les Apocryphes du Nouveau Testament. Paris: Librairie Letouzet et Ané, 1913.

Watson, Duane F. "Laodiceans, Letter to the." Page 790 in *Eerdmans Dictionary of the Bible*. Edited by D. N. Freedman. Grand Rapids: Eerdmans, 2000.

CHAPTER 23: EPISTULA APOSTOLORUM

Hannah, Darrell D. "The Four-Gospel 'Canon' in the *Epistula Apostolorum*." *JTS* 59 (2008): 598–633.

Hartenstein, Judith. *Die zweite Lehre: Erscheinungen des Auferstandenen als Rahmenerzählungen frühchristlicher Dialoge*. TUGAL 146. Berlin: Akademie, 2000.

Hill, Charles E. "The Epistula Apostolorum: An Asian Tract from the Time of Polycarp." *JECS* 7 (1999): 1–53.

Hills, Julian V. *Tradition and Composition in the Epistula Apostolorum*. 2nd ed. HTS 57. Minneapolis: Fortress, 2008.

Kiel, Nikolai. "Auferstehung des Fleisches in der Epistula Apostolorum." *VC* 74 (2020): 165–98.

Lindenlaub, Julia D. "The Gospel of John as Model for Literate Authors and Their Texts in Epistula Apostolorum and Apocryphon of James (NHC 1,2)." *JSNT* 43 (2020): 3–27.

Schmidt, Carl, with Isaak Wajnberg. *Gespräche Jesu mit seinen Jüngern nach der Auferstehung: Ein katholisch-apostolisches Sendschreiben des 2. Jahrhunderts*. Leipzig: J. C. Hinrichs, 1919. Repr., Hildesheim: Georg Olms, 1967.

Stewart-Sykes, Alistair. "The Asian Context of the New Prophecy and of Epistula Apostolorum." *VC* 51 (1997): 416–38.

Watson, Francis. *An Apostolic Gospel: The "Epistula Apostolorum" in Literary Context*. SNTSMS 179. Cambridge: Cambridge University Press, 2020.

———. "The Conversion of Paul: A New Perspective (*Epistula Apostolorum* 31–33)." Pages 195–211 in *Receptions of Paul in Early Christianity: The Person of Paul and His Writings through the Eyes of His Early Interpreters*. Edited by J. Schröter, S. Butticaz, and A. Dettwiler. BZNW 234. Berlin: de Gruyter, 2018.

———. "A Gospel of the Eleven: The *Epistula Apostolorum* and the Johannine Tradition." Pages 189–215 in *Connecting Gospels: Beyond the Canonical/Non-Canonical Divide*. Edited by F. Watson and S. Parkhouse. Oxford: Oxford University Press, 2018.

———. "On the Miracle Catena in *Epistula Apostolorum* 4–5." Pages 107–27 in *Gospels and Gospel Traditions in the Second Century: Experiments in Reception*. Edited by J. Schröter, T. Nicklas, and J. Verheyden. BZNW 235. Berlin: de Gruyter, 2019.

CHAPTER 24: SUNDAY LETTER

Bauckham, Richard. "Sabbath and Sunday in the Medieval Church in the West." Pages 299–309 in *From Sabbath to Lord's Day: A Biblical, Historical, and Theological Investigation*. Edited by D. A. Carson. Grand Rapids: Zondervan, 1982.

———. "Sabbath and Sunday in the Post-Apostolic Church." Pages 251–98 in *From Sabbath to Lord's Day: A Biblical, Historical, and Theological Investigation*. Edited by D. A. Carson. Grand Rapids: Zondervan, 1982.

———. "Sabbath and Sunday in the Protestant Tradition." Pages 311–41 in *From Sabbath to Lord's Day: A Biblical, Historical, and Theological Investigation*. Edited by D. A. Carson. Grand Rapids: Zondervan, 1982.

Beskow, Per. *Strange Tales about Jesus: A Survey of Unfamiliar Gospels*. Philadelphia: Fortress, 1983.

Burke, Tony, and Brent Landau, eds. *New Testament Apocrypha: More Noncanonical Scriptures*. 2 vols. Grand Rapids: Eerdmans, 2016.

Goodspeed, Edgar J. *Strange New Gospels*. Chicago: University of Chicago Press, 1931.

Haines, Dorothy, ed. *Sunday Observance and the Sunday Letter in Anglo-Saxon England*. Anglo-Saxon Texts 8. Cambridge: D. S. Brewer, 2010.

Laansma, Jon C. "Lord's Day." Pages 679–86 in *Dictionary of Later New Testament and Its Developments*. Edited by R. P. Martin and P. H. Davids. Downers Grove, IL: InterVarsity Press, 1997.

Lees, Clare A. "The 'Sunday Letter' and the 'Sunday Lists.'" *Anglo-Saxon England* 14 (1985): 129–51.

Miceli, Calogero A. "Epistle of Christ from Heaven." e-Clavis: Christian Apocrypha. www.nasscal.com/e-clavis-christian-apocrypha/epistle-of-christ-from-heaven/.

———. "The Epistle of Christ from Heaven: A New Translation and Introduction." Pages 455–63 in vol. 1 of *New Testament Apocrypha: More Noncanonical Scriptures*. Edited by T. Burke and B. Landau. Grand Rapids: Eerdmans, 2016.

Priebsch, Robert. *Letter from Heaven on the Observance of the Lord's Day*. Oxford: Basil Blackwell, 1936.

CHAPTER 25: APOCALYPSE OF PAUL

For a very detailed bibliography of the Apocalypse of Paul and its various translations in the East and West, see Jan N. Bremmer and Istvan Czachesz, eds., *The Visio Pauli and the Gnostic Apocalypse of Paul* (Leuven: Peeters, 2007), 211–36. Below, I list only those writings that have appeared afterward or that were missed in that bibliography.

Baun, Jane. *Tales from Another Byzantium: Celestial Journey and Local Community in the Medieval Greek Apocrypha*. Cambridge: Cambridge University Press, 2007.

Bremmer, Jan N. "Christian Hell: From the *Apocalypse of Peter* to the *Apocalypse of Paul*." *Numen* 56 (2009): 298–325. Updated on pages 295–312 of Jan N. Bremmer, *Maidens, Magic and Martyrs in Early Christianity*. Tübingen: Mohr Siebeck, 2017.

Bullita, Dario. *Páls leizla: The Vision of St Paul*. London: Viking Society for Northern Research, 2017. Norse translation.

Copeland, Kirsti. "'The Holy Contest': Competition for the Best Afterlife in the *Apocalypse of Paul* and Late Antique Egypt." Pages 189–207 in *Other Worlds and Their Relation to This World: Early Jewish and Ancient Christian Traditions*. Edited by T. Nicklas et al. Leiden: Brill, 2010.

Di Paolo Healy, Antonette. *The Old English Vision of St. Paul*. Cambridge, MA: Mediaeval Academy of America, 1978.

Meyer, Paul. "La descente de Saint Paul en enfer: poème français composé en Angleterre." *Romania* 24 (1895): 357–75, 589–91.

Micha, Alexandre. "Les Visions de saint Paul en vers." Pages 963–69 of vol. 2 of *Et c'est la fin pour quoy sommes ensemble: Hommage à Jean Dufournet*. Edited by J.-C. Aubailly. 3 vols. Paris: Champion, 1993.

Nicklas, Tobias. "Gute Werke, rechter Glaube: Paulusrezeption in der *Apokalypse des Paulus*?" Pages 150–69 in *Ancient Perspectives on Paul*. Edited by T. Nicklas et al. Göttingen: Vandenhoeck & Ruprecht, 2013.

Piovanelli, Pierluigi. *Apocryphités*. Turnhout: Brepols, 2016. See pp. 365–434.

Seymour, John D. "Irish Versions of the Vision of St. Paul." *JTS* 24 (1922): 54–59.

Williams, J. E. Caerwyn. "Irish Translations of Visio Sancti Pauli." *Éigse* 6 (1948–52): 127–34.

CHAPTER 26: APOCALYPSE OF PETER (GREEK)

Bauckham, Richard. *The Fate of the Dead: Studies on the Jewish and Christian Apocalypses*. NovTSup 93. Leiden: Brill, 1998.

Bausi, Alessandro. "Towards a Re-Edition of the Ethiopic Dossier of the *Apocalypse of Peter*: A Few Remarks on the Ethiopic Manuscript Witnesses." *Apocrypha* 27 (2016): 179–96.

Beck, Eric J. *Justice and Mercy in the Apocalypse of Peter: A New Translation and Analysis of the Purpose of the Text*. WUNT 427. Tübingen: Mohr Siebeck, 2019.

Bremmer, Jan N. "Orphic, Roman, Jewish and Christian Tours of Hell: Observations on the Apocalypse of Peter." Pages 305–21 in *Other Worlds and Their Relation to This World: Early Jewish and Ancient Christian Traditions*. Edited by T. Nicklas et al. JSJSup 143. Leiden: Brill, 2010.

Bremmer, Jan N., and István Czachesz, eds. *The Apocalypse of Peter*. Studies on Early Christian Apocrypha 7. Leuven: Peeters, 2003.

Buchholz, D. D. *Your Eyes Will Be Opened: A Study of the Greek (Ethiopic) Apocalypse of Peter*. SBLDS 97. Atlanta: Scholars Press, 1988.

Frey, Jörg, Matthijs den Dulk, and Jan G. van der Watt, eds. *2 Peter and the Apocalypse of Peter: Towards a New Perspective*. BibInt 174. Leiden: Brill, 2019.

Grünstäudl, Wolfgang. *Petrus Alexandrinus: Studien zum historischen und theologischen Ort des zweiten Petrusbriefes*. WUNT 2.353. Tübingen: Mohr Siebeck, 2013.

Helmer, Robert C. *"That We May Know and Understand": Gospel Tradition in the Apocalypse of Peter*. PhD diss., Marquette University, 1998.

Kraus, Thomas J., and Tobias Nicklas. *Das Petrusevangelium und die Petrusapokalypse: Die griechischen Fragmente mit deutscher und englischer Übersetzung*. GCS NF 11/Neutestamentliche Apokryphen 1. Berlin: de Gruyter, 2004.

Nicklas, Tobias. "Jewish, Christian, Greek? The *Apocalypse of Peter* as a Witness of Early 2nd-Cent. Christianity in Alexandria." Pages 27–46 in *Beyond Conflicts: Cultural and Religious Cohabitations in Alexandria and Egypt Between the 1st and the 6th Century CE*. Edited by L. Arcari. Studien und Texte zu Antike und Christentum 103. Tübingen: Mohr Siebeck, 2017.

Norelli, Enrico. "L'adversaire eschatologique dans l'Apocalypse de Pierre." Pages 291–317 in *Les forces du bien et du mal dans les premiers siècles de l'église*. Edited by Y.-M. Blanchard, B. Pouderon, and M. Scopello. Théologie historique 118. Paris: Beauchesne, 2011.

CHAPTER 27: APOCALYPSE OF THOMAS

Bihlmeyer, Pius. "Un Texte non interpolé de l'Apocalypse de Thomas." *Revue bénédictine* 28 (1911): 270–82.

Dando, Marcel. "L'Apocalypse de Thomas." *Cahiers d'Études Cathares* 28 (1977): 3–58.

Frick, Carolus. "Die Thomasapokalypse." *ZNW* 9 (1908): 172–73.

Geigenfeind, Matthias. "The Apocalypse of Thomas." Pages 580–604 in vol. 2 of *New Testament Apocrypha: More Noncanonical Scriptures*. Edited by T. Burke. Grand Rapids: Eerdmans, 2020.

———. "Audi Thomas, . . . Audi a me signa quae futura sunt in fine huius saeculi—Zum Textbestand und zur Überlieferung der apokryphen Thomas-Apokalypse." *ZAC* 20 (2016): 147–81.

James, Montague Rhodes. "The Revelatio Thomas Again." *JTS* 11 (1910): 569.

Nicklas, Tobias. "Die apokryphe Thomasapokalypse und ihre Rezeption der Offenbarung des Johannes." Pages 683–708 in *Die Johannesapokalypse: Kontexte-Konzepte-Rezeption*. Edited by J. Frey, J. A. Kelhoffer, and F. Tóth. Tübingen: Mohr Siebeck, 2012.

Sanchez, Sylvain Jean Gabriel. "L'usage de l'Apocalypse de Thomas au sein des Priscillianistes." Pages 259–69 in *Parcs et jardins au Moyen Age et à la Renaissance: L'Apocalypse*. Edited by C. Ridoux. Recherches valenciennoises 28. Valenciennes: Presses Universitaires de Valenciennes, 2009.

Santos Otero, Aurelio de. "Apocalypse of Thomas." *NTApoc* 2:748–52.

Seymour, John D. "The Signs of Doomsday in the Saltair na Rann." *Proceedings of the Royal Irish Academy* C 36 (1923): 154–63.

Swan, Mary. "The Apocalypse of Thomas in Old English." *Leeds Studies in English* 29 (1998): 333–46.

Wilhelm, Friedrich. *Deutsche Legenden und Legendare: Texte und Untersuchungen zu ihrer Geschichte im Mittelalter*. Leipzig: J. C. Hinrichs, 1907.

Wright, Charles D. "Rewriting (and Re-editing) the Apocalypse of Thomas." Pages 441–54 in *Écritures et réécritures: la reprise interprétative des traditions fondatrices par la littérature biblique et extra-biblique.* Edited by C. Clivaz et al. Leuven: Peeters, 2012.

———. "Vercelli Homily XV and the Apocalypse of Thomas." Pages 150–84 in *New Readings in the Vercelli Book.* Edited by S. Zacher and A. Orchard. Toronto Anglo-Saxon Series 4. Toronto: University of Toronto Press, 2009.

CHAPTER 28: FIRST APOCRYPHAL APOCALYPSE OF JOHN

Brannan, Rick. "1 Apocryphal Apocalypse of John." e-Clavis: Christian Apocrypha. www.nasscal.com/e-clavis -christian-apocrypha/1-apocryphal-apocalypse-of-john/.

———. *The First Apocryphal Apocalypse of John: A Greek Reader.* Appian Way Greek Readers. Bellingham, WA: Appian Way, 2017.

Court, John M. *The Book of Revelation and the Johannine Apocalyptic Tradition.* Sheffield: Sheffield Academic Press, 2000.

Kaestli, Jean-Daniel. "La figure de l'antichrist dans l'Apocalypse de Saint Jean le Théologien (Première Apocalypse Apocryphe de Jean)." Pages 277–90 in *Les forces du bien et du mal dans les premiers siècles de l'église.* Edited by J.-M. Blanchard, B. Pouderon, and M. Scopello. Théologie historique 118. Paris: Beauchesne, 2011.

Papadoyannakis, Yannis. "Instruction by Question and Answer: The Case of Late Antique and Byzantine Erotapokriseis." Pages 91–106 in *Greek Literature in Late Antiquity: Dynamism, Didacticism, Classicism.* Edited by S. F. Johnson. Burlington, VT: Ashgate, 2006.

Tischendorf, Constantinus. Pages 70–94 of *Apocalypses Apocryphae: Mosis, Esdrae, Pauli, Iohannis, Item Mariae Dormitio.* Leipzig: Mendelssohn, 1866.

Tóth, Péter. "New Wine in Old Wineskin: Byzantine Reuses of the Apocryphal Revelation Dialogue." Pages 77–93 in *Dialogues and Debate from Late Antiquity to Late Byzantium.* New York: Routledge, 2017.

Volgers, A., and Claudio Zamagni, eds. *Erotapokriseis: Early Christian Question-and-Answer Literature in Context.* Contributions to Biblical Exegesis and Theology 37. Leuven: Peeters, 2004.

Weinel, Heinrich. "Die spätere christliche Apokalyptik." Pages 141–73 in *ΕΥΧΑΡΙΣΤΗΡΙΟΝ: Studien zur Literatur des Alten und des Neuen Testaments.* Edited by H. Schmidt. FRLANT 36. Göttingen: Vandenhoek & Ruprecht, 1923.

Whealey, Alice. "The Apocryphal Apocalypse of John: A Byzantine Apocalypse from the Early Islamic Period." *JTS* 53.2 (2002): 533–40.

CHAPTER 29: NEW TESTAMENT APOCRYPHA

Burke, Tony, and Brent Landau. *New Testament Apocrypha: More Noncanonical Scripture.* Vol 1. Grand Rapids: Eerdmans, 2016.

Ehrman, Bart D., and Zlatko Pleše. *The Apocryphal Gospels: Texts and Translations.* New York: Oxford University Press, 2011.

Elliott, J. K. *The Apocryphal New Testament: A Collection of Apocryphal Christian Literature in an English Translation.* Oxford: Clarendon, 1993.

Hennecke, Edgar. *Neutestamentliche Apokryphen.* 3rd ed. Edited by W. Schneemelcher. Tübingen: Mohr Siebeck, 1959. (Originally published in 1904.)

Hennecke, Edgar, and Wilhelm Schneemelcher, eds. *New Testament Apocrypha.* 2 vols. English translation edited by R. McL. Wilson. Philadelphia: Westminster, 1963–1965.

Martin, Dale B. *Biblical Truths: The Meaning of Scripture in the Twenty-First Century.* New Haven: Yale University Press, 2017.

———. *New Testament History and Literature.* New Haven: Yale University Press, 2012.

Thomassen, Einar, ed. *Canon and Canonicity: The Formation and Use of Scripture.* Copenhagen: Museum Tusculanum, 2010.

SCRIPTURE AND OTHER ANCIENT LITERATURE INDEX

SUBJECT INDEX

AUTHOR INDEX